GERALD ALBAUM
University of New Mexico, USA

EDWIN DUERR
San Francisco State University, USA

JESPER STRANDSKOV
Aarhus School of Business, Denmark

INTERNATIONAL MARKETING AND EXPORT MANAGEMENT

FIFTH EDITION

FT Prentice Hall
FINANCIAL TIMES

An imprint of **Pearson Education**

Harlow, England • London • New York • Boston • San Francisco • Toronto • Sydney • Singapore • Hong Kong
Tokyo • Seoul • Taipei • New Delhi • Cape Town • Madrid • Mexico City • Amsterdam • Munich • Paris • Milan

Pearson Education Limited
Edinburgh Gate
Harlow
Essex CM20 2JE
England

and Associated Companies throughout the world

Visit us on the World Wide Web at:
www.pearsoned.co.uk

First published 1989
Second edition published 1994
Third edition published 1998
Fourth edition published 2002
Fifth edition published 2005

ISBN 0 273 686348

British Library Cataloguing-in-Publication Data
A catalogue record for this book is available from the British Library

Library of Congress Cataloging-in-Publication Data
Albaum, Gerald S.
   International marketing and export management/Gerald Albaum, Edwin Duerr and Jesper Strandskov, -- 5th ed.
     p. cm.
   Includes bibliographical references and index.

   ISBN 0-273-68634-8 (pbk)

   ISBN-13: 978-0-273-68634-7

    1. Export marketing--Management.   I. Duerr, Edwin. II. Strandskov, Jesper. III. Title.

   HF1416.I617 2004
   658.8'4--dc22

               2004053302

10 9 8 7 6 5 4 3 2
09 08 07 06 05

Typeset in $9\frac{1}{2} \times 11\frac{1}{2}$ Sabon Reg Justified by 25
Printed and bound by Ashford Colour Press., Gosport

The publisher's policy is to use paper manufactured from sustainable forests.

CONTENTS

Preface   viii
About the authors   xii
List of abbreviations   xiii
Guided tour   xviii
Publisher's acknowledgements   xxi

1 International marketing and exporting   1

1.1 Introduction   1
1.2 The nature of international marketing   5
1.3 Export marketing planning and strategy   15
1.4 The Internet, the World Wide Web, and e-business   22
1.5 The impact of technology   25
1.6 Entrepreneurial approaches to international marketing   28
1.7 The growth of nontraditional exports   31
1.8 Overview of the book   35
Questions for discussion   35
References   36
Further reading   38
Case Study 1.1 Export of art goods from Hungary   39
Case Study 1.2 Murphy Company Limited   39
Case Study 1.3 eBay, Inc.   40
Case Study 1.4 DaimlerChrylser AG   43

2 Bases of international marketing   51

2.1 Introduction   51
2.2 Potential benefits from export marketing   52
2.3 International trade theories   55
2.4 Export behaviour theories and motives   61
2.5 The development of export in the firm; internationalization stages   70
2.6 Exporting and the network model   73

2.7 Ethical/moral issues | 76
2.8 Social responsibility and the business environment | 80

Summary | 87
Questions for discussion | 87
References | 88
Further reading | 90
Case Study 2.1 Bridgestone Corporation | 91
Case Study 2.2 GlaxoSmithKline PLC | 94

3 The international environment | 99

3.1 Introduction | 99
3.2 Economic forces | 100
3.3 Socio-cultural environment | 106
3.4 Political/legal environment | 118
3.5 Economic integration | 136
3.6 Competition | 141

Summary | 144
Questions for discussion | 144
References | 145
Further reading | 147
Case Study 3.1 Supreme Canning Company | 148
Case Study 3.2 Ford Motor Company | 149
Case Study 3.3 Avon Products, Inc. (A) | 153

4 Export market selection: definition and strategies | 159

4.1 Introduction | 159
4.2 Market definition and segmentation | 161
4.3 Market expansion/selection process, procedure and strategy | 170
4.4 Foreign market portfolios: technique and analysis | 187

Summary | 191
Questions for discussion | 191
References | 192
Further reading | 193
Case Study 4.1 IKEA | 194
Case Study 4.2 Seven-Eleven Japan | 196

5 Information for international market(ing) decisions | 199

5.1 Introduction | 199
5.2 Sources of information | 202
5.3 Assessing market potential | 208
5.4 Export marketing research | 213
5.5 Using the Internet and e-mail for data collection | 226

Summary | 228
Questions for discussion | 228
References | 228
Further reading | 230
Appendix: Selected publications and web sites providing secondary data | 231
Case Study 5.1 Mariani Packing Company, Inc. | 235

Case Study 5.2 Aquabear AB   237
Case Study 5.3 Ford Motor Company Latin America   239

6 Market entry strategies   246

6.1 Introduction   246
6.2 Entry as a channel decision   246
6.3 Entry as a strategy   251
6.4 Factors influencing choice of entry mode   257
6.5 Managing the channel   264
6.6 Selecting the entry mode   265
6.7 Using free areas   267

Summary   267
Questions for discussion   267
References   268
Further reading   269
Case Study 6.1 Alcas Corporation   270
Case Study 6.2 Yang Toyland Pte, Limited   272
Case Study 6.3 Avon Products, Inc. (B)   277

7 Export entry modes   280

7.1 Introduction   280
7.2 Indirect export   282
7.3 Direct export   295
7.4 The Internet and e-commerce   309
7.5 Gray market exporting   313

Summary   315
Questions for discussion   316
References   317
Further reading   318
Case Study 7.1 HV Industri A/S   319
Case Study 7.2 Quint Winery   321
Case Study 7.3 Nestlé   323

8 Nonexport entry modes   326

8.1 Introduction   326
8.2 Alternative modes of entry   329
8.3 Manufacturing facilities   331
8.4 Assembly operations   341
8.5 Strategic alliances   344
8.6 Choosing between alternatives   357

Summary   358
Questions for discussion   358
References   359
Further reading   361
Case Study 8.1 Terralumen S.A.   362
Case Study 8.2 GG Farm Machinery Company   367
Case Study 8.3 VW in China   368
Case Study 8.4 Nu Skin Enterprises, Inc.   372

9 Product decisions 374

9.1 Introduction 374
9.2 Product policy 375
9.3 Product planning and development 377
9.4 Product mix decisions 391
9.5 Standardization vs adaptation 400
9.6 Packaging 407
9.7 Branding issues 410

Summary 415
Questions for discussion 416
References 417
Further reading 419
Case Study 9.1 Daewoo Corporation 420
Case Study 9.2 Supreme Foods of France 422
Case Study 9.3 BRL Hardy 426

10 Pricing decisions 431

10.1 Introduction 431
10.2 Determinants of an export price 433
10.3 Fundamental export pricing strategy 442
10.4 Relation of export to domestic price policies 447
10.5 Currency issues 453
10.6 The price quotation 454
10.7 Transfer pricing 460

Summary 464
Questions for discussion 464
References 465
Further reading 466
Case Study 10.1 RAP Engineering and Equipment Company 467
Case Study 10.2 The Capitool Company 467
Case Study 10.3 Strato Designs 470

11 Financing and methods of payment 472

11.1 Introduction 472
11.2 Export financing methods/terms of payment 473
11.3 Payment/financing procedures 479
11.4 Export credit insurance 497
11.5 Countertrade 498

Summary 502
Questions for discussion 504
References 504
Further reading 505
Case Study 11.1 Tainan Glass Manufacturing Company 506
Case Study 11.2 Arion Exports 507

12 Promotion and marketing communication 508

12.1	Introduction	508
12.2	Export marketing promotion and communication decisions	510
12.3	Alternative techniques of promotion	519
12.4	Promotional programs and strategy	538
12.5	Standardization or adaptation?	542
12.6	Advertising transference	549
12.7	Management issues	551

Summary 552
Questions for discussion 553
References 553
Further reading 555
Case Study 12.1 Adidas AG 556
Case Study 12.2 LEGO A/S 558
Case Study 12.3 Christa Clothing International 559
Case Study 12.4 Nove Ltd 563
Case Study 12.5 Eli's Cheesecake Company 565

13 The export order and physical distribution 570

13.1	Introduction	570
13.2	Handling the export order	574
13.3	Physical distribution	577
13.4	Structure of international physical distribution	584
13.5	A concluding comment	608

Questions for discussion 609
References 609
Further reading 610
Case Study 13.1 Jaguar Electronics, Inc. 611
Case Study 13.2 Megabox, Inc. 613
Case Study 13.3 Primex Marketing, Inc. 616

14 Organization of international marketing activities 619

14.1	Introduction	619
14.2	Main considerations of being organized internationally	620
14.3	Organizational structures	625

Summary 636
Questions for discussion 636
References 637
Further reading 637
Case Study 14.1 Asea Brown Boveri Limited 638
Case Study 14.2 Unilever 639

Glossary 647
Index 658

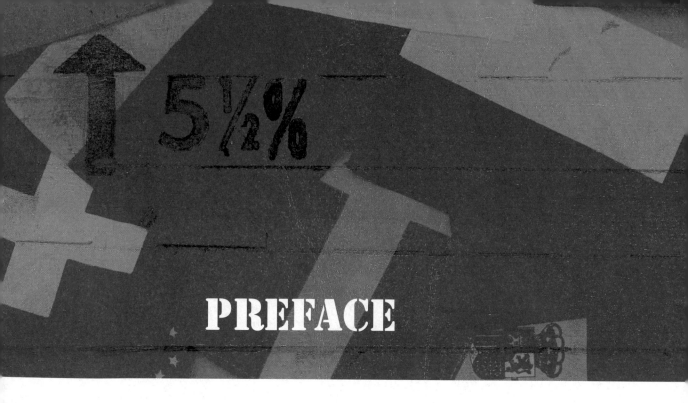

PREFACE

➡ Changing opportunities and challenges in international marketing

This major revision of *International Marketing and Export Management* has been made necessary by the continuing rapid changes in international marketing, and the increasing importance of international markets to companies of all sizes. While most of the factors that have driven change over the past decade are continuing, new opportunities and problems are emerging. There continue to be technological advances and lowered costs in communications, growth in e-commerce, improvements in transportation and logistics, lowering of barriers to trade and investment, growth of international strategic alliances, and increasing globalization of business. Now the internationalization of retail and other service-sector companies is escalating. The pace of innovation in products and services is increasing. The advances in communications are enabling people in some knowledge-based industries to remain in their home countries while performing their work for companies in other countries.

New challenges are arising. Marketing in deflationary economies is a new concern. The growth of China as an economic power and major exporter and its membership in the World Trade Organization is causing substantial changes in trade patterns. There are disruptions in trade flows, patterns and volumes being caused by concerns over terrorism, military action, and health hazards. There is increasing scrutiny of business behavior by customers, the public, and governmental agencies. This makes ethics, social responsibility, public policy, and company responses an essential concern.

Although many of these changes have created new problems that firms must address, all of these changes have opened new opportunities for businesses ranging from one-person operations to corporate giants. E-commerce has had a particularly strong impact in furthering the globalization of business, especially for smaller and medium-sized businesses. With a viable product or service, the smallest business can now find potential customers and means of distribution across the globe. The increased ease of entry has also resulted in new entrants creating increased competition in all marketplaces.

➡ New to the fifth edition

The changing opportunities and challenges in international marketing have led to increased emphasis on several topics in this fifth edition, including the following:

- the impact of the Internet, the World Wide Web, and e-commerce on the way the world does business and the way marketing is conducted;
- the increasing use of specialized software to assist in managing marketing functions, increasing efficiency in logistics, and coordinating and controlling enterprises;
- the impact of technological advances on international marketing;
- the growth of nontraditional exports;
- the changes resulting from China's rapid, export-led growth and from its entry into the World Trade Organization;
- the growing concerns with respect to social responsibility, and the costs of failure to meet societal expectations.

All of these factors are integrated through discussions in the text, exhibits, and cases.

➡ Aims and objectives

The basic aims and objectives of this fifth edition remain the same as those of the previous editions:

1. to provide a text in international marketing that will be as applicable and valuable for small and medium-sized enterprises as it is for large international corporations;
2. to provide an emphasis on exporting that is appropriate given its position as the major international activity of most small and medium-size businesses and its extensive use by virtually all global companies; and
3. to provide coverage of the nonexport modes of market penetration used by both expanding, smaller companies and corporate giants as a part of their overall international marketing strategy and channel management.

These emphases are a reflection of both the international marketing environment and the authors' view of exporting. In terms of the numbers of companies doing some type of international business, small and medium-sized companies are most prevalent. Most of these companies never diversify and grow to the size where being a multinational (or global) company is desirable or even feasible. The major activity of most small and medium-size companies is exporting. It is in this area that the transition from domestic to international marketing usually occurs, and in which knowledge of international dimensions of marketing is of critical importance. For the increasing number of enterprises that do expand into other methods of market entry, exporting typically remains a major activity. Even the largest multinational firms with global operations are involved in extensive exporting.

This book is focused primarily on the marketing decisions and management processes involved in developing export operations. The key procedural aspects and activities required in exporting, which the manager must know, are covered. Necessarily, a certain amount of descriptive material must be included. This is not, however, a 'how-to' treatment of technical details. As in previous editions, the emphasis remains on exporting as a marketing activity.

From a marketing perspective, the ideas underlying international market selection, information development, product development, and strategy, pricing, and promotion are often the same whether the mode of entry is export or nonexport. Thus export marketing and international marketing as a whole converge from both an educational and an operational/practice perspective.

As in previous editions, we approach the material from the perspective of the process by which a company – from any country – can creatively adapt to the international environments within which it can operate. To enhance the discussion of each topic, case studies are provided at the end of each chapter. We have added a number of new cases to provide coverage of emerging areas of opportunity and concern, such as e-commerce, changing strategies for market entry and development, and social responsibility. Some of the cases from the previous edition have been retained, and updated where appropriate. Most of the cases have been written expressly for this book. The experiences of the companies covered in the cases illustrate issues covered in the text and provide a vehicle for: (a) integrating material from throughout the book, and (b) illustrating key elements and concerns in making decisions.

This edition of *International Marketing and Export Management* has been rewritten and updated to cover the events and changes that have occurred since the fourth edition was published. Both increasing opportunities and challenges are addressed. While the exporting focus remains, more extensive material on other forms of entry and methods for evaluating market entry strategy are provided so that decisions can be made regarding economical and effective entry mode selection. As in previous editions, we continue to link the various topics to strategy.

➡ Target audience

This fifth edition of *International Marketing and Export Management*, is ideal for anybody wanting to acquire or increase his or her knowledge of international and export marketing. Ideal for undergraduate or postgraduate students who are taking courses in export management or international marketing, the book provides comprehensive coverage of the marketing mix, including all types of entry modes and channels.

In addition, the book is well suited for those in management education courses and other tertiary nonuniversity programs that cover export management and/or international marketing. The book also offers fresh insights for the export/international marketing practitioner that even the most experienced exporter might find useful.

➡ Authors' acknowledgements

The authors wish to thank the many people who have encouraged, or assisted in, the preparation of the book. In this short preface we cannot possibly acknowlege everyone by name. First and foremost however we are grateful to Juliet Dowd for making material available to us from the book *Introduction to Export Management*, written by Laurence Dowd and published by Eljay Press. We owe a great debt to the many scholars and business people whose articles, books, and other materials we have cited or quoted. Also, personal contacts with specialists in many of the subject areas have enhanced our knowledge.

We wish to acknowledge the following who were very helpful:

J. Andrzej Lubowski
J.H. Dethero
Dico de Jon, ABN AMRO Bank
James Fitzgerald, President, EFI Logistics
Daniel Scanlan, Bank of America
Steven Schafer, Fenestra Technologies Corporation

In particular, we want to thank Gordon Miracle from Michigan State University for making material available to us from work he did in the past with one of the authors of this book. We are also grateful to those who reviewed the fourth edition and previous editions of the book in part or in whole. We value their suggestions, even though we were not able to incorporate them all. Therefore any deficiencies remaining are ours. Reviewers include:

Michele Akoorie, University of Waikato
Jeremy Baker, London Guildhall University
Geraldine Cohen, Brunel University
Ofer Dekel, University of Derby
David Demick, University of Ulster
Nick Foster, Sheffield Hallam University
Collin Gilligan, Sheffield City Polytechnic
Raul de Gouva, University of New Mexico, Anderson School of Management
E.P. Hibbert, Durham University Business School
Valerie Isaac, University of Derby
Jürgen Reichel, University of Stockholm

Finally, the Marketing Publishing Team at Pearson Education, including Thomas Sigel, Senior Acquisitions Editor; Peter Hooper, Editorial Assistant; and Sarah Wild, Desk Editor; deserve our appreciation for their encouragement, support, and most of all, patience while we prepared the manuscript.

Gerald Albaum
Edwin Duerr
Jesper Strandskov
Summer 2004

ABOUT THE
AUTHORS

Gerald Albaum is Research Professor at the Robert O. Anderson Schools of Management at the University of New Mexico. In addition, he is Professor Emeritus of Marketing at the University of Oregon and a Senior Research Fellow at the IC^2 Institute, University of Texas at Austin. He received his PhD in 1962 from the University of Wisconsin-Madison and his MBA (1958) and BA (1954) from the University of Washington.

He is the author, or co-author, of 8 books, 9 monographs, more than 75 articles in refereed journals, 30 papers in refereed conference proceedings, 20 papers in other publications, and 14 book and software reviews published in the *Journal of Marketing Research*. His writings deal with issues in research methods, international marketing activities, cross-cultural/national research, and retailing (especially direct selling). Many of his studies are cross-cultural/national in nature.

Dr Albaum has presented seminars for such Danish companies as Danfoss, GfK Research, Novo Nordisk, and LEGO. He has also made presentations before industry groups such as the Northern Jutland Export Council in Denmark and the Hong Kong Institute of Marketing. He has given seminars for the Hong Kong Housing Authority and for Air China in the People's Republic of China.

Edwin Duerr is Professor Emeritus of International Business at San Francisco State University, where he has served as Department Head of International Business, Director of Graduate Studies in the College of Business, and Chairman of the Board of Directors of the SFSU Research Foundation. He has been a Visiting Professor at universities in Denmark, Germany, Japan, The Netherlands, and Sweden.

Dr Duerr obtained his BS in Engineering at the Illinois Institute of Technology. After working for several years in technical and management positions in multinational companies, and establishing (and later selling) a successful importing company, he received his PhD in Business Administration from the University of California, Berkeley.

He has had extensive consulting experience in Brazil, Japan, Spain, and the United States. He has written widely on comparative management, productivity improvement, and international marketing, and is a frequent speaker to business and educational groups in Europe, the United States, and Japan.

Jesper Strandskov is Professor of International Business at the Aarhus School of Business, and currently Head of the Department of Management and International Business. He has been a Visiting Professor at the Royal Institute of Technology, Melbourne, Australia and the University of Hawaii at Manoa, USA.

Dr Strandskov holds an MSc (Economics) from the University of Copenhagen and the Dr.merc. degree in Business Administration from the Aarhus School of Business. He has published 8 books and more than 100 journal articles and book chapters, and is the recipient of several academic awards. He is a consultant as well as a member of the Board of Directors in several Danish companies and institutions, with special emphasis on strategy and internationalization.

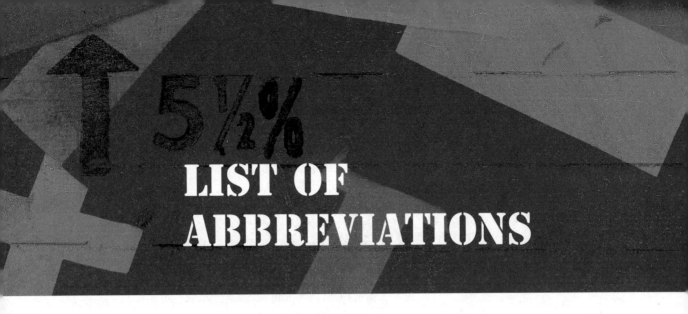

LIST OF ABBREVIATIONS

(excludes company names; *these are not spelt out in the text)

*ABS	antilocking brake system
AFTA	ASEAN Free Trade Area
AID	[US] Agency for International Development
ANZSCEP	Australia, New Zealand, Singapore Closer Economic Partnership
ASEAN	Association of Southeast Nations
ATM	automated teller machine
Austrade	Australian Trade Commission
B2B	business to business
B2C	business to consumer
BA	business area
BEMs	big emerging markets
BERI	Business Environment Risk Index
B/Ls	bills of lading
BPI	*Business Periodicals Index*
CACM	Central American Common Market
C&F	cost and freight
CalPERS	California Public Employees Employment System
CalSTRS	California State Teachers Retirement System
CARICOM	Caribbean Community and Common Market
CATI	computer-assisted telephone interviewing
*CATV	Cable Television
CCC	[US] Commodity Credit Corporation
CD	compact disk
*CD-ROM	compact disk read-only memory
CE	chief executive
*CEO	chief executive officer
CEPA	Closer Economic Partnership Arrangement [between Hong Kong and China]
CER	Closer Economic Relations [between Australia and New Zealand]
CFO	chief financial officer
CIF	cost, insurance and freight
CL	container loads
CMA	German Agricultural Marketing Board
COD	cash on delivery
COFACE	Compagnie Française d'Assurance pour le Commerce Extérieur
COMECON	Council for Mutual Economic Assistance
CPM	cost per thousand (*mille*)
CSM	customer satisfaction management

CTCs	commodity trading companies
D/A	documents against acceptance
*DDP	delivered duty paid
*DDU	delivered duty unpaid
*DEQ	delivered ex quay
DJVs	domestic joint ventures
D/P	documents against payment
*DVD	digital video disc
EC	electronic assemblies
ECGD	[UK] Export Credits Guarantee Department
ECIC	[Hong Kong's] Export Credit Insurance Corporation
EDI systems	electronic data interchange systems
EEA	European Economic Association
EFIC	[Australia's] Export Finance and Insurance Corporation
EFTA	European Free Trade Area
EJV	equity joint venture
EMC	export management company
EMDG	[Austrade's] Export Market Development Grant scheme
EMS	environmental management system
EMU	European Monetary Union
EPZs	export processing zones
ERP	enterprise resource planning
ETCs	export trading companies
EU	European Union
Eximbank	[United States] Export–Import Bank
EXW	ex works
FAS	free alongside
FCA	free carrier
FDA	[US] Food and Drugs Administration
FDI	foreign direct investment
FMGs	federated export marketing groups
FOB	free on board
FPA	free of particular average
FPA-AC	free of particular average American conditions
FPA-EC	free of particular average English conditions
FSCs	foreign sales corporations
FTAA	Free Trade Area of the Americas
FTZ	free trade zone
*GATT	General Agreement on Tariffs and Trade
GMO	genetically modified
GNI	gross national income
GNP	gross national product
GTCs	general trading companies
IATA	International Air Transport Association
IBRD	International Bank for Reconstruction and Development
ICAC	[Hong Kong's] Independent Commission Against Corruption
ICC	International Chamber of Commerce
ICFs	insulating cement forms
IJV	international joint venture
IMF	International Monetary Fund
*INCOTERMS	trade terms of the International Chamber of Commerce
IPO	Initial Public Offering
*IP	Internet provider
*ISIC	International Standard Industrial Classification of All Economic Goods
ISO	International Standards Organization
ISPs	Internet service providers

IT	information technology
JAG	[Australia's] Joint Action Group
JETRO	Japan External Trade Organization
JIT	just in time
L/C	letter of credit
LCL	less than container load
LNG	liquefied natural gas
LOV	List of Values
MA	mechanical assemblies
MATV	Master Antenna Television
MENA	Middle East and North African region
MFN	Most Favored Nation
MII	[China's] Ministry of Information Industry
MNCs	multinational corporations
MNEs	multinational enterprises
NAFTA	North American Free Trade Agreement
NICs	newly industrialized countries
NVOCCs	non-vessel operating common carriers
OBUs	[Avon's] Operating Business Units
OECD	Organization for Economic Cooperation and Development
OEMs	original equipment manufacturers
OLAP	Online Analytical Processing
*OPEC	Organization of Petroleum Exporting Countries
PAIS	Public Affairs Information Service
*PC	personal computer
PCT	Patent Co-operation Treaty
PLC	product life cycle
POP	point of purchase
POS	point of sale
PRC	People's Republic of China
PROEXPO	[Colombian] Government Trade Bureau
PSE	Personal Selling Ethics Scale
*R&D	research and development
RFID	radio frequency identifiction
RIP	Regulation of Investigatory Powers (Act)
*ROI	return on investment
RTA	ready-to-assemble
RTBs	regional trading blocs
RvA	Dutch Council for Accreditation
SAR	Special Administrative Region
SARS	severe acute respiratory syndrome
SBU	Strategic Business Unit
*SDR	Special Drawing Rights
*SITC	Standard Industrial Trade Classification
*SKUs	Stock Keeping Unit
SMEs	small and medium-sized enterprises
SRC	self-reference criterion
SUV	sports utility vehicle
SWIFT	Society for Worldwide Intra-bank Transfers
*SWOT	strengths, weaknesses, opportunities, threats
TGW	Things Gone Wrong
TPOs	[public sector] trade promotion organizations
TQM	total quality management
TRIPS Agreement	Agreement on Trade-related aspects of Intellectual Property
UNCTAD	United Nations Conference on Trade and Development
UNIDO	United Nations Industrial Development Organization
URL	uniform resource locator

VALS	Values and Life Styles
VAT	value added tax
VCR	video cassette recorder
VERs	voluntary export restraints
VRA	voluntary restraint agreement
WAPs	wireless application protocols
WFOE	wholly foreign-owned enterprise
WIPO	[UN] World Intellectual Property Organization
WTO	World Trade Organization
WWW	World Wide Web

GUIDED TOUR

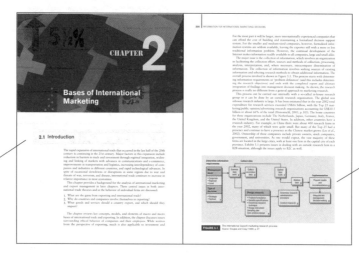

Each chapter opens with an **Introduction** which outlines the main themes and issues explored in the chapter.

Figures and Tables illustrate key points, concepts and processes visually to reinforce learning.

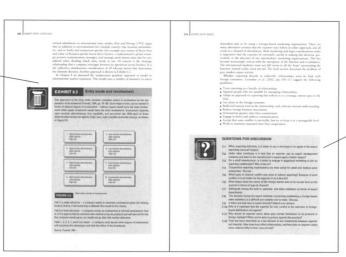

Exhibits elaborate and expand on specific topics and issues which are discussed within the text, often showcasing real-life examples from export management.

Questions for discussion at the end of every chapter enable students to test their understanding and help track progress.

Case studies at the end of each chapter feature some well-known international companies. They help to consolidate the major themes by encouraging the student to apply what they have learnt to real-life marketing and export scenarios.

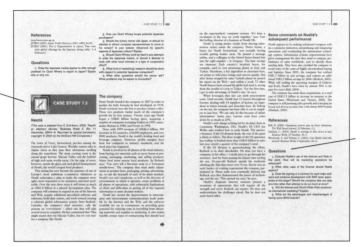

Additional **Case Questions** help test understanding.

Each chapter is supported by a list of **References** and additional suggested **Further Reading**, directing readers to further information sources.

A comprehensive **Glossary** at the end of the book defines the key terms related to international marketing and export management.

Companion Website and Instructor Resources
Visit the website at **www.pearsoned.co.uk/albaum**

For lecturers
- Complete, downloadable Instructor's Manual
- PowerPoint slides that can be downloaded and used as OHTs

PUBLISHER'S ACKNOWLEDGEMENTS

We are grateful to the following for permission to reproduce copyright materials:

Figure 1.1 adapted from *Internationalization of Finnish Firms and their Response to Global Challenges*, UNU/WIDER Research for Action 18. Helsinki. December. (Luostarinen, R. 1994); Exhibit 1.5 from *Marketing Management: Millenium Edition*, 10th edition, © 2000. (Kotler, P. 2000). Reprinted by permission of Pearson Education, Inc. Upper Saddle River, NJ; Table 1.1 adapted from 'Reducing the Impact of Barriers to Exporting: A Managerial Perspective' from *Journal of International Marketing*, 3(4), published by the American Marketing Association, (Shoham, A. and Albaum, G. 1995); Figure 2.2 Reprinted with permission from 'The Commitment Trust Theory of Relationship Marketing', *Journal of Marketing*, July 1994, 58, p. 21, published by the American Marketing Association, (Morgan, R.M. and Hunt, S.D. 1994); Figure 3.1 from 'Getting a leg up in China', *Business 2.0*, Jan/Feb, 69-70 (Caulfield, B. and Shi, T. 2004) © 2004 XPLANATiONS™ by Xplane.com®. XPLANATiONs are visual maps and stories that make complex business issues easier to understand. For more information visit XPLANE at www.xplane.com or call 1/800/750-6467; Tables 3.1 and 3.2 from World Bank website, International Bank for Reconstruction and Development, © The World Bank; Exhibit 3.1 reprinted with permission of The Conference Board, *Adapting Products for Export*, (Yorio, V. 1978); Table 3.6 and Exhibit 6.3 from *Experiencing International Business and Management*, 2nd edition, © 1994 (Punnett, B.J. 1994). Reprinted with permission of South-Western, a division of Thomson Learning: www.thomsonrights.com. Fax 800 730-2215; Exhibit 4.4 from 'Global Segments from Strivers to Creatives', *Marketing News*, 30(15), 20 July 1995, published by the American Marketing Association, (Miller 1995); Table 4.3 from 'Country and Method of Entry Selection for International Expansion' in *Dimensions of International Business*, No. 11, (Papadopoulos, N. and Jansen, D. 1994), with permission from N. Papadopoulos; Figures 4.2 and 5.1 from *International Marketing Research*, p.111 and p. 27 (Douglas, S.P. and Craig, C.S. 1983), published by Prentice Hall, Pearson Education Ltd., with permission from S. Douglas; Figures 4.3 and 8.2 from *Entry Strategies for International Markets*, 2nd edition, p. 56 and p. 155 © Copyright © 1994 John Wiley & Sons, Inc (Root, F.R. 1994). This material is used by permission of John Wiley & Sons, Inc; Figure 4.6 from 'Multinational Strategic Portfolios', *MSU Business Topics*, (Harrell and Kiefer 1981). Reprinted by permission of Eli Broad Graduate School of Business, Michigan State University; Table 5.3 from 'Manager's Guide to Forecasting', in *Harvard Business Review*, Jan–Feb 1986, p. 111 (Georgoff and Murdick 1986), © Copyright 1986 Harvard Business School Publishing Corporation, all rights reserved; Exhibit 5.4 and Figure 5.3 adapted from 'The value of practical ignorance in cultural research' from *Quirk's Marketing Research Review*, April, (Sack, M. C. 2000), reprinted with permission from the author; Table 5.5 from *Global Marketing Management*, 6th edition, © Copyright 1999, (Keegan, Warren J. 1999). Reprinted by permission of Pearson Education, Inc. Upper Saddle River, NJ; Exhibit 6.1 *from Blunders in International Business*, 3rd edition, Blackwell Publishers (Ricks, D. 1999); Figure 6.5b Dennis MacDonald/Alamy; Table 7.1 adapted from 'Toward a conceptualization of export trading companies in world markets' from *Advances in International Marketing*, Vol. 2, © Copyright 1987, reprinted with permission from Elsevier Science (Amine, L. 1987); Figure 7.2 reprinted with permission of The Conference Board from *Policies and Problems in Piggyback Marketing*, (Duerr, M.G. and Greene, J. 1969); Figure 7.3 from 'The Gray Market Threat to International Marketing Strategies' from *Marketing Science Institute Report*, No. 90–116, Marketing Science Institute (Bucklin, L.P. 1990); Figure 8.1 from *Strategies for Asia Pacific*, Palgrave Macmillan Ltd and NYU Press, (Lasserre and Schutte 1995); Figure 8.4 from 'Rupert's World', *Business Week*, 19 January, reprinted with permissions from McGraw Hill Companies, (Tang *et al.* 2004); Figure 8.5 from 'Building Transnational Alliances to Create Competitive Advantage', from *Long Range Planning*, Vol. 25, reprinted with permission from Elsevier Science (Gugler 1992); Figure 9.3 from 'International Product Positioning', *Journal of International Business Studies*, Vol. 16, No. 3, (J. Johansson and H. Thorelli 1985), used with permission of Journal of International Business Studies; Figure 9.4 adapted from a paper entitled 'Product Phasing: the Synchronous Deletion and Replacement of Products', with permission from the author, Professor J. Saunders; Table 9.3 from 'Global Products: when do they make sense?', *Proceedings*, published by the Academy of International Business (B. Rosen 1986); Figures 9.11 and 9.12 from *Trademarks*, (1995), courtesy of the LEGO Group; Exhibit 10.1 adapted from 'Cost transparency; The Net's real threat to prices and brands' in *Harvard Business Review*, March–April 2001 (Sinha, I. 2001) © Copyright 2000 by the Harvard Business School Publishing Corporation, all rights reserved; Table 10.3 from *International Dimensions of Marketing*, 2nd edition, © Copyright 1988 (V. Terpstra 1988). Reprinted with permission of South-Western, a division of Thomson Learning: www.thomsonrights.com. Fax 800 730–2215; Figure 11.2, An application for irrevocable letter of credit, reproduced with permission of ABN AMRO Bank, N.V.; Figure 11.3 adapted from *International Banking Services*, (Seafirst Bank 1988); Figures 11.4, 11.5, 11.6, 11.8 and 11.9, reproductions of Bank of America documents, reprinted with permission of Bank of America; Table 11.2 adapted from *Journal of Global Marketing*, Haworth Press (D. Paun and G. Albaum 1993); Table 12.1 adapted from *Elements of Export Marketing and Management*, 2nd edition, Thomson Publishing, (A. Branch 1990); Exhibit 12.1 adapted from 'Managing images in different cultures: a cross-national study of color meanings and preference' in *Journal of International Marketing*, 8 (4), reprinted with permission of American Marketing Association (Madden, T. J. et al. 2000); Table 12.3 from 'Blunders in International Marketing: fact of fiction?', in *Long Range Planning*, 17(1), © Copyright 1984 (D. A. Ricks and V. Mahajan 1984), with kind permission from Elsevier Science Ltd, The Boulevard, Langford Lane, Kidlington OX5 1GB, UK; Figure 12.4 from *Fair Play* (1995), courtesy of the LEGO Group; Exhibit 13.2 adapted from 'ACES update' and 'Moving into the 21st century', *Via International*, 44(11), 1992, the Port Authority of NY and NJ; Exhibit 13.4 adapted from 'Foreign trade advantage: an innovative way to trim costs', *Via Port of NY–NJ*, 43(1), 1991, the Port Authority of NY and NJ; Figure 13.8 Ocean/combined transport bill of lading, reproduced with permission of Unz & New Providence, NJ 07974.

Case study 1.4, reprinted with permission from Professor Joel Nicholson, Professor Nicholas Gurney and Mitsuko Duerr; Case study 3.1 reprinted with permission from Mitsuko Duerr; Case study 4.1 reprinted with permission from Sharen Kindel; Case study 5.3 reprinted with permission from Dr Michael F. Alioto; Case study 6.1 reprinted with permission from Mark George (President of CUTCO International, Inc.); Case study 6.2 reprinted with permission from Hellmut Schütte; Case study 7.2 reprinted with permission from Dr Neil Evans; Case study 7.3 reprinted with permission from McGraw Hill Companies; Case study 8.1 and Northeastern University logo reprinted with permission from Professor Nicholas Athanassiou; Case study 8.3 reprinted with permission from Min Zhao; Case study 9.1 reprinted with permission from Mitsuko Duerr; Case study 9.2 reprinted with permission from Professor Roger Kerin; Case study 9.3 reprinted with permission from Professor Richard Fletcher, Head, School of Marketing and International Business, University of Western Sydney and *Australasian Marketing Journal*; Case study 10.2 reprinted with permission from Gordon E. Miracle, © Copyright Gordon E. Miracle, Michigan State University; Case study 11.1 reprinted with permission from Mitsuko Duerr; Case study 12.1 reprinted with permission from Sharen Kindel; Case study 12.2 reprinted with permission from Copenhagen Business School Press, Svend Hollenson and Marcus J. Schmidt; Case study 12.3 reprinted with permission from Gordon Miracle; Case study 12.5 reprinted with permission from Marc S. Schulman (President of The Eli's Cheesecake Company); Case study 13.2 reprinted with permission from David Ronen; Case study 13.3 reprinted with permission from Mr Peter J. U. Reich (President of Primex Marketing, Inc.); Case study 14.2 reprinted with permission from Phillippe Lasserre.

In some instances we have been unable to trace the owners of copyright material, and we would appreciate any information that would enable us to do so.

CHAPTER 1

International Marketing and Exporting

1.1 Introduction

This chapter provides an introduction to international marketing, and covers the following:

- the reasons for the growing importance of international marketing to companies of all sizes
- an overview of the book's objectives, orientation and emphases;
- the nature of international marketing;
- export marketing planning and strategy;
- a discussion of the effects of the Internet, World Wide Web, and e-commerce on the way the world does business and how marketing is conducted;
- the impact of technology on international marketing;
- entrepreneurial approaches to international marketing;
- the growth of non-traditional exports;
- an overview of the book.

Four cases are provided at the end of the chapter. Two involve basic questions faced by small businesses considering exporting. The third case, eBay, shows how a combination of new technology and entrepreneurship created a new type of international marketplace. The fourth case, DaimlerChrysler AG, introduces a number of issues discussed more fully in subsequent chapters of the book, including reasons for exporting, market selection and entry modes, competition, and organization of international operations.

1.1.1 The growing importance of international marketing

In the 21st century, international marketing is proving to be of ever-increasing importance to companies of all sizes, to their customers, and to national economies. Worldwide, most companies are now selling to, using materials or equipment from, or competing with products from other nations. For many companies, small as well as large, international sales provide additional profits and are all that enable some companies to make any profits at all. Consumers worldwide are familiar with international brands and additionally are using locally produced goods that include materials or components supplied from abroad. National and regional economic health and growth have become increasingly dependent upon export sales as an engine of growth and as a source of the foreign exchange necessary for the import of the goods and services.

The increasing importance of international markets over the past 20 years has been the result of a number of interrelated factors:

- There has been a continuing lowering of barriers to trade and investment, through multilateral agreements and increasing regional integration. This has enabled more companies economically to expand exports and to establish production and sales operations overseas.
- Improvements in transportation and logistics have further lowered the costs of exporting and importing.
- Entrepreneurial innovations and technological improvements have resulted in the development of new goods and services with international appeal.
- Major advances in communications and the emergence of e-commerce have made possible the widening and linking of markets.
- Companies and industries in different countries have become increasingly linked and interdependent with respect to materials, parts, and business operations.
- Capital markets have become more international as regulation has decreased and cross-national linkages have increased.
- Excess capacity exists in a wide range of industries in many countries. This is partly a result of increased efficiency in production in new and existing facilities. It has also been created as national or local producers have expanded to achieve economies of scale, to meet peaks in demand, to market to new areas, to employ an oversupply of labor, or for other reasons. This has added to the pressures to increase international marketing and exporting efforts.
- Overall, world trade has continued to expand more rapidly than world gross national product, thus contributing further to the importance of international markets.

The international marketplace has become increasingly turbulent at the same time as globalization has progressed. China has emerged as a world-class manufacturing center, with low production costs and rapidly increasing industrial capabilities. Both trade and investment were accelerated when it joined the World Trade Organization in 2001. Its increasing exports are providing new and lower-cost competition for exporters in other nations, and are also creating additional competition for domestic manufacturers in countries throughout the world. Even small, local producers of handicrafts in Mexico have found that textiles made in China are replacing some of their products in local markets, while larger manufacturers are losing markets in the United States and elsewhere. At the same time, consumers in many countries are benefiting from lower prices. Deflation has occurred in Japan, China, and some other nations.

Diseases, terrorism, internal unrest in some countries, wars and threats of wars have all disrupted established trade patterns and/or raised costs. The threat from severe acute respiratory syndrome (SARS) reduced tourism, participation in trade fairs (particularly in China), and some exports. Bovine spongiform encephalopathy (mad cow disease) and variant forms of the disease led to the slaughter of hundreds of thousands of cows and more than 100 people died. It also resulted in embargoes on beef exports from some countries, reduced sales from other producers, and caused shortages in some traditional importing countries. In Japan, which banned US beef imports, restaurant chains specializing in beef and rice dishes were hard hit. Recurring avian flu (bird flu) outbreaks have had similar effects on importers, exporters, individual companies, and consumers. A recent epidemic resulted in the slaughter of over 80 million birds. Japan's suspension of poultry imports from Thailand and China opened up additional opportunities for producers in the Philippines and Brazil. In 2004 Kentucky Fried Chicken, the international fast food chain, took fried chicken off its menu in China and Viet Nam, replacing it with fish. The destruction of the World Trade Center in New York, bombings by terrorists in Bali, and wars and violence in other areas resulted in severe drops in air travel and tourism, which together account for over 10% of world GDP. A number of airlines and many tourist-related businesses had large losses, with some going bankrupt.

At the same time, entrepreneurial innovations and technological changes have resulted in the development of new products and services. Some of these have met existing market needs while others have created new demands. A very few of the many possible examples of the latter include the development of: new equipment and medicines to combat disease; new and improved electronic games and products for home entertainment centers; more capable computers; and new software that enables organizations to increase the efficiency and effectiveness of both their internal operations and their interactions with other organizations. All of these have served to increase overall levels of national and international economic activity.

The innovations and changes have created new opportunities for some individuals and companies, while creating challenges and threats to other companies. The lowered barriers to trade have increased the ability of producers of a wide range of items, from food products to appliances to industrial supplies and parts, to expand from regional or national markets to selling internationally. This has concurrently meant that producers formerly serving a local market protected by formal or informal barriers to trade are or will be exposed to new competition.

For many companies, the changing environment combines elements of both new products and services that add to their opportunities, and additional competition in existing and substitute products and services. Whatever the combination encountered, the importance of international marketing opportunities and threats is increasing.

The internationalization occurring may thus be seen as resulting from a combination of factors in the home country market, the (prospective) host country market, the global environment, and characteristics of individual firms. A small home country market and/or competition from outside tend to encourage companies to consider exporting or entering foreign markets in some other way, a sort of domestic push toward internationalization. Large and open host country (foreign) markets provide opportunities that encourage outsiders to enter, a sort of international pull. The global changes discussed above, such as improved communications and logistics, encourage exporting. Company specific factors, such as competitive advantage and interest in international activities, also encourage internationalization.

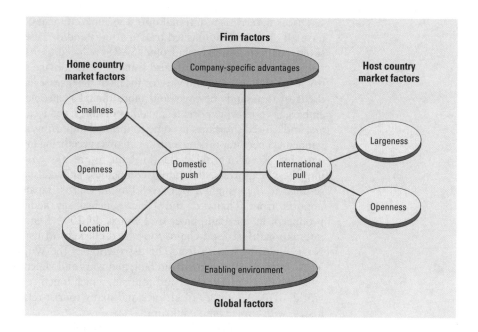

FIGURE 1.1

Factors explaining
internationalization
Source: adapted from
Luostarinen, 1994, p. 7

Figure 1.1 shows how the forces of firm factors, home country market factors, host country factors, and global factors explain the movement toward increasing internationalization.

1.1.2 Orientation of the book

This book is designed to provide a solid introduction to *international marketing*, covering all types of international marketing entry modes and activities, but with an additional emphasis on *export management*. The approach has been used in order to make the text as applicable and valuable for small and medium-sized companies as it is for large international or global corporations. Many of the smaller enterprises, which comprise most of the firms involved in international business, use exporting as their foreign market entry mode. All of the international giants do extensive exporting and importing.

The knowledge and understanding required for successful exporting provides a valuable foundation for undertaking any of the modes of market entry. Competence in domestic marketing, by itself, is a necessary (but not sufficient) condition for success in exporting and other modes of international marketing. Marketing across national boundaries, in any entry mode, requires interacting effectively with those in other cultures whose tastes, values, practices, economies, laws, and administrative systems may differ from your own. This involves a distinctive set of competencies that must be acquired. Thus the knowledge, examples, and cases in this book are applicable for all entry modes.

In addition to knowledge, competence, and experience in foreign markets, success also requires the proper attitude and commitment by company management. Kenneth Butterworth, chairman of Loctite Corporation, has stated that 'the biggest non-tariff barrier for Americans in the world is the attitude of the CEO.'

1.2 The nature of international marketing

1.2.1 Definition

The basic definition of international marketing is simple: *international marketing is the marketing of goods, services, and information across political boundaries.* Thus it includes the same elements as domestic marketing: *planning, promoting, distributing, pricing, and support of the goods, services, and information to be provided to intermediate and ultimate consumers.*

The process of international marketing, however, is typically much more complex, and interesting, than domestic marketing. The international marketer must deal with a number of key differences in foreign environments as compared to domestic environments. These may include differences in consumer tastes and needs, economic levels, market structures, ways of doing business, laws and regulations, and many other factors to be discussed in this book. Any one of these can make a company's domestic approach to marketing ineffective, counterproductive, and/or a violation of local law in the foreign market. Together, these differences require a careful and well-planned approach to entering and expanding in the international marketplace. There are facilitating organizations that can provide assistance in the process, but the marketing manager has the responsibility for developing an effective and efficient approach to marketing in other nations. This requires an understanding of all of the differences that must be accommodated.

The business activities that must be carried out in marketing, and adjusted to accommodate differences in the international market, include the following:

- the analysis of markets and potential markets;
- the planning and development of products and services that consumers want, clearly identified in a suitable package;
- the distribution of products through channels that provide the services or conveniences demanded by purchasers;
- the promotion of products and services – including advertising and personnel selling – to inform and educate consumers about those products and services, or persuade consumers to try new, improved, or different ways of satisfying their wants and needs;
- the setting of prices that reflect both a reasonable value (or utility) of products or services to the consumers, as well as a satisfactory profit or return on investment;
- the technical and non-technical support given to customers – both before and after a sale is made – to ensure their satisfaction, and thus pave the way for possible future sales that are necessary for company survival, growth, and perpetuation.

1.2.2 Internationalization and the global marketer

Internationalization may be thought of as: (1) a process, (2) an end result, and/or (3) a way of thinking. A firm becomes increasingly internationalized as it becomes more involved in and committed to serving markets outside of its home country. This may be a planned and orderly process, or arise from perceived new opportunities or threats.

For the international marketer, internationalization is most effective when developed as a carefully planned process for increasing penetration of international markets. In entering target markets, companies have traditionally begun with exporting, later developed a sales subsidiary abroad, and finally developed production facilities abroad. Licensing may be used as an initial entry strategy for some companies, and at later stages for others. Strategic alliances may be formed. Whatever the approaches used they should be carefully thought out, with advantages and disadvantages carefully analyzed, before implementation.

The terms international, multinational, and global are sometimes used interchangeably when referring to international operations in general or international marketing specifically. Even though it may seem to be mainly a matter of semantics, it is useful to distinguish between these terms since they imply differences in approaches to marketing.

International marketing refers to any marketing activity that is carried out across national boundaries. Thus it could include anything from exporting one product to one other country in response to an order, to a major effort to market a number of products to many countries. It thus provides an appropriate title for a book such as this one that addresses a wide variety of marketing objectives and approaches.

The term multinational marketing came into use to describe the approach used by companies with a strong commitment to international marketing. Additionally, in the minds of some, it became associated with companies that treated each foreign market as separate and distinct, developing differentiated products and marketing strategies specifically for each of the markets.

The term global marketing originally came into use as a result of Theodore Levitt's discussion of the move toward global corporations that would operate as if the entire world, or a major region of the world, were a single entity (Levitt, 1986, ch. 2). Such companies would sell the same product(s) in the same way everywhere. He noted that people all over the world were becoming more alike in their tastes. He argued that they would accept the same standardized products, in many cases, if the prices were low and the quality good. The economies of scale in producing and marketing a product in the same way worldwide would produce substantially lower costs, and thus allow lower prices that would overcome remaining differences in tastes. For some products, such as Coca-Cola, Mercedes-Benz automobiles (from DaimlerChrysler), and McDonald's fast food (in most of its markets), this appears to be substantially the case.

However, three factors have served to limit the general applicability of this approach. First, very significant differences in consumer demands and in marketing requirements exist from country to country for many products. Second, as incomes rise, many consumers tend to become less price sensitive and willing to pay more to get products and services that meet their specific individual needs. Third, a move toward more flexible production systems in some industries has lowered (though failed to eliminate) the cost advantage of very large-scale production.

Thus the term multinational came to be associated with adjusting products and practices in each country, with attendant relatively high costs. The term global implied standardized products and practices, with relatively lower costs. A more complete explanation of the assumptions underlying these two paradigms, and the implications for international marketing, is given in Hampton and Buske (1987).

In the first decade of the 21st century a combination approach of 'think globally, act locally' appears to be most effective for most companies. The global strategy is based on location-specific and competitive advantages (Roth and Morrison, 1994), operating without regard for national boundaries except as they affect the desirability of one course of action over another. However, adjustments are made as required to meet local requirements. Even companies noted for their overall global approaches do adjust their products and marketing methods to meet local requirements. At the same time, they strive to retain the distinctive competencies that provide competitive advantage.

Consumer products giant Procter & Gamble relies on continuing development and introduction of superior products, heavy advertising, and use of efficient distribution systems in all of its markets. But it adjusts product formulations, names, and packaging to meet local requirements. The General Manager of Procter and Gamble China has observed that 'The strategy that is guaranteed to fail in China is a one-size-fits-all approach' (Fowler, 2004). Even McDonald's fast food chain, long considered to have a global approach because of its use of similar production methods, menus, and store designs everywhere, has found that significant variations in presentation are the key to more rapid growth and improved profits in France. While continuing its efficient and economical approach to food preparation, it has changed store ambience, introducing chic interiors, music videos, and a fancier menu. Dennis Hennequin, the chief executive in the French unit, has stated 'We are upgrading the experience, making McDonald's a destination restaurant' (Matlack and Gogoi, 2003).

A long-range objective, for those companies that are large enough or have other characteristics that allow it, is to develop a global view in which they treat the whole world as their market. With this global view they increasingly move toward the following:

- evaluating and entering markets worldwide based on their potential both as individual markets and as a part of a worldwide strategy;
- procuring capital and investing funds on a worldwide basis according to costs and opportunities;
- purchasing raw materials, components, equipment, and supplies from sources worldwide;
- staffing their organizations with the managers and employees best suited to carry out their operations without regard to national origin.

1.2.3 Degree of internationalization

While a multinational or global approach is a desirable objective for some companies, most have relatively lower levels of international activities. Exhibit 1.1 lists some of the indicators that may show the level of internationalization of a particular firm. Measuring the degree of internationalization of a firm can be useful in encouraging management to think about how international the company is now, how international the company can be, and how international the company wants to be. This is the first step in determining what changes in internationalization strategy are appropriate for the company.

EXHIBIT 1.1	**The degree of internationalization of a firm**

There are some people who believe that it is important to be able to measure the degree of internationalization of a firm. A truly valid measure seems to have eluded those interested. Over the years, attempts have been made to infer degree of internationalization by looking at the evolution, structure, and process of relationships among a firm's demographic, strategic, market, organizational, product, and attitudinal characteristics of international expansion. Further, measures have included internationalization of the percentage of sales volume, production, profits, and assets. One attempt at measurement is provided by Sullivan (1994) who has developed a composite measure based on the following:

■ foreign sales as a percentage of total sales;
■ foreign assets as a percentage of total assets;
■ overseas subsidiaries as a percentage of total subsidiaries;
■ physical dispersion of international operations;
■ top managers' international experience.

Sullivan (1994, p. 336) believes that his measure meets statistical requirements and that the measure is an improvement over other measures. However, what is not indicated is the operational value of such a measure to a company.

A much more useful approach is that provided by Piercy (1982) who has developed a checklist to help a company assess the following:

■ how international it is now;
■ how international it can be;
■ how international it wants to be.

The end result is a so-called gap analysis covering the difference between where the company is now and where it wants to be.

There are a number of strategies for market entry and development available to a company that seeks to internationalize. These include exporting, establishing a sales subsidiary abroad, licensing, and establishing a production subsidiary abroad. Joint ventures may be used in establishing sales subsidiaries and production facilities. Though an approach beginning with exporting, progressing to opening a sales subsidiary, and finally establishing a production facility is common, any given company may start with any of the entry strategies and go on to other stages. Some firms use different strategies for different markets, only exporting or licensing to some smaller markets while establishing sales subsidiaries and/or production facilities in larger markets.

Small and medium-sized companies often go about internationalizing operations in a different manner and to a different extent than larger companies. Large companies may introduce their products/services globally, entering a number of markets quickly. Small and medium-sized companies are more likely to first enter markets that are close geographically and/or have the same language (such as the United Kingdom and the United States). Canada has been an appealing market for many first-time exporters in the United States because of its similar business culture, few language barriers in most provinces, and NAFTA (North American Free Trade Area) (Barrett, 1995, p. 99). When Mexico joined NAFTA, trade between Mexico and the United States increased rapidly based on the reduced trade barriers, their common border, and different comparative advantages in a number of products.

Companies that have success in nearby markets may then move on to more distant markets in Europe, the Asia/Pacific area, other Latin American countries, or elsewhere.

There are some small companies, and divisions of large companies, that become global because they are niche marketers that must sell worldwide in order to have an adequate market, or as a way of keeping ahead of imitative competitors. The $320,000 Phantom sedan, which was introduced in 2003, is distinguished by its high level of comfort, cost and exclusivity. In order to sell the 1000 cars that can be produced annually at the Rolls-Royce factory in Goodwood, England, the vehicle must be sold throughout the world to celebrities, wealthy business people, and others who are very rich (Taylor, 2004).

As companies expand their sales internationally, they may find it necessary to make purchases abroad and/or to make investments in overseas production facilities because of transport and/or production costs. While such actions are for sourcing rather than market entry, they may well be necessary for retaining existing overseas markets or entering additional ones.

1.2.4 International marketing management

International marketing management is faced with three basic decisions. The first is whether to engage in international marketing activities at all. Second, if a company decides that it wants to do business in international markets, then a decision has to be made concerning what specific individual markets are to be served. Finally, the company must determine how it is going to serve these markets – i.e., what method or system should be used to get product(s) into the hands of the consumers in foreign countries. This last decision can be called the basic marketing mix decision, and includes planning and strategy with regard to market entry, products, promotion, channels of distribution, and price.

International marketing management includes the management of marketing activities for products that cross the political boundaries of sovereign states. It also includes marketing activities of firms that produce and sell within a given foreign nation if (1) the firm is a part of an organization or enterprise that operates in other countries and (2) there is some degree of influence, guidance, direction, or control of such marketing activities from outside the country in which the firm produces and sells the product. Specifically, the major dimensions of international marketing are as follows:

- exporting: selling to foreign markets;
- importing: purchasing from foreign areas;
- management of international operations: all phases of business activity wherever undertaken, including such activities as operating marketing and sales facilities abroad, establishing production, assembly or service facilities in foreign areas, creating licensing arrangements and other types of strategic alliances, and engaging in countertrade transactions.

International marketing management involves the management of marketing not only to but also in foreign countries. From an overall perspective these dimensions relate to the broad area of foreign market entry strategy. Thus we see that export marketing fits into international marketing as one of the major dimensions and, as such, is a significant alternative entry mode.

The planned and coordinated combination of marketing methods or tools employed to achieve a predetermined goal is called a marketing program or the marketing mix. A central feature of marketing is consumer orientation. The marketing program should be formulated with the interests and needs of consumers in mind. It must be structured in such a way as to integrate the customer into the company and to lead to creating and maintaining a solid relationship between the company and the customer. A firm operating in this manner is said to be *market driven*, and is concerned with what the consumer will buy that can be made profitably.

Market-driven marketing is oriented toward creating rather than controlling a market. It is an ongoing process based on incremental improvement, not on simple market-share-based tactics, sales volume per se and/or one-time events. The real goal of marketing is to 'own' a market, not just to make or sell products (McKenna, 1991). When a company owns a market it develops products to serve that market specifically. A good example of this is Intel with its microprocessor. Intel developed what is essentially a computer on a chip, not a semiconductor, and created a new product category that it could own and lead as long as its technology stayed ahead of that of its competitors. Microsoft's Word for Windows has been so widely used that it has virtually taken over the market for word processing software, though it is being challenged on several fronts.

In contrast, some companies are product or technology driven. They believe in the old saying, 'If you build a better mousetrap the world will beat a path to your door.' While there are successful companies that are not market driven, these are often found in industries where market demand greatly exceeds industry productive capacity and there is less concern among competitors (if there are any) about consumers and market share than about product performance. Since conditions can change rapidly (i.e., markets change, competition grows, products become obsolete, etc.), product-driven companies cannot adapt as quickly or as easily as market-driven companies. A good example of this is the personal computer industry. At the outset, hardware and software companies could be product and technology driven. However, those that did not become market driven experienced severe problems or were forced out of the market by competition. IBM, Dell and Toshiba are examples of companies in this industry that are market driven. For an example of what one company did to become market driven, see Exhibit 1.2.

| EXHIBIT 1.2 | **Scandinavian Airlines:**
a customer-driven company |

In 2002 and 2003 Scandinavian Airlines (SAS) was adjusting its marketing approach to fit changing customer desires. For the previous 20 years SAS had followed policies instituted by Jan Carlzon after he took over the money-losing airline in 1981. At that time, rather than instituting further cost cutting and fare reductions, he had started a program to make SAS a customer-driven (market-driven) company. He began by trying to identify key customers, their needs, and what was needed to win their preference.

Carlzon decided to focus on *frequent-flying business people* and their needs and preferences. He recognized that other airlines were also trying to attract the same segment, offering wider seats, free drinks, and other amenities. SAS had to find a way to become more attractive in order to be the frequent business traveler's preferred airline.

Carlzon's approach was based on two key ideas. The first was the importance of the initial 15-second encounters between a passenger and the front-line people, from ticket agent to flight attendant. This 'moment of truth,' which occurs more than once during a single trip, is what sets the tone of the entire company in the mind of the customer. The front-line people who meet the customers are the most important people in the company. Managers are there to help the front-line people do their job well, and the role of the president is to help the managers support the front-line employees.

The second key idea was to increase the percentage of passengers traveling business class – a class of ticket yielding higher revenue than economy class (and much higher than discount tickets). An innovation in this regard was to start selling all tickets as business class (Euro-Class) unless the traveler specifically wanted economy class. This second idea would not work without an emphasis on making the customer's experience worth the cost.

In addition to emphasizing employee interactions with the customers, check-in systems were made faster, travelers staying at SAS hotels could have luggage sent directly from their hotels to the airport for loading, aircraft were chosen with the prefer-ences of the customers in mind, and SAS aircraft provided the greatest percentage of business class seats of any of the European airlines.

This approach had provided impressive results for two decades. SAS carried a higher proportion of business class passengers than any other European airline and enjoyed an outstanding passenger satisfaction index. Passenger traffic and revenue increased. Profits returned.

Then came the bombing of the World Trade Center and SARS, resulting in sharp declines in airline travel. At the same time discount airlines were rapidly capturing a greater share of the market. SAS incurred large losses in 2001, 2002, and 2003.

This led to changes in marketing policy at SAS. The main focus is still on business travelers, but has been widened to include the leisure travel market. Both of these target groups have become more price sensitive. In response, SAS has removed the business class sections and increased the number of seats on all planes operating on intraScandinavian flights, made selected fare reductions, and started a new low-fare Snowflake service in Europe. Costs were cut through reorganization, obtaining increased productivity (more hours of work) from pilots and cabin crews, reducing the number of employees, and relocating parts of accounting to India. Easier, more efficient, and less costly Web-based reservation services have been stressed. A strong effort was made to secure the cooperation of the front-line employees (and their unions) in maintaining the highest possible level of friendliness and service. The new president, Jorgen Lindegaard, and his team are counting on the new approach to meet the needs and preferences of their customers – and return the airline to profitable operations.

Sources: Carlzon, 1987, www.scandinavian.net (through March 2004), other published material.

The elements in the marketing program are interrelated and interdependent. Sometimes they are substitutes for each other; sometimes they are complements; sometimes both. For example, advertising in a business or trade publication with circulation in the United Kingdom may be an alternative to hiring two additional sales persons, one to be located in London, the other in Edinburgh; it may be used to supplement the efforts of existing sales personnel in these areas; or it could be used to perform both functions.

Since a marketing program consists of a set of interacting and interrelated activities, it can be viewed as a system. Marketing activities are the *controllable* (by the firm) variables, and the profusion of geographic, economic, sociological, politi-cal, and cultural circumstances (in both domestic and foreign environments) as well as certain firm characteristics are the *uncontrollable* (by the firm) variables. The state of the uncontrollable variables influences the composition of the marketing mix and the functional relationships between the elements in the marketing mix. A business firm engages in marketing activities to adapt to its environment in a way that the goals of the firm are being achieved. This is the essence of marketing man-agement, whether domestic or international (or export). The relationship between the controllable and uncontrollable variables was used by Warren Bilkey (1985) as the basis for formulating and testing a theory of the export marketing mix. A schematic model for analyzing such a marketing mix is shown in Figure 1.2.

This model can be supplemented and further explained by the following proposition:

- The *relative export profitability* of any marketing program or component is situation specific, and is influenced by the variables shown in Figure 1.2.
- Figure 1.2 itself does not indicate which components are most profitable for any specific situation.
- The export channel used will determine which export structure and dealer support is most profitable.

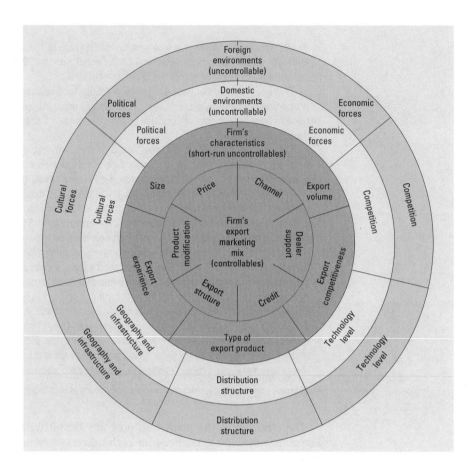

FIGURE 1.2

Schematic model of the
export marketing mix

1.2.5 Importing as inward internationalization

When one thinks of international marketing it is usually in the context of a sale
being made by penetrating a foreign market, either at the time or in the future.
However, in the previous section importing was included as a major dimension of
international marketing. The reason for this is that often there is a link between
importing and the means by which foreign markets are entered. Foreign sourcing
activity (inward internationalization) may precede and influence the development
of market entry and marketing activities (outward internationalization) in such a
way that the effectiveness of inward activities could determine the success of
outward activities (Welch and Luostarinen, 1993). Inward/outward relationships
can be classified on a continuum ranging from direct to indirect. In a direct relationship the outward actions are overtly dependent upon the inward internationalization process or vice versa. In contrast, there is relatively little dependence of
one movement on the other. For example, an indirect relationship may involve the
importer that gains knowledge of its suppliers' so-called 'network' – its suppliers
and even customers – such that at some later time there will be an outward export
to members of that network. In a more direct relationship, inward foreign licensing may be followed by outward technology sales. An illustration of how inward
action may precede outward activity in a company is provided by an Australian
company, Island Cooler Pty Ltd. Two Australian businessmen formed the
company after importing the concept of wine cooler drinks and purchasing the

formula from a California company. They obtained additional capital from an Irish company, and then subcontracted bottling and distribution to other Australian companies. Within two years they began exporting bottled drinks, eventually selling in New Zealand, Hong Kong, and Japan (Welch and Luostarinen, 1993). There are also many cases of companies, a number in Asia, that have imported machinery and/or technology in order to produce manufactured goods for export to Europe, North America, and Japan. Counter-trade arrangements and certain strategic alliances have also been set up with inward–outward links as a foundation.

1.2.6 Some similarities and differences

The task of international marketing managers is the formulation and implementation of a marketing program that will enable a company to adapt to its environment in such a way that its goals are attained as completely as possible. There are similarities and differences in all markets, domestic and foreign, but the concepts of marketing science are universally applicable. Basic marketing concepts such as the product life cycle and traditional marketing tools such as market segmentation are as applicable in Wales, United Kingdom, as they are in New South Wales, Australia.

The broad categories of environmental factors are the same (i.e., social, economic, political, and geographic). The broad approach to the solution of marketing problems is identical, namely, the consideration of various marketing methods to achieve the goals of the firm, in light of the firm's environment.

Therefore it may appear that experience in domestic marketing management will be transferable to international and export marketing (see Exhibit 1.3).

EXHIBIT 1.3	Some characteristics of export marketing executives

What characteristics and background qualify a person for export marketing management? In simple terms the answer is as follows:

- technical competence in marketing;
- specialized knowledge of the factors in the international environment that are dissimilar or absent from the domestic environment;
- the ability to utilize such knowledge in working with others, at home or abroad, to develop and implement sound marketing programs.

Technical competence and a specialized knowledge of environmental factors can be achieved in part in the classroom and, of course, by experience and international travel. Developing the ability to use such competence and knowledge to implement decisions may be more difficult. It has been argued by many that the essential ingredient in a person who will be successful in exporting is cultural empathy, not only being able to recognize cultural differences, but also being able to understand them in a manner that permits effective communication and effective direction of human efforts to implement marketing decisions.

Many have observed that there is a large distinction between understanding the need for cultural empathy and the ability to practice it well. There is some evidence that a knowledge of the need for cultural empathy can be obtained by studying anthropology and sociology. But skill in the practice of cultural empathy will most likely be best obtained through action-oriented case studies. However, such studies and case analyses are not entirely sufficient. There is no substitute for learning a language as a means of understanding another person's beliefs, way of life, and point of view. Further, more is required than only a superficial or a reading knowledge of a language. Cultural empathy may be achieved by the thorough development of the language skill to the point where a person can think, feel, reason, and experience emotions in a language other than his or her mother tongue.

A survey of 1500 senior executives from 20 countries revealed that ideally international marketing managers should have the following traits (Korn, 1989):

- global perspective and an international outlook;
- experience outside one's home country;
- knowledge of, or at least some training in, a foreign language.

In a brief review of studies conducted during the period of the mid-1970s through the early 1990s Gray (1995, p. 110) concluded that the most common elements (i.e., exporter manager characteristics/skills) are adaptability, cultural sensitivity, and language skills. Considering international marketing investment decision making, three personality variables seem to account for variances (Gray, 1995, p. 107):

- international experience;
- international orientation (this includes cultural empathy/sensitivity and language skills);
- international business commitment.

However, the evidence seems to indicate that only orientation and commitment have been consistently correlated with performance.

Factors in a foreign or domestic environment can be grouped so broadly that all are included in the same classification, but in a more detailed breakdown it will be noted that some factors are not present in domestic environments. For example, although both domestic and international marketing activities are conducted in a legal environment, the components of the legal environment differ; certain types of regulations and laws are found in some countries but not in others. Taxes and tariffs vary widely between countries, as do various restrictions on trade, such as quotas or exchange controls. Likewise, although both domestic and international transactions may be conducted in a currency, there are differences in the type and characteristics of currencies and in the exchange rates imposed by countries.

Although domestic business is conducted over intranational (e.g., state and county) political boundaries, international business is conducted over the boundaries of sovereign nations. Governmental institutions and banking systems vary widely from country to country and often have significant influences on marketing activities. These influences as well as those from the legal environment may be affected by the nature of political systems.

Other commonly recognized environmental differences arise from language, religion, customs, traditions, and other cultural differences, not to mention geographical distances and climate variations, and basic infrastructure. Thus the analysis and solution of international marketing problems requires skills, background, and insights in addition to those required to solve strictly domestic marketing problems.

So far we have discussed two basic dimensions of international marketing and, of course, exporting: the *environment* and the *crossing of national borders*. There is a third dimension that arises because *a company markets its products simultaneously in more than one national environment.* This results in problems as well as opportunities different from those associated with crossing national borders. The international marketer must analyze respective national market opportunities, and a decision must be made regarding who should perform marketing activities in the company. The company should relate its activities in multiple nations to each other such that the effectiveness of the individual national marketing programs is enhanced as well as the effectiveness of the total world marketing effort.

The approach to the solution of international marketing problems requires, first, an international (or *global*) outlook – viewing the world or relevant parts of the world as a single market consisting of a number of segments, defined in a manner appropriate to the product to be sold, and not necessarily along national boundaries. Second, market targets must be realistically assessed and the segments of the 'world market' to be exploited should be selected. Third, the relevant environmental factors in the market segments must be assessed, and fourth, a marketing program must be formulated. In going through this process, the size and extent of markets must be determined, customer behavior must be evaluated, domestic and foreign competition must be assessed, legal and political factors must be reviewed, and costs must be calculated.

1.3 Export marketing planning and strategy

From a broader planning and decision-making point of view, there is need to be concerned with both *strategic* and *tactical* issues as they relate to export marketing decisions. Strategic decisions concern such things as choice of countries, product markets, target segments, modes of operation, and timing of market entry. In contrast, tactical decisions are concerned with operations within a given country as they concern such things as product positioning, product adaptation, advertising copy adaptation and media selection, and specific promotional, pricing, and distribution decisions. An essential first step, particularly for the 'newcomer' to international markets, is for the company to assess its *readiness* to enter such markets (see Exhibit 1.4).

EXHIBIT 1.4	**Is a company ready to enter foreign markets?**

An essential first step in planning and strategy development is the company's need to assess its readiness to enter foreign markets. Any firm, regardless of its size and experience, must determine just how ready it is to make the move. Two expert systems – *Export Expert: Judging your export readiness* (Columbia Cascade, 1997) and *CORE* (Company Operational Readiness to Export) (Cavusgil, 1994) – are decision support tools that can be used to assist in determining readiness.

These expert systems are designed to provide an evaluation of *internal company* strengths and weaknesses in the context of exporting. Although the two pieces of software are not exactly the same, the major areas covered are quite similar:

- competitive capabilities in the domestic market;

■ motivation for going international;
■ commitment of owners and top management;
■ product readiness for foreign markets;
■ skill, knowledge and resources;
■ experience and training.

The end result of the analysis is a report that includes scores for each of the dimensions and overall readiness with an assessment of what this means to the company and what the company should do next.

Export Expert is somewhat broader as it helps to analyze risks, assists in developing an international business plan, and helps to define target markets.

The systems are especially useful for small and medium-sized companies considering initial export experience. However, they are also useful for larger companies that want to reassess their strengths and weaknesses regarding present international marketing activity.

Analysis of readiness to enter foreign markets – by export or any other form of international marketing such as strategic alliance – using evaluation systems such as these provides a good starting point for making the decision. But it should only be a start! A company should not base its decision solely on this type of analysis. The next step would be a comprehensive analysis of strengths, weaknesses, structure and competitive advantage and opportunity (i.e., a type of SWOT analysis). Competitive advantage can provide the niche needed to succeed in a new market.

At a very simple level, export planning and strategy development have three distinct components:

1. **Goal.** The company exporting will have certain objectives that it wishes to achieve, and which will serve as criteria for assessment of progress. The basis of company goals will be identifying and measuring market opportunity.
2. **Program.** This involves developing the marketing mix at both strategic and tactical levels.
3. **Organization.** Developing an organization means putting together company resources in order to operationalize the marketing mix. In short, the strategy and tactics are put to work.

Figure 1.3 summarizes what we have said about export planning as well as international marketing planning in general. These components, though distinct, are interrelated and thus dependent upon each other. For example, if a company for any reason cannot put together the organization needed to implement the program developed to achieve the selected goal, then either the program or the goal (or perhaps even both) will have to be changed. Underlying all this, including the initial decision to export in the first place, is the nature and level of *perceived risk* associated with such activities. There may be times, for instance, when the risk that is perceived to be associated with an export marketing program is too great for management to go ahead. When this occurs the program will be changed, the goals restated, and/or the organization adjusted. In all cases the desired result is perception of a level of risk that management will accept.

The export performance (i.e., its growth, intensity, etc.) of a company is affected by the firm itself, the company's markets and industry, and the export strategy chosen. Two major components of export strategy are product policy and market selection. The question of product strategy ultimately results in deciding upon the extent of product adaptation. This can range from no or minimum adaptation (i.e., selling what is essentially the domestic product) to developing a

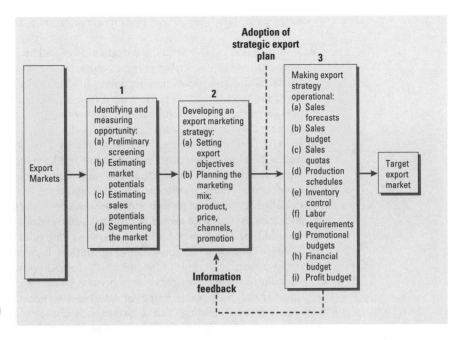

FIGURE 1.3

Export marketing planning
process

product specifically for export markets. Market selection concerns the countries
exported to, and the nature and level of segmentation within these countries.

1.3.1 Demand management

The role of marketing in business is often concerned with more than attempting to
increase sales. A number of factors have led to efforts to control rather than just
stimulate demand for some products. These factors include concerns over the
environment, pressures due to increasing populations and higher income levels
often leading to increased consumption of limited natural resources, the cost and
availability of resources (such as fuels and electrical power generation facilities),
changing regulations related to restrictions on automobile emissions and the mix
of traditional and low-emission vehicles required, conscious attempts to restrict
supply so as to keep prices at desired levels (as in the case of OPEC and petroleum
production), attempts to reduce waste and increase recycling, etc.

   In the case of temporary shortages of products or service capacity, a serious
concern is how to avoid damaging relations with present and potential customers.
The following are some examples of problems and efforts to solve them:

- In late 2003 and early 2004, unmet demand for the new Phantom luxury car
  had built up because of production problems at the factory in England. To avoid
  the danger of losing its potential customers, the company shipped vehicles to the
  United States by air.
- During the Christmas seasons in 1999 and 2000, some Internet marketers were
  unable to fill many orders because of lack of inventories and insufficient staff.
  Performance has improved since then as experience indicated requirements for
  staffing, inventories, and/or arrangements with suppliers. Some problems continue to exist (as they do with 'bricks-and-mortar stores') because of problems
  in predicting demand for particular items.
- Sony's first version of the AIBO pet robot sold out in 20 minutes, leaving many
  potential customers with a long waiting period until more could be produced. A
  reservation system was set up for the second version so that demand could be

more accurately forecast and production adjusted before actual introduction in 2001.

■ Sony also had trouble with the introduction of its PlayStation 2 because of problems in the manufacture of graphics chips. Many retailers and customers were irritated, and companies making games for the device had lower than expected sales. Because of the competitive need to introduce new products at the earliest possible time, more careful tracking and control of component development is the only way to avoid similar problems in the future.

■ Electric power companies, faced with excess capacity in certain periods and excess demand during other periods, have tried a number of methods of changing demand levels. These include charging higher prices at peak times, offering lower overall rates to customers that are willing to have power cut off in exceptionally high-demand periods, and contracts with suppliers from other areas or countries to exchange power at differing peak periods.

■ An additional approach for electric power companies has been to build a combination pumping station-generating station between reservoirs above and below a dam. In periods of low demand, electrical power is used to pump water back up to the higher reservoir. In periods of excess demand, water is released down through the same flumes and turbines to generate electricity. Where the terrain allows building such a system, it is cheaper to build and operate, and more environmentally friendly, than simply adding overall fossil fuel generating capacity that will seldom be needed.

In California, overall excess demand for electric power has resulted in power generating companies actively promoting conservation.

A concept of marketing management has evolved, namely that of the problem of regulating the level, timing, and character of demand for a company's products in terms of its objectives at the time. Eight different demand states can be identified – four states represent underdemand, two states make up adequate demand, and two states constitute overdemand. Each of these gives rise to a specific export marketing task, which varies because different variables, psychological theories, and managerial requirements are involved or emphasized (see Exhibit 1.5).

EXHIBIT 1.5   Various states of demand

1. **Negative demand** This is a state in which segments of a potential market dislike the product and may even pay a price to avoid it. This condition applies to a rather large number of products and services. The marketing task is one of conversion through changes in one or more of the marketing activities. This type of demand state often arises because of political actions and beliefs of national governments. Examples are consumer boycotts on products from certain countries (for example, South African gold coins), and tourism in countries where government is disliked. However, cultural and religious beliefs can also be a source of dislike, as with the Muslim feeling toward alcoholic beverages, or the strong opposition that arose against Nestlé baby formula.

2. **No demand** In this demand state, segments of a potential market are uninterested or indifferent to a particular product, service, or idea. The object of concern may be perceived as having no value per se, no value in the particular market, or may be an innovation, of which the market lacks knowledge. There is a need to stimulate the market by demonstrating product benefits. When attempts were first made to introduce modern farm machinery into certain underdeveloped countries, farmers saw little value in changing their methods.

3. **Latent demand** When a substantial number of people share a strong need for something that does not exist as an actual product, a state of latent demand exists. The marketing problem is that the right means of satisfying the need (that is, a product) must be developed. The development of a low-cost, high-protein food to help solve the malnutrition problem in many Latin American and African countries is an illustration. Again, there must be concern for any cultural and religious beliefs that exist.

4. **Falling demand** This state exists when the demand for a product is less than its former level and where further decline is expected unless changes are made in the target market, product, and/or marketing program. Something must be done to revitalize demand. An example is when a market becomes inaccessible due to government action, such as quota limitations, even to the extent of prohibiting all imports of a product because it is desired that a local industry be created. The marketing job in this case is straightforward – invest in production facilities (if allowed) or forget about the specific market and redirect efforts to other market areas.

5. **Irregular demand** In this type of situation concern is not with total demand, but rather with its temporal pattern in that seasonal or other fluctuations in demand differ from the timing pattern of supply. This is a very common occurrence in all national markets for many products, and can be easily illustrated by international tourism. The greatest period of demand by Americans and Canadians for travel to Europe, and vice versa, is the summer. The task facing hotels, transportation companies, and so on, is to convince tourists to travel during other times of the year. Lowering prices is one marketing technique that is widely used. Another example of irregular demand is foreign airline purchases of aircraft from companies such as Airbus Industrie (Airbus 330) and Boeing Aircraft Company (Boeing 777).

6. **Full demand** This is the most desirable situation for an exporter since the level and timing of supply and demand are in equilibrium. While such a state may be more ideal than real, products do achieve this condition on occasion. Unfortunately, a full demand state cannot be expected to continue indefinitely because needs and tastes change, and competition does not become passive. Consequently, the exporter with a highly successful product has no easy job in the task of maintaining demand.

7. **Overfull demand** For many reasons the demand for a product may be substantially greater than the level at which the seller wants to supply it. Consequently, the exporter deliberately attempts to discourage customers in general, or a certain group of customers. This involves marketing in reverse as the attempt is made to reduce demand by 'demarketing.' Perhaps the classic example in the international marketplace was the action of the oil-producing nations of the Middle East in the early 1970s. Their action was prompted by their desire to conserve their most important resource and foreign exchange earner, their desire to become more economically developed quicker, and perhaps even by a feeling of 'getting back' at the industrial nations that had exploited them for many years. Another example was the action of Wilkinson Sword (UK) during the introduction of stainless steel razor blades in the United States in the early 1960s, when the product was demarketed because the demand could not be met.

8. **Unwholesome demand** This is a state in which any demand is felt to be excessive because of the undesirable qualities associated with the product. In most situations of this type the attempt to destroy demand is generally carried out by a government agency or organized group(s) of concerned citizens. Vice products (such as alcohol, cigarettes, drugs) and military arms sales to certain parts of the world are examples. A company may deliberately try to destroy the demand for its own product when it has an innovation for which it wishes to develop a market.

Source: adapted from Kotler, 2000, p. 6. Reprinted by permission of Pearson Education, Inc, Upper Saddle River, NJ.

In assessing the significance to the exporter of the focus on demand management it is important to keep in mind the simple fact that different overseas markets may have different demand states. Thus export marketing potential will differ, perhaps necessitating different export strategies. Also, a company may be facing different demand states within any single national market because of differing reactions by individual major market segments. This can be especially relevant in national markets that are not culturally or socially homogeneous, such as Belgium, or economically homogeneous, such as Italy.

1.3.2 Obstacles to exporting

Some companies never take the first step and get involved in international marketing, particularly exporting, because they feel that there are obstacles or barriers that cannot be overcome easily enough. These obstacles may be real or may only be perceived to exist. Other companies may proceed at a slower pace in their international involvement because of the obstacles. For the most part, it is the smaller-sized (and to some extent the medium-sized) companies that have the hardest time handling these barriers.

Whether barriers exist, or are perceived to exist, for any given potential or actual exporter at any point in time is, of course, an empirical question. For our purposes, we address the issue by looking at potential barriers. These are the obstacles that have been reported by companies to have influenced their decision to export. Overall, a major obstacle that appears to affect many companies is the greater operational effort involved in export and foreign market penetration in

TABLE 1.1   Dimensions of export barriers

Barrier	Dimension of export barriers			
	Internal controllable I dimension	Foreign non-controllable dimension	Internal controllable II dimension	Local non-controllable dimension
Communication with foreign unit	✓			
Lack of export training (experiences and language skills)	✓			
Lack of market information	✓			
Controlling international activities	✓			
Documentation requirements	✓			
Foreign government attitudes		✓		
Foreign public attitudes		✓		
Trade barriers (tariffs, quotas)		✓		
Arranging transportation, packaging, etc.			✓	
Providing services			✓	
Higher than domestic risk			✓	
Financing sales				✓
No assistance from home government				✓

Source: adapted from Shoham and Albaum, 1995, p. 93

general as compared to domestic marketing. In particular, it is the 'mechanics' of export (e.g., means of payment, documentation, physical distribution, and terms of trade) that 'frighten' many companies. Also, there is the belief that the risk involved is greater.

Many of the barriers are controllable by the company while others are not; some barriers are foreign-market based while others are home-market based. Table 1.1 presents some results on underlying dimensions of export barriers that emerged from a study of Danish exporters. On an overall basis, all listed barriers were perceived to be not particularly important. However, this should not be surprising as the group studied was 'practicing' international marketers. In contrast, a study of small- and medium-sized US companies found that they tended to view many of these barriers as very important (Mahone, 1995). Moreover, trading companies felt that the barriers were more important than did manufacturers.

Both of the studies mentioned above dealt with perceived obstacles rather than 'documented' real ones. In the end it makes no difference whether obstacles are real or imagined as managers will make decisions on the basis of their perceptions of the situation that they face. Obviously barriers are important because of the impact they have on the behavior of potential and actual exporters at different stages of internationalization. Exhibit 1.6 gives some advice to small companies about how to cope with, and handle, some of the barriers that are perceived to exist.

EXHIBIT 1.6   How can a company cope?

Does a small company have to accept the barrier situation as it appears to it to exist? Of course not! There are many things that a small company can do to overcome any barriers, in addition to applying sound business practices. *Business Week* presents the following global guidelines for small business (Barrett, 1995, p. 97):

LOOK TO EXISTING CUSTOMERS. Many companies can penetrate foreign markets by selling products or services to their domestic customers' units overseas.

MAKE A COMMITMENT. Exporting is not a part-time effort. It requires extensive research. Foreign business should be run by seasoned managers.

SEEK ADVICE. Universities often have MBA students who work as consultants on exporting. Some consulting firms, such as Accenture (formerly Arthur Andersen), provide a free first-time consultation.

USE TRADE SHOWS. Trade promotions sponsored by government agencies abroad draw big crowds. Cost-conscious companies can send a product without attending.

PICK MARKETS CAREFULLY. While potentially lucrative, fast-growing markets can tank unexpectedly. Consider customer quality, not just nationality.

MANAGE GROWTH. It takes time to line up financing and expand an organization to handle exports. Many small exporters are overwhelmed by big orders.

USE LETTERS OF CREDIT. Some first-time exporters ship a product and hope they get paid. A letter of credit protects against default by a weak or shady buyer.

BE PATIENT. Many foreign customers do business based on relationships. Small companies must spend time cultivating contacts before racking up export orders.

CHOOSE PARTNERS CAREFULLY. An experienced freight forwarder at home is crucial for handling Customs paperwork. An inept distributor abroad can ruin a company's reputation.

1.4 The Internet, the World Wide Web, and e-business

The development of the Internet, and the World Wide Web system operating through the Internet, have resulted in the rapid growth of e-business and changes in all aspects of traditional business operations. The Internet provides greatly increased speed and lowered cost in communications. The World Wide Web is an easily used system for providing constantly available displays of information, leading to new opportunities for advertising and promotion, and a new form of interaction with customers and suppliers.

The Internet, because it is global and operates on a consistent protocol, is being more widely used than the variety of electronic data interchange (EDI) systems set up by specific sets of companies. They were useful primarily for large companies that had the resources and needs to justify setting up their own individual systems for electronic exchange of purchase information, orders, invoices, payments, etc. The high cost of these individual systems and the lack of a common standard that would permit interactions between different systems led to limited use. New EDI systems are being developed, however, since added security and improved software to support them has become available. Several large marketers such as France's Carrefour are now using EDI systems.

1.4.1 The Internet

The Internet itself is a worldwide telecommunications network that provides for rapid exchange of information in digital format, including files, written material, pictures, and sound. The information to be sent is automatically translated into digital format for transmission and translated back into its original form at the destination. The transmission of films is limited in some cases due to the capacity (bandwidth) required. As noted below, this limitation is easing as bandwidth is being expanded rapidly in segments of the communications system, supporting continually greater capabilities.

Users connect with the system through Internet service providers (ISPs). The connection to the ISP is made over telephone or cable lines using a computer and modem, or through cellular telephones. The amount of information that can be transmitted through cellular phones and the ability to display the information are currently limited. The ISPs are connected by a variety of electronic communications linkages, including telephone lines, cables, fiber optic lines, and/or wireless. A system of routers and switches attempts to select the best channel through the network for transmission of data from one point to another. Geosynchronous satellites also provide a two-way Internet.

Use of the Internet increased greatly with the development of the World Wide Web in 1995. An early form of the Internet had been developed in 1969, but was used primarily for e-mail (developed in 1971) and transferring large computer files. The use of e-mail is important to businesses in permitting the rapid and relatively inexpensive transmission of information, both domestically and internationally. It is inexpensive because users in most countries are able to send messages for just the cost of a local telephone call (to their local ISP) and a monthly fee, and because information is sent more rapidly than via fax. But the basic e-mail system has limited capabilities to present information on a continually available, easily accessible, and widespread basis.

The Internet has become more powerful with the growing use of broadband.

Broadband permits the rapid transmission of much greater quantities of information, including moving pictures. South Korea, Hong Kong, and Canada have led in this expansion with more than two-thirds of Korea's 15 million households having broadband service by 2002 (Moon, 2002; *The Economist*, 2003). By 2004, more than 152 million people in the United States were online with over one-third having broadband connections (Fost, 2004). The number of connections by businesses and individuals was growing rapidly. Internet use has also been increasing sharply in Germany, Britain, Italy, France and Spain. Communication using radio-based networks known as Wi-Fi appears to offer even greater potential for expansion of usage as broadband will become available almost everywhere a laptop computer can be taken (Mullaney *et al.*, 2003).

The number of Internet users worldwide has been projected to grow to over 1.2 billion by 2008, but actual growth is exceeding projections.

1.4.2 The World Wide Web

The World Wide Web is a service that operates on the Internet, displaying information on web sites in the form of web pages. Web sites have been established by individuals and by all types of organizations including governments, companies, universities, hospitals, clubs, and special interest groups. Approximately 4500 new web sites are added each day, and Wild *et al.* (2001) estimated that there would be 8 million web pages by 2002.

Addresses within the World Wide Web are arranged in a hierarchical or tree-like system, with different organizations responsible for assigning domain names within each branch of the tree. Each site has a registered address called a uniform resource locator (URL) within a domain. When an organization registers a domain name, the organization receives the right to use all web site addresses ending in the designated name. For example, if a US company registers the name foobar.org with the Public Interest Registry, the entity that has responsibility for all domain names ending in '.org,' the company has the right to use www.foobar.org, www.abc.def.foobar.org, home.foobar.org, and any other series of designations ending in foobar.org.

Each country has domain names ending in a country indicator, for example '.nl' for The Netherlands. The highest level domain names assigned to the United States do not end in '.us' (though within the country's overall domain names, there is a top level '.us' domain used primarily by government organizations). There are no restrictions on what a country can do with its top-level two-letter domain. Some of the implications of this overall structure are shown in Exhibit 1.7.

| **EXHIBIT 1.7** | **Implications of the WWW registry system** |

- **A caution**: Registering a name in the United States, such as 'foobar.org' does not prevent someone else from registering the name in another country under that nation's top-level domain designation. That is, someone else can register the name 'foobar.org.nl' in The Netherlands. If a company does business in, or is considering doing business in, other countries, it might be wise to register its name in those countries also. In some jurisdictions, another party registering a domain with your company's name would have the right to that address there and might gain the right to prevent your using your name there. (At the time of this writing, the law is unclear in some places.)

> ■ **An opportunity recognized**: The official two-letter designation of the nation of Tuvalu, a small cluster of islands in the South Pacific, is '.tv.' Sensing a marketing opportunity, the Tuvalese officials have set up a corporation whose sole purpose is to auction off domain names ending in '.tv' to the highest bidder. As of 2004, you could register the 'news.tv' domain name for $1,000,000, or 'cable.tv' for a mere $100,000.

To access a web site from a personal computer it is necessary to use a web browser such as Microsoft's 'Internet Explorer' or Netscape's 'Navigator' and to go through an ISP such as MSN. These serve to provide a guide as well as access to the web.

The large number of sites and web pages makes attaining visibility a problem for the smaller company advertising on the Web. Even a very well-designed set of pages is useless if too few potential customers find it. Methods for increasing the number of people visiting the site include registering the site with search engines online (Yahoo, Excite, Alta Vista, etc.), through partnerships with related web sites, and through traditional media campaigns. Companies need to be careful when marketing on the web. E-mail campaigns can be very successful in some cases, but must not be seen as 'spamming' (burdening and irritating the customer with unrequested e-mail). The gathering and usage of information from customers must be handled carefully in order to ensure its privacy.

One present limitation to the international use of the web is the dominant use of English. While many business people throughout the world speak English, half of the world's Internet users are not native English speakers. At the beginning of 2001 only a little over 5% of the material on the web was in languages other than English. However, web sites in other languages are being added at a rapid rate, and should increase the overall usefulness of the system. In Europe, 80% of corporate web sites now offer at least one language besides English.

There are several ways for prospective sellers to list goods and services, and prospective buyers to find them, on the World Wide Web. The prospective buyer may visit any of the many sites directly offering merchandise such as eBay, Amazon, Yahoo! Shopping, Wal-Mart and other stores, travel sites, etc. Alternatively, the buyer may go through a search engine such as Google, Yahoo! Search, MSN Search, etc. The latter allow comparison shopping, and have gone in to 'sponsored search' in which merchants pay to have a link to their sites displayed every time a potential buyer clicks on a certain word or phrase in an Internet search. The sponsored search business first started in the United States but is now spreading rapidly in other countries (Waters, 2004).

The multiple capabilities that the World Wide Web brought to the Internet have played an important role in the rapidly growing field of e-business.

1.4.3 E-business

Electronic business (or e-business) refers to the sale, purchase, or exchange of goods, services, or information over the Internet or other telecommunications networks. Functions that can be carried out include advertising, the publishing of a wide range of information, scheduling, distribution, payment, and service. E-business may also use systems outside of the Web or the Internet. When individuals use an automated teller machine (ATM), the verification and authorization information may be sent outside the Web via satellite, but the transaction is very rapid and most people give little thought to how it was accomplished.

In 2003, the global e-commerce market grew to a value of $3.9 trillion, and is continuing to increase. Transactions between businesses (B2B) comprise by far the largest portion of this, but business to consumer sales (B2C) have received the most attention from the general public.

The United States had the greatest investment in companies offering goods and services online. B2C sales have grown rapidly but, excluding travel and auction sites, still reached only $54.9 billion in 2003. This amounted to just 1.6% of US retail sales. If sales by travel and auction sites are included, the figure for online sales reached $123 billion (Fost, 2004). A number of companies that used business models relying solely on Internet sales went bankrupt in the period from 2000 to 2001. Others, however, have become profitable. For most large companies some combination of traditional marketing and Web-based marketing seems to be most successful. While some traditional store-based ('bricks and mortar') companies have reduced their Web-related activities, others have increased them. An increasing number of customers in some countries do a search for products online, and then visit a store (or stores) to actually see the article before making a purchase. Overall, B2C business continues to grow rapidly in the United States.

In Europe, the number of active Internet users has been increasing rapidly, with over 60 million people online. Internet sales for some organizations including the French railroad, Egg PLC of London, easyJet Airline, and the four non-US domains of Amazon.com Inc. in Britain, France, Germany, and Japan have risen as much as 70% year on year (Reinhardt and Passariello, 2002). For a number of entrepreneurs and companies the World Wide Web has been a key factor in increasing opportunities and sales to customers.

One of the problems for Internet retailers is consumer concern over the security of transactions and cybercrime. Though Internet transactions overall are safer than using a credit card at stores and restaurants, the perception limits growth for Internet retailers. The actual problem is much greater, and causes more losses, for the retailers because of fraudulent credit cards.

Business to business online spending continues to increase. B2B transactions often involve much more than simply buying and selling. Networks within and between companies use software that enables all parties involved to monitor the process of goods through the whole supply chain. Software has also been developed to perform many other marketing and broader business functions. Examples are given in sections 1.5 and 1.6 below.

The development and marketing of software to support e-business has become a major international industry, with major players in Europe, North America, and Asia. When properly designed and operated, e-business software improves coordination and communication, reduces the number of repetitive tasks required, and provides management with up-to-date information on key marketing information. It thus enables companies to improve marketing responsiveness, effectiveness, and efficiency.

1.5 The impact of technology

Advances in information technology and other areas of technology have affected international marketing in two ways. First, trade in technology-related products and services has grown rapidly. Secondly, the improvements in communications technology and organization have led to the development of new channels of communication, lowered costs, and an increased flow of information. This, in turn, has led to the development of increasingly efficient and responsive production and distribution systems.

Information technology (IT) related trade has reached over $1 trillion in value, amounting to approximately 16% of the total value of world trade. India's revenues from software and computer services have increased from approximately $4 billion in 2000 to a projected $27.5 billion in 2006. China's exports of software and computer exports, which amounted to less than $0.5 billion in value in 2000, are projected to grow to $27 billion in 2006 (Einhorn and Kripalani, 2003). Several of the EU member nations are major exporters of IT-related products and digital-related products account for approximately 26% of all exports from the United States.

Advances in communications technology have included increasing bandwidth, improved methods of compressing data, more secure connections, and sharply reduced prices. As an example, an executive at a French telecommunications provider has estimated that international rates to the world's biggest markets fell by 50% from 2003 to 2004. In some cases, costs have dropped even more sharply (Drucker, 2004). High definition TVs, cellular phones and wireless communications networks have changed the amount of information people receive, the way it is received, and what it costs. From the standpoint of international marketers, additional products are available, additional markets can be reached, and the costs of doing business are reduced.

Some international companies are applying developments in radio-frequency identification (RFID) systems technology to make supply chain management more efficient and effective. The RFID technology uses sensors that can be installed on containers, pallet loads, or even individual items. Uniform standards have not been agreed upon and various RFID producers are developing different systems. The sensors may be of different types, from microscopic microchips to postage-stamp-size for shorter-range communications and larger versions for long-distance communication via satellite to the user's network. They may be designed to provide various types of information from product information to real-time location and physical condition of containers. Using this system, users can determine the location of products and stock levels, and provide point-of-sale information. This has the potential for reducing inventory and out-of-stock costs, and improving coordination of steps in the supply chain. Wal-Mart is going to require 100 of its largest suppliers to start using some applications of RFID by January 2005 (Khermouch and Green, 2003). Germany's Metro Group AG expects its Chinese suppliers to use RFID for exported containers and pallets (Hutzler, 2004). In 2003, Benetton announced a plan to attach microscopic-size chips to track individual items of clothing from factory through sales floor to cash register. The chips will be made by Philips Semiconductors and will use microscopic antennas made by Lab ID, an Italian technology startup (Strasburg and Yi, 2003).

An indication of the scope of IT applications to health care in Europe, all requiring both hardware and software, can be seen from a very small and partial list:

- telemedicine and video-conferencing over the net;
- monitors on patients sending data to health research centers;
- privacy of patient information through the use of smart cards for EU citizens;
- UK-based B2B trading exchange for pharmaceuticals;
- wireless application protocols (WAPs) linking UK doctors with a US government database;
- computer-enhanced 3D imaging of the human body allowing less invasive surgery.

The development of new information about the human genetic system has provided additional tools in the search for and development of new medicines. These medicines have a worldwide market among the people and countries able to pay for them, and efforts are being made to increase their availability to those less able to pay.

The development of e-business software has had an important effect on international marketing. In addition to creating international markets for the software products themselves, it has enabled and encouraged companies and individuals to take entrepreneurial approaches to the international marketing process (as discussed in section 1.6).

Technological advances in traditional products and in manufacturing processes have also accelerated in recent years. While innovations in high technology often receive the greatest publicity, advances have been made in many fields and at many levels of technology. An indication of the range of advances is given in Exhibit 1.8.

EXHIBIT 1.8

Examples of international markets for products with various levels of technology:

- A plastic mechanical device that allows swimmers to talk to each other was invented by a US schoolboy. He patented it, formed a company, sold 5000 units of his 'Water Talkie' to Toys Я Us, and then developed other toys that he sold to retailers around the world. After three years, and with projected sales of a million units in 2001, he sold his business to a larger company for over $1 million.
- European builders developed construction techniques using insulating cement forms (ICF) to improve fire safety, increase sound insulation, reduce maintenance costs, and require less wood in smaller buildings. It is expected that the techniques will be used in 12.5% of US residential construction by 2003.
- An Italian firm developed a small-sized, lightweight floor polisher for hard-to-reach places. In 2001 it found an additional market in Japan where many buildings have relatively restricted spaces.
- Several German companies have developed recycling sorting processes, biological organic-based waste treatment systems, and other environmental technology with worldwide applications.
- A Belgian manufacturer of innovative wheelchairs designed for special types of disability now exports its products to 35 countries.
- A US producer of walnuts has found an export market for the shells, which are used by a Japanese producer of plant-based powders for industrial polishing, cleaning, and as a porosity adjuster for sharpening-stones.
- Combining mechanical and a number of electronic-related technologies, BioTrac of the United States has developed a magnetic bolus with attached microchip that may be inserted into cattle and other ruminant animals, with the same device used to administer large pills. It permanently identifies each animal, records its temperature, keeps track of its location, and can be read automatically at the slaughterhouse. It provides information of particular value to problems involving E. coli and mad cow disease.

Improvements in cargo ships and handling equipment, increasing containerization, applications of IT to scheduling and controlling shipments and to Customs procedures, new bridges and roads, high-speed trains, and a host of other technological advances and innovations have reduced the costs of international marketing of goods, services, and information.

The euro has lowered costs of international trade among member nations, eliminated exchange risks, and allowed more efficient cash management. Though its home base is outside the euro zone, the UK's Pilkington glass manufacturing company was able to reduce its European continental treasury operations from three offices to one central operation. This enabled it to substantially lower the amount of idle cash tied up in unbalanced loans and overdrafts, putting the money to work generating interest (Nairn, 2001).

Licensing of new and improved technology has become increasingly important for both large and small companies. The obtaining or sharing of technology is also being accomplished through acquisitions, mergers, and joint ventures, all of which have tended to stimulate trade.

In addition to contributing directly to an increase in international trade, technological advances have encouraged, and in some cases made possible, entrepreneurial approaches to international marketing.

1.6 Entrepreneurial approaches to international marketing

New approaches to international marketing are being undertaken by both small and large firms. Some of these have been made feasible by technological advances, particularly in communications, e-business, and logistics. Others have come about as emerging opportunities have been recognized or created.

E-business software has allowed companies to incorporate a number of key administrative functions online in a coherent system. These can include supply chain management and distribution chain management, expediting order and bill processing, providing cost and budgeting data, providing up-to-date sales information, and facilitating the analysis of sales trends and targeted markets. Specialized tools or programs are available to handle specific processes such as integrating online and offline sales channels, facilitating contract management, and handling online financial services. It is claimed that online applications can result in major cost savings, such as reducing the cost of processing payments from $1.00 each to $0.05 each, and reducing the costs of updating software licenses from about $220 to less than $20 (Kehoe, 2001). Some companies are specializing in developing integrating software; others are attempting to provide virtually the whole range of applications. Applications may also be designed to meet all of the information and interaction needs, outside of direct personal contact with the buyers, of specific business segments such as retail jewelers.

Specific software is available for developing and conducting customer relations programs. In 2000 sales of such software reached almost $8 billion. Sales of software programs for supply chain management amounted to over $5 billion.

1.6.1 Online marketplaces

The World Wide Web has allowed the development of online marketplaces. Automobile manufacturers Renault, Nissan, DaimlerChrysler, Ford, and General Motors, together with Japanese parts supplier Denso Corporation, set up an online global electronic market designed to increase efficiency and reduce costs in procurement. The system enables suppliers and auto manufacturers to show requirements, products, quantities, and delivery dates, with prices to be determined by bidding. With the addition of Toyota, Honda, Mitsubishi, and Mazda in

2001, it substantially changed the traditional exclusive automobile company–supplier relationships in the Japanese market. In 2000 food manufacturer General Mills Inc. teamed up with 16 competitors to set up an e-commerce network to work with transportation companies in combining shipments and in maximizing cargo space utilization. Chevron, Oracle, and a subsidiary of Wal-Mart teamed up to create an Internet exchange where convenience stores can order merchandise. Leading computer manufacturers created an online market where members can buy and sell computer components worldwide.

E-bay created an online marketplace where individuals can buy and sell items worldwide. This site is increasingly being used by businesses.

Online marketplaces thus are not restricted to large companies. Individuals and small companies around the world are finding new opportunities. Exhibit 1.9 shows how the World Wide Web has enabled small producers of handicrafts to join the international market.

EXHIBIT 1.9	**Novica: providing marketing opportunities for producers of arts and crafts**

The Internet and World Wide Web have dramatically increased opportunities for small and medium-sized companies to export their products and services worldwide.

Novica.com, a Los Angeles-based company, is making a business out of assisting artists and artisans from the developing countries to market their products. Before the advent of the Internet the marketing channels available to most small-scale makers of arts and handicrafts in the less developed countries were typically quite inefficient. In areas frequented by tourists, producers might set up small stands themselves, or they might sell directly to local stores run by others. Most artisans and artists, however, had to rely on local buyers and a chain of wholesalers that created high distribution costs. The small scale of operations made advertising of individual products unfeasible in most cases.

Through its web site (www.novica.com) Novica is now providing small producers with an additional, widespread, and efficient marketing channel connecting the makers with prospective buyers, both individuals and companies. Listing on the site is free, and more than 2000 artists were featured there by 2004. Novica evaluates the product to determine what it believes it can pay for it, and then estimates what the product can be sold for in the international market. Because of its efficiency in marketing through the Internet the company is usually able to raise substantially the amount paid to the producer and simultaneously offer prices to the international buyers that are much lower than they are currently paying for such goods. Novica makes its money on the difference between what it pays the producer and the price it charges for the product.

The operation is being financed by the venture capital arm of the *National Geographic* magazine and a number of individuals, institutions, and other venture capital firms. While at least some of the investors have social objectives related to assisting the artists and artisans in the developing world, the company is being operated as a business venture.

Small producers and individual artists and artisans who formerly had no economically feasible method to export can now use Novica's Web-based system to sell abroad.

Source: adapted from Craig, 2001, and Novica.com's Web site, 2004.

1.6.2 The virtual company

An interesting example of innovative approaches to business and marketing is the development of the virtual company. The virtual company is one that has no substantial physical headquarters or other physical facilities, and few or no employees. It contracts with other organizations or individuals to perform almost all business functions, such as design, procurement, production, warehousing, shipping, accounting, etc. The outside organization's employees and the independent contractors never need to visit the 'company'. In the ultimate example, the virtual company comprises only an individual with a desk, computer, communications linkages, and knowledge.

There are two factors that make the virtual company possible. The first is the owner's ideas, vision, knowledge, contacts, and ability to organize and coordinate the activities of others. The second is the Web-based communications linkages that permit the transmission of information, including pictures.

One example of a virtual company is Latcha & Associates. Mr Latcha used his knowledge and experience gained in working for advertising agencies dealing with automobile companies in setting up a one-person business. He started with organizing car displays at international automobile shows. Operating from the bedroom of his home, he used the Internet to post proposals and designs for his customers worldwide. Subsequently, he made a proposal to Ford Motor Company for changing the design and content of the brochures provided in dealers' showrooms. In 2000 he received a $10 million contract from Ford to produce brochures for the company. He then operated as a virtual advertising agency, linking himself with designers, photographers, and printers via the Web. All materials are sent digitally and all approvals made online (Simison, 2000).

A second example of a virtual company is an individual who organizes trade show arrangements for large real estate companies requiring display set-ups and logistics for the large number of its own employees who attend. A third example is an individual who develops curricula, organizes programs, and contracts with instructors to provide training for client corporations. All three operate from their homes. A number of consulting organizations in The Netherlands and elsewhere also operate in this manner.

1.6.3 Business–government alliances

Joint ventures and strategic alliances between government or quasi-governmental organizations and private businesses are being used more widely than before. In the year 2000 ten private–public joint ventures were formed in the United Kingdom. The largest of these alliances have been with national postal systems. Beginning in 1997 the German postal system, Deutsche Post, spent $3.1 billion acquiring stakes in 20 companies across Europe, the United States, and elsewhere. This included buying 97.4% of Danzas AG of Switzerland, the leading European logistics business, and an equity share in DHL, the US international package delivery system (Plehwe, 1999). In 2000 the US Postal Service began an alliance with DHL to provide a two-business-day service between 20,000 US postal locations and most addresses in over 200 foreign countries and territories. It also formed a partnership with Emery Worldwide aircargo company to deliver heavy items to homes. In 2001 the US Postal Service formed a strategic alliance with FedEx, valued at $6.3 billion over a period of seven years. It combines the complementary competitive strengths of FedEx's fleet of 665 aircraft worldwide with the coast-to-coast retail strength of the Postal Service in the United States.

1.7 The growth of nontraditional exports

Two types of non-traditional exports are becoming increasingly important in the first decade of the 21st century. One is the export of a new type of service. Of course the construction industry has a long history of sending employees overseas, and the travel and shipping industries provide services for both domestic and foreign individuals and companies. Now a new industry has arisen in the exporting of services of knowledge-industry workers who remain in their own countries while performing work for a wide variety of clients abroad. India and China are the major providers of such services but eastern European nations, smaller Asian nations, and other countries have also entered the market.

Secondly, a growing number of successful companies have found that the particular business models they have developed can enable them to successfully enter foreign markets. While business models have not traditionally been considered an export, it has become increasingly apparent that it is not only products or services per se that can give companies a competitive advantage abroad.

1.7.1 Exporting services of knowledge-industry workers

The improvements in communication technologies and capacities, together with sharply lower communications costs, have supported the development of cross-border sales of information services and software. Exports of local companies, such as India's large Tata Consultancy Services and Infosystems Technologies have been growing rapidly (DiCarlo, 2004). US and European companies have also set up offshore operations to supply their domestic and international operations.

The organizations in the lower-wage nations can hire well-educated but relatively lower-paid talent to provide the services at lower costs to the more highly developed and higher wage cost nations. India and the Philippines have been leaders in providing services to English-speaking countries. Now China is growing rapidly as a service provider for neighboring Asian countries as well as for North American and European firms. China has a comparative advantage in working with several nearby countries because of its large number of people who speak Japanese and Korean as well as Chinese dialects (Einhorn and Kripalani, 2003). Some EU companies have been outsourcing in nearby eastern European nations that have recently become EU members, where German and/or French and/or English are fairly widely spoken. A call center in Hungary services Swedish and US companies. Russia is also a rising power in information technology and customer support (Condon and Butler, 2003).

Initially, both India and the Philippines primarily provided call centers and back-office support for financial services, telecom, software, and retail companies. Increasing numbers of customers in the West who call their banks, telecommunications providers or other companies with questions about bills, for reservations, or for other information that can be handled by telephone have their inquiries answered from a call center overseas. The physical location of the call center is irrelevant as long as the employees of the call center have all the necessary records, information, access to reservations systems, etc., and the ability to speak the language of the callers. The only indication to the callers that the providers of the information are not nearby might be the accent of the respondent. In the United States, Canada, and a number of other countries accents are not necessarily indicative of where the call center is since even many domestic employees have accents associated with nations abroad. Routine accounting, order processing, and other administrative tasks were also handled by people overseas who were employees of local companies or, more frequently, employees of subsidiaries of the home country.companies.

The international provision of more highly sophisticated services is now growing rapidly. This has been made possible by the availability of a large number of highly sophisticated professionals in India and the Philippines, the comparatively low wage levels there, and the installation of high-speed fiber-optic networks in some major Indian cities. The cost of leasing a 128-channel telephone and data line from Los Angeles to Bangalore dropped from $58,000 per month in 2000 to $11,000 in 2004 (Drucker, 2004). Infosys Technologies in Bangalore hires well-educated Indians to develop software for companies including VISA, Northwestern Mutual Life Insurance, and Nordstrom (Millman, 2003). Radiologists in India can immediately receive and analyze CT scans and chest X-rays taken of patients in US hospitals. GE Capital's International Services unit has over 8000 university-educated employees in India providing a wide range of technical services. The accounting firm of Ernst & Young has 200 Indian accountants processing customized US tax returns. They plan to increase the number of their workers there (Schwartz, 2003). Small as well as large organizations are benefiting from the provision of services by knowledge-based workers abroad. One US company has only 3 employees in its Menlo Park, California home office, but employs 35 artists, designers, programmers, 3D modelers, animators, and Web developers at its subsidiary in India.

It has been estimated that the total number of US service jobs moving offshore will be 1.6 million by 2010 and 3.3 million by 2015. While approximately half of these are expected to be in back-office work, a wide range of fields including architecture, computers, law, medicine, and management will be affected. In a survey by DiamondCluster International Inc. of firms that already outsource some technology abroad, 86% planned to send additional jobs overseas (Kirby, 2004).

China is still primarily focused on back-office support for companies in a variety of fields including data entry for companies in Asia, multinationals doing business in the country, and even processing information for a Norwegian shipping line. As time goes on, however, more complex work is being done in China. A joint venture in China is developing a system to track production processes for the 14 North American factories of Sweetheart Cup Co. The Chinese government is working with international companies and Indian companies to train thousands of software specialists (Einhorn and Kripalani, 2003).

In general, European companies have been less aggressive than North American corporations in moving support services and jobs offshore. This is due to a combination of factors including a desire to achieve social outcomes, less flexibility in cutting domestic jobs, greater private and governmental concerns, and the less widespread use of some European languages. A Rand Corporation report has indicated that the flexibility and hospitable domestic environment will enable the US technology industry to maintain world leadership. Even in the United States, however, the loss of jobs in the technology sector worries employees in the industries affected, some economists, and some politicians, with some demanding legislation to slow or stop job exports (Konrad, 2003). There are also concerns in the United States about perceived potential risks of workers outside of US jurisdiction having access to detailed financial, medical and other information on US citizens. Possible identity theft and privacy issues are among the concerns (*San Francisco Chronicle*, 2003).

The concern over the loss of jobs in the United States has raised questions about the ethics of sending so much work overseas. It became a political issue in 2004 as national elections approached, with numbers of people calling for 'job protection'

(Shales, 2004). Chapter 2 provides some comments on how ethical issues may influence public policy when taken up by groups (unions, companies, politicians, etc.) that have or can gain political power.

While companies outsourcing work to firms overseas sometimes expected cost savings to be as high as 50%, the actual cost savings for many have been nearer 10–20%. Most, however, intend to do additional outsourcing (Kirby, 2004).

1.7.2 Exporting business models

Every company has a business model for what it does and how it does it. That is, each company offers some combination of products and/or services, develops methods for promoting, pricing, distributing, and supporting what it provides, and develops systems for management and control. In some companies the model is carefully thought out and its effectiveness periodically evaluated while in other companies it may simply be thought of as 'what we do.'

An organization that develops a new or different business concept, finds a better way of organizing its operations and doing business, identifies a potential new market and a way to exploit it, or develops some other innovative approach may gain a unique competitive advantage. The most valuable assets of highly successful Wal-Mart and Dell Computers are not stores or factories, but their business models using unique expertise in organizing their supply and distribution systems (Millman, 2003). The formation of Star Alliance, with its code-sharing, coordination of flights, and improved reservations and ticketing, generated greater traffic and higher load factors for each of the 14 member airlines that had joined as of 2004.

A number of companies that have developed improved business models have been able to successfully apply these models in expanding internationally. While their operations may include the export (or import) of products, it is really the model being used (exported) that gives the companies their competitive advantage. Exhibit 1.10 gives examples of innovative business models that have proved to be very successful in some markets outside of their home countries.

EXHIBIT 1.10

Examples of successfully exported business models:

- **E-Bay**. Company founders recognized that the Internet could be used to develop an entirely new type of market in which potential buyers and sellers could participate in online auctions without ever having to meet. It grew rapidly in the United States and then quickly spread overseas where its business method, organization, and size gave it a continuing competitive advantage. In 2003 its rapidly increasing sales volume exceeded $2 billion, 38% of it from overseas operations. (See Case 1.3).
- **Cirque du Soleil**. The Canadian-based circus without animals 'is one of the rare companies that utterly redefined their industries.' With a dozen full-time talent scouts searching the world for outstanding performers, heavy emphasis on research and development (about $40 million per year), elaborate staging and costumes, and New Age music, it has created 15 separate productions, none a flop. In 2004 five shows were touring the world and four were at permanent locations in the United States (Keighley, 2004).
- **Starbucks**. There are coffee shops and chains around the world, but Starbucks has successfully expanded to many countries by using a particular brand of 'lifestyle

Starbucks in Shanghai, China

marketing,' selling the 'Starbucks experience' rather than just their coffee (Sullivan, 2003). It aims to provide a community gathering place to enrich people's daily lives through its particular ambience, friendly service, and consistent quality of the coffee drinks and related products served. Started in the United States, the company now has over 7000 stores in 32 countries (Sewer, 2004).

- **Ikea**. The Swedish producer of high-quality furniture initially failed in its attempts to market its products overseas because of their high cost. The company lowered costs by developing ready-to-assemble products, reducing manufacturing costs through standardization and mass production, and going to international sourcing of materials. In a new and very successful effort at international expansion they emphasized very large stores with easy freeway/motorway access and plenty of parking. This enabled them to provide furniture that is accessible, approachable and economical. (See Case 4.1).

- **Seven-Eleven**. This chain of convenience stores was started when a store selling blocks of ice realized that their customers would be willing to pay premium prices for food products if the company would supply them at hours when traditional food stores were closed. It used this model, adding additional products and new locations, as it grew to become the world leader in convenience retailing. In 2004 it had over 24,000 stores operating in 18 countries. Seven-Eleven maintains its competitive advantage by making continual improvements in its demand tracking, stocking, and delivery systems to keep costs low and increase responsiveness to customer demands. The introduction of additional services and products serves to create additional customer traffic. (See Case 4.2).

- **McDonald's**. There were many hamburger stands and some chains of stores selling hamburgers in the United States before McDonald's was started. The McDonald's approach, unique at the time, was to organize the production and delivery (sale) of hamburgers and associated products (French fries, milk shakes, etc.) on the model of a factory assembly line. The products themselves, steps in production (assembly), and presentation to the customer were all standardized in order to produce food quickly, cheaply, and of consistent quality. Its initial advantage, coupled with a franchise system of opening new outlets, allowed it to expand rapidly. It remains the world's best-known fast food chain with over 30,000 company-owned and franchised outlets worldwide.

A business model that is successful in its home country will usually need some modifications to fit the differing economic, political, legal or cultural environments in other countries. In its international expansion of theme parks, Disney had to make a number of adjustments in Japan, and achieving success in France was even more difficult and tenuous. As with any international venture, management must carefully evaluate conditions abroad before entering new markets. Some concepts and approaches simply are not exportable to certain countries.

The companies introducing a new business model often lack the patents and particular technological advantages enjoyed by many exporters of products, though they typically have trademarks and brands that may become more valuable as they grow. In order to retain competitive advantage, they generally must rely on developing brand recognition, economies of scale, wide coverage, and/or innovations – as well as maintaining consistent high quality in service and products. The companies listed above, as well as many others, have continued to be very successful in some or all of their international markets, even when imitators or other competitors have emerged.

1.8 Overview of the book

While the basic principles of marketing are the same whether it is being done in a domestic or overseas market, the international marketer will find significant differences of degree, if not of kind. These differences, and any related difficulties, stem from the fact that environmental conditions vary, products are crossing national borders, and there may be marketing in two or more overseas areas at the same time.

The main focus of this book is on examining those marketing activities and institutions that are 'unique' to international and export marketing as well as activities that are involved but may not be unique. Chapter 2 looks at the bases of export marketing, both from a macro and from a micro perspective, and discusses ethical issues.

Chapter 3 is concerned with the international environment and examines effects of all the dimensions indicated previously in Figure 1.2. Since these dimensions are uncontrollable, adaptation to them is very important. Often business people tend to take for granted certain aspects of the environment such as culture, since this is generally well known in the domestic market. In export marketing this cannot be done since overseas markets represent unfamiliar cultures.

Chapter 4 covers the all-important market selection problem. Of concern are both strategies to employ and methods of assessment. This is the essence of market opportunity analysis. Chapter 5 deals with issues relevant to market(ing) research.

The components of the international marketing mix are discussed in Chapters 6 to 12. Chapters 6, 7 and 8 cover the various market entry modes and channel of distribution strategies. Chapter 9 looks at the product variable. Pricing a product for export markets and methods of financing transactions are the topics covered in Chapters 10 and 11. Finally, export promotion and market communication issues are discussed in Chapter 12.

Chapter 13 covers the practical aspects of the export order and shipment, and includes a broader look at physical distribution management. Where appropriate, strategic implications are discussed within the context of the particular topic of concern.

Chapter 14 looks at organizing for international marketing operations, and discusses some of the broad types of company organization structure.

QUESTIONS FOR DISCUSSION

1.1 Why has there been such an increase in interest by business firms in international and export marketing? Will this interest continue to increase? Why, or why not?

1.2 What is meant by internationalization and how does this relate to the global marketer?

1.3 Is taking a global view limited to companies that view themselves as global companies? Explain.

1.4 Is it meaningful to attempt to measure the degree (or amount) of internationalization of a firm? Explain.

1.5 What does it mean for a company to be 'market driven'? Is this really important in today's environment or can a company be successful without being so driven? Explain.

1.6 Explain the meaning of the following statement: 'If a company is to be successful in foreign markets its management must have a good understanding of all aspects of the environment within which it will be operating.'

1.7 Give two or more examples of how external factors (exogenous variables) in the international environment make export marketing more complex than domestic marketing.

1.8 What is inward internationalization? Explain the nature of the relationship between inward and outward internationalization from an individual company's perspective.

1.9 What are the three distinct components of export planning and strategy development and how are they related?

1.10 Identify the potential barriers (or obstacles) that face companies considering – or expanding – international marketing operations. Which are most important and which are less important? Explain.

1.11 When considering the ethical and moral issues underlying the behavior of an international marketer, should the manager follow the utilitarian, the rights, or the justice principle? Defend your position.

1.12 Is the role of the international marketer only to attempt to increase sales? Explain.

1.13 Is use of the World Wide Web appropriate only for large companies? Explain.

1.14 What is 'e-business'?

1.15 Are online marketplaces useful only to businesses? Explain.

1.16 Does e-business present a threat or an opportunity to traditional stores and wholesalers? Explain.

1.17 What factors have resulted in the rapid rise in outsourcing of jobs overseas?

1.18 Give an example of a 'business model' and how it can give rise to an opportunity to enter markets overseas.

REFERENCES

Barrett, A. (1995). It's a small (business) world. *Business Week*, 17 April, 96–101.

Bilkey, W. J. (1985). Toward a theory of the export marketing mix. Paper presented at the Academy of International Business Meetings.

Carlzon, J. (1987). *Moments of Truth*. Cambridge, MA: Ballinger.

Cavusgil, S. T. (1994). *CORE 4.0*. East Lansing, MI: Michigan State University.

Columbia Cascade (1997). *Export Expert: Judging your export readiness*. Computer software published by Columbia Cascade, Inc., Reston, VA.

Condon, C. and Butler, R. (2003). A chill wind blows from the east. *Business Week*, 1 September, 44–5.

Craig, J. (2001). Developing world artists' dot-com. *San Francisco Chronicle*, 29 January, B3.

DiCarlo, L. (2004). Software Sahib. *Forbes*, 15 March, 178.

Drucker, J. (2004). Outsourcing abroad becomes even more attractive as cost of fiber-optic links drops. *The Wall Street Journal*, 11 March, B1.

Einhorn, B. and Kripalani, M. (2003). Move over, India. *Business Week*, 11 August, 42–3.

Fost, D. (2004). Shoppers clicking, buying. *San Francisco Chronicle*, 24 February.

Fowler, G. A. (2004). Questions for ... Austin Lally. *The Wall Street Journal*, 21 January, B7.

Gray, B. J. (1995). Assessing the influence of attitudes, skills, and experience on international marketing investment decision-making: a behavioral/systems approach. *J. Global Marketing*, 8(3/4), 103–23.

Hampton, G. M. and Buske, E. (1987). The global marketing perspective. *Advances in International Marketing*, 2, 259–77.

Hutzler, C. (2004). China to draft standards for radio-tracking. *The Wall Street Journal*, 19 January, B4.

Kehoe, L. (2001). E-business to the rescue of the Valley. *Financial Times*, 21 February, 11.

Keighley, G. (2004). The phantasmagoria factory. *Business 2.0*, January/February, 103–7.

Khermouch, G. and Green, H. (2003). Bar codes better watch their backs. *Business Week*, 14 July, 42.

Kirby, C. (2004). Firms plan to send more jobs abroad. *San Francisco Chronicle*, 27 March, C1.

Konrad, R. (2003). US techs to continue to lead global sector. *San Francisco Chronicle*, 16 July, B4.

Korn, L. B. (1989). How the next CEO will be different. *Fortune*, 22 May, 157–8.

Kotler, P. (2000). *Marketing Management: The millennium edition*. 10th edn. Upper Saddle River, NJ: Prentice-Hall.

Levitt, T. (1986). *The Marketing Imagination*. New York: Free Press.

Luostarinen, R. (1994). *Internationalization of Finnish Firms and Their Response to Global Challenges*. UNU World Institute for Development Economic Research, Research for Action.

McKenna, R. (1991). Marketing is everything. *Harvard Business Review*, January–February, 65–79.

Mahone, C. E., Jr. (1995). A comparative analysis of the differences in perceived obstacles to exporting by small- and medium-sized manufacturers and traders. *The International Trade Journal*, 9(3), 315–32.

Matlack, C. and Gogoi, P. (2003). What's this? The French love McDonald's? *Business Week*, 13 January, 50.

Millman, G. J. (2003). Wake of the flood. *German–American Trade*, 14(2), 12–15.

Moon, I. (2002). A nation of digital guinea pigs. *Business Week*, 4 February, 50.

Mullaney, T., *et al.* (2003). The e-biz surprise. *Business Week*, 12 May, 60–8.

Nairn, G. (2001). A euro hub in Lancashire. *Financial Times*, 21 February, 11.

Piercy, N. (1982). *Export Strategy: Markets and competition*. London: George Allen & Unwin.

Plehwe, D. (1999). Why and how do national companies go 'global'? Berlin: Wissenschaftszentrum Berlin Für Sozialforchung.

Reinhardt, A. and Passariello, C. W. (2002). E-commerce starts to click. *Business Week*, 26 August, 56.

Roth, K. and Morrison, A. J. (1994). Implementing global strategy: characteristics of global subsidiary mandates. *J. International Business Studies*, 26(4), 715–35.

San Francisco Chronicle (2003). 14 July, 13.

Schwartz, N. D. (2003). Down and out in white-collar America. *Fortune*, June 23, 39–42.

Sewer, A. (2004). Starbucks to go. *Fortune*, 26 January, 61–74.

Shales, A. (2004). On trade, it's back to the Dark Ages. *Financial Times*, 23 February, 13.

Shoham, A. and Albaum, G. (1995). Reducing the impact of barriers to exporting: a managerial perspective. *J. International Marketing*, 3(4), 85–105.

Simison, R. (2000). New Technologies Give Small Advertising Firms the Edge. *The Wall Street Journal Europe*, 23–24 June, 32.

Strasburg, J. and Yi, M. (2003). Benetton to keep track of clothing with tiny transmitters. *San Francisco Chronicle*, 12 March, B1.

Sullivan, D. (1994). Measuring the degree of internationalization of a firm. *J. International Business Studies*, 26(2), 325–42.

Sullivan, J. (2003). Call it Starbucking. *San Francisco Chronicle*, 13 August, D1.

Taylor III, A. (2004). At $320,000 this Rolls is flying off the lot. *Fortune*, 26 January, 40.

The Economist (2003). Seriously wired. Page 7 in A survey of South Korea, 19 April.

Waters, R. (2004). A tussle for power in online shopping: the sites may have the goods, but the search engines have the eyeballs. *Financial Times*, 23 February, 11.

Welch, L. S. and Luostarinen, R. K. (1993). Inward–outward connections in internationalization. *J. International Marketing*, 1(1), 44–56.

Wild, J. J., Wild, K. L. and Han, J. C. Y. (2001). *International Business: An integrated approach*. Upper Saddle River, NJ: Prentice-Hall.

FURTHER READING

Miller, M. M. (1993). Executive insights: the 10-step road map to success in foreign markets. *J. International Marketing*, 1(2), 89–106.

The Economist (2001). A survey of globalisation. 29 September, 3–30.

Yoo, S. Y., Leone, R. P. and Alden, D. L. (1992). A market expansion ability approach to identify potential exporters. *J. Marketing*, 56 (January), 84–96.

Export of art goods from Hungary

A professor and her husband, while on vacation in eastern Europe, found some beautifully hand-crafted, fired-clay figurines for sale in Budapest. Displayed by the artist in a stall in a small open market near the Danube, the pieces were exquisitely fashioned in unique designs. In a long conversation with the professor, the maker commented that no one should buy one of the figures 'unless it spoke to him.'

During two visits to the market, and a trip to the artist's small studio in his home across the river, the professor bought three pieces. Two were different poses of a boy in a type of jester's costume and one a figure of a young woman in contemporary dress. The models, the artist's son and wife, were introduced at the studio. The studio contained a large number of finished individual pieces, no two alike. The artist indicated that he spent over half of his time at the stall selling his goods – time that he would rather spend creating. The relatively small number of tourists and the occasional local well-to-do individuals who visited his small open market stall simply did not provide enough customers.

Upon their return home, the professor and her husband displayed their new art pieces in their living room. They were surprised at how many of their friends admired the figures, and asked where they might obtain similar works.

Since the professor was teaching a course in international marketing, it occurred to her that she could use the development of a marketing plan for the figures as a classroom project. Such a plan could be either from the standpoint of the artist who wanted to sell his figures abroad, or from the standpoint of a dealer abroad who wanted to import and distribute the art goods. Such a plan would have to include at least a determination of potential demand, marketing channels to use, methods of promotion, export, import procedures, physical distribution, and economic feasibility.

Questions

1. How might a textbook such as this one be of use to: (a) the class in the assigned project, (b) the artist if he decided to try to export his works, and (c) a potential new importer in another country?

2. List some of the items that should be included under each of the major dimensions of a marketing plan for the art goods.

Murphy Company Limited

The Murphy Company Limited, located near Auckland, New Zealand, manufactured dishwashers and garbage pulverizers for home use, and cooking equipment and commercial pulverizers for restaurants. A relatively young company, its products were highly regarded by housing contractors and builders. The company had a reputation for quality construction and for good and prompt after-installation service.

Although sales were still growing, the managing director of Murphy, Bryan Murphy, realized that the New Zealand market was limited and would level off within a few years. There is a relatively small population and it is not growing appreciably. Therefore, he proposed exploring the possibility of exporting as a way to maintain growth.

The Export Institute was holding a two-day seminar in Wellington, the national capital, on opportunities for export by New Zealand companies. The director of marketing, Fred Murphy, along with his assistant Sam Murphy, decided to attend this seminar to see what these opportunities were and what types of assistance would be available to a company such as Murphy Company Limited, which had no export experience at all.

One of the presentations at the seminar was by Michelle Akory, an expert on export marketing and a university lecturer. Among the items that Ms Akory gave to the seminar participants was a listing of potential mistakes made by new exporters. This list is reproduced below:

1. Failure to obtain qualified export counseling and to develop a master international marketing plan before starting an export business.
   Correction: Get qualified outside guidance.
2. Insufficient commitment by top management to overcome the initial difficulties and financial requirements of exporting.

Correction: Take a long-range view and establish a good foundation or do not get involved.

3. Insufficient care in selecting overseas agents or distributors.

Correction: Conduct a personal evaluation of the personnel handling your account, the distributor's facilities, and the management methods employed. Remember, your foreign distributor's reputation is your company's reputation wherever he represents you.

4. Chasing orders from around the world instead of establishing a basis for profitable operational and orderly growth.

Correction: Concentrate efforts in one or two geographical areas at a time, then move on to the next selected geographical area.

5. Neglecting export business when the domestic market booms.

Correction: Make a long-term commitment to export business and do not neglect it or relegate it to a secondary place when the home market booms.

6. Failure to treat international distributors on an equal basis with domestic counterparts.

Correction: Do not isolate your export distributors from domestic programs. Expand institutional advertising campaigns, special discount offers, sales incentive programs, special credit-term programs, and so on, to include foreign distributors as equal partners. Otherwise, you run the risk of destroying the vitality of overseas marketing efforts.

7. Unwillingness to modify products to meet regulations or cultural preferences of other countries.

Correction: Modifications necessary to be legal and locally competitive are best made at the factory. If modifications are not made at the factory, the distributor must make them – usually at greater costs and, perhaps, not as well. As a result, the added cost may make your account less attractive for the distributor and less profitable for you.

8. Failure to print services, sales, and warranty messages in locally understood languages.

Correction: Print instructions, sales messages, warranty, and so on, in the local language. Just think how it would be if operating instructions on your new camera were in Japanese.

9. Failure to consider use of an export management company or other marketing intermediary.

Correction: If the company does not have the personnel or capital to invest in experienced export staff, engage an appropriate intermediary.

Questions

1. Does a small company such as Murphy Company Limited have the capability of exporting? Explain. Would it be better for the company to expand its product line for the New Zealand market?

2. Evaluate the nine 'common mistakes' in terms of their relative importance and impact on a company such as Murphy.

3. What should Fred Murphy recommend to Bryan Murphy?

CASE STUDY 1.3

eBay, Inc.

EBay was started in 1995 by an entrepreneur working from his home. It has developed into a business handling $24 billion of goods annually, with a net profit of $441.8 million on revenues of $2.17 billion per year (2003 figures, with amounts growing rapidly). Its phenomenal success has been based upon its use of the World Wide Web to create a new online marketplace. In essence, a market can be defined as the sum of all of the people who have possible interest in buying or selling a particular product or service and who are in contact with each other. The use of the World Wide Web has enabled eBay to broaden markets to include

people and organizations that otherwise would not have known of buying or selling opportunities. As could be expected, the expanded markets have usually provided benefits to both sellers and buyers. Meg Whitman, eBay's CEO, says 'At our core, we help make inefficient markets efficient' (Hof, 2003a).

The company quickly developed an international presence and now derives 40% of its earnings from overseas. EBay faces both opportunities and challenges in selection of additional markets to serve, types of services to be provided, security issues, growing competition, and further expansion of operations overseas.

An idea becomes a company

Pierre Omidyar, the founder of eBay, had been a computer science major at Tufts University when he moved to the San Francisco Bay Area and began working in the software engineering business. He had a combination of technical, creative, and entrepreneurial interests, and co-founded Ink Development Corporation. That company was subsequently sold to Microsoft. In 1995 his future wife, who collected Pez dispensers, complained that it was hard to find people in the area to trade with (Cohen, 2000). He decided that he could set up an auction site on the Internet and developed a simple and easy-to-understand mechanism for trading. In the autumn of 1995 he started AuctionWeb as a hobby on his home Internet service. The domain name was www.ebay.com (ebay.com web site). It was started as a free service but there was so much traffic on the site that he began to charge a small fee. Omidyar made money the first month and revenue kept going up rapidly (Cohen, 2000). As the volume grew and problems emerged, it became necessary to increase the capacity, adding equipment and making changes to the software.

With business booming, Omidyar brought in a Stanford University MBA. They hired technical people, customer-support staff, and finance people. He worked with a venture capital firm and arranged an Initial Public Offering (IPO), turning his CEO position over to Meg Whitman (who was a Hasbro Inc. executive before joining eBay). The IPO took place in 1998, and all of the staff members found themselves rich (Cohen, 2000). Every year since then, including the time of the dot-com bust, eBay revenues and profits have increased sharply (Kopytoff, 2004).

The number of employees also increased rapidly. The supporting software for the site, one of the most complicated applications ever created, had to be continually expanded and improved. Along with the rapid growth, there were some spectacular problems. In 1999 the eBay site went dark for 22 hours, resulting in lost fees of $4 million and a drop of $5 billion in eBay's market valuation. Maynard Webb was hired as president of eBay Technologies and Lynn Reedy was hired as senior vice-president for software development after the crash. There are now 640 people in the software department (Murphy, 2004). Technology became a core strength for eBay.

Making use easier and entering new markets

Ebay has continued to innovate, providing new sites and new services, and made acquisitions to support its online marketplace. It has also benefited as more individuals and organizations find that they can profitably offer items on eBay sites.

Ebay offers a wide variety of features that enable members to buy and sell on the site quickly and conveniently. In addition to the auction format for purchases, items may be purchased at fixed prices through the Buy-It-Now feature or through eBay's Half.com. The company offers a number of workshops and courses to teach people how to promote their products more effectively on eBay. They also provide discussion and chat boards to encourage open communication between members and the company. They have a feedback system in which buyers and sellers rate each other on each transaction, and the company watches for fraud. They have developed software to limit sales of merchandise such as guns and Nazi memorabilia (Hof, 2003b).

In spite of eBay's continuing efforts to make their site easier for customers to use, some people still hesitate to learn how to do it and to take photographs where appropriate. Separate companies with storefronts have been started where people can take items they want to sell. For a fee, these companies then take photographs and handle all other aspects of the listing for the customer. EBay does not discourage the formation of such companies, believing that any additional customers benefit eBay. EBay itself does not want to get into the business of opening stores.

Ebay purchased PayPal, a company that enabled users to send and receive payments through credit cards or bank accounts, for $1.5 billion in October 2002. This provided better service for eBay users than did eBay's previous system. Ebay shut down the handling of online gambling payments and some other activities of the newly-acquired PayPal unit. In 2003 eBay agreed to pay $10 million to settle US government charges brought against PayPal before it was acquired (*San Francisco Chronicle*, 2003). The PayPal unit is doing well, with its payments business up 64% in the first quarter of 2004 compared to the first quarter of 2003.

Ebay started a new Internet-postage venture with the US Postal Service in 2004 (Bandler, 2004).

After an eBay manager saw that some people were listing real cars in its category for die-cast model cars, the company developed a site for real cars (Hof, 2003a). EBay motors, launched in 1998, has since become the top online automobile site, with sales of over 4000 cars per month by 2003. It is used both by individuals and by dealers, for some of whom it provides the majority of sales. Advantages cited include wide selection, quick responses, and often lower overall transaction costs (Ross, 2003). Buyers can hire someone to inspect a vehicle offered for sale, but most rely on photographs and sometimes on e-mails to the sellers. One poll indicated that the majority of buyers believe the cars they purchased are as good or better than described, 47% find them slightly or significantly worse than described.

➡

Since the late 1990s parents looking for a hard-to-find toy have turned to eBay. In 2002, eBay kept in contact with toy makers and monitored its own sites to see which toys appeared to have high demand. They then supplied a list of the top 20 of these toys to regular sellers on eBay, mainly mom-and-pop merchants. The merchants then sold the toys on eBay when the toys became scarce in stores. A number of merchants did quite well in reselling these toys, though a few of the recommended toys did not sell well (Wingfield, 2002).

The types as well as the numbers of sellers on eBay have increased. Sears Roebuck & Co., Walt Disney Co., and others are selling brand-new items. These are often offered at fixed prices (Hof, 2003b). The site has not worked as well for corporations to move large stocks of unsold merchandise. One company found that when it offered more than a few dozen digital cameras or laptops, it tended to crash the price. EBay core merchants remain the small entrepreneurs for whom the site offers excellent opportunities (Wingfield, 2004b).

At least 12 state governments in the United States have found eBay an effective and profitable way to dispose of surplus items. Traditional auctions are often poorly publicized, inconvenient, and reach relatively few people. The result is that the governments typically receive very low prices for the goods. Sales through eBay commonly double or triple the prices received, and the government may even be able to sell something that appeared unsaleable. The state of Massachusetts had been trying unsuccessfully to sell a 128-foot lightship for a year and a half. They finally posted it on eBay, and it eventually sold for $126,100 (Whitaker, 2000). Everything from tools and furniture to confiscated jewelry is being sold.

Since 1999 billionaire financial guru Warren Buffet has offered himself once a year as a lunch companion to the highest bidder. The money goes to Glide Memorial United Methodist Church in San Francisco, an institution that provides many social services. Up until 2002 the bidding was done live at a fund-raising gala in San Francisco. Winning bids were in the range of $25,000 to $35,000 every year. In 2003 Buffett suggested that the auction be conducted on eBay. It was, and the winning bid in the five-day auction was $250,100 (Kopytoff, 2003b).

A home where former President Bill Clinton once lived was put up for sale on eBay, as was a whole small town in California (the latter bringing a much higher price than expected).

Small businesses may find the site useful for purchasing items from testing meters to bulldozers, lathes, and dental X-ray machines. The equipment, often surplus at another company, is generally available at a fraction of the cost of new equipment from the manufacturer. In 2002 sales of business products on eBay reached $1 billion, up 90% from the year before (Kopytoff, 2003c).

Expanding internationally

EBay currently receives 40% of its revenue from international operations. While its US business continues to grow rapidly, company executives emphasize potential for even more rapid growth overseas. EBay has local sites serving 17 countries in Europe, Asia, and in Australia and New Zealand. It also has a presence in Latin America through an investment in MercadoLibre.com. In December 2003 eBay launched a web site for Hong Kong residents, and increased its stake in South Korea's Internet Auction Co. It became a minority partner in EachNet in China in 2002, and took over complete ownership in July 2003. There is strong competition in some international markets and in 2003 the company shut down its web site in Japan where Yahoo is dominant (Kopytoff, 2004a). In the short term, Britain and Germany are expected to grow the most. In the longer term China, Korea, Taiwan, and other Asian nations are expected to provide more rapid growth.

Looking to the future

There are challenges facing eBay. Other online sellers and auction sites provide competition. Activists protest if items they deem offensive because of race or other reasons appear on the web site. Varying laws regulate what can be sold in various countries. Taxes on online sales have been imposed in some countries. Vigilance against fraud and non-payment are required. The high degree of market penetration in the United States would seem to indicate that more growth must come from other countries if eBay is to continue to expand at the present rates.

References

Bandler, J. (2004). Ebay chooses Pitney to provide technology for postal venture. *The Wall Street Journal*, 9 March, B6.

Cohen, A. (2000). World's biggest tag sale. *Reader's Digest*, July, 84–9.

Hoff, R. (2003a). Ebay rules. *The Business Week 50*, Spring, 172.

Hoff, R. (2003b). The eBay economy. *Business Week*, 25 August, 125–7.

Kopytoff, V. (2003a). EBay posts rosy results. *San Francisco Chronicle*, 23 April, B1, B4.

Kopytoff, V. (2003b). Buffett lunch bid not cheap. *San Francisco Chronicle*, 12 July, B1.

Kopytoff, V. (2003c). Businesses click on eBay. *San Francisco Chronicle*, 28 July, E1, E4.

Kopytoff, V. (2004). EBay's profit doubles. *San Francisco Chronicle*, 22 April, C1, C6.

Murphy, V. (2004). Control freak. *Forbes*, 29 March, 79–80.

Ross, Jr, B. (2003). EBay becomes national car dealership. *San Francisco Chronicle*, 21 July, E2.

San Francisco Chronicle (2003). PayPal to pay $10 million in gambling probe, 25 July, B2.

Whitaker, B. (2000). State governments are sold on eBay for surplus auctions. *San Francisco Chronicle*, 24 April, B6.

Wingfield, N. (2002). How eBay spurred sellers to grab hot toys. *The Wall Street Journal*, 13 December, B1.

Wingfield, N. (2004). As eBay grows, site disappoints some big vendors. *The Wall Street Journal*, 26 February, A1–A2.

http://pages.ebay.com

Questions

1. Evaluate eBay's marketing strategies to date. What changes, if any, would you suggest?

2. Evaluate its technical and personnel strategies. What changes, if any, would you suggest?

3. Has eBay really created a new kind of market?

4. Are eBay's efforts to increase and improve interactions with members worth the cost?

5. Is continued rapid growth desirable for eBay?

6. Where does growth appear to be feasible?

CASE STUDY 1.4

DaimlerChrysler AG

(This case study was written by Mitsuko Saito Duerr, Nicholas Gurney and Joel Nicholson, all of San Francisco State University.)

Introduction

In 2004 DaimlerChrysler's efforts to become a global car manufacturer were in serious trouble, and the company was considering a new Asian strategy (Mackintosh, 2004b). Its presence in the Asian market decreased when it abandoned its Japanese affiliate, Mitsubishi Motors, to bankruptcy or takeover. Its relations with Korean auto maker Hyundai Motors, in which it holds a 10% equity stake, had already broken down (Mackintosh *et al.*, 2004). In the United States its Chrysler arm was not performing to expectations, with an overall net loss since its acquisition. While the Mercedes division continued to make money, DaimlerChrysler overall had weakening profits and a small loss in 2001, primarily due to the Chrysler arm (Edmondson and Kerwin, 2003). This led to a 50% decline in the value of its stock (Mackintosh, 2004a). DaimlerChrysler's CEO, Jurgen Schremp, was under increasing criticism from stockholders, including the second largest asset management fund in Germany (Edmondson, 2004).

DaimlerChrysler AG had been formed in 1998 by the combination of Germany's Mercedes-Benz and the US's Chrysler Corporation. Originally described as a merger of equals, subsequent events demonstrated that it was actually an acquisition with power held by the German company. The acquisition, which had been strongly pushed by Mercedes-Benz CEO Jurgen Schremp, created the world's third largest automobile manufacturer, with Schremp as CEO. In 2000–1, DaimlerChrysler spent over $2 billion in acquiring a 37% (controlling) interest in Mitsubishi Motor Company of Japan, a 10% stake in Korea's Hyundai Motors, and outright purchase of Detroit Diesel Corporation, a US manufacturer of truck engines. The acquisition strategy fitted Schremp's vision of creating a global powerhouse offering a full range of cars. A number of other automobile manufacturers were also extending the breadth of their offerings during the same period.

The emphasis on providing a wide range of automobiles was a change from earlier in the 1990s, when the objective of a number of companies had been to produce a 'global car' that could be sold to specific market segments across all key world markets. Though several car companies including Mercedes-Benz had achieved varying degrees of success with this approach, it had limitations in a world with differing tastes and income distribution.

Entering the 21st century, the greatest opportunities appeared to lie in developing a 'global car *company*' or a 'world car *company*' that provides a mix of vehicles designed to capture a substantial share of the overall vehicle market in each of the world's key areas. The objectives were greater profits and the spreading of risks through the potential economies in research, product development, joint production, and marketing that larger size and breadth of coverage would allow.

Serious problems for DaimlerChrysler arose shortly after the merger. In the last half of 2000, the US

Chrysler division had a major drop in sales and profits changed to losses. The division lost $5.8 billion in 2001 (Edmondson and Kerwin, 2003), did not return to profitability until the second quarter of 2002, and then slid into a $360 million loss in 2003 (*Business Week*, 2004). Chrysler's share of the US passenger car market is continuing to decline (Fahey, 2003). In addition to worsening market conditions, clashes between US management and German headquarters arose over several issues. Some senior US executives quit, others were fired and replaced with German managers. Stockholders who had originally owned Chrysler shares filed lawsuits over misrepresentation of the acquisition as a merger, one group being paid $300 million by DaimlerChrysler and another has a $2 billion lawsuit pending (*Business Week*, 2004).

Mitsubishi Motors Corporation presented DaimlerChrysler with an unexpected problem after the acquisition. The company admitted to having covered up defects in their automobiles for a period of over ten years, and there were police raids on the company's headquarters (Ibison, 2004). The corporate climate in the company, and the lack of a sense of urgency made change difficult. An executive from the group of three other Mitsubishi companies (*keiretsu* members) that owned the controlling interest in Mitsubishi Motors Corporation before the merger now says 'We accepted DaimlerChrysler's capital participation in MMC because we cannot run a carmaker' (*The Nikkei Weekly*, 2004). In an effort to keep up sales in 2003, Mitsubishi Motors offered loans in the United States to customers with weak credit, resulting in very large losses on loans. When they tightened up credit, sales in the country dropped. For the year, sales fell 26% and the company had a loss of over $800 million for the six months ended 30 September (the end of the fiscal half year in Japan). In order to bring out new models necessary for its survival, the company needed a large infusion of cash. There were doubts that even such an inflow would solve their problems (Zaun, 2004). With the total amount of additional capital DaimlerChrysler felt was needed to bring Mitsubishi back to profit, and the amount that the other Mitsubishi companies were willing to put in, DaimlerChrysler decided simply to withdraw. It does not plan to sell its shares immediately.

Questions have been raised about both DaimlerChrysler's strategies and its management practices. There are several possible causes for the company's problems, including the timing of the acquisition and subsequent market changes, poor management of parts of the organization, possible difficulties in integrating managerial styles and motivating people, and/or problems in realizing potential economies and synergies. In order to understand the motivation of the company, why major problems arose, and what might

be done at this point, it is useful to look at several interrelated topics. These include: (1) the changing environment and structure of the worldwide automobile industry; (2) the differing and changing strategies of three historically successful producers (Mercedes-Benz/Chrysler, Toyota, and Ford); and (3) how DaimlerChrysler's present structure and strategy fit in with the competitive environment.

The changing worldwide automobile industry

The market for automobiles and automobile parts is already largely international, and becoming more so. Major US, European, and Asian producers are increasingly sourcing parts wherever they can be produced most economically, building production facilities abroad, and participating in joint ventures and other forms of strategic alliances. Market shares held by foreign automobiles in most European countries, North America, and some other countries have increased substantially in recent years. Among the industrialized nations, only Japan has had very limited penetration by foreign producers, held back by formal and informal trade barriers as well as by a lack of available distribution networks and consumer preferences. Countries that have attempted to isolate their automobile industries from the trend toward internationalization have generally produced only comparatively expensive cars that cannot compete in the world marketplace.

There is an estimated 25% excess production capacity in Europe and over 32% worldwide. This has put pressure on prices and created problems for smaller and over-extended producers. The escalating costs of developing more environmentally friendly and increasingly complex vehicles have made cooperation in research and development necessary for a number of companies. The overall result has been that the number of acquisitions, joint ventures, and strategic alliances among automobile manufacturers has increased sharply over the past decade and they now involve virtually every major producer and many smaller companies. At the beginning of the 1990s, 12 automobile companies accounted for 70% of the world market; in 2000, it only took four companies (GM, Ford, DaimlerChrysler, and Toyota) to do so.

The search for a 'world car'

During the late 1980s and most of the 1990s there was much interest in developing a 'world car' or 'global car' that could be sold in certain market segments throughout most of the world. Two opposing factors were at work in determining the feasibility of this strategy. On the one hand, as improved communications and increased interactions among people spread information and ideas worldwide, people become more alike in the general types of consumer goods they want. For example, throughout the world there is a small, long-existing market for luxury cars and a growing market for medium-priced cars. On the other hand, as people became more affluent, they tend to demand more variety and choice. Additionally, basic differences in consumer preferences remain because of cultural, economic, and institutional differences.

The challenge for automobile companies is to determine the product mix, the locations for design, development and production, and the marketing strategies that will most effectively and efficiently meet the demands of their targeted markets. Insofar as they are able to develop cars salable to a wide global segment, rather than just a segment in one country or region, they can enjoy substantial economies of scale in manufacturing and marketing. This, in turn, can increase the value of their brand franchise, their sales, and their profits. Yet they still need to obtain market segments sufficiently large to support the research and development efforts necessary to meet changing market demands.

Rolls-Royce was a clear example of a company that could sell the same automobile all over the world to the small segment of the very rich. However, this segment eventually proved to be too small to support the design and development efforts required for maintenance of the company's Rolls-Royce and Bentley marks and they were eventually sold off. Other comparatively small players formed strategic alliances, were taken over by larger players, or disappeared.

The change to the 'world car company' or 'global car company'

Concentrating on serving one market segment limited the size of a company, and thus limited the potential benefits from economies of scale in research, product design and development, production, and marketing. Larger profits seemed to require a 'world car company' or a 'global car company' that could compete successfully in a number of market segments in two or three of the world's major markets. Ford benefits from having major market shares in automobiles and light trucks in both the US and European markets, and strategic alliances worldwide. General Motors, though having lost market share continuously over a 30-year period, is still the world's largest automobile manufacturer, with operations worldwide. It has multiple relations with other automobile companies including Italy's Fiat; Japan's Suzuki Motors, Isuzu Motors, Fuji Heavy Industries; a joint venture in China; and others. Toyota has the largest market share in Asia, and large market shares in the United States and Europe, and is increasingly involved in strategic alliances with other companies.

Against this background, Mercedes-Benz embarked on its present strategy to become a global car company.

Three strategies

Three different strategic approaches are available for automobile manufacturers striving to become world car companies or global car companies, and any given enterprise may go through all of them over time. The strategy may focus on production in the home country, using exports to meet foreign demand. It may move on to producing as well as marketing in a number of countries, becoming multinational but maintaining a domestic orientation with research, development, and control functions all centered in the home country. Finally, a company may become global in orientation as it begins to design, develop, produce, and market products in whatever regions are most economically appropriate.

All three of the companies discussed in this case develop and produce a variety of types of automobiles that can be sold across large regions of the world, and have substantial sales in several market segments in at least two of the world's three major market areas. All three companies have also achieved generally good levels of profitability overall. Yet each of the companies is changing its strategies as new markets emerge and existing markets become increasingly competitive.

The experiences and evolving strategies of Ford, Toyota, and Mercedes-Benz before its acquisition of Chrysler illustrate some of the advantages and disadvantages of the different approaches. They also provide a framework for analyzing the appropriateness of the acquisition and other policies that led to DaimlerChrysler's present problems.

Ford and the quest for globalization

Ford has become the most globalized of the three companies, with research and design facilities as well as manufacturing and marketing operations around the world. The company, started in 1903, introduced the assembly line with interchangeability of parts to automobile manufacturing. With its advantages in low cost, high volume, and availability of parts for service, it was able to rapidly expand its market. It quickly moved from a domestic to an international and then to a multinational firm. The company set up a sales branch in France in 1908, built its first European factory in Britain in 1911, established Ford-Werke AG in Germany in 1925, and began production in Japan in the same year. Ford has factories in North America, Latin America, Europe, and Asia.

Where government policies, limited market sizes, or other factors have kept the company from developing wholly owned factories, they have used exports and/or joint venture production facilities to meet local demand. In 1971, Ford started buying trucks from Mazda for sale in the rest of Asia. When Mazda had financial difficulties in the mid-1970s, it turned to Ford for help and in 1979 Ford purchased a 25% equity share in Mazda primarily in order to gain knowledge related to small car development and production. The relationship was often a difficult one as the two companies tried to bridge national and cultural differences, different corporate cultures and styles, differences in objectives, and communications problems. Direct involvement of senior management, frequent meetings, and a willingness to seek mutually beneficial solutions helped the relationship to develop and strengthen over time.

The relationship assisted Ford in moving toward global design, manufacturing, and marketing. In the late 1980s, then Ford Chairman Donald E. Petersen had called for a 'global car,' one that could be engineered on one continent and then produced and sold in several. The objective was to avoid expensive duplication of development and engineering expenses. The 1991 Escort, with an exterior designed by Ford and the inside engineered by Mazda, was made for assembly in 12 locations and sale in 90 markets. The cooperative venture met the objectives of both companies and was estimated to have saved at least $1 billion in development costs. The Escort, with some variations in design between countries, became the best selling car in the world.

Ford has continued to work effectively with Mazda as a partner. They cooperated on development of 10 models, with one of every four Fords sold in the United States having some input from Mazda and two of every five Mazdas having some Ford input. When Mazda had additional financial difficulties during the 1990s, Sumitomo Bank asked Ford to take control of the company.

In 1995, in a continuing effort to impose a global mindset on all of the company's product-development activities, the company split its worldwide design and engineering effort into five separate 'vehicle centers.' Located in the United States, England, and Germany, each focuses on a particular market segment. The European Mondeo was designed in this manner and was also the basis for US-made cars. The Ford Focus, a more upscale car designed to replace the Escort, has become one of the best sellers in the world, being named Car of the Year in more than a dozen European countries and doing well in the United States.

Ford also has various types of strategic alliances with other firms in Europe, Asia, and Latin America, including a cooperative agreement with PSA Citroën to develop environmentally friendly, high-technology diesel engines. In 1999 the company opened a new research laboratory in Aachen, Germany, devoted primarily to developing new environmental technologies. Ford also continues to design new cars for particular regions.

Ford has four key strengths, as follows:

1. It is the most advanced in developing and integrating worldwide research, design, and production operations.
2. It has a wide range of models with the industry's most complete lineup of the highly profitable SUVs.
3. It has excellent brand recognition, particularly in the United States and in Europe where its long-term presence gives it the aura of a European company.
4. Ford's factories have the highest productivity of the big three in the United States and also the highest of the biggest four in Europe.

Ford's weakest position is in Asia, where the Japanese have 85% of the market. Its larger cars are not suitable for the roads and tastes of most Asian nations, and it does not have the reputation for quality and elegance enjoyed by the Mercedes mark. Toyota, with its reputation for quality and price in smaller cars and luxury models, and its longer-term presence in most Asian markets (excluding Korea and Taiwan) provides very difficult competition.

Toyota and changes in strategy

The Toyota Motor Company (then Toyoda Automatic Loom) began small-scale manufacturing of automobiles in Japan in 1935 and later began making trucks. After the destruction of World War II, and a crippling labor dispute in 1949, it was a small and struggling truck manufacturer selling only about 300 vehicles per month. Then orders for thousands of trucks came in from the US Defense Department for support of the Korean War. Profits from this sale gave the company money to finance the production of passenger cars.

Toyota had already developed a prototype small car, and had studied Ford's production lines. The company invested in modern manufacturing equipment, eventually succeeded in getting its workers to form an 'enterprise union', adopted the 'lifetime' employment system for its regular assembly workers, invited employee input in decision making, and introduced the 'just-in-time' inventory system. Formal and informal trade barriers provided Toyota, and other Japanese manufacturers, with a protected domestic market while they developed an increasingly efficient production system.

As the scale of production rose and costs declined, Toyota decided to try to export to the US market. The first cars were introduced into the United States in 1958, but failed in road tests and because of poor styling. A second entry into the US market, with redesigned automobiles and improved quality, was a success and they subsequently began exporting to Europe. The oil crises in 1973 and 1978–9 made Toyota's small, fuel-efficient automobiles very attractive in the United States, and their market share grew rapidly.

While preferring to continue to manufacture only in Japan and rely on exports to supply international markets, Toyota eventually felt compelled to begin production abroad because trade barriers limited their ability to increase market shares overseas. The rapidly growing Japanese automobile sales in the United States, accompanied by job losses for US workers and serious loss of market share for US manufacturers, had led to a 'voluntary restraint agreement' in 1980. This had seriously limited the export of Japanese cars to the United States. Continuing restrictions on imports by European nations limited Toyota's ability to increase exports to that area.

Toyota opened its first factory abroad in 1984 when it joined General Motors in a joint venture, New United Motors Manufacturing Inc., to produce cars in California. Toyota used the joint venture as much for a learning experience as for the cars produced. Their primary objectives included learning to work effectively with US labor and suppliers. They incorporated features into their managerial approach designed to appeal to US workers' egalitarian values while preserving the key elements of their highly productive manufacturing system. The success of this plant was followed by the establishment of a wholly owned factory in Kentucky in 1986, and the opening of plants in Canada and then in the United Kingdom in 1992. It has since added manufacturing bases in Thailand, Taiwan, Indonesia, the Philippines, and Brazil. By 2000, Toyota had five factories in North America, with a sixth to be started in 2001.

Toyota is today one of the largest automobile manufacturers in the world and has the largest market share in Japan. From an initial marketing niche of small and relatively inexpensive cars, the company expanded into more expensive models and eventually into luxury cars. It also produces particular cars for individual countries and areas.

It has moved from an international to a multinational company, and now has some of the characteristics of a global company. Approximately 14% of its sales are in Europe, 32% in the United States, 40% in Japan, and approximately 14% elsewhere. It sells more automobiles overseas than in Japan. Of the 1.7 million cars it sold abroad in 1995, 60% were assembled in local markets. Toyota still produces in Japan many of the parts it uses in overseas factories, but it is rapidly expanding the procurement and use of local components for these plants. Toyota continues to retain most design and development in Japan, while relying on its production system to ensure customer satisfaction through high quality and low cost.

The company's key strengths are its high productivity, reputation for quality, and unrelenting pressure for continual improvement in both areas. While still lacking as wide a range of vehicles as Ford, it has steadily increased the number of models it offers. Its advance into luxury cars was very successful. With over US$ 25 billion in cash and government securities, it has the economic strength to exploit new opportunities.

It is hard to find major weaknesses, though the ability to achieve additional market share in Europe has been limited by a failure to style cars specifically to meet European preferences. A stronger research and design effort in Europe should help to overcome this problem.

Mercedes-Benz's preference for an exporting approach

For many years before the formation of DaimlerChrysler, Mercedes-Benz relied heavily on exporting in serving the international market. Until the late 1990s, the company concentrated production in Germany while developing worldwide distribution channels.

The worldwide luxury car market has been Mercedes-Benz's niche since the 1960s and it enjoys a worldwide reputation for luxury vehicles with a classical style. Owning a Mercedes-Benz has become a symbol of success in developed, newly industrialized, and less-developed nations alike. It dominates the luxury car segment in almost every country in Southeast Asia. In 1982 it introduced its first compact car, the Mercedes 190. DaimlerBenz, the holding company of Mercedes-Benz, carried out a series of mergers and acquisitions after 1989 under president Edzard Reuter.

Until the 1990s Mercedes produced a relatively narrow range of models with comparatively infrequent model changes. Meanwhile, Ford was producing a wide range of sizes and styles of automobiles and frequent model changes in its major markets. Then Toyota extended the range of its exports to include higher-end models. When the luxury Lexus 400 was introduced in 1991, its sales surpassed those of Mercedes-Benz in the United States. It was also rated more highly in consumer satisfaction surveys than Mercedes-Benz. The resulting economic and competitive pressures forced

Mercedes-Benz to reconsider its strategies. Chairman Helmut Werner stated: 'We had to understand that the world had changed, and that the philosophy Mercedes had pursued so successfully had come to an end.'

The company reduced prices and succeeded in regaining US market share. It also began to produce more new models and designs. In 1995, Mercedes-Benz started marketing three new models of its E-class luxury car. This was the first time in 11 years that the company had introduced fully remodeled cars in the Japanese market. A new and relatively inexpensive compact, the A-class hatchback, was introduced in October 1997.

The high cost of producing automobiles in Germany, coupled with the increased competition from the Japanese, caused the company to begin producing overseas. A factory was opened in the United States in 1997 to produce a new SUV. The A-class was produced in Brazil as well as in Germany. Asian plants followed. The greatest shift in strategy, however, was the acquisition of the US's third largest automaker, Chrysler Corporation, and the creation of DaimlerChrysler. Other acquisitions followed.

The company's key strengths before the acquisitions were: (1) its core competencies in superior engineering, high-quality products, and time-honored designs; (2) its worldwide distribution network; and (3) its reputation. Its major weaknesses were: (1) the comparatively low overall volume of sales that somewhat limited resources available for design and development of new models; and (2) the lack of production and marketing capacity for high-volume cars that limited total company size and profits.

DaimlerChrysler's structure and strategy

The acquisition of Chrysler and the purchase of a controlling interest in Mitsubishi appear to be in keeping with the trend toward developing 'world car companies.' From a position of being the ninth largest producer in Europe, it has become the world's third largest producer with a global market share of 11% (compared to GM with 23%, Ford with 17%, and Toyota with 9%). There are a number of potential benefits in having substantial shares of several market segments in more than one major world market. These include the following:

1. permitting a higher level of spending on research and development;
2. supporting joint development and production of related products among its separate divisions;
3. reducing the risk of poor market acceptance of one product from seriously damaging overall results of the diversified company;

4. providing valuable additional information inputs regarding varying demands and manufacturing systems; and
5. allowing synergies in marketing.

DaimlerChrysler originally stated that it did not intend to take actions that might adversely affect its own premium status. It pledged to limit sharing Mercedes components with Chrysler and intended to move very cautiously in undertaking any cooperative endeavors with either Mitsubishi or Chrysler, though Mitsubishi and Chrysler might work together. This is now changing because of the losses at Chrysler and Mitsubishi.

Part of the current problems of DaimlerChrysler stem from timing and, possibly, lack of adequate knowledge of the US market. At the time of the acquisition of Chrysler, the US automobile market was strong and expanding. The years 1998 and 1999 were exceptionally good in both sales and profits. Chrysler was benefiting from the popularity of its minivans, the company was able to offer lower incentives to prospective buyers than GM and Ford, and marketing costs were comparatively low. Several problems emerged during 2000. Sales began to weaken, particularly in the latter half of the year. Chrysler had always been the weakest of the US's big three, and the first to suffer in a downturn. It had been saved from bankruptcy a number of years earlier by a US government loan, and had done well in recent years primarily because of its pioneering of minivans and its continued leadership in developing improved models. Other automobile companies were catching up in the minivan market, and Ford was the leader in developing and marketing the SUVs that were gaining an increasing share of the overall market. Industry wide, the offering of 'incentives' (discounts to purchasers) was increasing, reducing profits from sales. Chrysler was reluctant to cut production to meet current demand, so it was necessary to offer exceptionally large incentives.

There are other problems also. In spite of the launching of the 'smart car' and some other less expensive vehicles, Mercedes-Benz has traditionally benefited from its reputation as a producer of very high quality automobiles. Though it had to respond to the threat from Japanese luxury cars by lowering costs somewhat, its reputation made it unnecessary to compete primarily on price. It thus did not need to have the continual stress on productivity and price that drove the Japanese auto makers. The same approach was not appropriate at Chrysler, however. This division has to compete on price with larger US manufacturers that have a wider range of vehicles to offer, and with Japanese companies which continue to enjoy a cost advantage.

Nor did DaimlerChrysler foresee all of the problems that were to befall Mitsubishi Motors. As the fourth largest producer in Japan, Mitsubishi faced the same basic problems of the other smaller companies in the Japanese automobile industry due to the prolonged economic downturn, excess capacity, and redundant workers. It also had a group debt totaling over $16 billion at the end of 1999. However, the scandal resulting from the disclosure that Mitsubishi had been illegally covering up defects and recalls for 10 years could not have been foreseen. The accomplishments of Renault's Carlos Ghosn at Nissan, Japan's second largest automobile manufacturer, could not easily be duplicated at the smaller Mitsubishi.

Another problem that arose was the difference in management style at DaimlerChrysler and the two widely different styles at Chrysler and Mitsubishi. The parent company's managerial style is more authoritarian than the US style, and much more abrupt and less consultative than the Japanese style. When Ford took over control of Mazda, appointing a US president, Mazda was brought back from six successive years of losses to profits in 1998 and 1999, before again falling into the red. This relationship is substantially different than that faced by DaimlerChrysler. Ford had worked closely, cooperatively, and effectively with Mazda for several years in joint product development, production, and marketing arrangements before it took charge. Both sides learned a lot about shared and differing values and approaches during that period, and so were fairly well prepared for the new control arrangement. Ford also replaced the original person sent to be president of Mazda after he found himself in confrontation with the labor union for pushing too hard on a restructuring program.

DaimlerChrysler executives offended Mitsubishi board members in a country where arrogance and confrontation are abhorred. But some progress was made. DaimlerChrysler has begun marketing its new smart car in Japan, both through Mitsubishi dealers and its own dealers. It planned to develop additional models of the car jointly with Mitsubishi.

In the United States, Chrysler's top management made some miscalculations and mistakes during the period after the merger. They had incurred heavy expenses in launching their new minivans, and they had hoped to recover these costs by reducing incentives when the new model was released. Competitive pressures prevented them from doing this, incentives increased, sales weakened rather than increased, and inventory built up. It appears that top management did not realize how serious a loss would result, and failed to give accurate information to the German headquarters. Some US business periodicals suggested that the Chrysler unit should have taken strong action on its own, given the buildup of unsold vehicles and the escalating incentives.

Chrysler Group's CEO, James Holden, was fired after he informed DaimlerChrysler's CEO, Jurgen Schremp, of the need to temporarily idle seven factories at a cost of $350 million. Holden was replaced with a German executive who has some US experience, but no experience in the mass-produced automobile market. Additionally, several other senior executives have been fired and replaced by German nationals. These actions reinforced the feeling of some managers and workers that German management is too authoritarian. A number of key executives, including the designer responsible for some of the company's best-selling models, resigned.

Jurgen Schremp stated that he always meant Chrysler to be subordinate, in spite of the fact that during the negotiations he had said it would be a merger of equals. This was viewed as both duplicitous and arrogant. He also dissolved the DaimlerChrysler ad hoc shareholders' committee of which the company's third largest shareholder, the American Kirk Kerkorian, was a member. That resulted in unfavorable reactions in the press and from company personnel, and eventually led to the lawsuits against DaimlerChrysler.

Dieter Zetsche, the CEO who replaced Holden, worked to restructure Chrysler, focusing on adding flexibility and cutting costs in materials management, fixed costs, and operations. He also looked at possibilities of economies of scale and common designs with Mitsubishi and Hyundai.

A major opportunity to effect cost savings for both Chrysler and Mercedes would have been to move quickly to develop design, procurement, and manufacturing cooperation. This was impeded by Schremp's desire to avoid taking any actions that might adversely affect Mercedes premium status. Executives at Mercedes kept their designs secret and their parts different from Chrysler's to protect Mercedes' reputation or mystique. Engineers at Chrysler preferred to maintain what independence they could. An effort begun in 2001 resulted in the introduction in 2003 of a vehicle cooperatively developed. The companies are also working together on a set of components that can be used on a number of vehicles. Potential cost savings from such cooperation are very large (Boudette, 2003).

With control of Mitsubishi Motors now over, any cooperation with the Mitsubishi group will have to be on a mutually agreeable basis. Given the history of the relationship, and the very nonJapanese action taken by DaimlerChrysler in its sudden withdrawal, this would require a very careful approach by DaimlerChrysler.

Whether DaimlerChrysler can solve its Chrysler division problems remains to be seen.

References

Boudette, N. (2003). At DaimlerChrysler, a new push to make its units work together. *The Wall Street Journal*, 12 March, A1.

Business Week (2004). 12 January, 72–3.

Edmondson, G. (2004). Daimler's fumbles are firing up Europe's shareholders. *Business Week*, 19 April, 52.

Edmondson, G. and Kerwin, K. (2003). Stalled. *Business Week*, 29 September, 53–5.

Fahey, J. (2003). Celine Dion? Who's that? *Forbes*, 22 December, 58–9.

Ibison, D. (2004). Mitsubishi Motors reels as Daimler walks away. *Financial Times*, 24–5 April, 1.

Mackintosh, J. (2004a). Three on the starting line to follow Schremp at Daimler. *Financial Times*, 19 February, 16.

Mackintosh, J. (2004b). Daimler to 'reconsider' its Asian strategy. *Financial Times*, 24–5 April, 8.

Mackintosh, J., Ibison, D. and Grant, J. (2004). DaimlerChrysler cuts lifeline to Mitsubishi unit. *Financial Times*, 23 April, 1.

The Nikkei Weekly (2004). Mitsubishi group hits rough patch, 26 April, 2.

Zaun, T. (2004). Mitsubishi Motors needs a fill-up. *The Wall Street Journal*, 6 February.

Questions

1. What problems would Mercedes-Benz have faced if it had remained a niche player selling 'world cars' to the luxury market worldwide?

2. What are the key characteristics of Ford's approach to internationalization/globalization?

3. What are the key characteristics of Toyota's approach to internationalization/globalization?

4. Which of the three companies approached internationalization best? Explain.

5. Are there other approaches to internationalization/globalization that Mercedes-Benz could have taken rather than relying on large acquisitions? What problems might they have caused?

6. Should the potential problems at Chrysler and Mitsubishi have been foreseen by German management?

7. If Ford was so successful in working with Mazda, why should DaimlerChrysler have any concerns about working with Mitsubishi?

CHAPTER 2

Bases of International Marketing

2.1 Introduction

The rapid expansion of international trade that occurred in the last half of the 20th century is continuing in the 21st century. Major factors in this expansion include reduction in barriers to trade and investment through regional integration, widening and linking of markets with advances in communications and e-commerce, improvements in transportation and logistics, increasing interdependency of companies and industries in different countries, and rapid technological advances. In spite of occasional slowdowns or disruptions in some regions due to war and threats of war, terrorism, and disease, international trade continues to increase in relative importance in most economies.

This chapter provides a background for the analysis of international marketing and export management in later chapters. Three central issues in both international trade theories and in the behavior of individual firms are discussed:

1. What are the gains from exporting and international trade?
2. Why do countries and companies involve themselves in exporting?
3. What goods and services should a country export, and which should they import?

The chapter reviews key concepts, models, and elements of macro and micro bases of international trade and exporting. In addition, the chapter discusses issues surrounding ethical behavior of companies and their employees. While written from the perspective of exporting, much is also applicable to investment and strategic alliance decisions. In short, what is discussed is appropriate for all types of international marketing activity.

2.2 Potential benefits from export marketing

Ideally, export marketing occurs on the premise that it results in benefit to all participants and injury to none (other than perhaps competition), regardless of whether we are considering nations or individual firms. For the individual business concern this usually means that profits are realized, either directly in the case of the seller (exporter) or indirectly for the buyer (importer). The discussion in this section will be primarily in the context of international trade for it is here that the macro effects are more readily apparent.

Generally speaking, the benefit of international trade to a country is determined by its impact on consumption and production. No country is entirely self-sufficient in terms of its ability to satisfy effectively and economically the entire range of the ever-changing desires of its populace. Since consumption is the end of economic activity and production is but a means to that end, the most basic of all contributions of international trade is that to the welfare of domestic consumers. Active trade relationships among countries create employment opportunities, and consumers gain as employment is their source of purchasing power for both domestic and foreign goods and services.

2.2.1 The effects of imports

Interestingly, to economists the real benefits of trade lie in importing rather than in exporting. Thus the only real reason for exporting is to earn the funds to pay for imports. This was clearly stated almost 200 years ago by James Mill when he said the following: 'The benefit which is derived from exchanging one commodity for another, arises, in all cases, from the commodity *received*, not the commodity given' (cited in *The Economist*, 1997, p. 85). The nature of potential benefits of importing consumer goods are obvious – namely, lower price, an increase in the supply and variety of goods from which consumers can choose, and being able to access the results of technological developments and advancements. While not quite so obvious, the effect of importing industrial goods is the same. However, it is not a direct benefit, but depends on the impact that such imports have on the domestic production sector of the economy.

In the first place, importing certain industrial products, whether raw materials or capital equipment, brings about lower domestic costs of production than would be possible if the consumer goods manufacturer bought only from domestic suppliers. Another way of looking at some raw material imports is that they tend to conserve precious resources.

Second, importing many industrial goods, particularly certain raw materials such as copper and tin, enables the production of goods that depend almost exclusively, and in some cases entirely, on nondomestic sources of supply. It may be that a country has to import because it is not capable of supplying domestic buyers with all their requirements from domestic resources. Oil-producing countries of the West that also import from the Middle East are examples. Again consumers gain by paying lower prices but, in addition, gain through the greater quantity and variety of goods made available to them in the marketplace.

A major benefit of importing to a nation and to individual companies is the acquisition of technology to add to whatever innovations are developed locally. This happens in three ways (Sachs, 2000, p. 82). First, countries can *import directly* technology in the form of capital and consumer goods (e.g., cell phones, machine tools for use in industrial production, etc.). Second, they can *license* technologies from those who developed them. Third, a country can attract *foreign direct investment* (FDI), so that a multinational company can establish production facilities within its borders (e.g., Intel's plants in Ireland and Malaysia). Licensing and FDI represent a direct import of the technology itself, which is the preferred acquisition method of developing countries. In all cases, however, countries must also be successful as exporters in order to pay for the imports of technology or to pay dividends on foreign investment.

Clearly, there may also be adverse effects in the importing country. In order to pay for imports, there must be a capital outflow. Not only does this have a negative effect upon the country's balance of payments, but there would be a reduction in the amount of foreign exchange available for other needs. Increased competition to locally produced goods may exist, and labor could be affected if this competition led to lost sales and profits and redundancy in employment. Since a significant amount of imports into a given country can result from intracompany 'sales' this situation could occur more often than would be apparent.

On balance, the effect of imports will, in practice, vary on a country-by-country basis.

2.2.2 The effect of exports

In order to finance a country's imports in a way that does not adversely affect its balance of payments and cause a drain on its international monetary reserves, a country must export. Consumers have a stake in the exports of domestic firms to the extent that high volume creates economies in the production process which are then passed on. That is, selling abroad helps to gain economy in production at home, which means lower prices to consumers of domestic products. For the individual firm, a lowering of product costs tends to improve its competitive position both at home and abroad, and helps to diversify the risk inherent in conducting business.

Exports may also have an influence on, and be influenced by, the general business conditions of a country. During a domestic business downturn, exports generally tend to hold steady and sometimes even increase, thereby softening the effect of the recession. Since the business cycle in some countries is on the upswing while it is on the downswing in others, exports may even increase during a domestic recession. This occurred in Japan in 2004, based in part on the upsurge of orders from China, helping to improve Japan's weak economy.

In the late 1990s the so-called Asian crisis emerged. The currencies of Southeast Asian nations crashed to the extent that many were at less than one-half their old values against the US dollar. This would indicate that export prices from these countries would be lower and that exports would increase. However that did not happen, as many manufacturers in the countries of the region were so short of cash they could not buy the imported materials needed to produce the goods to fill the export orders that were out there 'for the grabbing.' Even though sharp falls in currencies lower labor costs, manufacturers still had to pay more for imported raw materials and components and they could not easily obtain the financing to fill export orders. This applied to all kinds of firms ranging from small Indonesian shoemakers to South Korea's largest conglomerates (Moore and Ihlwan, 1998).

Although, on balance, exports will tend to have a positive effect in a country, there may be individual countries that at certain times face negative effects as well.

Shortages of goods could exist, leading to higher prices for domestic consumers. In 2004 the United States considered placing an embargo on the export of scrap copper to Japan, its major market for the material. The rapidly rising export demand for scrap copper was felt to be hurting the US manufacturers that used the material. Many years before, the United States had also briefly imposed an embargo on soybean exports because of concerns over shortages and rising prices in its own market. In that case, it opened new markets for Brazilian producers. Some years ago Japanese companies set export prices lower than domestic prices on a number of products from automobiles to color television sets. The Japanese domestic market accepted the high prices and Japanese businesses were seeking more rapid market penetration of international markets through low prices (as well as high quality). The Japanese government, seeking a higher level of exports, approved of these policies. When such pricing policies are used now, they are likely to bring charges of 'dumping' (as discussed in Chapter 10). Some industries and companies, particularly those that are less export oriented, may find it difficult to hire qualified people if the export-oriented industries are growing. This has not been a serious problem for most of the more industrialized countries in recent years.

2.2.3 Increasing productivity and efficiency

The previous comments on imports and exports suggest that to some nations a substantial amount of international trade will primarily foster efficient use of productive resources. This means that trade is a way to increase, and perhaps even maximize, productivity. Industry and trade are dynamic. Methods of production and marketing are changing continuously. In old industries, new production techniques are developed and they migrate from one country to another. Furthermore, technological advancement creates entirely new industries all the time. These changes are transmitted around the world by international trade or through direct foreign investments or strategic alliances. This means that established domestic industries are constantly confronted with new competitors. In some instances new industries displace old ones. For example, nylon practically ruined the silk industry of Japan, while the development of synthetic materials, such as synthetic rubber, has limited the expansion of their natural counterparts and may, in some cases, entirely replace them. Transistors, silicon chips, and similar products have completely changed the electronics industry.

There is great interest throughout the world in *technology transfer*, which can be viewed as the sending of new products, processes, and production inputs from one country to another. Eastern European countries have been acquiring technology from the West, and at the same time have been supplying technology there. The developing countries of the world are constantly seeking technology from the developed countries. China, with the allure of its potentially huge market and its large purchases of industrial equipment, is being particularly aggressive in seeking technology transfer. General Electric, with potentially billions of dollars of orders at stake, is providing high technology. In 2004, in order to secure a $900 million contract for electrical generation turbines, GE agreed to provide advanced technology to two Chinese partners that eventually want to make such equipment themselves. Siemens AG is working with a Chinese academic institute to develop technology for a national mobile phone standard for the nation (Kranhold, 2004).

In addition to the technology per se, countries may benefit by employment opportunities for its citizens, housing, schools, and management development programs. Earlier, in addition to transferring technology and building a $720 million computer chip factory, Motorola Inc. built 2200 apartments and two schools for its employees – and provided a fast-track management training program for local Chinese (*The Economist*, 1996a, p. 48).

With industrial change, therefore, international trade becomes a potential engine of progress. Whether this potential becomes actualized, and productivity is increased, depends upon the response of domestic industries to the challenge created by competition from new industries and new methods. In the United States, for example, some industries such as bicycles and watches responded to rising competition from imports by seeking government protection. The semiconductor industry, on the other hand, virtually abandoned domestic production of high-volume standardized chips and turned to an emphasis on specialized and custom-made computers-on-a-chip. This enabled the US industry to regain its position as the world's largest supplier of computer chips (on a dollar-value basis). Some industries have been able to persuade their government to seek and obtain from foreign governments 'voluntary' reductions or limits in the amounts of products exported. When such government protection is granted to domestic companies the stimulus from import competition causes no gain in productivity because the reaction is negative; the situation in the protected industry is literally frozen.

Another type of response to the competition from imports that leads to increases in productivity is that of cost reduction. Incorporated by many industries in western Europe and the United States, that has been accomplished through improved management, automation, economizing in personnel, elimination of parts, and product simplifications.

2.3 International trade theories

The underlying influences that govern the trade among countries are complex and many. While it is clear that business firms and nations can benefit in many ways from trade, a more complete understanding can be achieved by briefly examining a number of international trade theories, all of which claim to offer distilled wisdom about what determines the patterns of trade among countries. None of them has proved to be the ultimate general theory applicable to all traded goods at all times.

The theories presented here are as follows:

- the classical theory of international trade;
- the factor proportion theory;
- the product life-cycle theory of international trade.

This section concerns only a short summary of the basic concepts and explanations of each of these. The discussion is limited to the question: 'What determines the nature and amounts of the goods that a country buys and sells in international markets?' A more comprehensive treatment of the subject is given in textbooks on international economics and in books on international trade theory covering one or more of these three theories.

2.3.1 The classical theory of international trade

What a country exports and imports is determined not by its character in isolation but in relation to those of its trading partners. The concept of *economic advantage* states that countries tend to specialize in those products in which they have an advantage, namely, lower cost of production. This means simply that a country produces for domestic consumption and for export those items that it makes better or more cheaply than other countries, and imports those products that it can acquire more cheaply from abroad than at home. The essence of the logic behind economic advantage is that any nation can only hurt itself by excluding imports that can be obtained more cheaply from abroad than at home.

Furthermore, this logic applies even if countries such as France and Germany, for example, may be able to produce domestically most kinds of products more cheaply than can be produced in foreign countries. In such circumstances, Germany and France will gain by importing those goods for which each has a *relative* disadvantage in production, and thus gain the opportunity to export goods for which each has a relative advantage, by reason of superior natural resources, labor and management skills, capital resources, manufacturing processes, or technology.

There are three different situations concerning international differences in costs that must be considered – *absolute* differences, *comparative* differences, and *equal* differences. The extent to which trade is carried on and its very nature depends on which of these three conditions exists in any given potential trading relationship and upon the nature of reciprocal demand structures. In the classical theory it is assumed that the supply price is the same as the money cost of production, that is, transport costs, marketing costs, and individual firm profits are not considered. In the real world, of course, these costs certainly exist, and are quite significant in most cases. But the concept of supply price remains unchanged; only absolute magnitudes are affected.

Absolute advantage

A condition of absolute advantage exists when one country has a cost advantage over another country in the production of one product (that is, it can be produced using fewer resources) while the second country has a cost advantage over the first in producing a second product. In a two-country two-product world, international trade and specialization will be beneficial to each country when the country is absolutely more efficient than its trading partner. For a given set of productive resources (capital and labor inputs), specialization and trade lead to a greater output of both products.

The absolute advantage theory also sought to explain why costs differ among nations. Cost differences exist because productivities of factor inputs (in particular labor) represent the major determinant of production cost in different countries. Such productivities are based on natural and acquired advantages – localization advantages. Natural advantages include factors relating to climate, soil, and mineral wealth, whereas acquired advantages include special skills, technical and marketing know-how, and so on. Another advantage in the 21st century is technology. With such advantages for producing an item, a nation would produce that item at lower cost than a trading partner without the same advantages.

Comparative advantage

In order for trade to be profitably carried on it is not necessary that a country have an absolute advantage over other countries. If one country has an absolute advantage over another country in the production of all products, trade will be beneficial if the domestic exchange ratios in each country are dissimilar; in other words, if the country with the absolute advantage has a greater advantage in producing one product than it has in producing another. This situation is known as 'the principle of comparative advantage.'

When this condition exists a country benefits by specializing in and exporting the product in which it has the greatest advantage, or a superior (comparative) advantage, and importing the product in which its advantage is less, or in which it has an inferior advantage (that is, a comparative disadvantage). Thus, the other country, even though it is at a disadvantage in producing all products, can benefit by specializing in and exporting the product in which its disadvantage is least. An illustration is presented in Exhibit 2.1.

EXHIBIT 2.1	**Comparative advantage: gains from trade**

To see how this theory works, think about why two countries – call them East and West – might gain from trading with one another (*The Economist*, 1997, p. 85). Suppose, for simplicity, that each has 1,000 workers, and each makes two goods: computers and bicycles.

West's economy is far more productive than East's. To make a bicycle, West uses 10 workers while East uses 100. Suppose there is no trade, and that in each country half the workers are in each industry. West produces 250 bicycles and 50 computers. East makes 125 bikes and 5 computers.

Now suppose that the two countries specialize. Although West makes both products more efficiently than East, it has a bigger edge in computer making. It now devotes most of its resources to that industry, employing 700 workers to make computers and only 300 to make bikes. This raises computer output to 70 and cuts bike production to 150, as shown in Table 2.1. East switches entirely to bicycles, turning out 250. World output of both goods has risen. Both countries can consume more of both if they trade.

At what price? Neither will want to import what it could make more cheaply at home. So West will want at least 5 bikes per computer; and East will not give up more than 25 bikes per computer (these are the *domestic exchange ratios* that set the limits within which the *international exchange ratio* must fall for gains to accrue to both trading partners). Suppose the terms of trade are fixed at 12 bicycles per computer and that 120 bikes are exchanged for 10 computers (the exact international exchange ratio will depend upon the existing reciprocal demand situation). Then West ends up with 270 bikes and 60 computers, and East with 130 bicycles and 10 computers. Both are better off than they would be if they did not trade.

TABLE 2.1

Comparative advantage: gains from trade

	Output and consumption under autarky		Output after specialization		Consumption after trade	
	Bicycles	Computers	Bicycles	Computers	Bicycles	Computers
East	125	5	250	0	130	10
West	250	50	150	70	270	60

In the real world, the power of comparative advantage seems weaker than this simple model of trade implies (*The Economist*, 1996b). For instance, countries specialize less than one would expect. There is much intra-industry trade – France sells cars to Germany and vice versa. Competition from foreign suppliers does sometimes lower wages in the importing countries. Clearly, geography and the role of similar but different products appealing to varying tastes also explain why trade occurs. In addition, comparative advantage is often the result of history and chance. A good example is the commercial aircraft industry of the United States (*The Economist*, 1997). There is no inherent reason why the production costs of large jets, e.g., the Boeing 747, relative to other goods/services should be lower in the United States than in, say, Japan. But, due to the early acceptance of air travel, airmail, and large purchases of military aircraft, such costs are lower. This suggests that comparative advantage can be created and that perhaps government should help create it. The European consortium Airbus Industrie is doing this with its new Airbus 380.

More complicated versions of this model help explain these apparent anomalies. Moving from two goods and countries to many goods and countries greatly complicates the mathematics, but otherwise changes little. In the real world labor is not the only factor of production. There is capital, human resources, etc. Thus, the domestic exchange ratio is not in general linear, but is curvilinear, bending outward in the middle. This in turn implies that complete specialization is unlikely. As the international exchange ratio or price based on reciprocal demand changes, a country shifts production slowly in accordance with comparative advantage to complete specialization.

Equal advantage

A condition of equal advantage exists when one country has an absolute advantage over another in production of all products but no superior advantage in the production of any one product.

This can be simply illustrated by the data for shoes and clothing in Table 2.2.

In producing both products Italy has an absolute advantage over Guatemala. In fact Italy is twice as efficient in both products. The domestic exchange ratio of

TABLE 2.2

Production costs for shoes and clothing

| Country | Production costs per unit (in hours of labor) | |
	Shoes	Clothing
Guatemala	30	60
Italy	10	20

shoes to clothes in each country is the same, 1 : 2. Using the reasoning above, there is no range of possible international trade ratios, which means that each country will neither gain nor lose anything by trading. Under such conditions, trade could not possibly exist as the incentive of gain is lacking.

It is reasonable to ask what the limitations and implications of this analysis are. The equal ratios for these two products might be the same for any number of reasons, such as better machinery being used in Italy. However, it seems unlikely that ratios of labor costs for all products in both countries would be the same. Therefore, while trade in some products might not be feasible, it might be advantageous for other products where the ratios differ. But could trade still be advantageous if Guatemala had higher costs in hours of labor for every product than Italy? The answer is yes. Over time the monetary exchange rates would change to reflect the differences in productivity in the two countries – not precisely, but enough to make trade feasible in some products in which Guatemala had less of a comparative disadvantage in labor costs.

2.3.2 The factor proportion theory

The classical trade theories argue that the basis for trade stems from differences in international production conditions and factor productivities, owing to domestic differences in localization advantages (natural and acquired advantages). But other than offering this general explanation, the classical theories do little to explain what causes discrepancies in comparative costs.

The factor proportion theory, in contrast, offers an explanation for the differences in comparative costs among trading partners. According to this theory, international differences in supply conditions, e.g., factor productivities and factor endowments, explain much of international trade. It is assumed that trading partners have the same tastes and preferences (demand conditions), use factors of production that are of uniform quality, and use the same technology. The productivity or efficiency of a given resource unit is thus identical for both trading nations.

The factor proportion theory argues that relative price levels differ among countries because (1) they have different relative endowments of factors of production (capital and labor inputs), and (2) different commodities require that the factor inputs be used with differing intensities in their production (factor intensities – capital/labour relationships). Given these circumstances the factor proportion theory can be formulated as follows:

> A nation will export that product for which a large amount of the relatively abundant (cheap) input is used, and it will import that product in the production of which the relatively scarce (expensive) input is used.

The principal explanation of the pattern of international trade lies in the uneven distribution of world resources among nations, coupled with the fact that products require different proportions of the factors of production. While the production of clothing, for example, is very labor intensive, the manufacturing of machines is much more capital intensive.

2.3.3 The product life-cycle theory of international trade

For various reasons, the traditional theories based on economic advantage or factor endowments have been shown to be deficient in explaining international trade patterns as they evolved starting in the 1960s. Because of rapid technological progress and the development of multinational enterprises, there has been a need to search for a new international trade theory to fit the changing realities of the trading world as it began to evolve and now exists. The product life-cycle theory of international trade has been found to be a useful model for explaining not only trade patterns of manufacturers but also multinational expansions of sales and production subsidiaries, that is, it has been useful in explaining certain types of foreign direct investment (Vernon, 1966; Vernon *et al.* 1996).

According to the product life-cycle concept, many manufactured goods, in particular technologically advanced products such as electronic products and office machinery, undergo a trade cycle. The essence of this process and how it affects a country's international trade flow is shown in Figure 2.1.

During the process, which can be described in various stages, the innovator country of a new product is initially an exporter, then loses its competitive advantage vis-à-vis its trading partners, and may eventually become an importer of the product some years later. The introduction stage of the trade cycle begins when the innovator company establishes a technological breakthrough in the production of a manufactured item. The country where the innovating company is located initially has an international technological gap in its favor, and is typically a high-income developed economy. At the start, the relatively small local market (home market) for the product and technological uncertainties imply that mass production is not feasible.

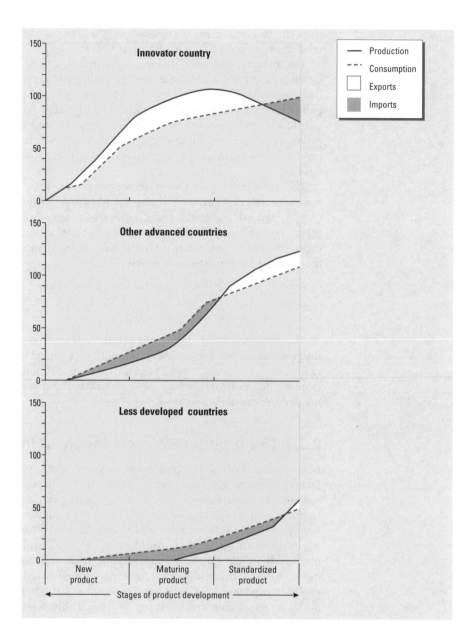

FIGURE 2.1

The product life-cycle
theory of international
trade
Source: Vernon *et al.* 1996,
p. 119

During the trade cycle's next stage, the innovator manufacturer begins to export
its product to foreign markets, which are likely to be countries with similar tastes,
income levels, and demand structures, i.e., other developed countries. The manufacturer finds that during this stage of growth and expansion, its market becomes
large enough to support mass-production operations and the sorting out of inefficient production techniques, which means that increasing amounts can be supplied
to world markets.

As time passes, the manufacturer realizes that to protect its foreign sales and
export profits it must locate production operations closer to the foreign markets.
The domestic industry enters its mature stage as innovating firms establish subsidiaries abroad, usually in advanced countries first. A major reason for this is that
the cost advantage initially enjoyed by the innovator is not likely to last indefinitely. Over a period of time, the innovating country may find that its technology

has become more commonplace and that transportation costs and tariffs play an important role in influencing selling costs. The innovator may also find that the foreign market is large enough to permit mass-production operation near the marketplace, either by a direct investment or strategic alliance arrangement.

Although an innovating country's monopoly position may be prolonged by legal rights (for example, patents and other intellectual property rights), it often breaks down over time. This is because knowledge tends to be a free item in the long run. The Internet contributes to this. Once the innovative technology becomes fairly commonplace, foreign producers begin to imitate the production process. The innovating country gradually loses its comparative advantage and its export cycle begins to experience a declining phase. The trade cycle is complete when the production process becomes so standardized that it can be easily utilized by all nations, including lesser developed countries. The innovating country may finally itself become a net importer of the product as its monopoly position is eliminated by foreign competition.

This model is 'fueled' by technology. As is well known, technology is less likely to converge (i.e., close the gap between rich and poor countries) than capital (Sachs, 2000). Innovation shows increasing returns to scale, meaning that countries with advanced technologies are best placed to innovate further.

At the individual company level, a situation that leads to the breakdown of monopoly positions based on patents and intellectual property rights is counterfeiting and piracy. In some cases governments become involved in order to assist national firms. A good illustration is the threatened sanctions by the US government over selected exports from China in 1996 over piracy of compact disk software for computers. The US government felt that the government of China was not doing enough to stop such piracy.

The product life-cycle model of international trade has been helpful in explaining the history of trade patterns of a number of products, particularly textiles, shoes, radios, televisions, semiconductors, automobiles, industrial fasteners, and standardized components for different uses. These products, available in the United States, western Europe, and Japan, are being imported from Korea, Taiwan, Hong Kong, India, Singapore, other newly industrialized countries (NICs), and China.

2.4 Export behavior theories and motives

Exporting is still the most common way for manufacturers to do business in foreign markets, especially in the early stages of internationalization. The export behavior of firms has received significant attention – by researchers and practitioners. Although conceptualization and theory development have been scarce, contemporary international business theory development considers exporting as a continuous process with the firm gradually increasing its level of foreign involvement and commitment. Export expansion is generally viewed as involving discrete changes in organizational structure as firms increase their commitment to serving foreign markets. The first is thus perceived as passing through a sequence of export entry modes which ultimately lead to direct foreign investment.

In contrast to the international trade theories as presented above, export behavior theories attempt to explain why and how the *individual firm* is engaged in export activities and, in particular, how the dynamic nature of such activities can be conceptualized. Export theories focus explicitly on the firm's motives and strategies of exporting (and not only economic rationales for exporting), the firm's marketing and other capabilities in exporting, and its interaction with the foreign market environment. Risk, uncertainty, and imperfect knowledge are important determinants in export behavior since companies engaging in foreign marketing activities often lack prior knowledge, experience, and adequate marketing information.

Why do firms engage in international marketing in general and exporting in particular? We can assume (realistically, we might add) that the driving forces for either starting or exploiting export activities are that the firm wants to utilize and develop its resources in such a way that its short-term and/or long-run economic objectives are served. As a consequence, export motives will be strongly connected to the basic goals of the company. Broadly speaking, companies expand abroad when they can no longer achieve, to their satisfaction, their strategic objectives by operating solely in the domestic market.

2.4.1 Basic goals

Every business firm has a major goal that it strives to achieve. This goal may be profit or nonprofit oriented. Profit-oriented objectives include those of return on investment, return on sales, profit maximization, growth, or stability. Objectives that are nonprofit in nature include a desired volume of sales, market share, preservation of the status quo, serving customers and specific markets, financial liquidity, security of existing management, and various humanitarian goals such as maintaining employment and producing products that the firm honestly believes are good for consumers.

Regardless of how the business firm explicitly states its major objective(s), if in fact an explicit statement exists, there is really only one basic or primary incentive – *to make a profit*. Thus, a nonprofit-oriented objective may be desired only to the extent that a profit is forthcoming, either directly or indirectly. It is only through the generation of profits that a firm can continue its operations and afford the luxury of having objectives that are nonprofit in nature. Export business, to those who are already exporting, is frequently the difference between a profit and a loss for the entire company. In addition, foreign operations, including exports, lead to stability of profits.

Samsung Electronics' current profitability is the result of a 1998 decision not to give greater emphasis to gaining market share than to profits. The Korean conglomerate decided not to pursue the opportunity to flood export markets during the economic crisis in Korea and Southeast Asia at the time. The company's president, Yun Jong Yong, stated that Samsung factories would produce only goods after orders were in hand and profitability assured. Putting profitability ahead of gross sales was a radical concept at Samsung and other Korean conglomerates (*Business Week*, 2000, p. 136). Samsung's actions stand in contrast to those of Daewoo, as discussed in Case 9.1 in Chapter 9.

For many companies a significant share of their sales revenue and earnings can come from export and other foreign operations. Examples abound. In 2003 BMW sold more automobiles in the United States than in Germany. As much as 80–90% of sales and profits of companies such as Sweden's Ericsson and Electrolux have come from exports and foreign subsidiaries. By 2000, Finland's Nokia was generating 96% of sales and French retailer Carrefour 44% of sales from foreign operations. Other examples of companies in which a significant share of earnings comes from international operations are not difficult to find: Coca-Cola, IBM, Unilever, Procter & Gamble, Motorola, Exxon, CPC, N.V. Philips

Gloeilampenfabrieken, Sony, Nestlé, C. Itoh, DaimlerChrysler, and Toyota. For many companies the bulk of foreign earnings comes from foreign-based operations rather than export sales.

2.4.2 Specific reasons

In addition to the basic objective of attaining profit, there may be specific goals underlying a firm's commitment to foreign markets, however strong or weak that commitment might be. As previously stated, each of these becomes a valid goal only to the extent that there is a contribution made to achievement of the basic goal. That is, underlying each of these specific goals is the expectation that profits will be enhanced in the long run.

A classification of specific export motives is shown in schematic form in Table 2.3. Basically, the schema suggests that different kinds of stimuli or influences cause a firm to engage in exporting. Two main distinctions can be drawn. First, the motivational factors are specified as either due to stimuli initiated from influences *internal* to the firm or due to stimuli originating from the company's *external* environment (home market or export markets). Second, the motives are categorized in terms of whether the export activity is due to *reactive* behavior, that is, the firm responds to internal or external pressures (push factors), and acts passively, or is a result of *proactive* and/or aggressive behavior based on the firm's interest in exploiting unique competencies or market possibilities (pull factors). Another way of looking at this is that the decision can be *innovation oriented* (i.e., there is awareness of the existence of a market opportunity) or *problem oriented*. Such a distinction may be important because it identifies the nature of the export decision task: is the foreign activity initiated because of the need for exports or is it initiated on a purely voluntary basis, to improve an already secure situation of the company? Exhibit 2.2 reinforces the importance of some motives.

TABLE 2.3		Internal	External
A classification of export motives	Proactive	■ Managerial urge ■ Marketing advantages ■ Economies of scale ■ Unique product/technology competence	■ Foreign market opportunities ■ Change agents
	Reactive	■ Risk diversification ■ Extend sales of a seasonal product ■ Excess capacity of resources	■ Unsolicited orders ■ Small home market ■ Stagnant or declining home market

EXHIBIT 2.2   Should a company market overseas?

How does a company decide whether foreign marketing is 'right' for itself and its product(s)?

The keys to achievement in foreign markets are *information*, *preparation*, and *commitment*. A study of successful medium-sized companies showed that success overseas was due to management commitment, quality, better marketing, innovation, and acculturation – *not* company size, financing, or a favorable currency.

A company's main incentive, of course, is opportunity for growth and profit. In addition, sales in foreign markets can aid in stabilizing revenue/turnover fluctuations whether these fluctuations are caused by seasonality, technology changes, saturated markets, or economic conditions. New markets help a firm to use its production capacity better, to extend the product life cycle, to increase competitiveness, and perhaps even gain tax advantages.

There are four steps to guide the decision whether to become involved internationally or not:

- *Make sure that there is sincere commitment and involvement* from the president down, and that such commitment becomes integral to business strategy.
- *Allocate research and evaluation time and resources.*
- *Gather information on which to base the decision:*
  - Study market characteristics (including need and propensity to buy), competition, possible entry barriers, export/import regulations, customs, and licensing considerations of targeted markets.
  - Evaluate company and product strengths and weaknesses by market.
  - Evaluate how to adapt products and services to meet local requirements, standards, and tastes. Anticipate export financing, pricing, payment methods, and the additional costs of doing business in foreign markets.
- *Audit the foreign marketing know-how, capabilities, and expectations of personnel, suppliers, and other stakeholders.*

Managerial urge

Managerial attitudes play a critical if not a major role in determining the exporting activities of the firms. Managerial urge reflects the desire, drive, enthusiasm, and commitment of management towards exporting and other types of international marketing. In smaller and medium-sized companies export decisions may be the province of a single decision maker; in bigger firms they can be made by a decision-making unit. Irrespective of the number of people involved in the export decision process, the choice of a foreign market entry strategy is still dependent on the decision maker's perceptions of foreign markets, expectations concerning these markets, and perceptions of the company's capability of entering those markets. This suggests that individual decision-maker characteristics may act at two levels: (1) information stimuli related to export activities are ultimately processed, and (2) the characteristics are related to subsequent decisions to engage in export activities or not.

There is a distinct relationship between individual decision characteristics and export behavior. Favorable attitudes toward foreign activities have been considered an essential prerequisite before firms go into or expand in international markets. Decision-maker characteristics, including cognitive and affective factors, can explain in certain instances the systematic differences between managers in attitude and behavior toward foreign activity.

A process of cultural socialization which exposes the decision maker to information and contacts with foreign markets is likely to make stimuli received from or related to foreign countries more familiar. Managers who either were born or have the experience of living or traveling abroad may be expected to be more internationally minded than other managers. Prior occupation in exporting companies and early socialization, and continued contact with external reference groups (such as membership in trade and professional associations) may also reinforce key decision makers' perceptions and evaluations of foreign environments.

Unique product/technology competence

There is a definite role that unique products and/or unique technology competence plays in stimulating exporting behavior. First, a firm producing superior products is more likely to receive inquiries from foreign markets because of perceived competence of its offerings. Several dimensions in the product offerings affect the probability that a potential buyer will be exposed to export stimuli. Although little is known on this issue, significant elements in describing the export product may be its degree of standardization, degree of complexity, and, where 'software' and 'hardware' are involved, the distribution of sales (turnover) between them.

Second, if a company has developed unique competencies in its domestic market, the possibilities to spread unique assets to overseas markets may be very high because the opportunity costs of exploiting these assets in other markets will be zero or very low. Explanations of why a unique competence leads to seeking the exploitation of exporting are usually based on the fact that there would have been certain sunk costs incurred in developing the competence or product.

Risk diversification

Many, but not all, exporting companies probably face less total market risk than nonexporting firms by virtue of their having diversified geographical markets. Typically, countries do not face the same type and timing of business cycle. The expectations are that an economic downswing does not manifest itself necessarily at the same time or with the same intensity in different foreign markets. Selling in several markets (market spreading) reduces the risk associated with declining sales and profits in any one market. Such diversification in markets helps the firm to cope with the ever-changing general business conditions in the domestic market. If the home market should be in the midst of a recession, export sales can still be made since world markets are seldom equally depressed at the same time. When the wood products industry in the Pacific Northwest region of the United States was depressed during the first half of the 1980s due to a quiet domestic building industry, some companies did better than others because they were able to export logs and wood chips to Japan. Companies that also developed competencies in cutting wood to the precise dimensions and configurations required by Japanese construction companies continue to have a market not open to US lumber mills which only cut to US specifications.

Foreign market opportunities

Revealing market opportunities abroad has often exerted a strong influence upon the firm's willingness to export. It is evident that market opportunities act as stimuli only if the firm has or is capable of securing those resources that are necessary to respond to the opportunities. In general, decision makers are likely to consider a rather limited number of foreign market opportunities in planning their foreign entry. Moreover, such decision makers are likely to explore first those overseas market opportunities perceived as having some similarity with the opportunities in their home market.

Change agents

Government agencies, industrial trade associations, banks, chambers of commerce, port authorities, and other organizations may be major promoters of export activities. Major export promotion activities include giving and guaranteeing loans, providing credit facilities and insurance, publishing basic market data on foreign markets, exhibiting at trade fairs and exhibitions, sponsoring and participating in trade missions, providing trade leads and reports on individual companies, and being party to a trade agreement or convention. For example, government stimulation measures can have a positive influence, not only in terms of any direct financial effects that they may have but also in relation to the provision of information regarding market opportunities in a foreign country.

Economies of scale

If scale economies exist in production, advertising, distribution, or other areas, a broader market scope created by exporting can give rise to a decrease in unit costs of products produced. The scale effect reflects the natural efficiencies associated with size. Through exporting, fixed costs arising from administration, facilities, equipment, staff work, and R&D can be spread over more units. For some companies a condition for exploiting scale effects on overseas markets to the fullest extent is that it is possible to standardize the marketing mix internationally. For others, however, standardized marketing is not necessary for scale economies; such companies can accrue economies on the basis of their size alone.

Foreign marketing advantages

Specialized marketing knowledge or access to information can distinguish an exporting firm from its competitors. A good and perhaps unique product, a strong sales force, an efficient marketing infrastructure, and a good service technical support system, for example, may act as incentives for exporting because a company has built up competitive marketing advantages. Past marketing success can be a strong motivator for future marketing behavior. Competence in one or more of the major marketing activities will often be a sufficient catalyst for a company to begin or expand exports. Doing any type of marketing job well, together with having a strong product and/or brand franchise, means that a company can be better shielded from competition in export markets. In short, marketing advantages can serve as entry barriers for potential competitors in foreign markets.

Extend sales of seasonal product

Some industries, for example textiles, clothing, sports equipment, tourism, and toys, may be less resistant to business cycles than others. Seasonality in production and demand conditions in the domestic market may be industry specific and can act as persistent stimuli for foreign market exploration. In the first place, export markets are likely to be pursued in order to remove fluctuations in the product cycle. Second, eroding of the home market may force pursuit of export markets to secure continued growth and profitability. Consequently, firms may be expected to pursue an appropriate strategic response to cope with such changes.

By selling seasonal products in countries where the seasons are opposite to those at home, a greater stability in sales can be achieved. This, of course, makes possible more balanced production throughout the year. For example, ski equipment and clothing from such companies as Saloman, Rossignol, Olin, Head, Columbia, and North Face have markets in the northern hemisphere (North America and Europe) during the months of November–March whereas markets in the southern hemisphere (Chile, Argentina, New Zealand, and Australia) would be best during the period May–September.

Excess capacity of resources

When the domestic market served by a company is unable or unwilling to absorb the output that the firm is capable of producing or is actually producing then export markets can serve as outlets for this surplus production or productive capacity. Both domestic and foreign competition in the home market often force a firm to seek overseas markets. In many cases additional production can be obtained from existing equipment and labor without adding greatly to cost, the effect being an increase in the productive efficiency of the firm. Such economy in production will enhance the firm's competitive position both at home and abroad.

There is one potential problem that should not be overlooked when engaging in this type of activity. Sometimes companies with excess inventories attempt to 'unload' them in overseas markets at attractive prices. When the price that is offered in the overseas market is lower than that at which a product is sold in its home domestic market, *dumping* occurs. Under WTO rules, investigations are made into antidumping charges on products that importing countries say are being sold at unfairly low prices and are harming their domestic industries (de Jonquieres, 2003). Many countries and groups of countries have enacted laws making dumping illegal or the dumped products subject to higher duty rates designed to adjust for the situation. Though usually lower, antidumping duties as high as 454% have been assessed. Not all of the national laws are the same, contributing to possible different interpretations of what actually constitutes dumping. US laws were written over 80 years ago and define dumping not only as selling in other countries at prices lower than those in the home markets, but also those selling at prices below the 'total cost' of production, and that are harming domestic industries. Examples of some recent charges of dumping, by both industrialized nations and developing countries, are given in Chapter 10, Pricing decisions, in Exhibit 10.2. Countries that do not have antidumping laws may simply frown on the practice of dumping with the effect that local importers are discouraged from buying products that are being dumped. In addition, the government involved most likely will not view very favorably a foreign company engaging in the practice. Consequently, any short-term immediate gain from dumping may be offset by adverse longer-term effects.

Under certain circumstances entire industries begin to produce a permanent surplus for export. This occurs when further growth of the domestic market is blocked, or when, because of lack of an adequate domestic market, price degeneration appears to be forthcoming unless new markets can be discovered and developed.

Unsolicited foreign orders

The receipt of an unsolicited inquiry for product, price, or distribution information may be a very common method by which firms become aware of opportunities in export markets. These inquiries can result from advertising in trade journals that have a worldwide circulation, through exhibitions, and by other means. The evidence has been overwhelming that in different countries for the majority of exporting firms their initial orders were unsolicited. Such an involvement may emphasize an unplanned or passive (reactive) export market entry, but unsolicited orders as an explanatory factor for export activities raises at least one fundamental question. Why should some companies receive more of these inquiries than others, if in fact they do?

In general, it seems to be too simplistic to attribute exporting behavior to any single order explanation. It should be expected that those factors that make a firm a likely target for an unsolicited order do not cease after it has started to export. So besides unsolicited inquiries, there must exist certain enabling conditions that facilitate export activities. In a study by Simpson and Kujawa (1974), there was evidence presented supporting the view that firms are differentially exposed by such external stimuli as unsolicited orders. In this study more than 80% of the exporting firms were exposed to inquiries from foreign customers in contrast to approximately 30% of the nonexporters being so exposed. This points out that there are firm- and industry-specific factors at work that provide an environment that encourages receipt of unsolicited foreign orders. Relevant characteristics may be related to the firm's technology, product mix, experience, and present exposure in the marketplace.

Small domestic market

A company may be pushed into exporting because of a small home market potential. For some firms, domestic markets may be unable to sustain sufficient economies of scale and scope, and these companies automatically include export markets as part of their market entry strategy. This type of behavior is likely for industrial products that have few, easily identified customers located throughout the world, or for producers of specialized consumer goods with small national segments in many countries. The strategy is also possible for firms producing consumer products that are targeted to international consumers with common lifestyles and disposable incomes.

Although domestic markets may be very large this does not necessarily imply that a firm would want to expand within its home market before choosing to export. For example, for some Canadian firms, markets in the United States might be far more accessible and economically feasible than markets in west Canada. For an Australian firm that has attained full expansion in its regional market, economic factors such as transport convenience may make Singapore, Japan or South Korea the most attractive market for entry rather than another Australian state.

Stagnant or declining home market

Market saturation can provide a major incentive for firms to search for new opportunities. Foreign expansion may become a feasible strategy if the home market is stagnant or declining. Home market saturation occurs when a company is, at best, receiving declining marginal revenues from its marketing effort, or, at worst, is in a situation where required incremental sales revenue is less than the costs of the related incremental marketing effort. But another perspective on market saturation is relevant for understanding why firms may expand overseas. Home market saturation suggests that unused productive resources (such as production and managerial slack) exist within the firm. Production slack is a stimulus for securing new market opportunities, and managerial slack provides those knowledge resources required for collecting, interpreting, and using market information.

Resources

The ability to undertake any form of international activity is clearly limited by the means available to the firm to carry out such activity. While export motives drive the process of internationalization, the resources that are available may limit the expansion at any point in time. There is more to the resources question than just production or financial capacity. Several critical factors in the ability to carry out chosen export activities are the possession of appropriate export knowledge, the ability to make personal contacts, and a greater willingness to take risks compared with doing domestic business.

Multinational, global, world companies

International marketing opportunities including export opportunities are the major reason for the existence of some companies whose operations are truly global in nature. These companies have been called different names (for example, multinational, transnational, global, world) and there are some differences in operating characteristics. However, they all share the common characteristic that decisions are made on the basis of comparative opportunities worldwide. Markets are not limited to the confines of any political entity and global resources are utilized. Such companies tend to be increasingly market driven in their strategic and tactical decision making.

Other relatively common characteristics are that these companies sell, market, and manufacture in many countries. This means that global business strategies are needed, including research and development in multiple areas. Global marketing means a fully integrated worldwide strategy based on consistent brand selling. These companies are progressive. The dynamic forces inherent in all progressive companies are logically directed toward growth and expansion. When the opportunities for growth become limited in domestic markets, for whatever reason, there is no place to turn but to foreign areas.

Examples of these types of companies are General Motors (US), Philips (Netherlands), Samsung (Korea), Intel (US), Unilever (Netherlands; UK), Nestlé (Switzerland), and Hitachi (Japan). Of course, not all such companies are as large as the ones mentioned above.

Other goals

In addition to the goals already mentioned, marketing internationally can enhance the development of management personnel and stimulate the development of improved products and methods. The successful handling of situations in different foreign countries gives managers the opportunity to show how capable they are, and brings into the open new ideas and techniques that have been designed to handle particular situations. Moreover, although technology is such that invention and innovation are distributed unevenly, no one has a monopoly on success.

Pyramid at Chichén Itzá, Yucatán, Mexico

Another goal for exports is to provide a source of supply for the home market. This is the phenomenon known as the 'offshore plant' and can be defined as a plant owned by a company in one country (usually an industrialized country) but located in a less developed country whose principal mission is to manufacture products to be exported to the home country. One type of offshore plant operation has been used in Mexico since the early 1970s by US manufacturers with the encouragement of the Mexican government. These are assembly plants, known as *maquilalora* operations, mainly in the electronics industry, that have been established in designated duty-free areas. Originally, these plants were established in areas along the US–Mexican border in Tijuana, Mexicali, Ciudad Juarez and Nuevo Laredo. However, due to rising labor costs along the border, firms located in the interior of Mexico, where labor costs are as much as 50% lower. For example, Motorola and Burroughs Corporation operate in Jalisco, near Guadalajara, and other similar facilities are in San Luis Potosí, Durango, and the remote Yucatán peninsula. Japanese manufacturers are also moving offshore, to lower costs. Regardless of the specific reason for investing in such ventures, for example intense import competition in the home market or the availability of extremely low-cost labor, the objective underlying the setting up of an offshore plant is the desire to export to the home market.

Related to the 'offshore production' phenomenon as an objective for exporters sourcing overseas is buying overseas (importing) from independent sellers simply because quality is better and/or prices are lower. For example, in 1989 a subsidiary of the US company Johnson & Johnson bought a water-purification system from a Finnish company because the system was better than anything available in the United States.

A concluding comment

To conclude our discussion on goals or objectives of individual business units it should be emphasized that companies usually operate with multiple goals in mind. However, one goal will most likely be primary, while the others will be secondary and set up so-called boundary conditions. Also, some goals may be 'given' to the export marketing executive by higher management, and he or she has to operate within the confines of such goals.

2.5 The development of export in the firm: internationalization stages

For most companies, export operations are the first step in internationalization. While some firms may first become international through other means of market entry, the process of export development is the key to increased internationalization for the majority of companies. The rates at which firms increase their international activities differ substantially. From the standpoints of both individual firms and organizations promoting exports, it is important to understand what factors determine the process followed and the rate at which it moves.

A number of studies of the export development process (i.e., the internationalization process) have been conducted over the past 30 years. From the viewpoint of the firm, internationalization is an evolutionary process in which foreign experience gained over time results in accumulated organizational learning. The learning cycles include processes by which the firm adjusts itself defensively to foreign markets as well as processes by which knowledge and experience are used offensively to improve the fit between the firm and its foreign market environment. Export development can be described as a stimulus–response process, in which experimental learning has been considered as an important determinant. Information activities, willingness to commit resources, and managerial risk-taking behavior are all essential in describing the process.

Within the research on export behavior, researchers have concentrated almost exclusively on finding industry and firm determinants of international activities. Relationships between market environmental variables and foreign activities have rarely been subject to systematic empirical analysis. In the 1970s and 1980s research dealt with identifying technology and product-specific variables as important structural factors contributing to the process of export expansion. Structural factors have often been regarded as critical determinants in the exporting activity of a firm, but the evidence to support the effect of size, product, and technology orientation is conflicting.

More recently, attention has been directed towards behavioral determinants of the process of internationalization. Research in this respect has been dealing with the role of the decision maker's perception of foreign markets, expectations concerning these markets, and the firm's capacity to enter such markets. The available research does give tentative support to the existence of individual managerial factors influencing the export behavior of firms.

Empirical evidence indicates that as companies increase their level of international involvement there is a tendency for them to change the methods by which they serve foreign markets. As well as increasing commitment, the pattern appears to be one of greater operational diversity as internationalization proceeds. This appears to be related not only to the greater experience, skills, and knowledge of foreign markets and marketing that develops within the firm, but also to the exposure of a wider range of possibilities and threats.

As the company increases its involvement in international operations there is also a tendency for its offering to foreign markets to become deeper and more diverse, whether through an expansion within an existing product line, a new product line, or by changing the whole product concept to include nonmaterial components such as services, technology, know-how, or some combination. In the same way, firms tend to export initially to those customer markets and/or countries that are familiar and/or similar (close psychological distance) in terms of history, culture, and industrial economic development, where barriers to information retrieval are low, and where resource commitment can proceed incrementally.

Theories of export behavior identify several stages in the process and, although each theory uses a different classification scheme, the theories all portray one common view: the decision to go international is a gradual process that can be subdivided.

It should be stressed that the concept of a sequential, cumulative process of internationalization does not necessarily mean a smooth, immutable path of development. The actual paths are often irregular. Commitments are frequently lumpy over time and particular steps are affected by the emergence of opportunities and/or threats that do not usually arrive in a continuous or controlled manner. The outcome tends to be derived from a mixture of deliberate and emergent strategies.

In an early stage-theory approach, Johanson and Vahlne (1977) used the market entry form as a criterion based on extensive experience with Swedish firms. The classification of firms consists of four broad stages in which the following international activities take place: (1) no permanent export, (2) export via agent, (3) export via a sales subsidiary, and (4) production in a foreign subsidiary. Another approach, Exhibit 2.3, outlines briefly the levels of exporting. Typically, a company will reside either in level 1 or level 2. This is particularly true when first starting to export.

EXHIBIT 2.3   Levels of exporting

Level 1: Export of surplus The firm is interested only in overseas sales of surplus products, or is without resources to fill overseas orders for most products on a continuing basis.

Level 2: Export marketing The firm actively solicits overseas sales of existing products and is willing to make limited modifications in its products and marketing procedures to accommodate overseas buyers' requirements.

Level 3: Overseas market development The firm makes major modifications in products for export and in marketing practices in order to be better able to reach buyers in other countries.

Level 4: Technology development The firm develops new products for existing or new overseas markets.

More recent empirical studies indicate that a stage approach is most effective in explaining the export development process when companies are grouped according to similarity in managerial attitudes, size of firm, or product orientation. Other studies, a number of which were based on research in Nordic companies, have confirmed that there is a general pattern of evolutionary development. An understanding of the importance of initial experiences and the learning process discussed above is important for smaller companies (and for smaller countries), especially for latecomers to internationalization.

There has been a growing critique of the stage-of-development approach to the theories of export behavior (Turnbull, 1987). There are interpretive, conceptual, and empirical problems that should be considered. First, there is the question of the fundamental theoretical validity of the approach. The theory's underlying assumption that firms develop mere formal structures for handling export markets as their dependence on these markets increases is extensively criticized. Every stage describing the development sequence is a result of the outcome of the activities of a previous stage and there is an influence of a later stage. This implies a deterministic description of company evolution over time.

Second, a conceptual difficulty arises when one tries to define a company's degree of internationalization. How should one measure the individual firm's *degree of internationalization*? Several measurements have been proposed (one approach was introduced in Chapter 1 by Exhibit 1.1). In general, the degree has been measured by quantitative indicators, such as the number of countries in which the firm is doing business, characteristics such as foreign earnings, sales, turnover, assets, the number of employees engaged in foreign activities, and so on. These quantitative indicators may be measured absolutely or relatively. The absolute component gives an indication of the amount of resources that a firm commits to foreign operations. The relative measure shows that a firm is strongly dependent on its foreign activities if it has committed a significant portion of its financial, technological, and human resources to foreign market activities.

The firm's degree of internationalization can also be described by qualitative indicators. Behavioral characteristics such as top management 'international orientation', the degree of foreign experience, and so on, are very appealing, but the use of such indicators involves many measurement problems and they are difficult to operationalize. It is almost impossible to ascertain exactly what is meant by top management 'thinking international' or 'looking at the world as our marketplace.' Whether a company weighs alternative marketing possibilities on a worldwide basis or does not discard a marketing opportunity abroad simply because it is not in the country where it has its production, is of importance in understanding a company's international behavior; such distinctions, however, are very difficult to make in practice.

A third criticism is that companies do not necessarily internationalize in an orderly way. Moreover, companies may stop at a particular stage without proceeding further, skip stages or even reverse the process by starting their internationalization at a later stage.

None of these criticisms invalidate the overall concept of development by stages. It is not necessary that a company go through all stages in order to be internationalized. What these 'criticisms' do is point out that a particular company may proceed through the stages in any way it wants. However, it has been shown empirically that the majority of companies proceed as specified by the theory. Where they stop in the development process depends upon their goals/objectives.

As mentioned earlier, for many companies exporting is only the first step in internationalization. A more comprehensive view of, say, the stages of manufacturing firms is:

1. export operation stage;
2. foreign sales subsidiary stage;
3. licensing and contracting alliances;
4. foreign production subsidiary or alliance stage.

Each of these modes is discussed in subsequent chapters of the text.

2.6 Exporting and the network model

Empirical research has demonstrated that firms in industrial markets establish and develop lasting business relationships with other businesses. This is known as *relationship marketing*; examples are shown in Exhibit 2.4. In particular, this is true in international markets, where a company is engaged in a network of business relationships comprising a number of different firms – export distributors, agents, foreign customers, competitors, and consultants as well as regulatory and other public agencies (see Figure 2.2). These business relationships are connected by networks, where the parties build mutual trust and knowledge through interaction, and that interaction means strong commitment to the relationships.

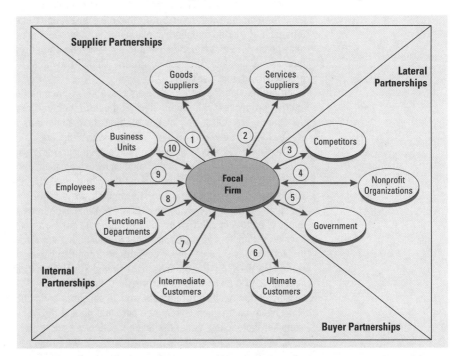

FIGURE 2.2

Relational exchanges in relationship marketing
Source: Morgan and Hunt, 1994, p. 21

EXHIBIT 2.4   Relationship marketing

Observers of the corporate scene in Europe and the United States might be forgiven for confusion (*The Economist*, 1994). On the one hand, firms are busy subjecting once-stable relationships within companies to market pressures, contracting out noncore businesses and forging 'profit centres' within firms to compete for cash. On the other hand, they are turning away from market transactions with outsiders in favour of gentlemen's agreements.

Traditionally, firms would force their suppliers and distributors to compete on the basis of price. Today they increasingly rely on informal partnerships. Instead of having many suppliers compete for their business, they are reducing the number of suppliers they use (in the space of just three years in the 1990s, Ford reduced the number of its suppliers by 45%, 3M by 64% and Motorola by 70%) and forming closer relationships with the ones that survive. They are even helping their suppliers to tackle difficult problems, from financing to design. At the same time, they are breaking down the traditional boundaries that divided one company from another.

Companies are realizing that, far from being the prerogative of a particular company, creating value is the responsibility of an entire chain of firms, starting with suppliers and ending with distributors. Firms should be willing to improve the performance of their distributors and their suppliers in addition to improving their own performance.

In the West, this started first in the car business. Humiliated by Toyota in the late 1970s, US and European companies began to study Japanese business methods. They discovered that the *keiretsu* system of long-term relationships between firms and their suppliers helped Japanese firms to outperform them on quality and timeliness, as well as price. Now partnerships are so established that the US's General Motors and Germany's BMW even allow their suppliers to help design their cars.

One advantage of partnerships is that they can reduce transaction costs. Dealing with a handful of trusted suppliers is much easier than negotiating with hundreds of potentially hostile ones. Companies need to put less time and effort into cultivating relations, forecasting demand, processing orders, filling in invoices and hoarding stocks as a precaution against disaster.

In the first phase of the business craze of 're-engineering,' firms focused on their internal processes, obliterating here and contracting out there. When they discovered that they were still losing money, or that their employees were overstretched, they started looking outwards, to their relations with suppliers.

The World Wide Web is making relationship marketing easier and more effective. A Special Report in *Business Week* listed many examples including: (1) Lockheed Martin is linking 80 major suppliers from around the globe in a $255 billion project to design and build a new type of stealth fighter. The company expects the networking of designers and engineers to reduce costs by an average of $25 million per year. (2) In 2002 Sony linked teams of editors in different countries in order to get *Lord of the Rings: The Two Towers* back on schedule. The cost was about $1 million, but enabled on-time completion of the project. (3) Bovis Lend Lease construction company had a $600 million contract to modernize 10,000 BP gas stations in the United States. In 2001 the vice-president of Bovis sent out 22,500 faxes just for parts orders. In 2002, he used Constructware software to coordinate the builders, architects, and 25 suppliers and subcontractors over the Web. The system has helped to reduce costs and double the pace of renovations. (4) Other examples include toy-maker Mattel connecting designers and licensees worldwide, IBM using an intranet for workers' brainstorming, and Eli Lilly drug company establishing a web site where scientific problems are posted and anyone solving one of the problems can receive a reward ($600,000 paid out in two years) (Green *et al.*, 2003).

Swapping electronic data, which allows customers and suppliers to share business documents in a few seconds, is proving so popular that many big companies are shunning nonusers. Tesco, a British supermarket chain, and Wal-Mart, the US super-retailer, will not deal with suppliers who are not part of their automated system for ordering and paying for products. At its most extreme this integration ignores corporate boundaries and manages suppliers as though they were subsidiaries. Sherwin-Williams, a paint company, lets managers from Sears, Roebuck help select people who would service the Sears account. Eastman Kodak, a chemicals and films group, allows outsiders to run one of its supply rooms. Xerox and General Electric send people to each other's in-house training sessions.

Though partnerships are the height of popularity at the moment, they are not without their problems. For a start, they entail a loss of those two crucial competitive weapons, confidentiality and freedom. A firm that hands its production schedule over to a supplier may see that supplier run off with a rival. The car firm that pays its supplier for what it uses may have reduced its paperwork but it has also made itself dependent on a supplier that may raise prices or go bust.

And partnerships are difficult to manage. If managing one firm is difficult, managing several, with different cultures and strategies, can be a nightmare.

Industries such as textiles, clothing, and machinery can be regarded as networks of business relationships. Often the specific firm in question will be involved in different industrial networks because it exports to several countries. However, different industrial networks may be more or less international to the extent that the connections between networks in different countries are more or less intensive. A global industrial network can be partitioned in various ways. Delimitation can be made concerning geographical areas, products, techniques, and so on.

When the grouping is made on the basis of national borders, different 'national nets' can be identified. Correspondingly, 'production nets' refer to relationships between those companies whose activities are linked to a specific product area. For example, it is possible to distinguish a 'heavy truck net' including firms manufacturing, distributing, repairing, and using heavy trucks. The firms in the net are linked to each other and have specific dependence relations to each other. The 'heavy truck net' can further be distinguished by its nationality, for example a French heavy truck net operates in France.

The network model has consequences for the meaning of internationalization of the market. For example, a production network can be more or less internationalized. A high degree of internationalization of a production net implies that there are many and strong relationships between the different national sections of a global production net. On the other hand, a low degree of internationalization of a global production net means that most national nets have few relationships with each other.

When relationships develop through interaction the people or companies in the local or international environment are tied to each other through a number of different bonds: technical, social, administrative, legal, economic, and so on. These bonds can be exemplified by, respectively, product and process adjustments, knowledge about counterparts, personal confidence, special credit agreements, and long-term contracts.

According to the network model, the internationalization characteristics of both the firm and of the market influence the process (Johanson and Mattson, 1988). In terms of networks, internationalization means that the firm develops business relationships in networks in other countries, that is, network positions. But the firm's internal assets (a unique product line, an efficient production process, and so forth) have a different structure when the company is highly internationalized than when it is not. Similarly, the competitive strength of the assets may differ if the market has a high or low degree of internationalization.

A basic assumption in the network model is that the individual firm is dependent on resources controlled by other firms. The companies get access to these external resources through their network positions. Since the development of positions takes time and depends on resource accumulations, a firm must establish and develop positions in relation to counterparts in foreign networks. This can be achieved by (1) *international extension*, through establishment of positions in national nets that are new to the firm, (2) *penetration*, by developing an existing foreign position, and (3) *international integration*, by increasing coordination between positions in different national nets. Which option the firm may choose depends on the internationalization degree of both the firm and the market.

In sum, the network approach of internationalization offers a model of the market and the firm's relationship to that market. The model stresses the cumulative nature of the firm's activities in developing international market positions and seems especially important in understanding key issues involved in cooperation in industrial systems and of global industry competition.

2.7 Ethical/moral issues

Marketing activities are being subjected to increasing scrutiny and challenges on ethical grounds. There are growing demands from consumers, special interest groups, and the public for companies to behave in a socially responsible manner. At the same time, governments continue to expand restrictions and requirements governing corporate behavior. For international marketers, meeting these expectations and demands is particularly difficult. With activities in more than one country, they frequently deal simultaneously with more than one set of ethics, different views of what constitutes socially responsible behavior, and different legal requirements. The issue is an important one. In the short run, failure to act in an ethical and socially responsible way may result in a wide range of problems including protests by customers or special interest groups, possible loss of markets/market shares, and/or lawsuits, penalties and fines. In the long run, failure to act in accordance with changing societal expectations results in additional laws and restrictions on business activities.

The objective of this section is to provide the export/international marketer with a basic understanding of the ethical factors that should be considered in evaluating proposed actions or activities. In doing so, it is useful to discuss what is meant by ethical behavior, some criticisms of the behavior of international companies, and possible ethical models to use in evaluating possible different courses of action.

2.7.1 Defining ethics

Ethical behavior, at its most basic level, is what most people in a given society or group view as being moral, good, or right. Some societies emphasize moral conduct based on abstract moral principles, the violation of which is expected to cause feelings of guilt. Other societies emphasize correct or proper conduct based on what is expected in the situation/relationship, the violation of which is expected to cause a feeling of shame (Sullivan, 1999). The judgement as to whether a decision is considered ethical is 'firmly anchored and steeped in a set of individual, corporate and social values, which derive from the cultural underpinnings of a society' (Sanyal, 2001, p. 150). Stated another way, what is considered ethical in one society may be considered unethical in another.

Three examples that illustrate these basic differences may be seen in the varying views of the paying of interest on loans, the attitudes toward women in the workforce, and differences regarding the payment of bribes. Lending money for the payment of interest is ethical in many societies, but considered unethical in some Islamic societies. Providing equal employment opportunities for women is considered morally right in many countries (and required by law in some), but is specifically prohibited by law in other countries. There are great differences in attitudes toward the payment of bribes or gratuities between countries.

In testimony before a Select Committee of the British House of Commons in 2001, Unilever and BP argued that small 'facilitating payments' or bribes are a commercial requirement in some countries (Mason, 2001). Even though their job requires it, Customs personnel may refuse to clear merchandise or other local government workers may refuse to process paperwork unless a small 'gratuity' is paid. Lower-level government officials are so poorly paid in some countries that they simply cannot survive without such payments. In some areas, gifts to local officials are traditional and considered ethical (if they are even thought about from this perspective). In other areas, the local people view them as unfair and exploitative, though perhaps necessary.

Large-scale bribery is more generally condemned, though it has been widely practiced, and is still a fact of life in some nations. It has been reported that leading exporters in the construction and arms industries have traditionally paid 10% or more of the value of a contract to a senior official or officials to obtain the contract (Mason, 2001). Payments made by international corporations, though sometimes legal in the countries in which they were made, are often considered unethical in the corporation's home country, and receive widespread unfavorable publicity in the international press. Such publicity resulted in the passage of the Foreign Corrupt Practices Act in the United States. This Act specifically prohibited the payment of bribes to foreign government officials, directly or indirectly, in order to obtain sales or contracts. However, in the 25 years since the passage of that Act, no other industrialized nation has passed such comprehensive and punitive anti-bribery legislation. This may change since in 1998 the OECD, together with five other nations, developed a proposed convention making bribery of public officials a criminal offence (Hershman, 1998).

The issue of making facilitating payments or bribes may present a difficult dilemma to the international marketer. To do so may violate his or her personal ethical code and the laws of the home country, and possibly those of the host nation. To fail to do so may, in some cases, result in lost sales, profits, and jobs for the company – and perhaps purchase by the host nation of inferior products from a company that will make such payments. The desire to remain fully competitive may account for the reluctance of most industrialized countries to pass laws against making facilitating payments abroad.

Companies have also been accused of unethical behavior in a number of other activities or practices. In 2000 Bridgestone Corporation of Japan was accused of failing to promptly recall defective tires that resulted in a number of accidents, injuries, and deaths in the Middle East, Latin America, and the United States (discussed in Case 2.1). An earlier case that received widespread publicity was Nestlé's introduction of baby formula in areas where breastfeeding was the norm and the product was improperly used by many mothers. Also widely criticized have been business activities that tend to support oppressive regimes where human rights are viewed as being violated, such as Royal Dutch/Shell in Nigeria and UNOCAL in Myanmar (Burma) in the 1990s. Charges have been raised that some companies are providing inadequate pay or poor working conditions to employees in the less developed nations, or buying products produced by foreign companies or government organizations that mistreat workers. In 2003 a lawsuit in the United States against two dozen large clothing retailers over alleged labor abuses in the Pacific island of Saipan was settled for $20 million. Also in 2003, for the first time, a dozen international companies that belong to the Fair Labor Association (www.fairlabor.org), including Phillips-Van Hensen, Reebok, Adidas, and Levi Strauss, made public labor audit findings on overseas factories that produce their products. This is expected to increase pressure on other firms to release information on conditions in their overseas factories (Bernstein, 2003).

An increasing number of companies, such as oil giant ChevronTexaco and Ford

Motor Company, have started issuing annual reports on their corporate social responsibility performance.

An issue of particular concern is the effect of business activities on the environment, including global warming, pollution, wasting of natural resources, the destruction of forests, destruction of animal and plant species, etc. Emphasis on these concerns tends to be greatest in the industrialized world, while many of the lesser-developed countries still focus primarily on promoting economic growth or other objectives. One way for the international marketer to operationalize its concern for the environment is to develop an internal environmental management system (EMS). At the international level in the late 1990s the International Standards Organization set a standard known as ISO14001 and companies could gain registration by meeting specified criteria. As discussed in section 2.8 below, conforming to ISO14001 is becoming necessary for many companies.

Larger international and global enterprises are the ones most often identified as violating ethical standards. This is due primarily to the fact that they are 'high-profile' companies. The effects on small and medium-sized businesses of failures to meet ethical (and legal) standards are often as damaging, or more damaging, than for the larger entities.

2.7.2 Possible bases for ethical decision making

The international marketer would like to have some guides to action regarding ethical behavior. Unfortunately, there is no universally agreed upon, or even widely accepted, standard or model that will always lead to decisions that will be viewed as ethical. Carroll and Buchholtz (2000) have provided a useful summary of a variety of approaches to ethics that may give helpful insights to decision makers. These include the following:

- **Principle of Utilitarianism:** the correctness of an action is determined by its results, such as the efficiency in use of resources or overall benefits to society. A weakness is that it may lead to a failure to consider the morality of the means used.
- **Principle of Rights:** individual or group rights should not be overridden simply because overall benefits to society occur. What is claimed as a 'right' by one individual or group may be validated by law or claimed on some other basis. Various rights may be in conflict (smokers versus non-smokers).
- **Principle of Justice:** fair treatment. Distributive Justice refers to the distribution of benefits and burden; Compensatory Justice refers to making up for past injustices; and Procedural Justice refers to fair treatment.
- **Additional approaches:** include the Principle of Caring, focused on people; Virtue Ethics, concerned with the development of virtuous people, and others including the Golden Rule.

Sanyal (2001, pp. 451–2) has discussed three extreme positions including individual relativism (based solely on what the individual decision maker thinks is right), cultural relativism (based on values in the host country alone), and ethical imperialism (based solely on home country values). He indicates that these extreme views indicate a need for universalism (based on core values and principles that are applicable everywhere). The core values that are universally accepted tend to be very general and subject to different interpretations in specific situations.

The different approaches will not always lead to the same conclusion or course of action. Thus the individual still must make decisions based upon his or her understanding of the way in which people in both the home and host countries will view the decisions from the perspective of ethics and morals.

2.7.3 Applying ethics in international marketing

Certainly international marketers need to be concerned with issues related to products (or services), promotion, and their customers. A number of the issues are also the subject of legal requirements in many countries. A more complete discussion of these issues is found in Maidment and Eldridge (2000, Ch. 14):

- The product (or service) should be safe and effective for use in the intended manner. Potential hazards or problems, both when used as intended and with possible misuse or use in other applications, should be identified. The product or service should not damage the people or the environment in the target market.
- In activities related to market entry and expansion, care should be taken to ensure that methods used do not conflict with either local or home country values, and will not be construed as including bribery.
- Advertising and promotion should honestly represent the product or service, avoiding misleading or confusing claims. The international marketer must also be aware of what approaches and subjects are considered as acceptable in the target market, and conform to local requirements. Control of activities by salespersons in the field is difficult, and efforts should be made to ensure that false claims and pressure tactics are not used. Proper training of field personnel is necessary, and sales incentives should be carefully designed to avoid putting pressure on people in the field to behave in ways not proper with respect to the product or customers.
- Prices should be set at a level that will be viewed as reasonable or fair, given the conditions in the target market. Both dumping (selling at below the cost of production or the cost of the product or service in the home market) and prices that will be viewed as excessively high should be avoided.
- Customers, employees, and suppliers should all be treated in a manner viewed as equitable and proper in their country.

Some specific 'dos and don'ts' are found in Fritzsche (1985, p. 95).

The international marketer must also be aware of ethical issues that are currently receiving increased attention. Some involve the marketing chain and others involve the procurement chain. One issue is the promotion of goods and sales to children of toys or games that may encourage or promote violence or other improper behavior. Another is the use of misleading advertisements and pressure tactics in selling to people who may be particularly impressionable or easily influenced (such as children and the elderly). Procurement activities are also of increasing concern, including the production of goods or the purchase of goods made by underpaid or unfairly treated workers, use of child labor, pollution of the environment in extractive or processing industries, and the waste or destruction of natural resources in procuring and manufacturing goods. In all company activities, the best practice is usually to base actions on the highest ethical standards, whether the standards are those of the host country or of the home country.

In brief, the international marketer needs to understand that his or her beliefs about what is right and wrong may not be shared by those in the countries in which this marketing occurs. Knowledge of the ethics, values, and customs in the overseas markets, as well as those in the home market, is necessary for successful marketing and avoiding possible problems. The great importance of the legal framework is dealt with in Chapter 3.

2.8 Social responsibility and the business environment

Traditional British and US views have held that the primary goal of business organizations was to maximize profits/returns to the stockholders. In much of continental Europe it was believed that businesses had broader obligations including specific responsibilities toward customers, employees, suppliers, and society as a whole. In Japan, the reason-for-being of private business organizations was to advance the interests of the nation, including economic growth, social and political stability, and international recognition. Stability of employment and market share were more important than the level of profits, values that are changing only slowly even in the 2000s. However, they are changing, particularly in foreign-controlled companies such as Nissan (Renault) and Mazda (Ford). Even in the traditional large Japanese companies, fewer employees are being covered by the lifetime employment system as companies rely more on temporary workers, and companies in serious financial difficulties have encouraged or even forced regular workers into 'early retirement.' Some new university graduates no longer seek 'jobs for life,' though most who are able to obtain regular employment with a large company do so. There is also a small cadre of university graduates who prefer to work for foreign companies that are believed to offer less security but greater opportunities.

Even in the United States, the foremost proponent of a laissez-faire economy with severely limited government intervention, the government has in fact been placing restrictions on businesses for social reasons for over 100 years. Laws were passed to protect the public and promote competition (1890s onwards), and later to promote social goals (1930s and 1950s onwards). Business as a whole opposed the majority of these initiatives, viewing them as impediments to maximizing profits.

A broader concept of corporate social responsibility began to receive widespread attention in the 1960s. Changing social values, and therefore a changing social environment of business, led to a discussion of whether companies should go beyond legal requirements and proactively attempt to improve society and the environment. There were a number of arguments in favor of companies going beyond what is required, including the following:

- Business must respond to changes in society and its demands/expectations.
- Profit maximization in the long run requires a socially and physically healthy environment.
- It was necessary to do so in order to avoid increasing government regulation.
- It would provide a better corporate image, with benefits in the ability to attract better employees, increased sales, improved access to capital, and improved stock performance.
- It might open up additional opportunities profitably to meet existing or emerging demands.

Arguments against companies going further than required in attempting to improve society included the following:

- It would reduce the company's ability to meet its primary objective of maximizing profits to stockholders.
- It would undermine free enterprise and result in business assuming functions that should be handled by the government or social institutions.

- It would place individual business leaders in the position of personally making nonbusiness-related decisions about spending corporate money.
- And the whole concept is fuzzy.

A more complete discussion of the arguments can be found in Buchholz (1986, pp. 23–30).

2.8.1 The stakeholder concept

An expanded view of what corporations should be responsible for doing was fostered by the recognition that businesses have more than just shareholders/owners. They also have 'stakeholders' who have an interest or some share in the undertaking. The shareholder/owner is a stakeholder with a legal right to certain treatment. Other stakeholders, such as employees, customers, suppliers, and the government, also have certain legal rights. In addition to these legal rights, stakeholders may claim moral rights. An employee may feel that he has a moral right to his job, beyond the requirements of the law, because of his long service to the company. A customer may feel that she has a right to have a product that is better or safer than the warranty specifies because of the money she spent on it.

Primary stakeholders who have a direct or financial interest in the firm usually exert the most influence. Owners/shareholders/strategic alliance partners, employees/managers, and customers have obvious interests. Governmental bodies, through regulation, collecting taxes, providing benefits, and acting as customers, are particularly influential.

While many small investors in stocks may feel that they have little influence, the institutional investors who now own 49% of US equities are becoming increasingly active in attempting to bring about changes in corporate behavior (*The Economist*, 2003). Public employee pension funds are at the forefront of this effort. CalPERS (the California Public Employees Employment System) and CalSTRS (the California State Teachers Retirement System), together with similar funds from Connecticut, New York, North Carolina, and Ohio, manage over $500 billion in assets. The majority of their funds are invested in equities in large US corporations, and their votes can be crucial in elections of corporate directors. CalPERS annually publishes a list of companies that it judges are poor performers and do not follow good corporate governance practices. It encourages them to change, and if they do not may take more direct action. Research indicates that a number of companies targeted by CalPERS in the past did take action to improve and, on average, have enjoyed substantial increases in returns (Earle, 2004). CalPERS also removes investments in whole countries from the list in which they will invest if the countries do not meet criteria regarding labor standards, press freedom, financial transparency, and shareholder protection (Engardio, 2002).

In March 2003 the six funds listed above worked together in declining to support the reelection of Michael Eisner, the president and CEO of Disney. Since no alternative candidates were listed on the slate proposed by the company, votes were simply withheld for Eisner on 43% of all shares. The Board of Directors acted quickly to split the positions of CEO and chairman, appointing a new chairman but retaining Eisner as CEO (Burt and Parkes, 2004). Since then, CalPERS has acted to nominate a critic of the New York Stock Exchange to its Board of Directors and, working with other funds, decided to withhold support for the CEO and six other directors of Citigroup, the CEO and two directors of Safeway, and the entire board of Pacific Gas & Electric (Raine, 2004; Brewster, 2004).

Secondary stakeholders may also exert significant influence. Competitors and potential competitors are of obvious importance. The media has a direct effect on public opinion, and also an influence on legislation affecting business. Special interest groups and individuals have become increasingly important in recent years, promoting causes and directly or indirectly influencing the media, the public, and legislators. Some of these groups/individuals are directly involved with business as a whole (such as labor overall that is concerned with unfair competition from poorly paid/badly treated foreign labor, and minority and women's groups concerned about discrimination and equal opportunities). Others are affected by the actions of business in which they are not direct participants (such as those living near sources of pollution). Yet others act out of overall concern for the environment, human rights (including labor), or other causes (such as animal rights). The stakeholder concept is discussed in detail by Carroll and Buchholz (2000).

2.8.2 Changing views of social responsibility

The actions of the media, educational institutions, special interest groups, and others have led to increasing public awareness of social, economic, and environmental problems, and increasing demands for businesses to act in a socially responsible manner. The definition of what is socially responsible, as with the definition of ethics, varies from society to society. However, the strong tendency is for societies to demand that companies act with increasing concern for the overall societal and environmental needs, as well as economic needs.

In free market economies, social responsibility for a company with widespread private ownership would seem to include, as a minimum, the following objectives:

- conducting business in accordance with the owners' desires, including
- maximizing profits, or at least returning a satisfactory level of profits, while
- conforming to the law in both the host and home nation, and
- conforming to the ethical values of both the host and home nation.

Even in free market economies, companies that are privately held, such as the US's Ben & Jerry's Ice Cream before its acquisition by Unilever, may be willing to sacrifice substantial profits in order to pursue social goals. Volkswagen AG, whose largest stockholder is the German state of Lower Saxony and with the apparent acquiescence of other shareholders, has always been more concerned about providing jobs for local workers than about profits and share prices (Miller, 2000).

Many large US and western European companies have developed codes of ethical conduct and/or social responsibility, though not all have made their codes available to every employee and the public. All leading business schools in the United States, and elsewhere, address the topics of ethics and social responsibility in their curricula. The United States leads the way in corporate giving to educational, humanitarian, and cultural organizations. European corporations have traditionally been less socially proactive, partly because the European governments tend to play a more central role. In Japan, there is no tradition of corporate giving and businesses have concentrated their efforts on protection of the company and its employees.

The international marketer must be aware of the need to act in a way that is viewed as socially responsible in both the host and home countries. The guidelines listed in the discussion of ethics above should be of help in evaluating current and proposed activities. An interesting account of the differences between Japan and the United States in legal practices, business–government relations, and views of the social responsibility of business is presented in Exhibit 2.5. What this illustrates is the need for companies entering markets with subsidiaries or with other modes to understand that things are most likely not as they are used to.

It is not inherent that social responsibility and corporate profit are incompatible. A good example of this is companies' signing on to the ISO 14001 standard that is concerned with the environment, and requires a specified type of environmental management system (Fielding, 2000; Lister, 1998). As market pressures start to dominate, more companies are considering the international environment standard a *necessary* business tool. As of the end of 2000, more than 10,000 companies worldwide have had their facilities registered to ISO 14001. Along with this, companies such as IBM, Ford Motor Co., Xerox, General Motors, and Honda of America are asking – even requiring – their suppliers to develop an environmental management system similar to ISO 14001 or be registered to ISO 14001. Many companies are finding that profits are increasing as costs such as those for energy go down due to ISO 14001.

| EXHIBIT 2.5 | Legal practices, business–government relations, and social responsibility in two countries |

Japan and the United States have significantly different legal practices, business–government relations, and views of the social responsibility of businesses. These differences need to be taken into account in company policies and practices of Japanese subsidiaries in the United States and US subsidiaries in Japan. While the Japanese public is becoming more concerned about corporate behavior than it has been in the past, companies there are still not subject to the detailed scrutiny or potential liabilities that they are in the United States.

Legal practices

The United States has the most litigious society of any industrial nation. Lawsuits are a widespread and accepted means of settling disputes between and among individuals, businesses, and government agencies. Judgements are made as to who was right and who was wrong, and often result in monetary awards for laws violated, losses incurred and/or punitive damages meant to punish an organization or individual for misdeeds. Penalties and monetary awards are often large, frequently in the millions and sometimes in the billions of dollars. A number of large US corporations, including Dow Corning, Johns Manville, and several asbestos-related companies, have been driven into bankruptcy by lawsuits claiming injury resulting from the products of the companies or exposure to environmental hazards at work. Lawyers may take cases on a contingency fee basis for plaintiffs seeking damages; the lawyers collect a part of the damages awarded if they win, and the clients pay nothing if they fail to win. This does give greater access to the legal system for individuals, particularly for individuals with limited financial resources, but also results in many additional lawsuits.

In Japan, recourse to the legal system is much less common than it is in the United States. The nation has less than one-twentieth of the number of lawyers per capita as the United States, 17 lawyers per 100,000 population in Japan compared to 352 per 100,000 population in the United States (Naohiro, 2000, p. 41). The Japanese public and neighbors react badly to lawsuits (Hendry, 2003, p. 237). There is an emphasis on conciliation, both informal and formal, rather than recourse to the courts. For cases that do reach the courts, the judge usually tries to satisfy both sides, not make declarations about right and wrong. An attempt is made to restore harmony. In Japan, all cases are decided by judges; the nation does not use the jury system available to most litigants in the United States. In criminal cases, apologies may serve to lessen sentences since the objective is to correct behavior and not to punish (Hendry, 2003, p. 235). For corporate failures or misdeeds, acceptance of responsibility and resignation of the president may be considered an adequate response by the company.

Examples of the relatively infrequent resort to courts and the small penalties are found in both governmental and private actions. The Japanese government imposed only a relatively small fine (by European and US standards) on Mitsubishi Motor Company for concealing automobile defects from the Japanese government for a period of over 30 years. Even major cases of product-related injuries and deaths do not usually result in a number of lawsuits. Payments for damages are rare and are usually relatively small. The Snow Brand recall, discussed below, provides an interesting example of a company that was sensitive to customer and public concerns, but acted in a very non-Western way. In recent years, there have been an increasing number of lawsuits between individuals resulting from automobile accidents, but even these are still very uncommon.

Business–government relations

While there are many ties between government and business in the United States, and companies often contribute to both major political parties' fund raising for elections, business–government relations are basically adversarial. Underlying the relationship is a societal emphasis on the rights of the individual, a strong belief in property rights (and profits), and a belief that free competition is both fair and results in the availability of more goods and services for consumers. The government, which has the objectives of protecting the public and promoting competition, has passed many laws, established agencies, and taken actions that most businesses have felt (at least at the time) have interfered with their property rights, efficient operations, and profit. With differences in some basic goals, business and government often tend to be in an adversarial relationship (Duerr, 1991, p. 51).

The United States enforces its laws through a bureaucracy that is usually aggressive in investigating violations of laws and regulations, and through heavy financial and sometimes criminal penalties for non-compliance. The government levies penalties and/or sues on its own initiative, and also acts on complaints or enters cases brought by individuals or organizations where it deems appropriate. The aggressiveness and adversarial stance taken by US government agencies, and the large penalties that may be assessed by US courts, is often a surprise to Japanese companies (and sometimes companies from other countries). Almost every large Japanese subsidiary in the United States, for example, has been charged with discrimination or sexual harassment, and many have paid multi-million dollar settlements. Most of the actions in which the companies engaged would not have been violations of Japanese law, and none would have been subject to large fines.

Business–government relations in Japan are so cooperative that many outsiders have viewed them as conspiratorial. The generally close cooperation, however, is actually based primarily on Japanese beliefs that cooperation is often more effective than competition, that the group is more important than the individual, that the nation is the most important group of all, and that strong industries are needed to promote national interests. Industry and labor, as well as the government, have shown a sense of national purpose in promoting economic growth and stability. Thus, similar objectives and mutual dependence are the basis of cooperation (Duerr, 1991, p. 48).

Japanese antitrust laws on the US model do exist – as a result of actions taken during the Allied Occupation after World War II – but are seldom enforced. Since the end of the Occupation in 1951 no significant legislation affecting business has been drafted and passed without substantial consultation with and input from businesses. Where business has had serious concerns about the effects of a proposed law, modifications are almost always made to the law before it is passed by the legislature. For example, in the case of the 1985 Equal Employment Opportunity Law that addresses the rights of women in the workforce, business pressure resulted in the law having no enforcement provisions at all.

The law can be, and is, violated without legal penalty by many companies (Duerr, 1997, p. 67; Nakanishi and Duerr, 1999, p. 130). In the relatively few cases where the government has taken formal administrative or legal actions against companies, penalties usually have been small or nonexistent.

Views of the social responsibility of business

The public in the United States shows a high level of concern over business behavior that affects consumers, workers, suppliers, minorities, the public, the environment, the community, international activities, and other areas. A study of over 22,000 people in 23 countries indicated that the United States has the highest percentage of consumers who say they have punished a company for not being socially responsible by refusing to buy its products or services (*San Francisco Chronicle*, 2000b). The media is active in investigating and publicizing corporate misdeeds or problems, including those related to unsafe products. A number of individuals and public interest groups have goals of putting pressure on companies to change their behavior in ways that are believed to be more socially responsible. The government, as noted above, is active in trying to at least ensure compliance with the law. The national legislature conducts hearings about problem areas, and additional laws believed to be in the public interest are enacted. Curricula in university schools of business address the topics of ethics and social responsibility. While the pursuit of profit remains a primary goal, most large companies have policies or statements regarding corporate social responsibility.

The Japanese public has generally shown much less concern with issues of the social responsibility of business. The primary responsibility of companies has been believed to be to provide jobs and economic growth, and business and government together have been credited with creating Japan's highly prosperous society and high level of employment. The greater importance of the group as compared to the individual, or the larger group (total company) compared to the smaller group (some workers or a small community) tended to make complaints seem selfish (Hendry, 2003, p. 58). The media in Japan has been less likely than their US counterparts to report certain types of misdeeds. Where serious corporate misbehavior has received public attention in the media, an apology or resignation by the president of the company has often been viewed as a sufficient response.

Changes are now occurring in Japan as a result of several factors. The economic slowdown and increasing unemployment during the last 10 years, the collapse of a number of companies due to mismanagement or bad judgement, and scandals involving payoffs to gangsters and bribes to government officials have reduced the faith of many Japanese in their government and companies. The June 2000 case of Snow Brand Milk Products, where nearly 15,000 people were made sick by contaminated milk from the country's biggest dairy, and the revelation that some of the recalled products were secretly reshipped to other stores, created distrust in the minds of many Japanese consumers. The response of the company to the problem was uniquely Japanese. Snow Brands made a payment to everyone who indicated that they had been made ill, without trying to evaluate the validity of the claim, and without lawsuits being filed. The company also paid a fine to the government. Additionally, a manager from the company personally visited every person who reported they had problems, and made a personal apology for the company's actions. Then the president, vice-presidents, and other senior executives of the company all resigned in apology. The process was time-consuming but consumer confidence was restored and the company enjoyed a rebound in sales. Though there were 18 food-contamination recalls in July 2000, the Japanese Consumers Cooperative claims that contamination is not on the rise but that the problem is just getting more attention (*San Francisco Chronicle*, 2000a). The increased media attention to such problems should also encourage change.

2.8.3 Effects on the political/legal environment

Any issues related to the social responsibility of business may result in changes in the political/legal environment discussed in Chapter 3. These will occur when some group is successful in identifying a problem/issue and proposal for change, developing support for their position, and finally obtaining legislative or administrative changes implementing the objective. The group may be comprised of members from any of the primary or secondary stakeholders. Changes impacting a large number of people usually trigger the push for change, and the media normally play a role in bringing the problem, related issues, and possible solutions to the attention of the public as a whole. Legislators and officials who can bring about changes in appropriate laws or regulations are affected both by the press and by their constituents.

Two issues currently receiving both media and legislative attention are: (1) spam, unsolicited bulk commercial e-mails that are unwanted by the recipients; and (2) the outsourcing of jobs (discussed in section 1.7.1., Exporting services of knowledge-industry workers). Both are of great concern, particularly in most of the industrialized nations.

Approximately 15 billion spam e-mails are sent every day, over 10 million per minute (Baker, 2003). Spam is of great concern to individuals and companies as it clogs the Internet, causes lost time for recipients, and leads to distrust among shoppers. Europeans are demanding that the United States does something to restrict spam originating in that country. Even though Europe has strong privacy laws that prohibit commercial e-mail unless the recipient requests it, 53% of e-mail there is unsolicited commercial bulk e-mail. Of the spam e-mails received in Europe 80% are in English and the same number appear to originate in the United States (Mitchener, 2004).

Spam is also of great concern to many US companies and individuals. Sales of anti-spam software reached over $600 million in 2003. Yet spam continues to be profitable, with 7% of US Web surfers saying they have purchased something from an unsolicited e-mail. A national law passed in 2004 criminalizes some tactics used by spammers, such as using deceptive subject lines or routing e-mails through third-party computers. It also allows civil suits against those who violate the law, and four of the largest US ISPs have filed hundreds of lawsuits against people accused of sending junk e-mails illegally (Morrison, 2004). More laws may be passed, though a European-style approach in the present US political environment will be difficult to achieve.

The outsourcing of jobs, discussed in Chapter 1, is another subject that has received much attention in the US media and by political candidates in advance of the November 2004 national elections. Unlike the earlier movement of manufacturing jobs overseas that involved mainly industrial workers, this is affecting many highly educated people employed in the knowledge-intensive industries that have been the United States' strength in recent years. In addition to the loss of jobs, there are also concerns over security of private health and financial information sent abroad for evaluation.

Arguments for avoiding restrictions on sending of work abroad revolve around the demonstrated resilience of the US economy to past changes, the benefits derived from past openness to change, and the expectation that new jobs will be created, as has been true in the past. For example, Peter Drucker has emphasized the number of jobs that have been created in the United States by foreign companies setting up facilities there, including 60,000 by Germany's Siemens and tens of thousands more by Japanese and European automobile manufacturers. US unemployment reached record lows after the implementation of the NAFTA trade agreement with Canada and Mexico, and remains the lowest among the Western industrialized nations (Drucker, 2004).

Some state and local restrictions on outsourcing of jobs have been passed, but the likely effects are small. Given the overall business and political environment, it would be difficult to pass legislation that would seriously impede the freedom of US business to increase outsourcing.

SUMMARY

This chapter has examined the bases and economic rationale for export marketing. In essence the thrust of the chapter has been to understand the motives that underlie company involvement in exporting. These motives are also the basis of the broad and specific goals and objectives that individual companies seek to achieve through export strategy.

Our first concern was with a more macro understanding. The potential benefits from exporting and relevant international trade theories were presented. Next we turned to micro considerations by exploring alternative theories of export behavior of the individual firm. This necessarily led to discussing the process by which companies can become 'internationalized.'

The nature of networks – i.e., business relationships among companies – was discussed from the perspective of national and international networks. Where the individual company fits in such networks and the alternative positions that a firm can develop in such networks were identified.

Finally, ethical and moral issues that potentially face all companies doing business in foreign markets were discussed. It is important to understand that what is 'right' and 'wrong' is not always easy to determine as there is no universally accepted code of behavior to aid decision makers. Knowledge of the home market and foreign markets is essential to arriving at one's own behavior code for each situation faced.

QUESTIONS FOR DISCUSSION

2.1 What are the benefits to consumers arising from international trade? Are they the same for industrial goods as for consumer goods? What costs to consumers arise from international trade?

2.2 Discuss how exports and imports help to increase productivity and efficiency.

2.3 The productivities of factor inputs with respect to different products are determined by a combination of natural and acquired advantages. Is the productivity of the Japanese due primarily to natural or acquired advantages? How about the French, or the Chinese? Explain.

2.4 **a** Briefly explain the different types of economic advantage for two countries, A and B, each able to produce two products, X and Y, and discuss the conditions for trade to be advantageous (assuming no transaction costs).

   b How is it possible for an individual business firm to have a comparative advantage?

2.5 Find an example of a country that is exporting a product for which it has an absolute disadvantage with a trading partner but where there is a comparative advantage. Explain the nature of this trading relationship.

2.6 Explain the product life-cycle concept as it relates to international trade and investment. What does the concept mean to the individual firm?

2.7 Export motives can be classified as internal or external and as reactive or proactive. What is meant by these terms with respect to export marketing? Give examples of each of the combinations of export motives.

2.8 Why might some companies be willing to undertake new or additional international/export marketing even though it apparently offers only similar (or even lower) levels of profitability?

2.9 What is meant by a 'change agent' in export marketing? Give examples of activities of each type of change agent.

2.10 How can a company determine how internationalized it is? Explain.

2.11 Find an example of a company that has expanded its export/international marketing activity, or started such activity, and determine the company's objectives for doing so and the results achieved.

2.12 How can a company make operational use of the network model and relationship marketing in planning and implementing international marketing programs?

2.13 There are many who believe that 'whatever is legal is ethical'. Do you agree with this belief as it might apply to the international marketer? Explain your position and give examples of behavior in the global marketplace that would support your position.

2.14 Is being 'right' or 'wrong' about moral issues in international marketing activities an absolute or is it relative? Explain.

2.15 With what particular issues must international marketers be concerned?

2.16 Are traditional views about the goals of business the same in Britain, the United States, and the continental western European countries? If not, how do they differ?

2.17 In general, are businesses becoming more or less sensitive to social responsibility issues? Why?

REFERENCES

Baker, S. (2003). The taming of the Internet. *Business Week*, 15 December, 78–82.

Bernstein, A. (2003). Sweatshops: finally airing their dirty linen. *Business Week*, 23 June, 100.

Brewster, D. (2004). CalPERS to oppose Citigroup directors. *Financial Times*, 13 April, 15.

Buchholz, R. (1986). *Business Environment and Public Policy* 2nd edn. Englewood Cliffs, NJ: Prentice-Hall.

Burt, T. and Parkes, C. (2004). A 'resounding victory' for shareholders. *Financial Times*, 5 March, 20.

Carroll, A. and Buchholz, A. (2000). *Business and Society: Ethics and Stakeholder Management* 4th edn. Cincinnati, OH: South-Western Publishing Co., Chs 3–5.

De Jonquieres, G. (2003). WTO points to halving of antidumping probes. *Financial Times*, 27 October, 3.

Drucker, P. (2004). Peter Drucker sets us straight. *Fortune*, 12 January, 115–18.

Duerr, M. (1991). Business–government relations in Japan. *SFSU School of Business Journal*, 45–52.

Duerr, M. (1997). Gender-based occupational segregation in Japan. *Occupational Segregation of Women Workers in Japan, the Philippines, and the United States*. Washington, DC: Philippine American Foundation, 60–74.

Earle, J. (2004). CalPERS plays policeman to great effect. *Financial Times*, 14 April, 25.

Engardio, P. (2002). The era of blind investment is over. *Business Week*, 11 March, 50.

Fielding, S. (2000). ISO 14001 brings change and delivers profits. *Quality Digest*, 32–5.

Fritzsche, D. J. (1985). Ethical issues in multinational marketing. In *Marketing Ethics: Guidelines for Managers* (ed. G. R. Laczniak and P. E. Murphy), Lexington, MA: Lexington Books.

Green, H. *et al.* (2003). The Web smart, *Business Week*, 24 November, 82–106.

Hendry, J. (2003). *Understanding Japanese Society*, 3rd edn, London: Routledge-Curzon.

Hershman, M. (1998). A blow against bribery. *Financial Times*, 23 February, 14.

Johanson, J. and Mattson, L.-G. (1988). Internationalization in industrial systems – a network approach. In *Strategies in Global Markets* (ed. N. Hood and J. Vahlne), New York: Croom-Helm.

Johanson, J. and Vahlne, J. E. (1977). The internationalization process of the firm – a model of knowledge development and increasing foreign commitments. *J. International Business Studies*, 8 (Spring/Summer), 23–32.

Kranhold, K. (2004). China's price for market entry: give us your technology, too. *The Wall Street Journal*, 26 February, A1.

Lister, N. (1998). ISO 14001: a European view. *Quality Digest*, December, 31–5.

Maidment, F. and Eldridge, W. (2000). *Business in Government and Society: Ethical, International Decision Making*. Upper Saddle River, NJ: Prentice-Hall.

Mason, J. (2001). Petty corruption set to move up agenda for multinationals. *Financial Times*, 11 January, 13.

Miller, S. (2000). VW starts work on a new model: profits. *The Wall Street Journal*, 13 December, A21–2.

Mitchener, B. (2004). Europe blames weaker US law for spam surge. *The Wall Street Journal*, 3 February, B1.

Moore, J. and Ihlwan, M. (1998). Not so fast. *Business Week*, 2 February, 48–9.

Morgan, R. M. and Hunt, S. D. (1994). The commitment-trust theory of relationship marketing. *J. Marketing*, 58 (July), 20–38.

Morrison, S. (2004). US Internet providers use new law to hit spammers. *Financial Times*, 11 March, 2.

Nakanishi, T. and Duerr, M. (1999). Improving conditions for women in the contingent workforce in Japan. *Contingent Employment of Women Workers in Japan, the Philippines, and the United States*. Washington, DC: Philippine American Foundation, 128–39.

Naohiro, Y. (2000). White Paper on international trade sheds light on domestic structural problems. *Japanese Journal of Trade and Industry*, November/December, 40–1.

Raine, G. (2004). Funds to yank votes from Safeway CEO. *San Francisco Chronicle*, 26 March, C1.

Sachs, J. (2000). A new map of the world. *The Economist*, 24 June, 81–3.

San Francisco Chronicle (2000a). Lizards in potato chips. 11 August, A22.

San Francisco Chronicle (2000b). US found most likely to punish socially irresponsible firms. 11 November, C1.

Sanyal, R. (2001). *International Management: A Strategic Perspective*. Upper Saddle River, NJ: Prentice-Hall.

Simpson, C. L. and Kujawa, D. (1974). The export decision process: an empirical inquiry. *J. International Business Studies*, 5 (Spring), 107–17.

Sullivan, J. (1999). *Exploring International Environments*. Boston: Pearson Custom Printing, ch. 12.

The Economist (1994). Tying the knot. 14 May, 73.

The Economist (1996a). Tough at the top. 6 January, 47–8.

The Economist (1996b). The miracle of trade. 27 January, 61–2.

The Economist (1997). Trade winds. 8 November, 85–6.

The Economist (2003). Open the club. 19 April, 11.

Turnbull, P. W. (1987). A challenge to the stages theory of the internationalization process. In *Managing Export Entry and Expansion* (ed. P. J. Rosen and S. D. Reid), New York: Praeger.

Vernon, R. (1966). International investment and international trade in the product life cycle. *Quarterly J. Economics*, 80 (May), 190–207.

Vernon, R., Wells, L. T. Jr. and Subramanian, R. (1996). *Manager in the International Economy* 7th edn. Englewood Cliffs, NJ: Prentice-Hall.

FURTHER READING

Business Week (2000). Up the ladder, global trade: can all nations benefit? 6 November, 78–84.

Donaldson, T. and Dunfee, T. (1999). When ethics travel: the promise and peril of global business ethics. *California Management Review*, 41(4), 45–63.

Dunning, J. H. (1988). The eclectic paradigm of international production: a restatement and some possible extensions. *J. International Business Studies*, Spring, 1–31.

Wartick, S. L. and Wood, D. J. (1998). *International Business & Society*. Oxford, UK: Blackwell Publishers, Inc., Chs 6–7.

CASE STUDY 2.1

Bridgestone Corporation

(This case study was written by Edwin C. Duerr, San Francisco State University.)

Introduction

On 31 March 2001 Bridgestone Corporation's president and three executive vice-presidents resigned. Though the company president denied that he was resigning because of the events at its wholly owned US subsidiary, Bridgestone/Firestone North American Tire LLC, the problems surrounding the recall of 6.5 million tires there had been a disaster. In the first seven months after the recall, the costs to the company's reputation and its direct financial loss had escalated beyond all expectations. The parent company's stock dropped over 50% on the Tokyo Stock Exchange. The $750 million dollars Bridgestone/Firestone had initially set aside to cover the direct costs of the recall and impending lawsuits proved totally inadequate, and Bridgestone had to inject more capital into the Firestone subsidiary. Sales of Firestone tires declined (though the parent company's Bridgestone brand tires continued strong). The recall eventually led to closures of some of the Firestone manufacturing plants in the United States. Relations with Ford Motor Company, a major Firestone customer, were strained and eventually the relationship was severed (though Ford honored existing contracts to buy tires from Firestone) (Nikkei Net, 2004). Approximately 60% of the recalled tires were on Ford Explorer sports utility vehicles (SUVs), and the recall and subsequent lawsuits and out-of-court settlements eventually cost Ford $3.5 billion.

Bridgestone's apparent slowness in identifying problems with their tires, their delay in taking action, and their lack of responsiveness to questions by the public and the media had led to sharp criticism. The US government, and governments in other countries where the tires had been sold, had launched investigations.

Much of the problem in handling the recall appeared to arise from an assumption by Bridgestone Corporation that Japanese business approaches could be applied in the same way in the United States. Responses to questions and complaints that would have been acceptable in Japan proved to be totally unsatisfactory in the United States. US customers who had been injured as a result of tire failures filed over 100 lawsuits, some leading to multimillion dollar set-tlements. In Japan, it is likely that few (if any) lawsuits would have been filed under similar circumstances, and awards (if any) would probably have been small. The US government took a proactive and adversarial stance that would not have been used by the Japanese government.

Background

The tire recall in the United States was ordered following reports of a number of cases in which tread separation on Firestone tires had led to vehicle rollovers, resulting in injuries and deaths. The tires recalled in the United States were all ATX, ATXII, and Wilderness AT model 15" tires made at Firestone's Decatur, Illinois factory. Most of them had been installed as original equipment on Ford's Explorer SUV, beginning in 1991. The same models of tire were also made at other US plants, but these were not recalled. Additionally, the same model of tire was made in various locations overseas and installed on Explorers sold in the Middle East and Latin America.

Under US law, the quality and safety of every part of an automobile except the tires is the responsibility of the vehicle manufacturer. The tire warranties are the sole responsibility of the tire manufacturer. All tires are coded and the manufacturers maintain detailed records of return rates so they are able to spot possible problems with particular models or manufacturing facilities. In some other nations, however, an automobile manufacturer may take responsibility for a recall of defective tires, either for legal or customer-relations reasons.

In 1992 the first lawsuits involving tires on the Explorer were filed against Firestone, but settlements were reached out of court and did not attract media or government attention.

The tire problems receive media attention

The first media reports of Firestone tire failures, with resulting vehicle rollovers and deaths, appeared in 1998 in Saudi Arabia. Ford said that the tire failures there apparently resulted from drivers deflating tires for better traction in the sand and then failing to re-inflate them when they returned to high-speed driving on tarmacked roads. The low tire pressure and high ambient temperatures combined to overstress the tires. Ford recalled approximately 45,000 vehicles in the Middle East and several other areas with extreme temperatures in 1999. In February of 2000 Ford recalled tires in Thailand and Malaysia, following that with recalls of 30,000 tires in Venezuela, Ecuador, and Columbia in May.

Initial recognition that there might be a problem with Firestone tires in the United States came from several sources. On 22 July 1998 a researcher at US insurance company, State Farm Insurance, sent an e-mail to the US National Highway Traffic Safety Administration (NHTSA) detailing 21 cases of Firestone tire failures. Of the 21 failures 14 occurred on Ford Explorers, very roughly in proportion to the percentage of the total number of tires that had been installed on the Explorers. For some reason, possibly problems in filing and retrieval, neither this nor two additional attempts by the researcher triggered an investigation.

Meanwhile, Firestone was sued by the family of a girl killed in 1998 when the car in which she was riding rolled over after tread separation on a Firestone ATX tire. In court, Firestone stated that it knew of only one similar case. However, in November 1999 a Texas state judge ordered Firestone to hand over to the family's lawyer any complaints or lawsuits against it regarding its tires, and employee depositions arising from those lawsuits. Possibly because of problems in gathering data, or for some other reason, Firestone did not hand over the last of the depositions until 22 June 2000 (after having paid a fine of almost $9000 for its delay). When cooperating lawyers finally totaled the updated number, they claimed there were 1100 incident reports and 57 lawsuits by February 2000.

In February 2000, a Houston TV station aired a report linking Firestone failures to deadly Ford Explorer rollovers. Media attention resulted in more people coming forward with complaints. NHTSA became interested in the problems in April and opened an investigation in May 2000.

The recall

On 9 August 2000 Firestone voluntarily recalled 6.5 million tires of three models made at their Decatur, Illinois plant. On 31 August NHTSA indicated that an additional 1.4 million tires were believed to be defective, but evidence was not conclusive and Firestone did not recall any of these.

With the additional publicity, the number of complaints continued to escalate. By October 2000 more than 3500 people had complained to NHTSA about tread separations, blowouts, and other problems with certain Firestone tires. More than 119 deaths and over 500 injuries were reported in the complaints. A number of complaints were received about other models of tire not included in the initial recall, and there was the possibility of additional lawsuits arising from problems with those tires.

The legislative branch of the US government was greatly concerned about the problem, and Congressional hearings were held beginning in mid-September of 2000.

It was not just in the United States that the companies were having trouble. On 1 September the Venezuelan government started a criminal investigation of an alleged cover-up by both Firestone and Ford.

Company responses to the problems

It is not completely clear when Bridgestone and Ford recognized that there was a serious problem with the tires in the United States. While neither company's actions appear to have satisfied either the US public or government, Ford does seem to have done a better job of its public relations. It did, of course, face an easier job than Firestone/Bridgestone that had the basic responsibility for tire performance and record keeping. Ford's comparative openness and relatively quick responses were also more appropriate in the US environment. Bridgestone's slow and inadequate response, at both the Firestone subsidiary and Bridgestone headquarters levels, appears to have been due to a combination of factors, probably the most important of which was a failure to understand US culture.

Slow recognition of the problem seems to have been due to a combination of poor data analysis, poor internal communications, and reluctance to release potentially damaging information. Problems recognized by engineering were not conveyed to marketing or senior officials. Though Firestone periodically did an analysis of warranty information on a plant-by-plant basis, it had not spotted the problem in the eight years since the introduction of the tire. Even after the beginning of the NHTSA investigation in May, it took the company almost three months to gather requested data. Ford did a computer analysis of Firestone's data in July, pinpointing a problem in the Decatur plant. Firestone said that it did not know of the Decatur problem until Ford identified it.

It was not until the month in which the NHTSA began its formal investigation that the US subsidiary first informed Mr Kaizaki, the president of Bridgestone, of the frequent occurrence of accidents involving Ford vehicles equipped with Firestone tires. Mr Kaizaki was told, however, that there were no problems with the tires. Mr Ono, the Japanese president of Firestone, apparently did not fully understand the gravity of the situation, was hesitant to talk to the press (which he had never had to do in Japan), or did not feel he had the authority to take strong action. Even after mounting pressure forced the tire recall Mr Kaizaki continued to avoid becoming involved in the situation. He maintained that the recall was an issue Firestone should handle by itself.

The recall itself did not start well. The company did not seem prepared for the number of calls from the media, and failed to give clear answers to questions. Since the company did not have adequate inventory to support a quick recall, their initial plans catered for a recall spread over a one-year period. It did not understand that US consumers simply would not stand for this. Mr Ono finally gave an interview to the *Washington Post* two weeks after the recall started. He said that the company was determined to 'resolve customers' concerns' but gave few specifics (Klein and Sugawara, 2000).

Part of the slowness and inadequacy of Firestone's response may have been due to the expectation that Ford would step in and accept part of the blame for the tire failure problems. In Japan, close relationships between companies may call for mutual support, and the penalty for accepting blame is primarily one of losing face. In the United States, however, if Ford had willingly accepted even partial blame, it would have meant that Ford would have invited even greater liabilities in lawsuits. Therefore statements by Ford placed all of the blame on Firestone. Even without accepting blame, Ford has been named as a party in many lawsuits that will end up costing millions of dollars.

Mr Ono was called to appear at the Congressional hearings held in September 2000. A Japanese television program noted that he had trouble in representing Firestone effectively. It was stated that in his whole career with Bridgestone Mr Ono had never had to make a speech until his appearance at the hearing. Additionally, English was a problem for him so he simply read a prepared statement. (The program was broadcast in Japan and also carried in overseas programming by NHK, the Japanese National Television channel, on 17 October 2000.) NHK also raised questions as to the extent to which the corporate headquarters and company practices in Japan might have been responsible for the disaster. Separately, headquarters in Tokyo said that Bridgestone did not have specific crisis-management rules for Firestone, such as reporting accidents to the head office. A Japanese lawyer was quoted as saying 'Japanese companies generally are not as sensitive to the risks of improper disclosure or delaying as US companies are. Because the penalty is far smaller in Japan, many companies don't [understand the seriousness of the problem]' (Klein and Sugawara, 2000).

As the Congressional hearing progressed John Lampe, executive vice-president of Firestone, took over the job of leading the company representatives. Firestone criticized the 26-pound tire pressure recommended by Ford in place of the 30-pound pressure Firestone originally recommended. Ford responded that Firestone tires on 1996 Explorers were involved in rollovers 15 times more often than Goodyear tires on the same vehicle (*San Francisco Chronicle*, 2000a). At a

subsequent hearing Mr Lampe admitted for the first time that Firestone had produced defective tires. He blamed the tire design and possible quality control problems in one plant as being the causes. He still indicated that the lower tire pressure may have reduced the margin of safety of the tires. His remarks concerned only one of three models recalled, and did not address the problems with the tires made in the Venezuelan plant (Alanso-Zaldivar, 2000).

Mr Kaizaki, the president of Bridgestone in Japan, relieved Mr Ono as president of Firestone. Mr Lampe was made president and CEO of Firestone. His more conciliatory stance was undermined by repeated statements by Mr Kaizaki that there were no problems with the Firestone products (Dvorak, 2001).

In November, Firestone was still analyzing data regarding the tires. The company said it had determined that another model of tire of the same size made at the same Decatur plant had only one-tenth the number of complaints as the recalled model. But overall there were more complaints about tires from the Decatur plant than from other US plants. Therefore it appeared that the failures were due to a combination of tire design and something plant specific (Ansberry, 2000).

Even with a new president, the company seemed to continue to have public relations problems. On 17 November a federal judge ordered Bridgestone/Firestone to stop destroying its recalled tires until plaintiffs and defendants could hold a conference about preserving some for evidence in lawsuits. A lawyer for Firestone said that he would pass the information to Firestone, but could not be sure how quickly the company could obey (*San Francisco Chronicle*, 2000b).

Additional lawsuits over tires made at other US plants besides Decatur have been filed against Firestone. Bridgestone officials have stated that there is no danger that Firestone will be driven into bankruptcy by the lawsuits and lowered sales. There is a possibility that they have underestimated the amounts which will be awarded to plaintiffs.

Ford has also faced lawsuits and some public relations problems. It has apparently minimized the public relations problems through a number of actions. It has steadfastly maintained that the rollovers are exclusively a tire problem and emphasized the overall good safety record of the Explorer. After the announcement of the recall, Ford launched a multimillion dollar public relations campaign to reassure customers that the company was moving quickly to replace the tires. On 28 August 2000 the CEO of Ford, Jacques Nasser, apologized to the public on television. In the Congressional hearings in September he stated that he would release all documents indicating what Ford knew and when they knew it (Eisenberg, 2000). In November 2000 Ford took out full-page advertisements in US newspapers, thanking the public for their patience during the difficult time, and stating that: 'Working around the clock with Michelin, Goodyear, Continental-General, Firestone, and other manufacturers, we now have all of the tires we need to replace the 6.5 million recalled Firestone tires' (*San Francisco Chronicle*, 2000c). Ford also decided to use Michelin as an additional supplier for the 2002 Explorer, and will stipulate in future contracts that it must have complete access to all warranty data from tire suppliers to ensure greater safety in the future (Eisenberg, 2000).

Ford has been moving with great speed to settle all individual lawsuits against it resulting from injuries and deaths in the rollovers in the United States. It has also made a practice of apologizing to the plaintiffs for equipping the Explorers with tires made by Firestone, indicating that Ford never intended for tires of this quality to be used on its vehicles. Thus, while Ford claims that it was not responsible for the problem, the company indicates that it is helping to solve the problem.

Firestone's responses, inadequate in the US environment, have placed its brand name, and perhaps even the future of the company, in jeopardy.

References

Alanso-Zaldivar, R. (2000). Firestone executive says firm takes blame. *San Francisco Chronicle*, 13 September, A3.

Ansberry, C. (2000). Firestone finds more problems in one line and left rear tire. *The Wall Street Journal*, 7 November, A4.

Dvorak, P. (2001). Bridgestone's CEO Kaizaki is resigning. *The Wall Street Journal*, 12 January, A15–A16.

Eisenberg, D. (2000). Anatomy of a Recall. *Time*, 11 September, 29–32.

Klein, A. and Sugawara S. (2000). Bridgestone tire crisis tests Japanese executive. *International Herald Tribune*, 24 August, 17.

Nikkei Net (2004). http://www.nni.nikkei.co.jp

San Francisco Chronicle (2000a). Firestone, Ford trade charges in hearing on Explorer tires, 22 September, A8.

San Francisco Chronicle (2000b). The Firestone recall is almost over, 26 November, D7.

San Francisco Chronicle (2000c). Judge halts destruction of flawed tires, 18 November, A3.

Questions

1. What appears to have caused delays by Firestone in recognizing and responding to the problem with the tires?

2. Why was the response of the company not adequate to satisfy the US public and government?

3. Should a company apply the ethical, behavioral, and legal standards of the home country or host country in its overseas operations?

4. In your view, and given the time frames indicated in the case, did Ford act as quickly as it should?

5. Given what is known today, should the US government have required that new cars must have tire pressure warning systems?

6. What ethical issues arose surrounding the situation in Venezuela?

CASE STUDY 2.2

GlaxoSmithKline PLC

(This case study was written by Edwin Duerr.)

Britain's GlaxoSmithKline, the second largest pharmaceutical company in the world, was formed on 27 December 2000 by the merger of Glaxo Wellcome PLC and SmithKline PLC. The merged company had over 7% of the world market for ethical (prescription) drugs. GSK had increases in both sales and profits in 2001, 2002, and 2003. Total sales in 2003 were £21 billion with profit before tax of £6.7 ($37.8 billion and $12.1 billion respectively at the April 2004 exchange rate of £1.0 = US$1.8). With a number of problems facing the whole pharmaceutical industry, GSK expects 2004 to be a year of transition before it returns to growth in 2005 (GSK, 2004).

Because of the international nature of the companies involved, the proposed merger had required approvals by three governments as well as the stockholders of the companies involved. The European Commission had granted approval in May 2000, stockholders of both companies had endorsed it in July, and both the US Federal Trade Commission and the British High Court had given their approvals in December 2000. As a condition of approving the merger, the three governmental authorities had required the companies to divest themselves of specific patents and drugs. These conditions were imposed in an effort to avoid reducing competition in pharmaceutical markets where the companies had overlapping products.

The companies expect that the merger will provide economies of scale and scope in marketing and production, spread the risks inherent in the high cost of new drug development and testing, and provide a smoother income stream as new drugs reach the market and the patents on older drugs expire. The chief executive of the new company, and former chairman of SmithKline, is Jean-Pierre Garnier. One of his major objectives is ensuring that customer loyalty is maintained so that as patents expire on older medicines they can be successfully marketed as over-the-counter medicines. This strategy worked well for SmithKline with its ulcer drug, Tagamet. While the merger and policies to increase customer retention can be very beneficial, they may not be sufficient to meet changes in the market.

A primary problem for GSK, as for other international pharmaceutical companies, is the worldwide challenge to their pricing practices. Though GSK is a British company that markets worldwide, much of its earnings come from the United States and are therefore subject to prices received there. The United States is the only industrialized nation that does not have price controls on prescription drugs. It accounts for 40% of the $350 billion sales of prescription medicines sold worldwide, and an estimated 60% of pharmaceutical company profits. Demand in the United States is growing at twice the rate of that in Europe as governments there attempt to limit their spending on drugs. However, there is growing dissatisfaction in the United States with the way in which the companies price their drugs. This presents not only a threat to the profits of the drug companies, but in the longer run may limit their ability to develop new drugs.

The problem arises from several interrelated factors: the basic cost structure of developing, testing, and producing drugs; the growing number of individuals who need high-priced drugs, but cannot afford them; the publicity given to these unmet needs, particularly but not exclusively related to the AIDS epidemic in Africa; and an increasing public acceptance of the idea that all people (or at least all people in their own country) are entitled to needed pharmaceuticals.

Even after offering the AIDS drug Combivir in Africa for less than 12% of its price in the United States, GSK continues to be criticized for high prices there and elsewhere. Garnier has commented: 'Do you want us to give away these drugs for free? Then there won't be any more drugs to treat AIDS or anything else. Isn't it ironic that the companies that brought the drugs to market are the ones being criticized for people dying?' (Harris and McGinley, 2001).

While the problem may be clear, what GSK should do about it is not apparent.

Costs of producing pharmaceuticals

The development of new drugs to the point where they can be marketed is both very expensive and risky. The marketing itself is expensive. The manufacturing costs, and particularly the marginal costs of production, are relatively low. In order to sustain (or increase) overall profitability, the drug companies must charge enough for their drugs to cover the high development costs. This has been possible primarily because of the patent system that allows the company holding the patent to set a far higher price than it could obtain if other companies could begin to manufacture and market it. Of course, some system allowing companies to recover research and development costs is necessary or the development of new drugs by private enterprise would cease.

The total cost of simply developing a single new drug, including research and testing, is estimated to range from $300 million to $600 million (Aoki, 2001). The cost of actually bringing a new drug to market, including meeting regulatory requirements and marketing, has risen to $1.7 billion (Flynn, 2004). The costs of both the initial research and the expenditure on trials may be lost if the drug proves to be ineffective or has serious adverse side effects. Approximately 80% of drugs in development never win FDA approval in the United States, though some are dropped before the expensive trials are conducted. Some drugs are banned after they have been in use for some time as side effects emerge that were not found during the trials.

New technologies for developing some additional drugs, including those designed to tap the potential of new knowledge of genetic triggers of disease, require extremely large investments. Application of bioinformatics, merging information technology and molecular biology, holds the promise of assisting in developing new candidates for pharmaceuticals. The great computing power and specialized software required are very expensive. The manufacturing equipment required for producing new drugs is also very costly when new technologies or additional capacity are needed. Once these are provided the marginal costs of manufacturing the medicines are relatively small compared to the fixed costs already incurred.

Pricing of pharmaceuticals

David Stout, the head of GSK in the United States, called the country the last free market in the world for pharmaceuticals (Shales, 2001). Most of the European countries have programs under which their citizens have some sort of entitlement to prescription drugs. Their national health systems have become monopsony buyers of pharmaceuticals exerting downward pressure on prices. The result is that patients in Europe pay one-third less for drugs than do Americans.

The low marginal costs of producing drugs, combined with the high prices that can be charged in the United States, have made pharmaceutical companies willing to supply drugs to markets outside of the United States at much lower costs than they charge within it – when they are forced to do so. That is, insofar as they can charge more than production costs, and sales to the outside market do not decrease sales in their primary market, they profit by selling abroad at lower prices than they obtain in the United States. This is, of course, the situation that gives rise to 'dumping' in steel and a wide range of other products. Even within the United States very large purchasers of pharmaceuticals can obtain lower prices when the alternative for the company is selling less product overall.

The result has not only been that drug companies make most of their profits in the United States. The country has also become the center for research on new drugs with companies working there spending $22 billion per year on research while those in the EU spend approximately $12 billion per year. This is in spite of the fact that the EU has a larger population and a bigger economy than that of the United States. Of the 17 antiretroviral drugs used in AIDS treatment, 13 were developed in laboratories in the United States.

Growing dissatisfaction

US drug companies have argued for many years that they must continue to have patent protection and be able to charge high prices in the United States for their current drugs in order to support the costs of research and development for new drugs. They have been successful to date, but face the increasing probability that a combination of factors will result in downward pressure on prices.

Public dissatisfaction with the prices of prescription drugs in the United States has been rising both because of the increasing prices and because of greater knowledge of what is charged for the same drugs in other countries, including Canada and Mexico. Increasing numbers of US residents who live sufficiently near to Canada are driving over the border to purchase their prescription medicines there. On average, brand-name prescription drugs cost over 60% more in the United States than they do in Canada, but importing them from Canada into the United States is technically illegal. US law forbids the importation of prescription drugs by anyone other than the original US manufac-

turer (who may bring them in from its plants overseas). Thus a US company can, for example, bring in drugs from its plants in Europe, but an individual or other company cannot buy the same medicines in Europe and legally bring them in. US pharmaceutical manufacturers imported $40.7 billion of drugs into the United States in 2002 (Barlett and Steele, 2004). The US national government has not, however cracked down on individuals bringing in prescription medicines.

Escalating prescription drug costs, coupled with an aging population increasingly in need of more medication, are a concern of governmental bodies at different levels as well as individuals and consumer advocate groups. In the United States, the amount spent on prescription drugs as a percentage of total health costs reached over 8% in 1999 and it is estimated that this will increase to almost 12% in 2006 (Aoki, 2001). It has been stated that the higher prices US residents pay for drugs in turn pay for half of the industry's research, and that US taxpayers also pay for most of the world's government-funded basic biomedical research. Commissioner McClellan of the US Food and Drug Administration has stated 'That is not a sustainable or fair situation' (Carey, 2003). Still, the US national government has not come up with a feasible solution to the problem, and is opposed to efforts by individuals, consumer groups, and some local governments to make imports of less expensive drugs easier. In addition to industry objections to easing imports, there are also potential problems with counterfeit drugs (as discussed below).

While the US national government has not stopped individuals from bringing in medicines for their own use purchased in Canada, it has warned that it will go after third parties assisting US residents in buying Canadian drugs (Colliver, 2003). A number of Canadian-based Internet companies are providing prescription drugs to US residents. The process is legal from the standpoint of Canadian law as long as a somewhat complicated procedure is used to obtain proper prescriptions. In spite of warnings by US officials, as of mid-2004 no action has been taken against the Internet companies (Parloff, 2004).

In 2003 GSK and several US pharmaceutical companies stopped selling to Canadian pharmacies that supply US patients. They indicated that they did so because it is illegal and is undercutting their business. A nonprofit organization in San Francisco then tried to organize a boycott of GSK products but the company indicated it had not felt any effects (Collier, 2003). In 2004, drug industry giant Phizer, Inc. threatened to cut off all sales of its products to Canadian pharmacies that help the cross-border trade. In Minnesota, where there is much opposition to US national government restrictions on imports, the state attorney general is looking at whether the actions by the companies constitute antitrust violations (Barry, 2004). Political pressure is building at both the local and national levels to allow such imports, or to find another solution to the high prices of drugs for US residents.

It is not only in the United States that the price of drugs has been criticized. Concern over the AIDS epidemic, and particularly the recognition that the drugs needed to fight the disease are too expensive for most of the population affected in Africa, has led to widespread criticism of the pharmaceutical industry. Strong public pressure resulted in a number of pharmaceutical companies, including GSK, offering lower-cost AIDS drugs for African nations. This action, or any other to reduce the costs of AIDS drugs for Africa, appears unlikely to do much to help the vast majority of people affected (Knickmeyer, 2001). Problems of distribution and education, and the reluctance of some African leaders to admit that there is a problem, are likely to limit the effectiveness of the efforts. It has been pointed out that even where medications have been available at low cost for other diseases in Africa, it has still not been possible to control the diseases. However, the extensive attention given to the problem by governments and the media has increased concern everywhere about the pricing of prescription medications.

Governments have also taken action to make lower-cost AIDS drugs available. The US government announced in February 2001 that it would not seek sanctions against poor countries that legalize the importation of generic copies of patented anti-AIDS drugs (McNeil, 2001). Some reputable drug manufacturers in India, Argentina, and other countries do not honor traditional patents, and produce properly labelled pharmaceuticals for sale outside the United States and Europe (Capell and Timmons, 2001). This practice is, of course, objected to by the original developers of the drugs.

Another potentially serious problem for the pharmaceutical industry was raised by an agreement negotiated by the World Trade Organization (WTO) in August 2003. It provides a method by which developing countries can overrule drug patents in certain cases. The Brazilian government threatened to use the procedures on a leukemia drug patented by Novartis of Switzerland before successfully negotiating a lower price from Novartis. In the meantime, a generics drug company in India has been given the right to produce a copy of the Novartis drug (Dyer, 2004).

Another critical problem, for both consumers worldwide and for pharmaceutical companies, is that of counterfeit drugs or substandard drugs originating in a number of less developed countries. Various studies have found drugs with no active ingredients and others with so little of the required active ingredients that they may serve only to increase the resistance of microbes to the active ingredients (Johnson, 2000). Some counterfeit drugs contain poisonous substances. The World Health Organization estimates that 8% of the bulk drugs imported in the United States are counterfeit, unapproved, or substandard (Capell and Timmons, 2001).

Critics of the pharmaceutical industry argue that it could lower cost without sacrificing innovation. They note that the industry is one of the most profitable in the United States. The industry is also criticized for the amounts it spends on advertising. Since the Food and Drug Administration began to allow the advertising of prescription drugs on TV and radio in the late 1990s, spending has increased rapidly, reaching $1.9 billion in 1999. The industry claims that advertising is an effective way to inform the public of advances in medicine. Critics complain that much of the money is going to promote heartburn, allergy, and hair-loss medicines, and even some expensive drugs that might be less effective than cheaper medicines. The growth in staff is also criticized. It is noted that the number of sales people employed by the top 40 drug companies grew from 36,500 in 1995 to 62,000 in 1999 (Barrett, 1999).

Others argue that the rising cost of health care is a result of the changing demographics of the population and the continuing search for new drugs to solve health problems previously untreatable. A contributing writer for the *New York Times Magazine* become a supporter of the pharmaceutical companies after he was diagnosed with HIV. Though his medications cost $10,000 per year, he argues that having effective drugs that are expensive is better for the health of the nation than not having the drugs at all. In the long run, as patents expire, cheaper generic versions will become available. He further argues that if Americans do not carry the burden of high drug costs, innovation will dry up (Aoki, 2001).

The pharmaceutical industry is now spending some of its advertising money on producing TV commercials featuring individuals whose lives have been saved or vastly improved by newly developed prescription medications.

It appears at this point that the US government will almost certainly move to increase prescription drug coverage under its Medicare system for older Americans. In this connection, or in separate actions, the government is also likely to attempt to find a way to force down the cost of some prescription drugs for at least a portion of the population. The United States will thus become less of a free market. How this will affect the pharmaceutical companies will depend upon how much volume will be increased by whatever scheme is used, and the policies followed by the pharmaceutical companies.

Some options for GlaxoSmithKline

In general, when patents expire and generic drugs become available, prices overall may drop as much as 90%. Companies selling prescription drugs on which the patents are about to expire have used various methods in attempts to maintain as much of their income stream as possible. One approach has been to actually raise the price of the product. Though some (or many) users will switch to cheaper generic products, others are relatively price insensitive. It may thus be more profitable to sell substantially less of the drug at a higher price rather than try to maintain a higher level of sales at much lower prices.

Another approach, which may be combined with the first, is for the company to introduce its own generic product before the patent expires. The company can then advertise the new generic product and gain a dominant position in the generic market before the competition is allowed to enter that market. Combining heavy marketing in the original drug with dominance in the generic market allows the company to continue to earn a high margin on the original drug while having most of the lost sales on that version go to its generic version.

The former SmithKline's policy of developing lasting customer loyalty for patented products, through a combination of advertising and pricing, may allow a company to continue to successfully market the product on an over-the-counter basis after the patent expires.

Pricing in a US market where the government is likely to take steps to force lower prices is a major challenge. While the pharmaceutical companies have been unwilling to provide data to the public on 'actual' manufacturing costs, careful internal consideration of this information is necessary in order to develop effective policies. Any government provision of prescription drug benefits, however structured, is almost certain to result in increased sales. If the pharmaceutical companies are able to influence the price levels set by the government, they may be able to partially or fully offset the lower prices with the increased volume.

References

Aoki, N. (2001). Rising drug costs a prescription for debate. *San Francisco Chronicle*, 2 April, B5.

Barlett, D. and Steele, J. (2004). Why we pay so much for drugs. *Time*, 2 February, 44–51.

Barrett, A. (2000). Crunch time in pill land. *Business Week*, 22 November, 53.

Barry, P. (2004). Crackdown in Canada. *AARP Bulletin*, February, 18.

Capell, K. and Timmons, S. (2001). What's in that pill? *Business Week*, 18 June, 60.

Carey, J. (2003). Drug R&D: must Americans always pay? *Business Week*, 13 October, 38.

Colliver, V. (2003). SF nonprofit escalates its boycott of Glaxo. *San Francisco Chronicle*, 14 March, B1, B8.

Dyer, G. (2004). Africa Aids crisis raises ethical questions over drugs deal. *Financial Times*, 3 May, 23.

Flynn, J. (2004). In two generations, drug research sees a big shift. *The Wall Street Journal*, 11 February, A1.

GSK (2004). *GlaxoSmithKline Annual Report*, available at http://www.GSK.com.

Harris, G. and McGinley, L. (2001). AIDS gaffes in Africa come back to haunt drug industry at home. *The Wall Street Journal*, 23 April, A1.

Johnson, E. (2000). Third World threatened by phony drugs. *San Francisco Chronicle*, 15 June, 18.

Knickmeyer, E. (2000). Cheaper AIDS drugs in 6 African nations won't reach many patients. *San Francisco Chronicle*, 12 April, A12.

McNeil, Jr, D. (2001). Bush won't block use of AIDS drugs. *San Francisco Chronicle*, 22 February, 19.

Parloff, R. (2004). The new drug war. *Fortune*, 8 March, 144–56.

Shales, A. (2001). America foots the bill for Europe's largesse. *Financial Times*, 3 July, 17.

Questions

1. Are the present pricing policies of the major pharmaceutical companies ethically justifiable? Explain your answer.

2. Are companies in less developed countries ethically justified in producing and selling generic copies of patented drugs without obtaining the permission (and paying) the patent holders? Explain your answer.

3. With Americans paying substantially higher prices for prescription drugs than people in other countries, are US consumers unjustifiably having to subsidize the development and sale of drugs to people in other countries?

4. Is the selling of drugs abroad at lower prices than in the United States actually a case of dumping? If not, why not? If so, why do other countries force 'dumping' of pharmaceuticals while they try to stop 'dumping' of steel?

5. Is advertising by pharmaceutical companies socially desirable?

6. What policies should GlaxoSmithKline adopt with regard to:

    a) pricing of patented products during the early years of protection and as patent protection is due to expire;

    b) attempting to influence public policy through advertising or lobbying?

CHAPTER 3

The International Environment

3.1 Introduction

As we have shown in Chapter 1 the international marketer operates within both a domestic and a foreign environment. Our concern here is primarily with the foreign environment, as this dimension might affect the international marketing/exporting business firm in unfamiliar ways.

There are many distinct components of the environment that can affect the international marketing company. We will limit our discussion to economic forces, socio-cultural forces, political–legal forces, and competition, as these are the major dimensions affecting behavior and, as such, are sufficient to provide the necessary environmental framework for subsequent discussions of international marketing mix variables. More complete discussions of these components as well as those of distribution structure, geography and infrastructures, and technology levels are presented in broader texts on international business. Social responsibility and the environment were covered in the previous chapter.

The international environment was very turbulent in the late 1980s and 1990s. The former Soviet Union disintegrated, the former Yugoslavia was replaced by a number of independent areas, but not without major fighting for territory, and Czechoslovakia peaceably split into Slovakia and the Czech Republic. Changes occurred in eastern Europe as a number of countries experimented with democracy and market economies. Another major event occurred in the European Union (EU) where the 15 member states have for the most part completed the creation of the internal market in accordance with the Single European Act of 1987 that was 'institutionalized' in the EC92 program that came into force on 1 January 1993. In addition, the Maastricht Treaty of 1991 dealt with major financial and currency matters, and the euro has replaced national currencies in all current (as of March 2004) EU countries but Denmark, Sweden, and the United Kingdom. A major issue now facing the EU is how to integrate the central and eastern European countries and Malta and Cyprus that joined the Union in 2004.

The turbulent environment is not limited to Europe. The People's Republic of China (PRC) has expanded, and continues to expand, its international trade, wholly foreign-owned enterprises, joint venture and other strategic alliance formations, and political contacts. Further changes will occur as Hong Kong, which transferred to PRC sovereignty in 1997 as a Special Administrative Region, and Macau, which reverted in 1999, become more integrated into China. China was granted membership in the World Trade Organization (WTO) in late 2001. So far, China has been used more for sourcing than for market penetration. In the late 1990s Asia faced a major financial crisis, from which it has emerged in the early 21st century. Major sources were Indonesia, Korea, Thailand and Malaysia.

Perhaps the single most significant phenomenon in the international environment in the early 21st century is the threat of terrorism. Although terrorism was with us continuously during the 20th century, it typically was limited to specific areas of the world – Indonesia, Turkey, Germany, Spain, the Philippines, Israel, etc. However, since the Islamic-based attack on the United States on 11 September 2001 and the United States' interventions (or invasions) in Afghanistan and Iraq, terrorism has become a world phenomenon that affects business and individual lives. World terrorism is now on a new level!

3.2 Economic forces

A major characteristic of the international marketer's world is the diversity of marketing environments in which business may be done. In particular, the economic dimensions of the world market environment are of prime importance.

Economic forces affect the international marketer by the impact that they have on market potential and, at any point in time, market actualization. In addition, economic forces in a country may be influenced strongly by the infrastructure that exists, including the communications, energy, and transportation facilities.

Significant variations in national markets originate often in straightforward economic differences. *Population* characteristics represent one major dimension. Of relevance are such attributes as total population and location of the population within the country (for example, degree of urbanization). The *income and wealth* of the people, both absolute magnitude and location, are relevant because they determine purchasing power. It is well documented that income is a major determinant of ownership of consumer durable goods. Of course, sales of some durable goods are affected by other factors such as climate and geography. For example, purchases of air conditioners and dehumidifiers are affected by climate as well as income. High-income people in Sweden can easily afford an air conditioner but are unlikely to buy one. In contrast, low-income people in Algeria have a need for an air conditioner but are unlikely to buy one since they cannot afford it.

Distribution of income and wealth and the affluence of particular groups in a nation or region are also of great interest. Even in a society with low average income, there may be a population segment with a high income level and the desire to purchase luxury goods. While the average income in Hong Kong is well below that in the major industrialized nations, it has the highest per capita ownership of Rolls-Royce automobiles in the world.

3.2.1 Market development

On a broader scale, the extent of *economic development* of a market influences the lines of business and methods by which business can be carried out in a country. Infrastructure is affected, as are all types of institutions within the country.

Foreign markets may be at different stages of economic development, each stage having different characteristics. A common way to group countries is as *developed* (for example Denmark, the United Kingdom, Japan, the United States) or *developing* (for example Malaysia, Costa Rica, Egypt, Uruguay). Several developing countries grew considerably more rapidly than most other such countries. These were called *newly industrialized countries* (NICs) – for example Brazil, Mexico, South Korea, Taiwan, and Singapore (Hong Kong is an NIC but is now a Special Administrative Region of the PRC) – and did not conform to the traditional model of developing countries as their gross domestic product (GDP) per capita exceeded US$3000, the majority of manufactured products were exported, and their industrialization process included locally owned companies as well as joint ventures with foreign multinational corporations. Such a grouping is, of course, highly simplified and represents the extremes.

Another approach to categorizing the world's economies is illustrated in Table 3.1, where the World Bank groups countries on the basis of gross national income (GNI) per capita as follows:

1. **low-income economies** (GNI per capita < US$735);
2. **lower middle-income economies** (GNI per capita ⩾ US$735 but ⩽ US$2935);
3. **upper middle-income economies** (GNI per capita > US$2935 but ⩽ US$9075);
4. **upper-income economies** (GNI per capita > US$9075).

A small number of countries in central Europe, Latin America, and Asia experienced rapid growth in the 1990s, and have been identified as having major marketing opportunities. These countries have come to be known as big emerging markets (BEMs). Ten countries generally recognized as BEMs are China (PRC), India, Indonesia, South Korea, Brazil, Mexico, Argentina, South Africa, Poland, and Turkey (Keegan and Green, 2000, p. 54). These countries cut across all stages of economic development as per capita income ranges from over US$11,000 in South Korea to less than US$400 in India. China is the largest with a population of over 1.2 billion and Argentina is the smallest with a population of 37 million. Some barriers to their emergence as major global players are their past behavior on human rights, environmental protection, and other issues of concern to potential trading partners. This grouping of countries overlaps somewhat with the grouping known as NICs.

These types of classification are of only limited usefulness to an international marketer and should not be used as the sole basis for deciding whether or not to enter foreign markets and how to market to such markets. Such classifications rest upon many factors involving trade-offs within this system. Thus, two countries that differ in many ways may be classified in the same group. An example of a classification schema developed by a company for its own internal use is shown in Exhibit 3.1. Although this schema is more than 25 years old, it illustrates what a company can, and often must, do when it has a specific need and there is nothing available that fits this need.

TABLE 3.1 Classification of selected countries by the World Bank based on GNI

Low-income economies	Lower middle-income economies	Upper middle-income economies	High-income economies
Afghanistan	Albania	Hungary	Andorra
Guinea	Guatemala	Panama	French Polynesia
Nigeria	Romania	Argentina	Netherlands
Pakistan	Algeria	Latvia	Germany
Azerbaijan	Guyana	Poland	Netherlands Antilles
Haiti	Russian Federation	Belize	Aruba
Papua New Guinea	Armenia	Lebanon	Greece
Bangladesh	Honduras	Saudi Arabia	New Caledonia
India	Samoa	Botswana	Australia
Rwanda	Belarus	Libya	New Zealand
Indonesia	Iran, Islamic Rep.	Seychelles	Austria
Bhutan	Serbia and Montenegro	Chile	Norway
Kenya	Bolivia	Lithuania	Bahamas, The
Senegal	Iraq	Slovak Republic	Hong Kong, China
Korea, Dem. Rep.	South Africa	Costa Rica	Portugal
Sierra Leone	Bosnia and Herzegovina	Malaysia	Bahrain
Burundi	Jamaica	St Kitts and Nevis	Iceland
Kyrgyz Republic	Sri Lanka	Croatia	Barbados
Solomon Islands	Brazil	Mauritius	Ireland
Cambodia	Jordan	St Lucia	Qatar
Lao PDR	St Vincent and the	Czech Republic	Belgium
Somalia	Grenadines	Trinidad and Tobago	San Marino
Cameroon	Bulgaria	Dominica	Bermuda
Lesotho	Kazakhstan	Mexico	Israel
Sudan	Swaziland	Uruguay	Singapore
Central African Republic	China	Estonia	Brunei
Liberia	Macedonia, FYR	Venezuela, RB	Italy
Tajikistan	Syrian Arab Republic	Gabon	Slovenia
Chad	Colombia	Oman	Canada
Madagascar	Maldives	Grenada	Japan
Tanzania	Thailand	Palau	Spain
Malawi	Cuba		Cayman Islands
Congo, Dem. Rep.	Marshall Islands		Korea, Rep.
Mali	Tonga		Sweden
Togo	Micronesia, Fed. Sts		Kuwait
Congo, Rep.	Tunisia		Switzerland
Mauritania	Dominican Republic		Cyprus
Uganda	Morocco		Liechtenstein
Côte d'Ivoire	Turkey		United Arab Emirates
Moldova	Ecuador		Denmark
Uzbekistan	Namibia		Luxembourg
Equatorial Guinea	Turkmenistan		United Kingdom
Mongolia	Egypt, Arab Rep.		Macao, China
Vietnam	Paraguay		United States
Eritrea	Ukraine		Finland
Mozambique	El Salvador		Malta
Yemen, Rep.	Peru		France
Ethiopia	Vanuatu		Monaco
Myanmar	Fiji		
Zambia	The Philippines		
Gambia, The			
Nepal			
Zimbabwe			
Georgia			
Nicaragua			
Ghana			
Niger			

Source: World Bank web site, www.worldbank.org/data.countryclass/, 2004. International Bank for Reconstruction and Development. © The World Bank

| **EXHIBIT 3.1** | **Economic development variable in countries' use of electricity and electrical goods** |

Occasionally, a company may develop its own schema. For example, the classification system once used by the General Electric Company is summarized below:

- *Less developed:* These countries have primarily agrarian and/or extractive economies. High birth rates, along with limited infrastructures, account for the low per-capita income and usage of electricity. Electrification is limited to the main population centers. Generally, basic electrical equipment is imported.
- *Early developing:* These countries have begun initial development of an infrastructure and have infant industries, especially mining and selected cottage manufactures. Target economic sectors may enjoy high growth rates even though per-capita income and electricity consumption are still modest. Progressively more sophisticated electrical equipment is imported, frequently to achieve forward integration of extractive industries.
- *Semi-developed:* These countries have started an accelerated expansion of infrastructure and wide industrial diversification. Thus, per-capita income and electricity consumption are growing rapidly. Increased discretionary income and electrification allow greater ownership of autos and electrical appliances among the expanding middle class. Larger quantities of high-technology equipment are imported.
- *Developed:* These countries enjoy well-developed infrastructures, high per-capita income and electricity consumption, and large-scale industrial diversification. They are also characterized by low rates of population and economic growth, as well as shifts in emphasis from manufacturing to service industries – notably transportation, communication, and information systems.
- *Communist:* The separate listing for these countries does not imply that they represent either a higher or a lower stage of economic development. They could have been distributed among each of the above four categories.*

This approach incorporates general country variables – e.g., geography, population, income, etc. – and industry-specific variables of interest, e.g., usage of the product, total imports, etc.

* Today, this category is obsolete.

Source: Reprinted with permission of The Conference Board from V. Yorio, *Adapting Products for Export* (1978), p. 11.

Any classification scheme assumes a certain homogeneity among markets in the same category, which often is not correct. Even the more traditional countries may have groups of people who, due to their income and other sets of values, will be a market for sophisticated products and services, while some of the developed countries still have portions of their population to some extent outside the money economy.

If complemented with the use of socio-economic, cultural, demographic, and structural data, then it becomes possible to use classifications to assess the existence of a potential market for a given product or set of products in a given country. However, the results of such analysis may yield nothing better than the knowledge that a market exists for the product *concept* without ensuring the success of any given marketing mix. At best, then, any classification schema is an indicator that further investigation is or is not warranted.

3.2.2 Some areas of change

One of the major areas of rapid growth and change has been Asia and the Pacific Rim countries. The countries of Asia are expanding trade, investment, and technology links by themselves, rather than depending on Europe or the United States as in the past. As shown in Table 3.2, Asian countries vary in population, and per capita GNP. Exhibit 3.2 reports that East Asian countries are counting heavily on high-technology industries to provide much-needed economic growth during the early 21st century (*Business Week*, 2000a, p. 134).

TABLE 3.2

Selected indicators for Asian areas (2002)[a]

Area	Population (millions)	Per capita GNI (PPP, US$)[b]
Hong Kong	6.8	26,810
South Korea	47.6	16,480
China	1,280.9	4,390
Singapore	4.1	23,090
Taiwan	n.a.[c]	n.a.
Malaysia	24.3	8,280
Thailand	61.6	6,680
Indonesia	211.7	2,990
Philippines	79.9	4,280
Vietnam	80.5	2,240
Myanmar (Burma)	48.9	n.a.
Cambodia	12.5	1,590
Laos	5.5	1,610

[a] Reported by World Bank, www.worldbank.org/data/, 2004.
[b] PPP is purchasing power parity, which accounts for price differences between countries.
[c] n.a. = not available.
Source: International Bank for Reconstruction and Development. © The World Bank

EXHIBIT 3.2	**East Asia's future growth industries**

East Asia is placing its hope for future growth on the following four high-technology industries:

- **Biotechnology**. East Asia has lagged behind the West in the life sciences. But the region's wealth of brainpower and low costs could make Singapore, Taiwan, China, and South Korea global centers for commercializing discoveries in genetics and molecular structure.
- **Wireless Internet Appliances**. East Asian electronics companies plan on being global players in many digital products that access the Internet.
- **Software**. Countries such as Vietnam and Indonesia hope to establish themselves as contractors to develop software applications, animation, and web services.
- **Specialty Chips**. South Korea, Taiwan, and Singapore have been major suppliers of commodity semiconductors. Now they hope to compete against US companies as producers of innovative and higher-margin multimedia chips.

During the past few years business people have been looking to China's large population as new potential customers. Consumer goods companies such as McDonald's and Kentucky Fried Chicken in fast foods, United Biscuits, Kraft Foods, and beer producers Australia's Fosters, Denmark's Carlsberg, and the

The Great Wall of China

Philippines' San Miguel have been aggressively marketing to Chinese consumers. Most consumer durable goods (electronics, appliances, stylish clothing) are out of the reach of most Chinese people, but this is changing relatively rapidly as the Chinese economy continues to grow and affluence begins to appear beyond the four major cities of the east coast – Beijing, Shanghai, Shenzhen, and Guangzhou. Wealth in 40 middle-tier urban areas such as Chongqing in western China and Tianjin near Beijing is appearing (Armitage, 2003). Overall, consumption growth is increasing. For example, it has been estimated that in late 2003 there were 260 million mobile telephone subscribers in China. The youth of China, those in their 20s who represent the group of 'only children' who were born after the introduction of China's one child per couple policy in the late 1970s, are a different kind of consumer who is not afraid to spend money (*The Economist*, 2004a). Related to this surge in spending is the emergence of multiple areas of economic strength, as shown in Figure 3.1. For example, the Pearl River Delta area in southern China

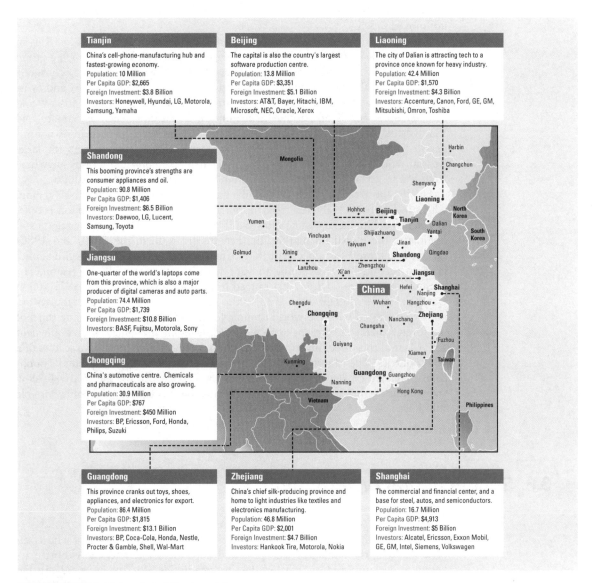

Tianjin

China's cell-phone-manufacturing hub and fastest-growing economy.
Population: 10 Million
Per Capita GDP: $2,665
Foreign Investment: $3.8 Billion
Investors: Honeywell, Hyundai, LG, Motorola, Samsung, Yamaha

Beijing

The capital is also the country's largest software production centre.
Population: 13.8 Million
Per Capita GDP: $3,351
Foreign Investment: $5.1 Billion
Investors: AT&T, Bayer, Hitachi, IBM, Microsoft, NEC, Oracle, Xerox

Liaoning

The city of Dalian is attracting tech to a province once known for heavy industry.
Population: 42.4 Million
Per Capita GDP: $1,570
Foreign Investment: $4.3 Billion
Investors: Accenture, Canon, Ford, GE, GM, Mitsubishi, Omron, Toshiba

Shandong

This booming province's strengths are consumer appliances and oil.
Population: 90.8 Million
Per Capita GDP: $1,406
Foreign Investment: $6.5 Billion
Investors: Daewoo, LG, Lucent, Samsung, Toyota

Jiangsu

One-quarter of the world's laptops come from this province, which is also a major producer of digital cameras and auto parts.
Population: 74.4 Million
Per Capita GDP: $1,739
Foreign Investment: $10.8 Billion
Investors: BASF, Fujitsu, Motorola, Sony

Chongqing

China's automotive centre. Chemicals and pharmaceuticals are also growing.
Population: 30.9 Million
Per Capita GDP: $767
Foreign Investment: $450 Million
Investors: BP, Ericsson, Ford, Honda, Philips, Suzuki

Guangdong

This province cranks out toys, shoes, appliances, and electronics for export.
Population: 86.4 Million
Per Capita GDP: $1,815
Foreign Investment: $13.1 Billion
Investors: BP, Coca-Cola, Honda, Nestle, Procter & Gamble, Shell, Wal-Mart

Zhejiang

China's chief silk-producing province and home to light industries like textiles and electronics manufacturing.
Population: 46.8 Million
Per Capita GDP: $2,001
Foreign Investment: $4.7 Billion
Investors: Hankook Tire, Motorola, Nokia

Shanghai

The commercial and financial center, and a base for steel, autos, and semiconductors.
Population: 16.7 Million
Per Capita GDP: $4,913
Foreign Investment: $5 Billion
Investors: Alcatel, Ericsson, Exxon Mobil, GE, GM, Intel, Siemens, Volkswagen

FIGURE 3.1 Hot spots in China to watch
Source: Caulfield and Shi, 2004, p. 70. © 2004 XPLANATiONS™ by Xplane.com®. From *Business 2.0*

(Hong Kong, Shenzhen, Guangzhou, Foshan, and Dongguan) has an integrated economic structure that makes it the 'world's workshop for everything from stuffed toys to cell phones to desktop PCs' (Einhorn *et al.*, 2003).

Another major area of change is Latin America, where a number of countries – such as Argentina, Chile, Mexico, Colombia and Peru – are growing rapidly and economic conditions have improved significantly. Industries such as utilities, manufacturing, construction, and telecommunications are still in their early growth stages in countries such as Argentina, Brazil, Chile, and Mexico. One indication of the appeal of Latin America has been the investment there by Asian companies. For example, South Korea's Kia opened a US$500 million automobile production plant in Brazil in 1995 while Samsung announced that it would expand its production of television sets and white goods in Brazil and Mexico. A Taiwanese textile firm, Nieu Hsing, and a manufacturer of batteries, CSB, announced plans to build factories in Mexico. A type of market revolution occurred across Latin America. Governments are privatizing and cutting tariffs and bureaucratic red tape, and markets are being opened to all. But some Latin American countries have not moved much.

Another area of change as we move into the 21st century concerns Russia, where a middle class is beginning to make itself known and 'heard.' Such a group is very appealing to international marketers as they have the income to consume. This group's influence is being boosted by a resurgent national economy and by its own efforts. The middle class is concentrated in the western cities of Moscow and St Petersburg, but is also found in major provincial cities such as Samara and Vladivostok. By profession, most are entrepreneurs who own their own businesses. Some are lawyers and accountants. Still others are managers for large Russian and multinational corporations. Depending upon definition, anywhere from 8% to 20% of the population is middle class (*Business Week*, 2000b).

Finally, the area known as the Middle East and North African (MENA) region, which includes 24 Arab countries and territories and almost 500 million people, has lagged behind in economic growth and globalization. Although the region still dominates the global oil market, the benefits from oil in the 1970s and 1980s failed to generate a sustained growth dynamic or bring about greater regional integration. Income levels continue to vary widely within the MENA region. For example, per capita GDI in 2001 ranged from an estimated high of US$27,900 in Qatar to US$350 in Djibouti (Abed, 2003, p. 11). However, MENA countries are poorly integrated with the world economy. The region receives only one-third of the foreign direct investment expected for a developing country of an equivalent size. Most of this direct investment tends to be concentrated in enclave sectors of a few countries. The March 2003 issue of the International Monetary Fund's publication *Finance & Development* examines the main causes of the relatively slow growth during the past 20 years, the problems this has caused, and some possible solutions.

3.3 Socio-cultural environment

The socio-cultural environment influences the behavior of customers who comprise markets, the managers who plan and implement international/export marketing programs, and the marketing intermediaries (for example advertising agencies and media) that participate in the international marketing process.

Culture should not simply be considered as an obstacle to doing business across cultures. It can provide tangible benefits and can be used as a competitive tool or as a basis of a competitive strategy. In short, cultural differences can, and should, be managed. To illustrate, the Japanese company Bridgestone's acquisition of the US tire maker Firestone did not proceed as smoothly as desired (Ricks, 1999, p. 99). The former chairman of Firestone, John Nevin, admitted that his style of management appeared abrupt and abrasive at times to the Japanese, whose manner tends to be much more subtle. He needed to be less direct and forceful with them and they had to become more aware of US-style directness. Both sides tried to adjust, but it did not work out and new managers had to be brought in. It is when cultural differences are mismanaged that problems arise and profits are adversely affected. Exhibit 3.3 provides some guidelines for managing multiculturalism.

EXHIBIT 3.3	**Managing multiculturalism**

Managing multicultural organizations is not easy. A recent paper (Vence, 2003) reported that Elmer Dixon, senior associate at US-based Executive Diversity Services, Inc. specified some vital characteristics of a manager for this task:

- *Cultivate self-awareness.* If a manager is to understand the styles and behaviors of other cultures he or she has to be able to understand his or her own actions and their cultural origins.
- *Work with differences.* A key question to ask is whether the difference in behavior or culture really makes a difference.
- *Learn various styles of communication.* To be successful and effective in a multicultural organizational environment a manager needs to be fluent in a number of communication styles, which are tied to individuals' experiences, values, and nuances in every culture. This includes cultures that one works with and markets to.
- *Ability to settle cross-cultural conflict.* Some conflict is inevitable within organizations, distribution channels, and the marketplace. A manager needs to be able to distinguish between misunderstanding and real differences.
- *Be curious.* One should be willing, in fact be eager, to seek out and be fascinated with information that is different.

Within organizations, and channels of distribution as well, managers from different cultures can have differing management styles, which can have a negative impact on relationships being successful. A management style is 'a recurring set of characteristics associated with the process of making decisions.' Research has been reported that shows such styles differ among managers from five European Union countries (Albaum and Herche, 1999) and among six Asia-Pacific region countries (Albaum *et al.*, 2004).

Socio-cultural characteristics of buyers – consumers and industrial buyers as well – which are influenced by external stimuli are but one set of factors that influence the buying decision process, albeit a very important set of factors. Included are such things as material culture, language, education, aesthetics, values and attitudes, social organization, and political–legal structure and philosophy. The purpose of this section is to illustrate some of the socio-cultural similarities and differences found in societies.

What has not always been understood is that foreign consumers differ from domestic consumers to some extent in all aspects of buyer behavior – the what, why, who, how, when, and where of buyer behavior. On a more general level, consumers in each country differ from consumers in every other country, and within countries as well. Countries such as the United States, Canada, Australia, and many European countries are truly multicultural in nature. This has been due largely to immigration. In effect, significant sub-cultures exist within many countries. In the United States, for example, there are large populations of Chinese, Vietnamese, Koreans, Hispanic/Latinos, African-Americans, Arabs, Native Americans, etc.

Export managers all too often lack cultural awareness that can lead to errors or loss of potential gains in marketing policies. For example, Ricks (1999, pp. 31–2) reports an example of use of multiple-unit packaging that backfired. A US golf ball manufacturer attempted to sell golf balls in Japan packaged in groups of four. Pronunciation of the word *four* in Japanese also sounds like the Japanese word for *death*. The number four, therefore, is considered undesirable and items grouped into fours simply do not sell well. As another example, Adler (1991, p. 25) cites the case where a North American expatriate manager in Hong Kong chose an office of large size, regularly shaped, and located next to the vice-president's office. Chinese customers were uncomfortable visiting him in this office as they felt that the office had bad *feng shui* and would create bad business. *Feng shui* reflects the belief that people and their activities are affected by the layout and orientation of their workplace and home, and the goal is to be in harmony with the environment. The manager's choice of office reflected his culture – maximize status and influence through office size and proximity. But to the Chinese, the office was unlucky because it lacked harmony with nature. Fortunately, the manager was sensitive to Chinese cultural values and changed offices.

Another illustration of cultural difference and its effect on the existence of a viable market is provided by the food product cookies. A gourmet cookie company in the United States produced top-quality cookies made from the best ingredients. These cookies were fairly large, beautifully presented, individually packaged, and were premium priced. A market that was identified as a potentially good prospect was Japan. However, with further research it was concluded that the size of the cookie was a negative feature in Japan. Unlike the United States, where 'bigger is better' and where value is equated with additional volume and quantity, in Japan smaller products are perceived to have more value because it is assumed that more design and engineering effort were dedicated to their creation (Pacheco, 2002). A jumbo-sized cookie is viewed as the antithesis of the Japanese cultural value regarding size.

3.3.1 The nature of culture

Cultural factors exert the major influence on consumer behavior as it is the most fundamental determinant of a person's wants and behavior. Since so much of success in international marketing depends upon an understanding of culture, one might ask: what is it? For anthropologists, culture has long stood for the way of life of a people, for the sum of their learned behavior patterns, attitudes, and material things (Hall, 1973, p. 21). In a real sense, culture is human-made. It is learned and, as such, is communicated from one generation to another. Culture is shared by members of a society, and the behavioral traits of which it is comprised are manifested in a society's institutions and artifacts. It is something that shapes behavior or structures one's perception of the world. In sum, culture is a shared system of meanings, it is learned, it is about groups, and it is relative (that is, there are no cultural absolutes); it is not right or wrong, inherited, or about individual behavior (Hoecklin, 1995, pp. 24–5). Thus, culture can be viewed as the homogeneity of characteristics that separates one human group from another (Griffith *et al.*, 2000, p. 304). Yet another view looks at culture as the collective programming of the mind that distinguishes one group or category of people from another (Hofstede, 2001, p. 9). Table 3.3 presents a set of indicators identified by Brislin (1993).

TABLE 3.3 Indicators of a person's culture	1. Concepts, values, and assumptions about life that guide behavior and which are widely shared by people. 2. The person-made part of the environment. 3. Ideas that are transmitted generation to generation, rarely with explicit instruction (by parents, elders, teachers, etc.). 4. This means that there will be identifiable childhood experiences that lead to the transmission of culture. 5. An image that may be helpful is to think of a group of 18–20-year-olds; respected elders can look at all the 18–20-year-olds and can make the summary judgement, 'Yes, that person is one of us,' or, 'No, that person is not one of us.' The people judged as 'one of us' have learned the culture. 6. Culture is not talked about – much of it is taken for granted (much as the air we breathe), and what is taken for granted is not discussed. Also, since culture is widely shared, it is uninteresting to talk about what everybody shares. This means, however, that people have little practice in discussing how culture affects their behavior, and so are ill prepared to explain their culture to people from other countries. 7. Behaviors influenced by culture are done for their own sake – people are not expected to defend these behaviors. 8. Practices strongly influenced by culture stay despite mistakes and slip-ups. 9. Culture becomes clearest when people interact with others from very different backgrounds. Culture becomes clear in 'well-meaning clashes.' People are engaging in proper behavior according to their own culture, but there is a clash when the interaction is between people from different cultural backgrounds. 10. There is an emotional (not just intellectual) reaction when cultural assumptions are violated. 11. Behaviors influenced by culture can sometimes be summarized in very clear pictures, or in short scenes (scripts) that are much like those in a movie. 12. Culture allows people to 'fill in the blanks' when faced with the basic elements of a set of behaviors familiar in their own culture. 13. Related to point 12, culture allows people to say 'and all that sort of thing' and 'you know what I mean' when the basics of familiar behaviors are mentioned. 14. People can reject aspects of their culture at one point in their lives and can move back into an acceptance of these aspects at other times in their lives. 15. Some culturally influenced behaviors can be summarized in very sharp contrasts (individualism–collectivism, punctuality, spatial orientation of people, theory vs. empiricism). 16. There is a feeling of 'this will be difficult and time consuming' when attempts at culture change are considered.

To understand a culture one must understand its origins, history, structure, and functioning; how its artifacts and institutions developed to cope with the environment; and the effects of the geographical environment on the culture, acculturation, and assimilation. Culture undergoes change over time, with change typically being slow to occur. Sometimes 'rapid' changes occur. These, however, are often not 'natural' but are due to outside pressures, for example from government or other groups such as religious organizations. When the Shah lost power in Iran and the religious leaders gained control of the government, the culture changed relatively rapidly from its 'Westernized' direction to a more fundamental Islamic orientation. A similar situation occurred in Afghanistan. Government influences culture in other ways that may not be as quick in becoming effective. For example, there are movements in many countries to develop a legal framework for cohabitating couples. If laws are passed that recognize these legally, unmarried couples would become eligible for many fiscal and legal rights now enjoyed by married couples. In the mid-1990s the percentage of all couples in European countries that were unmarried ranged from 20% in Denmark and 18% in Sweden to about 2% in Greece. Such 'legalization' would ultimately lead to a change in values about marriage. In 2004 some states in the United States began to allow legal marriage between same-gender couples. This practice, however, is being questioned in the courts. Needless to say there is, and will continue to be, strong opposition to this from religious groups. International marketing managers need to know how the culture changes, and also how their decisions interact with and sometimes serve as a change agent in the culture. Culture provides norms for behavior of buyers, consumers, and sellers, and these norms control behavior in ways that are not always well understood.

There are many dimensions to culture as summarized in Table 3.4. Some of the great religions of the world, for example, transcend national boundaries and thus contribute to cultural homogeneity among certain nations. Or the educational opportunities in 'developed' nations for people from 'developing' nations can contribute to similarity of habits and customs, tastes, and values. Foreign languages are often used by the educated classes of nations and contribute to cultural homogeneity. On the other hand, the diversity of languages, religions, education systems, and numerous other cultural factors contributes to different ways of life, habits, and customs. Even within nations there is great cultural diversity, for example between those from Hamburg or Munich in Germany, or as previously mentioned between the numerous ethnic and racial groups in the United States, or among the 14 or more major language groups in India and the seven major groups in China.

Another way to learn about cultures is to examine *cultural universals*, and seek generalizations that apply to all cultures. Murdock (1945) identified more than 70 cultural universals including such diverse things as athletic sports, education, feasting, games, language, mourning, music, status differentiation, and visiting. While the means of, say, *status differentiation* or the preferences for *music* may or may not be the same in each culture, every culture has some means of differentiation and some preferences for some kind of music.

Although one can study and compare cultures by seeking regularities or irregularities in cultural universals, this task is made difficult by the fact that much of the routine of living is governed by cultural characteristics of which people are only dimly aware, or perhaps even unaware. This phenomenon is known as the *iceberg principle*. There is a surface culture that includes the more obvious dimensions of music, art, food and drink, greetings, dress, manners, rituals, and outward behaviors. But the most powerful elements of culture may very well be those that lie below the surface and include so-called value orientations, which are preferences for certain outcomes over others – for example control of the environment over harmony with the environment. Illustrations of selected value orientations toward selected variables are shown in Table 3.5.

Learning about cultures is made even more difficult because societies or groups may share certain common culture traits, but there are also many possible *subcultures* with characteristic traits that explain variations in behavior within cultures.

TABLE 3.4

Cultural dimensions

Values and attitudes about
    time   wealth
    work   change
    risk taking achievement

Education
    formal education (primary, secondary, higher)
    literacy level
    vocational training
    human resources planning

Language
    spoken, written, official
    international languages
    mass media
    linguistic pluralism

Religion
    beliefs and norms   rituals
    sacred objects   prayers
    taboos   philosophical systems
    holidays

Law
    common law, code law   foreign law, home country law
    antitrust policy   overall regulation
    international law treaties

Social organization
    interest groups   kinship
    social mobility   social satisfaction
    social institutions authority structures
    status systems

Politics
    nationalism, national interests   sovereignty
    imperialsim   power
    political risk   ideologies

Technology and material culture
    communications, invention, science, etc.

Major subcultures may be based on nationality, religion, race or ethnicity, and geographical area. For example, the Catalonian Spanish are fiercely proud of their distinct culture that differs in many ways from the rest of Spain. Some people may share common cultural traits with citizens of other nations; but these same people may also have some distinctly different characteristics. Although members of the Catholic Church in France and Latin America have cultural similarities, there are other socio-cultural characteristics such as lifestyles associated with poverty or affluence that cause diverse behaviors in this religious group. As another example consider the clusters of countries formed on the basis of similarity of cultural

TABLE 3.5

Selected value orientations

Variable		Description of different value orientations toward variable
Environment	Control:	People can dominate their environment; it can be changed to fit human needs.
	Harmony:	People should live in harmony with the world around them.
	Constraint:	People are constrained by the world around them. Fate, luck, and change play a significant role.
Time	Past:	High value placed on continuance of traditions.
	Present:	Short-term orientation aimed at quick results.
	Future:	Willingness to trade short-term gain for long-term results.
Action	Doing:	Task-centered. Stress placed on productive activity in goal accomplishment and achievement.
	Being:	Relationship-centered. Stress placed on working for the moment, experience rather than accomplishment.
Communication	High context:	Shared experience makes certain things understood without them needing to be stated explicitly. Rules for speaking and behaving are implicit in the context.
	Low context:	Exchange of facts and information is stressed. Information is given primarily in words, and meaning is expressed explicitly.
Space	Private:	Individual orientation to the use of physical space. Preference for distance between individuals.
	Public:	Group orientation to the use of physical space. Preference for close proximity.
Power	Hierarchy:	Value placed on power differences between individuals and groups.
	Equality:	Value placed on the minimization of levels of power.
Individualism	Individualistic:	The 'I' predominates over the 'we.' Independence is highly valued.
	Collectivist:	Individual interests are subordinate to group interests. Identity is based on the social network. Loyalty is highly valued.
Competitiveness	Competitive:	Achievement, assertiveness, and material success are reinforced.
	Cooperative:	Stress is placed on the quality of life, interdependence, and relationships.
Structure	Order:	High need for predictability and rules, written and unwritten. Conflict is threatening.
	Flexibility:	Tolerance of unpredictable situations and ambiguity. Dissent is acceptable.
Thinking	Inductive:	Reasoning based on experience and experimentation.
	Deductive:	Reasoning based on theory and logic.

Source: adapted from Brake et al., *Doing Business Internationally*, Irwin Professional Publishing, 1995, pp. 46–7.

values as shown in Table 3.6. Although the countries within a cluster have similar values (or shared preferences) there are differences in other cultural characteristics. For example, in Cluster 4 the language of Finland differs from that of the others. A final example is from Asia. Asian values have been held by certain political leaders in the region such as the former Prime Minister of Malaysia, Dr Mahathir, and former president and Senior Minister Lee Kuan Yew of Singapore to be 'homogeneous' and to differ greatly from values of the West. Moreover, these same leaders asserted that these values were inherently superior and explained East Asia's economic success of the 1990s and prepared the region for future global dominance. As shown in Exhibit 3.4 the idea of Asian values and their worth can be questioned. In addition, the research of Hofstede (2001) indicates there is measurable variance among Asian nations in four of the five dimensions of culture he has identified. The one value dimension that has the most consistency in the index scores developed is individualism/collectivism. Asian countries are essentially collectivist in nature.

TABLE 3.6

Country clusters ranked on similarity of values*

Cluster 1 – Anglo:
    Canada, Australia, New Zealand, United Kingdom, United States
Cluster 2 – Germanic:
    Austria, Germany, Switzerland
Cluster 3 – Latin European:
    Belgium, France, Italy, Portugal, Spain
Cluster 4 – Nordic:
    Denmark, Finland, Norway, Sweden
Cluster 5 – Latin American:
    Argentina, Chile, Colombia, Mexico, Peru, Venezuela
Cluster 6 – Near Eastern:
    Greece, Iran, Turkey
Cluster 7 – Far Eastern:
    Hong Kong, Indonesia, Malaysia, Philippines, Singapore, South Vietnam, Taiwan
Cluster 8 – Arab:
    Bahrain, Kuwait, Saudi Arabia, United Arab Emirates
Independent (not closely related to other countries)
    Japan, India, Israel

* Countries within a cluster are considered similar with regard to their cultural values. Clusters are arranged in an approximate order of cluster similarity; i.e., the Anglo cluster is more similar to the European cluster (Germanic, Latin European, and Nordic) than it is to the Latin American, Near Eastern, Far Eastern, and Arab clusters.

Source: Punnett, 1994, p. 15.

EXHIBIT 3.4   **Asian values revisited**

To believe that Asian values caused either miracle or crash (i.e., the financial crash of the late 1990s) is to accept these two questionable premises:

1. there is a common core of distinctly Asian principles, and
2. this core has been accurately defined by the proponents and opponents.

The list of Asian values includes, but is not limited to: attachment of family as an institution, deference to societal interests, thrift, conservatism in social mores, and respect for authority. In addition, Asians are said to favor consensus over confrontation, and to emphasize the importance of education.

These values are held to justify government regimes that might be viewed as illiberal. By invoking Asian values, authoritarian governments claim they are only providing what the people want. Political leaders state that there is something different about Asian values, and that they, unlike Western ones, are *universal*. Asian values can change with time, but are believed always to be appropriate for the stage of economic development at the time. For the most part, these values are seen to be relevant for East Asia, not South Asia. Accepting a single set of values involves blending Confucianism, Buddhism, and Islam. There have been a number of authoritarian governments, and until the late 1990s some unusually high rates of economic growth.

Another view is that the region's economic downturn represents Asian values gone wrong. Attachment to the family becomes *nepotism*. The importance of personal relationships rather than formal legality becomes *cronyism*. Consensus becomes *wheel greasing* and *corrupt politics*. Conservatism and respect for authority become *rigidity* and an *inability to innovate*. Educational achievements become *rote learning* and a *refusal to question those in authority*.

The assertion of Asian values partly represents a desire to increase regional cohesion, both to ease tensions between the countries of the region, and to become more of a presence internationally. The Association of South-East Asian Nations (ASEAN) is diverse politically as it includes communist states (Vietnam and Laos), a military dictatorship (Myanmar), an Islamic monarchy (Brunei), and parliamentary democracies of various types. There are countries with Buddhist, Muslim, and Christian majorities.

Is there such a thing as a set of universal Asian values, and if there is, are these values inherently superior? An answer still awaits us.

Source: Adapted from *The Economist*, 1998a.

With regard to international marketing management, it seems best to study cultures not only from a broad perspective to learn about relevant patterns and themes, but also from a narrow perspective as behavior relates specifically to certain products or marketing efforts. This approach to studying culture can lead to information that will guide international marketing efforts, especially to determine when the same strategies and tactics can be employed in multiple countries and when they cannot. The example of cookies and Japan mentioned earlier in this chapter illustrates this point.

It may be well also to identify some of the limits of culture as an explanation of behavior. For example, linguistic relativity (or the Whorf hypothesis) is still cited in some circles, namely, that the world-view of individuals depends on the structure and characteristics of the language they speak; that different languages provide different segmentations of experience; and that perhaps language and thought are synonymous (Kess, 1976). Many nations are linguistically homogeneous and others are heterogeneous. Examples of linguistically homogeneous nations are the United Kingdom, United States, Korea, Japan, Costa Rica, Egypt, Norway, and Brazil. Nations where more than one language is spoken include Belgium, China, South Africa, India, Ivory Coast, Switzerland, Guatemala, and Canada. In linguistically heterogeneous countries, one language may still be predominant for certain uses. China provides a good illustration. There are seven major languages spoken in the country (*The Economist*, 1999). There is, however, a unified national language, *Putonghua*, which is based loosely upon the Beijing dialect of Mandarin. More than 60% of the population speaks Mandarin of one form or another. *Putonghua* is the universal language of government, and it is used in schools and universities (regional dialects are banned).

Those who have had experience with another language often find that certain ideas are difficult to translate, or the 'best' translation seems incomplete somehow. Ricks (1999, p. 90) cites an example of what can happen in translation of idioms and expressions. The English expression 'touch-toe' created an adverse reaction for a manufacturer of dental equipment. In a brochure written for the Russian market, the company featured the 'touch-toe' control of its dental chair equipment. The translator rendered the description of this feature in such a way that the Russians thought that the dentist had to be barefoot in order to operate the equipment. Some languages seem to express certain ideas, feelings or experiences more briefly or more clearly than others.

Research by the international marketer on these and related topics would be likely to have meaningful strategic and tactical applications in selecting brand names, or packages, or in designing advertising in multiple countries. Such information, for example, would be helpful in determining when brand names, packages and/or advertisements that are appropriate for one culture could also be appropriate for others (and when not).

At times government acts on business practices in support of cultural values. In 1996 the central government of the PRC announced that Chinese businesses could no longer use Westernized names as brand names if they were viewed as detrimental to Chinese culture and society.

3.3.2 Culture and communication

Each culture reflects in its language what is of value to the people. Language – whether written, spoken, or silent – becomes the embodiment of culture and is a means whereby people communicate to other people, either within their own culture or in other cultures. More broadly, communication includes any behavior that another person perceives and interprets. As such, it is one person's understanding of what another person means. According to Adler (1991, p. 64):

> Communication includes sending both verbal messages (words) and nonverbal messages (tone of voice, facial expression, behavior, and physical setting). It includes consciously sent messages as well as messages that the sender is totally unaware of sending ... Communication therefore involves a complex, multilayered, dynamic process through which we exchange meaning.

Behavior itself is a form of communication. Each culture may differ in the way that it experiences and uses such things as time, space, relationships, and a host of other aspects of culture. This form of communication is known as the *silent language*. In a general sense, Hall (1973) has defined so-called *primary message systems* as the means by which cultures communicate to their members and to other cultures. These primary message systems include the following:

- *Interaction:* the ordering of people's interaction with those around them, through language, touch, noise, gesture, and so forth.
- *Association:* the organization and structuring of society and its components.
- *Subsistence:* the ordering of people's activities in feeding, working, and making a living.
- *Bisexuality:* the use of sex lines to differentiate roles, activities, and function.
- *Territoriality:* the possession, use, and defense of space and territory.
- *Temporality:* the use, allocation, and division of time.
- *Learning:* the adaptive process of learning and instruction.
- *Play:* relaxation, humor, recreation, and enjoyment.

- *Defense:* protection against the environment, including medicine, warfare, and law.
- *Exploitation:* using the environment through technology, construction and extraction of materials.

More specifically, Hall (1960) has defined the major dimensions of the silent language as they operate within international marketing as being: (1) time; (2) space; (3) things; (4) friendship; (5) agreements.

These five dimensions can form the basis of a real understanding of foreign cultures. The international marketer must, if there is to be a successful and mutually profitable relationship, *know* how the persons whom he or she will be contacting use each of the languages. For example, it is essential to know that when communicating verbally, Middle Easterners and Latin Americans stand much closer to each other than do western Europeans.

Another example can be derived from how agreements are arrived at. Agreements involve negotiation, and cultural differences do arise in techniques of negotiating. In some countries in Asia, for instance, the specified price is often the starting point for negotiations, not a 'final figure' as in many western countries. In addition, the value of using logic or emotion when negotiating can vary among cultures.

Cultural context is important for understanding differences among cultures in their reactions to communication and behavior. High context cultures are those that need to know in what context you find a person or a product in order to evaluate it, or, in the case of language, how a word or words are used. By themselves words carry little meaning. In contrast, low context cultures can evaluate a product based on, for example, test results and without knowing what kind of people use it, when it is typically used, and so forth. With respect to language, in a low context culture most of the meanings are in the words themselves, and the meaning of a message can be isolated from the context in which the message occurs. Example of low context countries are those in Northern Europe and North America whereas high context countries are found in Asia and Latin America (Gesteland, 1999, pp. 38–40).

Finally, the international marketer needs to recognize that doing business in foreign markets involves cross-cultural communication in all aspects of the relationship. When the person from the other culture does not receive the sender's message in the manner intended, cross-cultural miscommunication occurs. The greater the differences between the cultures of the seller and the buyer, the greater the probability for cross-cultural miscommunication to occur. Miscommunication involves misunderstanding due to misperception, misinterpretation, and misevaluation. Thus, in becoming involved in a cross-cultural situation, the international marketer should heed the advice of Adler (1991, p. 67): '*assume difference until similarity is proven*' (emphasis added).

3.3.3 Self-reference criterion (SRC)

Lee (1966) coined the term 'self-reference criterion' as a useful concept to avoid cultural bias. He suggested that problems should be defined first in terms of the cultural traits, habits, or norms of the home society. Then they should be redefined without value judgements, in terms of the foreign cultural traits, habits, and norms. He indicated that the difference between these two specifications is an indication of the likely cultural bias, or SRC effect, which can then be isolated and carefully examined to see how it influences the concept or the problem. Following this examination, the problem is redefined with the bias removed. The value of this approach lies in forcing the manager posing the problem to make specific his or her assumptions about the cultural elements affecting the problem and to question whether or not they hold for another culture.

3.3.4 A concluding comment

Culture is a pervasive environmental variable affecting all international and export marketing activity (see Exhibit 3.5). Of concern to the manager are the influences of the religious, family, educational, and social systems of a society. Often these are manifested in the values, attitudes, and motivations of people and can affect business customs such as personal manners, colors, advertising, 'gift' giving and receiving, and pride and status. All too often in domestic transactions we have a tendency to take culture for granted and not explicitly incorporate its effects into our decisions. When dealing with the foreign markets, even those whose cultural distance from ours is not great, this should not be done.

EXHIBIT 3.5	**The pervasive effects of culture on international/export marketing**

The most apparent effects of culture may be on the types, designs, styles, and colors of products that can be sold in overseas markets. Pork products are not normally acceptable in Islamic cultures, although a US-owned international chain of barbecue restaurants received permission to import pork into Malaysia (which has a sizable nonIslamic Chinese population). Personal tastes, as well as road conditions, taxes, and income levels determine what colors, sizes, and horsepower are preferred in automobiles. The high-tech Japanese toilets, which feature heated seats, water sprays and warm-air drying, did not sell in Arabic countries because the seated individual had to operate it with the right hand. A Middle East company that made a similar toilet that was flushed with the left hand did find a ready market among the most affluent.

Culture also affects the themes and presentation of advertisements that will be most effective in selling products. In promoting diamonds, television ads that pictured a sophisticated man and woman in a romantic setting, which worked well in European countries and the United States, were not very effective in Japan. There, sales increased substantially when the theme was changed to a man in ordinary business dress giving a diamond to his wife, who indicated (very pleasantly) that he was stupid for spending so much money on her.

Methods of negotiation also are culturally influenced. US negotiators typically prefer direct statements, vigorous defense of their positions, agreements on a point-by-point basis, the covering of all contingencies in a written contract, and rapid progress toward a settlement. Japanese negotiators typically prefer to take time to get to know their potential associates first, prefer to avoid argument and confrontation, wish to consider the agreement as a whole, and need to concur frequently among themselves and with their colleagues at the company before agreeing to anything. If these differences are not recognized and allowed for, feelings of mistrust may cause failure in reaching agreements that would otherwise be beneficial to both parties.

Dealing with foreign managers or subordinates in overseas offices presents potential for misunderstandings and conflict. A senior US executive, visiting a large office in Italy, called a meeting for 8 a.m. (against the advice of his resident US manager). Only the resident US manager showed up on time, and everyone was greatly irritated: the Italian staff for the outsider's having called a meeting at a completely unacceptable hour, the US executive because people who 'worked for him' did not do as he told them to, and the

US manager because he was embarrassed. In some countries, the manager who invites suggestions from subordinates or gives them too much latitude in deciding how to do a job may be viewed as not doing his own job, as weak, or as incompetent. Managers and professional people from many European countries, Canada, and the United States expect a degree of individual freedom, discretion, and responsibility that they may not receive if assigned to work for someone from a country emphasizing a higher degree of collectivism and group cooperation. In the United States, the Japanese owners of gambling casinos in Las Vegas reportedly ran into problems when they tried to use Japanese management techniques – specifically, making decisions the Japanese way by consensus. The approach may work well in Japan, but it was deemed too slow and cumbersome in the fast-moving casino environment (Ricks, 1999, p. 99).

Understanding the effects of culture on dealing with people in other societies, whether they are customers, partners, employees, or subordinates, is necessary if one is to avoid costly mistakes. It is also valuable in helping one to avoid the feelings of discomfort and stress that occur when others do not behave in the way we expect, or fail to respond to us as we believe they should. Thus, culture influences the selection of foreign market entry mode especially when choosing among joint ventures, greenfield (new start-up) investments, and acquisitions (Kogut and Singh, 1988); influences the ability of businesses to effectively organize intra- and intercultural relationships with their international partners and whether or not the *process* of fostering and evaluating relationships can be globally standardized (Griffith, *et al.*, 2000); and through social ties can influence export initiation in small and medium-sized enterprises (Ellis and Pecotich, 2001).

Personal relations are an important input into social and economic life. If the international marketer wishes to be successful in doing business in China, for example, it is important that *guanxi* be established. *Guanxi*, which is based on reciprocity, refers to personal connections/relationships, which can range from strong personal loyalties to semi-bribery. One way to cultivate *guanxi* is to show respect for business partners and government contacts, especially in social settings. This gives them 'face.' Small gestures count. Avoid giving lavish gifts such as jewelry and avoid using white gift wrap. The former may appear to be bribery and the latter connotes death. In effect, having good *guanxi* amounts to having a good network operating in China. The realities of doing business in China, or with Chinese companies, are such that one cannot get anything done easily, reasonably quickly, or even at all without good *guanxi* (Davies *et al.*, 1995; Cheung, 1996). *Guanxi* has been a norm in China for hundreds of years.

3.4 Political/legal environment

The political/legal environment operationally equates with government although political philosophy and beliefs that may affect behavior of business firms may not be part of formal government policy. An example of the latter is *nationalism*, which can be viewed as the influence of collective forces in the form of a national spirit or attitude. Nationalistic feelings may be limited only to some subgroup within the nation or they may encompass the entire nation.

International marketing decisions by business firms are affected by the actions of government bodies at all levels – supranational, national, and subnational. The extent to which any government becomes involved in international marketing, and the specific nature of such involvement, depends in part upon the type of economic system in the country (e.g., capitalism, socialism, or communism), the type or form of government organization (e.g., monarchy, republic, or dictatorship), and the type of legal system (code law or common law). To illustrate, consider the differences between legal systems. The bases for common law (in countries such as the United Kingdom and Canada) are tradition, past practices, and legal precedents set by past court decisions. In contrast code law, which is found in most countries of the world, is based on a system of written rules of law that are considered to be all inclusive.

3.4.1 Role of government

As an environmental force affecting international/export marketing, government *intervenes* in a single country's (and the world) economy by being a participator, planner, controller, or stimulator. Such intervention activities can be categorized into the following three groups:

1. those that *promote* (i.e., encourage or facilitate) international/export marketing transactions;
2. those that *impede* such transactions;
3. those that *compete* with or replace international/export marketing transactions by private business firms.

These basic types of intervention activities exist to some extent at all levels of government, but with varying emphases. At the supranational level, the actions taken are primarily those whose effect is to encourage and facilitate international marketing relationships, especially exports. Illustrations include the many agreements and conventions that are made between countries, such as international commodity agreements, and bilateral agreements such as the agreement between Australia and New Zealand (Closer Economic Relations, CER) signed in the late 1980s, the free trade agreement between Singapore, Australia, and New Zealand (Australia, New Zealand, Singapore Closer Economic Partnership, ANZSCEP) that took effect on 1 January 2001, the United States and Vietnam bilateral trade agreement ratified in late 2001, the United States/Singapore free trade agreement signed in 2002 and covering investment, telecommunications, and financial services, South Korea's first-ever free trade agreement – with Chile – in 2004, and the Closer Economic Partnership Arrangement (CEPA) between Hong Kong and China. In fact there appears to be a 'movement' on the part of Asian countries – especially Singapore – to sign bilateral trade agreements with each other. One major reason is China and its growing economic clout (*The Economist*, 2004b).

On the organization level there are the various agencies of the United Nations, for example, United Nations Conference on Trade and Development (UNCTAD), United Nations Industrial Development Organization (UNIDO), the Organization for Economic Cooperation and Development (OECD), the International Monetary Fund (IMF), the World Bank (International Bank for Reconstruction and Development (IBRD)), and similar organizations. In the mid-1990s the GATT was converted to a formal organization called the World Trade Organization (WTO). As indicated in Exhibit 3.6, there are great expectations for the WTO. In December 2001 there was a major change in the WTO. China became a member. In addition to phasing in tariff reductions and eliminating some tariffs entirely, eliminating export subsidies, and increasing quotas, China agreed to open its telecommunications, financial services, distribution, and many other industries to foreign service providers (Adhikori and Yang, 2002).

Subnational (that is, state, province, and so on) government agencies tend to concentrate on promoting export marketing activities by private business firms.

There are, however, some instances where subnational governments place restrictions that act as impediments. For example, certain state governments in the United States may have restrictions against state agencies purchasing foreign-made products, which means that exports from other countries are adversely affected. In 1997, for example, the state of Massachusetts in the United States imposed trade sanctions on companies trading with Burma (Myanmar). The sanctions typically affect bidding on public contracts. Similar sanctions have been imposed by individual cities within the United States.

EXHIBIT 3.6   High hopes for the WTO

The World Trade Organization came into existence on 1 January 1995. A major task at the outset was to finish what the GATT had left undone. Negotiations over financial services, telecommunications, shipping, and other service businesses needed to be concluded. This is more than simply tying up loose ends – basic principles had to be developed and carried through.

There is a dispute resolution mechanism within the WTO. The process works in a way that makes the WTO act as a world trade court. There are four steps (Borrus and Javetski, 1995):

1. The WTO sends the two countries having a trade dispute back to the negotiating table.
2. If, after 60 days, there is no resolution, the WTO can appoint a three-person panel to decide the case. The panel has six to nine months to issue findings.
3. The panel's report may be appealed to another three-person panel to decide the case. The appeals panel has 60 days to issue its ruling.
4. The loser of the appeal must comply with WTO rules or negotiate compensation with the other country. If the countries cannot agree on compensation, the complaining country may retaliate with tariffs.

It seems obvious that the resolution mechanism has been set up to stall long enough to get both sides to negotiate a settlement.

Cases such as the following fit within the WTO's domain:

1. In 1998, on a technicality, the WTO ruled against a US import ban on shrimps caught in nets that also ensnare sea turtles. But the WTO panel did uphold the right of countries to waive WTO rules to protect health, safety, or the environment.
2. On three occasions, starting in 2000, the WTO, following a complaint raised by Europeans, ruled that the Foreign Sales Corporation, an offshore tax shelter used by US companies, constitutes an illegal export subsidy.
3. The US complaint that the benefits obtained by Chinese electronics exporters through the full tax refund from the government of an 8% tax amounts to an illegal export subsidy.

At the national level, governments engage in all kinds of activities and may or may not favor one category over another. Many of the specific intervention activities that national governments engage in, particularly those of an impediment nature, are indicated in Table 3.7. These activities bear directly on company operations and management and affect strategy formulation and implementation. Sociological and economic constraints – for example, nationalism, views toward foreigners, and balance of payments position – are also of concern since they may have a definite influence on how legal political constraints are implemented.

In addition to the many international constraints there are certain local

TABLE 3.7

Political–legal constraints

1. *Political ideology:* The political viewpoints of existing governments as demonstrated by the prevailing pattern of rule, philosophy of leading political parties, and similar factors.
2. *Relevant legal rules for foreign business:* The special rules of the game applied only to foreign-owned firms, including special discriminatory labor and tax legislation.
3. *International organization and treaty obligations:* Formal obligations of the country in terms of military responsibilities; political obligations; copyright, postal, and patent obligations; and similar matters.
4. *Power or economic bloc grouping:* Membership in formal and informal political, military, and economic blocs such as Communist, Marxist or neutralist groups; explicit and implicit obligations of such blocs.
5. *Import–export restrictions:* Formal legal rules controlling exports and imports, including tariffs, quotas, export duties, export restrictions, and similar matters.
6. *International investment restrictions:* Formal legal and administrative restrictions on investments by foreigners within the country.
7. *Profit remission restrictions:* Formal legal and administrative restrictions on remittance of profits of local operations to foreign countries.
8. *Exchange control restrictions:* Formal legal and administrative controls on the conversion of the local currency to any or all foreign currencies or gold.
9. *Membership and obligations in international financial organizations:* Obligations and responsibilities of the country toward international organizations such as the World Bank and the IMF; rights of the country as a member of such organizations.

Source: adapted from Farmer and Richman, 1984, p. 68

governmental constraints that come from an exporter's home country. For instance, a company may find that it cannot do business in a particular foreign market because its home government has political differences with the foreign government in question. The economic sanctions placed by certain western European governments against South Africa in the mid-1980s and the United Nations against Iraq in the early 1990s are examples.

Sometimes, foreign governments react to political decisions and feelings in an exporter's country. In 1996, China awarded a large order (US$1.5 billion) for commercial aircraft to the European company Airbus Industrie rather than to the US's Boeing. This was done, in part, because the United States has loudly criticized China's policies over, and behavior towards, Taiwan, human rights, intellectual property rights violations, and so forth. China's position has always been that political issues should be separated from trade matters.

3.4.2 Government controls

It will be noted from Table 3.7 that many of the government-derived impediments to international marketing in general, and exporting in particular, are in the form of restrictions and controls. There are different kinds of restrictions and controls that are specifically concerned with exports and imports. Such controls directly affect both the types and amounts of products that can be exported and imported. Other restrictive controls may indirectly affect trading relationships by directly influencing the advisability and/or profitability of individual transactions. Export controls typically are intended to restrict the shipment of defense products, protect the domestic economy from a drain of scarce materials, and enhance national security (physical and economic). Concerning the latter, increased terrorism and the events of 11 September 2001 in the United States have led to a drastic change in the world and in how governments treat people. Primary and secondary impacts have been on export earners such as airlines, tourism, transport in general, investment, global supply chains, etc. Responses by governments have included increased spending on security and more regulation of business practice and individual behavior. The extreme of this has been the restriction of rights or enforcing existing laws more harshly, with the net effect of restricting citizens' – and noncitizens' as well – freedoms. In short, in some countries there has been a considerable loss of liberty (*The Economist*, 2002).

Government controls are used as a tool to further both the foreign and trade policy of the government as well as controlling technology and resources. Although export controls may be important in isolated cases, import controls create the most significant barriers to export transactions by the firm. For example, in 1998 the government of Myanmar (Burma) banned the import of a range of products that could be produced locally – soft drinks, beer, alcohol, cigarettes, fresh fruit, biscuits, canned food, and seasoning powder. At the same time many products were banned for export including rice, sugar, minerals, rubber, and cotton.

Sometimes a company exporting to a specific country may run foul of laws governing marketing practice. In mid-1999 the Supreme Court of Germany ruled that Lands' End's use of its lifetime guarantee that it uses everywhere, 'Money Back Guarantee, No Matter What,' was a violation of law and represented unfair competition to German competitors.

In addition to export/import controls there are regulations that affect foreign operations and ownership resulting from direct investment and strategic alliances such as licensing arrangements. A country that regulates foreign direct investment does so in order to limit the influence of the foreign investor, typically a multinational (or global) corporation, and at the same time have a pattern of investment that contributes in desired ways to the achievement of the country's economic, social, and political objectives. Although not an exhaustive list, the following are areas that countries may regulate and limit within the broad dimension of foreign investment:

1. Decision making through procedures affecting selecting type of investment, control of takeovers, how mergers and acquisitions may be achieved, restrictions (including prohibition) of investment in certain industries, and similar matters.
2. Regulation of ownership, managerial control, and employment through local participation requirements in ownership, management, product content, and employment. In India, for example, companies are not allowed either to close down a factory or to sack workers without government permission. In Vietnam, foreign companies are now allowed to wholly own local subsidiaries or buy out joint venture partners. Full foreign ownership was technically possible as far back as 1987 but was effectively blocked.
3. Taxation and regulation of financial transactions, control of capital and profit movement and remittance, and sources and types of foreign and local borrowing.

Individual countries may regulate investment by placing limits on specific international marketing practices. For example, the government of India approved PepsiCo's request for establishing a joint venture bottling plant. Among the many conditions of approval imposed by the Indian government was one concerned with branding. PepsiCo agreed not to use its Pepsi brand name. The Indian government felt that global brands gave an international marketer an advantage over local companies.

There are government controls that affect all companies, foreign and local alike. In 1993 all tobacco advertising (including sponsorship of sports and cultural events) and most liquor advertising in France was banned. Most wines were excluded from the law. Similar laws exist in other countries including Australia, New Zealand, Malaysia, and Canada. In 1999 Nepal announced it was going to ban all alcohol and tobacco advertisements on television and radio. In Vietnam, Malaysia, and Hong Kong tobacco advertising by sponsoring sports events is banned. Going even further, alcohol company advertising is also banned by Vietnam for sports events, and both products are banned from cultural events. In a reversal, an appeals court in Sweden in 2003 reversed a 24-year ban on alcohol advertising, saying it was too intrusive to warrant an exception to European Union law.

For another illustration we turn to Germany and its packaging laws that regulate the management and recycling of packaging waste. On a broader scale are government programs that award *eco-seals* for products that are environmentally friendly. By early 1998 more than 25 countries offered independent seals of approval, some government based, some from nonprofit organizations (Ottman, 1998).

The latest area where regulation is becoming increasingly prevalent is companies' use of the Internet and the World Wide Web as means of exporting. This is an area of law and regulation that is continually evolving, and it will take years for the development of a cohesive legal/regulatory structure. An example of a law passed in 2001 that will have a great impact on Internet use is the Regulation of Investigatory Powers Act (RIP) in Great Britain. In essence, RIP requires public telecommunications services to install interception equipment to make their networks tappable, and it lets police demand decryption keys that unlock coded data. A warrant is needed, but the warrant is not issued by a judge but by a politician – the head of the Home Office. Any multinational company doing business in Britain is going to have to redesign its systems, or install special systems, if it has an ISP component to its work (Grossman, 2001).

There are differences in the approaches to e-commerce taken by the United States and the European Union. Broadly, concerns involve the extent of self-regulation within the industry, single market rules, and jurisdiction. The United States tends to favor self-regulation while the European Union desires more regulation, especially to protect consumers. Regarding jurisdiction, the United States tries to follow the traditional laws, meaning that the home state of the purchaser (the consumer) normally has jurisdiction. In contrast, in the past the European Union emphasized 'home country' control, meaning the seller's home country had jurisdiction. There is a European Union directive requiring each country to harmonize certain regulatory laws relating to e-commerce.

China represents an extreme case in this type of regulation as all Internet content is regulated and controlled by the government.

License requirements

One way in which various countries regulate the nature of their external trading relationships is by requiring that licenses be obtained before goods may be exported or imported. For products the government desires to restrict, licenses would not be granted or only granted for limited amounts. The extreme case is where there are specific prohibitions against exporting or importing certain products. For example, the United States controls the export of products that are deemed to have military value. Mexico prohibits the importation of selected products in order to encourage development and growth of local industry. The most comprehensive prohibition is when one country prohibits all trade with another country, usually for political reasons.

Tariffs

A tariff is a tax on imports, and is stated either as a percentage of value (*ad valorem*) or on a per unit basis. A government may have a system of tariffs for purposes of keeping products out of the country (*protective tariff*) and/or to generate tax revenue (*revenue tariff*). As might be expected, protective tariffs tend to be relatively high since they are designed to protect domestic industry. The purpose of a protective tariff also may be simply to bring the price level of the imported goods up to that of domestic substitutes. In contrast, revenue tariffs are often quite low since they are designed to generate maximum revenue for the government.

Governments may impose a tariff surcharge on their imports. Generally this is a somewhat temporary action taken when the government wants to discourage imports for some reason, such as the existence of an unfavorable balance of payments. A surcharge will be removed once the condition that led to it being imposed has been corrected. In 2001 Chile had a surcharge of up to 8% on semiconductors from Singapore.

A more permanent kind of surcharge takes the form of countervailing duties. These may be assessed to offset some special advantage or discount (e.g., an export subsidy) allowed by the exporter's government. The intent is to bring protection in the country of importation up to the level originally intended. For example, in 2002 the United States imposed countervailing duties averaging 27% on imports of softwood lumber and wood products from Canada, in response to subsidies given to Canadian exporters by their government.

Another type of countervailing tariff is one imposed as an *antidumping* measure. Dumping has been defined as selling in a foreign market at a significantly lower price than on the domestic market, or at below cost if there are no domestic sales. Antidumping tariffs are 'popular' in Australia, the European Union, South Africa and the United States, and the main targets have been China, South Korea, Taiwan, and the United States (*The Economist*, 1998b). India, Mexico, and Brazil have also been heavy users. The use of these duties has been increasing rapidly. Worldwide, during the period 1998–2002, 1581 antidumping investigations were filed with the WTO. Probably the most important factor in the rise of antidumping protection has been changes in international trade laws (Crowley, 2004). These tariffs are legal under WTO rules when domestic producers can show they are being harmed. In an extreme case, in 1997 the United States imposed a 454% tariff on supercomputers made by Japan's NEC. Although market conditions can change relatively quickly, these tariffs tend to be reviewed relatively infrequently. Proponents of these measures argue that they are needed to prevent *predatory pricing* (i.e., prices below domestic prices) that is used by foreign companies to drive domestic companies out of business, and after that occurs the foreign firms raise their prices to recoup their losses. The evidence seems to be that genuine predatory pricing is rare, and even if it exists higher prices will attract new competitors. Moreover, predatory pricing is not mentioned in WTO rules nor in US or European law. Antidumping laws do not take into account developments such as floating (rather than fixed) exchange rates that make dumping appear to be more widespread than it really is.

The impact of tariffs upon individual business firms is usually direct. Costs and prices of competitive products are affected. Companies often do things that they otherwise would not do, particularly in response to a protective tariff. On a more aggregate level, developing countries that export primarily agricultural and labor-intensive goods such as textiles and clothing are hard hit by industrial countries' tariff policies. In addition, tariffs on clothing and shoes harm consumers in industrial countries, especially lower-income groups.

Quotas

Quotas are specific provisions limiting the amount of foreign products that can be imported. In some countries they are also imposed on exports as part of national planning. The application of quotas may be global or on a country-by-country basis.

In general, quotas may be classified into the following three categories:

1. Most restrictive are *absolute* quotas, which limit absolutely the amount that can be imported. The most extreme case is the zero quota, or embargo. There are times when quotas may be changed. In mid-1998 the United States unilaterally reduced its import quotas for textile products from China. The government accused Chinese enterprises of illegally reexporting textile products to the United States. The Chinese government complained that the quota reduction violated a bilateral agreement on textile products that exists between the two countries.
2. *Tariff* quotas permit importation of limited quantities at low rates of duty, with any amount in excess subject to a substantially higher rate.
3. There are different types of *voluntary* quotas. These are known as *voluntary export restraints* (VERs) and are generally to protect domestic companies until they have had time to make necessary adjustments to regain external competitiveness.

One type of VER results from an explicit international agreement. Another type is unilateral in form but results from diplomatic negotiations, or other types of pressures at the governmental level. For example, during the period from the early 1980s until 1992 the United States 'persuaded' a number of foreign governments to limit steel exports to the United States.

A third type of voluntary quota is also unilaterally imposed by the exporting country, but as a result of an evaluation of the market situation in the importing country and without any commitment with respect to the amount or duration of the quota. To make it impossible for domestic traders to dump products abroad, China has a mechanism that requires exporters of a select group of products to buy the right to export (Lu, 1996). The scheme is one of public bidding for strict quotas for export. Major products covered by this scheme include gum resin, cashmere, ginseng, carpets, honey, and royal jelly.

All VERs arise from some pressure from an importing country. The inherent vice of all quotas is that their use creates confusion and frequently destroys normal marketing processes. Indeed, companies sheltered from the demands of competition by foreign companies because VERs exist have less reason to stay current and up to date in R&D, for example. Often, when governments guarantee an industry's survival regardless of performance, that performance is almost certain to worsen.

Yet there are times when quotas can work to the advantage of the export company and the organizations selling its products overseas. An illustration is the voluntary restraint agreement (VRA) that the Japanese government, under strong pressure from the US government, imposed on its own exports of automobiles to the United States beginning in 1983 (Duerr, 1992). When the number of automobiles that they could export to the United States was reduced below demand, the Japanese automobile companies responded by sending fully equipped automobiles at the top of their product lines. Because of the demand by US consumers, everything that was exported was sold at a premium price by the local retailers. This resulted in substantial increases in profits for both the Japanese companies and their US dealers. The losers at this time were the consumers who had to pay substantially more for their automobiles.

Quotas can have an impact on an international marketer's sourcing decisions. A Hong Kong-based manufacturer of textiles, Milo's Knitwear, moved its production of ramie and silk from China to Thailand to avoid having its goods barred from Europe due to the EU quotas on certain Chinese textile products that existed in 1994.

Extra taxes

Some countries have excise or processing taxes on certain products. Although such taxes are intended to provide government revenues from domestic sources, the manner in which they are levied can restrict imports and thus affect an exporter. For instance, European road taxes on automobiles have served effectively as a means of discriminating against US automobiles when they were of larger size, weight and horsepower.

A much broader form of taxation of importance to international marketers are the so-called border taxes that were levied on imports by European countries, which are in addition to tariffs. A border tax adjustment imposed by a country is intended to place a tax burden on imports equivalent to that which similar domestic products bear. Consequently, the rate supposedly is equal to the amount of internal excise and other indirect taxes paid by domestic producers of competing products. The idea behind border taxes is to put local goods and imports on the same competitive basis. Thus, the tax basically is a type of value-added tax, but one that does not affect domestic producers.

Qualitative controls

Although these controls limit the profitability of exporting, foreign products can be imported with few exceptions provided that the seller is willing to accept a lower net return and/or the buyer pays a higher price. In this way, they are far less restrictive than the various quantitative controls such as tariffs and quotas. Of importance are customs procedures, mark-of-origin regulations, and so-called 'buy domestic' legislation. Japan, for example, has very specific rules covering the shipping of containers into the country. 'Buy domestic' regulations are imposed also by subnational governments. In various ways, each of these can be used effectively to impede the importation of certain products.

Exchange controls

Government control over the supply of, or demand for, foreign currencies can be used effectively to restrict international/export marketing. Exchange controls limit the amount of foreign currency that an importer, for example, can obtain to pay for goods purchased and that an exporter may receive and hold for goods sold to a foreign country. Limitation of the ability to obtain foreign currencies effectively stops purchasing abroad, since the seller, with very rare exceptions, can engage in profitable business only if his or her own currency, or a currency other than the buyer's, can be secured in payment. In some instances the quantitative restriction is combined with a qualitative restriction of placing an unduly high price, or official exchange rate, on the foreign currency desired. By establishing a very unfavorable official exchange rate the actual domestic currency cost of an import may serve to price it out of a domestic market. Another option is illustrated in Exhibit 3.7.

EXHIBIT 3.7 **Are currency boards an answer?**

A currency board combines three elements: an exchange rate that is fixed to an 'anchor currency,' automatic convertibility or the right to exchange domestic currency at this fixed rate whenever desired, and a long-term commitment to the system. In effect, domestic currency can only be issued to the extent that it is fully covered by the central bank's holdings of foreign exchange.

Use declined throughout the 1980s. However, in the 1990s there was renewed interest in currency boards. By 1999 14 countries were using them. Three currencies were used as anchor currencies: US dollar (10 countries), Deutschmark (3 countries), and Singapore dollar (1 country). For example, the Hong Kong dollar has been pegged to the US dollar for more than 15 years.

The immediate obvious advantages of a currency board are economic credibility, low inflation, and lower interest rates (Enoch and Gulde, 1998).

When an exporter has an overseas sales subsidiary for certain markets, or has a direct investment or licensing arrangement, *profit or income remittance* restrictions may become of concern. These restrictions are part of a country's general exchange control program over the conversion of local currency to foreign currency. They pertain specifically to the remittance of profits or earnings of 'local' operations to the parent organization located in another country.

3.4.3 Other types of legal/regulatory activities

In addition to regulating trade, government also regulates other business activities, although not to the extent some would like. Major concerns include the environment, labor rights, human rights, intellectual property, tax policy, antitrust, and corruption.

Regarding the environment, issues of packaging and environmentally friendly products were briefly mentioned in the previous section. In December 1997, 160 nations meeting in Kyoto, Japan agreed to cut back emissions of carbon dioxide and other greenhouse gases during the period 2008–12 to about 5% below 1990 levels. Each country must still ratify what is known as the Kyoto Protocol and determine how it will implement it. Developing countries are not obligated to cut back their emissions. In early 2001 the new US president, George W. Bush, stated that the United States was withdrawing from the Kyoto Protocol. In addition to outright banning of products, an action that is unlikely to occur for many reasons, governments choose between two major instruments for reducing pollution – 'green' taxes and tradable permits – with taxes the preferred approach. These options are discussed in more depth by Norregaard and Reppelin-Hill (2000).

Regulation of labor and development of labor standards vary widely. In addition to wages and job security, freedom of association (i.e., forming of unions), and health and safety rules are issues of concern for governments. More broad is the matter of overall human rights, or how people are treated by their government. Countries that are reported to have poor records include China, Turkey, and Indonesia. In addition to individual country policy, there is an increasing call for multinational action and for the development of international standards. As globalization (i.e., free trade) increases, there will be stronger pressure for international agreements on these issues, including environmental issues. One proposal for labor standards includes the items shown in Table 3.8. These standards represent minimum standards for treating labor.

Protection of intellectual property is of concern to most governments, and there

TABLE 3.8

Proposed labor
standards

Do not use child labor
Provide a safe working environment
Respect workers' rights to unionize
Do not regularly require more than 48-hour work weeks
Pay wages sufficient to meet workers' basic needs

are patent and copyright laws 'on the books.' Looking at the process of obtaining a patent, standards for what is new, or even how to describe something new, vary widely, and the process involves a mass of paperwork. What is really lacking is a single global standard, something that will be necessary if globalization is really to take hold. Progress was made for such a standard in June 2000 when 43 countries signed – and 64 others were expected to sign – a new world patent-law treaty under the auspices of the United Nations' World International Property Organization (WIPO). The treaty, known as the Madrid Protocol, became effective in late 2003. Members of the Protocol include Australia, China, Japan, Korea, Singapore, the United States and most European countries. A trademark owner files a simple application with the home country, a 'basic' registration, and can designate extension of the registration to other member countries (Lansby, 2003). The most significant impact – in addition to standardizing forms, etc. – is the requirement that authorities of member states accept nationally any patent filed according to an international standard known as PCT, or Patent Co-operation Treaty (*The Economist*, 2000). This is a step towards filing a single patent according to a global standard.

International marketers are affected by national and subnational government tax policy. While most developed countries have an established tax system in place, developing countries face challenges when they attempt to establish efficient tax systems. In addition to taxes on imports (tariffs and other charges), there is a need to decide on excise taxes, value added tax (VAT), corporate income tax, and personal income tax. Another area of tax policy is tax incentives to promote foreign investment. These are common throughout the world and include such features as tax holidays, tax credits and investment allowances, accelerated depreciation, investment subsidies, and indirect tax incentives (such as exempting raw materials and capital goods from VAT). The evidence seems to indicate that the cost effectiveness of giving such incentives to promote investment is questionable. Not all such incentives are equally effective, and there is always a cost to the country giving them.

Along with globalization come an increasing number of mergers and acquisitions around the world. Mergers such as Boeing and McDonnell Douglas, Exxon and Mobil, and EMI and Time Warner's music arm have raised awareness of, and interest in, *antitrust* regulation. Of concern is concentration and possible monopoly power. While long popular in the United States, antitrust action seems to be on the increase in the European Union and elsewhere. Activities beyond mergers and acquisitions are coming under scrutiny. Pricing (including price fixing) and other marketing efforts are being examined more closely. For example, the European Union in 2001 started investigating Intel Corporation's business tactics, concentrating on possible exclusionary effects of the company's marketing efforts, including the 'Intel Inside' marketing subsidies. These incentives are alleged to have been used to reward computer makers that use Intel chips exclusively while punishing those computer companies using competitors' chips (Wilke, 2001). It is Intel's market power that is under observation and its situation is similar to that of Microsoft in the United States and the European Union. The European Commission dropped one of its inquiries into Microsoft's operations when the company agreed not to exercise 'undue influence' over two digital-TV companies in which it holds small shares – NTL, Inc. of the UK and United Pan-Europe Communications NV of the Netherlands (Shishkin, 2001). The Commission is still looking into allegations that Microsoft is unfairly leveraging its dominance in the market for personal computer operating systems in order to achieve a competitive advantage in the market for software used in servers. In addition, in 2004 Microsoft still faced another antitrust issue in the European Union regarding the market for media players. All these problems arise from the fact that Microsoft's Windows operating system runs 94% of the world's PCs. Another company that has been hit by antitrust probes is Coca-Cola. Mexico was concerned with the company's sales and marketing practices and Italy charged the company with abusing its marketing power to damage competitors. Coca-Cola also was charged in mid-1999 by the European Commission with abusing a dominant position in Germany, Denmark, and Austria. Fines levied on cartels can be quite high. In 2001 eight vitamin producers from three European countries and Japan were fined €855 million by the European Commission for fixing prices, and setting sales quotas. Because of 'abusively wielding its Windows software monopoly,' in 2004 Microsoft was fined US$613 million by the European Union. Also, Microsoft must offer a version of Windows without the company's digital media player, and must give accurate and complete information to rivals in the office server market so their products can work more smoothly with desktop computers running Windows. There is increasing antitrust activity in Asia as Japan, South Korea, and Indonesia have antitrust legislation in force, including anticartel laws. In contrast, Hong Kong and Singapore do not have laws against cartels.

A marketing activity that is coming under closer scrutiny is pricing. In 2000 the United Kingdom passed its Competition Act, which targets industrial cartels and the unfair pricing they engender, specifically price fixing. China has a Price Law that defines and bans unfair practices: price collusion, market dumping, price deception, price discrimination, exorbitant profit through high prices, concocting and spreading rumors of price increases to raise the price level, willfully raising or reducing prices, and any other pricing behavior prohibited by law (Li, 1998). We have presented only a small number of examples. Increasingly, company and industry marketing practice will be watched more closely by government regulators.

Corruption of officials is of concern to many throughout the world. Corruption can affect the international marketer in many ways, both positive and negative. Countries are using many measures to fight corruption with the intent of control, reduction, and ultimately elimination (Klitgaard, 2000). A role model of how to handle the problem is Hong Kong's Independent Commission Against Corruption (ICAC), which has been very effective in Hong Kong. A region where corruption has a long history is Southeast Asia, except Hong Kong. While there have been encouraging signs of effective counter-corruption measures, much remains to be done. This situation stems in part from a lack of laws, personnel, and money to fight corruption. But the resource in shortest supply is *political will* to tackle the problem (*The Economist*, 2004c). Transparency International, a nonprofit organization, monitors corruption worldwide and has a website (www.transparency.org) that has much useful information for business people. We will not discuss this issue further as our intent has been to identify this as an area of government action. Other discussions are presented in Pope and Vogl (2000) and Wolf and Gurgen (2000).

3.4.4 Promotional activities

The policies and programs adopted by governmental organizations to promote exporting are an increasingly important force in the international environment.

Many of the activities involve implementation and sponsorship by government alone while others are the results of the joint efforts of government and business. An example of the latter are the so-called company grouping programs that have evolved in a number of countries, often under the label of network schemes. Encouraged and facilitated by government, these schemes are designed for small and medium-sized enterprises (SMEs) and are used primarily – but not exclusively – for export activities. In general, an export grouping scheme provides the opportunity for member companies to spread the initial costs and risks of international market entry, to share information and experiences, and to pool resources to support stronger promotional efforts. Illustrative uses of network schemes are the 'export circles' in Finland which have the requirement that each circle be kept small and that the companies must be noncompetitive (Luostarinen, *et al.*, 1994) and the Joint Action Group (JAG) scheme in Australia which was initiated by the semi-government agency the Australian Trade Commission (Austrade) as a way of improving performance of Australian exporters (Welch, *et al.*, 1996a, 1996b). One requirement of such groups is that member companies must accept group-determined goals and activities, which is often difficult for smaller companies to do especially when the group comprises competitors. Two approaches have been used to form groups: (1) supply based, which starts with formation of a group and then seeks an opportunity, and (2) demand driven, which starts with an international prospect or opportunity and then the group is formed. The JAG approach is an example of the latter.

The Opera House, Sydney, Australia

In addition to becoming parties to agreements and conventions and being members of supranational organizations, national governments promote international marketing through so-called *regulatory supportive* activities. These activities generally fall within the political or legal jurisdiction of the national government, and are essentially regulatory-type activities that are used as promotional tools. By the use of such tools, a government attempts directly to make its country's products more competitive in world markets. Also, there is the attempt to encourage greater participation in exporting, particularly for smaller companies, as illustrated in Exhibit 3.8.

EXHIBIT 3.8   Assisting small business firms

Small and medium-sized businesses need assistance in international marketing that large companies do not. Very simply, the large companies have the resources and the expertise to develop and implement international marketing programs, especially export marketing programs.

Government, quasi-government, and private organizations offer various types of assistance. To illustrate, Austrade has a comprehensive program designed to assist Australian small businesses. Austrade is represented in more than 50 countries. An export counselor at a local Austrade office can do a quick market assessment of the level of demand for a company's product in a foreign market and provide information on all relevant regulations there. If the market looks promising more detailed research can be conducted covering market size, competitive situations, alternative marketing intermediaries to contact, and so forth. An overseas Austrade office will assist in getting appointments and providing information on practical aspects of doing business in that market. In addition, Austrade runs the Export Market Development Grant scheme (EMDG), which helps SME exporters locate and develop overseas markets. Grants of up to A$200,000 are given to SME exporters or intended exporters to pay for up to one-half of their overseas marketing and promotional costs incurred to earn export revenue.

Other aspects of the Austrade assistance program include trade fair participation, and grants and loans to assist in such activities as marketing and travel.

Another example of a national government agency that was created to assist small and medium-sized companies gain export markets is the Japan External Trade Organization (JETRO). Along the way, JETRO's major goal changed to import promotion: helping foreign companies sell their products to Japan. One thing did not change: the focus on small businesses.

JETRO offers companies interested in exporting to Japan many services. Information is one of the most basic services, and JETRO has long put special emphasis on collecting and making available accurate, high-quality, and up-to-date information. Individual trade inquiries are handled, seminars on how to export to Japan are held, and a broad range of publications on the Japanese market and business practices is published. JETRO also plays an active role in organizing and promoting trade fairs in Japan as well as in facilitating participation by foreign companies in such events.

One of the most innovative activities is the Senior Trade Adviser Program, under which seasoned Japanese business people are mobilized from private firms, such as trading companies, and dispatched to countries for periods of two years to assist local companies in developing their exports to Japan. Assistance is not limited to simply providing advice but also includes introducing customers in Japan, mediating technical tie-ups with Japanese companies, brokering individual transactions, and so forth.

An illustration of what subnational governments can do is provided by the Trade Division of the state of New Mexico in the United States. Its mission is to promote New Mexican products and services worldwide, primarily for the state's small and medium-sized companies. The four trade specialists in the Division, most of whom speak several languages, travel worldwide presenting New Mexico companies at trade shows and expos, and occasionally will accompany business people on trips. The Trade Division has two small offices abroad, both in Mexico, and has contracts with part-time consultants in Germany, Taiwan, and Israel. The Division's aims are as follows:

- support and educate state companies by giving seminars on doing business abroad;
- provide guidance, advice, and matchmaking;
- identify niche markets;
- showcase products at international trade shows.

The Division does not make actual business deals. Its role is strictly supportive.

Turning to the private sector, an illustration is the Rotterdam Distriport, which is a nonprofit foundation including 16 Dutch companies. These companies are active in The Netherlands in physical distribution, container handling, insurance, accounting, and banking, as well as in financial, legal, and fiscal areas. The prime objective of Rotterdam Distriport is to assist and support the foreign exporter to get the most efficient distribution to the markets of Europe by way of the Port of Rotterdam.

Sources: adapted from Matsutuji (1992), *VIA Port of NY–NJ* (1988), and Bullock (1995).

With respect to exporting, two types of government activity are of special significance: state trading and the granting of subsidies. When engaging in state trading, a government either directly involves itself in business transactions through buying and selling (by state-owned enterprises) or regulates export activities. Export subsidies are to the export industries what tariffs are to domestic industries. In both cases the aim is to assure the profitability of industries and individual firms that quite likely would succumb if exposed to the full force of competition. For export industries, revenue is supplemented by subsidies, or costs are reduced by subsidies to certain input factors. Subsidies can be given through such tactics as lower taxes on profits attributable to export sales, refunding of various indirect taxes (for example, some countries refund 'value added' taxes), lower transportation rates for exported merchandise, and manipulation of the system of exchange rates. Moreover, a subsidy may take the form of a direct grant, which enables the recipient to compete against companies from other countries that enjoy cost advantages, or may be used for special promotion by recipient companies. Subsidies should be used with care as many are illegal under WTO rules. The rationale for using subsidies and how they fit into export promotion schemes of the United States are discussed by Shelburne (1997). The theoretical reasoning applies to all countries.

In a broader sense, government export promotion programs, and programs for international marketing activities in general, are designed to deal with the following major barriers:

1. lack of *motivation*, as international marketing is viewed as more time-consuming, costly, risky, and less profitable than domestic business;
2. lack of adequate *information*;
3. *operational/resource-based* limitations.

These programs are quite popular in developing countries, where they are known as public sector trade promotion organizations (TPOs). In many instances TPOs have not proved suitable for the emerging needs of countries, particularly developing countries. However, such organizations can be effective in providing marketing assistance if the following apply (Keesing and Singer, 1992):

- they enjoy the support of the business community;
- they are adequately funded;
- they are staffed with qualified people who are paid salaries commensurate with the private sector; and
- they are somewhat independent of government.

More detailed explanations of export promotion and government programs will be found in the works by Seringhaus and Rosson (1989) and Milner (1990). Evaluations of government programs are provided by Shelburne (1997) for the United States and Crick (1997) for the United Kingdom. A more general discussion of evaluation criteria and implementation of evaluation and assessment to specific export promotion activities is provided by Hibbert (1998).

Financial activities

In some ways a national government assumes the role of an international banker. One way in which this role is carried out is through membership in international financial organizations such as the International Monetary Fund, the World Bank, and the International Finance Corporation. The granting of legal subsidies is another financial-based promotional activity of national governments.

Some national governments grant direct loans to business firms. For example, in the United States under certain conditions loans are available from the Export–Import Bank (Eximbank), the Agency for International Development (AID), and the Commodity Credit Corporation (CCC). Although Eximbank loans and AID dollar loans are granted to foreign sources, they must be used to purchase goods and services from US exporters. In Australia grants and loans are available to small business firms by Austrade.

One of the most vital determinants of the results of a company's export marketing program is its credit policy. Exporters throughout the world are finding that in today's highly competitive international marketplace the traditional factors that normally determine competitive advantage – price, quality, and speed of delivery –

are sometimes playing a secondary role. The supplier that can offer better payment terms and financing conditions may make a sale, even though the price may be higher or the quality of the product inferior to that of any competitors. For example, the Colombian Government Trade Bureau (PROEXPO) offers credit facilities to cover working capital needs as well as medium-term financing for infrastructure needs. These are used to encourage nontraditional exports (other than coffee and oil). In the United Kingdom, the Export Credits Guarantee Department (ECGD) guarantees credit and subsidizes export credit offered through commercial banks. Credit rediscounting is available in many countries including France, Korea, and Sri Lanka. Turkey has used an export credit subsidy.

As the credit terms necessary to make a sale are extended, the risks of payment increase, and many exporters are reluctant to assume the risks. Consequently, if a national government wants to encourage the growth of exports, it is necessary that it offers exporters the opportunity to shift the risk through credit insurance. Credit insurance and guarantees cover certain commercial and political risks that might be associated with any given export transaction. In Australia, for example, the Export Finance and Insurance Corporation (EFIC) provides payment risk insurance – or a guarantee – to a bank as well as improved access to working capital. Most of EFIC's clients are small exporters. Hong Kong has the Hong Kong Export Credit Insurance Corporation (ECIC), which provides credit insurance to exporters against the risk of nonpayment for goods and services; it also has a Credit Guarantee Scheme. On a regional basis in 2001 the African Trade Insurance Agency was created to provide insurance for exports to, from, and within Africa. Insurance is available for political upheaval, expropriation, and problems with exchange controls.

Information services

For a company to be successful in international marketing, its managers must be able to make the right decisions consistently. Over the long run, sound decision making is next to impossible without adequate and timely marketing information. Marketing information is indispensable in making such decisions as what market(s) to be in, when to be there, and how to be there. This is discussed further in Chapter 5. This includes both strategic and tactical decisions.

National governments can provide much of the basic information upon which international marketing decisions are based. Obviously not all business firms need to use such information services. Many large companies can collect the information they need themselves. Other firms, even if they do not possess the expertise to do their own research, can afford to hire outside research agencies to do the needed research or can turn to the Internet. However, there are a large number of companies that are not in a position to take either of these approaches. For these firms, generally smaller companies or newcomers to international marketing, their national government is the major source of basic marketing information. It should also be mentioned that there are many times when those companies that can do their own research or can afford to hire a research agency will utilize government information services. This will occur when the government is the only source of a particular type of information, a more common situation as the government expands its information services.

Although the information relevant for international/export marketers varies from country to country, the following kinds are available from a number of leading nations:

1. economic, social, and political data on individual countries, including the infrastructure;
2. individual reports on foreign firms;

3. specific export opportunities;
4. lists of potential overseas buyers, distributors, and agents for various products in different countries;
5. summary and detailed information on aggregate international marketing transactions;
6. information on relevant government regulations both at home and abroad;
7. sources of various kinds of information not always available from the government, for example foreign credit information;
8. information that will help the company to manage its operation, for example information on export procedures and techniques.

Most of the above-mentioned types of information are made available to business firms through published reports or documents. In addition, government officials often participate in seminars and workshops that are aimed at helping the international marketer.

Export facilitating activities

There are a number of national government activities for stimulating exporting that can be called export facilitating activities. These include the following:

1. Operating trade development offices abroad, either as a separate entity or as part of the normal operations of an embassy or consulate.
2. Sponsoring trade missions of business people who go abroad for the purpose of making sales and/or establishing agencies and other foreign representation.
3. Operating – or participating in – trade fairs and exhibitions. A trade fair is a convenient marketplace in which buyers and sellers can meet, and in which an exporter can display products.
4. Operating permanent trade centers in foreign market areas, which run trade shows often concentrating on a single industry.

From the point of view of the national government, each of these activities represents a different approach to stimulating the growth of exports. From the point of view of an individual company, they provide relatively low-cost alternative ways to make direct contact with potential buyers in overseas markets. Thus these services provide a way to expand overseas market coverage at a relatively low cost.

While promotion of exporting by the national government serves useful purposes, it is usually not directed to any specific political subdivision of a country. Political subunits such as states, provinces and municipalities in some countries (for example Canada, the United States, Germany) have actively moved into the promotion of international business with the purpose of aiding business firms located within their boundaries.

Both long- and short-range programs have been developed to tap foreign markets and grasp the many opportunities available. These programs have been aimed at helping those already active in export marketing as well as those to whom exporting may be an entirely new venture. Most of the subnational government activity occurs at the state or provincial level, but there is some activity at the local or municipal level (for example the Office of Economic Promotion for the City of Düsseldorf in Germany). The kinds of activities that subnational government agencies engage in are similar to those of national governments, including sponsoring trade missions and trade shows and operating trade development offices, but are targeted to more 'local' business firms (Wilkinson and Brouthers, 2000). For example, the Canadian provinces of Alberta, Quebec, and Prince Edward Island were operating trade offices in Hong Kong in mid-1996 as were the US states of New York and California. As previously mentioned, the US state of New Mexico operates overseas offices in Mexico and has part-time consultants in Berlin, Germany; Taipei, Taiwan; and Jerusalem, Israel. One success story is that in early 2000 the German circuit board manufacturer Sennheiser Electronic GmbH opened a manufacturing plant in the state.

Somewhat related to these activities are the government-authorized free trade zones, free ports, and free perimeters. A *free trade zone* is basically an enclosed, policed area without resident population in, adjacent to, or near a port of entry, into which foreign goods not otherwise prohibited may be brought without formal Customs entry or payment of duties. Examples are the Colon Free Zone in Panama and the Barranquilla free trade zone in Colombia. A *free port* encompasses a port or entire city isolated from the rest of the country for customs purposes. An example of a major free port is Hong Kong. Finally, a *free perimeter* is similar to a free port in the kinds of activities allowed, but is generally confined to a 'remote' underdeveloped region. Certain areas in Mexico extending about 7 km from the US border illustrate this type of operation. Since all these areas have the effect of encouraging and facilitating international transactions, the exporter may find them useful in the distribution of products not only to a single country but to an entire region. Hong Kong is a much used distribution center for the entire Far East.

Some developing, and newly industrialized, countries have established *export processing zones* (EPZs) as a vehicle for promoting industrialization. Examples are the Jakarta Zone in Indonesia, the Penang Zone in Malaysia and the Batran Zone in the Philippines. An EPZ is a relatively small, geographically separated area within a country, the purpose of which is to attract foreign investment in export-oriented industries. The EPZ allows imports of products to be used in producing exports on a bonded duty-free basis. An exporter can use such zones as a base for serving several markets.

Promotion by private organizations

Various nongovernmental organizations play a role in the promotion of international marketing. Many of the activities overlap and duplicate those of government agencies. Others, however, can be viewed as a supplement to government endeavors. A general listing of the types of nongovernmental organizations engaging in international marketing promotion is as follows:

1. chambers of commerce: local chambers of commerce; national chambers, national and international associations of chambers; national chambers abroad and bi-national chambers;
2. industry and trade associations: national, regional, and sectoral industry associations; associations of trading houses; mixed associations of manufacturers, traders, and other bodies;
3. other organizations concerned with trade promotion: organizations carrying out export research; regional export promotion organizations; world trade centers; geographically oriented trade promotion organizations; export associations and clubs, international business associations, world trade clubs; organizations concerned with commercial arbitration;
4. export service organizations: banks; transport companies; freight forwarders; export merchants and trading companies.

The types of assistance available to business firms include information and publications, education and assistance in 'technical' details, and promotion in foreign countries. Our discussion has, of necessity, been quite brief. A much more detailed exposition is provided by Seringhaus and Rosson (1989, pp. 44–56).

3.4.5 State trading

The extreme level of government involvement in international marketing is *state trading*, which is defined to include government engagement in commercial operations, directly or through agencies under its control, either in place of or in addition to private traders. Examples of countries with active state trading activities are China and Russia, and other countries where all exports and imports and exchange are handled by government monopolies or where individual state-owned enterprises are involved in international marketing activity. Many of these countries are now allowing or experimenting with some private trading activities either through joint ventures or as a result of privatization of state-owned enterprises. In addition, Australia and certain African countries have marketing boards to handle foreign trade.

In capitalist countries state trading is not a normal and regular activity of the state. It is undertaken to achieve specific objectives that are related to problems of a relatively temporary nature. Exceptions are activities of companies that may be owned by the state but which operate as if they were privately owned.

In general, whether communist or capitalist, a country may undertake state trading to achieve one or more of the following objectives:

- further its political goals;
- dispose of surpluses in various products;
- encourage export trade;
- enhance domestic planning programs by purchasing products needed to fill a gap in the plans;
- improve the country's balance of international payments;
- control foreign exchange;
- maintain national security and defense;
- acquire specific products, either because they can be obtained at lower cost or because they are scarce at home and/or abroad;
- help domestic interests by improving trade bargaining power or by protection against foreign competition.

Private business firms are concerned about state trading for two reasons. First, the establishment of import monopolies means that exporters have to make substantial adjustments in their export marketing programs. They cannot sell directly to markets and develop customer loyalty as in private enterprise economies. The state buying office buys certain goods to fill a gap in the total state plan, and the seller's marketing know-how cannot be used to the extent possible in private enterprise economies to influence or change the buying plan.

Second, if state traders wish to utilize the monopolistic power they possess, private international marketers are not really equipped to compete and deal with them. Backed by almost unlimited funds and untroubled by the need to operate at a monetary profit, they can be powerful bargainers, and they can extract payment from international marketers for marketing rights in their country.

3.5 Economic integration

Since the 1950s a key economic force affecting all forms of international business activity, especially exporting and FDI, has been the formation of regional economic integration arrangements, also known more generically as regional trading blocs or RTBs (Bryant and Unger, 2001). In its broadest sense, economic integration means the unification in some way of separate individual economies into a larger single economy. In effect, such integration goes beyond purely economic issues, and involves socio-cultural and political–legal matters as well. Consequently, we can view regional economic integration schemes as arrangements designed to promote closer economic ties within an area comprised of several politically independent countries, which minimize the economic consequences of political (and perhaps even cultural) boundaries.

Various schemes for achieving regional economic integration have been attempted, are operational, or have been suggested. These range from bilateral agreements to eliminate trade barriers (for example the Closer Economic Relations agreement between Australia and New Zealand) to complete economic integration with supranational institutions (for example the European Union). As shown in Table 3.9, the major types of integration schemes range from the least complex and exacting one of a *free trade area* to the most comprehensive *political union*. Illustrations of each type that exist today are presented in Table 3.10.

TABLE 3.9

Characteristics of economic integration

Characteristics	Free trade area	Customs union	Common market	Economic union	Political union
Removal of internal tariffs	X	X	X	X	X
Common external tariffs		X	X	X	X
Free flow of capital and labor			X	X	X
Harmonization of economic policy				X	X
Political integration					X

TABLE 3.10

Existing economic integration arrangements

Free trade area:

European Free Trade Association (EFTA)
- Iceland
- Liechtenstein
- Norway
- Switzerland

Latin American Integration Association
- Argentina
- Bolivia
- Brazil
- Chile
- Colombia
- Ecuador
- Mexico
- Paraguay
- Peru
- Uruguay
- Venezuela

Association of Southeast Asian Nations (ASEAN)
- Brunei
- Burma (Myanmar)
- Indonesia
- Laos
- Malaysia
- Philippines
- Singapore
- Thailand
- Vietnam

North American Free Trade Area (NAFTA)
- United States
- Canada
- Mexico

Customs union:

Benelux
- Belgium
- Netherlands
- Luxembourg

TABLE 3.10

continued

Common market:

European Union (EU)

Austria	Italy		
Belgium	Luxembourg		
Denmark	Netherlands		
Finland	Portugal		
France	Sweden		
Germany	Spain		
Greece	United Kingdom		
Ireland			

Admitted in 2004

Cyprus	Lithuania
Czech Republic	Malta
Estonia	Poland
Hungary	Slovakia
Latvia	Slovenia

Andean Common Market

Bolivia	Peru
Colombia	Venezuela
Ecuador	

Mercosur

Argentina	Chile*
Brazil	Bolivia*
Paraguay	
Uruguay	

Caribbean Community and Common Market (CARICOM)

Antigua and Barbuda	Jamaica
The Bahamas	St Kitts and Nevis
Barbados	St Lucia
Belize	St Vincent and
Dominica	the Grenadines
Grenada	Suriname
Guyana	Trinidad and Tobago

Central American Common Market (CACM)

Costa Rica	Honduras
El Salvador	Nicaragua
Guatemala	Panama

Economic union:

The closest is the European Union (EU). The creation of the so-called EU 'internal market' at the end of 1992 was a step towards fully integrated economic cooperation between the then 12 (now 25) member states.

Political union:

The Council for Mutual Economic Assistance (COMECON) was a hybrid involving the political union of economic affairs. Originally it was a forced union of the countries of eastern Europe with the USSR, but it evolved into a type of voluntary economic association including any nations that cared to be members.

The British Commonwealth of Nations can be viewed as a voluntary union. Similarly, the EU is moving in this direction under various provisions of the Maastricht Treaty, including the creation of a single currency, the euro.

* signed a free trade agreement

Regional integration schemes typically establish *Rules of Origin*, which include provisions for the amount of content that must be region based in order for a product to be exported/imported between countries in the region without tariff, or at a reduced tariff if tariffs have yet to be totally eliminated. Using NAFTA as an illustration, a company exporting a motor from the United States to Canada would have to prove that a specific percentage of the motor originated in one or more of the three countries in NAFTA. Various products may have different NAFTA content requirements. Rules of Origin are established to ensure that a nonmember country such as say, Taiwan, cannot get in 'through the back door' by first shipping a product to a warehouse in Mexico and eventually exporting it to the United States duty free. Other regional areas operate in a similar manner.

Exporting business firms may be affected in two basic ways by the formation of any type of regional scheme. There may be a *preference* effect and a *growth* effect. For exporters located outside any particular region a preference effect means that there will be a decrease in their exports to that region (perhaps even a total loss of market) because of the preferential treatment given to competitors located within the region. Of course, up to a point the 'outsider' can become more competitive by having a superior product, lower price, entering into one or more strategic alliances, or at the extreme by developing a production base within the region. In some situations the development of a production base is 'encouraged' by the integration group. ASEAN, for example, since its inception in the late 1960s, has had a program for complementary sectorial development of various industries. The governments promote foreign investment in 'approved' industries. Any action taken by an outsider to respond to the preference effect can necessitate a change in strategy and/or tactics by exporters to the region.

To an extent this preferential effect may be offset by the growth effect. Since a larger total market has been created, this together with the increased rate of economic growth means that consumers and industrial users will have more money to spend on products from abroad.

Preference and growth effects also touch companies located within the regionally integrated area. The results of economic integration to inside companies will probably be lower costs and increased sales. Input costs should decrease since inputs of all kinds become available from larger areas and without a tariff charge. Sales should increase because of expanding markets. Of course, not all companies will benefit to the same extent.

Economic integration can also be expected to result in the redistribution of economic activities to more efficient producers of goods and services. Less efficient producers, who were able to sell their products domestically only because of protective national barriers, will need to improve efficiency, combine with others, find new niches, or decline and go out of business. Companies already exporting when further integration occurs have already demonstrated their competitiveness and should be able to improve their positions.

One potential problem of the preference effect is that it may cause trade to flow in inefficient ways, a process known as *trade diversion*. In Chapter 2 we discussed comparative advantage as a basis of trade. If the United States imports Mexican televisions merely because the Mexican goods are tariff free, even if, say, Malaysia has a comparative advantage in television manufacturing, the main benefit of trade will be lost.

A second issue is that regionalism may block efforts to liberalize trade throughout the world. There is no clear-cut theoretical answer to the question of whether regional trade agreements are good or bad, and empirical results are disputed (*The Economist*, 1998c, 1998d). There is disagreement about the extent of trade diversion. One basis for judging regional arrangements is how much they discriminate between members and nonmembers. For example, there is evidence that Mercosur's high tariffs cause the countries to import from one another when it would be more efficient to buy products elsewhere. Given the mixed evidence, regionalism is not necessarily good or bad for free trade. In the end, the success of global efforts to liberalize trade depends mainly on whether governments want to move in that direction, not whether they seek or reject regional agreements.

It is tempting to think that, from a marketing viewpoint, a region (such as the EU) could be treated by an exporter as a single market area, and the EU has a single currency – the euro – in use in 22 member countries. The exporter that conducts operations using such a strategy will soon find that things are not as they seem. Within a region, separate markets do not cease to exist. The relevant demographic characteristics and social, legal, and cultural influences that define a market do not change just because a country is part of an area with free internal trade and perhaps even free movement of resources. In addition to variations in consumer needs and attitudes, other factors may still lead to such market differences – government regulations of marketing activities, distribution structures, and media availability, to mention just a few. Finally, there are many languages spoken within the EU, for example. Things will become even more diverse within the EU with the admittance of 10 countries in 2004.

Regional economic integration is a dynamic activity. Because of this it is not easy to describe and analyze what is happening throughout the world. What exists today may not exist tomorrow, at least in the same form. What is proposed today may never even come about. Examples of the dynamic nature of regional integration include the expansion of ASEAN by adding Laos and Burma (Myanmar) in 1997 despite the opposition of North American and European governments over Burma's entry. Cambodia's application was put 'on hold' due to the political strife and instability that arose in mid-1997. On a broader base the Free Trade Area of the Americas (FTAA) has been suggested, consisting of 34 countries including those in NAFTA, and Mercosur (Gouvea, 2002; Gouvea and Hranaiova, 2002). In addition, China has suggested a free trade agreement between itself and ASEAN; there have been negotiations between the ASEAN Free Trade Area (AFTA) and the New Zealand/Australia area; and a possible Northeast Asia Free Trade Area consisting of Japan, China, and South Korea is being examined, with a possible merger with AFTA to cover all of East Asia. A final example of the dynamics of regional integration is that of what has been happening in Africa during the past 50 years. By early 2001 there were at least nine different groupings of varying sizes.

It is in Europe where the most dynamic events have occurred. In 1987 the 12 nations of the European Union approved the Single European Act. This Act called for the implementing of 285 accords by 1 January 1993. The end result was to be the creation of the *internal market*. Although there already was free movement of products and resources within the community, there were gaps that needed to be closed. Moreover, all border controls and technical barriers to trade were to be removed, government purchasing was to be opened to nonnationals, and financial services were to be opened up competitively. These issues are covered in the Maastricht Treaty, which was finally ratified by all EU members in 1993. On 1 January 2002 the common currency, the euro, began circulation and its coins and bills replaced the currencies of the member countries of the European Monetary Union (EMU). All countries except Denmark, the United Kingdom, and Sweden are members of the EMU. The single currency has caused marketers to restructure pricing strategies and will lead to increased competition between firms in Europe as price comparisons are easier among countries. There will be cross-border trade due to differences in taxes. Not having to worry about foreign exchange costs and risks will also impact on supplier relationships and internal organization and investment. But it is in pricing where the most significant impact will be.

The long-run goal of EU leadership is to expand membership to other countries. Former EFTA members Austria, Sweden, and Finland entered in 1995. The EU and EFTA agreed on an alliance – the European Economic Association (EEA). A number of eastern European and Mediterranean countries joined the EU in 2004 – Czech Republic, Hungary, Poland, Estonia, Slovenia, Cyprus, Latvia, Lithuania, Malta, and Slovakia. In the next round of expansion Romania, Bulgaria and perhaps Turkey will make it in. This could be as soon as 2007.

Much of the business done by the EU is subject to majority voting among the member countries. But there are some areas where any national government can use its national veto power to stop the EU from adopting new laws or policy decisions, including: revision of EU treaties, admission of new members, defense, international agreements, use of EU money for promoting employment, new EU or national subsidies to industry, obligatory harmonization of national tax legislation, financial assistance to a member in serious economic difficulty, and external trade in services and intellectual property.

3.6 Competition

One of the most dynamic environmental forces affecting the marketing strategy of individual exporters is competition. Every firm must seek and find a function in order to maintain itself in the marketplace. Every firm occupies a position that in some respects is unique (for example, its location, product, customers).

Competition comes about because business firms, in their search for a niche in the economic world, try to make the most of their uniqueness. The result, hopefully, is the establishment of a *differential advantage* that can give the firm an edge over what others in the field are offering. It is this unending search for differential advantage that keeps competition dynamic. Hoecklin (1995) argues that understanding and *managing* cultural differences can lead to innovative business practices and sustainable sources of competitive advantage. Indeed on a broader level we see that more sustainable competitive advantages are changing from 'harder' efficiency sources to 'softer' effectiveness sources. Competitive advantage lies in doing the *right* things effectively, not in doing the 'wrong' things efficiently. However, knowing what the right things are in terms of consumer perception is central to strategic thinking. According to Haybyrne (1998), information used effectively is *tactical competitive advantage*. Thus, an international marketer must have a way to develop and manage knowledge as part of its competitive advantage. In determining what knowledge to manage, the marketer must first have a clear strategic direction for itself. This strategy becomes both a 'magnet' and a 'filter' – a magnet in terms of pulling relevant information into the company and a filter in terms of converting that information into usable competitive knowledge. This means that the international marketer must focus resources on core skills rather than trying to develop knowledge and skills in a broad range of categories. Nike, for example, concentrates on shoe design and promotion (Tiger Woods), and subcontracts (outsources) to others the rest of the value chain such as production and distribution. Nissan decided that it could gain competitive advantage by dedicating its knowledge base at the distribution and marketing points and concentrated on superior dealer service. It developed the most intensive dealer training program in the industry, involving everyone from salespeople to the receptionist, training them in identifying and meeting customer needs.

Sometimes competition is not 'fair.' A large German electronics company pays bribes to get export orders, France demands 20% of Vietnam's telecommunications market in exchange for aid, and a European aerospace company threatens to block EU membership for Turkey and Malta unless their national airlines purchase its planes. These and other practices have been reported to exist in the competitive arena for global business, and other evidence seems to be that such practices will increase, particularly in key sectors. Companies and governments seem to be more willing to use these unconventional methods to make a sale. Not all countries (or cultures) view practices such as these as illegal, or even unethical.

3.6.1 Nature of competition

Export marketing planning requires a knowledge of: (1) the structure of competition: the number and types of competitors; and (2) the action of competitors: the competitive tools available to marketing executives in the decision areas of product, channel, price, and promotion. Managers must be continually monitoring, for instance, competition in international markets.

This may concern products for which prices in various nations bear a known relationship, products that are standardized or graded according to accepted international standards, products that normally flow from one country to another in accordance with market needs and competitive conditions – in short, products for which there is a recognizable international market. Raw materials and semi-manufactured products (for example steel, coffee, rubber, textiles, industrial chemicals) are examples of such products. These products are homogeneous, or capable of being graded into homogeneous classifications; they are the 'components utilized in a wide variety of products by industries in virtually all nations.'

However, an international market also exists in some degree for products that are only somewhat alike, not quite homogeneous but sufficiently similar so that they may be considered to be acceptable substitutes; for example aspirin, razor blades, soft drinks, automobiles, clothing. Such products should to some degree be tailor-made and tailor-marketed to each market segment. For example, a foreign company producing automobiles will be more competitive in markets that drive on the left side of the road (the United Kingdom, Japan, Thailand) if they market right-hand drive automobiles. When an international market exists, producers must compete with those in other nations. If producers in one nation set the price too high or if they set the quality level too low, consumers may view foreign products as a superior 'buy' for the price. Often domestic producers or multinational firms producing for a given domestic market will recognize the boundaries within which they must remain in order that their products meet the needs of the local market more precisely than foreign products. Thus, a manufacturer of aspirin may market the product in different-sized packages in various national markets; a manufacturer of an orange soft drink might vary the formula (for example, amount of natural orange juice in the drink) according to various national consumer tastes. Although it may appear as if such products do not experience direct competition from similar but somewhat different products produced and marketed elsewhere, this conclusion is an illusion. Competition can exist in a meaningful sense.

3.6.2 Factors influencing competition

When products are homogeneous in the sense that the output of one producer is a good substitute for the output of other producers and when there is a sufficient number of buyers and sellers so that the actions of any one of them, acting alone or in concert with others, are of virtually no consequence to other buyers and sellers, the price of such products are determined by natural market factors. The quality and nature of the product (or product grades) tend to settle to a level that the market feels is consonant with the price, and physical distribution, selling, and advertising costs tend to be reduced to the lowest possible level. Under such conditions the structure of competition is the chief factor that exporters take into consideration when determining marketing policies. In a sense exporters need not have much more of a policy than to reduce product quality to the minimum acceptable level, reduce other marketing costs to a minimum, and offer their products for sale at the market price. The net result is that price tends to be forced down to average unit costs, low-cost producers tend to prosper and less efficient competitors (in a cost reduction sense) tend to be driven out of business or into other enterprises in which they are able to function more efficiently.

A key factor in the above described circumstances is the assumption of product homogeneity. For some products this is a reasonable assumption; for others it is not. Thus, as a practical matter, producers often find it desirable to distinguish their products from those of their competitors in ways that consumers find meaningful. Such efforts include not only physical changes in the product but also changes in the package, product line, marketing channels, personal selling, advertising, and price; that is, changes in any of the elements in the marketing mix. When sellers react in such ways, competition acquires new dimensions in addition to its structural aspects.

Sometimes competitive conditions evolve under which the needs of consumers are met adequately; but sometimes the needs and interests of consumers are subservient to the interest of sellers. In the latter instance laws or government regulations sometimes become necessary to protect the interests of society as a whole from the interest of 'minorities.' Laws or government regulations may be a substantial factor in promoting 'effective competition' or in some other way protecting society and competitors. Thus, laws or government regulations become factors that determine, in part, the nature of competition.

In summary, then, competition is influenced largely by: (1) general business, cultural, economic, and social conditions; (2) costs; and (3) laws and regulations. In addition, the activities and policies of *competitors* themselves affect competition. For example, in the Philippines in 1996 a local company, Jollibee Foods Corporation, had three times the market share of McDonald's – measured by hamburger restaurant visits. Jollibee's strength was its understanding of local tastes – heavy, sweet-spicy sauces, and rice offered with entrées. This success led McDonald's to offer its own Filipino-style spicy burgers. In the 1990s two of the largest producers of telecommunications equipment were from small Nordic countries – Finland's Nokia, in the mobile (cellular) telephone business, and Sweden's L.M. Ericsson, in mobile telephones and digital exchanges for mobile networks – supplied about one-third of the world market for mobile communications equipment. The success of these two companies offers the following lessons to all telecoms equipment firms everywhere and perhaps lessons for other industrial goods firms as well: (1) compete at home; (2) look abroad; and (3) invest in new technology.

From a marketing viewpoint, the exporter may compete on a *price* and/or a *nonprice* basis. Nonprice competition can be quite intense, particularly in markets where incomes and wealth are such that buyers can look for things other than the 'best buy.' At the same time domestic companies also compete on these bases. For example, in China a state-owned PC maker, Legend, dominates the market against such global leaders as IBM and Compaq. The company has done this by having low prices, a broad product range, helpful software, and a vast distribution network. Also contributing have been the company's strong links to the Chinese government, which accounts for about one-fourth of its sales, and its decision to offer state-of-the-art PCs, not yesterday's models. This allowed the company to remove the stigma associated with buying a local product. To keep its position Legend is forging a global strategy starting with Hong Kong and then moving into the United States and Europe. Its global brand is called Lenovo.

SUMMARY

This chapter has discussed major components of the international environment as they have a bearing on marketing efforts of international marketers. Our interest has centered on the economic, socio-cultural, political–legal, and competitive environments. Although each is distinct, each may also interact with one or more of the others. For instance, government policy may influence the competitive situation. It is imperative that the international marketer/exporter never forgets that 'a business firm is a product of its environment.'

QUESTIONS FOR DISCUSSION

3.1   Various classification schemes are sometimes used to give an indication of the potential of a particular foreign market/country. Explain why these schemes should or should not be used as a basis for deciding what markets to enter.

3.2   Explain the meaning of 'cultural universals.' Do these provide universal guides to behavior in all societies? How can the international marketer use these universals?

3.3   Do you agree that the international marketer does not need to study a culture from a narrow perspective but rather needs only a broad perspective to learn about general patterns and themes? Explain your answer.

3.4   Explain the meaning of the following statement: 'People are what make international marketing exciting but frustrating.'

3.5   What is the 'silent language' of international marketing and how does it relate to the concept of 'culture is communication'?

3.6   What is the self-reference criterion and how should the international marketer apply it? Explain.

3.7   Government can play many roles in international marketing. What are these roles and how does each affect individual business firms?

3.8   Why is it that some exporters would support voluntary export restraints agreed to by their government?

3.9   For a country of your choice, determine what its government does to promote exports and other international marketing activity.

3.10 What is regional economic integration, what is its objective, how is it supposed to achieve its objective, and what impact is there on individual exporters?

3.11 Should an economically integrated region be considered as one market area? Explain your answer. Would your answer vary for the European Union in contrast to, say, ASEAN?

3.12 Can the European Union become too big? Is there a point of diminishing returns for a regional economic area? Explain.

3.13 What is really meant by a company having a differential advantage over its competitors in one or more foreign markets?

REFERENCES

Abed, G. T. (2003). Unfulfilled promise. *Finance & Development*, March, 10–14.

Adhikosi, R. and Yung, Y. (2000). What will WTO membership mean for China and its trading partners? *Finance & Development*, September, 22–9.

Adler, N. J. (1991). *International Dimensions of Organizational Behavior* 2nd edn. Boston, MA: PWS-Kent.

Albaum, G. and Herche, J. (1999). Management style characteristics among five European nations. *J. of Global Marketing*, 12(4), 5–27.

Albaum, G., Yu, J., Wiese, N. and Herche, J. (2004). A cross-national study of the impact of culture-based decision makers' management style. *Proceedings*, Third International Business and Economics Conference, San Francisco, 8–11 January.

Armitage, C. (2003). Chuppies shop till they drop. *The Australian*, 8 December, 15.

Borrus, A. and Javetski, B. (1995). Who's afraid of the World Trade Organization? *Business Week*, 5 June, 35.

Brake, T., Walker, D. M. and Walker, T. (1995). *Doing Business Internationally*. Burr Ridge, IL: Irwin Professional.

Brislin, R. (1993). *Understanding Culture's Influence on Behavior*. Fort Worth, TX: Harcourt Brace Jovanovich.

Bryant, S. K. and Unger, M. L. (2001). European Union as a role model for regional trade development. *Global Economy Quarterly*, II, 201–14.

Bullock, G. (1995). How Austrade can help your export drive. *Sydney Morning Herald*, 6 June, 47.

Business Week (2000a). Asia's future, 27 November, 132–6.

Business Week (2000b). Russia's middle class, 16 October, 78–84.

Caulfield, B. and Shi, T. (2004). Getting a leg up in China. *Business 2.0*, January/February, 69–70.

Cheung, C. (1996). The cost of good connection. *South China Morning Post*, 26 May, 2.

Crick, D. (1997). UK SMEs' awareness, use, and perceptions of selected government export assistance programs: an investigation into the effect of the internationalization process. *The International Trade Journal*, XI(1), 135–67.

Crowley, M. (2004). The worldwide spread of antidumping protection. *Chicago Fed Letter*, 198 (January).

Davies, H., Leung, T. K. P., Luk, S. T. and Wong, Y.-H. (1995). The benefits of 'guanxi.' *Industrial Marketing Management*, 24, 207–14.

Duerr, M. (1992). New United Motor Manufacturing Inc. at Midlife: experience of the joint venture. In *Research in International Business and International Relations*, vol. 5, Greenwich, CT: JAI Press, 193–214.

Einhorn, B., Engardio, P. and Shari, M. (2003). Damage in the Delta. *Business Week*, 21 April, 56–7.

Ellis, P. and Pecotich, A. (2001). Social factors influencing export initiation in small and medium-sized enterprises. *J. Marketing Research*, February, 119–30.

Enoch, C. and Gulde, A.-M. (1998). Are currency boards a cure for all monetary problems? *Finance & Development*, December, 40–3.

Farmer, R. and Richman, B. (1984). *International Business* 4th edn. Bloomington, IN: Cedarwood.

Gesteland, R. (1999). *Cross-Cultural Business and Behavior* 2nd edn. Copenhagen: Copenhagen Business School Press.

Gouvea, R. (2002). Brazil and Mexico – partners sowing a Free Trade Area of the Americas. *Thunderbird International Business Review*, 44, 5 (September–October), 603–24.

Gouvea, R. and Hranaiova, J. (2002). Brazil and the FTAA: stategic trade options. *Multinational Business Review*, Fall, 33–41.

Griffith, D. A., Hu, M. Y. and Ryans, J. K. Jr. (2000). Process standardization across intra- and intercultural relationships. *J. International Business Studies*, 31(2), 303–24.

Grossman, W. (2001). Losing the company keys. *Smartbusinessmag.com*, February, 48.

Hall, E. T. (1960). The silent language in overseas business. *Harvard Business Review*, May–June, 93–6.

Hall, E. T. (1973). *The Silent Language*. Garden City, NY: Anchor/Doubleday.

Haybyrne, J. (1998). Get smart with strategy. *South China Morning Post*, 26 April, 13.

Hibbert, E. (1998). Evaluating government export promotion: some conceptual and empirical approaches. *The International Trade Journal*, XII(4), 465–83.

Hoecklin, L. (1995). *Managing Cultural Differences: Strategies for Competitive Advantage*. Wokingham, England: Addison-Wesley.

Hofstede, G. (2001). *Culture's Consequences*, 2nd edn. Thousand Oaks, CA: Sage.

Keegan, W. J. and Green, M. S. (2000). *Global Marketing* 2nd edn. Upper Saddle River, NJ: Prentice-Hall.

Keesing, D. B. and Singer, A. (1992). Why export promotion fails. *Finance & Development*, 29(1), 52–3.

Kess, J. (1976). *Psycholinguistics: Introductory Perspectives*. New York: Academic.

Klitgaard, R. (2000). Subverting corruption. *Finance & Development*, June, 2–5.

Kogut, B. and Singh, H. (1988). The effect of national culture on the choice of entry mode. *J. International Business Studies*, Fall, 19, 411–32.

Lansk, H. L. (2003). New law protects marks worldwide. *Marketing News*, 14 April, 10–12.

Lee, James A. (1966). Cultural analysis in overseas operations. *Harvard Business Review*, March–April, 44, 106–14.

Li, J. (1998). Price law will set benchmark. *China Daily*, 24 April, 4.

Lu, H. (1996). Quota rules fix exports. *China Daily Business Weekly*, 26 May–1 June, 1.

Luostarinen, R., Korhonen, H., Jokinen, J. and Pelkonen, T. (1994). *Globalization and SME*. Helsinki, Finland: Ministry of Trade and Industry, Studies and Reports 59/1994.

Matsutuji, T. (1992). Helping American firms sell in Japan. *VIA International*, 44(6), 22–3.

Milner, C. (1990). *Export Promotion Strategies: Theory and Evidence from Developing Countries*. New York: New York University Press.

Murdock, G. (1945). *The Common Denominator of Cultures: The Science of Men in the World Crises* (ed. R. Linton). New York: Columbia University Press, 123–42.

Norregaard, J. and Reppelin-Hill, V. (2000). *Controlling Pollution: Using Taxes and Tradable Permits*. Washington, DC: International Monetary Fund, Economic Issues No. 25.

Ottman, J. (1998). The debate over eco-seals: is self-certification enough? *Marketing News*, 2 March, 7–9.

Pacheco, J. (2002). 'The cookie lesson,' a study in culture. *Albuquerque Journal*, Business Outlook, 23 September, 7.

Pope, J. and Vogl, F. (2000). Making anticorruption agencies more effective. *Finance & Development*, June, 6–9.

Punnett, B. J. (1994). *Experiencing International Business and Management* 2nd edn. Belmont, CA: Wadsworth.

Ricks, D. A. (1999). *Blunders in International Business* 3rd edn. Oxford, UK: Blackwell.

Seringhaus, F. H. R. and Rosson, P. S. (eds) (1989). *Government Export Promotion: A Global Perspective*. London: Routledge.

Shelburne, R. C. (1997). Government export promotion expenditures: some cost estimates and practical considerations. *The International Trade Journal*, XI(1), 69–83.

Shishkin, P. (2001). EU drops one of its inquiries into Microsoft. *The Wall Street Journal*, 19 April, A12.

The Economist (1998a). What would Confucius say now? 25 July, 23–8.

The Economist (1998b). Unfair competition, 7 November, 75–6.

The Economist (1998c). A question of preference, 22 August, 62.

The Economist (1998d). Alphabetti spaghetti, 3 October, 19–22.

The Economist (1999). Chinese whispers, 30 January, 77–9.

The Economist (2000). Going global, 17 June, 83.

The Economist (2002). For whom the Liberty Bell tolls, 31 August, 18–20.

The Economist (2004a). Golden boys and girls, 14 February, 37–8.

The Economist (2004b). Everybody's doing it, 28 February, 39–40.

The Economist (2004c). Who will watch the watchdogs? 21 February, 39–40.

Vence, D. L. (2003). Cultural understanding of self, others vital for managers. *Marketing News*, 1 September, 21–3.

VIA Port of NY–NJ (1988). Holland's matchmaker, 40(10), 8–9.

Welch, D., Welch, L., Wilkinson, I. and Young, L. (1996a). Networks: a challenge for export promotion. Paper presented at International Business Workshop, 25–28 August, Vaasa, Finland.

Welch, D., Welch, L., Wilkinson, I. and Young, L. (1996b). Export groups: market development and group functioning. Paper presented at Academy of International Business Meeting, Banff, Canada.

Wilke, J. R. (2001). European antitrust officials study Intel. *The Wall Street Journal*, 6 April, A3ff.

Wilkinson, T. J. and Brouthers, L. E. (2000). Trade shows, trade missions and state governments: increasing FDI and high-tech exports. *J. International Business Studies*, 31(4), 725–34.

Wolf, T. and Gurgen, E. (2000). *Improving Governance and Fighting Corruption in the Baltic and CIS Countries*. Washington, DC: International Monetary Fund, Economic Issues No. 21.

Yorio, V. (1978). *Adapting Products for Export*. New York: The Conference Board.

FURTHER READING

Brekke, D. (2001). What you don't know can hurt you. *Smartbusinessmag.com*, March, 61–74.

Garten, J. E. (1997). *The Big Ten: The Big Emerging Markets and How They Will Change Our Lives*. New York: Basic Books.

Jovanovic, M. N. (1992). *International Economic Integration*. London: Routledge.

Nsouli, S. M., Bisat, A. and Kanaan, O. (1996). The European Union's new Mediterranean strategy. *Finance & Development*, September, 14–20.

Stotsky, J., Suss, E. and Tokarick, S. (2000). Trade liberalization in the Caribbean. *Finance & Development*, June, 22–5.

Terpstra, V. and David, K. (1985). *The Cultural Environment of International Business*. Cincinnati, OH: South-Western.

The Economist (1996). Mercosur survey. 12 October, 3–30.

Wijnholds, H. de B. and Little, M. W. (2001). Regulatory issues for global e-tailers: marketing implications. *Academy of Marketing Science Review* [online], September.

Yau, O. H. M. (1994). *Consumer Behavior in China: Customer Satisfaction and Cultural Values*. London: Routledge.

CASE STUDY 3.1

Supreme Canning Company

(This case study has been written by Mitsuko Saito Duerr, San Francisco State University.)

The Supreme Canning Company (the true name of the company is disguised) is an independent US packer of tomato paste and other tomato products (whole peeled tomatoes, chopped tomatoes, tomatoes and zucchini, ketchup, tomato paste, and pizza and other sauces). The company is located in the state of California. Although it produces some cans with its own-brand label, much of its output is canned for others and their brand names and labels are put on the cans. It produces shelf-size cans for eventual sale at retail, and gallon-size cans for use by restaurants and industrial users. It also packs tomato paste in 55-gallon drums, and in plastic containers holding approximately 0.7 cubic meters (with the flexible plastic container held inside a heavy shipping container). Supreme Canning Company's annual processing capacity is in excess of 100,000 tons of tomatoes (processed during an operating season of approximately three months).

The market for tomatoes is divided into three segments with distinct characteristics:

1. Fresh tomatoes are produced in many countries, with much cross-border trade and frequent trade disputes. Canadian and US farmers have had a series of trade disputes with each country claiming dumping by companies in the other of fresh tomatoes of different varieties at different times. In 2004 the year-round supply of fresh tomatoes from Mexico was depressing prices for US farmers (www.dailydemocrat.com/2004). Special varieties of hothouse tomatoes from The Netherlands are sold in other European countries and overseas.

2. Canning of tomatoes is carried out in fewer countries because of the market size required to support economically sized factories.

3. Even fewer countries (and packers within countries) produce the tomato paste used by other tomato canning companies to make end products such as tomato soup. Economical production of tomato paste requires an extremely large supply of tomatoes that could be harvested by machines (or very cheap labor) and easily transported to the processing facility. California's Central Valley was an ideal location for such processing because of its vast amount of relatively flat land, large farms, and good road network. China, with its low wage rates, was also a producer of tomato paste, and exported paste to Italy.

Italy is a major exporter of canned tomato products, but a net importer of tomato paste. The tomato paste is used along with domestic fresh tomatoes in making and canning various tomato products. Italy exports canned tomato products to many countries.

Supreme Canning Company, along with other US producers, was pressed by a combination of heavy competition from factories overseas (particularly in Italy) and inadequate domestic demand. Tri Valley Growers, California's largest agricultural cooperative and processor of 10% of the canned tomato products sold in the United States, had gone bankrupt in 2000. A surge in demand from Italy, which decreased its imports from China in 2003–4 when the SARS epidemic occurred, provided a temporary increase in demand for Californian tomato paste. But Supreme Canning Company still needed additional markets.

One potential bright spot for the Supreme Canning Company had been the possibility of getting into the Japanese market. Japan was reducing trade barriers and attempting to encourage imports. At the same time, the popularity of pizza and Italian-style foods and restaurants had grown rapidly, creating an increased demand for specialty tomato products. Because of the scarcity of land, the nation had not gone into the large-scale production required to support an economical domestic tomato-canning industry. The insistence of Japanese consumers (and companies) on high quality had resulted in relatively low sensitivity to the prices of food products.

An inquiry that had been received from a food packer and distributor in Japan indicated interest from that side. The Japanese firm handled a large number of products, was well known in Japan, and was much larger than the US firm. Since Supreme Canning Company did not have well-known brand names of its own, it was interested in acting as a large-scale supplier of products made to customers' specifications for use by the customer or distribution under the customer's label. Thus the inquiry from Japan was most welcome.

The Japanese company invited senior executives of the US firm to visit their production facilities and offices in Japan. Both the president and chairman of the board of Supreme Canning Company had a four-day visit with the executives of the company in Japan. The president of the US company, who had some knowledge of Japanese business practice from studies at Stanford University and from his widespread reading, attempted to act as a guide to Japanese business practice. The chairman of the board had little knowledge of Japan, and viewed himself as a decisive man of action. Although there were a few minor misunderstandings, the visit was concluded successfully and the Americans invited the Japanese to visit their plant in California for four days.

The Japanese indicated their interest in the signing of a mutual letter of cooperation. The chairman of the board of Supreme Canning was not interested in this, but rather wanted some specific agreements and contracts. As the time for the Japanese visit to the United States drew near, the Japanese indicated that their president would not be able to come. Some senior executives would be able to meet, but they would only be able to spend two days instead of four. The vice-chairman of the board of the Californian company wrote asking why the Japanese were not going to send their president, and inquiring why they could not spend four days instead of two, 'as we did in Japan.' The letter was frank and direct. The tone was that of a person talking to an equal, but not with any great deal of politeness. The Japanese company decided to cancel the visit, and no further negotiations or serious contacts were made.

Some months later, a local businessman of Japanese extraction asked the president of Supreme Canning Company if some representatives of another (and even larger) Japanese food products producer and distributor could visit the plant. Four Japanese showed up along with the local businessman, who acted as interpreter and go-between. The three middle-aged Japanese produced their *meishi* (business cards) and introduced themselves. Each spoke some English. The older man did not present a card and was not introduced. When the president of the US company asked who he was, the go-between said 'He's just one of the company's directors.' The visit concluded without discussion of any business possibilities, but this was to be expected in an initial visit from Japanese businessmen.

Supreme's president later found out the family name of the unknown visitor, and immediately recognized it as being that of the president of the Japanese company. He assumed that the president of the Japanese company had come but had hidden the fact. He felt that he had been taken advantage of. He telephoned the go-between and told him that he never wanted anyone from that company in his plant again.

From a description of the unknown visitor, a consultant to the company realized that the visitor was not the president of the Japanese company. Rather, it was the semi-retired father of the president. The father retained a position on the board of directors and maintained a lively interest in company activities, but was not active in day-to-day affairs. Unlike his son who was fluent in English, he spoke only Japanese. The consultant suddenly realized that the chairman of the board of the US company apparently did not understand:

- the Japanese preference for getting to know people well before doing business;
- the significance of a letter of cooperation (which could be expected to be a first step in concluding a long-term business agreement);
- the status relationship in Japan of little companies to big ones (larger companies have greater status, and their managers are shown greater respect);
- the status relationship in Japan of sellers to buyers (buyers have greater status, and their managers are shown greater respect).

Questions

1. Was the chairman of the US company wrong for not having found out in advance about Japanese business practice?

2. Were the Japanese wrong for not having found out about US business practice before they initiated contacts?

3. What should the president of the US company do now?

CASE STUDY 3.2

Ford Motor Company

(This case study was written by Edwin C. Duerr, San Francisco State University.)

Introduction

The Ford Motor Company issues a Corporate Citizenship Report each year. The first, *Connecting with Society*, was issued at its annual shareholders' meeting held in Atlanta, Georgia in May 2000. That report was unique in its recognition that the company face a dilemma because its most profitable products, sports utility vehicles, contribute to environmental problems and may be considered not socially responsible. In spite of these recognized problems the company stated that it intended to continue to manufacture and sell these vehicles. In an interview, Chairman William C. Ford, Jr. cited the Ford Explorer as an example: 'If we didn't provide that vehicle, someone else would, and they wouldn't do it as responsibly as we do.' He indicated that Ford Motor Company's approach combined altruism with a foundation for long-term planning. The press noted that Mr Ford had been one of the most enthusiastic supporters of the company's 1996 decision to introduce the full-size Ford Expedition, a SUV with a high gasoline consumption rate (Bradsher, 2000).

Ford's report and comments can be viewed in a number of ways: as an exceptionally honest recognition of the conflicting demands placed upon the international corporation by its various stakeholders (society, suppliers, customers, employees, and stockholders); as an admission that corporate interests in this case are in conflict with social responsibility; or as the foundation for building a corporate approach that will attempt to reconcile conflicting demands.

In evaluating the approach taken by Ford, it is useful to briefly review the company's overall approach to corporate citizenship and key stakeholders before looking at some of the specifics regarding the SUVs and their place in the product line.

Corporate citizenship and key stakeholders

With 114 factories located in 40 countries and selling to markets worldwide, Ford Motor Company operates within a wide variety of ethical, political, and legal systems to which it must adapt. The company's approach to international corporate citizenship has been influenced substantially by William Ford, who has been active in environmental causes since his school years. When he joined the Ford Motor Company Board of Directors in 1988, colleagues suggested that he drop his contacts with environmentalists. He refused to do so and indicated that he believed he could help build bridges and understanding between the company and environmentalists. In 1997, he chaired a newly established Environmental and Public Policy Committee of the Board of Directors. Since becoming Chairman of the Board of Directors in January 1999 he and Jacques Nasser, the President and CEO of the company, have been working to improve corporate citizenship and social responsibility.

Ford's *Connecting with Society* states that good corporate citizens are distinguished by their behavior, and by the social, environmental, and economic impacts of their actions. They should generate sustained profits from products that meet human needs with greater value to society and a smaller environmental impact. The company has established an administrative structure and strategic plans for developing a more comprehensive set of business principles, increasing interaction with all stakeholders, transforming goals into action, and providing transparency and verification of problems and progress. Specific problem areas have been identified, and the report provides a justification for

undertaking additional efforts in the area of social responsibility. In 2001 Mr Nasser reported that quality problems in new and redesigned vehicles launched in Europe and the United States in 2000 had cost the company over $1 billion in profit, and added 'That will never happen again' (White and Lundegaard, 2001).

The company is already a leader in many areas of social responsibility. Several years ago it lobbied for higher gasoline taxes in the United States (a position opposite to that taken by other automobile companies). Such taxes would, of course, encourage fuel conservation by consumers and influence manufacturers to make more fuel-efficient vehicles (as the high taxes in Europe already do). Ford is also increasing the amount of recycled materials in vehicle manufacture, using more than 2 million tons of recycled metals per year. It has indicated that it views the European laws requiring manufacturers to take back vehicles at the end of their lives as an opportunity rather than a threat. It has emphasized the development of new factories and the redesign of existing plants to reduce pollution well below the legal requirements of the countries within which it operates. The company has achieved ISO 14001 environmental management certification for all of its facilities and in 1999 became the first US automobile maker to develop a program requiring certification of all of its suppliers with manufacturing facilities. Ford has offered to support its suppliers in the United Kingdom, Germany, Australia, and the United States with assistance in ISO 14001 training. In Europe, the company works with more than a dozen environmental organizations, environmental investment funds, and other not-for-profit organizations focusing on transportation issues. Since 2000, Ford has designed all of its SUVs and its F-series pickup trucks to meet US standards for low emission vehicles, cutting smog-forming emissions by over 40% compared to government requirements. In 2000 Ford opened its newest research laboratory, devoted primarily to developing new environmental technologies, in Aachen, Germany. The company works cooperatively with local governments internationally in projects to address environmental concerns.

In its 2000 publication, *Connecting with Customers*, Ford indicated that its goals are to build shareholder value by putting customers first and enabling employees to develop their potential to the fullest. The company views its primary responsibility as meeting the needs of three major stakeholders: stockholders, customers, and employees.

Ford has also undertaken a number of initiatives with respect to the welfare of its employees. It has made efforts to show that they are economically justified, thus benefiting stockholders as well. In cooperation with part-supplier Visteon and the United Auto Workers, Ford will be opening 30 Family Service Centers in 14 states during the coming years. They will offer round-the-clock childcare, classes, and other services to employees. Jacques Nasser, Ford President, stated: 'It's not a low cost, but we're not wasting a cent.' He indicated that it would help both the company and the workers. 'This is an effort to attract talent and retain talent because turnover costs money' (Pickler, 2000).

Internationally, the company is attempting to help overcome the digital divide between the richer and less-developed countries. Ford indicated that companies and individuals that want to be successful in the 21st century will need to be leaders in using the Internet and related technologies. In 2000 the Chairman of the Board announced that employees worldwide will be provided with a computer, printer, and Internet usage at home for a small monthly fee, $5 in the United States (Ford, 2000). This effort is tied into the development of employees who will be more valuable in the changing international environment.

The company's marketing of SUVs is directly related to the interests of shareholders, customers, and employees. How well it fits, or does not fit, with the company's environmental objectives is discussed in the following two sections.

SUVs and major stakeholders

Ford pioneered the development of the modern sports utility vehicle market. The SUVs were designed to provide those who spent time in the outdoors, whether for work or for recreation, with a vehicle that could function effectively off regular roads and was more comfortable than typical pickup trucks. Eventually, the SUVs appealed to individuals who just wanted a sporty vehicle, as well as to the original target market of those who really needed off-road capabilities.

When Ford introduced its Explorer model in 1990 the vehicle quickly became the most popular SUV in the United States. It also proved popular in Latin America and in the Middle East. Over 3.5 million Explorers were sold and they brought in billions of dollars in profits.

US government regulations classed large SUVs as trucks, allowing them to emit 5.5 times as much smog-causing pollution per mile as automobiles do. (New rules will require that SUVs meet the same standards as automobiles by 2009.) This allowed companies to put larger engines in the vehicles, adding to their attractiveness to many buyers. The largest US auto makers all worked on developing larger SUVs that they priced so as to return a high level of profit. The major Japanese automobile manufacturers initially lagged behind in developing SUVs, but have caught up in some model

types and are continuing to develop new models and expand production capacity in the United States. European auto makers have similarly been expanding their line of SUVs.

In 1990, only 5% of Ford's sales were of SUVs. In 2000, SUVs accounted for 20% of its sales, and most of its profits. It has been estimated that Ford earns $10,000 to $15,000 on each Ford Expedition and Lincoln Navigator sold, and as much as $18,000 for each Ford Excursion (Bradsher, 2000).

Safety and environmental issues and viewpoints

Environmentalists and consumer groups have been critical of the SUVs with respect to three factors: (1) the high level of smog-causing pollution they create; (2) their high rate of fuel consumption; and (3) safety concerns. Both the high level of pollutants that SUVs are allowed to generate and their high rate of fuel consumption are being addressed by legislation, as are some safety considerations.

Ford's basic argument with regard to the development and marketing of SUVs is that customers want them and Ford produces vehicles that are more environmentally friendly and safer than those of their competitors. They have pointed out that all of their SUVs are certified Low Emission Vehicles, and that the Ford Excursion, a vehicle criticized by some environmentalists, produces 43% less contaminants than are allowed by US government standards. They continue to work both to improve fuel efficiency and reduce pollutants.

Safety is an issue because SUVs are generally designed with greater ground clearance and therefore higher centers of gravity, higher bumpers, and are heavier than automobiles of the same size. In collisions with automobiles, they tend to ride up over the bumpers of the cars and crush them. They have also been involved in a number of accidents in which the SUVs rolled over without being involved with another car. These rollovers may have occurred in some cases because of their off-road uses, in others because of the way they are sometimes driven on roads, and in still others because they are less stable than many automobiles.

It has been claimed that Ford could have made the Explorer safer by redesigning it before taking it to market, though this would have been costly and delayed its introduction by more than a year. This would have allowed other manufacturers to beat it to the market. Further, Ford has pointed out that the overall safety record of the Explorer is better than that of the comparable SUVs and passenger cars from other vehicle manufacturers. The car has a 26% lower rate of rollover fatalities than other SUVs (Levin, 2000). Thus it could be argued that delaying its introduction could have resulted in customers buying less safe vehicles from competitors.

In 2001 the US National Highway Traffic Safety Administration released its first report on the expected tendency for 43 types of vehicles to roll over. It was based on calculations involving the vehicles' track widths and heights of centers of gravity. Of the 19 SUVs analyzed, 9 received poorer ratings and 2 received better ratings than the 4 Ford models evaluated.

Another view regarding the safety of SUVs was provided by State Farm Insurance Company, the United States' largest insurer of vehicles. In December 2000, after an analysis of its claim rates, the company changed its pricing policy to give sizable discounts to drivers of SUVs, vans, and luxury cars. Their records indicate that these vehicles are safer. Consumer groups have countered that they may be safer to the occupants of the vehicles, but not to those in cars they may hit (Lazarus, 2000).

Both Ford and General Motors introduced new versions of their key midsize SUVs in 2001, redesigned to provide greater stability. Ford also redesigned the bumpers to reduce the danger of riding up on other vehicles in the event of a collision.

In the Chairman's Message in Ford's *2002 Annual Report* (published in 2003), William C. Ford, Jr. stated that the company would be producing the cleanest and most fuel-efficient SUV in the world by the end of the year (http://ford.com). In 2004 Ford signed cross-licensing technology agreements with Toyota for the purpose of further development of hybrid vehicles. Ford also plans to sell a limited number of a fuel cell-powered version of the Ford Focus for use in commercial applications (http://ford.com). In 2004 demand for SUVs in the United States continued to be strong, with Toyota enjoying an increasing market share on its entries in the market (Zaun, 2004).

It can be argued that continuing to produce SUVs, and developing new vehicles as new markets emerge or can be created, meets Ford's goals of building shareholder value and of putting customers first. It provides customers with a larger choice of vehicles from which to choose while also meeting stockholders' profit objectives. It also provides employees with a higher level of employment than they would otherwise enjoy. It could be further argued that by continuing to improve design, and exceeding government safety and pollution requirements, they are meeting their social responsibility to society.

On the other side, an argument could be made that the company should not make vehicles that pollute the atmosphere or which have potential safety hazards.

References

Bradsher, K. (2000). Ford admits SUVs are socially irresponsible. *San Francisco Chronicle*, 12 May, A1.

Ford Motor Company (2000a). *1999 Annual Report*, Dearborn, MI.

Ford Motor Company (2000b). *Connecting with Society*, Dearborn, MI.

Ford Motor Company (2000c). *Connecting with Customers*, Dearborn, MI.

Ford Motor Company (2003). *2002 Annual Report*, Dearborn, MI.

Lazarus, D. (2000). State Farm discounts SUVs. *San Francisco Chronicle*, 3 December, B2.

Levin, M. (2000). Low-tire pressure recommendation may hurt Ford. *San Francisco Chronicle*, 24 August, A3.

Pickler, N. (2000). Ford, UAW building 30 centers that make workers' child care job 1. *San Francisco Chronicle*, 22 November, B1.

White, G. and Lundegaard, K. (2001). Ford says last year's quality snafu's took big toll – over $1 billion in profit. *The Wall Street Journal*, 12 January, A3.

Zaun, T. (2004). Toyota posts 60% rise in profits. *The Wall Street Journal*, 6 February, A3.

Questions

1. Are Ford's report and comments:

a) an exceptionally honest recognition of the conflicting demands placed upon the international corporation by its various stakeholders (society, customers, employees, and stockholders);

b) an admission that corporate interests may be in conflict with social responsibility; or

c) a foundation for building an approach to research and development that will attempt to reconcile the conflicting demands?

2. Is Ford behaving in a socially responsible manner when it continues to make SUVs? Discuss.

3. Should the government be more aggressive in setting safety standards? Why or why not?

4. Should the governments of the world ban vehicle types that they consider unsafe or not socially responsible?

5. Should Ford oppose or support tighter environmental standards that would apply equally to all vehicle manufacturers? How should Ford react to varying environmental standards in different countries?

6. Is spending corporate funds on nonrequired socially responsible activities an unjustified expenditure, or a recognition that in the long run companies must exercise social responsibility in order to avoid societal or government actions that will damage them? Explain.

CASE STUDY 3.3

Avon Products, Inc. (A)

(This case study was written by Yim-Yu Wong and Edwin Duerr, both of San Francisco State University.)

Avon Products, Inc. (Avon), the US cosmetics giant, had considered China the keystone of its marketing effort in Asia. Years of effort and the development of a large direct marketing organisation in that country had made operations in China its most profitable and most rapidly growing market in Asia. On 21 April 1998 senior company officials from the New York headquarters and throughout Asia had gathered in Guangzhou for what was supposed to be a festive occasion. During the meeting William Pryor, Avon's head of China operations, was called away from his table to take a phone call. When he returned, it was with devastating news. The Chinese government had just announced an immediate ban on all direct selling.

In 113 years, Avon had used only direct selling and had no experience in traditional retailing. Thus the large financial investments they had made in China beginning in 1990, and the expected potential for growth in the Chinese market, were in immediate and very serious danger. While Avon had enjoyed eight consecutive years of profit in China, the implications went beyond the possible loss of the Chinese market itself. Avon had planned to use China as a manufacturing base for its export activities, thus strengthening its status as a global company. At corporate headquarters in the United States the ban not only demonstrated that regulatory and bureaucratic uncertainty continued to be a major problem for foreign businesses in China, but also provoked reconsideration by Avon of its strategic approach to the global market.

The company and its competitors

Avon Products, Inc. was founded in 1886 by David McConnell as the California Perfume Company. The name was officially changed to Avon Products, Inc. in 1939. In the late 1990s the company was operating in over 135 countries with a sales force of more than 2.3 million independent representatives. These representatives, called Avon Ladies, handled 650 million customer orders and generated more than US$2 billion in commissions per year.

The company is the world's largest direct seller of beauty and related products. A leader in skin care prod-

ucts, it is also a manufacturer of costume jewelry, and markets an extensive line of apparel, gifts, decorative items, collectables, and family entertainment products. Of these products, cosmetics account for over 60% of total sales. With US$4.8 billion in annual revenue, Avon was ranked 293 among Fortune 500's list of the largest US companies in 1998.

The vision of Avon is: 'To be the company that best understands and satisfies the product, service, and self-fulfillment needs of women – globally. The vision influences the company's research, product development, marketing and management practices' (www.avon.com).

Avon is in some of the most competitive consumer-product markets in the world. Their target market is women in a wide age range, from teens to the over 40s, in two different market segments. The Avon Skin Care line, targeted at the lower end of the mass market, offers modestly priced, daily-use-type products. This line is designed to be 'simple' and appeal to customers who prefer a 'less involved' skin care regime. It is expected to be a beginning step for some consumers' to skin care, and Avon hopes that these customers will eventually move to its higher-scale products. The major competitors in low-end skin care products are Oil of Olay (Oil of Ulan in China), Neutrogena, Ponds, Biore, Almay; there are many others. In coloring products, competitors include Mabelline, Cover Girl, Almay, Revlon, L'Oréal, Oil of Olay, among many others. Other products, such as Anew, target the lower end of the premium segment, where competitors include Estée Lauder, Lançome, Christian Dior, and Clinique. Two major direct marketing competitors, at both the domestic and international levels, are Amway and Mary Kay.

The high-end products have been developed through an ongoing research effort that has resulted in a number of innovations and new products. Avon scientists developed Anew, a skin care cream containing alpha-hydroxy-acid, which provided anti-aging benefits beyond what was available in other products. Its Bio Advance was the first product to use stabilized retinol, a form of vitamin A, and Collagen Booster facilitated the use of vitamin C. In the late 1990s the company obtained US Food and Drug Administration approval of the use of Parsol 1789 to fight damage caused by UVA rays. It used this material in a new Age Block Daytime Defense Cream. The company has 19 laboratories worldwide that develop products and packaging. In addition to its own research staff and independent experts, Avon uses focus groups in evaluating potential new products, and has company employees use the products.

In 1996 Avon spent US$30 million on an advertising campaign, which focused on the Avon Lady, the core of the company's success, and a new product image. Avon is now projected as having a contemporary product with a consistent, high-quality image in all markets. Its advertising program uses celebrities, such as fashion designer Josie Natori and Olympic athlete Jackie Joyner-Kersee. Avon moved away from mature, matronly appearance to updated, sophisticated, and glamorous images. The result is a more vibrant beauty image, similar to other US brand names such as Revlon, Mabelline, and Cover Girl. Also under this campaign, Avon advertised on television for the first time in 20 years, and began direct selling on the Internet in April 1997. Its web site now attracts 300,000 visitors per month.

Avon credits the maintenance of its competitive position to several factors including attractive product designs, high product quality, reasonable prices, company and product image, innovative products, guarantees, and commitment to product satisfaction. The personalized, friendly customer service offered by Avon Ladies is considered a key competitive strength.

Avon does not require its sales representatives to spend money in advance to purchase a starting kit and inventory. As a matter of policy, the company attempts to avoid having representatives use a hard selling approach or hard-core pressure tactics. There is an effort to create a relaxed, approachable, and friendly image through the Avon Ladies and a few gentlemen. The ability to attract and hold an effective direct sales force has been an important factor in Avon's success. For those who like interacting with customers, Avon Lady positions provide opportunities for women to be their own bosses in jobs with flexibility, simplicity, and low stress. For women who wish to move on to more responsible jobs, the company offers career positions and opportunities to move up in the organization. Avon is one of the few companies in the Fortune 500 that has six women on the Board of Directors.

The company emphasizes its international character. Under the Chairman and CEO, policy is developed by a senior management team called the Global Business Council. Members of the Council include the top executives of Avon's Operating Business Units (OBUs), the chief financial and administrative officer, and the president of global marketing. The company groups its operations, by region, into five OBUs: the United States; Asia-Pacific; Mexico-Central America-South America; Brazil-Colombia; and Europe. Each OBU has a headquarters within its respective region.

Avon overseas

Avon's first overseas operation was in 1954 in Venezuela. Its success there motivated the company to continue expansion. It went to Europe in 1957, Australia in 1963, Japan in 1969, Malaysia in 1977,

the Philippines and Thailand in 1978, Taiwan in 1982, and Indonesia in 1988. From 1990 to 1998 Avon entered 18 new markets, mostly in Asia, including China. Avon's products are distributed through subsidiaries in 45 countries and through other marketing channels in 89 additional countries.

Over 65% of Avon's sales earnings come from overseas operations, and the growth of overseas production and sales outpace those in the United States. Rising incomes in Asia during the 1980s and early 1990s led to a greater demand for beauty products there, and encouraged expansion in that area. Additionally, the importance of appearance to the increasing number of Asian women in the workforce added to the number of customers. Analysts also attribute Avon's success in foreign markets, particularly those in developing economies, to the earning opportunities the company offers to women who have little chance to work outside the home or even find a job. Increasing demand had been combined with an expanding number of women interested in direct selling, a key strength of the company.

Overseas operations continue to be Avon's first priority for growth. The economic crisis in 1997 in Asia did not frighten the company. Instead it planned to take advantage of the favourable exchange rate to invest between US$65 and US$75 million to construct manufacturing plants in the Philippines and China. Avon believed that the financial problem in Asia was short term whereas the company is in Asia for the long term.

Global strategies and products

Avon is an example of a company that 'thinks globally and acts locally.' That is, it pursues economies of scale and scope in manufacturing, logistics and marketing by selecting the most cost-effective facility locations and scales of operation on a worldwide basis. Product variations, which increase costs, are limited to those demanded by the various markets served. Overall, it balances the cost-saving potential of standardization with responsiveness to individual market needs in pursuing both profits and market share. Avon has production facilities in 45 countries and a market covering over 135 countries.

Beginning in the 1990s, the company developed 'global product' lines that could be sold in multiple markets, with only limited variations in packaging and marketing to meet differing national requirements. Avon's global products are first developed in the United States and tested in the mass US market. Next, the potential of the product's marketability is validated by Avon's Global Product Council and global market research. Some of the criteria for creating successful global products include market viability in at least six of Avon's major markets, the potential to be among the top three brand names in each market, and the potential to generate at least $75 million in annual sales. Most of Avon's global products are actually sold in 50 to 60 markets simultaneously.

The eight global product lines introduced in the 1990s (Avon Color, Far Away, Rare Gold, Millennia, Natori, Josie, Anew, and Avon Skin Care) have been highly successful. They accounted for 26% of Avon's total sales of cosmetics, fragrances, and toiletries in 1996 and 39% in 1997. Developing global products will continue to be a major emphasis of Avon.

China's overall market and business climate

The Chinese market has grown rapidly since China began its open door policy in the early 1970s. During the following two decades, foreign businesses increased investment and marketing activities in an attempt to attain first mover advantages in this nation of 1.2 billion consumers. The suppression of student protestors in 1989 at Tiananmen Square resulted in the cessation of almost all new foreign investment, but within two years both foreign and domestic investment were again booming.

Although there was a lack of accurate, reliable information on which to base economic forecasts, many economists and businesses believed that China was a promising consumer market in the long run. When Avon was considering a substantial commitment to marketing in China in the early 1990s, the per capita income was below $400 per year. However, there was a growing middle class with a high level of discretionary income. By the mid-1990s consumers in big cities, such as Shanghai, spent up to 80% of their disposable income on entertainment, clothing and cosmetics. According to US Department of Commerce statistics, retail sales in China reached US$297 billion in 1996 as many entrepreneurs, professionals in private companies, and workers in township enterprises became more affluent.

The common cultural background of Chinese people allows, to some extent, product standardization and coordination. Yet regional differences in levels of economic development, infrastructure, consumer purchasing power, distribution, and transportation logistics result in very different levels of market attractiveness in various parts of the country. Fortunately for foreign firms, the Chinese generally regard foreign-made products to be of better quality and a symbol of prestige and status.

One major challenge to foreign business in China is the regulatory uncertainty. New laws, reinterpretation of laws, disagreements between arms of the central government, and differences in national and regional regulations present continuing hazards. In 2001 the State Postal Bureau claimed a law gave them the exclusive right to deliver international express mail. The Ministry of Foreign Trade and Economic Cooperation indicated that a 1995 order by the State Council granted foreign freight forwarders, such as DHL, FedEx, and UPS, the right to do so. In the meantime, postal offices in some parts of China set up roadblocks and confiscated deliveries. In another example, as an inducement to capital investment, the government had offered tax breaks on imported capital equipment at one point, abolished the incentives in 1996, and then restored them in 1998.

The cosmetic and skin care market

Skin care products have a long history in China, but their use was discouraged, and at times prohibited, during much of the Communist period. But with reform and modernization women again began using make-up and skin care products. Cosmetics sales in China grew 40% from 1990 to 1995, reaching a level of US$1.5 billion annually. A department store in Shanghai found that sales in a 100,000-square-foot cosmetic department space were: 10–18% for fragrances, 60–70% for skin care, 20% for color cosmetics, and 0.5% for body care products. In 1996, 70% of cosmetics were sold through state-owned businesses or selling cooperatives. In 1998, 80% of women living in big cities bought cosmetics at large shopping malls and 16% at general department stores or supermarkets. One important factor in the growth of cosmetics sales was the introduction of more expensive, up-scale international cosmetic brands into China.

In spite of the inroads of foreign brands, high-quality local brands still dominate the market. There are around 2800 local cosmetics manufacturers in China, of which over 90% are small in size. Of these companies, 470 now have partial foreign direct investment. The official record of cosmetics imports is around US$23 million per year, but there is a large and unrecorded smuggling operation in southern China. Altogether, there are about 300 brands sold in China, of which the 28 largest dominate the market. Yue-Sai Han, a Coty-backed joint venture, is important in the cosmetic and skin care product market. Kan, the Chinese partner in that joint venture, is a television celebrity and is known as China's 'Barbara Walters.' A Hong Kong-based brand, Cheng Mingming, has also done well in China. Foreign brands are mostly the choice of the younger consumers whereas older or more conservative people prefer domestic brands. Other best-selling foreign brands include Estée Lauder,

Christian Dior, Lançome and Clarins.

Marketing tactics for foreign brands are similar to those used in the United States including the offering of free gift sets. However, while a five-piece gift set is commonly offered by cosmetic companies in the United States, seven-piece gift sets are offered in China. The primary advantage of Chinese-made cosmetics is their lower prices. China levies duties amounting to 120% of the landed price on imported cosmetics.

Direct selling in China

Direct selling is a relatively new concept in China. Avon pioneered direct selling in China beginning in 1990, and was followed by Amway and Mary Kay. The Chinese government knew very little about direct selling and therefore had virtually no control of or regulations on it. China appeared to be a promising opportunity for direct selling for several reasons:

- Direct selling is labor intensive, and China has an abundant supply of labour.
- Direct selling relies on personal contacts for promotion instead of extensive mass advertising (mass advertising does not reach the majority of Chinese consumers).
- Unlike traditional retailing, direct selling does not rely heavily on a well-developed infrastructure for transportation and delivery; China lacks a well-developed infrastructure.
- Direct selling allows China's long-suppressed entrepreneurial spirit and opportunity to develop and creates earning possibilities, especially for women.
- Direct selling is very flexible and the financially conservative Chinese do not have to risk their primary jobs.
- Direct selling relies on personal networking, which is already built into the Chinese culture.
- China has a very large group of financially stable people who are retired by the State in their early 50s but who are interested in seeking more activities that would improve their retired life.

Entering the Chinese market: *Ya fang daojia* (Avon calling home)

Although Avon had over 30 years of experience in a number of countries internationally, entering and operating in China offered new problems as well as successes. The company had experienced an indirect relationship with China since the late 1970s when it had established a regional headquarters in Hong Kong that sourced a wide variety of gifts and decorative products in China. In the mid-1980s, Avon's first attempt to open the Chinese market via official channels in Beijing failed due to a commonly cited problem: Chinese bureaucracy. In 1990, Avon adopted a cautious, short-term approach to China. Going through its Hong Kong connection, the company established a joint venture with the state-owned Guangzhou Cosmetics Company factory. Avon purchased 60% of that joint venture. It was estimated that 60 million people lived within a 100-mile radius of the factory, making it a convenient location for Avon Ladies to order and deliver products. Business in China was an overnight success. Avon sold what was estimated to be six months' supply of inventory in the first 30 days.

In the first year of its operation, 1 million units of cosmetics and skin care products were sold. Sales reached US$4 million in 1991, far beyond Avon's original US$1.5 million target. In 1992, sales grew to more than US$8 million, and 8000 women were working for Avon. Many of them earned 12 times more than typical Chinese women. At that time, Avon operated through a chain of 10 branches in the vicinity of Guangdong, but the area the Avon Ladies covered extended south to Hainan Island and northeast to Fuzhou. China became Avon's first priority in terms of market growth.

In 1994, Avon's sales in China grew to US$20 million. At that time Avon was building and training a 70,000-woman sales force with 15 sales branches in China's southern region. It was also the year in which Avon opened a distribution center in Shanghai as its first move into central China. In 1995, Avon's sales in China climbed to US$40 million and were expected to continue growing.

In 1996, Avon had 40 branches and 27,000 sales representatives, and a total of US$35 million invested in China. Nearly all of the products sold in China were made in China using local materials. Avon also planned another US$35 million investment for a new joint venture with a state factory, which would triple its production capacity in China. On 16 August 1996 Avon opened a branch office in Beijing, signifying further success and commitment to the Chinese market. China was now one of the most important markets for Avon in Asia, and Avon was enjoying government support at both provincial and local levels. In 1997 Avon's sales in China reached US$75 million.

By 1998 Avon had approximately 150,000 sales representatives and over US$200 million invested in China. The representatives in China recruited friends and colleagues, bought in bulk, and distributed products themselves. In the same year Avon extended its operations to Urumqi, the capital of Xinjiang, which later became Avon's fastest-growing market.

In China, Avon's target was the mass market consisting of teen to middle-aged women with adequate discretionary income. It succeeded in China, up until the April 1998 ban, for the following reasons:

- Avon had brand recognition throughout Asia. Many Chinese had learned about Avon from its television commercials in Hong Kong.
- In China, Avon was synonymous with direct selling. Its reputation also came from how it treated sales representatives and employees and its ethical business practices. Avon also taught hygiene, proper dress, and other values to the sales representatives and district managers. More important, Avon taught them personal empowerment and a balance between work and family responsibilities. The company was even able to attract college-educated women into becoming Avon Ladies.
- Avon distinguished itself from other direct selling companies. It used a single-level structure. There was no expensive starter kit that the sales representative had to buy. Avon district managers trained the sales representatives, and then the sales representatives functioned semi-independently afterwards. That is, they took orders, picked up products, and distributed them. There was no product-introduction party necessary or large motivational training conference involved.
- Avon in China specifically promoted the idea of using skin care or make-up products to bring fulfillment and self-confidence to women. Other marketing techniques included a nationwide talent contest. By Chinese standards, this was a rather bold approach. Although it was first greeted with suspicion or even rudeness, the public later accepted it. Avon also reached its goal of raising public awareness of the company.
- Avon in China had strong leaders and talents. For example, Bill Pryor, the former president of Avon in Japan, came out of retirement to work with the company's China sales effort. Andrea Jung, Avon's current President and Chief Executive Officer, was named eighth among *Fortune* magazine's list of the 50 Most Powerful Women in the United States.
- Avon in China had modern offices and facilities. The company imported modern technical and management know-how in production, packaging, computer, and delivery systems to manufacture and distribute products in China. Some of the company's operations incorporated offices, production workshops and warehouses to promote efficiency.
- Avon's ability to build businesses in the markets of developing economies was a key to its success.
- Avon provided enticing export opportunities for the Chinese government. The company planned to export products and ingredients from China to other Asia-Pacific countries, the United States and Europe.

- By manufacturing in China, Avon avoided paying high tariffs, which amounted to 120% of the wholesale cost. Other foreign brands did not always seek a similar advantage.

The company had to meet several challenges in developing its business in China. In its initial years in China, Avon was able to source only 10% of its suppliers from local manufacturers and had to absorb the resulting high import tariffs. Because direct selling was new to the Chinese, extensive training had to be provided. Due to the underdeveloped and unreliable nature of the Chinese transportation and postal systems, Avon had to use its own trucks for transporting supplies to the branch offices. These problems hindered Avon's business development. Another problem was the limited supply of qualified managers, and their fast turnover. Foreign companies in China often struggled with compensation problems for expatriates as demand for executives in China grows rapidly. Last but not least, bureaucrats at local, regional, and national levels had to approve company actions, and the various levels of bureaucracy were not always in agreement. The ground rules for doing business were frustrating and subject to unexpected changes.

Avon did enjoy great success in China, up to the 1998 crisis, as a result of a combination of business approach, attitude, appealing products, good timing, and an appropriate marketing strategy.

The 1998 crisis and its background

Because foreign direct selling companies were doing well in China from the early to mid-1990s, many local direct selling activities cropped up. The Chinese government gradually recognized the need to control this type of business. In 1995 China ordered all direct selling companies to register with the government, but this order was ignored by most of the indigenous companies. The unregulated market continued to concern the Chinese government because unscrupulous direct selling companies were deceiving the public. A number of companies started pyramid schemes. There were also schemes in which dealers sold products to distributors at inflated prices. A herbal-medicine 'dealer' cheated 2300 peasants out of US$170 each in a direct selling operation. In an incident in Hunan Province, 10 people died and more than 100 others were injured when disgruntled representatives in some direct marketing companies rioted. Many indigenous direct sellers went out of business, leaving their dealers with overpriced goods of no interest to consumers.

There were other reasons that the government was concerned about direct selling. First, the government thought that direct selling provided supervisors and district managers with too much freedom to travel around the country. Second, the Chinese government was concerned that there were individuals using the pyramid method to exercise influence on the public and perhaps engage in a scheme to establish sects and cults that could be a threat to the social order. Motivational seminars given by direct selling companies were criticized as superstitious and as encouraging 'excessive hugging'. Mary Kay had to eliminate the word 'God' from its promotional slogan in China and had to stop hiring teachers, soldiers, and party members. Third, the position of sales representatives was perceived to be of relatively low professional status in China. Pursuing such a job lowered the overall image of the primary professions of individuals holding other positions. Fourth, direct selling was enthusiastically received by women who worked in the traditionally more highly respected professions in China, such as education, health and medical care, and the civil service. The notion of earning extra income seemed to reflect dissatisfaction with their current income, and the desire for more money contradicted Communist economic ideology.

These events culminated in a State Council's decision to ban direct selling on 21 April 1998. The new regulation also required that these companies change into conventional retailing and that their distribution centers be converted into retail outlets by 31 October 1998, or they would lose their business licenses. An apparently contradictory existing government regulation, however, prohibited foreign companies from conducting retail business in China.

Charlene Barshefsky, the US Trade Representative, discussed the problem with both company executives and Chinese government officials on a visit to China shortly after the ban was issued. The US companies hoped that Secretary of State Madeline Albright would also discuss the subject with Chinese officials when she visited China, but this did not happen.

The Chinese government did subsequently indicate that it might again allow direct selling in the future. But this did not alleviate the immediate problem, and it is estimated that the ban against direct selling would cost US direct marketing companies a total of US$2 billion in sales.

In the meantime, the US direct sellers had to decide on both immediate courses of action and longer-run strategies in response to the ban. Avon chose to cease sales operations in China immediately, and concentrate on planning for a new approach. One of its competitors decided to continue its direct sales efforts temporarily, perhaps until the October cut-off date.

Questions

1. In what way does Avon follow a global strategy? Does this experience indicate that it should pursue a different strategy?

2. What options did Avon have in responding to China's ban on direct selling?

3. What effects will the use of traditional retailing in China have on Avon's overall marketing strategy?

4. What actions and organizational changes are required by Avon's new marketing strategy in China?

5. What are some other tactics and strategies that Avon could pursue in China?

6. What cultural dimensions of the Chinese people would affect the future success of Avon in China?

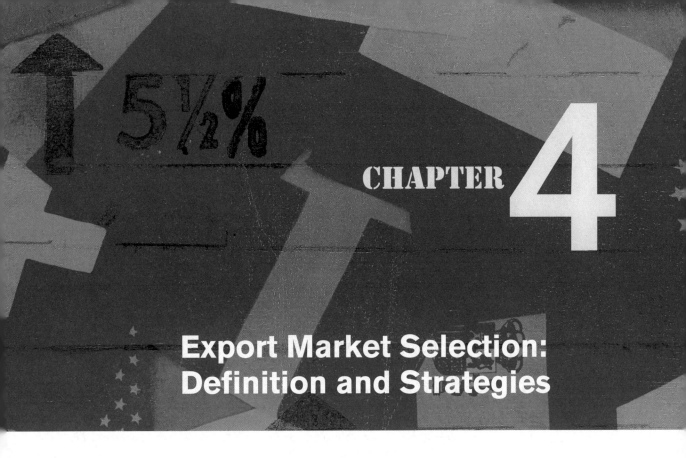

CHAPTER 4

Export Market Selection: Definition and Strategies

4.1 Introduction

The aim of this chapter is to describe alternatives of international, especially export, market strategy decisions and the base of export competition. It deals specifically with the company's selection of international markets, that is, the number and types of countries and market segments. Although the orientation of this chapter is strategic in nature and is aimed at export marketing, the discussion applies equally to non-export entry modes, when entry by such methods is for market penetration (i.e., serving a market) rather than for sourcing.

In ensuring an effective international and export marketing strategy, the process of market selection and direction has at least three major implications for export managers. First, the marketer should not focus only on individual products and their foreign markets; there is the need to consider the role of each product and/or market within a company portfolio. Second, in addition to the traditional focus on the detailed issues of segmentation and differentiation, the process of market selection needs to focus also on the broader strategic measures representing the overall attractiveness of a market and the overall competitive position of the company in that market. Third, export marketers have a key role in the strategic planning process, since many planning tools depend heavily on marketing concepts such as market share, market definition, segmentation, positioning, and the product life cycle. On the one hand, the export manager needs to contribute the more detailed view of foreign markets that strategic planners by necessity cannot have. But on the other hand, the export manager also has to use aggregated measures in order to communicate effectively with company strategists.

An important step in formulating an international marketing strategy is *export market selection*: 'The process of opportunity evaluation leading to the selection of foreign markets in which to compete.' This process requires an appraisal of the fit between a prospective market's requirements and a company's ability to meet those requirements (or conversely, the company's ability to alter the requirements of the market). In addition, market selection cannot be decided on purely marketing grounds; broader considerations of the company's skills, capabilities, and goals require that the market selection process has to be placed in the context of an overall strategy. Identifying the right market(s) for entry, either initially or as part of an expansion program, is important for the following three reasons (Papadopoulos and Jansen, 1994, p. 38):

1. Target market decisions are antecedent to the development of foreign marketing programs and, thus, costs of marketing.
2. The nature and location of its markets will affect a company's ability to co-ordinate them.
3. Establishing bases at appropriate foreign markets can be a major dimension in global positioning strategy.

Exhibit 4.1 presents some examples of insufficient and overlooked markets.

A second decision in marketing strategy, closely related to market selection, is *export market direction*. Should the company seek to *build*, *hold*, *divest* or *abandon* its position in a given foreign market? This decision is almost inextricable from that of market selection because the factors that determine a country's degree of attractiveness for selection are highly relevant to the decision on the company's direction in that market. Furthermore, the build option often leads to selection of additional export markets while the end point of the divest option is the dropping of a market altogether.

Together with strategies for and choices of market entry and operating decisions, market selection and direction are perhaps the most aggregate of export marketing issues. The marketing mix transforms these high level decisions into concrete policies. Segmentation, positioning, and differentiation are some of the traditional analytical tools applied in developing the marketing mix.

EXHIBIT 4.1   Insufficient and overlooked markets

One of the worst errors a company can make is failing to determine if a market exists for its product(s) or service(s) prior to market entry. The market may not be as promising as anticipated or there may have been inadequate market assessment studies performed. For example, Asia represents a problem in assessment in market size as the exact size of its middle class is difficult to measure as purchasing power and tastes vary. A widely quoted study in the late 1990s by the Marketing Partnership in Manila divided these consumers into three groups: *superhaves* with annual household income above US $30,000, *have-somes* with incomes above US $18,000, and *near-haves* who had newly crossed over the poverty line into consumption (Tripathi *et al.*, 1998). It was estimated that by the year 2000 there would be 16 million, 75 million and 150 million nonJapanese Asians in the superhaves, have-somes, and near-haves groups, respectively. By mid-1998 it was clear that such estimates were grossly overstated.

China (PRC) represents a country where a company can easily overstate market size. Many companies look at China as having more than 1.3 billion people in the marketplace. In the aggregate, this is probably so. But the real market for many products companies are selling is more like 200 million–250 million middle-class, urban residents in the major cities along the east coast (Andruss, 2001, p. 11).

The other side of this is *overlooked markets*. An example would be the 4 billion people worldwide who live in abject poverty, subsisting on less than US$1500 per year. To some foresighted companies such as Hewlett-Packard and Unilever, and Citibank, these are underserved markets in Africa, Asia, eastern Europe, Latin America and the Middle East where a profit can be made while having a positive impact on the sustainable livelihoods of people not usually considered potential customers. These people rarely have extra cash, often live in remote areas where they shop at small kiosks, and many have low literacy. In order to be successful, companies will be required to form unconventional partnerships – with entities ranging from local governments to nonprofit organizations to pop stars – to gain the community's trust and understand the environmental, infrastructure and political issues that may affect business. Being able to provide affordable, high-quality products and services often means new approaches to marketing – new packaging and pricing structures, and using unfamiliar distribution structures. In order to learn about this rather large global segment, traditional marketing research techniques will have to be modified and adapted to the population. For example, where literacy is low, researchers should use visual rather than numeric and verbal scales.

There are numerous examples of individual company mistakes based on insufficient markets (Ricks, 1999). One company tried to market aerosol spray furniture polish in a less developed country, based on analysis that average income levels were at a level that the population could afford the product. But the wealth was concentrated in the hands of relatively few so the average measure was misleading. A US company is reported to have shipped a large quantity of ketchup to Japan when it learned that the product was not available there. The size of the market and its affluence was very tempting. The firm had not determined why ketchup was not being sold in Japan. Had it done even elementary market analysis it would have found that the condiment of choice was soy sauce.

The lessons to be learned are few and simple. Never assume that a market is of sufficient size to make it profitable to enter just because it has a large number of people. There is no substitute for performing a formal analysis of a market. Formal market analysis is discussed in Chapter 5.

4.2 Market definition and segmentation

Market definition is not a mechanical exercise, but a crucial and complex component of export marketing strategy. Correct market definition is obviously crucial for the measurement of share and other indicators of performance, for the specification of target customers and their needs, and for the recognition of important competitors.

Issues of market definition lead inevitably into issues of *market segmentation*. Given the heterogeneity of most markets, segmentation means breaking down the market for a particular product or service into segments of customers that differ in terms of their response to marketing strategies. By doing so, the firm can tailor its marketing policies to the need of each specific segment, hoping to obtain greater profits than are possible by following a uniform strategy aimed at the entire market. For example, on the basis of language only, there are French, German, and Italian-based segments in Switzerland. As another example, consider the United

States where ethnic background is the basis for many potential segments in different areas of the country including Hispanic, Irish, African–American, Chinese, Italian, Korean, and other Southeast Asian areas. Yet another example comes from China where by 2002 average income per capita was US$1000 and rising. More than 25% of its 1.3 billion people earned more than US$2000. If purchasing-power parity is the measure, China's per capita income was US$5500 (*The Economist*, 2003, p. 53). There are wide differences within China. For example, in the year 2000, average income per capita of rural dwellers was less than US$300, but average income in Beijing was US$3000, and in Shanghai it was US$4000 (Andruss, 2001, p. 11). Obviously, using purchasing-power parity income would have been much greater in these cities. For China, it should be recognized that it is several fragmented, regional markets that can be further broken down into niche markets based on cities, rural vs urban, types of people, and income levels (Andruss, 2001, p. 11). A study in the late 1990s of China's urban consumers identified four market segments based on income: (1) working poor (55%), (2) salary class (25%), (3) little rich (15%), (4) yuppies (5%). These segments were distinctive in their demographics, psychographics, lifestyles, media usage, and consumption patterns (Ciu and Liu, 2001). One other characteristic to consider is accessibility. China's rural dwellers are not easily accessed. Nor are the 10 million (10% of the population) Indian people of Mexico. There are 19 major groups of indigenous people in Mexico, and 59 linguistic groups among them (*The Economist*, 2001, p. 33). Trying to take advantage of segmentation on these bases would, at best, be extremely difficult.

A major strength of market segmentation is that it can generate specialization. At the same time, segmentation involves costs, risks, and possible weaknesses in some cases, especially where accessibility is not easy.

In export marketing a common way of defining and describing markets is in terms of export countries. This is only one level out of an immense number of potential market levels. To be of value, analysis of market behavior should be conducted at multi levels including such dimensions as channels, customer segments, or use occasions as well as the geographic dimension. Market definitions are often made on the basis of only one dimension (e.g., customer groups) which may be in conflict with definitions based on other dimensions (e.g., product function). Competitors also define markets, and their definitions often may not coincide with each other. Ignoring competitors' definitions may result in both lost opportunities and bases for future competitive action. For yet another way, see Exhibit 4.2.

Eiffel Tower, Paris, France

EXHIBIT 4.2   What is a European customer?

Is there such a thing as a European customer? One would think there is on the basis of the Single European Act of 1987, which forms the foundation for the present European Union. It often refers to the creation and completion of the so-called *single market*. According to Lynch (1994, Ch. 4), to clarify the geographical market in which a company operates, it is useful to specify five positions along the continuum from local markets to global markets. These are shown in Figure 4.1.

As is shown, European customers fall into the three markets on the right of the figure.

Assume that these are European consumers; what does this really mean? Does it mean, for example, that there is a single market – even with a single currency in most of the nations – of millions of people who have homogeneous wants, etc.? This is highly unlikely! The concept of the European customer is one of *geographical location* only.

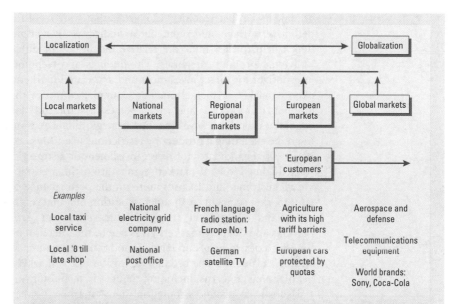

FIGURE 4.1

Continuum of geographic markets

From a marketing perspective there are pan-European market *segments* that are reachable, viable, and different. Each segment has common needs. For example, there is a Euroteen segment (Bertagnoli, 2001). These Euroteens are wearing US fashions, eating at US fast-food restaurants, listening to US music, and are concerned about what their peers think. But they also have strong national loyalties. There is a growing purchasing power of teens in Europe. The group is not homogeneous, and according to Marian Salzman, Global Director of Strategic Planning for the global advertising agency Euro RSCG Worldwide: 'it's virtually impossible to standardize findings across borders ... Generalizations [are] highly superficial at best and grossly inadequate at worst' (cited in Bertagnoli, 2001, p. 15). A key consideration in marketing to European teens is the differences in national attitudes that affect how marketing messages are received in different countries.

How useful are attempts to categorize Europeans? A major issue from the exporter's perspective is whether such groups can be reached. For example, how can one market to a Euro-moralist segment when many languages are spoken and different media 'used' by members of the segment? Such approaches to segmenting Europe are at best highly questionable. There is no evidence that decision making will get better and that the people's needs will be better served by export marketers.

To what extent will all this change with the expanded European Union that incorporates central and eastern European countries? At best, the area will become even more heterogenous!

An analysis of marketing a product or service should be undertaken within every relevant market segment and at higher levels of analysis across market segments, markets, and countries. Evaluating the company's performance or potential for a given product within the boundaries of a market segment provides an indication of the interrelationship among the products offered by a number of competitors. At this level of analysis interest is centered on the individual customer. The single market segment's perception is important to marketers for determining market boundaries. A narrow definition can satisfy the short-term, tactical concerns of the marketing mix.

Product mix (i.e., structural pattern of imports) may also define markets. Green and Srivastava (1985) used cluster analysis to group 80 nations on the basis of their imports (18 product categories, two-digit SITC, were used), and concluded that there are dangers in segmenting international markets on single geographic or demographic bases. The resulting 12 clusters that were identified are not to be viewed as definitive in their own right, but as indicative of complex interactions that occur which help to determine the relative magnitude of different national markets for individual product categories. The findings and techniques used in this study are appropriate for direct investment and associated marketing activities as well as for export market segmentation. For example, countries that import relatively large amounts of a product and which possess a sufficiently large market may represent candidates for direct investment or strategic alliances. Similarly, large countries that might be excluding a product by restrictions (e.g., Mexico's past behavior) may also be potential candidates for direct investment or a strategic alliance.

At higher levels of market segmentation the analysis tends to ignore the individual customer and focuses more on the performance of each product in its relevant market segment. A broader definition of a market then results in a dilution of effort and competence in the business's current activities. Defining product markets and country markets gives rise to the selection of the most attractive combinations of products and markets and thus to resource allocation of *a portfolio of strategic elements*. The broader definition of the market reflects long-term, strategic planning concerns, including changes in technology, price relationships, potential substitute products, potential 'new' markets, and so on. In identifying new opportunities or competitive threats, the market definition must not only reflect *the served market*, e.g., the customers to whom the business directs its marketing effort, but also those portions of the unserved market that in the long run are critical for the competitive success of the company.

4.2.1 Export market segmentation

The issues of segmentation are at least as important, and often more important, for export markets as for domestic markets. Because of differences in the economic, cultural and political environments between countries, international markets tend to be more heterogeneous than domestic markets. The range of income levels and the diversity of lifestyles and of social behavior are likely to be significantly greater when considering the world as opposed to a national market. The existence of such heterogeneity provides substantial potentials for identifying different segments.

Given limited financial and organizational resources, the export firm should try to identify the most attractive market segments that it can serve in terms of segment preferences, patterns of competition, and company strengths. This offers several benefits including better market opportunities in terms of competitive positioning, tailoring marketing programs to meet the needs of different customer segments, and clearer criteria in allocating marketing funds to the different segments in line with their likely levels of purchase response. But in identifying market segments these benefits have to be greater than the costs of reaching them with the company's marketing strategies.

There are many possible ways to segment on a worldwide basis, and applying mixed criteria can create the most meaningful segments. For example, in selling sewing machines the use of the level of economic development (measured by, say, GNP or GDP per capita) as a base for country segmentation could identify export markets with high purchasing power but with no or, at most, insignificant agricultural sectors. Thus, more complex and combined measures have to be used, including, for example, the importance and composition of the agricultural sectors, purchasing powers, education levels, level of technology, buying decision criteria, and so forth.

It is important to note that any decision to segment on a particular basis should be evaluated in terms of the following.

Measurability

Measurability is the degree to which segments can be *identified* and to which the size and purchasing power of the segments can be measured. In export marketing management, important qualitative indicators such as cultural characteristics are intuitively appealing bases for country segmentation, but difficult to use due to conceptual and measurement problems. Suppose a clothing manufacturer from Hong Kong wanted to export to the EU countries and was interested in the following two segments based on age: 16–24 years, 25–40 years. The company must be able to identify which potential consumers belong in each group and must be able to measure the size and, say, income of each group. If these age categories do not correspond to those used in the various countries, which may differ among themselves, then it would be difficult to assess the size and purchasing power of each group.

Accessibility

Accessibility is the degree to which the resulting segments can be effectively reached and served. In the case of China, for example, not only is it difficult to access per se its rural segment, but the composition of it also changes as there is migration from the country to the cities, particularly of younger people. Such migration is a characteristic of Asia in general, and is one of the eight megatrends identified for the region by Naisbitt (1996) in the mid-1990s. In export marketing, communication problems pose distinct difficulties in reaching the end user (often also the foreign distributor) because of inadequate language skills, nationalistic attitudes, the difficulties for an exporter in understanding foreign media systems (structure and format), and so on. Continuing with the Hong Kong clothing company manufacturer, are there media that can be used to reach the two segments efficiently and effectively? It is very unlikely there are print or broadcast media that are read or listened to, by only members of the segments. Thus, some promotion – or information providing – cost would be wasted. Moreover, as suggested in Exhibit 4.2, there are differences in the segments between the countries.

Profitability

Profitability is the degree to which the resulting segments are large and/or profitable enough to be worth considering for separate marketing attention. In export marketing there can be excessively high costs involved in segmenting markets because of necessary adaptation to local markets' specific needs and demands. Market conditional factors such as the imposition of tariffs or taxes on certain goods create a basis for product modifications. Product conditional factors, such as specific legal restrictions (patent agreements, quality standards, and controls) may also influence product specification and costs. The company has to realize that segmental export marketing is expensive, and there is a trade-off between profits and costs. If costs of export tend to be high, the segments may be approachable by investment or strategic alliance. For the Hong Kong manufacturer one question here is whether the two age segments in the European countries are large enough to warrant spending funds to market its product line.

Actionability

Actionability is the degree to which effective programs can be formulated for attracting and serving the segments. Segments that are measurable, accessible, and potentially profitable are 'worthless' as segments unless marketing programs can be developed and implemented for each of them. In addition, to be effective the segments need to respond differentially to marketing efforts. The Hong Kong clothing manufacturer needs to assess whether it has the resources and organization capable of developing and implementing the needed marketing program(s) for the segments. Profitability will depend in part on how responsive the two segments are to the company's marketing efforts.

4.2.2 Bases of segmentation

Ayers Rock, Northern
Territory, Australia

A classification scheme of various bases for export market segmentation is shown in Table 4.1. It is evident that the relevance of any particular criteria for segmentation will depend on the specific market situation and company characteristics, and the suggested criteria are only possible elements to be considered. Two types of segmentation variables are distinguished – *general market* indicators and *specific product* indicators – and these are viewed from both country and customer market levels. General market indicators are those that do not vary across purchase situations, whereas specific product indicators vary with the individual purchase situation or particular product.

It is clear that there are many different bases upon which international markets can be segmented. An example of psychographic segmentation is shown in Exhibit 4.3 which relates soft drink brands to lifestyle characteristics in the Australian market. In addition to 'specific' segmentation (i.e., for a product class or for a company), many schema have been proposed that are more general in nature. For example, a study in the mid-1990s by Roper Starch Worldwide, Inc. on global consumer trends identified the following four major shopping styles of consumers (Shermach, 1995):

- *Deal Makers* (29%): well educated, median age of 32, with average affluence and employment; this group concentrates on the process of buying.
- *Price Seekers* (27%): the highest proportion of retirees, the lowest education level, tends to be female, with an average level of affluence.
- *Brand Loyalists* (23%): the least affluent, mostly male, median age of 36, with average education and employment.
- *Luxury Innovators* (21%): seek new prestigious brands, are the most educated and affluent shoppers, mostly male, median age of 32, with the highest proportion of executives and other professionals.

Looking at specific areas of the world, deal makers predominate in the United States (with price seekers nearly as prevalent), Asia, Latin America, and the Middle East. In contrast, price seekers predominate in Japan and Europe.

TABLE 4.1	General market indicators	Specific product indicators
Bases for export market segmentation		
Country market level	Demographic and population characteristics Socio-economic characteristics Political characteristics Cultural characteristics	Economic and legal constraints Market conditions Product-bound culture and lifestyle characteristics
Customer market level	Demographic characteristics: age, gender, life cycle, religion, nationality, etc. Socio-economic characteristics: income, occupation, education, etc. Psychographic characteristics: personality	Behavioral characteristics: consumption and use patterns, attitudes, loyalty patterns, benefits sought, etc.

EXHIBIT 4.3	An illustration of psychographic segmentation

Export markets can often be segmented on the basis of psychographics including lifestyles. A study by a commercial research house of the Australian market for soft drinks examined 18 lifestyle dimensions and how each related to the brand of soft drink consumed most often. A total of 12 brands were identified. So-called 'lifestyle maps' were constructed that showed how consumers of particular brands rate the lifestyle characteristics. These maps were constructed by using factor analysis (three factors accounting for 78% of total variance of brand positioning), and a metric multidimensional scaling technique.

TABLE 4.2 Lifestyle characteristics and brands

	Lifestyle characteristic	
Brand	**Positively related**	**Negatively related**
Solo	Adventure seeker Fashion conscious Achievement motivated Impulsive Extrovert Australian chauvinist Upward mobility Quality experience seeker	Self-asserting Authoritarian Economic conservative Social conservative Job involvement
Loys	Social conservative Authoritarian Self-asserting Cynical	Upward mobility Quality experience seeker Australian chauvinist Achievement motivated Adventure seeker Critical consumer Environmentalist Fashion conscious Family cohesion Job involvement
Marchants	Thrifty consumer	Environmentalist Extrovert Economic conservative Quality experience seeker Impulsive Job involvement Cynical Upward mobility
Schweppes	Job involvement Economic conservative Environmentalist	
Shelleys	Environmentalist	
Swing	Cynical Extrovert Social conservative	Family cohesion Thrifty consumer Critical consumer Australian chauvinist
Tab	Thrifty consumer Family cohesion Critical consumer Job involvement Environmentalist Australian chauvinist	Cynical Extrovert Social conservative

Table 4.2 shows the lifestyle characteristics that were associated with the respective brands of soft drink in order of importance.

Other brands were included (Coca-Cola, Cottees, Fanta, Leed, and Torax) but were not closely associated with any of the lifestyle characteristics.

The market map for this study is for the total market covering all of Australia. Other bases for segmentation could have been used, such as demographics or geography.

The advertising agency Backer, Spielvogel Bates Worldwide identified five distinct consumer segments globally, based on studying 15,000 adults in 14 countries on five continents. The research they conducted found global similarities in values, attitudes, and actual purchasing patterns. The consumers were then defined by demographics. The first group, called *strivers*, has a median age of 31 and leads active lives. They are under stress most of the time and prefer products and services that are sources of instant gratification. Another group, *achievers*, is also young but its members have already found the success they seek. They are affluent, assertive, and society's opinion and style leaders. Achievers value status and quality in the brands they buy, and are largely responsible for setting trends. The *pressured* are mainly women, in every age group, who find it extremely difficult to manage all the problems in their lives. They have little time for enjoyment. A fourth segment are older consumers who live comfortably, the *adapters*. They recognize and respect new ideas without losing sight of their own values. They are willing to try new products that enrich their lives. Finally, *traditionals* embody the oldest values of their countries and cultures. They are resistant to change, and they are content with the familiar products.

Values have been used to define other broad schemes for consumer segmentation. Although these typically have been developed based on consumers in one country they are purported to be applicable to consumers in all countries. In fact, values tend to reveal cross-cultural differences. One approach to the use of values as a segmentation tool in international marketing involves using the List of Values (LOV), which measures eight values that people feel are relevant to them (Kahle *et al.*, 1987). These values are a sense of belonging, fun and enjoyment, warm relationships, self-fulfillment, being well-respected, a sense of accomplishment, security, and self-respect. Specific application areas for this schema, as well as others, include environmental scanning, product introduction and positioning, and advertising. Studies have been done in many nations of the world in Europe, North America, South America, and Asia (Kahle *et al.*, 1999; Albaum *et al.*, 2004). A similar schema based on values is shown in Exhibit 4.4.

EXHIBIT 4.4   Core values segmentation

Is it nationality, culture, or personal values that makes, say, Austria so different from China or the Philippines? The answer is: *It depends*. Each of the three factors plays a role in determining the nature and development of global consumer markets. But the relative importance of each depends upon the product/service category the international marketer is dealing with.

Core values are key ingredients in all of this. In a study conducted in the late 1990s Roper Starch Worldwide interviewed 1000 adults, residing in 35 countries (Miller, 1998). One task was for these adults to rank 56 values in terms of the importance they hold as guiding principles in their lives. Six global values segments were identified, residing in all 35 countries, but to varying extents in each. The segments are:

- *Strivers*: the largest group; slightly more likely to be male, and they place more emphasis on material and professional goals than the other groups; about one in three in developing Asia and one in four in Russia and developed Asia fall in this group.
- *Devouts*: 22% of adults are in this group, which includes more women than men; tradition and duty are very important; most common in developing Asia and the Middle Eastern and African countries; least common in developed Asia and Europe.
- *Altruists*: 18% of all adults fall into this group, with slightly more females then males; are interested in social issues and the welfare of society; median age is 44, making this group older; more live in Latin America and Russia than in other countries.
- *Intimates*: comprising 15% of the world's population, this group values close personal relationships and family above all else; about equally split between the genders; one in four Americans and Europeans fall in this group compared to just 7% in developing Asia.
- *Fun Seekers*: accounts for about 12% of the world's population, although found in disproportionate numbers in developed Asia; the youngest group, with males comprising about 8 percentage points more than females.
- *Creatives*: the smallest, with 10% of the world's population; have a strong interest in education, knowledge, and technology; more common in Latin America and Europe; has a balanced gender mix.

Some values cut across many categories and countries, although most people tend to fall into a particular category. People in different segments tend to engage in different activities, buy different products and use different media for information acquisition. This, of course, is the essence of segmentation, targeting and positioning!

Source: Miller, 1998

Sometimes companies will need to rethink strategies and adjust product/market portfolios when changes occur in market segments. To illustrate this phenomenon Vandermerwe (1990) studied the youth segment (15–24 years of age) in Japan, the United States, and Europe. Her research showed this group to be decreasing in size but having increasing money and influence in the marketplace. Using a 2×2 (new/existing) product/market mix a useful framework is provided for structuring and directing necessary changes. The four strategies are explained as follows:

1. **Increase penetration (existing products and markets).** This strategy is aimed at obtaining more young consumers by persuading them to switch brands or products. Particularly common in high-growth markets, this strategy requires a sophisticated understanding of purchase criteria and a competitive marketing effort aimed at carefully defined segments. Rather than mere promotion and 'hard sell,' a combination of all elements of the marketing mix is needed to gain a competitive edge. For example, banks in the United Kingdom in the late 1980s were fighting for market penetration, having seen the teenage savings market expand to £1 billion annually. They offered special accounts requiring no minimum investment, generous interest rates on balances, and free cash cards allowing teenagers to withdraw money around the clock. To entice these consumers to open checking accounts, they offered gifts such as free calculators or electronic personal organizers.

2. **Develop products (new products in existing markets).** The objective is to increase the youth market by improving product performance using new technologies. This approach requires carefully selected and planned research, development, and marketing programs for specific untouched niches. Companies

successful at this strategy have involved youth consumers in product design and other marketing decisions. In the early 1980s the Japanese electronics company Nintendo launched 'Famicon,' a family computer specifically for games. The selling price was ¥14,800, the amount typically received by Japanese teenagers on New Year's Day. Whittle Communications, in a joint venture with *Time*, launched a 12-minute news program specifically for the teenage audience, which was distributed through the schools.

3. **Extend markets (existing products in new markets).** To counter the decline of the youth market, some firms are entering new market segments with core product offerings. Because baby boomers are similar in many characteristics to youth consumers in many markets, this strategy is becoming increasingly feasible. As one executive from Benetton said, 'People are getting younger, acting younger, and dressing younger.' Levi Strauss developed a new line of jeans for those aged over 40 with styles adapted to heavier body shapes. Nintendo started making its products for a wider adult market group. Changes included making the games more sophisticated and varying advertising plans to reach adults.

4. **Widen activities (new products and markets).** When this is done a company is looking for new product and market opportunities. This strategy often requires the largest amount of investment and is most successful when synergies can be found with current operations. Kellogg, a cereal company once geared mostly to children, invested heavily in developing adult fiber products, new frozen foods for the dual-working family, and new diet products.

The advertising agency DMB&B studied the cultural attitudes and consumer behavior of more than 6500 teenagers in 26 countries (Miller, 1995). The results indicated that in the mid-1990s teenagers throughout the world led very similar lives. In fact, they could be viewed as truly global consumers.

This is a group that has grown up with MTV. Even though teenagers appear to be a global segment, there will still be regional and local differences that require subtle differentiations in marketing, as indicated in Exhibit 4.2. There are certain fundamental values that teenagers around the globe share, but opponents to the global teenager idea argue that the cultural differences are so prominent that it is very difficult to speak in one voice throughout the world.

4.3 Market expansion/selection process, procedure, and strategy

The choice of a market expansion policy is a key strategic option in export marketing and provides the foundation for decisions about the elements of the export marketing mix. Expansion strategies deal with issues on how the company identifies and analyzes the selection of export markets over time, determining the *number* of markets in which to operate and the desired *characteristics* of these markets. An expansion policy can be seen in several dimensions including the nature of market research activities in choosing export markets, the procedures of screening export markets, and the ways of allocating efforts and resources among different export markets. The purpose of this section is to present a framework for analysis of alternative market expansion strategies.

4.3.1 Market selection process: reactive vs proactive approaches

Many companies have moved into exporting and international marketing in a piecemeal and unplanned manner. The *reactive market selection* approach characterizes a situation where the exporter acts passively in choosing markets by filling unsolicited orders or awaits initiatives on the part of foreign buyers, foreign representatives (importers, agents, and so on) or other export change agents who indirectly select the market for the company. The selection process then remains very informal, unsystematic and purchase oriented, making export (and also other types of international) marketing more or less sporadic. With this approach, the exporter is *responding* to a situation that has emerged.

Typical approaches used with passive market selection are inquiries from foreign firms either through active buying on their part or through contacts established by indirect media used by the exporter in the home country for purposes of attracting the attention of foreigners. Exporters may advertise or be listed in national or subnational export directories; they may also participate in internationally oriented fairs and/or exhibitions in the home country. Developing company web sites is increasing in importance as we move further into the 21st century. In one survey of manufacturers in the United States it was reported that 41.1% of the responding regular exporters and 62.4% of sporadic exporters started export by reacting to an unsolicited inquiry or order from a buyer or intermediary efforts (Samiee and Walters, 1991). Also, for a small and open economy such as Denmark empirical evidence shows that Danish manufacturer exporters passively select export markets. In a study of such Danish exporters 42% of the responding companies started export by filling an unsolicited order (Strandskov, 1986).

Market selection by passive means has been primarily used by small and medium-sized exporters with little or no experience even though larger and more experienced exporters may find the strategy useful in certain cases (for example when an unsolicited order comes from a market never before exported to by the company). One of the driving motives is short-term profit, which is often provided very easily by the low costs usually associated with filling an unsolicited order.

The *proactive market selection* approach is, in contrast to the reactive approach, marketing oriented. The exporter is active in initiating the selection of foreign markets and the further customer segmentation of these markets. Since active market selection is systematic and formalized, rather heavy organizational burdens are put on the exporter requiring personnel with international experience and access to international market information, including using the Internet, to access potential buyers' web sites.

Proactive market selection is a *formal* process. As such it then may involve systematic market research, and even one or more visits abroad, such visits being to assess the potential market. There is another approach to finding markets that is used widely. More or less *informally*, an executive may select a foreign market on the basis of discussion with a business acquaintance who has experience in a particular market or the executive may 'stumble' on the opportunity while on holiday. For every new export market uncovered by systematic market research there are more that are developed on a more intuitive basis. With formal export market research being very costly this may not be such a bad way of finding some types of markets.

Obviously there are no clearcut divisions between the reactive and proactive approaches since many exporters will tend to apply the proactive strategy to what are considered primary markets and the reactive strategy to what the company considers to be secondary or marginal markets. Papadopoulos and Jansen (1994) report that many studies have shown that most managers, whether reacting to an inquiry or proactively seeking an opportunity, are heavily influenced by one or more of the following:

- *psychic distance* – feeling of uncertainty about foreign markets, and of the perceived difficulty of finding information about them;
- *cultural distance* – the perceived differences between the manager's own and the destination culture;
- *geographic distance* – proximity.

Exhibit 4.5 gives one viewpoint regarding distance.

EXHIBIT 4.5 Distance: psychic, cultural, psychological?

When considering which foreign markets to enter, the international/exporter marketer considers many variables. One such variable is how close the potential market area is to the marketer's home country. Although geographic proximity may be a keen determinant, often what has come to be known as *psychic, cultural,* or *psychological* distance may be even more important. Many exporters and other international marketers prefer to enter market areas that are not too distant from their home markets on these bases. To them, the risk is less when entering a market they might know more about because of similarities between it and the home country.

Over time, the use of these three concepts has become interchangeable by most authors. However, psychic and cultural distance – as originally defined – are distinct phenomena. Psychological distance has been developed as another name for psychic distance as it is now viewed. Psychic distance was defined as the difference in perceptions between buyer and seller regarding either needs or offers (Hallen and Wiedersheim-Paul, 1984), and is strongly influenced by culture. In contrast, cultural distance was meant to look at differences in language, political systems, educational levels, and other culture-based dimensions. Today, psychic (psychological) distance between countries encompasses differences in many things including culture, history, and economic and industrial development.

In the late 1980s Kogut and Singh (1988) devised a formula to measure psychic distance between the United States and various countries based on Hofstede's (2001) cultural dimensions of power distance, individualism/collectivism, masculinity/femininity, and uncertainty avoidance. Since then, Fletcher and Bohn (1998) have added the fifth cultural dimension – Confucian dynamism, now called long-term orientation (Hofstede and Bond, 1988) – and modified the formula to measure psychic distance between Australia and a number of countries. The smaller the index number the closer the country to Australia. Examples of the index are United States (0.1), Great Britain and Canada (0.6), New Zealand (0.7), Sweden (8.8), Japan (15.2), Hong Kong (20.5), and Panama (31.4).

4.3.2 Market selection procedures: expansive vs contractible methods

When implementing a proactive, or initiative-based, market selection policy, two distinct procedures for screening export markets can be applied: expansive or contractible methods.

Expansive methods

In general, this approach takes as its starting point the home market or the existing market core. Market selection over time is based upon similarities between the national market structures of a political, social, economic, or cultural nature, so that the export marketer expands from one market to the next, introducing a minimum of further adaptation to the product as well as other export marketing parameters. This is a type of experience-based market selection.

Among the national market characteristics either environmental proximity or trade policy proximity can determine the market selection process. In the first case, immediate neighboring markets seem to be the optimal expansion area because of a high degree of similarity in economic, political, sociological, and cultural standing, therefore making the marketing program more or less identical in these markets. Often this policy is referred to as the *nearest neighbor* approach, which is a type of clustering or grouping of markets based on geographic proximity. In marketing to a nearest neighbor the marketer may or may not adapt products and/or segments. The more general clustering market selection method presupposes that a company has one single market that can be treated as the base market area. The base market is selected either because it represents the company's strongest marketing center or because it is intended to turn into the focal point for export marketing. Therefore, the foundation for clustering markets is a marketing opportunity in its own right, often based on qualitative environmental factors measuring how close other markets come to the base.

Striking illustrations are the heavy trade propensity among neighboring countries in the Scandinavian area (Denmark, Norway, and Sweden), the British Isles (United Kingdom and Ireland), the South Pacific area (Australia and New Zealand), and the North American continent (United States, Canada, and Mexico). Other illustrative clusters can be the North African countries (Algeria, Egypt, Libya, Morocco, and Tunisia), Arab Gulf States (Bahrain, Kuwait, Oman, Qatar, and United Arab Emirates), the Andean countries (Bolivia, Chile, Ecuador, Colombia, and Peru), and different Asian countries (e.g., Malaysia and Singapore).

One final cluster can illustrate trade policy proximity as well. This cluster has established a common market and economic union structure. In a European context, the EU is a relevant illustration. Being located inside a trade bloc it is only natural for an exporter to look for market opportunities first in markets where Customs duties and other trade policy measures have been or are in the process of being harmonized or eliminated, before looking outside. From a trade policy point of view the exporter has essentially a home market situation in all member countries. Of course, other barriers may still exist, such as cultural and technical barriers.

In choosing a base for clustering markets other considerations are important. For example, if a company wants to penetrate simultaneously up to as many as five country markets, establishing an export sales branch in one of the markets should be seriously considered. In this case, tax conditions are important elements to look at. A sales office established in a small country such as Switzerland could function as an export base to markets such as Germany, France, Italy, and The Netherlands – each having a high market potential. Because of tax benefits, Switzerland could be the best location for a foreign sales branch but, as a benchmark for clustering markets, the choice may not be particularly good, due to the different national market characteristics that have to be served. On the other hand, choosing a large country such as China as a benchmark for clustering markets in Southeast Asia would be understandable. In marketing terms China is still a 'desert' in that it is difficult to measure, it is not fully accessible and purchasing power is quite low.

On a more formalized basis, the multivariate statistical technique of *cluster analysis* has been used to group countries that are similar. For example,

Papadopoulos and Jansen (1994) used 27 variables representing seven environmental factors to cluster 100 countries into four groups. This study involved use of the so-called *temperature-gradient approach*, in which countries are classified as *super hot*, *hot*, *moderate* or *cold*, on the basis of a composite evaluation of seven variables: political stability, market opportunity, economic development and performance, cultural unity, legal barriers, physiographic barriers, and geo-cultural distance. As one moves from super hot to the cold clusters, markets become poorer, GNP per capita declines, economic indicators such as steel and energy consumption decrease, ethnic homogeneity declines, legal and geographic barriers increase, and cultures tend to differ. Table 4.3 lists the countries by cluster.

TABLE 4.3			
Country placement in temperature-gradient clusters			

Super hot			
United States			
Hot			
Belgium	Ireland	Norway	
Denmark	Italy	Singapore	
France	Japan	Sweden	
Germany	Luxembourg	Switzerland	
Hong Kong	Netherlands	United Kingdom	
Moderate			
Argentina	Finland	Portugal	
Australia	Greece	Saudi Arabia	
Austria	Jamaica	South Korea	
Bolivia	Mexico	Spain	
Chile	New Zealand	Turkey	
Ecuador	Panama	Uruguay	
Egypt	Paraguay	Venezuela	
Cold			
Brazil	Malaysia	Peru	
Indonesia	Morocco	Philippines	
India	Nigeria	Senegal	
Kenya	Pakistan		

Source: Papadopoulos and Jansen, 1994, p. 42

Analyses such as these are quite general, and they are best suited as starting points for individual company analyses. A more product-specific study classified 173 countries and territories on the basis of market potential using seven screening criteria (Russow, 1992). The seven criteria are market size growth (product-specific), trade (product-specific), indirect market size, level of economic development, population density, infrastructure and capital spending. The analysis was done for six products. Cluster analysis applied to data pertaining to calculators, for example, generated eight country clusters.

Closely related to the proximity principles just presented is the analogy principle, which is based on similarities in market trends between markets as related to complementary or substitutable products. When direct market data cannot be collected, indirect data relevant for analogies can be introduced for market selection purposes.

Contractible methods

When using a contractible method the optimal market selection starts with the total number, or a large number, of national markets, which are eventually broken down into regional groupings on the basis of political, economic, language, or other criteria. Contractible methods involve a systematic screening of all markets leading to immediate elimination of the least promising markets and to further investigation of those markets that are more promising. In doing so, relevant elimination or 'knock-out' factors have to be stipulated. Two sets of factors, as discussed previously, are: (1) general market indicators and (2) specific product indicators. An example of a contractible method is presented in Figure 4.2.

Although the overall approach appears to be complex, the procedure involves three stages:

1. Preliminary screening criteria for examining countries are identified. The result is a list of feasible countries.
2. The second stage determines which country characteristics are to be used in evaluating marketing opportunities and how each should be weighted. Four

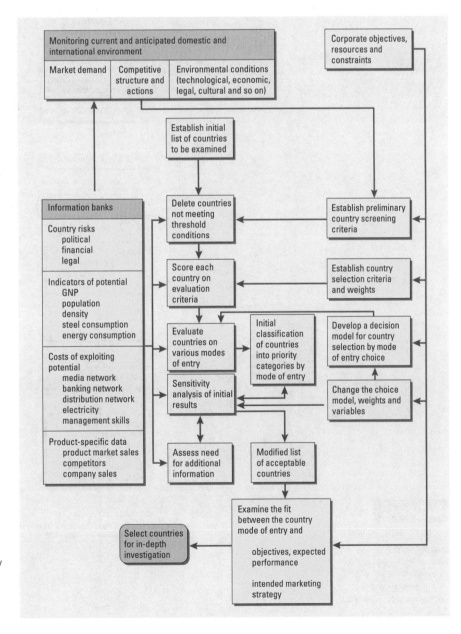

FIGURE 4.2

A conceptual framework for country/mode-of-entry selection: an illustration of a contractible method
Source: Douglas and Craig (1983), p. 111

types of variable are examined: operating risks, market potential, costs, and potential local and foreign competition.

3. Countries are evaluated on the basis of the criteria selected in the second stage, and they are rank ordered on the basis of scores derived.

The end result of this is an ordering of countries such that a number of these can be selected for further in-depth analysis. A similar process is advocated by Root (1994, pp. 55–71), which is based on identifying the country market with the highest sales potential for the company's generic product. Starting with the preliminary screening, industry market potentials are then estimated for a relatively small number of prospective target countries. The last stage is to estimate company sales potentials for the high industry market potential countries. This procedure is summarized in Figure 4.3.

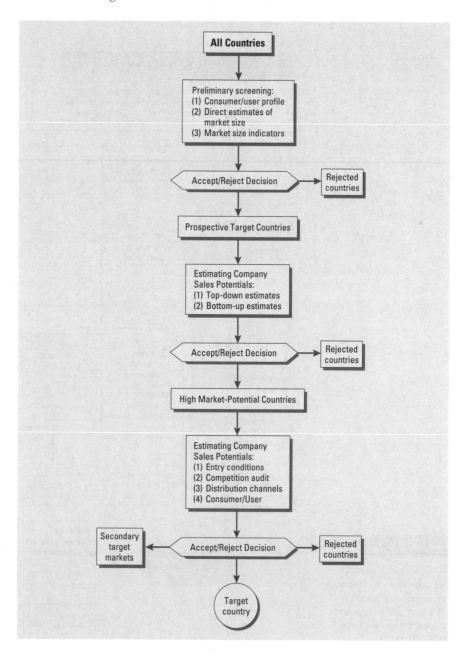

FIGURE 4.3

Model for selecting a target country
Source: Root, 1994, p. 56.
Copyright © 1994.
This material is used by permission of John Wiley & Sons, Inc.

An example of a market screening process is shown schematically in Figure 4.4. The screening of potential markets is organized in a systematic two-step procedure, starting with geographic market segmentation and ending with customer market segmentation.

Step 1: Geographic segmentation

The first screening stage can be further divided into an *information stage* and a *decision stage*, depending upon the proximity of the market and the degree of accumulated experiences the exporter has in collecting data on a set of general market indicators. In addition to geographic indicators as such, demographic, economic, political, and infrastructure market characteristics are also of interest. Since some of these characteristics fluctuate more than others, primary concern should be for the changes and perspectives rather than for past statistics per se. In a world of ever-changing economic policies by national governments and international authorities it is of the utmost importance that the exporter draws out of the vast information supply in this field what is relevant to the marketing situation faced in order to adjust strategies and policies accordingly.

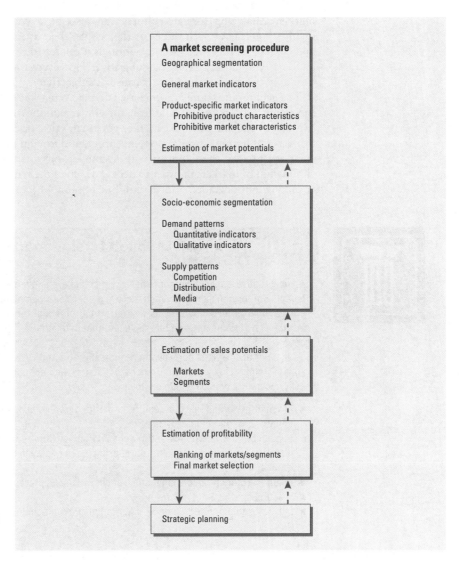

FIGURE 4.4

Export market selection: a market screening procedure

Apart from general market indicators, a set of product-specific market indicators have to be compared to secure optimal market selection. These data can be divided further into two sets of prohibitive factors: a set of *prohibitive product characteristics* (i.e., product-inherent factors that are obviously in conflict with the above general market indicators for climatic, cultural, religious, or other reasons), and a set of *prohibitive market factors*, that is, when the market itself for various reasons prevents or makes further investigations meaningless because of prohibitions, bans, boycotts, embargoes, import quotas, and prohibitive Customs duties and nontariff barriers. A prohibitive product characteristic would be illustrated by trying to sell a beverage or food product with alcohol in a country where religious beliefs prohibit its use. A prohibitive market factor is exemplified by a company wanting to export a product to Mexico that has embargoed its importation, or a company wanting to sell to another company in a country while UN economic sanctions were in force.

Specific consideration needs to be given to the economic, legal, and cultural environments. To a large extent the economic environment is the easiest to evaluate as there are quantitative indicators available. The legal environment can be very complex as it covers many areas and differs from one country to another. A company cannot extensively analyze all of the major laws in each potential market. Analyzing foreign cultures can also be a complex undertaking as it involves looking at such things as the people, their attitudes and values, customs and courtesies, lifestyle, and the nation as it relates to the culture. So much of the analysis will, of necessity, be subjective. However, the value of such analysis should not be understated just because of subjectivity.

The geographic segmentation based on macro market indicators reduces further the number of potential markets; for the remaining markets the total annual capacity of each market (i.e., market potential, sales, or demand) can be estimated by means of national production, inventory, and foreign trade statistics. These calculations present the exporter with a comparable quantitative basis for further elimination of markets in order to decide which of the remaining markets warrants collecting more detailed information (see Exhibit 4.6).

EXHIBIT 4.6   Detailed foreign market analysis

A number of so-called indicators (that is, variables) are relevant for evaluating the export potential of foreign markets. When there is a need for a complete and detailed analysis, each should be examined for its impact on the potential for a given market. In some instances a variable may not be relevant to that market, or its 'value' may not be significant.

In general, the value of an overseas market is affected by its physical characteristics, political tendencies, socio-cultural characteristics, and economic factors. More specifically, indicators would include the following:

- physical geography of the country (area, topography, climate, distances from other countries, geographical division);
- population characteristics and purchasing power (total population, gender and age distributions, income, wealth, purchasing power, social classes, urban and rural groups);
- cultural factors (religion, languages, habits, customs, preferences, values, attitudes);
- resources;
- industries (major ones, location, importance, growth of industrialization);

- foreign trade patterns and partners (exports, imports, patterns of development);
- competition (local, foreign);
- basic infrastructure including transportation and communication facilities;
- financial matters and credit conditions (currency, exchange rates, availability of capital, interest rates);
- marketing channels and business customs;
- government and its restrictions and regulations on trade;
- legal factors (copyright, trademark and patent protection, contract negotiations, etc.).

Relevant past, present, and expected future conditions should be assessed. All significant trends and changes must be included in the analysis.

Step 2: Customer segmentation

For the markets that remain under consideration after Step 1, a further segmentation on the basis of customer market data should be initiated in order to establish the final rankings of potential markets. Among customer segmentation indicators the demand and supply patterns are crucial, both being measured by quantitative as well as qualitative data.

On the demand side the characteristics differ considerably between consumer and industrial markets, although for both types of markets psychographic indicators such as behavior, lifestyle, attitudes, buying patterns, and decision making must be included. On the supply side competitors have to be characterized according to nationalities, capacities, activities, and so on. In addition, distribution channels have to be identified in terms of such characteristics as availability, capacities, and activities performed. Finally, also on the supply side the media situation has to be presented according to availability, costs, circulation, and priorities.

Having collected data on both the geographic and the customer market level, the exporter should then adjust the findings on market potentials to estimate market share (sales potential) leading to a final ranking based on estimated profitability. Market selection can then be made and those markets not selected can be held 'in reserve' for possible later entry. Specific techniques for assessing market potential are discussed briefly in Chapter 5.

4.3.3 Market selection strategies

The major strategic alternatives of market expansion are *market concentration* and *market spreading*. In previous presentations, the expansion strategy alternatives have been identified by the number of markets. A market concentration strategy has been described as a slow and gradual rate of growth in the number of markets served by a company. In contrast, a strategy of market spreading is characterized by a fast rate of growth in the number of markets served at the early stages of expansion. It is evident that these two strategies represent extremes on a continuum of different expansion alternatives.

The choice of a market expansion policy is a key decision in export marketing. First, different patterns are likely to cause development of different competitive conditions in different markets over time. For example, a fast rate of growth into new markets characterized by short product life cycles can create entry barriers towards competitors and give rise to higher profitability. On the other hand, a purposeful selection of relatively few markets for more intensive development can create higher market shares implying stronger competitive positions.

Second, the two market expansion policies lead to selecting different levels of marketing effort and marketing mixes in each market. With the same levels of financial and organizational resources, the allocation of resources to each market will be higher in the case of market concentration strategy than with the strategy of spreading. This has implications for the marketing mix investments in a marketing infrastructure, resulting in greater commitments and controls (and also risks) in the choice of market entry modes, heavy promotional outlays and so on. A strategy of spreading, on the other hand, implies less promotional expenditures and more reliance on foreign distributors (importers, agents, and so on).

Are concentration and spreading synonymous with few and many numbers of markets, respectively? In general, export market strategies and plans have been measured in terms of country markets. However, some conceptual and analytical problems with such measurement arise. First, which absolute approach to market numbers should be adopted? If a company is using a concentration strategy, does that mean it is serving only no more than, say, five target markets? A company's ability to sell to several export markets will vary according to the resources and capabilities of the firm, the existence and degree of export market differences, and the extent to which products and marketing efforts are differentiated by markets. Thus, market number can be viewed as a relative concept. For the smaller firm selling to more than, for instance, eight relatively heterogeneous markets, this would not be considered as adopting a concentration strategy. For the larger company, where adaptation costs have only a minor influence on the company's resource situation, eight markets could well represent concentration. Because there are differences – some great, some minor – between the small and medium-sized enterprise and the larger companies, an assessment of whether any company is following a concentration or spreading strategy must take into account the size of the company.

Second, how should the number of markets be conceptualized? In some cases real market differences may be unrelated to national boundaries. In other cases markets differ within national markets and this may be due to differences in socio-cultural characteristics and/or behavioral attitudes. For example, does a company that exports only to the United States – adapting the marketing program to regional and state differences in socio-cultural and economic characteristics – concentrate its effort in contrast to a company exporting the same product to Denmark, Sweden, Norway, and The Netherlands? In this example market numbers are of minor importance. The relevant issue is the degree of market differences affecting the resource allocation of marketing efforts between different target markets (geographical markets *and* market segments).

Instead of using the number of markets to characterize the different expansion strategies, it seems more appropriate to apply measurements on how the *size of the export marketing budget* is allocated between different types of country markets and market segments. There is, however, a positive relationship between numbers of country markets and amount of resources allocated to each market, which means that number of markets cannot be ignored.

Because it can be difficult to operationalize how marketing expenditures are distributed among export markets (the distribution of shared costs, costs of entry to various countries and markets, overall transaction costs, and so on), a company, alternatively, can calculate its *degree of export concentration* and compare it over time or with other firms, using the *Herfindahl index*. This index is defined as the sum of the squares of the percentage of sales in each foreign country.

$$C = \sum S_i^2 \quad i = 1, 2, \ldots, n \text{ countries}$$

where C = the export concentration index for the firm
          S_i = exports to country i as a percentage of the firm's total exports

$$\sum_{i=1}^{n} S_i = 1$$

Maximum concentration ($C = 1$) occurs when all the export is made to one country only and minimum concentration ($C = 1/n$) exists when exports are equally distributed over a large number of countries. In discussing factors affecting choice of market expansion strategy the following definitions are used.

A *market concentration strategy* is characterized by channeling available resources into a small number of markets, devoting relatively high levels of marketing effort and resources to each market in an attempt to win a significant share of these markets, for example to provide export growth by market penetration. After building strong positions in existing markets the company slowly expands the scope of its operations to other countries and/or customer segments.

A *market spreading strategy* is characterized by allocating marketing resources over a large number of markets in an attempt to reduce risks of concentrating resources and to exploit the economics of flexibility, for example to provide export growth by market development.

4.3.4 Considerations affecting the choice of export market expansion strategy

There are several major factors influencing the export market expansion strategy of the company. In most cases an explicit choice between market concentration and market spreading is not feasible to reach, because the balancing between various situational factors often leads to strategic decisions in between. But it is important that a company has an analytical framework to assess the match between its export position and the opportunities faced. Such a framework should provide an overall picture, showing whether the company's marketing situation favors concentration or spreading. It is important to note that although there are objective determining factors involved, the strategic option that the company may actually choose depends largely on management's subjective judgement of the degree and type of risk associated with the alternatives faced and with the nature of the company's objectives (profit vs volume). The perception of commercial (economic) and political risks in export marketing, and other types of international marketing as well, is a result of the management expertise in the firm, accumulated export experience, and the availability and quality of information of export market environments, customers, competitors, and so on. For example, doing business in very poor countries (such as the African countries Congo and Lagos) or in dangerous countries (such as Colombia) is perceived as involving such great risk that many firms tend to invest in projects that promise quick profits and/or where profit and return on investment is expected to be quite large (*The Economist*, 2000). Risks involved range from expropriation (including partial government ownership) to sudden changes in government (triggering changes in existing agreements) to economic implosion where needed resources (foreign currency, fuel, and so forth) are scarce and the infrastructure is in chaos, to terrorism and concern for physical security. Political risk, which can be viewed as the application of host government policies that constrain the business operations of a given foreign investment operation, has multidimensions. There are transfer, operational, ownership/control, and general instability dimensions. The company's objectives are primarily determined by the driving motives and reasons behind the current export activities.

Sometimes there are considerations that tend to override such risk. A case in point is Indonesia, where political turmoil and violence seem to permeate the nation. Foreign manufacturers ranging from Energizer batteries through Nike running shoes to General Electric lightbulbs to Renault cars seem to be 'thriving' amid the nation's chaos (Shari, 2001). The reasons for staying for purposes of both sourcing and market penetration are quite logical: Indonesia has some of the lowest costs in the world, a large domestic market, and is in great proximity to the rest of Asia. In order to reduce risk companies need to be patient, adaptable, and have the ability to think like a local.

Arguments for applying a market concentration strategy are drawn from the *power of market specialization, scale and market penetration, greater market knowledge,* and *higher degree of control* in export marketing. Improvement takes place through the export learning process and the experience curve. Simply, the company gets better at tasks because of improvement in knowledge and expertise dealing with a small group of markets. Gains arise because some problems are recurrent and have to be solved once the experience of export personnel develops, personal contacts are established, influence patterns emerge, and control is increased.

According to Attiyeh and Werner (1979), a marketing concentration strategy can be based on the concepts of critical mass and selectivity. *Critical mass* means that a minimum level of size and effectiveness has been achieved. Typically, profits tend to increase once critical mass has been reached and the exporter is better able to meet the competitive demands of the marketplace. As a company approaches the critical mass threshold, all that is needed to gain a substantial increase in sales and/or profit is a relatively small increase in time and resources. This can be illustrated by a home appliance manufacturer that put a great amount of investment and resources into several European markets, including Germany, with very low profit being earned. After analysis of the German market the company found that by making an additional investment in dealer support, training, and closing a gap in its product line – all of which was a small incremental outlay relative to its prior investments – there was a step-function improvement in profits. Companies typically have limited resources and this means that they cannot be successful in an unlimited number of foreign markets. Hence, there is need for *selectivity* in choice of markets. Over the long term, markets so selected should be developed in a sequence that will best balance resources to be used with requirements for critical mass.

After markets have been evaluated and selected there still remains the matter of how to proceed within each market. This may involve market segmentation. A company needs to specify a time schedule and the resources needed for reaching critical mass in each segment of a market. For example, a number of years ago a company exporting electrical equipment to France decided that the market had a number of distinct customer segments. The company's sequential market development plan, utilizing time and resources, was: (1) shipyards, (2) regional contractors, (3) small contractors, (4) indirect customers, and (5) original equipment manufacturers. For some segments the company set up a sales subsidiary or used regional sales offices, whereas for others assembly operations were established.

The rationale for market spreading is based on the weaknesses of market concentration. Market spreading offers a position of *greater flexibility, less dependence on particular export markets*, and *a lower perception of risk and uncertainty* in the international marketplace. Small market shares are gained at low costs.

In Table 4.4 we summarize many of the significant company, product, market, and marketing factors that bear on the relative attractiveness of expansion alternatives. Rarely will all the factors operating for a company point toward one strategy. Thus companies often arrive at a strategy through an evaluation process involving trade-offs.

TABLE 4.4	**Factors favoring market spreading**	**Factors favoring market concentration**
Export market concentration vs market spreading	*Company factors* High management risk-consciousness Objective of growth through market development Little market knowledge	Low management risk-consciousness Objective of growth through market penetration Ability to pick 'best' markets
	Product factors Limited specialist uses Low volume Nonrepeat Early or late in product life cycle Standard product salable in many markets	General uses High volume Repeat-purchase product Middle of product life cycle Product requires adaptation to different markets
	Market factors Small markets – specialized segments Unstable markets Many similar markets New or declining markets Low growth rate in each market Large markets are very competitive Established competitors have large share of key markets Low source loyalty	Large markets – high volume segments Stable markets Limited number of comparable markets Mature markets High growth rate in each market Large markets are not excessively competitive Key markets are divided among many competitors High source loyalty
	Marketing factors Low communication costs for additional markets Low order handling costs for additional markets Low physical distribution costs for additional markets Standardized communication in many markets	High communication costs for additional markets High order handling costs for additional markets High physical distribution costs for additional markets Communication requires adaptation to different markets

Source: adapted from Piercy, 1981, p. 64

Product factors

The nature of the product transaction (volume, frequency, and diversity), the degree of product specialization, standardization, software content, repeat purchase, and the stage of the product life cycle influence the choice of expansion strategy. High volume and low frequency products with nonrepeat purchase characteristics may be associated with market spreading. Selling, for instance, heavy industrial systems such as steel and cement plants requires a worldwide perspective in identifying export possibilities. On the other hand, for low-volume and high-frequency products (for example a broad range of common consumer goods) the concentration strategy may appear relatively more attractive.

For specialized products, where most countries have only small market segments, the adoption of a spreading strategy is requisite to gain a sufficient share of the market potential. The specialization character of the product can either be due to technology, service, or marketing features. For instance, the Danish company Radiometer, which sells scientific instruments to hospitals and laboratories, addresses its few product lines to a worldwide niche market, implying that export sales probably account for more than 90% of the company's total turnover.

The software content of the product, for example the service feature, is also important in assessing the market expansion strategies. If the need for customer advice, after-sales service, delivery arrangement, and warehousing is high, a company has to concentrate its resources and marketing efforts to encourage buyers to maintain a custom of repeat purchasing. Especially in industrial markets where buyer/seller relationships based on trust and confidence are important, a foreign manufacturer often has difficulties in gaining credence because of nationalistic buyer attitudes or *buyer ethnocentrism*. So in many cases only service-oriented efforts can compensate for not being a local company.

The position that the product holds in its life cycle in each geographical market has implications for the expansion choice. If positions differ largely over a broad range of countries, a successive concentration strategy, where the company penetrates and expands from one market to the next, may appear logical. On the other hand, if product life-cycle differences between markets do not exist, it is meaningful whether the product is in the earlier or later stages of the cycle. For example, in both the introduction and decline stages it seems advantageous to serve as many markets as possible, first to gain experience and volume, and later to maintain volume as the market declines. In contrast, market concentration appears more appropriate in the stages of growth and maturity where price competition becomes stronger.

Environmental factors

The nature of the markets (market size, growth, stability, the degree of market uncertainty, heterogeneity, competition, and loyalty of buyers to suppliers) affects the choice of an export expansion strategy. High market potentials with stable and mature characteristics tend to favor market concentration whereas low potentials together with new and unstable markets are more suited to a spreading strategy. In the same way, when the company can compete on its own terms effectively against competitors, and when major key markets are not dominated by strong international competitors, market concentration may be an appropriate choice.

Also the growth rate of each market is important. When the rate of growth of the industry in each country or market segment is low, a company can frequently achieve a faster growth by diversification into many markets. However, a spreading strategy at the same time can be advantageous for companies with limited resources. High rates of growth in many countries can be accomplished by relying on marketing efforts of independent sales agents, who are interested in promoting the firm's product in their own growing markets.

One environmental factor that can affect choice of strategy, although it tends primarily to affect specific market choices, is buyer ethnocentrism, or preference for local products and services. Such bias against imported goods can have a consequence of turning a desired spreading strategy into a concentration strategy or making a concentration strategy more concentrated. But companies can adapt. In the late 1990s during the Asian economic crises there was increased movement among the middle class in Thailand and Malaysia to buy local rather than imported products. In Thailand and Malaysia, Nestlé ran an advertising campaign that emphasized the company's decades-long links with the countries and affirmed its determination to remain there in good and bad times (Tripathi *et al.*, 1998, p. 14). Unilever, meanwhile, publicized the fact that it was aggressively purchasing more raw materials locally.

If there are not many fundamental differences in the environmental conditions (there is low market heterogeneity), market spreading appears to be the more attractive strategy. The same conclusion holds when barriers to entry of major markets (for example tariffs) are high and difficult to overcome, and when there is low buyer loyalty.

Export marketing factors

The costs of serving a market, and the nature of these costs, are probably the most important determining factors of the expansion choice. Marketing costs are a result of the nature of the product and the character of the market, and depend, in general, on the chosen entry mode of foreign operation and the need for adaptation to local conditions and demands. Considerations of market entry modes relate to the question of resource commitment to international markets and specify an essential element of distribution strategy in market expansion. Extensive use of independent agents is frequently associated with market spreading, while a resource commitment to sales subsidiaries is a more likely strategic element of market concentration.

However, a major consideration is how a company can achieve and generate the highest sales volume with the lowest marketing costs. This issue is associated with the sales response function for the marketing effort. To the extent that export managers have a good feel for (or knowledge of) relevant sales response of a given product, the better are the possibilities to formulate an effective expansion strategy. The sales response function describes the relationship between sales volume and a particular element of the marketing mix. Two alternative shapes of response functions are common: an S-curve function and a concave function, as shown in Figure 4.5.

The S-curve function (A) assumes that small efforts of penetration to a new market are beset by various difficulties and buyers' resistance. For example, small advertising budgets do not buy enough advertising to create more than minimal brand awareness. But when marketing efforts and expenditures reach a higher point, any increase in costs will produce a large increase in sales until diminishing returns to the increase of additional efforts are reached, for example, very large marketing expenditures may not produce much additional response because the target market is already familiar with the brand.

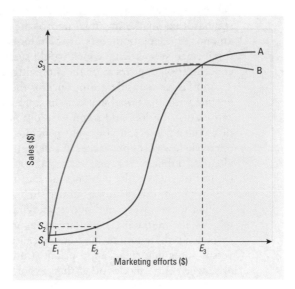

FIGURE 4.5

Sales response
functions: low share
vs high market
share strategies

The concave function (B) illustrates a situation where sales volume is increasing throughout but at a decreasing rate. This implies that the highest return on marketing effort comes from lower levels of marketing expenditures. This function relationship is based on the assumption that the markets under consideration include a number of customers who are particularly interested in the exporter's product. A unique product in terms of such things as quality, differentiation, and marketing program creates such an interest, but spending additional marketing expenditures only affects sales volume marginally over a given point.

What are the implications for the choice of market expansion strategy? Conventional wisdom often argues that if a company faces an S-curve response function, a market concentration strategy based on seeking a large market share of a few markets usually is preferred. This relies on empirical evidence that shows that higher market shares are associated with high profitability. To provide a high market share often requires a strong resource commitment to a sales subsidiary in export marketing. For many small and medium-sized exporters who are not in a position to increase marketing expenditures to a level where efforts lead to increasing returns in sales response, a concentration strategy may not be feasible. Facing an S-curve sales function, the smaller exporter may use its marketing resources more productively (see Figure 4.5) by spending E_1 costs for sales S_1 in several markets rather than spending E_2 for sales S_2 in one or two markets. This means that there may be advantages in accepting a low market share in a larger number of markets as opposed to pursuing market concentration even in the case of an S-curve function.

On the other hand, when a company believes that it faces a concave response function, there should be a strong motivation to follow a strategy of market spreading. Such a strategy is based on the premise that it is easy worldwide to capture a small (but acceptable) market share for very low marketing expenditures, for example by extensive use of independent agents. This is especially an attractive strategy for the small and medium-sized exporter where efficient use of a limited marketing budget creates a great market value and gives rise to particular advantages. A small market share over a broad range of export markets is not necessarily a handicap. It can be a significant strategic challenge that enables the smaller firm to compete in ways that are unavailable to its larger rivals.

The above discussion on the type of sales response function a company faces is determined first by the nature of the product itself. Other export marketing factors associated with the choice of expansion alternatives are largely a result of incremental costs and fixed costs of serving the export market. The degree of heterogeneity between various national markets and the possibilities to apply a standardized marketing mix approach determines the kind and the absolute amount of adaptation costs. If the international environment is characterized by fragmented submarkets, which would suggest a need for local adaptation, market concentration appears to be the more attractive strategy.

Another key consideration concerns the level of marketing costs associated with dealing with additional markets. In some cases the incremental costs of communication, distribution, and so on to additional markets may be low. For example, a firm with a good reputation may generate significant export business by using such relatively low cost approaches as international exhibitions, direct mail or sales catalogues, publicity through technical journals, and customer recommendations. Conversely, where the incremental and fixed costs for additional export markets are very high, it is necessary to use such approaches as establishing a sales office, running local advertising, and employing additional sales staff. In general, low incremental marketing expenditures favor market spreading and high incremental costs tend to reinforce market concentration. When examining concentration versus spreading as an appropriate strategy, the same considerations and issues arise when entry modes other than export are being used.

4.4 Foreign market portfolios: technique and analysis

As competition for world market shares intensifies in many industries, guidelines and systematic procedures for evaluating foreign market opportunities and threats, and for developing a strategic plan to take advantage of opportunities, are much needed. For the international or export-oriented firm, planning on a country-by-country or even regional basis can result in a spotty international market performance, especially for industries in which major companies are competing on a global scene. There is a need to adopt a worldwide perspective to determine the optimal combination of countries and market segments.

4.4.1 Standardized approach to portfolio analysis

Portfolio analysis is an excellent technique to evaluate the degree and nature of a company's involvement in international markets, where opportunities for improving profitability by reallocating resources and efforts across countries, product lines, and modes of operations, for example, can be assessed. Included among the portfolio models that have been proposed to guide the formulation of marketing strategies are the Boston Consulting Group (BCG) model, the business assessment array, and the directional policy matrix.

The BCG approach to product portfolio analysis is the best known and most widely used of these models. The BCG portfolio analysis centers on two determinants of marketing strategy:

- *market strength* – the relative market share (unit sales of the company's product divided by unit sales of the major competitor);
- *market attractiveness* – market growth rate.

In a formalized product portfolio analysis, each product in the portfolio is represented graphically on a relative market share/growth matrix by a circle, the diameter of which is proportional to the sales volume of the product. By classifying the products into the matrix, four broad categories are distinguished: *stars*, *problem children* (also known as *question marks*), *cash cows*, and *dogs*. Cash cows are expected to be cash generators and problem children are expected to be cash users, while stars and dogs should generally break even in cash flow.

Most of the standardized portfolio models are domestically oriented. The traditional models do not incorporate considerations such as:

- costs of entry to various countries and markets;
- shared costs in international (and export) marketing;
- the risks involved in foreign business operations.

These are all critical issues in developing international, including export, marketing strategies, and managers should consider them explicitly. On the *cost side* exporters may experience price escalating factors such as transport costs, costs of product adaptation, and restrictions to competition. Furthermore, overseas differences in wages, inflation, exchange rates, tariffs, and government subsidies may have a considerable effect on a company's competitive advantages. The BCG portfolio approach assumes that market dominance (measured by relative market share) is associated with high profitability explained by the existence of experience effects. Competitors with higher market shares are expected to achieve a greater profitability than competitors with lower market shares. However, in foreign markets the association between market power and profitability may not be as valid as in a home market.

Concerning *shared costs* in export marketing, a number of advantages can arise when a company operates in several countries. Prohibitively high R&D costs of developing a new product for an individual market might be spread out over a number of countries and create a higher return on capital of the R&D investment. Establishing an overseas sales subsidiary might function as an export base to other foreign markets, and lowering the entry costs might be economic for multiple product lines in contrast to a single product line.

In all of the standardized portfolio models, the *risk dimension* is not included. The political, financial, and commercial risks (foreign exchange, legal and regulatory risks, and so on) are increased when companies operate in international environments.

4.4.2 Applying a portfolio model to export market selection decisions

Given the limitations of applying the standardized models to international portfolio analysis and since there are some problems in applying such analysis to the needs of small and medium-sized firms (the typical exporting company), an export market portfolio approach should focus simultaneously across a broad range of foreign markets to help balance capital requirements, competitive economies of scale, entry costs, and profitability to gain stronger long-term market positions. An example of such an approach is shown in Figure 4.6.

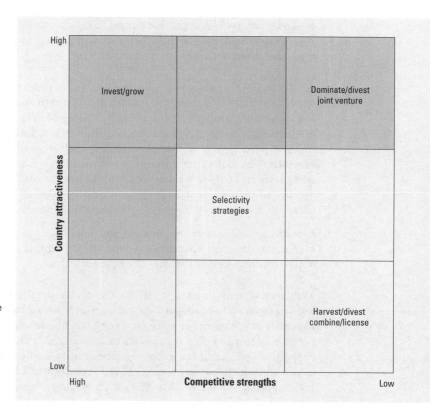

FIGURE 4.6

Market portfolio analysis: a country attractiveness/competitive strength matrix
Source: Harrell and Kiefer, 1981, p. 288. Reprinted by permission of Eli Broad Graduate School of Business, Michigan State University

This country attractiveness/competitive strength matrix can be used as an important tool in the process of export market selection and direction (Harrell and Kiefer, 1981). The *country attractiveness/competitive strength matrix* replaces the two single dimensions in the BCG growth-share matrix with two composite dimensions applied to export marketing issues. Measures on these dimensions are built up from a large number of possible variables as depicted in Table 4.5.

TABLE 4.5		
Dimensions of country attractiveness and competitive strength	**Country attractiveness**	**Competitive strength**
	Market size (total and segments)	Market share
		Marketing ability and capacity
	Marget growth (total and segments)	Product fit
		Contribution margin
	Market seasons and fluctuations	Image
	Competitive conditions (concentration, intensity, entry barriers, etc.)	Technology position
		Product quality
	Market prohibitive conditions (tariff, nontariff barriers, import restrictions, etc.)	Market support
		Quality of distributors and service
	Economic and political stability	

Using these variables, and some scheme for weighting them, countries are classified into one of the nine cells depicting relative market investment opportunity. The flexibility and comprehensiveness of this approach raises some distinct issues in application, as follows:

■ The relevant list of contributing factors in any given situation has to be identified.
■ The direction and form of the relationship have to be determined.
■ Some scheme, whether explicit or implicit, has to be used to weight the contributing factors in each composite dimension. One issue is whether the same weights are used for different countries or markets within the same company.

In using Figure 4.6 in practice each key country would be located on the market portfolio matrix based on the ratings assigned for country attractiveness and competitive strength.

Invest/grow countries

These call for company commitment to a strong market position. A dominant share in a rapidly growing market will require substantial financial investment. Equally important are the investments in people at the country level to sustain a strong competitive position. Product development and modification will be important to match products closely with specific market requirements. Foreign direct investment in sales and service facilities is often required for the sake of rapid market response, delivery, and service, because major competitors will also operate in such growth markets. Marketing support of all kinds should be expansive – related to personnel, advertising, and quality of services.

Harvest/divest/license/combine countries

These often call for strategies to harvest profits or sell the business. Generally, any cash they generate will be required to maintain share; therefore, share generally is given up for profits. Cash flow timing becomes critical. Since the company's market share and competitive position are probably low, and the market is relatively small and the growth low, plans should focus on harvesting near-term profits until the day the export activities are abandoned. Finance should concentrate on frequent cash flow calculations to ensure that variable costs are covered. Pricing policy will be keyed to short-term considerations. By increasing price and reducing the marketing costs, the firm generally can produce cash from those export sales that do occur. Exceptions to abandonment occur when several of these countries can be combined to give enough volume for a sizable export or subsidiary business.

Dominant/divest countries

These present a particularly difficult strategic choice because the firm is competitively weak but the market appealing. Movement toward stronger market positions requires long-term cash flow deficits; divestiture requires the presence of a buyer and cuts the company off from cash and profit opportunities.

The decision demands a careful analysis of cash requirements and cash availability, as well as most of the other factors pertinent to entering a new venture. It would be wise, for example, to match an export market environment with product design strength with one possessing distribution and marketing strength.

Selectivity countries

These present yet another problem. In some situations products in these sections generally are perfect candidates for milking. They produce strong cash flows. In general, in these countries market share will be difficult to maintain even if the company is in a second- or third-ranking competitive position. Competition is extreme and intense. These markets clearly suggest maintenance strategies that build cash flow. On the other hand, if technological and other advantages exist, the strategy may be on building market share.

An illustration of the use of the country attractiveness/competitive strength matrix is provided by the International Tractor Operations of Ford Motor Company. Using ratings assigned for each factor and a specific weighted model relating the factors making up each dimension, Ford Tractor located European countries on the matrix such that the UK was plotted as having high country attractiveness and high competitive strength, Germany was middle country attractiveness and low competitive strength, and Sweden was middle on both dimensions. Considering other key countries, Ford assessed Kenya and Pakistan as being high on both dimensions whereas Australia and Japan were in the middle on both dimensions. Although this actual application was used many years ago, the worthiness of the model is not invalidated by age. Moreover, it illustrates the creativity that any firm can use when developing analytical models for decision making.

Winchester Cathedral, UK

There seem to be several benefits deriving from using portfolio analysis of export markets. First, portfolio analysis combines the dimension of the company's internal strengths/weaknesses and the foreign market environment's opportunities/threats and focuses on interdependencies among various decisions and the forcing of a tool for resource allocation among alternative strategic market choices. Compared with the traditional model of market selection, where the focus is on a systematic screening of all markets leading to immediate elimination of the least optimal markets, the analysis of the company's strengths and weaknesses enters very late in the selection process, which may mean that some opportunities or threats are overlooked.

Second, the portfolio analysis helps to determine the primary role of each specific export market in the international context. The role may be, for instance, to generate cash, to provide growth, to contribute to production volume, or to block the expansion of competition. Once this role has been defined, objectives can be determined for each export market to ensure that country marketing strategies are consistent with the overall international marketing strategy. It should, of course, be noted that market portfolio analysis is a tool that only provides a part of the total export marketing picture, and therefore other analytical tools and considerations have to be included.

It should be noted that the approach discussed above is as applicable to investment and strategic alliance entry modes as it is to export.

SUMMARY

This chapter has looked at the foreign market selection decision. Export market strategy decision alternatives were discussed. Throughout the chapter available alternatives were presented as dichotomous. This approach was used to emphasize that continuums were involved and that only the opposite extremes were being presented. Individual companies will often develop strategies and policies that lie between these extremes. Indeed, many may seem to have features of each 'pure' strategy.

The chapter ended with a discussion of a type of portfolio analysis applied to foreign market selection and market direction decisions. This analysis is indicative of the kinds of 'creative' management that any company can use.

QUESTIONS FOR DISCUSSION

4.1 Strategic export planning requires the development of an effective marketing strategy, including market selection and direction (development). What major implications does this have for the company's export manager?

4.2 Explain the difference between export market selection and export market direction.

4.3 What is market segmentation, and why is it more complex for foreign markets than it is for domestic markets?

4.4 What is the practical value to a manager of accepting the belief that there are European customers, Asian customers, and North American customers, rather than customers from Europe, Asia, and North America?

4.5 What is the best way for segmenting export markets? Explain.

4.6 Give examples of global market segments and companies that are marketing on that basis. Can small and medium-sized enterprises market successfully to such segments? Explain.

4.7 Explain the difference between a proactive market selection approach and one that is reactive. Is one approach better than the other? Why?

4.8 Distinguish between expansive and contractible market selection procedures. If you were making a decision on such a procedure, which would you favor, and why?

4.9 Differentiate between market concentration and market spreading as expansion strategies. Is one universally better than the other for a given product?

4.10 If sales response functions are S-curves, is it more cost effective to expend a little marketing effort in each of several markets, or to concentrate efforts in fewer markets? What if the response functions are concave?

4.11 Using the variables shown in Table 4.5, develop operational measures of each, specify differential weights that you feel are realistic, and apply these to a matrix analysis (such as that shown in Figure 4.6) of the EU and ASEAN countries using a consumer durable product of your choice.

4.12 Repeat the exercise stated in question 4.11 for an industrial product. Explain any difference in the resulting matrix from that derived in question 4.11.

4.13 What changes would you make in the variables used in Table 4.5 to measure country attractiveness and competitive strength? Explain why you have added or deleted variables to those shown.

REFERENCES

Albaum, G., Yu, J., Wiese, N. and Herche, J. (2004). A cross-national study of the impact of culture-based values on marketing decision makers' management styles, *Proceedings*, Third International Business and Economy Conference, San Francisco, 8–11 January.

Andruss, P. L. (2001). Slow boat to China. *Marketing News*, 10 September, 1ff.

Attiyeh, R. S. and Werner, D. L. (1979). Critical mass: key to export profits. *Business Horizons*, 22(6) (December), 28–38.

Bertagnoli, L. (2001). Continental spendthrifts, *Marketing News*, 22 October, 1ff.

Ciu, G. and Liu, Q. (2001). Emerging market segments in a transitional economy: a study of urban consumers in China. *J. International Marketing*, 9(1), 84–106.

Douglas, S. P. and Craig, C. S. (1983). *International Marketing Research*. Englewood Cliffs, NJ: Prentice-Hall.

Fletcher, R. and Bohn, J. A. (1998). The role of psychic distance in the internationalization of the firm. *J. Global Marketing*, 12(2), 47–68.

Green, R. T. and Srivastava, R. K. (1985). Segmentation of export markets based on product mix. Unpublished Working Paper, Department of Marketing Administration, University of Texas at Austin.

Hallen, L. and Wiedersheim-Paul, F. (1984). The evolution of psychic distance in international business relationships. In *Between Market and Hierarchy* (ed. I. Hagg and F. Wiedersheim-Paul), Uppsala, Sweden: University of Uppsala, 15–27.

Harrell, G. D. and Kiefer, R. O. (1981). Multinational strategic portfolios, *MSU Business Topics*, Winter, 51–5.

Hofstede, G. (2001). *Cultures Consequences: International Differences in Work Related Values* 2nd edn. Beverly Hills, CA: Sage.

Hofstede, G. and Bond, M. H. (1988). The Confucius connection: from cultural roots to economic growth. *Organizational Dynamics*, 16(4), 4–21.

Kahle, L. R., Albaum, G., and Utsey, M. (1987). The List of Values (LOV) as a segmentation tool in international marketing research and product introduction. In *Proc. 14 International Marketing Research Seminar in Marketing*, Institut d'Administration des Enterprises, Université d'Aix-Marseille III, France.

Kahle, L, Rose, G., and Shoham, A. (1999). Findings of LOV throughout the world and other evidence of cross-national psychoanalysis: introduction. *J. Euromarketing*, 8(1/2), 1–14.

Kogut, B. and Singh, H. (1988). The effect of national culture on the choice of entry mode. *J. International Business Studies*, 19, Fall, 411–32.

Lynch, R. (1994). *European Marketing: A Strategic Guide to the New Opportunities*. Burr Ridge, IL: Richard D. Irwin.

Miller, C. (1995). Teens seen as the first truly global consumers. *Marketing News*, 29(7), 9.

Miller, T. (1998). Global segments from 'Strivers' to 'Creatives.' *Marketing News*, 30(15), 20 July, 11.

Naisbitt, J. (1996). *Megatrends Asia: Eight Asian Megatrends that are Reshaping Our World*. New York: Simon & Schuster.

Papadopoulos, N. and Jansen, D. (1994). Country and method-of-entry selection for international expansion: international distributive arrangements revisited. In *Dimensions of International Business, No. 11*. Carleton University, International Business Study Group, Spring, 31–52.

Piercy, N. (1981). Export strategy: concentration on key markets vs market spreading. *J. International Marketing*, 1(1), 56–67.

Ricks, D. A. (1999). *Blunders in International Business* 3rd edn. Oxford, UK: Blackwell Publishers.

Root, F. R. (1994). *Entry Strategies for International Markets new and expanded edn*. New York: Lexington Books.

Russow, L. C. (1992). Global screening: the preliminary identification of potential markets. *Proc. Conference Academy of International Business*.

Samiee, S. and Walters, P. G. P. (1991). Segmenting corporate exporting activities: sporadic versus regular exporters. *J. Academy of Marketing Science*, 19 (Spring), 93–104.

Shari, M. (2001). Staying the course, *Business Week*, 24 September, 112.

Shermach, K. (1995). Portrait of the world. *Marketing News*, 29 (28 August), 20–1.

Strandskov, J. (1986). Hvor internationale er Danske verksornheder. *Forlaget Management*, Copenhagen.

The Economist (2000). Risky returns. 20 May, 85–8.

The Economist (2001). One nation, or many?, 20 January, 33–4.

The Economist (2003). The great leap forward, 1 February, 53–6.

Tripathi, S., Dolven, B., and Daorueng, P. (1998). Asia's sinking middle class. *Far Eastern Economic Review*, 9 April, 10–15.

Vandermerwe, S. (1990). Youth consumers: growing pains. *Business Horizons*, 33(4) (May–June), 30–6.

FURTHER READING

Agarwal, M. K. (2003). Developing global segments and forecasting market shares: a simultaneous approach using survey data. *J. International Marketing*, 11(4), 56–80.

Baalbaki, I. B. and Malhotra, N. K. (1993). Marketing management bases for international market segmentation: an alternative look at the standardization/customization debate. *International Marketing Review*, 10(1), 19–44.

Backhaus, K. and Meyer, M. (1986). Country risk assessment in international industrial marketing. In *Contemporary Research in Marketing*, vol. 1 (ed. K. Möller and M. Poltschik), *Proc. 15th Annual Conference of the European Marketing Academy*, Helsinki, June.

Cathelet, B. (1993). *Lifestyles*. London: Kogan Page.

Robinson, R. and Goodman, D. S. G. (eds) (1996). *The New Rich in Asia*. London: Routledge.

CASE STUDY 4.1

IKEA

(This case study is adapted from Sharen Kindel (1997). IKEA: furnishing a big world, Hemispheres, February, pp. 31–4 – used with permission of the author; Business Week, 1997, IKEA's new game plan, 6 October, 99–102; Lisa Margonelli (2002). How IKEA designs its sexy price tags. Business 2.0, October, 106–12 and the company web site www.IKEA.com)

In 1943 a 17-year-old Swedish boy started what was to become a multibillion dollar company by selling work pants and other farm supplies door to door. Ingvar Kamprad began selling farm implements under the name IKEA, which is an acronym for his name and where he was born. Today Inter IKEA Systems BV is the owner and franchiser of the IKEA concept. IKEA retailers worldwide operate on a franchise basis. Most, but not all, IKEA retailers belong to the IKEA Group (154 stores), which includes IKEA retailers, the product development center IKEA of Sweden AB and IKEA trading and wholesaling companies. IKEA group activities are coordinated by IKEA International A/S in Denmark. The IKEA Group is owned by a charitable foundation in The Netherlands. IKEA of Sweden AB is responsible for the entire product range on behalf of Inter IKEA Systems BV. In 2002 the company had a turnover (sales volume) of US$10.8 billion. IKEA is the world's largest furniture and home furnishing retailer with 175 stores in 32 countries as of the end of 2002.

Company history

Well into the 1950s Sweden was a fairly poor country that was still struggling through sharp class differences. Kamprad, who grew up poor during that period, was struck by the notion that beautiful things should not be limited solely to the well-to-do, but should be available to everyone. With that appropriately egalitarian sentiment in mind, in 1950 he decided to add a line of well-designed, functional home furnishings to his list of farm products.

They were an immediate hit. To expand the territory he could cover, Kamprad soon added a catalog, and then a showroom. By 1955, as Scandinavian-designed furniture was beginning to enjoy a worldwide reputation, IKEA began designing its own furnishings. The first IKEA retail store opened in 1958 in Almhult, a village not far from Kamprad's boyhood home. By 1965, when IKEA opened its first store in Stockholm, a 450,000 square foot behemoth, thousands queued for a chance to sample the wares.

While those in the Scandinavian design community embraced Kamprad's ideals of furniture that is aesthetically meaningful *and* available to a wide, nonelite market, it was not until the postwar period that its members began turning out the designs that would win such prestigious international competitions as the Milan Triennale. The international acclaim led the Scandinavian countries to market their home furnishings seriously to the world at large. By this time furniture and household decorative arts that used simple, unadorned, geometric forms had become known as Scandinavian design.

Company operations: tactics and strategy

The problem with Scandinavian design, however, was that it was still too expensive for the average consumer. As a result, several attempts to market Scandinavian furnishings beyond Sweden's borders failed. Bonniers, the Swedish chain, and Design Research in the United States both came and went in the 1960s and 1970s. And today (the early 2000s), Scandinavian furniture is still very much an up-scale, niche market. But Kamprad, convinced that there was a broad, as yet unserved middle class that would want this beautiful furniture if it was reasonably priced, set out to cut his costs to the bone. In 1997 a line of children's furniture and toys was added.

Price had been the key competitive idea behind IKEA since its inception, but to drive prices still lower Kamprad turned the ready-to-assemble (RTA) concept into an art form by manufacturing parts that can be easily put together. Even today most IKEA furniture can be assembled with only one tool, an Allen wrench, which is generally included as part of the kit.

The RTA proposition also saves money for IKEA on shipping and storage. Most of the company's products are packed in flat boxes, reducing transportation costs, minimizing the risk of damage, and making them easy for the customer to take home. IKEA's RTA approach works, says Jan Kjellman, president of IKEA North America, because consumers realize that 'by doing half the job they will pay so much less than they would at a traditional furniture store.'

Thus IKEA recognized that the value added in making furniture was not necessarily in manufacturing. IKEA designed kits that put the consumer in the middle of the value chain, giving them lots of things to do that were traditionally done by the manufacturer. This took incredible amounts of cost out of its system.

IKEA further reduced its costs by becoming production oriented. The company strives to carry out product development on the shop floor. It sends its 10 in-house designers into its suppliers' factories to learn the capabilities and limitations of their machinery so that product designs can be adapted to the machines, instead of the other way around. 'Most designers look at the form and the function, but ours must also look at the price,' explains Kjellman. 'We don't want to make limited edition products. We want to mass produce them.'

Sometimes keeping costs down means that an IKEA design will be made of a lesser quality material. For example, the company does not hesitate to make a painted tabletop out of a lower grade of wood, or substitute a simpler material for a base that is not seen. And furniture that would be too expensive to make in birch is made out of pine.

While the company aims to provide a good quality product, price is still the main reason that people shop at IKEA. Its furniture, toys, and housewares typically are priced 20% to 30% below competitors.

International expansion

International expansion started in the 1960s when the company was forced to source products outside Sweden. Local Swedish furniture retailers felt that IKEA's low-price policy was unfair competition and they tried to prevent local manufacturers from supplying them with goods. Rather than raise prices, IKEA sourced their own designed goods outside Sweden. Today the company sources its products from 1800 suppliers in 55 countries and contracts for capacity rather than a set number of items from its manufacturers. In some instances IKEA has taken ownership positions in factories that supply it with furniture and household goods. In other cases it acts as a financier, especially in eastern Europe. IKEA also operates distribution centers worldwide.

It took IKEA 30 years to grow beyond its boundaries as a local, seven-store chain and penetrate foreign markets. When it was time to expand, explains Kjellman, 'We decided to go to the most conservative market we could find and that was Switzerland.' With success there, IKEA began a slow, steady expansion that has gradually taken it into northern Europe, especially Germany, central Europe, Australia and Canada. By 2002 the company had 154 stores operated by the IKEA Group and another group in additional countries run by franchises. The market expansion history indicating when the first store was opened in a foreign country is shown in Table 4.6.

During the 1980s IKEA was opening between 5 and 10 stores a year. But expansion slowed considerably in the 1990s as the company consolidated its holdings and

TABLE 4.6	International expansion of IKEA

Country	Year
Sweden	1958
Norway	1963
Denmark	1969
Switzerland	1973
Germany	1974
Australia	1975
Canada	1976
Austria	1977
Singapore	1978
The Netherlands	1979
The Canary Islands	1980
France	1981
Iceland	1982
Saudi Arabia	1983
Belgium	1984
Kuwait	1984
United States	1985
United Kingdom	1987
Hong Kong	1987
Italy	1989
Hungary	1990
Poland	1990
Czech Republic	1991
United Arab Emirates	1991
Slovakia	1992
Mallorca	1992
Taiwan	1994
Finland	1996
Malaysia	1996
Spain (mainland)	1996
China (PRC)	1998
Russia	2000

worked on increasing per-store sales and raising overall profitability.

Worldwide expansion has brought new challenges, among them the need to gauge demand and then stock accordingly. 'We have had a lot of shortages,' acknowledged Kjellman. 'One of the biggest problems we have faced as we have moved out of Sweden was having enough of the right product in the stores. We underestimated how much we would sell when we first entered the North American market.'

The US market

An even bigger problem that IKEA has had to overcome is its limited name recognition. 'The first thing we did when we entered the United States was to teach people how to pronounce our name,' Kjellman says. To do so, IKEA ran ads featuring an eye, a key, and a plus sign followed by the word 'ah.' After this initial campaign the company began advertising its value proposition of well-designed home furnishing at affordable prices in ads that featured the tag line: 'It's a big country. Someone's got to furnish it.' In 1990 IKEA expanded by acquiring five stores owned by Stor Furnishings International in California.

During the period 1985–2002 sales in the United States grew from US$50 million for one store to US$1.3 billion for 17 stores. Its first profit was not earned until 1993. In 2002 sales (turnover) in all of North America were about US$1.8 billion. A major reason for this growth is that US consumers view low prices as a given.

Realizing that the United States is a highly mobile society with a large rate of household formation and change, IKEA has changed its television advertising to link the value of its home furnishings to easy, affordable lifestyle choices. Kjellman understands that he is not just competing with other furniture chains, but with anyone vying for disposable income. 'We have to convince people that they should come to us to buy a new sofa,' he says.

While establishing its presence in the United States has not been easy, the company has no intention of leaving. The US furniture market is enormous and highly fragmented. In fact, the top 10 competitors account for less than 12% of retail volume, and IKEA is already well up in the top 10. In 1997 it started developing its first superstore in Schaumberg, Illinois, which was to be the prototype for a chain of much larger stores. It now has stores in 15 cities in the United States.

'The United States is the toughest market in the world, but we can learn a lot from it,' says Kjellman. The furniture trends that begin in the United States, such as home entertainment units or home office furnishings, gradually work their way to other parts of the world. By being where those trends are starting, IKEA can develop new designs to meet those trends and then amortize its costs by selling them into other parts of the world.

IKEA's appeal is that its furniture is accessible, approachable, and economical. 'We have met a need that nobody bothered about,' Kamprad says. 'And the response has been fantastic.'

Questions

1. Evaluate the market expansion approach taken by IKEA.

2. Is it better for IKEA to own its factories or to contract for its products?

CASE STUDY 4.2

Seven-Eleven Japan

(This case study was written by Margaret Kuo and Edwin Duerr, both of San Francisco State University.)

Introduction

The growth of shopping via the Internet had been viewed by Japan's Seven-Eleven convenience store chain as an opportunity rather than a threat. Because of conditions in the Japanese marketplace, Seven-Eleven Japan was not likely to be able to sell its own food and other products over the Internet. The company could, however, provide a service for the large number of Japanese who do not have credit cards or who do not have strong aversion to providing credit card information over the telephone. With over 10,000 outlets in Japan, Seven-Eleven has stores within a short distance of most of its customers and, in fact, of most Japanese. Their customers tend to visit the stores frequently for relatively small purchases.

Thus Seven-Eleven Japan developed a plan to serve as a distribution point for the products of other companies that were selling over the Internet. Customers who wanted goods from an Internet marketer could order the goods over the Internet, and the Internet marketer would ship the goods to a Seven-Eleven store near to the customer. The store would then give the goods to the customer when he or she came in, accept payment in cash (as most Japanese customers prefer) or by credit card, and remit the money to the shipper. The ubiquitous and efficient delivery services available in Japan would facilitate quick delivery to the stores, which would, in fact, be easier than locating the often difficult-to-find address of individuals. Seven-Eleven would collect a small fee for this service. More importantly, the stores would bring in additional potential customers, or bring in regular customers for additional visits. These customers might buy some of Seven-Eleven's own products in addition to picking up their Internet order.

In November 1999, the company started this system of handling merchandise for Internet marketers, delivering goods to customers from their stores, accepting payments from the customers, and remitting the payments to the sellers. They entered into agreements with Softbank Corporation, Tohan book wholesalers, Yahoo Japan, and others to create a venture to sell books and videos using a web site on Yahoo Japan. In February 2000 Seven-Eleven partnered with seven others, including Sony, NEC, Mitsui trading company, and Japan Travel Bureau, to distribute a wide range of products, to provide music and photos online, and to handle book and ticket sales. In another venture, they are involved with Internet automobile sales agencies. In July 2000 they opened a virtual mall named 7dream.com, allowing customers to order goods online and pick them up at the Seven-Eleven store of their choice. The services proved to be a great success, increasing the sales of their own products while they also collected small fees from the sellers.

In 2001 Seven-Eleven was extending this service to Taiwan. The service might also be offered in additional markets if successful in Taiwan, and if target markets had appropriate characteristics.

In 2004 the company opened its first outlet in China, a joint venture with local firms. Although a Hong Kong company operates several Seven-Eleven stores in southeastern China, this is the first time Seven-Eleven had made an equity investment and operated a store in the country. Seven-Eleven (Beijing) Co. expects to open 30 to 50 stores in the Chinese capital by mid-2005. By 2010 the company plans to have 500 stores in the nation.

Background

The Seven-Eleven chain has a long history of innovation and growth. It was originally a US company that was subsequently acquired by Japan's Ito-Yokado Co., Ltd. The original US Seven-Eleven, owned by Southland Corporation of the United States, was designed to meet the needs of the growing number of dual wage-earner families and single workers in the United States who worked nonstandard hours. These people often had difficulty in getting to large grocery stores and supermarkets during the hours that they were open. The increasing affluence in the United States, particularly among the target customers, suggested that they would be willing to pay something extra for the convenience of being able to shop at other times, and preferably 24 hours per day. The company opened a number of outlets, carefully selecting the items to be carried, used centralized purchasing to obtain low prices, monitored sales to improve the mix of products offered, carefully controlled inventories, and used frequent delivery to achieve high turnover in limited spaces.

In 1973 Seven-Eleven's parent company, Southland Corporation, saw an opportunity in the Japanese market where many other companies saw only potential problems. The Japanese distribution system was very complex with multiple levels of wholesalers and many very small 'Mom and Pop' stores. Compared to the United States there were twice as many wholesalers per capita and over twice as many retailers per capita in Japan. Though many of those in the distribution chain in Japan operated on very small margins, the multiple levels resulted in high distribution costs. Additionally, all participants in the distributions system were notoriously reluctant to change distributors or suppliers.

While many foreign markets viewed the Japanese market as too difficult to penetrate, Southland felt that they could set up their own marketing chain and operate it more effectively than Japanese competitors who retained their existing systems. Japanese society appeared to be ripe for the Seven-Eleven concept. The number of women in the workforce had increased, and most men worked such long hours that they could not visit stores during the regular hours of operation. The typical neighborhood food stores were small and carried a limited range of products, often specializing in only one type of food (fish, or vegetables, or rice, etc.) Traditional housewives were accustomed to visiting local shops once per day to get fresh foods, but the number of households where women had the time to do so was decreasing. Japan was becoming increasingly affluent and people had always been willing to pay extra for convenience. The concentration of the population in a few metropolitan areas, and the widespread use of trains and buses for commuting to major business districts, meant that there were many locations with high traffic volumes.

Japan was still viewed as a very difficult place in which to do business if you did not have the right connections plus detailed knowledge of the legal, political, and social environment. Southland therefore formed a strategic alliance with Ito-Yokado, a large Japanese supermarket chain operator. The joint venture was highly successful, with Seven-Eleven becoming the largest convenience store operator in Japan. In an attempt to avoid being acquired by a Canadian company in 1987, Southland sold its shares of Seven-Eleven Japan to Ito-Yokado. Seven-Eleven Japan thus became Japanese owned. Subsequent financial problems at Southland in 1990 led to the US company selling 75% of its stock to Ito-Yokado. In doing so it turned its approximately 7000 company-owned stores in 21 countries over to the Japanese company. (The name of Southland Corporation, now Japanese-owned, has been changed to Seven-Eleven, Inc.)

Under Japanese leadership

During the period of Japanese ownership from 1987 to the present, the company has enjoyed remarkable further growth and increasing profitability in Japan, and has expanded its overseas operations. The number of its stores in Japan has grown from 3304 in 1987 to over 10,000 in 2004. Sales per store have steadily increased, market share has increased, and earnings have grown rapidly, with a record profit of over US$1.6 billion in the fiscal year ended February 2004. On average, each store in Japan now attracts 950 customer visits per day.

Seven-Eleven Japan's performance is even more impressive when placed in the context of the whole industry. Several other Japanese companies, attracted by Seven-Eleven's early success, formed competing chains. Lawson Inc. is the second largest convenience store franchise operator, followed by Family Mart. While Seven-Eleven has prospered, the convenience store sector as a whole has suffered from a slowdown in sales growth. Seven-Eleven remains the market leader.

The company's success appears to have built on a commitment to innovation. It was the first in Japan to introduce a point-of-sale system (POS) for merchandising control. It was also the first to start accepting payments for utility companies, a service now earning commissions on US$6 billion of such payments per year. It subsequently started handling insurance company payments, payments for NHK (the national broadcasting company), and others. Also in 1987 they introduced a control system to keep prepared rice food products at 20 degrees Centigrade through factory, delivery, and in selling cases. They continually upgrade their information systems (fifth generation via satellite communications in 1997), and their warehousing and delivery systems. They continually track sales data so as to determine the best mix of products, and make changes in 70% of their products each year. The company develops tie-ins with manufacturers and producers, where mutual advantage can be attained in advertising or offerings. It is increasingly looking overseas for suppliers where superior products or lower prices for quality products can be obtained.

Taiwan and beyond

The overall social, economic, and geographic environment in Taiwan appear to offer excellent potential for a profitable extension of Seven-Eleven's delivery and payment service for items ordered on the Internet. Taiwan has an even higher population density than Japan, with 611 people per square kilometer in Taiwan compared to 333 people per square kilometer in Japan. Both countries also have most of their populations concentrated in a few major cities. The ratio of stores to populations is high in both nations, with over 10,000 stores in Japan with its population of 126 million, and over 3100 stores in Taiwan with its population of 22 million. Thus, in Taiwan as in Japan, there is easy access to Seven-Eleven stores for most of the population.

The per capita GDP in Taiwan is only approximately one-third that in Japan. However, the Taiwanese also have an aversion to giving out private information over the Internet. Many people cannot, or do not want to, stay at home waiting for delivery services. Thus it is easier for them to pick up items at the convenience stores.

Seven-Eleven Japan has outlets in 19 countries. Only 4 of these countries have more than 500 outlets per country. These are Japan, the United States, Taiwan, and Thailand.

Strategy in China

Seven-Eleven took a conservative approach in entering the Chinese market, determining market potential by licensing agreements with a Hong Kong firm that opened stores in Shenzhen and Guangzhou. When they decided to make an equity investment they did so in the capital city with local firms as partners. In operations they will be similar in some ways to the approach in Japan. The outlet will be open 24 hours per day. It will handle mainly prepared dishes and foodstuffs in lunch boxes, although handling about 20% fewer items. The per capita income in China is low, but it is growing rapidly and there are increasing numbers of busy people with comfortable incomes in the larger cities.

Questions

1. What factors accounted for Seven-Eleven's initial success in Japan?

2. What factors accounted for Seven-Eleven's continuing success in Japan?

3. Is Seven-Eleven Japan wise in extending its delivery and payment services to Taiwan?

4. If its extension of services to Taiwan is a success, should it extend such services to the United States, Thailand, or other countries? What factors should be taken into account in making such a decision?

5. Is the offering of more services in Japan, including banking, provision of in-store terminals for use by customers, etc., likely to cause problems for part-time workers in the franchises?

6. Does China offer good potential for Seven-Eleven?

7. Was Seven-Eleven's entry strategy appropriate for the country? Explain why or why not.

CHAPTER 5

Information for International Market(ing) Decisions

5.1 Introduction

In the last chapter we discussed the market selection problem and covered market selection processes, procedures, and strategies. A basic ingredient of any market selection program is the availability of market information. As a general observation, the sources of international market and product information can be characterized as overwhelming, the problem being to identify the relevant data when needed. For large-size exporters and other types of international marketers this identification problem can be partly solved through the establishment of computerized databases, which must be continually screened and updated. When selecting new markets, and to support ongoing decisions, many companies have developed *marketing decision support systems*. Such a support system should be able to provide data that are all of the following:

- *relevant*: have meaning for decision makers;
- *timely*: current and available quickly;
- *flexible*: available in the forms needed by management;
- *accurate*: valid information for the 'problem' at hand;
- *exhaustive*: data bank should be reasonably exhaustive as international marketing tactics and strategies can be affected by many things that do not enter into domestic markets;
- *convenient*: access and use must be relatively easy to accomplish (Czinkota *et al.*, 1995, pp. 55–6).

For the most part it will be larger, more internationally experienced companies that can afford the cost of building and maintaining a formalized decision support system. For the smaller and medium-sized companies, however, formalized information systems are seldom available, leaving the exporter still with a more or less traditional information problem. However, the continual development of the Internet makes information readily available to all companies, large and small alike.

The major issue is the *collection* of information, which involves an organization in facilitating the collection effort, sources and methods of collection, processing, analysis, interpretation, and, where necessary, intracompany dissemination of information. The collection of information involves seeking sources of existing information and selecting research methods to obtain additional information. The overall process involved is shown in Figure 5.1. This process starts with determining information requirements or 'problem definition' (and this includes determining the research objectives) and ends with the completed report and ultimate integration of findings into management decision making. As shown, the research process is really no different from a general approach to marketing research.

This process can be carried out internally with a so-called in-house research group or it can be done by an outside research organization. The global non inhouse research industry is large. It has been estimated that in the year 2002 total expenditure for research services exceeded US$16 billion, with the Top 25 marketing/public opinion/advertising research organizations accounting for US$10.5 billion or about 66% of the total (Honomichl, 2003, p. H3). The home countries for these organizations include The Netherlands, Japan, Germany, Italy, France, the United Kingdom, and the United States. In addition, other countries have a research industry. For example, in China there were about 400 research firms in the year 2002, many of which were quite small. But many of the Top 25 had a presence and continue to have a presence as the Chinese market grows (Lee *et al.*, 2002). Ownership of these companies include private owners, stock companies, government, and universities. As one would expect, the vast majority of these firms are located in the large cities, with at least one firm in the capital city of each province. Exhibit 5.1 presents issues in dealing with an outside research firm in a B2B situation, although the issues apply to B2C as well.

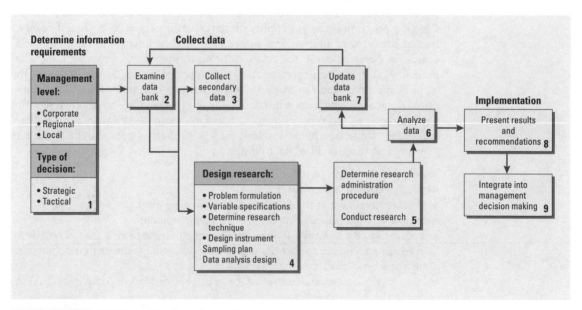

FIGURE 5.1 The international (export) marketing research process
Source: Douglas and Craig (1983), p. 27

EXHIBIT 5.1   Dealing with an outside research firm

When working with an outside research organization there are several things to consider. First and foremost, the international marketer should find an outside research firm that has expertise in acquiring and analyzing international data. Second, it has been suggested that for B2B marketers such a firm should be able to 'focus on the client's clients, manage language differences and negotiate the ins and outs of business culture in the target countries' (Vence, 2003). Project costs can be expensive, running into hundreds of thousands of US dollars, or they can be as low as a few thousand US dollars. Third, since it helps if the research firm has offices in, or established relationships with partners, in the client's target market countries, clients should be asking such questions as the following:

1. Which companies does the research firm have good relationships with?
2. How long have these relationships existed?
3. How much ongoing business does the research firm have with such companies?

The desired end result is global data consistency, or so-called *data equivalence*. This enhances comparisons between markets and potential markets.

It should be obvious that a critical aspect of this process is the first stage – determining what kind(s) of information is (are) needed. This is not to say that the other stages are not critical. It is just that if the needed information is not properly defined, it will not be obtained, thereby negating the value of the other stages. When analyzing potential markets, information is often needed on the various environmental constraints (and attitudes) facing the exporter/international marketer including *educational* (for example literacy level, higher education, attitude toward acquisition of knowledge), *sociological* (for example class structure and mobility; views toward authority, achievement and work, wealth and materialism, risk taking, change), *political–legal* (for example rules of the game, political stability, and organization), and *economic* (for example stability, factor endowment, market size) constraints.

More specifically, the major types of information needed for making decisions about what markets to enter, the appropriate mode of entry in a chosen market and the specific export (or other) marketing mix and strategy to use will include the following: (1) political, financial, and legal data; (2) data about the basic infrastructure of markets; (3) marketing data; and (4) product-specific data. Thus, the information needed goes beyond that directly related to marketing decisions and includes all other aspects of the company's operations. More specifically, exporters would find the following types of information extremely useful: reports on potential customers, identifying potential overseas agents, specific export opportunities, market reports, and information on export payments, transport, and distribution. Czinkota *et al.* (1995, pp. 22–5) provide a checklist of research questions on broad strategy issues, foreign market assessment and selection, and the marketing mix. They argue that the list of information requirements should be detailed and complete. Examples of such research questions are shown in Table 5.1. As we progress in the 21st century another research question that all firms are seeking an answer to is: 'How can the company best use the World Wide Web and the Internet in its international marketing activities?' This question involves use both as a research tool and as a marketing tool.

TABLE 5.1

Examples of international
marketing questions and
information requirements

Broad strategic issues
What objectives should be pursued in the foreign market?
What are the best product, place-distribution, pricing, and promotional strategies for the foreign market?

Foreign market assessment and selection
What is the market potential abroad?
Are there foreign markets that the company can serve?
Who are the firm's present and potential customers abroad?
What are their needs and desires?
Who makes the purchase decisions?
How are the products used?
How difficult are certain government regulations for the firm?
How well developed are foreign mass communication media?
Does the foreign market offer efficient channels of distribution for the firm's products?

Marketing mix assessment and selection
Which product should the firm offer abroad?
At which stage in the life cycle is the product in the foreign market?
At what price should the firm sell its product in the foreign market?
What should the firm do about product line pricing?
What are the characteristics and capabilities of the available intermediaries?
What are the costs of physical distribution?
What are the communication needs of the foreign market?
Are there foreign laws against competitive advertising?
Is there a need for personal selling to promote the product abroad?
What should the nature of foreign sales efforts be?

5.2 Sources of information

Sources of information can be classified according to internal or external sources. *Internal* sources include sales and cost records, and the acquired knowledge of company personnel, such as sales persons or company officers or technical personnel who obtain information in the course of their contacts with customers, competitors, personnel, or governmental officials. Unfortunately, many companies overlook, underutilize or ignore internal data sources. There are times when such sources can provide all the information needed to make the decision at hand.

External sources include both primary and secondary sources. The use of primary sources refers to the collection of information by observation, controlled experiments, surveys, and other techniques to obtain information directly from those on whom one desires such information. The use of secondary sources refers to any source of published information, including government pamphlets or books, news and trade papers and magazines, competitors' house organs, trade association publications, web sites on the Internet, and miscellaneous published research studies. It is well to keep in mind that others often have obtained from primary sources some or all of the information that the international marketer may need to solve a particular problem.

In the early stages of the market screening process, for example, the international marketer/exporter can benefit from (or be overwhelmed by) an abundance of secondary data. This especially holds for information on general market indicators, which can be obtained through regular reporting and special reports from national government agencies and international (supranational) bodies. Some of the major supranational organizations are the United Nations, the Organization for Economic Cooperation and Development, the European Union, Association of Southeast Asian Nations, the World Trade Organization, the International Bank for Reconstruction and Development, the International Monetary Fund, and the International Finance Corporation. In addition to reporting historical and current data, some of these organizations publish reports containing *forecasts*, *outlooks*, *trends*, and so on. Reports are available in print, on CD-Rom, or on an organization's web site. For example, among its many publications the IMF publishes a semi-monthly report, *IMF Survey* (with special supplements), Working Papers, and Policy Discussion Papers. Each is available on the IMF's web site (www.imf.org) as well as in printed form. These data, of course, do not remove the uncertainties of the future, but can provide the exporter with an improved decision platform.

National government agencies are a major source of basic data and other reports useful to exporters/international marketers. This includes the exporter's own government as well as governments of potential foreign markets. Both global indicators and specific country analyses may be available as well as studies done on specific business activities or problem areas. Contacting a *consulate* or *embassy* often is an early step in conducting foreign market analysis. A potential problem in foreign government sources may be language. For example, exporters from the English-speaking world (such as the United Kingdom, United States, New Zealand) would not have trouble with data from Denmark, Norway, and China as statistics from these countries are published in English. In contrast, statistics from Switzerland typically are available in French and German. This can be overcome somewhat if a company has a multilingual capability. Other useful government-provided data can come from subnational governments, such as states/provinces and cities. One active type of government agency is the *port authority*. Ports such as San Francisco (United States), Rotterdam (The Netherlands), Sydney (Australia) and Hong Kong (China) can be very helpful to exporters from other countries.

Nongovernment agencies also may be useful sources of information for the exporter. Large *commercial banks* and *investment houses* often have an international department that regularly collects and disseminates useful statistics. For example, the large US bank Bank of America has a *World Information Services* department that provides country outlooks, country data forecasts, and the country risk monitor. Similarly, Barclays Bank has available market information country data sheets. Also, the experienced personnel of these institutions are quite willing to provide assistance and guidance. For example, through an international network banks can provide advice and on-the-spot timely information about a foreign market. They may work closely with other service businesses such as *insurance* and *freight forwarding* firms that may also be helpful, especially to the newcomer to exporting. The service industries (such as transportation companies, advertising agencies, and large consulting firms), hoping to gain business in their own special areas, may be helpful in providing information not only on foreign markets and conditions, but also on the technique of exporting, financing, insuring, and shipping products to foreign countries. An example is the series of guides published by the large accounting firm Price Waterhouse (now PriceWaterhouseCoopers) on various aspects of doing business in countries where the company has offices or business contacts. Business, trade, and professional associations – including chambers of commerce – may be a source of relevant data.

For example, Business International Corporation in the United States and the Economist Intelligence Unit in the United Kingdom publish many reports, some as a regular series, that are useful to the international marketer/exporter. Commercial marketing research agencies do research for clients, at times preparing so-called *multiclient reports*. As an illustration, starting in 1997 CVSC-Sofres-Media, a joint venture between China's Viewers Survey and Consulting Centre and the French research group Sofres, began offering continuous TV viewing ratings in 62 cities of China, tracking the viewing habits of more than 40,000 people (12,200 households) through diaries the viewers completed (Campbell, 1998). Finally, universities and other educational institutions conduct technical and business-type research and make it available through various

EXHIBIT 5.2	A culturegram can provide an introduction

A culturegram is essentially an introduction to the people of a country. It is general and may not apply to all regions and peoples of the nation. The information included is 'a product of native commentary and original, expert analysis.' The editors state that statistics are estimates, and information is presented as a matter of opinion. Thus the document cannot be considered strictly factual. Still, it is a useful source of cultural information about a country and does give an overview of the situation in a country. It is updated annually.

Using a four-page format, the following types of information are among those included for each country.

I. Customs and courtesies
   - Greetings
   - Visiting
   - Eating
   - Gestures

II. The people
   - General attitudes
   - Personal appearance
   - Population
   - Language
   - Religion

III. Lifestyle
   - The family
   - Dating and marriage
   - Diet
   - Business
   - Recreation
   - Holidays

IV. The nation
   - Land and climate
   - History
   - Government
   - Economy
   - Education
   - Transportation and communication
   - Health
   - For the traveler

technical reports and other publications. As an illustration, the David M. Kennedy Center for International Studies at Brigham Young University in the United States has 'culturegrams' available for over 100 areas of the world. Updated yearly, a typical culturegram includes information about the people of a country – customs and courtesies, lifestyle, and so on (see Exhibit 5.2).

Secondary sources will not usually be sufficient (at least, they should not usually be relied upon as a sole source) for making international marketing program decisions. Nevertheless, available data from secondary sources should be collected, processed, analyzed, and interpreted, so that they can serve as a background for whatever primary research is necessary. Not only will money be saved by avoiding unnecessary primary research; but when primary research is imperative the background knowledge already available will be useful in planning and conducting the study. Often the problem of the international marketer will not be finding data, but selecting, evaluating, interpreting and using the data that are already available.

Use of secondary data is not without some limitations and potential problems. The major issues are data availability, reliability, and comparability. Data are not available from all markets in equal quantity and aggregation and detail. The developed countries typically provide much detailed data. Similarly, the reliability of data is not the same, even among developed countries. There are many reasons for this as individual firms are prone to not always reporting accurately to their government. The reliability issue applies also to data made available from supranational agencies such as the UN as these organizations rely on national governments to supply them with the statistics. Finally, when attempting to make cross-national comparisons, comparable data may not be found. The categories used, for example, may not be the same. Many countries do not use the same categories when showing the distribution of population by age. This should not be interpreted as meaning that all secondary data are bad. Rather, it means that the international marketer/exporter should try to assess who collected the data, for what purpose, and how. Answers to questions such as these will help an exporter to judge the 'value' of the data.

The 1990s saw the growth of the Internet as a quick, efficient, and relatively low-cost means of communication electronically. The databases available to the international marketer are vast, and the Internet has made available to business firms types of information that in the past were difficult to access (see Exhibit 5.3). Some words of caution about the Internet! There is variance among the sites regarding the accuracy, completeness, and currency of the information provided. Updating is not always done regularly. There are technical problems which arise regularly such that a given site may not be accessible when one wants it to be as the server is down. Moreover, the web sites themselves are somewhat fluid and what is operational today may not be tomorrow. New sites appear regularly. Consequently, the international marketer needs to continually monitor the Internet to ensure that the most recent and useful information is being provided.

EXHIBIT 5.3 Examples of web sites

One of the major sources of information for international marketers that 'took off' in the 1990s is the Internet. This provides instant access to global data online that are mostly accurate and up to date. Data are available that are useful to companies which are evaluating whether they should be doing business internationally, which specific countries are viable target markets, what mode of entry should be used, risks associated with doing business in foreign countries, alternative marketing strategies, and potential customers, suppliers, and partners.

For example, if an international marketer or exporter were interested in Asia the following Internet sites would be available (as of early 2004):

ASEAN countries

http://www.asean.or.id
Divided into several sections that cover the history of ASEAN and the economic and social indicators for each member country, and general news about the area.

Asian Business Watch

http://www.asianbusinesswatch.com
Provides updated links to Asian business news, stock market data, and recent headlines from major news sources.

Asia-Pacific.com

http://www.asia-pacific.com/links.htm
A useful site for locating sources for Asia-Pacific business research; there are links to hundreds of sites about business in the Asia-Pacific region. Included are country and company profiles, bank ratings, market research, trade reports, and so on.

AsiaSource

http://www.asiasource.org
This site covers various types of information about the countries of Asia. There are economic and other types of statistics, news, business resources, maps, etc., and links to other sites.

Doing business in Taiwan

http://www.tptaiwan.org.tw
Sponsored by the Bureau of Foreign Trade, Ministry of Economic Affairs of the Republic of China, and maintained by the Taiwan External Trade Development Council, Taiwan's major nonprofit trade promoter. This site covers trade and investment opportunities, access to suppliers in Taiwan, and deals with B2B e-commerce for SMEs.

Hong Kong home page

http://www.hongkong.org
History, shopping, and travel from the Hong Kong Government Trade Offices in the United States.

IndoExchange.Com

http://www.indoexchange.com/econit
Hosted by the information technology Indonesian Internet company Indoexchange.com, this site features integrated information technology solutions for numerous business requirements including: IT consulting, IT solutions, media solutions, and integrated e-business solutions.

Japan Cabinet Office

http://www.cao.go.jp/index-e.html
Gives links to other sites in Japan and covers various aspects of the Japanese government. Includes a link to the Economic and Social Research Institute of the Government of Japan.

Malaysia Information Network

http://www.jaring.my

A computer-based network for access to the Internet in Malaysia, it offers information on research and development, the economy, statistics, and the Malaysian Legal Code.

Political and Economic Risk Consulting Ltd (PERC)

http://www.asiarisk.com

Hong Kong based, this non-government site provides risk reports on each of the countries in the region, paying special attention to critical socio-political variables, together with key economic indicators, to subscribers. The site also has a list of business and financial links for Asia.

Singapore Trade Development Board

http://www.tdb.gov.sg

Information on doing business in Singapore and links to many government-affiliated organizations and private-sector sites.

Thai Government Online

http://www.nectec.or.th

Business information and links to more than a dozen ministries, research organizations, export bodies, and the Board of Investment.

The above listings should be viewed as illustrative. Similar data are available for other areas of the world from other Internet web sites, such as www.arabdatanet.com, which is a gateway site to the Middle East on the Web; and Euroguide (www.euroguide.org/euroguide/subject-listing/), which is a gateway to the web sites containing information about the European Union. Other sites are listed in the appendix to this chapter. Also, over time, the types of information available will change and the timeliness and quality of data provided will improve. For example, the Internet has made available thousands of databases for intelligence research – i.e., research on competitors. In addition, electronic databases carry marketing information ranging from the latest news on product development to new thoughts in the academic and trade press and updates in international trade statistics.

The Internet is here to stay. But it will not totally replace other sources of secondary data. Cost, currentness and availability will still be factors influencing a company's choice of secondary data sources.

The appropriateness of various sources of information depends on the type of information needed and how it is to be analyzed, interpreted, and applied. For example, if a company was considering a commitment to go into international markets, it would need an estimate of the political and legal situation, a knowledge of the financial institutions that are essential to the planned venture, and a large number of statistics on the various topics mentioned earlier in this chapter. Much information on these subjects is available from the various sources mentioned above.

In a study of small and medium-sized exporting companies (i.e., companies with less than 500 employees) in the United States, Yeoh and Jeong (1996) were able to classify sources of information into the following three categories:

- personal (including personal visits to foreign markets);
- professional (such as chambers of commerce, consulates, and so forth);
- documented (published material).

An obvious positive relationship between frequency of use of source and perceived usefulness was found to exist. In addition, these researchers found that although professional sourced information was perceived to be very useful, it may not be adequate to satisfy firms' information needs – there is a need to supplement it with personal and documented sources.

Formal systematic research is not always done when identifying foreign market opportunities. In a study of Hong Kong toy manufacturers that examined foreign market entry resulting from the exporter's initiative, an unsolicited order (buyer initiated), a third-party (e.g., a broker) suggestion, or a trade-fair chance encounter, Ellis (2000) provided support for the belief that formal search behavior is not necessarily done for this type of problem. Information sources used were categorized as either personal or impersonal. A key role is played by *social ties*, or so-called social networks. Information search activities appear to be selectively influenced by those existing social ties linking the initiating party (seller, buyer, or third party) with others that are in some way connected to a particular foreign market (Ellis, 2000, p. 448). This is a version of the Chinese practice of *guanxi*.

When information is needed to estimate the nature of competitors' activities, for example, some typical sources are the following:

- trade publications;
- competitors' house organs;
- salespeople, who are alert for information from the wholesalers or retailers they call on, and who may sometimes be given a specific task to ascertain certain information from such intermediaries;
- overseas-based agents and distributors;
- salespeople, engineers, and officers of the company, who participate in social or professional activities that bring them into contact with competitors' personnel in a way that may permit them to learn something about what competitors are doing;
- direct observation of competitors' activities – such as the introduction of new products and advertising campaigns.

To make product, channel, promotional and pricing decisions, data on consumer needs, attitudes, and other behavior influences are needed. Such information can be obtained in part from the literature of a nation, especially publications of sociologists, social psychologists, and cultural anthropologists who report the results of their research in scholarly journals and books. However, it is often necessary to have a great deal of detailed information, obtained specifically to solve the company's individualized marketing problems. Such information might be obtained from knowledgeable local specialists in the market, but often some kind of direct observation, experiment, or survey is required.

A listing of selected publications and web sites is presented in the appendix to this chapter.

5.3 Assessing market potential

Secondary data are often used to estimate the size of potential foreign markets. A number of techniques are available as described briefly in Table 5.2. Detailed explanations of these techniques (and others) and how they can be used will be

TABLE 5.2	*Demand pattern analysis*	This approach involves examination of industrial growth patterns in an industry.
Some techniques for estimating export market size	*Income elasticity measurements*	The relationship between demand for a product and changes in income in a country are assessed.
	Lead-lag analysis	This is a technique based on the use of time-series data from one country to project sales in other countries. It assumes that the determinants of demand in the two countries are the same, and that only time separates them.
	Estimation by analogy	When data are not available for a regular lead-lag analysis, estimation by analogy can be used. This is essentially a single-factor index with a correlation value (between a factor and demand for a product) obtained in one country applied to a target export market.
	Multiple-factor index	This type of index estimates demand by using two or more surrogate variables that are believed to be related to the potential market demand for the product of concern. Such indexes are best suited for making relative judgements based on rank orders of markets or submarkets within a larger market.
	Regression analysis	This is a powerful tool for estimating demand in export markets when appropriate data are available. One or more predictor variables are used to estimate the demand (that is, the dependent variable). Ideally, these predictors will explain a large amount of the variation in the dependent variable demand.
	Cluster analysis	The objective of this technique is to find groups of countries (clusters) that have similar characteristics. Then if potential is known for one or more countries in a cluster, this information can be used to assess the 'worth' of other countries in the cluster.

found in the works of Douglas and Craig (1983, pp. 114–24), Keegan (1999, pp. 185–8), Moyer (1968), and Kotler (2003, Ch. 5). To illustrate estimation by analogy, assume that:

X_G is the demand for product X in Germany

Y_G is a factor that correlates with demand for X in Germany, data from Germany

X_{UK} is demand for X in the UK

Y_{UK} is the factor that correlates with demand for X in Germany, data from the UK

Further assume that:

$$\frac{X_G}{Y_G} = \frac{X_{UK}}{Y_{UK}}$$

Since X_G, Y_G, and Y_{UK} are known, we can solve for X_{UK} as follows:

$$X_{UK} = \frac{(X_G)(Y_{UK})}{Y_G}$$

This is a very simple method of analysis that can provide useful estimates whenever data are available in at least one *potentially analogous* market for product sales and a single estimating factor. However, Keegan (1999, p. 187) provides the following caveats about the method:

1. Are the two countries for which the analogy is assumed really similar?
2. Have technological and social developments resulted in a situation in which demand for a particular product will not follow previous patterns?
3. If there are differences among the availability, price, quality, etc. associated with the product in the two markets, market conditions are not comparable so demand will not develop into actual sales.

When assessing market potential there are two key dimensions: (1) the number of possible users of the product, and (2) the maximum expected purchase rate. Market potential can be defined as *the amount of a product that the market could absorb over some indefinite time period under optimum conditions of market development*. Market potential is a useful measure for assessing the attractiveness of a market with respect to whether it should be entered. To an extent we can argue that the market potential and company sales potential should be the same, that is, all potential buyers and the amounts they could purchase are available to each and every company trying to sell there. Once specifics are brought into the picture, market demand becomes more relevant for strategic and tactical decisions to be made by exporters. Market demand for a product 'is the *total volume* that would be *bought* by a defined *customer group* in a defined geographical *area* in a defined *time period* in a defined *marketing environment* under a defined *marketing program*' (Kotler, 2003, p. 145). Once export marketing expenditures are brought into the picture, the exporter can think in terms of market and company forecasts. A market forecast is *expected* market demand, whereas a company sales forecast is the expected level of sales based on the marketing plan to be implemented and some assumed environment within which the exporter will be operating. Brief descriptions of selected methods of forecasting – based on judgement, counting, time series, and association/causation – are presented in Table 5.3. As indicated, the exporter has a wide range of alternatives. In a study of UK manufacturing companies that examined the popularity of different forecasting techniques and the factors determining the type of technique used in an export situation, the results showed clear preference for so-called judgemental techniques over a variety of forecasting levels (Diamantopoulos and Winklhofer, 2002). But, the choice of technique and the number of techniques did not seem to impact on forecast accuracy, implying that in order to improve forecast accuracy attention needs to go beyond technique choice and issues such as quality of data used, and the organizational practices associated with the export sales forecast process need to be considered.

Stonehenge, UK

There are many illustrations to support the importance of market analysis and assessment of potential before making a commitment of resources to entering a foreign market, among which are the following (Ricks, 1999, pp. 139–47):

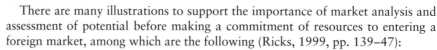

- A US manufacturer of cornflakes tried to introduce its product to the Japanese, but the attempt failed miserably. Since the Japanese were simply not interested in the general concept of breakfast cereals, how could the manufacturer expect them to purchase cornflakes?

TABLE 5.3 Brief descriptions of selected forecasting methods

Judgement methods	Counting methods	Time-series methods	Association or causal methods
Naive extrapolation: the application of a simple assumption about the economic outcome of the next time period, or a simple, if subjective, extension of the results of current events.	*Market testing:* representative responses to new offerings, tested and extrapolated to estimate the products' future prospects.	*Moving averages:* recent values of the forecast variables averaged to predict future outcomes.	*Correlation methods:* predictions of values based on historic patterns of covariation between variables.
Sales-force composite: a compilation of estimates by sales people (or dealers) of expected sales in their territories, adjusted for presumed biases and expected changes.	*Consumer market survey:* attitudinal and purchase intentions data gathered from representative buyers.	*Exponential smoothing:* an estimate for the coming period based on a constantly weighted combination of the forecast estimate for the previous period and the most recent outcome.	*Regression models:* estimates produced from a predictive evaluation derived by minimizing the residual variance of one or more predictor (independent) variable.
Jury of executive opinion: the consensus of a group of 'experts,' often from a variety of functional areas within a company.	*Industrial market survey:* data similar to consumer surveys but fewer, more knowledgeable subjects sampled, resulting in more informed evaluations.	*Adaptive filtering:* a derivation of a weighted combination of actual and estimated outcomes, systematically altered to reflect data pattern changes.	*Leading indicators:* forecasts generated from one or more preceding variable that is systematically related to the variable to be predicted.
Scenario methods: smoothly unfolding narratives that describe an assumed future expressed through a sequence of time frames or snapshots.		*Time-series extrapolation:* a prediction of outcomes derived from the future extension of a least squares function fitted to a data series that uses time as an independent variable.	*Econometric models:* outcomes forecast from an integrated system of simultaneous equations that represent relationships among elements of the national economy derived from combining history and economic theory.

TABLE 5.3 Continued

Judgement methods	Counting methods	Time-series methods	Association or causal methods
Delphi technique: a successive series of estimates independently developed by a group of 'experts' each member of which, at each step in the process, uses a summary of the group's previous results to formulate new estimates.		*Time-series decomposition:* a prediction of expected outcomes from trend, seasonal, cyclical, and random components, which are isolated from a data series.	*Input–output models:* a matrix model that indicates how demand changes in one industry can directly and cumulatively affect other industries.
Historical analogy: predictions based on elements of past events that are analogous to the present situation.		*Box-Jenkins:* a complex, computer-based iterative procedure that produces an autoregressive, integrated moving average model, adjusts for seasonal and trend factors, estimates appropriate weighting parameters, tests the model, and repeats the cycle as appropriate.	

- Unilever was forced to withdraw temporarily from one of its foreign markets when it learned the hard way that the French were not interested in its frozen foods.
- One company found that an inappropriate application of its product was the cause of poor performance. The company tried to market aerosol-spray furniture polish in one of the less developed countries. Analysis of the local average income levels suggested that the natives could afford the product. This type of data, though, is often misleading; in many countries, most of the wealth is concentrated and owned by a few. Therefore, average income levels erroneously indicate that many people in a population can afford a product. In this case, only the few individuals who enjoyed the high incomes could afford the 'luxury' of an aerosol-spray furniture polish. Even they, however, were not interested in the product; such labor-saving devices were not felt to be necessary for their servants.
- One company produced a product far superior to any similar product being used in a particular African nation. Since market tests indicated strong consumer interest, the product was introduced in the market. Shortly thereafter, word spread among the locals that the product was unreliable, although this was not true. The product broke down because buyers did not understand its maintenance requirements. They refused to oil it even though they were instructed to do so. Because this type of maintenance was not typical of their lifestyle, they returned to the earlier more primitive tools that required no special care. In effect, there was no market for such advanced products.
- A Swiss pharmaceutical company built a US$8 million manufacturing plant in Southeast Asia. Researchers had overlooked a very important feature of the market in their studies – the local black market. Because of this unexpected competition, the company experienced lower earnings than expected and found itself with a large excess production capacity.
- In the mid-1990s the Canadian-based shoe company Bata made a big mistake in India (McDonald, 1996). It overestimated the size of the market for its products. Bata assumed that India's middle class had money to 'burn' on more stylish branded products. The company's strategy had been to lift Bata's image from a supplier of cheap, serviceable shoes and sandals. Prices were increased and upgraded outlets in the more fashionable shopping centers were used. The plan was a flop. The white-collar workers on salary did not want to pay the extra cost for what was viewed as a routine part of their 'uniform.' The Indian middle-class consumers feel that if a cheaper product or service is available they will take it.

These illustrations have one theme in common. All involve the existence of an insufficient market. Had a proper market potential study been conducted, market entry most likely would not have been made – at least at the time.

5.4 Export marketing research

Our discussion of sources of information and analysis of potential markets has only scratched the surface. It is not possible to discuss all the sources of information nor all the techniques of market analysis available to exporters. Thus, only a few illustrations have been presented. Often the export marketing data collection effort is a more difficult and complex task than the domestic collection effort. However, the same principles and practices of conducting secondary and primary research that are available to domestic marketers are available, to a large extent, to export and other international marketers. There are a number of sources that discuss these techniques and we refer the reader to the books by Douglas and Craig (1983), Kumar (2000), and Smith and Albaum (2005).

5.4.1 Marketing research defined

Marketing research can be defined as the systematic and objective search for, and analysis of, information relevant to the identification and solution of any problem relevant to the firm's marketing activity and marketing decision makers. The process was outlined in Figure 5.1 earlier in the chapter.

Very broadly, the functions of international/export marketing research include *description* and *explanation* (which are necessary for *understanding*), *prediction*, and *evaluation*. More narrowly, the function of such research within a company is to provide the informational and analytical inputs necessary for effective *planning* of future foreign market marketing activity, *control* of international marketing operations in the present, and *evaluation* of results. One such type of research that can influence all three functions is customer satisfaction. Hewlett-Packard runs three programs as part of its overall personal computer customer satisfaction program in Europe and elsewhere: (1) customer feedback input, (2) customer satisfaction surveys, and (3) total quality control. So-called worldwide relationship surveys are run about every 18 months. These surveys include some product questions but ask how satisfied the customer is with the company as a whole and how Hewlett-Packard rates against its competition.

In European markets, European companies recognize the need to go beyond simply measuring satisfaction and identifying sources of dissatisfaction and view the goal of customer satisfaction management (CSM) programs as customer loyalty and retention. One of the major challenges in implementing CSM programs in Europe is comparing the results across countries (Sivadas, 1998). There are cultural differences across the countries that comprise the European Union, for example. Further, respondents in southern Europe tend to overstate their satisfaction while northern European respondents tend to understate it, making valid comparison of satisfaction scores difficult. In a similar manner, it is erroneous to assume that the same questionnaire can be used with consistent effectiveness in all countries. Rather, a set of core survey questions can be used, but the final instrument should be customized with the assistance of local, research firm partners or managers in an in-house operation. Data collection time and costs will vary across countries as there are differences in language structure and conversational habits. A 10-minute survey in one country may take 20 minutes in another.

In nonEuropean markets, studies of customer satisfaction are becoming recognized as valuable in the planning stages of sales and marketing activities. In some markets customers may actually be a type of 'barricade' as they are not used to being asked for their opinions and suggestions in customer satisfaction research. In doing this type of research one must resist the temptation to query all aspects of customers' buying behavior – customer satisfaction research should explore only those issues relating to the company product/services among current and former users. Service companies, particularly in the travel and tourism business, continually monitor customer satisfaction with a formalized questionnaire at both local and regional levels. At the B2B and B2C high technology sectors, Marketing Metrics, Inc., a US marketing consulting firm, has been doing customer satisfaction surveys in China since 1992 for Motorola and Rolls-Royce. It has a completion rate of more than 70%, which compares very favorably with a worldwide industry average of 30–60%. Such a response rate will not be retained. In China CSM is a new phenomenon, and it is also somewhat new to be able to offer constructive criticism. The Chinese business person likes the idea of being able to critique a supplier and to recognize that the supplier will listen and respond (cited in Andruss, 2000a).

Marketing research has many uses in export marketing. First, research is used to estimate demand, which is critical to the market selection and product positioning decisions. Second, it may be designed to help decide which bases of international market segmentation are most appropriate. Third, marketing research can be invaluable in assessing the merits and problems of alternative modes of market entry. Fourth, marketing research can be helpful in planning and implementing specific export marketing activities such as advertising and pricing. Often of interest is whether strategy should be aimed at standardization or adaptation to the specific needs of individual markets. Fifth, research can be helpful, if not essential, in times of crisis. For example, in 1998 Unilever Holdings Thailand had an ongoing program of consumer focus groups to assist in handling the Asian economic crisis at the time.

5.4.2 The export market(ing) research process

As we mentioned earlier in this chapter, the international/export market(ing) research process has several distinct, though often overlapping, dimensions to it (see Figure 5.1). We now discuss each briefly.

Problem formulation

In a very real sense, problem formulation is the 'heart' of any research process. As such it represents the single most important step to be performed. Problem formulation from the researcher's point of view represents translating the *management problem* into a *research problem*. In order for this to occur the researcher must understand the origin and nature of management's problem and then be able to rephrase it into meaningful terms from an analytical point of view. The end result is not only a management problem that is analytically meaningful but one that specifies the types of information needed to help solve the management problem.

Research method and design

Which method is appropriate to use for a research problem depends in large part on the nature of the problem itself and the extent or level of existing knowledge. Two broad methodologies can be used to answer any research question – *experimental* research and *nonexperimental* research. The major difference between the two methodologies lies in the control of extraneous variables and manipulation of at least one variable by the intervention of the investigator in experimental research. In nonexperimental research there is no intervention beyond that needed for purposes of measurement.

Once the methodology has been selected, the next step is to develop a research design. A research design is defined as *the specification of methods and procedures for acquiring the information needed*. It is a plan or organizing framework for doing the study and collecting the data. In short, research designs are unique to a methodology.

Data collection techniques

The research design begins to take on detailed focus as the researcher selects the particular techniques to be used in solving the problem formulated and in carrying out the strategy or method selected. There are a number of techniques available for collecting data, and these can be used with either methodology.

In general, data collection uses the process of either *communication* or *observation*. Communication involves asking questions and receiving (it is hoped) a response. This process can be done in person, by mail, by telephone, by e-mail, or by the Internet, and in most instances constitutes the broad research technique known as the *survey*. In contrast to this process, data may be obtained by observing present or past behavior. Regarding past behavior, techniques will include looking at secondary data (for example company records, published studies by external sources) and physical traces (for example, erosion and accretion). Research is known as 'qualitative' or 'quantitative' depending upon the extent of structure and directness (disguised or not) of questions asked.

Not all data collection techniques are necessarily usable in individual countries. For example, in Mexico it is almost impossible to use telephone surveys for general population research as telephone penetration is low – Mexico City 55–60%; Guadalajara and Monterey less than 50%; other cities as low as 35%. By far the best method for Mexico is the in-person, house-to-house survey (Namakforoosh, 1994). The situation of low telephone penetration in homes is common throughout Latin America. For example, it has been estimated that in Latin America as a whole in the year 2001 about 18 people out of 100 had telephones (Parmar 2003). There is no indication that this situation has changed. So, researchers typically conduct personal interview street intercepts. In China, both mail and telephone consumer surveys are less likely to provide generalizable data than the in-person survey, conducted either in the home or using some type of intercept-based method. For high-technology-based B2B and B2C relationships, Marketing Metrics is using e-mail and the Internet for contacting Motorola's customers. About 40% of Motorola's customers' e-mail addresses are available, which is relatively high for China. Although Internet penetration in China is low – less than 1% or about 11 million people – it is increasing. In Europe, due to differences among the countries, different 'favored' data collection methods can be found. According to Naresh Malhotra (cited in Andruss, 2000b), about three-quarters of the interviews conducted in Portugal are face to face. In the Nordic countries, however, the populations' higher education levels make mail interviews more common.

Another potential problem is making sure that data from different countries are compatible. For example, research methodologies in Europe will never match 100% perfectly because of the different cultures and customs that make people respond differently. By way of illustration, compared to people in the United States, Europeans tend to be less open to talking about personal information as it relates to certain aspects of their lives. In fact Europeans tend to be more formal in many ways (Andruss, 2000b). There are also legal issues. In Italy, for instance, researchers cannot use the mail to send product test samples to panel members (Miller, 1997, p. 22). There are strict privacy laws in European countries such as Germany that make customer lists and other lists less accessible to researchers than, say, in the United States.

In some parts of the world *gender* – of the person being asked, the person doing the asking, and the research manager – is a potential problem. This is particularly true in predominantly Islamic countries where, for example, female research managers or project directors can expect only limited acceptance. Females can head research projects in some liberal Islamic nations such as Egypt, but are barred completely from Saudi Arabia (Jarvis, 2002). Conducting focus groups in Islamic countries is another area where gender becomes an issue. For the most part mixed gender groups – if allowed – are not usually a good idea as males tend to be dominant and females will defer to them. When interviewing *is* done in these areas the interviewer and interviewee should be of the same gender. In time, use of the Internet for data collection will ease this problem, but at present Internet penetration in the Islamic nations of the Middle East is only 2–3%.

In order to communicate or observe there must be a means of recording responses or behavior. Thus the process of measurement and the development of a measurement instrument are closely connected to the decision of which data collection technique(s) should be used. The relationship is two-way. That is, while the structure and content of the measurement instrument can depend on the data collection technique, measurement considerations often influence technique selection. A study was conducted many years ago by *Reader's Digest* (Ricks, 1999, p. 147). A conclusion drawn from the findings was that more spaghetti was consumed by West Germans and French than by Italians. This 'false finding' was ultimately attributed to how the questions were asked. The survey questions concerned the purchase of branded and packaged spaghetti. Italians, however, tended to buy spaghetti in bulk. When dealing with a heterogeneous population that has not been exposed much to marketing – for example in developing countries – it is often useful to ask the same question(s) in different ways and in different sections of the instrument. This is one approach to quality control.

More generally, multiple methods should be used. Although the structured questionnaire is a familiar tool in marketing research, it may fail to capture key information regarding the intangible characteristics of a culture, resulting in the overlooking of important nuances. A structured questionnaire also can rarely account for contextual influences on purchase and consumption as it is typically based on assumptions about this behavior and what people can recall about it. In short, depth of understanding may be lacking. Combining qualitative methods with the more traditional quantitative ones will add some flexibility to the research process. One such approach is *ethnographic* research. Ethnography is a qualitative approach to research that studies human behavior within a cultural context. With its multiple methods, ethnographic research can pick up contextual information that is not always available through the more traditional reflective self-reports (Day, 1998). For consumer research, for example, ethnographic research attempts to enter the consumer's world directly as much as possible. Multiple methods are often used, including observation, interviews, documents, and material possessions such as artifacts.

A major concern in questionnaire design and research implementation is language. A potential problem arises when the study is conceived, and the questionnaire first written, by a person from one culture speaking one language for use in another culture that speaks a different language. The usual way of handling this is by applying the process of translation and back-translation. It is desirable to have 'outsiders' handle the back-translation and any further retranslations needed. This process may be time-consuming and costly, but it still works! Figure 5.2 shows the English and Chinese language versions of the first page of a questionnaire used to measure consumer ethnocentrism in Hong Kong. The questionnaire was first written in English and then translated into Chinese. The translation/back-translation process was done twice before a satisfactory translation into Chinese characters was achieved. Data were collected by self-report with an interviewer present.

There are times when knowing a language may be a hindrance rather than a benefit. Under such conditions, so-called image research based on visual language and symbols may be beneficial, as indicated in Exhibit 5.4.

Observation can be a useful technique for international marketers who are not familiar with the situation they are entering. Often it is difficult to assess behavior by asking about it – observing it is more revealing. For observing people, it is

A. Original English language

SURVEY ON ATTITUDES AND PURCHASE INTENTIONS

A. Original English language

SURVEY ON ATTITUDES AND PURCHASE INTENTIONS

1. Do you qualify for permanent residency in Hong Kong (i.e., lived here for more than 7 years)?

_____ Yes (continue with Question #2)

_____ No (thank person and terminate the interview)

2. What is your age? _____

If a person is aged 18–65, continue the interview. Otherwise thank the person who is under 18 or 65 and terminate the interview.

3. Attitudes

Following is a series of statements pertaining to consumer attitudes and behaviour. Please indicate the extent to which you agree or disagree with each statement by circling the appropriate number where

1= strongly disagree   4= agree
2= disagree   5= strongly agree
3= neither agree nor disagree   6= no opinion

		strongly disagree	disagree	neither agree nor disagree	agree	strongly agree	no opinion
a.	Hong Kong people should always buy Hong Kong made products instead of imports.	1	2	3	4	5	9
b.	Only those products that are available in Hong Kong should be imported.	1	2	3	4	5	9
c.	Buy Hong Kong made products. Keep Hong Kong working.	1	2	3	4	5	9
d.	Hong Kong products, first, last and foremost.	1	2	3	4	5	9
e.	Purchasing foreign-made products is un-Hong Kong.	1	2	3	4	5	9

FIGURE 5.2   English- and Chinese-language versions of a questionnaire

B. Final Chinese characters

<h2 style="text-align:center">《對產品意見及購買意欲問卷調查》</h2>

1. 閣下是否香港永久居民（即居港七年或以上）？

　＿＿＿＿＿ 是（繼續回答問題二）

　＿＿＿＿＿ 否（多謝被訪者，並終止訪問）

2. 閣下年齡是 ＿＿＿＿＿

　若該被訪者年齡介乎 18 至 65 歲之間，繼續訪問；若非，多謝被訪者，並終止訪問。

在回答本問卷時請注意：香港意指香港本土，並不包括中國；而中國則指中國大陸本土，並不包括香港。

3. 對產品之意見

　以下是一糸列有關消費者意見及行為之陳述句子。請在適當數字上劃圈表示您對該句子之意見。

1 ＝ 極之反對	4 ＝ 同意
2 ＝ 反對	5 ＝ 極之同意
3 ＝ 既非反對亦非同意	9 ＝ 無意見

	極之反對	反對	既非反對亦非同意	同意	極之同意	無意見
a. 香港人應該永遠只購買在港生產的貨品（港貨）而非進口貨	1	2	3	4	5	9
b. 香港應該只進口本土不能提供之貨品	1	2	3	4	5	9
c. 買港貨，保飯碗	1	2	3	4	5	9
d. 港貨永遠是最要緊的，應該永遠被放在第一位	1	2	3	4	5	9
e. 買外國貨等於反港	1	2	3	4	5	9

FIGURE 5.2　Continued

EXHIBIT 5.4   Using visual data

It is obvious that fluency in a language and familiarity with local idioms are helpful in collecting research data. But complete reliance on understanding verbal communication is based on the assumption that people can and will provide the information needed, an assumption that often does not hold. Words are not the only symbols available to the researcher. *Images* can overcome the weaknesses of words and effectively complement information verbally available. In some foreign markets low levels of verbal literacy can be a problem, whereas visual literacy is almost universal.

In verbal research there are usually at least 10,000 words that need to be understood to achieve cultural knowledge. A culture's visual language contains about 200 active symbols on any particular topic. Thus the visual language of a target culture on a given topic can be learned during the time frame of a typical normal project, unlike the spoken language. In this type of image research people can provide more information when selecting images. Therefore patterns emerge with greater clarity, and with smaller samples (and lower cost).

An example of this type of research is a study done to determine how to sell cosmetics to Muslim women in Indonesia. Data were collected from 150 respondents participating in 12 group interviews. Recruiting and moderating were done by native Indonesians in their own language. Each interview group completed ten picture-sort tasks on average, answering questions by selecting pictures from a set of more than 10,000 magazine images collected from throughout the world. The picture-sorts were developed to measure perceptions, values, and motivations regarding skin care products. One finding is that almost 80% of the images selected in answer to the question 'How would you most like to smell?' featured people, usually children. In the West, by contrast, the most fre-

FIGURE 5.3

quent image response would be flowers. The interpretation was that the people being studied are comfortable with natural human odor as well as their general appearance. Further, it was seen that youthful health was associated with a strong human 'fragrance' related to odor but totally consistent with a habit of smelling a child's head as a gesture of affection (see Figure 5.3). Additional images selected to represent the concepts of 'enhancing beauty' and 'repairs skin' were strongly associated with healthy eating and drinking (see Figure 5.4).

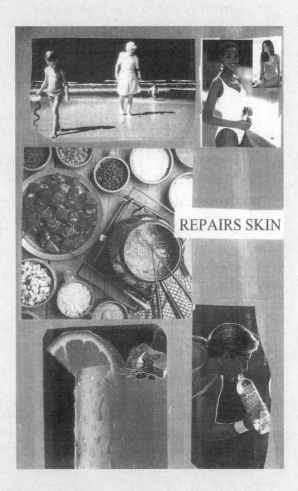

FIGURE 5.4

This approach to research in different cultures is based on a concept of *practical ignorance*. One starts with a lack of knowledge about language and cultural issues and moves on from there. Once the visual data patterns have been collected and interpreted, ignorance has to be left behind. Developing culturally appropriate marketing strategies and tactics requires a thorough understanding of relevant cultural values, messages, and communication channels.

Source: Adapted from Sack (2000)

important to realize that culture may play a major role in how people react to having their behavior observed. This can be especially important for consumer goods research using in-store research techniques.

Sample design

Rarely will a marketing research project involve examining the entire population that is relevant to the problem. For the most part, practical considerations (for example absolute resources available, cost vs value) dictate that a sample, or subset of the relevant population, be used. In other instances the use of a sample is derived from the trade-off between systematic and variable errors.

In designing the sample, the researcher must specify three things: (1) where the sample is to be selected from, (2) the process of selection, and (3) the size of the sample. The sample design must be consistent with the relevant population, which is usually specified in the problem formulation stage of the research process. This allows the data obtained from the sample to be used in making inferences about the larger population.

In sampling for research in multiple countries there is often a conflict between the need for within-country representativeness of each national sample and between-country comparability of the samples. Resolution of this conflict depends largely upon the type of research being done. Reynolds *et al.* (2003) have identified four types of international marketing research:

1. *Descriptive* research is focused primarily on understanding behavior and the market environment in a single country.
2. *Comparative* research is concerned with comparing attitudes, behaviors, etc. in two or more countries with the intent to identify similarities and differences between them.
3. *Contextual* research is concerned with studying cross-national groups, or so-called 'pan-cultural' research.
4. *Theoretical* research looks at the extent to which theories, models, methods, and constructs developed in one country are valid in other countries and cultural contexts.

Table 5.4 presents sampling choices based on these types of research in international marketing research.

When deciding on sample size, two important questions need to be answered (Ball, 2004): (1) Are the data going to be analyzed by the entire sample or by subgroups within the sample? (2) What is the desired level of accuracy?

A detailed discussion of sampling procedures that can be used in international marketing research is found in Kumar (2000, Ch. 12).

Implementing data collection

Once the previous steps have been performed, data collection can begin. Data collection, whether by communication or observation, requires the use of people, which then raises questions regarding the management of these people. Data collection can be costly.

Organizational issues center on: (1) the extent to which research is to be centralized or decentralized within the company, and (2) whether the research is to be done in-house or purchased from outside suppliers. Some major potential problems that can arise when using outside suppliers include communicating in different languages and translating project material. Other problems may be as follows:

- distance and time differences;

TABLE 5.4 Sampling choices in international marketing research

Type of international research	Research objective	Sampling characteristics		Preferred sampling method
		Sampling objective	Desired sample attributes	
Descriptive	Examine attitudes and behavior within specific countries	Within-country representativeness	Ability to estimate sampling error	Probability within each country
Contextual	Examine attributes of a cross-national group	Representatives of specific population of interest	Ability to estimate sampling error	Probability sampling of population of interest
Comparative	Examine differences or similarities between countries	Cross-national comparability	Homogeneous samples to control extraneous factors	Nonprobability acceptable
Theoretical	Examine the cross-national generalizability of a theory or model	Cross-national comparability	Homogeneous, or deliberately sampled for heterogeneity	Nonprobability acceptable

Source: Reynolds *et al.*, 2003, p. 82

- communicating the goals of the research to suppliers;
- maintaining quality control over data collection;
- locating and evaluating qualified overseas suppliers.

Problems facing outside research suppliers are the following:

- communication;
- difficulty with different methodologies;
- varying professional standards;
- low-quality suppliers.

A way to overcome these problems starts with defining the research and objectives using a bottom-up approach. The second aspect concerns defining the specific tasks to be carried out and incorporating them on to extensive specification sheets. Included are everything from the sample determination to analysis, including all aspects of translation and back-translation.

The centralization/decentralization issue is largely a function of whether standardized or adaptation strategies are being followed. It will also be influenced by the size of the exporting company and the significance of export sales. The question of in-house versus external purchase is also influenced by the size of the company. Additional considerations include the number of distinct national markets being serviced. Many exporters simply do not have the in-house expertise to design and conduct research for all their foreign markets. The need for familiarity with the local environment and multiple language capability means that purchase of outside research is necessary, unless of course a study is primarily desk research using secondary data. In addition, the amount of research to be done may not warrant the cost of having a permanent research staff.

Analysis and interpretation

The data that have been obtained must be analyzed. Once obtained, the data must be edited, coded, and tabulated before formal analyses (for example statistical tests) can be performed. The types of analyses that can be performed (that can be 'properly' performed) are a function of the sampling procedures, measurement instrument, and data collection techniques used. One thing to remember is to avoid using overly sophisticated analytical tools for unsophisticated data. The tools must be appropriate for the quality of the data. Just because a market is a developing country is not, by itself, sufficient reason for applying vigorous analysis for high-quality data.

Reporting results

The culmination of the research process is the research report. Everything that has been done should be included and the results, conclusions, and – whenever possible – recommendations for courses of action should be included and presented clearly, accurately, and honestly. Two critical attributes of the report are that it provides all the information that readers need using language that they understand (*completeness*) and that it be selective in what is included (*conciseness*). These attributes are often in conflict. A marketing research report – regardless of its length, beauty, use of pedagogical techniques, and so on – contains no information unless it has the potential for changing the state of knowledge of the reader.

5.4.3 Issues of concern

Regardless of its use in export marketing, a number of conceptual, methodological and organizational issues that impede data collection and the conduct of research have been identified. These include the following:

- the complexity of research design, due to operation in a multicountry, multicultural, and multilinguistic environment;
- the lack of secondary data available for many countries and product markets;
- the high costs of collecting primary data, particularly in developing countries;
- the problems associated with coordinating research and data collection in different countries;
- the difficulties of establishing the comparability and equivalence (construct, measure, and sampling) of data and research conducted in different contexts;
- the intrafunctional character of many export marketing decisions;
- the economics of export marketing decisions.

The issue of comparability takes on special importance. To an extent, each foreign market may be characterized by its own pattern of socio-cultural behavior patterns and values. This means that attitudes and behavior may be expressed uniquely. Relevant constructs and their measures will be unique to a particular country (i.e., culture specific). At the other extreme, there may be similarities (culture free). The existing situation determines the preferred research process. Equivalence should never be assumed to exist. To illustrate, a US company assumed that similar languages indicate similar tastes. When it tried to sell its after-shave lotion in England it failed because the average British male saw no functional value in the use of the product (Ricks, 1999, p. 144). Similarly, a Japanese bicycle manufacturer would find different functional views of its product in the United States (a recreational vehicle) and China (a vehicle for nonrecreational activities such as traveling to and from work).

As another issue in comparability and equivalence, consider how consumption is measured by PepsiCo in seven different foreign markets. As shown in Table 5.5, it would be difficult to make any cross-national comparisons of Pepsi Cola consumption except for Mexico and Venezuela. Other examples of problems concerning measure equivalence are shown in Exhibits 5.5 and 5.6.

TABLE 5.5

How consumption is defined by PepsiCo

Country	Definition
Mexico	Number of occasions product was consumed on day prior to interview
Venezuela	Same as for Mexico
Argentina	Number of drinks consumed on day prior to interview
Germany	Number of respondents consuming 'daily or almost daily'
Spain	Number of drinks consumed 'at least once a week'
Italy	Number of respondents consuming product on day prior to interview
Philippines	Number of glasses of product consumed on day prior to interview

Source: adapted from Keegan, 1999, p. 190. Reprinted by permission of Pearson Education, Inc., Upper Saddle River, NJ

EXHIBIT 5.5 **Lack of equivalence in Europe**

Is Europe uniform in its categorizations of data? Within the European Union the same standard definitions for categories of data are not employed by all governments, as shown in the following list:

■ *Demographic data* are not always collected by government bodies. Some countries use private research agencies, which do not have statutory authority or enforced participation, making the data less reliable.

■ *Educational levels* can be used as a measure of social status, but various means of defining levels exist throughout Europe: examinations, numbers of years at school, and college graduate status may all be employed.

■ *Marital status* can be important for identifying some household trends. Some Roman Catholic countries, such as the Irish Republic, recognize only three statuses: single, married, and widowed. This ignores those who are divorced or cohabiting or those who are members of a single-parent family.

■ *Country source* classification can be a problem with pan-European financial transactions. For example, a funds transfer in which an Anglo-American holding registered in The Netherlands takes up credit in Luxembourg to finance an acquisition in Spain will be recorded as a Dutch direct investment. If the credit is long term, it may also be recorded as a Luxembourg investment.

■ *Social class* is measured on different scales in EU countries, such as by occupation, educational attainment, and wealth. These will not necessarily produce the same ranking.

■ *Advertising and promotional expenditures* data, according to the European Commission, may be incomplete or doubtful in three ways:

   ■ some countries use estimates; others use actual data;
   ■ media coverage for compiling data is not always complete; for example, cinema advertising may be excluded, and print media may cover only major titles;
   ■ some countries include commissions paid to advertising agencies and costs of producing the advertising in turnover data; others do not.

So much for a single Europe!

With the recent expansion of the EU to include central and eastern European countries, the situation will become even more complex and mixed up.

Source: adapted from Lynch (1994), pp. 97–8

Scales of measurement that are used in international marketing research studies are developed in one country within one culture. Often, they are used in other countries without concern for equivalence. Are scales generalizable? Not always!

EXHIBIT 5.6 **Questions need to be pretested**

Although individual questions – indeed, entire questionnaires – should be pretested in all studies, the need is even greater for multicountry research. Concern is for uncovering poorly worded questions and questions that potential respondents do not really understand. In addition, the issue of *measure equivalence* – specifically *translation equivalence* – can arise in such studies. Among the concerns regarding translation equivalence is how perceptual cues are interpreted in a research context. Respondents may misinterpret stimuli because the associations evoked by the stimuli differ from one country or culture to another.

A good illustration of what needs to be done, and why, is cited by Oppenheim (1992, p. 48) when discussing an international study of health problems. The researchers decided to include a set of factual questions about domestic facilities available to respondents. These questions had been used in previous studies conducted in several countries. One of the items asked about was 'running water.' Results from pilot work (Oppenheim's term for pretest) indicated that respondents in developing countries often interpreted 'running water' to mean a river or a brook near their home. So the item wording had to be changed. It now became 'piped fresh water supply' and this new wording, too, had to be piloted – just to make sure.

It should be noted that if the pilot work had not uncovered this unintended interpretation, the item might well have been used in the main field work, since respondents found it easy to answer the question. Only much later, during the analysis phase, might the researcher have noticed a remarkably high proportion of respondents who apparently had no piped fresh-water supply; but by then it would have been too late. A poorly worded item is not necessarily one that causes respondents difficulties in answering; far more dangerous are apparently unproblematic items that, unwittingly, produce data that are not valid.

For example, Donoho *et al.*, (2001) assessed the 'transportability' of two measures – the Personal Selling Ethics Scale (PSE) and the List of Values (LOV) – across cultural boundaries associated with the United States, The Netherlands, Australia, and Canada and concluded that they are not easily transportable. Blindly transporting research measures and instruments from one culture to another may produce measures that are less useful in describing and explaining phenomena in the country of interest than developing a measure unique to that country.

5.5 Using the Internet and e-mail for data collection

The Internet and e-mail are emerging modes of data collection for international marketers. The Internet, which is a worldwide network of private, corporate, and government computers that gives users access to information and documents from many and distant sources, can be used for obtaining external secondary data – as we discussed earlier in this chapter – and for primary data collection by conducting surveys electronically. It can also be used when the research design is experimental and the data collection is by survey technique.

Through the Internet many databases, large and small, become available to an organization. A system of Internet servers known as the World Wide Web consists of computers supporting a retrieval system that organizes information into hypertext documents known as web pages. Many companies, government agencies, other organizations, and individuals have their own web pages. These are additional sources of secondary data. Anyone can access most web sites without prior approval – i.e., access is 'free.' However, many commercial sites require that the user be registered (often with payment of a fee) and have a password to access the site. From an external secondary information perspective, the Internet together with the World Wide Web is one large *library* – if not the world's largest library – for a potential user.

In its role of providing primary survey-based information to a company, the Internet becomes a vehicle for developing internal databases about customers, suppliers, and other things in the marketplace. This activity can assist a company in developing a *marketing information system* as part of a *decision-support system*. Software has been developed that allows a company to engage in *data mining*, which involves using internal customer-based databases and, perhaps, third-party databases, to obtain meaningful information about customers, such as purchasing patterns.

Using the Internet for *online research* (using survey techniques) is becoming an increasingly attractive alternative for international/export marketers. Although it operates much like a mail survey in that it is self-report and contact is usually unsolicited, there are some advantages over the mail survey. Data typically can be obtained *quicker* and at *lower cost*. For example, the very large US multinational Procter & Gamble estimates that using the Internet allows them to cut marketing research costs by anywhere from 50–70%; also, the time needed for concept testing is dropping from weeks to days (VanScoy, 2001, p. 74). Some nonsampling errors from data collection can be minimized, at least as compared to person-to-person and telephone surveys. Other characteristics of the Internet as a research tool are: extremely flexible questioning, a modest length questionnaire should be used, and there is no direct influence of an interviewer on answers.

There are however some problems in using the Internet for data collection. First and foremost is *sampling*. Users do not represent a research population or sample frame that is representative of the general population. Thus a random sample of the general population is not possible. This is particularly a problem in many countries where there is a lag in people coming online and access to the Internet. This is the problem of penetration, which is low in most parts of Asia, Latin America, and central and eastern Europe. Such a situation makes comparability across foreign markets problematic. While still a problem, the sampling issue is less damaging for B2B relationships.

Another problem area is *language*. For some markets such as China, Korea, and Japan software that uses the appropriate character set must be available. Also, other countries such as the Scandinavian countries and Turkey need special software as the alphabets differ from those in Europe and North America, for instance. Due to formatting and other technical problems as well as a lack of an interviewer being present, there is a high probability of the respondent *not understanding the question*. Finally, there is the matter of *respondent cooperation*. Since the Internet is relatively new as a research tool, there is little known about response behavior. Such behavior will vary by country, by web site (the source of the survey), and by sponsor (if known).

A discussion of information collection based on the Internet is given by Kleindl (2001, Ch. 7) and Smith and Albaum (2005, Ch. 6). Some useful sites for information are shown in the appendix to this chapter.

E-mail can be used in the research process in two ways. First, it is often the vehicle through which potential respondents are asked for their participation and are told about the web site containing the questionnaire. In essence e-mail serves as a means of preliminary notification. Second, it can be the direct vehicle by which the questionnaire is administered. When used this way, e-mail has characteristics similar to those associated with the Internet.

SUMMARY

This chapter has looked at issues relating to the types and sources of information used in market selection analyses and further examined briefly some key issues in export marketing research. The chapter introduced the use of the Internet and World Wide Web as tools for research. The methods involved in the research process tend to be technical and the reader was referred to specialized sources for detailed discussion.

QUESTIONS FOR DISCUSSION

5.1 How would you respond to a person making the following statement: 'As a general rule, the export marketing manager has few sources of information available for use in market selection.'

5.2 For three different products that are being exported, or are exportable, list the major sources of information on competitors' activities.

5.3 Select two foreign markets – one a developed country and one a developing country – and make a list of sources of information that might be helpful to you in assessing the probable market for an exportable product from your country (specify your product and country). Are web-based or nonweb-based sources preferable? Explain.

5.4 What is the market research process that the international/export marketer uses and what are the major issues that can arise to provide 'complications'?

5.5 Marketing research is beyond the capabilities and needs of the small exporter. Only larger companies doing business in many countries have need for research services.' Discuss.

5.6 Explain how the Internet may be a valuable source of information, for even the smallest-sized exporter.

5.7 How can an international marketer overcome the incompatibility of research methods usable in different countries when doing a comparative study?

REFERENCES

Andruss, P. L. (2000a). 1.3 billion potentially satisfied customers. *Marketing News*, 23 October, 41–2.

Andruss, P. L. (2000b). Going it alone: US research firms must put time, thought into European studies. *Marketing News*, 11 September, 19.

Ball, J. (2004). Simple rules shape proper sample size. *Marketing News*, 1 February, 38.

Campbell, A. (1998). Diaries help survey TV viewing habits. *South China Morning Post*, 6 April, Business 3.

Czinkota, M. R., Ronkainen, I. A. and Tarrant, J. J. (1995). *The Global Marketing Imperative*. Lincolnwood, IL: NTC Business Books.

Day, E. (1998). Researchers must enter consumer's world. *Marketing News*, 32(17), 17 August, 17.

Diamantopoulos, A. and Winklhofer, H. (2002). Export sales forecasting by UK firms: technique utilization and impact on forecast accuracy. *J. Business Research*, 56(1), 45–54.

Donoho, C., Herche, J. and Swenson, M. (2001). Assessing the transportability of mesaures across cultural countries: a personal selling context, Proceedings of the 8th Cross-Cultural Research Conference.

Douglas, S. P. and Craig, C. S. (1983). *International Marketing Research*. Englewood Cliffs, NJ: Prentice Hall.

Ellis, P. (2000). Socialties and foreign market entry. *J. International Business Studies*, 31(3), 443–69.

Georgoff, D. M. and Murdick, R. G. (1986). Manager's guide to forecasting. *Harvard Business Review*, 64(1), January–February, 110–18.

Honomichl, J. (2003). Acquisitions help firms' global share increase. *Marketing News*, Special Issue on Global Top 25, 18 August, H1–H32.

Jarvis, S. (2002). Status quo = progress. *Marketing News*, 29 April, 37–8.

Keegan, W. (1999). *Global Marketing Management* 6th edn. Upper Saddle River, NJ: Prentice-Hall.

Kleindl, B. A. (2001). *Strategic Electronic Marketing: Managing E-Business*. Cincinnati, OH: South-Western College Publishing.

Kotler, P. (2003). *Marketing Management* 11th edn. Upper Saddle River, NJ: Prentice-Hall.

Kumar, V. (2000). *International Marketing Research*. Upper Saddle River, NJ: Prentice-Hall.

Lee, B., Saklani, S., and Tatterson, D. (2002). Top prospects: state of the MR industry. *Marketing News*, 10 June, 12.

Lynch, R. (1994). *European Marketing: A Strategic Guide to the New Opportunities*. Burr Ridge, IL: Irwin.

McDonald, H. (1996). Bata finds promise of Indian middle classes wearing thin. *South China Morning Post*, 2 April.

Miller, C. (1997). Research firms go global to make revenue grow. *Marketing News*, 31(1), 6 January, 1ff.

Moyer, R. (1968). International market analysis. *J. Marketing Research*, 5 (November), 353–60.

Namakforoosh, N. (1994). Data collection methods hold key to research in Mexico. *Marketing News*, 28, 29 August, 18.

Oppenheim, A. N. (1992). *Questionnaire Design, Interviewing and Attitude Measurement* new edn. London: Pinter.

Parmar, A. (2003). Tailor techniques to each audience in Latin market. *Marketing News*, 3 February, 4–6.

Reynolds, N. L., Simintiras, A. C. and Diamantopoulos, A. (2003). Theoretical justification of sampling choices in international marketing research: key issues and guidelines for researchers. *J. International Business Studies*, 34(1), 80–9.

Ricks, D. (1999). *Blunders in International Business* 3rd edn. Oxford, UK: Blackwell.

Sack, M. C. (2000). The value of 'practical ignorance' in cultural research. *Quirk's Marketing Research Review*, April, 18–19ff.

Sivadas, E. (1998). Europeans have a different take on CS programs. *Marketing News*, 32(22), 26 October, 39.

Smith, S. and Albaum, G. (2005). *Fundamentals of Marketing Research*, Thousand Oaks, CA: Sage.

VanScoy, K. (2001). Can the Internet hot-wire P & G? *Smartbusinessmag.com*, January, 69–79.

Vence, D. L. (2003). Leave it to the experts. *Marketing News*, 28 April, 37.

Yeoh, P.-L. and Jeong, I. (1996). Export information source use: impact of perceived usefulness, entrepreneurialism, organizational and environmental characteristics. Paper presented at AMA Summer Educators' Conference.

FURTHER READING

Agarwal, M. K. (2003). Developing global segments and forecasting market shares: a simultaneous approach using survey data. *J. International Marketing*, 11(4), 56–80.

Gestland, R. R. (2000). *Cross-cultural Business Behavior*. Copenhagen: Copenhagen Business School Press, Chs 4, 7.

Hanson, W. (2000). *Principles of Internet Marketing*. Cincinnati, OH: South-Western College Publishing, Chs 4, 8.

Malhotra, N. K. (1988). A methodology for measuring consumer preferences in developing countries. *International Marketing Review*, Autumn, 52–66.

Roy, A., Walters, P. and Luk, S. (2001). Chinese puzzles and paradoxes: Conducting business research in China. *J. Business Research*, 52(2), 203–10.

Sharma, S. and Weathers, D. (2003). Assessing generalizability of scales in cross-national research. *International Journal of Research in Marketing*, 20(3), 287–95.

APPENDIX

Selected publications and web sites providing secondary data

The following is a selected list of various publications and web sites that are useful for the manager seeking reference sources in international and export marketing. The listing is divided into five parts:

- **A.** Indexes and guides
- **B.** Economic trends
- **C.** Special services
- **D.** Statistics
- **E.** Web sites.

A. Indexes and guides

1. CD-ROMS.
   There are different computerized databases available through compact disk (CD) technology. These databases allow people to create a customized bibliography on a topic of their choice.
   a) ABI/INFORM
      i) *Subjects covered*: accounting; banking; economics; finance; management; human resources; marketing and advertising; companies and products; business conditions and trends.
      ii) *Publications indexed*: 800 business journals.
   b) PAIS (Public Affairs Information Service)
      i) *Subjects covered*: public policy; social issues; international relations; political science; public administration; economics; federal, state, and local governments.
      ii) *Publications indexed*: journal articles, books, government documents, reports.
   c) World Development Indicators on CD-ROM. Produced by the World Bank, it contains 500 time series of development indicators for over 200 countries covering the years from 1970 to about two years prior to publication in most cases.
2. *Business Periodicals Index (BPI)*, monthly. Indexes all major business and economic periodicals. Somewhat weak on trade journals.
3. *Predicasts Funk and Scott Indexes*, weekly.
   a) *US Index of Corporations and Industries*, weekly. Excellent for searching for current US company, product, or industry information.
   b) *F & S Europe*, monthly. Companion index to the one above, covering articles or data in articles on foreign companies, products and industries.
   c) *F & S International Index*, monthly. See b) above.
4. *Public Affairs Information Source Bulletin*, semi-monthly. The index covers periodical articles, books, government documents, conference proceedings, and other publications that touch on topics of interest to public policy. Over 1400 journals are indexed. Also on CD-ROM (see 1. b) above).

B. Economic trends

1. *Asia Yearbook*, annual. Contains information on individual countries, plus finance, investment, economics, trade and aid, etc.
2. *Encyclopedia of the Third World*. Provides a compact balanced description of the political, economic, and social systems of 122 countries.
3. *Europa Yearbook*, annual. Includes history, economic affairs, economic statistics, constitution, government, etc. of individual countries.
4. *Organization for Economic Cooperation and Development: Economic Surveys of the OECD*, annual. Economic surveys of each of the 24 OECD member countries, containing information on current trends in demand and output, price and wages, foreign trade and payments, economic policies, and future economic prospects.
5. The World Bank, *Global Development Finance, I: Analysis and Statistical Appendix*. Annual review of recent trends in – and prospects for – financial flows to developing countries.
6. *International Monetary Fund Staff Country Reports*, in-depth economic analyses and data on more than 160 countries.
7. *World Economic Survey*, annual. A comprehensive picture of the economic situation and prospects for the world as a whole and for major world regions. Analysis of inflation, rates of interest, exchange rates, trade balances, commodity prices, and indebtedness are included.
8. *Euromonitor References*. A series of reports on consumer markets and products throughout the world. Some are in regional editions while others are for one country. Available on CD-ROM or printed.

C. Special services

1. *African Research Bulletin: Economic, Financial and Technical Series*, monthly.
2. *Asian Recorder*, weekly.

3. *Business International*, loose-leaf service.
   a) Business International *Loose-leaf Services*, weekly. This is a newsletter service that offers short articles on capital sources, economy, industry, exporting, foreign trade, management and marketing.
      These newsletters cover the following areas:
      i)   Business Asia
      ii)   Business China
      iii) Business Eastern Europe
      iv)   Business Europe
      v)   Business International
      vi)   Business Latin America
   b) *Financing Foreign Operations*, irregular. Current guide to help the business person find sources of capital and credit in 34 major markets.
   c) *Investing, Licensing and Trading Conditions Abroad*, annual. Covers Africa–Middle East; Europe; Asia; North America; and Latin America. Includes information on state role in industry; rules of competition; price controls; corporate taxes; personal taxes; incentives; labor; foreign trade.
   d) *Research Reports*, irregular. These are in-depth reports prepared by the BI service on various subjects and countries. 'Marketing in China,' 'Andean Common Market,' etc.
   e) *Worldwide Economic Indicators*, annual. Includes key economic indicators for over 130 countries. Includes GDP; demographic and labor force data; foreign trade; production and consumption data.
4. *Moody's Global Company Data*, annual. Provides financial and business information on more than 5000 major foreign corporations and national and transnational institutions in 100 countries.
5. *Graham and Whiteside Major Companies*. A series of directories on companies in different parts of the world. There are specialized directories for financial institutions, energy companies, chemical and petroleum companies, telecommunications companies, and food and drink companies. Available in CD-ROM and/or printed form from the UK-based company Graham and Whiteside.
6. *Kogan Page Publishers*. Has a global market briefings series of books on 13 central and eastern European countries and China.

D. Statistics

1. *Demographic Yearbook*, annual. Comprehensive collection of international demographic statistics. Includes population; demographic and social characteristics; geographical; educational; economic information.

2. UN Statistical Office, *Statistical Yearbook*, annual. Kept up to date by the *Monthly Bulletin of Statistics*. Comprehensive compendium of internationally comparable data for the analysis of socio-economic development at the world, regional and national levels.
3. The World Bank, *Global Development Finance, II: Summary and Country Tables*. Statistical data for 138 countries, as well as summary data for regions and income groups. Also available on CD-ROM.
4. International Labor Office, *Yearbook of Statistics*, annual. Includes total and economically active population, employment, unemployment, hours of work, wages, etc.
5. UN Department of Economic and Social Affairs, *International Trade Statistics Yearbook*, annual. Commodity trade statistics and direction of trade.
6. UN Statistical Office, *National Accounts Statistics*, annual.
7. UNESCO, *Statistical Yearbook*, annual. Contains tables grouped according to various subjects: population, education, libraries and museums, book production, newspapers and broadcasting, television and cultural expenditure. Over 200 countries or territories represented.
8. UN Statistical Office, *Yearbook of Industrial Statistics*, annual.
   a) Volume I, General Industrial Statistics: industry data for each country. Includes industrial activity, number of establishments, number of employees, wages and hours, cost of goods and materials.
   b) Volume II, Commodity Production Data: also for a 10-year period. Uses ISIC Code. Over 527 industrial commodities are covered in 200 countries or areas.
9. The United Nations has separate Economic and Social Commissions for each geographical region. Each publishes an annual report which surveys the economic and social trends of that area, including economic prospects, foreign trade, investments, oil industry and agricultural. These are supplemented and updated by periodicals.
10. Other international statistics.
    a) *Index to International Statistics*. Provides access to and description of statistical publications of international intergovernmental organizations.
    b) *International Financial Statistics*, monthly. Data on exchange rates, international reserves, money and banking, trade, prices, and production for all IMF member countries.
    c) International Monetary Fund, *Balance of Payments Statistics Yearbook*, annual. Five-

➡

year detailed balance of payments statistics for about 100 countries: includes statistics for goods, services, capital, SDRs, etc. Pay special attention to notes that accompany each table.

E. Web sites

There are thousands of web sites useful to the international marketer. It is not possible to list all that exist at a given time. Some sites fall out of use and new ones are created regularly. In addition, site names are changed. Listed below are examples of the kinds of sites that provide information helpful in decision making regarding such areas as market entry, marketing strategy, financial issues, and so forth.

1. *World Business Resources.Com: A Directory of 8000 International Business Resources on the Internet*. As its name states, this directory lists thousands of web sites providing information on all topics related to international trade, marketing, and business in general.
2. *World Information, Ltd* (www.worldinformation.com). A UK business information company's site that has useful information about countries around the world.
3. *Government web sites*. Most major governments and supranational government organizations have one or more web sites that provide information about the country or region or world. Some examples are:
   a) strategis.ic.gc.ca Canada's business and commercial site from Industry Canada.
   b) www.ita.doc.gov Site for the International Trade Administration of the US government.
   c) www.info.gov.hk/censtatd/ All about Hong Kong from the Hong Kong Census and Statistics Department.
   d) www.stats.govt.nz Basic data about New Zealand from Statistics New Zealand.
   e) www.imf.org The International Monetary Fund's site linking to reports online and to publications.
   f) www.europa.eu.int The European Union's main server providing links to sites within the EU and within individual countries.
   g) www.mercosur.org Links to web sites within Mercosur's member countries, many of which are in local languages – Spanish, Portugese. For example, www.brasil.gov.br is Brasil's site in Portuguese whereas www.indec.mecon.ar/i_default.htm gives – in English and in Spanish – Argentina's statistics from the National Institute of Statistics and Censuses. Also covers information related to Mercosur itself and gives links to other economic blocs.
   h) www.wto.org The site for the World Trade Organization. Information on trade topics, resources, documents, and news about the WTO. Reports such as *International Trade Statistics*, annual reports, and special studies can be downloaded. Is presented in three languages – English, French, and Spanish.
   i) www.stat-usa.gov This is a service of the US Department of Commerce providing access to statistics and other information. There is access to the National Trade Data Bank (there is a fee to subscribe), which is the US government's most comprehensive source of international trade data.
   j) www.oecd.org/eco/surv/esu.htm Economic surveys from the Organization for Economic Cooperation and Development.
   k) www.worldbank.org The site for the World Bank. Country data for more than 200 countries and other reports are found in www.worldbank.org/data and 800 development indicators organized into 85 tables are presented in Word Development Indicators (www.worldbank.org/data/wdi2000).
   l) www.unctad.org The web site for the United Nations Conference on Trade and Development.
4. Other sites
   a) www.investineurope.com Covers what an international marketer needs to know to invest and do business in Europe.
   b) www.going-global.com Has a most comprehensive list of resources available.
   c) www.fita.org The Federation of International Trade Associations site covering trade leads, publications, world trade news, web resources and other things. Provides a free (but one has to be registered) bi-monthly report titled Useful Web Sites (www.fita.org/useful.html). Can show locations of ATM machines (www.fita.org/marketplace/travel.html#atm).
   d) www.ibl.com Covers international business and law.
   e) www.kompass.com A B2B search engine from Kompass International of France.
   f) www.smartbiz.com/sbs/cats/ie.htm A comprehensive source providing links to current information about import, export, country facts, agreements, regulations, payments, translation, customs, language, foreign travel, WTO, regional economic blocs, etc.
   g) www.ibrc.bschool.ukans.edu A comprehensive set of Internet resources on international

business are presented by the International Business Resource Center at the University of Kansas in the United States. Has information links to country resources, top 10 resources, international business resources, trade statistics, and international news. There are similar sites from other universities in North America and Europe.

h) www.worldpop.org/prbdata.htm Eighty-five indicators for 221 countries are provided by the Population Reference Bureau.

i) www.euroguide.org/euroguide/subject-listing This is a gateway to web sites containing information about the European Union developed by a group of libraries.

j) www.europages.com A European Yellow Pages business that includes 500,000 companies in all business sectors in 33 countries. This is a good source for finding new clients/customers, suppliers and partners. It is available in English and 24 European languages.

CASE STUDY 5.1

Mariani Packing Company, Inc.

Mariani Packing Company, Inc. is in the business of growing, drying, and processing fruit. Headquarters are now located in Vacaville, California, in the United States. By far the greatest share of its sales (turnover) is made in the United States. However, Mariani has been involved in export business to a number of countries including Canada, Mexico, Australia, Germany, Norway, and the United Kingdom. Sales are made in bulk as well as in individual packages ready to be sold in retail stores. In the mid-1990s total corporate sales worldwide reached a level exceeding US$60 million.

Company history

Paul A. Mariani, Sr had launched a family business in 1906 in Santa Clara County (now Silicon Valley), California, buying fruit from Santa Clara orchardists for resale. The Paul A. Mariani Company was born.

Soon the Mariani Company was packaging and exporting dried fruit. By the mid-1920s the firm led the industry in the shipment of dried prunes to Europe and its export trade continued until World War II. Because of the war, when the European market was in disarray, Paul Sr. said to his son, Paul Jr., 'Go out and develop a domestic market.'

He did just that! By the mid-1940s he had taken charge of the company. Never one to wait for opportunity, he expanded the company operations to Australia and other parts of the world.

Among his many innovations Paul Mariani, Jr. is especially known for being the first to package 'moist pak' dried fruit, using a process he developed at the University of California, Davis. The Mariani 'Moist Pak' was the pioneer of ready-to-eat dried fruit in a see-through bag, introduced in 1947.

Mark A. Mariani, one of Paul Jr.'s seven children, has been the company's president since 1979. Under his leadership, the company constructed state-of-the-art production facilities, developed additional sources of dried fruit, new value-added products and innovative packaging to meet growing consumer demand. For Mark and his family Mariani is more than a brand name, it is a family name that for generations has passed on a strong commitment to quality, innovation, and service to its customers.

Current operations and organization

The company's name changed to Mariani Packing Company, Inc. and in the mid-1990s a facility that included headquarters, processing, packaging, and distribution was located in San Jose, California. Other processing facilities at the time included a 20-acre dry-yard and cutting facility in Kelseyville, California, and a modern dehydration plant and cold storage facility in Marysville, California. Distribution warehouses were located in 10 cities in the United States and there were sales offices in three cities nationwide.

The company sold a variety of dried fruit products that included the following:

Prunes	Pitted and unpitted
Cut fruits	Apricots, peaches, pears, nectarines, apples, mixed fruit, and fruit medley
Raisins	
Figs	
Snack fruits	Yogurt raisins, apricots, plums, raisins, fruit medley
Tropical fruits	Banana chips, papaya, pineapple, tropical fruit medley

Situation in Mexico

Although the company had been exporting to Mexico for some time, sales were in bulk only. The international department believed that with the passing of the North America Free Trade Agreement (NAFTA), there was real potential for exporting a complete retail product line (already packaged for sale). Mark Mariani made contact with Cascade Consulting Group and met with them to discuss a research project based on the following management problem:

> How can we [Mariani] efficiently, from a cost and time standpoint, penetrate the Mexican market with a broad dried fruit retail line?

Prior to his meeting with Cascade personnel to finalize the agreement for the project, Mark Mariani received the memorandum shown in Figure 5.5. Mark recognized that the concerns indicated in this memorandum 'involve research matters that would have to be handled in more than one project.' Accordingly, he thought he should work only with the more important questions that had direct bearing on the management problem at hand.

For the last fiscal year Mariani's exports of prunes to Mexico were 164 short tons, which was about 10% of all California exports of this product to Mexico. This share of the market was a decrease from the 25% share of the preceding year.

Questions

1. What are the most important concerns that need to be addressed in this first study?

2. What alternative sources of information are available for providing needed information?

3. Can the study be done entirely by use of secondary data? Explain.

4. Assuming primary data collection was needed, what research questions should be answered? Explain the methodology and data collection techniques that you would recommend be used to do the project.

MEMO

TO: MARK MARIANI   FROM: DIRECTOR, INTERNATIONAL DEPARTMENT
SUBJECT: CASCADE CONSULTING GROUP - FOREIGN MARKET RESEARCH

Mark,
In reference to your upcoming meeting with the Cascade personnel I would appreciate it if you could address the following areas regarding the situation for Mexico. Some particular points of interest are:

Products
1. What type of dried fruits are most popular in Mexico?
2. Are the dried fruit products available in Mexico considered high in quality and high in price or generally low grade and priced accordingly?

Packaging
3. What are the most preferred package types for dried fruits (cello bags, cartons, canisters, cans, etc.)?
4. Do the Mexicans prefer products packaged in original US packages or under a Spanish label?
5. In what net weight units are dried fruits commonly sold in the retail market?
6. Do the consumers look for specific features on the packages (visibility, reclosability, no double packaging due to environmental concerns, etc.)?
7. What are the particular labeling requirements for packages?

Place/Distribution
8. What type of distribution network is recommended, for example one national distributor, separate local distributors or direct sales handled by Mariani Packing out of the San Jose, California, office.
9. What functions would a potential representative of Mariani have to perform in Mexico? What would be your criteria when choosing your representative?
10. In which way do the individual supermarket chains request delivery of the ordered goods (to regional warehouses, direct store deliveries, etc.)?
11. Which areas (Mexico City, Guadalajara, etc.) have the greatest sales potential?

Importing
12. Current import requirements.
13. What are the duty rates for the individual dried fruits that shall be part of our product line for Mexico?
14. Are there other fees assessed by the Mexican government, customs, freight forwarders, or other instances? This is important in calculating selling prices.
15. What is the most efficient way for shipping goods to Mexico?

Prospects
16. Would you recommend to pursue working with the produce markets in the various Mexican cities or do you feel that Mexico's growth will be in retail?
17. In the grocery stores, which department are dried fruits commonly displayed in (grocery, produce, etc.)?

Promotions
18. What kind of promotional support are the retail chains seeking from the suppliers, if any?
19. What kind of in-store advertisement is most efficient in Mexico?
20. Do the Mexico retail chains promote their products through their own coop magazines?
21. Which methods of consumer advertising are most efficient (bill boards, TV, magazines)? Please specify.

Competition
22. Who is our current competition (foreign competition, California brands)?
23. Mariani wants to set itself apart from the competition. Would niche marketing be appropriate? If yes, what is/are the niche(s)? If no, what are the alternatives?

Consumers
24. How are the dried fruits most commonly consumed by the Mexican consumers?
25. What are the reasons consumers buy dried fruits in Mexico (health, traditions, meals, etc.)?
26. How can Mariani take advantage of the consumer trends in its marketing strategy?
27. Can the consumers be classified by income, age, sex?

Current Market Conditions
28. In which form are dried fruits mostly sold (bulk vs. retail, produce markets vs. grocery stores)?
29. Is a change in trends detectable? If yes, how?

FIGURE 5.5   Memorandum to Mark Mariani

CASE STUDY 5.2

Aquabear AB

Aquabear AB was founded in 1970 in Stockholm, Sweden, as a small private company that manufactured maritime leisurewear clothing. In 1975 the company started a line of ski clothing using the brand name Snowbear.

By the end of 2003 the company employed about 130 people. The sales volume for 2000 was about SKr175 million. (Assume an exchange rate of US$1 = SKr7.41. and euro 1 = 9.17 Kr.) The company has experienced a period of rapid growth in the past 10 years due to the market growth in sportswear and leisurewear and is financially sound. The Snowbear line of ski clothing has become the dominant product line due largely to the efforts of a creative designer (and skiing enthusiast) who joined the company in 1979.

Aquabear AB has all its manufacturing capacity in Sweden, and as a result of the previous year's success its plant and equipment in 2004 are up to date. In Sweden Aquabear sells directly to department stores and specialty retailers. The company has about 30 years' experience of export to the western European market, mainly Germany, Austria, and Switzerland. Aquabear exports directly by using agents in the respective countries.

The skiwear products

Aquabear AB's Snowbear line of ski wear consists of high-quality clothing for nordic and alpine skiers. Snowbear's trademark is a striking design in bold yet simple patterns and colors, a good cut, and high quality material and finish. The garments are very functional with details such as closures at neck, hands, legs, and pockets very thoroughly thought out. The Aquabear production/design has followed market developments in fabrics for skiwear closely as well as successfully keeping up with fashion trends. The company has even become something of a market trendsetter for some items.

The collection of jackets, vests, ski suits and ski pants for men and women are matching and can be mixed at will. A typical collection consists of a couple of models and colors of each garment, although there are more jacket styles since jackets are also bought for nonski winter wear.

The price level of the product line is in the upper ranges but not in the same top price bracket as the designer label ski wear collections. Approximate retail prices in Sweden during late 2003 were as follows:

	SKr
Ski suits	2,800
Jackets (alpine)	1,800
Jackets (nordic)	1,200
Vests	1,000
Pants (alpine)	1,100
Pants (nordic)	900

Management's search for new markets

Aquabear has been very successful in the past 10 years, especially with its Snowbear line of products. The increasing number of skiers, and the increased use of ski wear as winter and leisure wear as well as the Snowbear clothes' quality are the main reasons for this. The company's sales personnel judge that the primary customers are people of both sexes, both young and older people, belonging to middle- and upper-income groups, who rate quality and functional and original design higher than the price.

Ski wear is a seasonal commodity. In Europe the retail season is from late October until March, although this can vary with the weather. Encouraged by its success in the home and European markets, and a sound financial and organizational situation, management is interested in expanding its export markets to the southern hemisphere. The main advantage of this compared to entering new European or US/Canadian markets is expanding the market as well as being able to even out some of the seasonal variations in production and sales; the southern ski wear season complements the northern hemisphere season.

Selection of potential markets in the southern hemisphere

The countries in the southern hemisphere where skiing is possible and where the company is looking are: Chile, Bolivia, and Argentina in South America; Australia; and New Zealand. There is now a ski resort in South Africa catering to a rich, young clientele that may eventually prove of interest. The company has decided to exclude Bolivia because skiing is limited to one ski run (the highest in the world, however). The four remaining countries can be analyzed in terms of geographic, demographic, economic, and political data in order to select the most promising export market(s) in the southern hemisphere.

The export manager, Wil Hønacker, has done some

preliminary background research and has found that the ski season tends to run on average from May or June through September in Argentina, Chile, and Australia, while in New Zealand it may last as late as October or November. Each country has the following major ski areas:

Argentina: Cerro Catedral (Bariloche), Chapelco, Las Leñas and 7 additional areas.

Chile: Portillo, Valle Nevado, La Parva, Farellones-El Colorado, Termas de Chillán plus 10 other areas.

Australia: Thredbo Village, Perisher Valley, Blue Cow, Mount Selwyn, Charlotte Pass (all in the Snowy Mountains of New South Wales); Mount Buller, Mount Hotham, Mount Baw Baw, and 4 other areas in Victoria.

New Zealand: Treble Cone, Coronet Peak, Mt Hutt, Mt Ruapehu, The Remarkables, Cardrona and 4 other areas.

Mr Hønacker realizes that the process of market selection should include consideration of a number of characteristics. Accordingly he asks his assistant Harald Gornisson to do some further research. Mr Gornisson recently received his MBA from Simon Fraser University in Canada. After some searching, the basic information in Table 5.6 was obtained about the four countries from United Nations databases.

Mr Gornisson reported back to Mr Hønacker and stated that the above information included only general indicators useful for screening potential export markets. To obtain a more comprehensive analysis of the four potential target countries, many other kinds of data such as purchasing patterns of ski wear and competitive situations should be obtained, as well as consumer expenditure on clothing and footwear, con-

sumer expenditure on leisure, and tourist arrivals at frontiers. More specifically, the following types of information are suggested:

- number of skiing resorts, and number of active skiers;
- income level and standard of living;
- distance of skiing resort(s) from largest cities and other populated areas;
- customs duty, other import-related fees, and sales and value-added taxes;
- import restrictions such as import licenses and quotas;
- political situation (maturity, stability);
- extent of nationalism;
- growth potential of the market;
- language barriers that may exist;
- number (and source) of tourists;
- competition;
- transportation costs;
- foreign exchange situation.

When he was back in his office after meeting with Mr Hønacker, Mr Gornisson was thinking about what he had just done. He wondered why South Africa had not been included in the request made by Mr Hønacker. In the past few years one major resort, Tiffindell, and four other ski areas had been developed. In 2003, more than 5000 people visited Tiffindell during the winter season.

Questions

1. Should Aquabear AB enter southern hemisphere markets with its line of ski wear?
2. If so, which market(s) should it enter and why?
3. If not, why not?

TABLE 5.6 Economic and population indicators

	Chile	Argentina	Australia	New Zealand
Population (2005 est.)	16.18m	39.31m	20.09m	3.93m
Percentage of population in 15–64 years age group (2005 est.)	64.6%	63.2%	67.8%	66.0%
Gross National Income per capita (2002)	US$4,260	US$4,060	US$19,740	US$13,710

CASE STUDY 5.3

Ford Motor Company Latin America

(This case is adapted from a presentation at the 7th ESOMAR Latin American Conference, 12–14 May 2002, by Marilyn Parrett (Ford Motor Company) and Michael Francesco Alioto (The RDA Group), 'The use of "respondent-based intelligent" surveys in cross-national research.' Used with permission of the authors.)

Many of the major automotive manufacturers have developed a series of market research tracking programs that measure and report customer perceptions concerning price, financing options, brand, style, customer treatment during the sales and service process, and product quality. Of these critical characteristics, product quality remains among the top issues in terms of customer importance and is a major driver of customer satisfaction. Customers repeatedly identify product quality as a 'must have,' and can become quite rapidly unsatisfied when their expectations are not met. Things Gone Wrong (TGW), the major metric of automotive quality research, impacts customer satisfaction in a negative linear relationship.

Therefore, the automobile manufacturers perceive it to be in their long-term interests, if not their survival, to continuously identify quality problems and defects early in the ownership cycle. Their objective is to develop 'fixes' for erroneous manufacturing and production processes quickly to stem any customer satisfaction erosion due to product quality defects or variability.

Many of the major automotive manufacturers have launched product quality market research tracking programs on a global scale to aid in the collection, analysis, and comprehension of customer feedback on their product quality. This information provides critical dynamic 'report card'-level diagnostics of the manufacturing and production processes for the manufacturers. From this customer information fixes and adjustments are made to the automobile manufacturing and production processes where product quality defects are identified.

The challenge faced by all automobile manufacturers, and their partner market research agencies, is to collect the most accurate, timely and market sensitized data available, while eliminating or greatly reducing market research biases due to survey, methodological, cultural, and structural parameters. Ford Motor Company is no exception.

Quality and research objectives for Ford's quality research programs in Latin America

In 1994–5 Ford Motor Company redesigned its quality research system. Two main objectives were identified for the quality research program:

1. Collect detailed information from the customer on product quality in order to supply the Ford Quality Office and the plants with crucial customer feedback to support Ford's 'Find' and 'Fix' strategy. The 'Find' and 'Fix' strategy allowed Ford to seek and uncover problems in manufacturing and production operations and rapidly repair or correct defects using key 'customer-derived' input.
2. Compare and track Ford's rank and standing against the competition on overall satisfaction with the quality and ownership process, number of Things Gone Wrong, satisfaction with various vehicle and ownership attributes, as well as a number of key dealership, brand, and non-TGW issues.

In order for Ford to meet its quality objectives and tracking requirements, the company, in partnership with the RDA Group, a full-service market research firm located in Bloomfield Hills, Michigan in the United States, developed a global market research program, known as Global Quality Research System. The program was developed over a two-year period and was Ford's first real attempt at defining a truly global quality research program. The program included theoretical and analytical development and testing, first in the United States and then in Europe, South America, and Asia-Pacific. Ford's goal was to use the Global Quality Research survey and market research system wherever in the world Ford had production plants. Direct customer feedback on vehicle quality and ownership issues would be provided to the global quality offices and plants for direct and continuous assessment of both 'Find' and 'Fix,' as well as competitive benchmark tracking.

The design of the survey and its content contained a large number of survey attributes that allowed Ford and its Quality Office to uncover minute details of the customer's vehicle quality issues and provide Ford with the specific information they required to 'find and fix' quality concerns with their vehicles in a timely manner. After piloting the study in a number of markets, detailed vehicle assessment and ongoing tracking of Ford vs the competition was initiated. The Global Quality market research program was first launched in the United States in 1988 using a mail methodology.

Qualified Ford and competitive customers were identified through the use of state vehicle registration records. The mail survey was extended to the western European markets shortly after the launch of the program of the United States. Finally, the Global Quality Research program was launched in Latin America and Asia-Pacific by the middle of the same year. At any point in time, anywhere in the world, Ford could assess both its quality performance and competitive standing.

The Ford Global Quality Survey included overall product quality and ownership experience satisfaction measures, a 360-item TGW checkbox battery, a 60-item quality and ownership expectation battery, respondent demographics, and detailed respondent TGW verbatim comments. All of these survey attributes were extremely critical for Ford's understanding of their customers' satisfaction. The Ford Quality Office and Plants used the detailed TGW data and respondent comments for 'find and fix' solutions for their vehicles coming off the assembly line. Overall, satisfaction scores are tracked both over time and among markets/plants. The detailed satisfaction/expectation batteries are utilized in Ford's modeling strategy of assessing future customer 'needs' and 'wants' impacting future product redesign/development.

While methodology, survey wording, translations, and scales were modified for the local market and culture, the basic content, survey design, and administration of the survey were consistent with the approach in the United States. The idea was to retain as much of a consistent global approach as possible in order to enhance the use of the customer information cross-nationally. The most critical factor was the retention of the 'mail methodological appearance,' although it was administered in either street intercept or appointment-based interview format.

The Ford historical North American research approach in Latin America

As indicated, the original global quality survey was designed for the more stable mail methodologies of the industrialized North – the United States, western Europe (France, Germany, Italy, Spain and the United Kingdom), and Canada. Respondents in these countries could review the entire survey at their leisure and respond to the various sections within the relative comfort of their home or workplace. In these countries, respondents were then directed to return the completed survey in the postage-paid envelope that accompanied the original survey. The content of the survey was developed to reduce line item and order bias. The overall quality and ownership questions are ordered first, as 'top of mind.' The customer then proceeded

through the 360-item TGW checkbox, completing only those quality sections concerning his/her troubles with their vehicle. The respondent then proceeded on to the product and ownership satisfaction/expectation battery, completing all 60+ satisfaction and expectation questions. Finally, the customer completed the demographic section and completed the survey. Depending on the number of TGWs, a respondent could spend between 20 and 45 minutes completing the Global Quality survey. This is considered a fairly lengthy survey. Response rates for the United States are on average between 35% and 40%. The Global Quality surveys are administered at both Low Time in Service (three months in service) and High Time in Service (one or three years in service) in the United States, Europe, Latin America, and Taiwan. In Thailand and Malaysia the surveys were used only for three months in service.

Originally, the North American mail questionnaire, used also in Europe and Taiwan, was adopted for use in Latin America by modifying the research methodology. Since the mail systems in Latin America are either unusable or inefficient, personal street intercepts (Mexico, Venezuela, and Brazil) or personal appointments (Argentina and Colombia) were adopted. The questionnaires used are almost identical with modifications for language, vehicle options, and socio-demographic indicators. Given the political, socio-economic, and cultural environmental constraints within these Latin American countries (personal security issues, mixed socio-economic neighborhoods, restrictions on accessibility to A–B socio-economic groups, civil unrest/conflict, and the cultural limitations of completing market research surveys), the results from Latin America were mixed, at best. However, Ford perceived that it was receiving fairly reliable and valid results since customers approached for the interview typically completed the survey, if time permitted. The above-mentioned biases were viewed as 'common cause' variation since these biases were assumed to occur in non-systematic random occasions.

From 1998 until the year 2000 Global Quality surveys were conducted throughout Latin America using the personal-intercept/appointment methods. As Ford increased its emphasis in product quality and manufacturing/production fixes, it instituted a number of independent internal and external checks on the Global Quality Research system. At the same time, increases in personal security issues and other socio-political-economic environmental factors led to increasingly unstable results. Lower response rates, increasingly more incomplete surveys, the continued lack of accessibility to nonurban rural areas, and the limited accessibility for higher-level luxury or truck segments in addition to exceedingly long fieldwork time supplied Ford with incomplete and extremely dated findings. The result was customer information that was either misleading or incomplete. This situation practically paralyzed the plants because critical, accurate, customer-driven information was lacking.

It was apparent to all parties involved (Ford GCI, The Ford Quality Office, Ford plant personnel, and the RDA Group) that critical corrective actions had to be taken to address the methodological and cultural biases associated with the current Latin American Global Quality Research program. The difficult task was how to address the biases without compromising the global nature of the program. Ford's major manufacturing and production processes were highly dependent on all the information captured in the survey.

Methodological and result biases using the North American approach in Latin America

The first critical factor was to correctly identify the methodological and survey biases from the five Latin American markets that were using the Global Quality Research system and correctly comprehend their root causes. After a careful review of the previous two years of data from the five Latin American markets, and conducting a series of brainstorming sessions with both Ford market research and quality end users of the information, it was concluded that the biases were derived from two distinct but related aspects of the Global Quality Research method and survey processes: (1) the actual methodology itself; and (2) the responders who completed the studies. Table 5.7 indicates the particular biases within each of the identified categories, their root cause, and the effect they had on the final findings from the study.

Given the changes in the current state of the socio-political-economic environmental factors in Latin America, the biases were found to be systemic non-random in nature vs common cause variation that was originally thought to be the case. The conclusion was that methodological/responder biases were severely affecting both the study results and the actions taken by the plants to address quality issues.

The questionable results from the Global Quality surveys (for example reduction in TGW over time with no improvement in satisfaction) seem to indicate that respondent fatigue, responder bias, the lack of national level representation, and security/safety issues were having a major impact on the results. Inconsistent results with other Ford internal and external market research studies tended to confirm that the Global Quality Research biases were challenging the validity of the entire program. Finally, the extremely long field times associated with personal street intercepts and per-

sonal appointments hindered the usefulness of the data and findings. That is, by the time the findings were reported and analyzed at the Ford Quality Office and plant level, almost an entire year of vehicle production had been completed.

The main challenge facing Ford and the RDA Group was how to address and correct the methodological/responder biases in the Global Quality Research program without any help from the conventional market research literature, while at the same time retaining the content and structure of the Global Quality Research survey program in order to keep it consistent with the global program being conducted in multiple markets. Clearly there was a need to institute a major paradigm shift in the way Ford and the RDA Group conceptualized, operationalized, measured, collected, and analyzed the product quality data from Latin America.

The 'respondent-based intelligent' methodological approach

Ford GCI (Global Consumer Insights), in partnership with its global quality supplier, the RDA Group, set out to address both the survey content and methodological issues in Latin America. The intent was to not only solve the responder biases, but to formulate a product quality research system that would be both sensitive to the Latin American market conditions and provide results which could be used on a global basis.

One strategy was to review other market research projects being conducted throughout Latin America. Methodology, survey type, measurement criteria, operationalization of the concepts, etc., were reviewed. However, what was discovered was that many of the other market research studies focused on packaged goods, services or small durable goods that were sold across the socio-demographic spectrum (from A-through E-level socio-demographic groups). Given the wide variability in the socio-demographic construct of the customers, most market research studies appealed to the lowest common denominator, resulting in most studies using methodologies and approaches that were similar to the current approach used in the Global Quality Research program.

As part of its quality efforts, Ford has embraced the Six Sigma Breakthrough Methodology as a tool to aid in the addressing and fixing of defects and variability in the manufacturing and production processes. The main idea of the Six Sigma Methodology is to assess the 'needs' and 'wants' of its customers or the customer critical-to-quality aspects and bring these concepts to bear in the manufacturing/production processes. The strategy is to have these processes functioning within

TABLE 5.7 Methodological and responder biases inherent in the North American Global Quality Research approach to Latin America

I. Methodological Bias		
Bias	**Root causes**	**Effect on research program**
Responder bias	■ Survey length too long ■ Respondent skipping or not reading all survey responses	■ Biased results ■ Inaccurate results
Low response rates	■ Survey length too long ■ Vehicles in certain segments could not be located	■ Biased results ■ Insufficient sample size for certain segments
Respondent fatigue	■ Survey length too long ■ Respondent skipping or not reading all survey responses	■ Biased results ■ Inaccurate results
Nonnational representation	■ Only respondents from major urban areas included in the study	■ Biased results ■ Sample not representative of the population
Culturally inconsistent survey attributes	■ Attributes not fully specified in local dialect ■ Attribute definition not available in local language	■ Biased results
Nonresearch environmental issues (e.g., personal security, political, macroeconomic, etc.)	■ Changes or distributions in environmental variables	■ Biased results ■ Delays in field and reporting time
Delayed timing issues	■ Long field time to complete intercept methodology	■ Delays in field and reporting time ■ Out of date findings
II. Responder Bias		
Bias	**Root causes**	**Effect on research program**
Inconsistent results (Reduction in TGW with little or no change in satisfaction ratings)	■ Intercept methodology ■ Nonresearch environmental issues	■ Biased results ■ Inaccurate results
Global Quality Research results not consistent with other external research programs	■ Intercept methodology ■ Delays in field and reporting time	■ Biased results ■ Inaccurate results
Results not consistent with internal plant measures	■ Intercept methodology ■ Delays in field and reporting time	■ Biased results ■ Inaccurate results
Results not consistent across plants and markets	■ Variable methodologies ■ Nonresearch environmental issues ■ Delays in field and reporting time	■ Biased results ■ Inaccurate results

Six Sigma of the target. Product would leave the factories over 99.99996% error free, resulting in increased customer satisfaction and stronger customer/owner loyalty commitment. The Six Sigma Breakthrough Methodology has been embraced by a number of major manufacturing and service corpora-tions, and bottom-line cost savings due to reductions in variability/defects and increases in satisfaction have been tremendous.

While not defined as an official Ford Six Sigma project, Ford GCI and the RDA Group decided to employ the Six Sigma Customer Driven Breakthrough Methodology and body of knowledge toolset to the market research problem in Latin America. Customers would be contacted in order to assess what methodology to adapt and how to operationalize it for the Latin American market.

The first step was to identify Ford's customers, of which there were two:

1. *Internal customers:* the Ford Quality Office and the Plant Managers in Ford's South American markets. These customers were the users of the data and findings. They are the individuals who are charged with assessing vehicle TGW and developing fixes for the manufacturing and production processes. Their main requirements include detailed customer TGW, satisfaction, expectation, and verbatim comments that are highly accurate, detailed, valid, reliable, and delivered in a timely manner to impact the improvements on the assembly line.

2. *External customers:* the actual Ford customers who are interviewed during the survey process. These are the individuals who must complete Ford's surveys and provide the critical information for use by its internal customers. Their main requirements include surveys that are short, easy to understand, and which provide a linear communication flow to Ford for them to clearly communicate their TGWs

and quality/ownership satisfaction in the most expedient method possible.

The next step was to complete the design phase of the project. The main goal of this phase is to develop the purpose and scope of the project, as well as to collect critical information from both internal and external customers. This would be the key to the Global Quality Research system redesign efforts.

Once the scope of the project redesign was complete, the next step was to measure the current Global Quality Research system process across all of the markets where Ford conducted quality research in Latin America.

The main result of this stage of the redesign process indicated that Ford's current methodological approach (street intercept or scheduled appointment) was extremely cumbersome and difficult to administer to the customer, resulting in extremely high rates of interview refusal, incomplete, and biased results. Information collected from this measurement stage of the redesign process laid the foundation and provided guidance for reformulation of the program in Latin America.

Table 5.8 outlines the proposed survey and methodological redesigns for the Global Quality Research program in Latin America. The recommended changes impacted five critical areas: survey content, survey administration, methodology, timing, and information usage by the end client.

TABLE 5.8 Recommended changes for the Latin American Global Quality Research program based on internal and external customer requirements

Program category	Customer recommended changes	
	Recommended changes	**Proposed actions**
Methodology	■ Migrate from current street intercept/ personal appointment to telephone (CATI)	■ Switch methodology ■ Develop 'bridge factor' for historical trending
Survey content Incorporate/capture market uniqueness	■ Remove noncritical 'nice to have' and 'not needed' attributes ■ Clarify any misunderstood market-specific terminology or concepts	■ Survey was reviewed and revised
Survey administration	■ Migrate from respondent self-administered to interview administered	■ Completed during the migration to the CATI methodology
Field timing	■ Increase the number of program waves and dramatically reduce field time	■ Completed during the migration to the CATI methodology
End-client data usage	■ Added additional detail and content to the reporting process due to more complete customer phone records	■ Completed during the migration to the CATI methodology

The challenge was to implement the recommended changes while still retaining the main objectives of the global program. To do this, a sample of the Ford Quality Office and plant managers from the global markets were interviewed and a table of critical attributes was developed. These critical attributes were items that the Ford Quality Office and plant managers had to have to continually assess and fix their manufacturing and production processes. Other attributes were segmented into either 'nice to have' or 'not needed' categories. Anything that was 'not needed' was immediately dropped for retention consideration.

The 'respondent-based intelligent' systematic elimination of the methodological and responder biases

The result of customer assessment of the current Global Quality Research program was development based on a dual approach to redesigning the program consisting of the migration from a personal-based intercept/appointment to a CATI (computer-assisted telephone interviewing) methodology and the adoption of a 'respondent-based intelligent' survey. The 'respondent-based intelligent' survey allowed Ford to keep all the 'critical' and some of the 'nice to have' survey attributes, but respondents were only administered those questions that were directly related to their vehicle or their specific quality problems through the use of intelligent survey skip patterns.

In the redesigned survey, respondents were asked if they had any problems in 13 key vehicle function groups: key vehicle level attributes, such as brakes, interior vehicle components, steering/handling, etc. If the customer identified that he/she did indeed have a problem in one of the 13 groups, then a detailed series of related checkboxes and opportunities for verbatim comments would be administered to the customer. Unlike the mail survey format, the respondent-based intelligent CATI survey would not inundate the respondent with a large number of TGW checkboxes and verbatim prompts that were not pertinent to the customer's problems. At the same time, other customers who experienced TGW in other vehicle function groups would be administered those related TGW checkboxes. The result was that Ford was able to retain all the 360 TGW checkbox and verbatim prompts without having every respondent go through every TGW checkbox including those that are not pertinent to their problems. This methodological improvement allowed for a consistent Latin American regional application of the survey administration and reporting of the findings.

The other key implemented strategy was to split the Global Quality Research system into two distinct research programs. The 'find' and 'fix' element was conducted by CATI with Ford-only vehicles using a Ford-only name list. Ford would conduct as many or as few of these studies as needed, depending on sales volume, informational need, etc. The sample was large and could be conducted with a nationally represented sample. The competitive benchmark study was completed using a smaller Ford and selected competitive set of vehicles. The availability of competitive name lists is the key factor for this portion of the program. Where competitive telephone name lists are available, the study is completed in conjunction with the Ford-only 'find' and 'fix' study. Where competitive telephone name lists are not available, the study is completed using the traditional street-intercept methodology. Since the competitive benchmark portion of the Global Quality Research program is concerned with benchmark satisfaction and TGW level information only (not detailed TGW), this portion of the program is less susceptible to methodological and responder biases and can be completed in a more traditional manner.

Based on the results of interviews with the internal customers and the biases from the current Global Quality Research program, a proposed survey, CATI methodology, and survey administration were developed that addressed the critical biases of the old program with the critical 'needs' and 'wants' from internal and external customers. The results were the proposed redesigned survey, methodology, and program as presented in Table 5.9.

Although comfortable with the proposed redesign of the program for Latin America, Ford decided to apply a series of experimental designs to simulate and test the new approach. Experiments and simulations were pretested first in the United States and were then rolled out to the two largest and most diverse markets in Latin America where Ford conducts the Global Quality Research program: Brazil and Mexico. Selected vehicle lines and segments were chosen for simulations and experiments applying slightly different survey content and modified CATI approaches. The results confirmed which survey attributes were critical for Ford's quality research assessment.

Operationalization of the respondent-based approach for Latin America

The use of 'respondent-based intelligent' surveys accurately simulated the respondent interview process and greatly reduced respondent fatigue, respondent bias, and invalid responses. Interview time was reduced from 20–45 minutes to 15–30 minutes per interview.

TABLE 5.9	Final changes for the Latin American Global Quality Research program based on customer requirements and experimental design results

	Customer required changes	
Program category	**Biases from the old program**	**Final changes**
Methodology	■ Responder bias ■ Low response rates ■ Respondent fatigue ■ Inconsistent results	■ Migrate from current street intercept/personal appointment to telephone (CATI)
Survey content	■ Respondent fatigue ■ Culturally inconsistent survey attributes	■ Remove non-critical 'nice to have' and 'not needed' attributes ■ Clarify any misunderstood market specific terminology or concepts
Survey administration	■ Nonnational representation	■ Migrate from respondent self-administered to interview administered
Field timing	■ Delayed timing issues	■ Increase the number of program waves and dramatically reduce field time
End-client data usage	■ New additional use of the data	■ Added additional detail and content to the reporting process due to more complete customer phone records

Interviewing over the telephone eliminated many of the customers' personal comfort and security issues. It was discovered that customers interviewed on the telephone were much more relaxed and able to provide a more accurate and reliable assessment of their satisfaction with their vehicle/quality ownership experience, as well as their vehicle troubles.

Changes were made to the surveys to reflect both the migration from street intercept/personal appointment to CATI and the survey content changes recommended by the internal customers.

Brazil implemented three waves of interviewing per year, Mexico two waves, and Venezuela and Argentina one wave.

based survey effectively eliminated or greatly reduced the methodological and respondent-based biases from the traditional intercept surveys.

All Latin American markets launched the new Global Quality Research program in 2000. Initial findings and results from all the Latin American markets further verified the success of the new program and the 'respondent-based intelligent' surveys. Critical quality information has continued to flow into the Ford Latin American plants and has provided key information for both competitive benchmark tracking and quality 'find' and 'fixes.' A number of quality defects have been identified and fixed early in the manufacturing process throughout Latin America.

Assessment of the results: Mexico and Venezuela pilot tests

Once the final set of experiments from Brazil and Mexico was finished, Ford decided to complete pilots in the two markets that had the most extreme biases and skewed results: Mexico and Venezuela. The results from both the Mexican and Venezuelan pilots tended to confirm the assumption that the new respondent-

Questions

1. Evaluate Ford's use of different methodologies in its Global Quality Research program prior to 2000.

2. Evaluate Ford's decision to change to what is essentially a single global methodology for data collection, a CATI system.

3. What method should Ford and the RDA Group use in markets having low telephone penetration? Explain.

CHAPTER 6

Market Entry Strategies

6.1 Introduction

A market entry strategy consists of an *entry mode* and a *marketing plan*. The mode of entry is what is used to penetrate a target country while the foreign marketing plan is used to penetrate a target market. The entry mode is important as it determines the degree of a company's control over the marketing mix (program), and to an extent the degree of its commitment, in the target market. Implementing an entry strategy for each market is analogous to establishing a *channel of distribution*. This may be for initial or continued entry.

6.2 Entry as a channel decision

6.2.1 Channel structure

A company's international marketing channel is the path in the structure of distribution through which the products of the company reach the final consumer or user. From the company's point of view, the structure of distribution consists of the marketing channels currently available in a foreign market together with those channels by which the market is reached in the first place. Thus, the structure of distribution for reaching any foreign market includes all of the intermediary marketing agencies or institutions that are in use by all companies at any given time, their capacities and capabilities, and their geographic coverage.

In developing its entry mode(s) a company must plan for the flow of two things that are involved when its products pass through the structure of distribution: (1) the flow of transactions, and (2) the flow of the physical product. The transactions flow, also known as the flow of ownership, is accomplished by the series of sales transactions negotiated or facilitated by the channel members that ultimately transfers ownership of the product to the final buyer. The physical flow moves the product itself to the final buyer through a series of physical movements and storage points. Throughout international marketing channels these two elements tend to coincide, but exceptions do occur. For example, the use of an export broker involves only the element of transactions; but when an export merchant is involved both elements typically coincide. Of the two flows, that of ownership is perhaps more significant to management because ownership carries with it both risk and control. This is not to say that physical distribution (supply chain management, logistics) is unimportant. On the contrary, there may be instances where the physical flow has a definite impact on the transactions flow. A company may be able to make a particular sale only because the physical distribution system it uses gets the product to the buyer when and where it is wanted and at a reasonable cost, relative to other alternatives available to the buyer. In a similar manner, what happens after the sale is made (after-sales service) is also important as such service performance affects future export sales.

Many specific types of organizations may be involved performing the transactions and physical flows in a given international marketing channel of distribution. Of primary significance are the *marketing organizations* – independent companies of various types, overseas sales offices, and so on – that directly participate in these flows. They perform a direct role in the sales function. The independent companies, which may or may not take ownership of the products involved, are not under any direct control by the producer. In addition to marketing organizations there are other types of organization – for example banks, transportation companies, and advertising agencies – that provide useful and necessary services to the international marketer. Such institutions or agencies are not members of the marketing channel, but are *facilitating* or *service organizations*.

We can now define an international marketing channel of distribution as follows:

> a system composed of marketing organizations that connect the manufacturer to the final users or consumers of the company's product(s) in a foreign market.

Sometimes a channel is quite simple (or short), perhaps direct from a manufacturer to the final user or consumer. Often it is more complex (or long), utilizing many marketing organizations – independent or manufacturer owned.

6.2.2 Importance of the entry decision

In a number of respects the choice of entry modes or international marketing channels is important to management. Consequently a great amount of effort and patience must be provided by management when considering this decision.

Decisions on international marketing channels influence the price that final users or consumers will pay. For example, the margins required, and obtained, by independent organizations such as export merchants or wholesalers in the foreign market often constitute a significant share of the price paid by the final buyer. In some instances, if the marketing agencies can be eliminated from the channel, the price can be reduced. On the other hand, it should be recognized that eliminating such an organization may lead to an increase in price simply because the remaining channel members cannot perform certain activities as efficiently as a marketing agency that is able to specialize in the performance of these activities.

Policies concerning channels are related to production decisions. In the first place, location of production base (or sourcing) is the first channel decision that has to be made. Second, fluctuations in production may be reduced by proper selection of such channels. Greater production stability tends to eliminate or reduce problems of inventory control that face all the channel members. Moreover, production stability leads to security of employment, which is of increasingly great concern to individual workers, labor unions, and national governments both at home and abroad.

Another reason that entry mode selection is important is that the procedure of developing international channels can be slow and costly. The time and cost required in development can hinder a company that wants to expand its international operations by entering new foreign markets or a new industry. Also the future locational patterns and structural changes in distribution must be predicted, which may be difficult to do because of the great spatial distances involved and the limited availability of reliable data.

A typical manufacturer may do business in many countries, each one having a 'unique state' of general economic activity at any one period of time and each one exhibiting its own cyclical pattern of economic activity. The existence of such fluctuations, and their differences from country to country, makes the entry mode decision and the management of existing chemicals most difficult. For example, when there is a scarcity of supply in relation to demand (a seller's market exists), the practice of *selective distribution* (utilizing only the most profitable outlets and ignoring all others) may seem particularly inviting. However, for the long term this can be a dangerous practice to follow since a seller's market cannot last indefinitely. Unless management is continually aware of existing economic conditions in each of its foreign markets, it may find itself operating in a buyer's market without really knowing that conditions have changed. A policy of selective distribution may not provide the outlets needed to compete effectively in such a market.

Economic conditions can have a major impact on intermediaries in a market, thus affecting manufacturers and other international marketers as well. A case in point is the Asian situation that existed in the very late 1990s, as it impacted on international manufacturers/retailers and independent retailers, especially those dealing with luxury brands (*The Economist*, 1998). In Hong Kong, for instance, Gucci, Versace, Hugo Boss, Emporio Armani, and others had few customers. Yaohan, the Japanese department store chain, declared bankruptcy for its operation outside Japan, and closed many stores. Joyce Boutique, up to that time a very successful specialty store chain based in Hong Kong, closed its operations in Thailand, the Philippines, and South Korea, and severely cut back elsewhere. The 'pain' was felt by high-end and discount retailers alike. With adversity there is often opportunity. Wal-Mart, the US chain, bought discount superstores in South Korea and had plans to build more stores in China by the beginning of the new century; Tesco, a large British supermarket chain, entered Asia in 1998 by acquiring 13 superstores from CP Group in Thailand; Carrefour, a French hypermarket chain, continued to expand its presence in Asia during the 'crisis' period.

But not everything works out as planned. A case in point is the US retailer Wal-Mart, the world's largest retailer (and the world's largest company). In 2003, in addition to its stores in the United States it operated more than 1300 stores in 10 countries, ranking as the largest retailer in Canada and Mexico (Bianco and Zellner, 2003, p. 106). The road to success abroad has not always been smooth.

Wal-Mart's original ventures into Argentina, Indonesia, and Germany were 'failures,' resulting in large losses. In Germany, for example, in 1997 Wal-Mart acquired 21 hypermarkets from Wertkauf, and acquired 74 Interspar stores a year later. When they tried to introduce their 'normal' operating practices, German consumers resisted the Wal-Mart approach to service that is based on friendliness (Rubin, 2001). In short, Wal-Mart failed to understand Germany's retail culture, government regulations, and the competition among 14 hypermarket chains in a stagnant market (*Business Week*, 2001, p. 84). Things are going better now.

Entry mode is a vital part of the international marketing mix. Decisions on channels can limit the alternatives available to a manufacturer in the other activities making up the marketing mix, or at the very least constrain the tactical implementation of the other marketing variables. In exporting, for instance, if a manufacturer decides to use the services of an export management company, wholesalers, and retailers, the general nature of the pricing problem to marketing organizations is determined. Also, the selection of specific marketing channels reduces promotion alternatives. The need for promotion support might affect selected dimensions of the total promotion program. Sometimes an international marketer will eliminate intermediaries in a foreign market because they do not promote the product(s) to the extent desired. Such an action can turn out to be a mistake, as shown in Exhibit 6.1.

| **EXHIBIT 6.1** | **Eliminating wholesalers can 'backfire'** |

Warner-Lambert ran into major problems trying to sell its brands of chewing gum to the Japanese. Its wholesalers were not promoting the products to the extent desired, so a decision was made to change its strategy. The company attempted to eliminate its wholesalers from the channel of distribution. This turned out to be a big mistake. In addition to upsetting the wholesalers, the move created suspicions among the retailers, who often viewed companies as being unreliable if they switched business tactics. The decision was reversed, and Warner-Lambert asked its sales force to collect the retail sales orders for the wholesalers (Ricks, 1999, p. 113).

Finally, the relations between the manufacturer and marketing organizations, and between two marketing organizations at different levels – such as wholesalers and retailers – can create some difficult problems for both. The basic source of difficulty is the inherent conflict of interest between the two. The selling organization wants the buying marketing organization to sell as much as possible for the minimum possible margin. In contrast, the marketing company buying for resale wants to maximize its own profits. This conflict is compounded by the complication in relations that arise because the companies involved will come from different cultures, societies, political systems, and so forth. In general, however, the area of mutual interest is far greater than that of conflict.

6.2.3 The whole channel concept

Management should be striving always to select the 'best' international marketing channel; the one that comes closest to completely satisfying target customers, fits the entire international marketing mix, and still satisfies the company's overall objectives. In this endeavor, the channel of distribution should be viewed as an integrated system with the manufacturer on one end and the final user or buyer on the other end. This can be called the *whole channel concept*. For the international marketing channel system there are three basic components, as follows:

1. the *headquarters' organization* developed by the manufacturer to implement its international marketing operations;
2. the methods used or channels through which the products are sent to foreign markets – the *channels between nations*;
3. the means by which these products reach the target, final user or consumer in the foreign markets, assuming that the importers are not the final users or consumers – the *channels within nations*.

Company organization has a unique relationship with the entry mode decision. In the first place, it is the headquarters' organization that supervises the channels used, including any intermediary marketing organizations. As such, then, it is an integral part of the channel itself. Second, the specific channel alternatives used can influence the structure of the headquarters' organization. For example, a company that is relatively new to international markets and/or one that markets only one product will need a different (and simpler) organization than one that is an established international marketer selling in many foreign markets and perhaps also having many products. Similarly, a company engaged in only exporting will need a different (and perhaps simpler) organization than one that also has overseas operations such as licensing or production facilities. Third, companies with fairly rigid organization structures will find themselves in a position where the existing headquarters' organization can limit the alternative avenues to serve foreign markets. For a multiple subsidiary company, so-called internal (parent) *isomorphism* can have an effect on a subsidiary's (i.e., a Strategic Business Unit or SBU) foreign market entry mode decisions (Davis *et al.*, 2000). Isomorphism is a process that forces a subsidiary to resemble other company business units facing a similar environment. For any given company the nature of the interdependence between its headquarters' organization and international marketing channels and between the international channels themselves will depend on its present stage of internationalization development, and different managements find themselves at varying stages of development.

The international marketing channel is viewed as a two-phase system to emphasize the whole channel concept. This is particularly important when independent marketing organizations are part of the channel since many exporters think that their channels end with these organizations. Since a channel is only as good as its weakest link, international marketers should be concerned with *all* the links in the channel. To do otherwise is an invitation to trouble, particularly for the firm entering a foreign market for the first time. Certain actions of intermediaries, especially overseas 'domestic' wholesalers and/or retailers, may at best hinder and possibly even completely destroy the long-run profit potential of doing business in a market.

To illustrate, Nine West is a producer of women's footwear, handbags, and accessories. In late 2002 it had 850 outlets in 43 countries. Stores under its own name are either company owned or licensed. But its principal business is supplying other retailers. However, in the early 2000s it began expanding its own retail base, thus competing with its customers. Other manufacturers such as Nike and Guess have done likewise. To an extent, this movement has been 'fueled' by shrinking department store chains and shoe stores that are consolidating. In Canada, for example, Nine West lost a major client when Eatons Department Store chain closed in 1999 (Strauss, 2002).

6.3 Entry as a strategy

Entry into foreign markets, initially and on a continuing basis, should be made using methods that are consistent with the company's strategic objectives. From a strategy perspective, entry mode is influenced by the international strategy pursued by the firm for its foreign venture or market expansion. All market entries may not be motivated by the same international strategy. Thus, the choice of entry mode is made to facilitate the firm's international strategy for a particular foreign market entry. When a firm becomes committed to international markets (becomes more than a casual exporter) it is well on its way to becoming *internationalized*, even if limited only to export operations. Exporting may be the best international learning experience, something that takes a firm toward more and more sophistication and commitment to other modes of international marketing such as establishing a manufacturing facility in a foreign market.

6.3.1 The elements of entry strategy

(*This section draws upon material contained in Root, 1994, Ch. 2.*)
The strategy for how foreign markets are to be entered (the international marketing channel strategy) should be viewed as a comprehensive plan, which sets forth the objectives, resources, and policies that will guide a company's international marketing operations over some future time period which is of sufficient length that the company can achieve sustainable growth in foreign markets. For the firm new to international marketing or new to specific foreign markets it has been suggested that the entry strategy planning horizon be three to five years.

Rather than view entry strategy as a simple plan, in practice it is actually a summation of individual product/market plans. Each target market is unique in some ways and each product has unique market needs. Therefore managers need to plan the entry strategy for each product in each foreign market. In short, managers must think in terms of a *product/market* as the relevant unit for decisions. While the end result of this process may exhibit similarities one cannot assume that market response to a particular entry strategy will be the same for different products and country markets. In some national markets it may be necessary to vary, or at least consider varying, the entry strategy within the market itself, especially when the entry is to serve the market rather than for sourcing only. Very broadly, a foreign market entry strategy can be viewed as a plan for the marketing program to be used for the product/market. As such, then, it requires decisions on the following:

- the objectives and goals in the target market;
- needed policies and resource allocations;
- the choice of entry modes to penetrate the market;
- the control system to monitor performance in the market;
- a time schedule.

The dominant objective should be to build permanent market position and whatever resources are needed for this should be committed.

The last two decisions are part of a broader activity, namely, managing the international marketing channel. In addition, an international marketing plan should include an analysis of the target market and the market environment, a financial analysis, and an evaluation of competitive conditions. Yet such an approach may be useful for the 'newcomer' firm and to companies needing to gain export experience and greater confidence in their own ability.

In planning international/export marketing channels, the first step after delineating the target market(s) is to specify the objectives of the channel or channel group, that is, what it is the channel is to accomplish. After the target markets and channel objectives have been determined the international marketing mix to be used in serving the target markets must be outlined. There is a two-way relationship between channels and the international marketing mix. Ideally, all elements of the marketing mix should be determined simultaneously. In practice, however, some must be determined first, and it is these elements that provide the base upon which the others are determined. For example, in determining the price of products a manufacturer limits pricing alternatives once a channel has been selected. In the same way, if a price has been established first, then the alternative channels available from which one can choose may be limited severely.

6.3.2 Alternative market entry modes

An international market entry mode is an institutional arrangement necessary for the entry of a company's products, technology, and human and financial capital into a foreign country/market. To the international marketer, different entry modes represent varying levels of control, commitment, involvement, and risk. Concerning channels between nations, there are major alternative strategies for entering a foreign market as shown in Figure 6.1. The first decision that must be made concerns where the production base should be located – in the home

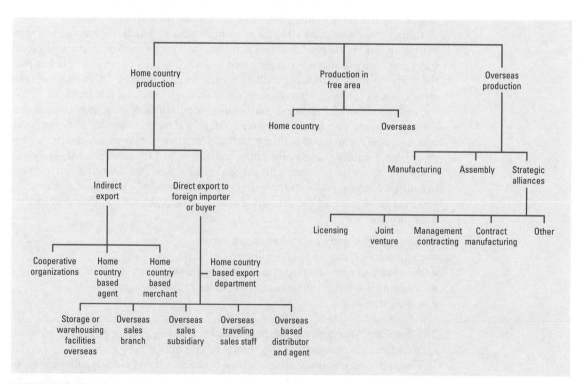

FIGURE 6.1 Outline of alternative basic international marketing channels

country, overseas, or in a free area (free port, trade zone, perimeter). After this decision has been made, a company must decide whether or not areas are to be served outside of the countries in which production facilities are located, and, if so, what channels between countries are to be used. We discuss briefly each of the major alternative entry modes. More detailed discussions are presented in Chapters 7 and 8.

Channels between nations

Exporting. Perhaps the simplest and easiest way to meet the needs of foreign markets is by exporting. This approach generally has minimal effect on the ordinary operations of the firm, and the risks involved are less than other alternatives. At the same time, many companies long involved in foreign markets still export on a regular and permanent basis. Nike and other casual shoe manufacturers, for example, use export to do business in North America and Europe, with products actually produced in China, South Korea, Indonesia, and Taiwan by contract manufacturers. Similarly, clothing manufacturers – including those with 'designer clothes' – have their products manufactured in China and other countries in Southeast Asia and Central America and use export to serve North American and European markets.

Management can choose from two broad avenues of exporting – *indirect* or *direct* export. These two basic forms of exporting are distinguished on the basis of how the exporting firm carries out the transactions flow between itself and the foreign importer or buyer. In indirect export the manufacturer utilizes the services of various types of independent marketing organizations or cooperative organizations that are located in the home country. When a manufacturer exports indirectly the responsibility for carrying out the foreign selling job is transferred to some other organization. On the other hand, in direct export the responsibility for performing international sales activities is in the hands of the producer. These activities are carried out and managed by so-called dependent organizations that are administratively a part of the manufacturer's company organization. In essence, then, the choice facing a company is whether market entry and/or expansion is to be handled by an integrated channel (captive or company owned) or by a channel that includes independent intermediaries (Anderson and Coughlan, 1987).

Increasingly, some companies are turning to the Internet as a means of exporting to foreign markets. This is *e-commerce*. The Internet has potential usefulness for companies that can sell direct to the foreign market or direct to intermediaries within the domestic market who would then handle the export transaction. The Internet seems to be better suited for B2B than for B2C marketing, although B2C will increase as the percentage of the population having Internet access increases. For example, in early 2001 it was estimated that only 2–3% of the Latin American population had access to the Internet; this was estimated to increase to as much as 14% of the population by 2005 (Strohmeyer, 2001). Internet penetration is also low in most parts of Asia, central and eastern Europe, and the Islamic nations of the Middle East. The Internet is open to all types of companies – manufacturers, wholesalers, 'regular' retailers, service companies, and companies that started as Internet based and which do all their business using this method (the so-called dotcoms), such as Amazon.com and eBay. This is a tool that either supplants or supplements other techniques such as direct mail or telemarketing, or even personal selling. However, as with all newer technologies, the international marketer who chooses to use the Internet should do so selectively, and with caution. There are still many legal issues to be resolved that could affect relationships consummated by this means.

Licensing.   One of the first means that a manufacturer can use in expanding international operations beyond exporting is licensing agreements. Licensing includes arrangements for the foreign licensee to pay for the use of manufacturing, processing, trademark or name, patents, technical assistance, marketing knowledge, trade secrets, or some other skill provided by the licensor.

Licensing is a viable means of developing investment footholds in overseas markets, and a complement to exporting and direct investment in manufacturing facilities. It often constitutes a prelude to a more permanent equity investment.

Contract manufacturing.   This strategy involves contracting for the manufacture or assembly of products by manufacturers established in overseas markets, while still retaining the responsibility for marketing. Under certain circumstances, for example in the book publishing field, the contractor firm may distribute the products through its own outlets. This method allows a company to break into international marketing without making the final commitment of setting up complete manufacturing and selling operations; yet the way is kept open for implementing a long-term development policy at an appropriate time. Often this approach is used for sourcing because of lower cost of production. Nike and other shoe producers, as mentioned earlier, use Asian contract manufacturers.

Management contracting.   In management contracting a local investor in a foreign market provides the capital for an enterprise, while a company from 'outside' provides the necessary know-how to manage the company. Such an approach to entering international markets is a low-risk way, if used with some type of purchase option. It allows a company to manage another company without equity control or legal responsibility.

Manufacturing.   The decision to manufacture abroad may be forced upon a company because of competitive pressure, market demands, government restrictions on imports, or government actions that would result in imports being at a disadvantage. For example, the completion of the EU's internal market originally scheduled for 1 January 1993 (resulting from the Single European Act of 1987) but not completed then, put companies outside the EU at a greater disadvantage than existed in the past. Or the decision may be part of a company's long-run plan to strengthen its international operations. Rarely should a company establish manufacturing facilities as its first international business operation. Exceptions exist, however, if the policies and regulations of the foreign government are such that the best way to enter the market is through direct investment in a manufacturing facility, which may be by 'starting from scratch' or by acquisition.

Assembly operations.   The establishment of assembly facilities represents a cross between exporting and foreign manufacturing. When following this strategy, a manufacturer exports components or parts. At the foreign assembly site these parts, often with those from other suppliers, are then put together to form the complete product. When a product is exported in this manner, savings may be realized in freight charges, various foreign government fees and in some countries (for certain products) Customs duties. Assembly has been widely used in the global automobile and personal computer industries.

Joint venture.   This strategy is followed in a foreign market when a nonnational company joins with national interests, or with a company from another foreign country, in forming a new company. The central feature of a joint venture is that ownership and control are shared. A company may be forced into a joint venture in a specific foreign market because of local government policies (for example in China), nationalistic feelings, or intense competitive pressure. Yet some companies select this approach voluntarily, because it is more profitable in the long run than other approaches. For example, in Mexico, the US shoe company Reebok used a joint venture – in contrast to Nike using a wholly owned subsidiary – because it is believed that local partners do better than US businesses (*Marketing News*, 1994).

Other.   An emerging type of alliance is the *outsourcing* of service work. Major countries where this is being done are India, China, and the Philippines. India, for example, is being used by US companies for creating call centers. India offers better-educated (college educated) workers than its US counterparts (high-school educated). More important, call center work is considered a lucrative, successful job in India, not a dead end (Brady, 2003). Annual turnover in call centers in India is one-sixth that in the United States.

China is rising fast as a services outsourcing hub. For example, near the Guangzhou airport a call center run by PacificNet of Hong Kong employs 2000 Chinese to service telecom and insurance companies in Hong Kong, Taiwan, and China. An Ernst & Young facility in Guangzhou, Cap Gemini, does everything from entering sales data for a Hong Kong convenience-store chain to processing cargo information for a Norwegian shipping company. In 2004, China's role has been largely focused on providing back-office support for financial service, telecom, software, and retailing companies in neighboring Asian countries (Einhorn and Kripalani, 2003). But companies from English-speaking countries are starting to look to China for call centers and back-office work. For example, Sweetheart Cup Company, a US manufacturer of plastic plates, cups, and utensils for customers such as McDonald's and Wendy's International, hired a consultant, E5 Systems of Waltham, MA, to develop a system to track production processes at its 14 North American manufacturing plants. E5 is doing the work in Shenzhen, China, where it has a joint venture.

Channels within nations

There are many different ways that a manufacturer's product can reach consumers or users after the product has entered the foreign market. Some broad alternative channels within a nation are shown in Figure 6.2.

When products are produced abroad these channel decisions are 'domestic decisions' in each market. Often a channel within a nation can be long and complex, as illustrated in Exhibit 6.2.

FIGURE 6.2

Some alternative channels within a nation
Source: reprinted by permission of the author from Root, 1982

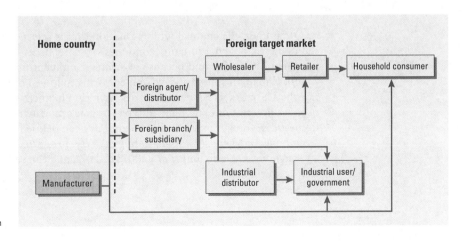

EXHIBIT 6.2   A complex channel within a nation

Among the many things Japan is noted for is its often complex distribution system. For many products there are layers of wholesalers that must be dealt with before getting to retailers and final customers. A simplified example is shown in Figure 6.3, which illustrates the distribution route for medicinal herbs. Imported plants go first to 'big wholesalers' either directly or through *sogo shosha* (that is, large trading companies).

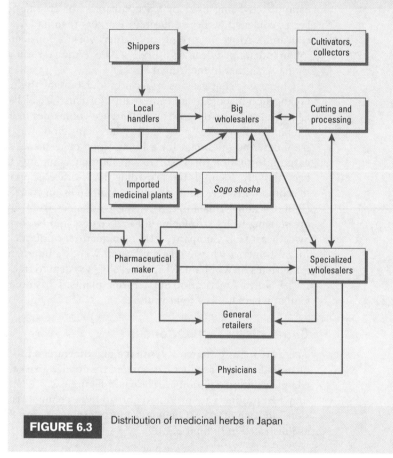

FIGURE 6.3   Distribution of medicinal herbs in Japan

Oftentimes, the channel within a nation that is selected is a result of *extending* the domestic channel to gain economies of scale, because product characteristics are generally similar and because of strategic momentum (McNaughton and Bell, 2000). Canadian software development firms followed this approach when entering the US market. Extension of distribution channels is one application of the broader practice of extending all types of marketing activities and strategies from domestic to foreign markets. Extension has been defined as *the amount of change from home market use of a marketing activity, program, or strategy when used in a foreign market* (Albaum *et al.*, 2003, p. 107), and can range from total extension to no extension at all.

6.4 Factors influencing choice of entry mode

The decision concerning what specific international marketing channels to use is not a simple one for the manufacturer. The existence of a great variety of types of international marketing organizations and the many ways they may be linked together have generated different types of alternative marketing channel systems, as we have just discussed.

Selection of mode of entry can be based on either or both of two broad approaches: through experience or through analysis. A company, through its own experience or that of other firms (competitive or otherwise), may decide that a particular entry mode is desirable for its product. In contrast, the same mode, or any other, may be arrived at after making an analysis of the marketing task, needs and buying habits of potential customers, and the competence of marketing organizations to perform various activities. In either approach, the end result is based essentially on needs and capabilities. Thus, the decision revolves around both internal and external considerations.

Regardless of the approach used in entry mode selection, the choice should be based on the alternative expected to give the greatest contribution to profit. Generally speaking, this may be easier said than done, particularly for those foreign markets where relevant data that normally are useful in making this type of decision are lacking. Many of the selection criteria are qualitative in nature, often defying any attempt at quantification. These criteria are relevant for the needed entry mode strategy decisions that have to be made. Such decisions involve formulating policies for the following areas:

- the type or kind of entry mode to be used, and, thus, the channel length;
- the selection of individual channel members;
- managing the channel, including relations with channel members and provision for feedback from the channel.

6.4.1 Type of mode

Questions about type or kind of entry mode or channel involve the types of marketing organizations, if any, to use. Thus, the international marketer decides how far its own organizational structure should be extended toward the consumer or user.

Target market

There are certain market-related factors that operate as international marketing channel determinants. These can be categorized into the following three groups:

1. the nature, size, and geographical distribution of customers;
2. the needs, requirements, and preferences of these customers;
3. the level of economic development of the market.

In addition, the question of 'market access' may arise in a given situation. The extent to which there is access to a market will depend upon other factors such as the location and needs of customers, the competitive situation and the infrastructure development and intermediary availability within the market. Finally, political stability and legal barriers can be significant entry mode determinants.

If potential buyers are diverse in character, if they are widely dispersed geographically, and if they buy frequently and in small quantities, there must be broad product availability, which would require the use of wholesalers and retailers (for consumer goods) within the market. Of course, were the opposite conditions to prevail, direct sale to retailers or industrial users would be more likely to be feasible. The more highly specialized the market and the more geographically concentrated it is, the shorter the channel is likely to be. At the same time, the preferences of customers cannot be ignored. If customers expect to find products in certain types of marketing organizations then they must be there, regardless of what the size and geographical concentration conditions indicate.

The level of economic development of a foreign market is an entry mode determinant in that it affects the overall organization of alternative channels, that is, the structure of distribution. Although this is a market-related factor, its impact is felt through the factor of availability of suitable marketing organizations within the target market.

Finally, the degree of political stability and extent of legal barriers that exist can affect the choice of channel in a target market. Both factors are derived from governmental policy and are attributes of a market. For example, a market with a high degree of political instability would involve a high degree of risk for a firm using direct export or production abroad in that payment (or profit repatriation) may be slowed or blocked altogether or desired currency may be in limited supply. If such a situation were to exist or be suspected, then indirect export (if a buyer could be found) would be better for the manufacturer.

Product

The nature of the product affects channel selection because products vary so widely in their characteristics (for example unit value, weight and bulk, technical complexity, and perishability) and use and because the selling job may differ markedly. For instance, the technical nature of a product may be such as to require service work both before and after sale. In many foreign market areas, especially in the developing nations, marketing intermediaries may not be able to handle such work. Also, the size and weight of the product or even the temperature, as in the case of frozen foods, may indicate the need for special handling facilities that marketing organizations might not have. These are situations where wholesalers are not likely to be used. Similarly, product perishability, either physical or in the form of fashion, often makes speed in distribution both necessary and desirable. Thus the international marketer will use a shorter channel than might otherwise be used, and direct export may be preferred.

The stage of development of a product as well as its relative newness to a foreign market can have a bearing on the channels to be used. If a company has a relatively unknown product, it might find it more beneficial to rely upon wholesalers and/or agents rather than try to sell direct. One exception to this would be when the product is part of a wider product line that is known to customers.

Availability of marketing organization

An international marketer's choice of entry mode is affected by the existing structure of distribution both in the home country and in the target market, and by the availability and competence of intermediary marketing organizations within the structure. An example of small retailers in a developing country is shown in Figure 6.4. Figure 6.5 shows examples of small retailers and larger 'designer' retailers in a more developed area. If 'good' marketing intermediaries do not exist or are already committed to handling competitive products, the international marketer/exporter may have to use a more direct mode of entry both between

FIGURE 6.4

For some consumer goods, local country markets are a major part of the structure of distribution. This is an example of the Indian market located in Chichicastenango, Guatemala

(a)

FIGURE 6.5

Retailers of all types are key to the successful marketing of consumer products in foreign markets. The images here depict (a) a street shopping area, Kowloon, Hong Kong, goods market and (b) a modern shopping directory
Source for (b): Dennis MacDonald/Alamy

(b)

nations and within the target market. In some instances the nonavailability of suitable marketing organizations may even be a deciding factor in a company's decision not to enter a foreign market.

Company considerations

A number of factors can be classified as company related. Most of these factors are influential in determining the marketing strength of the international marketer. Included are the following:

- marketing management capability and know-how;
- newness of the company to international marketing activities;
- size of the company and width of its product line;
- financial strength and ability to generate additional capital if needed;
- parent institutional norms.

Generally speaking, the greater the marketing strength, the better able, and more likely, a manufacturer will be to sell direct. A counterbalancing factor, however, is that the best and most aggressive marketing organizations often prefer to deal with established manufacturers that have marketing strength.

Another company-related factor that can affect the choice of a channel is management prejudice. There are times when influential executives have a preference for a particular channel. Regardless of their reasons, if these managers are truly influential, their choice will be selected even if analysis or experience indicates that some other alternative is more desirable. This is more likely to happen when choosing a channel between nations than when choosing channels within foreign nations. For example, the managing director of a Norwegian company may decide that the entry mode for Spain should be a sales branch or sales subsidiary, or some form of investment, perhaps even locating the facility along the Costa del Sol. This decision may have been influenced primarily by the executive's wish to have a nice place to visit on a business trip, particularly in the winter months. In a study of US service firms' foreign market entry mode choice, control (actual and/or desired) emerged as a useful basis for this choice (Erramilli and Rao, 1993). A conclusion reached was that all costs and benefits of obtaining and retaining control in a specific situation must be carefully weighed against each other.

Another company-related factor is the extent of control that is desired by the international marketer. This factor may affect the choice of both the channel between nations and channel within a nation. For the export mode of entry, for example, the use of indirect export gives weaker control over export sales than does exporting directly. Indeed, the truly integrated or captive channel gives the greatest control over export operations. For nonexport operations, the greatest control (and risk as well) is derived from a wholly owned overseas production (or service) facility.

A final company-related factor is related to the overall internal institutional environment that affects subsidiary behavior in a multisubsidiary company. This environment can place on individual SBUs in a company isomorphic pressures to conform with what other units in the company are doing. Results of a study of US firms competing in the paper and pulp industry indicated that business units that are highly influenced by their parent firm's institutional norms tend to use wholly owned entry modes, whereas business units that are influenced more by host-country environmental factors tend to use export as their entry mode (Davis *et al.*, 2000).

Governmental policies

There are many actions by national governments that can affect channel selection, particularly the channel between nations. General regulatory activities may discourage export entirely and dictate production abroad if the market is to be served effectively. Also, some governments regulate their foreign exchange and import licenses in a way that local importers cannot get enough foreign exchange (or the necessary license) to buy what they want from various countries. This may be due to a shortage of particular currencies or it may be that only a small amount is available for importing certain products that are not believed to be important in a country's overall development plan.

Another governmental factor in channel selection is the nature of any existing international business promotional program. Although governments tend not to promote imports, it may be that when such promotion is done it is carried on selectively, and certain products are excluded. Thus, although there may be no formal trade restrictions against its product, an international marketer may be forced to select a channel between nations that compensates for the discouragement by the government. The same type of situation may prevail in the international marketer's home country if its government's policies toward direct investment and/or export promotion are such that some form of export will have to be used, despite any greater value that can be obtained by using some other entry mode.

There may be actions by subnational government bodies that have an effect. For example, an exporter of Scotch whisky to the United States finds that in certain states the channel within a nation is predetermined; the product must be sold through a state-owned distributor and state-owned retail stores.

Finally, the actions of governments (regulations, etc.) on e-commerce and the Internet are evolving and changing, making it difficult for the international marketer using, or wanting to use, this method of market entry to gauge any effects upon its operations with any degree of certainty. The newness and rapid changes in technology have led to what amounts to a regulatory vacuum in many areas. In China, for example, the Ministry of Information Industry (MII) has issued many rules restricting what dot-coms can do and censoring what they can say (Einhorn *et al.*, 2000). In Europe, companies face a patchwork of conflicting local regulations. Europe's privacy laws, for instance, are much tougher than those in the United States. A digital signature may be legal in one country, but invalid in another. Thousands of different business and sales taxes are levied around the world. The globalization of the Internet is creating pressures to develop a globally accepted commercial code (Gleckman and Carney, 2000).

Concluding comment

The criteria for selecting export marketing channels that have been discussed in this section, while not all inclusive, are sufficient to show the complexity of the problem. Seldom, if ever, will the international marketer find the channel determinants all pointing in one direction. Management must find a balance among them and evaluate alternative systems. A good, and detailed, discussion is given by Root (1994, pp. 28–40).

Qualitative criteria can be used to limit the possible number of channel alternatives to a feasible few. Hopefully, these alternatives can then be evaluated on the basis of quantitative criteria. In the end, however, necessary trade-offs will most likely have to be made. This emphasizes the need to recognize that the determinant factors influencing firms' entry choice are interrelated. A study by Agarwal and Ramaswami (1992) based on the framework of Dunning (1988) provides evidence of interrelationships among a company's *ownership* (ability to develop differentiated products, size, and multinational experience), *location* (market potential and investment risk), and *internalization* (contractual risks) advantages when choosing among exporting, licensing, joint venture, and sole venture as a means of foreign market entry. Similarly, in a study comparing licensing, joint ventures, and wholly owned subsidiaries as international entry modes, Kim and Hwang (1992) argue that in addition to environmental (for example country risk, location unfamiliarity, and so forth) and transaction-specific (for example tacit nature of know-how and value of business-specific know-how) factors, a multinational's *global strategic posture* (concentration, synergies, and strategic motivations) must also be considered when deciding which entry mode to use. Of concern is the strategic relationship that a company envisages between its operations across borders. It is the collective, simultaneous consideration of all relevant factors that determines the ultimate decision. Another approach is shown in Exhibit 6.3.

In Chapter 4 we discussed the 'temperature gradient' approach or model to international market expansion. This model uses a number of measures to assess

EXHIBIT 6.3   Entry mode and involvement

One approach to the entry mode decision considers *extent of involvement* as the key question to be answered (Punnett, 1994, pp. 79–80). Each mode of entry can be viewed in terms of desired degree of involvement – indirect export would have the least involvement while equity investment would have the most involvement. Involvement depends upon location attractiveness, firm capability, and perceived risk. With each of these determinants having two options (high, low), eight possible scenarios emerge, as shown in Figure 6.6.

1. High location attractiveness High capacity High risk	5. Low location attractiveness High capacity High risk
2. High location attractiveness High capacity Low risk	6. Low location attractiveness Low capacity High risk
3. High location attractiveness Low capacity Low risk	7. Low location attractiveness Low capacity Low risk
4. High location attractiveness Low capacity High risk	8. Low location attractiveness High capacity Low risk

FIGURE 6.6   Alternative levels of involvement

Cell 2 is most attractive – a company wants to maximize involvement given the limiting factors; that is, if full ownership is allowed this would be the choice.

Cell 6 is least attractive – a company wants no involvement or minimal involvement; that is, if it is approached by someone who wishes to buy its products and will take all the risk the company would agree, but would not go after this market otherwise.

Cells 1, 3, 4, 5, 7, and 8 are mixed – a company must decide what degree of involvement will maximize the advantages and limit the effect of the drawbacks.

Source: Punnett, 1994

the attractiveness of a market's environment. Four categories of environments are identified ranging from 'super hot' to 'cold,' and there is a presumed relationship between market temperature and entry strategy. The results of a study of Canadian companies indicate that companies follow entry strategies involving greater control and commitment as the country's environment becomes hotter, which is what the temperature gradient model itself would predict (Papadopolous and Jansen, 1994).

In general, 'foreign entry mode' has tended to be viewed as a singular entity, even though companies often use multiple or mixed modes in the same foreign market. Firms that start with export to a market and then move to an alliance or manufacturing operation often continue to export to that market. Four forms of multiple entry modes have been identified, as follows (Petersen and Welch, 2002):

1. *Unrelated modes*: occurs when a company uses more than one mode in a foreign market, but there is no connection between their uses within that market. An example is a company that does business in different industries or markets and uses a different mode for each.
2. *Segmented modes*: occurs when a company uses multiple modes in the same industry or market to serve different segments.
3. *Mode complementarity*: multiple modes are used in a combined mutually supporting way to achieve the firm's objectives. The same segment may be involved, but different activities in the value chain are handled by different modes. For example, the manufacturing activity may be handled by licensee or contract manufacturer, but marketing is done through a sales subsidiary established in the country.
4. *Competing modes*: the different modes compete with each other by targeting the same segment(s) and performing the same activities. Ownership and location differ. The example of Nine West discussed earlier in this chapter is an example of this type of mixed mode.

Particular modes may be used in different ways to achieve different objectives such as supporting the impact of another mode or by achieving outcomes beyond that possible with a single mode. So-called *mode packages* have been used to increase revenues and foreign market penetration, and other benefits as well.

6.4.2 Channel members

Along with deciding upon the *type* of entry mode, the international marketer must select those marketing organizations that are to be members. While our discussion of selection criteria might lead one to believe that selection is autocratic, this is not the case. For at least two reasons the international marketer does not necessarily control the choice of individual firms in the channel.

First, in view of the realities of the competitive situation in the world's marketplaces, a marketing organization, particularly a good one, has many products from which to choose. Therefore such a company can be selective in the decision on whether or not to carry a product. This means that the channel to be used depends upon the relative strength of the international marketer, its product, and the marketing intermediary. An example of where the marketing organization can be the stronger party is with the giant Japanese trading companies, the *sogo shosha*.

A second reason that the international marketer lacks complete control over the members of the channel is that generally the international marketer can select marketing organizations only at one level in the channel. For example, in the distribution of consumer goods the selection of retail outlets typically is left entirely to those institutions selected at the wholesale level; the choice of wholesalers is left to the importers and/or export marketing organizations (if indirect export is used). The international marketer, however, can come closer to consumers or industrial users by selecting those exporter organizations, importers and/or wholesalers or distributors who sell to the kinds and quality of desired marketing intermediaries within the target market. Of concern to the manufacturer are such characteristics of the marketing intermediary as trading area covered, product lines carried, sales organization, potential sales volume of the manufacturer's product line, capacity to provide auxiliary services, financial strength to maintain inventories and extend credit to customers, and the willingness and ability to promote the manufacturer's product line. In the extreme case the international marketer can deal directly with the consumer.

Interpersonal links can play an important role in the selection of channel members. Foreign market entry by export essentially is a situation of exchange between companies and/or individuals. This exchange may be initiated by the exporter, the importer, a third party, or may be due to a chance encounter at a trade fair or some other type of meeting. In a study of Hong Kong toy manufacturers, individual exchange partners were commonly acquired via existing *social ties* (Ellis, 2000). An individual's social network and existing connections with others played a much stronger role than formal search behavior.

6.5 Managing the channel

In general, the overall task of managing the international channel involves finding ways to improve performance. A channel is viewed as a network and consists of a number of *stakeholders* – that is, independent or dependent companies that are interrelated and all have a stake in the success of the network.

6.5.1 Relations with intermediaries

Policies dealing with the relations between the international marketer and those marketing organizations that are members of the marketing channel revolve around the kinds of assistance *offered to* them and the cooperation to be *received from* them. The underlying premise is that whatever is done should be for the mutual benefit of all the parties concerned. This is the essence of the system concept.

One critical aspect of relations with intermediaries centers around international promotional activities of the intermediaries. In this regard three types of policy can be distinguished: gravity, push, and pull. A *gravity* policy is one of nonpromotion in that the international marketer merely sells to an intermediary and lets the product find its own way to ultimate consumers and users. A *push* policy is one of promotion through the marketing channel. Channel members must aggressively sell and promote the product to other channel members at lower levels. This policy is one that many companies in western Europe, the Americas, and Australia have come to accept and even in some instances demand. A *pull* policy is one whereby distribution is 'bought' by establishing consumer demand. The international marketer engages in mass advertising to the target market so that consumers are presold; consumers then 'pull' the product through the channel by demanding it from intermediaries. Such a policy is more appropriate for certain types of consumer goods than for industrial goods because it is difficult to presell the industrial user.

The problems encountered by the international marketer in attempting to establish proper relations with intermediaries are perhaps compounded because of certain communication gaps. Four such gaps – cultural, nationality, environmental, and distance – are relevant. The *cultural* gap comes from the problems associated with communication between people from groups with different values, social mores, and attitudes. The *nationality* gap is more obvious than cultural differences. Although there may be a few individuals who have a binational or multinational outlook, most people will clearly identify with the single country to which they have pledged their nationalistic loyalties. The *environmental* gap pertains particularly to the problems of individuals in one country attempting to make decisions that are best for another country, and other individuals. The *distance* gap comes about from geographic distance together with imperfections in existing communication media. Both time impediments and obstructions in the flow of information are engendered. These gaps must be overcome or closed if the international marketer is to have an effective, smoothly functioning channel system. Unfortunately there are no easy guidelines for international management to follow.

6.5.2 Channel feedback

The international marketing manager must develop an effective communication system within which 'feedback' information flows from channel members. This puts the manager in a position to evaluate rationally the channel's effectiveness. The manager must know how well the channel system is operating, in terms of such things as where sales are going, the adequacy of the quality of cooperation from channel members, and whether conflicts within the channel are causing tensions. At the same time marketing organizations may expect similar feedback. Thus the need is for two-way communication. Without feedback the task of evaluating results would be impossible.

6.6 Selecting the entry mode

We have now discussed the various entry modes that are available to companies that wish to take advantage of foreign market opportunities. At this point we are concerned with an answer to the question, 'How should a decision maker choose the foreign market entry mode for a product and target country market?' Three distinct decision rules for entry mode selection have been identified by Root (1994, Ch. 7), and can be distinguished by their degrees of sophistication: the *naive* rule (use the same entry mode for all foreign markets), the *pragmatic* rule (use a workable entry mode for each target market), and the *strategy* rule (use the right entry mode for each target market).

6.6.1 Naive rule

Managers follow the naive rule when they consider only one way to enter foreign markets, for example when a manager says 'We only export through foreign-based agents' or 'Once we are beyond export, we only use licensing as our overseas-based mode.' This rule obviously ignores the heterogeneity of individual foreign markets and entry conditions. A manager who uses this rule might be viewed as having 'tunnel vision.' At some point in time this manager will make mistakes of two kinds: either a promising foreign market that cannot be penetrated with their 'only entry' mode will be given up or a market will be entered with an inappropriate mode. The inflexibility of the naive rule prevents a company from fully exploiting foreign market opportunities. A special application of this rule is when the domestic channel is extended to foreign markets.

6.6.2 Pragmatic rule

An illustration of the pragmatic rule is the company that ordinarily starts doing business in foreign markets with a low-risk entry mode. Only if the particular initial mode is not feasible nor profitable will the company continue to look for a workable entry mode.

The pragmatic rule has certain advantages. The risk of foreign market entry with the wrong type of entry mode is minimized since unworkable modes are rejected. Also, costs of information collection and management time are reduced since not all potential alternatives are investigated once a workable mode has been found.

These advantages are not insignificant, but neither is the cost of lost opportunity. The fundamental weakness of the pragmatic rule lies in its failure to guide managers toward a determination of the entry mode that best matches the company's capabilities and resources with the market opportunity. In short, a workable entry may not be the best entry or the *right* entry.

6.6.3 The strategy rule

This decision rule simply states that the company should use the right entry mode. This approach requires that all viable alternative modes be systematically evaluated and then compared.

As we stated earlier in the chapter, a company's choice of foreign market entry for a given product/market is the result of evaluating many forces, which often conflict with each other. Comparing alternative approaches to entry may be complicated by the multiple objectives that a firm may have in each foreign market, and at times such objectives may appear to be inconsistent. Thus, trade-offs among objectives will have to be made. The end result of this analysis is a set of feasible entry modes that are then subject to further analysis.

Entry comparisons need to be made between projected costs and benefits over a future time period. Thus, *expected* costs and benefits are being estimated, and these are subject to changing uncertainties. Different entry modes are affected by different market and political risks.

An application of this decision rule would be to choose the entry mode that maximizes the profit contribution over the strategic planning period subject to: (1) the availability of company resources, (2) risk, and (3) nonprofit objectives. Since there is no objective procedure that results in a single number representing the profit contribution, risk, and nonprofit objectives analyses, decision makers have no choice but to use their own judgement in making the overall assessment.

6.7 Using free areas

A third major option for 'sourcing' for entering foreign markets is to use a free area. These areas are located in a particular country, but are considered to be outside the customs area of a country. Thus products may be brought into and exported from such areas easily, and other activities such as repacking, assembly, and manufacturing may be allowed. From an entry strategy and mode perspective, all options available for home country and overseas production may be available when a free area is used for a production site, depending upon the specific free area and market involved. Free areas may range in size from an entire port or perimeter to a specific zone. Free areas are discussed in more depth in Chapter 13.

SUMMARY

Our discussion of foreign marketing entry strategies has been in some detail. Although many different alternatives have been described and analyzed, by no means do these constitute the entire set of possibilities. The manner in which we have presented the material constitutes merely a subset of the possible alternative channels between countries, albeit a subset containing the most general and widely used alternatives.

It should be reemphasized that a particular manufacturer wanting to engage in international marketing may use more than one of these methods at the same time. The individual products within the product line may require different entry modes, as may the distinct foreign market areas. We discussed briefly the forms of multiple mode entry. It cannot be stated categorically which alternative mode is best. There are many conditions and criteria that affect the choice. The best we can do at this point in our discussion is to conclude that an international marketing channel should be 'form fitted.' That is, it should be unique and situation specific in the sense of being based on the requirements arising from the mix of the specific product, market, and manufacturer involved.

QUESTIONS FOR DISCUSSION

6.1 Explain how the flow of transactions and the flow of the physical product relate to foreign market entry mode.

6.2 Why is the decision regarding foreign market entry mode a particularly important decision for international marketing managers to make?

6.3 Discuss the nature of the 'whole channel concept.'

6.4 Evaluate the use of the Internet for export and other international marketing market entry modes.

6.5 Governmental regulations can affect the viability and effectiveness of a company using the Internet as a foreign market entry mode. Contrast the government regulations governing e-commerce in the United States, a European Union country (e.g., the United Kingdom or Germany), and an Australasian country. Is the Internet easier to use – regulation-wise – in one of the countries? Explain.

6.6 A number of alternative entry modes were identified in the chapter. Locate a company that uses export and one using overseas production or a strategic alliance. Describe their market entry strategies and determine why the companies differ in the entry mode being used.

6.7 Identify the major factors that have a bearing on the type of market entry mode that an international marketer might select. Is there any one or more that are more important than others? Explain fully.

6.8 Under what conditions would a strategy of multiple entry modes be most appropriate and when would it not be appropriate? Discuss.

6.9 Why should a company make a specific channel decision for each product going to each overseas market?

6.10 Select an industrially developed country (perhaps Japan or a European country) and a relatively less developed country (perhaps a Latin American or African country). Contrast the relative importance of the factors that should be taken into consideration by a foreign-based manufacturer of a low-unit priced packaged good selling in both markets, when determining policy on selecting appropriate channels of distribution in those markets. In which case is the managerial decision easier to make? Discuss.

6.11 Contrast the naive, pragmatic, and strategy approaches to choice of foreign market entry mode. Is any one superior to the others? Explain.

REFERENCES

Agarwal, S. and Ramaswami, S. N. (1992). Choice of foreign market entry mode: impact of ownership, location, and internationalization factors. *J. International Business Studies*, 23 (First Quarter), 1–27.

Albaum, G., Tse, D. K., Hozier, G. C. Jr., and Baker, K. G. (2003). Extending marketing activities and strategies from domestic to foreign markets. *J. Global Marketing*, 16(3), 105–29.

Anderson, E. and Coughlan, A. T. (1987). International market entry via independent or integrated channels of distribution. *J. Marketing*, 51 (January), 71–82.

Bianco, A. and Zellner, W. (2003). Is Wal-Mart too powerful? *Business Week*, 6 October, 100–10.

Brady, D. (2003). All the world's a call center. *Business Week*, 27 October, 43.

Business Week (2001). How well does Wal-Mart travel? 3 September, 82–4.

Davis, P. S., Desai, A. B., and Francis, J. D. (2000). Mode of international entry: an isomorphism perspective. *J. International Business Studies*, 31(2), 239–58.

Dunning, J. (1988). The eclectic paradigm of international production: a restatement and some possible extensions. *J. International Business Studies*, 19 (Spring), 1–31.

Einhorn, B., Webb, A., and Engardio, P. (2000). China's tangled web, *Business Week*, 17 July, 56–8.

Einhorn, B. and Kripalani (2003). Move over, India. *Business Week*, 11 August, 42–3.

Ellis, P. (2000). Social ties and foreign market entry, *J. International Business Studies*, 31(3), 443–69.

Erramilli, M. K. and Rao, C. P. (1993). Service firms' international entry-mode choice: a modified transaction-cost analysis approach. *J. Marketing*, 57 (July), 19–38.

Gleckman, H. and Carney, D. (2000). Watching over the World Wide Web. *Business Week*, 28 August, 195–6.

Kim, W. C. and Hwang, P. (1992). Global strategy and multinationals' entry choice. *J. International Business Studies*, 23 (First Quarter), 29–53.

Marketing News (1994). Nike chases shoe demand in Mexico, 10 October, 11.

McNaughton, R. B. and Bell, J. (2000). Channel switching between domestic and foreign markets. *J. International Marketing*, 9(1), 24–39.

Papadopolous, N. and Jansen, D. (1994). Country and method-of-entry selection for international expansion: international distributive arrangements revisited. In *Dimensions of International Business, No. 11*. Carleton University, International Business Study Group, Spring, 31–52.

Petersen, B. and Welch, L. S. (2002). Foreign operation mode combinations and internationalization. *J. Business Research*, 55, 157–62.

Punnett, B. J. (1994). *Experiencing International Business and Management* 2nd edn. Belmont, CA: Wadsworth.

Ricks, D. A. (1999). *Blunders in International Business* 3rd edn. Oxford, UK: Blackwell.

Root, F. R. (1982). *Foreign Market Entry Strategies*. New York: AMACOM.

Root, F. R. (1994). *Entry Strategies for International Markets* rev. and expanded edn. Lexington, MA: Lexington Books.

Rubin, D. (2001). Wal-Mart cheer meets a new match, *Albuquerque Journal*, 30 December, C2.

Strauss, M. (2002). Nine West steps closer across retail divide. *The Globe and Mail*, Toronto, Canada, 6 September, B5.

Strohmeyer, R. (2001). Way down south. *Smartbusinessmag.com*, January, 46.

The Economist (1998). Going cheap. 15 August, 55–6.

FURTHER READING

Business Week (2003). Relocating the back office, 13 December, 67–9.

Czinkota, M. R., Ronkainen, I. A. and Tarrant, J. J. (1995). *The Global Marketing Imperative*. Lincolnwood, IL: NTC Business Books.

Marshall, R. S. (2003). Building trust early: the influence of first and second order expectations on trust in international channels of distribution. *International Business Review*, xx, 1–23.

Tse, D. K., Pan, Y. and Au, K. Y. (1997). How MNCs choose entry modes and form alliances: the China experience. *J. International Business Studies*, 28(4), 779–805.

Wijnholds, H. de B. and Little, M. (2001). Regulatory issues for global e-tailers: marketing implications. *Academy of Marketing Science Review*, www.amsreview.org.

CASE STUDY 6.1

Alcas Corporation

Alcas Corporation is a company based in Olean, New York, which has manufactured and marketed CUTCO Cutlery, a very high quality kitchen cutlery, since its formation in 1949. Alcas was originally a subsidiary of ALCOA, but in 1982 four officers completed a management buyout and it is now privately held. Alcas exists essentially as a holding company. Its two major operating subsidiaries (wholly owned) are CUTCO Cutlery Corporation, the manufacturer of CUTCO Cutlery, and Vector Marketing Corporation, the direct sales marketer of CUTCO for all of North America. In 1994 the company established CUTCO International, Inc. as a subsidiary to handle the marketing of CUTCO on an international basis. As shown in Table 6.1, Alcas Corporation, for the past eight years particularly, has had strong and consistent growth. Since 1995 the average annual growth in total sales has been about 17%. International sales have not been a major component of that growth except perhaps for the year 2002. In fact, 2002 was the first year that international sales generated a meaningful profit. The company has a very strong balance sheet with a very low debt-to-equity ratio and a significant cash reserve.

| **TABLE 6.1** | Alcas Corporation sales history, 1990–2002 |

Year	Total consolidated sales (US$1,000s)	Total international sales (US$1,000s)
1990	59,197	0
1991	64,449	0
1992	72,228	1,055
1993	70,435	1,407
1994	66,275	1,961
1995	80,113	4,473
1996	101,889	9,007
1997	113,501	9,394
1998	123,746	9,968
1999	130,420	9,569
2000	152,946	10,160
2001	201,000	11,600
2002	253,000	15,200

The product

As a product line CUTCO Cutlery covers a broad range of food preparation knives, table knives, flatware, kitchen gadgets and hunting, fishing, and utility pocket knives (approximately 83 individual items; 180 SKUs counting gift packs and set combinations). The product line is identified as '*CUTCO the world's finest cutlery*' and testing against competitors' products worldwide consistently supports that claim. Product retail pricing is consistent with its identification as '*the world's finest cutlery*'; that is, it is at the high end of the price spectrum. The pricing is very comparable with the pricing of Henckels and Wustof knives, both of which are at the high end of the price range for cutlery products available in conventional retail stores. Product is sold as individual open stock or in a variety of gift boxed sets as well as a variety of wood block sets for the countertop.

Sales and marketing approach in the United States and Canada

CUTCO is sold by Vector Marketing Corporation through a 'one-on-one' in-home demonstration technique utilizing a sales force made up primarily of college students. Vector annually recruits tens of thousands of sales people, over 90% of them college students. The bulk of the sales force is recruited during the summer vacation months. Some of the students continue to sell during the school year and the business definitely exists as a year-round business (with September–April volume below the summer peak). The recruiting, training, and ongoing counseling of sales people (all of whom are independent contractors) are done via a totally decentralized approach utilizing approximately 220 district managers located in communities across the United States and Canada. During the summer months the company opens up more than 225 additional branch offices that are temporary summer offices run by college students with prior selling and management experience from previous summers. In 1990 the company set up Vector Canada as a separate 'international' marketing entity. It has been successful. It has been generally patterned after the US operations, and although it still exists as a separate corporate entity, its operation is managed by Vector US and the two are identified as Vector North America.

Current international sales activity

In 1992 the company established a Korean marketing operation, CUTCO Korea. Like the Canadian operation, it was set up using US-trained Vector managers and patterned after the US recruiting, training, and selling approach, but with managers being Korean born. The decision to enter Korea was in fact made because of the availability of US-trained Korean-born managers.

Whereas in Canada the transfer of US managers and US approaches took hold immediately and very effectively, the experience in Korea was one of only marginal success with this program. Due to heavy cultural differences regarding students, they needed to alter the approach in some fashion. CUTCO Korean management in 1995 instituted a revised structure utilizing Korean housewives as the recruiting base, and engaged a party-plan type group sales demonstration mechanism as a sales approach. This approach was immediately successful, with sales in 1996 reaching US$6 million. The Asian financial crisis in 1997 and 1998 took sales down below US$2 million in 1998 and CUTCO International came close to closing the Korean operation. A last-minute decision in November 1998 to 'hang in there' was the right one, as results for 2000 have returned sales to US$6.5 million and generated a profit for the first time. The Korean experience has been sobering in that the cost of entry has been far greater than expected (total costs to date, including operating losses for the years 1992–9 amounted to US$5 million). CUTCO management is very optimistic about the future of the Korean operation, barring a total political/military disaster with North Korea. Total sales of CUTCO Korea in 2002 were US$12.8 million.

In the spring of 1996 CUTCO International opened a sales operation in Germany (CUTCO Deutschland) with the sales program patterned generally after the Korean housewife/party plan program, which was then showing considerable success. The German operation initially showed every sign of being successful, but by 1999 CUTCO International had to make the decision to close it down as a company program. The reason for this was that although growing in sales volume, it was not growing fast enough to cover the total expenses of operating a company program in Germany. The sales operations in place at that point were converted to a distributorship which has since worked out very comfortably. The distributorship continues to grow slowly, but since there is no 'company program overhead' to carry, they are able to be profitable and the company benefits from the wholesale sales that are generated.

In the fall of 1996 CUTCO International opened a sales operation in Australia (CUTCO Australia) with five US Vector sales managers. It was patterned after the US Vector college program. The presumption was that the Australian culture was close enough to that of US culture for the program to work in Australia (just as it did in Canada). The first two years seemed to bear that out totally; in 1998 Australian sales were almost as high as Canadian sales. Then, in 1999 CUTCO International found that although it was advertising for recruits in the same fashion as in the United States, Australian regulations in that regard were particularly severe and imposed significant constraints covering the way recruiting advertising could be placed. These constraints resulted in a serious drop in recruiting volume and this in turn developed a chain of management problems. All of this brought about a downward spiral in sales and the year 2000 wound up at a level less than US$2 million in sales and caused CUTCO International to consider closing in Australia. In an early February 2001 visit to Australian headquarters by top company personnel, a decision was made to do some restructuring of the organization and 'give it another six months'. Unfortunately, CUTCO Australia was effectively closed in mid-2001. It now exists only as a customer service center to provide past customers with access to guarantee/repair service and customer service, in general. It may find its way back into CUTCO International's expansion plans.

In 1997 CUTCO International opened up a company operation in Costa Rica (CUTCO Costa Rica). Although Costa Rica is a very small country in terms of population (3 million), CUTCO International chose Costa Rica as its Latin American entry. The choice seemed appropriate, given the political and financial stability of Costa Rica, its strong culture and high levels of literacy among its population. CUTCO chose the US college program as the vehicle for entry and made this choice on the strength of the highly successful college program CUTCO had run in Puerto Rico for the prior three years. The presumption was that CUTCO managers from Puerto Rico could be utilized to start up and then help grow the Costa Rican operation. The Puerto Rico/Costa Rica connection did not seem to work out because there appeared to be significant though subtle cultural differences between the two peoples, and the company was unable to provide ongoing management talent to the operation. For this and other reasons growth in Costa Rica was very slow. CUTCO Costa Rica was closed and, on a trial basis, converted to a joint venture with another direct selling company manufacturing cookware. This joint venture was closed after about 18 months due to slow growth and an inability to merge two 'high ticket' items.

The questions being asked now by the corporation's board of directors and top management as it conducts its regular five-year strategic planning activity are as follows:

- Should the corporation continue to seek CUTCO sales in international markets?
- What criteria should the corporation use to select countries to target for entry?

- What type of market research will be required to make the selections intelligently?
- What type of country law, regulations, custom issues, etc. should be considered in making country choice decisions?
- What are the target countries, and what priorities and schedule should be developed for entry into each?
- Should it continue to use direct selling as its fundamental approach to these markets? If so, which specific direct sales approach should it use – the Vector US college program or housewife group sales program? Or both? If neither, what approach should be used?
- Are there any other concepts that should be considered for CUTCO International to expand its program internationally on a more cost-effective basis?

Question

1. How should the Alcas Corporation answer these questions in its five-year strategic plan?

CASE STUDY 6.2

Yang Toyland Pte, Limited

(This case study was written by Hellmut Schütte, Euro-Asia Centre, INSEAD.)

For Y. C. Yang the year was practically over at the end of August. He was heading Yang Toyland Pte, Limited, a small, family-owned toy manufacturer, which he ran together with his older sister and his younger brother in Singapore.

'This year's turnover will reach about S$14 million – an increase of about 20% over the preceding year,' he thought to himself, 'and profit will also be good – perhaps even reaching S$600,000.'

He did not expect any more major orders to come in. His customers from the United States and Europe had placed their orders, quite a substantial part of which had already been carried out and even shipped to arrive at their destinations in time for Christmas. There would be one or two additional orders within the next weeks, but after that his company would be able to turn its attention again to finding and developing ideas for new products.

Development of the firm

When his father died 13 years ago, the company had only eight people and had just launched its first toy car with an electric, battery-driven motor. The chassis and body were made of plastic with some metal used for parts such as axles, fixtures, tire caps, and so on. At that time Yang Toyland's turnover was below half a million dollars, and its profitability was very low. Y. C. and his younger brother had had difficulties convincing their father to add the motor to one of their existing models that they had produced for many years but which had become unattractive. He had finally given in when he saw that competitors were selling battery-driven cars like hot cakes while Yang Toyland's products were not moving.

Since those days they had regularly upgraded their product range of toy cars by adding features such as lights, sirens, and a steering system using a wire that connected the car to a small wheel fixed to a plastic box. The child held this box in his hand when following the car. Models ranged from fancy racing and luxury cars to trucks, pickups, police cars, and fire engines. Presently, their top-of-the-line product was a remote-controlled, four-wheel-drive jeep that could move forwards and backwards, stop and accelerate, turn to the right and left, and climb steep hills with a gradient of up to 40°. Control was exercised with the help of a telecommander that transmitted the various commands to the car. Both the transmitter and the car were equipped with antennae.

Y. C.'s brother, Paul, was the driving force behind the technological developments in Yang Toyland. As an electric engineer from Singapore's Ngee Ann Polytechnic, he spent 12–15 hours per day in the factory to deliver the goods that his brother had sold, and to look for new ideas on how to improve the production process and the products. Some sophisticated equipment and machinery had been introduced but in most cases the batch sizes for the various parts to be manufactured were too small to make automation or even semi-automation feasible, so that the whole process was still fairly labor intensive. Motors and the control system were purchased from outside. Most of the product ideas were derived from models found abroad or described in catalogs and trade journals. Paul's present dream was to come up with some innovations that would make use of cheap micro-electronics and increase the manoeuvrability of the toy cars.

The factory now employed some 40 people. Ten additional employees were involved in administration and sales. Y. C.'s sister, Rosy, was in charge of purchasing, personnel, finance, and general administration. Unlike her brother, she had initially insisted on making her own career outside the family firm in a bank. Later, when sales were growing rapidly and Y. C. and Paul had difficulties managing the firm, she acceded to the request of her brothers and joined the company. From that day on, many administrative problems become easier to handle and the relationship with the bank improved. Rosy also knew how to take advantage of various government programs set up to assist smaller firms and was able to obtain a long-term loan from the government at a very favorable rate.

Sales activities

Y. C. was responsible for sales. Over the years he had developed valuable contacts with buyers from the United States, Europe, and recently also Japan. He met many of the buyers in Singapore when they came around for shopping trips in the Far East, usually during the spring. Some of the bigger customers had buying offices in Hong Kong, two even in Singapore. The majority of his customers were wholesale importers. Others, especially from the United States, bought directly for their chains of specialized toy shops. So far he had obtained very few orders from department stores and other large retail groups. In terms of geographical spread, 55% of sales were shipped to the United States and 30% to Europe. Exports to Japan amounted to only 3% of total sales. The rest (12%) was sold in the local market. Some of the products found their way from Singapore into Malaysia, Indonesia, and other Asian countries.

Since his sister had joined the firm, it had been possible for Y. C. to go abroad twice a year for about two weeks each time, once to the United States and once to Europe. The trips were scheduled in such a way that he could attend the major international toy fairs and at the same time pay visits to his existing and potential customers. He had participated in a few fairs in which Singapore products were displayed, but considered a stand for Yang Toyland alone too expensive and thus not feasible.

At least twice a year he produced and dispatched a six-page color brochure in English that showed the company's products and prices. In each brochure it was pointed out that specifications of the various models could be slightly changed according to customers' demand, for which prices would be quoted on request. This gave Yang Toyland the flexibility to determine its prices according to the negotiation power of the potential buyer and their own capacity utilization. Apart from the brochures, Yang Toyland placed some advertisements in trade journals in Singapore, the United States, the United Kingdom, and Germany. Results from these were mixed.

The market

Competition in toy cars was very tough and came from multinationals such as Fisher-Price and Mattel as well as from a large number of smaller manufacturers in Asia, particularly in Hong Kong, Taiwan, and Korea. The industry was characterized by the sudden creation of bestsellers such as remote-controlled, four-wheel-drive cars that made other models obsolete within a very short time. It was therefore essential for survival to keep up with the market and to be quick to adapt to new trends. Singapore's higher wages in comparison with other Asian producers made it necessary to be at the forefront of technology, since older, standard models were sold only on price.

The fact that Yang Toyland had so far been successful in the business was, according to Y. C., due to its decision to concentrate on a narrow range of products. At the same time the company's specialization made it vulnerable to market changes. Y. C., however, did not rate this risk very high: 'Boys want cars, first as kids, later as adults. Toy cars are an essential part of the upbringing of boys – they are basic needs!'

Last year, Yang Toyland had 149 customer accounts. Two-thirds of those had placed orders of less than S$50,000 p.a. Only one customer, a chain store from the United States, had bought products for more than S$500,000 during that year (for further details see Table 6.2). This year the situation would not be very different. From experience Y. C. knew that only 50–60% of his customers would purchase from him again during the following year. This percentage was lower among smaller purchasers, which meant that stability of the business came mainly from the larger purchasers. It was not clear to Y. C. whether the high fluctuation among his customers was a problem specific to his company or the industry in general. His impression was that customer satisfaction had been relatively high in the past and that some of his former customers had returned to him after having bought from his competitors for a limited period.

TABLE 6.2 Distribution of account order volume

Order volume in S$ p.a.	Number of accounts
0–10,000	38
10,000–100,000	63
100,000–200,000	35
200,000–500,000	12
500,000–1,000,000	1
Total number of accounts	149

Contacts with direct mail order houses

Two years ago, Y. C. had started to attract orders from direct mail order houses. He had prepared special samples for them and arranged for various certificates to prove that his goods complied with the requirements and norms of the respective purchasers. He had met several times with the representatives in Singapore and visited three major direct mail order houses in the United States and two each in the United Kingdom and Germany. He remembered how surprised he was initially by the professionalism and the shrewdness of their buyers and their deep knowledge of the market. When, a year ago, he presented his latest model to a German direct mail order house, the buyer – a certain Herr Clausen – knew immediately from where his brother had adopted the design. It took him only four minutes to point out the weak spots in the construction and another three minutes to convince him that his asking price was indeed too high. But Herr Clausen had also given him some advice on how to improve certain aspects of the car and how to reduce costs. 'In 15 minutes I had learned more than I normally would in a year, but there wasn't even a hint of giving me an order,' Y. C. reported. His experience in the United Kingdom had not been more encouraging. Both companies there were basically interested in low prices to replace the models of competitors, which they considered too expensive.

In the United States the buyers seemed to be hooked on Taiwanese and Hong Kong producers with whom they had done business for many years. At Sears, the biggest mail order house in the world, he had not been able to see the person in charge of toy purchases. An assistant manager had talked about quantities that were much too big for Yang Toyland to handle.

Y. C. had developed the contacts further, especially with Herr Clausen from Gross-Versand and one of the British houses. Since Gross-Versand had a purchasing office in Singapore, communication with Germany had been relatively easy. But procedures for getting samples accepted were very time-consuming and tedious. The remote-control system in particular had created problems due to the strict frequency regulations in Europe. Although Yang Toyland imported the system from Japan where it was certified not to interfere with any radiowaves, Gross-Versand had insisted on special tests in Germany, the cost of which had to be shouldered by the Singaporean exporter.

The offer

It was on 3 September that Y. C. was invited to see Mrs Petra Müller, Gross-Versand's local representative, in her office in the Shaw Center. He had met her several times before and channeled most of his communication with Herr Clausen through her office. She had also been in his factory and had talked to his brother and sister. Y. C. was aware that she had tried to collect some information about Yang Toyland's reputation from banks, suppliers, and customers.

Mrs Müller opened the meeting with some good news for Y. C. Gross-Versand had accepted the samples of Yang Toyland and now wanted to buy two of their models for next year's autumn–winter catalog. The models selected were a four-wheel-drive jeep CXL and a Porsche 911 similar to their bestseller this year. Both products were especially designed, painted, decorated, and equipped for Gross-Versand. As discussed before, Yang Toyland would not be entitled to sell these models to anybody else, even if they proved outstanding market successes.

Gross-Versand estimated that it would sell 20,000 of the CXL and 120,000 of the Porsche cars, either directly or indirectly through their subsidiaries in Germany, Belgium, The Netherlands, Austria, and France. Because of the distribution throughout Europe some slight changes in the outer appearance were envisaged. This could be easily handled.

Gross-Versand wanted a firm commitment from Yang Toyland for the delivery of the total volume of 140,000 pieces by 30 October next year (arrival in Germany). However, the buyer himself would place an order for only 50% of the respective quantities with a delivery date of 31 July. The rest could be ordered by Gross-Versand later and had to be shipped as specified by the buyer within a very short period, the length of it depending on the volume ordered. Prices proposed by Gross-Versand were S$23.25 for the CXL and S$16.30 for the Porsche. These prices were about 25% below those quoted for similar models in Yang Toyland's brochure. They could not be altered for the duration of the contract.

Mrs Müller did not expect an immediate response from Y. C. Instead she announced that Herr Clausen would pass through Singapore in two weeks and wanted to finalize the contract with Yang Toyland. She also mentioned that her role would be confined to quality control while all contract negotiations would be the responsibility of headquarters. Mrs Müller further reminded Y. C. of the general purchase conditions of Gross-Versand that she had given to him some time ago (see Figure 6.7) and of the great value her company placed on long-lasting relationships with reliable suppliers. With this in mind, Y. C. left the office.

Three days later Y. C. met with Paul and Rosy to discuss 'Project Gross' as they called it. Y. C. brought with him a first production schedule for the next year based on orders received and further orders expected. Paul had all cost statistics to hand and some brochures of new machines that he wanted to buy and install once the contract was signed. Rosy had made some cost calculations and prepared a cash flow forecast. After seven hours of heated debate the following conclusions were reached:

■ The firmly placed order of 10,000 CXLs and 60,000 Porsche cars could be fulfilled without substantial investment in additional capital equipment. To cope with the workload, overtime would not be enough. Additional staff would have to be hired – not an easy task in Singapore. During the last two months before the dispatch of the products, no orders could be accepted in addition to those already received. Some of these they would try to reschedule by either delivering them earlier or later than requested. Bearing in mind the additional labor costs, and assuming constant prices for supplies, a profit of S$50,000 was expected.

■ Any order above the 50% level would create serious capacity problems for Yang Toyland given the assumption that orders from other customers would come in and had to be scheduled as they were this year. Additional machinery and equipment would be necessary, costing S$400,000–S$500,000. In order to have it installed before the peak season, orders would have to be placed soon. This investment could not be financed out of the cash flow but would require a bank loan or supplier's credit since their liquidity position would be very tight during the summer months.

■ Assuming a growth of their normal business of 10%

p.a. and the placement of orders amounting to 15,000 CXLs and 90,000 Porsches, the investment in additional capital equipment would just make sense. Rosy reckoned that the average profit on sales should go up slightly and 'Project Gross' should produce a profit of about S$75,000. Should 'Gross-Versand' order the full volume of 140,000 pieces and/or their business outside the mail order house grow by more than 10%, profitability would increase significantly. Should additional orders from Gross-Versand not materialize, and/or their normal business not grow as estimated, profits would quickly diminish.

Based on these calculations Rosy was not very keen on the contract with Gross-Versand. Paul, however, was excited and saw the order as a good incentive for improving their production capability. Y. C. himself had mixed feelings. He knew that even obtaining slightly better prices from Herr Clausen would not solve the dilemma in which Yang Toyland found itself. He also knew that Herr Clausen expected a clear answer from him in less than two weeks.

Questions

1. What advantages and disadvantages would you see for Yang Toyland in signing the proposed contract with Gross-Versand?

2. What should be Y. C.'s objective in his discussion with Herr Clausen?

3. What topics should Y. C. discuss with Herr Clausen and in which order?

---

1. Award of Contracts

For all contracts to be awarded only standard order forms shall be applicable. Verbal orders, supplements, amendments or any other agreements regarding orders already placed shall be binding only if agreed by both parties in writing and signed on their behalf.

2. Protection of Fair Competition

Prior to the expiration of the validity period of the catalogues for which the merchandise has been ordered, such merchandise shall not be supplied either in the same or in a similar form or make to any mail-order house. Trade-marked articles are excluded. Gross-Versand shall be entitled to deliver the merchandise to any enterprises with which it is associated.

3. Guarantee of Quality

During the validity of the Gross-Versand catalogues, the merchandise ordered to Gross-Versand shall be supplied as per sample, i.e., in accordance with the description, the sample submitted to and approved by Gross-Versand as well as in the same composition of materials, shape, manufacturing, presentation and guaranteed characteristics. If for any coercive reason, the supplier can no longer supply the merchandise in accordance with the

FIGURE 6.7   General purchase conditions of Gross-Versand (Germany) (shortened version)

original sample, the amended supply shall be subject to a previous approval in writing by Gross-Versand. The supplier undertakes to control the merchandise prior to dispatch.

4. Prices

The price stated in the order shall be inclusive of all packing requirements of Gross-Versand. The prices shall be binding during the validity period of the Gross-Versand catalogues for which the merchandise has been ordered.

5. Packing and Marking Requirements

Labelling, packing and shipment of the merchandise shall at all times comply with the packing and shipment instructions of Gross-Versand.

6. Delivery

All deliveries are to be effected in accordance with orders placed. The date of delivery stipulated in the order is always the latest shipping date (fixed date). Should the supplier be unable to deliver within the stipulated dates, Gross-Versand shall be entitled to raise the following claim:
(a) payment of damages for non-delivery plus accrued incidental costs;
(b) to have the ordered articles manufactured by third parties. In such event, the supplier shall be liable for any additional costs incurred to Gross-Versand;
(c) payment of damages for late delivery plus accrued incidental costs if Gross-Versand has advised the supplier without delay after the expiration of the stipulated date that it insists on performance.
Gross-Versand's right of cancellation of the order shall not be affected. Any extensions of time granted by Gross-Versand are to be interpreted strictly and no further extensions of time are to be implied. They do not affect the claim for damages for late delivery. Upon receipt of goods not delivered in time no express reservation need be made with regard to the damage caused by the later delivery.

7. Insurance of Merchandise

The supplier shall at his sole discretion arrange insurance of the merchandise during transit and he shall only be entitled to get the costs of such an insurance repaid in case it had been arranged at the special request of Gross-Versand.

8. Invoicing

Supplier shall submit invoices to Gross-Versand in quadruplicate at the address referred to below, and each invoice shall bear the address of the consignee. In the event that the merchandise is shipped to more than one consignee the supplier shall provide Gross-Versand with separate invoices.

The assignment of claims against Gross-Versand shall be allowed only in favour of the seller's supplier.

9. Payment

Payment shall be made by Gross-Versand in accordance with the terms and conditions appearing in the order. Payment shall be effected and time set for payment shall commence on receipt of merchandise and invoice only. Dispatch of a check or payment order to a bank is considered as due payment.

10. Warranty

Settlement of an invoice shall not imply any recognition that the goods thus paid for be free from defects, that they be in conformity with the contract or that the consignment be complete.

All quality defects and discrepancies in quantities, and measurements are covered by the supplier's warranty. The agreed warranty period will be 12 months.

The supplier is responsible under the rules of the Gerätesicherheitsgesetz (Equipment Security Act) and pursuant to the general product liability for the actual and consequential damages which are suffered by the end user. The supplier is, upon request, obliged to produce evidence of compliance with the Gerätesicherheitsgesetz (Equipment Security Act) (i.e., attestation or certificate of testing by a testing authority) and in case of orders of prohibition under the Gerätesicherheitsgesetz (Equipment Security Act) has to take back the article irrespective of any periods of warranty.

FIGURE 6.7 Continued

If the merchandise supplied is not in conformity with the sample, with the prescriptions as to quality, packing, dispatch, marking of the material, as well as with symbol instructions for care, the supplier shall compensate Gross-Versand for any handling and administrative costs caused to Gross-Versand by control of merchandise, ascertainment of the defects, sorting out, remodelling, etc. This also applies to any inspection tests to be carried out outside the premises of Gross-Versand.

The return of defective merchandise to the supplier shall be deemed to mean notification of default, but shall not entitle the supplier to replace same. Without prejudice to any further claims, especially those resulting from damages caused to third parties, Gross-Versand shall be entitled to deduct from the supplier's next pending invoice the value of the claimed merchandise plus costs in connection with the claim. In case such costs cannot be settled with invoices pending, then remittance of the claimed amount shall be due within ten days.

Instead of returning the defective merchandise to the supplier, Gross-Versand shall be entitled to claim a discount on the purchase price.

11. Industrial Property Rights

The supplier warrants that the offer and the sale of the goods do not infringe any rights of the third parties (Copyrights, Patents, Registered Designs or Design Patents, Trademarks, Licenses, claims under the law on competition, etc.) and will not violate any legal and government regulations. The supplier agrees to indemnify Gross-Versand as well as the enterprises associated with Gross-Versand against any claims by third parties and to make good the damage exceeding these claims and to give compensation for lost profits. The same applies, if the articles are offered and sold outside the Federal Republic of Germany, unless the supplier states on the Acknowledgement of Order that it is not permitted to offer and sell the goods abroad.

All drawings, sample designs, specifications and information supplied by Gross-Versand prepared or obtained by the supplier for and at the sole cost of Gross-Versand shall become and remain the property of Gross-Versand and shall be treated as confidential. They have to be returned to Gross-Versand after the contract has been fulfilled, and supplier is responsible not to have them mis-used in any way.

Supplier is not allowed to deliver merchandise bearing trademarks of Gross-Versand to any third party without written consent of Gross-Versand during winding up and after the expiration of the contract.

12. Applicable Law and Jurisdiction

This contract shall be governed by and construed in accordance with the laws of the Federal Republic of Germany.

FIGURE 6.7 Continued

CASE STUDY 6.3

Avon Products, Inc. (B)

(This case study was written by Edwin Duerr and Yim-Yu Wong, both of San Francisco State University.)

In 2003, Avon's sales in China reached $157 million, up 20% from the year before and over twice what sales had been in 1997. This was a major accomplishment for a company whose very existence in the Chinese market had been threatened when the Chinese government banned direct selling in April 1998. Direct selling was Avon's only sales channel in China, and the only marketing method it had ever used in the company's history. As a direct result of the ban, Avon's operations in China lost $110,000 per day in sales. Its 150,000 Avon ladies were out of jobs and the company had to lay off 20% of its regular staff. (See Case 3.3, Avon Products, Inc. (A).) The resurgence since 1998 was a result of the company's immediate response to the crisis, and the building of a new marketing structure.

Responding to the crisis

With the imposition of a ban on direct selling, Avon had the choice of changing its marketing model or withdrawing from the Chinese market. The company chose to go ahead immediately with developing plans to convert to new types of operation, pending Chinese government approval. It would operate as a wholesaler to Chinese retail stores, convert its 75 distribution centers into retail outlets to serve regular customers, and conduct limited direct selling activities. For the latter, representatives would not purchase and resell the product, but would work on commission. In short, sales representatives would become employees of Avon.

In early June 1998 Avon received government permission to resume operations as a wholesaler and to open retail outlets. They did not receive permission to resume any direct selling, though they could use sales representatives for delivery and service. The company was planning to apply for permission to use sales promoters or representatives on a commission basis when Beijing clarified how sales representatives would be allowed to operate. Amway did not receive permission to operate as a retail business until mid-July, but they also received permission to operate through representatives at that time. As of mid-July, Mary Kay still had not received approval of its application.

Avon was optimistic about the future. Since resuming operations in June, they had run a 'preferred customer' program under which individuals purchasing large enough amounts of products would receive substantial discounts. A number of former representatives were buying enough to become preferred customers, thus maintaining contact with the company. Avon was investing in advertising and point-of-sale material, and recruiting retail specialists in order to adapt to the new system.

Avon had a network of 80 sales centers in 14 provinces, but the sales centers were not designed and built for retailing so they presented some problems. Stores could be closed or added as appropriate, though government regulations regarding employment and facility openings and closures might present some legal and financial difficulties.

Building a new marketing structure

Avon (China) opened its first retail store in March 1999, and a flagship store in Beijing in October 2000. It followed with a group of concept stores in Beijing, Shanghai, and Guangzhou in 2002. It began Internet marketing, with primary coverage in Beijing's outer areas, in the same year. By 2004 Avon (China) Company Limited had 5000 franchise stores (beauty boutiques) and plans to add 500 more each year. It also had almost 2000 beauty counters in malls, shopping centers and hypermarkets in 74 large and medium-size cities.

Avon (China) uses its web page to communicate with the public. In addition to product information, the company includes its history, press releases, and franchisee success stories. *Business Week*'s selection of Andrea Jung, Avon's CEO, as one of the best managers in the world was reported. Other activities featured included Avon's donations to fight SARS, a modern dance program sponsored by Avon, and their annual Miss White Angel pageant (see below). Information about the company's corporate culture, guiding principles, operational objectives, managerial doctrines, and management styles is also posted. Avon lists its guiding principles as 'high quality, leading technology, and diversity, designed for Oriental women,' with the motto 'A Company for Women.' Potential new franchisees can find information on Avon China's web page about capital requirements, store size, applicant qualifications, and the type of lease that prospective franchisees are required to sign.

Currently Avon offers a wide range of products on the market in China, including skin care, cosmetics, personal care, fragrances, underwear, health foods, and others.

The company incorporates both Asian and western components in projecting its product image. It uses a research laboratory in Japan, a country known for its advanced technology, to make it more convincing that Avon products are made for Asian skin. At the same time, it selected a trendy English name, 'Up2U,' for a cosmetics line developed by that lab and intended to appeal to the mindset and attitude of younger Chinese women. Recognizing that the traditional concept of beauty in China favors fair, light skin, Avon offers a line of whitening products. It also sponsors an annual 'Miss White Angel' pageant in which a young lady is selected to be the spokesperson of the year. The program is broadcast on regional television channels. Additionally, since Caucasian women have features that are admired by many Asian women, most of the models used on Avon (China)'s web page are Caucasian. This also serves to present a prestigious image of Avon as a US company (that provides products suited to Asian skin).

Worldwide, Avon has undertaken several initiatives to increase sales, improve efficiency, and increase profitability. All of these are being developed over time. They will affect Avon (China) as they are implemented.

- Avon is continuing to develop its global operating model, pursing regional integration, harmonizing of products and marketing, and consolidating manufacturing.
- A major project, launched in 1994, is the develop-

ment of a 'next-generation' supply chain strategy designed to reduce costs while providing improved and faster service to Avon representatives and customers. Supply chain functions such as demand forecasting, sourcing, manufacturing, order filling, and logistics will be closely linked with the marketing functions of product design, product development, and merchandising.

- A program started in the United States to increase the number and performance of Avon representatives is being extended to other countries. Career-minded representatives have the opportunity to qualify for positions as Leadership Representatives in which they recruit, train, and motivate additional representatives as well as continue their own direct selling. The Leadership Representatives earn bonuses on the sales of those whom they have developed. In the United States, the program increased both the number of representatives and company sales. Avon is using the US program as a template, making adjustments for local needs and preferences, as it carefully expands into other countries. Of course no program for Leadership Representatives can be started in China until the government again authorizes direct sales.

- Avon continues to stress innovation and has opened a new $100 million research and development center. The company is a leader in anti-aging skin care, and is undertaking a comprehensive renovation of its color and fragrance lines. Other products are being developed or improved at the facility.

Avon's new marketing structure in China has been very successful, as evidenced by the growth in sales and profits. The company views China as its largest long-term opportunity. As of 2004, the government still had not authorized a return to direct selling in China. Avon expects, however, that the government will give permission in the future. It then expects to use the present outlets as hubs of a new direct selling business model. Even though the present system of distribution is providing good growth and profits, the company believes that distribution through independent Avon representatives will provide even greater growth and profits.

Questions

1. Does it appear that Avon's marketing strategy in China is working well? Might some other strategy have been more effective?

2. Discuss the probable usefulness of the development of the 'preferred customer' program in the short term and the longer term for Avon. How do you suppose the program might have been used by some of the 'preferred customers'?

3. What are the advantages and disadvantages of Avon applying some of the marketing models it developed in China to other markets?

4. Should Avon continue to experiment with new marketing approaches? What are the possible costs and benefits?

5. Should Avon return to its direct selling model in China if the government decides to allow it to? What are the possible costs and benefits?

CHAPTER 7

Export Entry Modes

7.1 Introduction

Alternative entry modes available to the export marketer were identified and categorized in Chapter 6 as indirect or direct. These two basic forms of exporting are distinguished on the basis of how the exporting firm carries out the transactions flow between itself and the importer or foreign buyer. In this chapter we discuss these entry modes in detail.

The decision between the two forms involves determining the level of vertical control desired by the exporter, and this involves considering two types of costs: (1) the costs of actually performing necessary functions, and (2) transaction costs that arise in the organization of an activity or of contracting with other parties.

As an illustration of the two approaches, Figure 7.1 outlines both indirect and direct export by a manufacturer of consumer goods. Exhibit 7.1 provides an interesting example (from Germany) that may be a model for similar companies elsewhere to follow.

EXHIBIT 7.1	Think small: export lessons from German *Mittelstand*

In order to get a good look at Germany's export strengths, one does not have to go any farther than the Glasbau Hahn factory on the outskirts of Frankfurt. Glasbau Hahn is the top of the line of glass showcases. Its products protect the world's most valuable art objects. Customers such as New York's Metropolitan Museum of Art and London's British

Brandenberg Gate, Berlin, Germany

Museum have paid up to US$100,000 apiece for custom-built wall-size showcases from Hahn, complete with heat-free, fiber-optic lighting and precision climate control.

According to Miller (1995), by the mid-1990s there were anywhere from 300,000 to 2.5 million small and medium-size companies such as Hahn – collectively dubbed the *Mittelstand*, meaning 'midranking.' Although large companies such as Daimler Benz (now DaimlerChrysler) and Siemens are best known abroad, it is these smaller ones with less than 500 employees or with a turnover between €25 million and more than €1 billion that produce one-half of Germany's business turnover, train eight out of every ten apprentices, employ four out of every five workers in the private sector and generate 20% of German exports (Fisher, 1998). They make everything from motors and machine tools to such consumer goods as camping equipment and high-fashion garments.

The *Mittelstand* companies are already important exporters, used to competing with the world's best companies. They know how to use innovation and applied research to overcome high labor costs and a strong currency that makes their exports more expensive. The best *Mittelstand* companies combine dynamism and flexibility on the one hand with caution and tradition on the other. More than 60% of them are among the world's top five in their niche, and hundreds are number one. Many, such as Haribo, a family firm that makes chewy sweets, enter a new market only if they can dominate it (*The Economist*, 1998).

Unlike Japan's export leaders, the *Mittelstand* have grown collectively big by thinking small. They work out of small plants often located in towns that are unknown to most people, and they target small but highly profitable niches in global markets. Investing large amounts of their revenue into research and development, *Mittelstand* companies routinely beat the large companies to market with new products. One reason is that they are mostly run by owner-managers. Nearly 40% are family owned. A study in the mid-1990s of 500 of the best *Mittelstand* firms reported that more than 65% are managed by their owners and their sales alone account for about 10% of the total German exports (*The Economist*, 1995b).

There are some *Mittelstand* companies that do not export directly, preferring to work through large companies. That is similar to the Japanese model in which smaller companies supply big exporters in their *keiretsu*, or industrial group. But in contrast with Japan, the vast majority of *Mittelstand* companies are fiercely independent. However, changes are occurring as companies go public and raise needed capital. In addition, professional managers are being hired.

Part of the *Mittelstand*'s success stems from the German business culture itself. Unlike US managers, *Mittelstand* members are not only concerned with quarterly earnings growth. Instead, they are devoted to quality, profits, and family ownership. In their terms, success means handing a healthy company on to the next generation. Although for more than 40% of *Mittelstand* firms, relatives take over when succession occurs, there is a problem in succession facing these companies as increasingly, the children of the owners do not want to run the firm (*The Economist*, 2001b, p. 55). Estimates in the late 1990s were that up to 25% of these firms would be sold in the next few years as families cash out.

Beyond the succession 'problem' there is another major concern for *Mittelstand* companies. Bank credit is getting harder to obtain. This has been attributed to international banking guidelines such as Basel 2 and Germany's large banks, which are believed by *Mittelstand* companies to have lost interst in small business (*The Economist*, 2001b). Their share of lending to craft companies ranging from hairdressers to builders has dropped by as much as 50% during the period 1991–2001. Banks claim to be interested in *Mittelstand* companies, but this generally meant to mean the larger ones.

Another feature is that the *Mittelstand* is beginning to create mini-conglomerates through mergers and joint ventures, a new activity that was frowned upon in principle. For example, in the late 1990s Hella, a car-headlamp producer, joined with radiator maker Behr to produce front panels for automobiles (*The Economist*, 1998, p. 68).

Finally, *Mittelstand* CEOs argue that it is their own efforts that make the difference between success and failure. These companies have good labor relations. The *Mittelstand* workforce is highly trained, in the past due to apprenticeship programs that ran from two to four years.

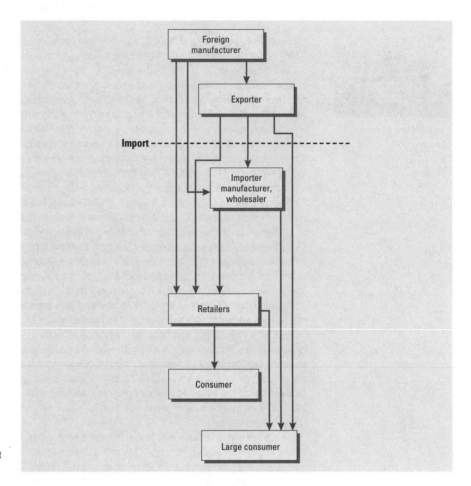

FIGURE 7.1

Indirect and direct export
of consumer goods

7.2 Indirect export

Indirect export occurs when the exporting manufacturer uses independent organizations located in the producer's country. In addition, the producer may have a dependent export organization (for example an export department) that works with the independent marketing organizations and coordinates the entire export effort. In this situation the dependent organization does not actively engage in any international sales activities.

There are two broad alternatives available to the manufacturer wanting to export indirectly: (1) using international marketing organizations, and (2) exporting through a cooperative organization.

7.2.1 Marketing organizations

In export marketing there are two basic types of independent wholesale marketing intermediaries: *merchants* and *agents*. The basic distinction between the two is that the merchant takes ownership of the products to be sold, while the agent does not.

7.2.2 Home-country based merchants

Export merchants

The domestic-based export merchant buys and sells on its own account. Generally engaged in both exporting and importing, it operates in a manner similar to a regular domestic wholesaler. When this type of marketing organization is used in an export marketing channel the marketing job for the manufacturer is reduced to essentially domestic marketing. All aspects of the international marketing task are handled by this merchant except for any needed modifications in such things as the product itself, its package, or in the quantity included in the unit package to meet any special needs of individual overseas markets. This also includes selecting the channels within foreign markets as well as activities relating to sales, marketing, merchandising, advertising, delivery, and services.

The export merchant company is free to choose what it will buy, where it will buy, and at what prices. The same freedom exists for sales. This type of company may have a far-flung organization that may include branch houses, warehouses, branch offices, docks, transportation facilities, retail establishments, and even industrial enterprises in foreign markets served. As a consequence, the export merchant is likely to be a powerful commercial organization, well able to exist without the cooperation or the products of any one manufacturer or any one group of manufacturers. In some instances this type of enterprise dominates the trade of certain localities or even certain nations.

There are some potential limitations to using export merchants. First, they may not be available for all markets. Export merchants are principally interested in staple commodities, which are generally open-market items not subject to a high degree of identification by the producer; and they are reluctant to undertake the development details and expense of the introduction and sale of any article that approaches the status of a specialty and which might require a considerable amount of sales effort.

The export merchant, occupying so commanding a position, is usually unwilling to allow the manufacturer much more than a manufacturing profit on any merchandise. The export merchant feels that he or she meets any terms of payment the manufacturer demands; that he or she performs every function connected with marketing and selling; and, finally, that he or she has all the manufacturers of a given line to choose from since their importance in the market gives them command of the outlets for any products that they may care to sponsor.

Trading company

In many countries export merchants known as *trading companies* are quite common. Different types of trading companies have been identified, as shown in Table 7.1.

Although international trading companies based in Brazil, Hong Kong, South Korea, Taiwan, Thailand, Turkey, and other countries, including some in Europe, have been active throughout the world, it is in Japan that the trading company concept has been applied most effectively and perhaps most uniquely. There are thousands of trading companies in Japan that are involved in exporting and importing, and the largest firms (varying in number from 9 to 17 depending upon source of estimate) are referred to as general trading companies or *sogo shosha*. This group of companies, which includes Mitsui & Co., Ltd., Mitsubishi Shoji Kaisha, Ltd., and Marubeni, handle a large share of Japan's exports and imports. While the smaller trading companies usually limit their activities to foreign trade, the larger general trading companies are also heavily involved in domestic distribution and other activities.

Type	Rationale for grouping
(1) General trading companies (GTCs)	Historical involvement in generalized import/export activities
(2) Export trading companies (ETCs)	Specific mission to promote growth of exporters
(3) Federated export marketing groups (FMGs)	Loose collaboration among exporting companies supervised by a third party and usually market specific
(4) Trading arms of multinational corporations (MNC-ETCs)	Import/export and trading activities specific in parent company's operations
(5) Bank-based or bank-affiliated trading groups (Bank-ETCs)	Extension of traditional banking activities into commercial fields
(6) Commodity trading companies (CTCs)	Long-standing export trading in a specific market, secretive, fast-paced and high-risk activities

Source: adapted from Amine (1987), p. 203

The Japanese general trading companies are engaged in a far wider range of commercial and financial activities than simply trade and distribution. They also play a central role in such diverse areas as shipping, warehousing, finance, technology transfer, planning, resource development, construction and regional development (e.g., turnkey projects), insurance, consulting, real estate, and deal making in general (including facilitating investment and joint venture of others). In fact, it is the range of financial services offered that is a major factor distinguishing general trading companies from others. These services include the guaranteeing of loans, the financing of both accounts receivable and payable, the issuing of promissory notes, major foreign exchange transactions, equity investment, and even direct loans.

The *sogo shosha* differ from multinational corporations chiefly in that their wide-ranging investments are all in some way directly connected with trade, with the broad aim of stimulating international business. They also differ from other companies in that they are not necessarily user or manufacturer oriented. Rather, they are supply/demand oriented and function as problem solvers. Recognizing demand for goods or services, the *sogo shosha* look for ways to supply it, either taking the intermediary role in trade deals between a number of parties or independently directing the flow of trade. To an extent these actions have been in response to the increased direct export activities of Japanese manufacturers such as Toyota, Hitachi, and Sony. Exhibit 7.2 illustrates many of these activities.

Some of the general trading companies, including C. Itoh & Co., Mitsubishi International Corporation, and Mitsui & Co., have established global sales networks consisting of branch offices overseas or wholly owned subsidiaries. For example, in Canada and the United States the subsidiary approach has often been used. C. Itoh America itself has more than 20 subsidiaries and affiliates in the United States – it imports Mazda and Isuzu automobiles, exports Beechcraft airplanes, and manufactures chain link fence and piping.

As another example of the far-reaching impact of trading companies consider

| EXHIBIT 7.2 | Japan's general trading companies |

In the mid-1990s Mitsui Bussan was among the largest of Japan's trading companies. It was also the central company of the Mitsui *keiretsu* – one of the groups of companies, held together by cross-shareholdings and directorates, that dominate Japanese business. Mitsui and the other leading general trading companies – Mitubishi, Sumitomo, Marubeni (which is part of the Fuyo *keiretsu*), Itochu (Dai-Ici Kangyo) and Nissho Iawai (Sanwa) – had turnover (sales) in 1994 of about ¥100 trillion; this was equivalent to about 25% of the GDP of Japan for that year.

But that large turnover yielded joint net profits of less than ¥45 billion for the year. To westerners these companies, known as the *sogo shosha*, seem to be prehistoric dinosaurs. Their core business of acting as middlemen is under attack from others as Japanese companies are increasingly willing to deal directly with suppliers and customers (*The Economist*, 1995a).

The *sogo shosha* are the world's largest 'jack-of-all-trades' with, somewhat questionably, an inability to master any of them. In short, they seem to be able to do a lot of things well, but few – if any – really well! At various times they act as commission agents, importing and exporting on behalf of clients; merchants, trading in their own right; middlemen in transactions between members of their *keiretsu*; financiers for smaller *keiretsu* members; investment trust managers; venture capitalists; project developers and managers; and consultants. They like their diversification into being oil companies, power generators, telecom operators, television stations, and even satellite communicators.

The companies, obviously, take on risks and management challenges that many western conglomerates would shy away from. But the *shosha* have a long history of entering new fields. Their core competence seems to have been built on their customers' lack of knowledge – of 'abroad' and what that meant. Once ignorance turns to enlightenment, as it did for many Japanese automobile and electronics companies in the 1970s, such business tends to dry up. This causes the *shosha* to move into new fields.

The old and the new

The *shosha* reduced their agency business in the mid-1990s, where gross margins tend to be no more than 3%, from about 80% of profits in 1980 to 40%; it is expected to decline to 20% by 2010. They also dropped their role as 'nonbanks' to the smaller *keiretsu* members. Instead they started buying and selling more on their own accounts, where margins can be as high as 20%, and moving directly into the businesses they used to service.

Many *sogo shosha* are becoming significant energy companies, building on their experience as oil traders. Mitsubishi's liquefied natural gas (LNG) plant in Brunei provided about one-third of the company's net profits in the mid-1990s. Other *shosha* also moved into energy where they had 21 oil and gas concessions producing or about to produce. Some of these are long-term gambles.

Another area where these companies have moved from being traders to operators is electricity generation. With support from the Japanese government they have been investing in power plants in other Asian countries. Despite the high yen value in the mid-1990s, Mitsubishi kept working with its *keiretsu* partner, Mitsubishi Heavy Industries, as its main equipment supplier. But Marubeni often works with foreign companies such as the Swiss-Swedish firm Asea Brown Boveri and the Anglo-French consortium GEC-Alsthom instead of its *keiretsu* partner Hitachi. The most dramatic move, however, has been the *shosha* rush into the communications industry.

Venturer merchants

The tendency to acquire and hang on to new businesses is being tempered by a new willingness to divest once they have matured. The *shosha* have always held large ownership stakes in other companies. Some are ownership in other *keiretsu* members and some are subsidiaries, which is how the *shosha* have preferred to run their noncore activities. Finally, some have been bought as investments.

Unless Japan changes and becomes totally 'westernized' the *sogo shosha* will continue doing things as they always have – adapting to fit whatever niche Japan's environment presents them with.

Jardine Matheson, the oldest trading company, or *hong*, based in Hong Kong (but legally domiciled in Bermuda). The group of companies is all over Asia, engaging in such activities as trading per se, retailing, hotel development and management, vehicle distribution, merchant banking, and mutual fund management. Unlike Japan, in the past trading companies in Hong Kong have not been directly influenced by government policy (Ellis, 2001). With Hong Kong now a Special Administrative Region (SAR) of China, Hong Kong-based trading companies, particularly the now foreign-owned ones such as Jardine Matheson, have to be sensitive to the effects that their decisions might have on the PRC government in Beijing. Operations in Hong Kong as well as China itself might be affected. China was 'upset' by such actions prior to the handover on 30 June 1997 as Jardine's moving its legal home to Bermuda and its delisting of its stock from the Hong Kong Stock Exchange and move to Singapore. One result has been delays in projects. The situation for Jardine has improved since the managing director made a public apology in early 1997 that Jardine regretted any offense caused in China by its actions.

Trading companies, whether the very largest from Japan or those increasingly emerging from such countries as South Korea, Brazil, countries within Europe or the United States, should be of concern to all export marketers. First, they may be necessary for market entry. This would include direct export by the export marketer as well as indirect export. It may be that in order to penetrate, say, the Japanese market the direct exporter would have to do business with a Japanese importing trading company. Second, since trading companies appear throughout the world they may be competitors to the export marketer. It is quite obvious that a trading company can be a very formidable competitor. Consequently, strategies may have to be changed in those markets where trading companies are major competitors. Exhibit 7.3 discusses the development of *sogo shosha*-type companies in China.

Ellis (2003) discusses how trading companies or what he calls 'international trading intermediaries' contribute to the economic development of host countries. This applies to both new foreign markets and offshore sources of supply. Three distinct contributions are identified:

- The efficiency of distribution in an economy is improved by minimizing costs incurred in overcoming barriers to trade – i.e., transaction costs are lowered.
- Productivity may be increased by opening new markets and finding new sources of supply. This creates international exchanges where none existed before.
- Marketing technology and credit may be introduced into local distribution channels, which is known as a catalytic contribution.

Export desk jobber

One type of export merchant often helpful to manufacturers deserves special note. This is the export desk jobber, who, because of the method of operation, is also known as an *export drop shipper*, and may be called a *cable merchant*.

| EXHIBIT 7.3 | Here come the Chinese |

In 1998 many Japanese and South Korean conglomerates were severely damaged or driven out of business due to the Asian financial crisis of the time. But China vowed to stick to its pilot drive to foster their large multiple-purpose trading houses – their *sogo shosha* (Zhang, 1998).

There were nine such trading giants in Japan and seven in South Korea. These companies held the great bulk of their respective country's total foreign trade volume. Between 1994 and 1998 China's central government approved two pilot *sogo shosha* – the China National Chemical Import and Export Co. and Orient International (Group) Co. Nie Gaomin, deputy director of the Circulation System Department under the State Commission of Economic Restructuring, said that the financial crisis in East and Southeast Asian countries would not prevent China introducing trading companies of this kind.

The central government plans to expand this pilot scheme. The China General Technical (Group) Holding Co., another trading giant resulting from the merger of the China National Technical Import and Export Co., the China Machinery Import and Export Co., the China National Instrument Import and Export Co., and the China National Corp. for Overseas Economic Co-operation, will be added to the pilot group.

Large trading companies should focus on their major business instead of dabbling too much in industry, Nie warned. 'Multiple-purpose doesn't mean multiple-industry, but means trade-oriented multiple-services,' he said. Considerable success has already been achieved by China's *sogo shosha*. The sales revenue and foreign trade volume of the China National Chemical Import and Export Co. are the best among all Chinese trading companies.

Used primarily in the international sales of raw materials, the desk jobbers never see or physically acquire the goods that they buy and sell. In all other respects, however, the desk jobber operates as a regular export merchant, except that goods are typically owned for a very short time. The manufacturer using this type of export merchant comes a little closer to direct export in that he or she is responsible for the physical movement (including documentation requirements) of his or her products to the desk jobber's customer. For example, a company in the United States may negotiate a sale of mercury to a buyer in Japan from a supplier in Spain. Title moves from the Spanish supplier to the US firm and then to the Japanese buyer. Actual shipment will be directly from Spain to Japan.

Export desk jobbers are specialists in knowing sources of supply and markets. They relieve the producer of the problem and risk of determining the reliability of the purchaser. However, they are not conducive to the establishment of continuous markets for a manufacturer's product. They simply conduct business too quickly for there to be any permanent market relationship.

7.2.3 Home-country based agents

There are several distinct types of wholesaler agents located in the country of export who are potentially available as members of a manufacturer's export marketing channel. When such an agent is used, the manufacturer generally assumes all financial risks.

Export commission house

The export commission house (export buying agent) is a representative of foreign buyers who resides in the exporter's home country. As such, this type of agent is essentially the overseas customer's hired purchasing agent in the exporter's domestic market, operating on the basis of orders or 'indents' (offers to purchase under conditions stipulated by the prospective buyer, including the price to be paid) received from these buyers. Since the export commission house acts in the interests of the buyer, it is the buyer who pays a commission. The exporting manufacturer is not directly involved in determining the terms of purchase; these are worked out between the commission house and the overseas buyer.

The export commission house essentially becomes a domestic buyer. It scans the market for the particular merchandise that it has been requested to buy. It sends out specifications to manufacturers inviting bids. Other conditions being equal, the lowest price gets the order and there is no sentimentality, friendship, or sales talk involved.

From the exporter's point of view, selling to export commission houses represents an easy way to export. Prompt payment is usually guaranteed in the exporter's home country, and the problems of physical movement of the goods is generally taken completely off its hands. There is very little credit risk and the exporter has only to fill the order, according to specifications. A major problem is that the exporter has little direct control over the international marketing of products.

Confirming house

The basic function of a confirming house is to assist the overseas buyer by confirming, as a principal, orders already placed, so that the exporter may receive payment from the confirming house when the goods are shipped. Some exporters may believe that confirming houses should be classified as financial institutions and not as a type of marketing organization. However, the confirming house does perform some functions usually performed by a commission house, even if it does not perform all the functions. The confirming house is not a common type of export enterprise everywhere in the world, but it is in Europe, particularly in the United Kingdom.

The confirming house interposes its credit between the buyer in the importing country and the exporter or manufacturer in the exporting country. It finds its greatest usefulness in those markets where credit conditions are uncertain or where the cost of money is high.

In addition to the payment aspects, the confirming house may also be involved in making arrangements for the shipper. Typically, all contact between buyer and exporter would go through the confirming house. Due to the functions that it performs, its greatest users would be small and medium-sized companies.

Resident buyer

Similar in operation to the export commission house are resident buyers. Resident buyers represent all types of overseas buyers and are domiciled in the exporter's home market. These buyers represent foreign concerns that want to have close and continuous contact with their overseas sources of supply, and are either sent to the market or are local people appointed as representatives. Large retailers utilize this type of intermediary extensively. Thus, retailers such as Galeries Lafayette (France), Harrods (UK), and Nordstrom (US) may have resident buyers in the clothing centers of Italy, Hong Kong, China, and wherever else clothing is produced. Although the resident buyer operates almost exactly like the commission house, that is, the buyer places an order, specifies the terms of sales, handles all shipping matters and other details of the exporting process, and either pays cash or furnishes the manufacturer with a low-risk means of financing – there is one important difference. Because resident buyers are 'permanently' employed representatives of foreign buyers, the exporting manufacturer has a good chance to build up a steady and continuous business with foreign markets. To a large extent, the existence of established brands, trademarks, and a historical record in the market do not count as heavily as being price competitive.

One advantage of an importer utilizing a resident buyer and of the exporter dealing with such a buyer is that any problems that might arise due to language difficulties and cultural and business customs differences are minimized, if not eliminated. It is especially important for the buyers to be fluent in the language of the exporter's country (or have translation help, which is not as desirable as first-hand knowledge) and be familiar with the local culture and customs. A resident of the exporter's country would have this knowledge. To illustrate what can happen when language is not understood, a buyer from Italy, who felt she knew English fairly well, was sent to Britain to purchase clothing (Ricks, 1999, p. 116). She found some appropriate sweaters at Bourne & Hollingsworth, and attempted to order 'four to five thousand pounds worth.' Upon her return to Italy it became clear that a major misunderstanding had occurred – delivery was made of the 'forty-five' thousand pounds worth that she had actually ordered.

Broker

Another type of home-country based agent is the export/import broker. The chief function of a broker is to bring a buyer and seller together. Thus the broker is a specialist in performing the contractual function, and does not actually handle the products sold or bought. For its services the broker is paid a commission by the principal. The broker commonly specializes in particular products or classes of products, usually staple primary commodities such as grains, lumber, rubber, fibers. Being a commodity specialist, there is a tendency to concentrate on just one or two products. Because the broker deals primarily in basic commodities, for many potential export marketers this type of agent does not represent a practical alternative channel of distribution.

The distinguishing characteristic of export brokers is that they may act as the agent for either the seller or the buyer. For example, an export broker in the lumber business may be contacted by a sawmill and asked if he or she can dispose of a quantity of lumber of a size and grade not readily salable domestically. The broker will then get in touch with potential foreign buyers with whom he or she is acquainted and either offer the lumber to them at a predetermined price or ask them to make an offer. When several foreign offers are received, the broker accepts the best offer or relays the information to the sawmill to ascertain whether the price is acceptable. When the transaction is successfully concluded the sawmill pays the broker's fee. Alternatively, the broker may be contacted by a foreign buyer and asked to secure quotations on a quantity of a certain size and grade of lumber. Quotations are then sought from sawmills with which he or she is also acquainted. If the broker is not authorized to place the order with the mill making the best quotation, the prices are sent to the foreign buyer for determination whether the price is acceptable. When the transaction is concluded successfully, the foreign buyer pays the broker's fee.

Export management company

Simply defined, an export management company (EMC) is an international sales specialist who functions as the exclusive export department for several allied but noncompeting manufacturers. That is to say, an EMC may serve five sailboat parts manufacturers, each making a different part. For the individual manufacturer the EMC is to exporting what the sales agent is to domestic marketing.

Although EMCs are independent intermediary organizations, as far as potential overseas buyers are concerned these firms are the manufacturing firm. Being the 'export department' of several manufacturers, the EMC conducts business in the name of each manufacturer that it represents. All correspondence with buyers and contracts are negotiated in the name of the manufacturer and all quotations and orders are subject to confirmation by the manufacturer. Different contractual arrangements with principals may be used.

In actual operation, the EMC in many instances is perhaps more a manufacturer's distributor or an export merchant than a commission representative since export managers often operate on a buy-and-sell rather than a commission basis. Many still work on a straight commission basis, but the majority today do their own financing, assuming all credit risks abroad and paying the manufacturer cash for every order. Thus the EMC often takes over all the risks and problems of export and the manufacturer just fills the orders.

The possible benefits to a manufacturer of using an export management firm in the channel of distribution are many. In the first place, a tailor-made export department is obtained without adding any extra selling expense. Since this export department is fully functioning at the time that it is obtained, using the EMC is one of the quickest ways for a manufacturer to enter foreign markets. In addition to handling the selling activities, the EMC does research on foreign markets, chooses the best type of channel within an overseas market and usually does its own advertising and promotion. Also, the EMC may serve as a shipping and forwarding agent, and may furnish its principals with legal advice such as patent and trademark situations. Second, where a buy-and-sell arrangement is involved, the manufacturer receives financing assistance. Even without buy-and-sell, an EMC is able to collect and furnish credit information on foreign customers to their principals. Third, the EMC offers experience, which is important in export marketing since no two foreign markets are alike. Being in daily contact with varying conditions in different foreign markets, the EMC knows which markets are receptive to a manufacturer's products and how to sell them in those markets. Fourth, specialization can lead to significant benefits. Handling a wide line of related but noncompeting products can help the sales of each individual product. If a buyer is interested in buying one product there may also be a need for other related products. Since many buyers prefer to work with as few suppliers as is practical, the fact that a supplier can offer a line of products may mean the difference in whether a sale is made or not. Specialization, of course, exists in degrees. Thus, if an EMC represents too many manufacturers, selling efforts may, of necessity, be extensive rather than intensive. Another potential benefit may be derived through savings on shipping expenses. By consolidating orders from different manufacturers into one shipment the EMC can help the overseas buyer make substantial savings. In short, using an EMC is a good way for a manufacturer to overcome any obstacles/barriers to exporting that exist or are perceived by companies to exist (Rameseshan and Soutar, 1996).

In retrospect, it appears that using an export management firm will perhaps be most advantageous to the small to medium-sized manufacturer. In general, however, these independent agents can provide valuable export marketing services to any manufacturer that either cannot afford to set up its own export marketing organization, that does not want to get involved in the more or less 'unique' problems found in export marketing, or that wants to let someone help break it into the business. There are reasons for the small or inexperienced firm producing a branded or specialized product to seriously consider utilizing an EMC. Export sales activities are handled by an expert. Since expenses of export promotion are shared with other producers, they are not unduly burdensome to anyone, especially in the developmental stages of export business. Representing only a limited number of accounts, the EMC pays adequate attention to each account. Since they accept accounts only from producers of related types of products, the danger of promotion of competitors' products is obviated. Small producers gain the prestige of association with related products. The experience and knowledge of the export manager provides the producer with immediate access to established foreign markets.

The truly successful EMC may expect and hope to work itself out of a job, as far as any single producer is concerned, by developing the principal's business to the point that it becomes preferable (cost wise or profit wise) for the producer to establish its own export department and perhaps even shift to direct export. Often the EMC will assist their principals in setting up such an export department.

Manufacturer's export agent

In contrast to an EMC, the manufacturer's export agent retains its own identity by operating in its own name. Also, the manufacturer's export agent is paid a straight commission and does not engage in buy-and-sell arrangements with the manufacturers represented. Because of these basic differences, the manufacturer's export agent does not offer a manufacturer all the services that an EMC does. Most notable is the lack of advertising and financial assistance. However, there are occasions when the manufacturer's export agent assumes foreign credit risks and charges a *del credere* commission in addition to the regular commission. With a *del credere* arrangement the export agent either guarantees payment for all orders sent to the manufacturer or finances the transaction.

The manufacturer's export agent may be most effectively used when the firm wants to sell small orders to overseas buyers, enter a new overseas market, or sell a product that is relatively new to consumers in overseas markets. Because this type of export agent retains its own identity, it usually desires to remain the foreign sales representative on a permanent basis. Thus producers are seldom encouraged to establish their own export departments.

7.2.4 Evaluation of marketing organizations

In assessing the various types of independent marketing organizations it must be recognized that often it is difficult to categorize a specific company completely into one of the types discussed. Frequently, over a period of time a single firm will perform the functions of several types. For example, an export merchant may on occasion participate in transactions in which it functions as some type of an agent, say, a broker. Similarly, a manufacturer's export agent may on a single transaction sell for its own account products it has previously bought. In addition, many marketing organizations may perform some or all of the services necessary to physically transport a shipment; in this case they operate as *freight forwarders* (see Chapter 13). Since the profit motive underlies the operations of independent export marketing organizations they may engage in all related functions from which profits may be forthcoming.

It should be apparent that by using some type of independent export marketing organization in the channel of distribution certain advantages accrue to a manufacturer. A minimum financial outlay by the producer is required, which is particularly desirable for the firm with limited financial resources or facing a small potential demand in foreign markets. Since these agencies are experts in export marketing they know foreign markets, have established contacts in foreign countries, and are able to pinpoint ready markets for certain products. Thus, foreign sales volume can be built up in a relatively short amount of time and seemingly out-of-the-way markets can be tapped. The best markets for particular products are not always the largest countries or those most developed economically. Finally, the manufacturer can determine the foreign potential for its product with a minimum of risk, something that is quite valuable to the company that is new to exporting.

There also are potential drawbacks to using independent marketing organizations. Because of the many different products handled, a marketing organization may not be able to promote the sale of any particular one. This is especially true for export merchants. Furthermore, since such agencies seek profits for themselves, they tend to handle only those products that appear to be the most profitable to them. If a more profitable product appears they will accept it and drop some other one. Thus a manufacturer may be in a position where its marketing channels are not permanent. In many instances the manufacturer may not be able to engage directly in sales effort and promotion. This can be a serious drawback if a product requires a great amount of specialized attention, since most marketing organizations are not able or willing to provide the needed effort. Finally, with the exception of the export management company there is a risk that product goodwill which is generated accrues to the intermediary marketing organization and not the manufacturer.

A matter of some concern to both the manufacturer and intermediary marketing organizations is the conflict that is to some degree inevitable. Conflicts can arise from many sources: (1) differences in major factors such as goals and objectives, desired target customers, desired product lines, and interpersonal relations; and (2) differences in channel design and channel policies. What really matters is not whether conflict exists, as it usually always will to some extent, but whether it is hurting the relationship and the channel and whether it can be managed.

7.2.5 Cooperative organizations

Cooperative exporting organizations represent a cross between indirect and direct export. For a manufacturer using this type of organization in an export marketing channel, indirect export is being engaged in since the specific cooperative organization is not administratively a part of the manufacturer's organization. On the other hand there is, in a sense, direct export occurring since a manufacturer can exert some 'administrative' control over the operating policies of the cooperative organization. There are two distinct types of cooperative international marketing organizations: (1) piggyback marketing, and (2) exporting combinations.

Piggyback marketing

Piggyback marketing, also known as 'mother henning,' occurs when one manufacturer (the 'carrier') uses its foreign distribution facilities to sell another company's (the 'supplier') products alongside its own. As shown in Figure 7.2 (Duerr and Greene, 1969, p. 5), there are alternative ways in which this can be handled. All types of products have been exported by this technique including textiles, industrial and electrical machinery and equipment, chemicals, consumer soft goods, and books.

Piggyback marketing is used for products from different companies that are noncompetitive (but related), complementary (allied), or unrelated. The particular relationship depends to a large extent upon the motives of the large, already exporting companies. In the past, some companies such as General Electric and Borg-Warner in the United States have viewed piggybacking as a way of broadening the product lines that they can offer to foreign markets. They feel that marketing allied products helps them to market their own products. Other companies engage in this type of operation in order to bolster decreasing export sales. Pillsbury Company, for instance, first began to sell the products of other

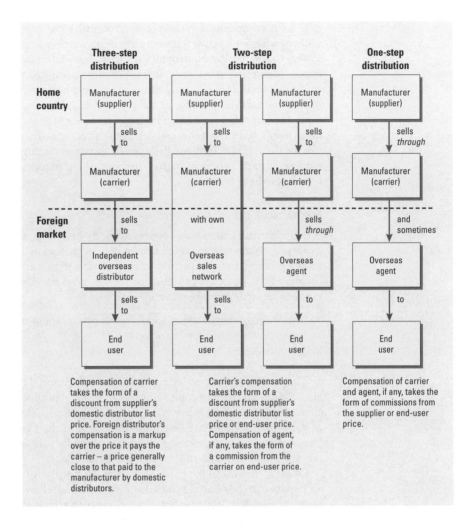

FIGURE 7.2

Chains of distribution in
piggyback marketing
Source: Duerr and Greene
1969, p. 5, reprinted with
permission of The
Conference Board

companies – packaged foods, farm machinery – when export sales of its flour
began to decline. Finally, some companies actively seek out smaller manufacturers
because piggybacking can be profitable. In general, the carrier's compensation
takes the form of a discount from the supplier's domestic distributor list price plus
a markup. The discount varies widely depending upon the product and the services
provided by the carrier. Although the usual arrangement is for the larger company
to buy outright the products of the smaller company, the larger company may
prefer to act as an agent and be compensated by a commission. Some companies
engage in this practice because of government encouragement or regulations. For
example, in the late 1980s Rhone-Poulenc, a French chemical company, sold the
products of hundreds of other companies through its extensive global sales
network (Karamally, 1998, p. 113). The French government encouraged this to
assist smaller exporters that lacked abilities to do extensive exporting. Another
example is Polymark Laundry Systems, which in the late 1980s marketed the
products of many other companies in Poland. Polymark was licensed by the
government and other firms did not find it worth the effort at the time to get the
required government approvals.

There may be differences concerning which company's name the product will
be sold under. Some companies have a policy of using either the actual manufacturer's name or creating a private label – but never their own name. Other

exporting companies have the policy of using the corporate name that is best known, whether its own name or that of its supplier.

Piggyback marketing provides an easy, low-risk way for a company to begin export marketing operations. It is especially well suited to manufacturers that are either too small to go directly into exports or which do not want to invest heavily in foreign marketing. As far as the smaller manufacturer is concerned, its transactions are domestic in nature. The larger firm can provide a well-established export department and export marketing channels geared to the needs of the smaller firm. Yet for the smaller company this type of agreement means that the control over the marketing of its products is given up, something that many firms dislike doing, at least in the long run.

Exporting combinations

A manufacturer can export cooperatively by becoming a member of some type of exporting combination, which can be defined as a more or less formal association of independent and competitive business firms, with membership being voluntary, organized for purposes of selling to foreign markets. There are two basic general types of exporting combinations:

1. marketing cooperative associations of producers or merchandisers that engage in exporting members' products;
2. export cartels.

The first type of exporting combination is the normal domestic marketing cooperative as is commonly found in certain primary product industries, for example citrus fruits, nuts, and other types of agricultural products. The export operations of such organizations are essentially the same as the export operations of manufacturers and intermediaries. A producer normally cannot join the cooperative for the sole purpose of entering foreign markets.

Of more interest to the manufacturer is the possibility of becoming a member of an export cartel or cartel-type arrangement. A cartel is said to exist when two or more independent business firms in the same or affiliated fields of economic activity join together for the purpose of exerting control over a market. More specifically, a cartel is a voluntary association of producers of a commodity or product organized for the purpose of coordinated marketing that is aimed at stabilizing or increasing the members' profits. A cartel may engage in price-fixing, restriction of production or shipments, division of marketing territories, centralization of sales, or pooling of profits. Three types of international cartels can be distinguished:

1. The traditional international cartel formed for the purpose of truly dominating a market for certain products. This type of cartel is perhaps best illustrated by pre-World War II steel and chemical cartels in Germany and the more current Organization of Petroleum Exporting Countries as well as the marketing of diamonds by the DeBeers Central Selling Organization.
2. International Commodity Agreements such as exist in wheat and tin. These differ from the pure cartel in that both selling and buying countries are parties to the agreement.
3. Cartel-type organizations engaged solely in exporting that are formed so that the individual members can compete more effectively in overseas markets. The Webb-Pomerene associations in the United States are of this type, as are certain cartels in Japan. Also, the same type of US export trading companies (perhaps with commercial bank participation) can be such a cartel.

Our major concern is with the type of cartel formed solely for the purposes of export. For a manufacturer, the cartel takes over all export responsibility. Also, there may be little or no direct competition from other 'domestic' manufacturers. There are, however, certain limitations to this approach to exporting. In the first place, the association may become ineffective because the members cannot agree on key matters. Thus cooperation may be missing. Second, if a manufacturer's products are branded or trademarked there is a measurable risk that the independent identity of both the firm and its products might get lost along the way. Finally, related to the last limitation are the difficulties inherent in this type of arrangement of adequately representing individual interests. However, a single manufacturer does not have complete freedom of choice. Either an association must already exist or a manufacturer must find others willing to form one, something that is often difficult to do. Other approaches are illustrated briefly in Exhibit 7.4.

EXHIBIT 7.4	**Privileged companies**

Some forms of cartel arrangements, or arrangements where would-be competitors may join together, may be per se illegal business practice in some countries such as the United States and countries of western Europe. But cartels are not illegal per se in other countries – Singapore and Hong Kong are examples. To overcome this a country may pass special legislation to allow such cooperative business ventures. These types of arrangements will vary by country. For example, in the United States so-called Webb-Pomerene associations and export trading companies formed under the Export Trading Company Act are exempt from antitrust regulation if they meet certain conditions.

Arrangements such as the above are encouraged by national governments that want to promote increased export business. Another approach to this is to use *tax incentives* by allowing certain types of organizational arrangements. The United States provides an example by its fostering of foreign sales corporations (FSCs).

The approach used by the United States could be viewed as a model for other countries that want to promote exports. However, it should be recognized that many of these special business formats have been considerably less than an overwhelming success.

7.3 Direct export

Direct exporting occurs when a manufacturer or exporter sells directly to an importer or buyer located in a foreign market area. Thus the actual transaction flow between nations is handled directly by a dependent organization of the manufacturer or a foreign-based marketing organization or customer. As we indicated in Figure 6.1, a manufacturer can export directly to a buyer domiciled in a foreign market in many different ways.

Although our discussion of these alternative methods of direct export will look at each individually, in addition to being alternatives they are also complementary. A manufacturer may use more than one to serve any specific foreign market. Perhaps the best example of this concerns the role played by the home-country based export department or division. Generally speaking, regardless of the method used, some type of home-country based department should exist.

Entry modes should not be viewed as sacred. When conditions change, so should the channel. In a more general sense the changing of export arrangements is evidence that export development occurs in stages (Exhibit 7.5), as we discussed previously in Chapter 2. There is some evidence suggesting that for small and medium-sized companies export does not necessarily follow a stages model. Rather, companies may be 'born global' in that their future involvement in export is to a large extent influenced by their behavior shortly after their establishment – i.e., their 'birth' (Moen and Servais, 2002).

| **EXHIBIT 7.5** | **'Stages' models of export development** |

Export development can be viewed as occurring in stages. One such model consists of at least six stages, as follows: (1) no interest in exporting, (2) fill unsolicited order, (3) explore feasibility of exporting, (4) export on experimental basis to psychologically close country, (5) experienced exporter to country of stage 4, (6) explore feasibility of exporting to other countries, ... and so on (Bilkey and Tesar, 1977).

In stage 1, management would not even fill an unsolicited order, whereas in the second stage, although an unsolicited order would be filled, there would be no attempt to explore exporting on a more formalized basis. It is at stage 3, which can be skipped if unsolicited orders are received and filled, that a formal commitment to export marketing is really being considered. At stage 4 the model postulates that it is most desirable to begin exporting to countries that are psychologically close to the exporter's own country. Such a country has the same culture, is at a similar stage of economic development, etc., as the exporter's country. Thus Australia is psychologically closer to most UK firms than is Mexico, even though the latter is closer geographically. In stage 5 the exporter has become experienced in dealing with psychologically close countries and is now ready to expand to countries more psychologically distant (stage 6). The model would then progress, presumably ending with the firm no longer being solely an exporter; some form(s) of overseas production base(s) would be integrated into the international operations.

Limited empirical tests of this model suggest that the export development process does indeed tend to proceed in stages; considerations that influence firms' moving from one stage to the next tend to differ by stage; and quality and dynamism of management tend to make size of firm relatively unimportant. Similar approaches have been proposed by Czinkota (1982), and Reid (1981).

Although somewhat old, these schema are as applicable today as they were when proposed.

7.3.1 Home-country based department

The manufacturer who wants to engage in direct export will most likely have to establish some type of export department or division in the home country. This dependent organization may either be involved directly in making export sales or serve as the home-based export marketing department to coordinate and control the activities of other dependent organizations located in foreign markets.

There are basically three different types of home-country based export organizations:

1. built-in export department;
2. separate or self-contained export department;
3. export sales subsidiary.

The specific type that is appropriate for any manufacturer at a particular point in time depends upon such factors as the nature of the product, the size of the company, how long the company has been exporting, the expected potential volume of foreign sales, the underlying management philosophy towards doing business internationally, the corporate organizational structure, and the extent to which either existing company resources can be allotted to export activities or additional needed resources can be acquired.

Built-in department

The built-in type of export organization is the simplest in structure and, thus, the easiest to establish. In its most simple form this organization will consist of an export sales manager with some clerical help. The primary job of the sales manager is to do the actual selling or direct it. Most other export marketing activities – e.g., advertising, logistics, credit, etc. – are performed by the regular domestic market-oriented departments of the company.

Although the built-in arrangement is simple in structure, and flexible and economical in use, these features may be more apparent than real. Many complications can arise when the export manager tries to coordinate activities that must be performed by organizational units not under his or her direction. Since these other departments are usually oriented toward domestic marketing activities there is the danger that they will view tasks associated with export marketing as something to be done only when there is spare time available. In addition, these departments may not be knowledgeable in the special intricate details connected with exporting and must be willing and able to learn them. Such conditions may lead to unnecessary delays and a disorganized and far from optimal export marketing program. So much depends upon the extent to which these domestic-oriented departments are permanently committed to the domestic end of the business, that is, upon the amount of 'capacity' that is available for export marketing tasks. Much of the success of this type of export organization depends upon the individual occupying the manager's job, and this person's ability to secure the cooperation of the other department managers.

Under the right conditions, a substantial amount of foreign sales can be adequately handled by this type of organization. Despite this, for direct export the built-in form is best suited – relative to the other types of departments – to a manufacturer operating under any of the following conditions:

- small in size;
- new or relatively new to export marketing;
- expected foreign sales volume (turnover) is moderate to small;
- management philosophy not oriented toward growth of foreign business;
- existing marketing resources capacity not fully utilized in the domestic market;
- either the company is unable to acquire additional resources or, if able to do so, *key* resources are not available.

In addition, this type of arrangement is potentially very useful for coordinating the indirect export activities of a manufacturer using that method to serve foreign markets.

Separate export department

Although the built-in type of organization may be adequate in the early stages of direct export market development, if sales continue to increase a point will be reached where a more fully integrated organization is needed. One way to meet this need is to set up a separate export department.

In contrast to the built-in type, the separate export department is a self-contained and largely self-sufficient unit in which most of the export activities are handled within the department itself, making it a relatively complete export marketing department. The separate export department may be structured internally upon the basis of function, geographic region, product, customer or some type of combination, depending largely upon how the export marketing task varies the most.

Most of the conditions that may cause trouble in the built-in form are eliminated when a separate department is established. In the first place, there is no inherent possibility for clash between the international and domestic sides of the firm regarding the time to be spent by domestic marketing personnel on foreign business matters. There is, however, a chance for conflict regarding allocation of resources to each side of the business. Second, export operations can be conducted on a full-time basis by personnel knowledgeable and specifically committed to exporting. Finally, the separate export department has a fairly high degree of flexibility in terms of where it is located. A built-in export department by its very nature must be located at the same place as the domestic departments with which it works. Yet there may be reasons that the export organization should be located not at the headquarters of the company but in one of the major centers of international business. For example, a manufacturer in The Netherlands may be located in Maastricht on the border with Germany, but have its export department in Rotterdam because of the need to keep close contact with the many specialist facilitating agencies with which it must work – banks, forwarders, consulates, and so on.

Export sales subsidiary

In attempting to divorce completely export marketing activities from domestic operations, some companies have established an export sales subsidiary as a separate corporation. Although an export sales subsidiary is wholly owned and controlled by the parent company, it is essentially a quasi-independent firm.

All authority and responsibility attached to export operations, including profit responsibility, may be 'assigned' to one subunit of the parent manufacturing firm. Thus, with this form of export organization, a manufacturer may be better able to ascertain the profitability of its foreign business. In addition, the chance of conflicting pressures arising from domestic departments is minimized.

In terms of its internal organization and the specific activities performed, the sales subsidiary differs very little from the separate export department. There is, however, one major difference that can cause top management some concern. Being a separate corporation, the export sales subsidiary must purchase from the parent manufacturer the products that it sells in overseas markets. This means that the manufacturer must develop a system of internal transfer pricing. There are numerous complexities and management problems associated with transfer pricing. These are discussed in Chapter 10.

Although the export sales subsidiary is in many respects similar to an export department, there are important reasons for its existence:

- *Unified control.* All authority relative to exporting is centered in one organization not subject to conflicting pressures from various domestic departments.
- *Cost and profit control.* Since all revenues and expenses are separated from the domestic organization, export costs and profits can be seen readily.
- *Allocation of orders in multiple plant enterprises.* The subsidiary company can place an order with the most suitable plant more readily and can supervise traffic management responsibilities more effectively.
- *Ease of financing.* Since the subsidiary is a separate corporation it is easier to ascertain its financial position. As a result, financial institutions may be more willing to advance funds for export purposes.

- *More complete line of products.* Being a separate company, it can purchase products from outside sources to offer overseas buyers a more complete line.
- *Tax advantages.* Corporate income tax laws in some countries may result in some savings in total corporate taxes.

The subsidiary export company can serve a variety of useful purposes, most of them corporate in character and comparatively unrelated to the practice of exporting.

7.3.2 Foreign sales branch

A manufacturer that has been exporting direct through some form of home-country based department, possibly even in conjunction with foreign-based distributors or agents, may reach the point where it is believed necessary to have closer supervision over the sales made in a particular market area. In this kind of situation the company can establish a foreign sales branch. This is essentially what Aerotek International, a producer of hydraulic hose repair systems used in industrial construction and mining, did in the late 1990s when it replaced 50 of its Asian distributors with a company it established in Singapore.

A foreign sales branch handles all of the sales, distribution and promotional work throughout a designated market area and sells primarily to marketing organizations (wholesalers and dealers) or, under certain conditions, industrial users. Thus, where used, the foreign sales branch is the initial link in the marketing channel within a foreign market. Often there will be storage and warehousing facilities available so the branch can maintain an inventory of the product itself, replacement parts, maintenance supplies, or operating supplies. Whether a storage facility is used or not, shipment may often be made direct from the manufacturing plant to the initial buyer, especially when large purchases of high value are involved. Thus, the operating characteristics of a foreign sales branch are much the same as those of a foreign distributor except that the manager is an employee of the company and is directly responsible to the home office. In fact, foreign sales branches are often established after a market area has been developed and built up by local distributors and agents. The point at which this transformation should occur is when the size of the sales volume (turnover) justifies the cost involved in establishing and operating a branch office, and it is believed that this turnover level will be maintained or will grow over time.

A foreign sales branch may serve other useful purposes. In the first place, where it is desirable for the manufacturer to display part or all of its product line, the branch office can set aside facilities for this purpose. The value of this as a marketing and sales promotion tool is obvious. Second, for many manufacturers a more important use of a branch office can be as a service center. For various reasons, many foreign business firms, particularly independent marketing organizations, are not willing or able to provide the service for products that might require it. If it is not made available by the manufacturer, the buyer will have to do it himself. While some buyers, particularly those of industrial equipment, prefer to do their own servicing and only require that the necessary parts and supplies be readily available, other buyers consider service as something to be handled by the seller.

Foreign governmental policy may exert an influence on the actual operations of a sales branch as well as on the decision to establish a branch. For example, adverse tax laws may exist and there may be problems involved in repatriating profits. This is particularly important when the sales branch is organized as a subsidiary. Equally troublesome, potentially, is the question of the personnel who staff the sales branch. In general, it is perhaps most desirable to have personnel, particularly at the managerial level, who have actually worked or been trained in the domestic organization. Ideally, these people should be nationals of the country in which the branch office is situated. In some countries the government requires that a minimum proportion of branch office staff be citizens. One final comment is that operating a foreign sales branch is a very costly activity. Consequently, this method of doing business overseas is usually best suited to the larger and financially established manufacturer, but there are numerous examples of smaller companies, for example Aerotek mentioned above, that successfully operate sales branches.

7.3.3 Storage or warehousing facilities

When it is necessary and profitable for a manufacturer to maintain an inventory in foreign markets, a storage or warehousing branch should be established. Such facilities may be part of a sales branch. If so connected, the buyer is afforded greater convenience and a potentially powerful marketing tool is created in that a greater volume of business may be generated than would be the case if storage facilities were absent. The same situation occurs when the warehousing branch is a separate entity, set up to fill orders made by foreign distributors or agents.

It is not necessary that a foreign storage or warehousing branch provide stocks for a single market area. In fact many manufacturers, as they increasingly apply the total cost concept to their physical distribution or logistics problems, are establishing such branches as central distribution points to serve a wide area. Where several market areas are to be served by a single storage or warehousing branch, it may be best for these facilities to be located in a free port or trade zone such as Hong Kong, New York, Rotterdam or Colon, Panama. By locating in a free area, it is relatively easy for a manufacturer to serve many markets since the usual Customs procedures and regulations of the country where the free area is physically located do not apply.

7.3.4 Foreign sales subsidiary

The foreign-based sales subsidiary is a variation of the home-country based export sales subsidiary. As such it operates much the same; it is also similar in operation to a foreign sales branch office. One major difference is the somewhat greater autonomy enjoyed by the foreign-based subsidiary because of its foreign incorporation and domicile. In addition, the foreign-based subsidiary in many cases has broader responsibilities and performs many activities beyond those of a foreign sales office. The foreign-based subsidiary is a flexible type of organization, and in terms of its physical facilities and operating activities can include anything from a complete operation to a small office set up merely to fulfill the residence requirements of the incorporation laws of the country in which it is incorporated.

The subsidiary type of organization can be used for many different functions (business activities) in foreign markets. When organized as a *sales subsidiary* (or when sales activities are performed) all foreign orders are channeled through the subsidiary that then sells to foreign buyers at normal wholesale or retail prices. The foreign sales subsidiary purchases the products to be sold from the parent company either at cost or some other price. This, of course, creates the problem of intracompany transfer pricing.

The reasons underlying the establishment of foreign-based sales subsidiaries as well as the reasons for choosing a particular country as the base for a subsidiary stem from two major sources: taxes and business practices. One of the major influences on the popularity of overseas-based subsidiaries has been potential tax advantages that can accrue to a company utilizing this form of organization in its international operations. This has been particularly important for companies headquartered in high tax countries. With proper planning, companies could establish subsidiaries in countries with low business income taxes and gain an advantage by not paying taxes in their home country on the foreign-generated income until such income was actually repatriated to them. Of course, the precise tax advantages that are possible with such subsidiaries depend upon the tax laws in the home country of the parent company. There are, moreover, potential tax advantages beyond tax deferral. These stem from the practice of the parent company having subsidiaries retain a large share of their profits and then using such funds for further expansion abroad either in the country in which the profits were generated or in other countries. This can be quite useful in areas such as the European Union.

Taxes have not been the only reason for establishing foreign-based subsidiaries, nor have they even been the major reason in many instances. In selecting a foreign base, companies look for good banking connections, good operating conditions, a stable political situation, clarity in legal rulings, and proximity to markets. Other characteristics considered in selecting a base for a foreign subsidiary include such things as ease and simplicity of incorporation, restrictions concerning ownership and operation of a business, and availability of adequate local staff and clerical personnel. Thus, business motives are intermingled with those of tax.

7.3.5 Traveling salesperson

A traveling export salesperson is one who resides in one country, often the home country of the employer, and travels abroad to perform the sales duties. In contrast, a resident salesperson is sent out of the home country to live and work in a foreign market. In essence the resident salesperson is a foreign sales branch of the company. Of course, the company may establish a formal branch office, to which a resident salesperson is assigned. However, a branch office often also employs as sales people nationals of the country in which it is located.

In making the decision whether to use traveling sales personnel in any particular foreign market, a company should consider just what the salesperson is to do. There are many types of sales jobs ranging from so-called order making to order taking. If a company finds that the type of sales job that it needs done in a foreign market tends toward the order-taking side of the sales-job pendulum, in most cases it probably would not be economical to use traveling salespersons. On the other hand, where the sales job tends toward order making, using a competent and well-trained salesperson may prove to be the best method. Much depends upon the relative costs and returns in the form of sales generated.

There are three basic functions that all sales personnel operating in foreign markets must perform, although the relative importance of each will vary depending upon such things as the nature of the product to be sold and the nature of the market. In the first place, there is the actual selling activity to be performed – the communication of product information to customers, and obtaining orders. Second, a salesperson is always deeply involved in customer relations. The sales force must at all times be concerned with maintaining and improving the company's position with customers and the general public. This is not always easy to do, and is one of the reasons that so many firms employ local nationals as sales personnel in a specific market. Where customer relations are critically important, the use of a traveling salesperson is less likely to be the best method of direct export. The reason is simply that there generally would not be enough customer contact. There is, however, one type of traveling salesperson whose main job is in the general area of customer relations. Sometimes called a *demonstrator* or *tutor*, this type of traveling salesperson works closely with foreign-based agents or distributors already representing his company. Since the sales task primarily is to help agents and distributors do a better job, the tutor operates more or less as a troubleshooter.

The third function performed by the field sales force, one that has often been neglected, is that of information gatherer and communicator. The salesperson is management's front-line intelligence agent, and, as such, is in a position to provide information on such things as what competitors are doing, what customers are thinking, how products are performing, and what the future is of any given market. In addition, the salesperson is often able to supply information pertaining to particular customers, and perhaps other types of information that might be useful in planning advertising and trade promotion programs. Where it is important that a salesperson provide information to the company regularly, then a resident, rather than a traveling, salesperson probably should be employed.

To a large extent the effectiveness of any salesperson in performing these three basic activities depends upon mutual *trust*. Ongoing trust is crucial to long-term relationships.

Obviously not all companies should be using traveling sales people. Although there are no ready answers to when they should be used, there are general criteria that can be evaluated and conditions that generally are most favorable to their use.

To a certain degree the nature of the product has an influence. If the product is technical in nature and the prospective buyer needs detailed explanation and demonstration, a traveling salesperson may be able to do the required job. In fact some companies have technical experts employed in specific foreign markets for this very purpose. If, however, servicing is required and a supply of parts, and so on, are necessary, the traveling salesperson is not as effective nor efficient a method of export as one involving some type of permanent overseas base.

Another criterion concerns the potential sales volume of a market. Since a selling trip can cost a great deal, a minimum sales volume must be possible for the use of traveling sales people to be profitable. Also relevant is whether the sales volume is spread out over a year or is seasonal. If seasonal, a traveling salesperson becomes a potentially more profitable vehicle since there would be no fixed costs to worry about in the slack periods.

Technology in the form of the Internet is playing an increasingly greater role in sales and is affecting the role of the salesperson, especially the traveling salesperson. This is particularly the case for B2B marketing. E-commerce, or Internet marketing, has a growing global presence, and is being used to complement or replace salespersons. Using e-commerce to replace a salesperson could be a mistake in situations where person-to-person interaction is crucial to a relationship, especially for the small and medium-sized enterprise. E-commerce is discussed further in section 7.4.

7.3.6 Evaluation of dependent organizations

Producers that have established their own organizations and have found them to be successful include the following among the reasons for doing so:

- *A full return from export sales.* As export business develops, there is no sharing of profits with other organizations.
- *Protection from neglect in active performance of the selling function.* There is complete control of marketing methods and sales promotion. Moreover, there is no worry that competing lines may be pushed at the expense of the producer's sales volume.
- *Thorough knowledge of foreign markets.* The producer can determine readily what adaptations of his or her product are necessary to fit the needs and desires of foreign buyers.

- *Export sales channels are permanent.* The producer does not have to worry that a marketing organization will suddenly drop its line in preference for that of a competitor.
- *Product goodwill accrues directly to the manufacturer* rather than to a marketing organization. This can prove quite favorable when new or different products are introduced into foreign markets.
- *Per unit cost decreases as sales volume increases.* Fixed costs are spread over growing sales volume rather than remaining a constant proportion.

There also are some potential drawbacks to the use of dependent organizations. A large initial monetary outlay is required to establish export markets, and this may be too large relative to sales volume. This includes provision for offices and equipment, salaries of personnel, costs of maintaining larger inventories necessary to fill foreign pipelines, and, most important, the costs of sales effort that may yield only insignificant returns.

The manufacturer is required to assume greater risks. There is always the chance that the product may not be acceptable in foreign markets or that foreign preferences may change suddenly. More important, the producer may be required to assume credit and financial risks.

Successful foreign marketing requires specialized knowledge that may not be available in the manufacturer's organization or may require excessive expense to obtain. Marketing techniques for successful foreign sales frequently differ materially from domestic sales and the techniques of export traffic and financial management are also considerably different.

Satisfactory sales volume may take an excessive time to build up, or it may never be achieved. Independent organizations have the contacts, knowledge, and experience necessary to develop export potential.

In general, the use of a dependent organization is preferable when the following conditions prevail:

- the product is differentiated, specialized, or has a brand appeal and requires particularized selling effort;
- there is an existing large and steady export sales volume; or export sales potential is concentrated in a relatively small number of markets so that available selling effort does not have to be spread too thin;
- future sales potential is growing and has an apparent large total volume;
- export costs can be spread over a growing volume so that per unit costs decrease as volume increases.

Although the discussion has been in the context of manufacturers, it should be recognized that marketing organizations such as retailers have exported their concept or operations abroad. Indeed some retailers such as Benetton from Italy and IKEA from Sweden use their retail operations expansion as the means of exporting products that they produce and sell in their own captive stores, as do many of the so-called designer label companies.

7.3.7 Foreign-based distributors and agents/representatives

So far our discussion of the various methods of direct export has been concerned with the use of dependent organizations. We now turn to a form of direct export involving independent marketing organizations – distributors and agents. This method of exporting is distinguished from the method of indirect export using similar type (in terms of operating characteristics) intermediaries in that when direct export is being conducted, the distributor or agent is foreign based. The terms 'distributor' and 'agent' are often used synonymously. This is unfortunate because there are distinct differences. For instance, a distributor is a merchant and as such is a customer of the exporter. An agent, on the other hand, is a representative (and is often referred to this way) who acts on behalf of the exporter and is not a customer. Thus the distributor actually takes title to the exporter's goods while the agent does not. In short, the distributor imports the products involved whereas an agent leaves importation to the buyers whose orders have been passed on to the principal. A second major point of distinction arises through the method of compensation by which each is paid. The agent is usually paid on the basis of a commission while the distributor's income comes from the margin taken as determined by the trade discount granted by the exporter. A third difference is that a distributor normally carries an inventory whereas an agent does not, except perhaps for showroom purposes. Root (1994, pp. 85–92) has suggested that selecting a foreign distributor or agent is a four-phase process, as follows:

1. drawing up a profile (see Table 7.2);
2. locating prospects;
3. evaluating prospects;
4. choosing the distributor or agent.

It has been suggested that there are at least six important selection criteria that are relevant for selecting foreign distributors:

- distributor's level of commitment to both product and market;
- financial strength of a distributor;
- marketing skills, including market knowledge;
- product-related factors such as the distributor's product line and its compatibility, complementary nature, and quality;
- planning abilities;
- facilitating factors, such as political ties of a distributor, language capability, and so forth.

Relatively recent research indicates that commitment and financial strength are the two most important criteria in the foreign distribution selection process (Yeoh and Calantone, 1995).

TABLE 7.2

Elements in profile of potential distributor or agent

Overall experience in the market
Market area(s) covered
Products handled
Size of company
Experience with exporter's product line
Sales organization and quality of sales force
Willingness and ability to carry inventories (if needed)
Capability to provide after-sales service (if needed)
Experience with, and knowledge of, promotion techniques
Reputation with customers
Financial strength and credit rating
Relations with local government
Language known
Willingness to cooperate with exporter

When distributors and agents are selected by the exporting manufacturer a formal contract or agreement between the parties should be used (see section 7.3.8). In most cases, the agent or distributor is a manufacturer's exclusive representative in a given foreign market area and is the sole importer. As such, the agent or distributor is granted sole rights for the sale of the manufacturer's products in the market area covered by the agreement. There are instances, however, where exclusive selling rights are not granted. For example, sales to foreign government agencies are often reserved for the manufacturer itself, who uses one of the other types of direct export involving a dependent organization. In this type of situation the agent or distributor receives no compensation. A second possible modification occurs when an agent is appointed as a general agent. In this case the manufacturer can appoint other agents in the general agent's market area. The general agent, however, is paid a commission – less than what would normally be received – on all sales made through the other agents.

The functions performed by distributors and agents are basically the same as those carried out by the domestic-based marketing agency of the same type or the manufacturer's own foreign-based organizations. However, some basic differences should be noted. First, since these foreign-based outlets are granted exclusive rights, there is every reason to expect that they will put extra effort into promoting the sale of a manufacturer's products. All the rewards of this extra effort accrue to them rather than having to be shared with other agencies. A second basic difference concerns the servicing of the manufacturer's products. If a product is of a type that may require service, the distributor stands ready to provide such service by having the proper facilities, well-trained personnel, and a complete stock of the necessary parts and materials.

In general, therefore, a manufacturer can usually expect better sales and related services from foreign-based outlets with exclusive market areas than if these outlets had to share markets. The activities performed and operating characteristics of foreign-based distributors and agents will vary greatly, and depend upon such things as the nature of the products, the characteristics of the market area, the particular type of foreign-based outlet chosen and its operating philosophy, and the general operating situation of the manufacturer. In addition, for the agent approach more than any other method, the extent of success rests largely on personalities and personal relationships. Although the exporter and its foreign distributor or agent are dependent upon each other, they are also separated by ownership, geography, culture, and law.

The general advantages and disadvantages of using these marketing organizations do not vary greatly from those associated with their home-country based counterparts. If a manufacturer is committed to direct export, then using exclusive agents or distributors is the easiest and least costly way of doing it. This method also appears to be the one most capable of development. For these reasons, manufacturers new to direct export often choose this way, particularly where only a moderate sales volume is expected in a market area. Many agents and distributors are so successful that they work themselves out of a manufacturer's marketing channel. After sales in a foreign market pass a certain level, the manufacturer may find it more effective and profitable to establish a sales branch or subsidiary. However, even if a large sales volume is generated, often there are good reasons why the agent or distributor should not be eased out of the manufacturer's channel. His or her intimate knowledge of the market and dealers and access to various sources may not be capable of being equaled by the manufacturer's foreign-based dependent organization. In addition, an agent or distributor may have political influence that can be of benefit to a manufacturer. This may be particularly helpful in a country such as China.

On the other hand, a manufacturer may not want to use an independent marketing organization as an exclusive distributor in a particular foreign market area. The possible reasons for this are many and varied, and may include such things as wanting to have complete control over the marketing channel between nations, and the nonavailability of a firm capable of assuming all the duties of an exclusive distributor. In addition, for both agents and distributors, the other product lines that they handle from other companies may make it difficult for an exporter to introduce new products into the foreign market. Much will depend upon the competitiveness of the new product(s) to those already handled by the intermediaries. In cases such as this, rather than entering into a contractual agreement the manufacturer may form a subsidiary to act as the sole importing distributor in a given foreign market area. This subsidiary may be wholly owned or jointly owned with nationals of the country involved.

A closer and tighter form of relationship between a manufacturer and its foreign representative than that obtained with the exclusive distributor or agent occurs when a *franchise* is given. The distinguishing features of the franchise are that it gives the holder the right to carry on certain manufacturing processes by which the product is prepared for the market, it delegates to the holder the right to use the brand name and trademark of the manufacturer's product for an unlimited period under stated conditions, and it is designed to be a long-term arrangement. These privileges make necessary the extremely meticulous protection that the manufacturer must have in order to safeguard its profit, property, and rights.

The franchise holder's business is characterized by a relatively small but exclusive territory. The best illustration of this type of representative in foreign markets is to be found in the nonalcoholic beverage industry, and includes companies such as Coca-Cola and PepsiCo where a major component of the product is exported by the manufacturer to the franchisee.

7.3.8 Relations with foreign-based distributors and agents

The importance of careful selection of overseas-based distributors and agents cannot be overstated. Not only are the usual business considerations involved, but there are some legal issues as well, namely those covering termination and compensation. Therefore it is essential that a good contract be developed, clearly covering all relevant aspects of the relationship and spelling out obligations of expectations of both parties. Having a contract is no guarantee that everything will work out as planned and that both parties will be 'happy.' A case in point is a bakery products firm that contracted to sell its entire line of goods through a sole distributor in a developing country (Ricks, 1999, p. 111). The distributor had really only been interested in carrying a few items and found the tie-in arrangement not to its liking. Relations between the manufacturer and distributor quickly degenerated to the point where there was little communication between them, and a major decline in sales occurred. Products were spoiled before the manufacturer became aware of the situation.

As mentioned previously, relationships are enhanced by mutual trust between the parties involved. Trust should be built early in all relationships within an international channel of distribution. Research has shown that building trust early is more dependent upon matching, rather than exceeding, a partner's expectations (Marshall, 2003).

As time passes some relationships between exporters and importers will end, or be cut back. The bakery example illustrates what is known as internally triggered dissolution (also known as a switch) of a relationship. An internally triggered dissolution occurs due to the inability of the partners to meet their mutual expectations regarding the business relationship – price, product quality, delivery, etc. (Shankarmahesh *et al.*, 2003). There is another type of dissolution, the externally triggered one. This can occur when there are changes in the global environment or the operating national environments of the partnering firms that make the cost structure of either firm noncompetitive, causing one of the firms to seek dissolution to remain profitable. The lesson here is that *relationships once formed should not be taken for granted.*

Essentials of a foreign representative agreement

The foreign representative agreement is the fundamental basis of the relationship between the exporter and its foreign representative. The purpose of the agreement is to define clearly the conditions upon which the relationship rests. *Rights and obligations should be mutually defined.* The spirit of the agreement must be one of mutual interest. With this 'spiritual' background the agreement should be written to cover the following provisions:

1. *Basic provisions*
   a Name of the exporter and the representative.
   b Lines or products covered by the agreement. If not all lines or products are to be included this should be clearly stated. If the agreement is to cover a broad working arrangement it can be stated that the agreement covers lines and products only that are specifically offered in the present agreement or as amended.
   c Territory assigned should be clearly defined. If exceptions are made, either as to locality or as to certain customer accounts, these should be definitely mentioned or provision made as to conditions under which such exceptions are to be made.
   d It should be clearly specified whether or not the agreement is mutually exclusive as to the sale of products and territory assigned.
   e Prices quoted to customers (by an agent) must be maintained as stipulated by the exporter. There should be no reductions in price without the exporter's prior approval of a change, or unless the exporter stipulates in the agreement the margin of such price reductions and the specific conditions of such reductions.
   f Provision for payment for samples and sample discount.
2. *Sales terms*
   a Terms of sale should be stipulated and it should be specified whether the offer is made to the representative as a buyer for his own account or as a salesperson on a commission basis.
   b Conditions of payment should be included, covering the following:
      i   the exporter's policy as to terms of payment, stating the limitation of tenor (time at which payment is due);
      ii reserving the right to approve terms of payment on orders obtained by the representative;
      iii requiring references or other satisfactory evidence of creditworthiness on all new customers' first orders;
      iv the conditions or limitations under which the representative has authority to grant the customer terms of payment, or the exporter may simply reserve the sole right to approve the terms of payment on receipt of the order;
      v   whether or not and under what conditions the representative stands *del credere* for customer payment.
   c Specify the nature and rate of the compensation to the representative – the distributor's discount or agent's commission – and the time and manner of payment.

d The exporter reserves the right to refuse all orders of customers that are not according to the exporter's quotations or not approved for credit, or impossible to fulfill for reasons beyond the exporter's control.

3. *General provisions*

a Provide for when and how the agreement goes into effect. Under international law the agreement is interpreted under the laws of the country where the agreement is consummated. If the agreement goes into effect when accepted and signed by the representative, the agreement will be effective under the laws of the representative's country.

b If the agreement is to be effective upon receipt of first order, a term of time should be stated as to how long the offer of representation is open and that meanwhile the exporter will not make any other offer of representation on the products quoted to any other representative in the territory.

c How disputes are to be handled. If arbitration is to be used, the exact details regarding how the arbitrator(s) are to be selected and where the arbitration hearing is to be held must be specified.

d Provide for the termination of the agreement. This is generally a provision for cancellation by either party after a definite period of time following notification, all obligations having been met under the terms of the agreement.

For most exporters, the three most important aspects of their agreement with foreign representatives are sole or exclusive rights, competitive lines, and termination of the agreement. Regarding exclusive distribution rights and competitive lines, there may be legal considerations in some countries. In the European Union antitrust regulations generally prohibit exclusive arrangements that restrict sales from one member country to another. Similarly, it is illegal in some countries for a manufacturer to 'require' that a distributor or agent not handle competing products as a condition of handling the manufacturer's product.

The exporter should make sure that it knows the relevant national and supranational laws governing relationships with distributors and agents. Legal issues arise also in cancellation of representative agreements that leads to termination of relationships between an exporter and its foreign distributors and agents. Termination laws differ from country to country and may change over time. Some have been overly protective, such as an indemnity being as much as five times annual gross profits plus the value of the agent's investment plus other payments. Or an agent can be given up to one year's commission based only on the fact that the agent has lost the right to represent the exporter and such agent does not have to prove that he or she gained clients for the exporter nor even that there were any clients at all.

Selecting a foreign representative

The exporter generally wants an agreement that is easy to cancel in the event that a foreign representative does a bad job in selling the exporter's product(s). In addition, ease in cancellation can provide the exporter with greater control over the marketing program. Yet it is in the best interests of the exporter that the representative feels good enough about the relationship to make a firm commitment to the exporter's product(s). Unsatisfactory relations with representatives can be reduced with proper selection of the foreign representative. Positive answers to questions such as the following will go a long way toward ensuring that the exporter ends up with the best possible representation in a foreign market:

1. Is the representative satisfactory in character, moral reputation, and integrity? Is it likely that he will live up to the agency agreement?

2. Is he able to promote sales effectively? Does he have proper facilities for storage, distribution, and service? How large a territory can he canvass successfully?

3. In the case of a commission representative, does he have good credit sense? Does he submit orders only from reliable firms that can be depended upon to pay in accordance with the sales terms? Does he adjust the sales terms to the creditworthiness of the customers?

4. In the case of a wholesale distributor, are his financial resources adequate both for normal times and for periods of business depression?

5. Has he represented his principals for a sufficient length of time to indicate that they are satisfied with his accomplishments?

6. Does he handle competitive products? Has he taken on too great a variety of lines, or has he specialized in a small group of related lines, thus making for more effective agency representation for each line of the group?

7. Is he progressive or conservative? Does he believe in and make use of up-to-date advertising?

8. Does his location have adequate transportation facilities with the rest of the territory?

9. What is the nationality of the agent; the names and nationality of his other principals; and the probable effect of his nationality on his attitude toward the manufacturer?

10. What is his position in the trade, and the attitude of the trade toward the agent? Will the trade deal with him?

11. Do his qualifications with respect to the features mentioned indicate that he will grow in importance in his own market?

7.4 The Internet and e-commerce

This section draws on material from Foley, 1999, Ch. 22.

One of the major technological impacts during the past few years on international marketing has been through the Internet. All phases of business from purchasing through supply chain management through sales and payments/financing have been impacted. The Internet is used more as a *source of information* than as a place to buy. All communication is immediate, and distance and length of communication have no impact on cost. As a source of information, the Internet is demand driven in that users have the option of getting the information they want – if it is available – when needed.

In addition to time and distance, other advantages emerging from use of the Internet are identified by Foley (1999, pp. 333–5) as follows:

■ *Low capital investment.* Access to the World Wide Web is relatively inexpensive and the cost of web site development can be less than that of developing a new promotional brochure.

■ *Small size makes no difference.* A company's web site becomes its public image. A small company typically can afford a site equal to one offered by a much larger company.

■ *Updates are easy and immediate.* Information can be updated and modified easily and quickly.

■ *Translating can be less expensive.* Because it is in electronic form, text is maintained separately from backgrounds and graphics and can be easily translated.

The Internet is at least cost competitive with other options (e.g., desktop publishing and traditional printing) and may be less costly.

- *More reliable.* This is a reliable means of communication and can become more so as countries increase their levels of Internet support. One potential problem can occur through technical breakdowns of, say, e-mail systems. But information can be sent again at little cost.
- *Audit trail.* Companies have full control over what can and cannot be sent over the Internet by the structure and controls built in to the web site.

The Internet is the base for international *e-commerce*, which refers to 'trade that actually takes place over the Internet, usually through a buyer visiting a seller's web site and making a transaction there' (*The Economist*, 2000a, p. 6). There are two levels of e-commerce: business-to-business (B2B) and business-to-consumer (B2C). B2B accounts for most of the business, perhaps as much as 80–90%.

While estimates of the present volume of e-commerce vary widely, it is clear that it is growing at a rate which is nearly exponential. By the year 2004, estimated combined B2B and B2C online sales in Europe were expected to have risen to US$1.5 trillion (Grossman, 2000). In addition, Internet access within Europe varies widely in terms of the percentage of the population having access.

Cellular telephone ownership and access is an important indicator of future Internet behavior as the technology is developing an increasing number of applications for wireless access to the Internet. This will be of increasing use in B2B international marketing, especially when the wireless technology and systems are uniform across countries throughout the world. B2B will grow much better than B2C within Europe as the common currency, the euro, removes exchange rate problems and business firms tend to be less hindered by the cultural and language differences issues that affect consumers.

E-commerce is also growing in Asia. B2B online transactions in the Asia-Pacific region reached US$31 billion in 2000, which is less than the US$244.8 billion generated in North America. Expectations were that revenues in the region would reach US$650 billion by 2005 (Belson, 2000). In addition, for most countries in the Asia-Pacific region, e-commerce revenues were expected to be at least US$5 billion by the end of 2002. One obstacle holding back e-commerce growth in Asia is the reluctance of Asian companies to outsource important functions such as accounting and billing, which is a key element in B2B e-commerce. In addition, supply-chain management programs require users to open their inventory and purchasing processes to suppliers and customers. This means that for some Asian companies sensitive information about them is on the Internet. Despite such concerns many companies are joining the e-commerce parade. For example, as the 21st century emerged two of Japan's largest trading companies – Mitsui & Co. and Itochu Corp. – formed a joint venture, e-Zaiko, to provide an online market for goods that are often quietly dumped or sold at a loss.

Often overlooked as a potential market area for e-commerce is Latin America. Countries such as Argentina, Mexico, and Brazil are affected by the Internet, and consumers there are becoming knowledgeable about it. In early 2001 only 2–3% of Latin Americans had Internet access. Estimates are that as many as 14% of the total population will have such access by the year 2005 (Strohmeyer, 2001). Specifically, estimates of the number of users by 2005 in selected countries are as follows (De Gouvea and Kassicieh, 2002, p. 107): Brazil (29.1 million), Mexico (12.7 million), Argentina (7 million), Colombia (4.4 million), Venezuela (3.8 million), Peru (2.4 million). Although expected users are a small proportion of the population they do represent a large increase over the numbers of users in 1999 – from fivefold to more than tenfold.

A number of business functions can be performed on the Internet (Foley, 1999, pp. 335–6):

- *Market research*. This was discussed in Chapter 5.
- *Expanding representation*. Distributors and agents have also established web sites. The exporter can develop marketing channels by identifying, profiling, and communicating with potential marketing intermediaries.
- *Customer and marketing support*. The Internet becomes a key link in maintaining relations with intermediaries and customers.
- *Advertising*. As a form of communication to the global marketplace, the international marketer has to be cautious in using Internet advertisements as many of these do not work too well. Advertisements that just pop up on the screen (interstitials) are viewed by many as annoying interruptions to the online experience and banner advertisements are being ignored. In contrast there are some who believe that banner advertisements that are being ignored are just poorly done, and that if the ad were targeted it would be more effective.
- *Trade leads*. The Internet is a good tool to generate leads and is complementary to a strong channel network.
- *Logistics*. The Internet is becoming a major logistical support tool used by transport companies as well as exporters and importers.

These functions have one thing in common. They all are based on using the Internet for communication. There is one additional function that is performed, one that can be the essence of e-commerce. In many instances *transactions* (i.e., sales) are consummated over the Internet and *payment* is made (for B2C in particular) by credit card, smart card, and so forth.

Companies intending to start e-commerce activities should look at the Internet as a means of enhancing international expansion. Although advantages and benefits exist for B2B, there also are some caveats to be recognized:

1. *No substitute for travel*. The Internet is not a substitute for international travel, despite its merits as a communication device. In the end, there is no substitute for regular face-to-face contact with marketing intermediaries and customers. The need for travel may be reduced, but it is not eliminated.
2. *Internet is not truly global*. Not everyone nor every company in the world has as much access as there is in the United States, Europe, and other developed countries.
3. *Imposters*. One never really knows who is at the other end of the Internet. There is a strong potential for fraudulent use.
4. *Open to misuse*. Access to a web site is open to many different companies and people. Thus the international marketer needs to control the information made available. Any truly sensitive and/or secret information should not be placed on a web site.
5. *No cure-all*. If a company is having problems in one or more foreign markets, shifting to an e-commerce approach is not necessarily the 'magic bullet' one would like it to be.

Another area of concern is government regulation, which varies widely. For example, in France all web sites aimed at French customers must be in French. In Germany, certain types of B2C promotions, such as 'two-for-one' may be illegal. In Sweden, toy advertising may not be directed at children. While regulations and laws such as these and others such as liability for faulty products apply to all modes of market entry, companies may fall into a trap of assuming they do not apply as long as the web site is in another country. The EU, for example, has a law where European consumers can sue EU-based Internet sites in their own countries, and this rule in mid-2001 was being considered to apply internationally. One area of law that directly affects e-commerce is *privacy* law and transfer of data. In Europe these are much stricter than in the United States and Asia. According to a directive issued by the European Commission, marketers must tell consumers what data they will collect and retain, exactly how it will be used in the future, and then give them the option of opting in or out of the process. The Commission, if it has not already done so, is likely to make opt-in the rule rather than opt-out. Opt-in is already the law in Germany, Austria, Italy, Denmark, and Sweden, and has been so since at least the early 2000s. Rules like those in the EU as a whole, and in indi-

EXHIBIT 7.6   How Nestlé does it!

1   Taking orders

How it works: Since July 2000 US storeowners have had the option of ordering Nestlé chocolates and other products via a new web site, NestléEZOrder.
The benefit: Nestlé hopes to eliminate most of the 100,000 phoned or faxed orders a year from mom-and-pop shops. That would reduce manual data entry and cut processing costs by 90%, to 21 cents per order.

2   Getting ingredients

How it works: Nestlé buyers have purchased cocoa beans and other raw materials on a country-by-country basis, with little info about how colleagues were buying the same products. Now they share price info via the net and pick suppliers that offer the best deals.
The benefit: Nestlé has reduced the number of suppliers by as much as two-thirds, and cut procurement costs by up to 20%.

3   Making the chocolate

How it works: Nestlé has traditionally processed its own cocoa butter and powder and manufactured most of its own chocolate. The web lets Nestlé better communicate with suppliers, making outsourcing a more viable option.
The benefit: In 1999 outside contractors in Italy and Malaysia won orders to produce raw chocolate. More such deals can be expected as Nestlé plans to sell or close a third of its 86 chocolate plants in the coming years.

4   Cutting inventories

How it works: In the past, Nestlé guessed at how many KitKat or Crunch bars it might be able to sell in a promotion. Today, electronic links with supermarkets and other retail partners give Nestlé accurate and timely information on buying trends.
The benefit: Nestlé is able to cut inventories by 15% as it adjusts its production and deliveries to meet demand.

5   Marketing the candy bars

How it works: Nestlé spends US$1.2 billion on advertising through traditional print and TV ads. Within two years more than 20% of that will go online.
The benefit: New marketing approaches include a chocolate-lover's web site with advice, recipes, and paeans to the pleasures of chocolate. Nestlé has similar sites for coffee, Italian food, and infant nutrition.

Source: Adapted from Echikson, 2000, EB48.

vidual countries, tend to make e-commerce more time-consuming and expensive, especially in B2C situations.

There are some things that governments can, and will, do – filtering and IP-address tracking (*The Economist*, 2001a). Filtering involves software installed on a PC, in an Internet service provider's equipment or in gateways that link one country with the rest of the online world that can block access to certain sites. Web sites themselves can block users by tracking the Internet service provider's 'IP address' to reveal where a user is. In a court ruling in late 2000 in France, Yahoo! was ordered to find some way to ban French users from seeing Nazi memorabilia posted on its US sites, or pay a stiff daily fine. IP-address tracking was judged to be able to spot more than 60% of French web surfers. Although not perfect, as there are ways to get around the blocking and address tracking, governments do feel they can help reduce the problems that arise. Moreover, given the rapid changes in technology, these techniques will improve relatively quickly.

An extreme case is that of China. By the end of 2004 there are expectations that there will be 81 million people online. B2B will be the major use as the country lacks a large base of affluent consumers and relatively few Chinese consumers have credit cards. In their desire to keep the Internet under State control, the government through the Ministry of Information Industry (MII) has issued a vast number of rules restricting what dot-com companies can do and censoring what they say (Einhorn *et al.*, 2000). The government is using blocking, banning use of foreign encryption software, Internet policing, and news monitoring (i.e., only news that has already been published by a State outlet is allowed on the Internet) to keep sites from the rest of the world with unwanted content from entering China's cyberspace (*The Economist*, 2000b). In effect, China has established an intranet that is isolated from the rest of the world. There are people who can get around these barriers. However, the majority of the people access the Internet from work or from a public place, where the government controls the software and can track what users do, and where they risk being seen if they go to an illegal site.

The Internet is clearly here to stay. But, like all new developments it will seek its place in the business world and level off. As a communication device it has no equal for speed, lack of distance effects, cost, and flexibility. But the international marketer must remember that it is not a panacea for ills and that it is only one 'weapon' in the arsenal that should be used with other market entry modes. Exhibit 7.6 illustrates how Nestlé is using the Web to market chocolate bars from KitKats to Butterfingers.

7.5 Gray market exporting

One type of channel conflict that can arise in exporting is that of *gray market* exports. Also known as parallel importation, gray market channels are those that are not 'authorized' by the exporter for a particular foreign market (see Figure 7.3). More formally, we can define gray marketing as the legal importation of genuine goods into a country by intermediaries other than authorized distributors. Distributors, wholesalers, and retailers obtain an exporter's product from some other business entity in another country. Thus, the exporter's 'legitimate' distributor(s) and dealers face competition from others that sell the exporter's product(s) at a reduced price. Sa Sa, a discount cosmetics retailer in Hong Kong and the largest cosmetics retailer there, in the late 1990s sourced about 10% of its make-up, perfume, and skin and haircare products from independent overseas traders and 90% from authorized distributors in Hong Kong. Another example of parallel importing into Hong Kong is the luxury-car market, including BMW, Mercedes-Benz, Lexus, and Jaguar. Cars destined for other Asian countries such as Thailand and Indonesia found their way into Hong Kong in the late 1990s, at prices up to 40% lower than those charged by authorized dealers. Of course, the economic slowdown in Hong Kong at the time helped fuel the appeal of gray market luxury cars. Although legal in a criminal sense, under Hong Kong law authorized distributors have the right to file civil charges against companies using parallel imports and sue for damages or compensation.

Parallel imports between European Union countries are legal. However, the European Court of Justice, with the support of the European Commission and many EU governments, has banned such imports into the EU. Thus companies can freely import Levi jeans into the UK from Greece, but not from the United States. Obviously consumers can benefit, while authorized dealers do not. Motorcycles provide another product where parallel importing is prevalent in the United Kingdom. Motorcycles such as a Honda 900cc Fireblade were available at a price as much as one-third less than the price at the authorized dealer. This parallel importing is legal as sourcing is from within the EU and it takes advantage of differing prices within the EU.

View of Victoria Harbor from The Peak, Hong Kong

Parallel importing is a concern in China. However, the concern relates more to smuggling of high-technology consumer products as they avoid payment of import duties, which have ranged from 20% for computer goods to 150% for automobiles, and VAT of 17%. A major source of such goods has been Hong Kong-based middlemen.

In 1998 New Zealand introduced a law making parallel importing legal. Local licensed dealers for products produced elsewhere would no longer hold a monopoly. Other businesses are able to import the same goods, potentially cutting prices on everything from cars to clothing and compact disks. Increased protection against piracy of such products as computer software, videos and CDs was added.

High-priced, branded consumer goods (for example, jewelry, cameras, watches, ski equipment) where production lies principally within a single country are particularly prone to gray market activity. Brand reputation is a critical aspect of the marketing mix and distribution is typically through exclusive wholesalers and

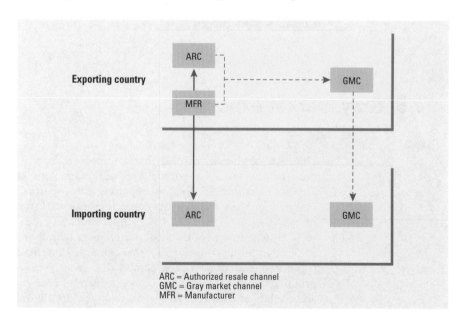

FIGURE 7.3

International gray market
Source: Bucklin (1990), p. 5

selected retailers. Would lower prices of prestige brands undermine the 'snobbery' of a brand? It is unlikely! For example, Calvin Klein products cost less in the United States than in the United Kingdom, but they still command a premium price. In the early 1970s authorized dealers in Germany for Minolta Camera Company faced competition from other dealers that had obtained Minolta products via gray market channels involving Hong Kong wholesalers.

According to Bucklin (1990, p. 2), the very conditions that foster global strategies also magnify the gray market opportunity. As products sold across national boundaries with the same brand name become more similar, the potential for gray market arbitrage becomes greater. A key question for the exporter of branded products is whether gray markets will cause global strategies to be less desirable.

Imports of gray market goods can potentially adversely affect manufacturers in at least the following four ways:

1. The trademark image can be damaged.
2. Relationships between manufacturers and dealers can be strained.
3. The manufacturer can incur unanticipated legal liabilities, especially when a product does not meet safety requirements in the country where it is being sold in the gray market.
4. The manufacturer's global marketing strategy can be disrupted.

Some reactive approaches that can be taken are as follows:

- *participation*, where dealers supported by manufacturers actually purchase goods from the gray marketer;
- *price cutting*;
- *supply interference*, where dealer or manufacturer finds where the goods are sourced and purchases there, depriving the gray marketer of a supply;
- *acquisition*, where a dealer acquires the gray marketer.

Potential proactive approaches include the following:

- offer unique features or benefits that the gray market product cannot;
- strategic pricing to encourage or deter gray market activity;
- dealer development;
- establish legal precedence;
- long-term image reinforcement to bond customers to existing dealers.

Obviously, the best solution is prevention, which means strong proactive actions.

Bucklin (1990, pp. 26–8) concludes that market shares held by gray operators need not be so large and that closer control over international marketing decisions can reduce these to a level where they are more a symbol of ineffective global marketing than a barrier to such a strategy. One key is better management of global marketing policies. The major appeal is lower prices.

SUMMARY

In this chapter the alternative modes of export were discussed in some depth. Indirect export was defined as involving the use of independent marketing organizations located in the exporter's home country. In contrast, direct export occurs when the exporter sells directly to buyers in foreign markets, either by its own dependent unit or by using a foreign-based marketing organization. There are many alternative avenues that the exporter may follow in either approach, and all result in a channel of distribution. Both marketing and legal considerations make it imperative that the exporter be extremely careful in making this decision, particularly in the selection of any intermediary marketing organizations. This has become increasingly critical with the emergence of the Internet and e-commerce. The international marketer must not fall victim to all the 'hype' surrounding the Internet; instead reality must prevail. The final section discussed the problem of gray market export activity.

Whether exporting directly or indirectly, relationships must be built with foreign customers. Leonidou *et al.* (2002, pp. 108–11) suggest the following guidelines:

- Treat exporting as a bundle of relationships.
- Appoint people who are suitable for managing relationships.
- Adopt an approach to exporting that reflects it as a strategic option open to the firm.
- Get closer to the foreign customer.
- Build and sustain trust in the relationship, and cultivate mutual understanding.
- Reduce foreign business uncertainty.
- Demonstrate greater inter-firm commitment.
- Engage in direct and indirect communication.
- Accept that some conflict is inevitable, but try to keep it at a manageable level.
- Work to maintain sustained inter-firm cooperation.

QUESTIONS FOR DISCUSSION

7.1 When exporting indirectly, is it better to use a merchant or an agent in the export marketing channel? Explain.

7.2 Under what conditions is it best that an exporter use an export management company and when is the manufacturer's export agent a better choice?

7.3 For a small manufacturer, is it better to engage in piggyback marketing or join an exporting combination? Why is this so?

7.4 'Cooperative exporting organizations are most suited for small and medium-sized enterprises.' Discuss.

7.5 What types of channel conflict may arise in indirect exporting? Because of such conflict, is it not better for the exporter to do it directly?

7.6 What impact does the nature of the foreign market area to be served have on the exporter's choice of type of channel?

7.7 Distinguish among the built-in, separate, and sales subsidiary as forms of export departments.

7.8 'The decision facing the export marketer concerning establishing a foreign-based sales subsidiary is a difficult and complex one to make.' Discuss.

7.9 Is there one best way to export directly? Defend your answer.

7.10 Why is it important that the exporter be very careful in the selection of foreign-based distributors and agents?

7.11 Why should an exporter worry about gray market distribution of its products in foreign markets? What can be done to protect against this practice?

7.12 Trust has been described as a key element of any relationship between exporter and importer. How does trust affect relationships, and how does an exporter adapt when cultures differ in their view of trust?

REFERENCES

Amine, L. (1987). Toward a conceptualization of export trading companies in world markets. *Advances in International Marketing*, vol. 2, pp. 199–238, Greenwich, CT: JAI Press.

Belson, K. (2000). Asia's Internet deficit. *Business Week E.Biz*, 23 October, EB105–11.

Bilkey, W. J. and Tesar, G. (1977). The export behavior of smaller-sized Wisconsin manufacturing companies. *J. International Business Studies*, 8 (Spring/Summer), 93–8.

Bucklin, L. P. (1990). *The Gray Market Threat to International Marketing Strategies*. Cambridge, MA: Marketing Science Institute, Report No. 90–116.

Business Week (2001). The net hauls in a big catch. 12 March, 32.

Czinkota, M. (1982). *Export Development Strategies: US Promotion Policies*. New York: Praeger.

De Gouvea, R. and Kassicieh, S. K. (2002). Brazil.com. *Thunderbird International Business Review*, 44(1), 105–17.

Duerr, M. G. and Greene, J. (1969). *Policies and Problems in Piggyback Marketing*. New York: The Conference Board, Managing International Business No. 3.

Echikson, W. (2000). Nestlé: an elephant dances. *Business Week E.Biz*, 11 December, EB44–8.

Einhorn, B., Webb, A. and Engardio, P. (2000). China's tangled web. *Business Week*, 17 July, 56–8.

Ellis, P. (2001). Adaptive strategies of trading companies. *International Business Review*, 10, 235–59.

Ellis, P. (2003). Are international trade intermediaries catalysts in economic development? A new research agenda. *J. International Marketing*, 11(1), 73–96.

Fisher, A. (1998). Rethink changes of style and substance. *Financial Times*, 20 August, 8.

Foley, J. F. (1999). *The Global Entrepreneur: Taking Your Business International*. Chicago, IL: Dearborn Financial Publishing.

Grossman, W. (2000). The outsiders. *Smartbusinessmag.com*, July, 70.

Karamally, Z. (1998). *Export Savvy: From Basics to Strategy*. NY: Haworth Press.

Leonidou, L. C., Katsikeas, C. S. and Hadjimarcou, J. S. (2002). Building successful export business relationships: a behavioral perspective. *J. International Marketing*, 10(3), 96–115.

Marshall, R. S. (2003). Building trust early: the influence of first and second order expectations on trust in international channels of distribution. *International Business Review*, 20, 1–23.

Miller, K. L. (1995). The *Mittelstand* takes a stand. *Business Week*, 10 April, 54–5.

Moen, Ø. and Servais, P. (2002). Born global or gradual global? Examining the export behavior of small and medium-sized enterprises. *J. International Marketing*, 10(3), 49–72.

Rameseshan, B. and Soutar, G. N. (1996). Combined effects of incentives and barriers on firms' export decisions. *International Business Review*, 5(1), 53–65.

Reid, S. D. (1981). The decision maker and export entry and expansion. *J. International Business Studies*, 12 (Fall), 101–12.

Ricks, D. A. (1999). *Blunders in International Business*. Oxford, UK: Blackwell.

Root, F. R. (1994). *Entry Strategies for International Markets* rev. and expanded edn. Lexington, MA: Lexington Books.

Shankarmahesh, M. N., Ford, J. B., and La Tour, M. S. (2003). Cultural dimensions of switching behavior in importer–exporter relationships. *Academy of Marketing Science Review* [online].

Strohmeyer, R. (2001). Way down south. *Smartbusinessmag.com*, January, 46.

The Economist (1995a). Japan's trading companies: sprightly dinosaurs? 11 February, 55–7.

The Economist (1995b). The *Mittelstand* meets the grim reaper. 16 December, 57–8.

The Economist (1998). *Mittelstand* or Mittlefall?, 17 October, 67–8.

The Economist (2000a). E-commerce survey, 26 February, 5ff.

The Economist (2000b). The flies swarm in, 22 July, 24–8.

The Economist (2001a). Stop signs on the web, 13 January, 21–5.

The Economist (2001b). Slipped disc, 15 December, 54–5.

Yeoh, P. L. and Calantone, R. J. (1995). An application of the analytical hierarchy process to international marketing: selection of a foreign distributor. *J. Global Marketing*, 8(3/4), 39–65.

Zhang, Y. (1998). Sogo shosha plan reaffirmed. *China Daily Business Weekly*, 22–28 March, 2.

FURTHER READING

Cavusgil, S. T. and Sikora, E. (1987). *How Multinationals Can Cope with Gray Market Imports*. Cambridge, MA: Marketing Science Institute, Report No. 87–109.

Cho, D.-S. (1987). *The General Trading Company*. Lexington, MA: Lexington Books.

Jausàs, A., ed. (1994). *Agency Distribution Agreements: An International Survey*. London: Kluwer Law International Ltd.

Karamally, Z. (1998). *Export Savvy: From Basics to Strategy*. New York: International Business Press.

Katsikea, E. and Morgan, R. E. (2002). Exploring export sales management practices in small- and medium-sized firms. *Industrial Marketing Management*, 32, 467–80.

Sirgy, M. J., Brown, J. R. and Bird, M. M. (2004). Importers' benevolence toward their foreign export suppliers. *J. Academy of Marketing Science*, 32(1), 32–48.

Tuller, L. W. (1994). *Exporting, Importing and Beyond*. Holbrook, MA: Adams Media Corporation.

Wells, L. F. and Dulat, K. B. (1996). *Exporting from Start to Finance* 3rd edn. New York: McGraw-Hill.

Wijnholds, H. de B. and Little, M. W. (2001). Regulatory issues for global e-tailers: marketing implications. *Academy of Marketing Science Review* [online].

CASE STUDY 7.1

HV Industri A/S

HV Industri A/S is a medium-sized company that processes fish using hermetics technology. It has its headquarters in Koge, Denmark, which is a few kilometers south of Copenhagen. The company's total turnover for 2003 was approximately DKr80 million. The annual growth in turnover averaged 5% during the early 2000s.

Within the fishing industry, hermetics is defined to include frozen fish, hermetically packed meals, hermetically packed shellfish, and sardines. The canned fish and shellfish industry is further defined by the WTO as including fish, crustaceans, and molluscs, prepared or preserved other than by freezing, salting, drying, or smoking, in airtight containers. Caviar and caviar substitutes, prepared or preserved fish livers, fish marinades, fish and shrimp paste and prepared snails, in airtight containers, are also included.

The company produces a high quality product. Only the best fresh fish are processed. HV's processing plant is modern and the quality of its canned products is very high. The company uses hermetical sealing for both cans and polybags.

The company sells mainly in Denmark. It has had limited exporting experience, primarily in Germany and Austria. In early 2004 the company's managing director and founder, Harald Vester, asked the marketing manager, Oli Viberg, to explore the possibility of HV Industri entering the UK market. What follows are observations made by Mr Viberg about the British situation.

The market

In general the British consumption of fish has been diminishing for some time. Since consumption is directed more and more against frozen and otherwise prepared fish products, conclusions should not be taken just from the aggregated supply of fresh fish. A glance at the development of the consumption during the first half of the 1990s confirmed the observation. Yet the reduction of about 6% (measured as share of total consumption of food and nonfood products over the period) was similar to the reduction in consumption of meat and bacon products and tells nothing in detail about what kind of products are consumed. That this trend is significant is verified by Retail Trade International, which clearly states not only that the number of fishmongers that sell fresh fish has been dramatically reduced, but also that the trade has shifted from fresh to frozen foods.

In the 1980s the International Trade Centre of GATT published a study containing data on the development of the market for canned fish and shellfish. It appears that this organization wanted to encourage the developing countries to export canned fish to Great Britain. For the period shown in this study, the total import of canned fish and shellfish increased 177% and 243% respectively. However, the general expenditure on fish increased only 173% during the same period.

Personal income in Great Britain tends to be unevenly distributed geographically, as does consumer expenditure. The average per capita and household disposable income and expenditure are highest in the southeast district around London, with Greater London as the unchallenged leader. Mr Viberg proposed that the southeast district be the target market area. Relevant data on consumer expenditure available from the *2001/02 Expenditure and Food Survey*, Office for National Statistics, and the Northern Ireland Statistics and Research Agency for 1999–2002 are shown in Table 7.3.

Distribution

The principal trade channels for imports of canned fish and shellfish in the United Kingdom are shown in

TABLE 7.3 Consumer expenditures, 1999–2002 (£ per week)

Area	Household Average total expenditure	Food	Per capita expenditure
North East	308.8	53.7	130.9
Yorkshire & Humberside	340.5	55.5	145.7
East Midlands	360.1	60.4	155.3
East	400.5	63.7	170.5
South East	443.0	65.3	194.4
Greater London	463.0	70.8	194.3
South West	366.4	58.6	158.5
West Midlands	360.3	58.8	148.5
North West	351.0	57.2	150.5
Wales	322.5	55.7	139.1
Scotland	344.7	59.8	150.2
Northern Ireland	347.3	68.2	132.7

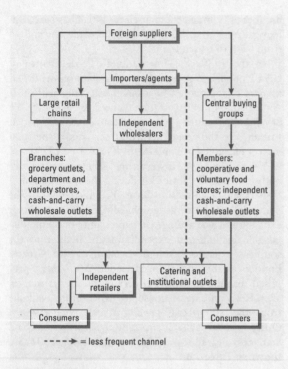

FIGURE 7.4 Trade channels

Figure 7.4. Normally, the import channels depend on the quantity of supplies required. Large-scale buyers such as the major retail chains prefer to procure their requirements, whenever possible, directly from foreign suppliers in order to avoid the costs of middlemen. Medium and small retailers tend to join central buying groups, which offer their members the possibility of grouping orders to attain sufficiently high quantities for direct procurement from foreign suppliers and the benefit of large-order discounts. In the United Kingdom the majority of such groups are voluntary or cooperative organizations.

A new kind of distribution seems to have grown in importance, namely the touring van. With increased margins, the touring van sells fresh fish as opposed to the frozen fish in superstores and supermarkets. Yet the van may be very well suited for distribution of hermetics, which do not substitute for fresh fish.

When it comes to institutional outlets, however, it was readily apparent to Mr Viberg that not much information about them is available. It is possible to supply hotels, restaurants, cafeterias, and caterers, chains and independents, by a British wholesale organization or perhaps a subsidiary of HV Industri. The advantage to HV of avoiding marketing intermediaries is more direct contact, with more personal communication with the institutions an end result. The disadvantage, of course, is greater demand(s) on resources.

Branding is of importance. Studies seem to indicate that the majority of the products in retail sales are branded, with a significant amount of these being private brands of the distributor. The British public does not consider private brands to be cheap or of inferior quality. The consequence of this is that although the producer wants to sell quality products under a producer-owned brand name, thereby creating brand loyalty, attractive offers from buying chains, which may insist on 'own brand,' should be evaluated positively as this does not necessarily mean a sacrifice of pricing policy and product image.

Competition

A large number of countries export fish and fish products to the United Kingdom. Two groups of countries are of special interest in this connection, namely the countries within the Commonwealth and those of the EU, where the developing and underdeveloped countries are associated through the Lomé Agreement and other countries or areas such as Norway and Greenland are associated via different bilateral agreements. EU members such as Portugal and Spain have a special position. Although Spain is believed to possess a large share of the total EU fishing fleet, it is still a large importer of fish.

The products of interest may be divided into those competing on price and those not able to use low price as a competitive parameter. The price-competing companies are most likely to be found in the developing countries. It is to be expected, however, that these countries will have problems not only in organizing export but also in maintaining quality and regularity of supply. Competition on quality can be expected from other Danish producers and from Norwegian producers. In general, the present EU market situation provides a good background for pursuing a policy of competition based on quality.

Based on his assessment of the potential in the United Kingdom, Mr Viberg feels that HV Industri could become a viable supplier by direct export. He feels that initial emphasis can be directed to restaurants, cafeterias, and catering establishments. Once established, HV can then turn its attention to retail outlets.

Questions

1. Should HV Industri A/S enter the UK market with hermetically packaged fish?

2. Is direct export the best initial entry mode? Why, or why not?

CASE STUDY 7.2

Quint Winery

(This case study was written by Prof. Dr Alfred Joepen, Fachhochschule Aachen, Germany, and Dr Neil Evans, San Francisco State University.)

Mr Michael Quint has recently taken over the family-owned, independent producer of quality wines in Germany's picturesque Mosel River Valley. With the enthusiastic support of his wife and the continuing support of his parents, he is developing new strategies for the winery to remain successful in the face of increasing competition. These strategies include new products, new packaging, and changing emphases in marketing. In all of these developments Mr Quint's objective is to retain the traditional and individual character of the company while increasing productivity, sales, and profitability. The rapid growth of the wine market in Japan, with its increasing emphasis on imports from countries around the world, may provide an additional opportunity for Quint Winery.

Background

The Mosel River Valley has been a producer of high quality wines since Roman times. The river has a series of low-rise dams that provide a broad, smooth surface reflecting the summer sunshine on to the shale-laden soil of the valley's steep slopes. Both the shale and the water itself absorb heat during the day, releasing it during the night. The result is a micro climate, in the valley alone, ideal for the production of high quality wine grapes. The suitability of the region for growing grapes was recognized by the Romans. They introduced viniculture, and wines have been the specialty of the river valley ever since.

The steep valley walls require that in some places winches and cables be used to move platforms from which cultivation and harvesting are carried out. This, together with the unsuitability of the climate above the valley walls for growing grapes, has resulted in a pattern of small, independently owned vineyards. In order to make the small-scale operations economically feasible, each family grows its own grapes, makes the wines, bottles them, and does the marketing themselves.

Many small German wineries market their wines directly to consumers. One of the major tools for attracting customers is the holding of 'wine tasting parties' in a traditional cellar bar close to the winery.

For a low package price, the participants have the opportunity to sample a variety of the winery's products along with a steak dinner. The owner of the winery additionally provides a tour of the vineyard and of the winery itself. The participants in such parties often buy bottles of wine on the spot, sometimes become long-term customers, and may recommend the parties to friends. This type of marketing approach has worked well in the past for small wineries with very limited funds available for promotion.

European integration and the move toward a single market have intensified competition. As a consequence, there are limits in the range of prices the wineries can charge for their wines, even if they are of high quality and unique. A number of wineries have experienced greater than desired carryover of stock from one year to the next, indicating that additional marketing efforts are required.

Strategies

Quint Winery specializes in higher quality wines with individuality in taste and flavor. The target market is people in the upper middle class, particularly those who appreciate excellent wines and are interested in information about wine, culture, and history. With his own background in the formal study of wine engineering, Michael Quint has a wealth of information that he enjoys sharing with others.

The overall strategy is to remain small, and use traditional recipes and processes. However, it is increasing productivity by outsourcing specialized bottling to others that have machinery which Quint cannot economically purchase. In adding to its product lines the winery is working with others that have core competencies which cannot be economically developed by Quint. These cooperative activities have allowed the winery to enjoy benefits of being both small and large at the same time.

Until the 1990s, a regulation issued by an archbishop several centuries earlier had prohibited the production of red wines in the region. Many vintners in the area still produce only white wines. However, when the restriction was removed, Quint winery began to produce some red wines whose production proved to be very successful and increased the range of their offerings. It subsequently began to produce sparkling wines, based on its white wines, in cooperation with a small subcontractor in the village. In the early 2000s it began to produce brandy, again with the assistance of friends who had technical expertise. The company has also been developing and experimenting with new bottle designs that will stress the Quint Winery brand while linking it to the traditions of the house.

Quint Winery's major marketing effort is still the holding of traditional wine tasting parties. Michael has added the family imprint by showing remarkable generosity in serving wines and food, and by providing interesting and informative presentations on the history, culture, and processes of wine making. He firmly believes in avoiding any sort of pressure to buy, letting the quality and individuality of the wines inspire a desire to purchase. In an unusual addition to typical service, he also offers to personally deliver the wines to his customers anywhere in Germany.

This approach has been working well. People attending the wine tasting events usually buy a number of bottles of the wines, and subsequently recommend both the events and the wines to their friends back home. In spite of the increase in customers generated by these activities, additional markets are desired.

A Japanese visitor, brought to a wine tasting by German friends, commented on the excellent quality of the wines. She believed that they might prove salable in Japan. If properly marketed, this should allow both increased sales and possibly greater margins. An initial step for Michael Quint would be to contact the Japan External Trade Organization (JETRO) office in Dusseldorf.

Information on marketing in Japan

There is much information available from JETRO on the wine market and wine marketing in Japan. Their *Japan Trade Directory* lists companies that import wine into Japan. The names of the top 10 Japanese importers of wine from Germany and their import volumes are available on the JETRO web page, http://www.jetro.go.jp. The JETRO office in Dusseldorf stands ready to assist potential exporters with information, contacts, and opportunities for participation in trade shows in Japan. German organizations that may offer assistance include Deutscher Weinfonds and CMA (the German Agricultural Marketing Board).

Wine consumption in Japan has increased substantially during the last 10 years. A red wine boom occurred in Japan in the late 1990s after researchers associated the drinking of red wine with a lowered incidence of cardiovascular disease. Germany, with its emphasis on the export of white wines, lost market share. Now white wines are growing in popularity again. JETRO has noted that 'Germany's wide variety of wines (especially white wines), its unique soils, and its North Country climate are what distinguish German wines from all others' (JETRO Marketing Guidebook for Major Imported Products, available on the JETRO web page, 2004). There is increased competition in the

Japanese wine market from South America, Australia, and the United States. However, there is still a good market for high quality white wines from Germany.

There are a number of channels available for selling wine to the Japanese market: direct sales to department stores and mass merchandisers, direct sales to wholesalers and discounters, sales to large trading companies, sales through joint venture projects, and sales in bulk or in bottles to domestic liquor producers. A number of small trading companies, specializing in or emphasizing wine, have opened. These small trading companies supply stores or restaurants which do not import directly, or that wish to supplement their own imports with small amounts from other producers. Together, these changes have substantially increased opportunities for small exporters abroad.

The market in Japan has become increasingly sophisticated. Larger department stores carry a wide variety of wines and may hold special promotions and displays. An increasing number of wine specialty stores have been opened. Several Internet wine shops are now serving the Japanese market, offering a very wide range of wines. According to JETRO, price is a key factor in wine purchase decisions, followed by taste, color, and brand. However, consumers have little interest in poorer quality wine.

JETRO offers several types of assistance to prospective exporters in foreign countries. It can help in arranging participation in government-sponsored trade shows of consumer goods. These allow potential foreign exporters to introduce their products to a wide range of Japanese consumers and companies. JETRO offices abroad provide information on markets and methods of penetration. JETRO Business Support Centers in Japan provide office space at no charge for up to two months to foreign business people seeking to export to or invest in Japan.

The possibility of marketing to Japan

Sales to a small Japanese trading firm or directly to a Japanese chain store might offer two advantages to Quint Winery. First, it could provide an outlet for current surplus production. Second, away from the intense competition in the domestic market, it might be possible to obtain a higher price for the unique and high quality wines, particularly if there were some way to inform the Japanese public of the history, romance, and culture of the Mosel River Valley vintners. It does not appear that Quint Winery could supply a whole container load of their own wine, nor could a smaller chain purchase a whole container load of one vintner's wine. What should Michael Quint do next?

References

http://www.jetro.go.jp

JETRO (2001). *Japan Trade Directory 2001–2002*, B-129.

JETRO (2001). *Pier J: Opportunities in Japan*, 'Fine wine club: global offerings for the Japanese dining table,' 3–4 (February).

Questions

1. Does the Japanese market appear to offer enough potential for Quint Winery to export to Japan? Explain why or why not.

2. How can Quint Winery locate potential Japanese purchasers?

3. Should the winery owner visit Japan, or should he attempt to attract company representatives to come to his winery? Is your answer influenced by specific aspects of Japanese culture? Explain.

4. Should Quint Winery work by itself in any attempts to enter the Japanese market, or should it attempt to work with other local wineries in a type of cooperative effort?

5. What kind of market(ing) research should be done with respect to potential Japanese consumers?

6. What other questions should the owner ask? What problems may he expect to encounter?

CASE STUDY 7.3

Nestlé

(This case is adapted from E. Echrikson, 2000, 'Nestlé: an elephant dances,' Business Week *E. Biz, 11 December, EB44–8. Reprinted by special permission, copyright © 2000 by the McGraw-Hill Companies.)*

The town of Verey, Switzerland, perches among the vineyards above Lake Geneva. Wealthy retirees take in Alpine vistas as they pass their afternoons strolling along the waterfront. The most exciting event is the annual grape harvest. Silicone Valley and the hubbub of high tech seem worlds away. On the edge of town, however, stands the glass and steel global headquarters of Nestlé, the world's largest food producer.

This setting has now become the epicenter of one of Europe's most ambitious e-commerce initiatives as Nestlé undertakes a plan to make the company more agile, more responsive to its customers, and more profitable. Over the next three years it will invest as much as US$1.8 billion in a phased development plan. The company will continue to expand its use of the Internet and Web, acquire additional specialized software and solutions, build data centers, and work toward creating a coherent global information system. Peter Brabeck-Lemathe, the company's chief executive, calls the process an 'e-revolution' – albeit one that will take several years to complete. He has commented that 'This might sound slow for Silicone Valley, but it's very fast' for a company like Nestlé.

The company

Henri Nestlé founded the company in 1867 in order to market the baby formula he had developed. In 1938, Nestlé scientists were the first to produce instant coffee. These two products fueled much of the company's growth for its first century. Twenty years ago Nestlé began a US$40 billion buying spree, acquiring a number of companies including Friskies in 1985, sauce-maker Buitoni in 1988, and Perrier in 1992.

Now, with 1999 revenues of US$46.6 billion, 509 factories in 83 countries, 230,000 employees, and over 8000 products, Nestlé is the world's leading food and beverage company. However, profits margins have been low compared to industry standards, and the stock price has stagnated.

Nestlé is involved in all phases of the food industry, from buying raw materials such as cocoa beans to processing, packaging, marketing, and selling products. Many food items remain local products. As Brabeck says: 'You can't sell a Bavarian soup to a Taiwanese noodle-lover.' The company thus must make adjustments to product lines, packaging, pricing, advertising, etc. to suit the demands of each of its many markets. Nestlé's size and complexity, as well as the diversity of environments in which it operates, create problems in all phases of operations, with substantial duplications of effort and difficulties in getting all of the required information to some decision makers.

Nestlé has viewed the improvements in intercompany and intracompany communications made possible by the Internet and the Web, and the software available for use in e-commerce, as providing great potential for reducing costs in everything from obtaining materials and supplies to marketing. It also makes feasible certain types of restructuring that should lead to improved responsiveness and control. 'For big companies like us, the Internet is particularly good because it shakes you up,' says Mario Corti, Nestlé's chief financial officer and head of its Internet offensive. In its e-commerce initiatives, Nestlé must practice a delicate balancing act: using the net to both reduce transaction costs and gain economies of scale while still catering to a variety of cultural preferences.

Nestlé's early e-commerce initiatives, coupled with restructuring efforts, led to an increase in net profit of almost 35% in the first half of 2000 (to US$1.7 billion). Now the company is undertaking a major additional effort in e-commerce.

Expanding e-commerce initiatives

In June 2000 Nestlé signed a US$200 million contract with German-based SAP to provide support in this effort. SAP is the world's largest provider of ERP (enterprise resource planning) software and solutions designed to support a broad range of integrated management systems including financials, supply chain management, e-procurement, customer relationship management, etc. For SAP, it was the largest sale ever. For Nestlé, the objective is to streamline the company's operations and give far-flung employees quick access to information from around the globe. This should enable Nestlé to better leverage its size by tying together long-independent national fiefdoms. Expected results are as shown in Table 7.4.

Although Nestlé is a consumer-driven company, most of the changes will be invisible to diners sipping Perrier or kids munching Nestlé Crunch bars. But behind the scenes, the way Nestlé buys, manufactures, and delivers its products is going digital. The company is a founder of online food-supply marketplaces Transora and CPGmarket.com, which aim to use the Web to streamline purchasing. The emphasis, though, will not be on slashing raw material prices or eliminating distributors. Instead, Nestlé wants to link its disparate operations, partner with suppliers to cut waste, and move its food products more quickly from farm to factory to the family dinner table. Rather than desiring to squeeze suppliers, these actions are designed to increase the company's internal productivity.

Nestlé's reinvention is a work in progress. The company's margins, while improving, remain a third lower than those of competitors H. J. Heinz, Cadbury, or Procter & Gamble. The giant SAP deal is at least three years away from giving all Nestlé employees access to information from other countries' divisions. Transora and CPGmarket.com are only now beginning operations, and online marketplaces in many other industries are encountering severe teething problems.

That is where the Web comes in. The first order of business has been linking to retailers. Since July, store owners in the United States have been able to order Nestlé chocolates and other products online at NestléEZOrder.com. The benefit for Nestlé: the system cuts out expensive manual data entry and slashes processing costs for each order from US$2.35 to 21 cents. Similar initiatives are on tap for other countries, which could trim as much as 20% from the company's US$3 billion in yearly worldwide logistics and administrative costs.

The net helps cut inventories, too. In the past, when Nestlé held promotions it had to guess at demand. By linking up electronically with its retail partners it can now adjust production quickly. In Britain, supermarket chains Sainsbury and Tesco send in daily sales reports and demand forecasts over the Web to Nestlé headquarters, while Nestlé managers check inventory levels

TABLE 7.4	Changes at Nestlé due to e-commerce development

Before e-revolution	After e-revolution
Technology mishmash: The company runs five e-mail systems and 20 versions of accounting, planning and inventory software. Country operations use different computer codes for the same products so it is hard to share supplies and data.	**Standardized software:** Nestlé is moving to one software package. The Web-linked program creates a single set of product codes, allowing buyers in one country short on, say, corn powder to get supplies from other Nestlé divisions.
Bad communication: Most employees have no access to production and sales figures from countries other than their own because they are not linked. A planner in France cannot see data about KitKat bars being made in a German plant – making it tough to adjust the order.	**Centralized data:** Nestlé is building up to a half-dozen data centers so employees can get quick access to information via the net. For the first time, Nestlé will know how much it is buying from suppliers with far-flung operations. That will let it negotiate better contracts, centralize production, and buy more across borders.

on the supermarkets' computer systems. 'It's been a revolution in the way we work together,' says Tom McGuffog, director of e-business at Nestlé UK.

Nestlé is seeing similar results from sharing information online inside the company. Pietro Senna, a buyer for Nestlé Switzerland, was recently having trouble getting kosher meat. He posted a message online, and a colleague in the United States found him just the right supplier – in Uruguay. The time savings are immense. Each country's hazelnut buyer, for example, used to visit processing plants in Italy and Turkey. Hazelnuts, a key ingredient in chocolate bars, are prone to wild price swings and uneven quality. But after Senna stopped by some Turkish plants he posted his report on the Web – and within a week 73 other Nestlé buyers from around the globe had read it, saving them the trouble of a trip to Turkey. 'For the first time, I get to take advantage of Nestlé's size,' he says.

When leveraged, that size can slash procurement costs. Until recently, Nestlé had 12 buyers throughout Europe, dealing with 14 suppliers of lactose, an ingredient in infant formula and chocolate bars. By linking via the net, the company has been able to cut its suppliers to just four. 'We can only do this because of online information,' Senna says. Lactose costs have come down by as much as 20%.

Nestlé's web charge is being led by its dairy farm in Carnation, Washington, USA. Nestlé's US CEO Joe Weller asks workers how to unify Nestlé. The answer: e-business. If the US division leads, the rest of the giant is likely to follow. The sheer weight of the US operation has wallop: it booked more than US$10 billion in sales last year, nearly a quarter of the company's total.

If the US division is quarterbacking the effort, Brabeck is its chief cheerleader. He does not have a computer in his office – e-mails have to go through his secretary. And far from passing his leisure time surfing the net, 56-year-old Brabeck spends his weekends climbing the Alps that tower over Vevey. But he was an early backer of e-tailing experiments the company participated in. Those trials were eventually shelved, but Brabeck says they demonstrated the power of technology and the net. 'This opened my eyes,' he says.

Nestlé's disparate Internet ventures present a mountain of opportunity that will require all the strength and savvy Brabeck can muster. He does not underestimate the challenges ahead. But he does not seem fazed either.

Some comments on Nestlé's subsequent performance

Nestlé appears to be making substantial progress with its e-commerce initiatives, streamlining and integrating operations, and overhauling the information technology systems. Information systems improvements have given management the data they need to compare performance of units worldwide, and to identify those needing help. They have also enabled the company to avoid some of the costs of highly decentralized buying and logistics. Since 2001, the company has realized US$1.5 billion in cost savings, and expects an additional US$2.5 billion savings by 2006 (Matlack, 2003). While still trailing the operating margins of Unilever and Kraft, Nestlé's have risen by almost 50% in the past five years (Ball, 2004).

The company has made three acquisitions, at a total cost of US$15.5 billion to increase its presence in the United States (Weintraub and Tierney, 2002). The company is still pursuing sales growth and is keeping its broad and diverse product line with about 8000 brands (Matlack, 2003).

References

Ball, D. (2004). Europeans narrow gap on share valuations. *The Wall Street Journal*, 25 February, C1.

Matlack, C. (2003). Nestlé is starting to slim down at last. *Business Week*, 27 October, 56–7.

Weintraub, A. and Tierney, C. (2002). Can Nestlé resist this morsel? *Business Week*, 2 September, 60–2.

Questions

1. Evaluate Nestlé's use of the Internet and Web to this point. How will its marketing operations be enhanced?

2. What other uses of the Internet should Nestlé explore?

3. Does the signing of a contract for such major software and solutions development with SAP seem appropriate at this stage? Should the company take one step at a time rather than attempt to do so much at once?

4. Will the Internet and World Wide Web revolutionize international marketing? Explain.

5. What are the advantages and disadvantages of having some 8000 brands?

CHAPTER 8

Nonexport Entry Modes

8.1 Introduction

Manufacturers have expanded their international marketing operations to include some type of production activity in foreign markets. Such expansion may be either a defensive or an offensive move, and it may be for reasons of market entry and/or sourcing. When the expansion is *defensive*, generally it is done to protect a profitable market or to maintain a beachhead in a potentially profitable market. In this case the manufacturer's action is not of its own choice but in response to pressure from some outside source – a foreign government, competition, or nationalistic-oriented buyers.

Government tariffs and other import barriers (including a ban on imports), currency restrictions, and general nationalistic attitudes may be such that if a firm wishes to do business in an overseas market it must establish either a partial or complete production base in that country. This, of course, may involve making some type of direct investment of capital or some other asset of the firm (for example, know-how). This is the reaction taken by many 'outside' companies to the developments of, and growth in, regional economic integration areas such as the European Union and NAFTA. Traditionally, the features that made a country a desirable place for such foreign direct investment (FDI) have been a favorable investment regime, market size, natural resources, market growth prospects, technology knowledge and development, and labor market conditions, depending upon whether the FDI was for purposes of market penetration or sourcing. China fits this profile. It has abundant cheap labor, many talented engineers, good infrastructure, and as a condition of joining the WTO, the large market will be open at some time soon to foreign competition. Many of these features are now 'taken for granted,' and companies are looking for places to invest that offer specific advantages, or *created assets*, including communications infrastructure, marketing networks, and intangibles such as attitudes toward wealth creation and business culture, innovative capacity, the stock of information trademarks, and goodwill. The created assets have become crucial for a firm's competitiveness and can make countries without more traditional advantages attractive locations for FDI. These advantages are sought by companies in the service industries and in distribution (such as retailing) as well as manufacturers. Thus much of what we will discuss in this chapter about nonexport modes of market entry will apply to investments of service and distribution companies. Many of these features also encourage companies to *outsource* business activities to a foreign country. For example, Germany's semiconductor maker Infineon Technologies has transferred its bookkeeping to Portugal. In addition, companies such as Intel, Texas Instruments, Oracle, and Cisco Systems have developed research and development laboratories and design centers for telecom and other high-tech products in India (Kripalani, 2002).

Competition exerts its influence in such a way that a manufacturer which relies on exporting may not be able to compete on price in foreign markets. In some instances a manufacturer's exports are priced out of foreign markets because of the tariffs that must be paid when the product is imported. Although tariffs may be significant, they alone do not always account for a difference in price. A manufacturer may lose out in competition with either or both domestic or foreign producers in a given foreign market because of the more favorable production costs enjoyed by these competitors. Consequently an exporting manufacturer often finds that it can remain competitive by making a direct investment in some type of production activity, or by forming a strategic alliance in a foreign market, or by outsourcing some business functions where it can take advantage of lower costs.

Finally buyers may be influential in that they tend to buy products of firms that they consider to be national. In some countries it may take a direct investment or strategic alliance to be considered a 'local' national manufacturer.

As an *offensive* device, expansion into overseas production operations is done for many of the same reasons outlined above. The difference, of course, is the attitude of management and the fact that such expansion is done by choice and typically according to a plan. A manufacturer that takes the offensive recognizes that it can go into certain foreign countries and beat its competition on their home ground with its greater experience, know-how, methods, and marketing ability and capacity. In addition, if a market appears to have good potential, this alone may be reason for foreign-based production. A manufacturer may reason that if it does not do this some other company eventually will. And there are always some benefits that accrue to the firm that is first (*first-mover advantages*), and some of these are never really lost when other firms appear on the horizon.

First-mover advantages include the following (Lasserre and Schutte, 1995, pp. 160–2):

■ Customer can be reached easily before he or she is bombarded by masses of conflicting messages.
■ Brand name may be established firmly in the minds of customers before other brands appear. In the extreme case, the first-mover's brand may become generic, such as Honda being the name used for motorcycles in Indonesia in the mid-1990s.
■ Distributors and retailers are more ready to carry new products when they have no alternatives. Also, these institutions are then not available to follower market entrants.
■ Entry barriers to later entrants can be set up by setting new technical standards, even by having them officially sanctioned.

Of course, being first does not guarantee continued market leadership. Constant adaptation and flexibility in marketing to changing demand and more aggressive competitors is needed to maintain first-mover advantages.

Typically, foreign direct investment involves companies from the more developed industrial areas of the world investing in both developed and developing countries. But major exceptions do exist, as evidenced by Chinese companies discussed in Exhibit 8.1.

| EXHIBIT 8.1 | The Chinese are moving 'silently but swiftly' |

When one thinks of China in the world economy thoughts go immediately to viewing it for sourcing purposes or as a large potential market to be penetrated. Both strategic alliances and partially and wholly foreign-owned enterprises are used for entry. In 2002, for example, foreign direct investment into China reached more than US$50 billion. Estimates for 2003 were that FDI into China would exceed US$60 billion, despite SARS and a less than 'smoking' world economy. Clearly, China is at present the world's number one destination for FDI.

But there is another side to FDI – Chinese companies investing outside China. At less than 1% of global FDI the amount invested is small, but it is growing. Only a small number of companies are large enough and have the resources to expand abroad. A report in 2002 by a consultancy company indicated that almost 75% of the mainland Chinese manufacturing companies surveyed had plans for foreign expansion. It is one thing to have a plan and another to implement it!

This 'charge' of Chinese expansion is being spearheaded by natural resource companies, who are still controlled by the government (*The Economist*, 2003). The big three oil companies – Sinopec, Petrochina, and China National Offshore Oil Company (CNOOC) – have invested in 14 countries, including Kazakhstan, Yemen, Sudan, and Myanmar. CNOOC is now the largest offshore oil producer in Indonesia after its acquisition of Repsol Indonesia in 2002. The natural resource companies are reacting to a government mandate to secure reserves abroad for meeting the country's growing needs.

Acquiring foreign know-how is also of interest to the Chinese. Shenzhen-based Huawei Technologies, a supplier of equipment to telecoms, has research facilities in Sweden, Germany, and the United States. In 2003 the company announced plans to invest about US$100 million in India to expand its Bangalore facility, which works on mobile phone software and broadband research.

There is a desire on the part of some Chinese firms to build their own global brands. Haier, China's electrical appliance manufacturer, has plants at 13 sites outside China, including Iran, Indonesia, and the United States. China's two major television manufacturing companies, TCL and Konka, have invested in plants outside China. However, such manufacturing investments have not really helped Chinese firms 'trade up' from cheap products. This has led to another strategy – buying established brands. Of interest are well-known brands from companies that are in 'trouble.' For example, D'Long Strategic Investments purchased Murray, a leading US company that makes lawnmowers and bicycles and it bought a stake in a jet aircraft project from the bankrupt German aircraft producer Fairchild Dornier.

There is a risk in Chinese FDI if it is successful. As the international fear of China increases, in the sense that it is viewed by many as an exporter of deflation and a destroyer of jobs in the West, the idea of Chinese firms buying increasing amounts of the world could lead to political ramifications (*The Economist*, 2003).

Inside the Forbidden City, Beijing, China

8.2 Alternative modes of entry

In Chapter 6 we defined an international market entry mode as an institutional arrangement necessary for the entry of a company's products, technology, and human and financial capital into a foreign market. Site of production base was identified as the first decision that had to be made, and foreign-market based production was a major alternative. Our discussion of production from a foreign-based location takes a broad viewpoint of the meaning of production. There are three basic alternative ways that a manufacturer can engage in overseas production (as shown in Figure 6.1 in Chapter 6):

1. a manufacturing plant can be established;
2. assembly operations can be set up;
3. a strategic alliance can be formed with one or more companies.

Although all forms of nonexport market entry mode involve some kind of an investment by the company entering the foreign market, a capital investment typically is required for the manufacturing plant and assembly operations options and may be necessary for a strategic alliance.

Figure 8.1 illustrates different potential modes of entry for the Asia-Pacific region based on extent of prior experience and type of market. According to Lasserre and Schutte (1995, pp. 34–5) the countries in Asia-Pacific roughly divide into five types: platform, emerging, growth, maturing, and established. Platform countries can be used at the start of the entry process as bases for gathering intelligence and initiating contacts. In emerging countries a company wants to establish an initial presence, and prepare itself for further development. Growth countries require that a significant presence be established quickly in order to take advantage of the opportunities available due to rapid economic development. The task at entry into maturing and established markets is to find a way to access the

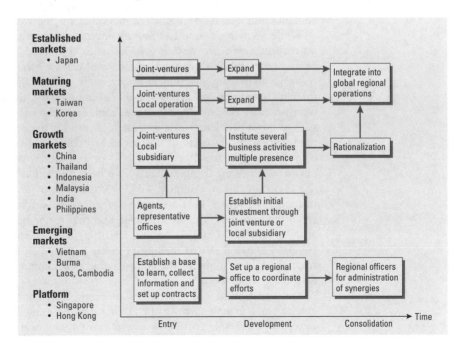

FIGURE 8.1

Entry modes and development in Asia-Pacific
Source: Lasserre and Schutte (1995), p. 35

operational capability necessary to catch up with already established competitors. Although this schema was developed for entry into countries of the Asia-Pacific region, it is applicable to market entry into other areas of the world where the markets can be similarly characterized.

As companies change their mode(s) of foreign market entry, either by evolution or deliberate and planned change, from export to overseas-based operations organized as an affiliate, their strategic orientation shifts in several respects from the country of origin to the host country. Meissner (1990, pp. 46–8) shows the relationship between involvement of management and infusion of capital in foreign activities and mode of market entry and extent to which the resources are invested in either the home or the host country. As management involvement increases toward emphasis on the host country and infusion of capital increases in the host country at the expense of the home country, the mode of market entry will follow a sequence: exports, licensing agreements, franchising, joint venture, foreign branch, production plant, and affiliate. The affiliate will have 100% management involvement in the host country with resources invested in the host country as well.

The *strategic focus* of companies that have nonexport foreign-market based operations also will vary, particularly when there are differences in attitudes toward profitability. Two opposite approaches to profit are expanding sales volume and improving productivity. In a study of 90 major US, Japanese, and British companies competing in the UK market in the early 1990s, there were distinct differences between companies in describing their strategic focus (Doyle *et al.*, 1992). Japanese managers believed in a long-run profit performance being enhanced by a focus on volume, by moving into new market segments, or by aggressive market penetration. With increased sales volume Japanese companies would be able to build competitive cost structures, generate the resources needed to sustain product development, and better control distribution channels in the future. The US and British companies, in contrast, felt that profits are improved best by focus on cost reduction and improved productivity. An advantage of concentrating on productivity, rather than volume, is that it can lead to fairly quick profit improvement. At the same time it can often lead to a longer-run decline of market position as reducing costs mean a reduced expenditure on new product development, building brand equity, and market support. If this is carried on long enough there would be a decline in market share and weaker distribution.

While many host countries provide incentives in order to attract direct private investment there are also many obstacles that tend to bother investors and obstruct, or at least slow down, the flow of private foreign capital. Some of these obstacles stem from government policy, such as exchange controls, restrictions on foreign companies and persons, political uncertainty, nationalistic attitudes, and unsatisfactory tax conditions. Others come from the nature of the economy itself, such as labor problems, inflation, and concern for the environment. For example, the Indonesian subsidiary of US-owned Freeport McMoran Copper and Gold has come under pressure from tribal leaders and western activists over its mining operations in West Papua. Claims have been made that the company is polluting the environment by dumping 200,000 tons of silt into local rivers every day, turning a 90-square mile area into a gray, treeless desert; that it is not sharing enough wealth with the local people; and that it has been aiding the Indonesian army's torture, detention and murder of civilians (*Business Week*, 2000a). The company states that it is making progress in changing things, but it is not clear what the future holds for the company in the remaining 40 years of its contract with the government.

The situation in China provides an example of another potential obstacle to investment – management of the labor force there. In western countries labor is viewed as a variable cost and workers can be temporarily or permanently let go when demand for products decreases, often at an extra cost to the company. In China, however, a business enterprise is viewed as a key unit in a giant social welfare system, and the worker's unit has an implied responsibility for the welfare of the worker. This is particularly so for joint ventures that may have to provide all the services needed by employees of the company – homes, stores, and schools. The joint venture is a *danwei*, the basic work unit in China (Pearson, 1991). Under these conditions, labor is in effect an overhead cost that must be covered regardless of fluctuations in demand. In some instances there are barriers to overseas investment placed by the government of the potential investor's country. Most generally this is limited to policies concerning the use of currency and taxes, although there have been cases where limitations on the absolute amount of investment have been imposed.

We now turn to a discussion of each of the alternative nonexport modes of entry into foreign markets. Before doing this we need to clarify a distinction between a joint venture and other types of investments that are not wholly owned. For the purposes of this text, a joint venture is a type of strategic alliance in which companies from at least two different countries, generally one being local, form a *new company* to manufacture/produce products or provide a service on a joint basis. This would involve what is known as a *greenfield investment*. This type of entity is quite different from one in which there is simply shared ownership in general, which usually involves an acquisition by one of the partners, although there are many overlapping characteristics.

Moreover, it must be recognized that companies may be using more than one approach. During a 12-month period in the mid-1990s, for example, the South Korean Samsung Electronics Company set up eight strategic alliances and acquired or took equity positions in six companies, mainly US and Japanese companies. This was done to have access to the technology needed to achieve the goals that it had set for itself. Similarly, in China the US firm Johnson & Johnson has successful pharmaceutical strategic alliances in the form of equity joint ventures (EJVs) and a successful wholly foreign-owned enterprise (WFOE) producing oral care, baby, and feminine hygiene products. The company has stated that all future investments will be WFOEs instead of EJVs unless a Chinese partner offers a very significant contribution (Vanhonacker, 1997).

The decision regarding which nonexport market entry mode to use cannot be entirely separated from the 'generic' decision to enter the market. Thus the bases of entry mode choice generally include the overall attractiveness of the market itself; costs of entering the market (i.e., what might be viewed as transaction costs); the timing and ability of a company to enter and develop necessary resources, assets, and competencies; local and home government requirements; the competitive situation; and political and operational risks that are involved (Lasserre and Schutte, 1995, p. 34).

8.3 Manufacturing facilities

8.3.1 General considerations

Rarely does a company set up manufacturing facilities as its first international business operation. Most often a factory is not established in a foreign market area unless and until the market has already been served by export channels, unless it is being set up purely for sourcing for other markets. Exceptions might exist, however, if a company is new to an area, and the policies and regulations of the foreign government are such that the best way to enter the market is through a direct investment in a manufacturing facility; or it might very well be desirable to form a strategic alliance either through a licensing agreement or a joint venture. In such cases it is desirable that the particular market offer great sales potential; however, in some cases it is adequate that the specific country is situated so that it serves as a good base from which surrounding foreign market areas can be served. For example, in the early 2000s Japanese, European, and US automobile manufacturers were using manufacturing facilities in Mexico as an export platform for some of the world's hottest cars (*Business Week*, 2000b). DaimlerChrysler's PT Cruiser was made only in Toluca; General Motors assembled the Aztek sports utility vehicle exclusively in Ramos Arizpe; Nissan's Sentra was centralized in Aguacalientes; and VW manufactured its new Beetle exclusively in Puebla. One thing that makes Mexico a very attractive place for an export base is that the country has signed free trade agreements with 23 countries during the past decade, as well as it being a member of NAFTA. Moreover, Mexico has long been used by US auto manufacturers as a sourcing production base for the US market.

Many of the possible reasons that companies establish manufacturing operations in a foreign market were discussed in Chapter 2 in the broader context of international marketing. At the same time it should be realized that a direct investment in manufacturing will require a significant investment in capital. In addition to the business risks involved there are personnel and other problems. For instance, there may be local labor laws to contend with, and often there is difficulty in repatriating profits and capital. These problems, while real, can be minor when compared to the many advantages that can emerge from having a foreign manufacturing facility. A few important advantages are: it offers control of sales policy and a flexibility not possible with a license; it provides product control of the market, including third countries; it seizes advantages offered by foreign governments as investment incentives; it makes the protection of trademarks and the building of a brand equity easier and creates a better image in the host country; it is much easier to use manufactured components in a worldwide integrated production program; it gives control of cost cutting, expansion programs, production policies and quality control; and it makes local financing easier and provides flexibility in currency agreements, etc.

Once the decision to manufacture in a foreign market has been made, then a company has three basic questions to answer. The first concerns where the manufacturing facility is to be located. Often this question is directly tied in with the decision to manufacture abroad. That is, the decision is made with a particular country in mind. Second, the question of degree of ownership must be answered. This involves deciding whether the operation is to be wholly owned or only partially owned. Finally, a company must decide what is the best way to implement its decision: should it start from scratch or acquire an existing firm located in the selected market? These three questions are in fact interrelated such that the answer to one will affect the answers to the others. Each company must establish a priority, which is not necessarily the order in which we have presented them. Thus, for some companies, the degree of ownership that it desires will be the controlling factor while for others the desired location will be of primary importance.

8.3.2 Location

The selection of one country over another calls for careful analysis of a host of important factors. These factors can be categorized under several broad headings, as follows:

1. **The climate for foreign capital**
   a political considerations;
   b economic and industrial dynamism of the people;
   c size of market and potential for growth;
   d geographic and climatic conditions;
   e financial considerations; taxation.
2. **Production considerations**
   a availability and cost of personnel and labor – skilled and unskilled;
   b availability and cost of personnel to perform managerial duties;
   c facilities;
   d availability and cost of water, power, transport, real estate, and so on;
   e availability and cost of raw materials, capital equipment, and so on.
3. **Special conditions** in respect to industry conditions and regarding one's own product line in particular, for example the competitive situation.

These are general categories. What is needed is a guide so that a more detailed analysis can be made of the potentialities offered by a particular country. Many checklists for this purpose are available.

The job of appraising a country is not easy. A great and important burden will be placed on many people in the company, particularly those involved in international marketing research. Many of the data sources discussed earlier in Chapter 5 will have to be utilized. For example, basic industrial surveys have been published for many areas, market reports and preliminary feasibility studies are often available, assistance in finding suitable partners for possible joint ventures is available, and fully serviced sites are available for industrial use. Finally, at some time during the appraisal process – though not at the beginning – the country should be visited.

It should be apparent that an appraisal will be costly – both in terms of time and money. However, it is better to spend the necessary time and money to make a thorough study and analysis than to invest in a manufacturing plant in the wrong place.

Often the choice of a location for manufacturing facilities is based on costs. According to Aliber (1993, pp. 127–8):

> Consider a firm with markets in fifteen or twenty countries. The key aspect of the sourcing decision for its managers is where each of the several stages of the value-added chain should be located so that the market in each country can be satisfied at a minimum unit cost ...
>
> Consider two corner approaches for the sourcing decision in the international context. One is the decentralization option: each product to be sold in each national market would be sourced exclusively within that country so that there are no cross-border flows of raw materials or components or final product between the parent and any of its foreign subsidiaries or among any of the foreign subsidiaries.
>
> The alternative approach, the centralization choice, is that each product sold by the firm and its subsidiaries in the various national markets would be sourced from one site, which might be in one of the countries in which the firm sells, or in some other country ...
>
> The manager's choice between the two approaches is likely to be based on a set of calculations about how best to minimize the firm's costs; the likely outcome is somewhere between these corner approaches.

As an example of cost orientation, in the early 2000s the South Korean company Goldstar was shifting as much production as possible of low-end and mid-range products to low-cost countries such as China and Vietnam.

For products that are higher in technology, other considerations such as the skill and education of labor are important. Computer companies such as the US's Intel

Corp., Japan's NEC Corp., Taiwan's Acer Inc., and the US's Cypress Semiconductor Corp. in the mid-1990s established operations in the Philippines. In addition to low wages, the Philippines is attractive to such high-tech companies because the labor force is well educated and well trained (DiCicco, 1996). China is a country where labor costs offer advantages for a production or simply an outsourcing site, and it is increasing its skill and education levels to attract higher technology investments. Motorola, IBM, and Microsoft have established research facilities. General Electric, Intel, Matsushita Electric and Siemens have shared technological know-how with the Chinese.

A special concern in the appraisal process should be for *political risk*. This can be defined as 'the application of host government policies that constrain the business operations of a given foreign investment' (Schmidt, 1986, p. 45). Political risk is multidimensional and includes the following (Root, 1994, pp. 150–7):

- *Transfer risk.* Risk arising from government policies that restrict the transfer of capital, payments, products, technology, and persons into or out of the host country.
- *Operational risk.* Risk due to host government policies, regulations, and administrative procedures that directly constrain the management and performance of local operations in production, marketing, finance, and other business functions.
- *Ownership-control risk.* Risk brought about as a result of host government policies or actions that inhibit ownership and/or control of the local operations of an international company.
- *General instability risk.* Risk that relates to the future viability of the host country's political system.

Such risks can be either macro risks in that all foreign companies are more or less affected the same, or they may be micro when only specific industries, companies, or projects may be affected.

A significant aspect of the evaluation of a proposed foreign investment is obtaining answers to many questions, including the following:

- What are the chances of there being general political instability in the country being examined over the relevant investment planning period?
- How long is the present government expected to be in power?
- How strong is the present government's commitment to its agreements with investors in light of its attitudes toward foreign investors and its power position?
- If a new government is to come to power, will it honor existing agreements and regulations or will changes be made?
- If changes in government policy are made, how will this affect the firm's profitability and safety of a project?

Answers to questions like these are not easily found, particularly when a proposed investment is to be in a developing country. In this situation political maturity as well as political stability needs to be assessed.

In order to evaluate the political risks of a proposed foreign investment, managers need information relevant to the situation and they need a structure for analysis. One such approach is shown in Figure 8.2, which is based on the four dimensions defined above. This structure looks at each dimension as a hurdle to be overcome, with general instability risk being first, and transfer risk being last. In order for top management to approve the investment it must pass all four political risk hurdles and, obviously, satisfy the desired rate of return. Another approach is to use a syndicated service measure such as the Business Environment Risk Index (BERI) discussed in Exhibit 8.2.

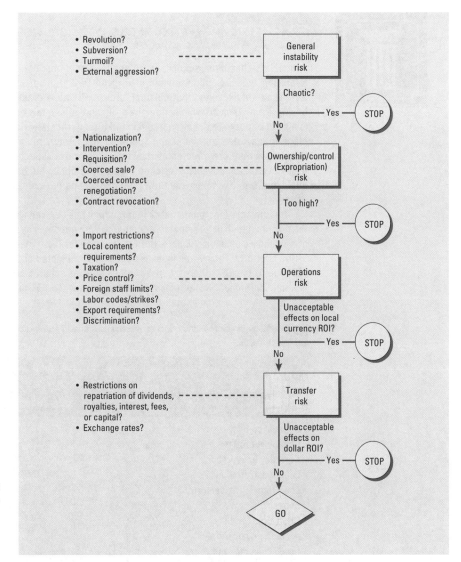

FIGURE 8.2

Evaluation of political risk
Source: Root (1994), p. 155
Copyright © 1994. This
material is used by
permission of John Wiley &
Sons, Inc

8.3.3 Ownership

The question concerning degree of ownership desired is basically that of deciding whether the foreign manufacturing facility is to be wholly owned (either as a branch or as a separate subsidiary) or only partially owned. If the foreign operation is to be only partially owned, then a decision is to be made concerning whether it will be a joint venture (i.e., a partnership arrangement with a foreign company or government), whether an acquisition is involved, or whether stock ownership will be made available to the nationals of the country in which the operation is to be located. In addition, where partial ownership is involved, the investor must decide between a majority or minority interest.

There are no ready answers to the question of how extensive ownership should be. Much depends upon such factors as the attitudes of management, the resources available, the nature of the market, the availability and capabilities of potential partners, and policies of foreign governments. Some companies will insist upon 100% ownership and there are advantages to this pattern, particularly that of

EXHIBIT 8.2   How can political risk be assessed?

Political risk has been defined as the application of host government policies that con-strain the business opportunities of a given foreign investment. This can be viewed further as the likelihood that political forces will cause drastic changes in a country's business environment which affect the profit and other goals of a business firm. Such risk is also of concern to the international marketer, particularly one with an investment in a plant or in a sales and marketing operation in a foreign country. Exporters and interna-tional marketers are affected also by the *transfer risk* aspect that includes risk derived from government policies restricting the transfer of capital, payments, products, and so on. In short, tariffs, taxes, nontariff restrictions, and payment for goods exported are of concern.

The Business Environment Risk Index, which has been available since 1972, measures the discrimination of foreigners as compared with nationals as well as the general quality of a country's business climate. BERI is reported for more than 40 countries and is pub-lished quarterly. The overall index is based on 15 weighted criteria, and ranges from 0 to 100 (see Table 8.1). Scores can be interpreted as follows: unusually stable (86–100), typical environment for an industrialized economy (71–85), moderate risk (56–70), high

TABLE 8.1   Criteria included in overall BERI and in sub-indices*

Criteria	Overall index	Political	Operations	Financial	Nationalism
			Weights		
Political stability	3	6			
Economic growth	2.5		5		
Currency convertibility	2.5		5	5	5
Labor cost/productivity	2		3		
Long-term loans/venture capital	2			5	
Short-term credit	2			5	
Attitude towards the foreign investor and profits	1.5	5			8
Nationalization	1.5	5			8
Monetary inflation	1.5	3		3	
Balance of payments	1.5	3		3	
Enforceability of contracts	1.5		4	2	
Bureaucratic delays	1	3		2	4
Communications: Telex, telephone	1		3		
Local management and partners	1		2		
Professional services and contractors	0.5		3		
	25	25	25	25	25

* Rating conditions: superior = 4, above average = 3, acceptable = 2, poor = 1, unacceptable = 0

risk (41–55), unacceptable business conditions (0–40). Four sub-indices also are derived: political, operations, financial, and nationalism. The desirability of using this index in business environmental analyses has been questioned on general grounds regarding risk indicators per se as well as poor empirical evidence to support one of the sub-indices. If risk indicators are to be used they should be supplemented by special information services and in-depth country reports.

Other country risk concepts have been developed by various market research institutes and economic magazines. These are described briefly by Backhaus and Meyer (1986), who in addition discuss their own approach to assessing risk based on factor analysis and then clustering countries with respect to their risk development.

retaining full control over the operation. However, if a company wishes to implement its decision to manufacture abroad by acquisition of an existing firm, complete ownership is often impossible. Furthermore, if operational control of the venture is the main criterion then this can be achieved by holding a majority interest and in some instances even a minority interest. In the latter case this can be accomplished by spreading the ownership throughout the public at large. In cases where political stability is an issue, then joint ownership – even as a minority owner – seems prudent, if the investment is even made. There are instances when the answers to the ownership question are somewhat automatically limited. When a company has limited resources (money, labor, and know-how) it will have to seek out a foreign partner. Also, government policy may limit the choice. For example, in the past, typically China has required shared ownership in many, but not all, ventures there. The Belgian brewer Interbrew owns 70% of K. K. Brewery, the leading beer maker in Zhejiang Province and US-owned Anheuser-Busch has an ownership interest in Tsingtao, China's largest brewer. With the exception of some industrial sectors where they are not allowed (such as assembly of automobiles and aluminum mining), increasingly China has been allowing WFOEs. More and more companies are pursuing the WFOE route rather than EJVs as good partners are hard to find, it takes less time to establish a WFOE, and regulations governing the two types of enterprises are much the same (Vanhonacker, 1997; Johnstone, 1997).

Sometimes government changes its policy about ownership after the investment is made. To illustrate, India in the late 1970s required Coca-Cola and IBM to transfer 60% of their equity to an Indian company. Rather than comply, both companies pulled out. As India's economy has opened more to foreigners, companies that left have been returning, including IBM. In 1993 Coca-Cola returned by establishing a strategic alliance with India's largest soft drink producer, Parle Exports Ltd.

There are times when 100% ownership is not advisable even when government regulations allow it. Ricks (1999, p. 124) cites the case of a US manufacturer of mixed feed for poultry that decided to enter the market in Spain. The company formed a subsidiary that was wholly owned even though local business people advised against it. A factory was built, technical staff were brought in, and operations were set up. Once the plant was running and feed was being produced, the company found it could not sell its products. It turned out that Spanish poultry growers and feed producers were a closely knit group, and newcomers were not welcome. To overcome this the company purchased some chicken farms, and discovered it could not sell its chickens either. If the company had understood the local business environment it would have entered the market in a shared-ownership arrangement, either by acquiring an interest in a Spanish feed producer or by entering into a joint venture agreement.

8.3.4 Implementation of the decision

As previously mentioned, implementation of the decision has only two basic alternative answers: (1) to start from scratch in what is known as a greenfield investment, or (2) to use the acquisition route. From the perspective of market entry, starting from scratch is at best time-consuming. Involved in this approach are such activities as setting up manufacturing facilities, recruiting and training labor, organizing a management team, and so forth. In short, all of the major internal management problems in international business are encountered. Furthermore, a major outlay of cash will be needed.

More and more companies today are turning to acquiring established foreign companies either wholly or in part, as the fastest and most economical way to enter a foreign market (see Exhibit 8.3). There are many examples of acquisitions that represent minority ownership, majority ownership, and total ownership. In the early 1990s in Japan, Eastman Kodak had a 20% interest in Chinon Industries (a supplier of cameras), a 51% share in Kodak Imagica (a photo-finisher), and wholly owned Kodak Information Systems, which had been part of a supplier called Kusuda. In the late 1990s the company was allowed to take over three local companies in China without any debt or labor obligations. Two limited-liability partnerships were formed. Kodak promised to bring to mainland China its best technology and management practices as well as a commitment to raise the country's photographic goods manufacturing industry to global standards. Another example comes from the beer industry in Hungary where the Dutch company Heineken NV acquired 51% of the company Komaron and the Austrian brewer Brau-Union purchased a 70% stake in Martfu and a 51% share of Sopron.

Big Ben, London, UK

| EXHIBIT 8.3 | Merger mania |

Some examples of cross-border mergers and acquisitions are presented below. These are not meant to be all inclusive, but are illustrative.

Following the financial crisis of 1997, cross-border mergers and acquisitions increased greatly in East Asia, particularly in the nontradable services sectors (Mody and Negishi, 2001). Triggering this activity were important policy changes, especially in Korea and Thailand. Although many had hoped this would speed up economic recovery in the region, this did not happen. At the same time such acquisitions were not predatory, although some were based on 'bargain' prices.

During the late 1990s multinationals looked to Latin America for companies to buy. Many so-called 'bargains' were available due to the economic volatility in the area. Some examples are the US-based energy group GPU, Inc. buying the Argentine electricity distributor Emdersa, the French supermarket chain Carrefour taking over Brazilian department store chain Lojas Americanas, Citigroup agreeing to purchase Chile's second-largest consumer fianance company, Corp. Financeria Atlas, and the Dutch bank ABN Amro looking to buy Banco Real of Brazil. Most acquisitions were for strategic, long-term reasons and buyers were looking to strengthen their positions in key markets (Katz, 1999).

European companies have been active in the United States. One of the major reasons is that the US market appears to have growth rate prospects two to three times that of Europe. In addition, taxes and labor rules are relatively less restrictive. Also, the European companies look to mergers and acquisitions as a means to solve many of their strategic challenges. Illustrative examples are the UK's wireless company Vodafone's acquisition of AirTouch Communications, Dutch insurer Aegon buying Transamerica, and the Daimler-Chrysler and British Petroleum-Amoco mergers.

Even in China mergers are on the increase, although most tend to be domestic consolidations. Where a cross-border merger is involved it has been the local Chinese company – state owned or otherwise – that has acquired the foreign company which already had a Chinese operation. Examples are Sanyuan Foods' purchase of the Beijing dairy operations of the US-based Kraft Food International and beer brewer Tsingtao's acquisition of a 75% stake in Danish Carlsberg's Shanghai brewery (Roberts and Webb, 2001).

Retailers have also been active in cross-border mergers, none more so than US-based Wal-Mart, the world's largest retailer. Its entry into Germany was made by acquiring the 21-store Wertkauf chain, which was then followed by its purchase of 74 Interspar hypermarkets. In 1999 Wal-Mart acquired the UK's third largest supermarket chain and leading discount marketer, Asda. It appears that Asda will be used as a base for a further assault on Europe as Wal-Mart sees acquisitions as the main route to take. In 2003 Wal-Mart acquired a controlling interest in Seiyu, a Japanese supermarket. Other examples of retailer acquisitions are the Dutch food retailer Ahold, which has acquired a number of chains in the eastern United States including Giant Foods, Stop & Shop, Tops Markets, and First National Supermarkets and the UK's Kingfisher, which in 2003 acquired control of a French DIY-chain, Castorama. In contrast, other retailers such as the Swedish home furnishing company IKEA and the UK's Marks & Spencer have entered foreign markets by 'greenfield' investments in starting stores from scratch, although Marks & Spencer once owned the US-based Brooks Brothers before selling it to Italian entrepreneur Claudio Del Vecchio in 2001.

Using the acquisition approach does not mean that internal management problems will not exist, because they most certainly will. Acquiring an established firm has perhaps greater advantages than starting from scratch – and there are advantages to both parties. From the point of view of the company doing the acquiring, such action may represent, in the long run, a lower cost despite the fact that it may need an initial cash outlay greater than would be needed to set up a new operation. The reason is simply that, if properly planned and executed, acquisition provides much more than just plant and production facilities. An established and effective marketing organization, market knowledge, overseas management ability, and good government and customer relations are but a few of the possible extras. A major reason underlying Ford Motor Company increasing its ownership in Mazda of Japan to 33.4% (from 24.5%) in mid-1996 was the expectation of great savings in development costs and extending its reach in Japan and Southeast Asia. Moreover, many acquisitions require relatively little cash while others may require none. In the latter case, the investor uses his own stock in payment. Immediate market share may be obtained and competition reduced, as was the situation for the MNC Procter & Gamble's acquisition of the Czech company Rakona.

Underlying many mergers and acquisitions is the wish to create a large enough market share in one principal business, or a small number of related businesses, in order to become a major factor in a market area. To illustrate, consider the situation of the UK company Thorn EMI. Through several acquisitions Thorn gained market leadership in the fragmented western European commercial and industrial light fittings market. More than 50% of its sales in these businesses came from outside its UK home market. Sometimes acquiring a number of companies in a market does not work too well. The Swiss watchmaker Asuag A6 needed to acquire technology and did this by purchasing 12 different firms in the United States. Although some of the companies were useful they did not seem to fit together well. Many were not even compatible. Eventually, all 12 were sold – at a big loss (Ricks, 1999, p. 125).

The advantages to the acquired company are just as real. A badly needed infusion of cash may be forthcoming, which can be used to finance R&D, market development, and similar activities. Needed expertise may also result from acquisition. Also, the acquired company may have access to a wide-ranging sales network.

There are, however, some potential limitations to the acquisition approach. To begin with, finding available companies is not always easy. Many of the potentially good ones are hard to convince that it would be advantageous for them to sell while those that are up for sale are quite likely to be in some type of distressed condition. Thus often an exhaustive study of the possibilities must be made and, once a candidate is selected, negotiations are entered into. There may be situations where prospects for acquisition simply do not exist, or where government policies make acquisition difficult, if not impossible. There is increasing scrutiny of mergers by the antitrust regulators in the United States and by the European Commission in the EU. For example, mergers blocked in the EU during the period 1998–2000 included MCI World Com/Sprint, Volvo/Scania, and Deutsche Telekom/BetaResearch.

In addition to the usual concerns in acquiring a company – paying a fair price, melding two management teams, and gaining the elusive 'synergy' that is supposed to add to profits – there are special risks and costs attached to cross-border mergers, as follows:

- Foreign acquirers usually pay more than a domestic buyer would, often with unrealistic hopes of future synergies.
- Differences of language and national and corporate cultures aggravate integration of two management teams, and possibly two headquarters.
- Misperceptions about the home market of the acquired company can lead to marketing mistakes.
- Vertical integration is much harder in cross-border deals than intracountry deals.
- Employees tend to be even more frightened of new management if bosses are from another country. This was a concern of Chrysler employees in the Daimler-Chrysler merger.

These challenges often involve wide differences in distance, language, and cultures that can lead to misunderstandings and conflicts.

There are two important potential problems that may arise. First, there is often a difficult problem of integrating practices and operating methods of the acquired company into the overall company structure and philosophy. This includes a need often to integrate *management styles*, or the patterns of decision making that exist in each company. In a study of Korean and Japanese management styles, Lee *et al.* (2000) found substantial differences in the two country styles. Albaum and Herche (1999) concluded that within the European Union there were differences in the management styles of Danish, Spanish, Dutch, French, and Finnish decision makers, using five underlying dimensions of decision making. In addition, a recent study reported differences in the management style of managers in six Pacific Rim countries – Australia, China, Vietnam, New Zealand, Hong Kong SAR of PRC, and the Philippines (Albaum *et al.*, 2004). The Pacific Rim managers differed from those in Europe.

Second, there may arise the problem of how to gracefully and diplomatically remove any former owners who may be impeding the development of the new company and who still own an important share of, or have some type of a contract with, the acquired company. These last two problems are avoided by starting from scratch. Furthermore, acquisition will seldom be the best route to take if a company wants to build its overseas operations according to the pattern of its home operation. However, a company must be careful here as it is not always desirable to extend a home country approach to a foreign-based operation.

A hybrid approach has been termed *brownfield* investment. A brownfield investment represents a special form of acquisition, and has been defined as:

> A foreign acquisition undertaken as part of the establishment of a local operation. From the outset, its resources and capabilities are provided by the investor, replacing most [but not all] resources and capabilities of the acquired firm (Meyer and Estrin, 2001, p. 577).

This form of entry is attractive if high transaction costs inhibit the more traditional approaches and if local resources are necessary, but not sufficient for the venture.

Needed resources include resources held by the local firms (assets, technology, etc.), the investor (managerial services, financial capital, transferable knowledge, etc.), and the markets (real estate, labor skills, etc.) The choice of entry is illustrated in Figure 8.3, which shows the conditions favoring the conventional acquisition, brownfield, and greenfield approaches.

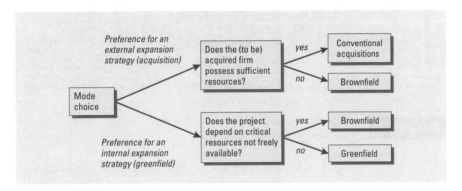

FIGURE 8.3

Entry mode choice
Source: Meyer and Estrin, 2001, p. 581

Regardless of the route generally favored by a company, it is quite important that the attitude and policies of management be flexible. Each foreign market area and each potential project is unique, and management must approach its decision making with an open mind.

An example of a global organization that was built largely by acquisition is Rupert Murdoch's News Corp. Figure 8.4 shows News Corp.'s worldwide distribution footprint for satellite and cable systems, including Direct TV, BSkyB, Sky Italia, Start TV, Innva, Sky Brasil, Sky Chile, Sky Colombia, Foxtel, and Direct TV Latin America. Adding the 175 newspapers published, News Corp. has a global media empire (Yang *et al.*, 2004).

8.4 Assembly operations

A manufacturer that wants many of the advantages associated with having overseas manufacturing facilities and yet does not want to go that far may find it desirable to establish overseas assembly facilities in selected markets. In a sense, the establishment of an assembly operation represents a cross between exporting and overseas manufacturing. Often it is difficult to distinguish assembly from full manufacturing, especially in industries such as automobiles and personal computers.

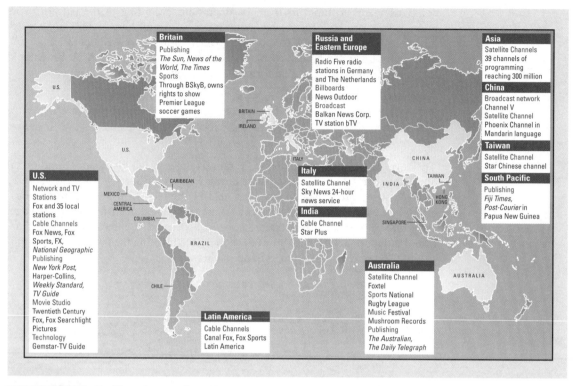

Britain
Publishing
The Sun, News of the World, The Times
Sports
Through BSkyB, owns rights to show Premier League soccer games

Russia and Eastern Europe
Radio Five radio stations in Germany and The Netherlands
Billboards
News Outdoor
Broadcast
Balkan News Corp.
TV station bTV

Asia
Satellite Channels
39 channels of programming reaching 300 million

China
Broadcast network Channel V
Satellite Channel Phoenix Channel in Mandarin language

Taiwan
Satellite Channel Star Chinese channel

U.S.
Network and TV Stations
Fox and 35 local stations
Cable Channels
Fox News, Fox Sports, FX, *National Geographic*
Publishing
New York Post, Harper-Collins, *Weekly Standard, TV Guide*
Movie Studio
Twentieth Century Fox, Fox Searchlight Pictures
Technology
Gemstar-TV Guide

Italy
Satellite Channel Sky News 24-hour news service

India
Cable Channel Star Plus

South Pacific
Publishing
Fiji Times, Post-Courier in Papua New Guinea

Australia
Satellite Channel
Foxtel
Sports National Rugby League
Music Festival Mushroom Records
Publishing
The Australian, The Daily Telegraph

Latin America
Cable Channels
Canal Fox, Fox Sports Latin America

FIGURE 8.4	The News Corp. media empire
	Source: Yang *et al.*, 2004, p. 54

In its purest sense, when engaged in foreign-market assembly operations a manufacturing company exports all or most of its product in a 'knocked-down' condition. That is, the various components or parts of the product are exported. At the foreign assembly site these parts are then put together to form the complete product.

When a product is exported in this manner in large quantities some potential cost savings may be realized (relative to what the costs would be if the item exported was the complete product). Often freight charges and various foreign government fees are lower; and in some countries for certain products Customs duties are frequently less for component parts than for the complete product. There is a cost saving in manufacturing at the home plant, especially costs permitted by automation or economies of scale. On the other hand the assembly operation may be labor intensive and lower wages abroad may permit a cost reduction. In addition to being cheaper, a company may prefer assembly because it allows most of the production, value added, and technology to remain at home where it can be better controlled.

Of course not all of this cost saving is realized by a manufacturer in the form of greater profit. The costs incurred in assembling the product at the overseas site may offset some, all, or more than the saving associated with this type of export. In addition, overseas assembly operations require a capital investment, although generally it will be much less than that needed to operate a branch manufacturing plant. For various reasons some of the component parts may have to be sourced either in the country where the assembly operation is located or in some other foreign location.

There is a certain amount of flexibility in foreign assembly that can be turned into a cost saving. By assembling its product overseas, a manufacturer is in a position to buy some of its manufactured components from local low-cost sources of supply. In fact it may be forced into using these sources if the nature of the foreign market requires that it modify its product in such a way that key component parts with the necessary operating characteristics are not normally available in its home country. From a cost point of view, therefore, it may be better for the manufacturer to export its product (either as components or as a semicomplete unit) and assemble it in the foreign market using parts from local sources than it would be to try to export a complete product by either importing the necessary parts, manufacturing them, or arranging for another firm in the home country to produce them. To illustrate, a German manufacturer of small appliances will have to modify its products when the foreign market uses 110 volt current. This will have an effect on the components to be put into the appliances. Under certain conditions this manufacturer will find it advantageous to assemble the product overseas, using components manufactured in the country where 110 volt current is being used.

Assembly overseas can, under the right conditions, be turned into a useful marketing tool. Much depends upon whether the assembly facility is regarded by the potential customers as being a national or indigenous company of the country in which it is located. This can be extremely important in those countries where there is a fervor of nationalism that leads to favoring national companies over foreign companies.

Nationalism can also exert its influence through foreign government attitudes and policies. Local assembly may satisfy the government so long as some local employment is created or a certain share of the finished product's content is of local origin. This, however, might indicate the need to eventually establish a full manufacturing operation, as some companies have found out!

Another dimension of government that can influence where an assembly facility is located is the tax code and the tax bureaucracy that goes along with it. This situation in Russia, together with the risks associated with the crime situation there, led the Taiwanese firm Acer Computers to establish in the mid-1990s its assembly facility for serving the Russian market in Finland. In addition to a relatively short time from start of assembly to being available in the marketplace, locating in Finland had the advantage of a special customs regime tailored to firms trading with Russia allowing them to bring in goods from outside the European Union and reexporting them to Russia with a minimum of formalities. Acer maintained a representative office in Russia. The products were to be sold to Russian distributors at the factory gate in Finland. These distributors had to arrange for the import into Russia. An incidental benefit to Acer was that Finnish assembly would make the product more desirable to Russian buyers than assembly in Russia would have done.

Whether by choice or by pressure applied from outside, foreign-based assembly may represent one stage in the evolutionary process of a manufacturer changing from a domestic-oriented company to a truly multinational marketer.

Foreign assembly points can be an integral part of a multinational or global manufacturer's worldwide marketing organization and can be tied directly to manufacturing plants, wherever these plants are located. Although foreign assembly costs much less than establishing a basic manufacturing facility, an assembly plant will not be good for every manufacturer or product. However, even when this type of operation has no production cost advantages the needs of the local market for product variations may make it desirable to assemble locally. In addition, one assembly plant can serve many nearby markets. If this is the case, then a manufacturer might find it advantageous to locate its foreign assembly facility in a free area. Whether this is practical, of course, depends upon relative tariff rates of the markets to be served by this facility.

An approach to assembling automobiles involving modular assembly is being used by Volkswagen and General Motors in Brazil. Both companies have their suppliers located at the assembly site where they manufacture their components. In the case of Volkswagen the employees of seven main suppliers are attaching their components to the cars on the assembly line. In short, they are directly involved in the final assembly of finished trucks and buses (*Business Week*, 1996). In contrast, the suppliers at the GM facility deliver pre-assembled modules to GM's line workers, who then piece the car together (Wheatley, 2000). In both cases these plants are viewed as potential models for assembly plants throughout the world.

8.5 Strategic alliances

8.5.1 Nature of strategic alliances

Licensing, contracting, and joint ventures are three types of activity between companies from two or more countries that have come to be known as *strategic alliances*. Other types include R&D consortia and partnerships, cross-marketing agreements, cross-manufacturing agreements, and cross-distribution agreements. All these can be considered strategic marketing alliances as they enhance marketplace leverage. Such alliances are increasing in incidence and will be prominent through the first decade of the 2000s as a way to operate in global markets. Examples are as follows: Boeing joined with the Japanese companies Mitsubishi, Fuji, and Kawasaki Heavy Industries to develop, manufacture, and market a small jet aircraft; AT&T, KDD of Japan, Singapore Telecom, and other Asian telephone carriers formed World Partners; British Telecom and MCI Communications formed Concert, which has distribution agreements with Norwegian Telecom, Tele Danmark, Telecom Finland, and Nippon Information & Communication; Korea's Samsung is acquiring technology from Japanese companies such as Fujitsu, Toshiba, and NEC. IBM and Germany's Siemens are sharing technology with Toshiba in its development of advanced, new generation semiconductors. As these examples show, alliances are formed between companies that can complement each other as well as companies that are competing in certain products, markets, or both. Such alliances are a necessity. There are so many different technologies changing the basis of competition in numerous industries, and changes occur rapidly, that no country, much less any single company is self-sufficient any more. Hence there is a recognition that sharing costs and resources has become a necessity and that marketing and distribution partnerships can be very attractive under the right conditions. Indeed, licensing and joint venture have been around for a long time. It is the label 'strategic alliance' that is relatively new.

There are many definitions of strategic alliance. Some examples are as follows:

- A formal and mutually agreed commercial collaboration between companies. The partners pool, exchange or integrate specified business resources for mutual gain. Yet the partners remain separate businesses (Business International, 1990, p. 27).
- A long-term collaboration between two or more companies that combine core competencies of the partners to build global advantages. Specific motivations of partners may be resource sharing or market access (Root, 1994, pp. 292–6).
- Linkages between companies from different countries to jointly pursue a common goal that have the following characteristics: independence of participants, shared benefits, and ongoing contributions in technology, products and other key strategic areas (Keegan and Green, 2000, p. 324).

A fundamental purpose of an international, or global, strategic alliance is to enhance the long-run competitiveness of the strategic partners. Such an alliance is founded on a belief that each party has something unique to contribute, for example technology, managerial know-how, market access. This requires that power and control be shared in the interest of mutual benefit.

Very broadly, the following advantages from interfirm agreements such as strategic alliances have been identified by Gugler (1992, p. 91):

- sharing of the large investments needed for specific activities such as in R&D;
- access to complementary resources such as technologies;
- accelerating return on investment through a more rapid turnover on the firm's assets;
- spreading of risks;
- efficiency creation through economies of scale, specialization and/or rationalization;
- coopting competition.

Any strategic alliance has certain core dimensions. If any of these are lacking, problems can arise and there can be conflict between individual company goals and alliance goals. These interrelated core dimensions are as follows (Spekman and Sawhney, 1990, pp. 6–9):

- *Goal compatibility*: each party's goals must be compatible to the extent that both alliance and individual party goals can be achieved.
- *Strategic advantage*: there must be a perceived benefit.
- *Interdependence*: each partner will be dependent upon the other and the relationship must be managed such that conflict is held to a minimum while cooperation emerges victorious.
- *Commitment*: trust is crucial to the long-run viability of an alliance and is vital to the pledge of relational continuity between partners that underlies commitment.
- *Communication and conflict resolution*: partners need to communicate with each other and there is a need to have a mechanism, other than legal, to resolve conflicts that inevitably will arise.
- *Coordination of work*: it is clear that work among the partners be coordinated without a bureaucracy and costs of ownership.
- *Planning*: the first things to plan are the structure and processes of exchange; then the substance of exchange can be tackled.

Other principles for success are illustrated in Exhibit 8.4, which looks at the auto industry in Asia. A key issue in partner selection is the degree of possible fit to the other partner's profile. The ideal partner for, say, a UK company may very well differ from that for a medium-sized Chinese company, or a small US high-technology company. The dimensions of fit are as follows (Lasserre and Schutte, 1995, pp. 180–90):

- *Strategic*. Are objectives compatible? How long a commitment will be made?
- *Resources*. Are the partners willing and able to contribute to the critical resources and competencies needed for success?
- *Cultural*. Do the partners understand each other, can they communicate, and do they share the same business logic?
- *Organizational*. How do the management styles fit and are they conducive to good communication and effective monitoring of the alliance?

The automobile industry offers an interesting illustration of how different companies active in global markets approach their markets differently:

1. **General Motors** prefers minority ownership or alliances, but did take full ownership of Saab. Holds 49% of Isuzu Motors, 10% of Suzuki Motors, 20% of Fuji Heavy Industries, makers of Subaru, and 20% of Fiat, and has a joint venture in the United States with Toyota.
2. **Ford** owns Jaguar and Volvo entirely, owns 33% and controls Mazda, and owns about 17% of Kia with whom it also has an agreement to take cars under the Ford name on a contract manufacturing basis.
3. **DaimlerChrysler** prefers outright ownership.
4. **Toyota** prefers alliances. Owns 51% of Daihatsu, has 33% of truckmaker Hino Motors, and builds cars in the United States with General Motors.

EXHIBIT 8.4 — How to succeed in a joint venture/strategic alliance

There have been many international joint ventures in the automobile industry. Often they did not make much profit. Because of that, and for other reasons as well, there have been dissolutions of the venture.

There is a major exception – Ford – Mazda. Their more than 30-year collaboration has weathered disagreements about specific projects, trade disputes between Japan and the United States, and allegations that Mazda and other Japanese companies engaged in dumping practices for minivans exported to the United States.

Ford and Mazda cooperate on new vehicles and exchange valuable expertise – Ford in international marketing and finance, Mazda in manufacturing and product development. For Ford, the payoff has been partly in the form of sales. But the alliance also taught Ford some practical lessons that it applied elsewhere in its business.

A major question is, why has this alliance been the success it has? According to the presidents of the two companies there are seven principles that have been followed (*Business Week*, 1992a):

1. **Top management must be continually involved:** Top management must set a tone for the relationship. If not, lower-level managers will resist sharing control of a project with a partner.
2. **Meet frequently, and often informally:** Meetings should occur at all levels and should include time for socializing. This is essential for building trust.
3. **Use a matchmaker:** A third party can mediate disputes, suggest new ways of approaching the partner, and be an independent 'listener.'
4. **Maintain independence:** Independence helps both partners to sharpen the areas of expertise that made them desirable partners in the first place.
5. **Allow no 'sacrifice' deals:** Every project must be viable for each partner. It is top management's responsibility to ensure that an overall balance is maintained.
6. **Have a monitor:** Someone must have the primary responsibility for monitoring all aspects of the alliance.
7. **Anticipate cultural differences:** They may be corporate or national. All parties should be flexible, and should try to place culturally sensitive managers in key posts.

The principles really are quite simple!

There is a wide range in complexity of strategic alliance relationships. On the one side there are the relatively 'simple' alliance structures as illustrated by the Star Alliance of United Airlines, Lufthansa, SAS, Thai and several other airlines, where they coordinate schedules (including flight code sharing), marketing, joint facilities, and other amenities for passengers. Somewhat more complex is the alliance formed in 1991 between the US pharmaceutical company Sterling Winthrop and the French firm Samofe. In the alliance, each company continues separate R&D operations. They then jointly develop, manufacture, and market any promising pharmaceutical compounds from these research efforts. At the other extreme are very complex networks involving many partners such as that found by the large Dutch electrical and electronics company Philips, as shown in Figure 8.5. Entire industries may be affected by strategic alliances such as that for the semiconductor industry (see Gugler, 1992), and the telecommunications industry.

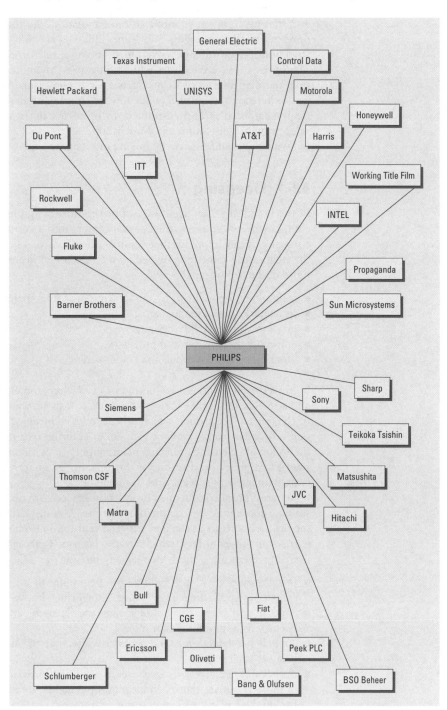

FIGURE 8.5

Philips' alliance network
Source: Gugler, 1992, p. 97

Strategic alliances are not static. They can be changing all the time. For example, the joint venture between Ford and Volkswagen established in the 1980s to service the Brazil and Argentina markets was dissolved in the mid-1990s. Another example comes from the global telecommunications industry. Telefónica de España, the largest communications provider in Latin America, and AT&T have both left an alliance with smaller European telecoms known as Unisource to pursue other interests. Telefonica joined with MCI Worldcom, but this alliance is reported to have accomplished almost nothing. The major problem with telecommunications alliances has been that partners are wary of integrating operations and sharing competitive information. Companies do not want to give up control of resources (Rocks, 1999). Sometimes alliances are changed due to pressures from stockholders, customers, government policy, and other 'outside' pressures. In 1996 PepsiCo severed all ties with its Burmese (Myanmar) bottler and all production and distribution of its products ended. The company stated that it took this action in recognition of US policy toward Burma and in deference to the desires of many shareholders and customers. In other instances alliances fail due to slow sales growth. For example in March 2003 Starbucks Corp. ended a joint venture in Switzerland and Austria by buying out its partners.

8.5.2 Licensing

In the broadest sense, licensing is a method of foreign market operation where a company in one country (the licensor) enters into a contractual agreement with a company or person in another country (the licensee) whereby the licensee is given the right to use something owned by the licensor. A license usually involves one or more of the following:

- technology, know-how, manufacturing processes (patented and nonpatented);
- trademark, brand name, logos;
- product and/or facility design;
- marketing knowledge and processes;
- other types of knowledge and trade secrets.

In his research monograph Contractor (1985) recommends to corporate planners and strategists that they view a license as a strategic wedge where technology can be the centerpiece around which other modes of business can be built. He suggests that a broader package might include, in addition to a technology license, any of the following elements: turnkey plant, supply of components to the licensee, contract assembly or production for third countries, guaranteed 'buy-back' in lieu of cash, management service, and so forth.

Where a branded or named product or service is involved, the licensee is responsible for marketing in a defined market area. Along with this responsibility go all the profits and risks associated with the venture. In exchange, the licensee pays the licensor royalties or fees, which are the licensor's main source of income from its licensing operations, and which usually include the following:

- *Initial payment*: a sum paid at the beginning of an agreement for the initial transfer of special machinery, parts, blueprints, knowledge, and so on.
- *Annual minimum*: the amount that the licensee must pay each year to the licensor as a minimum guarantee.
- *Annual percentage fee*: the actual royalty that the licensee agrees to pay the licensor each year.
- *Additional fees*: to cover expenses, a fee in the form of a prepaid royalty is used in those countries that prohibit initial payments. In addition, fees are also paid for any new plans, blueprints, and so on.

A license agreement may also be one of *cross-licensing* wherein there is a mutual exchange of knowledge and/or patents. In cross-licensing there may or may not be a cash payment involved.

Licensing is a cross between exporting and direct investment and involves a little of each. The licensor exports whatever the agreement is concerned with, but this export is in effect an investment.

A special type of licensing should be distinguished – *franchising*. Franchising is really incomplete licensing. In licensing, the licensor allows a foreign company to manufacture a complete product whereas in a franchise agreement the franchisor usually supplies an important ingredient (part, material, and so on) for the finished product. Franchise agreements are perhaps best known in the nonalcoholic beverage and retail fast food industries. For example, Coca-Cola has a worldwide network of franchised bottlers and supplies them with the syrup needed to produce its product. In the fast food field McDonald's golden arches are to be found throughout the world, including Russia and China. Similarly, Kentucky Fried Chicken is found worldwide. In many countries franchising will be combined with a joint venture. US-based Krispy Kreme Doughnuts opened its first store in the UK in the early 2000s and has plans to open more then 20 additional stores by the mid 2000s under a franchise agreement with both Cheshire and Kent, Ltd and Donald Henshall. The company also has plans for Australia and New Zealand.

Objectives and evaluation

Most companies have one or more of the following basic objectives in mind when they negotiate a license agreement and use licensing as a method of penetrating foreign markets:

- Obtaining revenue from company-owned patents, trademarks, and accumulated know-how.
- Gaining some tactical or strategic advantage in marketing its products in foreign markets.
- Acquiring reciprocal know-how and research developments from foreign companies.
- Gaining a foothold in the market to be used at a later date for a move into other types of foreign-market based marketing activity.
- Entering a market per se, or remaining in a market when conditions (including government action) make export undesirable or impossible.
- The company wants to have a foreign-market production presence but does not want, or may not be able, to make a capital investment.
- Contributing to economic development where needed.

Licensing offers many potential benefits to the licensor; at the same time, though, there are significant potential drawbacks. Probably the basic advantage in licensing as contrasted to other approaches is the ease and low cost of entering a foreign market. Large capital outlays are avoided as well as the expense of tying up personnel and production at home to satisfy unstable foreign markets. The licensor, in effect, uses the licensee's management, capital equipment, and knowledge (of the market and working environment) to exploit whatever markets are served by the licenses; royalty income can then be viewed virtually as a return of the technology alone. Thus, this method is particularly well suited to a small-sized manufacturer and others with limited financial and labor resources. For example, one of the reasons that Gerber Products Company, a manufacturer of baby food, entered the Japanese market through licensing when it did was that the company had a staffing problem; the company did not have enough bilingual people to operate a foreign subsidiary. Licensing is also advantageous in that it can be used to test a foreign market without the risk of capital loss should the market not be receptive to the manufacturer's product.

On the other hand, the greatest disadvantages to the licensor are that a potential competitor is set up, there is a lack of control over production and marketing, there may be incomplete market exploration, and there could be a loss in flexibility since it is often difficult to coordinate a licensee into a worldwide marketing plan. There are, of course, methods that a licensor can use to minimize the chances that a licensee will become a potential competitor. In the first place, if the arrangement is very profitable to the licensee, he or she will probably want things to remain as they are. Second, an option to buy into the licensee's company can be beneficial, and often rewarding if the operation is highly successful. This allows the licensor to become a partner, and the licensee is less likely to want to dissolve the agreement. Finally, probably the best way to maintain control and keep the arrangement intact is through marketing, particularly through innovation and product development. That is, the best way to keep a licensee happy and under control is to provide him with a continuing flow of innovations and product features or know-how that surpass what he could do personally. In this way the licensee receives something valuable on a continuing basis in return for the royalty that must be paid.

Policy decisions

Any company that is considering a new or expanded foreign licensing program is well advised to consider the company's interests and abilities to be a licensor, and to formulate certain basic policies before entering into any agreements. Included among those factors affecting the company itself are its existing stake and status in foreign markets, its objectives and future plans for foreign markets, alternatives for achieving the objectives, suitability of products for licensing, adequacy of existing organization and personnel to handle a licensing program, possible repercussions on the international and domestic operations, and the expected return in relation to effort, resources, and risks involved. All of these factors, and others as well, must be weighed in determining the feasibility of a licensing program. Moreover, a systematic and thorough evaluative technique should be used on prospective foreign licensees.

By broadly reviewing the factors just mentioned, a company will be able to make certain basic policy decisions. While such decisions cannot be applied automatically or inflexibly to specific proposed projects, they will provide a general frame of reference and set the general pattern for a program consistent with the company's objectives and other operations. Policy decisions must be made on the following issues:

- whether a licensing activity of any type is feasible and worth considering;
- purpose and main objectives of a licensing activity;
- place of licensing in present and long-range plans;
- relative emphasis to be placed on licensing activity;
- products, rights, and services to be available for licensing;
- market areas open to licensing activity;
- general type of agreement and relationship to be sought with licensees;
- attitude toward equity participation;
- management direction and responsibility for licensing;
- financial control and disposition of licensing income.

The importance of viewing a licensing agreement in the light of its short- and long-term implications to a company both at home and abroad cannot be overemphasized. To illustrate, consider the experience of one US company that initially exported to foreign markets. As the markets grew, local competition appeared. To combat this competition, the US company entered into a licensing arrangement with a leading European manufacturer. Extensive provisions for transmitting know-how were incorporated in the agreement. As foreign markets for the product became larger than the domestic market, the US company found itself blocked in planning any overseas expansion by its agreement to share design and production developments with what would be its European competitor. Furthermore, the European licensee had lower production costs than its licensor. The final blow came when the licensee set up its own marketing outlets in the United States and began to compete in the home market with the very company that had supplied it with know-how in the first place.

Why do licensees become involved with inward licensing? Some clues are available from a study of Australian licensee and nonlicensee companies in the engineering, pharmaceutical, and chemical industries (Atuahene-Gima, 1993). Compared to nonlicensee firms, those with license arrangements believed that major benefits of inward licensing are gaining a competitive advantage and increasing sales/market expansion. Other benefits perceived by licensees include quicker market entry, reducing new product development risk, and saving resources for internal use.

One final comment. All licensing agreements must have provisions for handling disputes between licensor and licensee, perhaps even allowing for arbitration. In addition, the conditions under which the licensor or the licensee can terminate the agreement must be specified, including what happens to any trademarks, patents, sublicenses, or other forms of intellectual property.

8.5.3 Contracting

In addition to licensing and franchising agreements, other contractual entry modes are *contract manufacturing* and *management contracting*. We discuss each briefly.

Contract manufacturing

This approach to foreign market entry is a cross between licensing and direct investment. A company contracts for the manufacture or assembly of its product(s) by manufacturers established in foreign markets, either targeted for sales there or elsewhere while still retaining the responsibility for marketing and distributing its products. Often the contract will call for a transfer of technology and provide for technical assistance to the foreign-market based manufacturer. Despite any transfers, this method of foreign market entry is purely a sourcing activity. In the personal computer industry in mid-1996, for example, Taiwan's Acer delivered a large number of its products to other computer makers such as Apple, which were sold under the buyer's brand names. More recently, Compaq signed an agreement to have the Chinese company Dawn produce computers with the Compaq name destined for the Chinese market. Finally, Best Buy, the largest electronics retail chain in North America, set up contracts in Asia in early 2002 to manufacture its new 'house-brand' computer, VPR Matrix. With the exception of Dell Computers, most of the world's personal computer manufacturing is handled by six Asian contractors (Malik, 2003).

The mobile phone industry is turning to contract manufacturing, or outsourcing the manufacturing of handsets. Sweden's Ericsson has gone entirely to contract manufacturing while the US-based Motorola is using this for most of its production. Even Finland's Nokia, the global leader, will outsource about 15% of its production. The major reason for this is cost.

As with all methods of serving foreign markets, contract manufacturing has its advantages and disadvantages. Although the disadvantages appear to be quite formidable, for many companies they are far outweighed by the advantages. Some of the major advantages are as follows:

- It requires minimum investment of cash, time, and executive talent – particularly desirable where the market is risky – and permits rapid entry into a new market.
- It gives control over marketing and after-sales service and protects a trademark.
- It avoids currency risks and financing problems.
- It is particularly desirable where a local production base is needed (that is, inside tight controls or high tariff barriers, or where the government requires local manufacture) but the size of the market does not warrant an investment.
- It allows labeling a product as 'locally made,' which is beneficial where nationalistic feelings are strong.
- It avoids intracorporate pricing problems that can arise with a subsidiary, foreign branch, or joint venture.

There are some potential drawbacks that must be acknowledged. First, the profit from manufacturing is transferred to the contractor. Second, like licensing, it trains a potential competitor that will have the know-how to manufacture a high-quality product. This is especially true when the agreement calls for exchange of research and know-how (which may sometimes benefit both companies). One answer is to develop better products constantly so that the contract manufacturer will not want to compete with only the old products and will extend the relationship. Third, it is often difficult to find a satisfactory manufacturer, and even then a transfer of technology may be required. Fourth, again as with licensing, there is little control of manufacturing quality, other than refusing to accept products that do not meet specifications. Finally, since many contract operations are done in developing countries, critics claim that workers are being exploited by low wages, poor working conditions, and no benefits. In China, where there is abundant cheap labor, plenty of engineers and good infrastructure, the charge has been made that subcontractors use prison labor, or that workers in other cases are mistreated by employers. In short, claims are made that so-called 'sweat shops' are being used. Often such claims are made by persons using a self-reference criterion and applying the employment situation in their own, usually a developed, country as a baseline. In the late 1990s Nike came under attack for its contract operations in Asia, especially Indonesia. Other companies such as Wal-Mart, Adidas-Solomon, Disney, Mattel, and Reebok have also been singled out. While such claims may have validity in some instances, in others it has been shown that workers are better off than those working for domestic employers not doing contract manufacturing. Still, those companies using Asian contract manufacturers have developed codes of conduct for their suppliers and have developed monitoring systems from self-policing to hiring outsiders (*Business Week*, 2000c; *The Economist*, 1999).

This method allows a company to have foreign-based sourcing without making a final commitment to establish both complete manufacturing and selling operations; yet the way is kept open for implementing a long-term foreign development policy when the time is right. These considerations are perhaps most important to the company with limited resources or wanting to measure more accurately the long-run profit potential of various foreign markets. Contract manufacturing allows a company to at least gain a beachhead with minimum risk when foreign markets are being more thoroughly evaluated. Thus, if it decides to enter a market permanently where it has previously contracted manufacturing, a company can do so with less difficulty and cost because competitive products would not be as firmly entrenched as they could be in the absence of such a contract arrangement.

Companies within the same industry do not always follow the same strategy regarding production. The retail clothing industry is a good example. Sweden's Hennes & Mauritz (H&M) outsources its production to suppliers in Europe and Asia, the US's Gap outsources all production, but Spain's Zara has the bulk of its production handled by the company's own manufacturing facilities in Spain.

Management contracting

In management contracting the international marketer operates a company in a foreign market for a local investor of the country in which the company is located. The local investor provides the capital for the enterprise, while the international marketer provides the necessary know-how to manage the company. The agreement between the two parties may give the international marketer an option to buy all or a part of the newly created company. A good illustration of this type of arrangement is the Hilton hotel system. Hilton manages hotels throughout the world. Another example is that, in the United Kingdom, London's southeast commuter belt rail service is being operated by a unit of the French company Générale des Eaux.

A specialized form of management contract is the *turnkey operation*. Such an operation typically calls for the construction of a plant, training of personnel, and the initial operation of the plant for a local investor. The client, in essence, acquires a complete operational system together with the skills and abilities to operate the system following its completion and initial operating experience.

For the 'outside' firm the use of management contracts as a mode of entering foreign markets offers a low-risk way into a foreign market, if used with some type of purchase option. It allows a company to manage, and in many ways control (in a functional sense), another company without equity control or legal responsibility. There is a 'guaranteed' minimum income from a joint operation, and unlike other types of joint foreign operations the return is quick. Also, exchange or other types of remittance controls are often avoided. Finally, a management contract arrangement establishes clarity in administration and decision making. By so doing, it tends to minimize the disputes that can arise between the partners in a joint operation, which can be a major problem in other forms of joint foreign operations. Thus the need for arbitration is lessened, which is a real advantage, since arbitration is usually very costly for all concerned, causes bad feelings among the parties involved, and seldom satisfies either side.

From the point of view of the international marketer, there are some important drawbacks to using management contracts. In the first place, the contract itself is a complex, expensive legal document, which must differ for each case. Because it is complex, many potential problem areas cannot possibly be foreseen in advance and these may lead to disputes and legal questions at a later time. More importantly, a management contract arrangement can limit future management and investment decisions depending upon the terms of the contract and the possibility of a conflict of interest arising. The international marketer is bound by the contract, which may not allow it to set up its own operations for a period of time, if at all. Finally, since the international marketer has to supply personnel to operate the local company, this can hinder the firm's other operations if there is a shortage of qualified management personnel available.

There is a resource investment involved – time, personnel, and managerial know-how. All of these are scarce. Consequently, a proposal for management contracting must be evaluated in light of the overall long-term objectives of the firm. This is of especial importance to an international marketer with a long-term interest in a particular foreign market. If there is no purchase option, or if it appears that the company should not exercise its option when one exists, then a potential formidable competitor has been set up. When the company finally decides to enter the market in its own way, the difficulty and cost of doing so will be that much greater.

8.5.4 Joint venture

As a way of engaging in international marketing by foreign production, joint ventures are quite popular. In some foreign markets this may be the only way to enter, except under very special circumstances. Joint ventures are favored by developing countries in general, but are widely used in developed countries as well.

There is a problem in defining just what is meant by joint venture. Certainly, the basic concept in the joint venture is that of partnership, which has two sides – *technical* and *emotional*. On the technical side, there is a joining of contributions; on the emotional side, there is a feeling of cooperative effort.

In the widest sense, any form of association that implies collaboration or cooperation for more than a very transitory period comprises a joint venture. For the purposes of this book at this time, we include only those ventures that involve the sharing of ownership and control in an economic enterprise. Moreover, it will be recalled that earlier in this chapter we defined a joint venture as occurring when companies from at least two different countries, generally one being local, form a *new company* to manufacture/produce products or provide a service on a joint basis. Excluded are other types of shared ownership, especially those involving an acquisition by one company of most or only a part of another company. Much of what was said about shared ownership is applicable to joint ventures as well. Furthermore, many of the advantages of the other types of strategic alliances are applicable, as are drawbacks and limitations.

One approach to identifying the ownership structure of international joint ventures (IJVs) is proposed by Makino and Beamish (1998). Using partnership nationality and partner affiliation, four distinct types of joint ventures are shown in Figure 8.6.

In this schema, home country refers to the foreign company and host country refers to the country where the joint venture is to be located and operated. The traditional IJV is where a foreign company joins with a local company in the market, and the two companies are not affiliated in any other way. This is a useful schema as it identifies joint ventures in a foreign market where neither of the partners are local (cross-national domestic joint ventures (DJVs) and trinational IJVs). There has been limited empirical research done on so-called nonresident-firm-based joint ventures. Pan and Tse (1996) studied this phenomenon in China regarding type of operation and level of control.

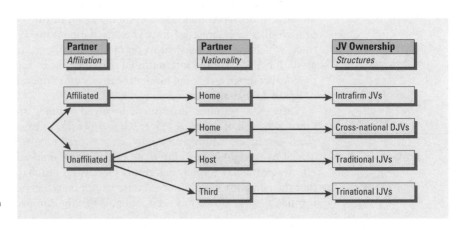

FIGURE 8.6

Joint venture ownership structure options
Source: Makino and Beamish (1998), p. 801

Joint ventures may be either specialized ventures or shared value-added ventures. Specialization ventures are generally organized around functions such as marketing or manufacturing. Each partner adds something unique that adds value – for example, one partner designs products while the other produces them. In shared-value ventures, partners equally engage in value-adding activities – for example, there is a designer team created (Gilroy, 1993, p. 156).

Every potential joint venture must be evaluated on its own merits. No categorical statement can be made concerning whether an international marketer should adhere to a policy of engaging in joint ventures. However, certain general comments can be made, which can point out possible conditions that should be considered by a firm in evaluating proposed projects.

Joint ventures are sometimes the best way to get started in an overseas market because they allow a company with limited capital and labor resources to enter more overseas markets than would be possible if the company established subsidiaries. Because of the resource savings and the potential ability to enter more markets, business risks can be minimized. Risk is also minimized because management skills and experience from a local partner allow easier adaptation to the particular dangers of an unfamiliar business environment. Moreover, risks are reduced because the project is generally less subject to the danger of adverse action by the host government. Sales and profits of the joint venture may be greater than those of a subsidiary, because the operation is looked upon with more favor by nationalist-oriented consumers than would be the case if it were considered a foreign operation.

While there are significant potential advantages associated with using joint ventures, there are potential limitations as well. The profit potential may be less, because all profits must be shared. Also, there are many things that can lead to disagreements between the partners, such as a dispute over dividend policies or differences in management philosophies. These can be resolved, however, if the partners can work together. For example, on the surface one might have concluded that the joint venture between Toyota and General Motors which created New United Motor Manufacturing, Inc. in the United States in 1984 could not succeed because of obvious differences in handling of profits and styles of management decision making. But the joint venture has been a success because each has gained what it really wanted from the alliance.

Being party to a joint venture can also affect operations in other markets. For example, problems can arise if the international marketer wants to create a new venture in a third market in which the joint venture has been selling. By creating such a new enterprise, the international marketer becomes a competitor while still being a partner. Competing with oneself is a policy that many companies in foreign countries have not yet accepted.

Regardless of policies, agreements, and so on, the real success of every joint venture is dependent upon the cooperation and communication between the partners. The extent to which such cooperation is forthcoming from each local partner depends upon the characteristics of each partner. Thus the selection of a local partner is *perhaps the single most important activity* involved in establishing a joint venture. Since it is extremely difficult to find compatible partners the situation can be eased somewhat if the partners attempt to anticipate all possible areas of disagreement and if they include specific phrases dealing with them in the joint venture agreement. In other words, the agreement should assist the partners in becoming, and remaining, compatible. Ricks (1999, p. 110) reports that one of the major reasons why Dow Chemical Company's joint venture in Korea failed was *poor communication*. Misunderstandings were everywhere and communication seemed to get nowhere. Dow made a mistake when it went public with complaints about its partner as Asians tend to keep problems very private. The

Korean partner felt it had no choice but to withdraw from the venture to avoid further loss of face.

The process involved in designing and implementing international joint ventures can be complex and time-consuming. One approach to the process consists of four phases: (1) solution–opportunity identification, (2) evaluation of the basic proposal for the international joint venture, (3) design of the IJV, and (4) implementation and results of operating the IJV. Each of the four phases can take one or more years. Using this process as a model, Woodside *et al.* (1991) analyzed retail joint ventures in Hungary. The decision process resulting in the first McDonald's fast food store in Hungary, with Babolna Agricultural Cooperative, involved a five-year time period. Similarly, the process involved in the Swedish company IKEA joining forces with the Hungarian company Butarker also took five years from first contact until the opening of a store in Budapest.

Often a joint venture agreement has a provision that the foreign partner buy out the local partner at some point in time. In short, the local partner has an option to sell at a fixed price. At the time the agreement is signed this may appear to be sound. But experience shows that the worst that could happen does, on occasion, happen (Keenan *et al.*, 2003). For example, in late 2001 AOL Time Warner had to pay its partner Germany's Bertelsmann US$6.75 billion for its half-share of AOL Europe. By April 2003 the value of the half-share was one-fourth the amount paid for it. To avoid this type of situation, and it may not always be possible to do so as it is hard to predict the world of business, agreements should be more flexible and spread the risk in the event of a breakup.

8.5.5 Other types of strategic alliances

In addition to licensing, contracting, and joint ventures there are other types of strategic alliance arrangements. These include marketing distribution agreements. Marketing agreements are best illustrated by the international airline industry. Among the many agreements (some of which involve an equity stake) are those between Northwest and KLM, Delta and Virgin Atlantic, Air Canada and Air France, and the Star Alliance mentioned earlier.

Alliances linked to R&D and technology are illustrated by the sharing of engineers between Mitsubishi of Japan and Daimler-Benz (now DaimlerChrysler) of Germany. Boeing and three Japanese partners in the 777 aircraft project created a trans-Pacific telecommunications system to link their design operations.

A distribution agreement existed in the late 1990s between Laura Ashley and Business Logistics Services (BLS), a subsidiary of Federal Express. BLS took over, in its entirety, Laura Ashley's global distribution operation. The agreement was designed to restructure, improve, and manage every aspect of the flow of goods and information within the Laura Ashley supply chain.

A *consortium* including Asea Brown Boveri (ABB) and Daimler-Benz Transportation received a contract in 1996 to build Singapore's first light-rail commuter line. On a broader scale, consortia have been created by European companies as a means of responding to international competition in general as well as competition from Japanese *keiretsus* and South Korean *chaebols*.

Yet another type of alliance is the *vertical alliance*, or supply-chain alliance. Companies forming these are seeking a long-term relationship with compatible partners. Volkswagen's assembly operation in Brazil, discussed earlier in the chapter, has many of the characteristics of this type of alliance.

8.6 Choosing between alternatives

As we stated in Chapter 6, the decision about what specific international marketing channel to use, including the phase of foreign market entry (or the channel between nations), is not a simple one for the international marketer. There are many factors that influence what might be the best choice for a company in a foreign market at a specific time. These factors also apply to choosing a nonexport entry mode from among manufacturing, assembly, and strategic alliance. It is clear that companies competing with each other directly in the same foreign markets do not make the same choice. As shown in Exhibit 8.5, this may be the situation even for competitors with the same home country.

Often, a company may use multiple entry modes and/or channels of distribution within a nation. A study of sales channels used in the European Union market for personal computers concluded that multiple channels, especially hybrid ones

| **EXHIBIT 8.5** | **Competitors from the same country approach Europe differently** |

Often assumptions are made that companies from the same country that produce and sell the same type(s) of products do the same things when entering foreign markets. There are statements made such as 'The Japanese do this,' 'The Germans have done that,' and so forth. Such behavior does not always hold in reality. As an example we can look at the three largest South Korean consumer electronics companies and their experiences in Europe in the 1990s. The companies – Daewoo, Goldstar, and Samsung – all tried assembly plants for TVs, VCRs, and microwave ovens as a way to overcome foreign market barriers. Even then, market share only got as high as about 5%.

Then, these Korean companies thought they had the answer. Starting in the early and mid-1990s the companies launched an all-out effort to become 'local players,' including direct investment and joint ventures. Being local was their way to lower costs and match European quality standards. It also avoided dumping charges.

Faced with high labor costs, increasing interest rates, and low-cost competition from Southeast Asian countries, Korean companies had seen their exports to Europe go flat. It appeared that a minimum share in each country was needed to remain a force in the market. The Korean products lacked clear brand identity and, as one Korean government official has stated, 'the image of Korea was of cheap, low-quality products.'

The new approach to Europe forced Korean companies to drop their nationalistic approach to foreign sales. 'Go European' was the theme for Daewoo Electronics Co. The company built a US$150 million, integrated color TV plant in France. The TVs were designed in France, and most of the components are European made.

In a key move, in mid-1992 Samsung announced it would buy Werk für Fernsehelektronik, a former East German picture tube maker. Samsung spent US$120 million to upgrade the plant, which could produce 1.2 million TV sets a year. The company negotiated to buy an even larger German TV maker, RFT. For more efficiency, Samsung has moved its Portuguese and Spanish color TV plants to Billingham, England, and its VCR plant from England to Spain. The company will use the Portuguese plant to make parts for all its European plants.

Goldstar focused on alliances to widen its market share. Its Italian venture, Goldstar-Iberna Italy, is a good example. Goldstar, Italy's Iberna, and Germany's Gepi collaborated to produce a refrigerator that was designed by Goldstar's Ireland facility and manufactured in Italy with parts and components supplied by Gepi. And Goldstar's color TV plant in Italy uses picture tubes made by Finland's Nokia.

As shown above, the three companies have taken different approaches to break away from production in Korea and export. One company made a greenfield investment, another company took the acquisition route, while the third emphasized strategic alliances.

where the manufacturer and the channel intermediary (or partner) share the marketing functions performed, may be an optimal solution for expanding sales volumes (Gabrielsson *et al.*, 2002).

SUMMARY

In this chapter we examined nonexport modes of entry into foreign markets. The use of direct investment, particularly in manufacturing, assembly operations, and strategic alliances was examined in enough depth to show how these represent viable alternatives for the international marketer. One thing is clear. There are no easy answers to which mode of entry is 'best' when a decision has been made to have a production presence in a foreign market area.

QUESTIONS FOR DISCUSSION

8.1　What are the major nonexport modes of entry into foreign markets? How does strategic focus relate to such market entry modes?

8.2　What are the major considerations taken into account by the international marketer in a decision to engage in some form of foreign area production?

8.3　If a company were contemplating establishing a manufacturing facility in a foreign market, why might it decide to wholly own the facility rather than partially own it? Similarly, why might it prefer partial ownership?

8.4　When developing manufacturing operations in foreign markets, is it better for the international marketer to seek out merger/acquisition possibilities or start from scratch (a greenfield investment)? Explain.

8.5　Why might an international marketer that is involved in foreign production still have problems concerning channel control and cooperation? Would such a marketer handle channel conflict differently than the international marketer that exports?

8.6　What is a strategic alliance? Why are these alliances so popular and who benefits?

8.7　What are the key essentials for a strategic alliance to be a success?

8.8　'Licensing seems to be a fairly safe way for a manufacturer to produce in a foreign market for the first time.' Comment.

8.9　Although licensing and contracting may appear desirable, they have drawbacks. What are the drawbacks?

8.10　Why might an international marketer prefer a joint venture to a licensing arrangement?

8.11　'In running a jointly owned facility in a foreign market (including a joint venture), it is not necessary to own more than 50% to maintain operational and management control.' Discuss.

8.12 Why are management style, and any cultural differences that exist in styles, important in all types of market entry modes involving partners?

8.13 Select a company that has chosen direct investment in a foreign market and a company that has established a strategic alliance abroad and analyze why each company made the decision it did. Explain why you would or would not agree with that decision.

8.14 Choose a company that has made both a direct investment in a foreign country and has become part of a strategic alliance in that same, or another, country and analyze why the company chose those particular modes of entry.

REFERENCES

Albaum, G. and Herche, J. (1999). Management style comparisons among five European nations. *J. Global Marketing*, 12(4), 5–27.

Albaum, G., Yu, J., Wiese, N. and Herche, J. (2004). A cross-national study of the impact of culture-based values on marketing decision makers' management style. *Proceedings*, Third International Business and Economics Conference, San Francisco, 8–11 January.

Aliber, R. Z. (1993). *The Multinational Paradigm*. Cambridge, MA: MIT Press.

Atuahene-Gima, K. (1993). International licensing of technology: an empirical study of the differences between licensee and non-licensee firms. *J. International Marketing*, 1(2), 71–87.

Backhaus, K. and Meyer, M. (1986). Country risk assessment in international industrial marketing. In *Contemporary Research in Marketing*, vol. 1 (ed. K. Möller and M. Poltschuk), Proceedings of the 15th Annual Conference of the European Marketing Academy, Helsinki, June.

Business International (1990). *Making Alliances Work: Lessons from Companies' Successes and Mistakes*. London: Business International, A Member of the Economist Group.

Business Week (1992). The partners. 10 February, 102–7.

Business Week (1996). VW's factory of the future. 7 October, 52 and 56.

Business Week (2000a). A pit of trouble. 7 August, 60–4.

Business Week (2000b). Car power. 23 October, 72–82.

Business Week (2000c). A life of fines and beatings. 2 October, 122–8.

Contractor, F. J. (1985). *Licensing in International Strategy: A Guide for Planning and Negotiations*. Westport, CT: Quorum.

DiCicco, M. (1996). Hi-tech hits the Philippines. *South China Morning Post*, 28 May, Business, 5.

Doyle, P., Saunders, J. and Wong, V. (1992). Competition in global markets: a case study of American and Japanese competition in the British market. *J. International Business Studies*, 23 (Third Quarter), 419–42.

Gabrielsson, M., Kripalani, V. H. M. and Luostarinen, R. (2002). Multiple channel strategies in the European personal computer industry. *J. International Marketing*, 10(3), 73–95.

Gilroy, B. M. (1993). *Networking in Multinational Enterprises: The Importance of Strategic Alliances*. Columbia, SC: University of South Carolina Press.

Gugler, P. (1992). Building transnational alliances to create competitive advantage. *Long Range Planning*, 25(1) (February), 90–9.

Johnstone, H. (1997). Foreign firms go it alone on the mainland. *South China Morning Post*, 13 July, Money, 3.

Katz, I. (1999). Snapping up South America. *Business Week*, 18 January, 60.

Keegan, W. J. and Green, M. S. (2000). *Global Marketing* 2nd edn. Upper Saddle River, NJ: Prentice-Hall.

Keenan, F., Welch, D., Black, J. and Fairlamb, D. (2003). Buyout pacts that backfire. *Business Week*, 7 April, 68–9.

Kirpalani, M. (2002). Calling Bangalore. *Business Week*, 25 November, 52–3.

Lasserre, P. and Schutte, H. (1995). *Strategies for Asia Pacific*. London: Macmillan Business.

Lee, J., Roehl, T. W. and Choe, S. (2000). What makes management style similar and distinct across borders? Growth, experience, and culture in Korean and Japanese firms. *J. International Business Studies*, 31(4), 631–52.

Makino, S. and Beamish, P. W. (1998). Performance and survival of joint ventures with non-conventional ownership structures. *J. International Business Studies*, 29(4), 797–818.

Malik, O. (2003), And the coolest new PC is made by ... Best Buy? *Business 2.0*, August, 47–9.

Meissner, H. G. (1990). *Strategic International Marketing*. Berlin: Springer-Verlag.

Meyer, K. and Estrin, S. (2001). Brownfield entry in emerging markets. *J. International Business Studies*, 32(3), 575–84.

Mody, A. and Negishi, S. (2001). Cross-border mergers and acquisitions in East Asia: trends and implications. *Finance & Development*, March, 6–9.

Pan, Y. and Tse, D. K. (1996). Co-operative strategies between foreign firms in an overseas country. *J. International Business Studies*, 26(5), 929–46.

Pearson, M. P. (1991). *Joint Ventures in the People's Republic of China*. Princeton, NJ: Princeton University Press.

Ricks, D. A. (1999). *Blunders in International Business* 3rd edn. Oxford, UK: Blackwell.

Roberts, D. and Webb, A. (2001). Buying binge. *Business Week*, 29 January, 48–9.

Rocks, D. (1999). A failure to communicate. *Business Week*, 11 October, 112–16.

Root, F. R. (1994). *Entry Strategies for International Markets* rev. and expanded edn. New York: Jossey Bass.

Schmidt, D. A. (1986). Analyzing political risk. *Business Horizons*, 29 (July–August), 43–50.

Spekman, R. E. and Sawhney, K. (1990). Toward a conceptual understanding of the antecedents of strategic alliances. *Working Paper 90–114*. Cambridge, MA: Marketing Science Institute.

The Economist (1999). Sweatshop wars. 27 February, 62–3.

The Economist (2003). Spreading their wings. 6 September, 57.

Vanhonacker, W. (1997). Entering China: an unconventional approach. *Harvard Business Review*, 75 (March–April), 2–7.

Wheatley, J. (2000). Super factory – or super headache. *Business Week*, 31 July, 66.

Woodside, A. G., Kandikó, J. and Vyslozil, W. (1991). Designing and implementing international joint marketing ventures: case research studies on new retail enterprises in Hungary. Tulane University, *A. B. Freeman School of Business Working Paper 91-MKTG-03*.

Yang, C., Capell, K. and Kripalani, M. (2004). Rupert's world. *Business Week*, 19 January, 52–60.

FURTHER READING

Beamish, P. (1996). Note on International Licensing. Richard Ivey School of Business, The University of Western Ontario, Case 9–96-G008.

Einhorn, B., Elgin, B., Himelstein, L. and Port, O. (2002). High-tech in China. *Business Week*, 28 October, 80–8.

Gallow, V., Devine, M., Horslip, W. and Holbeche, L. (2000). *Strategic Alliances: Getting the People Bit Right*. Horsham, UK: Roffey Park Institute.

Rosen, D. H. (1999). *Behind the Open Door: Foreign Enterprises in the Chinese Marketplace*. Washington, DC: Institute for International Economics.

Tse, D. K., Pan, Y. and Au, K. Y. (1997). How MNCs choose entry modes and form alliances: the China experience. *J. International Business Studies*, 28(4), 779–805.

United Nations (1989). *Joint Ventures as a Form of International Economic Cooperation*. New York: Taylor & Francis.

Woodside, A. G. and Pitts, R. E. (eds) (1996). *Creating and Managing International Joint Ventures*, Westport, CT: Quorum.

CASE STUDY 8.1

Terralumen S.A.  **Northeastern** UNIVERSITY

As Francisco Alvarez reclined in the Gran Clase cabin of the Iberia A320 flight to London on the morning of 11 January 2000, he began to recount the events of the past several months. This was Blue Ridge Spain's second directors meeting in six months, and Alvarez was beginning to think that his US joint venture partner, Delta Foods, wanted to end the partnership. But why? The past year had been profitable, and Blue Ridge Spain was poised to enter its most successful expansion year ever. Besides, he believed that it was his company, Terralumen S.A., that had contributed the most to the success of the joint venture, and that Delta would have a very difficult time running the company on its own.

Terralumen S.A.

Terralumen began as a family-owned agricultural company that later expanded into consumer products. Hernando Hidalgo, the founder, believed that the fastest way to acquire managerial expertise and brand equity was to establish joint ventures with US companies that were world leaders in consumer products. Over the years, Hidalgo had been very successful in gaining managerial control over the company's joint ventures. In his opinion, as long as a joint venture exceeded revenue expectations, most Americans were quite willing to cede control.

The joint venture

In 1983 a Barcelona banker, and friend of the Hidalgo family, contacted Terralumen to request a meeting on behalf of Gene Bennett. Bennett had come to Spain to evaluate opportunities establishing restaurant operations for Blue Ridge Restaurants Corporation, a highly successful US fast food company.

Francisco Alvarez, the most senior non-family executive in Terralumen, met with Bennett and had a favorable first impression. Bennett did not seem like the typical 'ugly American.' He not only spoke Spanish, but he seemed to enjoy learning about Spanish culture. Over the next few months Alvarez invited Bennett to family gatherings and other events in order to become better acquainted with Bennett and Blue Ridge. Over time, they developed a solid friendship.

In 1985 Terralumen established a joint venture with Blue Ridge to develop a restaurant chain in Barcelona. Blue Ridge contributed significant marketing expertise and a strong international brand name, while Terralumen contributed the knowledge needed to navigate Spain's complex real estate and labor markets.

Blue Ridge Restaurants Corporation

Blue Ridge was founded in Virginia in 1959 and quickly established a reputation for quality fast food. In the 1980s the company made its first major foray into international markets. The strategy at the time was to enter into joint ventures with local partners thereby allowing Blue Ridge to enter restricted markets and draw on local expertise, capital, and labor. Partnering also significantly reduced the capital costs of opening new stores.

The strategy of local partnering combined with Blue Ridge's marketing know-how and operations expertise quickly paid off in Australia, Southeast Asia, and the United Kingdom, where booming sales led to rapid international expansion. On the other hand, there had been some glaring failures. By 1987 Blue Ridge had had false starts in France, Italy, Brazil and Hong Kong, all places where infrastructure problems and slow consumer acceptance resulted in poor performance. When Blue Ridge was sold to Delta Foods in 1996 for US$2 billion it was one of the largest fast food chains in the world and generated sales of US$6.8 billion.

Delta was a leading soft drink and snack food company in the United States but, at the time of the Blue Ridge acquisition, it had not achieved significant success internationally. In the late 1990s Delta acquired the largest snack food companies in both Spain and the United Kingdom.

Blue Ridge Spain

In 1985 Alvarez chose Eduardo Rodrigo, a bright young Terralumen manager who spoke English, to head up Blue Ridge Spain as its managing director. Rodrigo was a refined and personable man who valued his late afternoon tennis with his wife. Alvarez and

Rodrigo both spent several weeks at Blue Ridge University in Virginia learning about the company's restaurant operations.

Rodrigo's eye for detail quickly became apparent as he mastered the new business's administrative and operating policies and procedures. He knew every detail of the first few stores' operating processes and had an equally detailed grasp of each store's trading profile. As a result, to the delight of both joint venture partners, Blue Ridge Spain began to show a profit unusually soon.

The Blue Ridge concept was well received in Barcelona. However, the leading consumer market in Spain was centered around Madrid, and Rodrigo, who was Catalan,[1] did not want to expand beyond his home base. He was also concerned that rapid growth would damage his impeccable profitability record in the short term.

In 1997 Alvarez transferred Rodrigo to a newly established pizza delivery business[2] and replaced him with Carlos Martin, who had just returned from a successful assignment in Venezuela. Martin was more proactive in growing the business than Rodrigo had been and, as a result, Blue Ridge began to prosper.

In Spain, securing good restaurant sites depended on personal relationships with real estate developers, property owners, bankers, and government officials. Due to the tight real estate market in Spain's rapidly growing cities, negotiations for new sites only succeeded in approximately one-third of cases. Therefore, if Blue Ridge wanted to develop 10 new restaurants in a given year, Martin had to be negotiating for about 30 sites, and each site involved multiple stakeholders. If a desired site was already occupied (which was often the case), Martin also had to negotiate directly with the current tenant, who often had to be paid a fee, known as key money, in order to vacate the property before negotiations could begin with the landlord.[3] Accordingly, Alvarez and Martin both contributed a good deal of their time to managing the relationships needed to obtain good commercial properties.

Another source of complexity was the Spanish labor market. In Spain, workers were typically hired on a full-time basis and paid full benefits, and the use of casual and part-time labor was uncommon. As a result labor could not be adjusted for fluctuations in demand. Low-volume restaurants were consequently less profitable, while high-volume ones often had difficulty meeting demand during peak hours.

Blue Ridge Europe

In contrast to Terralumen, which provided stable long-term management for the joint venture, Blue Ridge Corporation had a 'revolving door' of foreign managers, most of whom were Americans. Each time new managers were transferred to Blue Ridge European headquarters in London the Spaniards had to begin over again teaching them about the Spanish market. Most of these Blue Ridge managers were also beginning their first international assignments.

One of the few consistent faces from Blue Ridge Corporation was Yannis Costas. Costas was a US-educated Greek who joined Blue Ridge in the mid-1980s. He had worked with Gene Bennett from the inception of Blue Ridge Spain, and in 1988 he became European Regional Director, which included responsibility for Spain. Between 1993 and 1998 Costas served a term in Asia before returning to London to take up his previous role as European Director.

Alvarez was happy to be working with his old friend Costas again. Over the years Alvarez grew to trust Costas, inviting him and his wife to Alvarez family events, including their eldest son's wedding. The occasional disagreement between Costas and Alvarez was always amicably resolved. For his part, Alvarez always cultivated good relations with Blue Ridge managers in the United States, attending annual company conventions in Las Vegas and visiting the company's headquarters in Virginia.

In December 1998 Alvarez and Costas traveled to Virginia to personally present Blue Ridge Spain's strategic plan to Donald Kinsley, the newly appointed President of Blue Ridge's International division. Kinsley had formerly been president of another well-known family restaurant chain in the United States, but this was his first international assignment. Their presentation was followed by agreement on an aggressive five-year growth plan (see Table 8.2). Almost immediately upon returning to Europe Costas and Alvarez began working on the plan, which was to include a total of 50 restaurants by 2002.

In 1999 stores were opened in several prime locations, such as the prestigious Gran Via in Madrid, and Barcelona's famous Las Ramblas shopping district. Alvarez was exceptionally pleased with the company's progress.

The directors' meeting

In 1999 Delta began to take a more direct and active role in the management of Blue Ridge, replacing Blue Ridge senior managers with Delta managers or new hires with extensive experience in consumer goods companies. In Europe, Delta created a new regional vice-president position with responsibility for Europe, the Middle East and South Africa. Just before the joint venture directors' meeting in June, Delta announced that Mikael Södergran, a Finn who had worked as a

| **TABLE 8.2** | Development plan agreed between Terralumen and Blue Ridge restaurants as of December 1998 |

Blue Ridge Spain	**Estimates for year (US$000s):**					
	1998	2000	2001	2002	2003	2004
No. of Stores (Dec. 31)	12	24	37	50	65	80
Avg. Annual Sales	700	770	847	932	1,025	1,127
Gross Sales	8,400	18,480	31,339	46,585	66,617	90,189
Cost of Goods – Food	1,680	3,326	5,641	8,152	11,658	15,332
Cost of Goods – Direct Labor	1,680	3,696	6,268	9,317	13,323	18,038
Advertising/Promotion	504	1,478	2,194	3,261	3,997	5,411
Occupancy Costs	1,260	1,848	3,134	4,659	6,662	9,019
Fixed Labor	840	1,932	3,425	5,323	7,958	11,264
Miscellaneous	168	370	627	932	1,332	1,804
Royalties to Blue Ridge US	420	924	1,567	2,329	3,331	4,509
Contribution to G&A	1,848	6,199	10,677	15,873	23,019	31,125
Salaries and Benefits	875	1,531	2,641	3,493	4,580	5,899
Travel Expenses	120	240	300	375	469	586
Other	240	312	406	527	685	891
Occupancy Costs	240	720	828	952	1,095	1,259
Earnings Before Interest/Tax	373	3,396	6,502	10,525	16,190	22,490
% of Gross Sales	4.4	18.4	20.7	22.6	24.3	24.9
Office Employees (Spain)	10	20	30	35	40	45

Notes:
- This plan was agreed before Yannis Costas' appointment to Blue Ridge Europe in late 1998.
- End 2004 plan: 20 stores in Barcelona, 30 in Madrid, 30 in other cities.
- Capital Investment per store $700,000–$1 million.
- Site identification, lease or purchase negotiation, permits, construction: 18–24 months. Key money is a part of occupancy costs. It is a sum paid to a property owner at signing; varies by site $100,000 plus. Up to 1999, many owners wanted key money paid off the books, often in another country.
- Store Staffing (at the average sales level):
  - 1 manager, 2 assistants full time (larger stores 3–4 assistants);
  - 10–12 employees per 8-hour shift (40 hours/week); 980 employee hours per week.
- Store employees needed by end of 1999: 300; by the end of 2004: 2250 (approx.).
- Store employee attrition: approximately 25% per year.
- Dividends from earnings were declared periodically and then were shared equally between partners.

marketing manager for P&G in Greece, the Middle East and East Africa, had been hired as the new vice-president for Europe. He had no experience in restaurant management.

The board of directors planned to discuss a recently drafted consultants' report and to approve five-year growth targets (see Table 8.3). When Alvarez received the study a week before the meeting, he was amazed to see that it projected an expansion in Spain significantly higher than what had been agreed upon six months earlier. The report also projected a large expansion thrust in France and Germany, where Blue Ridge had no visible presence.[4] Yet, based on his prior experiences with Blue Ridge managers, Alvarez believed that the board would ultimately realize that these figures were not realistic. Besides, Kinsley had already agreed to the

current plan and the company was well on its way to achieving the previously agreed targets.

Among the joint venture directors, Delta-Blue Ridge was represented by Costas, Södegran, and Kinsley. Terralumen was represented by company president Andres Balaguer, Francisco Alvarez, and Carlos Martin. Martin began the meeting by protesting that his team of 10 managers could not handle the introduction of 30 more new stores a year. Alvarez also objected to Delta's suggestion that the contract should be renegotiated to introduce royalties and fees payable from the joint venture to the US partner in order to cover the cost of implementing new technologies, systems, and services (see Table 8.4). After all, the company's Spanish managers had contributed most to the success

TABLE 8.3 Consultants' recommendations on Blue Ridge European expansion (selected markets)

	1998	2000	2001	2002	2003	2004
Stores						
Spain	12	30	65	100	135	170
France	0	10	20	55	90	130
Germany	3	15	30	65	100	150
Total	15	55	115	220	325	450
Regional Managers (London)	1	15	20	22	24	26
Country Staff/Managers	12	40	90	180	220	250
Store Employees	215	1650	3450	6600	9750	13,500

TABLE 8.4 Blue Ridge Spain joint venture agreement exceptional term highlights

	Blue Ridge US-desired objective	Blue Ridge Spain – variance
Joint venture outlets		
Royalty	At least 4%	No royalty
Fees	$20,000	$5000
Term	10 years	5 years
Exclusivity	Avoid exclusivity	Spain, Canary Islands, Spanish Sahara, Beleares Islands
Advertising	5%, right of approval	No obligations
Outlet Renewal Requirements	Renewal fee at least $2000; Upgrading or relocation	No fee or other specific requirements
Delta Products	Required	No requirement
Development Program	Schedule for required development of territory	No requirement
Noncompetition	Restrictions on similar business	No provision
Assignment	First refusal right; approval of assignee	No provision
Sub-franchising		
Contract privity	Blue Ridge US should be a party and successor to franchisor	Blue Ridge cited; Blue Ridge succeeds on JV dissolution
Royalty	At least 4%	None
Fees	$20,000	None
Joint venture operation		
Equity Participation	More than 50%	50%
Profit Distribution	At least 50%	Additional 20% when profits are greater than 20%
Actual Management	Blue Ridge US should appoint General Manager	General Manager is from JV partner
Board Control	Blue Ridge US should have majority	Equal number of board members

of Blue Ridge Spain, nurturing a competent Spanish management team, developing the local market, and managing the relationships with the company's numerous stakeholders, such as customers, banks, developers, and city officials.

The meeting's cordial tone quickly dissolved when Södergran unexpectedly began to press the issue. His aggressive stance was not received well by Balaguer, who in turn questioned the ability of the consulting firm's young, freshly minted American MBAs to understand the intricacy of the Spanish fast food market. Balaguer simply brushed off the study as 'a piece of American business school cleverness.'

Södergran became visibly annoyed at Balaguer's refusal to consider Delta's targets. Alvarez was astonished when Södergran insisted that 'The contract says that you are required to grow the markets.' After all, Terralumen had already agreed to an aggressive growth plan. Furthermore, this was the first meeting with Delta's new vice-president, and he could not understand why Södergran was intent on beginning their relationship on such a sour note. He was less surprised when Balaguer, a tall, elegant man, rose from his seat with a sheaf of papers, and replied: 'If this is your contract, and if we rely on a contract to resolve a partnership problem, well, here is what I think of it and of you,' and then calmly dropped the papers into a waste paper basket. Upon returning to his seat, Balaguer softly commented in Spanish, 'If this meeting had been conducted in my language, you would have known what I *really* think of you.' But, since the US managers spoke no Spanish, the comment was only understood by Alvarez and Martin.

After a long pause Costas broke the silence by pointing out that Terralumen had already committed to considerable growth, and had therefore already come some way toward Delta's expansion goals. Alvarez knew Costas well enough to sense the embarrassment at his new boss's 'bull in a China shop' act, and that by siding with Terralumen he was only trying to avert permanent damage to the joint venture relationship. At this point the board agreed to adjourn the meeting until the two companies had more time to consider alternatives.

Emerging conflicts

Alvarez, while trying to keep an open mind with respect to Södergran, continued to travel to London for meetings with the Blue Ridge regional team. On one visit he was surprised that Södergran had moved to a new office two floors below the Delta-Blue Ridge offices. When he asked Costas what was going on Costas simply shrugged his shoulders and replied, 'He says he wants some peace and quiet.'

In October 1999 Delta sent Geoff Dryden, a finance manager from the Snack Foods division, to London for

his first international assignment as the company's new vice-president of finance for Europe. Up until this point Alvarez, Costas, and Martin, all of whom had finance backgrounds, jointly managed the company's finances.

A new strategy

Over the next six months the joint venture board of directors met four times. Alvarez insisted on sticking to the previously agreed growth rates. Higher growth, in his opinion, was simply unmanageable, but he agreed to make upward revisions to the plan if market conditions and real estate negotiations proved favorable. On the other had, he refused to consider revision of the royalty provisions.

By November 1999 Alvarez was becoming more concerned about Delta's new management team. Not only did they not respond to his latest offer, but Dryden ignored his repeated requests for a routine year-end transfer of funds to meet debt obligations to a major Spanish bank. Via fax, Alvarez impressed on Dryden the urgency of the funds transfer. If Blue Ridge Spain could not meet its debt obligations the partners were required to provide funds to avoid insolvency and the automatic dissolution of the company. When Dryden continued to ignore his request Alvarez began to grow impatient. Finally, he decided to sell one of the company's prime real estate properties to the bank and lease back the store over 30 years. This provided the necessary cash to keep Blue Ridge Spain in business for another year.

At the first opportunity Alvarez approached Costas to ask why Delta-Blue Ridge had withheld payment. Costas seemed as surprised as he was. Moreover, he was dismayed that Alvarez had sold a prime property given the tight real estate market. 'What else could I do?' replied Alvarez. Costas also wondered whether Alvarez had the legal right to sell the property without the consent of Delta-Blue Ridge. Alvarez replied that when Costas was in Asia he had been given power of attorney to make real estate transactions on behalf of the joint venture. Alvarez explained:

> Blue Ridge decided to give me this authority in order to reduce the amount of travel required by your managers from the US. Besides, as you know, it is not often that good properties become available, and when they do, we must act quickly.

Alvarez began to wonder if Delta was trying to force his company out of the joint venture. A few days before Christmas he shared his concern with Martin, who replied:

That would be crazy. Not only do they not speak Spanish, they do not have a clue about how to manage a Spanish restaurant chain. Besides, all the joint venture employees are ours. And if they try to take us to a Spanish court,[5] who do you think the judges will side with? We have complied with every clause of our joint venture contract!

'Well, they are definitely up to something,' Alvarez rejoined. 'But what?'

Next steps

The dark drizzly winter weather seemed appropriate as Francisco Alvarez arrived at London's Heathrow airport to attend the directors meeting. After all, the events that had transpired over the past several months could hardly bode well for the future of the joint venture company that he helped establish some 17 years earlier. Nevertheless, he now believed that, if Delta really was foolish enough to want 'out' of the joint venture, Terralumen was in a good position to dictate terms. After all, Södergran was going to be occupied with the impossible task of building new restaurants in France and Germany, and the last thing he needed was to start again in Spain.

Notes

1. Catalonia, a state in northeast Spain, has a distinct culture and language (Catalan).
2. A wholly owned subsidiary of Terralumen. In 1999 the subsidiary owned nearly 30 outlets.
3. Residential tenants essentially had occupancy rights in perpetuity under Spanish law.
4. Large restaurant chains served only 4% of fast food meals in Spain, compared with 15 for the rest of western Europe, and 50% for the United States.
5. The joint venture owned the rights to the Blue Bridge brand name in Spain and, in case of dissolution of the company, the court would have to decide ownership.

Questions

1. What should be Francisco Alvarez's position at the directors' meeting?
2. Can the joint venture between Terralumen S.A. and Delta Foods survive? What do the partners need to do to make this happen?
3. If Delta does want out of the venture, what terms should be set by Terralumen?

This case was made possible through the generous support of Darla and Fredrick Brodsky through their endowment of the Darla and Frederick Brodsky Trustee Professorship in International Business.

CASE STUDY 8.2

GG Farm Machinery Company

GG Farm Machinery Company is a French manufacturer of a specialized piece of machinery. Marcel Ger, the managing director of GG, was convinced there was a market in Australia for his machine and he wanted to explore in more depth how his company might do business there. Since GG was a relatively small company with less than 50 employees and an annual turnover in 2004 of approximately €30 million, the company did not have people available to make an appraisal. In addition, Marcel himself had little spare time for such an endeavor.

An international marketing consultant firm, Bonjoir Consulting Company, was hired to make an assessment of the Australian market for GG's machinery. Market entry mode was also to be examined and Bonjoir was to recommend whether an export or a licensing strategy would be the best approach to use in developing the market.

As part of the research effort, the project director assigned by Bonjoir to the GG project traveled to Australia where a number of potential distributors, licensees, and end users were visited. While in Australia, the project director discussed the issue of tariff and non-tariff barriers with Australian Customs officials.

The findings reported to Mr Ger by the consultant are summarized in Table 8.5.

Based on these findings, a decision was made by Mr

TABLE 8.5 Consultant's report to GG Farm Machinery.

| | | Strategy favored | |
		Licensing	Export
Product's Australian market potential	Excellent	either	
Service requirements	Minimal		yes
Transportation costs	High and difficult to reduce	yes	
Strength of French franc	Moderately strong	yes	
Import duties	Exist for some products	if duties are significant	in short run, no duties favor export
Patent protection	Exporter holds strong French and Australian patents	yes	
Capabilities and interests of potential representatives	Best candidate wanted to become a licensee, not a distributor	yes	
Price competitiveness	Price was sensitive issue: any duties would seriously damage export efforts	yes	

Ger to enter into a licensing agreement with an Australian manufacturer.

Questions

1. Do you agree with the decision made by Marcel Ger? Explain your answer.

2. What other modes of market entry into the Australian market might GG have considered? Why are these viable alternatives?

CASE STUDY 8.3

VW in China

(This case study was written by Min Zhao, University of Paris 1 Pantheon-Sorbonne, Paris. It is drawn from her much larger analysis of the comparative strategies of mutinational automobile companies in China.)

Volkswagen is the market leader in automobile manufacturing and sales in China. It has benefited from several strategies it has pursued: its early entry into automobile manufacturing in China; its effective adaptation to the business, political, and legal environments; the strength of its commitment; its development of management and employee training programs for local personnel; and changes in its product line as competitive conditions have changed.

Volkswagen began manufacturing in China in a joint venture with Shanghai Automotive Industry Co. (SAIC) in 1985, and formed a second joint venture with First Automobile Work Group (FAW) in 1991. Volkswagen has had rapid growth in production, sales, and profits in China. It has been the market leader since 1985 and retains that position though its market share is falling. Volkswagen held 58% of the automobile market in 1997, 50% in 2000, and 48% in 2001. In 2002, VW increased its sales by 42.8%, but its market share dropped to 38.5% as new competitors entered the market and existing competitors expanded production to meet rapidly rising Chinese demand. In 2003, VW's market share continued to fall, even as both sales and profits rose.

The operations in China are of great importance to the parent company, now Volkswagen's second largest market (after Germany). VW China contributed 15% of Volkswagen AG's total profit in 2002, and 22% in 2003 when demand in Europe fell and the company suffered a loss in North America.

Volkswagen is adjusting to the growing competition in China through expanding its product line, increasing production, and sponsoring activities to increase its visibility and reputation. The degree of success of these activities will affect both profitability and market share.

Government policies and regulations

A motor vehicle industry was started in China in 1955, primarily to produce trucks and military vehicles. After government policies changed in 1978, the economic growth rate increased and production of automobiles expanded. In 1985 the government declared the automotive industry a 'pillar' of industry, targeting it for financial and developmental assistance. The automobile industry was among the first Chinese industries to be backed by a formal state industrial policy. This policy was first formulated in 1987 and modified in 1994 with emphasis on three points: (1) shift the product mix of the industry from commercial vehicles to passenger cars; (2) increase economies of scale by restructuring the industry to bring about greater concentration; and (3) obtain technology from abroad by inviting the participation of multinational enterprises (MNEs).

A number of regulations were established in order to ensure the Chinese government's continuing overall control, encourage domestic production, and prevent possible abuses. The most important limitations on trade are high tariff and nontariff barriers on imports. Government approval of investments is required at central and/or local levels, there are limits on foreign investments, and there are local content requirements.

The limit on the percentage of foreign ownership allowed in a company depends upon the categories, types, and models of vehicles or components to be produced, and the size of the investment. Foreign companies planning to build a complete car or any of the three key components of a vehicle (motors, air bags, and ABS) are limited to a maximum of 50% of equity.

Foreign investments of over $30 million or involving key car components require approval at the national level by both the State Planning Commission and the Ministry of Foreign Trade and Economic Cooperation. Smaller investments not involving production of key components can be approved at the provincial level. Even with approved projects, barriers may still be encountered at the local level. Remittance of profits may still be difficult. In all arrangements,

with companies as well as with government officials, time must be taken to develop personal relationships and show the advantages to all groups involved.

In order to encourage local production and protect local industry, China has had very high tariff barriers, particularly on goods that are viewed as luxuries (such as automobiles). The tariff rate on automobiles was set at 180–220% before 1986. The import taxes were as high as 100% on complete vehicles and 60% for parts before 2000. Purchase prices of imported cars were therefore 250–300% higher than comparable prices abroad. China also has restrictions regarding the obtaining of licenses to import motor vehicles and parts. Thanks to government market-opening measures, tariffs for automobiles will be reduced to 25% by 2006. The tariff rate on other vehicles depends upon the cylinder capacity and ignition features of the vehicle, and ranged from 43.8% to 50.7% in 2002. In 2004, duties on passenger vehicles, vans, and minibuses were reduced to 34.2%, while the rates on other vehicles were reduced from 50.7% to 37.5%. The duties will drop further until they reach a stable rate of 25% in 2006. Import license restrictions and quotas will be phased out by 2005.

The government sets the duty rates on locally assembled vehicles according to the percentage of the value of locally made parts. In order to cut down on the nation's pollution problems, China's authorities give foreign car makers more favorable treatment if they bring in cars with advanced ecological technologies, such as catalytic converters, electronic fuel injection, and computer-controlled ignitions.

China's entry into the World Trade Organization in 2001 is resulting in the gradual liberalizing of trade and phased increases in the rights of foreign corporations regarding investment limits, property rights, and the ability to engage in distribution, finance, etc. Import duties will be reduced. Reduction of protection in the automobile industry over the next six years will present a challenge to domestic manufacturers. For the first time car makers can now set prices and introduce new models without obtaining formal government approval.

However, the Chinese 'domestic' industry is dominated by joint ventures. These, in turn, are partially owned by the same automobile MNEs that could increase exports to the Chinese market. For the MNEs, aggressive exports to China could 'cannibalize' the sales of their joint ventures, in which they have major investments. Thus these companies may voluntarily limit their exports to China.

The automotive industry in China is still fragmented, with over 3000 parts suppliers and over 100 final assemblers. The Chinese government has designated seven automobile companies as 'key firms' targeted for expansion. This is to be accomplished by enabling these companies to pursue alliances with foreign original equipment manufacturers (OEMs) and limiting new small investments.

Economic growth and the development of the automobile industry

China's economy has expanded rapidly since it opened up to investment by foreign companies in the early 1980s, with growth averaging 7% per year over the past decade. Since the country joined the WTO in 2001 foreign investment, exports, and GDP have grown even more rapidly. By the end of 2002 China was the world's second largest investment destination with an annual inflow of $33 billion and a $395 billion stock of foreign direct investment.

In the past 10 years the average annual growth in the production of motor vehicles in China has been 15%, compared to a world average of 1.5% in the same period. China produced and distributed 3.25 million vehicles in 2002 (Figure 8.7). China is now the fifth largest vehicle manufacturer in the world. Automobiles make up a growing proportion of total vehicle production. Improved quality and a wider selection of models, and more recently lower prices, have resulted from the technology and know-how brought in by foreign automobile manufacturers.

The number of privately owned automobiles in China grew from 0.8 million units in 1990 to 5 million units in 1999, a 23% annual growth rate. There were approximately 10 million privately owned cars on China's roads in 2003. With China's population at 1.3 billion people, this provides only about one automobile for every 130 people. The China National Automotive Industry Corporation has estimated that, by the year 2010, annual demand for cars and trucks will reach 5.5 million, making China the third largest automotive market in the world. According to the State Development Planning Commission, private cars are expected to comprise 70% of China's auto sales for the next 10 years.

Automobile sales to private parties have been rising faster than per capita income. This is partly due to a growth in the number of people in the middle and upper classes, and the recognition of the convenience, usefulness, and status value of the automobile.

The boom in the Chinese automobile market has attracted investment from almost all of the world's major automobile manufacturers. With sales stagnant or growing only slowly in their home markets, China has been viewed as a major source of growth. Toyota, Nissan, and Hyundai were latecomers to manufacturing in China, but now plan to invest a combined $3 billion there over the next few years. Five of the world's ten largest parts suppliers have established operations in China. There is a danger that the flood of investment may result in excess capacity. Automobile prices are already beginning to decline as competition increases.

Volkswagen's strategies in China

In spite of the high duty rates and other restrictions on imports, there was an increase in the demand for foreign automobiles in the growing market for vehicles in the 1980s. It was apparent, however, that importing would continue to be restricted. Thus achieving substantial sales in China would require an investment in manufacturing, at least in the assembly of vehicles, in China. The impediments and risks seemed high as government attitudes, policies and regulations were not always clear and could be changed abruptly. The division of authority and responsibility between the

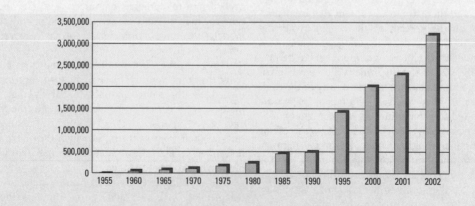

FIGURE 8.7 Growth of automotive industry production in China
Source: *China Automotive Industry Yearbook*

national, regional, and local governments was evolving, and not always transparent. Continued growth of the market was not assured.

Volkswagen had been able to export some automobiles to China and felt confident that they could sell enough of their least expensive models to justify undertaking local manufacturing. Because of the limits on foreign ownership on substantial investments, VW needed to find a domestic partner. The first step in the process was to develop relationships with government officials at all levels and with a potential partner. The Chinese emphasis on first developing trust, and the necessity of understanding the nontransparent but critically important informal relationships that influence both government and business actions, required both time and patience.

Volkswagen's first joint venture was with the General Corporation of Automobiles and Tractors of Shanghai, now the Shanghai Automobile Industrial Co. (SAIC). The joint venture, Shanghai VW (SVW), was formed in 1984 and started production in 1985. SAIC was the second largest vehicle manufacturer in China, one of the 'key firms' targeted by the national government for growth, and under the control of the local government. Its location in Shanghai put it in the main industrial and business center of the country. SAIC had an excellent industrial network for supplying parts. SVW invited the Bank of China to join the joint venture to ensure the ability to make foreign currency payments. The Chinese National Automobile Industry Co. (CNAIC), a firm controlled by the national government, became the fourth partner due to the importance of tangible and intangible support from the central government.

Zhu Rongji, the mayor of Shanghai from 1988 to 1991, set up a taxi company for the municipality that would be equipped with Volkswagen Santanas. VW moved its assembly lines for Santanas from South Africa to Shanghai. The efforts were mutually beneficial as sales rose for Shanghai VW, the local government encouraged foreign parts suppliers to establish joint ventures in China, more industrial workers were employed in the area, and SVW achieved an 85% local content rate by 1993.

Volkswagen's second joint venture was with First Automobile Work Group (FAW), forming FAW VW in 1991. FAW is under the direct control of the central government. The FAW VW joint venture was formed to produce the VW Jetta and the Audi.

The increasing competition in car production in China, and China's entry into the WTO, have caused Volkswagen to modify some of the strategies it adopted when it first began manufacturing in China. These include changes in manufacturing, changes in the product line and model introductions, and changes in marketing management.

Foreign automobile manufacturers entering China typically began by assembling cars from a set of imported components, with little or no use of locally made parts. They sometimes continued this policy for a number of years. Shanghai VW, with assistance from the local government, quickly adopted a program to increase the percentage of parts made locally. By 2004 Volkswagen had initiated the establishment of 160 joint ventures between foreign and Chinese suppliers of parts, approximately 100 license and know-how agreements, and 250 toll and equipment agreements.

VW modernized its production line and began to make its Passat model vehicle at the Shanghai facility in 2000, maintaining the same technical standard as that used in Europe (including processes such as laser welding). In 2002, the company successfully launched its Polo model car in Shanghai.

Productivity was improved by employee training programs from the beginning of the joint ventures, and by demonstrating to local employees that there were opportunities for advancement. In 1998 VW instituted a three-year program in which 40 key people from all sectors, including the factory lines, were sent to Germany. Since then, more than 1000 others have left Shanghai for various types of training in Germany. The joint venture is working hard to keep up with growing demand. Of the three production lines in Shanghai, two are on a double shift and one is on three shifts. The company has also spent $120 million on a new technology center.

The rate of introduction of new models has been greatly increased. For the first 10 years of SVW in China, it produced only one model, the Santana. In 1995, the more modern Santana 2000 was launched. Two other models, the Jetta and the Audi, were put into production at FAW VW plants. As the time of entry to the WTO approached, VW began production of Passats at its Shanghai plant. Today, with competitive pressure on all sides, it plans one or two new models every year, all of them to appear on the market within months of their European and US launches. Subsequently the Bora model was introduced. The choice of colors available has also been expanded.

While Volkswagen's main focus in China will remain on manufacturing locally, it will import specialized models that cannot be sold in sufficient numbers to justify local production. Examples include Volkswagen's super luxury Phantom and a Chinese version of its luxury SUV, the Touareg, introduced at the Volkswagen Forum Beijing in 2004.

Marketing is another area where changes have been made. In the 1980s, with market demand uncertain and Volkswagen desiring to concentrate on manufacturing, the joint venture agreement stated that the sales of assembled cars would be the responsibility of SAIC. With the expansion of the market VW has developed its own sales network under its control. VW has introduced a version of an incentive system for dealers that it uses in Europe. The system uses a computerized network that allows call center managers to monitor how dealers follow up on customer inquiries. Volkswagen is considering entering into car purchase financing.

The company is also increasingly engaged in promotional activities. In 2004 it sponsored a four-week Volkswagen Forum Beijing including a Volkswagen Masters–China golf tournament; a Women's Day Celebration; activities featuring German and Chinese artists, musicians and actors; and a Tree Planting Day.

Questions

1. Evaluate Volkswagen's strategies with regard to marketing.

2. What choices did Volkswagen have in market entry strategy, and did it make a wise choice?

3. Should Volkswagen make a strong effort to maintain market share?

4. Could selling the Phantom in China be useful for Volkswagen even if it does not make money there?

5. What benefits can Volkswagen expect from its promotional activities?

CASE STUDY 8.4

Nu Skin Enterprises, Inc.

(This case study has been adapted from Ellen Sheng, Tales of the tape: Nu Skin entry into China. Dow Jones Newswires, 7 October 2002; and Tom Locke, Nu Skin sees possible $20–$30M revenue from China. Dow Jones Newswires, 26 September 2002.)

Nu Skin Enterprises, Inc. was ready in 2003 to roll out a line of skin care products for 1.3 billion consumers in mainland China, a move that has many challenges but could pay off in a big way. The Provo, Utah company is the latest US skin care product maker to gain entry to China's large market. It has spent US$70 million and four years of development to gain approval to start selling its specially developed Chinese product line at 31 retail locations in 14 cities. It also has a manufacturing facility.

China represents an important building block in the company's plans. With some of its current markets, such as Hong Kong and Taiwan, already mature, the company needs to enter new markets in order to drive revenue and earnings growth. Nu Skin's biggest single market is Japan, which generates 50% of revenue. In fact, its home market, the United States, contributes only about 17% of sales and is seeing waning revenue.

Nu Skin anticipates breaking even during its first year in China with sales of US$20 to US$30 million. In five years, the company projects revenue of up to

US$300 million. Nu Skin's revenue totaled US$967.62 million in 2002.

Direct selling with Chinese characteristics

Nu Skin is entering territory already covered by Avon Products Inc., Amway Corp. and Mary Kay Inc. To succeed, Nu Skin must not only face off with its competitors, but must also deal with China's unpredictable regulatory and business climate. The company is confident it will do well in China because of its record of success in 'similar markets' such as Taiwan, Hong Kong, and Singapore. But mainland China has a very different business environment from neighboring Hong Kong or Taiwan.

To comply with China's current ban on direct selling, the company has established retail locations from which all sales must be conducted. Also, sales reps must be recruited by the company, and the company pays them a fixed salary plus a sales-based commission to comply with other Chinese labor laws. Nu Skin generally relies on its sales reps to recruit and train new members. For China, the company will use offshore foreign distributors to help recruit salespeople. The company pays its sales reps based on the number of products sold and people recruited. The company sells its products, such as skin care creams and vitamin packages, at a wholesale price to distributors, who then sell the products at retail prices. Distributors are also paid a 5% override commission on up to six layers of other selling distributors recruited underneath them. Those commissions add up to about 39% of Nu Skin's total sales. Nu Skin has 570,000 active distributors, and the number of distributors continues to grow. It has 27,200 executive distributors, who are committed to at least US$2000 a month in sales that are generated by them personally and through the organization of distributors they have recruited and trained. Asian countries appear to be more open to one-to-one selling than countries in North America and elsewhere. For that reason China appears to be a good prospect.

Rich Wood, Nu Skin's vice president of finance and new market development, said the current modified sales approach 'can be very successful.' Even CEO Steven Lund is optimistic that the current restrictions are temporary as China opens up to foreign competition, allowing Nu Skin to do even better. Under a World Trade Organization pact, 'They've agreed to allow direct selling by 2004, and so those regulations are coming online and we are comfortable that we will be able to do business in the regulatory scheme they are building,' Lund has said.

Direct selling, whereby salesmen sell goods door to door, is a relatively new idea in China and one that has been viewed with some suspicion. A proliferation of corrupt pyramid schemes tainted the reputation of even legitimate US companies in the late 1990s and resulted in a government crackdown on all forms of direct selling in 1998. Amway, a privately owned direct seller of personal care products, has had to change its business plan several times since it entered the mainland Chinese market in April 1995. When the Chinese government abruptly banned direct selling, Amway changed its model by launching retail locations. Then, when the government banned multi-level commissions, the company had to change its compensation structure as well. Amway's flexibility helped it bounce back from the ban, and today the company is turning a profit from its China operations. The company posted sales in China of about US$480 million last year.

Avon's operations in China were also abruptly shut down by the 1998 ban, but by working with government regulators and altering its business model the company finally posted a profit there last year. Avon's China operations reported sales of nearly US$100 million a year ago, and is expected to rack up sales of US$150 to $200 million next year.

Face off with rivals

As the newest player in the Chinese market, Nu Skin must also play catch-up with competitors that have larger distribution networks and more extensive product lines on the market. The rivals are all targeting the same population of women – those at the upper end of the urban market.

Nu Skin is starting small. Its Scion line is made up of 12 products featuring Cyprolix, a 'special ingredient complex' made up of hydrolyzed soy protein and willow bark extract. The line includes a facial cleansing gel for 60 yuan, or about US$7; scalp and hair treatment for 30 yuan or US$3.60 and hand and body moisture lotion for 48 yuan or US$5.50. Nu Skin intends to introduce its premium line of Nu Skin-branded products soon and then launch its line of vitamin supplements, Pharmanex, in two years.

Amway sells an extensive line of skin care products, Artistry branded cosmetics, home care products, and Nutrilite-branded food supplements. The company's 2000 employees are spread through distribution outlets in 22 provinces and a plant in the southern city of Guangzhou.

Avon sells several lines of cosmetics and skin care products through 5000 independent beauty boutiques in department stores and shopping malls. Products include 'whitening' face cream for 180 yuan or US$21, a 'Spa' line of fruity-smelling bath gels and lotions starting at 35 yuan or US$4 and an anti-static undershirt.

Mary Kay also sells a large line of cosmetics and beauty products. The company has 75,000 'independent beauty consultants' and reported double-digit sales and recruitment last year.

Questions

1. Should Nu Skin enter the Chinese market with a type of distribution that is new to the company? Explain.

2. If, and when, the government of China allows direct selling away from a fixed place of business, what are the expectations for Nu Skin using one-to-one selling in the home or elsewhere in light of Avon, Amway, and Mary Kay also being in the market? Discuss.

3. Evaluate Nu Skin's entry mode of direct investment in a manufacturing facility.

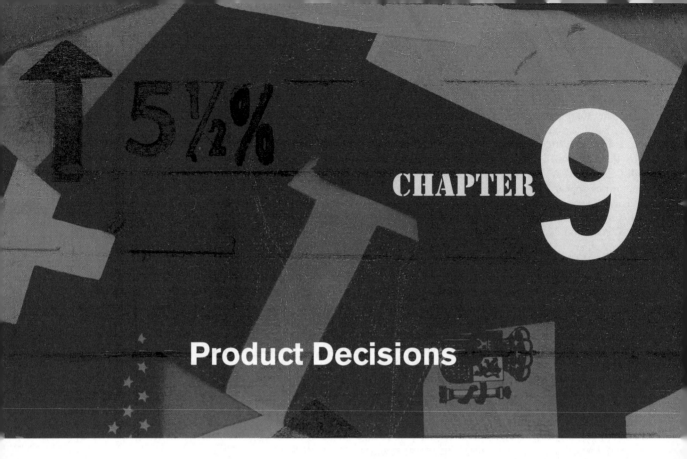

CHAPTER **9**

Product Decisions

9.1 Introduction

The product is the heart of the marketing mix. If the product fails to satisfy the end-user or the consumer in his/her needs, no additional efforts on any of the other ingredients of the marketing mix will improve the product performance in the marketplace. A washing machine that fails to perform satisfactorily will not become more attractive to the buyer just because large sums have been spent on an international marketing campaign extolling the virtue of the machine in question.

For a firm operating in multiple foreign markets, the problems of product planning and policies are extremely complex. Customers from different countries have varying requirements, and multinational decisions on product characteristics and containers or packages for products are necessarily quite complex. For example, Procter & Gamble's Vidal Sassoon shampoos contain a single fragrance worldwide but the amount of scent varies by country: less in Japan, where subtle scents are preferred, and more in Europe; General Foods blends different coffees for the British (who drink their coffee with milk), the French (who drink their coffee black), and Latin Americans (who prefer a chicory taste). There are examples from the automobile industry: Toyota's top-selling car in the United States is the Camry, a family sedan considered by many to be a bland design; its top-seller in Europe is a snub-nosed compact, the Yaris, which is Euro-styled and was designed by a Greek (Kerwin *et al.*, 2003).

9.2 Product policy

Product policy for international/export marketing has two major interrelated dimensions: (1) product planning and development, and (2) product strategy. These are applicable to both a single product itself and the total product mix. The product mix refers to the set (or assortment) of products that a company offers to customers. This assortment may consist of one or more product lines as well as individual products not part of a product line. Product lines are groups of products that are similar or have something in common – used together, sold to the same customer, handled through the same distribution channels; or are different versions (models) of the same thing. The important product policy questions facing the international marketer are as follows:

- Should the company keep a commitment to its existing product mix as the products reach maturity?
- How strongly should the firm follow a strategy of new product acquisition/innovation?
- What are the organizational requirements for following each of the above approaches?

In the case of export marketing, product strategy translates into policy regarding product adaptation or standardization (globalization). This is the extent to which the exporting company adapts (or customizes) its products to foreign markets. Product strategy together with market selection define the company's export marketing strategy and can be shown in the framework of a product/market matrix. The recent changing approach to product decisions in the case of Coca-Cola is illustrated in Exhibit 9.1.

| EXHIBIT 9.1 | 'Thinking local, acting local' – the new Coke formula |

The end of the 1990s was among the most traumatic in Coca-Cola's history, with 1999 as its *horrible year*. Profits declined, deals fell apart, and investors came to suspect that the firm had lost its way (*The Economist*, 2001).

Some of Coke's problems have been beyond the company's control, particularly the economic crises in Asia and growing disillusion with globalization in Europe. But others could be attributed to management. Pepsi was beating Coke in the United States, even as Pepsi shifted its focus towards salty snacks. Even worse, a poor approach to antitrust issues in Europe, a badly handled product-safety matter in Belgium, a racial discrimination case, and growing discontent among bottlers after big increases in syrup prices, had all adversely affected Coke.

One of the main problems for Coke was that the company had become a slow-moving, centralized bureaucracy, largely out of touch with local market trends. According to the head of European operations, 'If I want to launch a new product in Poland, I would have to put in a product approval request to Atlanta,' and it would be 'People who had never even been in Poland telling me whether I could do it or not.'

At the end of 1999 Mr Douglas Daft was appointed as new CEO of Coke. Mr Daft had spent nearly 30 years at Coke in Asia and was barely known at the firm's Atlanta headquarters. Mr Daft spent 2 years building the foundations for the return to Coke's glory days. The new strategy is to respond faster to changing consumer tastes by 'thinking local and acting local' and to boost growth by selling more of the noncarbonated products – such as ready-to-drink teas, coffees, waters, health drinks, and juices – that are taking market share from traditional sodas. It is a formula that served the new CEO well in Asia, where Coke now markets more than 250 different drinks.

The development of the noncarbonated business will require nothing less than a new business model centered on innovation and the invention of new brands. Europe, with its varied national markets, is a good test-bed for this. The company will be able to identify trends, incubate products, and get information back fast. Two recent examples of Coke's new approach are Fanta Exotic and Burn. Fanta Exotic was launched after a successful trial in just four months, compared with three to five years under the old system. And Burn, a new night-time energy drink for clubbers that was launched first in Australia, was launched in Britain within 60 days, using only word-of-mouth marketing. Higher management wants regional managers to think imaginatively when it comes to launching new 'short-cycle fashion brands,' and to overcome their fear of doing anything to damage their short-term financial targets.

We define a product as everything that the consumer or industrial purchaser/user receives when making the purchase or using the product. More formally, a product (or service) is:

> the sum of all the physical and psychological satisfactions that the buyer (or user) receives as a result of the purchase and/or use of a product.

Since a product includes everything that the buyer or user perceives as being part of the product, it can be viewed as having the following three major components:

1. the physical product core;
2. the product package;
3. auxiliary services.

Specific dimensions of each of these components are illustrated in Figure 9.1. In addition, price can also be regarded as part of a product, since buyers will view a product priced at €10 as being different from the same product (core, package, and auxiliary services) priced at €17. However, since price is important in its own right as an element of the export marketing mix it is discussed separately in Chapter 10.

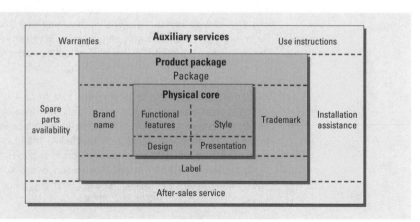

FIGURE 9.1

Dimensions of a product

9.3 Product planning and development

In international/export marketing there are four major forms of product development:

1. new product development or addition;
2. changes in existing products;
3. finding new uses for existing products;
4. product elimination.

All of these decision areas are important to the success of managing the product mix, although primary attention is frequently given to the problem of developing, adding, and modifying new products. Since any product may be at different stages in its life cycle in different national markets, concern for potential new uses and product elimination is as necessary as concern for the other facets of product development if a company is to operate effectively in foreign markets.

9.3.1 New products

There are many ways in which a company may add products to its product mix for marketing in foreign markets by exporting. The most obvious approach is to *export domestic products*. This strategy is easy to implement, at least initially, and may represent a relatively low-cost approach.

Another relatively easy way, though certainly not the most economical, is to *acquire a firm* or some operations of a firm that has products for which there are potential or existing overseas markets. The acquired firm may be a foreign firm whose products are designed for its home market and perhaps third markets, or it may be a company in the same country as the firm doing the acquiring. In the 1980s, and to an extent in the late 1990s, a great merger and acquisition movement spread throughout Europe which was aimed at creating companies that, among other things, would be large enough to engage in expensive product innovation programs. Such mergers included ones resulting in either greater market power in an industry or diversification. For example, Unilever and Nestlé created a joint venture for frozen foods, Dunlop and Pirelli's merger resulted in a stronger tire company for developing a market in the United States, and Ciba and Geigy merged to form a large chemical pharmaceutical company. More recently most of the mergers were more defensive, meaning that they were initiated in part because the company involved was under threat. Sometimes there was a change in the size or the nature of a particular market: McDonnell Douglas merged with Boeing for example, because its biggest customer, the United States Department of Defense, was cutting spending by half. Occasionally the threat lay in globalization, and its concomitant demand for greater scale: Chrysler merged with Daimler-Benz because, even as number three in the world's largest car market, it was too small to prosper alone. But, by late 2003 Chrysler was still struggling. Its models were unpopular, its factories were inefficient, and its brand image was weak. There are some who feel that this merger was a great mistake for Daimler-Benz, and that the company has been adversely affected (Edmondson and Kerwin, 2003).

Many acquisitions have cost a great deal of money, which seems to suggest that acquiring companies consider that it is cheaper in the long run to pay high prices for established brands than to invest in building new ones. For example, Ford

Motor Co. expanded its Premier Automotive Group by acquiring Europe's Jaguar, Land-Rover, Aston Martin, and Volvo (Kerwin, 2004). Although these examples are of very large companies, the acquisition approach is viable for any company that has the means to handle the acquisition.

A company can also add products to its offerings by *copying products* developed successfully by others. Many firms seem to follow this approach with varying degrees of success, although it is obviously not the approach used by a market leader.

Finally, a company can obtain its new products by *internal product development*. The process of internal product development can be viewed as an evolutionary process consisting of a number of stages. This is shown in Figure 9.2. As the process progresses from idea generation to evaluation to development to commercialization or introduction, each stage becomes progressively more expensive as measured in terms of both time and money. This is particularly the case for the development of drugs, where the time period of the discovery phase to the stage of realized sale often takes 10 to 15 years. The cost of making a wrong decision increases progressively from stage to stage. One characteristic of the process is the existence of a so-called decay curve of new product ideas whereby there is progressive rejection of ideas or projects at each stage. For example, the development process of a new drug by the Swedish company Pharma Swede resulted in one marketable drug product emerging from a starting set of 10,000 possibilities, and this occurred more than 10 years after the start of the process (Quelch *et al.*, 1994, p. 173). Similarly, in Figure 9.2 the number of arrows leaving each stage is less than that of the preceding stage. The invention of the micro compact car, the *smart*, a cross-border joint venture between Mercedes-Benz and SMH (Swatch) is shown in Exhibit 9.2.

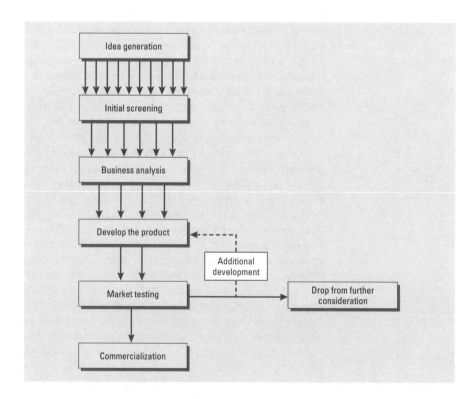

FIGURE 9.2

New product decision process

| EXHIBIT 9.2 | Inventing the *smart*: the micro compact car |

The whole adventure of the company MCC (Micro Compact Car) started in 1994 when Mercedes-Benz and SMH (Société Suisse de Microélectronique et d'Horlogerie SA) agreed on a rather unconventional cross-border joint venture in the automobile industry. Mercedes-Benz initially held 51% of the capital and SMH 49%. SMH was the company that made the world famous 'Swatch' line of products. The headquarters of MCC were located in Biel, Switzerland; the development premises in Renningen, Germany; and the production plant in Hambach, France. The marketing, sales, finance, and control functions were centralized in Biel. MCC Renningen started developing the car in March 1994, the site for the plant was selected in early 1995 and the plant received FF450 million in subsidies from the European Union as recognition for: (1) its environment-friendly production system, (2) creating a new market segment, and (3) inventiveness of the concept. Volume production was scheduled for July 1998.

'*smart*' was the name chosen for the new car, where *S* stands for Swatch, *M* for Mercedes, and *ART* to highlight the inventiveness of the total concept. Micro Compact Car was the name chosen for the company to evoke the revolutionary notion of a small city car. The joint venture was given extremely limited resources to carry out this experimental, yet rather ambitious, project.

The *smart* concept

Two major developments triggered the search for a new car concept. First, in Germany, consumers had since the early 1980s become increasingly sensitive to the societal costs of individual transportation, e.g., air pollution, energy, and material consumption. Second, individual car use was on the increase and the total number of registered cars as well as the average number of kilometers driven per capita had risen to alarming levels. In particular, the highly concentrated car park in urban areas was held responsible for negative effects on the quality of life, e.g., daily traffic jams, air pollution, shortage of parking space, and of course noise levels. Under strong pressure from consumer and environmentalist lobbies, governments were considering measures to restrict car pollution, control emissions and increase taxation on fuels.

What kind of car would people buy and how could you make money out of a venture such as this? These were the key questions for MCC. Since 1990, the Mercedes-Benz strategic design and car concept department had been working on a new concept to address these growing consumer concerns. The objective was to create a car with the following features: small size, yet maintaining a high level of passenger comfort and safety; low fuel consumption, using nontoxic, easy-to-recycle materials, and an environmentally friendly production process. However, further market research pointed out that consumers were not ready to acquire such a city car unless it offered additional qualitative and emotional utility. Therefore the car needed to provide the customer enhanced total driving experience to attract attention, a 'navigation system,' and customized design. To deliver distinct qualitative advantage the engineers were pushed to focus on three concepts: 'the pleasure to drive,' the 'mobility concept,' and the concept of a customized design.

The *smart* resulted in a significant departure from the usual product offerings from Mercedes-Benz, which traditionally focused on luxury cars. The car was supposed to create its own new market in the city car segment niche. It was revolutionary in its technological innovations and the way it was designed and produced. Only 2.50 m in length, 1.51 m in width, but 1.53 m high, the car was definitely designed to attract attention. The car had only two seats and customers could choose between two engines. To be on the market by October 1998, with a price tag ranging from DM16,000 to DM20,000, the *smart*

would first be distributed in Austria, Belgium, France, Germany, Italy, Luxembourg, The Netherlands, Spain, and Switzerland.

The *smart* was a tiny passenger car and safety was an even more important factor. MCC wanted it to be superior to other cars of this size. Its engineers were able to use the Tridion-frame technology invented by Mercedes-Benz, a steel-faced body for the car, around which the entire vehicle was designed. They also came up with the 'sandwich' design where the engine is located in the rear underneath the passenger compartment. The engine and the gearbox were designed as an integrated power unit decoupled from the passenger compartment. In the event of an accident the power unit would absorb the likely return shocks to which small cars are particularly prone. A crash box was installed in the front and in the back of the car and was able to fully absorb crashes at speeds of up to 15 kilometers per hour. Another key feature of the *smart*, likely to make it a market success, was its customized design and its 'mobility box' concept. The strategic design and car concept department aggressively pushed for shorter development time to allow for faster customer feedback and championed a 'modular' design that would allow complete customization. The customer, for instance, would walk into a *smart* dealership or visit the *smart* home page and custom design her own vehicle. She could independently choose from four colors for the body panels, two colors for the Tridion frame, or select one of the special colors and many other options. In addition, she could at any time after her purchase change any of these features very quickly and at low cost. The 'mobility box' offers individualized 'mobility' packages to include car navigation services, such as help functions, traffic information and assistance, and a mobile phone.

Today, the company is named Smart GmbH and is 100% owned by DaimlerChrysler. All management moved to Renningen, Germany in 1999. Smart is part of the Mercedes Car Group. By late 2003 the car was available in 28 countries throughout the world.

Four additional issues that are relevant to the internal development of new products merit brief discussion:

1. location of R&D facilities of firms;
2. the process of screening new product ideas;
3. the diffusion of new product innovations;
4. quality management.

Location of R&D

Research and development are major activities of the product development process. In general, one important issue facing the international operating company is to consider whether or not to locate R&D facilities abroad. Table 9.1 presents important criteria for considering overseas R&D locations. An important dimension in the evaluation process is the market orientation of the international company. Three possible 'market orientations' are considered: home market, host market, and world market. 'Home market' firms are primarily concerned with investing abroad for the purpose of serving their domestic market, while the foreign affiliate of the 'host' firms are oriented to the markets of the place where they are located. 'World market' firms are those foreign affiliates that are integrated to serve a standardized international market. These firms are typically organized to achieve economies of scale based upon high technology and a high degree of worldwide product standardization.

It seems that one important criteria for this evaluation is the 'critical mass' of the R&D resources. A 'critical mass' is the size necessary to ensure rich communications both within the group and between the group and its environment, to allow the degree of scientific and technical interaction among the group's personnel necessary to fulfil its mission.

TABLE 9.1

Important criteria for considering overseas R&D locations

	Home market firms	Host market firms	Worldwide market firms
Important criteria for considering an overseas R&D location	1. Proximity to operations 2. Availability of universities	1. Proximity to markets 2. Concept of overseas operations as full-scale business entities	1. Availability of pockets of skills in particular technical areas 2. Access to foreign scientific and technical communities 3. Availability of adequate infrastructure and universities
Important criteria for not considering overseas R&D locations	1. Products sold in the developing countries are not sophisticated 2. Lack of qualified scientists and engineers 3. Economics of centralized R&D	1. Increasing costs of doing R&D overseas 2. Economics of centralized R&D	1. Economics of centralized R&D 2. Difficulties in assembling R&D teams

Source: Behrman and Fisher, 1980

There seems to be considerable variation in the estimate of 'critical mass' for specific situations, but in general R&D laboratories in industries serving consumer markets (i.e., 'host market' firms) require a smaller R&D staff to reach 'critical mass' than do laboratories in science-based industries. Furthermore, R&D groups in consumer-oriented industries require less sophisticated personnel and less variety in personal specialization than do R&D groups in science-based industries.

For the larger multinational firms, in particular, the issue of location of R&D facilities involves answering two critical questions in implementing a global R&D policy (Zou and Ozsomer, 1999): (1) In how many countries should the R&D activities be located so that the locational advantages can be exploited? and (2) How should the R&D activities located in different countries be linked to benefit from cross-country synergies and improve the firm's global strategic position? The first involves configuration, or the pattern of a firm's R&D activities around the globe. Proper configuration enables the firm to exploit the comparative advantages of various countries, such that maximum efficiency can be gained. The second deals with coordination, which establishes concerted action among R&D activities and, therefore, is critical in managing interdependencies. Coordination of R&D activities is necessary to capture cross-national scope and learning benefits.

A recent study of subsidiary managers in seven European countries examined the degree to which commonly cited location advantages actually influence the incidence and level of subsidiary R&D (Davis and Meyer, 2004). Four aspects of the local environment were investigated: competitive conditions, supply conditions, scientific institutions, and government support. Major findings are: (1) only the presence of scientific institutions has a consistent, positive effect on the incidence and level of subsidiary R&D; (2) government support has a positive effect on the incidence of subsidiary R&D, but not its level; and (3) highly competitive environments have a negative effect, at least in small countries.

How is technology to be handled in terms of product and process? The two extremes seem to be 'incremental improvements' vs 'breakthroughs.' Many European and US companies tend to favor the latter and continually seek the technological breakthrough that will revolutionize things. In contrast, Japanese companies have tended to stress incremental improvements. Japanese companies seem to operate on the premise that technological leadership means gradual, perceived improvement (by consumers) throughout a product's life, while manufacturing processes are improved. Obviously, there are exceptions. For example, Sony had its blockbuster breakthrough with its Walkman. But Sony has also been able to refine repeatedly the original product that allows it to fend off the many imitators. Another example would be Intel and its incremental development of its processor chip, from the 8086 to the Pentium 4.

In the mid-2000s there is an even greater need for product and process R&D people to work as a team. By adapting a team approach to new product development, including design and manufacturing engineering, companies such as General Motors and NCR report that development time on new products is cut dramatically (Chiesa, 1995). Some companies even include marketing and sales personnel on such new product teams. By the early 1990s Ford Motor Company was using so-called 'centers of excellence' in the United Kingdom, United States, and Japan to develop common platforms for automobile models sold in different countries. Not all companies have been able to use the team approach effectively.

An integral part of research and development is product design. Often, companies establish design centers away from the home country, either to be market oriented or to have access to top product designers. For example, the Korean automobile manufacturer Hyundai opened a design studio in Fountain Valley, California in the United States in 1991. Increasingly, the company is moving its design process to the United States. Another example comes from China (Balfour and Roberts, 2003). Companies such as General Motors, Motorola, Siemens Mobile, LG Electronics, and Electrolux are using Chinese designers to create products tailored for China's domestic market. In addition, Chinese designers are working on new products such as automobiles, appliances, and electronic devices for export markets. These designers typically have worked on color and form, while conceptual work is done in Europe or the United States. With an increasing number of design graduates from its own schools and graduate programs abroad, China is moving toward a situation where 'Made in China' will be joined by 'Designed in China.'

Screening ideas

Since the cost of performing each stage in the product development process increases as an idea progresses from an idea to a product, careful attention must be paid to the screening of ideas. At this stage, the company should establish a system that is designed for either minimizing the chance that a 'bad' idea will be evaluated further, or minimizing the likelihood that a 'good' idea will be dropped.

Before any screening can occur, management must decide upon a set of criteria against which every idea can be judged and a model for applying the criteria. Such models as *ranking* ideas relative to each other or *scoring* each idea and seeing how each relates to a cut-off score are very useful in this stage of the product development process. Other models such as profitability indices or optimization models are better suited for the business analysis stage.

Management must be very careful in selecting screening criteria. Not every product type should be judged by exactly the same criteria. For companies that export products in diversified industries this means that multiple sets of criteria must be established. Or it may mean that a single master set of criteria may be developed and only selected criteria are used and/or are modeled differently, depending upon product type. Alternative approaches to modeling include the following:

- *Conjunctive model,* which uses all evaluative criteria. The product, in order to proceed for further consideration, must meet or exceed a minimum value for each of the criteria used.
- *Disjunctive model,* which is based on accepting a product that exceeds specified levels on one or a few key criteria, regardless of its score on the others.
- *Lexicographic model,* which is based on ranking the evaluation criteria in terms of their perceived importance. New product ideas are compared criterion by criterion until there is a superior idea. This may occur after the first criterion or after many criteria.
- *Linear compensatory model,* which assigns differential importance weights to each criterion and then determines a summated evaluation score for each product. Further analysis is conducted either on all products exceeding a minimum score or the one product scoring highest. This is perhaps the most widely used approach.

Table 9.2 shows one set of evaluative criteria that have been used to screen a wide range of product types. Screening probably is best utilized for dropping from further consideration the obviously inferior idea, rather than with identifying the superior idea per se.

Innovation and diffusion of products

Some companies, particularly multinational companies, often do not develop a product for their domestic market, but do so in response to opportunities in world markets. Consequently the company must select a strategy for the diffusion of the product from point of development to the market. The innovation and diffusion process is one of the most complex of all organizational processes. Past research has suggested a generic stages model that views the innovation process as consisting of sequential but also interaction subprocesses of sensing, response, and implementation. Nohria and Ghoshal (1997) have developed a typology of innovation processes of multinational enterprises that reveals four different patterns in terms of the location of sensing, response and implementation:

1. *The center-for-global innovation process.* Center-for-global innovations are those where the center – the parent company or a central facility such as the corporate R&D laboratory – creates a new product for worldwide use. Most instances of center-for-global innovations are technological innovations. Most involve no participation of the national subsidiaries except for the routine tasks such as marketing support at the implementation stage. The process by which L. M. Ericsson, the Swedish manufacturer of telecommunications switching and terminal equipment, created the AXE digital switch is one example of a center-for-global innovation. Impetus for the AXE digital switch came from an early sensing of both shifting market needs and emerging technological changes. The loss of an expected order from the Australian Post Office, combined with the excitement of a new digital switch developed by CIT-Alcatel (a French competitor), set in motion a formal review process within Ericsson's headquarters. The review resulted in a proposal for developing a radically new switching system. The new product was estimated to cost US$50 million, to require 2,000 worker-years of development effort, and to take five years before

TABLE 9.2

Evaluative criteria for screening new product ideas

1. *Societal factor*
    (a) Legality: product liability
    (b) Safety: usage hazards
    (c) Environmental impact: pollution potential
    (d) Societal impact: benefit to society

2. *Business risk factor*
    (a) Functional feasibility: work as intended
    (b) Production feasibility: technically feasible
    (c) Stage of development: prototype development
    (d) Investment costs: development costs
    (e) Payback period: time to recover investment
    (f) Profitability: profit potential
    (g) Marketing research: necessary market information
    (h) Research and development: production development

3. *Demand analysis*
    (a) Potential market: size of total market
    (b) Potential sales: economies of scale
    (c) Trend of demand: growth of demand
    (d) Stability of demand: demand fluctuation
    (e) Product life cycle: expected length of cycle
    (f) Product line potential: potential for additional products, multiple styles, and so on

4. *Market acceptance factor*
    (a) Compatibility: existing attitude compatibility
    (b) Learning: degree of learning for proper usage
    (c) Need: level of need/utility provided
    (d) Dependence: dependence on other products
    (e) Visibility: difficulty in communicating benefits
    (f) Promotion: cost to communicate benefits
    (g) Distribution: cost of distribution channels
    (h) Service: cost to provide after-sales service

5. *Competitive factor*
    (a) Appearance: perceived competitive superiority
    (b) Function: perceived usage relative to competition
    (c) Durability: perceived durability relative to competition
    (d) Price: selling price relative to competition
    (e) Existing competition: level of existing competition
    (f) New competition: potential level of new competition
    (g) Production: patentability or secrecy protection

it could be introduced to the market. The development was carried out entirely in Sweden. In 1976, the company had the first AXE switch in operation. By 1984, the system was installed in 59 countries around the world.

2. *The local-for-local innovation process.* Local-for-local innovations are created and implemented by a national subsidiary entirely at the local level. The sensing, response, and implementation tasks are all carried out within the subsidiary. Most of these innovations tend to be market led rather than technology driven and usually involve minor modifications of an existing technology, product, or administrative system.

    The ability of local subsidiaries to sense and respond in innovative ways to local needs and opportunities has been an important corporate asset for

The Blue Mosque,
Istanbul, Turkey

Unilever, for example. Advanced laundry detergents, a major product line of the company, were not appropriate for markets such as India where much of the laundry was done by hand in neighboring streams rather than at home in washing machines. A local adaptation that allowed synthetic detergents to be compressed into solid tablet form gave Unilever's local subsidiary a product that could capture a significant share of the traditional bar soap market. Similarly, in Turkey, where the company's margarine products did not sell well, an innovative application of Unilever's expertise in edible fats allowed the local subsidiary to develop a product from vegetable oils that competed with the traditional local clarified-butter product, *ghee*.

3. *The local-for-global innovation process.* Local-for-global innovations are those that emerge as local-for-local innovations, are subsequently found to be applicable in multiple locations, and are diffused to other organizational units within the multinational corporation. In other words, the initial sensing, response, and implementation tasks are undertaken by a single subsidiary, but then other subsidiaries participate in subsequent implementations as the innovation is diffused within the company.

   Such was the case when Philips' British subsidiary reorganized the structure of its consumer electronics marketing division based on an analysis of changes in its product line and a growing concentration in its distribution channels. The UK subsidiary abolished its uniform structure and organized the marketing department into three groups: an advanced-system group for technologically sophisticated, high-margin products (Laservisison and compact disk players); a mainstay group for high-volume mature products (color TVs and VCRs); and a mass-merchandizing group for older, declining products (i.e., portable cassette players). The new model for the marketing organization developed by the British subsidiary was clearly appropriate for other subsidiaries in Europe, and despite initial resistance the innovation was soon transferred to most other national organizations.

4. *The global-for-global innovation process.* Instead of finding individual local solutions or imposing a central solution on different subsidiaries, global-for-global innovations are created by pooling the resources and capabilities of many different organizational units of the MNC to arrive at a jointly developed general solution to an emerging global opportunity.

   One of the best examples of this mode of innovation was the way in which Procter & Gamble developed a global liquid detergent. Despite the success of liquid laundry detergents in the United States, all attempts to create a heavy-duty liquid detergent category in Europe had failed due to different washing practices and the superior performance of European powder detergents, which contained enzymes, bleach, and phosphates at levels not permitted in the United States. But P&G's European scientists were convinced that the liquid detergent's performance could be enhanced to match local powders. After seven years of work they developed a bleach substitute as well as a means to give enzymes stability in liquid form. Meanwhile, researchers in the United States were working on a new liquid better able to deal with the high clay soil content in dirty clothes in the United States, and the company's International Technology Coordination Group was working with P&G scientists in Japan to develop a more robust surfactant (the ingredient that removes greasy stains) to make the liquid more effective in the cold-water washes common in Japan. Joint effort on the part of all groups ultimately led to the launch of Liquid Tide in the United States, Liquid Cheer in Japan, and Liquid Ariel in Europe. Each product incorporated the best developments created in response to European, US, and Japanese market needs.

Postioning products. To a certain extent, how successfully a new product is diffused to an export market will be influenced by the product *positioning strategy* followed in a foreign market. Positioning is a communication strategy based on the notion of mental 'map.' Positioning refers to the act of locating a brand in the customers' minds over and against other products in terms of product attributes and benefits that the brand does or does not offer.

The conceptual foundation of international positioning is that a set of products can be viewed as different collections of attributes that can provide benefits to the buyer/user. When targeting specific market segments the marketer tries to develop those product attributes that generate the benefits matching the requirements of a targeted segment. This is a product design issue involving the product core, the package, and auxiliary services: the task is one of product positioning. Since it is the buyer/user perception of benefit-generating attributes that is important, product positioning is the activity that creates for a product a desired position in the buyer/user's mind. Whether a company is effective in positioning an export product where it wants depends heavily upon the extent to which any country-of-origin stereotype enters into the importing country's buyers' evaluation process. Past research has shown that the effect of country stereotype is to shift the position of a product in the perceptual space of buyers and thus alter the evaluation of its merits (Johansson and Thorelli, 1985). Figure 9.3 illustrates this for Japanese survey respondents' evaluations of automobiles. Figure 9.3(a) shows projections of the attributes underlying the evaluations. In Figure 9.3(a) the length of the vector for an attribute shows its degree of importance in determining the perceptual space. Color is not viewed as important, but durability is. By labeling the horizontal axis 'Performance' and the vertical axis 'Economy' we see that the Japanese view the US automobiles as relatively low on both dimensions. Figure 9.3(b) shows the misperceptions (stereotyping) by comparing actual and perceived positions in the perceptual space.

Quality management

Total quality management (TQM) became a major concern in the 1990s, and it will continue to be important. Company after company is finding out that managing for quality means more than just fine-tuning production controls. Total quality management is being used as a strategic weapon and companies are wanting to produce products of high quality at costs lower than competitors'. Japanese companies, for example, tend to use a preventive TQM approach that overhauls procedures in every function from R&D to marketing and service to avoid errors, while cutting costs anywhere from 10% to 50%. The idea is to get products to a market faster, with fewer defects, and at a lower cost. Companies adopting TQM often see dramatic results. For example, in the early 1990s the Swedish appliance manufacturer Electrolux reduced field-service repairs by 40% as a result of changes in design methods and other work processes.

In order to succeed in the international marketplace, particularly in the European Union, it is becoming necessary that companies adopt minimum standards set and administered by the International Organization for Standardization (ISO), known as ISO 9000. ISO 9000 specifies design, manufacturing, logistics, and other controls associated with producing quality products and services. ISO develops and administers standards; it does not register or certify companies (Paton, 2003). A company is issued a certificate of registration to, say, ISO 9001 by a registration/certification body, which is accredited by an accreditation body such as the Dutch Council for Accreditation (RvA). The European Committee for Standardization adopted it as the means of harmonizing the varying technical norms among EU member states. As shown in Exhibit 9.3 there exist five standards that collectively make up ISO 9000.

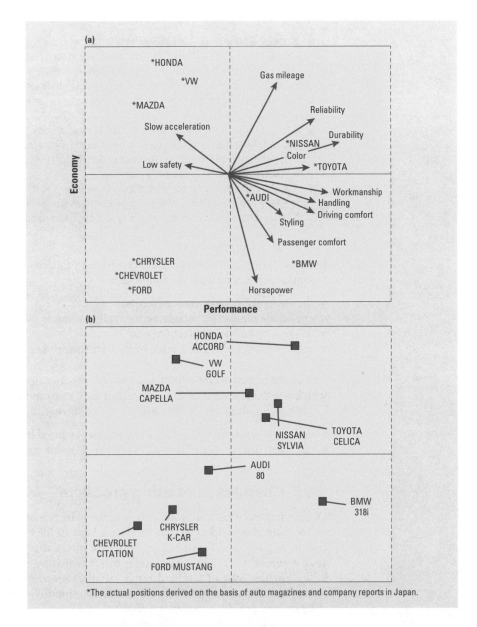

FIGURE 9.3

Perceptual space for automobiles: Japanese respondents.
(a) Interpreting the space;
(b) Misperceptions: actual positions (squares) vs perceived
Source: Johansson and Thorelli, 1985, pp. 66–7

EXHIBIT 9.3   The five standards of ISO 9000

The five standards that collectively make up the ISO 9000 are as follows:

- *ISO 9000.* This is the road map for the series. It is the overall term covering the other four standards in the series: 9001, 9002, 9003, and 9004.
- *ISO 9001.* This is the most comprehensive of the standards. It is a quality assurance that requires the demonstration of a supplier's capability to fulfil the requirements during all phases of operation: design, development, production, installation, and servicing.

- *ISO 9002*. This standard is a subset of ISO 9001 with the areas of design and development of the product removed. The standard is sometimes used as an interim standard before expanding to the more comprehensive ISO 9001. It is also the most common standard used by service companies. The quality guidelines are used to ensure that the service is provided using a consistent process that is described in the quality documents.
- *ISO 9003*. This standard provides a standard of quality assurance for firms only involved in final inspection and testing of products. Firms using this standard are basically performing the inspection function of the product that would normally be done by the customer when the product is received.
- *ISO 9004*. This standard provides a set of guidelines by which the management of a company can implement and develop an effective quality management system. There is heavy emphasis on meeting company and customer needs.

In short, ISO 9000 is primarily concerned with quality management, or what an organization does to fulfil the following:

- the customer's quality requirements;
- applicable regulatory requirements, while aiming to
- enhance customer satisfaction; and
- achieve continual improvement of its performance in pursuit of these objectives.

Closely related to ISO 9000 as it affects product development is ISO 14000, which is a 'family' of standards concerned with environmental management. This is what an organization does to achieve the following:

- minimize harmful effects on the environment caused by its activities, and
- continual improvement of its environmental performance.

9.3.2 Changes in existing products

Often a product that is in trouble or is in the market maturity or decline stages of its life cycle (discussed in section 9.4.3) can have its life extended by making modifications. Such modifications may be in the physical product core, the package, and/or auxiliary services. To an extent this may involve making a decision related to the broader issue of standardization or adaptation, an issue that we discuss in section 9.5. However, the need for considering modifying the product may arise independently of this broader question.

To an extent product modification, particularly at the outset of export to foreign markets, will be concerned with changing the product from that marketed in the domestic market. Unfortunately this is not done too often. At the present time foreign buyers are in a position to choose from a wide assortment of offerings from many sellers in many countries. Consequently they do not have to accept products that may represent offerings resulting from a company's surplus capacity, relative to its domestic market, or which may represent an outdated generation of a technology-based product. For the export marketer this means that products must be designed as specifically as economic and environmental considerations will allow for each specific overseas market being considered. For example, US, Swedish, and German automobiles exported to the United Kingdom, Australia, New Zealand, and Japan should be right-hand drive even though the home and other export markets are left-hand drive countries. Similarly, Japanese automobiles exported to western Europe (other than the United Kingdom) must be left-hand drive.

Often a company will need to continually change and improve its product(s) in order to maintain, and hopefully increase, its market share/position vis-à-vis competitors. This is the approach used by Sony for its Walkman personal stereo. Sony's ability to gain back market share it lost to other Japanese companies producing similar products is due to bringing out a stream of new and better models. It continually introduces new features to meet changing tastes.

9.3.3 New uses for existing products

Finding new uses for existing products can be an important approach to extending the life cycle for a product. For example, a home garden tractor marketed in an industrialized country such as the United States can be used commercially in a less developed country where farms are smaller and incomes lower.

Finding new uses for products may be difficult in foreign markets because of the distances between markets and the product planning and development activity of a company. Such distances can be great for the smaller company and for the company that relies primarily, if not solely, on exports. Also, a new use may also require some modification in the product. New uses may arise out of product research, consumer research, or chance. Regardless of the method by which new uses may arise, certain guidelines can be suggested, as follows:

- Is there a related application (for example, an insecticide for ants may be used for bees in Latin America)?
- A product sold to women may be sold to men and vice versa (such as deodorants).
- Can the product be used differently when used with another product (for example an after-shave lotion used as a pre-shave lotion with an electric razor)?
- Consumer products may have an industrial market and vice versa (such as garden tractors).
- Does the nature of attributes and/or ingredients suggest new uses (for example, the light weight and strength of balsa wood)?

Although chance can often play a meaningful role in success, it must be recognized that products are not always used in foreign markets for their intended purpose.

9.3.4 Product elimination

While primary attention is often given to the other forms of product planning and development, less emphasis is usually placed on deleting 'old' or weak products. This is unfortunate since keeping weak products can add substantially to overhead costs. In addition, company resources are often diverted from more profitable uses. One manifestation of carrying weak products in the product line is the *disproportionality phenomenon* in which a certain percentage of products in the product mix and product lines brings in a disproportionately greater or lesser percentage of sales and profits. This phenomenon is more popularly known as the 80–20 principle, although research evidence suggests that the empirical relationship is different. One study found that one-third of the products accounted for about three-quarters of sales and profits. The existence of this phenomenon alone does not necessarily mean that any given product should be deleted. There may be a valid reason that a product is not presently contributing as it should and it may contribute meaningfully in the future.

The existing product mix should be continually evaluated or monitored. For some export operations this can put a tremendous burden on the communication and information system of the firm. Nevertheless, monitoring of products should be done to examine their relevancy and contribution in the light of changing customer needs, competitive products, and environmental conditions. This is particularly important to the firm active in international markets because often the breadth and depth of the worldwide product line is greater than in the domestic market and the rate of change in international market conditions can be more rapid.

There is a need, then, for a procedure for the systematic review of products. As in screening new product ideas, criteria have to be established and a model developed for applying the criteria. For example, normal sales and cost analysis can provide the background data needed about a product. Then it can be evaluated by rating it along dimensions such as its future market potential, possible gain by modification of product and/or marketing strategy, alternative opportunities available to the company, its contribution to the sale of other products, and so on. Some type of rating value, weighted or unweighted, can then be used to guide the decision about elimination.

Once a product has been evaluated as being weak, thus becoming a candidate for elimination, decisions must be made as to *when* to withdraw it from foreign markets and, further, when to eliminate it from the company's product line. This again poses a number of issues concerning the uniformity of the worldwide product line. One approach is to withdraw products in potentially weak markets while retaining them in profitable markets. Alternatively, one could consider the withdrawal of the product from all markets. The appropriate approach depends on opportunity and other costs associated with carrying the product in a limited number of countries, and the autonomy of product management decisions in relation to other export marketing decisions.

There are times when the export marketer may find it desirable to replace a withdrawn product with a new one. The set of strategies for the synchronization of old product deletion with entry of a new product is known as *product phasing*.

		Product		
		No change	Modified	Technology change
Marketing	*No change*	**No change** • No change	**Face lift** • Appearance • Costs	**Inconspicuous substitution** • Technology • Materials • Manufacturing
	Re-mix	**Remerchandizing** • Name • Promotion • Price • Distribution	**Relaunch** • Costs • Promotion • Price • Distribution	**Conspicuous substitution** • Technology • Materials • Manufacturing • Name • Appearance • Promotion • Price • Distribution
	New market	**Brand repositioning** • Name • Promotion • Price • Distribution • Target • Competitors	**Product repositioning** • Name • Appearance • Costs • Promotion • Price • Distribution • Target • Competition	**Innovation** • Technology • Materials • Manufacturing • Promotion • Price • Target markets • Competition

FIGURE 9.4

The phasing continuity matrix
Source: adapted from Saunders (n.d.), p. 25

When a new product replaces an old one there is a choice in the element of the product/marketing mix that can be continued or discontinued. As shown in Figure 9.4, discontinuity increases from the 'No change' corner (upper left) to 'Innovation' (lower right).

There are many phasing strategies that can be used to implement the replacement of an old product. These include the basic *butt-on* approach where the replacement product is made available immediately after the old product is deleted, the *low season switch* where replacement occurs while demand is low, the *high season switch*, and *fudging*, where, in order to reduce discontinuity, overlapping occurs and there is no special market announcement about the replacement and replaced products.

9.4 Product mix decisions

Determining the export product mix involves making decisions with regard to the *breadth and length* of the product mix sold in a company's foreign market areas. Our major concern in this section is with those factors that affect such breadth and length. When these factors are used in product mix determination the analysis should be individual product-market situational. That is, they often act as limits to the expansion of a product line or the total mix, in one or more foreign markets. It must be remembered that these factors will help answer the question: 'Can a product be sold in a way that objectives are met?' Exhibit 9.4 discusses some major issues regarding managing consumer products in the international marketplace.

We discuss now an analytical approach to determining product line and then the specific considerations that go into determining the product mix.

EXHIBIT 9.4	**Managing a line of consumer products**

The cost of operating in the world market for consumer goods has increased greatly, and more companies are choosing to drop out. The cost now goes far beyond advertising budgets. It includes research to understand shifts in consumer attitudes; intertwined manufacturing and logistics networks providing superior retail service at lower cost; retaining information processing capability; and product discovery and development geared to speed new products.

The large companies in consumer goods categories amortize capabilities across related businesses and continually look to expand the definition of their categories. These companies apply a consistent set of principles, as follows (Silverstein, 1992):

- *Focus* resources on a broadly defined category across all core North American, European, and Asian markets.
- *Acquire* products to fill out the line.
- *Adapt* the world brand to local tastes.
- *Conduct* deep and thorough consumer research to understand all the possible segmentation dimensions and furiously hurl product at the most promising targets.

- *Control* the retail shelf and promotional program with value-added category management.
- *Recognize* profitable market share gain as a critical performance measure.
- *Behave* as if the category 'belongs' to them.

Only a few companies are rigorously applying the above principles, including Procter & Gamble in detergents and toiletries, Unilever in margarine, Philip Morris in tobacco, Coca-Cola soft drink in some markets and channels, PepsiCo in the remaining segments, Toyota in cars and light trucks, and Sony in consumer electronics.

Clout will come from focusing on winning categories, margin dollars that fund investment in behavior tracking, in-store activities, new product launches, new promotional schemes, and acquisitions that further consolidation. Companies will steadily expand their volume through brand development, clever consumer promotion, a stream of new products that respond to new consumer needs, and products that deliver superior performance.

9.4.1 Analytical approaches

Product portfolio

One approach that has been suggested for achieving an optimal export product mix, both within and across countries, is the *product portfolio* approach (Kotler and Armstrong, 2004, Ch. 2). The major assumptions of this approach are as follows:

- The two most relevant characteristics of a product portfolio are its expected return and its riskiness.
- Managers will choose to hold efficient portfolios that are defined as either maximizing expected returns for a given risk or minimizing risk for a given expected return.
- It is theoretically and operationally possible to identify efficient portfolios by a systematic analysis of information for each of *n* products.

The analytical procedures used in portfolio analysis can range from simple graphs to the use of calculus or complex mathematical programming. Given international management's preference for a trade-off between expected return and risk, the end result of the analysis could be a suggested proportion of the total product mix that should be allocated to each product and market in order to achieve efficiency.

In Chapter 4 we discussed the use of product portfolio approaches for market selection. Of particular note was the Boston Consulting Group approach in which products are classified as stars, question marks, cash cows, or dogs on the basis of relative market share and market growth rate, as illustrated in Figure 9.5. Relative market share, which is a surrogate measure of competitive strength within an industry, is computed by dividing a company's (or business unit, or brand) absolute market share by that of the leading competitor in an industry. Cash is generated via market share and is used to respond to market growth, and to survive in the long run a company needs a balanced portfolio where cash cows generate sufficient funds to support question marks and stars, which hopefully will become cash generators themselves at a later point in time.

The BCG portfolio approach has been criticized intensively, because it is not equally useful in all circumstances. In particular, for small and medium-sized companies involved in exporting (the largest group in terms of numbers of companies) the BCG approach will often lead to inappropriate and misleading applications.

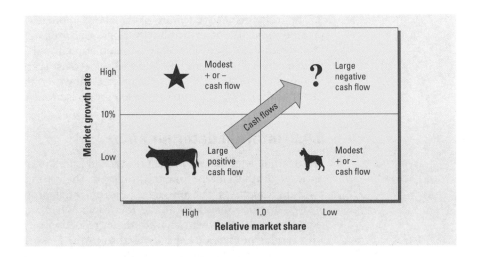

FIGURE 9.5

BCG portfolio matrix

First, the basic assumptions concerning the experience curve mechanism, that is, the links between market share and profitability, and the product life cycle as the driving force of market evaluation, are violated. Second, the measurements are questionable. How much market segmentation? Which level of geography? Should the definition of the product market be broad or narrow? These questions are important for measuring the relative market share and market growth rate, and so are the interpretations of the strategic bases for resource allocation.

Other issues relevant to the use of portfolio analysis by small and medium-sized exporters include the following:

- Do such companies even have a portfolio of strategic product/market combinations?
- Do these exporters have the environmental information needed to apply the approach, including strategically relevant information related to actual and future rate of market growth, market size, and market share?
- The key factors determining the success of these types of exporters are not necessarily based on costs, prices, and market shares (and therefore on economies of scale and experience-curve effects) but very often on other things such as quality, service, innovation capabilities, and a specific technology.

Since it is very difficult to implement the product portfolio approach, its major immediate value would seem to be in suggesting a framework for evaluating alternative product and/or market mixes.

Decision theory

Another approach involves the use of *statistical decision theory*, which provides a framework for improving not only the clarity of thought that is employed in the analytical process, but also a vehicle for quantifying certain aspects of the process (Moore and Thomas, 1976; Wright, 1984). Although this approach usually requires the use of probabilities and payoffs, and poor estimates are likely to lead to poor decisions, it could be argued that the method has some merit:

- It serves to focus attention on critical issues.
- It forces one to be explicit about alternative courses of action and their consequences.
- It provides a systematic procedure for quantifying and evaluating the consequences of alternative courses of action.

The really distinctive feature of the above approach is the personalistic interpretation and use of probability notions. Unfortunately, it is more difficult to utilize statistical decision theory in international and export product decisions than in domestic decisions; the degree of subjectivity is greater due to a greater lack of knowledge of the necessary probabilities. However, the framework for thought (if not analysis) is just as relevant to export decisions.

9.4.2 Internal determinants

The internal determinants of the breadth and length of the export product mix are those factors that emerge from the firm itself. These are collectively concerned with company objectives and resources, and potential profitability. Of concern are answers to such questions as the following. What are the firm's objectives in export marketing: growth, market share, reduction of risks, exporting products with surplus production capacity, and so forth? Does the product line make the best use of company resources and differential advantages, for example superior technology or management and marketing skills? Related to this is the philosophy of management regarding how serious they are about international/export marketing. Is permanence a desire of management? This question is analogous to making a distinction between sales and marketing. A sales approach would involve selling a product of which there is an excess in the hope that it can be found useful overseas. In contrast, the marketing approach dictates that a company assesses the needs of an overseas market and then attempts to find the product that best satisfies those needs.

The other elements of the export marketing mix can have an effect upon, and be affected by, product mix decisions. The mode of export entry abroad can be used as an illustration. If indirect export channels are to be used, a company may be able to concentrate on a limited number of the most profitable products. On the other hand, offering a broad range of products may be necessary for the profitable operation of direct export, for example for an overseas sales subsidiary. Similar concerns arise for nonexport market entry modes. For example, with licensing, only selected products from the overall product mix will be involved, and usually only a small number of them.

9.4.3 External determinants

External factors are those deriving from outside the company that affect product line decisions. We now take a look at some of these factors.

Customer influences

The nature of customer needs and wants in each relevant market affects the effectiveness of any marketing effort. Certainly, looking at these together with customer characteristics and interests provides the basis for determining which products should be, in the first place, considered and, second, which products should constitute the product mix. However, different assortments and quantities of products may be desired and purchased in various countries. One factor that often causes such differences is patterns of use, which may vary among market areas. For example, in the United States a bicycle is used primarily for recreation while in various parts of Europe and Asia the bicycle is used primarily for non-recreational transportation.

Cultural and social values that underlie market behavior can explain why some products can be marketed profitably in some foreign markets, but not in others.

Values influence a wide range of behavior, including product purchase and use, because they are central to people's lives. For example, as we discussed in Chapter 4, one approach to examining values uses the List of Values, which includes the following eight values: self-respect, sense of accomplishment, being well respected, security, warm relationships with others, sense of belonging, fun and enjoyment in life, and self-fulfillment. LOV is potentially useful in new product development as well as international market segmentation (Kahle *et al.*, 1987). The LOV has been used in consumer and management research settings in a variety of countries, including Japan, Scandinavian countries, the United States, the former USSR, Israel, Venezuela, Australia, PRC, Hong Kong, the Philippines, and Vietnam (Kahle *et al.*, 1999; Albaum *et al.*, 2004).

Earlier in this chapter we discussed country stereotypes in the context of positioning. Now we turn to so-called 'built-in' images that reflect the tendency for people to associate certain quality and products with certain countries (for example Swedish steel, French wines, German and Danish beer, US airplanes, English textiles, and Japanese consumer electronics). Research has shown that a product's country of origin is used by consumers as an attribute of the product, much as are specific product attributes, and probably has an independent influence on product evaluation (Shimp *et al.*, 1993).

Country of origin effects refer to the extent to which the place of manufacture influences product evaluations. The country of origin affects consumer perceptions of product quality (Chao, 1993) and has a significant influence, beyond advertising and marketing techniques, on the acceptance and success of a product. The goal of global marketers is to take advantage or benefit from positive, and to neutralize negative, country of origin biases.

Country of origin based stereotyping may be universal in nature; however, the degree to which it is applied and the prominence given in the evaluation of the product varies. This is, consumer sensitivity to the country of origin image diverges from one country to another (Papadopoulos *et al.*, 1987), may be hierarchical by country, and varies by the level of consumer knowledge. Studies have also concluded there is a tendency for consumers to more favorably evaluate their own home country products. This is known as *consumer ethnocentrism*. Ethnocentric views can lead to bias in favor of domestic products, but this will vary by country and product category. In short, while ethnocentrism often impacts on consumer purchasing of products, within the context of the world its impact is variable.

Cordell (1991) suggests that consumer preferences are more product specific for industrialized than for less developed countries. That is, a negative country of origin effect is evident when the home country of manufacture is less developed than alternative sources of goods. Also, research suggests that country of origin is used to evaluate a new product and give minimum consideration to product attributes (Maheswaran, 1994).

Some country of origin studies have measured country quality as a summary construct, rather than as a defined set of items that infer quality. Others viewed country image as a multidimensional or summary construct, of which perceived quality is but one dimension. To assess country image, four dimensions are common among the research. These dimensions are defined as follows:

- *Innovativeness* – the inclusion of new technology and engineering advances in a product.
- *Design* – the appearance, style, color(s), and variety.
- *Prestige* – the exclusivity, status, and brand name reputation.
- *Workmanship* – the product's reliability, durability, craftsmanship, and manufacturing quality.

Images based on perceptions of 'Made in "X" country' can lead to bias as it relates to national origin of products, and, thus can affect the desirable product mix offering of a company. At the very least these images can be formidable obstacles that can affect brand image strategy even to the point where manufacturers of foreign products should not stress their origin. Consumers' perceptions are affected by familiarity and availability of products together with the stereotype of the country. For instance, the image 'Made in Japan' would be strongly influenced by Sony, Toyota, and Nikon. However, although several studies have found that featuring Japan as a country of origin leads to favorable perceptions of product quality, other evidence shows that Chinese consumers might not purchase Japanese products because of World War II based animosity towards Japan (Maheswaran, 1994), and this judgement is independent of their judgements about the quality of Japanese products (Klein *et al.*, 1998). In particular, war animosity toward a particular country (e.g., Chinese consumers toward Japan and Dutch consumers toward Germany) reinforces consumer ethnocentrism and has a direct effect on reluctance to buy foreign products. In contrast, economic animosity due to feelings of economic dominance or aggression affects reluctance to buy indirectly through consumer ethnocentrism (Nijssen and Douglas, 2004). An example of economic animosity is the sensitivity of consumers in European countries to the economic power of Germany. In a study of this issue in eastern European countries, it was found that the country of origin played a dominant role in the decision making process of Russian and Polish consumers but relatively little emphasis was placed by Hungarian consumers (Ettenson, 1992).

A study of Canadian, British, and French consumers about products from the United States, Canada, Sweden, Japan, and their own country presents the following implications for export marketing strategy (Papadopoulos *et al.*, 1987):

- Attitude has three components – cognitive, affective, and behavioral – and a country's products may be judged favorable on one component but not so on another.
- There will be variation, country to country, in how ease of entry may be affected by how concerned the country's consumers are about product origins.
- Consumers do not always view their domestic products as being best across all evaluative dimensions.
- Export marketing strategies that stress the country of origin may meet with varying levels of success in different countries.
- It may be hard for new exporters to increase their international presence, given the dominance of foreign markets at present by a small group of major exporters.

These findings are illustrative of the many studies that have been conducted. One complicating factor is based on the increasing complexity with which multinational (or global or transnational) companies, and others as well, are expanding their international operations. Many companies are now using multi-country input to the design, sourcing, and manufacturing of a single product. It becomes difficult to assess just what the country of origin is for a given product. For example, if a product is financed in Japan, designed in Italy, and assembled in the United States, Mexico, and France using components invented in the United States and fabricated in Japan, what is the country of origin? Many companies often market products that have such a background.

So-called global outsourcing – buying products, components, materials, services, and so on, in foreign countries – is a contributing factor to the dilemma over country of origin. Major reasons that companies have increased purchasing from foreign sources include lower price, better quality, more advanced technology, more consistent attitude, and more cooperative delivery than domestic sources. Outsourcing has become a political issue and a matter of national concern in some countries, e.g., the United States, where it is claimed, often erroneously, to cause the export of jobs. In some cases the foreign source may be the only one available or it is done to fulfil a countertrade agreement (Davis, 1992). Another practice that can confuse matters is that of 'outward processing'. This occurs when a company exports components and parts for construction, and then reimports the constructed product for finishing.

A related effect is derived from ownership changes. Many companies, and their products, are still perceived to have an origin in their country of 'birth' even though they may be foreign owned. The following are some examples:

- Häagen-Dazs ice cream (US) is British owned.
- Arrow shirts (US) is French owned.
- Godiva chocolate (Belgian) is now a US company.

What can an international marketer/exporter do to overcome any such bias or predispositions that are due to 'built-in' images? Promotion may be used to overcome some bias, but predispositions are difficult, at best, to change by such means. Another possibility would be to use price as a means of overcoming attitudes. The effect of any existing origin-of-product bias on the selection between similar goods from different countries may be offset by manipulating price differentials. However, the exporter must be careful not to go too far as such a strategy could backfire if the exporter misreads any price/quality beliefs held by consumers.

Competition

Of concern are answers to questions such as the following. What is the type and range of products offered by competitors in the target market countries? Has the demand for a given product already been satisfied by competitors? If competition is strong the cost of market penetration for a given product may be very high, perhaps so high that it would not be worth the effort of trying to penetrate the market. For example, one US firm does not sell margarine in Europe, although it is one of its main domestic products, because of the strong position that Unilever has in margarine sales throughout Europe. A Swiss pharmaceutical company entered the Southeast Asian area by building a plant. From this plant the company would export to countries in the area. However, sales were less than anticipated (leading to excess capacity) because an important aspect of the competition was overlooked: the local black market controlled by government officials (Ricks, 1999, pp. 145–6).

To a large extent competition can be overcome by marketing specific products to selected segments of the market. The success of VW and Toyota are illustrations. Even here, though, the segment(s) may not be large enough nor have enough growth to sustain a new entrant into a market already dominated by competitive firms. CPC learned this lesson the hard way when it tried to market a successful European product, dry Knorr soup, in the United States. Not only was Campbell the dominant company (with Heinz a distant second), but the expected growth in the segment that used dehydrated packaged soups never materialized.

Product's stage in the life cycle

In Chapter 2 we discussed the product life cycle (PLC) as a theory to help explain and predict export trade. We now look at the concept at a more micro level, and see how it might affect a company's export product mix.

The product life cycle guides the development of product programs; it can be

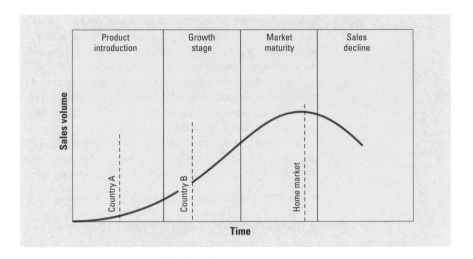

FIGURE 9.6

Product life cycle

used in the strategy of both existing and new products and can be involved in both product addition and elimination decisions. The life cycle can be a useful planning device, and is an essential methodological element of strategic international marketing. The development of products in various countries can be phased to the product cycle and growth of demand. Four distinct stages of the cycle can be delineated, as shown in Figure 9.6. In foreign markets, the time span for a product to pass through a stage may differ among the markets, and perhaps be longer than in the country of origin. In addition, a given product may be in a different stage in different countries. This is illustrated in Figure 9.6 by the product being in the market maturity stage in the home market, the introduction stage in country A, and the growth stage in country B.

A useful feature of the life-cycle concept is its emphasis on impending *change*. The PLC indicates quite clearly that the future will differ from the past and the present, although there may be some similarities. Another feature is that it alerts management to the strategic importance of timing, as the right strategy for one phase may not be appropriate for another phase. The product life cycle can also be used across markets. One approach would be to view markets as leader and follower countries. Figure 9.7 shows how leader and follower strategies vary by stage in the PLC. It is interesting to note that as the product enters stages 3 and 4 there are pressures to establish production facilities abroad, although the nature of countries differs for each strategy.

In both strategies company location is important. While there is a tendency for companies to introduce new products first in their home countries, such is not always the case. For example, Japanese color television producers exported to the United States before marketing them in Japan. Similarly, Hitachi exported video disks to the United States before selling them at home.

Depending upon its organization, a company may find it difficult to operate in more than one or two of the stages of the life cycle at any one time for any given product. Thus, *where* a product is in its life cycle in a foreign market can affect its inclusion in the product line being offered in that market. The differing characteristics of the PLC stages – for example advertising needs, competition, price behavior – illustrate why it would be difficult to operate in more than two stages at any one time.

Advanced planning should be directed at extending the life of the product. This means that export management should be thinking of later actions that may be necessary in the cycle even before a product is introduced into a foreign market. One or more of the following may be used to expand sales:

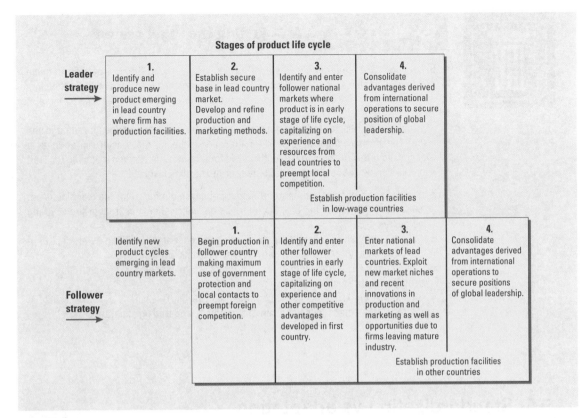

Stages of product life cycle

Leader strategy →

1.
Identify and produce new product emerging in lead country where firm has production facilities.

2.
Establish secure base in lead country market. Develop and refine production and marketing methods.

3.
Identify and enter follower national markets where product is in early stage of life cycle, capitalizing on experience and resources from lead countries to preempt local competition.

4.
Consolidate advantages derived from international operations to secure position of global leadership.

Establish production facilities in low-wage countries

Identify new product cycles emerging in lead country markets.

Follower strategy →

1.
Begin production in follower country making maximum use of government protection and local contacts to preempt foreign competition.

2.
Identify and enter other follower countries in early stage of life cycle, capitalizing on experience and other competitive advantages developed in first country.

3.
Enter national markets of lead countries. Exploit new market niches and recent innovations in production and marketing as well as opportunities due to firms leaving mature industry.

4.
Consolidate advantages derived from international operations to secure positions of global leadership.

Establish production facilities in other countries

FIGURE 9.7 Leader and follower strategies across the product life cycle

- Promote more frequent use among current users.
- Develop more varied use among current users.
- Create new users.
- Find new uses for the product.
- Make changes in the product.

Other external factors

A variety of other external factors may affect the breadth and length of the international product mix. Included among these are the following:

- the existing marketing structure of distribution, including facilitating agencies;
- government regulations on product content or packaging;
- import regulations including tariffs and nontariff barriers;
- climatic and other physical conditions;
- the level of economic development in markets.

Exhibit 9.5 gives an example of the problem facing Coca-Cola with its soft drinks vending machines in the Russian market.

EXHIBIT 9.5   **A Coke and the legal system**

In a country that regards beer as a soft drink, selling flavored fizzy water at premium prices is inevitably a bit of a challenge. Coca-Cola, which has invested millions of dollars in Russia since the collapse of communism, faces interesting challenges (*The Economist*, 2000).

Dealing with Russian teenagers' preference for alcohol over caffeine and sugar is one issue. The Russian legal system is another. For example, the western director of a Moscow advertising company recently asked for a Coca-Cola vending machine. His staff soon warned him about some of the bureaucratic hurdles involved:

- Giving Coca-Cola a square meter of floor space free of charge for the machine is not allowed: article 575 of the Civil Code forbids commercial entities from giving anything away free.
- Subletting or subleasing without the landlord's consent is forbidden by article 615 of the Code. In any case, this company's lease explicitly precludes it.
- The company risks the wrath of tax inspectors, as the machine will be operating on its premises without an official cash register.
- Selling soft drinks counts as retail trade in foodstuffs. This means potential trouble in the form of fire inspections and sanitary, medical, and trading standards.

9.5 Standardization vs adaptation

Closely related to the product mix decision is the issue of standardization or adaptation of individual products comprising the product mix. An overview of the broad issue of standardization of marketing programs, including the product dimension, is given by Delene *et al.* (1997), Solberg (2000), and Theodosiou and Leonidou (2003). Standardization or adaptation can occur for the physical product core (for example size, function, color), package, and auxiliary services. At one extreme a company will standardize by offering only one version of a product and this may be essentially the same product as that marketed in the domestic market. This approach is the essence of what is called a *global* product strategy.

A so-called global product is one designed to meet one of two standards: (1) the preferences of consumers in the domestic home market, or (2) the lowest common denominator of the export markets. At the other extreme, adaptation can be carried to the point of individualization whereby a company customizes products or services to meet the unique needs of individual buyers or groups of buyers in foreign markets. It has been suggested by Japanese officials, for example, that in order to exploit their market properly, companies should sell products that have been specially tailored to Japanese requirements. Examples of companies that have done this include Ore-Ida with frozen potatoes in smaller packages and with low salt content, and Triumph International producing women's underwear to fit Japanese women, who are smaller than Europeans.

The issue does not usually involve one extreme or the other. Of course, standardization is common for certain agricultural products, raw materials, and processed commodities sold to industry. Likewise individualization of products or services is common for certain kinds of buildings, plants, and equipment, as well as for certain services. But, although a policy may be primarily one of standardization or individualization, export product decisions usually have to be a compromise between these extremes. Adaptation can be *mandatory* or *voluntary*. Mandatory adaptation may be required because of such things as language differences, differing electrical systems, differing measurement systems and product specifications, and government requirements. A lumber mill in the United States, Vanport Manufacturing, produces lumber only for export to Japan by sizing its lumber exactly to the metric sizes used in Japan. Voluntary adaptation occurs when the exporter decides solely by itself to modify one or more products. For example, Switzerland-based Nestlé SA offers its popular instant coffee brand Nescafé with 200 variations – more variations than the number of countries that Nestlé sells coffee to.

Should an exporter try to globalize or standardize its products? It is not clear that there is a definite answer to this question, nor even that it is possible to completely standardize. Certainly it is possible to standardize a product concept such as fast food, convenience in use, state-of-the-art electronics, and so on. In general, however, some type of mandatory adaptation may have to be made or a voluntary change (minor or major) may be beneficial. Examples of global products are Coca-Cola, Sony television, McDonald's restaurants, Levi jeans, and Kentucky Fried Chicken. In fact each of these has required some adaptation to foreign market conditions:

Product	*Adaptation*
Sony TV	Voltage, broadcast standard
McDonald's	Menu, decor of restaurant
Levi jeans	Size mix, fabric, cut
Coca-Cola	Brand name (China), package
Kentucky Fried Chicken	Menu

From a buyer's standpoint a product should not be almost what the buyer wants, it should be exactly what he or she wants. This suggests a policy of individualization of products. However, from a seller's standpoint it is often possible to reduce costs by standardization. The key question then becomes: to what degree can the interests of producers in cutting costs be reconciled with the interests of buyers in having individualized products? Significant cost savings can come about from product design by offering the same basic product in several markets; often, however, with minor differences. Nestlé found it could reduce product variations in its KitKat line of chocolate bars worldwide when product testing showed that KitKat's particular combination of milk chocolate and wafers went over well across cultures. The differences were mainly in the raw materials, which are often purchased locally, and the packet sizes.

Cost savings can also come from packaging, as illustrated by a food processing firm selling prepared soups throughout Europe, which standardized packaging from the 11 different packages previously used. Another example, also from the packaged food industry, is Kellogg, which lowers packaging costs by using a multilanguage package for its individual-sized cereal packages in Europe.

While there definitely are production cost savings to be obtained from standardization, whether this should be viewed as one piece of evidence of the eventual emergence of global markets that consume and use global products is debatable. Wind and Douglas (1985) have argued that the cost of production is only one, and often not the critical, component in determining the total cost. In addition, they point out that there is no evidence supporting two other critical assumptions underlying the growing emergence of a standardization strategy:

1. Homogeneity of world wants, and an increase in the number of global market segments.

2. People are willing to sacrifice specific preferences in product features, functions, design, and so on for lower prices at higher quality.

Nevertheless, some companies do standardize to a greater or lesser degree. To illustrate, results from a study in the mid-1980s of adaptions made to 143 consumer nondurable goods transferred from domestic markets in the United States or the United Kingdom to four groups of nationally different country markets showing common cultural, economic, or political backgrounds indicate there is significantly different adaptation behavior among the different product dimensions. Overall, the percentages of adaption for different aspects of the product ranged from a low of 23% for usage instruction to a high of 71% for labeling.

The degree to which standardization is acceptable to the market – or to which individualization is necessary – depends in part on the kind of product involved. Figure 9.8 arranges a sample of products along two dimensions. The horizontal dimension, the consumer's preferred product, classifies products along a continuum from standardized to customized. The vertical dimension, rate of change of product, covers a spectrum from slow to fast.

For example industrial goods, such as steel and petrochemicals, may be homogeneous throughout the world. Certain consumer durables may be fairly well standardized except for technical characteristics such as different kinds of electrical plugs or internal components to handle different voltages. Consumer nondurables often require greater individualization due to more widely varying tastes, habits, attitudes or shopping behavior.

One of the most difficult products to standardize is food. Most of these are also slowly changing. For example, US-style Betty Crocker Cake Mixes were introduced unsuccessfully in England. Campbell's soup was reported to have lost US$10 million in Germany trying to change wet (canned) soup habits. Sara Lee, a large US packaged foods company, reportedly did not do very well in London with products developed in the United States. General Foods attempted to sell Jell-O (a brand of gelatin) in England in powder form (the US version) rather than jelled 'jelly' (the local form) and failed in its test market. Food is a difficult product class because food habits are deeply and emotionally ingrained in the culture of a people. And there are substantial differences not only regionally and internation-

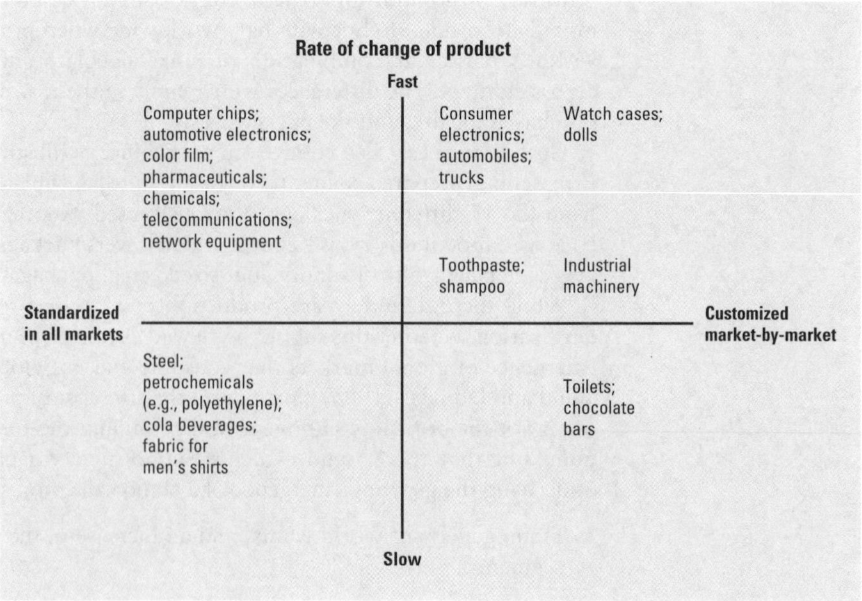

FIGURE 9.8

Market requirements and product characteristics

ally, but even from one community to the next. Often overlooked by food processors and packagers is that the key ingredient for a cook might be ritual. Therefore, convenience-based foods might not be readily accepted.

On the other hand, product policies on certain durable goods or industrial products are relatively easy to formulate. Perhaps the only change that needs to be made in the domestic model is to adapt the wiring for differences in electric current, or to change the size of the product. Automobiles may be designed in one country, exported, and meet fairly well the needs of drivers in another country. However, varying styling tastes, driving conditions (left or right side of road), as well as road and climate conditions, increasingly require some individualization.

Products requiring art work or creative designs ordinarily are relatively good candidates for standardization. Some forms of art and styles – such as are required by furniture, silverware, or china manufacturers – tend to be universal, with certain market segments in numerous countries. For example, Rosenthal-Porzellan AG, the large German china and glass producer, has stressed leadership through design. The company employs artists and designers from dozens of countries and lets them loose to produce their best work. They turn out products that meet both a high international level of taste and all the variations of taste within that level. Other types of artistic/creative products, especially for the consumer market, may be individualized, as shown in Figures 9.9 and 9.10.

For many products the world is not divided into national or regional markets. Rather it is divided into segments that transcend political or geographical boundaries of many countries. Therefore it sometimes is not necessary to adapt products

FIGURE 9.9 Designing pottery in Malaysia

FIGURE 9.10

Jewelry making in Bali,
Indonesia

to national markets. A good example is music. The musical tastes of teenagers in Tokyo are more nearly like the tastes of teenagers in London or Rome than they are like the tastes of their parents. There are products that have a small share of any given national market, but are successful in world markets, for example, Scotch whisky and quality cameras. This could involve being a niche marketer (see Exhibit 9.6).

| EXHIBIT 9.6 | Megacorp, Inc. vs Niche Ltd |

As we moved through the 1990s, two categories of market-oriented companies seem to have emerged from the marketing 'wars' of the 1980s – *Megacorp, Inc.* and *Niche Ltd* (*The Economist*, 1989). These types of companies continue to flourish in the 2000s. In most instances these companies are involved in the marketing of 'packaged consumer goods'. But the concepts underlying these companies can apply to firms producing and marketing any type of product where multiple branding is feasible.

Megacorp's approach is to sell a wide variety of brands throughout the global marketplace and, as such, is concerned with the global aspects of marketing. There are obvious economic benefits in producing the same product worldwide, then marketing it in the same way everywhere. This is the essence of having a *global product*. But such companies have found that if they wanted to sell their branded goods they need to be adapted somewhat to local markets. Very few exceptions exist – Coca-Cola and Marlboro are two examples.

As a result, the marketing managers of Megacorp companies put emphasis on *thinking global, but acting local*. In some instances this can mean altering the product's image. For example, Schweppes tonic water was advertised as a mixer for alcoholic drinks in the United Kingdom, but as a soft drink (such as Coca-Cola) in France. In other situations it is the product itself that is changed. Unilever's shampoo Timotei was marketed with the same image throughout the global marketplace, but the product was changed to suit the different ways that people in different cultures and nations wash their hair. In a similar manner, Procter & Gamble tried to develop products with a technology that could be applied globally but in forms suited to local needs. For example, its Japanese sanitary pad, Whisper, was lighter than its US product, Always.

During the 1980s most Megacorp-type companies changed their organization structure from a so-called *national* system where country managers controlled things towards a *product-driven* one where all sales are controlled from the head office, allowing country managers to benefit from the experiences of other countries. But even this did not seem to work. So companies have organized as 'transnational' companies, mixing the national and product-driven approaches.

Niche Ltd-type companies seem to have a simpler challenge – to survive! These are small, highly flexible companies that tend to specialize. Some specialize in luxury markets which have a demand structure that is so elastic it tends to be insensitive to price. In such markets the economies of scale of Megacorps have no effect. Other Niche companies operate in specialized industries with such high market barriers that Megacorp companies are not interested. A Niche Ltd company is always *defending* its market as it is concerned with a takeover, a decline in its market, or a chance discovery by a Megacorp that would make its product obsolete.

Government regulations, taxes, and political conditions can also be a factor. When Orange Fanta was introduced around the world it was found that there were many different legal requirements on the percentage of real orange juice that food products must contain if the word 'orange' is used. The differing regulations by the respective ministries of health required that Orange Fanta vary either the product formula, the name of the product, or the advertising messages. Likewise, the horsepower of automobile engines tends to be lower in countries where cars are taxed according to engine power. Also, pharmaceutical companies frequently encounter varying legal requirements of purity or tests of efficiency before a product can be introduced to a market.

There seem to be numerous conditions under which a policy of either standardization or individualization is desirable (see Table 9.3). But there seems to be no way to truly generalize on this matter except that the desirability of the policy depends on analysis of the market, buyer behavior, competition, government or legal regulations, and the numerous other factors in the relevant economic, social, and political environment. However, since modern transportation and communication media have made people in various countries more aware of the tastes of those from other areas, market segments with similar needs and wants tend to develop. This circumstance tends to make a policy of standardization feasible. At the same time, as local economies and citizens become more affluent, they demand greater variety. Thus the problem of meeting diverse needs and wants tends to intensify somewhat. These trends and countertrends, and the forces behind them, suggest that making good export product decisions is becoming increasingly difficult.

It is possible for individual companies to do both more standardization and greater individualization of products going to foreign markets. This seeming contradiction is explained as follows:

1. A policy of market segmentation can be followed to serve market segments that are similar in many nations and at the same time large enough in number to permit a simultaneous policy of standardization among such market segments.
2. Manufacturers from many countries increasingly have the ability to handle short production runs economically; to 'custom-make' goods to meet the increasingly individualized demands of markets as they become more affluent.

	Globalize when:	Adapt when:
Competitive factors		
Strength of competition	Weak	Strong
Market position	Dominant	Nondominant
Market factors		
Homogeneity of consumer preferences	Homogeneous	Heterogeneous
Potential for growth of currently small segments	Low	High
Consumer purchasing power	Uniform	Varied
Willingness of consumers to pay for differentiated products	Low	High
Need satisfied by product in markets served	Shared	Individual
Conditions of use	Uniform	Varied
Product factors		
Importance of scale economies in manufacturing	High	Low
Opportunities to learn from small-scale production of innovative products	Low	High
Type of product	Industrial	Consumer
Codes and restrictions	Uniform	Varied
Companies factors		
Scope of international involvement	Many or large markets	Few or small markets
Company resources (financial, personnel, production)	Limited	Abundant

Source: Rosen, 1986

Despite the potential benefit of standardization, there are and will continue to be some important obstacles arising from such sources as the physical environment (for example climate), stage of economic development (for example income levels), culture, competition, stage of product life cycle, availability of distribution outlets, legal restrictions, and even differences in consumer use. An example of the latter comes from the cellular phone industry. Finland-based Nokia found that mobile phone users in Finland and other countries in western Europe used the text-messaging capability of the cellular phone for communication. In contrast, users in the United States prefer voice communication. Although text messaging is being promoted in the United States this is a push strategy for promoting the feature itself.

9.5.1 An approach to determining standardization

How does an exporter determine the extent to which a product should be standardized across foreign markets? An approach that involves a certain amount of subjective judgement on the part of the decision maker is to select one country or market area as a 'benchmark' country and then evaluate all other markets in relation to it. Usually the benchmark will be the home country of the exporter, but it could very well be the country where success has been the greatest. A 10-point numerical rating scale, with 0 representing no hope for standardization and 10 indicating that standardization is quite feasible, can be used. The benchmark country is assigned the value of 10. If a manager decided that any point on the scale higher than 6 indicates that standardization should be considered seriously, then the profiles can reveal quickly which markets would warrant a closer look.

TABLE 9.4 Product–communications strategy alternatives

Strategy	Product function or need satisfied	Conditions of product use	Ability to buy product	Recommended product strategy	Recommended communications strategy	Relative cost of adjustments	Product examples
1	Same	Same	Yes	Extension	Extension	Low	Soft drinks
2	Different	Same	Yes	Extension	Adaptation	Medium	Bicycles
3	Same	Different	Yes	Adaptation	Extension	Low	Gasoline
4	Different	Different	Yes	Adaptation	Adaptation	Medium	Cards
5	Same	–	No	Invention	New communications	High	Hand-powered washing machine

To illustrate, a UK company is examining a number of markets. It decides to use its home market as the benchmark. The following ratings are made: Canada (8), France (8), Brazil (5), United States (10), Belgium (7), and Mexico (3). Using a cut-off value of 6, this example indicates that a similar product might be appropriate for Canada, France, Belgium, and the United States. This general approach can be used for the other marketing elements. As such, this approach can be useful in formulating market segmentation strategies.

9.5.2 Effect of other marketing variables

The issue of product standardization vs adaptation often cannot be resolved in isolation. Rather, product decisions of this type are often likely to be made with decisions regarding other export marketing variables. To illustrate, consider product and promotion policies. Five alternative strategies that can be identified are summarized in Table 9.4 (Keegan and Green, 2003, Ch. 11).

9.6 Packaging

Packaging is probably the cheapest, quickest, and easiest way to adapt a product to make it more suitable for foreign markets. Such adaptation goes beyond the matter of language and involves the question of altering appeals. The issues relevant to marketing revolve around the relative importance of the package's dual roles of *protection* and *promotion*. While protection is important, a package's promotional power cannot be ignored. Since the same product sells in different countries often for different reasons, package design can do much to express and present a product in a way that is preferred by customers in each market. The package must be convenient and easy for buyers to use. In addition, it should help sell the product by attracting the buyer's attention, identifying the product, and providing a reason to buy. Another way of looking at this is to apply the VIEW test in each market:

V – *Visibility*: the package must be easily distinguished from the visual competition.

I – *Information*: the package must quickly communicate the nature of its contents.

E – *Emotional impact*: the design must create favorable impressions in the mind of the consumer.

W – *Workability*: the package must function as protection and must also be efficient in home use.

Some amount of standardization is desirable, particularly for consumer goods that may be sold by self-service. Language may or may not be a problem. In various parts of Europe, such as Denmark, it is not uncommon to find products from English-speaking countries packaged using English. However, in some countries (for example Germany and the United States) you may need to use the country's language if you really want to tap the full potential of the market. The Canadian market requires bilingual packaging: English and French. In still other areas a company can export to selective markets using its own language because it is similar to that of the market. For example Danish, Swedish and Norwegian companies can use their own language in the other two markets.

Multilanguage packaging is becoming more and more prevalent for consumer goods. As previously cited, Kellogg's Corn Flakes, produced in Germany and distributed throughout Europe, in the past used 14 languages on a small individual package to convey contents and serving instructions. For its package of 3.5-inch diskettes, 3M shows opening instructions in five languages. A Danish company, Scandinavian Marzipan Factory A/S, uses French, English, and German on its Denmark brand of cookies, even those sold in Denmark. The French-made EKS model 38 diet and kitchen scale uses nine languages – Swedish, English, German, Finnish, Portuguese, Dutch, French, Italian, and Spanish – for showing capacity and other information about the product.

The Little Mermaid, Copenhagen, Denmark

Using standardized dimensions for packages leads to reductions in cost and generates some benefits. Some of these are as follows:

- Reduction of dimensions to a few standard sizes facilitates the machine packing of merchandise.
- Standardized package sizes reduce inventory investment in packaging materials, and facilitate mass production of the fewer types of packages and shipping boxes.
- Standardization permits full utilization of storage space at the factory and all levels of distribution.
- Uniform package dimensions permit a balanced format for display and for self-service selling.
- Standardized sizes simplify, expedite, and cut the cost of handling and shipping.

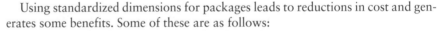

Standardization may be advantageous from the point of view of facilitating consumer convenience in purchasing, and possibly disadvantageous in terms of consumers' abilities to evaluate the characteristics of products of different producers, when such products come in identical package sizes. While products such as textiles lend themselves relatively readily to standardization, other products may cause problems. If cost savings are real, an exporter may be able to lower prices of the exported product(s), thus becoming more competitive and more appealing to consumers. For example, the Konica Corporation, a Japanese producer of film, uses the same blue package design in the United States, Europe, and the Far East. The goal is to be able to communicate multilingually and position itself against Kodak with its 'yellow box' identity worldwide, and Fuji with its 'green box' identity worldwide.

A potential problem is that countries may differ in their preferences for different packaging materials. The relative role of paper, plastic, glass, wood, and metal can vary in foreign markets. Unit size and internal packaging may also differ. In the United States food products such as crackers are sold with multiple paper-wrapped packages inside a box whereas in other parts of the world the tendency is to use bulk packages within the box. In the European Union all products sold within its borders must be labeled and specified only in metric measurement. Nonmetric measurements cannot be used in product advertising, catalogs, technical manuals, user instructions, and packaging design. Dual measurements on product labels – such as listing both ounces and liters on a soda bottle – are also prohibited.

A study of US multinational companies doing business in India concluded that packaging standardization is more often used in the early stages of entry into the market, when the firm's level of commitment is relatively low (Griffith *et al.*, 2002). This suggests that desire for cost efficiencies in packaging drives companies when first entering the market. Over time, however, companies may find that they are better able to achieve a competitive advantage by adapting packaging, and other forms of promotion as well, to more closely match consumer tastes in the local market.

Another issue regarding packaging arises through ecological problems. This has an impact on materials to be used and how they are used. Environmental policies are paramount in the EU and in other countries such as the United States. The EU has a directive on packaging and packaging waste. This directive aims to harmonize national measures concerning the management of packaging and packaging waste in order to reduce their impact on the environment. Within a few years after the directive has been implemented in the member states, the EU countries must ban packaging that is neither reusable nor recyclable and part of an established return channel. All packaging placed on the market in the community is included: sales packaging (primary), grouping packaging (secondary), and transport packaging (tertiary). All reusable and recoverable packaging must bear the appropriate marking(s) either on the packaging itself or on the label.

An issue related to packaging is *labeling*. A label is a means whereby information about the product (e.g., brand name and trademark, company name, etc.) is communicated to potential buyers and consumers. Throughout the world there is growing concern about the impact of products on the environment. This has led some companies to engage in so-called *green marketing* – i.e., matching the environmental performance of products and production processes to the current and future environmental concerns of consumers and other stakeholders. *Eco-labeling* has emerged. Eco-labeling is the identification of products that cause less harm to the environment than others in their category – i.e., products that are environmentally preferable to competing products (Bhatia, 1999, p. 106). Eco-labeling schemes exist in the European Union, Canada, the United States, Japan, and elsewhere, and may be administered by public sector (Europe) or private sector (United States) organizations. The end result for a company interested in identifying their more environmentally friendly products is that they have a recognized accreditation for a particular product. By meeting specified criteria, a label or seal can be attached to the package indicating this. This is closely related to the Green Dot program in Germany for recycling packaging and packing materials (discussed in Chapter 13).

In addition to the environment there is concern for safety requirements. A case in point is the European Union, where New Approach Directives are replacing national regulations. If a product falls within any of the EU's New Approach Directives it must have *CE marking* if it is to move freely throughout the EU (Brooks, 2002). CE marking on a product is a manufacturer's assertion that the product complies with the essential safety requirements of relevant European regulations for each country in which the manufacturer intends to market the product. There are CE marking directives for such diverse products as toys, machinery, medical devices and lifts.

9.7 Branding issues

A brand is anything that identifies a seller's goods or services and distinguishes them from others. A brand can be a word, letter, group of words, symbol, design, or some combination of these. A brand name is the spoken form of the brand. A trademark is a brand, or part of a brand, which is protected (in that others may not use it) by law. There are millions of names registered as trademarks in countries throughout the world, and the number increases every year.

Many companies have more than one trademark for their products, often having multiple trademarks for the same product. Figure 9.11 shows the many trademarks used by the Danish company LEGO.

The primary function of a brand is to identify the output of the owner of the brand – a manufacturer, exporter, agent, wholesaler, or retailer – so that buyers can distinguish it from other comparable merchandise. A brand indicates the origin of the product; it carries the assurance of quality; it serves as a warranty; it permits consumers to buy those products that satisfy their needs well and to avoid those that do not. A brand permits the manufacturer or seller or exporter to tell the market about the product and it helps purchasers to obtain what they want. In short, branding is necessary from the standpoint of both seller and buyer.

FIGURE 9.11

LEGO of Denmark uses many trademarks for its products
(Used by courtesy of the LEGO Group)

Branding is important to other elements in the marketing mix. Importers, wholesalers, and retailers in the importing country order by brand and promote brands in conjunction with their advertising and selling activities. Branding is one of the essentials that makes much advertising and selling not only desirable, but feasible. Without branding, manufacturers and exporters would find far fewer opportunities to advertise profitably. Without such opportunity undoubtedly some products would not even be introduced to the market. Manufacturers find that branding permits pricing policies, which assist both the price setter and the consumer in determining the appropriate price/value relationship. Although this discussion has been in the context of consumer goods, branding may also be important to the export of industrial products.

9.7.1 Brand protection

Brand protection is offered first at the national level, second at the regional level, and third at the international level. Virtually all countries, even those among the lesser developed in Africa, Asia, and Latin America, have some form of system for registering and protecting trademarks for foreign, as well as domestic, nationals. The EU has a directive that allows Community trademarks.

The nature of the protection afforded brands depends on the national legislation of each country. Most countries are 'code law' countries and follow the 'priority in registration' doctrine. In such countries the date of registration rather than prior use (with certain exceptions) determines who shall have the rights to use the brand. However, an increasing number of countries with such laws require continued use for a trademark to maintain protection. Included among the many countries following this doctrine are Bolivia, France, and Germany.

Some countries, however, protect brands even though they are not registered as a trademark. These countries, even though they may have codified their trademark law, have retained the 'priority in use' doctrine of the English common law tradition. Thus the rights to a trademark (with certain exceptions) depend upon priority in use. This approach is found in Canada, Taiwan, the Philippines, the United States, and other countries. In some countries a 'compromise' approach may be used. For example, in Israel either the first applicant or prior user will be entitled to registration, whichever is earlier. In Japan, although the first applicant is entitled to registration, another company that has been widely using the mark prior to the application can continue to use it. Also, even though France and Germany are 'first applicant' countries, exceptions are made for marks that are already well known as belonging to someone else.

There are a number of international, as well as bilateral, agreements that amplify and extend national legislation so as to provide protection for foreigners. The most important agreement is the International Convention for the Protection of Industrial Property (Paris Union) to which more than 70 countries adhere, including all major western European countries and the United States. Under this convention each country is required to extend national treatment to businesses of the other member countries. Another convention is the Madrid Agreement for International Registration of Trademarks. Under this agreement, the owner of a trademark registration in one of the signatory countries can have it filed and registered in the others. There is also the Agreement on Trade-related Aspects of Intellectual Property (TRIPS Agreement) of the World Trade Organization, which requires governments to create an effective deterrent against counterfeiting. Unfortunately, this agreement is vague on what this really means, and it does not have to be implemented by a country until 2006. There are also regional conventions, such as Inter-American conventions for western hemisphere countries.

Information on most of the trademark laws of the world is generally available to a firm from its national government, particularly in the industrialized nations. However, the many complexities in international trademark protection suggest that export marketers should consult legal counsel at an early stage when they plan to sell products abroad. In fact it has become routine among many large concerns to register trademarks abroad at the same time as they are registered in the home country. Smaller companies also should consider such a practice. If a company does register a trademark in foreign countries, it must not forget that the registration will be cancelled if the mark is not used within a specified period of time, which varies among countries. Also, use must be continuous.

Although every marketer would like its brand name and trademark to become a 'household word' this could lead to loss of the use of the trademark if it became *generic*. When a trademark becomes generic the trademark owners lose the exclusive right to use the mark in association with its products, because a court has found that the word, symbol, logo, or design no longer indicates to the public the source of the owner's goods. Instead, the mark now describes a *type* of goods. Examples of once famous trademarks that are now generic names are aspirin (in the United States), cellophane, escalator, octane, yo-yo, nylon, corn flakes, and thermos. There are some things that can be done to protect trademarks from this happening, discussed by Retsky (2001).

Owners of trademarks must be on the continual lookout for imitation or even outright piracy of brands that are exported to foreign countries. This is the growing problem of *counterfeit trade*, which is the practice of attaching brand names or trademarks to 'bogus' products or services, thereby deceiving customers into believing that they are purchasing the legitimate brand name or product of the owner of the trademark. As shown in Figure 9.12, at first glance it is often difficult to distinguish the copy from the 'real' product. The range of products for which this occurs is wide, as is the range of countries from which the products are exported. National governments are concerned with this problem, but it is difficult to resolve. To a large extent the exporter itself will have to 'police' its foreign markets in order to detect counterfeiting of its products. Then government can step in. For example, in 1998 Microsoft asked the Customs officials in Germany to seize a large shipment of counterfeit software entering the country from a plant in the United Kingdom, which they did. The owner of the plant, an American, was arrested when he entered Germany to check on the shipment. In 2003, Nike helped Vietnamese police seize 25 truckloads of fake shoes and shoe parts.

The piracy issue is one of violation of intellectual property rights. Particularly vulnerable are industries such as publishing and computer software. Various countries in Asia, such as China, Vietnam, and Indonesia, are known to be centers of this illegal activity. Often the existence of such activity affects relations between nations; for example, computer software piracy, particularly CD-ROM, has been an issue in the past in China's annual application to the United States for Most Favored Nation (MFN) status. China has been making concerted efforts to solve this problem, but it is not that easy to do. Tens of thousands of counterfeiters are at work in China today. They operate at all levels, from low-end products such as soap and shampoo through midrange (batteries, film), high-end (motorcycles), and top of the market. Companies that are 'favorites' include Procter & Gamble, Gillette, Bestfoods, Yamaha, Nike, Microsoft, Anheuser-Busch, DaimlerChrysler, and Epson (*Business Week*, 2000).

Lack of legislation is not the problem. China, Vietnam, and Indonesia all have laws covering intellectual property. All too often these laws are not enforced. Unfortunately results can be devastating. For example, in 2003 many infants in China who were fed fake formula died, while others have not had normal growth

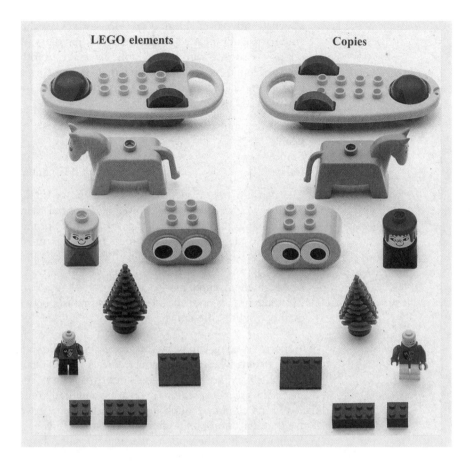

LEGO elements   Copies

FIGURE 9.12

Counterfeit products often do not meet the quality and safety standards of the genuine product, and this can lead to consumer confusion and dissatisfaction. These examples are from the Danish company LEGO. (Used by courtesy of the LEGO Group)

or health (Bodeen, 2004). Hopefully, over time enforcement will occur at a greater rate than it has in the past.

9.7.2 Branding decisions

Branding and trademark problems can be grouped into two major categories: (1) selecting a good brand, and (2) determining how many brands should be in the company's product line. Branding policies are important, since they may be used to accomplish a variety of important objectives. For example:

1. A single brand, or family brand, may be helpful in convincing consumers that each product is of the same quality or meets certain standards. Or, when the language of two or more countries is the same, a single brand may be used to make advertising more efficient. For example, a single brand may be useful for Austria and Germany, particularly when advertising crosses the border.

2. Individual (local) brands may be used in different national markets to meet unique market needs. For example, the New Zealand Dairy Board, a large exporter of dairy foods, uses the following brand names for its milk powder: Anchor and Fernleaf (Malaysia), Fernleaf (the Caribbean area), Magnolia (Singapore and the Philippines), and Mainland (Australia). Similarly, in Malaysia the Board uses the brand name Fern for its butter, although the name Anchor is its flagship brand. The reason that Anchor is not used for butter and is not promoted for milk powder in Malaysia is that the same name is used by

a widely advertised local beer. Housewives in the predominantly Muslim country are not inclined to buy their children dairy products that they subconsciously associate with an alcoholic beverage. Another example is the Dutch brewer Heineken, which operates in 170 countries and uses multiple brands throughout its markets. In 2003 the number of brands used within a country varied as follows:

The Netherlands	5	United States	4
China	2	Singapore	2
France	4	Germany	3
Italy	3	Poland, Panama, and Nigeria	2

The flagship brand, Heineken, is used in six of the countries listed above. Another brand, Amstel, is also used in six of the countries.

3. Multiple brands may be used as part of a policy of market segmentation: to sell essentially the same physical product to different market segments within a national market. Turning again to the New Zealand Dairy Board we find that more than one milk powder brand is used in Taiwan to meet the requirements of a highly segmented market where more than 30 brands compete.

4. Multiple brands may be used to distinguish between products of varying quality or with different characteristics.

In short, branding can be an integral aspect of the standardization versus adaptation decision. Even if the product core is not standardized, the brand may be used to satisfy export management's desire to achieve consistency with customers. There can be great cost savings in creating a unified brand across national borders. Such a brand eliminates duplication of design and art work, production, distribution, communications, and other related issues.

A company has the option of using the same brand in most or all foreign markets or in using individual, 'local' brands. There are certain cost and marketing advantages to using the same brand. However, local brands may also have advantages as well. The factors bearing on this choice include the following:

- customer needs;
- distribution and promotion methods to be used;
- competitive market structure;
- economies of scale in production and distribution;
- legal constraints;
- operational structures.

Despite the problems, companies still like using global branding. However, the products and/or markets should be related for maximum effectiveness. Sara Lee, a broad-base consumer goods company, extends a successful brand name to related products. Dim, a leading hosiery brand in France, has been extended to men's underwear and T-shirts. Gerber products uses the company's brand name in three product categories: food and formula (where it started), baby-care products, and clothing. The key is that all three product categories are aimed at children under the age of four.

Selection of a brand or trademark for use in multiple countries involves essentially the same considerations as when selecting a brand for use in a domestic market. Many companies today are taking a global perspective in selecting brands. Such a perspective requires a careful search among languages for unexpected meanings of words or phrases. In the past, companies with well-established brands have sometimes found it necessary to change their brand because of an unfortunate meaning in another language. For example, Vick's Chemical Company changed to

Wick's in Germany because the company name is an obscene word in the German language. Chinese exporters have tried to market to the West such products as Fang Fang lipstick, White Elephant batteries, and Pansy underwear for men. Situations such as these occur when the exporter tries to use its domestic brand. When a company has a name that is somewhat descriptive of the product there can still be translation problems. A company marketed a piece of equipment under the name Grab Bucket. In Germany this was translated as 'cemetery plot flowers.'

The so-called 'global brand' is typically positioned the same way in every market. For example, Carlsberg beer is positioned around the world as a premium beer. The Carlsberg brand is the global premium beer, with the specific objective of creating growth on a worldwide basis through a more widespread distribution supported by increased resources for communication and general market cultivation. Regional brands such as Tuborg are developed in the relevant regions around the world, whereas strong local brands such as Tetley's Super bock, Okocim, Falcon, Koff, etc. create the basis for strong local business systems in close contact with local consumer preferences. Similarly, Gucci bags are positioned as premium-priced bags. Benetton does similar positioning, but goes further by segmenting on the basis of age. Thus, within age group segments Benetton positions itself the same everywhere. A global brand is also marketed the same way in all markets, including following the same strategic principles, although the specific marketing mix may be modified to fit local market conditions – both consumer and competition.

A global brand does not just appear. It is created by international marketers. But it should be 'driven' by consumer considerations, not business convenience. On balance it is easier, and perhaps safer as well, to create a global brand from scratch than it is to reposition and rename an existing national brand. Based on a measure of brand value, the world's 10 most valuable global brands, in order, are (*Business Week*, 2003): Coca-Cola, Microsoft, IBM, GE, Intel, Nokia, Disney, McDonald's, Marlboro, Mercedes. All are brands of US companies except Nokia (Finland) and Mercedes (Germany). A good discussion of consumer preference for global brand is given by Steenkamp *et al.* (2003).

Choosing a brand name involves both legal and creative issues. In many countries there are specialist companies that can handle each of these aspects, such as advertising agencies to work on the creation of names.

SUMMARY

In this chapter we have discussed the broad area of product decisions. Of concern to international marketers/exporters are planning and developing of products for foreign markets and the strategies followed. Product strategy concentrates on policies regarding standardization or adaptation.

A product is defined as everything that the consumer or industrial purchaser/user receives when making the purchase or using the product. Relevant decision areas for product development were identified as new products, changes in existing products, new uses for existing products, and product elimination. Each of these was discussed, with emphasis given to new product considerations.

We next turned to product mix decisions and our concern was for those external and internal determinants affecting the breadth and length of a company's export product mix. Some discussion was denoted to analytical techniques, especially the product portfolio analysis.

A central issue facing all exporters that do business in multiforeign markets is whether to standardize a product for these markets or adapt it. There are no ready answers to this question. In reality, a company may have to compromise between the extremes. Sometimes adaptation is mandatory while at other times it is voluntary. A key question that arises is to what degree the interests of producers and exporters in cutting costs (by standardizing or globalizing) can be reconciled with the interests of buyers in having individualized products. In a way, market segmentation allows a company to do both. A final consideration is that the question often cannot be resolved in isolation since other export marketing variables interact with the product.

The final sections of the chapter dealt with packaging and branding issues. The matter of standardization or adaptation is also relevant for these two decision areas. Regarding packaging, there is also the issue of environmental impact, and this was discussed briefly in the context of what has been happening in Europe. Finally, the problems associated with counterfeit products were addressed briefly.

QUESTIONS FOR DISCUSSION

9.1 Explain the major product policy questions facing the exporting company. In what ways, if any, does size of company affect the relative importance of the question?

9.2 Discuss what you consider to be the best way for a company to acquire new products for its export product mix.

9.3 What is the relationship between a company's product development policies and its implementing a product positioning strategy?

9.4 Can an exporter realistically follow the strategy of product phasing when replacing a product in the product mix being exported to a foreign market? Explain.

9.5 Evaluate an exporter's use of the product portfolio approach in decisions about its product mix.

9.6 Is standardization or adaptation of individual products the most desirable policy for an exporter? Why or why not?

9.7 Explain briefly the alternative product/communications strategies available to an exporter.

9.8 For export packaging and branding considerations, discuss how language may be significant, particularly to the multimarket exporters.

9.9 Discuss the importance of using 'ecologically correct' packaging materials and the main impact of the packaging policy.

9.10 What can an individual exporter do about counterfeit products being sold as its own?

9.11 Find a company exporting its product under the same brand name in all (or most) countries and a company that uses a variety of brands. How do these companies differ and are these the reasons for different branding policies? Explain.

9.12 Is global branding limited to certain products, product classes, and/or companies, or can any company selling any product pursue global branding? Explain.

REFERENCES

Albaum, G., Yu, J., Wiese, N. and Herche, J. (2004). A cross-national study of the impact of culture-based values on marketing decision makers' management style. *Proceedings*, Third International Business and Economy Conference, San Francisco, 8–11, January.

Balfour, F. and Roberts, D. (2003). China's dream team. *Business Week*, 1 September, 50–1.

Behrman J. N. and Fisher W. A. (1980). Transnational corporations: market orientations and R&D abroad. *Columbia J. World Business*, 15(4), 55–60.

Bhatia, M. L. (1999). Eco-labelling: some perspectives. *Paradigm*, 2(2) (January), 104–11.

Bodeen, C. (2004). Fake formula kills babies in China. *Albuquerque Journal*, 21 April, A14.

Brooks, P. (2002). The global marketplace and CE marking. *Quality Digest*, July, 44–7.

Business Week (2000). China's piracy plague. 5 June, 44–8.

Business Week (2003). Brands in an age of anti-Americanism. 4 August, 69–78.

Chao, P. (1993). Partitioning country of origin effects: consumer evaluations. *J. Int. Business Studies*, 24(2), 291–313.

Chiesa, V. (1995). Globalizing R&D around centers of excellence. *Long Range Planning*, 28(8), 19–28.

Cordell, V. V. (1991). Competitive context and price as moderators of country of origin preferences. *J. Academy of Marketing Science*, 19(2), 123–9.

Davis, E. W. (1992). Global outsourcing: have US managers thrown the baby out with the bath water? *Business Horizons*, 35(4), 58–65.

Davis, L. N. and Meyer, K. E. (2004). Subsidiary research and development, and the local environment. *International Business Review*, 13(3), 359–82.

Delene, L., Meloche, M. S., and Hodkins J. (1997). International product strategy: building the standardization-modification decision. *Irish Marketing Review*, 40(1), 47–54.

Edmonson, G. and Kerwin, K. (2003). Stalled. *Business Week*, 29 September, 54–6.

Ettenson, R. (1992). Brand name and country of origin effects in the emerging economies of Russia, Poland, and Hungary. In *Proc. Int. Conf. Assoc. Consumer Research*, Amsterdam, June.

Griffith, D. A., Chandra, A. and Ryan, J. K., Jr (2002). Examining the intricacies of promotion standardization: factors influencing advertising message and packaging. *J. International Marketing*, 11(3), 30–47.

Johansson, J. K. and Thorelli, H. B. (1985). International product positioning. *J. Int. Business Studies*, 16(3), 57–75.

Kahle, L. R., Albaum, G. and Utsey, M. (1987). The list of values (LOV) as a segmentation tool in international marketing research and product introduction. In *Proc. 14th Int. Research Sem. Marketing*, Aix-en-Provence, France.

Kahle, L., Rose, G. and Shoham, A. (1999). Findings of LOV throughout the world and other evidence of cross-national consumer psychographics: an introduction. *J. Euromarketing*, 8(1/2), 1–14.

Keegan, W. J. and Green, M. (2003). *Global Marketing* 3rd edn. Upper Saddle River, NJ: Prentice-Hall.

Kerwin, K. (2004). Ford learns lessons of luxury. *Business Week*, 1 March, 116–17.

Kerwin, K., Palineri, C. and Magnusson, P. (2003). Can anything top Toyota? *Business Week*, 17 November, 114–22.

Klein, J. G., Ettenson, R. and Morris, M. D. (1998). The animosity model of foreign product purchase: an empirical test in the People's Republic of China. *J. Marketing*, 62, January, 89–100.

Kotler, P. and Armstrong G. (2004). *Principles of Marketing*. 10th edn. Upper Saddle River, NJ: Prentice-Hall.

Maheswaran, D. (1994). Country of origin as a stereotype: effects of consumer expertise and attribute strength on product evaluations. *J. Consumer Research* 21(3), 354–66.

Moore, P. G. and Thomas, H. (1976). *The Anatomy of Decisions*. London: Penguin.

Nijssen, E. J. and Douglas, S. P. (2004). Examining the animosity model in a country with a high level of foreign trade. *International J. Research in Marketing*, 21, 23–8.

Nohria, N. and Ghoshal, S. (1997). *The Differentiated Network*. San Francisco, CA: Jossey-Bass.

Papadopoulos, N. G., Heslop, L. A., Graby, F. and Avlonitis, G. (1987). Does 'country-of-origin' matter? Some findings from a cross-cultural study of consumer views about foreign products. Report 87–104, Marketing Science Institute, Cambridge, MA.

Paton, S. M. (2003). An 1S0 primer. *Quality Digest*, June, 4.

Quelch, J., Kashani, K., and Vandermerwe, S. (1994). *European Cases in Marketing Management*. Burr Ridge, IL: Irwin.

Retsky, M. L. (2001). Protect brands staunchly, but don't panic. *Marketing News*, 9 April, 8.

Ricks, D. A. (1999). *Blunders in International Business*. 3rd edn. Oxford, UK: Blackwell.

Rosen, B. N. (1986). Global products: when do they make sense? In *Proc. Academy Int. Business*, London.

Saunders, J. (n.d.). Product position phasing: the synchronous deletion and replacement of products. Working Paper.

Shimp, T. A., Samiee, S. and Madden, T. J. (1993). Countries and their products: a cognitive structure perspective. *J. Acad. Marketing Science*, 21(4), 323–30.

Silverstein, M. J. (1992). Companies that meet higher ante will win global marketing pot. *Marketing News*, 26(7), 30 March, 13.

Solberg, C. A. (2000). Educator insights: standardization of the international marketing mix: the role of the local subsidiary. *J. International Marketing*, 8(1) 78–98.

Steenkamp, J.-B. E. M., Batra, R. and Alden, D. L. (2003). How perceived brand globalness creates brand value. *J. International Business Studies*, 34, 53–65.

The Economist (1989). Still trying. 7 October, 92–3.

The Economist (2000). A Coke and a frown. 5 October.

The *Economist* (2001). New formula Coke. 3 February.

Theodosiou, M. and Leonidou, L. C. (2003). Standardization versus adaptation of international marketing strategy: an integrative assessment of the empirical research. *International Business Review*, 12, 141–71.

Wind, Y. and Douglas, S. (1985). The myth of globalization. Working Paper, New York University Graduate School of Business Administration.

Wright, G. (1984). *Behavioral Decision Theory*. Beverly Hills, CA: Sage.

Zou, S. and Ozsomer, A. (1999). Global product R&D and the firm's strategic position. *J. Marketing*, 7(1), 57–76.

FURTHER READING

Aaker, D. (1991). *Managing the Brand Equity: Capitalizing on the Value of the Brand Name*. New York: Free Press.

Balabanis, G. and Diamantopoulos, A. (2004). Domestic country bias, country-of-origin effects, and consumer ethnocentrism: a multidimensional unfolding approach. *J. Acad. Marketing Science*, 32(1) (Winter), 80–95.

Chang, H. F. L. (2003). International standardization strategies: the experiences of Australian and New Zealand firms operating in the Greater China markets. *J. International Marketing*, 11(3), 48–82.

Czinkota, M. R., Ronkainen, I. A. and Tarrant, J. J. (1995). *The Global Marketing Imperative*. Lincolnwood, IL: NTC Business Books, Ch. 7.

Klein, J. G. (2002). Us versus them, or us versus everyone? Delineating consumer aversion to foreign goods. *J. International Business Studies*, 33(2), 345–63.

Paliwoda, S. (1994). *The Essence of International Marketing*. Hemel Hempstead: Prentice-Hall, Ch. 4.

CASE STUDY 9.1

Daewoo Corporation

(This case study was written by Mitsuko Saito Duerr, San Francisco State University.)

In 2005 Daewoo Corporation, once Korea's second largest *chaebol*, no longer existed. The company's former Chairman, Woo Choong Kim, was under indictment for financial and accounting irregularities and was reportedly hiding out somewhere overseas. Some of Daewoo's component companies had gone bankrupt and been shut down, others had been reorganized under creditor supervision and were operating as independent enterprises, and some had been acquired by other Korean or foreign firms (using the name Daewoo, or other names). A controlling interest in the bankrupt Daewoo Motor Company in Korea, and a number of its overseas sales units, was purchased from its creditors by General Motors and partners in 2002. GM is now trying to rebuild the Daewoo brand in Europe. In 2004 Daewoo's automobile plant in China was purchased by General Motors and a Chinese partner.

There had been strong economic and political reasons for trying to keep Daewoo's component parts operating even after the corporation had been forced into a debt restructuring program by its creditors in 1999. Daewoo Corporation had subsidiaries in all major Korean industries, including consumer electronics, appliance manufacturing, steel making, shipbuilding, heavy machinery production, construction, textiles, securities, automobile manufacturing, export marketing, and others. The company was a major employer with 150,000 workers, accounted for 5% of Korea's gross domestic product and 13% of the nation's exports, and had 6000 suppliers. Most of its creditors were state-run banks with weak balance sheets that could not afford to have more nonperforming loans on their books. Many business people thought that Daewoo Corporation was so important that it could not be allowed to fail. However, with accumulated debts of $80 billion by 1999, and growing evidence of financial irregularities, it was forced into bankruptcy.

Even after Daewoo went bankrupt the creditor banks provided an additional $2 billion to keep the component companies operating. By February 2001 half of the *chaebol*'s remaining subsidiaries were for sale and the other half were under its creditor's control.

Daewoo's early marketing policies and expansionist approach had enabled the conglomerate to attain rapid growth into the 1990s. In the late 1980s and early 1990s the company reevaluated and changed its marketing approach. The costs of these changes, associated changes in investments, continued expansion during the Asian economic crisis of 1997, and changing Korean government policies, combined to lead to its downfall.

Early development and marketing policies

Daewoo was founded as a small exporter of textiles in 1967 by Woo Choong Kim. In 1969 and 1970 the United States became concerned about the threat to domestic textile manufacturers posed by rapidly increasing imports from Asia and considered imposing quotas on the imports. While most foreign exporters viewed the possibility of the United States imposing quotas as a threat, Mr Kim recognized it as an opportunity. He assumed that if quotas were imposed they would be allocated on the basis of historical performance. He thus made every effort to export as much as possible to the United States, regardless of profit, in the period before imposition. The result was that when the United States did impose quotas in 1971 Daewoo received a very large quota.

Because of the import quotas, prices of textiles eligible for entry to the United States doubled in the next six months, and then kept right on climbing. Daewoo became one of Korea's most profitable firms. The company expanded into textile manufacturing, purchasing modern equipment and quality control equipment identical to that used by US retailing giant, Sears. The company opened sales offices in London, New York, and Singapore, and was successful in obtaining orders from large chain stores. Their textiles were custom made and labeled with the brand names desired by the customers. The growing profits from textile manufacturing and exporting allowed Daewoo to expand into other industries.

As Chairman Kim's managerial reputation grew, he was asked by the Korean government to take over other ailing companies. In a desire to promote exports, and with the cooperation of the country's government-controlled banks, the Korean government provided relatively easy access to funds, tax incentives, and export incentives to companies with good export potential. The government also provided protection against imports for a number of products, and had policies that kept labor costs low during the early years of Korean development. Daewoo purchased 14 other firms and became part owner in additional companies, eventually having subsidiaries in most of Korea's major industrial sectors. Joint ventures were started with foreign companies that could offer technology and/or marketing channels. Daewoo also spent substantial sums on research and development, hired large numbers of qualified engineers, and concentrated on growth through being a world-class, low-cost, high quality manufacturer.

Most of its products were either components sold to original equipment manufacturers (those whose name plates appeared on the final products) or finished goods sold under another company's brand name. A visitor to the shipping room of its computer plant would find many cartons bearing German and other European brand names, and many US labels, but only a few with the Daewoo label. Its automobiles were marketed in the United States by General Motors as the LeMans (though sold in Korea under the Daewoo brand). The company produced fork lift trucks through a joint venture with Caterpillar, which then provided much of the marketing. Its television sets were sold in Europe, the United States, Japan, and elsewhere by domestic companies that put their names on the products.

The marketing strategy of letting others do much of the marketing under their private labels had served Daewoo very well from its founding up through the 1980s.

Changing marketing strategies in the 1990s

Reliance on the efforts of others to do much of its marketing came to be seen as potentially limiting growth for the conglomerate. It was recognized that doing its own international marketing would be expensive, entail some risks, and require additional skills that Daewoo had not yet adequately developed. It would require a great deal of time, effort, and attention from top management – scarce resources that would have to be diverted from other activities. Extensive advertising would be required to establish the Daewoo brand name in most lines; new marketing channels would need to be set up and foreign employees hired, paid, motivated, and controlled; warehousing space would have to be obtained; and other links in the distribution chain established. There was the danger of loss of sales to companies currently purchasing Daewoo products for distribution under the company's own name. In the case of automobiles, marketing under the company's own name would be a particularly expensive undertaking because of the dealer and service network that would have to be built up as well as the extensive advertising likely to be required.

The company had not held back from challenges in the past, and did want to be in control of its products down to the final user. Daewoo was particularly concerned that it should not miss out on opportunities in the expanded European market of 1992. The sales of Korean companies in some of the developed countries were weakening due to perceived problems in quality and after-sales service. In promoting the automobile brand abroad, Daewoo had to compete with the already established Korean car brand names of Kia and Hyundai.

Opportunities in eastern Europe, Latin America, and central Asia also seemed attractive. In order to expand under its own brand name in the Third World, the company began to invest in local production plants by buying failing domestic companies or building new plants. This gave it local visibility, influence with local governments, tax and other incentives, and access to low-cost labor. In 1993 alone Chairman Kim committed $8 billion to manufacturing and selling goods in Third World countries. By 1998 Daewoo was the largest single foreign investor in Poland, Romania, Vietnam, and Uzbekistan. It gained almost 30% of the automobile market in Poland.

Chairman Kim was particularly interested in expanding the sale of automobiles under the Daewoo Motor subsidiary name. For a period of time he relinquished the Chairmanship of the parent corporation (though apparently not his actual power) and moved to Europe to personally direct the automobile company expansion.

Changing economic and political environments

An Asian economic crisis in 1997 resulted in a sharp drop in demand for Korean exports by Third World countries and a deep cut in Korean domestic demand. Daewoo automobile sales in Korea fell by 56% in 1998. At the same time, sales in eastern Europe were substantially below projections and plants there were running at a loss. Operations in India were losing money and sales in the United States were below target. As market share was apparently viewed as more important than profits, some products were sold at a loss in order to increase sales.

In 1998 a reform-minded Dae Jung Kim became president of Korea. He promised to open the Korean market to foreigners, cut the collusive ties between big business and the government, and break up the *chaebol*. He repeatedly urged all of the *chaebol* to slim down and reduce their debts. Chairman Woo Chong Kim, however, continued to promote growth. In 1998 Daewoo issued bonds and increased its total debt by 40%, giving it a debt equal to 5.1 times its equity.

In spite of President Dae Jung Kim's desire to dismantle the conglomerates, the prospect of a bankruptcy by Daewoo threatened to plunge Korea into further problems as it emerged from the effects of the Asian economic crisis. Thus the government-controlled banks continued to roll over loans to the conglomerate until continuing losses caused the debts to reach totally unmanageable amounts in 1999. The debt restructuring program and breakup of the *chaebol* followed. Government investigations provided alleged evidence of widespread financial and accounting irregularities by a number of senior Daewoo officials, including the chairman. It was charged that they had illegally inflated the *chaebol*'s assets by $33 billion in order to hide financial troubles and persuade banks to make additional loans. Illegal diversions of funds were also charged. Seven of the top officials were arrested in February 2001 and Chairman Woo Chong Kim disappeared from the country.

Questions

1. What were the advantages and disadvantages of Daewoo's original strategy of manufacturing goods for marketing by other companies under the brand names of those companies?

2. Was Daewoo's original model out of date for a company in a rapidly industrializing country?

3. What were the advantages and disadvantages of expanding production as well as marketing overseas?

4. Should Daewoo have expanded its own marketing of Daewoo brands to so many countries in a short period of time? If not, how should they have chosen the markets into which they would go?

5. Was Daewoo's collapse due to internal policies, the external economic environment, or the Korean government's changes in attitude/policy?

CASE STUDY 9.2

Supreme Foods of France

(This case study was written by Professor Roger A. Kerin, Edwin L. Cox School of Business, Southern Methodist University, USA. All company data are disguised. Reprinted by permission of the author.)

Late in April 1993 Andre Belq had to prepare a budget for Spurt, a fruit-flavored concentrate that could be sprayed into a glass of water to produce a fruit-flavored beverage. The budget, which had to include forecast costs and revenues for Spurt for 12 months beginning 1 June 1993, was due on 15 May. The budget could include: (1) costs for further consumer research, (2) expenditures for a test market based on a tentative plan that had been submitted to Mr Belq by the firm's advertising agency, or (3) forecast revenues and costs for a national introduction in the United States.

The company

Supreme Foods of France (SFF) is a vertically integrated multinational firm that produces and markets a wide variety of convenience and commercial foods throughout western Europe. In addition, the company sells a variety of specialty products in the United States. These products are usually sold in the gourmet section of supermarkets.

SFF has shown consistent growth over the past decade. The company recorded sales of US$700 million in 1992. Although most company sales were generated from European operations, sales in the United States had shown a sizable increase. The growth of US sales was attributed to the increased popularity of gourmet foods, the popularity of French products, and the broadened distribution in supermarkets in the United States. In 1992 Supreme Foods of France sold its line of specialty food products through 50,000 US supermarkets and specialty food stores through a network of food brokers.

SFF was organized into three divisions: the Commercial Foods Division, the Consumer Foods Division, and the International Division. Each division was managed by a director, to whom several product managers and marketing support managers reported. In addition, a New Ventures Department operated at the corporate level, with the responsibility for identifying ways that the company could launch new products with high growth and high profit potential. The primary tasks of the New Ventures Department consisted of exploring new markets for the company and preparing market studies. These studies also identified possible means of entry and possible positions of new products in particular markets.

History of Spurt development

Development of Spurt began in late 1991, when the director of the International Division met with New Ventures Department executives to discuss opportunities in the US$46 billion beverage market in the United States. During the course of their discussion frequent reference was made to the apparent success of innovative package designs in launching new products in mature markets. For example, the director of the International Division noted that the Check-Up brand of toothpaste captured a sizable percentage of the toothpaste market because of the unique pump dispenser package. Gillette successfully launched Brush Plus – a device that dispenses shaving cream through a brush – and achieved a respectable share of the market. In each instance the unique packaging was considered at least partially responsible for the success of the product.

The meeting concluded with a consensus opinion that an opportunity existed for a new package design for dispensing beverages. Accordingly, the New Ventures Department went about searching for such a container.

Product development

In early 1992 the New Ventures Department came upon a container that appeared promising. The container, which had existed in France for five years, was used for dispensing a variety of fruit-flavored concentrates. The container held 15 oz of concentrate and made 6 qt of a beverage when added to water. A metered valve on the container assured that each time the valve was pressed, sufficient concentrate was squirted to produce an 8 oz drink (including tap water). Six fruit flavors were available: orange, grape, cherry, strawberry, raspberry, and fruit punch. The concentrate contained a vitamin C additive as well.

Further investigation revealed that the container and concentrate were generally well received. The product had a long shelf life and was ideal for storage since one container held the equivalent of 24 8 oz drinks and required no refrigeration. Both features were welcomed by French households. Furthermore, both children and adults appeared to like the flavors. Although actual sales statistics were not available, the product did have wide distribution in major metropolitan areas.

Informal discussions with the container's producer indicated that a licensing arrangement was possible whereby SFF would be given exclusive rights to market the product in the United States. SFF would obtain the product from the container's producer and would not have to build its own production facility since production capacity of 1.5 million cases (24 cans to one case) was available at the producer's plant. SFF sought and received approval to begin consumer research on the product in the United States. The tentative name given to the product was 'Spurt.'

Consumer research

In late June 1992 the New Ventures Department commissioned a series of focus group interviews on Spurt under the direction of Todd Anthony, an independent consultant in the United States. The primary aim of these studies was to obtain qualitative information on consumers' reactions to Spurt and to learn how they viewed it relative to canned fruit drinks such as Hi-C, carbonated soft drinks, and powdered soft drinks of the Kool-Aid variety. Anthony's report of the results were as follows:

1. Spurt is conceived as a children's drink but also, secondarily, as an all-family drink because of its excellent quality.
2. After mixing their drinks and before tasting, about half the respondents would buy Spurt, and half would not. Those who said they would buy the product were even more favorably disposed toward Spurt after tasting the product than before tasting it.
3. Spurt appears to be conceived as a high-grade Kool-Aid for day-to-day use, especially in the summer, rather than as a soft drink or canned fruit drink.
4. Consumers believe that the container may in general cause many problems: it can get plugged up, kids make a mess with it, and mothers will not know how much is left.
5. The present flavors produce excellent quality with little noticeable aftertaste. However, further taste testing will be required to optimize the quality of the drinks.
6. The need for a vitamin C additive in fruit-based drinks is recognized by all consumers.
7. Users, especially children, appear to enjoy squirting Spurt into a glass of water.
8. Although 99 cents for 24 servings is considered a fair price, there is some doubt whether the can would actually produce 24 servings.

In summary, Anthony remarked, 'We appear to have a "superior Kool-Aid" product that would be thought of as primarily for kids' consumption, but not exclusively so, at a reasonable price. The container appears to arouse misgivings among some mothers.'

In late August 1992 Todd Anthony conducted four focus groups with female heads of households with at least one child between 3 and 14 years of age. After a general discussion of fruit-type drinks, each group was asked to read a concept card describing the characteristics of the product, including its price, flavors, and cost per serving. Anthony summarized his inferences from the focus groups in four points:

1. Two groups were negative in their reaction to Spurt; two groups offered a positive response. The latter two said they would buy it for their children for a special treat. They did not say that the product would necessarily become a regular item.
2. The operation of the metered valve was a mildly pleasant surprise to the respondents. For many, it had a 'fun' element. However, continued use indicated that Spurt was a children's product, one that would likely be bought only with children in mind.
3. With initial trial of this product there would be tremendous variation in the amount used of the concentrate, the use of ice, and the need to stir. The wide range of colors in the final beverage indicates that consumers will be drinking very different drinks, depending on concentrate usage. As for ice, some use it and some do not. The addition of ice to the water before spraying the concentrate necessitates stirring. Many women stirred even if no ice was used.
4. From our studies, four distinct categories of beverage are evident: juices, nutritious fruit drinks, carbonated soft drinks, and Kool-Aids. Spurt falls into the Kool-Aid category. In comparison to Kool-Aids, Spurt wins on two points – more fun to use, and a better drink – and loses on two points – expensive (24 servings is not a believable figure) and on messiness.

In his summary, Anthony recommended that these findings represented a warning to move slowly on the project because it appeared that Spurt was potentially a one-time novelty that even children might not have the power to perpetuate. Soon after these results were submitted Mr Andre Belq, a product manager in the International Division, was assigned to the product.

To supplement the research being carried out by Anthony, Mr Belq commissioned SFF's advertising agency in the United States to study the relationship between Spurt and powdered soft drinks and consumption data related to consumer preferences and shopping behavior. In-home tests conducted by the agency indicated that Spurt was highly favored over powdered soft drinks for the fruit flavors. However, when the fruit punch flavor was tested alone against Hawaiian Punch, a canned fruit drink, Spurt lost on such features as taste, color, and aftertaste. Additional consumer tests by the agency on product positioning revealed that Spurt was most similar to carbonated soft drinks, not canned fruit drinks or powdered drinks. Furthermore, consumers expected to find Spurt located in the carbonated soft drink section of the supermarkets (see Table 9.5). Agency researchers considered this finding

TABLE 9.5	Product positioning and in-store location

	%
'Spurt most similar to …'	
Carbonated soft drinks	60
Canned fruit drinks	21
Powders	19
Total	100
Expected store location:	
With carbonated soft drinks	64
With canned fruit drinks	20
With powders	16
Total	100

important, since consumption data on beverages indicated that powdered soft drinks sales peaked in April and May and carbonated soft drinks sales in June and July. Moreover, the agency estimated that carbonated soft drinks captured 65% of the US$46 billion beverage market, powdered soft drinks captured 12%, and canned fruit drinks captured 23%. Based on shopping behavior patterns, shelf location, consumer preference tests, a newspaper coupon program, and a media expenditure level of US$5.5 million, agency researchers estimated that Spurt's introductory-year volume be 1.048 million 24-can cases.

Mr Belq's reading of the consumer test prompted him to commission another independent research agency to study Spurt. The research agency was instructed to determine the trial and repeat purchase rates for Spurt, given a sales price to consumers at 99 cents and two different advertising expenditure levels – US$5.5 million and US$7.9 million. Spurt would be tried by 15% of the 58 million households with children. The trial rate would increase to 20% at the US$7.9 million advertising expenditure level. The repeat purchase rate would be 35 or 40% of those households that tried the product. The report also noted that the average purchase for trial households would be one can. The average additional sales per repeat household per year would be three cans.[1]

Mr Belq continued to be plagued by the question of how to position Spurt. Should he position it against powdered soft drinks, canned fruit drinks, or carbonated soft drinks? Furthermore, he was not sure whether or not he had a product with long-term appeal or a novelty product that might be tried only once. The results from the consumer research studies were conflicting, and he was not sure whether the volume forecasts would make a profitable product introduction. A price–cost plan prepared by Mr Belq set the price to consumers for Spurt at 99 cents per can. The price per can to supermarkets was set at 72 cents, or US$17.28 per case of 24 cans. These cost and price figures, plus shipping costs, food broker commissions, and licensing fees, indicated that SFF could achieve a gross margin of US$6.50 per case. The only relevant fixed cost assignable to Spurt would be the advertising expenditure.

Options in April 1993

In late April 1993 Mr Belq received notice that he would have to prepare a budget for Spurt for 12 months beginning 1 June 1993. This budget would be based on a marketing plan that could include a test market, further consumer research, a full-scale introduction of Spurt in the United States, or some combination of these actions.

SFF's advertising agency executives advocated a test market for Spurt. The test market would be conducted in two cities and would run for 10 months beginning 1 July 1993. The agency recommended that Spurt be test marketed to evaluate marketplace performance with two strategies, under the assumption that even though Spurt was primarily a children's product, there might be an opportunity for substantial volume from consumers over 12 years old. In one city, a lower level of advertising spending (equivalent to US$5.5 million per year on a nationwide basis) would be put into appeals directed toward children, with minimal reinforcement of product advantages to the rest of the family. Consequently, advertising would be directed to Saturday morning cartoon shows and Sunday comic strips. The agency proposed a higher level of spending (equivalent to US$7.9 million per year on a nationwide basis) in the second test city. This test market would include an exact duplicate run of the advertising program in the first city, plus appeals directed toward an all-family audience, televised at prime evening time. In both cities redeemable coupons, which applied to the purchase of Spurt, would be inserted in Sunday comic strips and on a direct-mail program. Consumer panel data would be gathered in both cities to assess advertising effects and trial and repeat purchase rates to be used in drafting a national introduction program. The cost of the test market would be US$537,000.

Todd Anthony advocated further consumer research. He believed it was necessary to replicate his and the advertising agency's studies, since the agency's results conflicted with his observations. He believed the positioning issue was unresolved and improper positioning could result in Spurt's failure. Further consumer research would commence 1 June, and be completed 1 August 1993, at a cost of US$15,000.

Senior executives in the New Ventures Department advocated a national introduction. They reasoned that sufficient research had been conducted and that the advertising agency's test market plan could be easily expanded to a national program. Furthermore, they noted that the container producer was talking with a US-based food products firm about the possibility of using the container for a similar type of product. Failure to act with dispatch could forever eliminate the opportunity Spurt provided.

Note

1. The estimates made by the advertising agency and the independent research firm are based on what are called *pretest* market test computer models. These models incorporate such variables as advertising expenditure, promotion programming, and distribution coverage in a series of equations to estimate trial and repeat rates, as well as volume forecasts. Firms that have developed these models report that the models can reduce the failure rate in test markets by as much as 50%. For a nontechnical description of the use, benefits, and limitations of these computer models see R. Goydon, Easy numbers, *Forbes*, 23 September 1985, 180–1, and A. Stern, Test marketing enters a new era, *Dun's Business Month*, October 1985, 86–90.

Questions

1. Which action, or combination of actions, should Mr Belq recommend in his marketing plan? Why should he recommend this course of action(s)?
2. Discuss any other alternatives that should be considered by Supreme Foods.

CASE STUDY 9.3

BRL Hardy

(This case is adapted from an article written by Mary Pugh, Marketing Project Manager at the New South Wales Police, Australia, and Richard Fletcher, now at the University of Western Sydney, Australia. It was first published as 'Green international wine marketing,' Australasian Marketing Journal, 10(3), 2002, pp. 76–85.)

Introduction

One of the major challenges facing Australian firms in the international marketplace is how to differentiate their products from those of competitors. The global wine market is highly competitive and characterized by multiple players, labels, and products. One such player is BRL Hardy, Ltd.

Although by 2002 Australia had captured only 5% of the world's wine market, Australian wines were the fastest growing import category in key markets such as the United Kingdom and the United States, taking market share from traditional 'old world' wine producers such as France, Italy, Germany, and Spain. Australia's success to date stems not only from its comparative advantage of producing quality wines at reasonable prices but the ability of Australian wine companies to build brands to compete internationally.

BRL Hardy has identified a unique global market segment of a wine targeted at the environmentally conscious. The case covers the initial stages of the implementation of the strategy to position its Banrock Station brand of wines in the environmentally conscious segment, through to a promotional program of 'green' international wine marketing.

Background

BRL Hardy, Ltd was formed after a 1992 merger of South Australian-based wineries, Berri Renmano Ltd and Thomas Hardy and Sons Pty Ltd. It is now one of the top four wine producers in Australia and one of the top 10 largest wine groups in the world. Its Banrock Station brand, produced from grapes mostly grown in the Riverland region of South Australia, is the rising star of the company's wine portfolio. The first wine stock was produced as recently as 1995, and now production is 2.4 million cases a year.

In 1994 BRL Hardy acquired Banrock Station with 250 hectares of good soil for producing premium grape varieties. The rest of the property is made up of 900 hectares of wetland and 600 hectares of protected Mallee Woodland eco system. The property was suffering from the impact of prolonged farming and grazing. BRL Hardy, together with Wetland Care Australia, undertook a huge revegetation program to remove stock, install fish barriers and reintroduce natural wetting and drying cycles in the wetland. This has resulted in the native birds and fish, water plants, frogs, and insects returning to restore the health of the River Murray.

The 250 hectares of new vineyard are used to produce five major wine varieties. As Table 9.6 shows, red wines are more favored than white wine varieties.

The vineyard's total yield per year is 5000 tons, which converts to 3,500,000 liters of wine or 380,000 cases. The additional tonnage required to meet domestic and export demand of over 2 million cases comes from purchasing other grapes from local producers in the Riverland.

Australia and the global wine market

Market conditions are ripe for Australian wine producers to increase exports. The 'old world' wine producers such as France and Italy, which have historically held a large market share of the global export market, are in decline. Throughout the 1990s the 'old world' producers represented 67% of the export wine market. However, it is the 'new world' wine producers such as Australia, New Zealand, Chile, and South Africa who are experiencing growth. While only holding a relatively small market share of export volume, they are stealing share from the 'old world' producers.

TABLE 9.6 Banrock Station major wine varieties

Variety	Number of hectares planted
White wine	
Chardonnay	33
Semillon	43
Red wine	
Merlot	20
Cabernet	
Sauvignon	48
Shiraz	59

Source: BRL's Banrock Station

Following centuries of quality wine being associated with the 'old world' wine producers, Australian wines are now at the forefront of a new consumer trend led by 'new world' producers – the supply of good quality, good value, ready to drink now, good tasting, fruity wines. By the year 2000 Australia was ranked at No. 4 on export value and was the market leader in 'new world' wines.

Australia's remarkable success in the UK market is being demonstrated by delivering wine products that are relevant to everyday living and enjoyed by all. The wine brand 'Australia' is leveraging the effect of country-of-origin image in transferring favorable perceptions of quality fruit and a relaxed lifestyle to its food and wine. This positioning in the UK and US markets has stimulated demand for 'premium' category wines (i.e., those that are categorized above basic 'good quality/good value' wines).

Australian wine exports have grown substantially since the mid-1980s. At the end of the 2000/1 financial year. Australia exported 339 million liters, which was a 17% increase on the previous year. The export market volume for Australian wine is projected to double in size over the next 10 years to 676 million liters, accounting for 61% of production compared to 47% at

TABLE 9.7 Australian domestic market vs international market growth

| Year | Million liters | |
	Australian domestic	International markets
1990	301	42
2001 (current)	369	339
2010 (forecast)	437	676

Source: Adapted from Wine Federation of Australia and Australian Wine and Brandy Corporation, 2000

present. This is illustrated in Table 9.7.

There are five key quality/price segments in the wine industry. The principal driving force behind increased export sales is considered to be in the branded premium wine segment estimated to account for 34% of world wine sales. Australian brands in relation to these segments are shown in Table 9.8. As Table 9.8 shows, Banrock Station falls into the premium category (above 'basic', and below 'super-premium').

TABLE 9.8 Quality segments in the Australian wine industry

Segment	Price range	Volume market share	Illustrative brands
Icon	US$50 AU$50 £20	1%	Penfolds Grange Henschke Hill of Grace Leeuwin Chardonnay Petaluma Coonawarra
Ultra-premium	US$14–49.99 AU$15–49.99 £5–6.99	5%	Wolf Blass Grey Label Orlando St Hugo Brokenwood De Bortoli Yarra Valley Pipers Brook
Super premium	US$8–13.99 AU$10–14.99 £5–6.99	10%	Penfolds Koonunga Hill Jamieson's Run Rosemount Diamond Label Leasingham Bin Range
Premium	US$5–7.99 AU$5–9.99 £3–4.99	34%	Barramundi Banrock Station Jacobs Creek Lindeman's Bin Range Oxford Landing Hardy's Nottage Hill
Basic	US$<5	50%	

Developing an international strategy

The challenge for BRL Hardy is how to secure additional export sales in an increasingly competitive market. BRL Hardy needs to examine the following threats regarding the global marketplace for Australian wines:

- *New entrants*: There is a likely threat from new entrants, especially from large global liquor giants such as Diageo and Allied Domecq of the United Kingdom and LVMH and Pernod Ricard of France, who see the wine sector as a faster growing business compared to other liquor categories such as spirits, beer, and champagne with which they are historically associated. They are aggressively embarking on acquisitions and are interested in Australian wineries.
- *Suppliers*: There is a low threat from suppliers of grapes as these have little bargaining power apart from those supplying Merlot and Verdelho who have more clout due to some shortage of these varieties. Over-planting of red wine grapes has given Australian wineries scope to obtain higher-quality product at a competitive price.
- *Buyers*: The threat from buyers is high as securing distribution in a crowded market is difficult, especially when the distribution channels in major overseas markets are largely dominated by supermarket and major liquor chains. There is some evidence that distributors are becoming more favorably disposed towards Australian wines due to their consistent quality and availability.
- *Substitutes*: Although there are other alcoholic products that compete with wine, wine is the fastest growing alcoholic beverage on a global basis. Australia has a comparative advantage in producing innovative, high quality wines, because they can be consumed without aging, attract new wine consumers and young drinkers in 'old world' countries.

BRL Hardy countered the reaction of industry competitors to overseas market entry. It differentiated itself by pursuing a niche market strategy in its target overseas markets. This was achieved by positioning the Banrock Station brand initially in the two major markets of the United Kingdom and United States as a 'green' wine that supports conservation activities. This involved looking at the market from a different perspective and looking at areas to create value to differentiate the selected brand from the competitive pack. The key to discovering new value was asking four basic questions, as outlined in the Kim and Mauborgne model (1999) shown in Table 9.9.

Addressing these key questions has allowed BRL Hardy to create Banrock Station – a wine that can be simply positioned as 'good wine, good earth, good living.'

Creating a 'green' brand

Creating a 'green brand' meant tapping into the values and beliefs of wine buyers. As a starting point, BRL Hardy recognized that their investment in and achievement of restoring the magnificent Banrock Station wetlands might be shared with their customers. This strategy has proven to be successful in Australia. With every bottle of wine sold, a portion of the sale proceeds

---

TABLE 9.9 Creating a new value curve

Key questions	Areas for innovation
1. Reduce – What factors should be reduced well below the industry standard?	■ Price ■ Length of time to markets from the vine to the table ■ Alcohol content
2. Create – What factors should be created that the industry has never offered?	■ A representation of healthy living ■ An environmentally friendly wine ■ A relationship with the brand
3. Raise – What factors should be raised well above the industry standard?	■ Flavor and wine quality ■ Innovative wine styles ■ Interesting brands
4. Eliminate – What factors should be eliminated that the industry takes for granted?	■ Standard labels/packaging ■ Snob factor ■ Wine speak

➡

is donated to conservation projects to ensure environmental havens are restored and preserved for future generations. All proceeds in Australia go to Wetland Care Australia and Landcare Australia.

An analysis of the demographics of wine consumption in developed country markets such as Australia indicates that the bulk of wine consumers typically fall into the age group 40 and 60 years with a skew towards women. This generation is often referred to as 'Baby Boomers' and represents about 24% of the Australian population and around 33% of the US population. It is a group that is sensitive to environmental concerns. They were the original activists and are pro-environmentalists. They created the first Earth Day back in 1970. However, the values of this group have not previously been tapped as far as wine marketing is concerned.

For this strategy to be implemented, it must be conveyed to the customer via the brand. The brand is a bond with the customer, as it is perception in the mind of consumers' beliefs that gives values, and personalities to products. Strategically, it has been *brands* that have made Australian wine producers successful over market competitors – not the name of the wine producer. Successful wine, the brand, and the attitude it engenders, must relate to the wine consumer's own sense of individuality and unique style. For a 'green' wine, the brand image should appeal to consumers who are seeking a product that fits with their values of good living, being healthy, and their desire to act in an environmentally friendly way. Wine buyers are thinking about the quality connection – where the product comes from and what they are purchasing.

Although quality, price, and convenience are still uppermost in consumers' purchasing decisions, a fourth attribute, environmental compatibility, that is a product's greenness, has fast become a key determinant of purchase. By linking Banrock Station's brand attributes of good value, quality wines, that are ready to drink now, with a conservationist personality it is intended to create a new source of competitive advantage for BRL Hardy's Banrock Station brand. The brand slogan 'good earth, fine wine' easily identifies Banrock Station with supporting the environment. Additional in-store promotional material highlights Banrock Station wines' conservation initiatives – for example, a bottle flyer with a pelican. This saves the consumer time in evaluating other brands and helps them to distinguish easily the point of difference in retail outlets. In addition, Banrock Station's green brand image is reflected in the advertising, good news stories about conservation projects, packaging, point-of-purchase promotions, wine shows, and on the web site, where consumers can take a virtual tour of Banrock Station (see www.banrockstation.com.au).

Application of 'green' brand equity to international markets

As the 'green' marketing approach was successful in Australia, BRL Hardy decided to apply it to selected overseas markets that were considered to offer long-term growth potential. The eight selected international wine markets were the United States, The Netherlands, Canada, Sweden, New Zealand, the United Kingdom, Finland, and Denmark. All are developed markets with environmentally sensitive 'Baby Boomers.' In these markets, BRL Hardy aimed to build strategic alliances with local conservation groups, as they did in Australia. A key to the market entry strategy was establishing strategic alliances with 'green' groups so as to increase consumers' confidence in and credibility of the brand's environmental claims. In each case a certain percentage of profit from sales of each bottle of wine would go to the alliance partner to fund environmental projects. Implementation of this international approach was facilitated by hiring an environmental scientist, Tony Sharley, who manages the Banrock Station Wine and Wetland Center in Australia. In this role, he manages conservation projects with organizations in key international markets and can verify Banrock Station's 'green' credentials.

High on the agenda was Australia's number one wine market, the United Kingdom, where BRL Hardy sells a number of successful brands. In the United Kingdom Banrock Station wines and the Wildfowl and Wetlands Trust are working together to save wetlands and wildlife. Funds from Banrock Station wines are being used to support the continual monitoring and maintenance of 4000 acres of wetland reserves and their wildlife.

In Canada, BRL Hardy established its own organization to coordinate environmental projects to help conserve and protect endangered birds and wetlands (the Banrock Station Wine Wetland Foundation, Canada). In the United States, Banrock Station has partnered with the Arthur R. Marshall Foundation to champion restoration and preservation of America's Greater Everglades ecosystem and sponsored Cypress Tree Planting Day in an effort to restore the Everglades ancient forest.

In Europe, Banrock Station wines are working with the Swedish Wetland Fund, with proceeds supporting Oster-Malma, Lida and other wetlands in the area; in Finland, with Liminganlahti Bay, a high-profile and highly regarded wetland region in the north of Finland; and in The Netherlands Banrock Station wines, Staatsbosbeheer and Wetlands International are working together to save wetlands. Recently Banrock Station commenced a partnership with Danish Nature, which will use the funds to restore wetland in the Langelands region.

Closer to home, Banrock Station wines have combined with the environment group Wetland Care New Zealand to sponsor wetland restoration projects throughout New Zealand. The first year's proceeds under the sponsorship helped to develop a wetland within the widely acclaimed Karori Sanctuary in Wellington, followed by the creation of a wetland at Masterton in the Wairarapa region.

International sales growth

In Australia, Banrock Station was positioned in the premium wine category offering good value for money. A similar price positioning has been adopted in selected overseas markets. As such, it is priced below some of its major Australian competitors. In the United Kingdom, BRL Hardy has had to contend with a distribution system where the retailers are gate-keepers and 10 accounts can represent 70% of the market. Here, buyer label (i.e., private brand) wines account for a considerable share of the market. To counter this it is necessary for Banrock Station to create an awareness of its own brand. This is being achieved via the use of cinema and outdoor advertising, including the London Underground. By contrast, in the United States the distribution of wines approximates that of fast moving consumer goods and there is little wine sold under the labels of buyers. The value-for-money claim is being augmented in all markets with the 'support conservation theme' and point-of-sale support that reinforces the conservation image. It is this support that provides the brand with its unique selling proposition.

This approach has proved to be a deciding factor at the point of purchase amongst the growing number of environmentally conscious consumers in the United States and the United Kingdom. Banrock Station wines are proving to be an outstanding performer for BRL Hardy in international markets.

There is no doubt that much of this success has been due to the 'green' international wine marketing of Banrock Station wines. Future growth is dependent upon maintaining and building the brand through continued investment in conservation projects and the development of new markets with significant segments of environmentally friendly wine buyers.

References

Kim, C. and Mauborgne, R. (1999). Creating new market space. *Harvard Business Review*, January–February, 83–93.

Wine Federation of Australia and Australian Wine and Brandy Corporation (2000). *The Marketing Decade 2000–2010*, November (www.awbc.com.au).

Questions

1. Evaluate BRL Hardy's decision to market its Banrock Station brand as a 'green product' in international markets.

2. Is this a good strategy for a market such as the United Kingdom, where buyer label (private brand) wines have a dominant position?

3. Should BRL Hardy consider buyer labels for its green product?

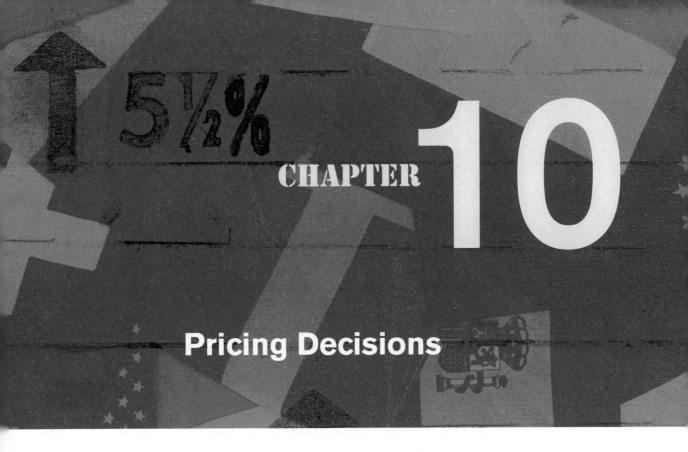

CHAPTER 10

Pricing Decisions

10.1 Introduction

Pricing for international marketing involves: (1) export pricing and (2) pricing within national markets when some form of nonexport market entry mode has been used, such as investment or assembly. Exporters themselves are often concerned with pricing within a national market. If direct exporting is being used to enter a foreign market the exporter may have to additionally price for other levels in the distribution channel. For example, the export of a consumer good may represent a wholesale transaction to the exporter's 'captive' wholesale organization within a foreign market. When the product is further sold to a retail organization, this involves pricing within a market. On a more general level, the exporter should always be concerned about pricing practices and strategies relevant to the product as it moves to ultimate consumer or industrial user. Pricing within a national market is domestic pricing. From a technical perspective it makes no difference which national market is the object of interest.

The management of prices and price policies in export marketing is somewhat more complex than in domestic marketing. Due to increasing complexity of markets, price decisions are becoming more critical than ever. All markets are becoming more segmented, which results in firms having to broaden their product lines with different products aimed at different types of customer. Gone are the days when Coca-Cola could offer a single brand to everyone; today it has Coke, Diet Coke, Caffeine Free Coke, Cherry Coke, etc. Successful B2B marketing is similarly shifting from commodity selling to speciality products. Of concern to the export marketing manager are the following:

- pricing decisions for products that are produced wholly or in part in one country and marketed in another (exports);
- pricing decisions that are made on products produced or marketed locally but with some centralized influence, from outside the country in which the products are produced or marketed;
- the effect of pricing decisions in one market on the company's operations in other countries.

The philosophy and practice of establishing an export price is fundamentally no different to establishing a price for the domestic market. The customer must feel that he or she has received full value for their money. At the same time the export marketing manager must seek profits, either short run or long run, depending upon the company's overall objectives and the specific decision situation at hand.

Broadly speaking, pricing decisions include setting the initial price as well as changing the established price of products from time to time. Changing a price may involve a discount or allowance or anything that represents a deviation from the so-called base price. Price decisions must be made for different classes of purchasers, that is, prices must be set for sales to the following:

- consumers or industrial users;
- wholesalers, distributors, or other importing agencies;
- partners in strategic alliances;
- licensees (when parts or components are exported);
- one's own subsidiaries or joint ventures, whether minority or majority interest or wholly owned subsidiaries.

Pricing for the last type of purchaser involves the use of transfer prices. Other pricing decisions include the following:

- determining the relationships between prices of individual products in a product line and between products in the product mix;
- whether to offer bundle pricing or price by individual product or component;
- deciding, in larger companies, on the type and amount of central control to be exercised to ensure that the price to ultimate consumers and users is maintained at a certain level;
- establishing a geographic pricing policy, for example whether or not to quote uniform delivered prices, or free on board (FOB) factory prices.

The issue of differential pricing is important with regard to most of these decisions, especially the differential between export prices and domestic prices. Decisions must be made on the relationships between the prices of products sold in multiple national markets, that is, whether the price to customers in one foreign market should be the same, lower, or higher than in other foreign markets or in the domestic market.

There are five distinct facets to the pricing problem facing the export manager, at least three of which are unique to exporting. These five facets, each of which will be discussed in the following pages, are as follows:

- fundamental pricing strategy;
- relation of foreign price policy to domestic policy;
- currency issues;
- elements in the price quotation;
- transfer pricing.

As a way to bridge the gap between domestic and export pricing matters, we first discuss the nature of a price and arrive at what we call the anatomy of a price.

10.2 Determinants of an export price

No other marketing tool has such a powerful and immediate effect on a firm's sales and profitability record as pricing. The consequences of price changes are more direct and immediate than those of any other of the elements of the marketing mix, as they result in subsequent customer and, in most cases, competitor reactions. Given their power, pricing issues have attracted surprisingly little research interest compared with other marketing tools (Stottinger, 2001). What applies to a single market-setting holds even more true for the global marketplace, because additional context factors increase complexity.

In order to understand the structure of a price we need first to examine those basic factors that influence the setting of an export price. These factors include the following:

- costs;
- market conditions and customer behavior (demand or value);
- competition;
- legal and political issues;
- general company policies, including policies on financial matters, production, organization structure; and on marketing activities such as the planning and development of products, the product mix, marketing channels, sales promotion, advertising, and selling.

10.2.1 Costs

Costs are often a major factor in price determination and there are a number of reasons to have detailed information on costs. Costs are useful in setting a price *floor*. In the short run, when a company has excess capacity, the price floor may be *out-of-pocket* costs, that is, such direct costs as labor, raw materials, and shipping. However, in the long run *full costs* for all products must be recovered, although not necessarily full costs for each individual product. The actual cost floor, therefore, may often be somewhere *between* direct cost and full cost.

Some years ago a large chemical company sometimes sold products abroad on an incremental cost basis whenever excess domestic capacity existed. The company's price floor was direct cost, since every unit sold at a price in excess of direct cost would contribute to net profit. This company illustrates a technique known as *marginal* pricing, based on the accounting concept of contribution margin. *Direct costs* are those that are incurred by the decision that is made. When used in export pricing, this technique suggests that only those costs that are necessary to produce export revenues are relevant and should be matched against export revenues when assessing profitability. In addition to excess capacity, marginal or incremental pricing may be used for the purposes of entering an export market on a competitive level, or retaining an existing competitive position. Other reasons for pricing exports at less than full costs include: to assist dealer organization growth; to keep a group of employees working together; to sell a special product outside the usual export line; to supply a manufacturing prototype to a subsidiary or licensee; orders for large volumes; the product sold in the domestic market at less than full cost; the export customer provides his or her own installation and services; and significant incremental sales may result.

Costs are also helpful in estimating how rivals will react to setting a specific price, assuming that knowledge of one's own costs helps to assess the reactions of one's competitors. Costs may help in estimating a price that will keep out or discourage new competitors from entering an industry. Internationally, however, costs are often somewhat less helpful for this purpose than in the domestic market, since they may vary over a wider range from country to country.

The developments of e-commerce, e-trade, etc. seem to lower the price differentials between countries. Economic theory might suggest the Internet would reduce price competition. Prices becoming more transparent, consumers and competitors having fuller information at a very low cost are all factors conducive to industry cooperation.

However, what makes price competition rather more than less likely is the lowering of barriers to entry. New entrants do not need to invest in expensive stores or international channels of distribution. This could increase the number of firms and the differences among them, making high prices more difficult to sustain. New entrants with no brand name will find it necessary to compete on price to get a toehold in the market. Further, the reduction in search costs and the ease with which consumers can compare prices on the Internet will encourage consumers to switch to lower price suppliers. Search and switching costs may be so low that negotiated prices become the norm. It may be much easier for customers to play suppliers off against each other, obtaining price quotes through e-mail and making offers and counteroffers among a large number of sellers.

The Internet challenges price quotations and strategies for most exporting companies due to what economists call price and cost transparency, a situation made possible by the abundance of free, easily obtained information on the Internet. All that information has a way of making a seller's prices and costs more transparent to buyers – in other words, it lets them see through those costs and determine whether they are in line with the prices being charged (see Exhibit 10.1).

EXHIBIT 10.1   The net's threat to prices and brands

The most prevalent form of information available on the Internet is about prices. Consumers know that they can often find lower prices for books, CDs, computers, and airfares by clicking online rather than by standing offline. But they can do much more than compare the prices of an Internet store against those of a traditional retailer. They can log on to price-comparison sites such as Pricescan.com and shopping agents such as Bottomdollar.com to compare the prices and features of more than 10,000 products available on the Web. Every time a customer takes advantage of a cheaper price from an online discounter such as Buy.com or Onsale.com, she unlearns her long-held rules of thumb about how price and cost are related for the product she has just purchased.

Therefore, the Internet represents a threat thus far to a company's ability to extract price premiums from buyers, to brand its products, and generate high profit margins. Everyone knows that the Web makes price comparisons much easier. The Web is increasing price and cost transparency in several ways:

■ *The Internet makes a buyer's search much more efficient.* Anyone can use web-based shopping agents or bots to research products quickly. With a few clicks of the mouse a consumer can find out, say, who's selling washing machines, at what prices, with what features, and what kind of warranty. Thus an online shopper with, say, US$400 to spend can know in a matter of minutes what the best deal is.

■ *The Internet encourages highly rational shopping.* The Internet presents a very different shopping experience, one that appeals to people's cognitive facilities instead of affective behavior. It encourages dispassionate comparisons of prices and features. It also puts shoppers in control – it is up to them to consciously navigate through the net's maze of pages and links. The information-rich nature of Web shopping will encourage people to make decisions based on reason rather than emotion.

■ *The Internet encourages buyer-led pricing and reverse auctions.* Buyer-led pricing and reverse auctions allow consumers to see the 'price floor' more easily than they can with traditional shopping. Thanks to sites such as Priceline.com and eBay, consumers have started to believe that the prices of even the best-known brands are open to negotiation. Priceline requires that buyers name the price they are willing to pay for hotel rooms, air tickets, home financing, cars, etc. It then lets companies decide if they want to meet the quoted price. A buyer whose price is accepted may be motivated to bid even lower the next time. Sooner or later, she will come to know the price floor – the lowest price for which the company is willing to sell a product or service.

■ *The Internet erodes 'risk premiums' experienced by the buyers.* Through the Web people can, in effect, always find an expert to provide information about a product or service. In the past, buyers had relatively few sources of information about a brand's quality or about variations in quality from brand to brand vis-à-vis the price of the product.

A growing number of sites maintained by individuals and organizations offer reliable and independent information about products and services, as well as stories about them from consumers around the world. For example, people who need medical treatment can research their ailments on the Internet. Moreover, health care consumers can even find out if the charges being levied by their health maintenance organization are in line with prevailing rates. Such easy access to information helps prospective buyers – whether of digital cameras or surgery – to see through a risk premium and make better decisions about the premium's justification.

Source: Adapted by permission of *Harvard Business Review* from 'Cost transparency; The Net's real threat to prices and brands' by I. Sinha in *Harvard Business Review*, March–April 2001. Copyright © 2000 by the Harvard Business School Publishing Corporation; all rights reserved.

In the new reality of price and cost transparency the seller or manufacturer can take several steps to mitigate the effects brought about by the Internet's trove of information; however, companies won't be able to avoid it. First, companies can pursue price options that go beyond just cutting their prices. One strategy involves 'price lining'. This is a well-known practice of offering different products or services at various price points to meet different customers' need. For example, the US telephone operator ANC offers many plans at different prices and rates for its customers worldwide according to the level of subscriber usage.

Second, companies may implement *dynamic pricing*, in which the prices they charge vary from one market to another, depending on the market conditions, differences in costs, and variations in the way consumers value the offering. By forcing the customers to enter their zip codes before they can view prices, companies can earn higher profits than those that have only one price for every market they serve. However, the companies should tread carefully when thinking about dynamic pricing. Because the Internet allows customers to share information with one another easily, dynamic pricing is likely to create widespread perceptions of unfairness that may prove devastating to business in the long run. Consumers will be unhappy if they believe they have paid more for a product than someone who was more persistent, more adept at bargaining, or just plain lucky.

As a third and better solution, companies should look towards innovating and improving the benefits that their products or services offer. Bundling – packaging a product with other goods and services – can make it difficult for buyers to see through the costs of any single item within the bundle. It focuses buyers on the benefits of the overall package rather than the cost of each piece. Also consumers will reward makers of new and distinctive products that improve their lives.

The basic categories of cost incurred to serve domestic and export customers are the same, for example labor, raw materials, component parts, selling, shipping, overheads. But their relative importance as a determinant of price may differ greatly. For example, the cost of marketing a product in a thin market thousands of miles from the production plant may be relatively high. Such items as the cost of sales people, ocean freight, marine insurance, modified packaging, specially adapted advertising, and so forth may raise the price floor. Also, the location of foreign customers affects either the time needed to ship products or the need for maintaining local inventories, thus influencing either the cost of transportation – for example relatively expensive shipments by air cargo – or the costs of carrying and financing local inventories. Special legal requirements may influence production costs; for example automobile safety requirements or legislation affecting food and drugs. To illustrate, in 2000 a right-hand drive model of a Jeep Cherokee vehicle produced in the United States and destined for Japan needed to have adjustments made to adapt it to Japanese regulations. Chrysler, the manufacturer, needed to show compliance with 238 regulations. It is no wonder that costs can easily mount up.

Any consideration of costs requires knowledge about volume. The allocation of nonescapable costs on a per unit basis varies in accordance with the number of units sold. Thus if volume is increased in a situation where nonescapable costs are a substantial proportion of total costs, the cost floor will drop relatively rapidly. On the other hand, if direct costs are high, say 80% or 85% of total costs – a realistic figure for a broad range of products – a substantial increase in volume is necessary before the amount of nonescapable cost allocated to each unit will be reduced appreciably. Thus, since for most products a high percentage of costs are direct, the cost floor is often influenced primarily by direct costs.

10.2.2 Market conditions (demand)

The nature of the market determines the upper limit for prices. The utility, or *value*, placed on the product by purchasers sets the price *ceiling*. When a manager attempts to establish the value of a product in an export market, the manager in essence is attempting to establish a demand schedule for the product. Values should be measured in terms of product utility, translated into monetary terms. Thus pricing can be viewed as a continuous process of adjusting the price of the export product to the fluctuating utility of the last prospective buyer so as to make him a customer. In June 1988 Isuzu Motors Limited of Japan increased its base price in the United States for its sports utility vehicles and pickup trucks. Although the company claimed that the price increase was due to the currency exchange situation caused by continuing pressure of the Japanese yen on the US dollar, the facts were that the dollar/yen exchange rate was the same as it had been six months earlier and the trend seemed to be for the dollar putting pressure on the yen. What did justify higher prices was a higher demand. Purchases of Isuzu vehicles were more than 6% above those a year earlier, while purchases of Japanese-produced competing products all declined. Since US consumers seemed to prefer Isuzu over competitors' products, it can be argued that the company made a good decision in raising the price to take advantage of that preference. In effect this amounted to assessing customers' price sensitivity or price elasticity. Although techniques such as conjoint analysis can be used to estimate elasticities, Dolan

TABLE 10.1

Factors affecting price
sensitivity

Customer economics:

Will the decision maker pay for the product himself?

Is the cost of the item a substantial percentage of the total expenditure?

Is the buyer the end user? If not, will the buyer be competing on price in the end-user
market?

In this market, does a higher price signal higher quality?

Customer search and usage:

Is it costly for the buyer to shop around?

Is the time of the purchase or the delivery significant to the buyer?

Is the buyer able to compare the price and performance of alternatives?

Is the buyer free to switch suppliers without incurring substantive costs?

Competition:

How is the offering different from competitors' offerings?

Is the company's reputation a consideration? Are there other intangibles affecting the
buyer's decision?

Source: adapted from Dolan, 1995, p. 178

(1995) suggests that a simple starting point is to examine the important factors
that affect sensitivity, as shown in Table 10.1.

When estimating a demand schedule the market can be stratified, which
involves estimating the number of customers who will buy at several levels of
price. The exporter can then select the strata of interest, which gives the last
prospect an amount of utility equal to the price charged while all other buyers will
have surplus utility in that they would be willing to pay a higher price. Value may
be determined by *asking* people, by some type of *barter* experiment, by *test market
pricing*, by *comparison to substitute products*, or by *statistical analysis* of historical price/volume relationships.

The basic factors that determine how the market will evaluate a product in
foreign markets include demographic factors, customs and traditions, and economic considerations, all of which are related to customer acceptance and use of a
product. However, the nature of demand as expressed in terms of price elasticity,
income elasticity, and so forth, often varies widely from country to country.
Diverse religions, differences in the cost of borrowing, varying attitudes on family
formation and living habits, to mention just a few factors, create wide differences
in the willingness and ability of customers to pay a given price.

Often a critical determinant to estimating demand is the availability of information. The obtaining of such information can be extremely difficult and costly in
many countries, particularly developing countries. The lack of published statistics
and the lack of competent local marketing research agencies in some countries,
added to the cost of conducting marketing research in distant markets, may make
it relatively difficult to determine how the market will respond to different levels
of export pricing.

10.2.3 Competition

While costs and demand conditions circumscribe the price floor and ceiling, competitive conditions help to determine where within the two extremes the actual
price should be set. Reaction of competitors is often the crucial consideration
imposing practical limitations on export pricing alternatives. Prices of competitive
products ('substitute' products) have an impact on the sales volume attainable by
an exporter. The decision is whether to price above, at the same level as, or below
competition.

In addition to present competitors, potential competitors must be considered. Of relevance is the extent and importance of the barriers to entry and competition – how easy and cheap it is to get into the business and compete effectively. Barriers that an exporter can use to provide 'shelter' from competition include having a *product distinctiveness*, a *brand prominence with high brand equity*, and a *well-established channel of distribution* both between countries and within a country that can provide greater dealer strength. Obviously, the more significant the barriers, the more pricing freedom there is.

Under conditions approximating *pure competition*, price is set in the marketplace. Price tends to be just enough above costs to keep marginal producers in business. Thus, from the point of view of the price setter, the most important factor is costs. If a producer's cost floor is below the prevailing market price, the product will be produced and sold. Since the exporter in such a market has little discretion over price, the pricing problem is essentially whether or not to sell at the market price.

Under conditions of *monopolistic* or *imperfect competition* the seller has some discretion to vary the product quality, promotional efforts, and channel policies in order to adapt the price of the 'total product' to serve preselected market segments. For most branded products and even for some commodities (when the export marketer and its reputation for service, dependability, and delivery are known) exporters have some range of discretion over price. Nevertheless, they are still limited by what their competitors charge; any price differentials from competitors must be justified in the minds of customers on the basis of differential utility, that is, perceived value. The closer the substitutability of products, the more nearly identical the prices must be, and the greater the influence of costs in determining prices (assuming a large enough number of buyers and sellers so that conditions of oligopoly do not exist).

There are times when an exporter in such a competitive structure ignores competitive prices. To illustrate, a few years ago one manufacturer of capital equipment for mining and earth-moving operations sold primarily on a cost plus 'fair profit' basis. The company sold in foreign markets at domestic factory list prices plus costs of exporting. The company paid little attention to the utility of the equipment and to competitors' prices, mainly because foreign products were not good substitutes. However, many branded industrial products must also be priced competitively (for example electronic data processing equipment, machine tools, and road-building equipment) since purchasers are often keenly aware of the comparative cost/value relationship among feasible product alternatives.

Under conditions of *oligopoly*, without sufficient product differentiation to give a seller a monopoly position, the point between the cost floor and price ceiling at which products will be priced depends upon the assessment of each oligopolist of the others' reactions to his decisions. If there is price leadership, conscious parallel action, or collusion, the price will probably be somewhat above the cost floor, and competition is likely to be based to a great extent on product variations, quality, services, and promotional activities.

A good illustration of the effect of competition on prices is the reaction of Eastman Kodak to competition by Japan's Fuji in the US film market. In 1994 Fuji was priced such that Kodak's main product, Kodak Gold, was priced at 17% above Fuji. Since Fuji could easily, and would, match any price cut, Kodak chose to introduce a new low-priced product, Funtime film, in larger package sizes and limited quantities. On a per-roll basis Kodak was priced lower than Fuji. Fuji continued using price as a competitive tool, but in 1997 it cut prices in the United States by as much as 50% on multiple-roll packs of color film (*Business Week*, 1997, p. 30). Kodak lost market share. Kodak's problems were aggravated by the loss of exclusive rights to parts of Wal-Mart's photo-developing business and problems with its film-developing agreements with Walgreen Co., the US's largest drugstore chain (Bandler, 2004). Kodak's film sales through these outlets has been hurt by its diminished visibility. In 2004 Kodak announced that it would cease selling traditional film-using cameras in its move into digital cameras, and the effect that this may have on its film sales is unknown. Sales of all brands of film have been declining for several years, but it is still a major market that Kodak cannot afford to lose.

10.2.4 Legal/political influence

The manager charged with determining prices must consider the legal and political situations as they exist and as they differ from country to country. Legal and political factors act primarily to restrict the freedom of a company to set prices strictly on the basis of economic considerations.

Today it is widely recognized that sovereign nations have the right and obligation to take action that protects and fosters the prosperity and wellbeing of their citizens. Although there is often disagreement as to whether specific types of governmental actions are proper (whether or not they advance the long-run interests of their citizens), managers with pricing responsibility nevertheless must usually accept the situation as it exists, taking account of antidumping legislation, tariffs, import restrictions, and so forth.

Officials of some countries will not issue import licenses if they feel that the price is too high or too low. One company in Brazil needed a product that Brazilian manufacturers were unable to supply due to lack of capacity. Brazilian authorities, presumably to foster local production, would not permit importation of the product from Japan or the United States because it was available from these countries at a lower price than ordinarily charged by Brazilian manufacturers.

Sometimes foreign officials use pricing guidelines as a criterion for granting foreign exchange to the buyer of foreign merchandise. In some countries the government is concerned with the relationship between the amount paid and the social benefits of the purchase. Even though the customer may be willing to pay a high price, the government may refuse to grant adequate foreign exchange for what it considers to be nonessential imports.

Most industrialized countries have antidumping legislation. Dumping is the practice of selling in foreign markets at prices below those in the domestic market. Antidumping legislation is ordinarily enacted in nations that wish to protect certain industries from temporary or abnormal price fluctuations that would disrupt local production. Thus, antidumping legislation sets a price floor. It should be noted that antidumping legislation is particularly relevant for firms from less developed countries wherein a Catch-22 situation often arises. Competitive advantage for firms from less developed countries centers on their low-cost base; firms run the risk of being reported in export markets for 'unfair' pricing and dumping. While promoting exports is essential to less developed countries improving their economic performance, in some cases they may be prevented from utilizing their competitive advantages in the most effective way. The fact that sales are made at lower prices for export does not mean that antidumping action will be initiated in a foreign market. Under the laws of most countries, no dumping occurs if the exporter's price is above that of the country's current market price, even if the exporter's price to that country is lower than its selling price in its domestic market. Exhibit 10.2 gives some recent examples of antidumping actions.

Another area of potential concern is how to handle rebates, discounts, allowances, and even price escalation or guarantee against price decline clauses in contracts. An importer may ask for, and the exporter may give, one of these price

EXHIBIT 10.2 Recent antidumping actions

The United States, European nations, and Canada have a long history of imposing antidumping penalties on products from developing nations and other industrialized countries. By the year 2000, 1175 penalties were in effect worldwide (Magnusson, 2002). The steel industries and chemicals industries in various countries, which are particularly import sensitive because of their relatively high fixed costs and low marginal (direct) costs, file a large number of antidumping petitions. Recently the developing nations have overtaken the industrialized nations as the most active users of antidumping policy, bringing over 700 filings in the second half of the 1990s (de Jonquires, 2003). India and China have been active in levying penalties against both the United States and the EU. In 2002 US exporters were subject to 89 penalty tariffs by other countries, with over 90 active investigations pending.

In the United States, antidumping duties are imposed if the US Department of Commerce finds that products were dumped and the US International Trade Commission determines that US producers were injured. In 2003 the United States imposed antidumping duties ranging from 44.66% to 63.88% on catfish from Vietnam, and tariffs of up to 44.71% on computer chips from South Korea (the amount varying according to the particular company producing the chips) (*The Japan Times*, 2003). In 2004 antidumping investigations were being held on shrimp exported from Vietnam. In some earlier examples, Canada imposed antidumping tariffs on carbon steel plate suppliers in seven European countries and Brazil. Canada also imposed antidumping duties on US exporters of cold-rolled steel in retaliation for the filing of antidumping petitions by US steel producers against Canadian steel exporters (and exporters in 18 other countries) (Mercado *et al.*, 2001).

US laws define dumping more broadly than those in many countries, but Congress does not want the rules reformed (Magnusson, 2002). Accusations have been leveled against the EU that its rules and methods for determining the existence of dumping are unfair and lack transparency. WTO rules state that dumping must be determined on the basis of conclusions drawn from fair comparisons of the export price and the domestic price in the exporting country (Mercado *et al.*, 2001).

concessions. By themselves such concessions are not illegal, but they may become so in the exporter's and/or the importer's country if they are not disclosed to the appropriate governmental agency (Johnson, 1994, p. 82).

Since tariff levels vary from country to country there is an incentive for exporters to vary the price somewhat from country to country. The incentive changes, depending on the nature of demand in each market and how much customers are willing to pay (that is, the price elasticity of demand). Thus, in some countries with high Customs duties and high price elasticity, the base price may have to be lower than in other countries if the product is to achieve satisfactory volume in these markets. Consequently the profitability of the product will be reduced. On the other hand, if demand is quite inelastic, the price may be set at a high level, with little loss of volume, unless competitors are selling at lower prices.

Import tariffs can influence decisions on sourcing, thereby influencing costs and prices. If import duties in a country are high on finished products, relative to duties on materials or component parts, from a total cost standpoint it may be desirable to import materials or components for local manufacturing or assembly.

When the government intervenes in currency markets the competitive situation may change. If a government devalues its currency exporters to that market might have to lower prices in order to compete with domestic producers. At the same time the country's exporters would find themselves able to do better in export markets as their prices become lower. An exporter in such a situation might find itself able to improve its competitive position in selected foreign markets. Currency issues are discussed further in section 10.5.

10.2.5 Company policies and marketing mix

Export pricing is influenced by past and current corporate philosophy, organization, and managerial policies. Ideally, all long-run and short-run decisions should be recognized as interrelated and interdependent, but as a practical matter some decisions must be made first and must serve as a basis for making subsequent decisions. For example, the company organizational structure must be established and maintained for a period of time. During this period other activities must be conducted within the constraints of the structure.

Pricing cannot be divorced from product considerations. Management must take the customer's point of view and evaluate a product in terms of its quality and other characteristics relative to its price. Decisions on the nature of the product, package, quality, varieties or styles available, and so forth influence not only the cost, but what customers are willing to pay, as well as the degree to which competitors' products are considered acceptable substitutes. For example, there are numerous manufacturers of such products as industrial machines, tools, and equipment, which are able to export at higher prices than foreign competitors because of a design advantage.

So-called national stereotypes and buyer attitudes toward particular countries of origin (as discussed in Chapter 9) can affect the way in which export prices are interpreted in foreign markets. Customer reactions to price and the judgements that customers make will be conditioned by their perceptions and attitudes toward the country of origin of imported goods. For example, if the image of the exporting country held by buyers is favorable and the price of a product from there is low, it will be viewed as 'good value for the money.' If the price was high, a product from there would be perceived as 'high quality.' With an unfavorable country image the perceptions would be 'low quality' and 'poor value for the money,' respectively. Such perceptions are thought to be more true the less the market knows about the products themselves and the suppliers. In short, this situation is most likely to face the new exporter as well as the smaller company with a limited market reputation.

The channel of distribution utilized also affects price. Certain channels such as export merchants may require a higher operating margin than a manufacturer's export agent, depending, of course, on the nature of the product, the markets served, and the cost of performing the required functions. Thus, if dual channels are used and if the price to marketing intermediaries is uniform, the price to ultimate users will probably vary. However, if the prices to intermediaries are varied in approximate proportion to their different costs of operations (or operating gross margin), it would be possible to achieve some degree of uniformity in prices to ultimate consumers or users. But such a price structure would be complex and difficult to implement and maintain.

Utility of a product depends not only on its physical characteristics but also on how it is sold and serviced. For example, a manufacturer of a diversified line of electrical control products and other electrical equipment once found that a price disadvantage (vis-à-vis foreign competitors) can often be overcome by the following:

- careful appointment and training of technical representatives;
- continued analysis and comparison of product features with competitors' products and exploitation of design advantages by demonstrating to customers superior performance characteristics, ease and low cost of maintenance, long life, and ease of installation;

- prompt delivery, which is in some cases facilitated by maintaining inventories abroad.

Thus such factors as the type of channels selected, the relations with foreign representatives or dealers, the distinctiveness of the product, and the services provided determine the price that customers are willing to pay.

Promotional policies are also interrelated with pricing. Communication activities (for example, advertising, personal selling, and sales promotion) should be designed to provide customers with appropriate information and persuasive appeals. The cost of preparing and conducting international promotional activities helps to set the price floor; such costs also contribute to the utility of the product and thereby influence the price ceiling.

10.2.6 Summary

We now summarize what has been said in this section of the chapter. The value of a product to the last prospective customer fixes the ceiling on price while cost sets the floor. However, there are two cost floors: one set by direct or relevant costs (the lowest floor) and one set by full costs. In any export price decision the appropriate cost floor depends upon the company's goals or objective in pricing. Between the cost floor and demand ceiling is a gap. Where in this gap to set the price depends upon such factors as the nature and type of competition, the legal/political situation, and the overall export marketing program.

10.3 Fundamental export pricing strategy

All too frequently export marketing managers rely entirely on costs as a basis for establishing foreign market price policy. In some instances they attempt to cover full costs at all times even though such a policy may result in substantially less than optimum sales volume or may encourage competitors to enter and steal the market. In other instances a rough approximation of marginal (direct) cost pricing is utilized. In this situation the price is based primarily on the variable, or direct, costs of production with only a minimum part of fixed costs added. Such a technique assumes that profits will be made on domestic sales and that they will be larger than otherwise because of the utilization of fixed equipment and labor for a larger volume of production, thus reducing fixed costs per unit. Foreign markets may be used to dispose of surplus production (or use excess capacity) priced at no more than the direct costs. Unfortunately, such strategy may prove short sighted since it gives rise to the frequent international complaint of dumping, which may result in foreign governments imposing arbitrary restrictions on the import of the commodity. In addition, there is a chance that the strategy may be viewed as predatory pricing, which might be a violation of the foreign country's antitrust law.

The relationship between cost and volume is critical to an approach to pricing known as *experience-curve pricing* (Dolan and Simon, 1997). Based on the Boston Consulting Group's work, unit costs are expected to decline as accumulated volume (that is, total units produced of a product) increases. The decline in costs is attributed to changes in production efficiency. Initially, prices are set below unit cost so as to gain a price advantage over competitors. Efficiency increases through

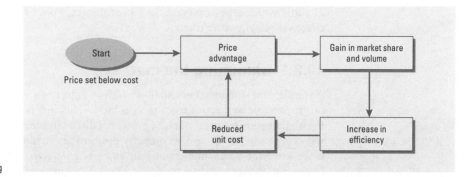

FIGURE 10.1

Experience-curve pricing

market share increase, leading to a reduction in cost, and these lower costs then exceed price reductions. The essence of the cyclical nature of experience-curve pricing is illustrated in Figure 10.1.

Strategies of basing prices on costs, whether full cost or marginal cost, over-simplify the pricing process in export marketing. There are a number of different pricing strategies that may be used effectively in export markets (Stottinger, 2001). Pricing is not the simple problem of establishing a selling price somewhere between cost and the maximum that the traffic (market, customers, or consumers) will bear. It is not one of mathematical precision, but one of statistical probabilities. The problem of the pricing executive is much like that of the player in a card game. His or her play is determined by the moves and countermoves of opponents. This anticipating and reacting to opponents or competitors is known as strategy and is as important in pricing as in card games.

It is the gap between cost and value that makes it possible to have a pricing strategy. Which strategy is appropriate for a company depends upon the objective underlying strategy choice. That is, just what is it that export management wants to achieve by using price as a marketing tool? There are many objectives in pricing (see Table 10.2) and as many strategies. For example, in a recent study of international pricing practice that was based on a series of 45 qualitative interviews with seasoned international business executives from five different countries, the author concludes that the respondent exporting firms did not employ seperate objectives for pricing decisions (Stottinger, 2001). Interestingly, the responding firms stated either financial or nonfinancial goals as key objectives for their international business. More explicitly, maintaining market share or increasing international market coverage ranked first. Only one-third of the firms in the sample were using financial goals to measure performance. What seemed in particular to influence the price goals were the company's experience in exporting and the distribution system in which the company was operating internationally.

TABLE 10.2

Alternative pricing objectives

Satisfactory return on investment
Maintaining market share
Meeting a specified profit goal
Largest possible market share
Meeting a specific sales goal
Profit maximization
Pricing at the high end of the price range
Highest return on investment
Prices are set at a high level and then lowered after a certain period has elapsed
Meeting competition

The following sections present the more important price strategies that can be used effectively in export markets.

10.3.1 Skimming the market

A simple, and somewhat unusual, objective might be to make the largest short-run profit possible and retire from the business. This involves the strategy of getting the highest possible price out of a product's distinctiveness in the short run without worrying about the long-run company position in the foreign market. A high price is set until the small market at that price is exhausted. The price may then be lowered to tap a second successive market or income level. However, little thought is given to the company's permanent position in the field. This strategy may be used either because the company feels that there is no permanent future for the product in a foreign market or markets or that its costs are high and a competitor may come in and take the market away.

10.3.2 Sliding down the demand curve

This resembles the above strategy except that in this case the company reduces prices faster and further than it would be forced to do in view of potential competition. A company pursuing this strategy has the objective to become established in foreign markets as an efficient producer at optimum volume before foreign or domestic competitors can get entrenched. This is primarily used by companies introducing product innovations. Here the strategy involves starting out with almost the entire emphasis on pricing on the basis of what the market will bear and moving from this point toward cost pricing at a measured pace. The pace must be slow enough to pick up profits but fast enough to discourage competitors from entering the market. Companies following this strategy are seeking to recover development costs as they become an established entity in the market.

10.3.3 Penetration pricing

This strategy involves establishing a price sufficiently low to rapidly create a mass market. Emphasis is placed on value rather than cost in setting the price. Penetration pricing involves the assumption that if the price is set to bring in a mass market, the effect of this volume will be to lower costs sufficiently to make the price yield a profit. In an industry of rapidly decreasing costs, penetration pricing can accelerate the process. The strategy also involves the assumption that demand is highly elastic or that foreign purchasers buy primarily on a price basis. This strategy may be more appropriate than skimming for multinational companies facing the demand conditions of the less developed countries.

An extreme form of penetration pricing is *expansionistic* pricing. This is the same as penetration pricing except that it goes much lower in order to get a larger percentage of the customers who are potential buyers at very low prices. This strategy assumes: (1) a high degree of price elasticity of demand and (2) costs extremely susceptible to reduction with volume output. This may be based on experience-curve pricing.

10.3.4 Preemptive pricing

Setting prices so low as to discourage competition is the objective of preemptive pricing. The price will be close to total unit costs for this reason. As lower costs result from increased volume, still lower prices will be quoted to buyers. If necessary to discourage potential competition prices may even be set temporarily below total cost. The assumption is that profits will be made in the long run through market dominance. This approach, too, may utilize experience curves.

10.3.5 Extinction pricing

The purpose of extinction pricing is to eliminate existing competitors from international markets. It may be adopted by large, low-cost producers as a conscious means of driving weaker, marginal producers out of the industry. Since it may prove highly demoralizing, especially for small firms and those in newly developing countries, it can slow down economic advancement and thus retard the development of otherwise potentially substantial markets.

Preemptive and extinction pricing strategies are both closely associated with 'dumping' in international markets. Actually, they are merely variations of the dumping process, depending upon the domestic or 'home' market price. Although they may serve to capture initially a foreign market and may keep out, or drive out, competitors, they should be used only with extreme caution. There is the ever-present danger that foreign governments will impose arbitrary restrictions on the import and sales of the product, consequently closing the market completely to the producer. More important, once customers have become used to buying at low prices it may prove difficult, if not impossible, to raise them subsequently to profitable levels.

Exhibit 10.3 provides examples of some pricing strategies used, and the results achieved.

EXHIBIT 10.3	Some pricing strategies and results achieved

- *Successfully using premium prices.* Louis Vuitton has opened its 46th store in Japan, where the combination of its status-symbol name and high prices appeal to a growing market segment of young, educated single women still living with their parents. They splurge on products with cachet while cutting costs on other items. Louis Vuitton sells more than twice as many handbags in Japan as in all of Europe. Maintaining high prices that support their positions as status symbols Vuitton, Chanel and Hermes do well while the overall market for luxury goods in Japan has been falling since 1996 (Katz, 2003).
- *A problem in failing to meet price competition.* With the weak dollar failing to adequately cover high euro prices for labor and parts in Germany, Volkswagen AG adopted a strategy of reducing discounts on cars being sold in the United States. Their US sales fell 30% in the first two months of 2004, and VW then resumed offering competitive discounts (White, 2004).
- *Successes in using low price strategies.* Ryanair of Ireland and Southwest Airlines of the United States are two very successful airlines that were both founded on the premise that they could provide low-cost scheduled air service at prices below those charged by the major airlines. They maintain substantially lower cost structures for personnel and overheads than the traditional international airlines, and fly only routes where they can attain high load factors for the aircraft they use. Most past attempts to challenge traditional carriers have failed (Szuchman and Cary, 2004) due to over-expansion, failure to reach and maintain an adequate number of customers, letting

costs rise, or failing to meet emerging competition from other low-cost airlines or changes by the traditional carriers. In 2003 Ryanair was very profitable and had a market capitalization exceeding that of British Airways, Lufthansa and Air France combined (Capell, 2003). Southwest's earnings in 2003 exceeded the combined totals for all of the US's other airlines combined (Serwer, 2004).

- *Pricing to capture an additional market segment.* Ten years ago, mid-priced Gap Inc. clothing company launched a less expensive chain of stores, Old Navy, to appeal to customers who wanted cheaper prices. With good merchandising and its current emphasis on cheap chic, Old Navy stores have been very successful, occasionally selling more clothes than the Gap stores (Strasburg, 2004).

- *An experiment in pricing.* Procter & Gamble has traditionally focused on in-house development of new products, setting initial prices at a high level to cover development costs and advertising, and then cutting prices as competitors move in. But in January 2001 they took a new approach in acquiring a low-cost battery-powered toothbrush from outside entrepreneurs, who they also hired to assist in marketing. Focus groups and the prior experience of the entrepreneurs in selling the electric toothbrush to selected retailers indicated that, with a toothbrush design that would appeal to children and with proper packaging, advertising would not be necessary for the product launch. The price was set at $5, far below the prices of $50 or more for most electric toothbrushes and one-fourth the cost of a recently introduced low-priced electric toothbrush. The SpinBrush was a great success and, in P&G's quickest global rollout ever, posted global sales of over $200 million in 2001 (Berner, 2002).

- *Changing competition, changing strategies.* Toys "Я" Us grew rapidly in the United States and overseas based on a low-price strategy. It was able to do this through high volume that allowed them to obtain low prices from manufacturers. Now, faced with growing competition from Wal-Mart in the United States, they are closing US stores, emphasizing some different product lines, and increasing their operations in smaller overseas markets that do not have extremely large competitors such as Wal-Mart.

- *A disaster in pricing.* In 1997 McDonald's Holdings Co. (Japan) was the market leader in hamburger chains, a position it had held since entering the market. The chairman of the company came up with a plan to increase that share by offering a burger for the extraordinarily low price of ¥59, far below that of any competitor. He was able to do this because he had contracted for a large amount of beef priced in dollars shortly before a substantial increase in the value of the yen. He expected to be able to continue to get beef at a very low price. The company enjoyed initial success as greatly increased volume raised profits in spite of the drop in prices. However, the temporary advantages gained from lower prices disappeared under a combination of price cuts by competitors, a drop-off in customers as the novelty wore off, and an inability to gain long-term cost advantages in using forward purchases of foreign exchange. McDonald's subsequently raised prices to a point part-way between the original prices and the lowest prices, but profits suffered. In 2003 McDonald's Japan had its first loss in 30 years and the chairman resigned (Tanaka, 2003).

10.3.6 Summary

These pricing strategies can be classified as either high price or low price. A high price with limited international market objective has merit under the following conditions:

- The product is unique in character and is well protected legally both domestically and in foreign countries so that no direct or indirect competition may be expected.

RELATION OF EXPORT TO DOMESTIC PRICE POLICIES | **447**

- Foreign market acceptance of the new product will require considerable educational or promotional effort, and at best product acceptance will be slow.
- The ultimate size of the foreign market is expected to be small and of insufficient size to attract competition or to justify extensive market promotion.
- The manufacturer has limited financial resources and, therefore, is unable to expand rapidly in international markets.
- Output cannot be expanded rapidly to satisfy probable foreign demand because of technical difficulties.

In the final analysis there are different approaches to pricing strategy; and there is no one master policy or procedure that should be used under all circumstances or in all foreign markets (see also Myers and Cavusgil (1996)). Pricing strategy is a matter of having as much information as possible about costs and the value of a product to various classes of consumers in different markets. With this information and intelligent application the danger of an exporting company pricing itself out of potentially profitable markets is considerably reduced. Given the importance firms attach to international pricing, however, it is a wonder that most exporting companies do not apply more systematic approaches to price-related issues. In the above-mentioned study on international price practices (Stottinger, 2001) the overall impression of how industrial exporters deal with international pricing issues was as follows: anchored around the strategic price position, managers set a certain, implicit price level. This price level serves as a guideline and overall benchmark. For setting prices, firms choose either a fixed or a flexible cost-plus approach. The calculation approach and the goals that are set are a matter of international experience. The size and the design of the firms' international distribution systems will mediate the final solution. The price decision is most likely taken centrally under the supervision of top management. Furthermore, the study concludes that the importance of pricing compared with other marketing decisions was at least highlighted by the responding exporting firms.

10.4 Relation of export to domestic price policies

The second aspect of price policy for the export marketing manager is the relation of export price policy to the company's domestic policy or policies. The manager must decide whether to price at higher levels, the same level, or lower levels than domestic prices. There are arguments for and against each of these alternatives.

10.4.1 Export prices lower than domestic

One argument for export prices lower than domestic prices is that the manufacturer's product is probably less well known in foreign markets than domestic. To secure market acceptance and initial purchase the lowest possible price should be quoted. Furthermore, as part of securing market acceptance the manufacturer should be willing to absorb any additional expenses such as transportation, marine insurance, and on occasion even the foreign import duties.

Others believe that export prices should be lower because foreign competitors can manufacture more cheaply due to lower labor costs, government subsidies, or other advantages that they are said to enjoy. Still another argument advanced in favor of lower export prices is the lure of increased sales volume in order to assist in absorbing manufacturing and overhead costs. A further argument is that the manufacturer has incurred certain necessary expenses in initiating its business that have been disbursed and cannot be escaped. Therefore, any export business is in a sense plus business and should not be charged with this burden.

It may be that the export price turns out to be lower than the domestic price simply because the manufacturer feels that domestic customers are nationalistic and will pay the price for a domestic product. For example, in 1999 the price of a Volkswagen Passat cost 25% more in Germany than it did in Denmark.

A potential problem that may arise by following this policy is that the exporter may be considered to be dumping. Consequently, the exporter should watch for 'local' government reaction in export markets.

10.4.2 Export prices higher than domestic

One of the arguments most frequently advanced in favor of higher export prices is that the increased initial cost of equipping an organization to enter the export field is considerable. The probability is that selling expense may be higher than in the domestic market due to the complexities of procedure, difficulties in language, differing commercial customs, and varying legal needs and tastes of customers in export markets (Exhibit 10.4). There is frequently extra investment and added expense in preparation of special documents and forms in packing, preparation, and alteration of the products. Some believe that the cost of extending credit to and financing foreign accounts means a slower turnover of invested capital and higher expense. Some manufacturers and producers feel that there is added risk in doing business abroad due to unsettled economic and political conditions, and that this risk should be compensated for in the form of a higher price.

EXHIBIT 10.4 Price escalation

Price escalation in exporting is a phenomenon that occurs all too often. If the exporting firm does not pay conscious attention to the conditions that lead to price escalation it may find itself in a situation where it prices itself out of a foreign market. In general, it is the physical and economic distance between the initial manufacturer and the consumer (or user for industrial products) that provides the environment for price escalation to emerge. These distances may mean that a longer channel of distribution with more intermediaries is needed than in the domestic market. In addition, there are other costs involved such as documentation and import duties.

Export price escalation occurs when there is a significant increase in the price of a product as it goes from the exporting manufacturer to the industrial user or ultimate consumer. Since usually exporting is more complex (in terms of stages) than is domestic marketing and each stage has a fixed cost, the final price in export markets can be much greater than in the exporter's domestic market. For example, in 1995 a Jeep Cherokee vehicle produced in the United States at a factory cost of US$19,100 had a retail price in Japan of US$31,372. A comparable model was priced in the United States at US$20,698 (WuDunn, 1995).

A short example illustrates this point. In Table 10.3 we show relative illustrative cost figures for a domestic sale and an export sale of a consumer product. The various markups and so on are not unusual. It is quite clear that there can be an escalation in the export price such that it ends up more than 50% higher than the comparable price in the domestic market. Obviously, there are situations where escalation will be less than that shown in the example; there may also be situations where it is greater.

Whenever there is escalation such as that illustrated the exporter is almost bound to price higher than in the domestic market. In trying to overcome the problems that arise with this phenomenon, Terpstra (1988, p. 138) has indicated that the exporter can consider at least four possible strategies, as follows:

1. shipping modified or unassembled products that might lower transportation costs and duties;
2. lowering its export price at the factory, thus reducing the multiplier effect of all the markups;
3. getting its freight and/or duty classifications changed for a possible lowering of these costs;
4. producing within the export market to eliminate the extra steps.

The last option amounts to sourcing for the foreign market within the market itself by making a direct investment in manufacturing facilities, or by forming a strategic alliance through licensing, joint venture or contract manufacturing.

TABLE 10.3	Cost figures of a consumer product	
	Domestic market	**Export market**
Factory price	$10.00	$10.00
Domestic freight	1.00	1.00
	$11.00	$11.00
Export documentation		0.75
		$11.75
Ocean freight and insurance		2.25
		$14.00
Import duty (10% of landed cost)		1.40
		$15.40
Wholesaler markup (15% on cost)	1.65	
	$12.65	
Importer/distributor markup (25% on cost)		3.85
		$19.25
Retail markup (50% on cost)	6.32	9.62
Final consumer price	$18.97	$28.87

Source: Terpstra 1988

10.4.3 Export prices on a par with domestic prices

The policy of carrying the domestic price into the export market has much to commend it, particularly to the manufacturer or producer who is entering export for the first time and who has not yet explored all the varieties of conditions that may be found later in the foreign markets. There are several arguments in favor of this policy. It enables the manufacturer to fix export prices that costs and experience in the domestic market have indicated are necessary and fair. It gives the manufacturer a feeling of safety upon entering the export market when the opportunity for marketing research, knowledge of competitive conditions, and previous experience are still lacking. It dispels any fear the manufacturer may have of becoming involved in antidumping regulations that exist in many foreign countries. It is a policy that can be easily altered when the manufacturer gains experience and acquires a more comprehensive knowledge of export markets.

This approach is easy to implement but may not be suitable if the domestic price is low because of unusual circumstances, such as intense competition. Before following this approach, or pricing lower than domestic price for that matter, the export manager should be certain that the domestic price is, in fact, the usual or 'normal' price. Exports priced the same as domestic assumes that objectives are similar. It should be recognized, however, that company objectives and market conditions may not be the same across markets.

10.4.4 Differential pricing

Since the market and competitive conditions and other environmental factors vary from one foreign market to another, possibilities arise for setting a different export price to each market. However, in a study of pricing practices of US multinational corporations (Samli and Jacobs, 1994), the findings indicate that 70% of US firms standardized their prices in most markets. Much has been said and written in conventional international economics textbooks about the conditions under which price differentials occur among foreign markets. The most important conditions are: (1) differential elasticities of demand, and (2) effective separation of markets.

Differential elasticities of demand are necessary if there is to be a profit incentive for the exporter to set a higher price in one market than another. High price elasticity suggests low prices; price inelasticity suggests high prices.

Another necessary condition for differential pricing is that the relevant markets must be separated effectively. Unless tariffs, transportation costs, or reexporting costs are higher than the price differential, or unless other restrictions on the free transfer of goods across political boundaries exist, products sold in a low-price market may find their way into a high-price market. In the case where export prices are higher than domestic prices, the exporter must guard against setting the differential so high that foreign customers or their representatives find it attractive to enter the domestic market and perform the exporting functions for themselves. Within the European Union, prices of automobiles vary by country. For example, in 2000 the price for a Volkswagen Golf (made in Germany) varied from a low of US$8290 in Finland to a high of US$13,040 in the United Kingdom. In Germany, the price was US$11,040 (*Business Week*, 2000). In some instances the differential was greater than differences in taxes, etc. This has been called 'pricing to the market.' In addition, there have been reports that the manufacturers have been 'encouraging' dealers not to sell to people in other countries. Currency differences even arise in the EU, where not all countries have adopted the euro. The euro is supposed to equalize prices, but they may vary as much as 30% from country to country for the same model of automobile. In 1999 the price of a BMW 318i was priced in the United Kingdom in pounds at 30% more than the euro-denominated price, converted to pounds, in The Netherlands. The higher price in the United Kingdom was partly due to the pound's appreciation against the euro.

This is the issue of the price of goods obtained through parallel imports or the so-called *gray market*, which was discussed earlier in Chapter 7. If buyers in one country are able to purchase at a lower price than in another country, there will be an incentive for customers in the lower price market to divert goods to the higher price market in order to make a profit. Obviously the exporter's distributor and dealers in the higher price country will complain about such unauthorized imports since they represent a loss in sales to them. According to Johnson (1994, p. 83), the laws of many countries including those in the EU and Japan *encourage* such parallel imports as a means of stimulating competition and forcing the authorized distributor to reduce its price. In the EU, any attempts to prohibit a distributor from selling outside its country, but within the EU, can be a violation of law. Hermann Simon, CEO of Prof. Simon & Partners in Bonn, Germany, believes that it is likely that price differentials will not disappear quickly even with concerted effort by exporters such that parallel imports will continue to exist, and perhaps a small amount is not all bad if it allows better profits in the individual countries (Simon, 1995).

Smuggling, however, is a crime. In 2001 the EU accused several large US tobacco companies of complicity in cigarette smuggling by selling oversupplies to neighboring nonEU countries. At the same time smuggling of cheap imitations of Philip Morris's Marlboro cigarettes made in China, South America, and eastern Europe were causing approximately $100 million in lost profits to Philip Morris International. It was estimated that smuggling costs the EU $1 billion annually in lost taxes. In 2004 Philip Morris agreed to a settlement with the EU in which the company will work with the EU to fight smuggling, and will pay the EU $1 billion over a period of 12 years. Part of the money will be used to hire and train more Customs officers and buy equipment and technology (Geitner, 2004). If the newly available RFID (Radio Frequency Identification) equipment is used it should be relatively easy to determine if checked cross-border shipments of cigarettes are actually legal, and if cigarettes delivered through legitimate distributors are authorized.

The exporter considering differential pricing must also look at other factors, including local competition in each market, the company's products' fixed-cost/variable-cost ratio, the stability of demand in the domestic market, and the overall marketing strategy to be employed.

Reasons for following a policy of differential pricing often arise because the marketing strategy varies from market to market. For example, in one country a policy of intensive distribution coupled with heavy advertising may go hand in hand with a low price to serve a mass market. In another country a direct marketing channel with little advertising may call for a high unit price to serve a small number of high-income persons.

Product line considerations may also contribute to the desirability of differential pricing. For example, so-called full-line considerations can be important. If customers expect to buy certain products from a common source the exporter that does not have all of the expected items in the product mix is likely to have difficulty selling any of the mix. The buyer might reason: 'Why should I split my orders among two or more suppliers when I can order all of my requirements from one supplier at one time, thus saving both time and effort?' Under these conditions it may be necessary for a seller to include an item in the product mix that cannot be sold at as high a price as in other markets; thus the price of the item must vary from country to country.

Product line pricing in another sense may also contribute to the desirability of differential pricing of certain items in the line. The products in a line often must be priced so that there is a reasonable relationship between them. For example, tractors of varying sizes and specifications may, to some degree, be substituted for each other. But the degree to which they are not substitutes, that is, the evaluation by customers as to the degree to which one product is better or more suitable than another, should correspond approximately to the price differential. Since groups of customers in diverse markets may evaluate products differently, the appropriate differences in the prices of items in the line will vary; thus it may be desirable for prices of identical products to vary from country to country.

A policy of differential pricing may also be desirable on an occasional basis. In industries that require heavy fixed investment it may be expedient, when there is periodic overcapacity due to short-term fluctuations in demand, to lower prices in foreign markets if such sales make some contribution to fixed costs.

Although the selection and exploration of nonhomogeneous marketing targets require varying marketing strategies, there is the possibility that a firm may try to select similar market targets from within the varying segments in each country. For example a manufacturer may make a product that appeals to persons of a certain economic or social position, regardless of nationality. National markets may be segmented on the basis of income, education, family size, leisure time, and so forth, and such segments of the markets of Canada, Denmark, France, Germany, Australia, Japan, and other nations may have similar motivations or needs, which a standardized product and marketing strategy can satisfy. Customer requirements in certain market segments for such products as household furniture, airline service, or automobiles may be quite similar in many respects. Likewise the marketing strategy, including price, may be similar.

On the other hand, the greatest opportunities for growth often exist in new or developing market segments that have not been reached or served adequately in the past. In fact, one of the frequently stated objectives of differential prices is to enter 'new markets' or attract a new class of buyer. This objective can sometimes be achieved by selecting an additional marketing channel, which may provide a different mix of functions and reach additional segments of the market. Such a channel is likely to have a cost structure different from other channels and thus will require a different operating margin. The operating margin required by marketing channels may vary for many reasons, including costs of market development (for example the need for heavy advertising in some areas, light in others), labor costs, or margins offered to marketing agencies by competitors. Either the manufacturer's price or the marketing intermediary's price, or both, should differ from prices in the previously established normal channel. In view of the great diversity among foreign markets and foreign marketing channels, therefore, a policy of differential pricing is often logical.

The size of an exporter and its share of market also has a bearing on the desirability of following a policy of differential pricing. A small exporter is likely to feel that there is greater flexibility since the company may have a relatively minor share of the total world market. If customers are small and scattered widely, customer pressures for equal prices may be minimal.

However, a large exporter, depending on large customers for a significant percentage of volume, may find that customer pressures call for uniform prices in order to avoid customer discontent. Also, in the cases where markets are not effectively separated by transportation costs, tariffs, or other barriers to trade, large customers are likely to make purchases in low-price countries. Or, if the product is important in a market, perhaps marketing intermediaries will purchase the product in the low-price market and sell it in the high-price market under the price umbrella provided by a manufacturer that sells at inordinately large price differentials.

Differential pricing may also be advisable seasonally or cyclically. For example, if a product has a seasonal sales pattern in the northern hemisphere it may have just the opposite pattern in the southern hemisphere. Thus a manufacturer in the north may find South American markets during the domestic slack season. It may be that price variations seasonally may contribute to the proper exploitation of both markets.

10.5 Currency issues

One of the most difficult aspects of export pricing can be the decision of which currency to specify. The exporter can choose its own currency, the buyer's currency, or some 'third party' currency. To a large extent, which of these should be used will be dependent upon a number of factors including buyer preferences, exchange rates per se, and whether they are floating or fixed, freedom of exchange, the availability of currencies in the importer's country, and government policies. If they are floating rates then their stability becomes a concern. Exhibit 10.5 shows the potential effects of changes in currency valuations. Another consideration is whether the exporter needs a particular currency. For example, exporters in developing countries often need foreign currency in order to purchase capital equipment that enables them to remain in business in the first place.

EXHIBIT 10.5	**The effects of changes in currency valuations**

Changes in currency valuations affect the ability of exporters to maintain competitiveness in foreign markets. In 2003 the Japanese government spent over ¥20 trillion (almost $200 billion) in a massive intervention in the foreign exchange markets attempting to keep the value of the yen low. The attempt was partially successful in the short term, but the government found it necessary to increase the amount of intervention in the market in the opening months of 2004 (*The Nikkei Weekly*, 2004). It was concerned that the rising value of the yen would reduce the competitiveness of Japanese exports to the United States, and their competitiveness with US exporters in third countries. Meanwhile, exporters in the United Kingdom were concerned about the competitiveness of their exports as the value of the British pound rose against the dollar and the euro. Exporters in the eurozone, and the nations whose currencies were linked to the euro, were concerned about their competitiveness as the euro rose to record highs against the dollar. Japan, the United Kingdom, eurozone countries and the United States were all concerned that the controlled Chinese currency was undervalued, giving Chinese exporters an unfair advantage in their rapid penetration of world markets.

Exporters from countries with more highly valued currencies do face a dilemma. If they raise prices in foreign countries to maintain profits they may lose market share (or lose out in some markets altogether). If they do not raise prices they may lose profits and may even be unable to cover their costs. The exporters from countries with lowered currency valuations will find that they can lower prices to increase market share, or maintain prices and reap more profits, as long as the currency imbalance remains. In 2004 the continuing high value of the euro resulted in European automobile companies increasing the prices they charged in the United States, in turn leading to reduced exports (White, 2004). At the same time wine exports from California to Europe surged, with California displacing Italy as the third largest exporter to the United Kingdom (Emert, 2004). Earlier, in the exchange rate changes in Europe in 1992, the currencies of Germany and France had increased in value relative to the currencies of Britain, Sweden and Spain. Some German and French exporters found their exports sharply reduced and some companies had to lay off workers or close plants. Companies in Britain, Sweden and Spain benefited (Rossant, 1992).

Currency devaluation does not always result in increased exports, as was illustrated by the Asian financial crisis of 1997. Exporters in some countries whose currencies had fallen sharply were unable to obtain export financing because of the financial crises within their countries, and their exports actually fell. The financial crisis and banking system problems in Argentina in 2003–4 also resulted in some companies being unable to obtain bank financing for exports.

A currency crisis in one country may spread to others (*The Economist*, 1996). This was a problem that occurred in the Asian financial crisis. Macro economic similarities may spread a crisis as countries similar to the one under crisis could face problems generated largely by expectations rather than concrete phenomena. Short-term investors may pull money out of similarly situated countries, resulting in devaluation in those countries. Trade is another possible channel through which a crisis may spread, as countries that have not devalued find exports falling and their economy suffers.

There is a strong tendency for devaluation of a currency to lead to inflation as raw materials cost more. It should be noted, however, that the value of a freely convertible currency is determined by other factors besides trade. Short-term investment flows, driven by interest rates or concerns over safety and other factors, are many times larger than trade and long-term investment flows. Thus currency levels do not necessarily follow trade balances even over fairly long periods of time.

The currency in which the price of a product or service is quoted can have a great effect upon company performance in a foreign market. Exchange rate changes between the time of the price quotation in foreign currencies and receipt of funds can also affect profitability in the short run unless some form of hedging is undertaken.

If avoidance of any foreign exchange risks were critical then exporters would prefer to receive their own currency and importers would prefer to pay with their currency. If, however, either party had to accept the other's (or a third country's) currency it could protect itself against exchange loss by entering the forward exchange market and hedge its open position (see Branch, 1990, pp. 144–7). Not all companies believe that hedging is a good practice, even though a company can lose money in the short run. The reason why companies such as Exxon, Kodak, and 3M do little, if any, hedging is that currency fluctuations can help profits as often as they hurt them. Large companies can usually ride out negative currency moves without having to cut back on plans. In addition, hedging can be costly (*Business Week*, 1998). Another way to lessen risk is to extend credit for a shorter period of time, if credit has been extended. This limits the extent of risk.

It cannot be said categorically which currency is best under all conditions. It should be noted, however, that if necessary, price can be used to an extent to compensate for potential exchange losses. This is one situation where a price escalation provision may be used.

10.6 The price quotation

A third phase of export pricing should be based upon some examination of the elements included in the price quotation. Such a determination should be made by the exporter in conjunction with the customer abroad.

Export prices are quoted in various ways. The two major systems available for use in quoting prices are known as *trade terms*. The use of such terms as FOB, FAS, C&F, and CIF (see page 457) are important with regard to specifying not only where the exporter's responsibility and liability end (and the buyer's responsibility and liability begin), but they determine the costs that the exporter will bear. Thus it is customary in the calculation of a price quotation to add the appropriate costs to the basic price.

There are two systems of definition that are used by exporters throughout the world – INCOTERMS 2000 (developed by the International Chamber of Commerce) and Revised American Foreign Trade Definitions – 1941 (originally developed by the Chamber of Commerce of the United States and two other trade organizations).

Trade term definitions generally have no status at law unless there is specific legislation providing for them, or unless they are confirmed by court decisions. If sellers and buyers agree to their acceptance as part of the contract of sale, the definitions become legally binding on the parties to the sale. In Europe, while the application of INCOTERMS 2000 is voluntary, courts and arbitration bodies tend to apply them even if not explicitly stipulated.

10.6.1 Comparison of terms

The Revised American Foreign Trade Definitions – 1941 and INCOTERMS 2000 are shown in Table 10.4. As a means of comparing the different sets of terms as well as the different terms within a set, Figure 10.2 shows for each term the point at which the exporter's liability, costs, and responsibilities cease. A more detailed breakdown of responsibilities and risks associated with activities is presented in other sources (Hall, 1983, pp. 46–9; International Chamber of Commerce, 2000).

Although the detail is beyond the scope of this book, below we present a brief description of the major general trade terms.

TABLE 10.4 Comparison of trade terms	**INCOTERMS 2000**	**Revised American Foreign Trade Definitions – 1941**
	EXW (ex works)	Ex (point of origin) or ex mill
	FCA (free carrier), named place	FOB (named inland carrier) Free on board at named point of departure
		FOB (named inland carrier – freight prepaid)
		FOB (named inland carrier – freight allowed)
		FOB (named inland carrier at named point of exportation)
	FAS*	FAS (Free alongside) vessel
	FOB*	FOB vessel
	CFR (Cost and freight)*	C&F (Cost and freight)
	CIF*	CIF (Cost, insurance and freight)
	CPT (Carriage paid to)	
	CIP (Carriage and insurance paid to)	
	DAF (Delivered at frontier)	
	DES (Delivered ex ship)*	
	DEQ (Delivered ex quay)*	Ex dock
	DDU (Delivered duty unpaid)	
	DDP (Delivered duty paid)	FOB (named inland point in country of importation)

* Sea and inland waterway transport only.

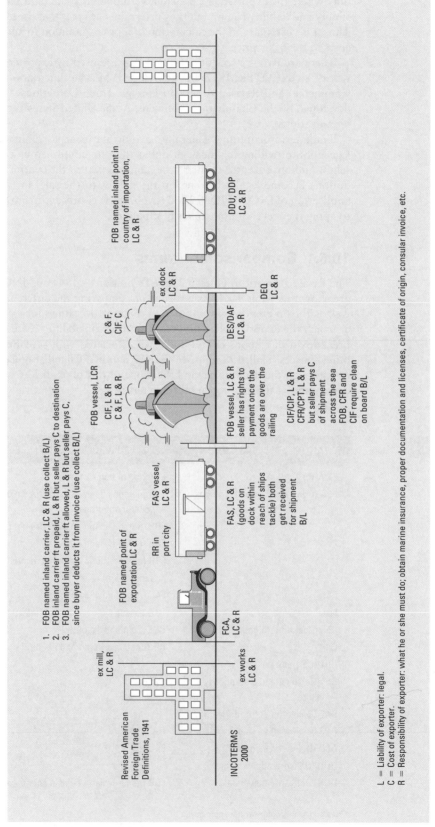

FIGURE 10.2 Point of expiration of exporter's liability, costs, and responsibilities

1. **Ex** (point of origin). This term is referred to as ex factory, ex mill, ex mine, ex works, ex warehouse, and so on (point of origin). The seller's responsibility and costs end at this point in his home country.

2. **Free on board** (FOB). In general, FOB means free on board a transportation carrier at some named point. There are a wide range of FOB terms, all but one of which specify a named point in the country of exportation. The comparable INCOTERM designation is FCA (free carrier) and is used for rail or air transport. The seller's responsibility and cost end in most cases when the goods are loaded on the appropriate carrier and a clean bill of lading has been issued. A clean shipping document bill of lading is one that bears no superimposed clause or notation that expressly declares a defective condition of the goods and/or the packaging. The one exception to this is when the named point is inland in the country of importation. In this case the seller is responsible until the goods arrive on a carrier at the appropriate place in the overseas market. For INCOTERMS this would involve use of DDU or DDP.

3. **Free alongside** (FAS). Under this term the seller must provide for delivery of the goods free alongside, but not on board, the transportation carrier (usually an ocean vessel) at the port of shipment and export. Thus this term differs from that of FOB since the time and cost of loading are not included in the FAS term.

4. **Cost and freight** (C&F). The C&F (or CFR, CPT) term means that delivery costs are extended beyond the country of export. Although the seller's liability ends when the goods are loaded on board a carrier or are in the custody of the carrier at the port of exportation, she is responsible for providing and paying for transportation to the overseas port of discharge. However, the buyer must still provide for the necessary insurance.

5. **Cost, insurance, and freight** (CIF). This trade term is identical to C&F except that the seller must also provide the necessary insurance.

6. **Ex dock**. The ex dock (and DEQ) term goes one step beyond CIF and requires the seller to be responsible for the cost of the goods and all other costs necessary to place the goods on the dock at the named overseas port, with the appropriate import duty paid.

10.6.2 Selection of trade terms

In deciding when to use each term exporters should consider the following factors:

- Whether shipment will be made on domestic or foreign carriers.
- Availability of insurance coverage.
- Availability of information on costs.
- Exporter's need for cash (reason against C&F and CFR/CPT).
- Needs of importers to have quotes from several suppliers that can be readily compared (reason for CIF and CIP).
- Currency convertibility problems. FOB vessel is often desirable so that the buyer pays freight in his own currency. Of course, the carrier still has the convertibility problem, unless it is from the buyer's country.
- Requirements of the government of the importing nation. For example, some developing nations require FOB point of exportation as a condition for receiving an import license. This allows them to foster their own developing merchant marine and insurance companies since the importer has the responsibility to arrange for insurance and transportation, and he may find it convenient (or required) to use certain facilities. Many importers request CIF (or CIP) terms so that they may compare alternative prices, and then they place the order in FOB point of exportation terms.

Price quotations can be a meaningful part of export marketing strategy. Ideally, the price quote should be in a form that customers find suitable, and at least as convenient for the customer as those offered by competitors. Often this requires a CIF or CIP quote since it is the only quote (among those commonly used) that permits the buyer to compare prices easily from alternatively located suppliers.

10.6.3 CIF quotations

Only one of these quotations represents any considerable difficulty in reaching an accurate figure: CIF. This is one of the most commonly used quotations in export trade. It indicates that the terms of the quotation include the cost of the merchandise delivered on board the vessel, plus the cost of the insurance to destination, plus the freight charges to the named destination. A CIF quotation indicates that no other charges will accrue to the account of the buyer before the shipment arrives at the port of destination.

The reason that the CIF quotation is more difficult to figure accurately is that it is customary in the export business to add a fixed percentage, usually 10%, to the insured value to take care of extra expenses and losses not covered by the simple CIF value. Therefore the insured CIF value is the sum of the cost, the freight to destination, and the insurance premium on 110% of the CIF value. Inasmuch as the premium is figured on the entire CIF value, the difficulty presents itself in figuring the I.

There are two methods of ascertaining insured value when the total C&F value has been determined in a CIF calculation. A widely practiced method is the approximation or estimate method. The other is the formula method.

The estimate method

The exporter employing the estimate method simply adds 10% (or some other percentage) to the C&F value. Then, if the insurance rate is X%, he takes X% of the C&F value and adds it to the 10%. The resulting amount is then added to the C&F value.

The formula method

The most accurate method of computing a CIF quotation involves the use of a formula. The formula, which in this case is used for calculating the CIF price when 10% is added to the C&F value, is as follows:

$$CIF = \frac{C\&F}{N(1 - 0.011R)}$$

where

C = FAS value
F = total freight charges
N = total weight to be shipped (or other unit of measure, e.g. volume, pieces)
R = insurance rate (per $100).

To obtain the insured value the following formula is applied (assuming a 10% addition):

$$\text{Insured value} = \frac{110(C\&F)}{100 - 1.1R}$$

There is no reason that only 10% should be added for insurance purposes, except that this is the general custom. Many firms add 15%, in which case 15% may be substituted in the above formula for 10%. As a matter of fact, any percentage that the exporter decides upon may be added and the formula changed accordingly. An example of a CIF calculation is shown in Exhibit 10.6.

Computation of ocean freight

In general, ocean freight is calculated either on the weight or on the measurement of the shipment, carrier's option. The standard unit is the long ton, which weighs 2,240 lb and measures 40 cubic feet. In quoting a price, care should be taken to distinguish between terms that seem to be the same but may be different. For example, the ton may be a short ton (2,000 lb), a long ton (2,240 lb), or a metric ton (2,204.62 lb); a gallon may be a US gallon or an imperial gallon, which is five US quarts. A British hundredweight is equal to 112 lb US weight.

EXHIBIT 10.6   CIF calculation

An apple packer located in the Okanagan valley in British Columbia, Canada, received an inquiry from a potential buyer in France for 4000 boxes of apples, five-tier, 175/215s, combination of extra-fancy and fancy. The request asked for a firm price, CIF, Le Havre, France.

The apple packer proceeds by examining relevant costs (in Canadian currency) as follows:

	$
Current price FOB, Penticton	7.50 per box
Rail freight to Vancouver	1.00 per box
Wharfage and handling	0.25 per box
Ocean freight (Vancouver to Le Havre)	4.80 per box
Marine insurance (coverage of cargo in refrigerated space)	0.20 per $100.00
French consular invoice fee	10.00 per invoice

To determine the CIF price, the packer wants to insure the shipment for a value that is the CIF price plus 10%.

The formula for calculating the CIF price is as follows:

$$CIF = \frac{C\&F}{N(1 - 0.011R)}$$

where C = FAS value, determined as

		$
FOB	=	30,000.00
Rail freight	=	4,000.00
Wharfage, etc.	=	1,000.00
Consular fee	=	10.00
FAS	=	35,010.00
F = ocean freight	=	19,200.00
R = insurance rate	=	0.20 (per $100)
N = total number of boxes	=	4,000

Now, we determine the CIF, Le Havre price per box to be:

$$CIF = \frac{35,010.00 + 19,200.00}{4,000(1 - 0.011 \times 0.20)}$$

$$= \$13.58 \text{ per box}$$

10.7 Transfer pricing

Prices must be set not only on products sold to independent customers, but also on products transferred to foreign subsidiaries or transferred to foreign operations in which the seller has part ownership. For our purposes, prices to wholly or partially owned operations are defined as transfer prices.

The problem of establishing international transfer pricing policies is in a broad sense essentially the same as the problem of establishing domestic transfer pricing policies. However, upon close examination it can be observed that not only are the details of international transfer pricing more complex than domestic transfer pricing, but additional factors influence the decision making process (Carter *et al.*, 1998; Schmitz and Korner, 2000; Elliott and Emmanuel, 2000).

10.7.1 Decentralization and profit centers

At the outset it must be made clear that the need for transfer pricing arises only when a company decentralizes managerial authority and responsibility, making each unit responsible for operating profitably. The reasons for such decentralization may be both legal and managerial. Laws relating to corporate organization, taxation, and other matters may make it desirable for certain units or divisions of a company to be incorporated separately. Under such conditions the financial records of the unit must be kept in such a way that the company appears to operate as a profit center, if for no other reason than to satisfy foreign and domestic tax authorities.

Indeed, transfer pricing has been viewed by many primarily as a means for controlling divisional performances and coordinating cash and income flows from foreign subsidiaries. However, there is strong evidence that transfer pricing, including export transfer pricing, can be used for marketing decisions. Transfer pricing has great potential for helping marketing managers achieve strategic objectives in changing international environments.

10.7.2 Transfer pricing to wholly owned foreign subsidiaries

For a company with wholly owned foreign subsidiaries such factors as distance, expense of communicating, and decentralization of authority to the local level complicate the process of setting export transfer prices. Also, a complex set of taxes, tariffs, and governmental regulations affect the decision. Since competitive and market conditions vary from country to country, it is difficult to develop a policy that can be applied uniformly.

In the case where 100% ownership is held, a company has complete freedom to decide who will control the establishment of transfer prices, for example company management, the selling units, competitors (by the market price), the buying unit, or some combination. The determination of who should set the transfer price, and the method to be used, depends in part on the needs of the company for cost and profit information. Typically this information is used for such decisions as whether to 'make or buy,' determining the price of the end product, deciding whether to add or drop products, and determining the budget for capital expenditure.

The problem of transfer pricing has two dimensions: (1) how (by what method) should transfer prices be set, and (2) who should establish transfer pricing policies and set specific transfer prices? These questions are interrelated, since whoever sets the price will have some influence on deciding which factors to consider and the relative weight to give each factor.

How should transfer prices be set?

A number of methods of setting transfer prices have been tried and tested by companies of various sizes and product lines. Out of this experience have come a number of guidelines. Nevertheless, as yet, there is no general agreement as to which method of setting transfer prices has the most merit. No one method is best for all circumstances since the 'best' method for a company depends on the characteristics of the company and the purpose of the transfer price.

The factors that influence transfer prices fall into three general categories:

1. **competitive market prices**, including competitor's list prices or bids;
2. **costs**, including production costs, physical distribution costs, foreign and domestic tariffs, and corporate income taxes;
3. **legal restrictions**, including political policies, governmental controls, and foreign laws against practices such as price discrimination and dumping.

If the purpose of transfer pricing is to provide profitability data, then it is necessary that an accurate profitability figure be obtained. Such decisions must be made on the basis of alternative rates of return on investment, in the short run as well as in the long run; opportunity costs also must be considered. Thus it may seem desirable to base the transfer price on the competitive market price, or the best estimate of a market price, and to require the purchasing unit to buy internally. Under this policy, if the selling unit has unduly high costs, its profits will suffer, and the divisional manager will soon have to correct the situation or face corporate management with a poor profit record.

If the purpose of the transfer price is to assist management in setting the cost floor for prices of the end product, or if the purpose is to shift profits to the foreign operation, the use of costs is desirable as a means of determining the transfer price. There are different relevant cost concepts to consider. In the short run, marginal costs may be the relevant minimum, since any amount over such costs would result in a direct contribution to net profit. In the long run, full costs or standard costs may be closer to the ideal minimum that will help management to determine whether or not the resources of the corporation are being used to maximize profits, and if not, how to correct the situation.

The views of foreign Customs officials (for purposes of valuation of goods and assessment of duties) are also important. To minimize Customs duties, it is often desirable to set the price as close to cost as possible. However, some countries require that the Customs duty valuation be the 'fair market value,' or some concept of value related to the market price of the item in the country of exportation.

Domestic and foreign tax regulations and enforcement of those regulations also influence whether or not cost can be used as the basis for prices. Tax rates vary from country to country. When the home country corporate income tax is higher than the tax rate in the country in which the subsidiary is located, the recommended procedure is to set transfer prices as close to costs as permissible. Income tax authorities, however, may object to using taxes as a criterion for setting transfer prices.

Cost-plus transfer pricing has disadvantages beyond not being able to set a price that assures maximized profits, if that is the objective. Prices set in this way may not provide sufficient incentive for the producing unit to reduce costs to the absolute minimum. However, standard costs may be satisfactory as a basis for cost-plus transfer prices if the standards are proper.

A transfer pricing method that uses both costs and competitive market prices may permit the accomplishment of desired objectives without incurring the disadvantages of either method when it is used alone. For example, a system might be set up whereby the transfer price is set at cost, but the selling unit is credited with a certain percentage of the net profit that results from any further processing and the ultimate sale. Such a system could be used to minimize taxes and tariffs and at the same time generate profitability data.

It is desirable that some degree of flexibility in the process of formulating transfer prices be maintained. If flexibility is to be maintained, and if the interests of the buying and selling units as well as the corporate entity are to be considered, a system of *negotiation* or bargaining is required.

Negotiation also has some disadvantages. Discussions can be long and tedious and they may erupt into unharmonious interdivisional squabbles. Even though the negotiations and agreements must be reviewed periodically, the amount of time spent in negotiation can be kept within acceptable limits. Perhaps the greatest disadvantage of negotiation, on the other hand, is the occurrence of disputes. If the dispute is resolved on the basis of strength of personality or power position within the company, healthy, cooperative intracompany relations may be destroyed. If transfer prices are imposed on managers, this may also hamper morale and the profit incentive.

The desirability of each type of transfer pricing system is related to the characteristics of a company and the products it sells. A relatively small company with only a few foreign operating units, staffed by managers who are well acquainted with each other, can often operate on a somewhat more flexible basis than a large company. The size of the company is also related to the number and types of products in the company's product mix. Since the transfer price of different products should sometimes be set by different methods, the situation faced by large companies is complex.

Generally, most authorities on transfer pricing feel that if profitability data from profit centers are used to accomplish management purposes, the pricing policy must be aimed at setting 'competitive' transfer prices. Another reason for using competitive transfer prices is that tax laws are often written to prevent the arbitrary shifting of income among taxable units of companies in order to evade taxes. A key test seems to be whether a transfer price is *reasonable* rather than arbitrary. One of the strongest pieces of evidence that a price is fair and reasonable is that the price is not only at the market value, but that it was established by dealing at 'arm's length.' The arm's length requirement is also a strong argument in favor of permitting the price to be set by bargaining between the selling and buying units, with the buying unit free to buy outside if it desires.

Since competitive prices may differ from market to market, a company that bases transfer prices on competitive conditions in each market may have to set a different price for each market. Not only would such a pricing schedule be complex and costly to administer, but disagreements may arise among company units. Moreover, tariff authorities may object if they feel that valuation should be based on the price in the seller's home market. Last, but certainly not least, foreign and domestic income tax authorities may object if they feel that differential transfer prices may operate to shift profits from one nation to another and thereby affect taxable income.

The so-called *business purpose* test requires that there be a demonstrable managerial purpose for the adoption of a particular method of transfer pricing. Where different but equally satisfactory methods of transfer pricing are available, a business firm is not precluded from choosing the method that is to its advantage tax-wise. However, in general, the business purpose must be paramount. Thus it seems that transfer pricing methods would be acceptable to governments if the method meets either the arm's length or the business purpose test and is not for the purpose of avoiding payment of taxes.

Who should set transfer prices?

The power to set the transfer price can be retained by company management or delegated to the selling or buying unit. A compromise may be to permit the selling unit to set the price, but to permit the buying unit to buy outside if it desires. Or, management may prefer that the buying and selling divisions negotiate the transfer price. When this is the policy, corporate management enters into the negotiations only if a dispute arises.

10.7.3 Transfer pricing to partially owned foreign enterprises

It is relatively common for companies to have only a part interest in a foreign operation in partnership with either a foreign concern or with another firm domiciled in the same home country. When only a partial interest is held, or in the case of a joint venture, the seller cannot dictate prices to the same degree as if it were an internal transfer. The independent nature of the buyer requires that the price be set so as to take account of the interests of the other owners or partners in the venture.

Setting transfer prices to foreign operations that are not wholly owned involves some considerations in addition to those that are relevant for pricing to wholly owned subsidiaries. There is little reason to set the transfer price as close to cost as possible since the 'shifting' of profits abroad would mean that the foreign partner would share in them. Likewise, it would not be reasonable for transfers to be made at prices higher than the competitive market price. In fact, there may be pressures on the part of the foreign partner to reduce the transfer price below the 'outside' price. The transfer pricing process under such circumstances is similar to the process of pricing to third parties. The normal practice is likely to be arm's length negotiation, with the buyer having the freedom to buy outside.

However, if a joint venture has been formed for some special purpose, perhaps to produce an item not available elsewhere, the transfer price may be set on the basis of factors in addition to those already discussed. For example, suppose a joint venture is entered into by two noncompeting German firms to produce abroad a component that both of them need in their foreign products. Equal amounts of capital funds for the establishment of the foreign plant may be contributed by both parties. Thus, any profit that the firm would earn would be either paid out equally to the two stockholders or retained in the business. As long as each partner also takes exactly 50% of the output of the joint venture, both firms are benefiting equally from it. Under such conditions, in order to minimize income taxes on any profits that the joint venture might earn, it may be well to operate the plant on a break-even basis. Prices charged to its two customers by the joint venture might be set just high enough to cover costs. But, if one of the partners takes a disproportionate share of the output of the joint venture, one partner will benefit more from the joint venture than the other partner.

If the joint venture's product requires components that are produced by one of the partners, the situation is even more complex. Generally, under this circumstance, the partner selling the component to the joint venture would want to set a high price for it. The other partner would desire a low price.

SUMMARY

This chapter has examined pricing for export. The major issues covered include the determinants of price, pricing strategy, how foreign prices are related to domestic prices, the elements of the price quotation, and transfer pricing. Although export pricing issues are in many ways similar to domestic price considerations, there are elements that are unique to export marketing. The issues facing an exporter become more complex when a number of often quite diverse export markets are to be served.

In the future, export pricing is likely to gain rather than lose importance. As most markets reach saturation, companies will find it increasingly difficult to achieve higher sales without actively using pricing as a competitive tool. At the same time, communication technologies such as the Internet lead to more transparency, rendering it more difficult for firms to establish and maintain price differentials across markets. Disappearing retail price maintenance and shortening product life cycles add pressure for more sophisticated pricing practices to achieve quicker payback times. Finally, trade liberalization and growing economic integration render traditional market-per-market pricing obsolete and require improved pricing strategies.

QUESTIONS FOR DISCUSSION

10.1 What is the meaning of the 'anatomy of a price' as it refers to an export price?

10.2 Explain why export prices should or should not be established using the same methods and according to the same criteria as prices set in the domestic market.

10.3 Discuss the relationship between objective and strategy in pricing.

10.4 What alternative pricing strategies are available to the exporter and what objective(s) does each seek to achieve? Is any one more desirable than the others? Explain.

10.5 Can a small exporter use experience-curve pricing? If so, how? If not, why not?

10.6 Under what conditions might an exporter establish a policy of differential pricing for foreign markets?

10.7 'Since all trade terms are basically the same, there is no need for using them in export sales contracts.' Discuss.

10.8 Under what conditions might an exporter prefer to use INCOTERMS for a price quotation and under what conditions might this exporter prefer to use Revised American Foreign Trade Definitions – 1941? Does an exporter always have the choice of which trade term schema to use?

10.9 What factors must the exporter consider when making a decision on price quotation?

10.10 From the perspective of the 'parent' company, is it better to use a low export transfer price or a high price? What effect does extent of ownership of the importing unit have on your answer? Explain fully.

10.11 How does the nature of the product involved affect what might be a desirable transfer pricing policy?

10.12 Discuss what you consider to be the ideal approach for establishing an export transfer price.

10.13 Explain when the export firm should no longer be concerned about the pricing of its products.

REFERENCES

Bandler, J. (2004). As Kodak eyes digital future, a big partner starts to fade. *The Wall Street Journal*, 23 January, A1, A8.

Berner, R. (2002). Why P&G's smile is so bright. *Business Week*, 12 August, 58–60.

Branch, A. E. (1990). *Elements of Export Marketing and Management* 2nd edn. London: Chapman & Hall.

Business Week (1997). A dark Kodak moment. 4 August, 30–1.

Business Week (1998). Perils of the hedge highwire. 26 October, 74ff.

Business Week (2000). The end of a free ride for carmakers? 26 June, 70.

Capell, K. (2003). Ryanair rising. *Business Week*, 2 June, 40–1.

Carter, W. K., Maloney, D. M., and Van Vranken, M. H. (1998). The problems of transfer pricing. *Journal of Accountancy*, 186(1), 37–40.

De Jonquieres, G. (2003). WTO points to halving of antidumping probes. *Financial Times*, 27 October, 3.

Dolan, R. J. (1995). How do you know when the price is right? *Harvard Business Review*, September–October, 174–83.

Dolan, R. J. and Simon, H. (1997). *Pricing Power?* New York: Free Press.

Elliott, J. (1998). International transfer pricing: a survey of UK and nonUK groups, *Management Accounting*, 76(11), 48–50.

Elliott, J. and Emmanuel, C. (2000). International transfer pricing, searching for patterns. *European Management Journal*, 18(2), 216–22.

Emert, C. (2004). For California wine exports, it was a very good year. *San Francisco Chronicle*, 27 April, A1, A10.

Geitner, P. (2004). EU, Philip Morris near deal on smuggling. *San Francisco Chronicle*, 6 April, C3.

Hall, R. D. (1983). *International Trade Operations: A Managerial Approach*. Jersey City, NJ: Unz & Company.

International Chamber of Commerce (2000). *INCOTERMS 2000*. Paris: ICC.

Johnson, T. E. (1994). *Export/Import Procedures and Documentation* 2nd edn. New York: AMACOM.

Katz, R. (2003). Too rich for their own good? *The Oriental Economist*, May, 3–4.

Magnusson, P. (2002). A US trade ploy that is starting to boomerang. *Business Week*, 29 July, 64.

Mercado, S., Welford, R. and Prescott, K. (2001). *European Business* 4th edn. Upper Saddle River, NJ: Prentice-Hall.

Myers, M. B. and Cavusgil, S. T. (1996). Export pricing strategy-performance relationship: a conceptual framework. *Advances in International Marketing*, 8, 159–78.

Rossant, J. (1992). One day panic: next day sales. *Business Week*, 3290, 26 October, 49–50.

Samli, A. C. and Jacobs, L. (1994). Pricing practices of American multinational firms: standardization vs. localization dichotomy. *J. Global Marketing*, 8(2), 51–74.

Schmitz, A. E. and Korner, G. (2000). Recent developments in transfer pricing. *Corporate Finance*, May, 41–3.

Serwer, A. (2004). Southwest Airlines: the hottest thing in the sky. *Fortune*, 8 March, 86–102.

Simon, H. (1995). Pricing problems in a global setting. *Marketing News*, 29(21), 9 October, 4ff.

Sinha, I. (2000). Cost transparency: the Net's real threat to prices and brands. *Harvard Business Review*, March–April, 43–50.

Stottinger, B. (2001). Strategic export pricing: a long and winding road. *Journal of International Marketing*, 9(1), 40–55.

Strasburg, J. (2004). Retailer's cheap thrills. *San Francisco Chronicle*, 29 February, I1, I4.

Szuchman, P. and Cary, S. (2004). Trouble in low-fare land. *The Wall Street Journal*, 13 February, W.

Tanaka, Y. (2003). Red ink sparks McDonald's shuffle. *The Nikkei Weekly*, 10 March, 2.

Terpstra, V. (1988). *International Dimensions of Marketing* 2nd edn. Boston, MA: PWS-Kent.

The Economist (1996). Are crashes catching? 31 August, 64.

The Japan Times (2003). US ruling says that exporters dumping catfish, chips. 19 June, 13.

The Nikkei Weekly (2004). Yen faces upward pressure despite massive intervention. 12 January, 1.

White, J. (2004). Prices rise on European cars. *The Wall Street Journal*, 18 March, D1, D4.

WuDunn, S. (1995). Cost of Jeep driven skywards when it leaves US shores. *Sydney Herald*, 18 May.

FURTHER READING

Clark, T., Kotabe, M. and Rajaratnam, W. (1999). Exchange rate pass-through and international pricing strategy. *J. International Business Studies*, 30(2), 249–68.

Czinkota, M. R., Ronkainen, I. A., and Tarrant, J. J. (1995). *The Global Marketing Imperative*. Lincolnwood, IL: NTC Business Books, Chs 8–9.

Gaul, W. and Lutz, U. (1994). Pricing in international marketing and western European economy. *Management International Review*, 34(2), 101–14.

Huang, L.-H. (2000). The development of a framework for understanding global pricing. *International J. Management*, 17(4), 540–7.

Myers, M. B. (1997). The pricing of export products: why aren't managers satisfied with the results? *J. World Business*, 32(3), 277–89.

Raymond, M. A., Turner, J. F. Jr. and Kim, J. (2001). Cost complexity of pricing decisions for exporters in developing and emerging markets. *J. International Marketing*, 9(3), 19–40.

Theodosiou, M. and Katsikeas, C. S. (2001). Factors influencing the degree of international pricing strategy standardization of multinational corporations. *J. International Marketing*, 9(3), 1–18.

Walters, P. G. P. (1989). A framework for export pricing decisions. *J. Global Marketing*, 2(3), 95–111.

CASE STUDY 10.1

RAP Engineering and Equipment Company

This company, located in Seattle, Washington, in the United States, is a distributor of engineering equipment and machine tools. The company receives an order from the Matens Company in Portugal for 10 light earth-moving machines. Since the company does not normally carry this number in stock, the export manager, Mr Green, places an option on 10 machines with the CPPC Manufacturing Company in Akron, Ohio, and requests a firm price quotation to be held in force for 90 days. The CPPC Company agrees to this and quotes a price of US$4500 ex warehouse, Akron, Ohio, for each machine.

Mr Green checks with his traffic manager and is told that railroad freight from Akron to Seattle for these machines will average approximately US$750 per machine. Other costs are as follows:

	US$
Trucking and handling	5.00 per short ton
Export packing	70.00 per machine
Shipping to pier	4.20 per short ton
Wharfage and handling	3.30 per 40 cubic feet (cf)

Heavy lift charges: (applicable to items weighing over 5000 lb)	17.00 per 2000 lb
Ocean freight: Seattle to Lisbon	142.50 per 2000 lb or 40 cubic feet, weight/measure
Marine insurance:	
shipped under deck	1.70 per $100
shipped above deck	2.50 per $100
Portugal consular invoice fee	20.00 per invoice
Seattle Engineering & Equipment Company markup	20% of machine cost

Weights and measurements

10 crates containing chassis, each	6400 lb, 180 cf
10 boxes containing rails, chains, and parts, each	6000 lb, 50 cf
10 bundles containing wheels and tires, each	240 lb, 20 cf

Questions

1. Calculate the C&F Lisbon price per machine and the CIF Lisbon price per machine.

2. At what point in time, or place, will RAP's responsibilities for arrangements of the shipment end? When does RAP's legal liability end and when does it acquire the right to payment?

3. How would your answer to question 2 change if the terms of sale were FOB vessel (FOB) or ex dock (DEQ)?

CASE STUDY 10.2

The Capitool Company

(This is an abridged version of a Capitool case study, originally written by Gordon E. Miracle, Michigan State University. All monetary figures have been adjusted to disguise the actual values. For the most part, the relationships between numbers were maintained.)

The Capitool Company, with headquarters and main manufacturing plant in Racine, Wisconsin, in the United States, produces a line of capital equipment for use in a variety of industries, especially for auto-

mobiles, trucks, farm equipment, and construction equipment. The company was founded over 70 years ago, with sales (turnover) growing slowly to about US$60 million by the end of World War II, and since then more rapidly to more than US$3 billion in the mid-1990s. After-tax profits have grown correspondingly, usually amounting to about 3–4% of turnover.

Capitool has been a leader in offering an advanced line of products. Heavy research and product development expenditures coupled with customer orientation have enabled the company to achieve a dominant position in the US market.

In order to continue to grow rapidly and profitably Capitool decided in the mid-1950s to move into foreign markets. The company had exported a number of products for many years, but increasing foreign demand made it not only feasible, but desirable, to establish manufacturing facilities abroad. Within a 10-year period Capitool had wholly owned manufacturing plants in New Zealand, England, and Germany; joint ventures in Germany and Italy; and licensees in England, Argentina, and Turkey.

In addition to manufacturing facilities, Capitool has sales branches in England, Argentina, and Turkey to handle the marketing of the products of licensees in those countries. Since the licensees take only a part of their output of the licensed products for use in their own end products, the remainder is marketed to third parties by the Capitool sales branches.

In areas of the world not served by Capitool manufacturing or licensing affiliates, Capitool Exports Ltd, a wholly owned subsidiary incorporated in Bermuda, functions as an 'offshore' trading company. Capitool Exports Ltd has 20 regional offices located strategically to serve about 100 independent distributors who act as sales and service outlets in more than 100 countries.

The German subsidiary company

The Capitool Company GmbH, a wholly owned manufacturing subsidiary in Germany, is responsible for the operation of two factories, one in Duisburg and one in Düsseldorf.

The Düsseldorf plant manufactures components for various items of capital equipment, and has customers throughout Europe. Sales are concentrated in Germany, with a large proportion going to a joint venture with a large US automobile manufacturer; the joint venture is incorporated under the name Genforsler-Capitool GmbH.

The Duisburg plant manufactures a piece of equipment that is a mainstay in the Capitool line in the United States and worldwide. The prices of this piece of equipment range from US$90 to US$700, depending on the size and performance characteristics of the item. The Duisburg plant and three major German competitors account for over 95% of sales of the piece of equipment in Germany.

The fact that the Duisburg and Düsseldorf plants are part of the same company permits a 'tax loss carry forward' from the Duisburg plant to be used to minimize the total German tax obligation. By itself, the Düsseldorf plant is quite profitable. Recently the Duisburg plant has also become profitable. The 'tax loss carry forward' is expected to be depleted within the next three or four years.

The total Capitool investment in the Duisburg plant since the mid-1950s has been US$10,500,000. The plant has an area exceeding 221,000 square feet and employs over 1100 people currently. Capacity to produce exceeds demand by about 20%. Within three years demand is expected to exceed capacity, and expansion will be required.

The output of the Duisburg plant is sold throughout the European continent, England, Canada, and Mexico. Annual sales of the Duisburg plant exceed US$10 million.

Although the Duisburg plant is a manufacturing operation, only 35% of the contents of the product are actually manufactured at the Duisburg plant or in Düsseldorf. Local German suppliers furnish about 30% of the finished components, and the remaining 35% are imported from one of Capitool's divisions in the United States. Components are purchased from the United States when one or more of the following conditions apply to a specific component:

- technically adequate manufactured components are not available in Germany;
- the total of the US transfer price (as defined below) plus freight, insurance, and duty is less than the purchase price in Germany;
- delivery from the United States is faster than from the German supplier, and the need warrants use of the fastest source.

Transfer pricing policies

Corporate policy on transfer pricing is as follows:

- If there is a market price for the item, the basis for establishing the transfer price will be the market price.
- If the product is available elsewhere but there is no market price, the basis is negotiation between the selling and buying division. Negotiation is guided by (a) costs, and (b) outside competitive bids, if realistic bids are available. If not available, an estimate of a realistic outside quote is made.
- If the product is not available elsewhere, that is, if it is a unique part which is made only by Capitool, the basis for establishing the transfer price is negotiation based on: (a) costs, (b) anticipated volume, and (c) an 'equitable' markup.

The policy with regard to 'international' transfer pricing is basically the same, but with some additional complications. A major additional consideration is to minimize unnecessary Customs duties and taxes. In addition, the policy depends in part on the types of overseas operations, for example:

1. If the transfer price is to a subsidiary that is 100% owned, the policy would be to price as near to cost as possible. The policy is designed to accomplish two objectives: (a) to minimize Customs duties, and (b) to let the maximum amount of profit be taken by the subsidiary so as to minimize taxes, while at the

same time satisfying the US Internal Revenue Service authorities that there is no intent to avoid legitimate taxes by shifting profits abroad.

2. In the case where products are sold to a 50–50 joint venture, the policy is to set the price as high as possible, but to keep it competitive (since the joint venture could buy outside). This policy permits the profits to be earned by the Capitool Company rather than shifting it to the joint venture so that the foreign partner shares it. The joint venture is in this way limited to the profits that are properly earned as a result of its operations and efficiency.

A limiting factor is the trade-off in taxes or in duties. For example, if the duty is exceedingly high, the Capitool Company share of joint venture profits might be enough to make a low transfer price more profitable than a high transfer price.

In some cases, the transfer prices are covered in the joint venture contract; that is, an upper limit may be set. When there is a specific price ceiling it is renegotiable periodically.

However, in the special case of the Genforsler-Capitool joint venture (special because Genforsler-Capitool produces machines for sales only to Genforsler and to Capitool) the philosophy is for Genforsler-Capitool to develop a high-volume operation by operating just above the break-even point, and charging both Genforsler and Capitool as low a price as possible while earning enough profit to satisfy German tax authorities.

In the case of a joint venture in which the transfer price has not been specified, the policy is to take as much of the profit as possible in the transfer price.

Since the company goal is to maximize corporate profits rather than divisional profits, there inevitably arise situations where a domestic division must take a reduced profit (by lowering the transfer price) in order that the International Division may capitalize on a favorable tax or Customs duty situation, or vice versa. Usually, the division that must give up the profits sees the reason clearly, and there is no friction. However, in complex situations, transfer price negotiations between divisions can result in disputes. When such an occasion arises, and when the dispute cannot be resolved satisfactorily, it is referred to the Control Committee. This committee consists of the financial vice-president of the corporation (the chairman of the committee), the corporate controller, the controller of the domestic division that is involved, and the International Division controller.

Company officials are reviewing their transfer pricing policy on components shipped to the Duisburg plant. When the original policy was established, the following considerations were evaluated in determining the transfer price:

- At what price would corporate profits be greatest? Capitool GmbH is in a 'tax loss carry forward' position.
- What price would be most advantageous for computing shipping insurance, freight, and duty? These costs are estimated at 40% of the FOB US price.
- What transfer price would the US Internal Revenue Service consider adequate for determining taxable income for the Capitool Company?
- What transfer price would the German authorities consider adequate for determining the taxable income of Capitool GmbH?
- What transfer price would the German authorities consider adequate for determining a duty base?
- Should the company encourage Capitool GmbH to seek maximum indigenous content through high transfer prices?
- What is the relative quality of German-sourced components versus US components?
- What transfer price is necessary to keep the landed cost of components at a level that will allow Capitool GmbH to price their machines competitively and obtain a satisfactory gross margin?

Currently the FOB US transfer price on components shipped from the US plant to the Duisburg plant is the sum of:

- actual direct material;
- actual direct labor;
- full manufacturing expense;
- 14.2% markup on cost.

This formula has been reviewed and approved by the United States Internal Revenue Service and the German Income Tax and Customs Authorities as the lowest acceptable basis for determining: (a) taxable profits at each location and (b) the value to be used in assessing Customs duty payments.

Company officials have been concerned about the meaning and usefulness of transfer prices. In the past the policy has been one of decentralization of authority to managers that head profit centers. Profit centers have been used both as a managerial incentive (so that a manager can see the profits for which he can take credit), and as a method of measuring the performance of executives. Under such a system, whenever there are intracompany transfers of products, a 'transfer price' must be established. Company officials are concerned that there are inequities in the system, since maximum corporate profit may not be achieved simply by letting divisions maximize profits individually.

One company official went so far as to suggest that perhaps it would be better to determine all transfer prices at headquarters; and that the 'profit' centers should be changed to 'cost' centers. The general manager of each cost center would have no control over centrally administered transfer prices; he or she would simply be forced to accept them as they are set by headquarters. Under this arrangement managers would be evaluated not on profits but according to other measures, for example share of market, sales increases, cost reductions, and so forth. The company's tax counsel pointed out that this policy would cause problems with tax and Customs authorities.

Another company official expressed the view that managers of cost (or profit) centers should be permitted to buy wherever landed cost is lowest, except when the corporate interest is served by 'buying' internally, for example: (1) when there is excess capacity (probably there would be no difficulty in this regard if the 'selling'

division were willing to set the price as near to marginal cost as necessary to be competitive), or (2) when tax or duty factors make it desirable to transfer at a 'higher than competitive' price.

Questions

1. What should be Capitool's general policy on the formulation of international transfer prices?

2. What methods should be used to set Capitool's transfer prices and who should be involved in the process?

3. Should Capitool have a system of multiple transfer prices: (a) for different products, (b) to different countries, or (c) to different classes of customers?

CASE STUDY 10.3

Strato Designs

Exchange rate fluctuations between the Japanese yen, the euro, and the US dollar posed serious problems for Strato Designs (the name of the company is disguised) during the period 1999–2004. The California company produces graphics components for 9 of the top 10 PC makers, other specialty logic chips for PCs, and modems. Approximately 35% of its sales are to Japanese companies, and approximately 10% to European companies.

Japanese customers require that prices be quoted in yen, and many European customers are now requiring that prices be quoted in euros. Payments in foreign currencies could, of course, be converted to dollars at the spot (current) exchange rate when received. However, when the yen or euro has increased in value between the time of price quotation and the receipt of payment, it means a windfall profit for Strato Designs. A decrease in the value of the yen or euro means an exchange loss that might exceed the margin on the sale, resulting in a loss on the sale.

The fluctuations in exchange rates during this period were substantial and unpredictable. From its launch in January 1999, the euro lost 30% of its value relative to the dollar by October 2000. It rallied, fell again, and then increased greatly. By January 2004 the euro had reached a value of $1.29, an increase of 53%

against the dollar from its low in October 2000 (Fairlamb, 2004). Daily fluctuations were sometimes substantial. During 1999–2004, the yen moved up and down within a range of about 25%. Fluctuations in the value of the yen were dampened somewhat by massive Japanese government interventions in the foreign exchange market.

Overall margins in the industry are not high enough to allow Strato Designs to make quotations to cover possible losses due to a weakening of a foreign currency. Even windfall profits from a strengthening foreign currency could be a problem for the company. Foreign customers who contracted for products when their currencies were weak, and subsequently paid when their currencies were strong, would realize that they were paying high prices in dollars. They might ask for rebates if Strato Designs' competitors were offering products at lower prices based on revised exchange rates.

Company officials discussed the problem with their bank, and with other companies facing similar problems, using the yen as an example. At least six strategies are available:

1. The company could enter into a forward exchange contract to sell the yen for dollars at a specified date in the future for a specified price. The date for sale of the yen (purchase of dollars) would be set for the time when the yen would be received from the Japanese importer of the goods. Such a contract, available at a relatively low price and usually with a rate very near to the spot rate, would lock in the profit. But it would also prevent Strato Designs

from benefiting from a windfall profit. Further, it would not solve the potential problem of having a dissatisfied customer if the yen became stronger during the period between the sales contract and the time of payment.

2. The company could purchase an option to sell the yen (buy dollars) at a specified rate at the date when the yen are due to be received. With an option, Strato Designs would not have to sell the yen to the option provider. It could do so if the yen had become weaker, or it could simply not exercise the option and instead sell the yen at the spot rate (current rate) if the yen had become stronger. The disadvantage of this method is that options are relatively expensive to purchase.

3. Strato Designs might be able to arrange a swap of currencies at a predetermined rate with a US-based exporter who will need to pay yen at the time that Strato Designs will receive yen.

4. Depending upon Strato Designs' need for parts or other goods from Japan, it might be able to partially or totally offset potential exchange losses/gains from export sales with balancing gains/losses from import purchases at the same time.

5. Strato Designs could make contracts or purchase options only when it believes that the yen will become weaker. When it believes that the yen will become stronger, it could simply wait to sell the yen

when received, thereby making an additional profit.

6. Strato Designs could simply not take any advance action, accepting exchange losses or gains as they might occur.

From these possible models, Strato Designs has to decide upon a specific system to use.

Reference

Fairlamb, D. (2004). Why Europe may be forced to drive the Euro down, *Business Week*, 26 January, 60.

Questions

1. Are the Japanese customers of Strato Designs likely to be willing to accept price quotations in dollars? Discuss.

2. What should be the company's objective in managing the exchange rate situation?

3. What model or system would you recommend that Strato Designs use? Defend your choice!

4. Is your choice in question 3 something that the company should do for all the foreign currencies that it might have to manage or only for the Japanese yen? Explain.

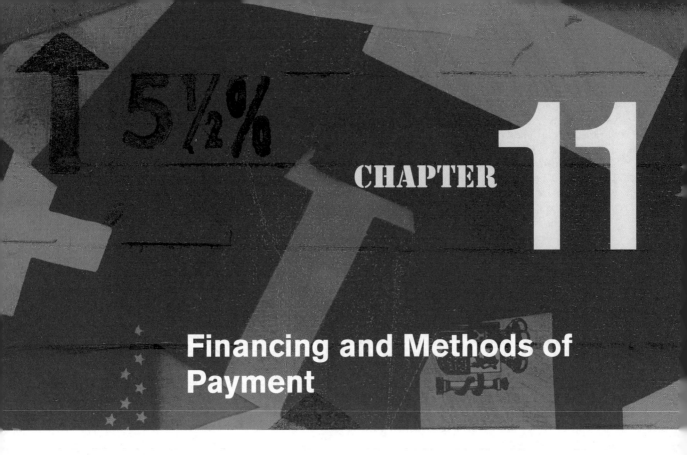

CHAPTER 11

Financing and Methods of Payment

11.1 Introduction

Financing and payments are issues directly tied to export pricing. Export prices are not set in isolation but must consider how payment is to be made. The financial procedures that have been developed, although rather complicated, provide export marketers with the services and tools essential to control payment for internationally traded merchandise. Although banks engage in international finance for the purpose of making profits, the services they furnish are indispensable aids to the export manager. In the following pages the methods, procedures, and tools of export financing and methods of payment, including some of the services offered by banks, will be described. In addition, various types of countertrade arrangements, which may or may not involve a monetary payment, are discussed. Necessarily, however, these descriptions will be brief. For more detail see the publications by Bank of America (2004) or similar publications by banks with international banking departments.

Advances in electronic communications have had a substantial impact on both bank interfaces with customers and inter-bank operations. Some customers still fill out paper application forms for letters of credit and other financial transactions. However, most companies now conduct much of their business online, sending EDI (electronic data interchange) and/or other files, using web-based application forms, etc. These forms, for international as well as domestic transactions, are usually in the language and format of the country in which the bank is located. In the past, letters of credit and other forms were sent internationally in full-language text in hard copy or electronically. Differences in formats and the meanings of terms sometimes resulted in delays or confusion in translating the forms into the language and format used in the receiving country. This procedure has been changed by the development of SWIFT (Society for Worldwide Inter-bank Transfers).

Over 90% of inter-bank financial transfers are now made through SWIFT, a proprietary electronic network owned by banks. It is also used for inquiries, settlements of various types of transactions, and commercial payments. For the various forms commonly used, messages are sent in a structured format that has all of the necessary information in standard locations (Scanlan, 2004). The cost of sending a letter of credit using the structured message is less than one-fifth of the cost of sending a full-text message, and greatly reduces the potential for mis-understanding. In the world of satellite and other means of wireless communi-cations, banks have various methods for conducting other types of transactions.

While the personal relationship of customers and their banks continue to be of great importance, routine transactions are often done online.

11.2 Export financing methods/terms of payment

Financing methods are determined to a large extent by the degree of control that the exporter desires to retain over the merchandise, as well as the time limit that has been placed upon the extension of credit.

In exporting, there are seven different ways in which credit is extended and pay-ments made. These are discussed more or less in ascending order from the least secure to the most secure – from the seller's/exporter's point of view – regarding risk of nonpayment. This ordering also corresponds to ascending costs to the importer from least expensive to most expensive. Generally, the exporter would prefer the most secure method, while the importer would prefer the least expensive. Since the extremes for each are on opposite ends of the ordering, it is obvious that some form of compromise may be needed.

11.2.1 Consignment

When this method is used, demand for payment is usually made by means of a clean draft (no documents attached), drawn on the consignee/importer by the exporter. Payment typically occurs after the products have been resold by the buyer/importer. The timing and procedures for payment will depend on the prior arrangements made between the buyer and seller. The seller may draw a clean draft (no documents attached) on the buyer for the value of a particular shipment or shipments. Alternatively, the buyer may simply make periodic payments, such as monthly, with or without receiving a clean draft, on the balance owed. Actual remittance (payment) is made by check, bank draft, or electronic transfer. Consignment business, in many countries, can be dangerous for three reasons: first, the laws are not always clear on the ownership of the consigned merchandise; second, it is difficult for the seller to keep a watchful eye on the consigned mer-chandise when it is physically in a far country; and third, exchange controls may preclude payment by the consignee.

11.2.2 Open account

Business done in export trade on open account is handled by the same procedure and methods as in domestic trade. An exporter would normally be willing to use this method only when he has confidence in the creditworthiness of the buyer. Exhibit 11.1 shows how use of this technique may be enhanced.

Theatre of Roman Ruins at Efes, Turkey

EXHIBIT 11.1	Factoring is an alternative

An exporter's ability to use open account can be enhanced by the use of factoring. Factoring is the purchase of a company's accounts receivable by a financial institution, which may be a bank or a specialized institution. Ideally, the exporter should go to the factor before any contract is signed and shipment made and secure its willingness to buy the receivable. The factor will check out the credit rating, and so forth, of the prospective buyer(s) typically by having a correspondent in the importer's country do the necessary checking. Thus the factor acts as a credit approval agency as well as a facilitator and 'guarantor' of payment.

According to the manager of Faktofins Company, an affiliate of Iktisat Bank of Turkey – the pioneering institution for factoring in Turkey – anything that can be made, sold, and forgotten without warranties can be factored. All consumer goods payable in 90 days and without a guarantee involving after-sales service are suitable for factoring. Warrantied goods whose deficiencies are not readily apparent complicate disputes over the quality of the goods traded. Iktisat Bank, as are many other factoring organizations, is a member of Factor Chains International (FCI), one of the major international factoring organizations. FCI has a set of rules of arbitration to determine whether a dispute is justified and to deal with it efficiently. Once shipments are made, the exporter takes the necessary documents to the factor for payment. The correspondent obtains the payment from the importer and transfers the funds back to the exporter through the factor. This process is illustrated in Figure 11.1. According to one expert, a factor can provide three major services to the exporter, as follows (Batchelor, 1990):

1. Immediate cash (up to 85% of the value of the invoices) can be given to the exporter. The remaining funds less service fee and interest charge for the advance are paid when the customer pays.
2. The factor, if desired, can take over administration of the client's sales ledger, sending out invoices and ensuring that payment is received.
3. The factor can assess credit risks and insure clients against the possibility of bad debts.

A related practice is forfait financing. Forfaiting is the transfer of a term debt obligation from an export sale in which the exporter sells the debt to a third party, usually without recourse to the exporter. This debt typically is guaranteed by foreign banks and/or governments. The exporter receives its money, at a discount, when the 'forfaiter' purchases the bill of exchange or promissory note written out by the exporter's customer. Ideally, after a predetermined time period the forfaiter collects payment from the customer. The forfaiter's profit is the difference between full payment received and the discounted amount paid to the exporter. In some cases the forfait house converts the receivables bought into commercial paper, which is salable.

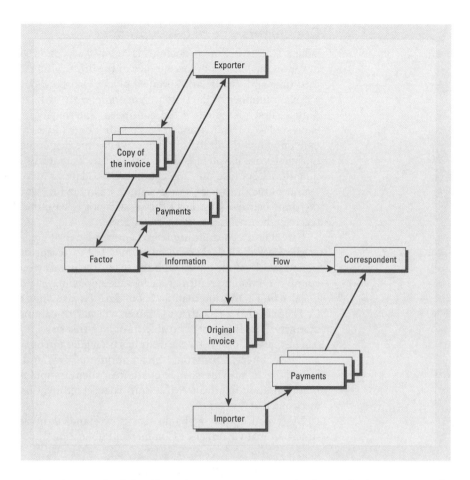

FIGURE 11.1

Exporter's use of factoring

Another method for financing open account sales is to obtain export credit insurance, as discussed in section 11.2.8, and then obtain financing from your own bank. Depending upon the country in which the exporter is located, export insurance may be obtained that covers political risk, nonconvertability of currency, and even commercial risk. Where this method can be used it may be less expensive than factoring.

11.2.3 Documentary collections

Exporters may obtain a greater measure of assurance of payment, beyond that of open account, by ensuring that the importer cannot obtain the shipment until he/she agrees to pay by a certain time (documents against acceptance D/A), or until payment is actually made by the importer (documents against payment D/P). The exporter does this by sending the documents the importer needs in order to get the shipment to a third party, almost always a bank or collecting agency, along with a draft demanding payment. The bank is instructed to deliver the documents to the importer only when the payment conditions are met.

Drafts may be sent to the importer's bank for collection, without the bank itself having provided any guarantee of payment. A greater level of security for the exporter is provided if the importer has arranged a letter of credit providing the exporter's bank's guarantee of payment as discussed in section 11.3. The importer may be unwilling or unable to arrange for a letter of credit from his/her bank.

Documents against acceptance

When a draft is drawn documents against acceptance credit is extended to the buyer on the basis of his acceptance of the draft calling for payment within a specified time and usually at a specified place. The specified time may be expressed as a certain number of days after sight (*time draft*), which means after the date the draft is first presented to the consignee. Alternately, the specified time may be expressed as a certain number of days after date (*date draft*), which means that the date on which the draft is drawn serves as the beginning day of tenor (i.e., length of time before payment is due) of the draft. Date drafts are generally preferred to time drafts because they indicate the exact date of maturity of the draft. In most countries the drawee of a draft cannot examine the merchandise before accepting the draft because Customs officials will not release the shipment until they have received the documents from the importer.

If a seller uses a draft not issued under a letter of credit, whether D/A or D/P he or she faces the risk that the buyer may fail to accept the draft. While this would leave the title of the goods with the seller, the goods would already be in a foreign country. Obtaining return or sale of the goods may be difficult and/or expensive. Legal action across international boundaries is also often difficult and/or expensive.

There is also a risk that the buyer will not or cannot honor (pay) the draft at maturity. The buyer may be able to reduce this risk by stipulating that the goods can be released only after the draft has been guaranteed by the buyer's bank as well as by the buyer. This would be an additional cost and, since the bank may not be willing to provide such a guarantee, such a stipulation should be used only if agreed upon in advance. If a draft is accepted by a bank it may be more easily discounted.

Most collections by banks are now handled in accordance with the ICC (International Chamber of Commerce) Publication 52.

Documents against payment

Here the buyer must make payment for the face value of the draft before receiving the documents conveying title to the merchandise. This occurs when the buyer first sees the draft. Sometimes, with instructions from the drawer, the buyer may be given a certain limited period within which to make payment. In the meantime, the merchandise remains in the name of and in the hands of the collecting agency, which is usually a bank. It should not be assumed, however, that the drawee must make immediate payment. It is the custom, in most foreign countries, for the drawee of the draft to make credit arrangements with his own bank, at point of destination, to advance the funds with which to pay the full face of the draft or some part of the draft against delivery to the buyer of a proportionate amount of the merchandise.

In some countries it is also customary that the drawee defers payment until the arrival of the goods. It is not customary to allow part payment of the draft against proportional release of the merchandise. The collecting agent must have specific instructions from the drawer in order to allow this.

In some countries also, no drafts are used in the case of sight transactions where payment is actually made upon delivery of the goods. Drafts are not really necessary when collections are made by the transportation company or the bank actually collects the money before delivering the goods to the importer.

11.2.4 Letter of credit (L/C) Documentary credit

Under a letter of credit, the buyer establishes a commercial credit through his or her bank and specifies the conditions under which payment may be made to the named seller (the exporter, who is called the 'beneficiary'). Upon arrival of the credit, usually electronically, the exporter's bank notifies the exporter that the credit is available and gives advice of the terms. To receive payment, the seller presents to the negotiating or paying bank the specified documents covering the shipment. Attached to the documents is a draft drawn on a bank and this draft can be either a sight, time, or date draft. If the documents are in order and if they have been presented on or before the expiry date, they are accepted by the bank and the exporter receives payment in full. Then, as far as the exporter is concerned, the transaction is closed. It should be noted, however, that each and every condition set forth in the letter of credit must be meticulously fulfilled by the beneficiary. It is not unusual for even experienced exporters occasionally to get into difficulties by overlooking some small but important provision in the letter of credit.

The letter of credit is a documentary credit as defined in ICC Publication 500, to which the vast majority of credits are subject.

In the case of an L/C of a usance type where delivery of the documents is made against acceptance of the documents rather than against payment, the beneficiary (exporter) will not receive payment immediately, but only at maturity.

If an L/C has not been confirmed by the importer's bank, that bank has no obligation to pay the importer if it does not receive payment from the exporter's bank.

11.2.5 COD (cash on delivery)

International COD transactions are sometimes used in connection with air transport, and may also be used where there is road transport or inland water transport between countries (as in Europe and elsewhere). In general, it is a convenient method in those cases where the goods are to be delivered to the buyer, the goods are not covered by a document conveying title (a bill of lading), and the carrier is set up to accept payment. Numerous airlines have facilities at their terminals for making delivery of merchandise against cash payments by the consignee. Where these facilities are available, a convenient method is afforded shippers for collecting payment. It should be noted, however, that the sight draft, D/P, is to all intents and purposes a COD payment.

11.2.6 Cash with order

Cash or part cash with order, also referred to as advance payment, is sometimes demanded by sellers. Often this may be required because of potential risks in obtaining payment or foreign exchange. When this method is used it is normally part cash, with the amount being sufficient to cover the transport costs to the point of import and back to the point of export.

A summary of the key aspects of these methods is shown in Table 11.1. Of the seven methods of payment used in export marketing, consignment, open account, and sight draft, D/A involve the extension of credit by the seller to the buyer. With any of these three the seller loses complete control of the merchandise and places it in the custody of the buyer.

With the letter of credit, cash on delivery, or cash with order the seller extends no credit to the buyer. In fact, with cash with order, the seller receives payment before delivering or even shipping the merchandise. Using sight draft, D/P, the seller does not lose possession or control of the merchandise because the buyer must pay for it before taking possession. In other words, this method is, in effect, cash on delivery. There is still the risk that the buyer will not accept the documents and thus not pay if draft was not under a letter of credit.

TABLE 11.1 Key features of export payment methods

Method of payment	Time of payment to seller	Goods available to buyer	Risk to seller	Risk to buyer
1. Consignment	Upon presentation of draft, usually after all or part of the goods have been sold by the importer	Upon delivery	Full reliance on buyer to pay the drafts	None
2. Open account	Upon payment of invoice made	Upon delivery	Full reliance on buyer to pay invoice when due	None
3. Time draft for collection ■ Documents against acceptance (D/A)	Upon maturity of time draft, or trade acceptance	Upon acceptance of time draft	Same, but buyer has possession of the goods	Same as time L/C
4. Sight draft for collection ■ Documents against payment (D/P) ■ Cash against documents	Upon presentation of documents	After payment	Possible nonpayment of draft due to commercial or political risk	Same as sight L/C
5. Letter of credit (L/C), or usance documentary credit	Upon maturity of time draft, or upon discounting of the bankers' acceptance	Upon his or her bank's acceptance of the documents	Possible nonpayment due to political risk	Actual payment is due after receipt of documents, but must be made regardless of product quality
6. Sight letter of credit (L/C), or sight documentary credit	When conforming documents are presented to the negotiating or paying bank	Upon settlement	Very little or none, based on condition in the L/C	Has assurance of shipment but relies on seller to ship goods as described in the document
7. Cash in advance	Prior to shipment	After payment	None	Full reliance on the exporter to ship goods as ordered

11.2.7 Long-term financing

Major projects, large capital equipment sales, and special exports such as agricultural commodities moving under governmental programs may require long-term financing. A number of governmental, banking, and private organizations have programs to facilitate such transactions. These generally allow the producers to receive funds in the near future while allowing the purchaser to spread payments over several years. In addition to direct loans, such as that provided by the Export–Import Bank of the United States, government agencies such as the Export Credits Guarantee Department in the United Kingdom, the Foreign Credit Insurance Association in the United States, the Hong Kong Export Credit Insurances Corp. and Compagnie Française d'Assurance pour le Commerce Extérieur (COFACE) in France provide for their exporters insurance protection against credit and political risks. Similar organizations exist in developing countries as well as developed ones (see Fitzgerald and Monson, 1987). Export credit and investment insurance companies from more than 30 countries are members of the International Union of Credit and Investment Insurers (the Berne Union). The Berne Union acts as the global coordinator of national credit insurers and maintains an extensive international databank of credit risks of private and public sector buyers. Such a source of credit risk data can be very useful to the exporter facing a decision about providing long-term financing.

11.3 Payment/financing procedures

It is clear that the export marketer has a large array of payment procedures from which to select. In common usage, however, the procedures may be classified into two general categories: (1) letters of credit and (2) drafts or bills of exchange.

There are many varieties of letters of credit, depending upon the provisions set forth in the letters themselves. But they have one objective in common: providing the credit of a bank or banks in place of the credit or risk of the importer or exporter.

Several varieties of drafts are also commonly utilized, depending upon requirements concerning documents and conditions of payment. In fact, even with letter-of-credit financing, a draft is invariably used. Drafts, too, have a common objective, which is to make a specific record of the financial aspects of the transaction in such a form that it can be used to obtain financing from the banking system.

11.3.1 Letter of credit

A commercial letter of credit, or documentary credit, may be defined as

> an instrument, usually issued by a bank, at the request and for the account of its client, which indicates that the bank agrees to pay to the named beneficiary a sum of money upon the presentation of certain documents or written representations as stipulated in the letter of credit.

When issued by a bank on behalf of one of its customers, the letter of credit adds the bank's name, integrity, and credit to that of their customer.

The use of letters of credit for financing export shipments has long been popular with exporters. They have found that this means of arranging payment affords a high degree of protection against the risk inevitably arising in export business. This is particularly true when the letter of credit is issued in irrevocable form and is further confirmed by a bank of unquestioned standing in the exporter's country. *A letter of credit is only as good as the bank that issues it* and, if confirmed, the bank that confirms it.

Except in their general form and phraseology, letters of credit vary greatly because each one is drawn to cover the requirements of an individual transaction. Such credits, however, have certain characteristics in common. All contain authorizations for the seller of goods to present required documents to a specified bank that promises to honor those documents in accordance with the stipulations in the credit, although in the case of revocable credits this promise is contingent upon the

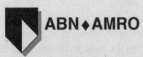

International Trade Services
200 W. Monroe Street, Suite 1100
Chicago, Illinois 60606-5002
(312) 904-8462   fax (312) 904-6303

L/C no. _____
(For Bank Use)

APPLICATION FOR IRREVOCABLE COMMERCIAL LETTER OF CREDIT

Subject to our Master Letter of Credit Agreement with yourselves, please issue an irrevocable Commercial Letter of Credit (L/C) substantially as set forth below, and
☐ send the original L/C directly to the Beneficiary
☐ send the L/C to the Advising Bank indicated or your chosen correspondent, as applicable (for delivery to the Beneficiary)
by ☐ airmail. ☐ courier. ☐ cable (SWIFT/telex/cablegram). ☐ other: _____.

Advising Bank (optional)	Applicant (name & address)
Beneficiary of L/C (name & address expected to appear on invoices)	Amount (U.S. dollars unless otherwise indicated) up to: plus or minus ____%
	Expiry Date of L/C (month in words, day, year) in the country of the Beneficiary unless otherwise indicated

Please make the L/C subject to the Uniform Customs and Practice for Documentary Credits (UCP) currently in effect.
Documents must be presented within _____ days after shipment (21 days if not otherwise specified) but, in any case, within the validity of the credit.
Draft(s) must be drawn at (specify "sight" or other tenor)_____ for _____% (100% unless otherwise specified) of Commercial Invoice
value drawn on you or (specify other drawee)_____ and accompanied by the following documents:

☐ Original and _____ copy(ies) of Commercial Invoice covering (describe goods as in the Beneficiary's proforma invoice but only in generic terms, omitting details as to
grade, quality, etc.): _____
  ☐ EXW (Ex Works, Ex Factory At) _____ (place)
  ☐ FCA (Free Carrier At) _____ (place)
  ☐ CPT (Carriage Paid To) _____ (place)
  ☐ CIP (Carriage & Insurance Paid To) _____ (place)
  ☐ FOB (Free On Board At) _____ (port of loading) (for port-to-port ocean shipments only; otherwise use FCA)
  ☐ CFR (Cost & Freight Paid To) _____ (port of discharge) (for port-to-port ocean shipments only; otherwise use CPT)
  ☐ CIF (Cost, Insurance & Freight Paid To)_____(port of discharge) (for port-to-port ocean shipments only; otherwise use CIP)
  ☐ Other terms_____

☐ Marine Cargo Insurance Policy or Certificate (for CIP and CIF shipments) in negotiable form for at least _____% (110% unless otherwise specified) of Commercial
  Invoice value, endorsed in blank and covering the following risks:
  ☐ All risks warehouse-to-warehouse
  ☐ All risks warehouse-to-warehouse including war risks and strikes, riots and civil commotions
  ☐ Other (specify)_____
☐ Copy of a cable or fax message addressed to the Applicant giving date and means of shipment and description and value of the goods shipped, bearing the
  Beneficiary's original signed certification that "This is a true and accurate copy of a message sent as addressed within two days of shipment of the described goods"
  (for insurance purposes on EXW, FCA, CPT, FOB, and CFR shipments).

☐ Full set of Multimodal Transport (Door-to-Door) Bills of Lading showing place of receipt as _____ and place of
  delivery or final destination as _____consigned to the order of the shipper, endorsed in blank.
☐ Full set of Port-to-Port Bills of Lading showing port of loading as_____ and port of
  discharge as _____, consigned to order of shipper, endorsed in blank.
  ☐ Transshipment prohibited (only applies to Port-to-Port Bills of Lading).
☐ Original Shipper's Copy of Air Waybill, showing airport of departure as _____ and airport of
  destination as _____, consigned to _____.
  ☐ Beneficiary's certificate that "one extra set of documents is accompanying the air shipment" (not applicable to ocean shipments).
The above Bills of Lading, Air Waybill or other transport documents are to be marked and evidence:
  Freight: ☐ Collect   ☐ Prepaid   Notify Party:_____
  Partial shipments: ☐ Allowed   ☐ Not allowed   Shipment not later than: _____
☐ Forwarder's Cargo Receipt issued by _____ showing merchandise received
  no later than _____, consigned to or held at the disposal of the Applicant.

☐ Original and _____ copy(ies) of Packing List.

☐ Original and _____ copy(ies) of Certificate of Origin.

☐ Original and _____copy(ies) of_____.

SPECIAL CONDITIONS/INSTRUCTIONS
☐ Please make the L/C transferable in full or in parts by any bank.
☐ All bank charges other than those of the Issuing Bank are for the account of the Beneficiary.   ☐ All bank charges are for the account of the Applicant.
☐ Discount charges, if any (applicable only to drafts other than "sight"), are for the account of the   ☐ Beneficiary.   ☐ Applicant.
☐ All documents are to be sent to you in one lot by   ☐ Courier.   ☐ Airmail.
☐ Other conditions/instructions: _____

_____
Account Party name (if different from Applicant name above)

Authorized signature	date	phone number	fax number

FORM NO:TP3263

FIGURE 11.2   Application for irrevocable letter of credit

letter of credit not having been cancelled. The bank thus places the security of its name behind the buyer; and in case of irrevocable credits this security cannot be taken away except with the consent of the beneficiary. Here lies the main point of attractiveness of letters of credit from the seller's point of view. The exporter is assured of obtaining payment for his or her goods, provided that the terms specified in the letter of credit are met.

The 'advising' bank which notifies the exporter that a letter of credit has been established to the seller's credit takes no risk in the transaction unless it agrees to confirm the letter of credit. The letter of credit, therefore, protects the exporter because it guarantees payment; it serves the best interests of the buyer because the buyer's money is not paid out until a clean on-board bill of lading evidencing shipment of merchandise is presented to the negotiating or paying bank, along with all other documents required under the letter of credit. Of course, if the letter is unconfirmed and the bank in the importer's country is unable to send payment because of actions of its government, or for other reasons, the exporter is not protected. The letter of credit does not protect the importer from mistake or fraud in the case that the merchandise is not as described/shown on the bill of lading.

Figure 11.2 shows the English language version of an application for irrevocable letter of credit from ABN-AMRO, the large international bank headquartered in The Netherlands. (The meanings of the terms used are explained in the remainder of this chapter.)

Figure 11.3 shows the operation of a letter of credit and the roles that each party plays. A correspondent bank's notification of the opening of a letter of credit

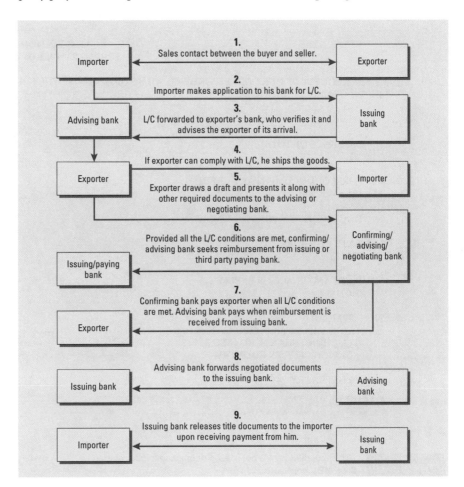

FIGURE 11.3

How a letter of credit operates
Source: adapted from Seafirst Bank, 1988, p. 10

Bank of America

DATE: DECEMBER 15, 2003

ADVICE OF IRREVOCABLE DOCUMENTARY CREDIT

ISSUING BANK'S NUMBER: 3ALLH205788-0822
OUR REFERENCE NUMBER: XXXXXXX

SEND TO	ISSUING BANK
BANK OF AMERICA, TRADE FINANCE	GOOD CORRESPONDENT BK
800 FIFTH AVE. WA1-501-31-01	325 CHUNG HSIAO E. ROAD
31 FLOOR	SEC 4, FL 3
SEATTLE, WA 98104	FOREIGN CITY, FX COUNTRY

BENEFICIARY	APPLICANT
VALUED EXPORT INC	GOOD IMPORTER CORPORATION
ANY USA STREET	113 CHUNG SHAN N. RD., SEC.2
ANYCITY USA 97290	FOREIGN CITY, FX COUNTRY

AMOUNT
USD 15,400.00
FIFTEEN THOUSAND FOUR HUNDRED
AND 00/100'S US DOLLARS

EXPIRATION
FEBRUARY 10, 2004 U.S.A.

AT THE REQUEST OF OUR CORRESPONDENT, WE HEREBY ADVISE THE FOLLOWING
LETTER OF CREDIT DETAILS:

QUOTE:

:27 : SEQUENCE OF TOTAL
:   : 1/1
:   :
:40A: FORM OF DOCUMENTARY CREDIT
:   : IRREVOCABLE
:   :
:20 : DOCUMENTARY CREDIT NUMBER
:   :
:31C: DATE OF ISSUE
:   : 031215
:   :
:31D: DATE AND PLACE OF EXPIRY
:   : 040210USA
:   :
:50 : APPLICANT
:   : GOOD IMPORTER CORPORATION
:   : 113, CHUNG SHAN N. RD., SEC.2
:   : FOREIGN CITY, FX COUNTRY
:   :
:59 : BENEFICIARY

Bank of America, N.A. Trade Operations
Mail Code: CA9-703-19-09
333 S. Beaudry Avenue, 19th Floor, Los Angeles, CA 90017

00-35-0202NSB 9-1999_CA9 19

FIGURE 11.4	Correspondent bank's notification of opening a letter of credit.
	Source: Bank of America, 2003

Bank of America

THIS IS AN INTEGRAL PART OF ADVICE NUMBER: XXXXXXX

```
:   : VALUED EXPORT INC
:   : ANY USA STREET
:   : ANYCITY USA 97290
:   :
:32B: CURRENCY CODE, AMOUNT
:   : USD15400,00
: :
:41D: AVAILABLE WITH ... BY ...
:   : ANY BANK      IN USA
:   : BY NEGOTIATION
:   :
:42C : DRAFTS AT ...
:   : SIGHT
:   :
:42A : DRAWEE
:   : TACBTWTP
:   :
:43P : PARTIAL SHIPMENTS
:   : ALLOWED
:   :
:43T : TRANSHIPMENT
:   : PROHIBITED
:   :
:44A : LOADING ON BOARD/DISPATCH/TAKING IN CHARGE AT/FROM ...
:   : U.S. PORT
:   :
:44B : FOR TRANSPORTATION TO ...
:   : KAOHSIUNG
:   :
:44C : LATEST DATE OF SHIPMENT
:   : 040131
:   :
:45A : DESCRIPTION OF GOODS AND/OR SERVICES
:   : 110 MTS OF WASTE PAPER
:   : KRAFT MULTIWALL BAG WITH POLYETHYLENE POLY
:   : COATED AND/OR ASPHALT INTERLEAF CONTENT 20PCT
:   : MAX., OUTTHROWS INCLUDING WET STRENGTH
:   : PAPER 5PCT MAX.,MOISTURE 13PCT MAX, COATED
:   : BAGS/SHEETS/CUTTINGS 25PCT MAX.
:   : USD140.00/MT
:   : CFR KAOHSIUNG (INCLUDING DESTINATION T.H.C.)
:   :
:46A : DOCUMENTS REQUIRED
:   : +MANUALLY SIGNED COMMERCIAL INVOICE IN SEXTUPLICATE
:   : INDICATING NUMBER OF THIS CREDIT.
:   :
:   : +FULL SET OF CLEAN ON BOARD OCEAN BILLS OF
:   : LADING MADE OUT TO THE ORDER OF SHIPPER BLANK ENDORSED,
:   : NOTIFYING APPLICANT WITH FULL ADDRESS
:   : AND MARKED " FREIGHT PREPAID"
:   :
:   : +PACKING LIST IN SEXTUPLICATE.
```

Bank of America, N.A. Trade Operations
Mail Code: CA9-703-19-09
333 S. Beaudry Avenue, 19th Floor, Los Angeles, CA 90017

00-35-0202NSB 9-1999_CA9 19

FIGURE 11.4   continued

Bank of America

PAGE: 3

THIS IS AN INTEGRAL PART OF ADVICE NUMBER: XXXXXXX

```
    : +BENEFICIARY'S CERTIFICATE STATING THAT
    :  ONE COMPLETE SET OF NON-NEGOTIABLE DOCUMENTS
    :  HAVE BEEN SENT DIRECTLY TO THE APPLICANT BY REGISTERED AIRMAIL
    :  WITHIN 5 DAYS AFTER SHIPMENT.
    :  :
:47A: ADDITIONAL CONDITIONS
    :  +ALL DOCUMENTS AND DRAFT(S) MUST BEAR THIS CREDIT NUMBER.
    :  +DOCUMENTS PRESENTED FOR NEGOTIATION LATER THAN 21 DAYS AFTER
    :   THE DATE OF SHIPMENT BUT WITHIN THE VALIDITY OF THIS CREDIT
    :   ARE ACCEPTABLE.
    :  +SHIPMENT EFFECTED PRIOR TO THE ISSUING DATE OF THIS CREDIT
    :  :
:71B : CHARGES
    :  ALL BANKING CHARGES, INCLUDING
    :  REIMBURSEMENT COMMISSION, OUTSIDE
    :  FX COUNTRY  ARE FOR BENEFICIARY'S A/C.
    :  :
:49  : CONFIRMATION INSTRUCTIONS
    :  WITHOUT
    :  :
:78  : INSTRUCTIONS TO THE PAYING/ACCEPTING/NEGOTIATING BANK
    :  +DOCUMENTS UNDER THIS CREDIT MUST BE SENT BY COURIER SERVICE
    :  +A DISCREPANCY FEE OF USDXX SHOULD BE DEDUCTED FROM NEGO
    :  AMT FOR EACH PRESENTATION IF DOCS DO NOT COMPLY WITH.
    :  +UPON RECEIPT OF DOCUMENTS ALONG WITH DRAFT(S) STRICTLY
    :  COMPLYING WITH TERMS OF THIS CREDIT WE WILL REMIT THE PROCEEDS
    :  TO YOU AS INSTRUCTED.
    :  +ONE FOLD OF NON-NEGOTIABLE B/L IS REQUIRED FOR OUR FILE.
    :  :
```

    UNQUOTE

THIS CREDIT IS NOT CONFIRMED BY US AND THEREFORE CARRIES NO ENGAGEMENT
ON OUR PART.

DRAFTS MUST BE DRAWN ON GOOD CORRESPONDENT BK TAIWAN COOPERATIVE
BANK, FOREIGN CITY, FX COUNTRY

THIS LETTER OF CREDIT IS SUBJECT TO THE UNIFORM CUSTOMS AND PRACTICE FOR
DOCUMENTARY CREDITS (1993 REVISION), INTERNATIONAL CHAMBER OF COMMERCE
PUBLICATION NO. 500.

DRAFT (IF REQUIRED) TOGETHER WITH THE DOCUMENTS SHOULD BE PRESENTED TO
BANK OF AMERICA, TRADE FINANCE, 800 FIFTH AVE. WA1-501-31-01, 31 FLOOR, SEATTLE,

Bank of America, N.A. Trade Operations
Mail Code: CA9-703-19-09
333 S. Beaudry Avenue, 19th Floor, Los Angeles, CA 90017

00-35-0202NSB 9-1999_CA9 19

FIGURE 11.4   continued

Bank of America

WA 98104

PAGE: 4

THIS IS AN INTEGRAL PART OF ADVICE NUMBER: XXXXXXX

DOCUMENTS RECEIVED AFTER 3:00 PM LOCAL TIME WILL BE CONSIDERED AS PRESENTED ON THE NEXT BANKING DAY.

THE ORIGINAL LETTER OF CREDIT (OPERATIVE CREDIT INSTRUMENT) MUST BE SUBMITTED WITH EACH PRESENTATION OF DOCUMENTS. ALSO, PLEASE PROVIDE ONE COPY OF EACH DOCUMENT FOR OUR FILES.

SHOULD PAYMENT BE EFFECTED BY WIRE TRANSFER OR CHECK, A USD 35.00 HANDLING FEE WILL BE DEDUCTED FROM PROCEEDS. THIS FEE DOES NOT APPLY WHEN YOU MAINTAIN AN ACCOUNT WITH US AND PAYMENT IS CREDITED TO THIS ACCOUNT.

PRESENTATION OF DOCUMENTS(S) THAT ARE NOT IN COMPLIANCE WITH THE APPLICABLE ANTIBOYCOTT, ANTI-TERRORISM, ANTI-MONEY LAUNDERING, AND SANCTIONS LAWS AND REGULATIONS IS NOT ACCEPTABLE. APPLICABLE LAWS VARY DEPENDING ON THE TRANSACTION AND MAY INCLUDE UNITED NATIONS, UNITED STATES AND/OR LOCAL LAWS.
SHOULD ANY OF THE TERMS OF THE CREDIT BE UNACCEPTABLE TO YOU, PLEASE CONTACT YOUR CUSTOMER SO THEY CAN INSTRUCT THE ISSUING BANK TO AMEND THE CREDIT.

IF YOU REQUIRE ANY ASSISTANCE OR HAVE ANY QUESTIONS REGARDING THIS TRANSACTION, PLEASE CALL 206-358-7411 .

AUTHORIZED SIGNATURE

Bank of America, N.A. Trade Operations
Mail Code: CA9-703-19-09
333 S. Beaudry Avenue, 19th Floor, Los Angeles, CA 90017

00-35-0202NSB 9-1999_CA9 19

FIGURE 11.4 continued

Bank of America

PAGE: 1

DATE: MARCH 10, 2004

IRREVOCABLE DOCUMENTARY CREDIT NUMBER: XXXXXX

BENEFICIARY
PACIFIC BENEFICIARY
2050 ANY STREET
ANYTOWN, CA 92507

APPLICANT
VALUED CUSTOMER
1278 GLORIOUS ST. NO.1200
SWEET TOWN, CA 92651

ISSUING BANK
BANK OF AMERICA, N.A.

AMOUNT
NOT EXCEEDING USD 49,541.10
NOT EXCEEDING FORTY NINE THOUSAND
FIVE HUNDRED FORTY ONE AND 10/100 US
DOLLARS

EXPIRATION
APRIL 5, 2004 AT OUR COUNTER

WE HEREBY ISSUE THIS IRREVOCABLE DOCUMENTARY CREDIT AVAILABLE WITH BANK
OF AMERICA N.A. BY PAYMENT AGAINST PRESENTATION OF THE ORIGINAL OF THIS
LETTER OF CREDIT AND YOUR DRAFTS AT SIGHT DRAWN ON BANK OF AMERICA, N.A.,
LOS ANGELES, CA FOR 100 PERCENT OF INVOICE VALUE, BEARING THE CLAUSE "DRAWN
UNDER BANK OF AMERICA N.A., LETTER OF CREDIT NUMBER XXXXXXX", AND
ACCOMPANIED BY THE DOCUMENTS DETAILED BELOW:

MERCHANDISE DESCRIPTION:

50,000 COMPUTERS PER PO NO. ABC, CFR LOS ANGELES PORT

DOCUMENTS REQUIRED:

+ ORIGINAL AND 2 COPIES OF COMMERCIAL INVOICE.

+ ORIGINAL AND 2 COPIES OF CERTIFICATE OF ORIGIN.

+ ORIGINAL CERTIFICATE OF INSPECTION DATED PRIOR TO SHIPMENT
  DATE, PURPORTEDLY SIGNED BY A REPRESENTATIVE OF TRUSTED
  THIRD PARTY INC, STATING THAT MERCHANDISE HAS BEEN INSPECTED
  AND IS ACCEPTABLE.

+ BENEFICIARY'S SIGNED STATEMENT CERTIFYING THAT ONE SET OF
  COPIES OF ALL DOCUMENTS HAS BEEN FAXED TO VALUED CUSTOMER
  AT FAX NO. 800-XXX-XXXX.

+ ORIGINAL AND 2 COPIES OF PACKING LIST.

+ FULL SET OF ORIGINAL OCEAN BILL OF LADING CONSIGNED TO THE ORDER OF
  SHIPPER, BLANK ENDORSED MARKED FREIGHT PREPAID NOTIFY VALUED CUSTOMER
  FORWARDERS AT ANY TOWN ANYWHERE, USA.

Bank of America, N.A. Trade Operations
Mail Code: CA9-703-19-09
333 S. Beaudry Avenue, 19th Floor, Los Angeles, CA 90017

00-35-0202NSB 9-1999_CA9 19

FIGURE 11.5 Opening bank's letter of credit notification.
Source: Bank of America, 2004

Bank of America

THIS IS AN INTEGRAL PART OF LETTER OF CREDIT NUMBER: XXXXXX

PARTIAL SHIPMENTS NOT ALLOWED

TRANSHIPMENTS ALLOWED

ADDITIONAL CONDITIONS:

INSURANCE TO BE EFFECTED BY THE APPLICANT.

THIS LETTER OF CREDIT IS TRANSFERABLE, TRANSFER OF THIS CREDIT IS
SUBJECT TO THE PAYMENT OF OUR USUAL TRANSFER COMMISSION ACCOMPANIED
BY BENEFICIARY'S INSTRUCTIONS SATISFACTORY TO US ON THE ATTACHED
FORM.

AS A MATTER OF U. S. LAW, PLEASE BE AWARE THAT U. S. BANKS CANNOT PAY
LETTERS OF CREDIT IN FAVOR OF OR TRANSFERRED TO PARTIES LOCATED IN,
ANY COUNTRY SUBJECT TO THE FOREIGN ASSET CONTROL REGULATIONS OF THE U. S.
DEPARTMENT OF THE TREASURY. NEITHER MAY ANY PARTY BE IN THE
UNITED STATES AND SUBJECT TO A DENIAL OF EXPORT PRIVILEGES PURSUANT
TO SANCTIONS ISSUED BY THE U. S. DEPARTMENT OF COMMERCE. WE ARE
OBLIGATED TO CHECK THE NAME OF THE SECOND BENEFICIARY AT THE TIME WE
RECEIVE BENEFICIARY'S REQUEST TO TRANSFER THIS CREDIT.

ALL BANK CHARGES, OTHER THAN THOSE OF THE ISSUING BANK, ARE FOR THE
ACCOUNT OF THE BENEFICIARY.

DOCUMENTS TO BE PRESENTED AT PLACE OF EXPIRY WITHIN 15 DAYS AFTER
SHIPMENT BUT WITHIN VALIDITY OF CREDIT.

DOCUMENTS MUST BE FORWARDED TO BANK OF AMERICA, N.A. 333 SOUTH
BEAUDRY AVENUE 19TH FLOOR, CA9-703-19-13 LOS ANGELES, CA 90017 ATTN
TRADE BANK SECTION IN ONE LOT BY COURIER.

THIS LETTER OF CREDIT IS SUBJECT TO THE UNIFORM CUSTOMS AND PRACTICE
FOR DOCUMENTARY CREDITS (1993 REVISION), INTERNATIONAL CHAMBER OF
COMMERCE PUBLICATION NO. 500.

AN ADDITIONAL HANDLING FEE OF USD XX.00 WILL BE DEDUCTED FROM
PROCEEDS FOR EACH SET OF DOCUMENTS PRESENTED WITH DISCREPANCIES. IF
DISCREPANT DOCUMENTS ARE PRESENTED TO US, AND IF THE APPLICANT WAIVES
THE DISCREPANCIES AND WE ACCEPT THAT WAIVER, THEN, NOTWITHSTANDING
OUR NOTICE OF REFUSAL TO THE PRESENTER AND NOTWITHSTANDING THE
PROVISIONS UCP500 SUB-ARTICLE 14(D), WE RESERVE THE RIGHT TO RELEASE
THE DOCUMENTS TO THE APPLICANT AND MAKE PAYMENT TO THE PRESENTER,
WITHOUT FURTHER NOTICE TO THE PRESENTER, UNLESS, PRIOR TO OUR FINAL
ACCEPTANCE OF THE WAIVER, WE RECEIVE CONTRARY INSTRUCTIONS BY
AUTHENTICATED TELETRANSMISSION OR A SIGNED LETTER FROM THE PRESENTER.
ANY SUCH RELEASE OF DOCUMENTS TO THE APPLICANT PRIOR TO OUR RECEIPT OF
CONTRARY INSTRUCTIONS FROM THE PRESENTER SHALL NOT CONSTITUTE A FAILURE
ON OUR PART TO HOLD THE DOCUMENTS AT THE PRESENTER'S DISPOSAL, AND WE
WILL HAVE NO LIABILITY TO THE PRESENTER OR ANY OTHER PARTY IN RESPECT OF
SUCH RELEASE.

SHOULD PAYMENT BE EFFECTED BY WIRE TRANSFER OR CHECK, A USD 45.00
HANDLING FEE WILL BE DEDUCTED FROM PROCEEDS. THIS FEE DOES NOT APPLY
WHEN YOU MAINTAIN AN ACCOUNT WITH US AND PAYMENT IS CREDITED TO THIS
ACCOUNT.

IF YOU REQUIRE ANY ASSISTANCE OR HAVE ANY QUESTIONS REGARDING THIS
TRANSACTION, PLEASE CALL 213-345-6614.

Bank of America, N.A. Trade Operations
Mail Code: CA9-703-19-09
333 S. Beaudry Avenue, 19th Floor, Los Angeles, CA 90017

00-35-0202NSB 9-1999_CA9 19

FIGURE 11.5   continued

is presented in Figure 11.4. In this case the Bank of America is the advising, confirming, and accepting bank. This letter of credit is a usance credit (or acceptance credit) as time drafts are to be drawn and payment is to be made at some future time. When the importer's bank directly notifies the exporter that a letter of credit has been opened, a form such as that shown in Figure 11.5 is used.

11.3.2 Types of letters of credit

Letters of credit can take many different forms. Some of the major distinguishing characteristics are described in this section.

Revocable and irrevocable

The distinction between revocable and irrevocable letters of credit rests upon the ability of the establishing bank to revoke the letter of credit before expiry date. The great majority of letters of credit are irrevocable in that they cannot be unilaterally cancelled or amended by the importer or the opening bank. In contrast, a revocable letter of credit may be changed or cancelled at any time without notice to the beneficiary. However, if the account party (i.e., the issuing bank's client) wishes to revoke the credit, he must give the bank timely notification. If a payment has been made to the beneficiary before a notice of revocation is received the funds will not be recalled. It is obvious that the privilege of revoking a letter of credit can put a temptation in the way of an unscrupulous buyer when prices decline.

It is not necessarily the case that revocable letters of credit are of no value. It is true that they may be terminated at any time by the establisher or the establishing bank, provided that payment has not been made. On the other hand, the establishment of the revocable letter of credit has cost the establisher a fee, sometimes a considerable one. He or she has therefore given the seller his assurance in the form of a revocable letter of credit that he or she intends to make payment. Furthermore, in countries where exchange controls exist, the revocable letter of credit may be one way of indicating to the exporter that he or she can obtain the necessary foreign exchange for payment.

Under the 1993 Revision of the International Chamber of Commerce Publication 500 (International Chamber of Commerce, 1993), all letters of credit are irrevocable unless they specify that they are revocable.

To the exporter who is concerned about payment for the merchandise sold, the confirmed irrevocable letter of credit gives the best assurance that can be obtained, other than actual cash, that payment will be made.

Confirmed and unconfirmed

If the bank in the exporter's country announces its confirmation, words to the following effect are to be found in the letter of credit: 'We confirm this credit and thereby undertake that all drafts drawn and presented as above specified will be duly honored by us.' If the credit does not require that drafts be drawn, the wording will be adjusted but still must state that the bank has added its confirmation to the credit.

It must not be assumed that unconfirmed letters of credit should necessarily be viewed with suspicion. The letter of credit that lacks confirmation by a local bank may simply lack it because the establisher was unwilling to pay the additional fee for confirmation. Irrevocable but unconfirmed letters of credit are as good as the credit status of the establishing bank and the willingness of the buyer's country to allow the required use of foreign exchange. Yet there are many banks and so-called banks whose irrevocable letters of credit are no better than the importer's order. A revocable letter of credit will not be confirmed by any bank because revocation would place full responsibility for making payment upon the confirming bank. On the other hand, the confirmation of an irrevocable letter of credit by a bank gives the shipper the most satisfactory assurance that the ultimate payment will be made for the shipment. It should be noted in this connection that confirmation of a letter of credit is not simply a guarantee by the confirming bank but becomes its primary obligation. This adds great strength to the confirmed letter of credit. It means that the exporter does not have to seek payment under any conditions from the establishing bank – invariably located in some foreign country – but has a direct claim on the confirming bank in his home country. Thus the exporter need not be concerned about the ability or willingness of the foreign bank to pay.

Clean and documentary

A clean letter of credit is one in which payment is made to the beneficiary against a clean draft or receipt for funds. Most commercial letters of credit, however, are documentary and in these cases payment is made by the notifying bank against documentary drafts accompanied by delivery of the full set of documents called for by the terms of the letter of credit.

Transferable and nontransferable

A transferable letter of credit is one that allows transfer of all or part of the letter of credit to some other party. A nontransferable letter of credit is one that may not be transferred by the beneficiary. A letter of credit is nontransferable unless the credit expressly stipulates that it is transferable. Thus if the exporter (beneficiary) desires a transferable letter of credit, he or she must arrange with the buyer to have this done.

There are three main reasons why an exporter may request a transferable letter of credit: (1) the beneficiary/exporter may actually be a 'middleman' who is purchasing the goods from someone else; (2) the beneficiary/exporter may be providing only a part of the goods; or (3) the beneficiary may be the buyer's/importer's agent, and may not yet know who the actual supplier will be. The transferable letter of credit is particularly advantageous to the small exporter who finds it difficult to finance purchases of merchandise from suppliers. A request for a transferable letter of credit may be seen by the buyer in a foreign country as indicating that he or she is dealing with an exporter who is financially weak, or is a broker or intermediary. This may not be acceptable to the buyer.

Under a transfer, the second beneficiary has all the rights to his portion of the letter of credit.

Assignment of proceeds

Subject to the policy of the advising bank, a beneficiary may assign the proceeds due to him or her to another party. This is a legal procedure similar to the assignment of rights under any contract. The original beneficiary remains responsible to perform under the letter of credit. If the original beneficiary cannot or will not perform, no proceeds will be available to the assignee even though he or she may have delivered merchandise or performed service.

Revolving letters of credit

The revolving letter of credit was devised to meet the needs of firms whose business transactions are more or less regular and continuous. It provides a certain assurance of regularity in a series of business transactions. For example, a firm in Mexico that expects to buy a substantial amount of fertilizer in the United States over a period of four, six, or more months, may find it convenient to establish a revolving letter of credit, permitting the US supplier to ship certain quantities every one or two months or at other regular intervals. The two most common types of revolving letters of credit are as follows:

1. A credit indicating the maximum amount of drawing that may be outstanding at any one time. When this maximum is reached the paying bank may negotiate fresh bills only to the extent that those previously negotiated are paid.

2. A credit providing for a specified maximum payment in any one month (or in some other period). It is a normal precaution in establishing such credits to indicate that if a credit is not drawn against during any period, the amount not drawn against cannot be drawn subsequently. This is known as a *noncumulative* revolving credit. In contrast, a *cumulative* credit allows unused shipment/credit amounts to be added to the amount allowed in a subsequent time period.

Deferred payment credit

A deferred payment credit is a form of letter of credit under which the exporter is to be paid at specified dates after shipment. This type of credit is used when a single shipment is to be paid for by a number of payments. In countries where there are expensive stamp taxes on drafts it avoids these expenses since drafts are not required. In the United States it is generally used only where payment is to be made in 180 days or less. Bankers' acceptances of more than 180 days cannot be discounted through the banking system. (In countries other than the United States the 180-day limit may not apply.)

There is a substantial difference between a usance credit available by negotiation and one by acceptance or deferred credit. A usance credit by negotiation is usually negotiated by the exporter with his bank after presentation of the documents. That is, the exporter receives credit from his own bank, immediately receiving his money less a deduction for the interest for the usance period. A usance credit by acceptance occurs when the bank upon which it is drawn adds its acceptance, creating a banker's acceptance which is easily discountable by that bank or any other bank. A usance credit by deferred payment is usually accomplished by the bank itself agreeing to make the stipulated payment when due. In this case, no draft is required and the engagement is not discountable. Recent court cases have indicated that the only obligation of the bank is to honor/pay at maturity, and not before.

Standby letter of credit

A standby credit is distinguished from a commercial letter of credit by function performed rather than form (see Figure 11.6). A commercial letter of credit is used to finance the movement of goods whereas a standby credit lends the credit of the issuing bank in *other* types of transactions usually guaranteeing the account party's performance. Once issued, this type of letter of credit is irrevocable. More specifically, a standby letter of credit is an obligation to the beneficiary by the issuing bank of the following:

- to repay money borrowed by or advanced to the account party; or
- to make payment on the account of any evidence of indebtedness undertaken by the account party; or
- to make payment on account of any default by the account party in the performance of a contractual obligation (performance or bid bond).

Bankof America

PAGE: 1

DATE: FEBRUARY 10, 2000

IRREVOCABLE STANDBY LETTER OF CREDIT NUMBER: XXXXXXX

BENEFICIARY	APPLICANT
ANY TOWN FOREST SERVICE	VALUED CUSTOMER, INC.
14931 BROAD RIVER ROAD	P.O. BOX 791230
ANY TOWN USA	35740 NEW ROAD, SUITE B25
	ANY TOWN USA

AMOUNT
USD 46,000.00
FORTY SIX THOUSAND AND 00/100'S
US DOLLARS

EXPIRATION
APRIL 20, 2004 AT OUR COUNTERS

WE HEREBY ESTABLISH IN YOUR FAVOR OUR IRREVOCABLE STANDBY LETTER OF
CREDIT NUMBER XXXXXXX WHICH IS AVAILABLE WITH BANK OF AMERICA, N.A.
BY PAYMENT AGAINST PRESENTATION OF THE ORIGINAL OF THIS LETTER OF
CREDIT AND YOUR DRAFTS AT SIGHT DRAWN ON BANK OF AMERICA, N.A.,
ACCOMPANIED BY THE DOCUMENTS DETAILED BELOW:

A WRITTEN STATEMENT FROM THE BENEFICIARY THAT FOOTHILLS FOREST
PRODUCTS, INC. HAS FAILED TO COMPLY WITH THE TERMS OF CONTRACT
NO ABCDEFG AND INDICATING THEY ARE DRAWING UNDER THIS LETTER OF
CREDIT BY REFERENCING THIS LETTER OF CREDIT NUMBER XXXXXXX.

THIS LETTER OF CREDIT IS SUBJECT TO THE INTERNATIONAL STANDBY
PRACTICES 1998, ICC PUBLICATION NO. 590.

IF YOU REQUIRE ANY ASSISTANCE OR HAVE ANY QUESTIONS REGARDING THIS
TRANSACTION, PLEASE CALL 213-345-6632.

| -------------------------- | -------------------------- |
| AUTHORIZED SIGNATURE | AUTHORIZED SIGNATURE |

THIS DOCUMENT CONSISTS OF 1 PAGE(S).

Bank of America, N.A. Trade Operations
Mail Code: CA9-703-19-09
333 S. Beaudry Avenue, 19th Floor, Los Angeles, CA 90017

00-35-0202NSB 9-1999_CA9 19

FIGURE 11.6 Irrevocable standby letter of credit
Source: Bank of America, 2000

In a sense, the standby credit is similar, but not legally identical, to the bank guarantees. These are flexible credits and are useful in a variety of situations including performance and/or bid bonding. Importers may find these useful in supporting purchases from exporters by open account. Exporters, on the other hand, may be required by importers to issue such credits that guarantee performance under a contract (Seafirst Bank, 1988, p. 21). This type of letter of credit cannot be changed or modified without the consent of all parties involved: the applicant, the issuing bank, and the beneficiary.

11.3.3 Drafts

A draft is an unconditional order in writing prepared by one party (drawer) and addressed to another (drawee) directing the drawee to pay a specified sum of money to the order of a third person (the payee), or to the bearer, on demand or at a fixed and determinable future time.

In export transactions drafts are generally drawn on either of two bases. The seller (drawer) may initiate the draft as provided for in the contract of sale. In such cases the drawee is the purchaser or other person or agent mutually agreed upon. When this method of trade financing is used it is known as collection draft financing, and final payment rests upon the ability to pay and reliability of the drawee rather than a bank. In order for payment to occur the exporter submits the draft and all other documents to its bank for collection as illustrated in Figures 11.7 and 11.8.

When letter of credit financing is used a draft may or may not be required. If required, the draft is drawn by the beneficiary under the terms of authorization in the letter of credit and in strict conformance with the conditions stated.

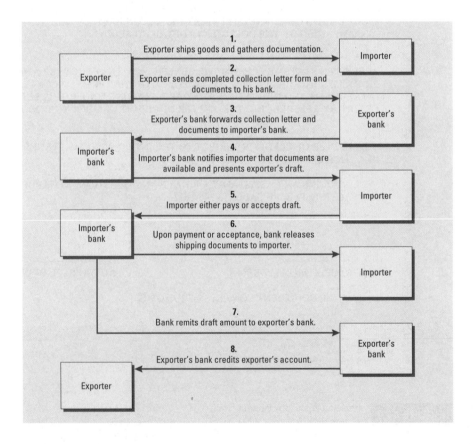

FIGURE 11.7

The process of foreign collections

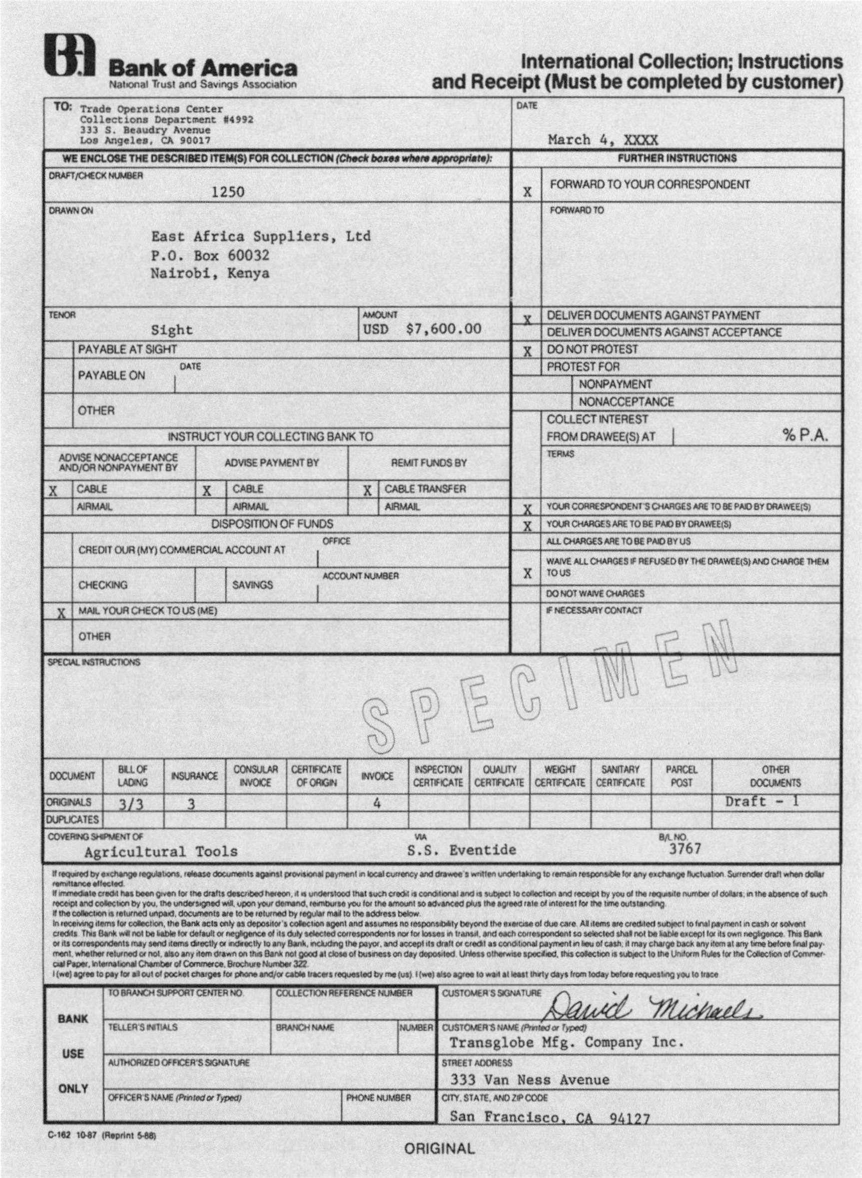

Bank of America
National Trust and Savings Association

International Collection; Instructions and Receipt (Must be completed by customer)

TO: Trade Operations Center
Collections Department #4992
333 S. Beaudry Avenue
Los Angeles, CA 90017

DATE: March 4, XXXX

WE ENCLOSE THE DESCRIBED ITEM(S) FOR COLLECTION *(Check boxes where appropriate)*:

DRAFT/CHECK NUMBER: 1250

DRAWN ON: East Africa Suppliers, Ltd
P.O. Box 60032
Nairobi, Kenya

TENOR: Sight
AMOUNT: USD $7,600.00

PAYABLE AT SIGHT
PAYABLE ON — DATE
OTHER

INSTRUCT YOUR COLLECTING BANK TO

ADVISE NONACCEPTANCE AND/OR NONPAYMENT BY		ADVISE PAYMENT BY		REMIT FUNDS BY	
X	CABLE	X	CABLE	X	CABLE TRANSFER
	AIRMAIL		AIRMAIL		AIRMAIL

DISPOSITION OF FUNDS
CREDIT OUR (MY) COMMERCIAL ACCOUNT AT — OFFICE
CHECKING — SAVINGS — ACCOUNT NUMBER
X MAIL YOUR CHECK TO US (ME)
OTHER

FURTHER INSTRUCTIONS
X FORWARD TO YOUR CORRESPONDENT
FORWARD TO
X DELIVER DOCUMENTS AGAINST PAYMENT
DELIVER DOCUMENTS AGAINST ACCEPTANCE
X DO NOT PROTEST
PROTEST FOR
NONPAYMENT
NONACCEPTANCE
COLLECT INTEREST FROM DRAWEE(S) AT — % P.A.
TERMS
X YOUR CORRESPONDENT'S CHARGES ARE TO BE PAID BY DRAWEE(S)
X YOUR CHARGES ARE TO BE PAID BY DRAWEE(S)
ALL CHARGES ARE TO BE PAID BY US
X WAIVE ALL CHARGES IF REFUSED BY THE DRAWEE(S) AND CHARGE THEM TO US
DO NOT WAIVE CHARGES
IF NECESSARY CONTACT

SPECIAL INSTRUCTIONS

SPECIMEN

DOCUMENT	BILL OF LADING	INSURANCE	CONSULAR INVOICE	CERTIFICATE OF ORIGIN	INVOICE	INSPECTION CERTIFICATE	QUALITY CERTIFICATE	WEIGHT CERTIFICATE	SANITARY CERTIFICATE	PARCEL POST	OTHER DOCUMENTS
ORIGINALS	3/3	3			4						Draft - 1
DUPLICATES											

COVERING SHIPMENT OF: Agricultural Tools
VIA: S.S. Eventide
B/L NO.: 3767

If required by exchange regulations, release documents against provisional payment in local currency and drawee's written undertaking to remain responsible for any exchange fluctuation. Surrender draft when dollar remittance effected.
If immediate credit has been given for the drafts described hereon, it is understood that such credit is conditional and is subject to collection and receipt by you of the requisite number of dollars; in the absence of such receipt and collection by you, the undersigned will, upon your demand, reimburse you for the amount so advanced plus the agreed rate of interest for the time outstanding.
If the collection is returned unpaid, documents are to be returned by regular mail to the address below.
In receiving items for collection, the Bank acts only as depositor's collection agent and assumes no responsibility beyond the exercise of due care. All items are credited subject to final payment in cash or solvent credits. This Bank will not be liable for default or negligence of its duly selected correspondents nor for losses in transit, and each correspondent so selected shall not be liable except for its own negligence. This Bank or its correspondents may send items directly or indirectly to any Bank, including the payor, and accept its draft or credit as conditional payment in lieu of cash; it may charge back any item at any time before final payment, whether returned or not, also any item drawn on this Bank not good at close of business on day deposited. Unless otherwise specified, this collection is subject to the Uniform Rules for the Collection of Commercial Paper, International Chamber of Commerce, Brochure Number 322.
I (we) agree to pay for all out of pocket charges for phone and/or cable tracers requested by me (us). I (we) also agree to wait at least thirty days from today before requesting you to trace

BANK USE ONLY: TO BRANCH SUPPORT CENTER NO. — COLLECTION REFERENCE NUMBER — TELLER'S INITIALS — BRANCH NAME — NUMBER — AUTHORIZED OFFICER'S SIGNATURE — OFFICER'S NAME *(Printed or Typed)* — PHONE NUMBER

CUSTOMER'S SIGNATURE: David Michaels
CUSTOMER'S NAME *(Printed or Typed)*: Transglobe Mfg. Company Inc.
STREET ADDRESS: 333 Van Ness Avenue
CITY, STATE, AND ZIP CODE: San Francisco, CA 94127

C-162 10-87 (Reprint 5-88)
ORIGINAL

FIGURE 11.8

International collection instructions and receipt
Source: Bank of America, 1994, p. 34

Fundamentally, the letter of credit is formal authorization for the beneficiary/exporter to draw a draft or drafts, in the amounts specified, and guaranteeing that they will be honored (paid) when presented for payment under the conditions specified. The draft must include the name of the issuing bank and have the credit number shown on its face. The draft is drawn as a:

- sight draft on the issuing bank (negotiation credit);
- usance draft on the issuing bank (usance negotiation credit);
- sight draft on the advising bank (payment credit); or
- usance draft on the advising bank (acceptance credit).

The usual forms of the draft used in letter-of-credit financing are shown in Figure 11.9 while those used in popular draft financing are shown in Figure 11.10. It will be noted that in letter-of-credit financing the draft is drawn on a bank

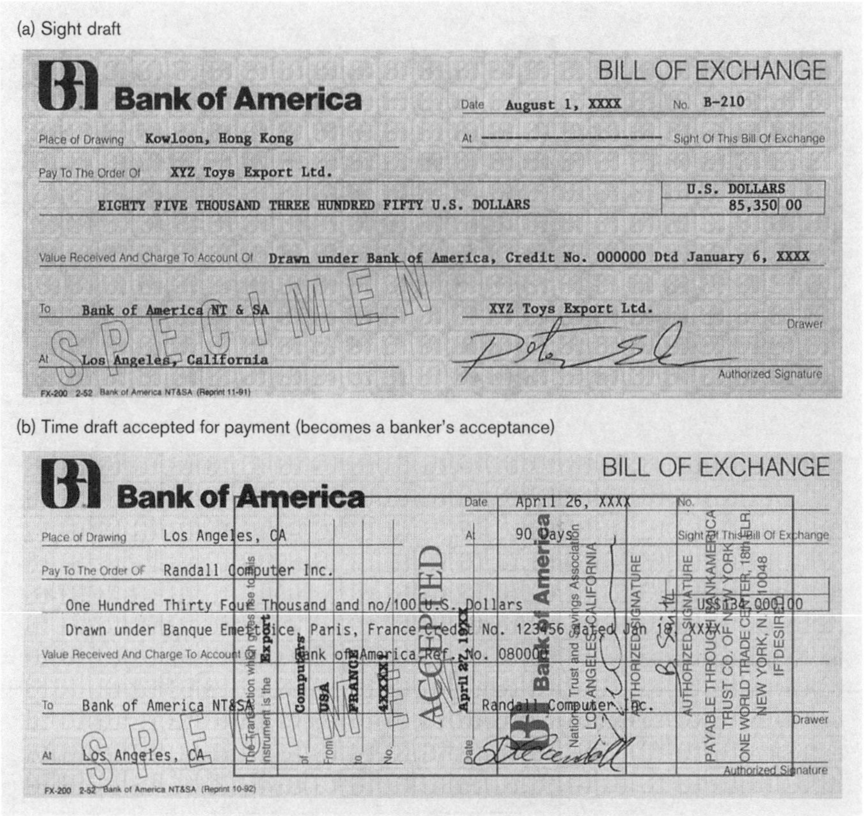

FIGURE 11.9

Drafts drawn under letter
of credit
Source: Bank of America,
1994, p. 24

whereas in draft financing it is drawn on the buyer. In some countries the draft is
said to be 'drawn to the account' of the bank or buyer.

Acceptance

The term 'accepted' is frequently used in connection with a draft, or *bill of
exchange*, as it is also known. An accepted time draft is called an acceptance.

The use of time drafts and acceptances provides a means by which the exporter
can grant credit to the importer without losing the protection of a letter of credit.
This is done by having the importer obtain a letter of credit specifying that drafts
will be paid at a specified future time (as discussed in section 11.3.4). In order to
obtain the shipping documents from the bank, the accompanying draft is
'accepted' by the addressee. This is usually done by the addressee writing or stamp-
ing across the face of the draft the date and the words 'accepted; payable at
_____' and thereafter affixing his or her signature.

Letters of credit specifying time or date drafts often state that the drafts are to
be drawn on the issuing or the advising bank, not the importer. If this is the case
there is no need for the importer to sign the draft; the bank is performing this function. Normally, when applying for a documentary credit (letter of credit), the
importer is required to sign a commitment that it will reimburse the issuing bank
for honoring the documents. When a draft is paid, the issuing bank may require
the importer to accept a draft drawn by the issuing bank on the importer. If this is
done it is outside of the terms of the letter of credit itself, and the practice varies
from country to country.

A draft that has been accepted by a company is called an *acceptance*, and if
countersigned by a bank, is called a *banker's acceptance* (see Figure 11.10). If an

acceptance has been issued or endorsed to the order of a person or company, it is a negotiable instrument. It is more easily negotiated or discounted if countersigned by the bank.

A draft is payable to bearer when it is made out to him or her when the endorser or the last endorsement is in blank. This endorsement in blank is one in which only the name of the addressee is shown with the name of the signer and his or her title.

Delivering documents

The most important element on the face of a draft besides the amount to be collected is the statement of whether the documents are to be delivered against the acceptance of the draft (D/A) or against payment of the draft (D/P). This is usually indicated in the bank's instructions for collection, as shown previously in Figure 11.8.

When a draft is drawn D/A, the drawee may obtain the documents evidencing title to the merchandise from the collecting bank by accepting the draft. The accepted draft, now bearing the word 'accepted' and signed by the buyer, is called

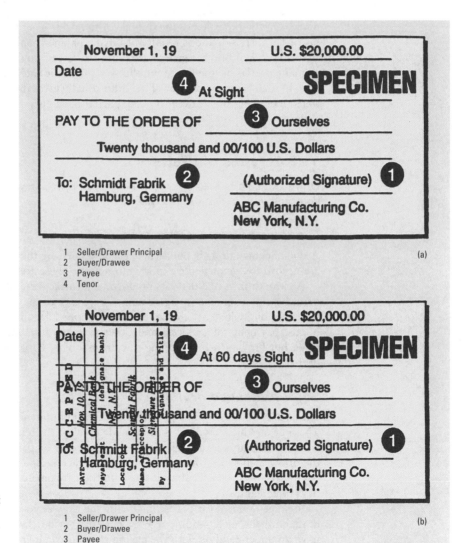

FIGURE 11.10

Sight and time drafts. (a) Sight draft. (b) Time draft accepted for payment (becomes a trade acceptance)
Source: Chemical Bank, 1987, p. 48

a *trade acceptance*. If the bank adds its assurance of payment by writing 'accepted' and signing the face of the draft, the draft becomes a *banker's acceptance*.

When the buyer has accepted this draft, the shipping documents are delivered to the buyer and possession of the merchandise can be obtained. In this case the shipper or the drawer of the draft extends credit to the drawee, usually the consignee, for the length of time indicated by the number of days specified in the draft.

When a draft is drawn D/P, the drawee may secure the documents of title only when the amount shown on the face of the draft is paid. In this case, the exporter does not extend credit to the consignee or the payee. If the draft has a tenor of several days, the collecting bank keeps control of the merchandise, usually warehousing it at the expense of the consignee, and accepts payment plus accumulated charges when the consignee pays the face value of the draft.

The requirement, however, is not quite as hard on the payee as it may appear. It is the practice, wherever drafts drawn D/P are used, for local financial institutions to advance the required amount to the drawee. The transaction then becomes a matter of credit extension between the local bank and the drawee. In this case, the drawer of the draft is fully protected because the collecting bank that is his or her agent retains possession of the merchandise until payment in full has been made. On the other hand, the drawee of the draft has the merchandise placed at his or her disposal; and is required to make payment only at the end of the tenor of the draft. It is also the general custom with respect to such drafts for the drawee to make partial payment and withdraw a proportionate amount of the merchandise. In such cases the drawer of the draft usually gives the collecting bank instructions permitting the drawee to make partial payments and to take proportionate deliveries.

11.3.4 Types of drafts

Drafts can be classified by type as *clean* or *documentary*, *sight* or *usance*, *time* or *date*, and *with* or *without recourse*.

Clean or documentary drafts

A documentary draft is one that is accompanied by the relevant documents that are needed to complete the export transaction. These are discussed in Chapter 13.

A clean draft is one that has no documents attached and is usually handed to a bank for collection in a foreign country. Such a draft may be drawn for many purposes, among which are the collection of an open account, the sale of stocks and bonds, payment for services, and other transactions that arise in international trade but for which no shipping documents exist. Bank drafts are usually clean drafts.

Sight or usance drafts

Drafts may be drawn to be payable either at sight or at some specified future time. The time at which payment is to be made is called the tenor or usance of the draft. As its name implies, the sight draft is supposed to be paid when it is first seen by the drawee. In some countries, however, a grace period of a specified number of days is allowed. Time drafts are those that specify payment at a certain number of days after sight.

In some countries it is customary for the drawee to delay payment of a sight draft until the merchandise arrives. For this reason the exporter should always have an understanding with the customer as to whether the customer will accept or pay a sight draft immediately or whether acceptance or payment may be delayed until the arrival of the merchandise.

Time or date drafts (usance drafts)

The only difference between a time draft and a date draft is that the time draft provides for payment a specified number of days after sight, whereas the date draft specifies that it is to be paid a certain number of days after the date on which the draft is drawn. The date draft is used when the drawer wishes to extend some credit to the drawee. The great advantage to the drawer of a date draft is that the date on which the draft should be paid is known.

With or without recourse

When financing is *without recourse* this means that the purchase by a bank or other financial institution of drafts is made with the understanding that the bank has no recourse to the drawer of the drafts if such drafts are dishonored. In other words, the bank that purchases drafts or bills of exchange assumes full responsibility for payment, discharges the exporter of his obligation as guarantor, and looks to the consignee to accept the draft and to pay it at the due date.

The term *with recourse* means the exact opposite – i.e., the bank does not, in the usual sense of the term, buy or purchase the draft or bill of exchange. The transaction is simply that the bank lends a certain amount of money to the exporter against a clean or documentary draft. If the consignee fails for any reason to meet the draft at the due date, the bank immediately has recourse to the original drawer of the draft. When the draft or bill of exchange is discounted or sold with recourse, the drawer assumes full responsibility for the payment of the draft.

11.4 Export credit insurance

Export credit insurance is available to most exporters through governmental export credit agencies or through private insurers. Such insurance can usually be obtained to cover political risk and nonconvertability of currency. It may even be available to cover commercial risks associated with nonpayment by buyers. Export credit insurance is based on three basic principles (Ghose, 1993):

1. *Co-sharing of risks*: The insurers provide about 80–95% cover against commercial and political risks, leaving the rest to be borne by the exporters.
2. *Spread of risk*: Like any other insurance, export credit insurance is based on the law of averages so that risk is widely diversified. Hence, exporters are usually required to insure their entire export portfolios rather than only the riskier ones. This type of cover is known as 'whole turnover' or 'comprehensive' policies. However, the insurers may exclude particular buyers or countries, at their discretion. Spread of risk is also necessary to provide cover at a reasonable cost.
3. *Reduction of risk*: By keeping an ongoing and current credit rating portfolio of overseas buyers, credit risk can be substantially reduced. However, it is beyond the capacity of individual exporters or even financial institutions to achieve this objective effectively. On the other hand, export credit insurance agencies are in a far better position to gather and exchange updated credit information through the central 'clearing house' of the International Union of Credit and Investment Insurers (the Berne Union).

Exporters may be able to use credit insurance to enable them to grant more liberal credit terms or to encourage their banks to grant them financing against their export receivables. In fact, the principal advantage of this type of insurance is that it encourages exporters to diversify and extend competitive credit terms at minimal commercial and political risks.

The costs of such insurance are often quite low in many markets, ranging from one-half of 1% to less than 2% of the value of the transaction. Specialized insurance brokers handle such insurance.

There are some disadvantages associated with credit insurance. Exporters still have to assume part of the credit and political risks. Claims may take a long time to be settled. There are restrictions that are attached to coverage. For example, for medium- and long-term commitments ceilings are often put on total exposure in a particular importing country. Coverage can be suspended in specific situations such as the Gulf War and the Bosnian crisis.

11.5 Countertrade

Countertrade techniques are used as a means of financing exports in both the industrialized and developing countries of the world. Countertrade is a generic term used to describe a variety of trade agreements in which a seller provides a buyer with products (commodities, goods, services, technology) and agrees to a reciprocal purchasing obligation with the buyer in terms of an agreed-upon percentage (full or partial) of the original sales value. In short, what is involved are parallel business transactions that link a sales contract to a purchase contract in addition to, or in place of, financial settlements. This means that each party is both a buyer and a seller at the same time. Such techniques are appealing to buyers in countries that lack sufficient foreign hard currencies to pay directly for exports. But, as shown in Table 11.2, there are many other objectives that buyers may seek to achieve (other than conserve hard currencies) and there are objectives that sellers have in engaging in countertrade. Often such agreements are made by governments rather than private companies. For example, at the end of the year 2000, in an attempt to export rice through state-owned trading houses, the Indian government asked its embassies to find out if government-to-government exports were possible. It was ready to exchange rice for other commodities, preferably oil. Indonesia and the Philippines, two large Asian importers of rice, were obvious potential markets (Bose, 2000). In some situations governments may 'mandate' that countertrade be part of a transaction or it may be 'voluntary' on the part of the contracting parties.

Some so-called voluntary countertrade, for example, is the result of a government creating conditions (such as restrictions on foreign exchange or on repatriation of funds) that stimulate firms to use countertrade. In contrast, other firms may voluntarily use countertrade for commercial reasons such as tax avoidance, developing relationships, disposing of excess inventory, and so forth.

While it is difficult to measure accurately the actual magnitude of countertrade in overall world trade, due to the lack of or inconsistencies in reporting systems, estimates range from 5% to 40% upwards. The increasing importance of world trade, the magnification of global competition, and the expanding Russian and east European markets suggest that the use of countertrade will increase. Indeed, in the early 1990s there was a shortage of cash (and currency) in many countries of the world. This led to increased usage of countertrade techniques (Miller, 1992).

Source: adapted from Paun and Albaum, 1993

Seller's objective	Buyer's objective
Increase profits	Generate goodwill
Capitalize on strong bargaining power	Acquire badly needed products and technology
Help countertrade partner conceal a price cut	Help conceal price cut
Signal a high quality product	Secure access to critical sources of supply
Increase sales volume and market share	Free blocked funds
Establish long-term relationships with new trading partners	Make purchases without deteriorating the balance of trade
Secure government contracts	Conserve hard currencies
Gain entry into new or difficult markets	Reduce heavy debt burdens
Fuller use of production capacity	Bypass trade restrictions
Generate customer goodwill	Establish long-term relationships with new trading partners
Dispose of surplus, obsolete, or perishable products	Circumvent an overvalued currency
Gain access to marketing networks and expertise	Secure low cost sources of production or raw materials
	Collection of existing debts

TABLE 11.2

Seller's and buyer's objective in international countertrade

The major types of countertrade are described briefly below. More detailed discussion is in the works of Francis (1987), Korth (1987), Hammond (1990), and Fletcher (1996).

11.5.1 Pure barter

This involves a simple direct exchange in that the exporter agrees to accept products from the importer as payment for the original export transaction. For example, in 2002 DaimlerChrysler joined General Motors and Toyota in accepting grain in payment for automobiles in Argentina. Problems in the banking system there made payment in cash very difficult for consumers, but grain collected could be sold by the automobile companies to farm-commodity exporter Louis Dreyfus Group at current market prices (*The Wall Street Journal*, 2002). In another case, PepsiCo had an agreement with the former Soviet Union to supply Pepsi-Cola syrup from its British subsidiary for bottling and sale in the USSR. For the syrup, for training and supervising Soviet workers, and for use of its trademarks, PepsiCo agreed to take Stolichnaya vodka as payment. In another transaction, General Motors agreed to supply the USSR with US$100 million worth of earth-moving equipment in exchange for timber.

Sometimes the barter process can become complicated. In the early 1990s SGD International, a US-based bartering company, supplied latex rubber to a Czech company in exchange for 10,000 yards of finished carpeting. SGD then traded the carpeting to a hotel for room credits. The rooms were then traded to a Japanese company for electronic equipment that was then bartered away for convention space. The 'cycle' ended when SGD traded the convention space for advertising space. Similarly, in the mid-1990s, the Paris-based Barter International Group (BIG) in France exchanged engines for advertising, then sent the engines to eastern Europe in return for cars, then exchanged the cars in Africa for cotton and sugar.

A number of so-called corporate barter companies operate throughout the world to assist companies that have no need for the product offered by potential buyers in a barter transaction. These companies buy the unwanted product (that is, they take actual title to the goods), and in exchange provide such things as advertising media space and time, air travel, hotel rooms, sales meetings, air freight, car rentals, and similar services. Operating in this manner, corporate barter companies help manufacturers to sell goods and services in foreign markets, even when a country does not have the hard currency with which to pay for the goods or services (Lund, 1997).

Technology is finding its way into barter. Online barter through 400 regional exchanges on the Internet is already available in the United States. It would seem that a next logical step is to globalize such exchanges. At the very least such an international exchange could be used as a focal point for information about barter opportunities.

11.5.2 Clearing arrangements

This system of barter occurs where two countries agree to exchange a number of products, some generally not easily sold on the open market, during a specified time period. The parties agree on the quantities and values to be exchanged, and the final settlement date when any surpluses must be cleared up, either by accepting more goods or by paying a penalty. When the transactions are between governments, any balances are known as 'clearing accounts,' whereas when the transactions have been between organizations they are known as 'evidence accounts.' In 1974, Russia and Morocco negotiated an agreement in which Russia agreed to build a phosphate plant in return for long-term phosphate supplies. Tied to this agreement was a commitment by Morocco to import petroleum products, timber, and industrial equipment, in exchange for Russia taking citrus fruit.

11.5.3 Counter purchase

This approach involves two separate exchanges: (1) an exporter sells its products to an importer for cash or credit, and (2) the exporter agrees to purchase (with the cash or credit) and market products from the importer or other companies in the importer's country. Often the products 'purchased' are not related to the original exporter's product line. As an example, in the late 1970s Volkswagen agreed to buy coal, oil, and machines from East Germany in return for selling 10,000 automobiles.

A US producer of mine safety equipment agreed to sell some units of a compact breathing apparatus to a Polish manufacturing and distributing firm in exchange for metal components that it could use in its US assembly operations (Reade, 1990). The Polish company obtained units for which it could not pay hard currency, and the US company obtained parts at a low cost while also penetrating a new market. In 1990 the US company's sales expanded rapidly as the Polish company began distributing the product to other eastern European and Third World countries.

11.5.4 Switch trading

Often, one party to a barter or counterpurchase arrangement has goods that the other does not want. If this is the case, then switch trading can be used, often with the help of a switch specialist. The original transaction can be completed and a firm will accept payment in the form of clearing currency units. These clearing currency units represent a bookkeeping unit that is universally accepted for the accounting of trade between countries and parties whose commercial relationship is based on bilateral agreements. When the unwanted goods are sold by the switch trader, the company with clearing currency units receives its hard currency payment. Or, it may be that the switch specialist buys the clearing units at a discount before reselling the goods. As an illustration of this system, consider the following hypothetical example.

A German firm agrees to trade machine tools worth €1 million to Brazil in exchange for coffee with an equivalent open market value. The equipment is shipped to São Paulo, and the coffee is ready for shipment to Hamburg. But the German firm does not really want the coffee. So, with the help of a switch specialist, the coffee is sold to a Canadian company for €925,000. The German company gets its hard currency, less a commission paid to the switch specialist. Since the German company would know in advance that the coffee would have to be sold at a discount, it could build this into its price for the equipment.

11.5.5 Buy-back

In the buy-back, or *compensation agreement*, a company agrees to supply technical knowledge to build a plant, or actually builds the plant or licenses the use of a trademark, in exchange for the production output of the plant. For example, Levi Strauss had such an agreement with Hungary; Levi's took part of the output of jeans produced in Hungary and exported them to western Europe. Another example of this type of countertrade is provided by three European companies that had jointly agreed to build two petrochemical plants in the former Soviet Union. Their payment was to be in petrochemicals that they would sell on the world market. In the late 1980s an Australian company undertook the rehabilitation of outdated coal washeries in Vietnam. Payment was made by Vietnam's National Coal Export–Import and Material Supply Corporation in anthracite coal.

11.5.6 Offsets

This involves an arrangement whereby the seller is required either to assist in or to arrange for the marketing of products produced by the buyer. When governments make large purchases from foreign companies they may insist that the purchase be offset in some way by the seller. The seller is expected to source some of the production locally, increase its imports from that country, and/or transfer technology. It is mainly used in defense-related and commercial aircraft sales. For example, McDonnell Douglas, subsequently acquired by Boeing, agreed to buy airframe components and other goods from Canadian companies in exchange for a US$2.4 billion commitment from Canada to buy fighter jet planes.

Although some offset transactions are similar to counterpurchase they are viewed as an offset because of the industry and parties involved. Moreover, offset transactions often involve the 'seller's' purchase of components from the 'buyer' to be used in producing the seller's product(s).

In addition to formal offset agreements connected to specific purchases, companies may enter into procurement arrangements designed to influence sales in a potential market. Japan Airlines, partially owned by the Japanese government, has been a major purchaser of aircraft from Boeing Company. When Boeing began development work on a next-generation B747 superjumbo jet aircraft, it brought three large Japanese companies into the venture. These companies anticipated providing components worth between 15% and 20% of the value of the jet, and the project was viewed by the Japanese press as a sort of 'national effort' in the civilian aircraft field. When Boeing suspended development work on the project in 1997, Airbus Industrie said that it would welcome Japanese participation in development of its own A3XX (now A380) project to develop a new jumbo jet. There seem to be implications for future purchases by Japan Airlines.

11.5.7 Concluding comment

Countertrade agreements are used for two general purposes. Barter contracts are used to avoid using money or to avoid setting a money price. Offset, buy-back, and counterpurchase agreements are used to impose reciprocal commitments.

Needless to say, barter/countertrade can become quite complex. The larger companies can often handle such transactions by establishing in-house organizational units for this purpose. The smaller, infrequent exporter will most likely find it more economically feasible to use independent barter/switch companies. Such firms act as agent intermediaries in much the same way as happens with regular exporting.

SUMMARY

This chapter covered export financing and methods of payment. For the most part the discussion involved describing methods, instruments used, and alternatives available. Primary emphasis was placed on letters of credit (which do not involve exporter financing) and drafts or bills of exchange (which often involve exporter financing). These are summarized in Table 11.3. The chapter concluded with a brief discussion of the major techniques of international countertrade.

While this chapter deals primarily with export financing for products and services, individuals can benefit from some advance knowledge about transferring and exchanging money in foreign countries, as illustrated in Exhibit 11.2.

TABLE 11.3

Outline of payment procedures

I Letter of credit
A Regular or ordinary letter of credit
1. Revocable: transferable, nontransferable
2. Irrevocable
a confirmed transferable
b unconfirmed nontransferable
B Revolving letters of credit
1. Revocable
a transferable
b nontransferable
2. Irrevocable
a confirmed transferable
b unconfirmed nontransferable
3. Cumulative, noncumulative

TABLE 11.3

continued

II Drafts (bills of exchange)
  A Payer of draft
    1. Bank draft, payable on presentation to the branch or correspondent of issuing bank (similar to a cashier's check)1
    2. Letter-of-credit draft, drawn under the authority of issuing bank's letter of credit and so indicated on the face of the draft
    3. Commercial draft (trade bill)
  B Documentary drafts
    1. Documents against acceptance
      a Time drafts, payable a specified time after sight
      b Time drafts, payable a specified number of days after a date drawn (also called date drafts)
    2. Documents against payment
      a Sight drafts, payment due on presentation
      b Time drafts, payment due on a specific date
  C Clean drafts
    1. Sight drafts
    2. Time drafts

EXHIBIT 11.2   Money transfer and exchange rates for individuals

The number of business people, students, and tourists traveling and living abroad is increasing every year. In their travel and temporary residence abroad, many individuals have encountered two problems. First, depending on the channel used, transferring small amounts of money can involve high percentage charges and may involve lengthy delays. A small check denominated in a foreign currency may cost more to negotiate through the bank than the value of the check itself. Government regulations may place restrictions on the transfer of funds. Second, depending upon the country and the channel used, the exchange rates on currency or travelers' checks may vary widely. The rates given by banks, money changers, and retail establishments are often quite different.

The spread of international retail banking with credit and ATM cards has made it possible to avoid high costs on many exchange transactions, and has facilitated the transfer of funds. Exchange rates on credit card charges are usually computed at very favorable rates. Where it is necessary to use local currency, an ATM card can be used to withdraw local currency directly from the user's bank account in the home country. In this case also, the bank usually uses a very favorable exchange rate between the two currencies in determining the charge to the user's home bank account. In many foreign countries the establishment of an account at a foreign branch of your home country bank may enable you to deposit local funds locally and later withdraw them in your own currency in your home country using an ATM card. Of course, local banking laws and regulations must be checked.

As an example, while teaching in Germany, one of the authors of this book who has an account at Citibank in the United States established an additional account at the local branch of Citibank. This enabled him to deposit Deutschmarks locally, and then draw out funds in Deutschmarks while in Germany and US dollars when back in the United States. He was also able to use his ATM card to obtain funds in local currency while traveling in most other countries of eastern and western Europe, and could have used it in many other areas of the world. The ATM card from the United States drew on the deposit there, while the ATM card from Germany drew on the deposit there. This allowed him to obtain money from whichever account he preferred at the most favorable exchange rates possible in each location.

QUESTIONS FOR DISCUSSION

11.1 Compare and contrast the seven methods of financing exports that are presented in this chapter.

11.2 Explain how factoring can enable an exporter to use open account when making payment arrangements with buyers. How does this differ from forfaiting?

11.3 What are the major differences between using letters of credit and bills of exchange (drafts) as a procedure for financing exports and receiving payment?

11.4 'An exporter gets the same protection from using a bill of exchange as from using a letter of credit.' Discuss.

11.5 Is there one best type of letter of credit? Explain.

11.6 When draft or bill-of-exchange methods are used, is it better to have the terms 'documents against acceptance' or 'documents against payment'? Defend your position.

11.7 'With export credit insurance the exporter can eliminate all risks of nonpayment by foreign buyers.' Discuss.

11.8 Compare and contrast the alternative techniques for countertrade. Is there one best form for a seller and one best form for a buyer? Explain.

11.9 To what extent are the objectives of sellers and buyers in countertrade transactions in conflict with each other and to what extent are they in harmony with each other?

REFERENCES

Bank of America (2004). *Trade Banking Services*. San Francisco: Bank of America.

Batchelor, C. (1990). Exporters see the light. *Financial Times*, 4 June, Section III-3.

Bose, K. (2000). India desperate to export rice. *Financial Times*, 21 December.

Chemical Bank (1987). *International Trade Guide: Financial Services for Importers and Exporters*. New York: Chemical Bank.

Fitzgerald, B. and Monson, T. (1987). The efficiency and effectiveness of export credit and export credit insurance programs. Internal Discussion Paper 4, Latin American and the Caribbean Region Series, The World Bank.

Fletcher, R. (1996). Countertrade and the internationalisation of the Australian firm. Unpublished PhD thesis, University of Technology, Sydney.

Francis, D. (1987). *The Countertrade Handbook*. New York: Quorum.

Ghose, T. K. (1993). *Export Credit Insurance: A Hong Kong Perspective*. Hong Kong: City Polytechnic of Hong Kong, Monograph 93301.

Hammond, G. T. (1990). *Countertrade Offsets and Barter in International Political Economy*. New York: St Martin's Press.

International Chamber of Commerce (1993). *Uniform Customs and Practices for Documentary Credits*, ICC Publication No. 500.

Korth, C. M. (ed.) (1987). *International Countertrade*. New York: Quorum.

Lund, B. B. (1997). Corporate barter as a marketing strategy. *Marketing News*, 31, 3 March, 8.

Miller, C. (1992). Worldwide money crunch fuels more international barter. *Marketing News*, 26, 2 March, 5.

Paun, D. and Albaum, C. (1993). A conceptual model of seller and buyer's pricing strategies in international countertrade. *J. Global Marketing*, 7(2), 75–95.

Reade, M. (1990). For barter or worse. *North American International Business*, June 16.

Scanlan, D. (2004). Interview with D. J. Scanlan, Senior Vice President and Global Products Manager-Trade, Bank of America, 2 March.

Seafirst Bank (1988). *International Banking Services*. Seattle, WA: Seafirst Bank.

The Wall Street Journal (2002). Daimler allows Argentines to pay with grain, 22 November.

FURTHER READING

Branch, A. E. (1990). *Import/Export Documentation*. London: Chapman & Hall.

Hennart, J.-F. (1990). Some empirical dimensions of countertrade. *J. International Business Studies*, 21(2) (second quarter), 243–70.

Verzariu, P. and Mitchell, P. (1992). *International Countertrade: Individual Country Practices*. Washington, DC: US Department of Commerce, International Trade Administration.

Wells, L. F. and Dulat, K. P. (1996). *Exporting: From Start to Finance* 3rd edn. New York: McGraw-Hill, Chs 19–29, 35–8.

CASE STUDY 11.1

Tainan Glass Manufacturing Company

(This case study was written by Mitsuko Saito Duerr, San Francisco State University.)

The Tainan Glass Manufacturing Company of Taiwan (the name of the company is disguised) produces large glass sheets for windows, display cases, and industrial uses. It is one of two manufacturers in Taiwan.

Odd-sized pieces left over from cutting sheets to order are made into glass louvers for use in jalousies. Jalousies, which are windows or doors made of slats that can be rotated open to allow air to flow through or closed to keep wind and rain out, are very popular in a number of countries with hot climates.

Unless made into louvers, the odd-sized pieces are scrap of no value. In effect, this makes the raw material free, and the only additional cost of making the louvers is the cost of cutting to exact size and polishing the edges. When demand for louvers is exceptionally high, however, full-size sheets are sometimes cut into louvers. This requires the use of full-cost raw material as well as labor, and the sales prices of the louvers normally reflect total cost for glass as well as labor.

For a number of years Tainan's major customers for the louvered glass had been several importers in Nigeria. However, three years ago economic problems in that African country had made it impossible for importers to arrange for foreign exchange to pay for the glass imports, unless the importers had special arrangements with the Nigerian government. None of the glass importers had been successful in making such arrangements, so Tainan has had to suspend exports to Nigeria. Unfortunately, except for some small buyers in the state of Hawaii in the United States, no other potential customers appeared. Tainan continued to make the louvers from scrap, rather than waste the odd-sized pieces of glass. They accumulated a large inventory of glass louvers.

Recently Tainan received an order for 200 container loads of louvers from a trading company in Nigeria. (Tainan ships the glass in ocean-going containers 20 feet long. Use of larger containers is not economical since it is the weight of glass rather than its volume that determines how much can be put in a container. Even a 20 ft container cannot be filled to its volumetric capacity.) The order was so large that it would not only use up the inventory, but also require some production from full-sized sheets.

Prolonged negotiations ensued, with the Nigerian company indicating that they could not provide a letter of credit because of government regulations, and Tainan arguing that without an L/C they would be running too large a risk of not receiving payment in US dollars. Tainan was very anxious for the sale to be made because of their large inventory, but did not let the Nigerian company know this. Tainan's bargaining position improved when representatives from some other Nigerian trading companies arrived and offered to buy smaller amounts (two or three container loads) for cash, US dollars paid in advance in Taiwan. This led Tainan to believe that there was a strong demand for the louvers in Nigeria.

The large Nigerian customer finally agreed to provide an L/C drawn in US dollars on a Hong Kong bank. The buyers did require that the invoice be undervalued because they said the duty in Nigeria was very high. Since the Nigerian government required that an independent firm certify the value of the shipment, Tainan had to pay an additional fee to that firm in order that they would certify the value which the Nigerian importer wanted.

The letter of credit did not arrive until two days before the shipment was due to be made, but it did arrive, the sale was completed, and payment received.

Questions

1. Why did the Nigerian company arrange for payment from a Hong Kong bank rather than a Nigerian bank?

2. In what ways may the Nigerian company have obtained hard currency?

CASE STUDY 11.2

Arion Exports

Arion Exports, a South Korean company that special-izes in producing automative replacement parts, had decided to enter the Canadian market. Raymond Lee, the general manager, turned his attention initially to specific arrangements for finance and shipment.

Arion's intention originally was to have the cus-tomers of its Canadian agent, the Peterson Trading Company, finance shipments by letters of credit. On the first order received from Peterson, the letter of credit was delayed. Lee had wanted to make prompt shipment to show the Peterson organization and its cus-tomers the fast service and deliveries they could expect from Arion. For this reason he did not wait for the tech-nicalities involved with the letter-of-credit delay to be resolved but proceeded with the shipment, using a 'to order' bill of lading to retain title and control of the merchandise.

As matters turned out, the shipment arrived in Canada before the letter of credit was received in South Korea. When it did arrive, Arion presented it and ship-ping documents to the South Korean bank involved. The bank promptly made payments in won and air-mailed the documents and clearances to its correspon-dent bank in Canada, where they were relayed to the customer.

Lee had quoted the lowest export prices possible on the order and had advised the Peterson Trading Company of its commission percentages as agent, and the terms of sale: letter of credit from the local cus-tomer. Since Lee had discovered that Peterson's cus-tomers would buy on a delivered-price basis, Arion had to give its new agent a fairly accurate basis for estimat-ing CIF charges on each of the lines. On some of the early quotations following the first order, Peterson's CIF estimates were too low, and its customer's letter of credit did not cover all costs; Peterson's account was charged for the balance. Conversely, when the estimate from Peterson Company's account was too liberal for CIF charges, the difference was credited to its account. By trial and error, Peterson improved its CIF quota-tions and, after several shipments, they corresponded closely to the exact shipping charges.

After a series of orders had been received from the Peterson Company, the financial delays showed clearly that wholesalers in Canada were having considerable trouble getting letters of credit. The reason was that the importer had to make a full deposit of the amount with the local banks before they would open letters of credit. Since a period of about 90 days was required – after the credit was opened, and the order placed – before the goods were received in Canada, a severe strain was being placed on the working capital of the auto-parts importers.

In view of this, Lee believed that, if practical, other financial arrangements should be made to replace the particular letter-of-credit procedure being used. The delays in opening letters of credit might have to be accepted as a necessary evil – a condition of doing busi-ness in Canada. On the other hand, it might be possible to effect other terms of payment.

Questions

1. What other financial and payment methods might Arion use in exporting to the Canadian market?

2. Which one of these would you suggest be used by Arion? Explain.

3. Should Mr Lee necessarily drop using the letter-of-credit procedure? Why or why not?

CHAPTER 12

Promotion and Marketing Communication

12.1 Introduction

Communication is a major part of international marketing activities. It is not enough to produce and make available a product or service; it is also necessary to provide information that buyers need to make purchasing decisions. International/ export marketing communication is cross-cultural communication; that is, communication between a person in one culture and a person or persons in another culture. In addition it is possible that, insofar as cultural differences occur within a single nation, advertising within that nation might also be cross-cultural in varying degrees. For example, many major languages are spoken in India, and, since language is an important part of the culture, cross-cultural communication can occur within the political boundaries of a single nation.

It is also possible for certain segments of markets in different nations to be culturally similar. Thus certain similar socio-economic market segments in Europe might have very similar personal characteristics and habits that might permit an advertiser to regard them as essentially a homogeneous market. For example, youthful motorcyclists in a number of different European cultures may be influenced to purchase motorcycle accessories by essentially identical advertising appeals, copy, illustrations, and layout. Or, farmers in several European countries, who use tractors for the same purposes and under the same conditions, may be influenced by nearly identical advertisements.

The nature of the communication task and some of the potential problems facing promotion by export marketers are illustrated in Figure 12.1. Although we will discuss these barriers in varying degrees throughout this chapter, some comments are in order at this point.

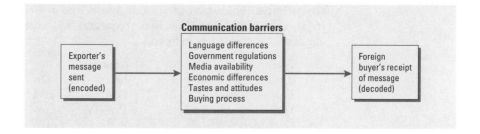

FIGURE 12.1

Some barriers to export
marketing promotion

These barriers (problems) may interact with each other as well as have independent effects. For example, there are some countries where government regulations prohibit the use of a foreign language in promotion activities. There may be exceptions. For instance, in Germany an advertisement can be run in English for a raincoat made in the United Kingdom, but not for one made in Germany. Other regulations may affect production of promotional materials. International Playtex, Inc. moved to an approach of global advertising (discussed later in this chapter) in order to sell its Wow bra in 12 countries. The single advertisement was developed in one of the markets, Australia, because of a regulation that no imported film could be used there except when a full Australian crew has taken part in the production: in short, at the time Australian television would only run commercials produced there. Similarly, in the United Kingdom a national crew had to be present at a filming (and be paid), but was not required to do the filming. Other regulations may affect the type of promotion that can be done. In South Korea, for example, comparing two different products in advertising is illegal. In addition, an increasing number of countries are prohibiting the promotion of tobacco products at sporting events. In India provisions of the Cable and Television Networks Act state that no advertisement will be allowed which derides any race, caste, color, creed, and nationality. Moreover, women cannot be portrayed in a manner that emphasizes passive, submissive qualities and encourages them to play a subordinate, secondary role in the family and society. In 2003 the government directed television channels not to air an advertisement for Fair & Lovely fairness cream (a skin lightening cream), a product marketed by the Indian subsidiary of Unilever plc (Parmar, 2003). It was claimed the commercial was racist, it promoted son preference, and it was insulting to working women.

Other regulatory barriers relate to market segments. For example, there is increasing concern about advertising aimed at children, particularly in Europe. As of mid-1999 there has been a ban on all television advertising to children under the age of 12 in Sweden and Norway; Greece banned television advertising of toys; and the Flemish region of Belgium banned advertising aimed at children for five minutes before and five minutes after children's programs (Stewart-Allen, 1999). In Hungary, advertising law bans any ad that may harm children's and juveniles' physical, moral, or intellectual development. This law was used in 1997 to ban advertising posters for the Hungarian edition of *Cosmopolitan* magazine that showed a semi-naked woman with a man's hands cupping her breasts from behind, under the caption 'The Cosmopolitan reader's favorite bra.' In the United Kingdom, in contrast, there is self-regulation within the advertising community. The British Independent Television Commission states that ads targeting children must not take advantage of their natural credulity, lead them to believe they will be inferior if they do not have the advertised product, harm children, or force them to pester their parents.

Promotion and communication by exporters is tied intimately to consumer and buyer behavior. But not all cultures will necessarily respond to marketing promotion in the same way, following the same sequence with respect to hierarchy of effects in the dimensions of attitude and behavior – cognitive (*learn*), affective (*feel*), connative (*do*). Four basic sequences by which advertising influences consumers are shown as follows:

Hierarchy	*Sequence*
Traditional learning	Learn – Feel – Do
Low involvement	Learn – Do – Feel
Dissonance attribution	Do – Feel – Learn
Dependency	Feel – Do – Learn

For the most part, the first three seem to be characteristic of western cultures. In contrast, Miracle (1987) argues that the *feel – do – learn* sequence appears to be appropriate for Japan and is, in fact, characteristic of television advertising there. Japanese consumers want to know that they can *depend* on the brand or advertiser. It has been suggested on more than one occasion that native-born Japanese tended to be less left-brain dominant than the American native-born. Such differences in the relative importance of left- vs right-brain dominance appear to explain why successful Japanese advertising campaigns are usually based on 'subtle sell' and not 'hard sell.'

12.2 Export marketing promotion and communication decisions

The promotion decisions faced by export marketing management can be reduced to the following:

- What messages?
- What communications media?
- How much effort or money to spend?

These decision areas are interrelated. Export marketing promotion takes various forms:

- *Personal selling*: sales people are used to communicating primarily face to face with prospective customers.
- *Advertising*: a nonpersonal presentation of sales messages through various 'mass' media, paid for by the advertiser.
- *Sales promotion*: all sales activities, which supplement and strengthen personal selling and advertising. Activities usually are nonrecurrent and have a relatively short-run 'life.'
- *Publicity*: any kind of news about a company or its products that is reported by some media, and is not paid for by the company.

Although much of the discussion in this chapter, and many of the examples given, will refer directly to advertising, the reader is cautioned to keep in mind two points: (1) general principles are applicable to all communication activities, including personal selling by an exporter's salesperson or the marketing intermediary in the export channel, and (2) advertising is viewed as only one of several components in the broader communication or promotional mix.

Finally, even though the discussion is presented in the context of export marketing, the general principles, concepts, and practices apply to other international market entry modes (such as strategic alliance or direct foreign investment operations), as appropriate.

We must also keep in mind that, in a broad sense, the question of what mix of promotion activities to employ is the question of whether to emphasize a 'push' or a 'pull' strategy. A *pull* strategy is defined as preselling the product so that buyers seek it out or ask for it at the point of purchase. A *push* strategy is defined as working with resellers or assisting them in selling the product at the point of sale; when a push strategy is required, buyers are not presold and they depend on the advice or guidance of the salesperson.

In the extreme case of a pull strategy a buyer would be firmly presold on a product before he reaches the place of purchase. In the extreme case of a push strategy a buyer would have no previous knowledge of a product and would make up his mind entirely at the point of sale. Obviously, most situations fall somewhere between these two extremes. Where an exporter finds itself with regard to emphasizing push or pull will affect the relative importance and desirability of the several methods of communicating marketing information to the target market.

The export/international marketer needs to have guidelines for selecting which promotion activities to use and in which combinations. There are a number of factors that will influence the decision regarding the mix of promotion activities. These are shown in Table 12.1.

TABLE 12.1 Factors affecting promotion mix	1. Availability of funds for promotion. Different activities have different costs per unit of activity. 2. Cost of promotion activities. 3. The degree of competition, both short and long term. Usually, the greater the degree of competition, the higher the budget allocation per forecasted product sale. 4. The type of product involved, its seasonality, and its price. 5. Mode of market entry. When distributors, agents, and partners in alliances are used for entry, they may share the promotion costs with the exporter. 6. The type of market. In a highly industrialized country more sophisticated promotion techniques can be used compared with countries of lower educational standard, where there is more reliance on radio communication and illustrated poster sites. Demographic characteristics are relevant. 7. The nonmonetary resources available within the company to handle the promotion and their adequacy and cost. 8. Size of market, and sizes of various market strata. 9. Media availability.

Source: adapted from Branch, 1990, pp. 68–70

12.2.1 Export marketing promotion as communication

Earlier in this chapter export marketing promotion was discussed in the context of communication wherein the exporter sends messages to the target market to *inform* prospective buyers (including intermediaries) about a product, to *persuade* people to become buyers, to develop *positive attitudes*, and to cause other *changes* in people's thinking and behavior that will be beneficial to the exporter. As suggested by Figure 12.1, there are obstacles to effective promotion and these can be formidable when attempting to communicate with people in foreign countries whose values, attitudes, and behavior patterns have been developed from different cultural backgrounds.

Communication problems are not limited to promotion that is *verbal* (spoken or written) in nature. *Nonverbal* communication problems can also arise. As we mentioned in Chapter 3, nonverbal communication exists in many forms; some kinds supplement verbal communication while others are used when verbal communication is not possible (see Table 12.2). Any one of these forms of nonverbal communication may lead to different interpretations and responses in different cultures (Gesteland, 1999, Ch. 7). This results in different messages being received. For example, sloppy attire (appearance) may be more offensive in some countries than in others. French and Italian people use their hands (kinesics) more than Americans do. South Americans and Greeks feel more comfortable when standing or sitting closer to others (proxemics) than do people from other cultures and nationalities.

In export marketing and promotion the communicator must learn about the audience, define the market as precisely as possible, and study background and motivational influences before beginning preparation of a promotion strategy and campaign. There are many who believe that the appeals, illustrations, and other features of advertising and other forms of promotion need not be changed from market to market. They have observed that, in many respects, consumers in diverse markets are similar and that human nature is basically the same in most societies. People everywhere require satisfaction of physiological and psychological needs. These people favor standardization of advertising programs.

TABLE 12.2 Nonverbal communication	Appearance: includes physical attire and grooming Chronemics: the timing of verbal exchanges Haptics: the use of touch while conversing Kinesics: the movement of part of the body to communicate Oculesics: the use (or avoidance) of eye contact Olfaction: the action of smelling Orientation: the angles at which people position themselves in relation to each other Paralinguistics: the nonverbal aspects of speech (such as accents) Posture: the many bodily positions of standing, sitting, lying, and so on Proxemics: the use of space in communication

However, it can be argued that a communicator should rightly take cognizance of the differences between consumers in his or her own country and those in other countries. They not only may speak another language, but they adhere to other religions, philosophies, and traditions; they differ with regard to family patterns, childhood training, and the role of members in the family. The occupational hierarchy varies among nations; climate and geography and other aspects of consumers' physical environment are diverse; consumers engage in a wide variety of sports, hobbies, and other forms of amusement and entertainment. These environmental differences play an important part in shaping the demand for specific types of goods and services and in determining which promotional appeals are best. Consequently, adaptation or individualization of advertising programs may be needed.

Another barrier to communication is social or class structure. In societies where social status attitudes are quite rigid, a salesperson from the middle class is usually not effective if the job requires selling to upper-class factory owners, since he will not know how to behave in the new social environment.

One conclusion that can be drawn from this discussion is that appeals, illustrations, and other advertising and promotion features often must differ from market to market. We discuss this issue later in the chapter in the context of standardization vs adaptation (the globalization) of export marketing promotion.

Another aspect of communication/promotion concerns the use of foreign settings, actors/characters, and written language in advertising in specific markets. The extent to which foreign elements are used varies across countries. In Japan, they find widespread use. In contrast, relatively few foreign elements are present in US advertising while their use in South Korea seems to be associated with features of the country's history, culture, and economic development (Taylor and Miracle, 1996). The feasibility of using foreign elements in advertising in a country has direct implications for standardization and/or transference of advertising campaigns or parts of campaigns.

If Exporter A wishes to communicate effectively with Buyer X, they must somehow put themselves in each other's shoes. This involves the process of *empathy*. Effective communication requires that they have a common set of meanings and definitions. Such a common set of meanings derives not only from the language, but refers more broadly to the pattern of beliefs, codes, and feelings on the basis of which people learn to live with their environment.

12.2.2 Symbols

The successful communicator depends upon symbols as a means of establishing empathy with another person. Thus, the export marketer must choose with care the symbols used in promotion for a foreign market. Color is one type of visual symbol that possesses emotional and psychological properties (see Exhibit 12.1). It is important that the exporter remember that specific colors may not have the same meaning and significance among cultures. In China, for example, light and bright colors are chosen by young people, and plainer and deeper colors by their elders. Yellow has always been the imperial color; originally its use by the masses was prohibited, and it is still not used extensively except for religious purposes; it suggests grandeur and mystery. Purple is a noble color in Japan, but in Myanmar (Burma) and in some Latin American countries it represents death. The color of mourning in Japan is black and in Iran it is blue; thus these colors are not likely to be well received in marketing promotion in these countries. Green symbolizes nationalism in Egypt and this color should be used only with great care by the exporter to that country.

Because of these differences in traditions, customs, religions, and related cultural features of a society, extreme care must be exercised in selecting symbols that can convey the intended message and that do not offend the sensibilities of the audience. For example, comparing people to animals, or utilizing animals in cartoon advertisements to portray human beings, may be quite unacceptable to Buddhists, who believe in reincarnation. An advertisement comparing people to animals also runs the risk of being offensive to an Arab. ('A beast is a beast and a man is a man. Allah says so.') Thus the use of animals to illustrate human behavior may not be attractive, even though understandable.

In a similar manner, the advertiser must be careful about the use of animal symbols and company logos in advertising illustrations (Ricks, 1999, pp. 58–9). These, too, can be misinterpreted and 'mistranslated.' For example, in Brazil a US company used a large deer as a sign of masculinity. The word 'deer' turned out to be a Brazilian 'street name' for a homosexual. Another company used an owl in promotion to India. To an Indian, the owl is a symbol for bad luck. The company was not successful.

Regarding layout of advertising, it is obvious that it should match the reading patterns of the target market. A laundry detergent company marketing in the

EXHIBIT 12.1   Color, culture and consumption

One marketing cue that export managers can use regardless of location is color. A rose by any other name may still be a rose, but the color of the rose may make a difference. Japanese consumers prefer white, whereas consumers from Hong Kong prefer red. Evidence shows that color ranks among the top three considerations, along with price and quality, in the purchase of an automobile. Color is also an important component of many corporate and brand-building cues such as logos, packages, and displays.

For example, the use of appropriate color in international B2B advertisements can profoundly impact the success of an advertised product. A study by Clarke and Honeycutt (2000) compares the usage of colors in business advertisements in France, the United States, and Venezuela. The findings conclude that Venezuelan ads use significantly more red, orange, and green, while ads from France and the United States use higher proportions of black and brown. The United States also utilized significantly more black-and-white ads than either France or Venezuela. These findings differ from prior theories of color preferences, indicating that cultural meanings may influence business's color selections for advertisements.

Color is one of many marketing tools that exporters use to create, maintain, and modify brand images in customers' minds. A good example of this comes from the consumer film industry. Kodak's packages are in yellow, Fuji FIlm's packages are in green and Konica uses blue for its packaging. Use of these colors allows consumers to quickly identify a brand. The significance of color to convey meaning is evident from the existence of the Lanham Act in the United States, which protects product colors as trademarks.

However, to what extent can international marketing managers strategically use color to communicate desired images and reinforce them to consumers?

The effect of color on choice

Carlton Wagner, the creator of the Wagner Institute for Color Research, contends that colors are associated with certain images. For example, blue is associated with wealth, trust, and security; gray is associated with strength, exclusivity, and success; and orange denotes cheapness. These associations may explain why banks are more likely to color their logos and collateral using blue or gray rather than orange. Wagner put his theory into practice with Wienerschnitzel, a hot dog restaurant with 350 locations in the United States. Wagner advised Wienerschnitzel to add a little orange to the color of its buildings to convey the message that the chain sold inexpensive hot dogs. After the change of color, Wienerschnitzel reported a 7% increase in sales.

Associations and meanings of colors

Color influences both human behavior and human physiology. Evidence shows that red is more often associated with exciting-stimulating, orange with distressed-disturbed-upset, blue with tender-soothing, purple with dignified-stately, yellow with cheerful-jovial-joyful, and black with powerful-strong-masterful.

Recently the Xerox Corporation launched an image and repositioning campaign in which the company's logo and trademark were changed from blue to red. The reason was to change customer perceptions of Xerox from a traditional copier company to a more diversified technology company that offers printers, scanners, faxes, and imaging equipment other than copying machines.

Culture and color preferences

Some studies have assessed the preference of colors across cultural borders. The results have demonstrated that people of different cultures have various preferences for color. Cultural differences in color meanings and associations have also been identified. One study surveyed respondents from 20 countries, asking them to rate seven colors on 12 semantic differential scale items. Blue was the most highly evaluated color, followed by green and white. The most potent colors were black and red. Red was the most active color, whereas black and gray were the most passive colors.

Another study asked respondents from four cultures (Japan, China, South Korea, and the United States) to state which one of eight colors was most closely associated with 13 words often used to describe consumer products. The results indicate some similarities and differences across cultures. All four cultures associate blue with high quality and red with love. Purple is associated with expensiveness for subjects from Japan, China, and South Korea. In contrast, respondents from the United States associate purple with inexpensive. Black is consistently associated with expensiveness and powerfulness across countries.

Although reactions to color are considered highly individualized, universal color preferences are thought to exist. For example, blue is the color most frequently chosen by adults. However, there are exceptions. A study in the late 1980s reported that African–American subjects like colors in the red-blue-black range, whereas white subjects prefer blues and greens. Similarly, blue is the color most often chosen, except by respondents from Senegal and the Transkei, who prefer red and black. In India, Hindus consider orange the most sacred color, whereas the Ndembo in Zambia do not even consider orange a separate color.

The effects of culture on the meaning associated with marketing cues such as color are critical for international marketing managers. If the meaning associated with a color or combination of colors is different across cultures, markets may benefit from pursuing a customized strategy with respect to the color associated with the brand, package, and so on. In contrast, when color meanings are similar across preference, a standardized strategy is more viable.

Source: adapted from Madden *et al.*, 2000

Middle East had all of its advertisements structured with pictures of soiled clothes on the left, soap in the middle, and clean clothes on the right. Since people in that part of the world read from right to left many potential customers interpreted the message to indicate that the soap actually soiled the clothes.

The exporter should also be sure that the symbols to be used are accurate and up to date. A number of years ago McDonnell Douglas Corporation had an unexpected reaction to a brochure sent to potential aircraft customers in India. An old photo was used that depicted turbaned men who turned out to be Pakistani men, not Indians.

When using an object (including a person) as a type of symbol the export promoter must be sure that the symbol means something to the target audience. Ricks (1999, pp. 51–4) provides two excellent illustrations of this.

In Japan, a cosmetics company tried to sell its lipstick through a television advertisement that depicted Nero coming to life just as a pretty woman wearing the lipstick walked by. Unfortunately for the advertiser, many Japanese women had no real idea who Nero was.

In the past, Marlboro cigarette advertisements were popular and successful in the United States and Europe, where the Marlboro man projected a strong masculine image. This approach was not successful in Hong Kong, where the urban people did not identify with horseback riding in the countryside. The advertising was changed to reflect a Hong Kong-style Marlboro man; a virile cowboy who is younger, better dressed, and owns a truck and the land he is on.

These examples illustrate the need to be more 'local' oriented in using symbols, including using locally known historical figures. Other examples are shown in Exhibit 12.2.

Moulin Rouge, Paris,
France

EXHIBIT 12.2 Promotion blunders are no joke

It is not difficult for a company doing business in foreign markets to make mistakes in promoting its products, including its use of advertising. Sometimes these errors result from applying concepts that worked in the home market. Even though errors are made, the blunder will not necessarily cause a company to lose out. Using the analogy of a race, the company can have a bad start and still win the race.

A case in point is Nike, the large US athletic shoe company (Cone, 1990), which was chasing the long-time leader Adidas in the very lucrative European sports footwear market.

Nike's blunder was its US$21 million European advertising campaign, which centered on US gridiron football and baseball star Bo Jackson. While the advertisement spots were deservedly popular in the United States – where Jackson was a superstar and the tag line from an earlier advertisement 'Bo knows ...' had become a pop culture reference – they did not go over well in Europe.

The problem was simple: a joke with a punch line that has to be explained is never funny, and Jackson was relatively unknown in Europe. One evening in 1990 at a crowded Paris cinema only one man – evidently the only American in the building – laughed as a slickly produced Jackson advertisement was shown to the French audience. Printed advertisements featured the muscular athlete with a note telling readers exactly who he is.

In February 2000 Adidas was hitting back at arch-rival Nike's campaign, which was launched a week before (*Marketing*, London, February 2000). Nike's ad was styled on a video game featuring Nike stars Andre Agassi, Michael Jordan, and Ronaldo alongside cyberbabe Lara Croft. The Adidas campaign employed humor to make its brand image more colorful for the youth market. Rugby star Jonah Lomu, tennis player Anna Kournikova and athlete Ato Boldon were shown performing successfully in their sports wearing Adidas clothing and footwear. The ads were intended as a tongue-in-cheek dig at products that claim to change people's lives. Adidas's television and poster campaign was shown across Europe, Latin America and Asia simultaneously.

TABLE 12.3

Examples of promotion blunders of the 1980s

Company (product)	Location	Reported blunder	Company response	
			Did it happen?	Comments
Otis Engineering (oil well equipment)	USSR	Promotional sign incorrectly said product was good for sex	No response	
Parker Pen (ink)	Latin America	Advertisement statement 'Won't leak in your pocket and embarrass you' gave false impression that the product helped prevent pregnancies	Yes	Blunder due to poor translation. In Spanish, it came out as 'Won't leak in your pocket and impregnate you.'
Pepsi Cola (drink)	West Germany	Advertisement was translated from 'Come Alive with Pepsi' to 'Come out of the grave with Pepsi'	No response	

TABLE 12.3

continued

Company (product)	Location	Reported blunder	Company response	
			Did it happen?	Comments
Exxon (gas)	Thailand	Used meaningless (locally) tiger symbol in advertisements	No	Nothing was wrong at all with using 'tiger' symbol in Thailand
General Mills (breakfast cereal)	England	Oriented advertisements to kids in a country that considered it improper to promote products in that manner	No	Not involved in the English ready-to-eat cereal market
General Motors (autos)	Belgium	Translation error made 'Body by Fischer' say 'Corpse by Fischer'	Vague	Considering the number of decisions made every day, our record for accuracy is a good one
Goodyear Tire & Rubber Co.	West Germany	Made illegal claims of superiority	Yes	We ran into problems because competitors used laws to restrict competition. We could prove our claims, but had to change advertisements anyway
McDonnell Douglas (aircraft)	India	Advertisements mistakenly depicted Pakistani men rather than Indians	No response	
Warner–Lambert (mouthwash)	Thailand	Advertisements depicted loving in violation of accepted local customs	Problem: yes Blunder: no	The advertising was in good taste, but the law changed. The commercial has now been revised to meet the new law
Unilever (detergent)	Germany and Austria	Firm did not coordinate promotion of its product resulting in confusion	Yes (sort of)	Report was not entirely correct. Small amount of overlap. Advertising did not cause much confusion

Source: adapted from Ricks and Mahajan, 1984; Ricks, 1999; and Cone, 1990

As with earlier examples of concepts that worked at home but flopped when transferred to other countries – such as Chevrolet's use of the word Nova in Mexico, where *no va* means 'it doesn't go' – Nike's mistake did not prove fatal.

A wide variety of companies in many different countries may have made promotional advertising mistakes for a wide variety of reasons. Table 12.3 shows some of the more publicized errors that were reported through the 1980s. As shown, not all reported mistakes were acknowledged by the company as having happened. Also, those that did happen were not always viewed as a blunder. Whether an event actually happened and whether a company accepts it as a mistake is not the issue. These events can happen and they can have unintended and adverse effects on a company's performance in foreign markets.

Going a step further, multinational corporations are increasingly directing advertising toward various parts of the world, which is being tailored more and more to specific differentiated audiences and markets. This, of course, is consistent with a philosophy that an increasing number of companies seem to believe in – 'think global, but act local.' The Dutch company Heineken typically tailors its beer advertising to each market. In France and Italy, for example, which are traditional wine cultures, Heineken is marketed as a drink for all occasions. It has been successful there. Farther east, Heineken targets young professionals, promoting its products as a taste of refined European culture. In the United States, Heineken is promoted as a status symbol, an upscale European beer. For Saudi Arabia, Heineken developed an alcohol-free version of its low-alcohol Buckler brand (Gesteland, 1999, p. 114). More recently Audi, the German prestige car maker, was kicking off an aggressive pan-European advertising campaign for its new A4 model launch with a £6 million expenditure in the United Kingdom over the first two months of 2001.

How a symbol is used (the context in which it is shown) can vary among countries. For example, Americans tend to show something including a product in action if at all possible. In contrast, the French are relatively more likely to look for an idea or symbol per se.

Cultural differences also may vary considerably over very short distances. For example, one might expect considerable homogeneity in language, traditions, and customs in Germany. But there are marked differences between Germans from different regions. Villagers from Schleswig-Holstein and Bavaria have great difficulty in communicating with each other in their native dialects, although both are German. Even in small countries like Denmark and Norway, with about only 5 million inhabitants, cultural differences occur. For example, Danish people from the western part of the country, Jutland, often have difficulty in communicating with people from Copenhagen and its surrounding area.

12.2.3 A concluding comment

Communication with buyers in export markets may not be effective for a number of reasons. Of particular importance to export marketing communication are the following:

- *The message may not get through to the intended recipient.* Either the medium may not reach the recipient, or the message may not be perceived for some reason, perhaps because the person is not interested in the message at the moment, or other distractions may take the intended recipient's attention away from the message. Such difficulties may be due to lack of knowledge about which media are appropriate to reach foreign target audiences, and lack of knowledge about when to reach them (for example scheduling difficulties).

■ *The message may not be understood in the way intended by the sender.* Because of lack of knowledge of the factors that influence how persons from different cultures will interpret messages, it is possible for a message to be perceived and interpreted incorrectly.

■ *The message may not induce the recipient to take the action desired by the sender.* Although a message may be perceived correctly, lack of knowledge about foreign cultural factors that influence attitude formation, purchasing behavior, and so forth, may cause communication to fail in producing the desired effect. Such failure may be due to lack of knowledge on such matters as consumer motives, reference group influence, or consumers' economic circumstances.

12.3 Alternative techniques of promotion

Earlier in this chapter we defined briefly the various major forms of export promotion; personal selling, advertising, sales promotion, and publicity. In this section we discuss further each of these activities.

12.3.1 Personal selling

The objective of any export marketing operation in the final analysis is only achieved through people. It is the *personal aspect of marketing* that can least readily be duplicated by competition. An enterprise must rely for survival and progress on the personal qualification of those who make up its personnel and direct its destinies.

Personal selling is person-to-person communication between a company representative and a prospective buyer. The seller's communication effort is focused on informing and persuading the prospect with the goal of making a sale. The salesperson's job is to understand the buyer's needs correctly, attach those needs to the company's product(s), and then persuade the customer to buy.

A well-selected, well-trained, well-compensated, and well-supported salesperson can, and in most instances will, make the difference between successful and unsuccessful foreign sales volume. For example, a key aspect in the Japanese approach to selling products is their reliance upon support materials and data. Sales representatives carry well-designed brochures, big notebooks of data, micro photographs, and other material. This allows them to respond quickly to questions with substantive answers (Leslie, 1990). Sales promotion, including advertising, will arouse interest in the company or the product. But the final sale will not be closed until the actual purchasing decision is made, and personal contact is usually essential for this.

There is little difference in kind between managing export and domestic marketing sales people; they have to be recruited, hired, trained, organized, compensated, supervised, motivated, and controlled (see Usunier, 2000). In global selling it is absolutely essential for a salesperson to understand cultural norms and proper protocol. Therefore a common theme in sales training is the notion of active listening; naturally, in global sales verbal and nonverbal communication barriers of the type presented in Table 12.2 may arise. As we discussed in

Chapter 7, there are three basic functions that all sales people operating in foreign markets must perform:

1. **The actual selling activity.** The communication of product information to customers, and obtaining orders.
2. **Customer relations.** The salesperson must at all times be concerned with maintaining and improving the company's position with customers and the general public.
3. **Information gathering and communicating.** The salesperson is often able to provide information that might be useful in planning advertising and trade promotion programs.

The personal selling process is typically divided into several stages: prospecting, pre-approach, problem solving, approaching, presenting, handling objections, closing the sale, and follow-up. It is important to realize that the relative importance of each stage can vary by country or region.

For example, an experienced Danish company operating with its own sales force in the United States knows that persistence in personal sales is often very important in that country compared with sales in the home market. Therefore, 'Don't take "no" for an answer' in the US market; in Denmark, however, 'A "no" means mostly a "no".'

Patience is also required if a global industrial marketing effort is to succeed; in some countries this means a willingness to patiently invest months or years before the effort results in an actual sale. For example, a company wishing to enter the Japanese market must be prepared for negotiations to take place over several years. This also is true for China.

Personal selling is a popular communication tool in countries with restrictions on advertising and in countries where low wage rates allow large local forces to be hired. In such countries it may be the only way to communicate effectively with potential buyers.

12.3.2 Sales promotion

Earlier we defined sales promotion as including all sales activities that supplement and strengthen personal selling and advertising. For the most part sales promotion activities are of a relatively short-run duration that add tangible value to the product or brand. The tangible value created by the sales promotion may come in various forms, such as price reduction or a 'buy one, get one free' offer. The purpose of a sales promotion may be to stimulate nonusers to sample a product or to increase overall consumer demand. Also, sales promotions are designed to increase product availability in distribution channels.

Of the wide variety of activities classed as sales promotion devices, the exporter must choose those best adapted to the company's products, the markets that are to be developed, and what the company can afford. Some devices that have lost their pulling power and have become worn out in the domestic market or some foreign markets may be effective in other foreign markets. However, sales promotion in Europe is highly regulated, although most popular in some countries, for example the Nordic countries. Promotions such as cash backs, free draws, lottery, and in-pack premiums are permitted in some countries but not in others.

Differences in promotional packages can be considerable in a European setting. Even in cases where there are no language problems, differences in promotional packages can be useful in order to elicit a strong regional response from consumers. If, as expected, such regulations are relaxed as an internal market develops in the EU and regulations are harmonized, companies may be able to roll out pan-European promotion programs.

For example, in Scotland promotional campaigns are often different from those used elsewhere in the United Kingdom. This can be illustrated by the Brooke Bond tea promotional policies. In most of the United Kingdom Brooke Bond PG Tips is marketed; in Scotland this product is called Scottish Blend. Although similar promotional tactics are used there are significant differences, including a distinctive Scottish-oriented advertising package.

In the vast array of devices, six should be discussed because of special factors significant for foreign market development. They are the foreign catalog, samples, the export house organ, the motion picture/video or slide film, trade fairs and exhibitions, and point-of-purchase materials. For the most part these activities are used for export to business firms rather than to the ultimate consumer. However, there are types of sales promotion materials designed for ultimate consumers that the export/international marketer must be concerned about, such as point-of-purchase materials, samples, and new direct promotion techniques such as coupons, contests, and so on.

Foreign catalogs

The foreign catalog is the ever-present, silent, accurate, all-knowing sales tool. The customer in a foreign market may be located quite a distance from the closest sales office. When prepared with this in mind, the foreign catalog can be extremely effective. It must be able to close the gap between buyer and seller. Independent of personal selling, it must attract attention, arouse interest, impel action, and make that action easy by supplying all the needed information from sizes, colors, and quantities to packing, approximate shipping time, terms, forms of payment acceptable, and, if feasible, duties. Prices, too, must be clearly stated, whether FOB, FAS vessel, or CIF port of destination.

Therefore, the purposes of the foreign catalog are as follows:

- *Create interest and attract readership.* A colorful cover, as much color as possible in the body of the catalog, and a well-printed and easily read text are 'musts.'
- *Mirror the personality of the manufacturer or exporter.* An introduction giving years in business, the array of products, number of plants and their locations, the company's status in the industry, and similar information is invaluable to the buyer. To supplement this impression, the catalog must also be well bound, logically arranged, and attractive.
- *Carry the reputation of the manufacturer or exporter into world markets.* Often this includes a statement regarding trademarks, for the exporting manufacturer must realize that domestic product names are often unknown abroad.
- *Make buying easy.* The foreign catalog must answer all questions that a buyer might want answered about the product, terms, and so on. It should make ordering easier for the foreign dealer.
- *Create the desire for ownership.* This can be achieved through action-packed illustrations or ultraclear photographs of the product in use.
- *Supply all the facts that a salesperson would present in person.* These include the features of the product that make it desirable to the consumer and the salesperson's arguments, and how complaints and later questions are to be handled.

The foreign catalog has the potential to be even more convincing than a salesperson. Nothing speaks more loudly or more effectively than the printed word, for dealers in other countries know that what a dependable company puts in print is apt to be true and is often more reliable than a salesperson's claims.

Preparation of this type of catalog is, of course, not an easy task. A foreign catalog cannot be merely a domestic catalog put into another language. The text must be completely edited for world markets, and all idioms, colloquialisms, and trade nomenclature used must be understandable in the target market. The products' qualities and qualifications must be clearly stated, and the best selling points presented. Adaptation to a specific foreign market is greater for consumer catalogs than B2B catalogs (Robles and Akhter, 1997).

Four hot international markets for catalog sales have been identified (*Catalog Age*, February 1997): Japan, the United States, Germany, and Canada. The four popular markets are mature, however, without being saturated. In fact, the more build-up the catalog infrastructure in a foreign market, the easier it is for exporting mailers to do business there. For example, the United Kingdom has long been a favorite foreign destination of US mailers. Germany on the other hand is by far the largest market in Europe, with a highly developed catalog infrastructure.

In addition to catalogs, other types of literature may be good sales tools (Wiklund, 1986, pp. 103–5). *Brochures* of various types are especially useful for sales people, distributors, dealers, and agents. Since sending printed sales aids to export markets can be very expensive, the exporter should carefully assess the needs of marketing intermediaries *before* sending vast quantities of such materials. The language will depend upon product and target markets. Translations (from the language of the domestic market) should be done in cooperation with overseas agents and/or distributors. The most effective brochures are those that are informative and which are written for a reader who knows nothing about the exporter's product(s).

Samples

A sample can give the potential foreign buyer an idea of form and quality that cannot be attained by even the most graphic picture. Foreign customers are often situated a long distance from where a product is manufactured and consequently any mistakes in ordering or misunderstandings over styles, sizes, models, and so on, are apt to prove serious and costly. Samples, as many successful foreign sales people recognize, are a means of avoiding such difficulties.

The use of samples will, of course, vary with the product and the markets involved. The most common is *direct sampling* by mail, express or courier, by which means the export marketer sends a specimen of its product(s) to the distant individual buyer or even the ultimate consumer. Second, and steadily growing in importance, is the use of samples by *residential agents*, *branch office managers*, and *travelling sales people*. Then there is the use of samples at sample *fairs*, import fairs, and similar demonstrational and promotional enterprises for buyers. In some places sample fairs take the form of a permanent display of manufacturers for buyers to look at the available offerings.

Direct sampling, preferably by mail, is usually practical only in the case of small or relatively inexpensive articles such as food products, medical preparations, toilet articles, and so on, where the size can be kept down so that the expense involved is not formidable, and where the samples can be tried out by the recipient under normal conditions of consumption. In the case of articles where the value can be measured only by the services rendered rather than by their appearance, such as various mechanical devices, samples are not satisfactory. Manufacturers of bulky objects such as furniture, ranges, and refrigerators are, however, able to use samples by putting them in permanent trade exhibits at commercial centers.

When planning to use samples, or any sales promotion material, direct to consumers the international marketer should look at national regulations. Laws pertaining to sales promotion activities differ greatly across countries. These laws govern both the types of promotion that are allowed and the manner of presentation. For example, in Malaysia a contest may be used, but it must involve a game of skill and not chance. In Germany, only full-value coupons may be used in a consumer promotion; in The Netherlands and Switzerland, although they are legal, major retailers refuse to accept coupons. Within the European Union the creation of the internal market did not call for harmonization of country-specific regulations on sales promotions. As of the end of 2000 only *free samples*, in-store demos, and reusable packages were allowed in all EU countries. Other sales promotion activities that are allowed or not allowed in selected European Union countries are shown in Table 12.4.

TABLE 12.4 Legality of selected sales promotion activities (as of mid-1999)	Activity	Germany	France	UK	Netherlands	Belgium
	On-pack price reductions	Legal	Legal	Legal	Legal	Legal
	Extra product	a	Legal	Legal	a	a
	Money-off vouchers	Not legal	Legal	Legal	Legal	Legal
	Free prize contest	Not legal	Legal	Legal	Not legal	Not legal
	In-pack gift	a	a	Legal	a	a

ᵃ Being reviewed

House organ and company-published magazines

Also important in sales promotion is the house organ, either offline or online. Such publications can serve as an effective means to provide company, distributor, or agent personnel with knowledge of the success of other distributors or agents. House organs may be a vehicle for promotional ideas, company news, the results of contests, employee commendation, and so forth, and may be an important device to stimulate enthusiasm and effective sales performance abroad. Unlike the catalog, this type of publication is not limited to an accurate description of the product, but can cover almost any phase of the business. Its articles can be so written as to convey information to the foreign customer. An exporter's house organ is especially suited to goodwill building and institutional advertising. It should endeavor to sell the entire organization as well as its merchandise.

Most companies prepare, edit, and produce house organs in the home country, but a few companies with well-established export operations may have separate foreign editions, prepared and produced locally, with only a minimum of central direction and control of content. Of these, probably the most successful are those in which there is a systematic or planned sharing of information and interchange of ideas among the various foreign editions.

Films, slides, and personal computers

One of the potentially best sales aids in foreign markets is the motion picture, video tape, and DVD. Though expensive, particularly the motion picture, such aids perform the essential task of telling the manufacturer's entire sales story to the foreign customer who may never have seen the products or factory, and may never have been to the manufacturer's country. The motion picture/video/DVD combines the illustration with the spoken word, but its effectiveness is dependent on the skill with which it has been made and used, and the extent to which it is adapted to the company's purpose. Films can show selected audiences of potential customers a comprehensive story of the exporter's product, organization, or even the manufacturing process.

A motion picture/video tape/DVD has many advantages. This method of presentation is still relatively new and unusual in many markets, some of them major ones, and buyers are often willing to take the time to watch, when they would not be willing to spend the same amount of time listening to a conventional sales talk. It adds novelty to the presentation of the company's message. The sales message is told in exactly the language that the exporter wishes to use and stresses exactly those points that it wishes to stress. The story is completely told, and no valuable points are inadvertently omitted. It serves to refresh the memory of the distributor and/or agent, aiding the intermediary to keep in mind the major points of manufacture. It supplies the marketing intermediary with a sales medium that saves energy for the all-important closing of the sale, attracts attention from clientele, and helps greatly in creating a desire for possession.

Slide films, though much less expensive to produce than films and videos, have definite limitations by comparison. Where cost is a major factor they do present a solution, for they can be more economically produced, easily presented, and readily transported. The opportunities for their use and the inherent problems are, however, similar to films, video tapes and DVDs.

Due to the technological revolution, the personal computer can be used in a manner similar to films and slides. Laptop and notebook computers are easily carried by salespersonnel and distributors, and companies can develop the appropriate software to present their promotion and sales message. The Internet has expanded the potential uses of the personal computer. In addition to sales promotion, it is increasingly becoming a basic advertising medium. Similarly, the fax machine is also being used for promotion purposes.

Trade fairs and exhibitions

Trade fairs and exhibitions are another medium that is extremely important for some industries and some countries. Often a trade fair is the first communicative step in the process of export development of the small and medium-sized company. A trade fair is a concentrated exhibition of the products of many manufacturers/exporters. They are of two general types: (1) the broad, general-type, well-established annual affairs, and (2) the specialized type, for products in specialized groups or industries. An example of the general fair, the largest of its kind, is the annual Hanover Fair in Germany, which attracts thousands of exhibitors in 20 major industry categories. Similarly, Colombia has its biannual Bogotá International Trade Fair that draws participation from more than 25 nations including countries in the western hemisphere, Europe, and Asia. An illustration of the more specialized fair is the annual Paris Air Show.

Trade fairs have become a big part of the selling process for many companies and industries. Although selling at a trade fair requires the same skills and knowledge as other selling, there are some elements of the process that are unique: (1) gathering names; (2) demonstrations; (3) prizes; and (4) client promotions. Gathering names of a trade fair's attendees makes up a list of potential buyers. A product demonstration not only involves a prospect with the product but also gives the exporting firm the opportunity to engage the potential buyer in a conversation about his or her needs and objectives. Prizes and client promotions are means that might generate a tremendous amount of traffic, but at the same time could made it almost impossible for the booth, or the one next to it, to conduct any business.

Trade fairs are used to buy and sell products, sign contracts, and arrange for international distributorships and agent relationships. Trade fairs can be valuable not only to well-established firms – for purposes of prestige, public image, introducing new products – but also to new firms that might have no other readily available way of getting their products displayed before the right audience, at low cost.

Sometimes trade fair participation is by invitation only. Such is the case for the semi-annual Chinese Export Commodities Fair held in Guangzhou, China. When participating in such a fair, advance preparation is crucial, including contact initiation and translation of materials into the language of the host country. Advance planning for trade fair participation and what to do during the fair are discussed by Wells and Dulat (1996, pp. 143–50) and Smith (1998).

A different type of fair is the annual month-long Christmas Market in Aachen, Germany. It is a consumer market that attracts about 1 million visitors from Europe and as far away as the United States. Figure 12.2 shows an exhibition of replicas of German cathedrals, castles and other buildings. Many of these items are designed in Aachen, custom-made in Lithuania, and sold in the Christmas Market.

FIGURE 12.2

An exhibit at the Christmas Market, Aachen, Germany

Point-of-purchase materials

Manufacturers and exporters of packaged consumer goods such as cosmetics, paper-tissue products, or proprietary pharmaceuticals sometimes find it useful to provide point-of-purchase (POP) literature and displays to sale subsidiaries, agents, distributors, and retail dealers. Successful POP merchandising ideas in one country can often be applied, directly or in modified form, in another country. Local POP materials can sometimes also be tied in with advertisements run in local media. Such materials may also contribute to, and be in harmony with, a uniform worldwide image that a manufacturer/exporter may want to achieve. Some companies prepare POP materials domestically in rough form for shipment abroad. Local foreign representatives usually handle production and printing. In the rare event that the POP materials are produced in the home country, the copy would most likely be left blank so that the local distributor or agent can silk-screen or overprint the copy in the local language.

Consumer promotion materials

Throughout the world international marketers of consumer goods, either through their subsidiaries, affiliates, partners, distributors, or dealers, are increasingly using various types of sales promotion devices to stimulate sales. This is particularly so for companies in the packaged consumer goods product categories such as Unilever, Procter & Gamble, and Nestlé. For the most part the larger companies have left sales promotion in the hands of local managers since it does deal with motivating local consumers and members of the trade to act – try the product, repurchase, buy more, switch brands, and so on. However, there will be differences among countries due to differing levels of economic development and market maturity, culture-based consumer and trade perceptions of promotional incentives, regulations, and trade structures (Kashani and Quelch, 1990).

Recent studies in developing countries have shown that free samples and demonstrations are by far the most widely used consumer promotion tool. In contrast coupons, which are widely used in the developed countries, are rarely used. Even in Japan coupons do not have widespread use. Coupons are distributed differently in various countries. In the United States freestanding inserts account for the major share of coupon distribution while in-ad couponing (for example, coupons within a grocery retailer advertisement) is the favorite in Canada. Newspapers and magazines are the most popular means in the United Kingdom while Spain and Italy utilize in/on-pack promotions for their coupon distribution. In some European markets coupons are distributed door to door.

The international/export marketer needs to address many issues concerning its relationship to local management of promotion activities. Headquarters should be concerned with how to help improve local practices; to upgrade local performance in terms of their overall impact, productivity, and, where needed, contribution to the building of an international brand franchise. What is needed will depend to an extent on whether the brands involved are local and do not need international coordination (for example Nestlé's Excella coffee in Japan), global with a widespread international presence and a high degree of uniformity in worldwide brand promotion (for example Swatch, Benetton, and Coca-Cola), or are regional using regional uniformity in promotion (for example Polaroid's Image System used in Europe). Obviously the major coordination task is for regional and global brands.

12.3.3 Publicity

Publicity, which is any form of nonpaid significant news or editorial comment about a company, its practices, its personnel, or its products, is a major component of the *public relations* activities of a company. Public relations is the marketing communications function that carries out programs designed to earn public understanding and acceptance: it should be viewed as an integral part of the export marketing effort. There are, of course, some exceptions but the trend is toward closer coordination of public relations activities, which are designed to accomplish marketing objectives.

The marketing purpose of public relations activities is to achieve objectives that cannot be achieved by other means or achieved as cheaply by other means. For example, if a company wants to gain recognition as one with social responsibilities in foreign locations, this objective may often be accomplished much more effectively by a carefully planned campaign to receive favorable editorial mention than by using paid advertisements. The context and source of the message may play an important role in how it is perceived and interpreted and whether or not it has the desired impact on attitudes of consumers, government officials, or other persons with whom a company wants to have a favorable reputation.

Among the most widely used tools of public relations are press releases and prepared editorial material. Such material is often prepared for new products, the opening of new plants, the achievements of the company, the activities of company personnel in community or governmental activities of locally recognized merit, the favorable impact of the company on the local economy, the role of the company as a local employer, or the contribution that a company makes to the country.

In many companies public relations materials for international use originate from the domestic operation. A few, however, attempt to solicit ideas and materials from foreign operations. For example, a clipping service may be maintained to demonstrate the success of local public relations activities. Or a story may be written on the successful application by a foreign customer of the company's product; in such cases pictures may be taken, and the material offered to an appropriate trade journal as editorial content. Reprints of such material may then be utilized by sales people in other export markets.

It should be remembered that publicity is not an export promotion activity in the same way as the others are. Although an exporter can attempt to influence the reporting of news about itself and its activities, the decision to carry out such reporting is out of the hands of the exporters. As companies become more involved in global marketing and the globalization of industries continues, it is important that a company recognizes the value of international publicity.

Public relations practices in specific countries can be affected by cultural norms, social and political contexts, and economic environments. Often there are large differences in such practices. In the developing countries the best way to communicate might be through the market square, or the chief's court. In most of the industrialized countries local, regional, and national newpapers, television, and so on, are the traditional mass media for public relations. The technology-driven communication revolution that has ushered in the information age, however, makes public relations a profession with truly global reach in the future. Faxes, satellites, high-speed modems, and the Internet allow public relations professionals to be in contact with media virtually anywhere in the world.

12.3.4 Advertising

Advertising may be defined as any paid message placed in a medium. International or global advertising is the use of the same advertising appeals, messages, art copy, stories, and so forth, in multiple country markets.

There seem to be several reasons for the growing popularity of international advertising. International campaigns attest to management's conviction that unified themes not only spur short-term sales but also help build long-term product identities and offer significant savings in production costs of a campaign. Regional trading areas such as the EU are experiencing an influx of internationalized brands. Second, the potential for effective global advertising also increases as companies recognize that some market segments can be defined on the basis of global demography – youth culture, life styles, and so on, rather than ethnic or national culture. Global advertising also offers companies economies of scale in advertising as well as improved access to distribution channels.

It is a rare exporter who does not use advertising of some type, even if it is no more than being listed in an export directory. In various countries government regulations may limit the type of advertising and the media to be used. But most foreign markets are open for advertising of some type. Even in the People's Republic of China the doors are increasingly open to advertising by exporters. But advertising there must be deeply rooted in Chinese cultural values and social and economic practices that the government considers nonthreatening. Consumer advertisers, for example, are focusing on the younger population segments that have greater spending power (Zhou and Meng, 1997). In 1999 an agreement was made between the government-run broadcaster Chinese Central Television

(CCTV) and an Australian company, Bo Long International, which opened the door for Australian companies to advertise on Chinese television. Australian advertisers were offered ad slots in and around a program called *World Sports*, which was to began airing in early 2000. The program focuses on Australian sports. Prior to this arrangement only advertising campaigns initiated in China or by Chinese agencies were allowed on CCTV.

An interesting form of advertising is through sponsorship of sports and sports teams. Regarding the latter, European soccer (football) teams in the various national leagues in Europe have been sponsored for years by multinational companies such as Philips Electronics and Siemens. The Chinese mobile phone manufacturer China Kejian Co. sponsors Everton, a team in the English Premier League, and China's Yanjing Beer, through its US distributor Harbrew Imports, has a sponsorship arrangement with the US National Basketball Association team the Houston Rockets. A key player on the Houston team is China's Yao Ming. On a larger scale in China, Adidas-Salomon sponsors the national soccer team, Coca-Cola sponsors the national basketball team, Siemens backs the first division soccer league, and Philips Electronics sponsors the national women's soccer team and the university soccer league (Balfour, 2003). Other multinationals are sponsoring other sports activities in China: Pepsi sponsors teen soccer; Adidas funds camps dedicated to the sport; and Nike has started a high school basketball league.

Climate for advertising

To a large extent the potential viability and effectiveness of export advertising depends upon the *climate* for that advertising in the foreign markets of concern. The climate for advertising is the result of a set of factors operating within a socio-economic and cultural system that determines if the system views advertising as a desirable activity, and reacts accordingly, or if it views advertising as a threat or a waste, and reacts negatively (Exhibit 12.3).

EXHIBIT 12.3	Dimensions of the climate for advertising

The climate for advertising is evaluated best through a review of underlying economic, social, and cultural conditions, popular attitudes, and legislation related to advertising.

The underlying economic, social, and cultural factors

- *Economic system.* A liberal economic system based on a market economy is more favorable to advertising than a centrally planned economic system. However, even a centrally planned system may, once in a while, use advertising to adjust demand to planned production.
- *Social structure.* Modern social structures tend to accept advertising because it fits within their dynamic outlook of the future; traditionally oriented societies do not accept advertising easily because it is viewed as a dangerous change agent, upsetting the status quo.
- *Cultural background.* Among modern societies the acceptance of advertising is not the same everywhere; some countries have a cultural background that fosters individualism while others are more prone to foster gregariousness. There is no evidence that advertising is more successful in one surrounding than another, but it seems that people in relatively individualistic societies are likely to view advertising as an invasion of privacy and tend to be more vocal in their criticism of advertising.

- *Religious climate.* Countries that are dominated by very dogmatic religious groups (and for that matter by dogmatic groups of any kind) tend to feel more negative toward advertising than those where a climate of benign tolerance exists (dogmatic groups tend to be found in traditionally oriented societies).

The underlying legal and political factors

- *State monopoly.* Certain countries own and operate all or part of the mass media, especially broadcast media.
- *Censorship.* The practice of controlling the content of mass media is widespread, especially in socialist countries, dictatorships, and in most of the developing countries. Censorship affects the media in terms of reach, program content, and cost structure.
- *Restrictions on advertising.* Restrictions may be total or partial and may affect all mass media, or only selected ones. Restrictions may affect certain product categories and not others. For example, in the early 1990s all tobacco advertising (including sports sponsorship) and most liquor advertising (except for most wines) were banned in France. Similar laws exist in Australia, New Zealand, Canada, and Vietnam. Prior to its sovereignty change, Hong Kong passed legislation that banned tobacco advertising at sports events. Since 1999 print and display advertisements cannot be used. In effect, this ban effectively stops tobacco sponsorship of major sporting events there. Some countries permit radio advertising but restrict television advertising. Other countries restrict the advertising of certain products, for example alcoholic beverages and cigarettes, on television. Furthermore, other countries restrict advertising by taxing it or by putting a ceiling on advertising deductions for income tax purposes. Still another form of restricting advertising is the practice of limiting the number of advertisements broadcast per day over certain media, for example television. Some Latin American countries have legislation discriminating on the basis of the origin of advertising copy. Other countries such as Germany restrict severely the techniques that can be used in advertising, such as prohibition of the use of superlatives or comparisons. Almost all countries have some legislation dealing with the truth of advertising claims. In Saudi Arabia business executives have endorsed the regulation of advertising aimed at children or dealing with products potentially harmful to the public, whereas the Singapore government in the mid-1990s banned all advertising that included gifts, special discounts, and incentives for credit card holders. Within the EU, Sweden is the first country to introduce a ban on advertising to children under the age of 12. Similarly, the Flemish region of Belgium bans advertising aimed at children for five minutes before and five minutes after children's programs. Greece bans television advertising of toys.

The number, type, and characteristics of media vary considerably from country to country. There are two broad categories of media of interest to the export marketer: (1) *international* media – those media that circulate, or are heard or seen, in two or more nations, and (2) *foreign* media – local, domestic media. For contiguous countries, such as Germany/Austria or Canada/United States, local media from one country may be heard or seen in the other.

International media

The term 'international media' is often used in reference to business and consumer magazines and newspapers that circulate in many countries. International media attract a relatively minor share of the advertising expenditure of exporters; the great bulk is spent in local, foreign media. Nevertheless international media are important for some companies.

International print media originate from a number of countries, primarily in Europe and North America. For example, *Time* and *National Geographic* magazines and *The Wall Street Journal* newspaper have a US home base, while the *International Herald Tribune* is published in Europe and elsewhere, but is owned by US companies. *The Wall Street Journal* also has a regional version, *The Asian Wall Street Journal*, published in Hong Kong. The *Financial Times* and *The Economist*, in contrast, come from the United Kingdom.

Technical business publications are also of great importance in certain industries such as agriculture, automobiles, construction, farm equipment, electronics, frozen foods, medical and pharmaceutical products, metalworking, petroleum, paper and pulp, plastics, and transportation. Technical publications aimed at engineers and scientists sometimes cut across a number of industries.

International print media are often published in several languages. Thus regional or country 'buys' are frequently available. They sometimes have surprisingly high readership as well as an excellent reputation as a source of information on foreign products.

Television is no longer only a local medium as in the 1980s, because technology and satellite transmission have created the potential for expanded use of television as international media. In Europe, pan-European television stations exist nearly everywhere, for instance in the United Kingdom, Germany, France, Italy, and The Netherlands. Their coverage extends beyond the EU to include eastern Europe, and the western part of Russia. Reception is obtained through cable television, either CATV (Cable Television available from commercial companies covering sections or all of a community) or MATV (Master Antenna Television, which is localized cable in apartment houses or hotels). Obviously satellite television has led to many changes regarding availability of television in countries that prohibit the use of this medium for advertising or which limit the times, days, and when during a program advertising can be used. In Chapter 8 we identified the media empire of News Corp., which includes satellite and cable television channels throughout the world.

Foreign media

The availability and suitability of local advertising media vary considerably from country to country. But, with the exception of broadcast media, major types exist in virtually all markets. Some of the lesser developed countries have no television at all; and in some developed countries television and radio are not available for commercial advertising of branded products. This situation is changing rapidly, however, as regulations are being liberalized, especially in Europe.

Media patterns differ from country to country because of cultural, sociological, economic, and even psychological differences between countries. We will discuss here, briefly and generally, each of the major media categories. It should be recognized that within a country there will always be some overlap between the audiences of the available media.

There is a great deal of variety in the types of *newspapers* and the reading habits of people from country to country. In countries where literacy is high, such as Canada, the United States, and the developed countries of Europe, the great majority of the population reads a daily newspaper. In other countries – those characterized by low educational levels, a low rate of literacy, and low consumer incomes – coverage of consumer markets by the press is very poor. Readership of the press may be limited to small portions of the market in the middle and upper socioeconomic groups. Some countries have national daily newspapers whereas in other countries newspapers are local.

When using newspapers in a foreign country, or any print medium for that matter, the advertiser should make sure that the readership class matches the appropriate target market. Some time ago a New Zealand company using a national newspaper in the United Kingdom (the *Daily Telegraph*) ran a mail order campaign similar to one done in their home market. The campaign was not successful because they should have been appealing to readers of the *Daily Mirror* and the *Sun*.

Foreign *magazines* are often a difficult medium for export advertisers to use. In Europe, for example, there are literally hundreds of consumer magazines, each with a very limited circulation compared to, say, the national magazines in the United States. Technical and business magazines, which are often considered an important part of the media mix for industrial advertising in such countries as Canada, the United Kingdom, Germany, and the United States, do not exist in many markets. Often either the lack of periodicals or the excessive number of small circulation periodicals forces export advertisers to rely less heavily on these media than they would otherwise prefer. Yet there are exceptions.

Posters, *signs*, and *car cards* (forms of outdoor and transportation media) are used quite frequently in low income countries, such as those in Latin America. In European countries posters are quite popular, especially on kiosks or the sides of buildings. Large billboards, which are particularly appropriate for viewing by a motorized populace, are not common in most countries, except for use near main traffic arteries in major metropolitan centers. Much outdoor advertising is designed for viewing by pedestrians or those who use public transportation. Buses and streetcars are major means of transportation and reach large, important audiences. Posters are usually intended to be read by people who are going somewhere and are preoccupied with other matters; they are designed to attract attention to, or to serve as a reminder of, the product.

Dandy, a large Danish confectionery company specializing in chewing gum, focuses its advertising in Russia on outdoor advertising primarily with billboard posters of their chewing gum brand, Dirol. In Russia, Dandy is one of the dominant confectionery competitors with high market share. Colgate Palmolive, on the other hand, started its toothpaste advertising in Russia by placing ads on buses. The Colgate advertisements were part of a strategy to develop increased awareness of its products among consumers and dentists. Finally, as illustrated in Figure 12.3, Vodafone uses buses to promote its company in Sydney, Australia.

FIGURE 12.3

Bus advertising in Sydney, Australia

The *cinema* is an important advertising medium in some countries (for example Italy and Denmark), especially in those without top quality press or broadcast advertising facilities. However, the importance of this medium is decreasing. Many cinemas, especially in small countries, sell commercial time. And, since attendance is often very high, even in poor countries, cinema advertising can be used to reach a high percentage of urban audiences. An attractive feature of cinema advertising is that an accurate estimate of the audience exposed to the commercial (attendance) can usually be obtained either from government tax records or from the files of theatrical film distributors. Cinema advertising can be useful to introduce new products requiring demonstration, or when color is important. It has a captive audience, which is not distracted by competing messages or other ongoing activities. Generally the impact can be considered high.

Radio can be an important advertising medium for products with a broad market. Radio tends to be used more widely in Latin America than in Europe. In Europe, the radio medium seems to be of greater interest in local and/or regional markets. Also, the medium is of special value when the literacy rate is low. It penetrates to the lowest socio-economic levels, reaching at reasonable cost otherwise inaccessible potential market segments.

Television is well developed as an advertising medium in an increasing number of countries. The greatest progress has been in the relatively affluent countries that permit commercial television to operate with a minimum of restriction. Some countries in which television is government owned permit television advertising, but restrictions are usually severe and have limited effectiveness. For example, in some countries commercials are bunched together and shown only at certain times. In other countries advertising may not be shown after a certain time in the evening and may not be shown on certain days or on holidays. In still other countries some products such as alcoholic beverages, tobacco, and pharmaceuticals may not be advertised by this medium.

The markets reached by television in many countries are relatively small and include primarily the privileged few. Television advertising is especially useful for packaged consumer goods and widely used consumer durables in which rapid technological developments and changing fashions or tastes play an important role in successful marketing. Television is especially helpful in demonstrating product benefits or to show the product in use. The number of major commercial television channels in Europe, for example, continues to grow.

The growth of new forms of mass communication, by satellite television and the integration of telecommunications and computer systems, will in the future not only create new 'buying systems' but will also increase the potential for the encouragement of a new cultural setting, which will reformulate the company's use of the television media. For example, in 2003 Honda had developed an unusual television commercial, a two-minute film called *Cog*, that it released on the Internet. This commercial shows 86 distinct parts from a Honda Accord dancing around using a roll, pirouette, and flying along the floor. Honda UK tested *Cog* on BSkyB's fledgling interactive television system in England. A relatively small number of people saw the film. However, more than 10,000 viewers requested additional information on the car. To obtain this kind of response through regular direct mail, Honda would have had to spend close to US$1 million. On BSkyB it spent about US$32,000 (Battelle, 2003).

Direct marketing can often be a useful part of a sales and advertising program. It can be useful as a direct action vehicle, to solicit orders directly, or in a supporting capacity; it can be useful to members of the export marketing channel, as a dealer or agent stimulator or aid, or to reach ultimate consumers. Direct marketing can take many forms – mail, letters, catalogs, technical literature, telephone, fax, Internet – and it can serve as a vehicle for the distribution of samples or premiums. A major problem in the effective use of direct marketing is the preparation of a suitable contact list or database. At the household level, for example, it should be recognized that there are big differences between countries in the levels/volume of direct marketing contacts, even within as developed an area as the EU. Consequently, response rates and effectiveness of direct marketing campaigns will differ between countries.

Users of direct mail in a direct marketing campaign aimed at households have to contend with regulations regarding acquisition and use of information about people and households. This concerns the purchase and sale of 'mailing lists.' Increasingly, governments are concerned over privacy rights of individuals. The European Commission, for example, is attempting to devise common guidelines on data use and protection across the countries of the EU. There is a directive stipulating that consumers should be told, at the time of collection or the first opportunity thereafter, about all possible uses of their personal details. The use of these data must be compatible with the need for the data. In addition, the consumer must have the express opportunity to be excluded from any such list.

Ordinarily direct mail and telephone/telemarketing can be handled best by local foreign distributors, or agents. The objectives of such campaigns are usually local objectives, for example to provide samples, to tell customers where they can get the product, or to announce a special sale. At the same time, however, direct mail and telemarketing can be a major tool for the exporter to use in reaching potential overseas customers and distributors, as can fax and the Internet.

Online advertising

Advertising on the World Wide Web is generally acknowledged to take place when an advertiser pays to place advertising content on another web site. It can be contended that each web site is in itself an advertisement since it can inform, persuade, and remind customers about the company or its products and services. However, a company web site is not strictly an advertisement in the conventional sense since money is not exchanged to place the content of the web site on a medium owned by a third party.

Advertisements placed on sites usually take the form of *banner advertisements*. These are so called because they are usually placed across the top of the web site. The power of banner advertisements is that they can be targeted at a particular audience. Companies will pay for banner advertisements for two main reasons: (a) in the hope that the customer will click on the advertisement and then will be exposed to more detailed brand information on the company's web site, (b) all visitors to a page will see an advertisement, either noting it consciously or viewing it subconsciously. This may help to establish or reinforce a brand image. Amazon (www.amazon.com) for example, advertised extensively on the Internet to help raise awareness of its brand. In the early 2000s the Mexican Tourist Board used banner ads that link back to its web site and posted these ads on various travel-related sites such as Orbitz and Expedia to increase traffic and awareness of the destination and activities available in Mexico.

Banner advertising is often thought of simply in terms of its function in driving traffic to the web site. There are, however, several outcomes that the international marketing manager may be looking to achieve through a banner advertising campaign. Cartellierie *et al.* (1997) identify the following objectives:

- *Delivering content.* This is the typical case where a click on a banner advertisement leads to a corporate site giving more detailed information on an offer.
- *Enabling transaction.* This is the case if a click through leads direct to a sale.
- *Shaping attitudes.* An advertisement that is consistent with a company brand can help build brand awareness.

- *Soliciting response.* An advertisement may be intended to identify new leads or as a start for two-way communication. In these cases an interactive advertisement may encourage a user to type in an e-mail address. The use of interactive banners is increasing and might for example include entering the amount of loan required to give an indication of its costs or entering the destination of a flight to show the cheapest fare available.
- *Encouraging retention.* The advertisement may be placed as a reminder about the company and its service.

Banner advertising is typically paid for according to the number of web users who view the web page and the advertisement on it. These are the 'ad impressions.' Cost is typically calculated as CPM or cost per thousand (*mille*) ad impressions. Some representative CPMs vary from US$20 to US$80 depending on the site; however, the rates are under pressure (*Forbes*, 2000). More expensive sites are likely to have a more specialist audience with a higher disposable income or to be related to specific keywords, as in the case of Yahoo!

The exporting company can place its banner advertisements through *advertising networks*. Advertising networks are collections of independent web sites from different companies and media networks, each of which has an arrangement with an advertising broker to place banners. For example, one of the best-known advertising networks is DoubleClick, which operates in the United States and through worldwide franchises. The network offers advertisements in a range of different areas such as automobiles, finance, health, and entertainment.

In contrast to advertising networks, an *affiliate network* is a collection of web sites that link to an online retailer in exchange for commission on purchases made from the retailer. The Amazon Bookshop is the best exponent of this online marketing technique. According to Chaffy *et al.* (2000), Amazon has over 300,000 affiliates, which offer small banner advertisements on their sites that when clicked on will take the user of their site through to the Amazon site. The network includes many major portals, for example Yahoo! Each partner earns up to 15% commission every time a customer clicks on the advertisement and then buys a book or other item at Amazon. Links to Amazon also occur on search engines such as AltaVista, where links to Amazon are given according to the kind of keywords typed in.

Many international advertisers such as Kraft, Heinz, Coca-Cola and Unilever that have prospered by advertising in traditional media are concerned as to how they can exploit the new medium. Lately, several consumer goods companies have created online communities on the World Wide Web for their brands, and are thereby building new relationships with their customers that enable consumers to communicate with each other. Many famous brands have developed online communities through bulletin boards, forums, and chat rooms, such as Disney (http://family.go.com/boards), the Shell International Petroleum forums (www.shell.com), CNN (http://community.cnn.com), and Bosch tools forum on www.boschtools.com. Heineken (www.heineken.com) allows individuals to establish their own virtual bars, where as bartender they can chat with other visitors or meet their friends.

In traditional brand relationships communication flows between the marketer and the consumer. Lately, brand-based online communities have demonstrated the potential benefits of dialogue flowing between consumers via two utilities: real-time 'chat' taking place in 'chat rooms' and discussions that play out over days, weeks, and even months in discussion forums or bulletin boards. Brand-based online communities have a distinctive focus. The audiences may be geographically dispersed in time, but they share common interests that are perhaps difficult to serve profitably through other international media. The online sites thrive because they offer their participants the following:

- a forum for exchange of common interests;
- a sense of place with codes of behaviour;
- a meeting place for specialists;
- the development of stimulating dialogues leading to relationships based on trust;
- encouragement for active participation by more than an exclusive few.

The popularity of interactive communication gives the brand web site an abundance of 'free' content from the consumer community. Consumers' benefit from their ability to recognize in each other 'people like me' and to form genuine relationships with like-minded people. Both the content and possibility of forming relationships with other buyers and with the brand's managers act as a magnet, drawing consumers back to the site on a frequent and regular basis. This enables further commercial opportunities for the brand owners and legitimizes the investment in web site development and maintenance. In this respect, connecting the brand site and the social aptitude of community participants potentially creates a new marketing tool.

By making sure that consumers can interact freely with each other and build a friendly online community, marketers can follow consumers' perceptions about and feelings toward the brand in real time. The value lies precisely in the volume of communication and interaction generated between consumers. The more communication and interaction, the stronger the community, and the better the feedback. Interactive online media will enable marketers to sense market forces with unprecedented accuracy and efficiency, overcoming the limitations of today's one-way research methods.

Any brand can develop an online community. However, not all brands allow for much customer involvement. Some brands enjoy a natural focus by virtue of their high-involvement product offerings. For example, Bosch, a German manufacturer of power tools, hosts a forum for trades people and do-it-yourself enthusiasts to swap information and suggestions, including prices, which brand of power tool to buy, and how to fix cracks between walls and ceilings (www.boschtools.com).

Other large consumer companies have built popular communities around associated interests. On its family.com site, Disney operates one of the liveliest bulletin boards targeted at mothers. Its discussion topics deal with parenting, marriage, health, food, education, holidays, and many other issues. CNN hosts many discussion forums and chat sites, generated in part from viewers of its broadcasts and in part from its regular audience that seeks out CNN when traveling. Not surprisingly, CNN has an active community of business travelers who share tips about packing, rate worldwide restaurants, and debate the hand luggage policies of various airlines (community.cnn.com).

Media mix

In terms of general effectiveness in accomplishing advertising objectives (see Exhibit 12.4), the capabilities of media in various countries are similar. Newspapers are a good medium to indicate where and at what price a product is available; magazines are suitable for reaching specialized audiences or for promoting products that require considerable explanation or perhaps display in color; outdoor or transportation advertising is good for brief visual messages; television and cinema are appropriate to demonstrate a product in use, especially when it is mechanical or when a demonstration is desirable.

International print or broadcast media are often useful as part of a corporate

EXHIBIT 12.4   Media objectives

Media are often evaluated in terms of the following:

- *reach* (the number of individuals or households reached);
- *frequency* (the number of times a message is delivered to target audiences);
- *continuity* (the pattern of message delivery);
- *size* (the space or time unit employed);
- *availability* (the extent to which a medium can be used and how it can be used).

Selection of media on the basis of whether or not they accomplish the objectives of desired reach, frequency, continuity, size, or availability is a somewhat mechanistic approach. Also to be sought are measures of the qualitative characteristics, for example the credibility and reputation of the medium, and general impact of messages that are carried by the medium. Some media are better suited to demonstration of a product in use while others are better suited to portray the color or other physical characteristics of a product. Thus different media may assist an advertiser with different communication objectives. Finally, there is the matter of costs. The media plan must be feasible within the limits imposed by the budget.

advertising program, designed essentially to accomplish broad objectives relating to the reputation and nature of the company as a well-known, responsible producer of certain products or as a respected member of the business community, serving the needs of society and the economy. International media audiences are often relatively influential, either as members of the middle and upper socio-economic groups or as specialized professionals in a given industry. Therefore international media may be used to enhance a company's reputation or prestige, or to reach opinion leaders, high-level government officials, foreign corporate executives, scientists, and others who may be in a position to influence the climate for the company's products or services.

International media may also be useful in reaching markets in which local foreign media are unavailable or, if available, are not sufficiently developed or suitable to provide coverage of and impact on the relevant persons in a market. For example, farm equipment manufacturers may advertise in international print media that are read by farm equipment dealers.

International media may also be useful to develop a uniform or at least a harmonious image in a number of relevant foreign markets. For example, an automobile manufacturer, an airline, an oil company, or a tire manufacturer – in view of the fact that significant segments of their markets frequently travel from country to country – may wish to advertise in international media in order to develop a uniform reputation throughout foreign markets.

Although international media can be used to accomplish specific promotional objectives, it does not follow that they can often be used to the exclusion of foreign media. In fact, companies are coming to depend more and more on foreign media, while continuing to refine their knowledge of the particular role that international media can play as a part of the total promotional program.

12.3.5 A concluding comment

Each of the forms of export (or international marketing) promotion discussed in this section has special strengths, but each also has significant weaknesses. For the most part these characteristics should be viewed as *relative* rather than necessarily absolute.

Personal selling can often be the most effective form of promotion in the context that the ratio of sales made to number of prospects contacted is usually higher than in nonpersonal promotion. In contrast, the major disadvantage of personal selling is its high cost per sales contact as compared to other forms of export promotion. Export sales people often travel great distances and remain away from home for long periods of time. Expenses 'on the road' are quite high.

It is difficult to generalize about sales promotion because it takes so many forms. Many techniques (sales aids, displays, training, and so on) are used to improve the sales performance of channel members or personal sales people. Participation in trade fairs and exhibitions is frequently successful for export marketers because it combines, in one place and in a short time period, personal contacts by company representatives with a large number of potential buyers. Sales promotion activities may also coordinate advertising and personal selling by helping both company sales people and channel members (for example distributors and agents).

A major advantage of publicity is its credibility. People who do not believe advertising claims about a product or company often believe the same claims when they are exposed to them as a news item.

In contrast to personal selling, advertising has the advantage of reaching many potential buyers at a relatively low cost for each contact. It is the form of promotion best suited for mass promotion. For example, *sponsorship of events* – sporting, cultural, and so on – has been successful for many companies. It is difficult to attend a major international sporting or cultural event in Asia without being aware of the presence of large tobacco companies such as Philip Morris (motor sports and the arts), RJR (tennis and rock concerts), and BAT (track and field, and the arts). Because of increasing government regulation tobacco sponsorship is on the decline. Other sponsorship activities include European schoolroom campaigns targeting children beyond traditional television as follows (Stewart-Allen, 1999):

- Procter & Gamble sponsors 3-on-3 basketball as a way of keeping fit on its European Sunny Delight bottles.
- News International and Walkers potato chips sponsor books for schools, where schools collect coupons from News International newspapers and the chip packets in exchange for books.
- Unilever's Stork margarine has its 'Make it, Bake it' program to promote baking in home economics classes.
- Earlier in this chapter we mentioned that Pepsi, Adidas and Nike are sponsoring youth sports in China.

A major limitation of advertising is its all-too-frequent failure to convince a significantly large share of the people exposed to it to buy the advertiser's product. In all fairness to advertising, it should be recognized that certain approaches are designed to have a longer-run impact and, as such, advertising's impact may be cumulative.

Also, sometimes the objective of advertising may be one of communication only, such as creating awareness. Finally, it is difficult to measure the true impact of advertising on sales because the individual main effects of all marketing variables cannot be separated.

Advertising as mass promotion is used most with the export of consumer goods to create brand/product acceptance in a broad target market. Industrial advertising uses specialized media to contact relatively smaller numbers of prospects. Often its main purpose is simply to 'open the door' for personal selling.

Sometimes companies engage in unorthodox forms of promotion in their search for brand loyalty. Coca-Cola is a case in point (Foust and Grow, 2004). In the

United States the company has targeted teens by testing 'teen lounges' in Chicago and Los Angeles, where teenagers can watch music videos, listen to music, play video games – and, of course, buy Coke drinks from a see-through vending machine. In the United Kingdom the company has launched the 'myCokeMusic.com' web site, where more than 250,000 songs can be legally downloaded. In Venezuela Coca-Cola has taken a prominent role in the popular television show *Who Wants to Be a Millionaire?*; players are asked Coke trivia questions that are integrated into the show's content. These are illustrations of Coke's apparent movement away from its traditional 30-second TV advertisements.

12.4 Promotional programs and strategy

Although the export (international marketing) promotional program is an integral part of the export (international marketing) marketing mix, it can be visualized separately as a subsystem (a collection of interrelated activities) that we will call the promotional mix or a promotional program. A promotional program is a planned, coordinated, integrated series of efforts built around a single major theme or idea designed to achieve predetermined communication objectives. A promotional program may include such activities as consumer product advertising, corporate advertising, personal selling, sales aids, and a wide variety of sales promotional activities. Promotional programs may be geared to either *prototype standardization*, in which minor modifications are made to some basic strategy, or *pattern standardization*, whereby a strategy is designed from the start to accept modification to fit local conditions, yet still keeping sufficient common elements to minimize the drain on resources and management time.

An example of globalizing the brand image of Unilever's ice cream business is shown in Exhibit 12.5.

EXHIBIT 12.5	Globalizing the brand image of Unilever's ice cream business

Unilever, world market leader in the ice cream business, was competing globally with a multidomestic strategy. At the beginning of 1997 the company considered globalizing its ice cream operations in the 130 countries where its products were marketed. In Europe there was a separate Business Group for ice cream and frozen foods. In North America ice cream was handled by a Business Group that was in charge of all Unilever's food products categories. In the rest of the world the Business Groups responsible for ice cream were also responsible for all other corporate products, including cleaning and personal grooming articles.

Reasons for changing Unilever's international image
There were four main reasons why Unilever started thinking about changing its ice cream brand image: market trends, new consumers, life styles, and individual brand images in different countries.

The ice cream market had undergone significant changes through the 1990s. Competitors were going global, placing more emphasis on their global brand name than on local brands. A good example of this was Mars' and Nestlé's global repositioning. Unilever was not benefiting from this globalization (i.e., tourism, overspill media, etc.) due to the use of different brand names and logotypes in different countries. In Europe, for example, Unilever used different brand names, although the same products and product brands in most of its subsidiaries had been gradually introduced over the last decade. Miko was the Unilever brand in France, Ola in Portugal, Wall's in the United Kingdom, and in Italy Unilever sold its ice cream under the Algida brand.

Furthermore, production was becoming increasingly highly concentrated. The industry's largest groups were unifying their production centers and reducing the number of suppliers to one or two for each ingredient.

In a situation such as this advertising was becoming tremendously important in the ice cream industry. Winning a single percentage point in market share translated to sizable profits for the large groups. The value of brand name products was becoming far greater than the value of local products.

Market studies carried out in various European countries revealed the weak points of Unilever's different ice cream brands. Among the shortcomings reported were the following:

- The brands had a seasonal image and were largely associated with summer.
- Customers perceived the brand images as somewhat out of date.
- The logotypes of the various brands were perceived as less than dynamic and somewhat old.

Market studies further revealed that although consumers were familiar with Unilever's different brands they did not associate them with the parent company. It seemed as though the time had come to search for a more uniform global brand.

However, not all Unilever's European subsidiaries were convinced that ice cream products in a single brand were such a good move. There was considerable reluctance on the part of some subsidiaries. Some local companies had logotypes of their own, which were quite strong in their particular markets, and they were therefore less than enthusiastic about any change in the corporate image.

'The best provider of the best ice cream product'

After carefully studying the situation, the group's management team thought it was time to radically change the different brand images. Their aims were to:

- shape a more up-to-date image that would strengthen Unilever Group's position as a market leader;
- transmit a more dynamic, natural, and fresh image;
- reduce costs through synergies attained;
- give the image an international identity.

There were many different options, given that the group manufactured in 80 countries and distributed its products in an additional 50. There were doubts about how many countries should be affected by the change in image, how the new image should be focused, whether one of the existing brands could be extended to other markets or whether an entirely new brand should be created. There were also doubts about whether a single image would be globally accepted, the different sorts of impact this image would have in individual countries and the consequences and implications of any major change.

At this point Unilever decided to get in touch with a London-based corporate design specialist. With the go-ahead of its advertising agency, McCann Erickson, Unilever commissioned the specialists to design a proposal that would enable the company to achieve the following goals:

- obtain a clear international brand position based on the following proposal: 'The best provider of the best ice cream products, providing the perfect ice cream to suit everyone's needs and moods every time';
- reinforce the corporate image;
- change the corporate communication strategy;
- shape a contemporary image that would give the brand the relevant position in the market;
- create a friendly, dynamic, and innovative image;
- develop an image associated with fun, happy moments when ice cream is an appetizing choice.

The Unilever decision: a new global brand image and local brand names

A new logotype was introduced in 1998 as the house brand of Unilever's ice cream products throughout the world. But this logotype was to be combined with each subsidiary's local brand name, so the high awareness of each local brand in its corresponding market would not be lost. This decision aimed to gain most of the benefits of using a global brand and avoid some of the drawbacks. Unilever was attempting to place stronger emphasis on the logotype, as Nike does with its 'swoosh.'

An implementation plan with different stages was designed. It was decided to change to the new global image in different stages: the countries in the northern hemisphere were to use the new global image starting in February–March 1998, the countries of the southern hemisphere had to adopt the new image as of September–October 1998. The exception was those countries in which a local subsidiary had been recently acquired.

By mid-1998 market research studies were conducted to measure consumer acceptance of the new logotype. The results were quite positive: the new logotype was regarded as dynamic, modern, distinctive, innovative, etc. It was reported that the new image had problems in two places: some Arab countries and the Basque country (in Spain). In some Arab countries the new logotype has a certain resemblance to the graphic writing of 'Allah' and was therefore rejected. In the Basque country the rejection of the logotype was for political reasons. The red and yellow colors used are the same as the colors of the Spanish flag. Using a different Pantone color closer to orange than to yellow solved this problem.

In all, the new general global logotype was successfully introduced. Some awareness studies conducted in Europe after the campaign revealed that brand awareness in most countries was similar to what it had been before the introduction.

At times a company whose identity, though strong at home, is relatively unknown in foreign markets finds it advantageous to attach its company identity to a known, respected entity in its targeted foreign market(s). This would involve what is called co-promotion. For example, when the US-based FedEx wanted to increase its name recognition in Europe, the company teamed up with Benetton, an established name there. FedEx sponsors one of Benetton's Formula One racing cars in Europe. In dual sponsorships, companies need to join with an overseas partner that has a common objective with them. FedEx joined with Benetton's racing team because their image fit with its brand, which connotes the image of speed and high technology. Another example is shown in Figure 12.4.

Planning export promotional strategy involves the following:

- setting promotional objectives;
- deciding on the types of advertising and promotional messages;
- selecting media;
- determining how much time, effort, and money to spend.

FIGURE 12.4 Co-promotions are beneficial when both parties deem their products or services suit each other, as in these examples of LEGO joining with Kellogg's and McDonald's (used by courtesy of the LEGO Group)

The possible objectives of promotional efforts are indeed large in number. For example, they might include not only creating an awareness and interest in a company's products, but also creating a favorable name and reputation in the minds of customers, distributors, suppliers, or even foreign governmental officials or regulatory agencies. Usually it is best to establish specific attainable goals. While it may sound fine to support the marketing of a product around the world, it is much better to try to accomplish specific objectives such as these:

- to convince buyers of the durability of a product;
- to illustrate the effectiveness of the product in satisfying a particular want;
- to create an image of the company as a dependable supplier.

Preliminary steps in the planning of an export promotional program include an assessment of the size and extent of markets, customer behavior and buying habits, and competitive circumstances. Consideration must be given to the channel(s) of distribution that a company uses (including original entry strategy) both between nations and within each foreign market; a promotional program may vary according to whether a company sells direct or through wholesalers; or it may vary according to the type of retail channels utilized, especially regarding the cooperation to be expected from channels. The nature of the product line, brand policies, the price of the product, and other aspects of the overall marketing effort must also be considered.

With the appropriate information at hand on markets, competition, channels, product characteristics, and price, a company can formulate its general promotional strategy. For example, the company can decide whether to depend mainly on consumer advertising to presell the product and pull it through the channel of distribution, or to depend mainly on distributors, agents, or dealers to give the product satisfactory push to help customers make up their minds at the point of sale. Then the company can decide on the advertising platform and the timing of the several stages of the campaign; and the company can make decisions on specific advertisements and media. Finally, the company can add up probable costs to arrive at the total cost of the program: a proposed budget. Then, the budget can be examined to be sure that it is within general company guidelines. If not, it will have to be justified to the satisfaction of management, or the promotional campaign will have to be revised.

Since advertising is the dominant form of sales promotion, we discuss in the remainder of this chapter two major issues facing export marketers in planning advertising strategy and tactics: (1) whether to standardize across markets, and (2) transference of a successful campaign from one market to another.

12.5 Standardization or adaptation?

An overriding issue facing export marketers is whether standardized advertising can be used across countries or whether each market is so unique that it needs to have advertising developed solely for it (individual market adaptation). There has been a great deal of discussion and research about the issue, but no consensus for an answer.

In a review of the, at the time, nearly 40-year debate on standardization or adaptation in international advertising, Agrawal (1995) concluded that practitioners alternated between the adaptation approach and the standardization approach. A preference for localization in the 1950s, due to a lack of familiarity with international consumers and markets, shifted toward standardization in the 1960s as knowledge of international markets improved. This was followed by a reversal toward greater adaptation in the 1970s as a result of the rising nationalistic forces and some well-publicized advertising blunders that occurred during the 1960s. Then there was the second reversal toward standardization in the 1980s, which witnessed the rise of multinational advertising agencies. In the last decade of the 20th century the trend was more diffuse, however; the few surveys on multinationals report the use of a combination strategy or adoption of a more localized strategy (Yin, 1999). A recent study of wholly owned subsidiaries of US, European, and Japanese multinational corporations in China, Hong Kong, Singapore, and Taiwan found that patterns of advertising standardization varied based on national origins of the MNCs (Samiee *et al.*, 2003). The subsidiaries of US-based companies are likely to pursue a standardized advertising approach, whereas the Japanese are least likely to standardize.

There are different schools of thought regarding the standardization vs adaptation issue. At one extreme is the belief that basic human needs, wants, and expectations today transcend geographical, national, and cultural boundaries. Consequently, any differences between countries are viewed as being of degree, not of direction. The values and lifestyles of people in different countries may be similar. One approach to measuring this is the Values and Life Styles (VALS) methodology developed by Mitchell (1983). Nine distinct VALS categories of people have been identified and these represent market segments based on lifestyle variables, values, and demographics as shown in Table 12.5.

At the other extreme is the view that even though human nature is the same everywhere a Dane will always remain a Dane, and an Australian will always remain an Australian. In the view of this group, different cultures create different needs, although there may still be similar *basic* needs. This means that people may not be satisfied with similar products and communication appeals and approaches. For example, Polish people have been reported as being irrational, sensitive, and

TABLE 12.5

VALS categories

Need-driven groups (poverty-stricken people with no real economy and unhappy with life)
1. Survivors: tend to remain depressed
2. Sustainers: continue to struggle to get ahead

Outer-directed groups (oriented toward others and the environment)
3. Belongers: conservative, traditional, family oriented, and happy with life
4. Achievers: successful, self-reliant, and happy; they have arrived!
5. Emulators: striving to be as successful as achievers, but have difficulty reaching this goal, are low in self-confidence, and dissatisfied with life

Inner-directed groups (internally motivated)
6. 'I-am-me's': in transition and tend to be young, active, and innovative
7. Experientials: seek direct, vivid experiences, tend to be experimental, self-reliant, and happy
8. Societally conscious: concerned with social issues and living in harmony with nature

Combined inner–outer directed group
9. The integrated: psychologically mature and tolerant

emotional, so in advertising to them these qualities have to be appealed to. Similarly, Asian countries have been characterized as each country being an 'individual minefield of social factors.' Strategies appropriate for Indonesia will not work in South Korea. A number of successes by companies following each extreme indicates that the approach to use is largely situation specific, particularly among product type. In some ways each person in the world is the same, and yet no two people are exactly the same.

Thus, each person is a cultural *communicator* and a cultural perceptor. When export advertising is being done the advertiser's cultural background affects message form whereas the recipient's cultural background determines message perception (Hornik, 1980). Another possible confounding aspect may be whether the respective cultures differ in context. Differences between low-context and high-context cultures have major implications for the export advertiser.

In high-context cultures (for example much of the Middle East, Asia, and Africa), the meaning of a message cannot be understood without its context. In contrast, in low-context cultures (North America and much of western Europe) the meaning of a message can be separated from the context of use and understood by itself. Such differences suggest that advertising messages developed for low-context cultures may not be effective in high-context cultures and vice versa.

The appeal of standardized export advertising is that it provides a number of opportunities to the company doing the advertising:

- *Present a worldwide company/product/brand image.* In the early 1990s the Italian apparel firm Benetton created a very controversial worldwide advertising campaign. This campaign replaced the 50 different campaigns that the company had in 50 different countries. The advertising was to create a message directly from the company without showing a product. This campaign included ads showing people of different races laughing, hugging, and kissing; and photos of an oil-coated bird, a newborn child with the umbilical cord still attached, and a man dying of AIDS. According to Luciano Benetton, chairman of the company, these ads were a consequence of the company seeing the world as a whole. It wanted to touch themes that were common to countries worldwide. This advertising has been both award-winning and banned (Lynch, 1993).
- *Lower costs of preparing advertisements and implementing an advertising*

program. In the mid-1990s Colgate Palmolive, a large US-based packaged consumer goods firm, saved a lot of money when it replaced 20 separate local advertising campaigns for laundry detergent with a series of successful commercials developed in France. This single campaign ran in 30 countries (*Business Week*, 1996).

■ *Reduce message confusion in areas where there is media overlap* (for example Canada/United States, Germany/Austria, Denmark/Germany) *or country-to-country consumer mobility* (for example throughout western Europe).

These opportunities may still be possible without adherence to a strict interpretation of standardized advertising.

One reason, perhaps even the major reason, that there is such controversy regarding standardization, and no consensus in research evidence, is that the concept of standardized advertising has been used too simplistically. It has been suggested that a more realistic approach to defining standardization would be to recognize that it has two versions, as mentioned briefly previously in this chapter (Onkvisit and Shaw, 1999). One version is *prototype standardization*, in which the same advertisement(s) or campaign(s) are used in multiple export markets with the only difference being language translation, and perhaps even a few idiomatic changes (see Exhibit 12.6). Even if prototype standardization is the goal of management, differences in product line, size of market, and media availability may influence the actual degree of standardization used. Based on a worldwide survey Exhibit 12.7 shows how foreign corporations advertise in China.

EXHIBIT 12.6   Wow goes global

Some years ago, Grey Advertising, Inc., a large advertising agency located in the United States, was involved in the development of an advertising campaign to help market the Wow bra in 12 countries. Wow was a product of International Playtex, Inc. The idea was to create a standardized campaign that would work in all the countries. That is, Grey wanted to develop a global advertising campaign based on a single commercial that could be used with minor changes wherever the product is sold. Such a campaign can save an advertiser a large amount of money in the production of advertising. At one time in the past Playtex had 43 different versions of advertisements being used throughout the world.

Major problems in creating a global advertisement include logistical problems and management resentment. Managers responsible for operations in individual countries may resent having an advertising plan and campaign imposed on them. In addition, government regulations and varying industry standards in different countries make sound logistics management critical. All this means that it is, in many ways, more complicated to develop a global advertisement than to produce advertisements in different languages.

It is essential that the advertising be based on the idea that specific versions of the product vary in their appeal. For example, lacy bras were the preference of French women whereas Americans favored plainer, opaque styles. The appropriate product version could then be inserted into the advertisements for each market. Although the style of the product varied for each market, the advertising message was the same. A single product feature was emphasized, which it was felt had universal appeal – extra support and shape without the use of underwires.

Included among the major changes for individual markets were that in some markets (for example the United States and South Africa) fully clothed women showed the product rather than modeled it directly. Also, some of the television advertisements were

20 seconds in length while others were 30 seconds.

This global campaign allowed Playtex to present one unified message in the markets of concern. At the same time the company was able to save money. The total cost of the single global advertisement was US$250,000. In the past, the cost of producing a single advertisement for the US market was US$100,000.

The start of versions run in Britain, Germany, and Spain had minor differences. There were subtle differences in the nonverbal communication (via positioning) of the three models in each version. Yet all versions covered the three basic hair-colors (red, blonde, brunette) and the dresses worn were the same and were appropriate for the models' hair color.

| EXHIBIT 12.7 | International advertising strategies in China |

China with its 1.2 billion people has become the largest emerging market in the world. The advertising industry has boomed, and international advertisers have also rushed in for a bigger share of the market.

A survey of international advertisers in China (Yin, 1999) investigated how international corporations advertise to the Chinese, what advertising strategies they use, and what factors influence the determinations of advertising strategies used in China. Out of 873 international companies that reported advertising in China in 1996 189 responded to a self-administered mail questionnaire. These were companies from 16 countries that engage in 13 types of business. The survey reported the following results:

- *A combination strategy was the popular choice.* A predominant majority of the companies surveyed use a combination strategy, that is, partly standardized and partly localized.
- *International advertising agencies were the favorites.* Of the seven types of advertising agencies, international agencies were the ones used most, followed by home-country agencies and corporate in-house agencies. This suggests that foreign advertisers in China need the experience of the international agencies in foreign markets.
- *Localized language was rated the most important.* Of the seven advertising components studied, localizing language to blend with local culture was rated as most important in advertising transferability. Next in order of importance were the need to localize product attributes, models, colors of advertisements, humor, scenic background, and music.
- *'Acceptance of the brand name' was perceived to be the key to advertising transferability.* Of the 20 environmental factors surveyed, acceptance of the trademark or brand name was rated as the most important in effecting transferring foreign advertisements to China. Next in importance was the group of factors concerning the Chinese economy, the market, and the advertising industry. Last in order of importance was the group of factors concerning Chinese cultural values, level of government regulation, attitudes toward spending money, and degree of nationalism in China, etc.

The survey also showed that the advertising strategy used was related to the rated importance of localizing language and localizing product attributes, and the rated importance of 3 out of the 20 environmental factors studies: attitudes toward the country of product origin, attitudes toward collective needs, and attitudes toward authority.

Chung (2003) reports on the experiences of New Zealand and Australian firms regarding standardization of marketing strategies in Greater China markets.

In contrast to prototype standardization is *pattern standardization*, which is more planned and flexible. Under pattern standardization the export advertising campaign, including its overall theme and individual components, is designed at the outset for use in multiple markets and is developed to provide a uniformity in direction, but not necessarily in specific detail. Thus pattern standardization need not differ significantly from a policy of individual market adaptation. In 1992 Colgate Palmolive was extremely successful (the product sold out in the country in two weeks) in adapting a global television commercial for Ajax all-in-one cleanser for use in Poland during the product's initial launch there. In late 2003 McDonald's launched a new global advertising campaign in more than 100 countries that is designed to increase business with a younger image and a new slogan – 'I'm lovin' it.'

A number of different aspects of international advertising are subject to standardizing, including the following components:

- target markets;
- product positioning;
- campaign objectives, campaign themes;
- media objectives;
- basic media mix, media schedules;
- creative execution – visual and copy.

12.5.1 Appeals

Export advertising appeals must be in accordance with tastes, wants, values, and attitudes; in short, in harmony with the prevailing mentality of the market.

For example, the health appeal varies in effectiveness from country to country. Belgians are hard working, earn a good living, and spend freely. They appreciate the good things in life. They desire comfort in clothing, heating, and home facilities. They are fun loving and appreciate radio, television, beer, wine, and other products that add to the enjoyment of life. To a Belgian, 'good for you' means pleasurable. He or she will buy if the taste pleases, even if it is bad for their health. Likewise, in France, the suggestion that the use of a certain toothpaste will help prevent dental caries is likely to be less effective than in the United States, since the French are not as inclined as Americans to be concerned about the numbers of cavities in their teeth.

In The Netherlands health attitudes are quite different. The Dutch show greater concern about their health than the French. To the Dutch the vitamin content and energy value of some foods are more important than taste. At the same time, however, vitamin content and energy value have the connotation of health food, for example sprouts, alfalfa, and muesli. Very stolid eaters, the Dutch like fresh, traditional foods such as farm products, for example, ready-scrubbed new potatoes, where freshness and presentation are very important. Some may question whether strong coffee, spirits, high-fat meats, cheese, and potatoes – all favorite foods of the Dutch – constitute a very healthy diet. What this can suggest, however, is that the effectiveness of an appeal in a foreign market may vary within the country and product class.

For products that are identical physically but which are used differently from one market to the next – for example corn starch, cake mixes, instant coffee, margarine, and many other food products – the advertising message may have to be adapted for each market segment. However, a number of years ago Campbell Soup, in order to show active people on the move around the world and at the same time to underscore the universal appeal of Campbell Soup, commissioned the filming of a 60-second film spot that included a high-speed train in Japan, a market scene in Singapore, and a children's playground in Puerto Rico. It was dubbed into a number of languages, including Cantonese, Spanish, and Creole, for cinema presentation in 20 countries.

12.5.2 Illustrations and layout

Illustrations and layout are perhaps more likely to be universal than other features of advertisements. Certain types of illustrations can be used in several nations. For example, many years ago advertisements for Canadian Pacific Airlines (now known as Canadian Airlines International) that were created in Mexico City appeared not only in US and Canadian publications but also in newspapers in such places as Tokyo and Hong Kong. The advertisements were originally planned for people in cities along the company's Latin American routes, but the airline found much of the work also suitable for worldwide use. A company spokesman said: 'It's one of the best campaigns we've got going. It's too good to limit it to Latin America. A slight change in copy, and we find it does the job as well for us in Vancouver or Hong Kong.'

The campaign to which the Canadian Pacific Airline spokesman referred had several features that may account, at least in part, for its wide suitability. The advertisements displayed large attention-grabbing photographs, usually with no more than 20% of the space used for copy. For example, a picture of a Canada goose, a symbol of the airline, was captioned, 'He knows the best routes south, so does Canadian Pacific.' Short and simple copy with the same message, of course, can be written for other routes. More recently, a three-minute television advertisement for Chivas Regal whisky was created by an advertising agency in Thailand and shot in western locations, for example in jazz clubs. The actors were Eurasian who looked western and therefore glamorous but were also eastern and therefore familiar. Since the Eurasians are not really identifiable as Thai, Chinese, or Malay, a pan-regional approach was used in running the ad in Thailand, Hong Kong, Taiwan, and Singapore. In the previously mentioned campaign of Benetton in the early 1990s, the same controversial pictures were used throughout the world.

Perhaps some forms of artwork are understood universally, and hence sometimes the same illustrations may be appropriate in different markets. Playtex used the same illustration of three models at the start of its commercial in the United Kingdom, Germany, and Spain, changing only the brand name Wow, shown in the background, to fit the language.

On the other hand cultural influences may dictate that illustrations for the same product must differ from country to country. In German and Danish magazines an advertisement for cheese might show a large foaming glass of beer with the cheese, which would whet the appetite of a Bavarian and a Dane. But in France an advertisement for cheese would more appropriately substitute a glass of red wine for the beer.

Sometimes an advertisement – or a campaign – may use a celebrity as an illustration. Sports figures and actors are often used. An unusual example is that of an Australian car rental company that ran advertisements a number of years ago featuring Monica Lewinsky, who was well known throughout the world because of her relationship with the then president of the United States, Bill Clinton. The ads showed her picture with the words '... no frills' coming from her open mouth and the headline, 'half the rate.'

12.5.3 Copy

There is considerable diversity of opinion with regard to the translation of copy from one language to another. On the one side are those who warn against translations. They point out that while mistakes can be made in any language, even by local copywriters, it is more likely that they will be made if advertisements are prepared in one country, translated, and inserted in international or foreign media without review by competent local linguists. Procter & Gamble attempted to market Pampers disposable nappies (diapers) in Thailand by stressing their convenience. This was a direct translation of the campaign developed in the United States. After some research it was discovered that Thai women worried that using the product might identify them as bad mothers, interested more in their own comfort than that of their babies. The campaign was changed to emphasize night-time use of Pampers, and that the disposable nappy would stay drier than cloth ones, resulting in babies being more comfortable at night. This approach has been successful in getting Thai women to buy Pampers.

With regard to whether to prepare new copy for a foreign market or to translate the domestic copy, it seems reasonable to conclude that an advertiser must consider whether the translated message can be received and comprehended by the foreign audience to which it is directed. Anyone with a knowledge of foreign languages realizes that it is usually necessary to be able to think in that language in order to communicate accurately. One must understand the connotations of words, phrases, and sentence structures, as well as their translated meaning, in order to be fully aware of whether the message will be received and how it will be understood. The same principle applies to advertising, perhaps to an even greater degree. Difficulty of communication in advertising is compounded, because it is essentially one-way communication, with no provision for immediate feedback. The most effective appeals, organization of ideas, and the specific language, especially colloquialisms and idioms, are those developed by a copywriter who thinks in the language and understands the consumer at whom the advertisement is directed. Thinking in a foreign language involves thinking in terms of the foreigner's habits, tastes, abilities, and prejudices; one must assimilate not only words but customs and beliefs.

There are things that the export marketer can do in trying to avoid translation errors (Ricks, 1999, pp. 154–9). First, even if a company has a good translator nearby, it is desirable that a local person also be hired as a supplementary translator, one familiar with the local slang and unusual idioms. Second, use the technique of back-translation when developing advertising messages. Its value is illustrated by the situation faced by an Australian soft drink company entering the Hong Kong market. The company had its successful slogan 'Baby, it's cold inside' translated into Chinese. When back-translated into English, the message read 'Small mosquito, on the inside it is very cold.' 'Small mosquito' was a local colloquial expression for a small child, but it did not convey the intended English slang word 'baby' to refer to 'woman.' Third, under certain conditions it may be possible to use the language of the exporter. For example, in Denmark one finds much cinema advertising presented in English. Obviously, a significant proportion of the target market must understand the exporter's language.

12.5.4 Some generalizations

Generally speaking most advertising people would agree that it is unlikely that standardization can be successful for all products, for all countries, and in all export markets. Thus the critical question is: when will this approach be successful and when not; and what criteria can be used to make a judgement on this question?

The factors that will influence the appropriateness of standardized advertising for various export markets and market segments include the following:

- *The type of product.* There are certain universal selling points for some products – for example razor blades, electric irons, automobile tires, ballpoint pens – that are sold primarily on the basis of objective physical characteristics.
- *The homogeneity or heterogeneity of markets.* When aggregate characteristics such as income, education, and occupation are alike, individual consumer characteristics such as needs, attitudes, and customs may also be alike, thus suggesting that the advertiser use the same selling points.
- *The characteristics and availability of media.* For example, if specific media are available in one country but not in another, certain messages and materials may not be usable.
- *The types of advertising agency service available in each market segment.* For example, if in some markets only poor service is available, a firm may be forced to rely on centralized control of advertising.
- *Government restrictions on the nature of advertising.* For example, some governments prohibit certain types of messages.
- *Government tariffs on artwork or printed matter*, which might offset a cost advantage of centralization.
- *Company organization.* If a company is organized to conduct business on a multinational basis, and if personnel are available, the standardized approach to advertising may be feasible; for example, if a company has subsidiaries it can often control advertising better than if it relies on independent licensees.

People the world over have the same needs – such as food, safety, and love. But they sometimes differ in the ways in which they satisfy their needs. Just as it is important to provide physical variations in products to meet the varying demands of diverse market segments, it is also important to tailor advertisements to meet the requirements of each market segment. But it is the demands of the market segments that are diverse, not the approach to planning and preparing marketing programs. It is only the specific methods, techniques, and symbols that sometimes must be varied to take account of diverse environmental conditions. Therefore international advertisers may be well advised to export their approach to planning and preparing export advertising; but before making final decisions on copy or media they should be sure to consult personnel who know the foreign market intimately.

12.6 Advertising transference

Closely related to the issue of standardization is that of *transferability* (or extension) of a successful campaign from one market (domestic or export) to another market. Whereas standardization occurs when a marketing activity is conducted the same way, or a marketing strategy is the same, in all (or a set of) foreign markets, it does not refer to *how* the commonality was achieved. Transference, which refers to how a marketing activity or strategy 'arrived' in a foreign market, can be defined as the extent to which a marketing activity or strategy is performed the same in a foreign market compared to the market from which it came, usually the home market. Three factors have been identified as having a bearing on whether transfer is a viable alternative (Sheth, 1978). These factors are as follows:

1. The expectations and criteria that people use to evaluate a product class in various countries. In other words, what benefits do people expect to get from

the purchase and consumption of a product class? This factor influences *appeals*.

2. The mechanics of encoding and decoding symbolic communications. This represents both the production and consumption of advertising and is reflected by: (a) media availability differences, (b) differing laws and regulations that affect advertising, and (c) cross-cultural differences in receptivity and acceptance of advertising.

3. The 'silent languages' of each country. These affect the background settings for the message to be conveyed.

A simple model of transference assumes that two countries are either the same or different for each of these factors, and this leads to eight different types of extension–adjustment combinations. These strategies are defined as follows:

- *Complete extension*. Under this strategy a successful advertising effort is transferred to other countries without any modification either in content or in media choice. We do find the strategy of complete extension operating in clusters of countries, among Scandinavian countries, for example, and in North American countries.
- *Symbolic extension*. Successful advertising is extended to other countries with modifications only in the background situations. Only minimal modification must be made, since both the appeal and the medium remain the same. A good example of symbolic extension is the substitution of a boy for a girl in the Vicks VapoRub commercials when extended to Arab countries, where boys are more the object of parental affection.
- *Literal extension*. This strategy is most common when buyer expectations and silent languages are the same but encoding/decoding processes are different. In this strategy different media may be used or the same medium may be used differently in the foreign country. This strategy is usually developed in response to differing legal restrictions. For example, cinema houses are a common medium for advertising in Scandinavia but seldom used in the United States.
- *Symbolic and literal extension*. It is probably more common to see both symbolic and literal extensions than either of them alone when a company is marketing a universal product to developing countries. A company such as Coca-Cola, IBM, or Unilever can conceivably create a worldwide advertising effort with the use of this strategy.
- *Simple adjustment*. In this strategy the medium and the background of advertising remain the same while the product is promoted on a different appeal. There are a number of instances in export marketing in which the same product is promoted on widely different appeals. For example, the bicycle is promoted as a commuting vehicle in developing countries as well as in Scandinavia, whereas in the United States it is promoted as a leisure or sports item.
- *Symbolic adjustment*. Under this strategy both content elements, appeals, and background are modified. We find numerous examples of this type of transfer of advertising in most developing countries. For example, a number of prepared or processed foods (such as instant coffee) are advertised on the basis of being modern rather than convenient.
- *Literal adjustment*. This strategy calls for the appeals themselves to be changed and different media chosen to convey them. To illustrate, in the past the advertising appeals used by Gillette in Sweden were directed to compete against dry shaving, whereas they were directed toward encouraging self-shaving in Greece and toward superiority of Gillette compared to other blades in the United States.
- *Complete adjustment*. This strategy suggests a completely fresh approach in a foreign country. Blue Diamond Growers has a practice that even if a

commercial or campaign promoting its almonds is a tremendous success in the home market (the United States), it is not used in any other country. Messages are tailored for each of the 94 foreign countries to which it sells and local people are used to direct advertising.

The United States brewer Anheuser-Busch in 2004 introduced its 'Ants' campaign – not seen in the United States since the late 1990s – into China, where it was a hit. Busch's former US campaigns are also being used in Great Britain, Ireland, and Canada. These campaigns are modified to fit each country's cultural tastes.

12.7 Management issues

Control over planning promotion strategy and selecting media for advertising depends on such considerations as the objectives of the promotional program, the availability of information on the relevant possible promotion forms including media selections, the knowledge and experience of company personnel, and the degree to which promotion, particularly advertising, must be supervised locally to insure proper performance.

For example, objectives that are company-based in nature, rather than local, suggest that control is likely to be centralized at the company level. Or, if relevant detailed information on certain media is available only on the local level, decisions are more likely to be made on that level. Similarly, if local media must be monitored closely to insure proper performance, company representatives and any cooperating organizations (for example an advertising agency) at the local level are more likely to be involved in both planning and control of media strategy.

The situations described above often vary from one part of the world to another, from time to time, from company to company, and from product to product. Thus it is only reasonable to expect that generalizations on the proper control policies should vary accordingly. And the question of centralized vs decentralized control has no universally applicable solution. Regarding media, however, we can identify types for which certain kinds of control are frequently desirable. International media are often used for company advertising and may be used for product advertising to reach markets not adequately served by the local media or in markets in which the exporter does not have representatives to handle local media advertising. For these reasons programs using international media are often planned and controlled at the company level, rather than locally. Also, international media provide extensive information regarding their publications, the markets they reach, circulation breakdowns, and so forth; therefore it is possible for personnel at a central location not only to develop expertise, but to maintain it.

In contrast, the original selection of foreign media is usually left to local personnel. Since media conditions differ greatly between countries, any centralized direction concentrates on policy guidelines on the use of, and criteria for the evaluation of, foreign media.

The basic reasons that those on the local level can do the media selection job better are as follows:

- They know the market better and which media will influence it effectively.
- They know the true costs, fee structures available to local advertisers, and local taxes that apply.

- They know at once whether an advertisement is running at the right time and place and can make necessary corrections without costly delay.
- They can get an advertisement into media with limited time or space, which can be extremely important. In the case of television, time is severely restricted in some countries.

On the other hand, centralized selection of media facilitates utilization of the latest and most sophisticated media selection techniques (if they can be used with the limited data available), coordination of regional or worldwide campaigns, and effective use of information on competitors' activities throughout the world as a base for appropriate counter strategies. Company, product, and brand image as it relates to country of origin is of increasing concern.

The availability of resources, especially technically competent marketing promotion personnel, make it desirable for some degree of centralization in order to be able to integrate and coordinate the major elements in export marketing promotion programs. The emergence of large international advertising agencies with offices throughout the world has facilitated this centralization. Perhaps the idea that a company exporting to many markets should aim for would be the following:

1. centralized strategic planning and policy making, based on information provided by foreign personnel as well as knowledge of company objectives;
2. decentralized planning and execution of advertising and promotional campaigns, with the guidance and assistance of central personnel or successful experience and ideas from other countries.

SUMMARY

In this chapter we have looked at communication and promotion as major activities in export (international) marketing. We started with general comments about communication per se and then looked at export promotion as a form of communication.

Next we looked at the alternative techniques available for export promotion. Specifically we covered personal selling, sales promotion techniques (catalogs, trade fairs, and so on), publicity, and advertising. Most of our attention was devoted to advertising since it is the form of export promotion that is most likely to be used in one way or another by all exporters. The climate for advertising and media types was discussed in some depth.

A short general discussion of promotional strategy was presented and this led to examining the one advertising issue that faces all companies exporting to two or more markets – standardization or adaptation – and the presentation of one model of the advertising transference phenomenon. We concluded the chapter by examining briefly some management issues relating to centralization or decentralization of promotion planning and control.

QUESTIONS FOR DISCUSSION

12.1 What is your interpretation of the term 'climate for advertising'? What factors cause the climate for advertising to differ among countries? Select one foreign country and explain how the climate for advertising in that country is important to an exporter.

12.2 From an exporter's standpoint, what kinds of objectives should promotional messages be designed to accomplish?

12.3 It can be argued that sometimes export marketing promotion activities appropriate for one foreign market are also appropriate in other foreign markets. Do you agree or disagree? Explain.

12.4 Which type of media can be most effective: international or foreign? Explain.

12.5 Explain why individual sales promotion activities might be more effective in some markets than in others.

12.6 In what ways does culture affect export marketing promotion and communications?

12.7 As an export marketer becomes more or less 'permanent' in doing business in multiforeign markets, it almost inevitably faces the issue of standardization vs adaptation of its advertising program. Discuss what you consider to be the best approach for an exporter to use.

12.8 Discuss the main issues involved in deciding whether to centralize or decentralize the planning, developing, and controlling of export promotion strategy and tactics.

12.9 Go to the library and search out print media (that is, magazine and newspaper) advertising by a company, or one of its products or brands in different countries. Does this company use standardized or individualized advertising? Explain.

12.10 What do you see as the 'future' for the Internet as a basic advertising medium and/or a means for implementing sales promotion in foreign markets?

12.11 Go to a European company's web site, an Asian/Pacific company's web site, and a US or Canadian company's web site and evaluate each in terms of its use for marketing communications about the company's product(s). What can you conclude about the promotion strategies of the web sites?

REFERENCES

Agrawal, M. (1995). Review of 40-year debate in international advertising. *International Marketing Review*, 12(1), 26–48.

Balfour, F. (2003). It's time for a new playbook. *Business Week*, 15 September, 56.

Battelle, J. (2003). Downloading the future on TV advertising. *Business 2.0*, July, 46.

Branch, A. E. (1990). *Elements of Export Marketing and Management* 2nd edn. London: Chapman & Hall.

Business Week (1996). Make it simple. 9 September, 97–100.

Cartellierie, C., Parsons, A., Rao, V. and Zeisser, M. (1997). The real impact of Internet advertising. *The McKinsey Quarterly*, 3, 44–63.

Catalog Age, February 1997.

Chaffy, D., Mayer, R., Johnston, K. and Ellis-Chadwick, F. (2000). *Internet Marketing: Strategy, Implementation and Practice*. Harlow, UK: Pearson Education.

Chung, H. F. L. (2003). International standardization strategies: the experiences of

Australian and New Zealand firms operating in the Greater China markets. *J. International Marketing*, 11(3), 48–82.

Clarke, I. and Honeycutt, E. D. (2000). Color usage in international business-to-business print advertising. *Industrial Marketing Management*, 29(3), 255–66.

Cone, P. (1990). How to shoot yourself in the foot and still win the sales race. *The European*, 9–11 November, 22.

Forbes (2000). Digital rules, 22 December.

Foust, D. and Grow, B. (2004). Coke: wooing the TiVo generation. *Business Week*, 1 March, 77–80.

Gesteland, R. R. (1999). *Cross-Cultural Business Behavior*. Copenhagen: Copenhagen Business School Press.

Hornik, J. (1980). Comparative evaluation of international vs national advertising strategies. *Columbia J. World Business*, Spring, 36–44.

Kashani, K. and Quelch, J. A. (1990). Can sales promotion go global? *Business Horizons*, May–June, 37–43.

Leslie, G. (1990). US reps should learn to sell Japanese style. *Marketing News*, 24, 29 October, 6.

Lynch, C. (1993). The new colors of advertising: an interview with Luciano Benetton. *Hemispheres*, September, 23–6.

Madden, T. J., Hewett, K. and Roth, M. S. (2000). Managing images in different cultures: a cross-national study of color meanings and preference. *J. International Marketing*, 8(4), 90–102.

Miracle, G. E. (1987). Feel – do – learn: an alternative sequence underlying Japanese consumer response to television commercials. In *Proc. 1987 Conf. American Academy of Advertising* (ed. F. G. Feasley), R73–R78.

Mitchell, A. (1983). *The Nine American Life Styles*. New York: Warner.

Onkvisit, S. and Shaw, J. J. (1999). Standardized international advertising: some research issues and implications. *J. Advertising Research*, 39(6), 19–24.

Parmar, A. (2003). Objections to Indian ad not taken lightly. *Marketing News*, 9 June, 4ff.

Ricks, D. A. (1999). *Blunders in International Business* 3rd edn. Oxford, UK: Blackwell.

Ricks, D. A. and Mahajan, V. (1984). Blunders in international marketing: fact or fiction. *Long Range Planning*, 17(1), 78–82.

Robles, F. and Akhter, S. H. (1997). International catalog mix adaptation. *J. Global Marketing*, 11(2), 65–91.

Samiee, S., Jeong, I., Pae, J. H., and Tai, S. (2003). Advertising standardization in multinational corporations. *J. Business Research*, 56(8), August, 613–26.

Sheth, J. N. (1978). Strategies of advertising transferability in multinational marketing. In *Current Issues and Research in Advertising* (ed. J. Leigh and C. R. Martin Jr.), pp. 131–41. Ann Arbor, MI: University of Michigan.

Smith, M. A. (1998). Working effectively with the international customer. In *More Secrets of Successful Exhibiting* (ed. V. A. M. Demetros), pp. 183–98. Lake Placid, NY: Aviva Publishing.

Stewart-Allen, A. L. (1999). Rules for reaching Euro kids are changing. *Marketing News*, 7 June, 10.

Taylor, C. R. and Miracle, G. E. (1996). Foreign elements in Korean and US television advertising. *Advances in International Marketing*, 7, 175–95.

Usunier, J.-C. (2000). *Marketing Across Cultures* 3rd edn. Harlow, UK: Prentice Hall.

Wells, L. F. and Dulat, K. B. (1996). *Exporting: From Start to Finance* 3rd edn. New York: McGraw-Hill.

Wiklund, E. (1986). *International Marketing: Making Exports Pay Off*. New York: McGraw-Hill.

Yin, J. (1999). International advertising strategies in China: a worldwide survey of foreign advertisers. *Journal of Advertising Research*, 39(6), 25–35.

Zhou, N. and Meng, L. (1997). *Marketing in an Emerging Consumer Society:*

Character Images in China's Consumer Magazine Advertising. Chinese Management Center, Faculty of Business, City University of Hong Kong, Working Paper No. RCCM97-07-0.

FURTHER READING

Chaffy, D., Mayer, R., Johnston, K. and Ellis-Chadwick, F. (2000). *Internet Marketing, Strategy Implementation, and Practice.* Harlow, UK: Pearson Education.

de Mooij, M. K. (1994). *Advertising Worldwide: Concepts, Theories, and Practice of International, Multinational and Global Advertising* 2nd edn. Englewood Cliffs, NJ: Prentice-Hall.

Fill, C. (1999). *Marketing Communications: Contexts, Contents, and Strategies* 2nd edn. Upper Saddle River, NJ: Prenctice-Hall.

Griffin, T. (1993). *International Marketing Communications.* Oxford, UK: Butterworth-Heinemann.

Miracle, G. E. (1998). Cultural effects on marketing communication. Paper presented at the American Marketing Summer Education Conference, Boston, MA, August.

Theodosiou M. and Leonidou, L. C. (2003). Standardization versus adaptation of international marketing strategy: an integrative assessment of the empirical research. *International Business Review,* 12, 141–71.

CASE STUDY 12.1

Adidas AG

(This case is adapted from Sharen Kindel, 1996, Making a run for the money: Adidas AG, Hemispheres, February, pp. 47–50. Used with permission of the author.)

In 1993 Robert Louis-Dreyfus, former head of the British advertising group Saatchi & Saatchi plc, along with a group of investors, acquired Adidas AG, the German shoe maker headquartered in Herzogenaurch, near Nürnberg. The following year Louis-Dreyfus and his associates unified all operations by acquiring control of Adidas International Holding GmbH, which owns 96% of Adidas AG. At the time of its acquisition Adidas AG was operating like a ship without a rudder due to lack of continuity in its management. Former management had cut marketing expenditures as a percentage of sales in order to show a profit. The result was that brand image was adversely affected.

Brief company history

In the 1920s a German shoe maker, Adolf Dassler, decided to make shoes especially for runners and soccer players. As early as 1928 Olympic athletes started winning medals in Dassler's shoes. This led to the creation of a mystique that grew into legend and helped turn his company into the world's largest sporting goods company.

And then one day the legend, along with Dassler, died. First his wife, Kathe, and then his son, Horst, tried to carry on the company name, trademarked as Adidas in 1948 (the beginning letters of Adi Dassler's first and last names), but Horst died unexpectedly at the age of 51. And during the time Horst struggled to keep the company going as a firm that made excellent shoes for real athletes, the trend of athletics shoes as fashion statements for weekend athletic 'wannabes' came of age, and Adidas was left in the marketing dust of new companies called Nike and Reebok.

All of Dassler's 700 patents for shoe technology turned out essentially to be for naught in the face of Nike's marketing savvy and ability to rapidly bring new products to market and shift manufacturing from the United States to the Far East. Rudderless, Adidas continued along its old path, until finally, in 1990, the remaining Dassler heirs sold the company in a leveraged buyout to French corporate raider Bernard Tapie.

But even while the company was bumbling along, management made a couple of smart moves which ultimately saved it. The first was to buy out four warring distributors in the United States and create a single marketing entity called Adidas USA. Although Adidas had remained relatively strong in international markets, more than half of world athletic shoe sales are in the United States, so any corporate strategy had to be built around stemming the flow of red ink in the critical US market.

The second smart thing that Adidas did was to hire Robert Strasser and Peter Moore as consultants. Strasser and Moore had been high-ranking executives at Nike until they resigned to form Sports Inc. in 1987. As consultants, Strasser and Moore conceived of a new line of shoes for Adidas, called Equipment. Their success persuaded Adidas to buy Sports Inc. and make Strasser CEO of a new company, called Adidas America, in February 1993. For a brief while things began to look up. Then Strasser died suddenly, and the company was once more adrift.

The turnaround

When Louis-Dreyfus took over he realized that he only needed to do a couple of things to turn the company around: (1) sell Adidas's shoe factories in Europe, (2) move production to the Far East, and (3) increase marketing expenditure.

Indeed, the first thing Louis-Dreyfus did before settling in at Adidas's headquarters in Germany was to go to the Far East to meet with the companies that manufacture most of the world's athletics shoes. The outcome of those meetings was the outsourcing of all production and a revamped logistics unit at Adidas to manage these new relationships. Louis-Dreyfus also streamlined production by reducing the number of items in Adidas's line, which increased the overall profitability of the company. In the late 1980s Adidas produced small quantities of everything needed for every kind of sport. By eliminating some items, and shoring up the productivity of others, company margins increased.

Since Adidas's products are shipped from factories to warehouses that the company maintains in most of its markets before being sent on to local retailers, restructuring sourcing also had the effect of improving Adidas's on-time delivery record, which had been poor for many years. 'What has changed the delivery problem has been getting the whole logistics process correct: better relations with the factory, better quality control, better delivery from the factory to the warehouse,' explains Thomas Harrington, Adidas AG's senior vice-president for marketing communications.

The next thing to do was to change the marketing attitude of the company in order to improve and enhance brand image.

Promotion activities

But selling its factories, outsourcing production, and becoming a marketing organization like Nike and Reebok was the easy part. Reclaiming the brand's image and heritage proved more difficult, in part because Adidas's heritage as the professional athletes' footwear of choice had been usurped by Nike, especially in the US market. Management believes strongly that creating the image that its shoes are authentic and worn by key athletes is critical to its growth and success. One had only to see what Nike did with Michael Jordan to confirm such a belief.

Having a former advertising person at the helm proved to be exactly what Adidas needed to get back into the marketing race. One tactic that paid off worldwide was Adidas's use of what it calls grassroots activities, a euphemism for guerrilla marketing that stretches limited advertising budgets. Says Adidas's Harrington, 'Adidas is not going after the top, high-ticket items, but is doing a lot of activities at the lower levels of sports.'

One event that attracted a lot of attention outside the United States was the creation of the 3-on-3 outdoor basketball tournament to give kids around the world a place to compete with each other. The first world championships were held last September on the steps of the palace in the center of Barcelona. Over 200,000 people watched as teams from 51 countries competed in the two-day event. 'It's things like this that really help drive the brand,' says Harrington. And street ball, along with the sponsorship of the largest high school basketball camp in the United States also helped Adidas chip away at Nike in the sport where it is the strongest.

Adidas had also moved into the area of entertainment cross-promotions. Its Los Angeles-based entertainment division has placed Adidas products on top-rated television shows like *Baywatch* and *Beverly Hills 90210* and slotted them into movies geared to teens such as *The Big Green*. Adidas has outfitted the rap groups Run DMC and Naughty by Nature. Its shoes are even turning up on the feet of people like Madonna and Elle Macpherson.

Its advertising has had to work harder, too. Because the German firm cannot match the advertising spending levels of its US competitors, it has taken a nontraditional path to reach young, urban consumers and persuade them to buy the product with the familiar three stripes. In the United States, Adidas has targeted key metropolitan areas such as New York and Miami and used subway car cards and graffiti-style painted walls to build its image. Adidas changed its approach to advertising in Europe, too. In 1993 the company consolidated advertising, which had previously been done on a country-by-country basis, at the agency Leagas Delaney. Since then the British firm has created pan-European image-building ads that air on Europe satellite TV stations such as MTV Europe.

These innovative tactics had people talking about the brand again, and sales grew. 'The foundation of our business is sports promotion,' says Harrington. 'You have to be seen on real players to get credibility.' But the company realizes that the perception of sports and athletes differs from country to country. That is why the marketing tactics used to achieve that goal vary with the geography.

The situation in the mid-1990s

Although Adidas has not yet regained its place as the oldest, most respected, and most enduring brand of athletic footwear, it is back in the game and gaining ground. Explains Harrington, 'There was a time when we were afraid to talk about the heritage. When the brand was in trouble it made us look old and boring. But now that we're successful again the heritage gives us authenticity.'

And it has paid off in real sales growth. Adidas made a dramatic comeback in the United States, moving from barely 2% of the market in 1991 to 5% in 1994. That does not sound like much, but in 1994 the US athletics shoe market, at $8 billion wholesale, accounted for more than half of the $14 billion world market, so a shift of three percentage points was worth nearly a quarter of a billion dollars in incremental sales.

The company expected double-digit growth through the 1990s and was aiming for 8% share of the US market by 1998. On top of that, Adidas has been able to maintain its leadership position in many of the world's other markets, most notably Germany, Japan, and Argentina while dominating the rapidly growing markets of eastern Europe and the Far East.

Adidas in the mid-1990s was number three behind Nike and Reebok. But it had begun the long march back and could depose the number two, Reebok, at any time.

Questions

1. Evaluate Adidas's decision to source its products in the Far East by contract manufacturing. Is there not a conflict of interest in using companies that its competitors also use? What other sourcing alternatives might have been just as viable?

2. Should Adidas continue with its so-called guerrilla marketing (promotion) activities worldwide? What other alternatives can the company use?

3. Can advertising and promotion activities be standardized? If so, explain why you would favor prototype or pattern standardization. If not, why must such activities be market specific, i.e., individualized?

CASE STUDY 12.2

LEGO A/S

(This case is adapted from one originally written by Svend Hollensen and Marcus J. Schmidt, Scener fra dansk erhvervsliv, *Copenhagen Business School Press, Handelshojskolens Forlag, 1993. Used by permission of the authors and publisher.)*

In 1932 the LEGO company in Denmark began making high quality wooden toys, including stacking and building bricks. In 1947 the company added to its product line by manufacturing plastic toys, including building bricks. The present-day concept was developed in 1949 when the bricks had studs on top. In 1958 a patent was given for a brick that had tubes inside which provided strong clutching power and stability. This is essentially the brick as it is today.

In the mid-1990s the LEGO product was sold in about 60,000 shops in more than 130 countries and over the past 30 years had established itself as one of the leading names in the toy business. Between 200 million and 300 million children and adults play or have played with LEGO bricks. In 1995 the range consisted of 378 sets and no fewer than 1720 elements, of which 481 are DUPLO elements, 968 are LEGO SYSTEM elements, 174 are LEGO TECHNIC elements, and 97 are LEGO DACTA elements – all of them different. The LEGO Group continues to market new ideas: new sets, new components, new ways of building, new ways of playing. But everything is adapted to the children's fundamental needs. High priority has been given to technical quality, product safety, play value, and educational value.

Co-promotion and licensing

In the 1990s LEGO has a well-established brand name. This has enabled it to achieve an annual turnover exceeding DKr10 billion. One thing that has always been very important to the company is its trademarks. Its most common trademarks are: DUPLO, LEGO,

LEGO SYSTEM, LEGO TECHNIC, and LEGO DACTA. The marks are used in ordinary type style and in a particular stylized form. The company is also very protective of its company name and how it is used.

In the early 1990s the company board of directors received the results of consumer surveys which they had commissioned. The 'image power' survey of Landor Associates represented 10,000 adults between the ages of 18 and 65 and was conducted in the United States, Japan, and many parts of Europe (Belgium, France, Italy, Holland, Spain, the United Kingdom, and Sweden).

Image power was defined as a measurement of a brand's strength or impact, combining the consumers' awareness of the leading (global) brands with their perception of the brands' quality. When the survey results were collated they revealed that in the United States and Japan the LEGO brand was not placed among the top 10, but the European results were encouraging. LEGO was fifth in the rankings after four automobile brands – Mercedes-Benz, Rolls-Royce, Porsche, and BMW – and ahead of brands such as Nestlé, Rolex, Jaguar, and Ferrari.

In the United States, the five top brands were IBM, Disney, Coca-Cola, Duracell, and Levis. In Japan they were Sony, Panasonic, Seiko, Canon, and Honda. In addition, an American survey carried out in Europe, the United States, and Japan shows that LEGO ranked thirteenth overall, while a similar survey by a German market analysis firm shows that LEGO, with a score of 67%, is the best-known brand of toy in Germany. Matchbox ranked second with a score of 41%.

The board of directors at LEGO decided to take advantage of this strong brand power and hired a vice-president for a new business area, LEGO Licensing A/S. The purpose of this company was to generate royalties from appropriate business partners that use the LEGO brand name in marketing their own products. The board had learned that Coca-Cola, for example, earned more than DKr3 billion in royalties using a brand-milking strategy, where the brand name, in certain product areas, was sold to the highest bidder.

In addition to licensing the use of its name, LEGO believes in joining other companies that are known and respected leaders in their line of business in co-promotional activities. The company insists on a clear distinction between its products and trademarks and those of its co-promotional partners so as to avoid confusing consumers.

Questions

1. Evaluate LEGO's use of licensing its brand name to others outside Denmark. What type(s) of products would be appropriate?

2. What conditions should be met in choosing an appropriate licensee company?

3. What benefits can accrue to LEGO by engaging in co-promotion activities in markets other than Denmark?

4. What type(s) of products would be most appropriate for co-promotion in foreign markets?

5. What type(s) of promotion activities can LEGO use for such co-promotion activities?

CASE STUDY 12.3

Christa Clothing International

(This case study is adapted from the case Kleider International Clothing, written by Gordon Miracle, Michigan State University.)

Company history

Christa Clothing International is a well-known international company headquartered in Blusen City, North Carolina in the United States. Christa specializes in fashion clothing for men and women.

In 1991 two 30-year-old former university classmates founded an importing business. They purchased cheap fabrics from Indonesia and the Philippines and sold them to garment makers in the United States. These two men, Frank Carmino and Saul Green, built their importing business rapidly and profitably. They soon decided to expand into the fashion business. In 1990 Christa launched two new brands of its own, 'Bluse' for women and 'Jacke' for men. In 1993 they merged the two into an international brand, Blujac. The brand change was made in anticipation of entering European markets.

Christa's success in the United States provided a firm foundation for expansion into Belgium, Germany, and The Netherlands in 1995; followed by Sweden, Finland, Canada, and France in 1996; Denmark, the United Kingdom, Switzerland, and Norway in 1997; Austria in 1998; Spain and Italy in 1999; and Portugal in 2000.

In 2003 company sales (turnover) were more than US$500 million in the North American and European markets. This level of sales was almost 400% greater than sales in 1994, indicating that company growth had been rapid.

Potential expansion

Christa is contemplating Asian markets as a source of future growth, especially Hong Kong, Singapore, Thailand, Malaysia, Japan, and Korea. Recently Mr Carmino visited Korea as a tourist. He was not sure that Korea was necessarily the best choice to enter first, but he had a favorable impression from his visit and from the general characteristics of the Korean market, which he felt had great potential. The economy seemed to be growing vigorously, and competition for fashion did not appear to be as strong as in the relatively more mature markets of Japan and Australia. It seemed to be the right time to move into this growing market.

Before doing any further planning, Mr Carmino felt he needed further information. He knew that the World Bank had reported population and the purchasing power parity measure of gross national income per capita in these countries to be approximately (in 2002):

	Population (million)	GNI per capita (US$)
Hong Kong	6.7	35,060
Singapore	4.1	23,090
Thailand	61.6	6,680
Malaysia	24.3	8,280
Japan	127.1	26,070
Korea	47.6	16,480

Mr Carmino ascertained that the Korean market was open to foreign products, and that several large, well-known international advertising agencies had branch offices or joint ventures with Korean agencies in Seoul. Korea has well-developed mass media and more than 1% of gross national product is spent on advertising. Korean GNI per capita continues to rise as recovery from the Asian crisis continues. Its population in 2002 was 47.6 million and is expected to be 50.3 million by 2015, according to estimates by the World Bank.

Mr Green, who had headed the European expansion, was a little concerned that the Korean cultural, economic, legal, political, and social conditions were somewhat different from those with which he was familiar. For example, he was aware of the following somewhat different cultural, legal, and political conditions: (1) Korea has experienced somewhat peaceful changes in government through what some were willing to recognize as democratic elections; (2) the Korean culture differed from the US culture with respect to language patterns, religions, the level of individualism vs collectivism, the desire for harmony vs confrontational behavior, and so forth. Mr Green had some experience with these kinds of differences and similarities in Europe, but knew he would need specialized help to enter Korea and other Asian markets.

In addition to population, income, and age statistics, market potential in each country depends on many other factors such as local habits and customs of consumers regarding purchasing and use of clothing, availability and consumer use of mass media, and the role of clothing as symbols of the lifestyles of young people.

Recently, Mr Green met Cathy Peters, a young vice-president of a New York advertising agency. She was born in Germany, has a degree in economics from the University of London, and had lived for several years in Japan as a teenager (where her father headed a US–Japanese joint venture advertising agency). She had several years' experience working as an account executive for US products sold in Korea and had been to Korea several times in a coordinating capacity. Her agency has had a joint venture arrangement in Seoul with a Korean agency for some years. Mr Green and Mr Carmino felt that Ms Peters' multicultural background and Asian experience were such that she would be an ideal person to head Christa's expansion into Asian markets.

Ms Peters was hired and given a mandate to study the situation and prepare recommendations to proceed. She began a broad program of desk research to make use of available published statistics and other information available from published sources. She was aware that some companies had tried 'global' branding, advertising, and marketing, and that some had failed while others had succeeded. She was determined to think carefully about the conditions under which advertising objectives, strategies, and executions should

or should not be standardized, transferred (or extended) from existing markets to new markets in Asia, and controlled from headquarters or controlled in local markets (see Table 12.6).

TABLE 12.6	Dimensions of international advertising to be considered for standardization/localization

I.	Advertising objectives
	Communication tasks
	Defined target audience
	Specified periods of time
II.	Advertising message strategies
	Theme
	Appeals
	Positive vs negative approach
	Benefits or product/service attributes
	Information amount and types
	Image vs product attributes
	Comparisons vs no comparisons
	Spokesperson vs voice-over color mix, etc.
III.	Advertising media strategies
	Choice of media categories and vehicles
	Size and length of advertising materials
	Scheduling patterns: continuity, flighting, pulsing
IV.	Advertising budgets
	Heavy, medium, or lightweight
	By product
	By market area
	By customer classification
	By selected media
	For selected creative or message approaches
	Match or not-match competitors
	Contra-cyclical or not
V.	Advertising decision processes

The fashion business

The fashion business is complex. There are many suppliers. Brands emerge and vanish rapidly. The average fashion brand life cycle is normally a maximum of seven years. Market offerings consist of manufacturer brands, fake brands (counterfeit labeled products), private brands, and unbranded products.

Distribution tends to be broad, varying somewhat from country to country, but often including shops (which can vary from cheap, shabby-looking outlets to high-fashion stores or boutiques), chain stores, street markets, mail order, and even selling from the back of a car.

Transactions between traders and retailers are still often made in cash. This fact, combined with the diversity of brands and manufacturers, makes accurate tracking studies of fashion sales, such as Nielsens's, difficult indeed.

Company organization and functions

Christa Clothing is organized to facilitate centralized control of coordination and planning functions. Local offices translate international guidelines and strategies into local strategies and tactics. Headquarters is responsible for:

1. corporate objectives, policies, planning, organization, and finance;
2. design and styling;
3. coordination of production and distribution;
4. marketing and advertising services.

The Christa subsidiary in Manila, the Philippines is responsible for production, quality control, physical distribution, and coordinating production in Indonesia and the Philippines.

There are two main types of country offices in Europe: (1) Christa wholly owned subsidiaries; (2) Locally owned distributors, such as agents or traders that deal with fashion products. Christa prefers wholly owned subsidiaries in larger markets, using locally owned distributors, especially to get started, in new markets.

Local country offices, both subsidiaries and distributors, have the following local responsibilities: sales, physical distribution, pricing, and coordination of advertising and other marketing communication.

Products and market segments

Christa offers fashion collections of casual wear that are coordinated with respect to design. Target groups are teenagers and young adults, mainly 'followers.' These target groups consist of those who are urbane, outgoing, and cosmopolitan. They shop for garments that fit their lifestyle, which is one of an attitude of fun, freedom, and individuality. With Christa, people buy a 'way of life.' It is a reflection of people's need and desire to be different. Therefore Christa emphasizes people's personalities with expressions of freedom, personal responsibility, and individuality. Christa fashion casual wear is leisurewear for young, dynamic, colorful, daring, and internationally oriented people.

Christa has not advertised in the mass media for over a year. The company felt its brands were well known and could depend on the support of retailers. However, brand awareness, liking, and preference have weakened compared to competitors. Christa may have to consider relaunching its brand or replacing it. Further, there is increasing demand for high quality in fashion, and

Christa feels its relatively low quality image may put the company at a competitive disadvantage.

The planning cycle is critical to Christa's success. In the fashion industry it is common practice for retailers to buy the next year's collections approximately six months in advance. Thus the manufacturer knows what has to be produced. The advantage is that there is no inventory problem. Everything produced has already been sold. The only problem is to get the goods delivered on time, as promised. One or two weeks' delay can be disastrous. Often delayed shipments are refused by the retailer. Because of the efficiency of its planning cycle, Christa has a delivery guarantee of 95% while other brands in the market often do not reach 70%.

For fashion casual wear, designs and styles change every few months. Christa offers a broad range of products from basics (simple trousers, shirts, and sweaters) to more stylish and extrovert clothing. They are not really 'designed' products, but, more accurately, are the commercial translations of top designers. The company originally targeted its collections at 15–25 year olds but recently split its primary target markets as follows: 20–30-year-old women and men, and 10–19-year-old girls and boys.

Seasonality

The fashion business is based on four seasons: Spring; High summer-transition; Fall; and Holiday, early spring. Spring and Fall are the major seasons, contributing approximately 80% of total sales.

Physical distribution

International distribution is handled by the Manila office. The local country offices, in turn, distribute the goods to local retailers. In general, Christa casual wear is available in regular shops and large chain stores; often the latter have a shop-in-shop. This means that a special counter or corner is reserved for a particular brand with a selection of its products, providing the opportunity to dress or merchandise the corner in the brand's style. Additionally, large countries (in terms of sales volume) have one or two pilot shops, which stock the entire Christa collection. In addition they offer the opportunity for both retailers and consumers to see, experience, and enjoy the Christa lifestyle.

Pricing

In most countries the Christa collections are moderately priced; not really expensive, not really cheap. Although there is a fixed price the local subsidiary or distributor can adapt prices to the local situation, as long as the unit operates within headquarters' profitability guidelines.

Communication

Christa Clothing International starts with catalogs of the available collection and distributes them to retailers. In 1996 Christa started advertising in Europe and the campaign proved successful. The creative theme was 'Streetlife,' which portrayed young people in the hectic atmosphere of big cities of the world. They are young people who are happy to meet each other and kiss. But the kissing does not denote a love relationship. It is more of a friendly kiss. The fashion is adventurous and extrovert. Christa's expenditure on advertising during the period 2000–3 are shown in Table 12.7.

TABLE 12.7	Christa Clothing International total advertising expenditure (US$000)			
	2000	**2001**	**2002**	**2003**
TV	500	500	1000	1000
Magazines	2100	3900	4100	4900
Newspapers		2000*	400	700
Cinema		400	600	1000
Outdoor	200	200	300	400
Total	2800	7000	6400	8000

* In 2001 a large newspaper campaign was used to achieve brand awareness

Competition

Competition is fierce, with many brands and manufacturers competing in the marketplace. Companies (and brands) competing with Christa include:

1. *Ciao*, a well-established, Italian brand. Ciao advertising is well known: 'United colors of the world.' Usually two completely different young people are shown next to each other, dressed in the Ciao style. Ciao's primary advertising media are magazines and outdoor.
2. *Derci*, the second brand of the Ciao company. It is small but has a distinctive image and lifestyle. Derci's use of media was striking, though expensive. It used the last five or six pages in magazines and turned its advertisements upside down, thus giving the impression that Derci had a magazine of its own. Derci used only magazines.
3. *Eureka*, a well-known US (California-based) brand. The company's collection is targeted at women in all age brackets. It is one of the largest companies in this segment. Eureka advertising campaigns show

beautiful, attractive people and radiate a kind of purity. The main media are magazines and outdoor.
4. *Mode/Statique*: Mode for women, Statique for men. This is a Danish company, mainly European oriented. Its products are middle-of-the-road, not extrovert. The creative aspects of its advertising campaigns have differed greatly over the last few years. The main media have been magazines.
5. *New Male*, a French company. This line is male oriented and comparable to Statique. Media expenditures have been low.
6. *Canonel*, a recently established Italian company, which uses an approach similar to Ciao. However, its products are somewhat more daring. Advertising expenditure is low but includes television.

Ciao, Derci, and Eureka have advertised consistently over the years. The others, including Christa, have been less consistent. Other competition consists mainly of many local brands.

The future

Christa expects to continue international expansion and to become a truly global company. The general preference is for standardization of product design, production, brand image, advertising, and other promotional efforts. In developed countries competition has been fierce, with many brands competing in each market. With the expansion of the European Union internal market in 2004 competition is expected to intensify.

Although Christa has utilized local advertising agencies in each market in the past, it is possible that global advertising may require a global advertising agency. However, one of the big unknowns is how similar consumer-purchasing behavior and product desires are in nonEuropean and nonNorth American markets. On the one hand, certain brands of jeans sell well worldwide. On the other hand, there is great diversity in cultures with respect to the naming of colors, preferences for particular styles, standards of modesty (or immodesty), types of leisure activities, climate, hair and skin colors, what is considered attractive, and so forth.

Questions

1. Should Christa Clothing International enter Asian markets? If so, in which countries, and in what order? If not, why not?
2. Assuming Christa decided to enter one or more of

the Asian markets, what should be the company's advertising objectives, message strategies, media strategy, and budget?

3. Can the company standardize its advertising or must it individualize? Can the company transfer advertising from other markets? Defend your answer.

CASE STUDY 12.4

Nove Ltd

Nove Ltd is a large concern located in Hong Kong that manufactures a line of household appliances in which sales expansion in the past has been very rapid. Actual manufacturing takes place in mainland China. Since Hong Kong is a Special Administrative Region (SAR) of China, the export takes place from Hong Kong while the country of origin of the products exported is China. For certain new products the increase in sales has been so fast that production capacity could not keep up with demand. For one of the new products – electric (dry) shavers – management foresaw and provided for more than normal commercial expansion. Production capacity for these articles has been enlarged to the extent that even in the face of a rapid sales growth, a sufficient number of dry shavers could be manufactured. In view of the enlarged production facilities, more effective sales effort became necessary. Total 2003 sales amounted to 7 million shavers. The 2004 sales target was set at 7.5 million pieces.

In order to put the planning indicated above into effect, a more intensive marketing communication campaign was considered desirable. In countries A, B, and C (countries so designated for purposes of disguise) particularly favorable results were expected from a stepped-up advertising campaign. The approved advertising budget for these countries was therefore separated from the normal sales budget and determined individually. The company's advertising manager felt that for the most effective results, the advertising budget should at least be doubled. In view of the enormous amounts planned for advertising, the management suggested a preliminary investigation in the countries concerned to ascertain why dry shavers in general, and the company's own brand, 'Nover,' in particular, were purchased. Nove intended to obtain arguments that might best be used in its advertising and get some tips for sales promotion.

Consumer investigation

Before the investigation, Nover enjoyed a strong market position in the three countries. Otex was its largest competitor while Porde accounted for an insignificant market share.

Shaving habits

From the answers about shaving habits it appeared that in Country A approximately 100% of the men shaved themselves, while in Country C an important number (23%) went to the barber shop for a shave. The portion of men who shaved themselves daily varied from 13% in Country C to 77% in Country A. The majority of dry shavers were found among the men who shaved themselves daily. To stimulate sales it might thus be useful to promote the habit of shaving daily.

Following a request to indicate the advantages of dry shaving, the most frequent reactions were: ease, speed, and absence of skin irritation. All wet shavers were asked why they had not yet switched to dry shaving. Between 40% and 50% replied that dry shavers were too expensive.

Characteristics of the dry shaver

Table 12.8 indicates, in percentages of total dry shavers, replies made to the question: 'Why do you shave electrically?'

TABLE 12.8	Reasons for shaving electrically		
Arguments	**Country A**	**Country B**	**Country C**
Ease	52	84	80
Speed	38	52	50
Absence of skin irritation	24	52	30
Other arguments	76	64	30
Total	190	252	190

How did users obtain their dry shavers?

It appeared from the market research that an important part of the dry shaver owners had received the shaver as a gift – in Country A, 52%; in Country B, 40%; and in Country C, 40%.

The greater part of those receiving gifts (approximately 65%) had expressed the desire for a shaver themselves. Usually it was a gift from a wife or fiancée (in approximately 60% of the cases). It was also important to determine the place of purchase. Most dry shavers (75% to 80%) were bought in radio shops and electrical appliance stores. An entirely different situation, however, appeared to exist in Country A. There, radio shops and electrical appliance stores accounted for only 30% of sales. Most dry shavers in this country were bought in barber shops and department stores.

Choice of brand

In the process of buying, it is important to know what portion of future buyers has gained information in advance about various brands. It appears that more than 50% of the buyers had in fact formed an opinion in advance about the brand to be selected and intended to ask for additional information. Factors that favored the purchase of a certain brand are expressed in Table 12.9 in percentages of the total answers recorded.

Further investigation of brand choice was based on brand distribution among the shavers in use. The brands in use in each country are shown in Table 12.10.

TABLE 12.9 Factors favoring brands

Motive	Country A	Country B	Country C
Seen in shop and advertisement	28	22	18
Advice of acquaintances	23	26	20
Price of shaver	13	12	10
Advice from shopkeeper	10	11	10
Other reasons	26	29	42
Total	100	100	100

TABLE 12.10 Brands in use

Brand	Country A	Country B	Country C
Nover	24	64	50
Otex	33	8	30
Porde	1	1	2
Miscellaneous	42	27	18

Familiarity with the three brands is shown in Table 12.11.

TABLE 12.11 Brand familiarity

Brand	Country A	Country B	Country C
Nover	67	88	79
Otex	80	33	60
Porde	4	2	15

Replies to a question about the best brand generally favored Otex, rather than Nover.

Results indicated that brand loyalty is very important. In the case of Otex, this loyalty seems to be somewhat stronger than for Nover. In Country C, however, a larger percentage of Nover users seem to be willing to switch brands than among Otex users. Relating the findings about brand switching to the results concerning the best brand (as expressed by wet and dry shavers), it can be concluded that there is a greater preference for Otex than for Nover by the wet shavers. This last observation could be an important aspect in attacking the potential market. Subsequently, the question was raised: 'Which brand are you likely to buy?' Reactions are expressed in Table 12.12 in a percentage of those intending to buy and who at the same time mentioned a brand name.

TABLE 12.12 Brands most likely to purchase

Brand	Country A	Country B	Country C
Nover	14	55	44
Otex	57	22	34
Porde	1	1	11

Factors that favor the purchase of a certain brand

Seen in shop and advertisements

It is known that advertising and sales promotion are important influencing factors. The extent to which this has affected dry shavers, however, has not yet been determined. The number of men, both wet and dry shavers, who have noticed advertising for dry shavers, is expressed in percentages of the group in Table 12.13.

TABLE 12.13 Who notices advertising

Brand	Country A	Country B	Country C
Wet shavers	60	48	28
Dry shavers	67	58	39
Both groups	62	51	30

It thus seems that dry shavers are more quickly aware of dry shaving advertising than wet shavers. This could be explained by the concentration of shaver owners in the higher income brackets. This group reads more, and consequently is confronted with more publicity and advertising matter than the lower-income classes. In view of the high percentage of shaver owners remembering publicity, it is probable that shaver owners in general have an active interest in dry shaving publicity. Of the replies to the question, 'Where, or in which media have you noticed dry shaving advertising?,' those favoring Nover were divided among publicity media as set forth in Table 12.14.

TABLE 12.14 Advertising media used by those preferring Nover

Brand	Country A	Country B	Country C
Newspaper	62	67	29
Weekly magazine	44	39	54
Shop	26	39	46
Posters	3	25	8
Movie	–	8	8
Folders, etc.	3	6	3

Price of shaver

Wet shavers generally regard price as an objection to buying a dry shaver. However, the influence of price in brand selection was not unfavorable for Nover, compared with other brands. In percentages of total Nover shaver owners, price was important in their selection of Nover to 12% in Country A, 17% in Country B, and 12% in Country C. This factor plays an important role in the gift market, where traditionally the cheaper brands are favored.

Questions

1. Explain why Nove Ltd can or cannot standardize its advertising in countries A, B, and C.

2. If advertising can be standardized, what would the advertising program be?

3. If advertising cannot be standardized, what advertising programs should be developed in each country?

CASE STUDY 12.5

Eli's Cheesecake Company

(This case study was written by Mitsuko Duerr and Edwin Duerr, both of San Francisco State University.)

In mid-2004 the president of Eli's Cheesecake Company, Mr Marc Schulman, was reviewing the policies that had guided the international expansion of the firm. In the 1990s the company had recognized the potential for increasing international sales provided by the Internet and the improvements in logistics. The company had moved quickly to exploit that potential.

Eli's opened its first web site in 1995. This helped support the company's policy, 'follow your customer,' by making it easier to continually provide up-to-date information to existing and potential customers, and to facilitate ordering and service processes. It resulted in accelerated growth, both domestically and internationally, and Eli's now exports its products to over 20 countries. In 2003 the state of Illinois gave Eli's its 'Exporter of the Year Award.' In 2004, annual sales passed US$35 million. In addition to its primary business of selling 50,000 cheesecakes per day in over 100 flavors and sizes, the company also offers tie-in products such as sweatshirts that help to spread the company name.

Mr Schulman was now planning to expand into additional overseas markets. This raised questions about selecting the countries into which to expand, possible changes in customer selection procedures, and the possibility of using additional marketing channels or entry modes. Whatever he did, he wanted to be sure that it would be consistent with the original vision for the company and the policies that had resulted in their success to date. In order to assist in the effort, Mr Schulman had asked their former US Sales Manager, Walter Babian, to come back from retirement to be Senior Vice-President of International Sales. Mr Babian was living in Arizona and continues to reside there, an option made feasible by the Internet and fax. While he spends a substantial amount of time traveling overseas to develop and maintain relationships, and some time at the Chicago headquarters, his home can be anywhere.

Company background

Marc Schulman had founded Eli's Cheesecake Company on 4 July 1980, in part to fulfill a dream of his father, Eli Schulman. The senior Schulman was a 48-year veteran of the restaurant business, who had eventually opened a fine restaurant in Chicago, 'Eli's the Place for Steak.' In addition to operating the restaurant, Eli Schulman took a great interest in civic affairs. He participated in and sponsored civic events, provided appropriate (and legal) gifts to organizations and dignitaries, and was host to and photographed with a wide range of important individuals including presidents of the United States. His activities and personality resulted in widespread recognition of, and a great deal of favorable publicity for, his restaurant.

At the restaurant, Eli developed an exceptionally rich and creamy cheesecake that customers began referring to as 'Chicago's Finest.' He had a vision of selling something outside of his restaurant that would carry his name, and his signature cheesecake seemed to be the appropriate product. Eli's vision became a reality when his son, Marc, founded Eli's Cheesecake Company.

The new venture grew steadily through the 1980s following four principles: Always provide high-quality food. Always give great service. Always maintain good relationships with customers and employees. Develop new products, varieties, flavors, and sizes to meet expressed and possible changes in consumer tastes.

The company uses all natural products and is able to avoid the use of preservatives because it can ship by refrigerated containers. As fast and reliable cargo

service has become available to more places, Eli's potential market has grown. They now ship primarily by United Airlines cargo, and also enjoy other relationships with the carrier as noted below.

As a small company with 220 employees, Marc Schulman believes that family-owned Eli's Cheesecake Company is big enough to have the resources to do things, and small enough to be nimble. At a speech at Crain's Small Business Forum in 2000 he indicated that a small business must have focus and passion. The owners are on the hook financially and personally and have a commitment to making it work with a longer-term perspective.

Marketing and sales organization

The company has three people in the marketing department, including the senior vice-president, Mr Babian, plus seven in sales. The senior vice-president spends all of his time on international accounts, reflecting Mr Schulman's objective of increasing sales in overseas markets. Mr Babian is assisted by a representative in England.

Domestic sales presently account for 85% and international sales account for 15% of total sales. International sales, however, are growing at approximately twice the rate of domestic sales. Domestically, 60% of sales are for foodservice operations and 40% are for eventual sale at retail.

Within the United States, the company uses 50 brokers as well as selling directly to some very large customers and selling directly to the public. Internationally, 70% of sales are for foodservice operations and only 30% for eventual sale at retail. Sales through retail outlets in some countries abroad have been limited because of costs and problems in meeting multiple labeling requirements for the relatively small markets. In each of the European countries, they need to have different packaging for their products that will be sold through retail outlets. Internationally, brokers are used in some areas but not in other areas, depending upon conditions and the market structure. Eli's does not generally need to modify their ingredients or recipe by country since they already offer a wide variety of cheesecakes. They have had testing done in France for GMO-free certification (product free from genetically modified ingredients).

Sales in Asia are growing rapidly with the increasing demand for premium American products. Europe is a large overseas market for Eli's Cheesecake. The company is working on a major project with a Japanese company. In spite of conflicts in the Middle East, sales in some areas are continuing. A market has been developed in Iceland.

Overall sales are affected, to some degree, by the level of tourism, and the destruction of the twin towers in New York in 2001 decreased both international and domestic travel. Total attendance at food product and service trade shows has decreased, but the increasing globalization of business has resulted in attendance at most major shows by representatives from companies in many countries. The continuing consolidation of food companies is also providing additional marketing opportunities for medium sized producers such as Eli's.

Mr Schulman sees expansion of international sales as requiring a serious commitment of time and effort. Without such a commitment there is a tendency to fail to respond to the inquiries from abroad because they entail additional attention and effort beyond that involved with domestic orders. This also means that a company must be careful in its international expansion. Because there are so many things going on at the same time, including dealing with many new regulations, developing new packaging for each market that requires it, and possibly developing new channels for sales and shipping, there is a high cost in time, effort, and managerial attention. In efforts to expand overseas the company must not only find customers who want their product, but must communicate effectively and get the product there when promised and in perfect condition. While Eli's takes great pride in the quality of its products and in its service, it has found that overseas customers – particularly in Japan, Hong Kong, and other Asian countries – are very demanding in all respects. The Eli brand name, and what it has come to represent, is what gives the company the advantage over others.

Personal relationships are of particular importance in international dealings. Eli's objective is to meet with each major customer four times per year, visiting each of them twice and having them visit Eli's twice. Both internationally and domestically, Mr Schulman feels that it is essential never to lose the focus on the customer, and face-to-face meetings cannot be replaced by telecommunications alone. Location in Chicago is an advantage for the company since many trade shows are held there. Most major food product distributors and food service companies send representatives to attend shows in Chicago at least once per year.

Product promotion

While Marc Schulman credits the Internet and improved logistics for his company's rapid growth since 1995, it is apparent that the company's policies and his skills in promotion were what made it possible for the company to take advantage of these advances. Mr Schulman has commented that traditionally bakers are not very marketing oriented, but that he comes from a foodservice background where marketing is extremely important.

A major method by which Eli's attracts customers is through participation in trade shows. In addition to participating in US trade shows, Eli's frequently has exhibits at both candy and food product expositions in Europe. They also attend some trade shows in Asia. The US government, and some state governments, have effective programs to assist small and medium-size companies to export. As a part of these programs, companies can obtain places in the US pavilions at many international trade shows. Eli's has had such places at a number of shows, and has found this very useful. Retailers and food service companies that visit their exhibits contact their importers or make direct inquiries to Eli's.

The company does not pay for advertising, except for printing brochures and mini-catalogs, and using its web page. However, it has been extremely effective in gaining recognition through its promotional activities as well as through the quality of its cheesecakes.

Major promotional activities include producing special cakes for special events and for celebrities. It provided Eli's cheesecake at the 1985 Superbowl. In 1987, it provided a 1000-pound cheesecake for Chicago's 150th birthday celebrations, and subsequently provided big cakes for Crain's 20th, the *Chicago Tribune*'s 15th, Chicago's 153rd, Steppenwolf's birthday, DePaul University's 150th anniversary, and many others. In March 1992, then Governor Clinton and Hillary Clinton visited in connection with a program to help associates earn General Education Diplomas. (People working at Eli's are referred to as 'associates' rather than employees.). Eli's provided Inaugural Birthday Cheesecakes in Washington in 1993 and 1997, in Chicago for Hillary's 50th birthday, and at the White House in 1999. A visit to the company's bakery by President Clinton led to a cover story in the *New York Times* and an appearance on *Face the Nation*. The company produced an event for the Gore-Liberman campaign in 2000. Other Eli's Cheesecake fans noted in the company's web site include Jay Leno, The Backstreet Boys, the Italian design team of Dolce and Gabbana, Donna Karan, and Bonnie Hunt. The company participates in various civic activities in Chicago, and provides the use of its parking lot for Chicago's Farmers' Market during the summers. It has partnerships with Wright College, Chicago High School for Agricultural Sciences, Norman Bridge School, New Horizon's Center, and the Chicago Public Library.

Eli's has expanded its partnership with Wright College, one of the community colleges of Chicago, to provide training opportunities for its people. Classes include sales training, database management, regulatory and costing issues and communications through a new City of Chicago Program called TIF Works that funds training through a portion of the real estate taxes paid.

United Airlines (Eli's primary carrier, as mentioned above) has featured Eli's cheesecakes on many of its flights, and an article about the company appeared in the United Airlines publication, *Hemispheres*, in September 2000. In the year 2000 alone, additional articles about Eli's appeared in *eCommerce Business*, *Modern Baking*, *Bon Appetit*, *Chicago Tribune*, and *eCFO*. Excellent reviews have appeared in *Parade*, *The New York Times*, *Chicago Sun-Times*, *News City*, and *Cooks Magazine*.

Eli's also provides a tour of its bakery in Chicago, including a slice of cheesecake, for $3 per person (price in 2001), and will provide luncheons for groups. It has tie-ins with the restaurant, Eli's the Place for Steak, and there is even an Eli's Cheesecake Fan Club that people may join. All of these promotional activities have provided a foundation for exploiting the Internet and modern information technology.

Using the Internet and the World Wide Web

Since Eli's Cheesecake established their first web page in 1995 they have frequently updated it to make it more 'user friendly' and effective as a marketing tool. As of 2004, the web page is in its fifth generation, and is still in English only in the US. Distributors in the United Kingdom and Germany have large web page set-ups devoted to them, with the latter in the German language.

The company's web page, http://www.elicheese cake.com, provides three basic services:

- information about the product, answers to questions most frequently asked by customers and potential customers, the story of Eli Schulman (in keeping with one of the original purposes of forming the company), the company's history, company activities in the greater community, and reviews and comments about the company and its products;
- a way for retail customers to order online and telephone numbers for customers who prefer to call;
- a way for existing Foodservice Partners to access the company's communications network regarding new products, merchandising, recipes, and promotions; a way for potential Foodservice Partners to obtain a username and password to the network.

The material is colorful and attractive, complete without being wordy, and easy to navigate. The *Direct Hit Search Engine*, which analyzes the sites that millions of Internet searchers have visited, gives the Eli web site the highest of its five ratings for relevance and satisfying searchers' requests.

The use of the Internet and commercial software for information and planning purposes has also improved Eli's Cheesecake's efficiency and effectiveness. In 1998, there had been only one Eli employee who knew how to work with their Microsoft Access database, and he had been overwhelmed with requests for reports. Then the company went to an Online Analytical Processing (OLAP) system that lets businesspeople query databases without knowing much about their underlying architecture. This allowed Mr Schulman and several other key users to obtain information and spot trends more easily (Liebs, 2000). This was a step forward in improving the flow of information, reducing the need to make multiple entries, and tying the ordering, producing, warehousing, shipping, and billing functions together. These advances facilitated the accommodation of additional international and domestic customers and sales information and processing. It still did not do the whole job and it was seen that additional steps would be needed. Now the company uses Cognos, a multi-dimensional data warehouse system for keeping track of sales and sales opportunities that provide a basis for future planning. All of their efforts are aimed at developing and maintaining ever closer contacts and relationships with customers and potential customers.

In the overall strategy of increasing international sales, Mr Schulman will be looking at criteria for selecting additional markets, customers, and distribution channels.

References

Interviews in 2000 and 2004 with Mr Marc Schulman, President, Eli's Cheesecake.
http://www.elicheesecake.com
Liebs, S. (2000): 'Store and deliver,' *eCFO*, October.

Questions

1. What factors/actions/characteristics of Eli's have made its web initiative so effective?
2. Evaluate the company's use of promotion vs traditional advertising in light of the type of business it is in. Would another mix of promotion and advertising more efficiently or effectively meet its objectives?
3. Are the apparent objectives of Eli's Cheesecake the same as those you would expect to find in a large conglomerate?
4. What appears to be the emphasis on short-term versus long-term objectives?

5. What channels should Eli's consider in its international expansion?

6. How should Eli's go about identifying potential new markets?

7. How should Eli's go about finding potential new distributors or large customers?

8. Should Eli's consider other methods of market entry such as joint ventures or establishing production facilities abroad?

9. Will the present web page be adequate for the next several years? Why or why not?

10. Should Eli's consider expanding its product line? If so, what additional products might it consider? What would be the advantages and disadvantages of its doing so?

CHAPTER 13

The Export Order and Physical Distribution

13.1 Introduction

The success or failure of the export business of a firm depends entirely upon securing orders from buyers, delivering products in good condition at the correct time, and, most important, receiving payment. This depends upon the correct handling of export procedures. All documents and procedures must be carefully followed in order to avoid violations of the laws of the countries involved and/or refusal of the financial organizations to honor demands for payment. Errors in paperwork (documentation) in export transactions can cause major delays or losses.

Successful handling of the export order and physical distribution depends upon much more than the filling out of paperwork. Decisions must be made regarding the management of all steps and processes in the supply chain that are under the control of the exporter. This, in turn, requires extensive knowledge of the characteristics and costs of alternative methods of packing, transportation, storage, and processing. The availability, costs, and benefits of using facilitating organizations, such as foreign freight forwarders and customs house brokers, must be understood and evaluated.

In the first decade of the 21st century two disparate trends are affecting the costs and speed of international physical distribution. The first is the continuing advance in systems and equipment that is making physical distribution faster, easier, and more efficient. There are continuing improvements in ports, handling equipment, and transportation equipment. There are also improved communications systems and technology including the evolving Radio Frequency

Identification Equipment (RFID) systems, briefly discussed in Chapter 1, for tracking and identifying problems with shipments.

The second is the increased concern over security and the prevention of terrorist acts. This has led to new requirements regarding documentation and to additional inspections. In 2004, truck-sized mobile gamma-ray detectors to spot nuclear materials were already in use at US seaports, and more sophisticated 'second-generation' X-ray machines are scheduled for installation. New equipment to detect particular chemicals and products inside containers is also being used. The eventual objective is to have all containers screened before they are shipped or while they are at sea (Armstrong, 2004). US Customs officials are now being stationed at key ports overseas, with the permission of the host governments. Cargo being shipped to the United States will not be loaded unless the manifest documents are presented to the carrier (and, by extension, to Customs) 24 hours prior to loading. In 2004 similar requirements were being considered for exports from the United States. Both exporters and importers must now take into consideration that deliveries may be delayed as agencies of various governments increase their scrutiny of cargo and choose to inspect more containers.

13.1.1 Differences in customs and practices

It should be noted that customs and practices differ from country to country, and even to some extent in different parts of the same country. A consular invoice (discussed below) is required by some countries but not by others. Dock receipts (discussed below) are used in the United Kingdom and on the United States East Coast, but are not used on the West Coast of the United States. Shipping conferences and rate agreements (sometimes called discussion agreements), designed to control rates and schedules on particular trade routes, are organized, become stronger or weaker, and may be disbanded in certain areas or at certain times. Inbound and outbound freight between the same two ports of the same type or classification of merchandise may pay widely differing rates.

Changes in government regulations may have substantial effects on procedures and costs in distribution. In 1995 the EU removed the requirements for Customs clearance at borders between member nations. This reduced both time requirements and costs for intraEU shipments. In 1996 the United States was the only nation still requiring international ocean carriers to file a tariff (schedule of rates and terms) with the government and use these rates for all customers. A shipping act passed in the United States in 1998 has given shippers and carriers much greater flexibility in arranging and implementing service contracts.

13.1.2 Purpose and organization

The purpose of this chapter is to discuss the successive steps and documents involved in the export procedure. In the following sections each step will be taken up in turn. Some of the essential documents required for order confirmation, shipment, and payment will be exhibited, and the more important aspects of their use and preparation will be discussed. The overall procedure is illustrated in Figure 13.1.

The first part of the chapter will cover the steps involved in receiving and confirming the order. The second part covers the physical distribution aspects – i.e., the options, requirements, procedures, and documents used in shipping the goods. Exhibit 13.1 describes briefly alternative means of communicating internationally.

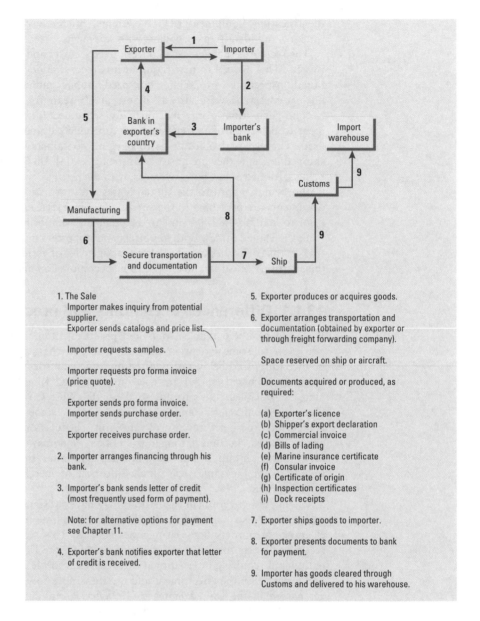

The export procedure

Technology, in addition to providing quick and efficient means of communication between buyers, sellers, and facilitating organizations such as transport companies, also offers new ways to make errors. Some of these errors are simply due to not fully understanding the technology, but sometimes the error happens because the normal or usual ways to detect mistakes do not always work. Thus new technology requires the development of new ways to detect errors (Ricks, 1999, p. 9). For example, in using the Internet it is very important that the web address is completely accurate. If the slightest error is made the resulting address may access a site that is totally inappropriate.

EXHIBIT 13.1 International communications

Rapid changes in communications technology have affected every step in the process of obtaining orders, scheduling and tracking shipments, and receiving payment. As discussed in earlier chapters, the Internet and the systems available on it have had a profound impact on all phases of marketing.

Transportation companies and the parties with which they interface are now being connected by electronic means on single platforms that allow mutual coordination of all phases of their operations. Savings in time and costs are substantial, while errors, delays, shortages, and excess inventories are reduced.

Because of ease of use and speed, e-mail has become the predominant form of general communications in international business. Text messages, files, documents, and forms can all be sent electronically. Electronic signatures are valid in some jurisdictions. Where electronic signatures cannot be used, agreements can be confirmed in paper copies sent via international courier or postal services.

Much of the world's information transmission is now accomplished electronically through Internet-based e-mail or other electronic communications networks. Some of the more traditional means, including courier services, telephone, and postal services, continue to be used. Fax machines connected to telephone lines continue to be used for sending letters and pictures.

International courier services

The use of international courier services is steadily increasing. These services provide door-to-door service, are very quick, highly reliable, and can be used to transport bulky documents. It is becoming increasingly common to see letters of credit which require that documents be forwarded to the buyer by courier service.

Telephone

Telephone rates have been greatly reduced in recent years in most areas, though telephone calls are still more expensive than e-mail in most places.

The advantages of telephone calls are that they provide some level of personal contact, and allow for a discussion with immediate answers to questions. These advantages may become disadvantages if the parties involved are not all fluent in a common language. In such cases misunderstandings may occur more frequently in oral communications than in written communications. Agreement reached via telephone must be confirmed in written documents (or electronically transmitted documents where permitted).

Postal services

Postal services are still used to some extent in international correspondence. Because of time considerations, air rather than surface mail is used. Inadequate reliability or speed of the postal systems in some countries may dictate the use of couriers, fax, or e-mail.

13.2 Handling the export order

13.2.1 The inquiry and response

The initial inquiry or order for goods from a prospective foreign buyer may be unsolicited, or may come from the efforts of an export management company, agents, or a company's own efforts. No matter in what form it may be received, every inquiry should be handled seriously with the expectation that it may lead to a profitable sale. A leading business executive in one of the largest South American countries made it a practice to make regular tours of inspection of his various activities. When he was advised of the need for a piece of machinery, for additional raw materials, or other items, he would rapidly scribble a letter of inquiry on a blank page of a pad of paper he carried with him, slip it into an envelope, and have it mailed. There was no letterhead or other means of identification other than the return address on the envelope. More than one exporter receiving one of these hastily scribbled letters in the writer's own language, sometimes even with smudged fingerprints on it, would promptly throw it away as having been written by some irresponsible person and not worthy of an answer. Those firms that carefully observed the fundamental rule that all inquiries should be answered seriously made considerable profitable sales.

The response to the inquiry should normally be in polite, business-like letter format. If the request for information is general, the response should include catalogs and price lists, and/or an offer to have a sales person or representative call. If the prospective order is a very large one the inquiry may serve primarily to open the way for negotiations. Major transactions often require some face-to-face communications, and business people in a number of cultures place less value on contracts and more value on personal relationships.

13.2.2 The order

Order received directly from prospective importer

There is no such thing as a standard order form. Some companies merely use a letterhead; others have regularly printed forms with spaces provided for all necessary information. As long as the order contains the essential facts concerning the desired merchandise and how it is to be shipped, no special form or procedure is necessary.

When the actual order is received, the exporter will normally send a *confirmation of receipt*, followed by a commitment to fill the order if the exporter finds all of the terms and the payment arrangements acceptable. If there are any problems the exporter should not agree to the sale until the problems have been resolved.

It should be noted that the acceptance of an order without modification creates a contract that is binding upon both parties. If, however, the manufacturer or exporter (or for that matter any seller) indicates to the prospective buyer that he or she wishes to make some modification in the terms of the order, there is no contract. But if the prospective buyer then confirms and accepts the proposed modification, a contract is created.

A *pro forma invoice*, as illustrated in Figure 13.2, may be prepared by the exporter to indicate the terms that have been agreed upon (or are proposed). The pro forma invoice normally shows the type and amount of merchandise, unit costs and extensions, expected weights and measures, and terms of sale and payment (INCOTERMS). If accepted by the prospective buyer, it may serve as a contract.

Order received from branch or representative overseas

Where the exporter has an overseas representative who visits the prospective customer the representative may use a combination order form and sales contract.

```
                                        XYZ Manufacturing
                                        22 Canton Road
                                        Hong Kong

       ABC Importers
       San Jose, CA
       USA


                                        Purchase      Order Date:
                                        Invoice Date:
                                        Invoice Ref. No.: PRO FORMA 0001

                                        Terms of payment:Confirmed
                                        Irrevocable Letter of Credit
                                        Payable in US dollars

       Invoice To:
       Ship To:
       Forwarding Agent:

                                   Country of
       via:                         Origin:           China
       _____

       QUANTITY         DESCRIPTION      PRICE EACH    TOTAL PRICE

       1000             Male shirts      $15.00        US$15,000.00

       Inland freight, export packing &
       forwarding fees                                 $     300.00

                                                       $15,300.00
            Free alongside (FAS) Hong Kong             $ 1,000.00
            Estimated ocean freight                    $   150.00
            Estimated marine insurance

                                                       US$16,450.00

            CIF San Francisco
       Packed in 5 boxes, 100 cubic feet
       Gross weight 1000 lbs.
       Net weight 900 lbs.
       Payment terms: Irrevocable letter of creit confirmed by a
       Hong Kong bank. Shipment to be made (2) weeks after
       receipt of firm order.
       We certify this pro forma invoice is true and correct.
                                 Woo Yuk Shee
                                 President
```

FIGURE 13.2

Illustration of pro forma invoice

When the sales representative has received approval from the exporter to accept the order the form is completed and signed by both the seller and the buyer. All the terms of the contract are printed on the reverse side of the form and may be considered legally binding unless changed by prior agreement.

An order received by an exporter based on a contract of sale negotiated between the final purchaser and an overseas-based branch office or distributor of the exporter is referred to in international trade as an *indent order*.

Performance of a contract

In the export business generally it is difficult to enforce performance of a contract. At the very least litigation between the nationals of two countries is so expensive as to make it virtually prohibitive. Both buyers and sellers, therefore, are likely to disregard a breach of contract if no monetary obligation has been created or if no considerable damages have been created or inflicted. But, and this is of grave consequence in export trade, if a contract has been created between a buyer and a seller both parties are honorbound to perform.

Commercial disputes are often hard to avoid in exporting. When such disputes do occur, their resolution is often complicated by the great distance between exporter and buyer and by the differing business customs and laws that exist in their respective countries. One approach to settling disputes is commercial arbitration (Keegan and Green, 2000, pp. 192–5). The usual arbitration procedure is for the parties involved to choose a disinterested and informed person or persons as a type of referee to determine the merits of the case and make a judgement that both parties agree to honor. It is desirable that a contract include an *arbitration clause* specifying that arbitration is to be used when there is a dispute between exporter and buyer.

Most international arbitration is done under the auspices of a formal arbitration organization. For example, in the western hemisphere there are the Inter-American Commercial Arbitration Commission (handling disputes between the businesses in more than 20 North and South American republics) and the Canadian–American Arbitration Commission for Canadian and United States businesses. In the United Kingdom, the London Court of Arbitration is limited to situations that can be legally arbitrated in the United Kingdom. Finally, the American Arbitration Association and the International Chamber of Commerce deal with disputes on a worldwide basis.

Questions sometimes arise concerning whether awards made in one country are enforceable in others. More than 60 countries have signed a United Nations Convention on the Recognition and Enforcement of Foreign Arbitral Awards. This convention provides for legal enforcement in a signatory country of private arbitral awards granted in other countries that are parties to the convention. However, some large countries are still not signatories of the convention.

13.2.3 Export licenses

No contract to supply goods or services should be accepted until the potential exporter ascertains that the material can be legally exported. Export regulations are presently in a state of flux with changes occurring frequently. Individual countries have their own export laws, and may control the export of products to specific countries for reasons of national security, foreign policy, short supply, preservation of cultural property, assisting of industries using domestic products, and revenue purposes.

The potential exporter must contact the appropriate government offices before accepting an order to assure that the goods can be exported. Then the proper license must be obtained before the goods are actually shipped. Foreign freight forwarders (discussed later in the chapter) can provide valuable information and assistance in this area.

To avoid potential problems for the importer, the potential exporter could also check that the goods can be legally imported into the country of destination, though this may be difficult and is often not done.

13.2.4 Financing/payment and other terms of sale

A key element for the exporter in any transaction is assuring that payment will be made by the importer. With the difficulties of international litigation, collection of overdue international accounts may simply become impossible. In Chapter 11 we discussed the options for obtaining payment.

The importer and exporter must agree on the dates when the items are to be shipped, whether all the goods must be sent in one shipment or if partial shipments are allowed, and so on. These terms are usually specified in the letter of credit if that approach is used for payment.

The importer, or the exporter in some instances, will also normally specify which party is to be responsible for making the following arrangements:

1. getting the merchandise from the exporter's plant to the port;
2. getting the merchandise through outbound customs;
3. getting the merchandise aboard ship (or other mode of transport);
4. paying for the freight;
5. paying for insurance.

These are aspects of the trade terms discussed previously in Chapter 10. It should be remembered that the trade term agreed upon also indicates when and where legal title to the goods changes.

13.3 Physical distribution

Having received the order, ensured that the terms of sale and payment are satisfactory, and then accepted the order, there is the need to arrange for shipping, insurance, and preparation of the multitude of required documents. In short, the physical distribution (i.e., supply chain management or logistics) of the product must be attended to. From the standpoint of the individual exporting company, physical distribution (and its management) can be viewed as encompassing the movement and handling of products outward to points of consumption or use. To a large extent physical distribution activities associated with shipments to foreign markets are much the same as those for shipment to domestic markets (Coughlin *et al.*, 2001, Chs 4–5). But the processes, procedures, and documents required in export shipments are relatively more complex because of the following three factors:

1. the passage of goods across national boundaries, with attendant legal requirements;
2. shipment by ocean-going vessels or international airlines, with attendant security needs and specific documentary requirements;
3. the time and distance required to complete the transaction, with attendant needs for ensuring payment.

13.3.1 Importance to management

There are many reasons that export marketing managers should be concerned with the physical distribution of their companies' products.

The price that the ultimate user in foreign markets has to pay is strongly influenced by the way in which the product is physically moved from the manufacturer/exporter. That is, in distributing the product to the place where the user wants it and at the time it is wanted, certain costs are incurred that ultimately are borne by the user. Included are inventory holding costs, warehouse costs, transportation and handling costs, and order processing costs. Thus, *the cost of physical distribution can constitute a significant portion of the selling price*. In an export shipment, for example, additional packing or crating beyond the standard pack used for domestic shipments may be necessary. In addition, there may be added costs because of the need to utilize the services of freight forwarders or other specialized organizations to avoid complex export problems such as documentation. Another example of an additional cost item is the need for special transportation insurance if full protection is to be had.

According to Anna Lin, Executive Director of the Hong Kong Article Numbering Association, which is a member of EAN International, a global organization (with more than 600,000 member companies in 85 countries) that sets, manages, and promotes a system for the identification and communication of products, services, utilities, transport units, and locations, supply chain management (physical distribution), simply, is all about balancing the right supply of goods to match demand, using enabling technologies such as bar coding. One of its major objectives is to make information flow more efficiently and accurately. Ms Lin states, 'if we can better manage the supply chain by integrating processes, communicating better with each other and streamlining some of the unnecessary procedures, *we will be able to take some of the costs out of the supply chain* [emphasis added]' (Russell, 1998). As business firms become increasingly reluctant to carry large inventories, the need for a fast and easily monitored international supply chain is obvious.

Monitoring of goods from manufacturer to final delivery to the industrial user or retailer is being made much easier by the development of radio-frequency identification systems, discussed briefly in Chapter 1. Depending upon the system used, sensors installed on ocean or air containers can provide real-time information on the location of a container, detect unauthorized entry, or monitor conditions within the container. The basic system includes a sensor or sensors in the container that have the ability to communicate that information via radio or satellite to the user. One such system, developed for the US Department of Defense, is presently tracking about 25,000 containers a day (Machalara and Pasztor, 2004). For the user, the costs are those of the equipment itself plus the cost of running the system. The benefits are knowledge of the real-time status of shipments with resulting potential for reducing inventory and out-of-stock costs, coordination of steps in the supply chain, and possibly easier movement through customs.

Another reason that physical distribution deserves the diligent attention of managers is that it is an aspect of export marketing where *increased profits can be generated directly* – through either reduced costs or increased sales. Technology and automation have had a great impact on costs. For example, order processing and inventory control have been made more efficient through the use of electronic data processing equipment (see Exhibit 13.2); transportation costs have been lowered through technological improvements such as containerization; and warehousing and materials handling have become more efficient because of the automated systems that have been developed for this purpose.

EXHIBIT 13.2 — Technology facilitates physical distribution

In late 1992 the Port of New York and New Jersey in the United States and the ports of Bremen/Bremerhaven in Germany initiated an Electronic Data Interchange system. The interchange involves the New York/New Jersey Port's Automated Cargo Expediting System (ACES) and Bremen/Bremerhaven's TELEPORT undertaken for Beck & Co., brewers of Beck's beer, which is headquartered in Bremen. The nature of the link is shown in Figure 13.3.

User's Information	BREMEN – teleport					NEW YORK			ACES		
	BECK & CO	dbh SIS	BLG CTOS	GERMAN CUSTOMS	OCEAN CARRIER	DRIBECK	HUDSON	MAHER TERMINAL	US CUSTOMS	OCEAN CARRIER	TRUCKER
SAILING SCHEDULES											
SPACE RESERVATION											
CONTAINER BOOKINGS											
BOOKING CONFIRMATION											
PORT ORDER											
CONTAINER ANNOUNCEMENT											
CONTAINER STATUS INFO											
BILL OF LADING (ECB)											
BILL OF LADING (ECB)											
COMMERCIAL INVOICE											
PACKING LIST											
CUSTOMS ENTRY/RELEASE								ABI-link			
ARRIVAL NOTICE											
FREIGHT RELEASE											
CARGO STATUS MESSAGE											
DELIVERY ORDER											
STATUS REPORT											

----------- planned in step 2

FIGURE 13.3

EDI-Link Bremen – New York for Beck & Co.

Key: **TELEPORT ACES** flow chart links Bremen and the bistate port. Users found in headings of chart include:

dbh SIS: German information services company that developed the EDI system for the ports of Bremen/Bremerhaven.
BLG CTOS: Bremer Lagerhaus Gesellschaft, the operating company of the Port of Bremen/Bremerhaven.
DRIBECK: US importer of Becks beer.
HUDSON: Hudson Shipping, Customs Broker.

Under this system Beck and the companies involved in getting its beer to the United States are linked in an information system. Beck's offices in Bremen send invoices, packing lists, and bills of lading via the link to Hudson Shipping, the customs broker for the company's importer in the United States Dribeck. Teleport and ACES serve as communication interfaces with Hapaq-Lloyd, the container terminal in Bremerhaven and Maher Terminals in the New York/New Jersey Port, each integrated into the network. By being able to enter an order only once, handling is expedited and the occurrence of errors reduced. The information about a shipment will be sent by EDI as soon as the vessel sails from Germany, instead of several days later when transported by courier.

EDI networks are not limited to only these two ports. Indeed, the ACES network is not solely a New York system. ACES services' subscribers are located throughout the world. Moreover, in 1997 the major port operators of Hamburg, Germany, announced that they were working towards introducing a standardized, paperless container dispatch system throughout Hamburg's container terminal. EDI will be replacing the documents. The ultimate goal is to extend the 'paperless port' to all customers, including shipping companies, agents, forwarders, shippers, and railways, as well as to other ports, authorities, and institutions. In 1998 a company was set up to establish an EDI system of international standard for the Shenzhen, China ports.

> EDI networks are not limited to ocean carriers. The Scandinavian airline SAS uses EDI when dealing with agents and forwarders.
>
> Source: adapted from 'ACES update,' *Via International*, 44(11) (November 1992), 4–5 and 'Moving into the 21st century,' *Via International*, 44(11) (November 1992), 18–19

Physical distribution can have a positive effect on a company's sales volume through the service provided. Service encompasses many things such as the following:

- the speed with which a product can be provided to a customer;
- the reliability with which the average speed of service is achieved;
- the degree of immediate availability of the product;
- the arrival of the product in good condition.

Thus an exporter may be able to make a specific sale only because the physical distribution method it uses gets the product to the buyer when and where it is wanted and at a reasonable cost, relative to other alternatives available to the buyer.

How a company structures its physical distribution system can determine whether it succeeds or even survives, as we move through the 21st century. For companies operating in Europe, for example, the protocols or directives of the European Union internal market have caused changes in the 'ground rules' of transportation, warehousing, and production and the role of logistics (i.e., supply chain management) will be even more crucial to success (Down and Anderson, 1990, p. 23).

A final major reason that export marketing managers should pay particular attention to physical distribution is that *national governments exert pressures that can affect the manner in which certain physical distribution activities are carried out*. These pressures emanate from the implementation by national governments of policies to stimulate national industrial development and achieve full and stabilized employment or the pressures may be due to political relations between governments. The result is that a company engaged in export marketing may find itself constrained and limited in its attempts to manage the availability and flow of materials, products, services, facilities, and other resources. For example, national government controls over exports and imports through the use of licenses, quotas, tariffs, etc., can influence the planning and control of a manufacturer's inventory. Moreover, national governments can affect inventories and movements of goods within and between nations through their buying practices – in many markets they are a major (if not the largest) customer. National government policies can affect the means of transportation used to move a product from a seller to a buyer by requiring that importing business firms must use land, sea, and air transportation companies owned by 'local' firms, as well as harbor facilities belonging to the importer's government. Finally, the political relationship between the exporter's and importer's countries may have an effect. Using the year 1996 as an example, there was a lot of indirect trade between companies in China and Taiwan. However, the Taiwanese government prohibited containers of the Chinese Ocean Shipping Company (COSCO) from entering the island (Engbarth, 1996). As a result, goods destined for Taiwan had to be removed from their Chinese containers in Hong Kong and repacked in containers belonging to non-Chinese shipping companies before being reexported to Taiwan. One estimate of the added cost per container was HK$4650 (US$600). This is no longer true for all shipments between China and Taiwan as there is limited direct service between Xiamen in Fujian province in China and Kaohsiung in Taiwan, with increased trade probable in the near future.

13.3.2 Decision areas

As suggested above, physical distribution embraces many specific activities concerned with product movement, storage, and related activities. We comment briefly on each of the major activities.

Nature of the shipment

To be decided are such things as the minimum size of the unit pack, the quantities to be shipped, the type and method of packing to be used to protect the product from damage in transit (i.e., its protective packaging rather than the immediate package in which the product is sold), the identification markings to be placed on the outside packing container, and so forth.

Transportation

The basic concern is with the external movement of the product, which usually involves choosing the route that the shipment is to follow, selecting the mode(s) of transportation, and providing adequate insurance coverage to protect the shipment while it is in transit, especially marine or air insurance for products in transit between countries.

Warehousing

This activity involves more than just storage. In addition to storing products in anticipation of consumer demand, warehousing encompasses a broad range of other activities, such as assembling, breaking bulk shipments into smaller sizes to meet customer needs, and preparing products for reshipment. Of importance to export marketing management is the need to determine: (1) the number and type of warehousing facilities to employ, and (2) their spatial arrangement.

Materials handling

Provision must be made for the internal movement of products within plant and warehouse facilities.

Carrying inventory

There are many different cost elements involved in managing an inventory – storage, interest on capital tied up, taxes, lost sales, materials handling, and so forth. Since these costs may sometimes be sizable, management must be concerned about inventory control. This involves determining the proper level of inventory to hold so that a balance is maintained between customer service and inventory cost.

Order processing and documentation

Procedures must be established to process orders in as routine a manner as possible. Correct documentation is essential to the successful physical movement of a shipment. Many overseas shipments have been delayed due to errors in documentation. Davies (1984, p. 66) has summarized the so-called 'problem of documentation' as consisting of five main components. These are as follows:

1. **Complexity**: numbers of documents and correspondents.
2. **Culture**: language, currency, law.
3. **Change**: changes in requirements.
4. **Cost**: costs of preparation.
5. **Error**: consequential costs of error and cost of correction.

In addition to the usual documents used in a business transaction, such as a commercial invoice and bill of lading, there are other special documents – for example, consular invoice, certificate of origin, export declaration, and Customs declaration – that may be necessary in selling to a foreign country. The complex and rather technical nature of documentation requirements and procedures necessary to obtain permission for a shipment to cross national boundaries has fostered the emergence and growth of two special types of international marketing intermediaries: the foreign freight forwarder (for the exporter) and the custom-house broker (for the importer). In most countries the laws allow companies to perform both types of services.

Within the EU, documentation requirements have been greatly simplified for shipments from one country to another. Since the mid-1990s most border stations have been closed, and all countries ultimately will be using the same single document covering shipments that cross national borders.

13.3.3 Logistics and the systems concept

The complexity of physical distribution and the key decision areas discussed above have indicated one of the reasons that export marketing managers must take a broad view of their job. The growing internationalization of business and increased competition have additionally resulted in the need for export marketing managers to view their function as an integral part of an overall production/storage/distribution *system*.

Logistics, or *supply chain management* as it is often called, is the study of the management of relationships, decisions, and activities among production, storage, and distribution so as to minimize total final cost to the user. For many years production and distribution managers have used economic order quantities and economic lot sizes to indicate the optimum amounts to be made, purchased, and held, given their production system. More recently ideas originally developed by the Japanese, and now widely used in many countries, have focused on just-in-time (JIT) manufacturing and flexible manufacturing. This approach has demonstrated advantages to producing in smaller lot sizes with more frequent shipments and reduced amounts held in storage. Flexible manufacturing, in which more versatile equipment and systems permit the production of more than one model of product on the same line with low changeover times, has changed the run size–cost relationship even further (Marsh, 2003). At the very least, these approaches require that a company examine the trade-offs between costs of inventory, transportation, and time.

Implicit in the systems concept is that the physical distribution alternatives considered by the export marketing manager must be alternative systems. In selecting from among the alternatives, the *total-cost approach* can be applied. This means that an attempt is made to optimize the cost–profit relationship of the various alternatives after considering the total cost of physical distribution, rather than looking separately at the costs of individual activities. A manager of a company in, say, Canada, that uses air freight to transport its products to Spain may want to reduce the transportation expense by changing to ocean transportation. This manager, however, must recognize that such a cost-reducing action may result in increases in inventory, warehousing, and packaging expenses that more than offset the saving in freight costs. Thus the total cost of operating the system may be increased.

In addition to *direct* physical distribution costs – such as the costs of transporting, warehousing, carrying inventory, packaging, packing, insurance – there is another group of costs that can have a pronounced effect on profits. These can be classified as *hidden* or *distribution-related* costs, and include such cost categories as lost sales, distributor–customer dissatisfactions, cost of time in transit, inventory losses, foreign warehousing, and losses from not being fully insured. Although the total-cost approach may sound simple and easy to implement, this is not necessarily the case. The nature of the various cost elements that have been identified suggests that even a relatively simple problem in physical distribution system development can involve great quantities of information that interact in an even greater number of ways. Fortunately, analytical techniques such as mathematical programming and simulation are available to handle this information and such complex interrelationships.

There are many instances in which relatively simple analytical techniques provide operational solutions to physical distribution analysis problems. One such technique is break-even analysis. To use break-even analysis (which is a *least-cost* model) one need know only the total fixed cost and average variable cost associated with each alternative system. For each alternative, such costs are assumed to be constant over the range of possible amounts of the product to be moved to an overseas market area. Given this information, it is relatively easy to determine the volume at which one is indifferent as to which alternative to use. For all volumes up to the point of indifference, one system has a lower total cost, while for all volumes beyond this point the other system is the least costly. The analysis can be easily expanded to include any number of alternative systems of physical distribution for specific overseas markets. An alternative system must not have both a higher fixed cost and higher average variable cost than the other alternatives. If this situation exists, there can be no point of indifference. An illustration of the application of this approach is summarized by Figure 13.4, which presents a graphical analysis of four alternative systems. The heavy line represents the minimum cost curve at any volume level. Because of its simplicity, this approach is easy to use. Also, it allows one to plan in advance for possible system changes. That is, the export marketer will know that as volume to a given market approaches a certain point, making a change in the system being used must be considered if minimizing cost is the objective. Referring to Figure 13.4, as volume approaches 2500 units the exporter should prepare to change from distribution system I to system II.

The total-cost approach is not limited to minimizing costs. Performance, or customer service, must also be considered. One objective may be to *maximize service* provided to a foreign market area. This may be accomplished by minimizing the

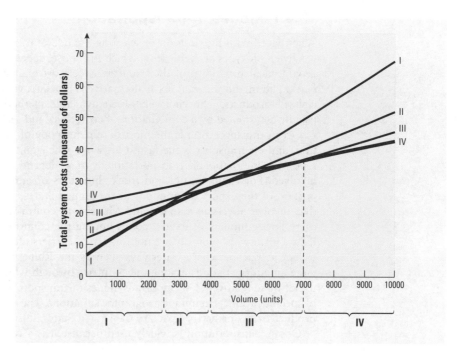

FIGURE 13.4

Total-cost analysis for multiple distribution alternatives

time involved in order processing and delivery. Although a greater service model will have some positive effect on revenue, additional costs will be incurred. Service played a key role in the physical distribution strategy of companies as they adapted to the changing environment of the 1990s. For example, General Electric viewed its physical distribution (logistics) operations as essential to achieving its global strategy of expansion and product leadership (Down and Anderson, 1990, p. 24). The company changed its logistics focus from price to service, using a single logistics agent rather than a number of different carriers, and using real-time rather than historical information as the basis for logistics decision making. Similar emphases are being placed as we progress in the 21st century.

Finally, the system may try to *maximize competitive advantage*. With this policy, management is interested in creating competitive cost advantages such that revenue will be positively affected.

It should be obvious that the objectives stated above are not consistent. For example, how can service be maximized and at the same time cost minimized? Also, how can costs be reduced and yet the system still provide maximum information feedback? The answer lies in recognizing that there is still another possible objective, to *maximize profits*. This policy involves optimizing service and costs to arrive at the best balance among them. In short, what is involved is a process of cost and service trade-offs.

13.4 Structure of international physical distribution

To facilitate the flow of products across national boundaries there has evolved a complex structure of specialized marketing institutions, organizations, and services.

13.4.1 Modes of transportation

When faced with the decision of selecting a mode of transportation, the exporter has five basic types available from which to choose, depending, of course, upon the geographical proximity of the countries of export and import: ocean, air, rail, truck, and inland water. A sixth alternative is pipeline, which transports very specialized products. The choice between available methods of transportation is usually determined by a combination of cost, time, and security.

Ocean transportation is the most dominant mode of international transportation, and air transport is the fastest growing. The significance of the other basic types of international transportation varies depending upon the countries involved. For example, rail and truck shipments do not constitute a significant portion of the export transactions of the United States, except perhaps for those that involve buyers in Canada and Mexico. In contrast, these transport modes carry large amounts of export goods among the countries of Europe. Similarly, inland waterways typically are not important carriers of goods between countries except in Europe where waterways such as the Rhine and Danube rivers carry large amounts of goods among the countries through which they flow. Often the use of these relatively less important modes of transport depends upon the nature of specific products in unique geographic situations. The use of trucks to haul fresh produce from northern Mexico to the United States illustrates this practice.

Ocean transportation is widely used because it is a relatively low-cost way to

FIGURE 13.5

A container vessel that is not fully loaded in Auckland, New Zealand harbor

transport goods, and it can easily handle large shipments. In addition, certain geographic conditions may make it impossible to use overland transportation to some foreign markets and infeasible to use it to others (see Figure 13.5). Exhibit 13.3 shows an interesting contrast between the two largest ports in the world.

EXHIBIT 13.3 The major ports of the world

As shown in Table 13.1, the two largest ocean transportation ports are Hong Kong and Singapore. Although both are entrepôts – i.e., ports that developed into commercial centers with related industries – there are some major differences between the two. One major difference is that in Hong Kong almost all the containers handled are driven from or into mainland China. Thus, for exports, it serves as a reexport port for products from China. In contrast, in Singapore as much as 80% of the containers entering the port leave it the same way – by boat. Singapore is a 'trans-shipment' hub, whereas Hong Kong is a 'local' port (*The Economist*, 2001). An explanation for this is geographic location. Singapore sits at the bottom of the Straits of Malacca, and almost everything moving between Europe and East Asia passes through these Straits. Hong Kong is located at the mouth of the Pearl River in southern China, which is the world's largest manufacturing region.

Another difference is that cargo terminals are run by private interests in Hong Kong and by the government in Singapore. The Singapore arrangement has led to some problems with carriers that wanted to run their own terminals. Because the government has resisted this, near the end of 2000 the Danish company Maersk, which provided 11% of the port's volume, moved its port operations to the nearby Malaysian port known as PTP.

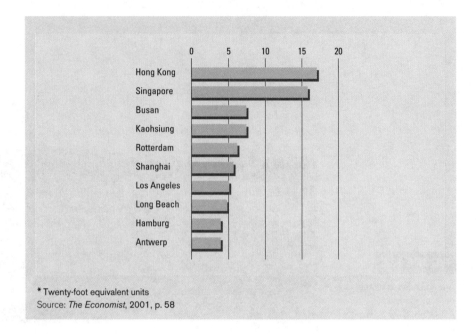

TABLE 13.1

The top ten ports in the world in the year 2000 (millions of TEU*)

* Twenty-foot equivalent units
Source: *The Economist*, 2001, p. 58

There is continuing pressure to reduce the costs of ocean transportation, and to meet changing logistics requirements. Container ships have traditionally been limited in size to allow passage through the Panama Canal. Now the traffic on the Asia–US route has grown so that there is no need for some ships to be able to transit the Canal. Much larger ships that carry more than 8000 20-foot-long containers will enter service in 2005 with another 95 scheduled to be launched in the remainder of the decade. The senior vice-president of Hyundai Heavy Industries Co. has commented that 'China's role as a global factory is reshaping transportation logistics' (Ihlwan, 2003).

Many diverse types of products are being transported to foreign markets by air in large volume: computers, office machines, electrical and electronic equipment, automobile parts, television sets, pharmaceuticals, certain metal manufactures, and clothing, to name but a few. Thus, even with existing technology, it is evident that air cargo movements are no longer confined to fast shipments of emergency supplies, goods of high value (for example jewelry), and perishable products (for example fresh-cut flowers), although it is widely used for such products.

Time in transit is but one of the so-called *hidden costs* that may be relevant. For example, Seagate Technology, which has an unpredictable global demand, uses air transportation to ship its computer disk drives from its plants in Singapore and Thailand to customers throughout the world in a very short time period. Thus, inventory-carrying costs are reduced and the company is able to predict better and with greater confidence when a buyer's order will arrive.

Exporters may send small shipments by international parcel post, air parcel post, or air courier service (such as FedEx, UPS, and DHL) rather than pay the higher minimum bill of lading charges for ocean freight or air shipments. Most large shipments of goods are sent by sea and are charged on a per-container basis, with a maximum weight allowed per container. Less-than-container loads will be charged on the basis of weight or measurement, whichever is greater. Very small shipments are charged a set fee because of the costs involved in documentation and handling. Bulk shipments of petroleum, grain, coal, etc. are carried in specialized vessels and may be charged per voyage.

Internet technology may make things easier for shippers of smaller shipments.

For example, there is a web site in the United States (www.intershipper.com) that offers a service for helping a US exporter compare rates among eight carriers (FedEx, Air Net, DHL, Airborne Express, BAX, UPS, Emery Worldwide, and the US Postal Service). A company can enter the size or weight specifications of a package and the site analyzes all shipping options and guaranteed delivery times and dates. The site also helps choose the best rate, call for a package pickup or locate a drop-off location, track shipments automatically, or notify the exporter or the recipient when the package is delivered, or if it is delayed. At present, the service is free. Similar sites may appear elsewhere in the world.

There are times when a combination of transportation methods are used. One commonly used arrangement is air–sea, wherein cargo is transferred between air and ocean carriers, usually without the same intermodal container. Containers used by each of these types of carriers have characteristics that are incompatible with the other. The intent in using such an intermodal combination is to take advantage of the speed and cost efficiencies of each. Although there are different routes where this combination is used, major ones include the Far East (Asia-Pacific). For example, one route is to ship from Southeast Asia by ocean to Singapore and the Persian Gulf. From there, air is used to Europe. Products that are particularly well suited for the air–sea arrangement are higher value, larger volume consumer electronics, automated office equipment, and high-technology components that are less time sensitive than other products using air freight.

A land–sea combination is often used in the United States. For example, fresh California grapes destined for Europe may be shipped by truck or rail to the East Coast, then loaded aboard ocean vessels bound for Europe. This combination greatly reduces the transit time compared to shipment by all-water service.

The method of transportation is usually selected by the importer. The route selected for the export shipment may be determined either by the exporter or the importer.

13.4.2 Facilitating organizations and services

In addition to the transportation carriers, other types of organizations providing service to the exporter are freight forwarders and public warehouses. Most companies can benefit at one time or another from utilizing the services of such facilitating organizations. This is particularly true for those companies whose export marketing operations are small or irregular, and for the firm located away from the main exit or entry ports of its country. Functioning as integral parts of an export marketer's physical distribution system, these facilitating organizations can often be powerful marketing tools in that their existence in a system can make the difference in whether a particular transaction is consummated.

Freight forwarders

Foreign (export) freight forwarders or consolidators, now designated in the United States as *ocean transportation intermediaries* under the US Shipping Act of 1998, have two principal classes of function. One group is concerned with the forwarding of an export shipment from the point of origin to the ultimate destination in some foreign market; the other is concerned with the engaging of space on transportation carriers.

The services that foreign freight forwarders perform in carrying out these basic functions are many. Although a forwarder can usually perform every necessary physical distribution service from the time that an order is placed until the shipment is delivered at the foreign destination, perhaps a forwarder's major contribution lies in the taking over of traffic (arranging for shipping to the port, booking space on the carrier, and arranging insurance) and documentation work on international freight movements. In addition, by being able to consolidate small shipments into larger ones, the forwarder is in a position to secure lower transportation rates than any single shipper could get directly from the carriers. Such savings in freight charges can then be passed on to the shipper. Some freight forwarders may also offer advice on markets, government regulations, and potential problems. The forwarder can track the movement of goods, warehouse inventory, and process Customs documentation electronically.

More recently, forwarders have expanded their activities to include production planning, inventory management, parts assembly, distribution warehousing, real-time tracking, wheels-up clearance, and electronic reporting. For example, in its center in The Netherlands, Air Express International (AEI) has its personnel perform simple repairs to electronic assemblies. AEI views this not as a concession to a customer but as a logical extension of being a forwarder. In Malaysia, AEI manages the entire inventory and distribution of Intel's plant, saving Intel millions of dollars and halving the delivery time of microchips.

Forwarders can function as nonvessel operating common carriers (NVOCC), though in the United States these are now officially designated simply as another type of *ocean transportation intermediary*. To the exporter an NVOCC is a transport carrier and to a carrier it is a shipper. The NVOCC issues a bill of lading to the exporter and is the responsible party to the exporter. The carrier, on the other hand, issues a bill of lading to the NVOCC. Air freight consolidators work in a manner similar to the ocean freight NVOCC.

The relationship between the exporter, the foreign freight forwarder, and the carrier may vary. The forwarder may perform some of the functions of an export house, particularly for companies fairly new in exporting. Sometimes more experienced exporters may choose to take over some of the forwarder's usual duties, especially documentation. The degree to which exporters take on some of the traditional forwarder's duties seems to be related to the export effort of the company, as measured by the number of orders or consignments rather than export volume or value.

In addition to exporters taking on forwarding activities, transportation companies themselves have done likewise. For example, DFDS, a Danish sea transport company, views itself as a total transport company operating multimodes of transport that are concerned with logistics management. It handles all the physical distribution for a number of companies, small, medium, and large. Thus DFDS has absorbed freight forwarding activities. The company has created a network in Europe based on strategic alliances formed in Germany and France. The company has allocated Europe among itself and its two partners as follows:

- DFDS Home (Scandinavia, Benelux, United Kingdom, Portugal);
- DFDS/THL Germany (Germany, Switzerland, Spain);
- French partner (France, Austria, Italy, Greece).

There clearly is a trend toward consolidation between carriers and freight forwarders to offer companies a total logistics and transport package. By forming long-term alliances with airlines and shipping companies, and by making the necessary investment and accepting the risks that go with it, forwarders can take on overall responsibility for the entire transport chain. This seems to be more viable than simply forming larger and larger forwarders.

Although all foreign freight forwarders will handle shipments by air transportation as a routine service, some specialize in air cargo. In the same way as regular forwarders, these special air freight forwarders provide complete services from point of origin to point of destination.

A special type of forwarder is the *shippers' agent*. This type of facilitating organization handles inland movement of international freight. As intermodal experts they offer valuable assistance to exporters, importers, ocean transport companies, railroads, and trucking companies. They aim to put together a cost-effective (through lower inland rates), quality intermodal transportation package (Ambrosino, 1994).

Warehousing

When it is necessary and profitable for an exporter to maintain an inventory in foreign markets a storage or warehousing branch can be established. Such facilities may be part of a foreign sales branch. If so connected, the buyer is afforded greater convenience and a potentially powerful marketing tool is created in that a greater volume of business may be generated than would be the case if storage facilities were absent. The same situation occurs when the warehousing branch is a separate entity, set up to fill orders made by overseas distributors or agents.

As an alternative to establishing branch warehouses in foreign markets, the exporter can utilize the services of public warehouses. A branch warehouse may not be practical because of irregular demand for warehouse space or, if such demand is regular, its magnitude is not large enough to support the investment required and the regular operating costs incurred. Many public warehouses are being established in the various free areas of the world.

International public warehouses provide all the usual services of warehousing: unloading, storing, packing, and so on. Such warehouses in many foreign markets may offer other services, as illustrated by a company in The Netherlands that offers customer freight forwarding, packaging, insurance, and transportation service to all of Europe and the Middle East. For at least one customer it has coordinated promotional material. In addition, many such warehouses are designated as *Customs-bonded warehouses*, which means that goods from abroad may be stored there, and certain manipulations performed on the goods, without payment of duty until such time as they are released from storage and delivered to a buyer. The manipulations may include manufacturing activities, although such activities may be allowed only if the finished products are exported. The activities carried on in bonded warehouses are under strict supervision of Customs authorities.

It is not necessary that a foreign storage or warehousing operation provide stocks for a single market area. In fact, many exporters, as they increasingly apply the total-cost concept to their physical distribution or logistics problems, are establishing such branches as central distribution centers to serve a wide area. For example, in the early 1990s a housewares company sourcing from the United States consolidated its seven European warehouses to two, while a computer manufacturer with a plant in Ireland stopped carrying inventory in each national market and shifted to direct delivery from the plant. Freight forwarders handled local distribution. Where several market areas are to be served by a single storage or warehousing branch, it may be best for these facilities to be located in a free port or trade zone such as Hong Kong, New York, or Colon. By locating in a free area, it is relatively easy for a manufacturer to serve many markets since the usual Customs procedures and regulations of the country where the free area is physically located do not apply. In addition to free areas, an exporter doing business in Europe might have one or more warehouses to serve the entire EU. These could be located in any member country.

Two additional types of facility need to be identified – Distriparks and Districenters. *Distriparks*, which are located in the major ports of the world such as Rotterdam and Singapore, provide a place where the supplier/exporter/shipper can lease warehouse space in the port area and assemble, process, and label products with a meaningful savings in cost. More comprehensive, in terms of what is done in them, are the *Districenters*. In effect, a Districenter offers the complete logistics system and effectively is a process whereby the manufacturer/ exporter/supplier contracts out of distribution and transport. The operator of the center handles the complete management of the flow of goods and information and provides additional services such as invoicing, packing, sorting, and inventory control. An early user of the concept was Nedlloyd Flowmaster in Europe. A new Districenter opened in Panyu, Guangdong Province, China in late 1997. It serves as an entry point into China. Tenants are allowed to buy, sell, and manufacture. The center offers one-stop-shop services, including licenses for distribution in Panyu, free business consultation, banking and transportation, business registration and help in hiring personnel (Tang, 1998). Since manufacturers can display products Chinese wholesalers and retailers can meet with the manufacturers for immediate cash-and-carry sales. The Panyu Districenter represents a new concept for distribution into China and has circumvented laws regulating such distribution. Interestingly, the center allows foreign buyers to bypass intermediaries, and if the concept catches on in China may reduce Hong Kong's role as an entrepôt for reexport of Chinese goods.

Free areas

Two distinct types of free areas can be found throughout the world. They are similar in that all are considered to be outside the Customs area of a country. Products may be brought into and exported from such areas easily. In addition, other activities may be allowed, such as repacking and manufacturing.

As we showed in Chapter 3, a *free trade zone* is basically an enclosed, policed area without resident population in, adjacent to, or near a port of entry, into which foreign goods not otherwise prohibited may be brought without formal Customs entry. The Barrenquilla Free Zone in Colombia, Shannon in Ireland, and Honolulu in the United States are examples. Sometimes the zone may be only one company's plant or warehouse. E. R. Squibb & Sons, a global manufacturer of pharmaceuticals and health-care products with 29 plants in 27 countries, has its New Brunswick, NJ, plant designated as such a zone. With such status Squibb will lower its costs significantly through tariff payment deferral, elimination of duties on waste products and reexports and by paying lower tariffs for finished products than it would pay for new materials. In a similar manner, 'free warehouses' in Denmark, operated by the Danish government in Copenhagen and other cities, function like a free zone. These are a variation of Customs-bonded warehouses that can be found in such European cities as Antwerp and Rotterdam. Exhibit 13.4 illustrates potential benefits from using a free zone.

Both BMW of North America and Mazda utilize a free trade zone in the United States to benefit from duty deferral on imported automobiles admitted into the zone. These companies use the zone to process their vehicles with domestic-status accessories and they are able to store them on site. Another example is Magnavox, which uses a free trade zone in the United States to store a marine navigation system product, a Navigator, which is manufactured in Denmark. This zone serves as an inventory center for sales made in the United States and abroad as well.

A *free port* encompasses a port or entire city isolated from the rest of the country for Customs purposes. Important free ports still operating as such are Hong Kong and Singapore. These areas exist primarily to facilitate reexporting and thus can be central distribution centers. A variation is the *free perimeter*, which is generally confined to a remote underdeveloped region of a country. At many points along its border with the United States, for example, Mexico has established such areas.

EXHIBIT 13.4	How companies can benefit from a free trade zone

A reason that many companies use a free trade zone (FTZ) facility is for cash flow savings. Realized savings can be accrued on lower cost items as well as high cost products. To show how savings can be significant, a hypothetical situation is depicted in the table below:

Activities in the FTZ	Examples of savings	
Duty is deferred on imported goods admitted to zone	*Constant inventory savings*	
For storage, manipulation such as packaging, marking, labeling, repackaging, etc. or for assembly/ manufacturing. Cash flow is improved.	Amount of average durable inventory	$40,000,000
	Average duty rate	10%
Zone user pays duty only when goods leave the zone and enter the market.	Duty deferred on permanent basis	$4,000,000
	Cost of money (est.)	13%
Zone user improves cash flow position by shortening the time between payment of duties, and receipt of income from sale of goods.	Annual savings (est.)	$520,000
Zone user achieves a major reduction in its capital requirements for financing.		
No duty is assessed when reexporting from zone	*Export savings*	
Goods imported duty free into zone may be processed several ways: inspected, assembled into finished products, repackaged, or warehoused, then exported to markets outside the country with no assessed duties.	Amount of imports exported annually from the zone	$20,000,000
	Average duty rate (est.)	6%
	Annual savings (est.)	$1,200,000
Processing goods within the zone can eliminate or lower tariffs	*Manufacturing/assembly/ processing savings*	
A company that imports parts into the zone and assembles them into finished products can reduce or eliminate tariffs by shipping finished products from the zone.	Annual duty that would have been paid on imported components/materials, etc.	$750,000
	Duty on finished goods due to lower rate on duty thereon	450,000
	Annual savings (est.)	$300,000
Duties can be avoided on defective damaged goods by inspecting and testing imported goods within a zone	*Defective/damaged/waste/ obsolete savings*	

➡

Segregate rejects for return to shipper or other duty-free disposition	Total dutiable imported goods	$20,000,000
	Percentage of defective material	15%
And no duty is due for any accountable losses including evaporation, seepage, spoilage, impurities, damage, defects, or obsolescence	Value of dutiable goods that became defective, etc.	$3,000,000
	Average duty rate (est.)	8%
	Annual savings (est.)	$240,000
Savings of 10% to 25% have been realized in total transport insurance from foreign shipper's plant to importer in a zone vs importer outside a zone	Fire and theft insurance	
	Average annual value of duty-paid inventory	$44,000,000
In addition to fire and theft insurance savings, which depend upon shipment method, air/ocean, containerized/ noncontainerized, nature of goods, etc.	Fire and theft insurance (7c per $100)	$30,800

Source: adapted from (1991) Foreign trade advantage: an innovative way to trim costs, *Via Port of NY–NJ*, 43(1), pp. 12–15.

A related type of area is an *export processing zone* (EPZ), which is an area where foreign manufacturers enjoy favored treatment on the import of intermediate goods, taxes, provision of infrastructure, and freedom from industrial regulations applying elsewhere in the country. Developing countries use these areas as a means of stimulating exports as a route to industrial development. In order to be successful, such zones should have adequate physical infrastructure and be close to good transport and commercial support services. Since the mid-1960s EPZs have spread rapidly throughout much of East and South Asia, the Caribbean, and Central America. Some western European countries, including France and the United Kingdom, have also accepted the idea (UNIDO, 1995).

Transportation insurance

One of the more important risks involved in an export transaction is that of loss or damage to goods during their physical movement from seller to buyer. In most instances full protection from this risk can be provided through special transportation insurance, such as *marine insurance*. Protection can be provided to cover all transport risks from the time the goods leave the seller's warehouse or factory – whether located inland or at a port of exit from the exporter's country – until they reach the final destination stipulated by the foreign buyer. In its most basic form such insurance provides the means to reimburse the owners of goods being transported to overseas markets for any losses or damages incurred for which the carriers cannot legally be called upon to make payment. In addition to legal owners, nonowners often have an interest in seeing that a shipment is adequately protected.

From the point of view of the parties involved in an international marketing transaction – the seller and buyer – a deciding factor in the question of who needs transportation insurance, and when to insure, is *insurable interest*. Generally speaking, insurable interest depends upon whether a company will benefit from the safe arrival of the carrier and its cargo or whether the firm will be injured by its loss, damage, or detention. This covers a wide range of situations in that not only do the owners of the carrier and cargo have such an interest, but so may certain nonowners. For instance, in some situations the seller can have an insurable interest as a nonowner even though the buyer has already become the legal owner of the goods.

The liability of the transportation carrier in international trade is severely limited. Additionally, the owner of cargo on board a vessel is a participant in a 'joint venture' and may become subject to a *general-average* claim which is liability for loss or destruction of merchandise of other persons which is sacrificed to save the vessel (see Exhibit 13.5). Therefore, shipments on ocean-going vessels are invariably covered by marine insurance. Most frequently coverage is secured by the shipper or exporter; however, importers customarily also maintain coverage to provide protection if for any reason it is not provided by the exporter. So universally is marine insurance necessary that most firms engaged regularly in export business maintain an open policy with a reliable marine insurance company.

EXHIBIT 13.5   Marine insurance coverage

When acquiring marine insurance there are a number of perils that the exporter wants to insure against. Major perils include fire, perils of the sea (weather, waves, damage by sea water, etc.), jettison (throwing items overboard), assailing thieves (forcible taking), and barratry (willful misconduct of captain or crew, including theft). In addition, the exporter can obtain insurance coverage for other perils and hazards, including theft by other than crew.

The perils specified govern the nature of the loss and damage recoverable under the insurance. The *average* terms cover the extent of coverage. As used in insurance, average refers to 'loss less than total.' A *particular average* loss is one that affects specific interests only, whereas a *general average* loss is one affecting all cargo interests on a particular vessel plus the vessel itself.

The narrowest form of coverage is 'free of particular average' (FPA) which means that in addition to total losses, partial losses from perils of the sea are recoverable, but only if the carrying vessel has stranded, sunk, burnt, been on fire, or been in a collision. Under English conditions (FPA-EC), any one of these conditions must have occurred but it is not necessary to show that it actually caused the loss. In contrast, under American conditions (FPA-AC), the event must have caused the loss.

A more inclusive coverage is 'with average'. Partial damage is recoverable, sometimes with a deductible being applied depending upon the specific event that occurred. The most inclusive coverage would be 'all risks.' At times the all-risk coverage may exclude specific types of damage to specific products.

When a CIF price is quoted to a buyer the exporter must furnish marine insurance. If no special coverages are requested by the buyer, the exporter provides that which is customary and which has been found necessary or desirable for that particular type of shipment.

Shippers by air may obtain insurance coverage for their shipments from the initial air carrier or through the shipper's insurance broker. Airlines provide a limited amount of insurance coverage on shipments of selected products. If insurance coverage is made by the airline concerned, it should be noted that the insurance company usually imposes a maximum limit upon the value of merchandise that may be carried on any one flight. This fact sometimes accounts for the refusal of an airline to carry some physically small, but highly valuable shipment.

Insurance is also furnished by the air freight forwarder. Merchandise, therefore, may be covered from the time of pick up to the time of delivery at the airport.

The regular form of open or floating policy used for marine insurance is also used for insurance of air cargo, but air insurance requires a special rider, which is attached to the open policy. If the exporter makes regular shipments by air, it is to his or her advantage to obtain an open policy covering all shipments. Such a policy can be arranged to cover door-to-door shipments from exporter to importer.

A comprehensive discussion of this subject is provided by Rodda (1970).

Export packing

Distinct from packaging is the activity of packing. Sound export packing is not just the operation of putting a piece of merchandise into a container so that it will arrive at its destination in good condition. Additional objectives are to economize shipping space, to save expense by employing economical packing materials, to prevent pilferage, and to insure the lowest assessable Customs duties.

The type of packing that will deliver the commodity in good condition to the foreign customer will vary with the product concerned, the port of destination, length of journey, climate of the place of delivery, and the heat and moisture conditions to which the goods may be subjected en route. Only experience and experimentation can determine the type of container or packing best suited to the particular conditions of a given shipment. A US company, Ekkwill Tropical Fish Farm, Inc., annually exports a few million live fish. Air transportation is used to service Canada, Mexico, and markets in Europe, Asia, South America, and the West Indies. Special shipping and packing precautions are needed for such a perishable product. Thus the company uses the latest technology including tranquilizers and top-quality water. Proper packing for export has a great impact on this company's reputation in diverse world markets.

Transportation space is expensive, and unless care is taken to use this space most efficiently, the cost to the exporter may quickly mount. Sound packing methods involve the use of economical packing materials. This is not synonymous with the use of either heavy or first-class packing materials. One exporter used heavy paper cartons to ship electric refrigerators with enamel exteriors to the west coast of South America. This is virtually a contradiction of every rule of sound packing, but it was successful because the amount saved in packing materials and in shipping space far outweighed the losses that occurred due to the fragility of the packing.

Another consideration is environment based. Throughout the markets of the world there is increasing interest in recycling packages and packing materials. In Germany, for example, there is the Green Dot program that covers recycling of packaging and packing materials. This program, or something similar, is very likely to become the norm in the European Union. The German law underlying this program is that all links in the distribution chain must take back and reduce or recycle used transport, sales, and secondary packaging. Since all packaging materials must be recyclable, only the following materials are allowed: paper, cardboard, wood, foils, packaging strips, stryrofoam, glass, tinplate, laminate board, and aluminum. Material used in packing export shipments is covered by this program.

Closely identified with packing is the marking and labeling of shipments being exported. In this matter there are three interested parties: transportation companies, Customs authorities, and importers. The requirements of these interested parties differ. Consequently, the manufacturer/exporter should be aware of the requirements for each individual export shipment. Careless marking and labeling can be a great stimulus to pilferage. Proper labeling conceals the contents of the shipment to outside parties and, at the same time, makes the contents identifiable to those who must know. Labels should also show the country of origin, number of packages contained in each case, destination and any special handling instructions.

13.4.3 Documents required

Table 13.2 describes briefly nine of the most common documents used in export shipments. One of the major documents required is the *bill of lading*, which is discussed in the next section. The other important documents are discussed now. At the present time there is a great amount of paperwork needed to complete an export transaction. Figure 13.6 illustrates the complexity of documentation as it identifies the main lines of communication in international trade. Each contact between the exporter/forwarder involves one or more documents. There is a great deal of work being done to standardize and simplify documentation, including development of EDI systems and networks.

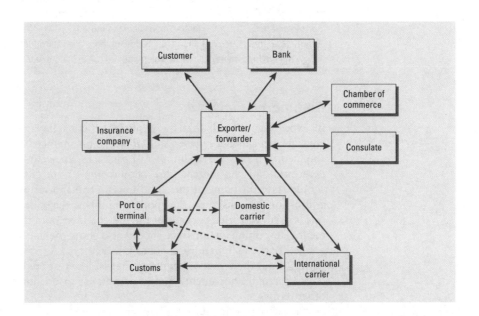

FIGURE 13.6

Main lines of communication in trade
Source: adapted from Davies, 1984, p. 67

Export license and export declaration

In addition to any required export license, the shipper may be required to complete a *shipper's export declaration*. Most countries require that shipments abroad be accompanied by such a declaration. This document is prepared by the exporter, given to the shipping company, and then filed with Customs officials at the port of export. In some countries, for example the United States, the document can be filed electronically with the proper government agency by the exporter or forwarder. The export declaration lists the descriptions, quantities, and values of the various types of merchandise in the shipment. It also lists the name of the shipper, the name of the agent of the shipper, and the destination and consignee. It is a basic document used in the collection of statistical data on exports and is also used by governments for control over exports. It is now an essential document for security purposes.

TABLE 13.2

Common export
documents

Transportation documents:
  Bill of lading. A receipt for the cargo and a contract for transportation between a shipper and a transport carrier. It may also be used as an instrument of ownership.
  Dock receipt. This is the document acknowledging receipt of the cargo by an ocean carrier.
  Insurance certificate. Evidence that insurance is provided to cover loss or damage to the cargo while in transit.

Banking documents:
  Letter of credit. A financial document issued by a bank at the request of the importer guaranteeing payment to the exporter if certain terms and conditions surrounding a transaction are met.
  Draft. A demand for payment from the exporter to the importer or his or her bank.

Commercial documents:
  Commercial invoice. This is a bill for the products from the exporter to the buyer.

Government documents:
  Export declaration. Includes complete information about the shipment.
  Consular invoice. This is a document signed by a consul of the importing country that is used to control and identify goods shipped there.
  Certificate of origin. A document certifying the origin of products being exported so that the buying country knows in which country the products were produced.

Commercial invoice

In exporting, the bill that the exporter or consignor sends to the importer or consignee is called a *commercial invoice*. This invoice lists full particulars of the shipment. The marks, the number of packages, an accurate packing list, and a full description of the merchandise should appear on the commercial invoice. It should state the name of the ship (if ocean transportation is used), the name and address of the consignee, the contract number, the code word for the contract if one is used, the price per unit of the merchandise, and the total price of the shipment. The commercial invoice should also show the nature of the price quotation – whether the merchandise is sold FOB factory, FAS vessel, or CIF port of destination – and the terms of payment (that is, letter of credit, sight draft, 60 or 120 days after sight, documents against acceptance or documents against payment, or other terms).

Various countries differ widely in the number of copies of the commercial invoice required with each shipment. The general practice is to send at least two copies to the bank with the other shipping documents and with the draft drawn either against letters of credit or filed with the bank for collection (drawn directly on the buyer). Many exporters send at least two copies of the commercial invoice direct to the consignee by separate mails. Other copies of the commercial invoice in large quantities are frequently required by consular officers of the importer's country.

In those countries that use common law, the commercial invoice generally carries no legal title to the merchandise and is, therefore, not a negotiable instrument. At best, it is evidence of the intentions of the parties and is a notification to the consignee of all the facts and the amount to be paid. In those countries where civil law is used, however, the commercial invoice is of much greater importance in determining the passage of title. In such countries, it may even become evidence of the fact that title has passed.

The commercial invoice is also important in connection with insurance claims and is frequently filed with underwriters and surveyors when claims for damages are made.

Consular invoice/special Customs invoice/factura

Another essential shipping document for shipments to some countries, but not all, is the *consular invoice*, 'special Customs invoice,' or *factura* (as it is called in some Spanish-speaking countries). This is a document obtained by the exporter in the home country from the governmental representative of the importer's country. Thus, the exporter must prepare and have certified before the foreign consul or representative a document containing all essential details of the sale. After certification the document is forwarded to the buyer for presentation to Customs with the Customs declaration, ostensibly for use in determining the amount of tariff to be levied. Figure 13.7 is an example of a consular invoice that has been used by the Republic of Haiti. Although specific formats will vary by country, this example shows the type of information that is requested.

The fees charged to certify the document by the consul of the foreign government vary widely from country to country. Some fees are nominal, but a few countries, particularly some of the less developed nations, have found that the consular invoice can be a good source of revenue.

Where they are required, consular invoices must be filled out with meticulous care. Some countries will not accept a form containing erasures or corrections of errors. When errors are detected by Customs officials a substantial fine may be levied, or the shipment may be subject to confiscation.

Packing list

The packing list is sometimes shown on the commercial invoice, or it may be a separate document, depending on the number of packages and the complexity of the list. It should contain, item by item, the contents of cases or containers in a shipment. The items should be listed separately with their weight and description set forth so as to make a complete check of the contents of each package possible upon arrival at the port of destination or the Customs office. This information is also useful for the consignee. Any variation in description from the commercial invoice or consular invoice usually subjects the consignee to large fines, which are then passed on to the exporter.

Certification and other documents

There are a number of other documents that may be necessary for a complete set of shipping papers. Among the most important are certificates of origin and special certificates.

Certificates of origin are documents certifying the place of origin of the merchandise. Figure 13.8 is an example of a general certificate of origin for the United States. Although specific formats may vary, this certificate is representative of those used by most countries. All ask for essentially the same types of information. They are required by some countries for all products and by other countries for only certain types of product or only for products originating in certain countries. In addition to such general certificates, special certificates may be required for shipments between countries with special arrangements. For example, there is a separate certificate for US shipments to Israel that are covered by the US–Israel Free Trade Area Agreement.

In some countries, the certificate of origin is the only special document required. In other countries, a combined consular invoice and certificate of origin is

FACTURE CONSULAIRE
CONSULAT DE LA   REPUBLIQUE D'HAITI
CONSULAR INVOICE
B. L. No. ————

Marque (Masque) and Country of Origin

Merchandise Shipped on the S. S.: ————
Marchandises expédiées sur le SS.
Nationality - Name (nom) ———— on le ———— Date of Sailing ————, Haïti
Sailing from the Port of ———— for ————
Partant du port de ———— Pour
Name and Address of Shipper ————
Nom et adresse de l'expéditeur
Consigned to order of ———— of ————
Consignées à l'ordre de
Notify ———— of ————, Haïti
Notifier ———— de

Numbers Numéros	Number of pieces Nombre de colis	Nature of Packing Nature de l'emballage	Denomination and Details of Each Article (Quantity, Quality, Measure, Yardage, etc.) in Terms of the Haitian Tariff. Dénomination et détails de chaque article (quantité, qualité, mesure, yardage, etc.) dans les termes du Tarif Haïtien.	Weights in Poids en		Values in U.S. Currency Valeur en Monnaie des E.U.
				Gross Brut	Net Net	

We affirm that this invoice is a correct and faithful expression of the truth, J'affirme que cette facture est l'expression sincère et fidèle de la vérité, that it corresponds in every particular with our books, and that neither the qu'elle est en tout conforme à mes livres, qu'aucune dénomination usuelle, usual designation, nor the weights, nor the quantity or quality, nor the value ni le poids, ni la quantité ou la qualité, ni la valeur, ni l'origine des articles and origin named therein are in any way altered, and are thereof exactly the qui y sont portés, n'ont été altérés et sont, en conséquence, les mêmes que same than those appeared on our Export Declaration No. soumise à la Douane des Etats-Unis. submitted to the U. S. Custom House. ceux accusés sur ma déclaration No. of (date) du

———— Date ———— 19 ————

———— For Account of
Name of forwarding agent, broker or commissioner, etc.

Shippers ————
Expéditeurs
Per: ————
Signature

NOTE:—In all cases where the merchandise is taxed at net weight, the weight to be taxed of said merchandise will include all interior or immediate packing, including the paste board boxes or objects made of paste board, not subject to a higher tax. (Article 29, Law of July 26, 1926.)

Dans tous les cas où les marchandises sont taxées au poids net, le poids imposable des dites marchandises comprendra tous les emballages antérieurs ou immédiats, y compris les cartons ou objets en carton, non soumis à un droit plus élevé (Article 29, loi du 26 Juillet, 1926.)

ARRANGEMENT OF DOCUMENTS:

3 Consular Invoices and 3 Original Bills of lading clipped or stapled together, the invoice on top.

To each of the remaining Consular invoices a copy of signed B/L must be stapled and the whole set clipped together.

Value of merchandise ————
Valeur des marchandises
Packing (if not included in the value of the merchandise) ————
Emballage (s'il n'est pas compris dans la valeur des marchandises)
Inland Freight. Bill of Lading. Wharfage and Trucking Charges ————
Frêt et frais du connaissement, embarquement et camionnage.
Total F.O.B. Value ————
Brokerage fees ————
Commission d'achat
Interest ————
Intérêts
Export Duties paid at Port of Origin ————
Droits d'exportation acquittés au port d'origine
Ocean Freight and Bill of Lading Expenses (including embarking and disembarking) ————
Frêt et frais du connaissement, embarquement et débarquement compris
Insurance ————
Assurance

Consular fees: *2% of F O B value $ ————
Droits consulaires: Stamp on Inv. ($1.20) ————
B/L visa ($2.00) ————
Stamp on B/L ($1.20) ————
Other expenses
Autres frais

Total amount of invoice ————
Montant total de la facture

CONSULAR INVOICE FEES
*For any merchandise being shipped by boat to Haiti and whose value FOB is inferior to $200.00 — the fee is $3.00 plus B/L visa and Stamps ———— 7.40
Over $200.00 — the fee is 2% on the value FOB plus B/L visa and Stamps
Visa for Certificate of Origin $2.00 plus Stamps $1.20 ———— 3.20
Visa for Commercial Invoice if requested $2.00 plus Stamp $1.20 ———— 3.20
ADDITIONAL FEES :
Visa on Consular Invoice requested after 4 p. m. ———— 2.00*
Visa on Consular Invoice requested on holidays ———— 4.00*

FIGURE 13.7   Consular invoice for the Republic of Haiti

CERTIFICATE OF ORIGIN

The undersigned . . . .
(Owner or Agent, & c)

for . . . . declares
(Name and Address of Shipper, etc)

that the following mentioned goods shipped on S/S . . . .
(Name of Ship)

on the date of . . . . consigned to . . . .

. . . . are the product of the United States of America.

MARKS AND NUMBERS	NO. OF PKGS., BOXES OR CASES	WEIGHT IN KILOS GROSS NET		DESCRIPTION

Sworn to before me

Dated at . . . . on the . . . . day of . . . . 19 . . . .

this . . . . day of . . . . . . 19 . . . .

. . . .
Signature of Owner or Agent

The . . . . , a recognized Chamber of Commerce under the

laws of the State of . . . . , has examined the manufacturer's invoice or

shipper's affidavit concerning the origin of the merchandise and, according to the best

of its knowledge and belief, finds that the products named originated in the United

States of North America.

Secretary . . . .

FIGURE 13.8

Certificate of origin from
the United States
Source: Form 10-900P
Certificate of Origin.
Reproduced with permission
of Unz & New Providence,
NJ 07974

required. In still others, a separate certificate of origin is required in addition to the consular invoice.

The certificate of origin is not treated, generally, with anything like the formality of the consular invoice. The form is generally filled out by the consignor or an agent, and is then certified by officers of a local commercial organization, not consular officials. In some cases a consular official has to authorize the signature of the local commercial organization person.

Special certificates include a wide variety of special inspection certificates issued by various authorities and may be required by the importer to meet his own or government requirements. These documents certify as to purity and absence of disease, and are issued to cover food products, plants, seeds, and live animals. Frequently, they must be visaed or legalized by the consular representative of the importing country. Food products are those for which sanitary certificates are most often required.

Special certificates are also issued for certain types of merchandise, to certify a required composition or the existence of specific ingredients. Some types of steel, for example, are sold on analysis. Certain chemical mixtures must be analyzed and certified with respect to the presence of desired constituents.

The importer can be expected to specify what special certificates may be required, and the exporter must provide them. All required certificates should be attached to the commercial invoice and forwarded to the importer together with the other shipping documents.

13.4.4 Ocean transportation and bills of lading

The ocean bill of lading

The bill of lading used in ocean transportation is a document that serves three distinct purposes:

1. It is the contract of carriage between the shipper and the transportation company.
2. It is a receipt for the goods issued by the steamship company.
3. It is evidence of title to the merchandise.

Different types of bills of lading are described in some detail in Exhibit 13.6. An example is shown in Figure 13.9 on page 603.

The conditions under which the ocean carrier company accepts goods for con-

EXHIBIT 13.6　Types of bills of lading

Bills of lading (B/Ls) may be classified on several bases relating to title to the goods and the type of receipt.

Signed and unsigned B/Ls

Bills of lading are frequently prepared in as many as 25 copies. Sometimes even more may be required. Only those signed by the master of the vessel or his authorized agent are legally binding documents. In the case of a to-order bill of lading (discussed below), each of the signed copies carries with it the title to the shipment. Any one may be used by the shipper, the consignee, or his agent, or by some person or persons to whom the merchandise has been conveyed for claiming ownership and taking delivery. However, when any of the signed copies is presented the others automatically become void (only one copy can be presented to the carrier to claim the shipment). Signed nonnegotiable copies, issued in the case of straight bills of lading (discussed below), are used as proof of shipment.

Unsigned copies of the bill of lading have no legal status, yet they are essential. Several are needed for the files of the shipper and the consignee; a number are used by the steamship company for recording and billing purposes; and others may be necessary for purposes such as preparing and settling insurance claims, and by banks participating in the financing or collection process.

Straight and order B/Ls, and datafreight receipts/seaway bills

Ocean bills of lading may be either *straight* or *order*. A straight bill of lading is made out to a specifically named consignee at the destination, who is the only person authorized to take delivery. An order bill of lading may be made out to the order of the shipper, a bank, an agent, or merely 'to order.' Whoever legally holds the document may take delivery of the shipment.

The straight bill of lading is nonnegotiable. By its provisions the transportation company accepts receipt of the freight and contracts to move it from the point of shipment to the point of delivery. Anyone who holds the arrival notice of a shipment and can establish the fact that he or she is the consignee, or represents the consignee, may obtain possession of the merchandise. This could be a bank, a custom-house broker, or an agent.

An order bill of lading is a negotiable instrument, and the surrender of the original, properly endorsed, is required for delivery of the merchandise. Title remains with the person to whose order it is made out – if made out 'to order,' title remains with the shipper – until it is endorsed. The ultimate recipient is usually shown as the person or organization to be notified of arrival at the destination by the carrier.

Documents generally called datafreight receipts in most European countries and seaway bills in the United States and Asia are often used in place of straight bills of lading. Under this system no original bills of lading are issued. The arrival information is simply forwarded to the carrier's agent at the port of discharge.

Received for shipment and on-board B/Ls

Unless the bill of lading specifically shows on the face that the cargo has been loaded on board the vessel, it is no more than a *received-for-shipment bill of lading*. This may be done when space on the vessel has not been reserved in advance and the carrier agrees to load it only if space should be available. Received-for-shipment bills of lading are only used when there is no urgency in delivery of the shipment to its destination and when other than letter-of-credit or draft financing is used.

On-board bills of lading carry with them the legal guarantee by the master of the vessel, acting as agent for the carrier, that the goods have actually been loaded on the vessel.

Clean or foul B/Ls

Cargo checkers inspect shipments carefully when they are delivered to the pier and when they are loaded on board the vessel. If any damage is observed or if the quantity is less than that specified when the goods are delivered to the pier, a notation is entered on the dock receipt, and the shipper is usually given the opportunity to make repairs or complete the quantity. If any exception to the apparent good order of the cargo is noted when the cargo is loaded on the vessel a notation is made on the bill of lading, which then becomes a *foul bill of lading*. If, however, the merchandise is in apparent good order and there are thus no notations, it is referred to as a *clean bill of lading*.

Special types of B/Ls

A special type of bill of lading, used more frequently than generally supposed, is the *accommodation bill of lading*. If the shipper is well (and favorably) known to the steamship company and wants a bill of lading dated on a certain day and the merchandise has not yet been delivered at the pier, the shipper may be issued a bill of lading in the regular form and properly signed by the company. This is an accommodation bill of lading. There is, however, no evidence on the face of it to indicate its character. The shipper might want the bill of lading in order to meet the expiry date in a letter of credit and may be willing to give such guarantees as the steamship company may require.

Forwarder's and NVOCC B/Ls

Another form of bill of lading that is sometimes used is the *forwarder's bill of lading*. The reason for the use of this particular form is the fact that most steamship companies have a minimum bill-of-lading fee. This imposes a heavy charge on the shipper who wishes to send a single box, crate, or small lot of merchandise. The export freight forwarder can combine several small shipments from individual shippers and send the lot under one bill of lading to a destination. At the destination, the forwarder's branch office or correspondent breaks out the shipment and delivers the individual pieces to the several consignees. At the time of shipment, the foreign freight forwarder delivers a forwarder's bill of lading to each of the original exporters.

This consolidation function is often performed by the ocean transportation intermediary formerly known as a nonvessel ocean common carrier. The NVOCC is authorized to issue regular bills of lading. The development of the NVOCC arose largely because of containerization that makes consolidation into much larger amounts desirable from the standpoints of cost, ease of handling, and security.

Uniform through export B/L

Use of this special form of bill of lading simplifies matters for inland manufacturers and exporters. This type of bill of lading replaces two documents: the railroad (or truck) bill of lading and the steamship bill of lading.

veyance are stated on the ocean bill of lading. Although the contract between the ocean carrier and the shipper of the merchandise is set forth in great detail, it is rare indeed that the shipper reads all of its conditions. Every sentence has been interpreted in courts, and a great body of law now surrounds and interprets this contract. The shipper's rights are fully protected.

As a result of these years of litigation, ocean carriers are almost completely exempt from the responsibility of loss of the shipment through theft or by pilferage, or its damage by breakage, water, or fire. The only responsibility ordinarily assumed by ocean carriers is the damage arising out of their own or their employees' negligence or for failure to make sure that the vessel is seaworthy before it leaves port.

Selecting the route and getting the merchandise to the port

The exporter should keep two major factors in mind when selecting the route of an ocean shipment. These are: (1) the route that will bring the shipment to its port of

MAERSK LINE

COMBINED TRANSPORT BILL OF LADING

B/L No. SFOL22983

Shipper/Exporter (complete name and address): NAF INTERNATIONAL INC. ONE WATERS PARK DR., STE 120 SAN MATEO, CA 94403	Booking No. SFO953929 Export references 1071010 NKL-859
Consignee (complete name and address) NKL FRESH FRUIT DEPT. POSTBOKS 21 HAUGENSTUA 0915 OSLO 9 NORWAY	Forwarding agent - reference FMC 0087 CHB 5118 J E LOWDEN & CO ONE EMBARCADERO CTR SUITE 1950 SAN FRANCISCO, CA 94111-3701 Point and Country of Origin CALIFORNIA USA
Notify Party (complete name and address) NKL FRESH FRUIT DEPT. POSTBOKS 21 HAUGENSTUA 0915 OSLO 9 NORWAY	Domestic routing/export instructions

*Precarriage by	*Place of Receipt NEW YORK	
Vessel MAREN MAERSK	Voy No. 9212	Port of Loading NEW YORK	Onward inland routing
Port of Discharge ROTTERDAM	*Place of Delivery OSLO	

CARRIER'S RECEIPT

PARTICULARS FURNISHED BY SHIPPER - CARRIER NOT RESPONSIBLE

Container No./Seal No. Marks and Numbers	No. of Containers or pkgs.	Kind of packages; description of goods	Gross Weight	Measurement
NKL-829 MAEU5504758 ML-US0346891 6451630	1	40' CNTR SAID TO CONTAIN 1540 PACKAGES FRESH GRAPES 38500# 1445' "NO SED REQUIRED, SECTION 30.39 FTSR, C.A.S. - JL." SHIPPERS LOAD, STOW AND COUNT FREIGHT COLLECT CY / CY STOWED IN A REEFER CONTAINER SET AT SHIPPERS REQUESTED CARRIAGE TEMPERATURE OF 34 TO 34 DEGREES FAHRENHEIT COMM CODE: AN10 0800000271	KGS 17463	CBM 40.894

These commodities licensed by the United States for ultimate destination NORWAY Diversion contrary to US law prohibited

Freight & Charges	Rate		Unit	Prepaid	Collect
BASIC FREIGHT	208.00	USD	MTON		3632.30
ARBITRARY CHARGE	200.00	USD	HIGHCUBE		200.00
CURRENCY ADJ. FACTOR	22.00	USD	SS		843.11
BUNKER ADJ. FACTOR	80.00	USD	HIGHCUBE		80.00
TERMINAL HANDLING CH	500.00	USD	HIGHCUBE		500.00
CONT SERVICE CHARGE	780.00	NOK	HIGHCUBE		780.00

Declared Value Charges (see clause 6) for Declared Value of US $	Total Prepaid		
Number of Original B/s/L 3/THREE	Total Collect		
Place of Issue SAN FRANCISCO	Date NOV 17 92	LADEN ON BOARD NOV 16 1992 MAERSK INC.	
*Applicable only when document used as a "Combined Transport Bill of Lading" MAERSK LINE U.S. CUSTOMS CONTAINER BOND NO. 1065-20581	By	As Agents for the Carrier	
M-1000 1/92			BLANKBL/1MM/2406/1/92/DR

FIGURE 13.9 Ocean/combined transport bill of lading

Source: reproduced with permission of Maersk Line and J. E. Lowden and Co.

destination in the shortest possible time, and (2) the route that will be most economical. Frequently the quickest route is not the most economical.

Frequency of sailings from a given port is more important than the actual duration of the voyage. When a shipment just misses one sailing and has to be held over for the next, several days or weeks later, demurrage (charges for the use of the freight car or container in which sent) and storage charges may accumulate. This is one of the reasons that, in spite of possible higher port costs for individual shipments, major ports are usually the best to use for shipment.

When the products to be exported are delivered to a railroad (or trucking company) at an inland point, either a railroad (trucking) bill of lading or a through bill of lading is issued. If just a railroad (trucking) bill of lading is issued, a second bill of lading will have to be issued at the port for the ocean portion of the shipment. Upon arrival of the merchandise at the port, a notice referred to as an *arrival notice* is sent by the railroad to the domestic consignee at port of shipment. The representative of the exporter then accepts the merchandise from the rail (trucking) carrier and makes delivery to the ocean carrier. The representative of the shipper then becomes responsible for all details connected with starting the merchandise on its ocean journey.

Freight rates and space reservations

Ocean freight rates may be obtained directly from shipping lines or through the foreign freight forwarder. In some countries the shipper is faced with the question of whether to use independent carriers or ocean carriers belonging to a conference or rate agreement. Referred to briefly earlier, shipping conferences are associations of ocean transportation companies. They are organized by formal agreement, with governmental sanction, primarily to set freight rates and sailing schedules over specified routes. A shipper may make an annual contract with the conference to ship all of the company's cargo to places served by the conference on vessels operated by conference companies. By signing such a contract the shipper gets a lower rate than shippers who do not have a contract. Independent carriers may also offer discounted rates for shippers that are willing to sign annual contracts. While both conference carriers and independent carriers have government-approved schedules of rates (tariffs) by which they must abide, the independent carrier's rates are often lower. The lower rates must be balanced against the possibly less frequent sailings available from one or a few independent carriers as compared with the often greater number of conference members. A third type of carrier, which often offers the lowest rates, is the so-called *tramp vessel*. Used largely in carrying bulk cargos, this type of carrier does not follow an established schedule. Rather, it operates on a charter basis.

Whether the carriers involved are members of a conference or independent, outbound and inbound rates between two points for the same product are often not the same. To illustrate, in the mid-1990s the rate for sporting goods going through base ports in continental Europe was $85 per ton for inbound cargo and $145 for outbound cargo.

Once the decision is reached as to the particular ocean transportation company to use, the next task is to secure a freight space reservation on a particular ship. An inland shipper may secure space by contacting the line or its agent. However, as sailing schedules to the destination are usually not known, it may prove better to contact a foreign freight forwarder, who will make the space reservation at no cost to the exporter.

Container shipment

Some years ago many commodities were shipped 'break bulk,' that is, in individual

FIGURE 13.10a

A modern container facility, Auckland, New Zealand

FIGURE 13.10b

A container vessel being loaded in Melbourne, Australia

packages individually handled. Now most merchandise that is not handled in bulk, such as petroleum or wheat, is packed in large, standard-sized containers. Figure 13.10a shows an example of a container facility in a major port and Figure 13.10b shows a vessel being loaded with containers. Containers may be filled on the dock before loading on the vessel, or they may be filled at the exporter's plant. Some ocean transport companies will provide containers to producers within a reasonable distance at a lower charge than usual inland freight rates (Hall, 1983, pp. 215–21).

Dock receipt

In some places, when the shipment has been delivered to the pier the receiving clerk signs a dock receipt. At the time that the shipment is checked at the pier, the packages are examined to determine whether they are all in good condition. Any that are not are noted on the dock receipt. If any such notices appear on the dock receipt, it is then described as a 'foul dock receipt' and these notes will, if not eliminated by the required repairs, appear later on the bill of lading. Dock receipts for full containers show only the condition of the container, which is not opened for inspection of contents.

13.4.5 Air shipments and air waybills

With the rapid expansion of international air freight, an ever-growing number of shippers are utilizing this means. Moreover, considering savings in inland freight, packing, inventories, and working capital investment, some shippers are finding that movement by air is actually cheaper even though air freight rates are somewhat higher. In short, following a total-cost approach to physical distribution may lead an exporter to use air transport.

Up to the point of overseas movement, the procedures for an ocean shipment and an air shipment are usually similar. One difference that may prove significant is that some international air carriers, such as Lufthansa and KLM, serve inland points; hence, no trans-shipment at an export point is necessary.

The major difference in procedure arises at the time that the shipment is turned over to the international air carrier. International airlines have been able to eliminate some of the routine of export procedure required of ocean carriers. Most important, an *air waybill* (variously designated as an 'air waybill,' 'airway bill,' 'international airwaybill,' or 'air consignment note') is used rather than a standard bill of lading (see Figure 13.11). In some cases the air waybill may also replace the commercial invoice, the consular invoice, the certificate of origin, and the insurance certificate. These simplified procedures have been devised and promoted by the International Air Transport Association (IATA), which has brought about a high degree of uniformity in the international use of the air waybill.

The application and use of the air waybill differs in different countries. Usually the abbreviated procedure applies only to shipments of small value. In some countries consular invoices and certificates of origin are still required, whereas in others they are not. In certain cases the shipper may elect to use his or her regular marine insurance coverage, especially where warehouse-to-warehouse protection is desired; in other cases insurance provided by the airlines is sufficient.

When foreign freight forwarders prepare the air waybill for the shipper from information furnished to them, the information usually includes a description of the merchandise conforming to the export declaration and any other shipping documents, and whether or not insurance coverage is desired. The shipper must also make a statement of value for carriage and Customs purposes.

The value for carriage serves three purposes:

1. It may be required for computing the transportation rates when a special commodity rate is based on value.
2. It is the limit of liability of the carrier for loss or damage to the shipment.
3. It is the amount on which the carrier's valuation charge and insurance premium will be computed.

As a general rule, the shipper uses as the value for carriage the amount declared as value for Customs, plus shipping charges, plus 10%. Although the shipper may

Shipper's Name and Address	Shipper's account Number	Not negotiable
		Air Waybill* (Air Consignment note) issued by
		Copies 1, 2 and 3 of this Air Waybill are originals and have the same validity
Consignee's Name and Address	Consignee's account Number	It is agreed that the goods described herein are accepted in apparent good order and condition (except as noted) for carriage SUBJECT TO THE CONDITIONS OF CONTRACT ON THE REVERSE HEREOF. THE SHIPPER'S ATTENTION IS DRAWN TO THE NOTICE CONCERNING CARRIER'S LIMITATION OF LIABILITY. Shipper may increase such limitation of liability by declaring a higher value for carriage and paying a supplemental charge if required

Issuing Carrier's Agent Name and City	Accounting Information

Agent's IATA Code	Account No.	

Airport of Departure (Addr. of first Carrier and requested Routing)

to	By first Carrier	Routing and Destination	to	by	to	by	Currency	CMGs	WT/VAL		Other		Declared Value for Carriage	Declared value for Customs
									PPD	COLL	PPD	COLL		

Airport of Destination	Flight/Date	For Carrier use only	Flight/Date	Amount of Insurance	INSURANCE if carrier offers insurance and such insurance is requested in accordance with conditions on reverse hereof, indicate amount to be insured in figures in box marked amount of insurance

Handling Information

No. of Pieces RCP	Gross Weight	kg lb	Rate Class / Commodity Item No	Chargeable Weight	Rate / Charge	Total	Nature and Quality of Goods (incl. Dimensions or Volume)

Prepaid	Weight Charge	Collect	Other Charges
	Valuation Charge		
	Tax		
	Total other Charges Due Agent		Shipper certifies that the particulars on the face hereof are correct and that insofar as any part of the consignment contains dangerous goods, such part is properly described by name and is in proper condition for carriage by air according to the applicable Dangerous Goods Regulations
	Total other Charges Due Carrier		
			Signature of Shipper or his Agent

Total prepaid	Total collect	
Currency Conversion Rates	cc Charges in Dest. Currency	.... Executed on Date at (Place) Signature of issuing Carrier or its Agent
For Carrier's Use only at Destination	Charges at Destination	Total collect Charges

COPY 5 (FOR AIRPORT OF DESTINATION)

FIGURE 13.11   Air waybill

declare any value, the carrier's maximum liability may be limited to the actual value plus 10%.

The air waybill is not negotiable. It is not, therefore, a complete substitute for an ocean bill of lading. The air waybill serves as a shipping contract and receipt to the shipper, providing evidence that the airline has accepted the goods, as listed, and agrees to carry the consignment to the airport of destination. International shipments made by air cannot be financed in exactly the same way as the majority of shipments made by surface carriers; modifications must be made. The elapsed time between dispatch and delivery is so short that financing during the transportation period is normally unnecessary. Generally, airlines will not deliver or change consignment without the original or shipper's copy of the air waybill. Finally, consignees always have the privilege of specifying that the air waybill shall be acceptable as the document against which payment will be made.

Since most airlines provide COD facilities as a service to shippers, this method may be utilized if the shipper requires quick reimbursement. Also, arrangements can usually be made for electronic notification of collection to the home office of the airline which can then issue a check immediately to the shipper.

If the importer has a satisfactory reputation and it is desirable to extend credit, a clean time or acceptance draft can be used. When used, the draft would be forwarded for collection in the usual manner.

These methods, however, can only be used in sales to countries in which there are no foreign exchange restrictions. For those countries in which exchange controls are still in effect, the letter of credit would still have to be used with necessary modifications in document specifications so as to permit utilization of the nonnegotiable air waybill.

If the shipper believes that credit protection is necessary, the merchandise may be consigned to a bank, an agent, or a foreign freight forwarder with instructions regarding conditions of delivery to the buyer. This method is similar to that used for surface shipments to those countries that do not permit the use of the order bill of lading.

13.5 A concluding comment

The ramifications of international marketing described in the preceding chapters and of export procedure and physical distribution described in this chapter may seem to be quite involved and somewhat complicated for the business firm considering foreign sales. Actually, export marketing management is not significantly more cumbersome than good domestic business management; and each particular function and institution fills a well-recognized need. Each individual document also covers some specific function in long-established export procedure. Once thoroughly learned, tasks and responsibilities become simple and routine.

Nevertheless, the omission of any management function or the omission of any document in the actual export procedure may create problems for either the seller or buyer, if not both. Wise business people frequently review both management responsibilities and procedures and, even more important, they keep up to date with changes in today's dynamic international business world, such as developments in Internet and other technology.

QUESTIONS FOR DISCUSSION

13.1 What are the main issues that are of concern to the exporter regarding inquiries and orders?

13.2 Why might the cheapest form of transportation not be the most economical?

13.3 Discuss the various ways in which a company might minimize its export marketing costs by paying proper attention to physical distribution matters.

13.4 Explain the meaning of the 'total-cost concept,' and illustrate how break-even analysis might be used to solve an export physical distribution analysis problem.

13.5 Why does an exporter often need the services of a foreign freight forwarder?

13.6 A typical export shipment requires many documents. Identify those that are generally required for all shipments and those that may be required only for specific shipments.

13.7 Why is the bill of lading an important document in an export transaction?

13.8 Distinguish between the alternative types of free areas that are potentially available for use by an exporter and/or importer. Is any one type better than the others? Explain.

13.9 How has the rapidly changing technology of the late 1990s and the early 2000s affected the physical distribution of products from one country to another?

13.10 How have security concerns affected physical distribution?

REFERENCES

Ambrosino, L. (1994). Facilitators par excellence. *Via International*, March, 4–5.

Armstrong, D. (2004). SF Oakland ports to get high-tech security. *San Francisco Chronicle*, 7 February, B-1, 2.

Coughlin, A. T., Anderson, E., Stern, L., and El-Ansery, A. I. (2001). *Marketing Channels* 6th edn. Upper Saddle River, NJ: Prentice-Hall.

Davies, G. (1984). *Managing Export Distribution*. London: William Heinemann.

Down, J. W. and Anderson, D. L. (1990). Logistics strategies for the New Europe. *Europa 1992*, 2(6), 23–6.

Engbarth, D. (1996). Move to lift ban on mainland containers. *South China Morning Post*, 18 April, 14.

Hall, R. D. (1983). *International Trade Operations: A Managerial Approach*. Jersey City, NJ: Unz.

Ihlwan, M. (2003). Monsters on the high seas. *Business Week*, 13 October, 58.

Keegan, W. J. and Green, M. S. (2000). *Global Marketing* 2nd edn. Upper Saddle River, NJ: Prentice-Hall.

Machalara, D. and Pasztor, A. (2004). Thinking inside the box: shipping containers get 'smart.' *The Wall Street Journal*, 15 January, B-1, 6.

Marsh, P. (2003). Speed puts tools on the cutting edge. *Financial Times*, 21 October, 11.

Ricks, D. A. (1999). *Blunders in International Business* 3rd edn. Oxford, UK: Blackwell.

Rodda, W. H. (1970). *Marine Insurance: Ocean and Inland* 3rd edn. Englewood Cliffs, NJ: Prentice-Hall.

Russell, M. (1998). Industries can save $9b a year. *South China Morning Post*, 19 May, 26.

Tang, R. (1998). New distribution concept challenges SARs gateway role. *South China Morning Post*, 9 April, 4.

The Economist (2001). Ports in a storm. 14 April, 57–8.

UNIDO (1995). *Export Processing Zones: Principles and Practices*. Vienna: United Nations Industrial Development Organization.

FURTHER READING

Branch, A. E. (1990). *Import/Export Documentation*. London: Chapman & Hall.
Johnson, T. E. (1994). *Export/Import Procedures and Documentation* 2nd edn. New York: AMACOM.
Wells, L. F. and Dulat, K. B. (1996). *Exporting: From Start to Finance* 3rd edn. New York: McGraw-Hill.

CASE STUDY 13.1

Jaguar Electronics, Inc.

(This case study is derived from one written by Frank C. Burinsky and Michael A. McGinnis, Shippensburg University. The company name, product and component names, overseas locations for selling the products, and shipping costs have been changed to protect the actual company name and reflect changes in trade agreements and shipping practices.)

Jaguar Electronics, Inc. is a specialized electronics firm located in Charleston, South Carolina in the United States. The company was founded in 1965 and has enjoyed success and modest growth as a supplier of components to large manufacturers of specialty electronic-mechanical devices. Recently the company's management has decided to begin manufacturing and marketing a product called the 'Airflow'. The Airflow is manufactured by assembling two component parts: (1) mechanical assemblies (MA), which are purchased from a company in Belgium; and (2) electronic assemblies (EC) manufactured by Jaguar Electronics at its Charleston facility.

Jaguar Electronics has manufactured and supplied the electronic assemblies to several national manufacturers of products similar to the Airflow for several years. Most of the consumer demand for the final products comes from areas enjoying a relatively warm climate throughout the year. Accordingly, the manufacturers of those products have sold their goods with great success throughout the southern and southwestern United States. The population and economic growth in these areas have contributed greatly to the success of this type of consumer product.

The man largely responsible for Jaguar Electronics' proposed move into manufacturing and marketing Airflow is the company president, Mr Smith. He has spent his entire career in the electronics industry and was with Jaguar Electronics for several years before becoming its president. His reign as president has been very successful. However, he has viewed the impressive sales growth of EC units with mixed feelings. As a supplier of EC components, Jaguar Electronics has prospered from the growth in sales of products such as Airflow. However, Smith has always felt that his company was not reaping all of the benefits available in sales to the consumers. At the same time he felt that Jaguar Electronics did not have the resources to compete successfully with the large firms that dominate the US market.

Smith employed a consultant to determine where increasing consumer demand for Airflow-type products would approach a level sufficiently high to justify entering these smaller markets. After reviewing the consultant's recommendations, Smith decided that Jaguar Electronics should target two of the higher-income countries in Latin America, Country 1 and Country 2. These nations, because of the income levels in particular cities, had the potential to be lucrative markets for Airflow. The consultant estimated the potential demand for Airflow to be 20,000 units per year in Country 1, and 40,000 units per year in Country 2.

The consultant had also recommended four options available to Jaguar Electronics as to how the widgets could be produced and distributed to these markets:

1. Assemble the widgets in Charleston and distribute them from that point.
2. Assemble them in a free trade zone in Country 1, and distribute them from that point.
3. Assemble them in Country 2 (which had no free trade zone).
4. Assemble them in a free trade zone in another country, Country 3, which had no significant potential domestic market for Airflow, but a lower labor cost.

Smith held a meeting to brief his production manager, Daphne R. Feldblum, and his distribution manager, Karl Q. Winklepleck, on the proposed Airflow venture and the consultant's recommendations. Both had been with the company for several years.

After briefing the two managers, Smith asked: 'What course of action would you recommend?' Feldblum replied: 'We should probably assemble them where the labor cost would be lowest.' Winklepleck commented: 'We should also consider transportation rates, insurance rates, import duties, and free trade zones.' Smith decided that Feldblum and Winklepleck should work together to compile the information necessary for making the best possible decision.

Two weeks later the information shown in Tables 13.3 and 13.4 had been compiled.

With the data available, Smith had a meeting with Feldblum, Winklepleck, and a member of the corporate legal staff to discuss what should be done. The meeting went poorly. Feldblum still believed that the company should locate assembly in the place with the lowest labor cost. Winklepleck realized that he should have provided a spreadsheet indicating total costs associated with each approach. In order to avoid having the meeting end in confusion, he decided to show on the conference room whiteboard how the calculations should be made.

TABLE 13.3	Cost, demand, weight, and tariff data

Annual demand in Country 1	20,000 units
Annual demand in Country 2	40,000 units
Labor costs for assembly	
in Charleston	$5.00/unit
in Country 1 free trade zone	$4.50/unit
in Country 2	$4.00/unit
in Country 3 free trade zone	$3.75/unit
Cost of components	
MA, FOB Brussels (Belgium)	$25.00/unit
EC, FOB Charleston	$30.00/unit
Product weight	
MA	60 lb/unit
EC	40 lb/unit
Airflow	100 lb/unit

Import duties as a percentage of price paid (excluding transportation and insurance costs from port of embarkation to port of entry)

United States	5%
Country 1	10%
Country 2	10%
Country 3	25%

TABLE 13.4	Combined rates for transportation and insurance between respective points

(Note: Projected sales volumes would justify shipping by container load. Though shipping rates would actually be charged per container load, for ease of calculation the rates below are shown as dollar costs per hundred pounds ($/cwt). If products were shipped in less-than-container loads, rates would be much higher.)

From	To	Rate, $/cwt
Belgium	US	1.65
Belgium	Country 1	3.50
Belgium	Country 2	3.00
Belgium	Country 3	3.75
US	Country 1	2.50
US	Country 2	2.25
US	Country 3	3.00
Country 1	Country 2	1.25
Country 2	Country 1	1.25
Country 3	Country 1 or 2	2.00

Footnote by Winklepleck: Ocean freight shipments from Belgium to Country 3 are very infrequent.

He gave the following figures for assembly in Charleston & shipping to Country 1:

$25.00	Cost of MA
0.99	Trans. + Ins., MA to Charleston (1.65 $/cwt × .60 cwt = $0.99)
1.25	Duty (5% of $25. Check to see if US government will rebate when finished goods are exported)
30.00	Cost of EC
5.00	Assembly
2.50	Trans. + Ins., US to Country 1 (2.50 $/cwt × 1.0 cwt = $2.50)
6.22	Duty in Country 1: 10% × $(25.99 + 30.00 + 5.00 + 1.25)
$70.96	Total landed cost in Country 1

The corresponding figures for assembly in Country 3 and shipping to Country 1:

$25.00	Cost of MA
2.25	Trans. + Ins., MA to Country 3 (3.75 $/cwt × .6 cwt = $2.25)
–	No duty in free zone on goods to be exported
30.00	Cost of EC
1.20	Trans. + Ins., EC to Country 3 (3.00 $/cwt × .4 cwt = $1.20)
3.75	Assembly in Country 3
2.00	Trans. + Ins., Country 3 to Country 1 (2.00 $/cwt × 1.0 = $2.00)
6.42	10% duty on all costs to Country 3 & Assembly in Country 3
$70.62	Total landed cost in Country 1

Winklepleck hoped that his quick calculations did not contain any errors. The total cost figures for assembling in Charleston and Country 3 appeared to be very close. If it was possible to obtain some type of free trade area in Charleston, or if the US government could refund duty on the component MA when the finished product was exported, Charleston would actually be less expensive. In any event, figures for all of the combinations should be carefully calculated.

Winklepleck also had some questions in his mind that he wondered if he should raise. They seemed to be important, but the president might not be pleased to have them brought up. If assembly were to be done overseas, how would quality be controlled? Should the company consider making a product for export that it thought it couldn't market successfully in the United States? Did the company have the resources needed and was it prepared to make the effort required to begin marketing internationally: establishing marketing channels, product promotion, etc? How long would it take to reach the projected sales overseas, and what would be needed to promote the product? How sure could they be that they could ever sell the expected number of units in each of the two overseas markets?

Questions

1. Calculate the costs if the Airflow is assembled in Country 1 and if it is assembled in Country 2. Note that Country 1 has a free trade zone and Country 2 does not. Note also that calculations should be done for total sales to the two countries rather than on a per-unit basis since the costs will differ depending upon destination as well as assembly point.

2. Is Jaguar Electronics likely to be able to compete overseas with a new product that it feels will not be competitive in its home market? Why or why not?

3. Should Winklepleck bring up the questions that are bothering him. If so, when?

4. What do you recommend?

CASE STUDY 13.2

Megabox, Inc.

(This case study was written by David Ronen, University of Missouri St. Louis)

Megabox, Inc. is a major manufacturer of color television sets and video cassette recorders (VCRs) with its major production facility and final assembly plant in the western Pennsylvania region of the United States. Competition from Far Eastern manufacturers has compelled the company to trim its product line and to concentrate on a limited number of quality products while attending to the needs of specialized market segments.

The leap of the oil-producing Middle Eastern countries into the contemporary consumer society has made them important markets to Megabox products. TV broadcasts have been introduced into those countries during the last two decades, but VCRs are newcomers to these markets, and their sales have been growing fast during the last couple of years.

As Joe Perez, the distribution manager of Megabox, was reviewing the coming year's sales forecasts, he was concerned about transportation of the products to Zumburu, one of the larger Middle Eastern markets. The government of Zumburu never seemed to have an economic policy, and with the recent drying up of oil revenues he was concerned that the government might suddenly impose higher import duties, or limits on imports in a different manner, in order to control the outflow of foreign currency. Since he had insufficient space available in cargo airlines serving Zumburu, he was considering entering into a 12-month contract with a carrier that would provide him with more space, but he had to commit himself to ship at least 4000 ft^3 per week during the contract period, and was concerned about erratic changes in demand due to the possible government action.

For distribution planning purposes, the product lines of Megabox have been divided into four characteristic products, three television sets and a VCR, as can be seen in Table 13.5.

TABLE 13.5	Products' distribution characteristics

Product line	Shipping volume (ft^3/unit)	Shipping weight (kg/unit)	Selling price (FOB plant $/unit)
TV1	16	18	360
TV2	10	15	230
TV3	2	4	120
VCR	3	7	300

The sales forecast (Table 13.6) was prepared by the marketing department and Joe used to discount it by 10%, because he knew from past experience that these forecasts were actually marketing goals which were seldom met. Sales were expected to peak in the second quarter (the camel racing season), and to be somewhat below the quarterly average in the third quarter.

TABLE 13.6	Zumburu sales forecast (units)

Product line	Quarter				
	I	II	III	IV	Total
TV1	3,000	5,200	2,200	2,800	13,200
TV2	2,200	3,200	1,800	2,000	9,200
TV3	1,200	2,400	1,400	1,200	6,200
VCR	6,300	11,100	6,500	7,200	31,100

Shipping services to Zumburu were available by air or by sea. Scheduled air cargo flights left JFK Airport in New York three times a week, and Joe could secure at least 3000 ft³ per week on these flights (more space could be used on space-available basis). If need be, Joe could use charter cargo flights at a cost 20% higher than the scheduled service. (On a full load basis, at least 4000 ft³ per shipment, these flights did not have return cargo.)

Sea service was provided by a weekly sailing of a conference container vessel, on which Joe could get as much space as he needed, but was limited to shipping in 40 ft container loads (CL) or in less than container load (LCL). Due to the high sensitivity of the products to pilferage, loss, and damage, Joe did not consider using general cargo vessels (which were also 40–50% slower than container vessels). Lately he had been approached by outsiders (ship operators that are not members of the conference) who offered him use of their semi-monthly container service to Zumburu, using 20 ft containers at 15% discount over the conference freight rates.

At Joe's request, his assistant has compiled several tables of pertinent data, in consultation with their freight forwarder. Transit time estimates for the various modes are given in Table 13.7. (Joe suspected that some of these estimates, especially those for the labor-intensive operations, were somewhat optimistic.) Information concerning sizes of sea containers is provided in Table 13.8.

TABLE 13.8 Sea containers' sizes

Nominal length	Outside measures	Inner volume*
20'	8' × 8' × 20'	1100 ft³
40'	8' × 8' × 40'	2000 ft³

* Due to package sizes incompatibility, only about 90% of the inner volume can be utilized for cargo.

Air shipments were trucked from the assembly plant to the carrier's terminal where they were stuffed by the carrier into air containers. The carrier unstuffed the containers at the other end of the trip, and the products were stored at an air cargo terminal until they were cleared through Customs and shipped to the local distributor.

Sea shipments required containerization (CL shipments) or crating (LCL shipments), and these operations take place at a packer's facility close to the loading port. Joe wondered if he should not move these operations into the assembly plant, thus saving on handling and transportation. Equipment incompatibility (truck box trailers are 40–50 ft long, sea containers are 20 ft or 40 ft long) made such analysis complicated, but possible use of rail service to move full sea containers to the loading port may make such an alternative attractive.

After containerization/crating, the shipment would be trucked to the loading port, where it would wait for the next ship. Although the average interval between sailings of conference ships was one week, there were frequent delays, thus that interval ranged from 3 to 10 days. At the other end, after the shipment was unloaded, full container shipments were trucked to the distributor (after clearing Customs). LCL shipments were unstuffed in the port and then, after Customs clearance, moved to the distributor.

Although CL shipments are cheaper, not all the shipments are large enough to fill a container. In the past year 70% of the volume of sea shipments went in CL, and the rest in LCL. Joe estimated that this ratio will shift to 90% CL by using 20 ft containers.

Megabox was selling its product to its local distributor in Zumburu on CIF (cost, insurance,

TABLE 13.7 Transit time (days)

| | Air (scheduled) | Sea (conference) | |
		CL	LCL
Plant	1	1	1
	–	1	1
Export packer/ container stuffing	–	4	7
	1	1	1
Loading port/ airport	1	4	4
Vessel/airplane	1	18	18
Discharge port	1	3	2
	–	–	1
Unpacking/ unstuffing	1	–	5
	1	1	1
Consignee	2	3	2
Total	9	36	43

freight) terms and, thus, Joe was concerned with the reduction of all the transportation-related costs and the cost of in-transit inventory. (Megabox used 28% for inventory carrying cost, 15% of which was the cost of capital.) Megabox paid all the expenses up to the storage point at the destination port, where title on the goods was transferred, and the local distributor paid for the shipment within 30 days after receiving the shipment's documents.

Some of the shipping costs may be allocated on the basis of the volume shipped, and these are presented in Table 13.9.

| TABLE 13.9 | Distribution costs breakdown (in $/shipped ft³) |

| | Air (scheduled) | Sea (conference) | |
		CL*	LCL
Transportation to packer	–	0.50	0.50
Packing/container stuffing	–	1.80	2.40
Transportation to port	0.50	0.20	0.20
Freight**	9.60	2.00	2.80
Unpacking/ unstuffing	–	–	0.70
Transportation to consignee	0.40	0.40	0.40

* In 40 ft containers.
** Freight rates are on 'liner terms' and include handling in ports on both ends.

Other associated costs are as follows:

1. Consular fee (1% of FOB plant price) – for Zumburu import license (used to finance the operations of their embassy in the United States).
2. Cargo insurance – 1% of (CIF value + 10%) for air shipments, 1.4% for CL and 1.6% for LCL (larger losses and damages).
3. Documentation – $220 per shipment is paid to the forwarder for the preparation of the US export documentation and the import documents of Zumburu.
4. Wharfage – charged by the unloading seaport at 2% of the shipment's landed value (CIF value).
5. Customs duties – 40% of value at the exit gate of the port (excluding port storage charges, but including wharfage).
6. Storage fees at destination ports – 0.24 $/kg per day for air cargo and 0.02 $/kg per day for sea cargo.

The distributor who receives the goods is interested in receiving frequent small shipments to reduce his average inventory, i.e., air shipments. Moreover, on air shipments he pays lower Customs duties (no wharfage included in the value for Customs duties calculations), thus Megabox grants the distributor a 2% discount on sea shipments (off CIF prices, which are: TV1 – $496, TV2 – $317, TV3 – $165, VCR – $432).

Bearing all these facts in mind, Joe was contemplating whether he should enter into the 12-month contract with the air carrier (which required freight rates 10% below scheduled carriers). In addition, he thought that it was worthwhile to have a comparative analysis of the costs of the different shipping alternatives which will take into account the cost of inventory in transit in addition to the direct shipping costs.

Questions

1. Evaluate the alternative physical distribution systems available for Megabox to use in its exporting activities to Zumburu.

2. Which system should Perez select? Why?

CASE STUDY 13.3

Primex Marketing, Inc

(This case study was written by Edwin C. Duerr and Mitsuko Saito Duerr, San Francisco State University.)

Primex Marketing, Inc., formed in 1982, is an international niche marketer of Roleez® wheels and a limited line of products using the wheels. The patented wheels use very low pressure, soft, wide, and pliable tires mounted on flanged hubs to disperse the weight of a load over a wide surface area. This permits carts, dollies and wheelchairs equipped with the wheels to be moved easily over sandy beaches and soft soil where regular wheels sink into the ground. The wheels also offer a level of protection to muddy turf and environmentally sensitive terrain.

Most of Primex's wheels are sold to other manufacturers for use in making sports, recreation, industrial, construction, and health assistance equipment. In addition to the Roleez® wheels Primex manufactures and markets a limited line of products using its wheels. These include push carts, sports caddies, four and six wheel dollies for moving jet skis, and two wheel carts and totes for canoes and kayaks using its wheels. The company also sells winch kits, hitch kits, and low-pressure tire gauges.

Resorts, and companies that supply products to them, are an important market for Primex. The resorts use large numbers of carts and dollies that must be operated over beaches and rough terrain in providing services to guests. Wheelchair manufacturers are another growing market, and additional uses in the industrial and construction sectors offer great potential.

In addition to continuing to provide quality products and service, on time and economically, the company has four additional marketing objectives. In order to continue to grow and to increase profitability, it is working to: (1) locate additional customers for its present products in current types of use; (2) find additional applications for its products; (3) develop modifications and innovations of present products for existing and new customers; and (4) extend its line of end products.

Mr Peter J. U. Reich, the president of Primex and the related company, Roleez Wheels, Inc., is an entrepreneur with a global view of all functions including marketing, manufacturing and distribution. Brought up and educated in what was then East Germany, he

moved to West Germany. Working for companies there, then in Canada, and finally in the United States, he developed personal contacts in a number of countries. He also began to explore new business opportunities.

In the mid-1980s Mr Reich became interested in windsurfing and recognized a business opportunity. Becoming increasingly involved in the sport, he eventually served on the board of the US Windsurfing Association. In addition to the demand for masts, booms and sails, the Association recognized the need for two additional products for surfers: helmets, and carts to make the transport of surf boards and other gear easier. These products did not bring the anticipated sales among surfers.

The carts did appeal to kayak/canoe enthusiasts and, in 1992, L.L. Bean™ approached Primex about providing a large number of carts. In 1997–8, as the Primex kayak/canoe carts became more widely used, the company received comments about the wheels sinking in the sand. Primex tried many types of wheels, but none of them were completely satisfactory. Then one of its customers said it should try Roleez® wheels.

At the end of 1998 Mr Reich contacted the inventor of the Roleez® wheels, a dentist in Virginia. The inventor was having problems in manufacturing and other areas of his business, and was open to developing a cooperative agreement with Primex. Mr Reich flew out to Virginia and they developed a 2-page letter of intent. This was subsequently turned into a carefully worded 28-page agreement by their lawyers. Under the agreement, Mr Reich took over the manufacturing, marketing, and other functions of Roleez® wheels under the Primex Marketing, Inc. umbrella.

In looking for a new manufacturing base, Mr Reich spent some time in Thailand, but decided that it was not ideal for what Primex needed for Roleez. A German friend in Thailand suggested that he talk to one of his contacts in Taiwan. This was not a problem since Primex had already been doing business in Taiwan for many years. The Taiwan contact then suggested that he talk to an individual in Hong Kong. Eventually, through additional contacts in the United States, Taiwan, Hong Kong and China, he located the Chinese companies that now work for Primex.

Marketing

The company employs several approaches in making itself and its products visible, and providing information to potential customers. By attending trade shows, it finds potential customers, and gains information about products that might use Roleez® wheels. Trade shows of particular interest include those concerned with travel and leisure, equipment for medical and rehabilitation use, and materials-handling equipment. Potential customers include a wide range of manufacturers and service providers. An Italian firm providing equipment for resorts worldwide is interested in carts for use outside, including beach access. A Japanese company uses the Roleez® wheels in its wheelchair designs. Those designs are licensed back to another US manufacturer for marketing. Several other small manufacturers are also using Roleez® wheels on newly designed wheelchairs. A US company dominates the worldwide market for service carts, and is a potential customer.

Primex uses the World Wide Web both to identify companies throughout the world that might be potential customers for its products, and to provide information on its products to present and potential customers. Potential customers are contacted, usually by e-mail, referred to the Roleez web site, sent literature as appropriate, and contacted further by e-mail as appropriate. In some cases a meeting at a trade show or a visit by a company representative is arranged, or prospective customers are invited to the company main office or its Shanghai office.

The Roleez web site was set up by a provider in Sacramento in consultation with Mr Reich. It is kept completely up to date by an outside support person in southern California. It provides information, including specifications, pictures, and costs for the company's products. Additionally, it provides information for ordering and for becoming a dealer.

The Roleez web site provides cross-links to a wide number of other sites of companies that handle its products and/or offer products for which Roleez® wheels would be advantageous. The company also makes arrangements to be on the web sites of other companies and in catalogs as appropriate. For example, it is on the web site of a provider of castor wheels.

Public relations and promotion are important elements in the overall marketing plan. In the Summer 2003 issue of *Access Today*, a publication of the National Center on Accessibility, a front page photograph showed four kinds of wheelchairs for use on beaches, all of which use Roleez® wheels. Primex is working with an outside company to prepare a press release targeting wheel-using markets where terrain requires Roleez balloon tires.

Cards, brochures, and instructions are printed in China. Advertising, except in areas of special interest, appears to be too expensive to be justified.

The company's present customer base includes over 400 companies worldwide. Mr Reich's marketing efforts are concentrated on extending this base, as well as selling more to existing customers.

Organization, logistics, and manufacturing

Primex is making maximum use of outsourcing, advances in communications and logistics, and working with others. This is serving to maintain flexibility, keep costs low, assure effectiveness, and minimize financial risk. The company has only five people at its main location in Benicia, California: the president (who spends much of his time traveling); a sales manager; a person handling order processing; an office manager (with responsibilities for accounting service and computers); and one person for warehousing and shipping. The company has both FedEx and UPS terminals in their office.

The company has a sixth employee, located at its Shanghai office, who handles arrangements there. The Benicia office, however, does the invoicing, handles collections/receivables from customers, and makes payments to suppliers in China. Primex has issued import and distribution rights for their products to Off The Road Wheel Systems, NL, for The Netherlands, Belgium, and Luxembourg. The company currently relies on importers in Australia, Germany, Japan, South Africa, and the United States. Companies in other countries are being contacted.

Customers overseas send their orders, including advance payment, directly to Primex's bank in the United States, either by electronic transfer or by credit card. The bank forwards the order to Primex after it has verified payment. If the payment is by credit card, the bank charges (usually about $2\frac{1}{2}$%), but the simplicity and assurance of payment is considered to be worth the cost. Payroll and tax services are contracted out.

The originally Roleez company in Virginia used polyvinylchloride (PVC) in making the tires, but testing indicated that polyurethane was a better raw material. Primex Marketing, Inc. changed to the polyurethane. The type required by Primex is produced at only one plant in the world, a Bayer facility in Marysville, West Virginia. Primex buys the raw material from Bayer through an agent, and has it sent directly from the West Virginia plant to a factory in China. The tires are then made in China at one of three companies, each of which is located in a different area of China. When the factory in China completes the order it sends the product directly to the customer who ordered it. Depending on the size of the order, the wheels are sent by 40-foot or 20-foot container, or by the pallet load. The latter substantially increases the shipping cost per wheel. At each stage of exporting and importing, required documentation is handled by foreign freight forwarders or custom house brokers for the local companies involved.

Mr Reich personally visits each of the factories frequently, working directly with each company's management regarding quality control, payment issues, and in some cases, product development. The meetings are conducted in English, and while most of the managers do speak English, it is easy for misunderstandings to arise. Mr Reich has found it useful to carefully watch the eyes of the people with whom he is speaking to see if they seem to understand, or if he is talking too quickly or is unclear.

Through the careful development of relations with his providers of products, Mr Reich has been able to arrange with all of them to accept payment after the products have been shipped. He thus does not have to prepay or arrange letters of credit.

Innovation and product development

It is the very low tire pressure in the Roleez® wheels (.069 bar or $1\frac{1}{2}$ psi, as compared to 20 to 35 psi for many pneumatic tires), and the wide surface coming in contact with the ground, that allow them to move over soft ground without sinking in. This also allows them to move easily over rough terrain and curbs. The largest wheel presently in production has a tire 49 cm (19.3 inches) in diameter with a tire width of 15 cm (5.9 inches) mounted on a 25.4 mm axle. In addition to the axle-mounted wheels, castor-type wheels, both rigid and swivel models, are made. Most of the Roleez® wheels currently being produced are used on carts and dollies, but the wheelchair market has great potential.

Additional development work needs to be done to expand the market for wheelchairs. The wide tread of the Roleez® wheels makes standard wheelchairs too wide to go through standard residence doors. Though the soft tires enable wheelchairs to be used at the beach, some assistance must be provided to the wheelchair occupant by another person. To meet the desire for greater independence by those in wheelchairs, there is a need to develop a motorized wheelchair to be used with these tires. The same concern does not arise with the use of carts and dollies since these all require human or motorized assistance in any event. Various new applications in industry will require other adaptations.

Research and development is an ongoing activity at the company, drawing on ideas from within Primex, from outside inventors, and from users and potential users of the products. Five small companies are designing wheelchairs specifically for Roleez® wheels. One of these companies is already building some, but the costs are high because each is made individually. Larger-scale production will be needed to bring the costs down. An inventor from outside of the company is looking at the feasibility of developing an adapter to allow Roleez® wheels to be used on standard-width wheelchairs.

Mr Reich is continually developing ideas of his own, which he writes down on anything handy, from pads of paper to napkins. He has found that the Chinese companies from which he buys wheels have very good product development people. Though he did employ an engineer as a product development person in his Benicia office for a year, he has now developed a synergistic relationship with the Chinese companies that is more satisfactory. His ideas, and those from others that may be appropriately handled in China, are sent there for development.

The company has patent protection in all major markets. Though obtaining patent protection is expensive and time-consuming, it is necessary for a product that can be relatively easily imitated. As Roleez develops new products, the company needs to assure itself that these also are covered by patent protection.

Looking to the future

Meeting all of the opportunities and challenges facing Primex and Roleez at this time can be expected to continue to place a heavy burden on Mr Reich's time and abilities. The company's future success will remain heavily dependent upon his knowledge of markets and needs, his selection of key employees and partners, his capacities for planning and coordination, and his ability to gain cooperation and useful input for all of those with whom he interacts.

Questions

1. Do the methods used to locate, contact, and work with prospective customers appear to be appropriate? What other actions might be undertaken?

2. What are the advantages and disadvantages in Primex's requirement for having payment in advance, and for having a bank handle incoming payments?

3. What are the advantages and disadvantages of contracting out services such as payroll (including handing of required taxes) and Web page updating?

4. What are the advantages and disadvantages of having others make international shipping arrangements?

5. What problems can the companies expect to face as they grow in size and expand product lines?

Organization of International Marketing Activities

14.1 Introduction

How should a company bring together its international operations to structure an integrated global enterprise system? How should it organize its export operations and international activities to best exploit market opportunities throughout the world? How should the company group its diverse activities? How should it coordinate and control them?

The way in which an international marketing organization is structured is an important determinant of its ability to exploit the opportunities available to it effectively and efficiently. It also determines the capacity for responding to problems and challenges. The major components in organization structure include the assignment and groupings of functions and other business activities, the authority and responsibility of individuals and groups, the locus of decision making, and the lines of communication and control.

In the early stages of international marketing activity, typically some type of export activity, the company may simply use intermediaries or set up a small export department to handle the foreign sales of its standard products. As export activities grow, and international competition increases, there is heightened pressure for improved responsiveness to the needs of foreign customers. There is also concern about coordination and control of foreign market activities. New types of management skills and sensitivities are required. Changes in the location of key functions, and in the decision-making structure, are sought in order to balance responsiveness to local needs with requirements for centralized and uniform direction. Decisions must be made as to whether to organize primarily along functional, product, geographical, or perhaps even customer lines.

The Internet and Web technologies are making it possible for companies with widespread operations to more quickly and easily determine the status of many aspects of their business operations. This can facilitate coordination, cooperation and control within the company's functional, product and geographical divisions or groupings. It can also improve effectiveness in working with suppliers, partners, and customers. However, the systems and the organization structure used must be compatible, and must be appropriate for use in the company's international operations.

The objective of this chapter is to discuss the issues that top management faces in developing an organizational structure suited to its needs and opportunities. The threats and opportunities facing an organization change over time, and the organizational structure similarly must change over time if the company is to remain competitive.

14.2 Main considerations of being organized internationally

There is no single correct organizational structure for international marketing. Geographical diversity is a consequence of a strategy of international expansion. The effect of operations in different countries and areas is to present a major new dimension of required response to the organization. A geographically dispersed company, in addition to its knowledge of product, function, and home territory, must acquire knowledge of the complex set of social, political, economic, and institutional arrangements that exist within each international market.

At the most basic level, the problem of organization design can be reduced to three closely related issues. The first involves the definition of organizational subunits based on the key functions and dimensions of the firm's operations. Closely related, the second involves the choice between centralization and decentralization for individual tasks and functions. Finally there is the issue involving the assignment of reporting and control systems. The result of these exercises determines the overall structure of an organization.

14.2.1 Definition of organizational subunits

The most basic issue is the relative degree of emphasis on the product, area, and functional dimensions of the organization. To be effective, an international organization must bring to managers three fundamental competencies at the times and places they are needed for decision making: *functional* (marketing, *production*, finance, and so on), *product* (including allied technology), and *geographical*. The important question in organization design, therefore, is how line operations should be subdivided according to these major dimensions. A wide range of internal and external variables influence this decision. Internal variables stem from company characteristics such as firm strategy, goals, key functions, diversity, and size. External variables are mostly related to the general environment and the industry, and include technological change, competition, customers and so forth. These are also known as contingency factors. Determining priorities for product, area, and functional elements of the organization requires careful analysis of the characteristics of all these elements.

First, environmental considerations have been widely discussed in relation to organization design. For example, the level of change and the degree of differentiation in the environment are related to structural needs, and to the effectiveness of different types of organizational structures. This, in particular, has important implications for a company operating across several different national and cultural environments characterized by different demand structures including growth rates, consumer habits, and competitive situations. The more complex the environment, the more complex the organization design. This is so because the company's response to different national and cultural environments may mean greater diversity, not only structurally but also functionally.

Many of the structural characteristics drawn from an analysis of the international environment are first translated into strategic imperatives. If corporate strategy is responsive to environmental realities, organization structure can largely be designed to fit strategy. 'Structure follows strategy.' But the interaction between structure and strategy cannot be isolated from other influences, such as history, size of the company, management philosophy, markets and technology of the organization.

Second, the goals underlying the corporate strategy hold important implications for structure. Emphasis on long-run profitability will require sophisticated management systems and a profit-center definition. Emphasis on rapid growth determines not only the nature of international marketing issues, production and finance activities, but also how they should be coordinated and integrated. This implies that corporate goals are translated readily into key organizational functions and tasks.

Third, several elements of the strategy are particularly important in designing the structure. A company's diversity of operations both in product and area dimensions represents a strategic choice with implications for organization. Diversity largely dictates the firm's ability to adapt a product, functional, and area orientation in its operations. Backward (upstream to R&D, manufacturing, and so forth) or forward (downstream to the channels of distribution) vertical integration represents another strategic issue with important implications for structure. Vertically integrated companies require extensive coordination, communication, and control mechanisms, often focused on functional activities. Also, an international sourcing strategy represents an organizational challenge and determines an important aspect of the choice between centralization and decentralization.

Consideration of all these variables will help to accomplish three things, as follows:

1. to identify the key dimensions around which to organize internationally;
2. to define organizational subunits;
3. to decide how to link the various elements of the structure through coordination and control mechanisms and management systems.

14.2.2 Centralization vs decentralization

The issue of centralization vs decentralization is an old, basic theme in international marketing. The arguments about centralization or decentralization depend upon what kind of central or regional/divisional authority is proposed. In practice, most companies must delegate daily operations to local management. To do otherwise could lead to a situation where headquarters become immobilized with too much information, and too many decisions requiring local knowledge. However, what is delegated and the kinds of structural relationships that emerge are questions for top management to decide.

The question of whether a company should centralize or decentralize its international operations depends to a great extent on the company's management philosophy and style. Those who argue for centralized control suggest that the conditions arising from the cross-national, multiculture, and diversity nature of international/export marketing have the potential for wasteful duplication of efforts. The attainment of efficiency and maximization of worldwide profits can only be achieved through tight central decision making. Those managers in favor of decentralization claim that strong central control often means constant delay in reaching decisions internationally. Centralization lacks sufficient flexibility to permit immediate reactions to local problems.

One means of analyzing a company's need for centralization is to examine the characteristics of its business area, the market and the industry. A wide range of criteria can be used to make this assessment. In Table 14.1 product, market, and financial variables are examined for three businesses: dairy products, aircraft machines, and watches. The cell values – high, medium and low – are values of the criteria that favor centralization.

The benefits of centralization are substantial in businesses with rapid rates of technological change. Innovation and manufacturing are performed more efficiently at central locations in such industries. The economics of manufacturing

TABLE 14.1

A business area-based framework to analyze centralization vs decentralization

Criteria	Benefits of centralization		
	Aircraft machines	Dairy products	Watches
Market characteristics			
Degree of standardization in:			
Product design	High	Low	Low
Product usage	High	Low	High
Buying behavior	High	Low	Low
Distribution	High	Low	Low
Nature of customers:			
Global/local ratio	High	Low	Low
Nature of competitors:			
Global/local ratio	High	Low	High
I/Advertising rate	High	Medium	Low
Product characteristics			
Rate of technological change	High	Low	High
Manufacturing:			
Minimum efficient scale	High	Low	High
Scope of cost curve	High	Low	High
I/Tariff rate	Medium	n.a.	Medium
Value/weight	High	Low	High
Capital intensity	Medium	Low	High
Financial characteristics			
Fixed assets/sales	Medium	Low	Medium
R&D/sales	High	Low	Medium
Cost of goods sold/sales	High	Low	Low
Value-added/sales	High	Medium	High
Inventory/sales	Medium	Low	High

also play an important role in organization design. The potential to exploit economies of scale in manufacturing, procurement, marketing, and so forth benefit from centralized management.

Businesses that are highly standardized in world markets in terms of product design, usage, buying behavior, and distribution outlets can realize advantages from centralization. If the principal customers for the product are multinational companies, or the same lifestyle end user with similar demands and needs, centralization of marketing management to insure coordination of prices, design specification, terms, and quality is essential. The presence of multinational competitors in an industry requires centralized management to guarantee an integrated global strategic posture. Also, some financial characteristics can give a general indication of the need for centralization. Businesses with high R&D/sales ratios and high value-added/sales will often benefit from centralization.

The dairy products industry presents an example of a business where centralization is not possible, because product standardization across markets is not pervasive. For all foodstuff products in general, and dairy products in particular, tastes, buying behavior, and channels of distribution vary widely in different foreign markets. Customers for such products are locally oriented. Within the border of France alone, for example, there are more than 200 specialized local cheeses available in the marketplace. The number of product varieties is also great in other countries because of a fragmented demand structure. For instance, within the European dairy industry there are more than 2000 producers.

Production of dairy products is neither capital intensive nor characterized by a high technology content. Even more importantly, shipment and storage of dairy products are limited because of freshness and handling requirements. The financial characteristics of the dairy business also suggest that centralization will not provide significant benefits; asset-to-sales ratio, the cost of goods sold, and inventory/sales are all low indicators.

In contrast, the aircraft industry provides a perfect example of a business that benefits greatly from a centralization policy. Standardization of products is quite high around the world. Customers are few in number. Customers also tend to be larger companies with international operations. The principal competitors in the industry are larger companies with multinational activities. At the manufacturing level, the rate of technological change is extremely high, requiring close contact between central research activities and the manufacturing function. The economies of production are capital intensive. The cost curve is volume sensitive, and the minimum efficient scale of production is rising sharply. All these factors contribute to the need for centralized management of such a business.

The watch industry provides a third example of the issues of centralization vs decentralization. The level of product standardization in this industry is not high. There exists a great deal of variety from national market to national market in, for example, preferences for digital versus hour-hand faces, frames, size, price, and power supply. Distribution channels and buying behavior also vary in the industry. The rate of technological change was for a number of years very rapid, but now the industry finds itself in a time period where consolidation is occurring. The economics of production are increasingly capital intensive and volume intensive. However, the watch industry does not give a clear-cut answer to the issue of centralization in organizational design.

While dairy industry products and aircraft industry products clearly demand a specific structural solution, watches present a more complex picture. One way to design an organization to fit the needs of the watch industry is to emphasize the role of functional dimensions in the centralization issue. We have been using the product and area dimensions to reflect the two extremes of the centralization aspects. In the case of the watches, it seems clear that the marketing function requires a decentralized approach to ensure responsiveness to unique local marketing conditions. On the other hand, R&D activities and manufacturing of watches require a centralized approach. By defining a centralized manufacturing unit and decentralized market units, an organization can be designed to meet the needs of this business.

14.2.3 Communication and control systems

For the international company, the need to manage people in different nations and cultures brings more attention to an appropriate design of the communication and control systems. The dichotomy that exists between central management (headquarters), and foreign unit management (subsidiary managers, relationships with sales agents, distributors, and so on) is not too dissimilar to that traditionally existing in any organization between staff and line personnel, that is, neither believes that the other understands the problems and, as a consequence, cooperation and communication sometimes suffer. This problem is increased because of the distance to the foreign market, culture, language, and differences in nationality that occur in international marketing.

When organizing units and making decisions about management control there are two major questions. What are the information-sharing needs of the departments and the international subunits? What are the communication needs of managers and groups within the international organization? One must not forget that organizations have to be run by human beings, and in an international setting this aspect gains enormous complexity.

One of the difficult problems to solve in organization design, especially when subunits are located across national borders with both large cultural and great geographical distances, is how to cope with both the work flow and the informal social needs, while maintaining a rational set of formal relationships that allows for the efficient use of resources.

Comparative studies of different countries typically focus on main institutional determinants of differences between countries, such as laws, regulations, state institutions, and the process by which economies are regulated. These institutional factors are often a result of differences in cultural norms and traditions and these variables influence the corporate policies, organizational mechanisms and working practices adopted.

This can be illustrated by the variations in control systems used by different forms of ownership in France, Germany and the United Kingdom. In Germany there are single- and two-tier systems available. In the two-tier system there is a supervisory board in control of a management board whose membership is not shared. In the United Kingdom the directors, whether executives of the company or not, sit on the same board; this is also the case with smaller private limited companies in Germany. German supervisory boards include bankers and directors of suppliers and customers, while in France the Conseil d'Administration of the large limited companies is very much the creation of the Président Directeur-Général (chairman of the board), who has considerable centralized power, often being the only management representative on the board. Family control is also still important in France, including in some of the larger companies, and the hierarchical nature of work relations and the emphasis on functional separation may be greater in French companies than in the United Kingdom.

Communication and control issues arise when reorganization takes place. A good example of this is the experience of Hewlett-Packard Co. (HP), the global computer and printer company. Starting in 2000 HP embarked on a major corporate reorganization that was spearheaded by its new CEO, Carlton 'Carly' Fiorina (Burrows, 2001). The company went from 83 product divisions to two product development units (computers, printers) that work with two sales and marketing units (corporate, consumer). Improvements in performance have not worked out exactly as planned, although there are indications that eventually the reorganization will have very positive effects. One reason is that the reorganization was rushed into place before the company's information systems were redone to reflect the organizational changes. Along with this was that fewer spending controls were in place than in the past when division chiefs had control. The result was that expenses increased greatly during the last quarter of 2000. A later change went more smoothly. In May 2002, HP acquired Compaq Computer Corporation after a bitter proxy fight within HP. This time there was a lot of advance planning and the development of detailed integration plans (Burrows, 2002). There was concern about potential layoffs among HP employees, and investor concern over possible negative effects of the merger on the HP image, but the initial results have been positive. In the HP Annual Report for 2003, Chairman and CEO Carlton Fiorina noted that the company achieved $3.5 billion in merger integration and cost savings, exceeding the goal by $1 billion, and finishing one year ahead of schedule.

14.3 Organizational structures

We now turn to a brief description of the principal organizational alternatives for the export, international, or global company. International organizational structures can be based on: (1) functions, (2) product groupings, (3) markets or customer groupings, (4) geography, and (5) mixed approaches, that is, matrix approaches. Because they are based on different competencies, each of these options has its advantages and drawbacks.

14.3.1 Functional export department (built-in or separate export unit)

Firms initially manage foreign operations through the creation of either a built-in unit in the marketing organization or separate export unit in the company's organization, as discussed in Chapter 7. For the inexperienced international company selling to only a few export markets, one person, or a few in the beginning, can handle all the elements of the export marketing operations. By hiring an export marketing manager who reports to the domestic marketing manager, the company starts building up a special expertise in export selling and marketing.

In most cases practical experience shows that export responsibilities should not be given to someone within the organization whose main job lies in the domestic area. This will not give the specialized functional export competence, technical and administrative insights in foreign operations (export documentation, language ability, handling, and so on), and experience needed in starting in international business. An export manager may be a way of organizing into a built-in exporting unit, reporting to the marketing manager of the company.

However, as the company's international activities grow, the complexity of coordinating and directing these operations extends beyond the scope of a single person. Pressure is created to assemble a staff group that will take responsibility for coordination and control of the foreign activities. This may lead to the creation of a separate export department.

In both of its forms the functional organization fosters the professional identity of the international marketing task and challenge, and is particularly useful for deploying specialized skills and training in the beginning stages of the internationalization process of the company with minor product and area diversities. This structure is easy to supervise, it allows maximum specialization in trained occupational skills, and other departments have good access to these specialized skills.

However, the functional approach to organization of foreign operations creates difficulties for coordinating among different departments and subunits and often creates conflicts in the allocation of tasks, resources, and money. Too much duplication of resources among departments may also arise.

The functional export department design is particularly suitable for small and medium-sized firms, as well as larger companies, manufacturing standardized products, that are at the early stages of developing international business, with low product and area diversities. The latter companies could come from the extractive industries, for example mining and petroleum. As small and medium-sized exporting firms gradually grow and enter a large number of countries, they may choose to introduce regional export managers. Regional managers may be assigned to specific geographical territories with specific reference to working with local distribution channel members (for example foreign agents, distributors, and importers) by assisting them in introducing new products, building up service and showroom facilities, and training their sales representatives and personnel.

14.3.2 International division structure

In Figure 14.1 we show an organization structure similar to the functional export department structure. For companies working in large home markets the beginning of foreign operations may often involve relatively large sales volumes and may be very complex, especially when using different entry modes such as traditional exporting, joint ventures, or sales subsidiaries. Multiproduct companies that are already organized by domestic product divisions respond most commonly to

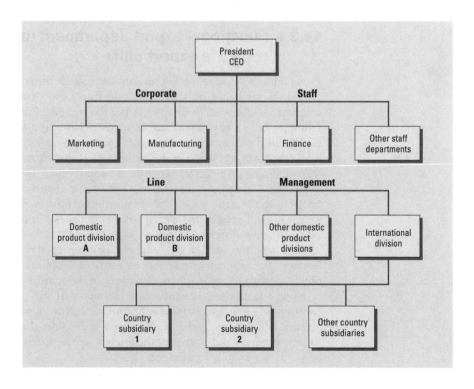

FIGURE 14.1

International division structure

overseas expansion by creating an international division at the same corporate level as domestic divisions.

The international division coordinates and controls the activities belonging to the division, acting as a representative of the higher management group. The international vice-president reports directly to the president (CEO). Since it is often established as a profit center, the international division structure has an additional advantage of encouraging a worldwide view of foreign operations, thus resulting in concentration of tasks and resources. This structure makes it possible to have a single, coordinated management of international business across product lines and countries.

Often it is claimed that the international division structure is only a transitory stage in organization, particularly for those companies that strongly increase the scale and scope of their international operations. This is due to its separation from the domestic product divisions and from corporate staff, and from its lack of key product/technology competencies and skills. Over time, the international division may not be able to fully support its foreign units (its distributors, sales and/or production subsidiaries, and other types of units).

14.3.3 International organization structure based on product

Highly diversified companies with several dissimilar product lines or business areas can gain advantages by adopting an international structure based on product. The main objective of this approach is to satisfy the special requirements of products and their supportive technologies. The whole idea behind the product-based structure is to treat product management as the heart of the marketing task. So viewed, it makes good sense for this subfunction to be centralized. This structure is shown in Figure 14.2.

As an example of this type of organization structure, in the late 1990s Procter & Gamble changed its organization structure from one based on geographic area

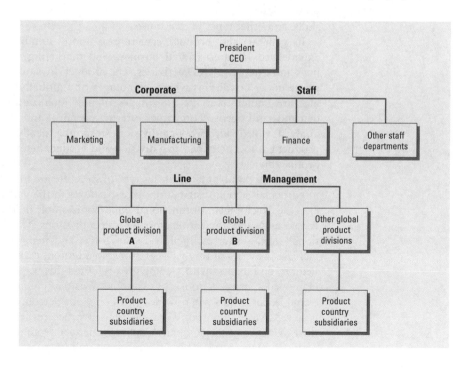

International structure based on product lines

to one based on product when it created seven global business units organized by product category (e.g., baby care, beauty care, and fabric and home care). The global business units develop and sell products on a worldwide basis. This was a major change from the old organization where country managers set prices and handled products as they saw fit. One positive effect of this reorganization was shown by the company being able to introduce an extension of its Pantene shampoo line in 14 countries in six months – it took two years to get the original shampoo into stores abroad. A major force behind Procter & Gamble's change was its largest chain-store customers, such as US-based Wal-Mart and French-based Carrefour, who wanted this to match their own global expansion. To these customers globalized pricing, marketing, and distribution allowed them to plan more efficiently and save money (*Business Week*, 1998). Subsequent changes have been made to increase the effectiveness of this structure based on product category. President and CEO A. J. Lafley is focusing on making the company more consumer and marketing oriented, and has outsourced some manufacturing (to a Canadian company) and IT services (to Hewlett-Packard Co.). He is stressing freer and less formal internal communications, training, and the development of managers. Symbolically, the five product division presidents have been moved from the senior executive's floor to the floors where their staffs are located. The company is now getting more of its ideas and new products from outside the company, and working on some joint development projects with other companies. (Berner, 2003).

An international product-based structure simplifies the coordination task, enables growth of the organization without losing control, and provides a stronger motivation to divisional heads. Marketing strategies and programs for the different product lines are developed, coordinated, and implemented by the 'local' staff. Economies of scale within each product line can be better exploited.

This structure facilitates international product positioning, when product division managers (often vice-presidents) become responsible for the production and marketing of their respective product lines throughout the world. Foreign agents and country sales and production subsidiaries report directly to a corporate product division, from which they receive product and technical information, skills, and other types of assistance.

In general, the product structure is more suitable for companies more experienced in international business and marketing with diversified product lines and extensive R&D activities. The product division structure is most appropriate under conditions where advantages of a globally standardized marketing mix are higher than the advantages of individualization to regional or local demands and needs. Companies offering chemical and electrical products often apply a worldwide product division structure. Ideally there should be some product homogeneity within a division and product heterogeneity between global product divisions.

The main disadvantages of this type of structure are that it duplicates resources, in particular selling/distribution infrastructures in the various countries, discourages the development of functional skills (for example marketing and finance) and encourages suboptimization among product divisions. The duplication of the functional staff, resources, facilities, sales force, and management can significantly increase the costs of foreign operations. In addition, many customers feel it is difficult to do business with a company organized this way as they are contacted by many salespersons from the various divisions. Using the Hewlett-Packard example, customers will now deal with only one person, regardless of the product involved. More importantly, product-based structures fragment the expertise and the experience of the company's activities derived from other product lines across national boundaries. This can result in failure to learn from mistakes, and embarrassing inconsistencies in divisional activities and procedures. Furthermore, it can give rise to underutilization of sales or distribution facilities abroad.

Another weakness of this structure is that quite often product groups tend to develop a total interdependence on each other in world markets. For example, a global product division structure may end up with several subsidiaries in the same foreign country reporting to different product divisions, with no one at headquarters responsible for the overall corporate presence in that country. A marketing organization based on a decentralized product orientation can also create poor communication among various marketing units throughout the world. It is often a great disadvantage that considerable creativity will be lost through this kind of structure. Local units may struggle to maintain their independence. They may resist decisions made at the corporate product division level (the 'not invented here' syndrome). Product development ideas, marketing ideas, and so forth created in one market can be lost unless a special system is established for transmitting ideas, methods, and skills from country to country.

A number of years ago a study of multinational corporations by Davidson and Haspeslagh (1982) reported the following about the global product structure:

- Cost efficiency in existing products for existing markets was promoted.
- Companies were helped in consolidating their positions in mature and stable markets, but the transfer of resources abroad – especially technology – seemed to be held back, not facilitated.
- Companies were forced into a defensive competitive position.
- Lower foreign sales performance resulted.
- Extensive attention to the need for international experience, responsiveness, and advocacy was required.

Many of these problems can be addressed through the use of a coordinating mechanism as, for example, the use of product-line coordinators – through the planning system or through direct communication at the senior management level. In several international companies using a product division structure, profit center managers meet as a group every month to review unit performance, activities, and plans. These meetings provide, among other things, a top management level forum for the solution of coordination and integration problems and a forum for promoting resource sharing and consistency in foreign operations. Other companies emphasize the formation of a 'leadership role' to the largest or most experienced foreign subsidiary in terms of product development, marketing methods, or skills in coordination between product divisions internationally.

The product-based organization is discussed further by Kramer (1994a).

14.3.4 International structure based on geographic area or customer groupings

A market- or area-based structure is useful for companies that have a wide geographical spread and mature, standardized products (Figure 14.3). Typically, the world is divided into regions (divisions) such as Europe, North America, the Middle East, and so forth.

Regions can also be subdivided in turn into areas or simply into countries where there will be a country subsidiary. The important feature is that the regions are fairly self-contained and possess their own functional infrastructure with respect to marketing planning and research.

A regional operating unit such as, for example, the European division, typically is organized as follows. The vice-presidents of manufacturing (if the company has foreign direct investment in production facilities), marketing, and so on report to

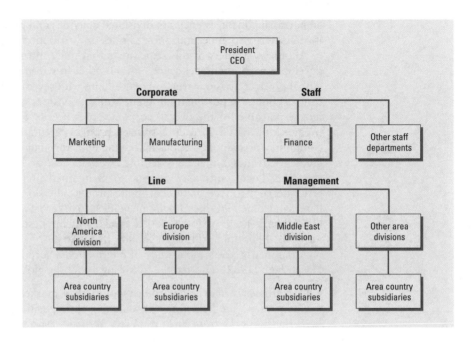

FIGURE 14.3

International structure based on geographic area

an area president. The area president coordinates functional inputs such as capital planning and distribution, manages the region's existing products, interacts with government officials and agencies, and has direct personal contact with the corporate board. Area presidents have line responsibility for profit and performance.

Each product line in a region is managed by the head of a product management team composed of marketing, manufacturing, and technical service managers. The product manager reports to the regional vice-president. The various teams set strategies and, subsequently, plans and goals for specific products. In their daily jobs they are expected to implement these strategies. In general, each geographic area has full internal staff support, although such support is often thin in some highly specialized functions such as R&D competencies and marketing research; these teams must borrow (at a cost to them) such expertise from corporate staff or another regional division.

The area-based organization is an ideal structure for companies with a single product or a homogeneous range of products that need fast and efficient country-wide distribution. Companies with product lines that have similar technologies and common end-use markets are attracted to this type of international organization. Many food, beverage, automobile, and pharmaceutical companies use this type of structure. The area-based organization simplifies coordination among different functions, and permits growth without losing control. One main advantage is its ability to respond easily to the environmental and market demands of a national, regional or cultural area through minor modifications in product design, pricing, market communication and packaging. Therefore, the structure encourages adaptive international marketing programs. Also, economies of scale can be achieved within regions.

The principal difficulties of the geographic organization arise when the company has a range of diverse products. This is a characteristic of Procter & Gamble. This is true for both international division structures and worldwide regional organizations. The tasks of coordinating product variations, transferring new product ideas and marketing techniques from one country to another, and optimizing the flow of product from source to worldwide product markets are not easily handled.

In the geographic organizational framework, companies traditionally complain that it is difficult or impossible to do the following:

1. make a consistent effort to apply newly developed domestic products to international markets;
2. avoid duplication of line marketing and product managers and staff managers, especially at the regional level;
3. conduct planning on a worldwide scale;
4. coordinate R&D and marketing plans on a global basis.

Consequently, the area-based structure has a tendency to foster area autonomy, posing obstacles to the creation of truly global marketing strategies. As a result, product lines will proliferate, product standardization will deteriorate and competition for export markets between areas and/or subsidiaries can occur.

Further discussion of geographic-based designs will be found in Kramer (1993).

The world can also be divided into customer groups: clearly defined user groups such as industries or end-user segments. Thus construction, packaging, or chemical industries are customer groups for companies selling machines, components, and technical support to the industrial segment. Schools, hotels, hospitals, and defense are customer groups in selling to the institutional market. Products are normally designed to meet the needs of specific geographic markets or customer groups and their specific characteristics. The market- or customer-oriented structure seeks to ensure that these needs and demands are accurately identified and acted upon. Much of what was said above about regions also applies to customer groups.

14.3.5 International mixed structures; the matrix organization

Most organizations in general, and international companies in particular, do not adopt purely simplistic structures based on either functional, product, area-based or customer dimensions. Often, the organizational design results in mixed structures (see Exhibits 14.1 and 14.2). As the task of managing becomes more complex, because the diffusion of technological and managerial competencies internationally give rise to more vigilant competition, there is a tendency for new organizational approaches to managing international business and marketing activities to be developed.

The so-called *matrix approach* seeks to combine two or more competencies on a worldwide basis; geographic knowledge, product knowledge, functional competence, or the knowledge of the customer or industry and its needs. The desired result is a matrix organization that stimulates sharing of resources, expertise, and information. It brings together the objectives set by corporate management. The matrix organization, in principle, also balances and integrates technology (product) and market forces in a project-oriented arrangement.

A way to illustrate the matrix concept is by looking at a simple case. Northern Pumps, Inc. manufactures a range of industrial machines and components that fall into three main categories: water pumps, heating electronics, and air ventilators. The company supplies these products to a large number of foreign markets. However, the main users come under three industry headings: construction, aircraft, and the marine industry. Furthermore, the company markets its products in many countries. Now, the problem is how to organize Northern Pumps internationally.

Organizing by products would mean that the needs of the specific markets served may be neglected. It is not possible for all product lines to have in-depth

EXHIBIT 14.1	**Hewlett-Packard's reorganization: will it work?**

In 2000 Hewlett-Packard (HP) embarked on a major reorganization plan that, among other things, was designed to provide sales growth of 20% starting in the year 2002 (Burrows, 2001). The intent of this action is to transform all aspects of HP at once, without any precedent that it will work for a company as large and complex as HP. This means that strategy, structure, culture, and compensation will be affected – everything from how to spark innovation to how to streamline internal processes. The 'new' HP is to excel at short-term execution while pursuing long-term visions that create new markets. It should increase sales and profits together rather than sacrifice one to gain the other. HP will emphasize technology, software, and consulting in every aspect of computing.

The key to all this is a complete overhaul of the organization structure from one based on products to a matrix or mixed organization. In the past, HP was essentially a confederation of 83 autonomous product units, each with profit responsibility, reporting through four groups: (1) home PCs, handhelds, laptops; (2) scanners, laser printers, printer paper; (3) ink cartridges, digital cameras, home printers; and (4) consulting, security software, unix servers. The company is now organized into two 'back-end' divisions, one developing printers, scanners, etc. and the other computers. These report to 'front-end' groups that market and sell HP's products (corporate sales and consumer sales). The organization is structured as shown in Figure 14.4.

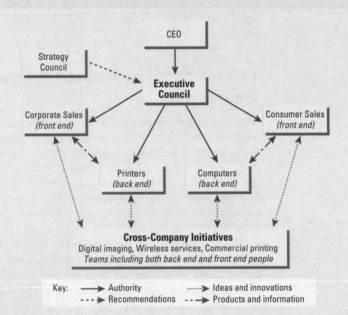

FIGURE 14.4	Hewlett Packard Organization

The functions of the major units are:

1. *Strategy Council.* Nine managers who advise the Executive Council on allocating money and people to growth industries.
2. *Executive Council.* Eight top managers, including heads of the back- and front-end groups.
3. *Corporate Sales.* Sell technology solutions to corporate clients. Keep back-end units abreast of what is hot.

4. *Consumer Sales.* Sell consumer gear. Let back-end know of must-have products and features.
5. *Printers.* Build new printing and imaging products to ensure HP's long-term growth.
6. *Computers.* Focus on future success by making computers that companies and consumers want, with sales input from front end.
7. *Cross-company Initiatives.* Personnel from back- and front-end groups work together to identify new markets that will create growth.

No one knows for sure whether such an organization will work as there is no 'model' to look to. Some expected benefits are happier customers, increased sales, products can be sold as solutions to problems, and financial flexibility. Concerning the latter, with all corporate sales under one roof, HP can measure the total value of a customer. There are some risks, however. With so much being made and sold by just four units, executives could be overwhelmed by their duties. There could be poorer execution as the front-end and back-end units will coordinate their plans with such a time schedule that quick response to changes will not be possible. Since profit and loss responsibility is shared between the front- and back-end groups, no one person is accountable. Finally, there will be fewer controls over expenditures.

This clearly is an ambitious direction being taken by HP.

EXHIBIT 14.2 **Marketing organizations: consequences of the EU movement to the internal market**

Changes in market structure of many industries along with the EU's efforts to reduce physical, technical, and fiscal barriers will lead to significant changes in marketing organizations and programs. In general, there will be a shift away from the assumption that a marketing program should necessarily be adapted to each country's special needs. The reforms in the EU in 1992 made individual country markets more accessible, but not more identical. Most of the cultural, historical, institutional, and economic differences among EU countries have survived. They will, however, indirectly over time promote more commonality in customer behavior across national boundaries.

The emphasis is on the search for similarities rather than differences across national boundaries so that adaptation costs can be minimized and scale economies maximized. Standardized market research tools will be needed to monitor changes in consumer attitudes and brand preferences across Europe, to permit (and to identify) cross-border, pan-European consumer segments. As the similarities in consumer behavior across national boundaries increasingly outweigh the differences, geographic segmentation is likely to give way to pan-European lifestyle segmentation. This shift has important implications for the organization of a company's European marketing operations.

The growing significance of pan-European marketing programs suggests the need for different organization approaches. Multinational companies such as Nestlé, Procter & Gamble, Kraft Foods, Gillette, and many others have already signaled a power shift from country to region in marketing decision making. Newly empowered regional managements are now deciding the marketing strategies for pan-European brands with the benefit of country management input. The companies are expanding the responsibilities of their European headquarters beyond the financial control function that has been central to their role in most decentralized multinationals. Some implications for organizational design, authority, and responsibility are assumed to arise within the European market, as follows:

- An increase in regional headquarters' role should permit a corresponding reduction in staff overheads in the company's country organizations, as unnecessary duplication of decision making is reduced and scale efficiencies are capitalized on.
- Country subsidiary offices will increasingly become sales and service facilities as marketing decisions are more and more centralized. In addition, computer technology can permit paperwork to be handled centrally. It may be expected that sales forces increasingly will be organized by product line; lower cost and more efficient travel within the EU will enable more specialized sales people to represent fewer products across larger territories.
- The shift of authority to the European regional level is also expected to have implications for executive development. Local country nationals will be fewer in number. Increasingly, promotion and advancement will go to marketing executives with experience in multiple business functions and cultures.
- Training and career programs will aim to create a pool of marketing managers with these broader skills. Gradual harmonization of professional qualification requirements within the EU countries will further facilitate international career pathing.

However, the ongoing shifts in marketing organizations in recent years have not only been fueled by the actions of the EU itself. The globalization of competition has motivated several companies to shift line authority from geography-driven organizations to worldwide business units.

expertise of the three markets. Organizing by geographic markets or by customer groups (industries) makes sense from a marketing point of view, but the needs of the products and the specific technology knowledge demanded for selling the products will not be covered adequately. The construction marketing manager and his other sales staff, who mostly sell water pumps and heating electronics to the construction industry, may have a blind prejudice against air ventilators, which typically are sold to the aircraft and marine industries.

A functional structure seems totally inappropriate because it will develop little or no marketing orientation on either products or markets. A geographic area-based structure will divide the world into different economic and political country groups, where each acts as a highly result-oriented profit center, but little or no development progress will be achieved for new applications. The matrix structure seeks to solve the organizational dilemma. Figure 14.5 illustrates the matrix organization.

In the case of Northern Pumps, Inc., the main implication of adopting this structural concept is that there are nine functional intersections. At these points one gets the benefits of maximum knowledge and expertise of a product group and a market group.

This means that the marketing staff work both as members of a product group (water pumps, air ventilators, and heating electronics) and as members of a project team based on a market dimension (customer group). They are therefore likely to have two different managers. We can further add the international dimension as a third geographic axis on the chart, representing the responsibility for the marketing coordination within a region or individual country.

In general, as with all types of structures, the matrix organization has its advantages and disadvantages. The structure is useful for companies that are both product diversified and geographically spread. By combining a product management approach with a market-oriented approach one can meet both the needs of markets and of products. As a result, the matrix structure exhibits sharply different patterns of product know-how, market knowledge, and technology transfer.

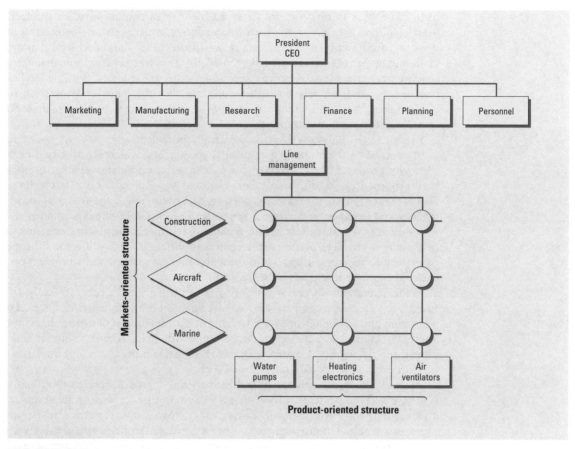

FIGURE 14.5   International mixed structure

Many know-how and service-based companies and technology-intensive firms use the matrix format.

Under this approach, instead of designating national subsidiaries, geographic area divisions or product divisions as profit centers, they are all responsible for profitability. National organizations are responsible for country profits, geographic area divisions for a group of national markets (North America, Europe, Latin America), and product divisions for worldwide product profitability.

Compared with the pure organizational forms, the matrix format provides a different internal financial and political environment in decision making. Area managers are responsible for the efficient use of local and regional resources. Their incentive systems encourage efficient allocation of local resources to investment projects. Product and functional managers will seek to maximize efficiency as well as allocate and apply resources to investment projects. This balances the powers of product managers and geographic managers. The economics of projects will appear more favorable as a result.

One of the disadvantages of the matrix structure mentioned often is the unclear decision-making structure. By giving equal importance to product, functional, and geographic competencies, the principle of unity of command with single lines of authority is abandoned. Because there is a widespread dislike of 'working for two or more masters,' matrix structures are often criticized.

In the matrix, authority and influence are based on professional competence in technology, marketing, and so forth, rather than on formal authority. This, in turn, has a built-in tendency to act as a generator of conflict between product, functional, and area managers. Because the different managers are involved from the start, decision making becomes a slower process, but those decisions that are made might be more quickly implemented. In a matrix organization managers have to accept the need to resolve issues and choices at the lowest possible level of management and not rely on higher authority. For the matrix organization to work, managers from different departments must be willing to participate in much committee and team management.

Kramer (1994b) discusses matrix designs in more depth.

In contrast to the above organizational approaches, which are all based on a hierarchy principle, the concept of the *heterarchical* multinational structure has been proposed by Swedish researchers Hedlund and Rolander (1992). The basic idea is that corporate management does not worry too much about logical inconsistency and elegance of the formal structure. The important thing is whether the structure is practical, coherent, and flexible over time. Among other elements, a heterarchy is characterized by many centers of different kinds, different strategic roles for foreign subsidiaries, coalitions with other companies, and a problem orientation behavior that tends to be 'radical'.

In the heterarchical structure, headquarter centers are more geographically diffused. For example, a company may have a financial center in Brussels, a regional marketing unit in Hong Kong with the role of coordinating activities in the whole Southeast Asia area, an Italian production unit with global responsibility for component supply, an R&D center in Denmark for certain products, and the largest product division headquartered in New York.

Also, in contrast to this traditional hierarchical approach, foreign subsidiaries can have specific strategic roles within a function, product line, or geographical area not only for 'their' company in Germany or Sweden, say, but for the corporation as a whole. The growing number of international strategic alliances between companies that face direct competitive positions vis-à-vis each other may also have an influence in the direction of more 'loose' or ad hoc organizational solutions.

SUMMARY

This chapter has presented some important considerations for organization of international operations. Three closely related issues have been discussed, namely the definition of organizational subunits, the choice between centralization and decentralization, and the assignment of reporting and control systems.

The chapter has also discussed advantages and drawbacks of the principal organizational alternatives for the international company. The structural alternatives are: (1) functional, (2) product groupings, (3) market or customer groupings, (4) geography, and (5) mixed approaches.

QUESTIONS FOR DISCUSSION

14.1 What kinds of variables influence how line operations should be subdivided into organizational units?

14.2 Define the concept of centralization and discuss the conditions favoring the centralization of a company's international operations.

14.3 Discuss the advantages and disadvantages of a centralized organizational structure.

14.4 Explain why a company in the early stage of its process of internationalization often uses a functional export department.

14.5 Why do companies choose an international organizational structure based on product lines? Explain.

14.6 Give examples of product types or lines where a company must expect to choose a geographic area division kind of international structure.

14.7 'The matrix structure is the best way to organize an international company operating in turbulent and diverse environments.' Discuss.

14.8 Is there a 'best' way for a company to bring together its international operations to structure an integrated global enterprise? Explain.

14.9 Is it wise for a company to drastically change its international organization at a time when the world economy is in a downturn? Explain.

REFERENCES

Berner, R. (2003). P&G: How A. G. Lafley is revolutionizing a bastion of corporate conservatism. *Business Week*, 7 July, 52–63.

Burrows, P. (2001). The radical bold management experiment at HP. *Business Week*, 19 February, 70–80.

Burrows, P. (2002). What's in store for this happy couple? *Business Week*, 20 May, 45.

Business Week (1998). P&G's hottest new product: P&G, 5 October, 92–6.

Davidson, W. H. and Haspeslagh, P. (1982). Shaping a global organization. *Harvard Business Review*, July–August, 125–32.

Hedlund, G. and Rolander, D. (1992). Action in hierarchies. In *Managing the Global Firm* (ed. C. A. Bartlett and I. Doz), Ch. 1. London: Routledge.

Kramer, R. J. (1993). *Organizing for Global Competitiveness: The Geographic Design*. New York: The Conference Board, Report No. 1034.

Kramer, R. J. (1994a). *Organizing for Global Competitiveness: The Product Design*. New York: The Conference Board.

Kramer, R. J. (1994b). *Organizing for Global Competitiveness: The Matrix Design*. New York: The Conference Board.

FURTHER READING

Johansson, J. K. (1999). *Global Marketing: Foreign Entry, Local Marketing, and Global Management*. Chicago: Richard D. Irwin, Ch. 17.

Keegan, W. J. (2002). *Global Marketing Management* 7th edn. Upper Saddle River, NJ: Prentice-Hall, Ch. 17.

Kramer, R. J. (1995a). *Organizing for Global Competitiveness: The Asia-Pacific Regional Design*. New York: The Conference Board, Report No. 1133–95-RR.

Kramer, R. J. (1995b). *Organizing for Global Competitiveness: The Business Unit Design*. New York: The Conference Board, Report No. 1110–95-RR.

Kramer, R. J. (1996). *Organizing for Global Competitiveness: The European Regional Design*. New York: The Conference Board, Report No. 1151–96-RR.

Kramer, R. J. (1997). *Organizing for Global Competitiveness: The Country Subsidiary Design*. New York: The Conference Board, Report No. 1180–97-RR.

CASE STUDY 14.1

Asea Brown Boveri Limited

(This case study is based on material contained in K. E. Agthe, Managing the mixed marriage, Business Horizons, 33(1) (January–February 1990), 37–43; W. Taylor, The logic of global business: an interview with ABB's Percy Barnevik, Harvard Business Review, 69(2) (March–April 1991), 91–105; and The ABB of management, The Economist, 338(7947) (6 January 1996), 56.)

Asea Brown Boveri (ABB) is a global organization headquartered in Zurich, Switzerland. The company was founded in 1987 when the Swedish firm Asea merged with the Swiss company Brown Boveri. At the outset the merged company consolidated operations based on layoffs, plant closings, and product exchanges between countries. The company also expanded through acquisition. The company is organized in a way that combines global scale and world technology with emphasis on local markets. The overall ABB management philosophy applied worldwide is: 'Think global, but act local.'

ABB is one of the world's largest electro technical corporations with annual revenues (turnover) exceeding US$25 billion. More than 240,000 people are employed worldwide. These employees work in more than 1300 companies that operate in 140 countries. These companies are organized into 5000 profit centers.

ABB is a global organization of much business diversity. Yet its organizing principles are simple. Along one dimension, the company is a distributed global network. Executives around the world make decisions on product strategy and performance without regard for national borders. Along a second dimension, it is a collection of traditionally organized national companies, each serving its home market as effectively as possible. ABB's global matrix holds the two dimensions together.

At the top of the company sit CEO Percy Barnevik and 12 colleagues on the executive committee. The group, which meets every three weeks, is responsible for ABB's global strategy and performance. The executive committee consists of Swedes, Swiss, Germans, and Americans. Several members of the executive committee are based outside Zurich, and their meetings are held around the world. Only 135 people work at the Zurich headquarters.

Reporting to the executive committee are leaders of the 50 or so business areas (BAs), located worldwide, into which the company's products and services are divided. The BAs are grouped into eight business (product) segments, for which different members of the executive committee are responsible. For example, the 'industry' segment, which sells components, systems, and software to automate industrial processes, has five BAs, including metallurgy, drives, and process engineering. The BA leaders report to Gerhard Schulmeyer, a German member of the executive committee who works out of Stamford, Connecticut.

Each BA has a leader responsible for optimizing the business on a global basis. The BA leader devises and implements a global strategy, holds factories around the world to cost and quality standards, allocates export markets to each factory, and shares expertise by rotating people across borders, creating mixed-nationality teams to solve problems, and build a culture of trust and communication. The BA leader for power transformers, who is responsible for 25 factories in 16 countries, is a Swede who works out of Mannheim, Germany. The BA leader for instrumentation is British. The BA leader for electric metering is an American based in North Carolina.

Alongside the BA structure sits a company structure; ABB's operations in the developed world are organized as national enterprises with presidents, balance sheets, income statements, and career ladders. In Germany, for example, Asea Brown Boveri Aktiengesellschaft, ABB's national company, employs 36,000 people and generates annual revenues of more than US$4 billion. The managing director of ABB Germany, Eberhard von Koerber, plays a role comparable with that of a traditional German CEO. He reports to a supervisory board whose members include German bank representatives and trade union officials. His company produces financial statements comparable with those from any other German company and participates fully in the German apprenticeship program.

The BA structure meets the national structure at the level of ABB's member companies. Percy Barnevik advocates strict decentralization. Whenever possible, ABB creates separate companies to do the work of the 50 BAs in different countries. For example, ABB does not merely sell industrial robots in Norway. Norway has an ABB robotics company charged with manufacturing robots, selling to and servicing domestic customers, and exporting to markets allocated by the BA leader.

There are 1300 such local companies around the world. Their presidents report to two bosses: the BA leader, who is usually located outside the country, and the president of the national company of which the local company is a subsidiary. At this intersection,

➡

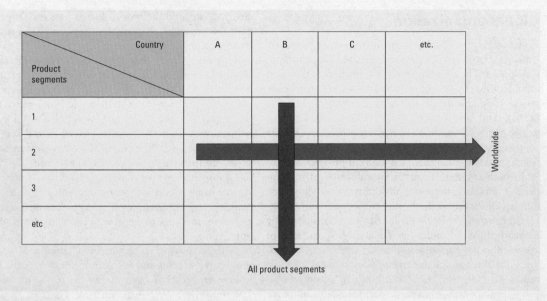

Country Product segments	A	B	C	etc.	
1					
2					Worldwide
3					
etc					

All product segments

FIGURE 14.6 International matrix organization

ABB's 'multidomestic' structure becomes a reality.

ABB's organization has been viewed by company officials as a matrix organization, as illustrated by Figure 14.6. There are many who feel that an international company active in many countries and with different business areas (product groups) has no other alternative but to operate within the framework of a matrix organization.

Questions

1. Evaluate the use of a matrix organization by ABB. What benefits accrue to ABB by having such an organization and what costs are there to the company?

2. Why would not a 'straight' product-based, or geographic-based, or perhaps even an international division-based organization structure do the job?

CASE STUDY 14.2

Unilever

(This case study was written by Charlotte Butler, Research Associate, in collaboration with Philippe Lasserre, Professor of Strategy and Management at INSEAD, Euro-Asia Centre.)

Founded in the 19th century, Unilever is one of the world's largest producers of branded consumer goods. Its products are manufactured in 75 countries and sold through subsidiaries operating in Europe, Latin America, Africa, and Asia for a total turnover of £23 billion.

In the early 1990s, with a combined turnover of about £1.5 billion, growth in the Asia-Pacific area had exceeded the corporate average over the previous 10 years. The group's positions in Thailand, Indonesia, Taiwan, Korea, and China were considered well established with China in particular having registered 'phenomenal success'. In Japan, Unilever was one of the relatively largest foreign companies but was still a small player in Japanese terms.

The Asia-Pacific region is considered an area for future growth, but the region generates only 7% of corporate sales, although 20% of the world markets are in Asia. According to Morris Tabaksblat, co-chairman of the company, because of a lack of experienced managers, 'Unilever is meeting its limits there.'[1]

Global organization

Consistently profitable throughout its history, Unilever's main strengths have been size and geographical spread. The core of Unilever's business is the local manufacture of branded and packaged consumer goods: food and drinks (50% of turnover), detergents (25%), and personal products (15%). Besides consumer goods, its other major activities include products for trade and industrial customers' agri-business operations, specialty chemicals, and medical products.

In each country, Unilever's products usually comprise a mix of internationally known brands and a number of local brands.

Unilever's worldwide businesses are coordinated by its head office in London, which acts as a 'reservoir of knowledge and expertise and as an agency for spreading ideas throughout the group.'[2] Six nationalities are represented on the main board, which comprises 18 people, each director having a specific responsibility for different sectors of the business.

Unilever's management structure is described as 'tight but free flowing,' with 'only four layers between the chairman of the group and the lowliest brand manager in the furthest corner of the world.' Over 95% of all Unilever's managers are nationals of the country in which they work. Their understanding of the nuances of local cultures is regarded as a great strength.

Unilever's operations are directed through a three-dimensional structure based on products, territories, and functions such as finance and marketing.

Product management groups, known as Coordinations, are each headed by a director. The Detergents and Personal Products Coordinations have responsibility for companies in Europe and the United States and act in an advisory capacity in the rest of the world. The Speciality Chemicals and Agribusiness Coordinations are run on a global basis.

The Foods Executive, consisting of three directors, is responsible for the worldwide strategy and global performance of Unilever's foods interests. From January 1991, each of the three became responsible for foods activities in a specific region (northern Europe, southern Europe, and the United States). They also have a close advisory relationship with the foods business in the rest of the world. The three are supported by five product groups, each one responsible for the strategy and performance of a particular category of food products worldwide.

Unilever's organizational heritage is basically one of strong, local, self-sufficient operations. Traditionally the group's highly decentralized organization, built on 'short communication lines and delegation,' gave its companies wide scope to act within an overall company plan, while its management philosophy placed great emphasis on decision making by its operating company chairmen around the world. In the past this approach gave the group great strength in terms of local responsiveness and knowledge.

However, from the 1960s on several forces for change led to a modification of this approach. First, the belief that 'the science, the knowledge, the know-how lies in the product Coordinations' led to a move from geography toward product. This was followed by the realization within the company that, as the speed of change increased, 'the windows of opportunity are small and move past very quickly.' In the past, the group had moved slowly and taken a long-range view, a luxury it decided it could no longer afford. This realization coincided with the perceived need to globalize, in order to be in a position to grasp global opportunities.

A third moving force was the changing balance of the world's economic structure. Historically, Unilever's strength has been in Europe (60% of sales in 1989) followed by North America. The East Asia and Pacific zones were of relatively small importance in its portfolio. However, the rapid opening of consumer markets in the developing world, and particularly in Asia-Pacific, altered Unilever's perception of the region's importance, and made it appreciate the need to 'push hard' in the region.

Unilever's overall strategy in response to this new environment has been to change its structure, in order to achieve a balance between 'powerful country managers and global product managers' the better to sell goods globally. The aim was to capture the synergies that came from operating in a multicountry fashion, without cutting the group off from the local roots that were 'the wellspring of our market understanding, which is the foundation of our strength today and, we believe, will be essential for operating tomorrow.'

Accordingly, Unilever modified its structure to achieve 'uniquely flexible organizations that are sensitive to local tastes, while at the same time deploying technologies and concepts globally.' On the other hand, 'We believe truly global opportunities and brands will be very rare. The global village academic discussion and "global vs local" are not relevant – the reality will be a lot of inconveniently sized things in between.'

Within this context, Unilever's approach to operations outside its two main markets (Europe and North America) has changed both in substance and style.

Until the early 1980s Unilever had a 'steamship approach' to the operations it labelled 'the rest of the world.' These were run by an overseas committee of three or four people, of whom two or three were on the main board. Each member was responsible for two or three countries in Latin America, Africa, or Asia, but there was no attempt to group countries with similar characteristics together. The strategy was one of 'divide and conquer.' Each country was a largely self-sufficient, autonomous unit reporting to the centre, and there was no attempt to forge lateral contacts between neighbors.

With slight modifications, this structure remained in place until 1985, when a major study of Unilever's organization recommended changes that led to the establishment of three regional management groups. They were as follows:

- East Asia Pacific (Thailand to New Zealand, including mainland China);
- Africa excluding South Africa and the Middle East;
- the rest of the world, consisting of Latin America, South Africa, and the Indian Subcontinent.

A main board director was put in charge of each group, supported by a staff. The group was fully responsible for profit for the region, and for specialist expertise on brands, marketing, and so forth, and drew on other Coordinations within the company. In 1990, this was the organization of the group's Asia-Pacific operations. All 12 companies in the Asia-Pacific region reported to the board member responsible for their profit and growth, who was based in London.

Unilever's development in Asia

Unilever has no set policy on how to enter a country and establish a presence. Generally it prefers to 'go it alone,' and have full control of its operating companies by retaining 100% of equity, provided that it can get access to good local people. Equity partnerships with local businesses, with the government, or with the investing public in the host country, are entered into where appropriate, for example in India and Indonesia.

Unilever's colonial past gave it an early presence in the region. Typically, a foothold was established in a country through the sale of soaps and soap powder, followed quickly by local production and then the steady expansion of products and ranges as the markets developed. Personal products, foods, and other activities developed on the back of the detergents and soap businesses. As it was often the first into these markets, Unilever's products gained a dominant position. In many cases this position was subsequently reinforced through acquisition.

At the beginning of the 1990s the group operated in 12 countries through its subsidiaries, and manufactured locally everywhere except Singapore and Hong Kong. The chronological development is described in Figure 14.7. Table 14.2 summarizes Unilever's presence in the region.

Throughout the 1980s Unilever had also largely succeeded in maintaining and often developing strong positions in soaps and detergents. The new emphasis on 'sharing ideas' and 'moving concepts around quickly'

had led to the transfer of a successful marketing idea for a detergent from Australia to the United States, where the product then became number two in the market.

It had also been generally successful in building strong positions in some personal products, especially hair products. Brands had been launched in one country after another following local adaptation. Unilever's main strength in Southeast Asia was its sale of one-shot sachets of toothpaste and shampoo.

> You can find these anywhere in any village. And this means a fantastic logistic and sales system, we are producing millions of these sachets ... we sell three a week to the same consumer. So you have to know their tastes, and you have to be locally entrenched. You have to have deep roots in the market ... the driving force of our marketing unit in Indonesia, in the Philippines, in Thailand ... Our marketing people are local people, with some expats to train and lead them.

| **TABLE 14.2** | Unilever's presence in Asia Pacific |

	Food	Detergents	Personal products
Philippines (1927)	Wholly owned subsidiary 1 factory		
Thailand (1932)		Wholly owned subsidiary 1 factory	
Malaysia (1930)	Jointly owned subsidiary		70% Unilever
Singapore (1954)	Wholly owned subsidiary		
Hong Kong (1924)	Wholly owned subsidiary		
China (1924 ... 87)	Joint venture	Joint venture	Joint venture
Japan (1964)	Wholly owned subsidiary		
Taiwan (1984)	Acquisition		
Korea (1985)		Joint venture	
Australia (1888)	Wholly owned subsidiaries		
New Zealand (1919)			

Australia: The company began distributing soap products throughout Australia in 1888, and local manufacture began in 1898 in Sydney. By 1990 most of the group's interests were organized under a holding company operating through the main group subsidiary. Activities covered all product groupings, except for the agribusinesses. The company employed over 4700 people, and over the years had invested heavily in management training and development. Many of Unilever's brands in the detergents and personal products fields enjoyed market or near market leadership.

New Zealand: Unilever's market leadership in detergents dates from 1919, when local production began. After 1945 the company expanded into foods and personal products, where good positions were won in the dental, hair, and skin-care markets. Overall, food activities were unsuccessful until 1988, when acquisitions enabled the group to establish a major presence. As a result, by 1990 foods represented more than 50% of Unilever's sales in New Zealand. Operations were directed through a wholly owned subsidiary.

The Philippines: Unilever's presence here goes back to 1927. In 1990 the company was one of the top 25 in the country in sales turnover. The subsidiary was wholly owned. The company's activities covered the whole range of packaged consumer goods, and it was particularly strong (market leader or second) in personal products.

Thailand: Unilever was granted a royal warrant at the turn of the century and opened its first factory in 1932. Consistently profitable and a leader in the soaps, detergents, and latterly personal products markets, in 1990 Unilever was the largest consumer goods business in the country. A key objective for the future was the development of a foods business.

Malaysia: Unilever began operating here on an import basis in the early 1930s, and in 1952 became the first foreign manufacturing company to start local production. The country is still an important supplier of raw materials to the group. Personal products manufacture began in 1963, and the 1980s saw an expansion of the foods business through acquisition. By the end of the decade the company's activities covered a full product range in most businesses, and it was the leader or second in its markets. Of the company's total sales volume, 25% was exported. In line with Malaysian law the subsidiary was 70% owned by Unilever, 30% by local institutional shareholders.

Indonesia: Activities here began in 1933 with the establishment of a soap factory, followed in 1936 by the manufacture of edible fats and cooking oils. The year 1941 saw diversification into toothpaste and other personal products. In 1980 all the companies were consolidated under one subsidiary that, by 1990, was the largest consumer goods company operating in Indonesia.

Singapore: Unilever's presence in this small market began in 1954, with the opening of a branch office for the Malaysian operation. Sales were conducted through agents until 1959, when a sales force was recruited to sell a limited range of soap and detergent brands. After independence in 1965 a plant was opened to manufacture detergents and edible fats, but it was closed in 1987. The personal products business started in 1976 and foods in 1979, following an acquisition. By 1990 most product areas of interest to Unilever were virtually saturated, and the competition was intense. With one exception, all products sold were imported from the region and from the rest of the world. However, Singapore's central location made it 'a good regional base.'

Hong Kong: Prior to 1949, Unilever's Hong Kong subsidiary was the depot for its Shanghai soap company that opened in 1924. After 1954 its assets and expatriate management were transferred to the Hong Kong company, which handled exports into China. Later, joint ventures with China were handled directly from London. After a sluggish period in the 1960s and 1970s the businesses took off in the 1980s, mainly due to exports to China. In 1989 the Hong Kong and Chinese activities were brought together under the chairman of Unilever's Hong Kong subsidiary. A year later, although the marketing for China was still being led from Hong Kong, increasingly the office was becoming a supporter of Unilever's activities in China. As the gateway to China, 'its whole focus is changing fast.'

China: In 1990 Unilever had three joint ventures in Shanghai, all reporting into Hong Kong. The first, established in 1987, was for the manufacture of soap and detergents; the second (1990) was for the manufacture of skin-care products, while the third (1989) manufactured margarine and ice cream (foods). Unilever showed its commitment to China by increasing its investment despite the events in Tiananmen Square (1989). By 1995 it was expected that Unilever's first joint venture investment would be paid back.

FIGURE 14.7 Unilever's chronological development in Asia Pacific

Japan: A subsidiary was established here in 1964 as a joint venture. In 1974 Unilever increased its shareholding from 45% to 79.9%, and in 1986 it became a 100% Unilever subsidiary, signaling a more aggressive posture. In 1990 the company manufactured on three sites and had achieved high growth since the mid-1980s, establishing a significant presence in the markets for hair care, fabric conditioners, and frozen foods. In recognition of Japan's importance in the world and the region, the company was committed to substantial future investment there.

Taiwan: In 1984 Unilever bought a 50% interest, on a foreign investment approved basis in a company that produced and sold detergent powders and toilet soaps. Further share purchases at later stages left Unilever holding 92.2% of the shares. Personal products brands were launched in 1988, followed by some foods products.

Korea: A joint venture was established in 1985, primarily for the sale of detergents. A wholly owned business was established in 1993.

FIGURE 14.7 continued

The group had been singularly unsuccessful in building a foods business in East Asia. While foods represented 50% of Unilever's total business, in Asia it was about 15% of the company's total Asia business.

This was primarily attributed to the fact that Unilever's knowledge was based on western European markets. However, the group had recently begun to try to 'use our market understanding in Asia and turn it towards foods and how people feed their families – and try to link it with our basic know-how in order to create value-added opportunities.'

However, the company had been encouraged by the success of an ice cream business in Thailand, where a greenfield operation was going well. Attempts would be made to try to repeat this success elsewhere.

As far as Unilever's other, highly successful products were concerned, 'Everyone is investing in Asia Pacific and we, as the guys in possession, are being targeted by new entrants. So we are not complacent.'

In the past the Unilever heritage of local autonomy meant that products were often adapted unnecessarily, 'past the law of diminishing returns.' While the basic R&D was usually carried out in the United Kingdom, the Unilever approach had always been, 'more than product adaptation ... I would say we are absolutely locally led in each country.'

In personal products, for example, 'We design our products for the local market ... We craft products by testing them to the liking of Indonesians and Thais, so we are doing much more than product adaptation.' However, faced by the trend towards 'large-scale economies, rapid innovation and flexible response to market trends, top management realized that such an approach was a handicap.'

The conclusion was that 'maybe we have gone too far from time to time.' By the end of the 1980s the new objective was to try to start with a Southeast Asian idea, and then adapt it marginally for the Philippines,

Indonesia, and so on. 'It used to be thought that selling detergent in the Philippines was like nowhere else on earth. Now we see that shampoos or concentrated detergents are essentially similar issues in all countries. Fine tuning only is needed.'

Organizational approach to Asia

Organizational structure

In 1990 the East Asia Pacific Group, to which the 12 operating companies in the region reported, was located in London. It was composed of a main board member, an operations member, a personnel and a finance member who was responsible for finance, accounting, logistics, buying, and computing for all the companies. In 1991 a foods member was appointed, indicating a 'wish to push it.'

The role of the Asia-Pacific group was as follows:

1. To ensure support for the operating companies.
2. To capture synergies, i.e., through regional and subregional strategies, and so 'prevent country divisions becoming walls.'
3. Strategic planning and resource allocation. To make plans and key appointments, and decide on major investments.

There was no operational headquarters in Asia. In each of the 12 Asian countries in which Unilever had an operating company, it was run either as a wholly owned subsidiary or as a joint venture according to local legal requirements. The head of the operating company was responsible for all Unilever's activities in that country. He reported to the East Asia Pacific Group in London.

The operating companies implemented standard policies, but a great deal was left to local management discretion. Although the local chief executive (CE) still had a lot of freedom in key decisions about the product, there was now more emphasis on the role of the Coordinations. In each of them, people who were 'part of the product heartland' were appointed as marketing and liaison members with specific responsibility for the companies in the region: 'These people have a lot of autonomy to go and tell them what they think they [the companies] should do.'

For example, 'If you're sitting in Bangkok and suddenly you see the invasion of a competitor and you want to react, there is a dotted line to the liaison member in the relevant Coordination who might say 'Look, what do you think we should do, why don't we have a meeting ... and we can develop a strategy together.' The main board member will be informed of the demand, and will receive a report about the advice given by the liaison member.'

Information and intelligence collection

There was no analysis bureau, or any specific intelligence collecting activity peculiar to Asia. As a global consumer goods business, Unilever believed the differences between the regions were of degree, not kind. The emphasis was more on a common language and systems globally than on local differentiation.

The reorganization of the Asia businesses had made everyone more aware of regional activities. Each of the 12 chairmen received data informing them in minute detail of what other operations were doing, and which products were being sold in the rest of the region. There was much more intercountry travel and managers knew each other. The 12 regional chairmen met once a year; their commercial directors also met regularly.

In subgroups, managers saw each other four or five times a year (the chairmen plus the commercial directors, or the chairmen plus the marketing managers, and so on). Each person probably saw his colleagues in other countries four or five times a year.

This had resulted in much more comparison of notes and recognition of the fact that 'the similarities in products and product problems are greater than the differences.' This was 'a dramatic change for the group.'

Planning and budgeting

For new markets there was a country strategy detailing what resources and what products were to be allocated. The local CE prepared a strategy for the regional management, who consulted with the relevant Coordination. Issues were then debated with the chairman and the eventual framework development plan was an amalgam of Unilever's central long-term strategy plus the country plan and the Coordination's input.

Within the corporate unit, in 1990 the Asia-Pacific region had greater emphasis as 'The 12 countries are regarded by Unilever as more attractive than any other 12 countries.'

Integration mechanisms

According to the operations member, the search for synergies represented the most interesting contrast to Unilever's old way of running its regional operations. The members of his group spent most of their time trying to stimulate a multicountry approach, to get more push behind products or better resource allocation.

On this basis, the aim of the group was to find ways of operating that seized opportunities at local, subregional, regional, multiregional and global levels.

> This requires a degree of flexibility that will not be met by either viewing the world as a set of countries, or a single village. We have to make simplifying assumptions, and so we do draw lines on maps, which may be different lines for different purposes.
>
> So, if we look at Southeast Asia we see basically the ASEAN countries. But for some purposes we may include Taiwan, while Greater China will often include Singapore plus the Chinese-influenced Southeast Asian countries.
>
> We are trying to establish a set of institutions and processes that are multicountry by nature (as opposed to the single-country dominance of the Unilever heritage) in order to identify common needs, and to organize resources on a task force basis, which may not always involve the same group of countries.

An example of this task-oriented approach was the move to try to develop ethnic Chinese human resources. For this, the focus was on Taiwan, Hong Kong, and Singapore.

Multicountry projects were implemented via task forces, which might be cross-country or cross-discipline, permanent or temporary. In recent years five or six individual subregional specialists had been developed to provide an efficient service to all 12 operating companies. Some were peripatetic. For example, a Tokyo market researcher spent half his time in Japan and the rest of his time advising other countries on market research techniques. However, in order to avoid empire building or adding cost, such individuals were not provided with a staff.

Clearly, such an approach required that the people running the country businesses be more open-minded than they had hitherto been. Where historically their task was to maximize progress in their country, they now had an additional responsibility to 'take off the blinkers.'

However, the group had not yet gone so far as to try to break down country barriers altogether. Organizationally, for example, Unilever could run its operations on a product division plus CE basis that ignored national boundaries. The group was moving towards that in the sense of 'looking for professional leadership per product group across national boundaries, but we see that as a supplement to strong local market understanding and an ability to deal with the retail trade and so on.'

Another internal factor to be considered was that Unilever 'still tends to think in terms of countries.' Within the East Asia grouping, from Thailand to Korea, not one of them was yet dominant (although China would be). This contrasted with the rest of the Unilever world, where Brazil dominated Latin America and India dominated the Indian subcontinent, and both acted as dynamos for their zones. Lacking an obvious dynamo for the Asia-Pacific zone, to be able to exercise internal clout and get attention from central R&D, the East Asia Pacific group was obliged to add together Thailand, the Philippines, Indonesia, and others.

The corresponding external point was that in dealing with suppliers and buying similar materials, often on world markets, there was a need to exercise clout as a group.

All this meant that 'national boundaries are becoming more porous, which creates problems for a company with our heritage and means change – which could be a threat or an opportunity.'

In the long term, believed the operating member, 'We need to create some picture of where we want to be before we put resources into place. So we are formulating notions of what our "mini dynamos" should be, and then we will invest.'

To this end the group members were collecting information. The tendency was to extrapolate, but 'the world operates by discontinuities, so we have attempted some leaps of imagination. However, at the end of the day we will probably be conservative about acting on insights – there is always the risk of being wrong.'

It was felt that there was still too much dependence on a particular individual's knowledge, which the company was not good at capturing and making available to a wider audience. There was also concern that all the information and expertise was in the heads of expats, and so was lost when they returned to England or went elsewhere. In future, the group hoped to ensure that it would be kept in the business by having local management. Although these local managers might become international, they would spend the bulk of their careers in their own country. For certain countries the company was evolving a scheme that would allow expats to work longer in one country.

Knowledge was becoming increasingly systemized, although the process was still in the early stages. In a unique experiment, the company was trying to promulgate Japanese knowledge and expertise on key subjects – on technology, for example – to the rest of the region.

Symbols and signals

Unilever's top management was very aware of what was happening in Asia, in fact the companies in the region felt that they suffered from too many visits by interested parties within the group, and by 1990 were almost at saturation point. Visits by the chairmen, board members and special committees had increased markedly during the last three years, a sign of the region's increased importance. Statements on the group's Asian businesses were frequent, and all the key business brands were there. Products representing leading Unilever technology, concentrated detergents for example, progressed further in the East than elsewhere.

Notes

1. 4 July 1994.
2. All quotations are drawn from interviews with company executives.

Questions

1. Evaluate the organization structure used by Unilever in Asia.
2. How should Unilever organize for optimum results?
3. Explain why a matrix organization approach would work or would not work for Unilever in Asia.
4. Should Unilever have restructured its organization as Procter & Gamble did in the late 1990s? Why or why not?

Some additional comments on Unilever's subsequent actions and performance

In the first decade of the 21st century, Unilever has undergone additional restructuring. Except as noted below, the information in these comments is taken from the Unilever Annual Review 2003, http://www.unilever.com, with page numbers noted as appropriate in brackets.

The company's operations are now organized into two global divisions, a Foods Division and a Home & Personal Care Division, each headed by a Divisional

Director. The structure is designed to provide appropriate focus at both regional and global levels, allow faster decision-making, and strengthen capacity for innovation by more effectively integrating research into the divisional structure. (20)

A Path to Growth is being carried out to simplify the business and to rationalize manufacturing and the supply chain. There is a target of annual savings of €3.9 billion. The brand portfolio is being reduced from 1,600 to 400 leading brands, releasing more resources to support the bigger brands. It is expected that most of the goals will be met by the end of 2004. (4) Acquisitions, divestitures and changes in joint venture arrangements are being made in support of these goals. Leading brands may use different names in different countries to meet local needs and preferences. (14)

During the past five years, Unilever has increased its operating margin by approximately 50% (Ball, 2004). While turnover in euros and British pounds has decreased in each of the past two years, operating profits have increased. Turnover as well as profits increased when calculated in US$ because of exchange rate changes.

The Asia-Pacific region accounted for approximately 17% of total Unilever turnover in 2003. (13)

References:

Ball, D. (2004). Europeans Narrow Gap on Share Valuations. *The Wall Street Journal*, 25 February, C1.

Unilever Annual Review 2003, http://www.unilever.com

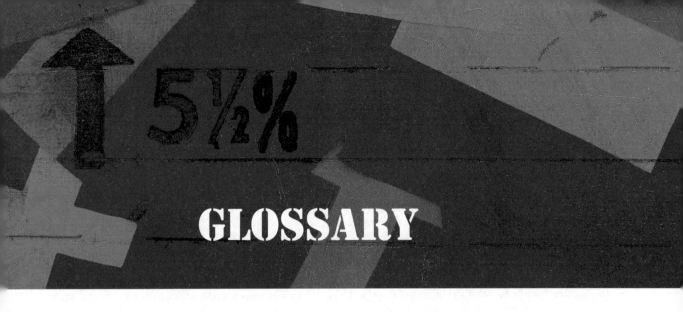

GLOSSARY

absolute advantage The case where one country or firm has a cost advantage in one product (or service) and another country or firm has a cost advantage in another product or service.

acceptance Time draft that has been accepted for payment.

adaptation A company offers different versions of the marketing program or individual elements of the program (such as a product) to each foreign market.

advertising Nonpersonal presentation of sales messages through mass media, paid for by the advertiser.

advertising network Collection of independent web sites from different companies and media networks.

affiliate network Collection of web sites that link to an online retailer in exchange for commission on purchases made from the retailer.

agent Independent marketing organization that represents the exporter when making a sale, and is paid a commission. May be foreign based or home country based.

air waybill Bill of lading used in air transport; it is a nonnegotiable document.

Andean Group A common market in South America that includes Bolivia, Colombia, Ecuador, Peru, and Venezuela.

antidumping duties Taxes imposed on an import that is being sold at a price lower than its cost of production or lower than the price at which it is sold in its home market.

antitrust regulation Government regulation of business behavior that is concerned with concentration of economic resources and possible monopoly power.

arbitration An approach to settling disputes in which a third, disinterested party acts as a type of referee to determine the merits of the case and make a judgement that both parties agree to honor.

ASEAN (Association of Southeast Asian Nations) A regional economic integration scheme that includes the countries of Brunei, Indonesia, Malaysia, the Philippines, Singapore, Thailand, Vietnam, Myanmar (Burma) and Laos.

assembly operations A foreign market-based facility that uses mostly imported components and parts to put together a final product.

auxiliary services When applied to a product includes warranties, use instructions, installation help, after-sales service, and spare parts availability.

banner advertisements Advertising paced on web sites.

barter A form of countertrade that involves a direct exchange of goods or services between two parties, which may be business firms or governments.

bases of segmentation Variables (criteria) used to segment a foreign market into specific components.

Berne Union The global coordinator of national credit and investment insurers from more than 30 countries. Formally known as the International Union of Credit and Investment Insurers.

bill of exchange Draft drawn on an importer. See *draft*.

bill of lading A document that is the contract of carriage between the shipper and the transportation carrier, a receipt for the goods issued by the carrier, and/or evidence of title to the goods.

border tax Used primarily in Europe, this tax was imposed on imports in addition to any tariffs and is designed to place a tax burden on imports that is equivalent to that borne by similar domestic products.

brand Anything that identifies a seller's goods or services and distinguishes them from others.

broker A home country-based agent whose chief function is to bring a buyer and seller together. May act as the agent for either party.

brownfield investment A foreign acquisition in which resources and capabilities are provided by the investor, replacing most resources and capabilities of the acquired firm.

built-in export department A company unit consisting of an export sales manager with some clerical help, and most of the export marketing (except sales) is done by the regular domestic marketing company units.

bundle pricing Pricing for all components, and/or products in a group, together.

Business Environment Risk Index (BERI) An index that measures the discrimination of foreigners compared with nationals as well as the general quality of a country's business climate.

buyback A form of countertrade where a company agrees to supply technical knowledge to build a plant, or actually builds the plant or licenses the use of a trademark, in exchange for a portion of the production output of the plant.

Caribbean Community and Common Market (CARICOM) Common market that includes 13 nations within the Caribbean area.

cartel An association of producers formed with the objectives of coordinating and controlling the production and marketing of a product and improving profits.

cash on delivery (COD) Payment is to be made in cash when the shipment is delivered to the buyer.

cash with order Payment, in whole or in part, for an order is to be made at the time of the order. Also known as cash in advance.

CE marking Used in the European Union to indicate that a product meets essential safety requirements of those countries where it will be marketed. It is required for products that fall within any of the EU's New Approach Directives.

center of excellence A technical-based center within a multinational or global company in which development of products or components of products is centralized for the entire company. Also known as competence center.

Central American Common Market (CACM) A common market that consists of Costa Rica, El Salvador, Guatemala, Honduras, Panama, and Nicaragua.

centralization Organization pattern where decision making and control for international operations are concentrated at headquarters.

certificate of origin A document that certifies the country of origin of products being exported.

change agent A government or private organization that promotes export activities of business firms.

civil-law (Roman Law) country A country in which the legal system is based on the codes that are considered to be the completely comprehensive, all-inclusive source of authority that 'regulates' behavior.

clean bill of lading Bill of lading that has no notation of damage indicated.

clean draft A draft with no documents attached.

clearing arrangements Type of barter where surpluses are cleared up either by accepting more goods or by one party paying a penalty.

climate for advertising Views about advertising in general held by people and institutions in a socio-economic, cultural, and political system.

commercial invoice A bill from the exporter to the importer for the product(s) that is being exported.

common-law country A country in which the legal system relies on past judicial decisions, or cases, to resolve disputes or 'regulate' behavior.

common market A group of countries that has formed an integration scheme in which internal barriers to trade are eliminated, external barriers are common, and free movement of factors of production internally is allowed.

communication/promotion barrier Anything that adversely affects, or potentially affects, a foreign buyer's receipt of a message sent by the international/export marketer as originally sent.

comparative advantage The case where one country or firm has absolute cost advantages in the production of all products and services compared to another country or firm, but has a greater cost advantage in some products or services than in others.

compensation agreement See *buyback*.

confirmed letter of credit Letter of credit where a bank in the exporter's country takes on the legal obligation to honor (pay) all drafts drawn under the letter of credit.

confirming house An agent who assists the overseas buyer by confirming, as a principal, orders already placed.

consignment The exporter ships to the buyer who pays after the products have been resold.

consolidator See *foreign freight forwarder*.

consular invoice A document signed by the consul of the importing country that is used to control and identify products shipped there.

contract manufacturing A form of strategic alliance where a company contracts for the manufacture/assembly of its product(s) by manufacturers established in foreign markets, while still retaining responsibility for marketing and distributing these products.

contractible market selection Systematic screening of all potential markets leading to elimination of the least promising and further investigation of the most promising.

co-promotion Joint promotions of two products that are compatible.

cost and freight (C&F) Trade term indicating that price includes costs for the goods to be on board a carrier plus the freight costs to a named foreign port.

cost, insurance, and freight (CIF) Trade term that includes the costs of C&F plus transportation insurance.

counterfeit trade The practice of attaching brand names or trademarks to bogus products or services, thereby deceiving the customer into believing that they are purchasing products/services of the owner of the trademark or brand name.

counter purchase A form of countertrade where an exporter sells its products to an importer for cash or credit and agrees to purchase (with the cash or credit) and market products from the original importer's country.

countertrade Parallel business transactions that link a sales contract to a purchase contract in addition to, or in place of, financial settlements. A seller provides a buyer with products/services/technology and agrees to a reciprocal purchasing obligation with the buyer.

countervailing duty Tax (a tariff surcharge) imposed on an import that is designed to offset some special advantage given to the exporter by the exporter's government.

country-of-origin image Views of foreign products held by consumers (users) in an importing country based on their perceptions of the country of export.

cross-cultural communication Communication between a person in one culture and a person or persons in another culture.

cross-licensing Mutual exchange of knowledge, processes, and/or patents between companies in different countries.

cultural distance See *psychic/psychological distance*.

cultural empathy The capacity of a person for understanding cultural differences to an extent that allows the person to see a situation from the standpoint of those in the other culture.

culture The sum of the knowledge, values, beliefs, and attitudes that are shared by a particular society or group of people.

customer organization Company structure organized on the basis of customer groups (industry, end users, and so on).

Customs-bonded warehouse A warehouse in which goods from foreign countries can be stored, and certain manipulations performed on the goods, without payment of duty until the goods are released from storage and delivered to the buyer.

Customs union A group of countries that have abolished tariffs among themselves and have adopted common external tariffs.

danwei The basic work unit in China where a joint venture is responsible for providing all the services needed by employees of the company – homes, stores, schools.

date draft A draft where payment is due a specified number of days after a specific date.

decentralization Organization pattern where decision making and control for international operations are delegated away from headquarters to subdivisions of the organization, often to local management.

deferred letter of credit Letter of credit under which the exporter is to be paid at specified dates after shipment.

del credere An extra commission paid to a manufacturer's export agent who either guarantees payment for all orders sent to the exporter or finances the transaction.

desk jobber A type of export merchant who does not ever physically possess the product sold in a foreign market. Also known as a drop shipper or a cable merchant.

devaluation of currency The price of a national currency in terms of another is lowered either by market forces or by government decision.

differential pricing Relationship of prices for products in a product line. Also used for relationship of prices for a single product in different markets.

diffusion of product Movement of a product from the point of development to the market.

direct export(ing) Selling directly to an importer or buyer located in a foreign market area.

direct marketing Marketing by mail, letters, catalogs, telephone, fax, and the Internet.

disproportionality phenomenon A certain percentage of products in the product mix and/or product lines brings in a proportionately greater or lesser percentage of sales and profits.

distinctive competence An ability or quality that gives an organization a unique advantage over its competitors.

distributor Independent merchant marketing organization that buys from the exporter and resells to other marketing organizations. May be foreign based or home country based.

dock receipt A document given to the shipper by the transport company indicating that goods have been received for shipment.

documentary credit See *letter of credit*.

documentary draft Draft accompanied by the relevant documents that are needed to complete a transaction.

documents against acceptance (D/A) A term used with a draft to indicate that the documents attached to the draft are to be given to the importer upon his or her acceptance of the draft for payment within a specified time.

documents against payment (D/P) A type of draft where documents are given to the importer when he or she pays the amount specified on the draft.

draft Type of check drawn on the importer by the exporter specifying that a sum of money is to be paid to the exporter. When used with a letter of credit the draft is drawn on a bank.

dumping The selling of a product or service by an exporter in a foreign market at below its production cost, or below its price in the domestic market.

duty See *tariff.*

e-business (e-commerce) Sale, purchase, or exchange of goods, services, or information over the Internet or other telecommunications networks.

eco-labeling Identification of products that cause less harm to the environment than others in their category: A seal or label indicating this is issued by a recognized national accrediting organization.

economic advantage Classical trade theory stating that countries tend to specialize in those products in which they have an advantage (i.e., lower cost of production).

economic environment Economic dimensions of the market environment, including population, income and wealth, extent of economic development, and so forth.

economic integration The unification in some way of separate individual national economies into a larger single (or internal) market.

economic union A group of countries that have eliminated tariffs among themselves, established common external barriers, allow free flow of factors of production, and coordinate and harmonize economic and social policy within the union.

emic Human behavior that is culture bound (specific).

empathy Process of a person looking at something from the point of view of another person. See *cultural empathy.*

endogenous variables Factors that can be controlled by the company.

entry strategy A company's strategy for how foreign markets are to be entered, and the plan for the marketing program to be used for a given product/market. Also known as international marketing channel strategy.

equal advantage A situation where one country or company has equal relative cost advantages over another country or company in all products and services.

etic Human behavior that is culture free.

ethical behavior Behavior that most people in a society or group view as being moral, good, or right.

ethnocentrism A buyer's preference for domestic (i.e., local) products and services, and bias against imported goods.

euro See *European Monetary Union.*

European Economic Area (EEA) Free trade area encompassing the EU and EFTA countries.

European Monetary Union (EMU) A union of the members of the European Union – excluding Denmark, Sweden, the United Kingdom, and the new members joining in 2004 – that have adopted a single currency, the euro, to replace their national currencies.

European Free Trade Association (EFTA) Free trade area consisting of Iceland, Liechtenstein, Norway, and Switzerland.

European Union (EU) Economic union consisting of Austria, Belgium, Denmark, Finland, France, Germany, Greece, Ireland, Italy, Luxembourg, the Netherlands, Portugal, Spain, Sweden, and the United Kingdom. In 2004 the following countries became members: Cyprus, Czech Republic, Estonia, Hungary, Latvia, Lithuania, Malta, Poland, Slovenia, and Slovakia.

ex dock Trade term that includes CIF plus all costs to place the goods on the dock at the port of import, including payment of duty.

exchange controls Government limitations on the ability of companies or persons to obtain foreign currencies, or import or export currency.

exogenous variables Factors outside the control of the company, such as culture, laws, and so forth.

expansive market selection An approach to selecting foreign markets that starts with the home market or existing market core as a base and expands from there on a market-by-market basis.

experience-curve pricing Pricing based on the relationship between cost and volume of production/sales as production/sales increase.

export(ing) The sale of products/services to foreign markets.

export commission house An agent representative of foreign buyers who resides in the exporter's home country. Also known as an export buying agent. See *resident buyer.*

export controls Restrictions by the exporter's government over the export of products.

export credit insurance Insurance from a government or private insurer that covers nonpayment by importers due to political risk, nonconvertibility of currency, and commercial risk.

export declaration Document required by an exporter's government showing complete information about a shipment. Used for statistical data and control over exports.

export development Process by which a company advances from not exporting to being a committed exporter.

export license Government document allowing a product to be exported. See *export controls*.

export management company (EMC) An international sales specialist that functions as the exclusive export department for several allied but noncompeting manufacturers.

export market direction Decision of company whether to build, hold, divest, or abandon its position in a foreign market.

export market selection (expansion) The process or opportunity evaluation leading to the selection of foreign markets in which to compete.

export merchant A company that engages in export and buys and sells on its own account.

export processing zone A free area in which foreign manufacturers are provided with incentives for investment, which will produce products for export.

export sales subsidiary A separate company unit located in the home country that operates as a quasi-independent firm.

export subsidy Direct or indirect financial contribution to the exporter by its government.

exporting agent An intermediary that does not take title to the products to be sold in a foreign market.

exporting combination A cooperative organization that is a more or less formal association of independent and competitive business firms, with membership being voluntary, organized for purposes of selling to foreign markets.

extinction pricing Price is set very low (close to direct cost) in order to eliminate existing competitors from foreign markets.

facilitating payment A type of gratuity or 'bribe' that is a commercial requirement in some countries in order to get things done.

facilitating/service organizations Institutions or agencies that are not members of the marketing channel, but provide useful and necessary services to the international marketer. Examples are banks, transport companies, and advertising agencies.

factor proportions theory A nation will export that product for which a large amount of the relative abundant (cheap) input is used and it will import that product in the production of which the relatively scarce (expensive) input is used.

factoring The purchase of a company's accounts receivable by a financial institution.

factura Consular invoice used in some Spanish-speaking countries.

first-mover advantages Benefits that accrue to the firm that is first in the industry to enact certain behavior in a foreign market, such as setting up a production facility.

foreign direct investment (FDI) Investment in ownership in firms in foreign countries with the object of gaining some degree of control.

foreign freight forwarder An independent firm specializing in arranging for the physical movement (forwarding) of an export shipment to a foreign market, and/or arranging for space on transportation carriers. Also known as a consolidator.

foreign media Advertising media that are unique to a single country. Also known as local, domestic media.

foreign representative agreement Defines the conditions upon which the relationship between the exporter and its foreign-based representative (distributor, agent) rests.

foreign sales branch An office located in a foreign market that handles all the distribution and promotional work in a designated market area and sells primarily to marketing organizations and industrial users.

foreign sales subsidiary A foreign market-based separate company operating as a quasi-independent firm.

forfait financing Transfer of a term debt obligation from an export sale by an exporter to a third party.

foul bill of lading Bill of lading making note that there is damage to the goods, or the packing container of the goods, that have been loaded on a transport carrier.

franchising Type of licensing where the company giving the right to use something supplies an important ingredient (parts, materials, and so on) for the finished product.

free alongside (FAS) Trade term indicating that goods are delivered free alongside, but not on board, a transportation carrier.

free area An area within a country considered to be outside the Customs area of the country.

free on board (FOB) Trade term indicating that goods are free on board a transportation carrier at some named point.

free perimeter A type of free area generally found in a remote underdeveloped region of a country, often along a border.

free port Customs-free area that encompasses a port or entire city.

free trade area An economic integration schema whereby member countries abolish tariffs between themselves, but each maintains its own tariffs for nonmember countries.

free trade zone Enclosed, policed area without resident population in, adjacent to, or near a port of entry, into which foreign goods not otherwise prohibited may be brought without formal Customs entry.

functional export department See *built-in export department* and *separate export department*.

General Agreement on Tariffs and Trade (GATT) See *World Trade Organization*.

general average A type of loss during shipment on an ocean carrier affecting all shippers on a particular vessel plus the vessel itself.

generic brand Trademark that has become the description of a type of goods and where the original owner no longer has the exclusive right to use the mark.

geographic organization Company structure organized regionally on a market or area basis.

global advertising Use of the same advertising appeals, messages, art copy, stories, etc. in multiple country markets. See *standardization*.

global corporation A company operating with such consistency across its markets or areas of operation that it appears to treat the world, or major regions within the world, as a single market.

global marketers Companies that are using an integrated worldwide marketing strategy based on consistent brand selling for their product(s), making only minor changes required by differing markets.

global outlook Viewing the world, or relevant parts of the world, as a single market consisting of a number of segments defined by the product(s) to be sold.

global outsourcing Buying products, components, materials, and services in foreign countries.

globalization Process of moving from individualized marketing programs for specific foreign markets to development of programs to market products/services on a worldwide basis.

gravity promotion policy A policy of nonpromotion. The international marketer sells to an intermediary and lets the product find its own way to consumers and users.

gray market export channel A marketing channel that is not authorized by the exporter for a particular foreign market. Also known as parallel importation.

greenfield investment Foreign direct investment in a manufacturing facility that 'starts from scratch.'

guanxi Personal relationships and connections, or a network, between people in China.

Hanover Fair General trade fair held annually in Hanover, Germany, covering at least 20 major industry categories.

hedging Use of techniques involving buying and selling currencies at about the same time to reduce exchange rate exposure by ensuring that the loss of one currency position is offset by a corresponding gain in some other currency position.

Herfindahl Index A measure of the degree of export market concentration of a company.

heterarchical organization structure Multinational structure that is characterized by many centers of different kinds, different strategic roles for foreign subsidiaries, coalitions with other companies, and a problem orientation behavior that tends to be radical.

high-context culture A culture in which the meaning of a message or behavior is dependent upon the situation or context in the message or behavior performed rather than on the words or acts themselves.

host country The foreign country within which a company operates.

house organ A company's in-house publication that presents promotional ideas, company news, employee commendations, and so forth.

import(ing) The buying of products from a foreign area.

INCOTERMS 2000 System of trade terms developed by the International Chamber of Commerce.

indent order An order received by an exporter based on a sales contract negotiated between a purchaser and an overseas-based branch office or distributor.

indirect export(ing) Using the services of independent marketing organizations, or cooperative organizations, located within the home country in exporting.

internal product development An evolutionary process consisting of a number of stages starting with idea generation and ending with commercialization.

international division Organization structure in which all international marketing activities are separated from domestic business operations and placed in a single division.

international marketing Marketing of goods and services across political boundaries.

international marketing channel The system composed of marketing organizations that connect a manufacturer to the final users in a foreign market.

international marketing strategy The sum of the basic marketing decisions regarding product and market selection, entry mode, and other marketing activities.

international media Advertising media that circulate, or are heard or seen, in two or more countries.

internationalization A process, end result, and way of thinking whereby a company becomes more involved in and committed to serving markets outside its home country.

Internet marketing See *e-business*.

inward internationalization Foreign-area sourcing.

irrevocable letter of credit Letter of credit that cannot be unilaterally cancelled by the importer or the opening bank.

ISO 14001 A standard set by the International Organization for Standardization (ISO) that sets criteria for a company's internal environmental management system (EMS).

ISO 9000 Minimum standards set by the International Organization for Standardization (ISO) that specifies design, manufacturing, logistics, and other controls associated with producing quality products and services.

joint venture Type of strategic alliance in which companies from at least two countries, generally one being local, form a new company to produce products/services on a joint basis.

Latin American Integration Association Common market that includes Argentina, Bolivia, Brazil, Chile, Colombia, Ecuador, Mexico, Paraguay, Peru, Uruguay, and Venezuela. See also *Andean Group* and *Mercosur*.

letter of credit Commercial credit established through a bank by the buyer that specifies the conditions under which payment is to be made to the beneficiary (the exporter). It is a type of credit with the backing of a bank or banks.

licensing A strategic alliance in which a company in one country gives the right to use something it owns (technology, trademark, etc.) to a company or person in another country.

List of Values (LOV) A set of nine value dimensions that characterize people.

Little Dragons Asian areas of Korea, Taiwan, Hong Kong, and Singapore.

location-specific advantages Advantages to a company that result from the specific location of its business activity.

logistics Management of relationships, decisions, and activities among production, storage, and physical distribution.

low-context culture A culture in which the meaning of a message or behavior resides primarily in the words or behavior themselves, rather than in the setting or context.

management contracting Strategic alliance where a foreign-based company operates a company in a local market for a local investor.

management style Pattern of decision making that exists in a company and/or country. It is also viewed as a recurring set of characteristics associated with the process of making decisions.

manufacturer's export agent A representative of a manufacturer who functions as a salesperson and is paid a commission.

maquiladora An offshore assembly plant established in designated duty-free areas of Mexico.

marginal pricing Pricing based on contribution margin wherein the only relevant costs are direct costs.

marine insurance Insurance for the protection of risk of damage to goods during their physical movement from exporter to buyer.

market concentration Market selection strategy involving a slow and gradual rate of growth in the number of foreign markets served by a company.

market demand The total volume of a product/service that would be bought by a defined customer group in a defined geographical area in a defined time period in a defined marketing environment under a defined marketing program.

market-driven firm A company that is customer oriented and is concerned with what the customer will buy that can be made profitably.

market entry mode The means that a company uses to penetrate (enter) a foreign target country. See *international marketing channel*.

market forecast Expected market demand.

market potential The amount of a product (or service) that the market could absorb over some indefinite time period under optimum conditions of market development.

market segmentation Process of identifying and categorizing groups of customers and countries according to common characteristics.

market spreading Market selection strategy characterized by a fast rate of growth in the number of foreign markets served by a company at the early stages of expansion.

marketing mix (program) The planned and coordinated combination of marketing methods or tools used by a company to achieve a predetermined goal.

marketing organizations Independent companies that directly participate in the transactions and physical flows in an international marketing channel.

marketing research The systematic and objective search for, and analysis of, information relevant to the identification and solution of any problem relevant to the firm's marketing activity. See *research process*.

matrix organization A mixed structure that combines two or more competencies on a worldwide basis.

mechanics of export The practical, everyday details of an export transaction and shipment.

media mix Combination of different advertising media used by a company.

MENA (Middle East and North Africa) A region consisting of 24 Arab countries and territories having a population of almost 500 million.

merchant exporter An intermediary who takes title to the products to be sold in a foreign market.

Mercosur A common market including Argentina, Brazil, Paraguay, and Uruguay.

multinational corporation (MNC) A company that operates in a number of countries and adjusts its products and practices to each country or group of countries.

multinational marketing Companies treat each foreign market as separate and distinct, developing differentiated products and marketing strategies specifically for each market. See *international marketing*.

NAFTA (North American Free Trade Area) Free trade area consisting of the United States, Canada, and Mexico.

nationalism The influence of collective forces in the form of national spirit or attitude.

nearest neighbor Type of clustering or grouping of foreign markets based on geographic proximity.

network model Approach to B2B marketing whereby a company is engaged in networks of business relationships comprising a number of different firms.

niche marketer International marketer who markets primarily to a generally small and specialized segment of the overall market.

nontariff barriers Government regulations on trade that are other than duty or tariffs on imports.

nontransferable letter of credit Letter of credit that may not be transferred by the beneficiary to another party.

nonvessel operating common carrier (NVOCC) Designation given to foreign freight forwarders that issue a bill of lading to the exporter, and which are the responsible party to the exporter.

offset A type of countertrade where the seller is required to either assist in or arrange for the marketing of products being produced or sold by the buyer.

offshore plant A plant owned by a company in one country but located in another country whose principal mission is to produce products to be exported to the home market.

open account Payment is to be made to the exporter either on a specific date or within a specified number of days after a date indicated on the export invoice.

opening bank Bank in the importer's country that opens a letter of credit for an importer.

outdoor media Advertising posters, signs, and car cards that are placed on the sides of buildings, public transportation vehicles, and stand-alone sites.

outsourcing See *global outsourcing*.

packing list Contains, item by item, the contents of cases or containers in a shipment.

Paris Union The International Convention for the Protection of Industrial Property in which signatory countries extend national treatment to business of other member countries in the protection of trademarks, patents, and so on.

particular average A loss during ocean shipment that affects specific shippers only.

pattern standardization Promotion strategy that is designed from the start to accept modification to fit local national-market conditions, yet still keeping some common elements across all foreign markets.

penetration pricing A strategy where a price is established that is sufficiently low to rapidly create a mass market.

personal selling Person-to-person marketing communication between a company representative and a prospective buyer.

physical core of product Functional features, style, presentation, and design.

physical distribution The movement and handling of products outward from the exporting country to points of consumption or use. See *logistics*.

piggyback marketing One manufacturer uses its foreign distribution facilities to sell another company's products alongside its own.

point-of-purchase materials Sales promotion materials by manufacturers and exporters of packaged consumer goods used at the point of purchase to appeal to consumers.

political risk Application of host government policies that constrain the business operations of a given foreign investment. Includes risk based on transfer, operations, ownership control, and general instability.

positioning A strategy of marketing communications to a foreign market whereby the attempt is made to locate a brand in the customers' minds over and against other products in terms of product attributes and benefits that the brand does and does not offer.

preemptive pricing Price is set low (close to total cost) to discourage competition.

price escalation The tendency for the price of a product to increase significantly as it moves from the exporting manufacturer to the user or consumer.

price sensitivity Consumers' (buyers') reactions to price changes. Also known as price elasticity.

primary data Data collected through original research pertaining to the particular research question asked.

primary information sources Collection of information by observation, controlled experiments, surveys, and other techniques to obtain information directly from those on whom one desires such information.

Primary Message Systems (PMS) The means by which cultures communicate to their members and to other cultures.

priority-in-registration doctrine Concept of law granting the rights to use a trademark to the firm or person who first registers it with the proper agency.

priority-in-use doctrine Concept of law granting the rights to use a trademark to the firm or person that has first used it.

proactive behavior Aggressive behavior based on a company's interest in exploiting unique competence or market possibilities.

product Sum of all the physical and psychological satisfactions that the buyer or user receives as a result of the purchase and/or use of a product.

product differentiation Perceived uniqueness of a product.

product-driven firm A company that is guided in its decision making by technology and product concerns.

product life cycle The stages followed by a product from its birth (product introduction) to its abandonment (sales decline).

product life-cycle theory Theory explaining stages where an innovator country of a new product is initially an exporter, then loses its competitive advantage vis-à-vis its trading partners, and may eventually become an importer of the product some years later.

product line Group of products that are similar or have something in common.

product mix The set (assortment) of products that a company offers to customers.

product organization Company structure organized on a product basis where product divisions have global responsibility.

product package Includes package itself, trademark, brand name, and label.

product phasing Set of strategies for the synchronization of old product deletion with entry of a new product.

pro forma invoice A preliminary invoice prepared by the exporter that shows the terms of a transaction agreed upon, or being proposed.

promotion mix Combination of different marketing promotion activities used by the export/international marketer.

promotion program Planned, coordinated, integrated series of efforts built around a single major theme or idea designed to achieve predetermined communication objectives.

prototype standardization Promotion strategy in which the same advertisement(s) or campaign(s) are used in multiple foreign markets with language being modified for the local markets.

psychic/psychological distance Applied to countries, this is distance between countries as assessed by looking at culture, stage of economic development, history, etc.

psychographic segmentation Segmentation of a market on the basis of psychographic variables, such as lifestyle, personality, and so on.

publicity Any kind of news about a company or its products that is reported by some media, and is not paid for by the company.

public relations Marketing communications designed to gain public understanding and acceptance of a company and its business activities.

pull promotion policy/strategy Consumer demand is established by promoting directly to the consumer who will then 'pull' the product through the channel by demanding it from intermediaries.

push promotion policy/strategy Promotion through the marketing channel. Channel members promote a product to other channel members at lower levels.

quotas Legal restrictions limiting the amount of a product that can be imported from a particular country.

reactive behavior A company responds to internal and external pressures and acts passively.

regulatory-supportive activities Regulatory-type activities used by a government to promote international marketing by local business firms.

relationship marketing Marketing by a country based on lasting relationships with buyers. See *network model*.

research process A process of obtaining information that starts with 'problem definition' and ends with the completed report and ultimate integration of findings into management decision making. See *marketing research*.

resident buyer An agent representing foreign buyers domiciled in the exporter's home market. See also *export commission house*.

Revised American Foreign Trade Definitions – 1941 System of trade terms originally developed by the Chamber of Commerce of the United States and two other organizations.

revocable letter of credit Letter of credit that can be cancelled at any time by the importer or the opening bank.

Rules of Origin Established by regional economic integration schemes to specify the amount of content that must be region based for a product to be exported/imported between countries in the region without tariff.

sales forecast The expected level of sales of a company based on the marketing plan to be implemented and some assumed external environment.

sales promotion All sales activities that supplement and strengthen personal selling and advertising.

sales response function Relationship between expenditure on marketing efforts and the sales response in a foreign market.

secondary data Data available from secondary information sources.

secondary information source Any source of published information and information previously collected for purposes other than the present need.

self-reference criterion (SRC) Judging a foreign market's cultural traits, habits, and norms on the basis of the cultural traits, habits, and norms of the home society.

separate export department A self-contained and largely self-sufficient company unit in which most of the export activities are handled within the department itself.

shippers' agent A facilitating organization that handles the inland movement of international freight.

shipper's export declaration See *export declaration*.

shipping conference Association of ocean transportation companies providing service on specific routes.

sight draft A draft indicating that payment must be made when the buyer first sees the draft and it is presented for payment.

silent language Nonverbal communication, including time, space, relationships, and other aspects of culture.

skimming the market Pricing strategy where a high price is charged until the market at that price is exhausted; the price may then be lowered and/or the company sold.

sliding down the demand curve Pricing strategy where a high price is set and then reduced in anticipation of competition so the company can become established in foreign markets.

socio-cultural characteristics Factors that influence the buying decision process and include material culture, language, education, aesthetics, values and attitudes, social organization, and political–legal structure and philosophy.

sogo shosha Large Japanese general trading companies engaged in a wide range of commercial and financial activities in addition to trade and distribution.

standardization A company offers one version of the marketing program or individual elements of a program (such as a product) to all foreign markets. Also known as globalization.

state trading Government engagement in commercial, business operations, either directly or through agencies under its control.

strategic alliances Long-term agreements for collaboration and/or cooperation in specific areas of international marketing activity between companies from two or more countries.

structure of distribution All of the intermediary marketing agencies or institutions in a foreign market that are in use by all companies at any given time, and their geographic coverage.

subculture A culture within a broader culture that may be based on nationality, religion, race, or geographical area.

supply chain management See *logistics* and *physical distribution*.

switch trading A type of countertrade to dispose of goods used when one party to a barter or counter-purchase transaction does not want what the other party is offering.

targeting Process of evaluating market segments and focusing marketing efforts on a country, region, or group of people.

tariff A tax (duty) on imports. A schedule of rates and terms for transportation of goods is also called a tariff.

tariff surcharge Temporary tariff placed on a product to discourage its importation. See *countervailing duty*.

technology-driven firm See *product-driven firm*.

time draft Draft where payment is due a specified number of days after sight.

total quality management (TQM) Managing for quality in which companies strive to get products to a market faster, with fewer defects, and at a lower cost.

trade fair Concentrated exhibition of the products of many manufacturers/exporters.

trademark A brand, or part of a brand, that is protected by law.

trade mission Government- or industry-sponsored activity where a group of business people go to a foreign market for the purpose of making sales and/or establishing relationships.

trade terms System for quoting export prices, indicating exporter's and buyer's liability, costs, and responsibility.

trading company A type of export/import merchant.

transfer price   Price quoted to wholly or partially owned foreign subsidiaries.

transferable letter of credit   Allows the transfer of all or part of the letter of credit to some other party.

transference of advertising   The process of moving an advertising campaign, or some of its components, from one market (domestic or foreign) to another market.

traveling salesperson   Salesperson for an exporter who resides in one country (often the home country) and travels to foreign markets to perform sales duties.

turnkey operation   A management contract calling for the construction of a plant, training of personnel, and the initial operation of the plant for a local investor.

unconfirmed letter of credit   Letter of credit where a bank in the exporter's country does not take on a legal obligation to pay (honor) drafts drawn under the letter of credit.

usance letter of credit   Letter of credit where delivery of documents is made against acceptance of the documents rather than against payment.

Values and Lifestyles (VALS)   A system for representing the values and lifestyles of people in a country or culture.

VIEW test   A way to assess the effectiveness of packaging by examining visibility, information, emotional impact, and workability.

voluntary export restraint (VER)   Agreement, typically unilateral, by a company or a country to limit its exports of a specific product, or product class, to a particular foreign market.

whole channel concept   An integrated system with the manufacturer on one end and the final user or buyer on the other end. Basic components are the headquarters organization of the international marketer, the channel between nations, and the channel within a nation.

World Trade Organization (WTO)   A multinational, supranational organization providing a forum for negotiating, at the national government level, issues affecting international business. Includes a mechanism for resolving disputes.

INDEX

Entries in **bold** are defined in the Glossary

ABB *see* Asea Brown Boveri Limited
abbreviations xiii–xvi
absolute advantage 56
acceptance 494–5, 496
acquisitions *see* mergers
adaptation
    advertising 542–9
    communication 542–9
    products 400–7
Adidas AG, case study 556–8
advertising 510, 527–36
    adaptation 542–9
    China 545
    climate 528–9
    copy 547–8
    foreign media 530–3
    generalizations 548–9
    international media 529–30
    management issues 551–2
    online 533–5
    standardization 542–9
    strategy 542–9
    transference 549–51
advertising networks 534
affiliate networks 534
agents, indirect export 282, 287–91, 303–9
air shipments, physical distribution 606–8
air waybills 606–8
Alcas Corporation, case study 270–2
altruists, core values segmentation 169
Andean Common Market 138
antitrust legislation 128–9
appeals, advertising 546–7
Aquabear AB, case study 237–8
Arion Exports, case study 507
art goods, case study 39
Asea Brown Boveri Limited (ABB)
    case study 638–9
    organization 638–9
ASEAN *see* Association of Southeast Asian
    Nations
Asia
    Asian crisis 53, 421–2

economic forces 104–6
economic integration 137, 140
growth industries 104–6
Unilever 641–6
values 113–15
see also named countries
assembly operations
    market entry strategies 254
    nonexport entry modes 341–4
assignment of proceeds 489
association methods, forecasting methods
    211–12
Association of Southeast Asian Nations
    (ASEAN), economic integration 137,
    139
attitudes, CEOs 2–4
Avon Products, Inc., case study 153–8,
    277–9

banks/banking
    government 132–3
    World Bank 101–3
    see also finance; payment methods
banner advertisements 533–4
barriers
    communication 508–9, 512
    exporting 20–1
    small companies 21
barter 437, 499–500
BCG approach, portfolio analysis 187–91,
    392–3
Beck's beer, physical distribution 579
Berne Union, finance 479
bill of exchange 474, 492–7
bill of lading 477, 595, 600–2, 603
blunders, promotion 516–18
branding
    brand protection 411–13
    counterfeit trade 412–13
    decisions 413–15
    and lifestyle characteristics 167–8
    products 410–15
    segmentation 166

Bridgestone Corporation, case study 91–4
BRL Hardy, case study 426–30
brokers 289
built-in export department 297
bundling, pricing 435–6
business-government alliances 30
business-government relations, social
    responsibility 83–5
business models, non-traditional exports
    33–4
buy-back 501
buyer ethnocentrism, market expansion
    184–5

C&F, pricing 455–9
CACM *see* Central American Common
    Market
canning business, case study 148–9
Capitool Company, case study 467–70
car industry
    case study 43–9, 149–52, 239–45,
        368–72, 420–2, 506
    positioning 387
    products development 378–80
    smart car 379–80
    strategic alliances 345–6
**Caribbean Community and Common Market
    (CARICOM)**, economic integration
    138
cartels 129
case study
    Adidas AG 556–8
    Alcas Corporation 270–2
    Aquabear AB 237–8
    Arion Exports 507
    art goods 39
    Asea Brown Boveri Limited (ABB)
        638–9
    Avon Products, Inc. 153–8, 277–9
    Bridgestone Corporation 91–4
    BRL Hardy 426–30
    canning business 148–9
    Capitool Company 467–70

car industry 43–9, 149–52, 239–45, 368–72, 420–2, 506
China 153–8
Christa Clothing International 559–63
clothing 559–63
communication 556–8, 558–9, 559–63, 563–5, 565–9
cosmetics 153–8, 277–9, 372–3
cutlery 270–2
Daewoo 420–2
DaimlerChrysler 43–5, 48–9
direct selling 153–8
eBay 40–2
electronics 470–1, 611–13, 613–15
Eli's Cheesecake Company 565–9
engineering 467, 467–70
environment 148–9, 149–52, 153–8
export entry modes 319–20, 321–3, 323–5
export market selection 194–6, 196–8
export orders 611–13, 613–15, 616–18
farm machinery 367–8
finance 506, 507
fish processing 319–20
food industry 319–20, 323–5, 422–5, 565–9
Ford Motor Company 45–6, 149–52, 239–45
GG Farm Machinery Company 367–8
glass manufacture 507
GlaxoSmithKline 94–8
HV Industri A/S 319–20
Ikea 194–6
Jaguar Electronics, Inc 611–13
Japan 148–9
Korea 421–2
Latin America 239–45
Lego A/S 558–9
Mariani Packing Company, Inc. 235–6
market entry strategies 270–2, 272–7, 277–9
marketing research 235–6, 237–8, 239–45
Megabox, Inc. 613–15
Mercedes-Benz 47–8
Mexico 235–6
Murphy Company Limited 39–40
Nestlé 323–5
nonexport entry modes 362–7, 367–8, 368–72, 372–3
Nove Ltd 563–5
Nu Skin Enterprises, Inc. 372–3
organization 638–9, 639–46
pharmaceuticals 94–8
physical distribution 611–13, 613–15, 616–18
pricing 467, 467–70, 470–1
Primex Marketing, Inc 616–18
products 420–2, 422–5, 426–30
Quint Winery 321–3
RAP Engineering and Equipment Company 467

restaurants 362–7
Seven-Eleven 196–8
shavers 563–5
shoes 556–8
skiwear 237–8
social responsibility 91–4, 94–8
Strato Designs 470–1
Supreme Canning Company 148–9
Supreme Foods of France (SFF) 422–5
Tainan Glass Manufacturing Company 506
Terralumen S. A. 362–7
tires 91–4
Toyota 46–7
toys 272–7, 558–9
Unilever 639–46
Volkswagen 368–72
wheels 616–18
wines 321–3, 426–30
Yang Toyland Pte, Limited 272–7
cash cows, portfolio analysis 187–91
cash with order 477, 478
causal methods, forecasting methods 211–12
Central American Common Market (CACM), economic integration 138
centralization/decentralization, organization 621–4
certificates of origin, physical distribution 597–600
certification, physical distribution 597–600
CFR (cost and freight), pricing 455–9
change
    economic forces 104–6
    social responsibility 82–5
change agents, export behavior theories/motives 65–6
channel decision, market entry strategies 246–56, 263–5
China
    7-Eleven 198
    advertising 545
    case study 153–8
    culture 118
    environment 100
    FDI 328
    growth industries 104–6
    guanxi 118
    hot spots 105–6
    pricing 129
    state trading 136
    trading companies 287
Christa Clothing International, case study 559–63
CIF (cost, insurance and freight), pricing 455–9
CIP (carriage and insurance paid to), pricing 455–9
Cirque du Soleil 33
classical theory, international trade theory 55–8
clean draft 473, 489, 496
clearing arrangements 500

clothing, case study 559–63
cluster analysis
    market potential 209
    market selection 173–4
clusters, culture 112–13
co-promotion 540–1
Coca Cola 375–6, 400
COD (cash on delivery) 477
color, communication 514–15
commercial invoice, physical distribution 596–7
communication 508–69
    adaptation 542–9
    barriers 508–9, 512
    case study 556–8, 558–9, 559–63, 563–5, 565–9
    color 514–15
    culture 115–16, 513–18
    decisions 510–19
    export orders 573
    international 573
    nonverbal 512
    organization 624–5
    socio-cultural environment 115–16
    standardization 542–9
    symbols 513–18
    VALS (Values and Life Styles) 542–3
    see also promotion
company considerations, market entry strategies 258–60
company policies, pricing 441–2
comparative advantage 56–8
compensation agreement 501
competition
    environment 141–3
    factors influencing 142–3
    nature of 142
    pricing 437–9
    products 397
confirming houses 288
consignment, payment method 473, 478
consular invoice, physical distribution 597, 598
consumer ethnocentrism 395
consumer promotion materials 525–6
container shipment, ocean transportation 604–5
continuum, geographic markets 163
contract manufacturing 351–3
    market entry strategies 254
contractible market selection 174–9
contracting *see* **contract manufacturing; management contracting**
control systems, organization 624–5
cooperative organizations, indirect export 292–5
copy, **advertising** 547–8
core values segmentation 168–70
corporate citizenship, stakeholders 150–1
corruption 129
cosmetics, case study 153–8, 277–9, 372–3
costs, pricing 433–6

counter purchase 500
counterfeit trade 412–13
countertrade 498–502
counting methods, forecasting methods
    211–12
countries
    classification, GNI 101–3
    market selection 174–7
    portfolio analysis 187–91
CPT (carriage paid to), pricing 455–9
creatives, core values segmentation 169
CSM see customer satisfaction management
cultural distance, market selection 172
cultural empathy 13–15
culture
    China 118
    clusters 112–13
    communication 115–16, 513–18
    dimensions 110–11
    indicators 109–10
    marketing research 216–24
    nature of 108–15
    pervasive effects 117–18
    value orientations 110–13
    see also socio-cultural environment
culturegrams, marketing research 204–5
currency boards, exchange controls 127
currency issues, pricing 453–4
customer groupings based organization
    629–31
customer satisfaction management (CSM)
    214–15
customer segmentation, market selection 179
customs-bonded warehouses 589
cutlery, case study 270–2

Daewoo, case study 420–2
DAF (delivered at frontier), pricing 455–9
DaimlerChrysler, case study 43–5, 48–9
data collection
    e-mail 226–8
    Internet 226–8
    marketing research 215–28
data equivalence, marketing research 201
date draft 497
DDP (delivered duty paid), pricing 455–9
DDU (delivered duty unpaid), pricing 455–9
deal makers, segmentation 166
decentralization, pricing 460
decision making 199–245
    physical distribution 580–2
    see also information; marketing research
deferred payment credit 490
demand curve, pricing 444
demand management 17–20
    demand states 18–20
demand pattern analysis, market potential
    209
DEQ (delivered ex quay), pricing 455–9
DES (delivered ex ship), pricing 455–9
desk jobbers 286–7
devouts, core values segmentation 169

differential pricing, pricing 450–2
diffusion, products 383–6
direct export 295–309
    evaluation, dependent organizations
        302–3
    home-country based 296–9
    stages 296
direct mail, case study 274
direct marketing 532–3
direct selling, case study 153–8
disproportionality phenomenon, products
    389–91
distance, market selection 172
distribution, physical see physical
        distribution
distributors, indirect export 303–9
dock receipt, ocean transportation 606
documentary credit see letter of credit
documentary draft 489, 496
documentation, physical distribution 581–2,
    595–600
documents against acceptance (D/A) 475–6
documents against payment (D/P) 475–6
dogs, portfolio analysis 187–91
domestic/export policies, pricing 447–52
domestic market limit, export behavior
        theories/motives 68
domestic marketing management, cf.
        international marketing management
        13–15
drafts 474, 492–7
    types 496–7
drugs companies see pharmaceuticals
dumping
    pricing 439–40
    tariffs 124
dynamic pricing 435

e-business 24–5
e-commerce
    export entry modes 309–13
    market entry strategies 253
    Nestlé 312, 323–5
e-mail, data collection 226–8
eBay 33
    case study 40–2
economic advantage 55–6
economic forces
    Asia 104–6
    change areas 104–6
    environment 100–6
    market development 101–3
    socio-cultural environment 106–18
economic integration
    characteristics 137
    environment 136–41
    EU 138, 139–41
    existing arrangements 137–9
economic trends, marketing research 231
economies of scale, export behavior
        theories/motives 66
EDI see electronic data interchange

efficiency, export marketing 54–5
EFTA see European Free Trade Association
electronic data interchange (EDI)
    physical distribution 579
    see also e-business; e-commerce; e-mail
electronics, case study 470–1, 611–13,
    613–15
Eli's Cheesecake Company, case study 565–9
EMCs see export management companies
engineering, case study 467, 467–70
entrepreneurial approaches
    business-government alliances 30
    international marketing 28–30
    online marketplaces 28–9
    virtual companies 29–30
entry, market see export entry modes; market
        entry strategies; nonexport entry
        modes
environment
    case study 148–9, 149–52, 153–8
    competition 141–3
    domestic cf. foreign 13–15
    economic forces 100–6
    economic integration 136–41
    international 99–158
    legal 86–7, 118–36
    political 86–7, 118–36
    socio-cultural 106–18
    see also social responsibility
environmental factors, market expansion
    184–5
equal advantage 58
estimation by analogy, market potential 209
ethical/moral issues 76–9
    applying ethics 79
    decision making 78
    defining ethics 76–8
    see also social responsibility
EU (European Union)
    economic integration 138, 139–41
    marketing organizations 633–4
European customers 162–3
    uniformity/non-uniformity 225
European Free Trade Association (EFTA),
        economic integration 137
excess capacity, export behavior
        theories/motives 66–7
exchange controls
    currency boards 127
    government 126–7
exchange rates, money transfer 502–3
executives
    CEOs 2–4
    export marketing executives 13–15
    international marketing managers 14
exhibitions 524–5
expansionistic pricing 444
expansive market selection 172–4
experience-curve pricing 442–3, 444
export behavior theories/motives 61–70
    change agents 65–6
    domestic market limit 68

economies of scale 66
excess capacity 66–7
foreign market opportunities 65, 66
global marketing 68–9
goals 62–70
managerial urge 64
resources 68
risk diversification 65
seasonal extension 66
unique product/technology competence 65
unsolicited foreign orders 67–8
export commission houses 287–8
export credit insurance 475, 497–8
export declaration 595–6
export desk jobbers 286–7
export/domestic policies, pricing 447–52
export entry modes 280–325
case study 319–20, 321–3, 323–5
direct export 295–309
e-commerce 309–13
gray market 313–15
indirect export 282–95
Internet 309–13
export licenses 576–7, 595–6
export management companies (EMCs) 289–91
export market direction 160–1
export market segmentation 164–70
export market selection 159–98
case study 194–6, 196–8
defining 160
definition 159–98
foreign market portfolios 187–91
market definition 161–70
market expansion 170–86
market segmentation 161–70
market selection 170–86
portfolio analysis 187–91
strategy 159–98
export marketing
efficiency 54–5
exports effect 53–4
FDI 53
imports effect 52–3
planning 15–21
potential benefits 52–5
productivity 54–5
strategy 15–21
export marketing executives, characteristics 13–15
export marketing factors, market expansion 185–6
export marketing research 213–28
see also marketing research
export merchants 283
export orders 570–7
case study 611–13, 613–15, 616–18
communication 573
contract performance 576
customs/practices 571
export licenses 576–7, 595–6

handling 574–7
inquiries 574
organization 571–3
payment methods 577
pro forma invoice 574–6
procedure 571–2
purpose 571–3
export processing zones (EPZs) 135, 592
export sales subsidiary 298–9
exporting
barriers 20–1
development 70–2
internationalization stages 70–2
levels 70–2
network model 73–6
obstacles 20–1
relationship marketing 73–6
exporting combination 294–5
exports effect, export marketing 53–4
extinction pricing 445–6
EXW (ex works), pricing 455–9

factor proportion theory, international trade theory 58–9
factoring 474, 475
falling demand 19
Far East *see* Asia
farm machinery, case study 367–8
FAS (free alongside) vessel, pricing 455–9
FCA (free carrier), named place, pricing 455–9
FDI *see* foreign direct investment
finance 472–507
Berne Union 479
case study 506, 507
long-term financing 478–9
see also payment methods
financial activities, government 132–3
first-mover advantages 327–8
fish processing, case study 319–20
FOB (free on board), pricing 432, 455–9
food industry, case study 319–20, 323–5, 422–5, 565–9
Ford Motor Company, case study 45–6, 149–52, 239–45
forecasting methods, **market potential** 211–12
foreign-based sales subsidiary 300–1
foreign catalogs, promotion 521–2
foreign direct investment (FDI)
China 328
export marketing 53
foreign market opportunities, export behavior theories/motives 65, 66
foreign market portfolios, **export market selection** 187–91
foreign media, advertising 530–3
foreign sales branch 299–300
forfait financing 474
FPA *see* free of particular average
franchising 349
free areas, physical distribution 590–2

free of particular average (FPA), insurance 593
free on board (FOB) 432, 455–9
free perimeters 135, 590
free ports 135, 590
free trade areas 137–8, 267
free trade zones 135, 590–2
freight forwarders, physical distribution 587–9
freight rates, physical distribution 604
full demand 19
fun seekers, core values segmentation 169
functional export department, organization 625–6

general-average claim, insurance 593
General Electric Company, countries classification, GNI 103
geographic area based organization 629–31
geographic distance, market selection 172
geographic segmentation, market selection 177–9
Germany
export entry modes 280–1
Mittelstand companies 280–1
GG Farm Machinery Company, case study 367–8
glass manufacture, case study 507
GlaxoSmithKline, case study 94–8
global marketers, internationalization 5–7
global marketing
defining 6–7
export behavior theories/motives 68–9
global outsourcing 396–7
glossary 647–57
GNI *see* Gross National Income
goals, export behavior theories/motives 62–70
government-business alliances 30
government-business relations, social responsibility 83–5
governmental policies, market entry strategies 260–1
governments
banks/banking 132–3
controls 121–7
exchange controls 126–7
export facilitating activities 134–5
financial activities 132–3
information services 133–4
information source 203
labor standards 127–8
license requirements 123–4
promotional activities 129–35
qualitative controls 126
quotas 125–6
role 119–21
state trading 136
tariffs 124–5
tax 126
gray market
export entry modes 313–15
pricing 450–1

greenfield investment 331
Gross National Income (GNI), countries
	classification 101–3
growth industries, Asia 104–6
guanxi, China 118

hedging, pricing 454
Herfindahl index, market selection 180–1
heterarchical multinational structure 636
Hewlett-Packard, organization 632–3
Hong Kong 585–6
HV Industri A/S, case study 319–20

ice cream, Unilever 538–40
Ikea 34
	case study 194–6
importance, international marketing 2–4
importing, inward internationalization
	12–13
imports effect, export marketing 52–3
income elasticity measurements, market
	potential 209
INCOTERMS 2000, pricing 455–9
indirect export 282–95
	agents 282, 287–91
	cooperative organizations 292–5
	evaluation, marketing organization
		291–2
	merchants 282–7
	piggyback marketing 292–4
information
	collection 200
	examples 202
	external sources 202–3
	government sources 203
	internal sources 202–3
	international marketing decisions
		199–245
	nongovernment sources 203–8
	sources 202–8
	sources, pricing 460–3
	see also decision making; marketing
		research
information services, government 133–4
Information Technology (IT) 22–5
	examples, international markets 27
	impact 25–8
	knowledge-industry 31–3
	RFID 26
	scope 26–8
	see also Internet
innovation, products 383–6
insufficient markets 160–1
insurance
	FPA 593
	general-average claim 593
	particular average loss 593
	physical distribution 592–4
integration, economic *see* economic
	integration
intellectual property 127–8
internal product development 378–80

international division structure, organization
	626–7
international marketing
	defining 5, 6
	entrepreneurial approaches 28–30
	importance 2–4
international marketing management 9–12
	dimensions 9
	cf. domestic marketing management
		13–15
	drivers 9–10
	marketing mix 10–12
international marketing managers, traits 14
international media, advertising 529–30
international trade theories 55–61
	classical theory 55–8
	factor proportion theory 58–9
	product life-cycle theory 59–61
internationalization
	degree of 7–9
	factors 2–4
	global marketers 5–7
	stages 70–2
	strategies 7–9
Internet 22–3
	data collection 226–8
	e-business 24–5
	e-commerce 253, 309–13
	e-mail 226–8
	export entry modes 309–13
	market entry strategies 253
	online marketplaces 28–30
	pricing 434–5
	virtual companies 29–30
	World Wide Web 23–4, 74
	see also websites
intimates, core values segmentation 169
irregular demand 19
irrevocable letter of credit 488
ISO 9000, quality management 387–8
IT *see* Information Technology
Italy, culture 117–18

Jaguar Electronics, Inc, case study 611–13
Japan
	business-government relations 83–5
	case study 148–9
	culture 117–18
	keiretsu 74, 285
	Seven-Eleven 196–8
	SMEs, assisting 131
	sogo sosha 283–7
	trading companies 283–7
	wholesalers 249
joint ventures 30
	market entry strategies 254–5
	nonexport entry modes 331, 346, 354–6
judgement methods, forecasting methods
	211–12

keiretsu 74, 285
knowledge-industry 31–3

Korea
	case study 421–2
	Daewoo 421–2
	nonexport entry modes 357–8

labor standards, government 127–8
latent demand 19
Latin America, case study 239–45
lead-lag analysis, market potential 209
legal environment 118–36
	social responsibility 86–7
legal influence, pricing 439–41
legal practices, social responsibility 83–5
Lego A/S, case study 558–9
letter of credit 475–6, 476–7, 478, 479–92
	defining 479
	types 488–92
license requirements, government 123–4
licenses, export 576–7, 595–6
licensing
	market entry strategies 254
	strategic alliances 348–51
life cycle, products *see* product life-cycle
lifestyle characteristics, **branding** 167–8
logistics, physical distribution 582–4
long-term financing 478–9
luxury innovators, segmentation 166

McDonalds 34
Madrid Protocol 128
magazines, promotion 523
management contracting 353–4
	market entry strategies 254
management issues, **advertising** 551–2
management styles 340–1
managerial urge, export behavior
	theories/motives 64
manufacturer's export agents 291
manufacturing facilities
	implementation 338–41
	location 332–5
	nonexport entry modes 331–41
	ownership 335–7
manufacturing, market entry strategies 254
marginal pricing 433
Mariani Packing Company, Inc., case study
	235–6
marine insurance
	FPA 593
	general-average claim 593
	particular average loss 593
	physical distribution 592–4
market concentration, market selection
	179–81, 183
market conditions (demand), pricing 436–7
market definition 161–70
market development 101–3
	strategy 169–70
market entry strategies 246–79
	alternative 252–6
	assembly operations 254
	case study 270–2, 272–7, 277–9

channel decision 246–56, 263–5
company considerations 258–60
e-commerce 253
elements 251–6
factors influencing 257–64
free trade areas 267
governmental policies 260–1
Internet 253
involvement extent 262–3
joint ventures 254–5
product factors 258
selecting entry mode 265–6
target market 257–8
market expansion 170–86
buyer ethnocentrism 184–5
environmental factors 184–5
export marketing factors 185–6
market share strategies 185–6
product factors 183–4
strategy 181–6
market potential
assessing 208–13
defining 210
forecasting methods 211–12
illustrations 210–13
market segmentation 161–70
accessibility 165
actionability 165–6
bases 166–70
continuum, geographic markets 163
European customers 162–3
export market segmentation 164–70
measurability 165
product mix 163–4
profitability 165
market selection 170–86
analysis, foreign market 178–9
cluster analysis 173–4
contractible 174–9
countries 174–7
customer segmentation 179
distance 172
expansive 172–4
geographic segmentation 177–9
Herfindahl index 180–1
market concentration 179–81, 183
market spreading 179–81, 183
nearest neighbor 173
proactive 171–2
reactive 171–2
screening 177–9
strategy 179–81
temperature-gradient approach 174
market share strategies, market expansion
185–6
market size *see* market potential
market spreading, market selection 179–81,
183
marketing communication *see*
communication
marketing decision support systems 199–202
marketing management, international *see*

international marketing management
marketing mix
international marketing management
10–12
pricing 441–2
SAS 10–12
schematic 12
marketing research
analysis 223–4
case study 235–6, 237–8, 239–45
culture 216–24
culturegrams 204–5
data collection 215–28
data equivalence 201
defining 214–15
economic trends 231
export 213–28
guides 231
indexes 231
interpretation 223–4
issues of concern 224–6
outside research firms 201
primary sources 202–3
problem formulation 215
process 199–202, 215–24
questionnaires 216–19, 226
reporting results 224
research methods 215
sample design 222, 223
secondary sources 202–3, 231–4
special services 231–2
statistics 232–3
visual data 217–22
websites 205–7, 233–4
see also decision making; information
markets
insufficient 160–1
overlooked 160–1
matrix organization 631–6, 638–9
media mix 535–6
Megabox, Inc., case study 613–15
Megacorp, Inc. vs Niche Ltd 404–5
Mercedes-Benz, case study 47–8
merchants, indirect export 282–7
Mercosur 138
mergers 128–9
examples 338–41
products development 377
Mexico, case study 235–6
Microsoft 128–9
Mittelstand companies, Germany 280–1
mix *see* marketing mix; media mix; product
mix
money transfer, exchange rates 502–3
moral issues *see* ethical/moral issues
motion picture/video/DVD, promotion
523–4
motives, export behavior *see* export behavior
theories/motives
multiculturalism 107–8
multinational marketing, defining 6
multiple-factor index, market potential 209

Murphy Company Limited, case study
39–40

NAFTA *see* North American Free Trade
Agreement
nearest neighbor, market selection 173
negative demand 18
Nestlé
case study 323–5
e-commerce 312, 323–5
network model, exporting 73–6
News Corp. 341, 342
Niche Ltd vs Megacorp, Inc. 404–5
no demand 18
non-traditional exports
business models 33–4
growth 31–4
knowledge-industry 31–3
nonexport entry modes 326–73
alternative 329–31, 357–8
assembly operations 341–4
case study 362–7, 367–8, 368–72,
372–3
joint ventures 331, 346, 354–6
Korea 357–8
manufacturing facilities 331–41
strategic alliances 344–56
nontransferable letter of credit 489
**North American Free Trade Agreement
(NAFTA)**, economic integration 137,
138
Nove Ltd, case study 563–5
Novica.com 29
Nu Skin Enterprises, Inc., case study 372–3

objectives, pricing 443
obstacles, exporting 20–1
ocean transportation
bill of lading 600–2, 603
container shipment 604–5
dock receipt 606
freight rates 604
physical distribution 600–6
ports of the world, major 585–7
ports transport 602–4
space reservations 604
offsets 501–2
oligopoly 438
online advertising 533–5
online marketplaces *see* Internet
open account 474–5, 478
organization
Asea Brown Boveri Limited (ABB) 638–9
case study 638–9, 639–46
centralization/decentralization 621–4
communication 624–5
control systems 624–5
customer groupings based 629–31
EU, marketing organizations 633–4
functional export department 625–6
geographic area based 629–31
heterarchical multinational structure 636

organization *(continued)*
    Hewlett-Packard 632–3
    international division structure 626–7
    international marketing activities 619–46
    matrix organization 631–6, 638–9
    products-based 627–9
    structures 625–36
    subunits 620–1
    Unilever 639–46
overfull demand 19
overlooked markets 160–1
overview, this book's 35

packaging
    products 407–10
    standardization 407–8
packing list, physical distribution 597
particular average loss, insurance 593
Patent Co-operation Treaty (PCT) 128
pattern standardization 538
payment methods
    bill of exchange 474
    bill of lading 477
    cash with order 477, 478
    clean draft 473
    COD (cash on delivery) 477
    consignment 473, 478
    documents against acceptance (D/A) 475–6
    documents against payment (D/P) 475–6
    drafts 492–7
    export credit insurance 475
    export orders 577
    factoring 474, 475
    forfait financing 474
    letter of credit 475–6, 476–7, 478, 479–92
    open account 474–5, 478
    sight draft 477, 478
    see also finance
PCT *see* Patent Co-operation Treaty
penetration pricing 444
personal selling 510, 519–20
pharmaceuticals
    case study 94–8
    social responsibility 94–8
phasing continuity matrix, products 390–1
Philips, strategic alliances 347
physical distribution 577–618
    air shipments 606–8
    air waybills 606–8
    case study 611–13, 613–15, 616–18
    certificates of origin 597–600
    certification 597–600
    commercial invoice 596–7
    consular invoice 597, 598
    decision making 580–2
    documentation 581–2, 595–600
    export declaration 595–6
    export licenses 576–7, 595–6
    export packing 594–5
    facilitating organizations 587–95

free areas 590–2
freight forwarders 587–9
    importance 578–80
    insurance 592–4
    inventory 581
    logistics 582–4
    marine insurance 592–4
    ocean transportation 600–6
    order processing 581–2
    packing list 597
    ports of the world, major 585–7
    structure 584–608
    supply chain management 582–4
    technology 579
    transportation 581, 584–7
    warehousing 581, 589–90
    see also ocean transportation
piggyback marketing 292–4
planning
    barriers 20–1
    components 16–17
    demand management 17–20
    export marketing 15–21
    process 16–17
    products 377–91
PLC *see* product life-cycle
point-of-purchase (POP) materials 525
political environment 118–36
    social responsibility 86–7
political influence, pricing 439–41
political risk 334–7
portfolio analysis
    BCG approach 187–91, 392–3
    countries 187–91
    export market selection 187–91
    products 392–3
ports of the world, major 585–7
ports transport, ocean transportation 602–4
positioning, products 386, 387
pre-emptive pricing 444–5
price escalation 448–9
price seekers, segmentation 166
pricing 128–9, 431–71
    barter 437
    bundling 435–6
    case study 467, 467–70, 470–1
    China 129
    company policies 441–2
    competition 437–9
    costs 433–6
    currency issues 453–4
    decentralization 460
    demand curve 444
    determinants 433–42
    differential pricing 450–2
    domestic/export policies 447–52
    dumping 439–40
    dynamic 435
    expansionistic pricing 444
    experience-curve pricing 442–3, 444
    export/domestic policies 447–52
    extinction pricing 445–6

gray market 450–1
hedging 454
INCOTERMS 2000; 455–9
information sources 460–3
Internet 434–5
legal influence 439–41
marginal pricing 433
market conditions (demand) 436–7
marketing mix 441–2
objectives 443
oligopoly 438
penetration pricing 444
political influence 439–41
pre-emptive pricing 444–5
price escalation 448–9
profit centers 460
quotations 454–9
skimming 444
strategy 442–7
strategy results 445–6
trade terms 454–9
transfer pricing 460–3
primary sources, marketing research 202–3
Primex Marketing, Inc, case study 616–18
private organizations, promotional activities 135
pro forma invoice 574–6
proactive market selection 171–2
problem children, portfolio analysis 187–91
product factors
    market entry strategies 258
    market expansion 183–4
product life-cycle (PLC) 397–9
    international trade theory 59–61
product mix, market segmentation 163–4
production, organization 620
productivity, export marketing 54–5
products
    adaptation 400–7
    branding 410–15
    case study 420–2, 422–5, 426–30
    characteristics 402–3
    competition 397
    consumer 391–2
    consumer ethnocentrism 395
    decisions 374–430
    development 377–91
    diffusion 383–6
    dimensions 376
    disproportionality phenomenon 389–91
    elimination 389–91
    existing 388–9
    external determinants 394–7
    global outsourcing 396–7
    innovation 383–6
    internal determinants 394
    internal product development 378–80
    market requirements 402–3
    Megacorp, Inc. vs Niche Ltd 404–5
    mix 163–4, 391–400
    new 377–88
    new uses 389

packaging 407–10
phasing continuity matrix 390–1
planning 377–91
PLC 59–61, 397–9
policy 375–6
portfolio analysis 187–91, 392–3
positioning 386, 387
R&D 380–2
screening 382–3, 384
standardization 400–7
statistical decision theory 393–4
strategy 404–7
TQM 386–8
products-based organization 627–9
profit centers, pricing 460
profit, incentive 62
programs, promotion 538–42
promotion 508–69
    blunders 516–18
    decisions 510–19
    programs 538–42
    strategy 538–42
    techniques 519–38
    see also communication
promotional activities, government 129–35
prototype standardization 538
psychic distance, market selection 172
psychographic segmentation 167–8
public relations 526–7
publicity 510, 526–7
pull strategy, communication 511
push strategy, communication 511

qualitative controls, government 126
quality management 386–8
    ISO 9000 387–8
question marks, portfolio analysis 187–91
questionnaires, marketing research 216–19,
    226
Quint Winery, case study 321–3
quotas, government 125–6
quotations, pricing 454–9

R&D *see* research and development
RAP Engineering and Equipment Company,
    case study 467
reactive market selection 171–2
regression analysis, market potential 209
regulation *see* government; legal
    environment; political environment
relationship marketing, exporting 73–6
representatives *see* **agents; distributors**
research *see* marketing research
research and development (R&D) 380–2
resident buyers 288–9
resources, export behavior theories/motives
    68
restaurants, case study 362–7
revocable letter of credit 488
revolving letter of credit 489–90
RFID, IT 26
risk

export credit insurance 497–8
    political risk 334–7
risk diversification, export behavior
    theories/motives 65
Russia, state trading 136

sales promotion 510, 520–6
sample design, marketing research 222, 223
samples, promotion 522–3
Scandinavian Airlines (SAS), marketing mix
    10–12
screening, market selection 177–9
screening products 382–3, 384
seasonal extension, export behavior
    theories/motives 66
secondary sources, marketing research
    202–3, 231–4
segmentation
    branding 166
    core values 168–70
    psychographic 167–8
    see also export market segmentation;
    market segmentation
selecting export markets *see* **export market
    selection**
self-reference criterion (SRC), socio-cultural
    environment 116–17
separate export department 297–8
Seven-Eleven 34
    case study 196–8
    China 198
    Japan 196–8
    Taiwan 198
shavers, case study 563–5
shipper's export declaration 595
ships *see* ocean transportation
shoes, case study 556–8
sight draft 477, 478, 495, 496
Singapore 585–6
skiwear, case study 237–8
small and medium sized enterprises (SMEs),
    assisting 130–1
small companies, barriers 21
smart car 379–80
SMEs *see* small and medium sized enterprises
smuggling 451
social responsibility 80–7
    business-government relations 83–5
    case study 91–4, 94–8
    changing views 82–5
    legal environment 86–7
    legal practices 83–5
    pharmaceuticals 94–8
    political environment 86–7
    stakeholders 81–2
    see also ethical/moral issues
Society for Worldwide Inter-bank Transfers
    (SWIFT) 473
socio-cultural environment
    communication 115–16
    culture, nature of 108–15
    economic forces 106–18

multiculturalism 107–8
    self-reference criterion (SRC) 116–17
sogo sosha, Japan 283–7
space reservations, physical distribution 604
stakeholders
    corporate citizenship 150–1
    social responsibility 81–2
standardization
    advertising 542–9
    communication 542–9
    packaging 407–8
    pattern standardization 538
    products 400–7
    prototype standardization 538
standby letter of credit 490–2
Starbucks 33–4
stars, portfolio analysis 187–91
state trading, government 136
statistics, marketing research 232–3
strategic alliances 30
    advantages 345
    car industry 345–6
    core dimensions 345
    defining 344–5
    fit 345–8
    nonexport entry modes 344–56
    Philips 347
    successful 345–8
strategic focus 330
strategies
    advertising 542–9
    barriers 20–1
    components 16–17
    demand management 17–20
    export market selection 159–98
    export marketing 15–21
    internationalization 7–9
    market development 169–70
    market entry strategies 246–79
    market expansion 181–6
    market selection 179–81
    market share 185–6
    pricing 442–7
    products 404–7
    promotion 538–42
strategy results, pricing 445–6
Strato Designs, case study 470–1
strivers, core values segmentation 169
supply chain management, physical
    distribution 582–4
Supreme Canning Company, case study
    148–9
Supreme Foods of France (SFF), case study
    422–5
SWIFT *see* Society for Worldwide Inter-bank
    Transfers
switch trading 500–1

Tainan Glass Manufacturing Company, case
    study 506
Taiwan, 7-Eleven 198
target market, market entry strategies 257–8

tariffs
  dumping 124
  government 124–5
tax 126, 128
  tariffs 124–5
technology
  impact 25–8
  physical distribution 579
  technology transfer 54–5
Terralumen S. A., case study 362–7
time draft 495, 497
time-series methods, forecasting methods
      211–12
tires, case study 91–4
total quality management (TQM), products
      386–8
Toyota, case study 46–7
toys, case study 272–7, 558–9
TPOs *see* trade promotion organizations
TQM *see* **total quality management**
trade diversion 139
trade fairs 524–5
trade promotion organizations (TPOs) 132
trade terms, pricing 454–9
trading companies 283–6
  China 287
  Japan 283–7
  typology 284
transfer pricing 460–3
transferable letter of credit 489
transference, advertising 549–51

transportation, physical distribution 581,
      584–7
traveling export salesperson 301
turnkey operations 353

uniformity/non-uniformity, European
      customers 225
Unilever
  Asia 641–6
  case study 639–46
  ice cream 538–40
  organization 639–46
unique product/technology competence,
      export behavior theories/motives 65
United States
  business-government relations 83–5
  culture 117–18
unsolicited foreign orders, export behavior
      theories/motives 67–8
unwholesome demand 19
usance draft 496–7

VALS (Values and Lifestyles) 542–3
value added tax (VAT) 128
value orientations, culture 110–13
values, Asia 113–15
venturer merchants 285–6
VERs *see* voluntary export restraints
virtual companies *see* Internet
visual data, marketing research 217–22
Volkswagen, case study 368–72

voluntary export restraints (VERs)
      125
voluntary restraint agreements (VRAs)
      125–6

warehousing
  customs-bonded warehouses 589
  physical distribution 581, 589–90
websites
  marketing research 205–7, 233–4
  see also Internet
wheels, case study 616–18
wholesalers
  Japan 249
  market entry strategies 249
  see also indirect export
wines, case study 321–3, 426–30
WIPO *see* World International Property
      Organization
with/out recourse 497
World Bank, countries classification, GNI
      101–3
World International Property Organization
      (WIPO) 128
World Trade Organization (WTO) 120
World Wide Web 23–4, 74
  see also Internet
Wow bra 544–5

Yang Toyland Pte, Limited, case study
      272–7